Lecture Notes in Computer Science 11423

Advanced Research in Computing and Software Science

Subline of Lecture Notes in Computer Science

More information about this series at http://www.springer.com/series/7407

Luís Caires (Ed.)

Programming Languages and Systems

28th European Symposium on Programming, ESOP 2019
Held as Part of the European Joint Conferences
on Theory and Practice of Software, ETAPS 2019
Prague, Czech Republic, April 6–11, 2019
Proceedings

Springer Open

Editor
Luís Caires
Universidade NOVA de Lisboa
Caparica, Portugal

ISSN 0302-9743 ISSN 1611-3349 (electronic)
Lecture Notes in Computer Science
ISBN 978-3-030-17183-4 ISBN 978-3-030-17184-1 (eBook)
https://doi.org/10.1007/978-3-030-17184-1

Library of Congress Control Number: 2019936299

LNCS Sublibrary: SL1 – Theoretical Computer Science and General Issues

This Springer imprint is published by the registered company Springer Nature Switzerland AG
The registered company address is: Gewerbestrasse 11, 6330 Cham, Switzerland

ETAPS Foreword

Welcome to the 22nd ETAPS! This is the first time that ETAPS took place in the Czech Republic in its beautiful capital Prague.

ETAPS 2019 was the 22nd instance of the European Joint Conferences on Theory and Practice of Software. ETAPS is an annual federated conference established in 1998, and consists of five conferences: ESOP, FASE, FoSSaCS, TACAS, and POST. Each conference has its own Program Committee (PC) and its own Steering Committee (SC). The conferences cover various aspects of software systems, ranging from theoretical computer science to foundations to programming language developments, analysis tools, formal approaches to software engineering, and security.

Organizing these conferences in a coherent, highly synchronized conference program enables participation in an exciting event, offering the possibility to meet many researchers working in different directions in the field and to easily attend talks of different conferences. ETAPS 2019 featured a new program item: the Mentoring Workshop. This workshop is intended to help students early in the program with advice on research, career, and life in the fields of computing that are covered by the ETAPS conference. On the weekend before the main conference, numerous satellite workshops took place and attracted many researchers from all over the globe.

ETAPS 2019 received 436 submissions in total, 137 of which were accepted, yielding an overall acceptance rate of 31.4%. I thank all the authors for their interest in ETAPS, all the reviewers for their reviewing efforts, the PC members for their contributions, and in particular the PC (co-)chairs for their hard work in running this entire intensive process. Last but not least, my congratulations to all authors of the accepted papers!

ETAPS 2019 featured the unifying invited speakers Marsha Chechik (University of Toronto) and Kathleen Fisher (Tufts University) and the conference-specific invited speakers (FoSSaCS) Thomas Colcombet (IRIF, France) and (TACAS) Cormac Flanagan (University of California at Santa Cruz). Invited tutorials were provided by Dirk Beyer (Ludwig Maximilian University) on software verification and Cesare Tinelli (University of Iowa) on SMT and its applications. On behalf of the ETAPS 2019 attendants, I thank all the speakers for their inspiring and interesting talks!

ETAPS 2019 took place in Prague, Czech Republic, and was organized by Charles University. Charles University was founded in 1348 and was the first university in Central Europe. It currently hosts more than 50,000 students. ETAPS 2019 was further supported by the following associations and societies: ETAPS e.V., EATCS (European Association for Theoretical Computer Science), EAPLS (European Association for Programming Languages and Systems), and EASST (European Association of Software Science and Technology). The local organization team consisted of Jan Vitek and Jan Kofron (general chairs), Barbora Buhnova, Milan Ceska, Ryan Culpepper, Vojtech Horky, Paley Li, Petr Maj, Artem Pelenitsyn, and David Safranek.

The ETAPS SC consists of an Executive Board, and representatives of the individual ETAPS conferences, as well as representatives of EATCS, EAPLS, and EASST. The Executive Board consists of Gilles Barthe (Madrid), Holger Hermanns (Saarbrücken), Joost-Pieter Katoen (chair, Aachen and Twente), Gerald Lüttgen (Bamberg), Vladimiro Sassone (Southampton), Tarmo Uustalu (Reykjavik and Tallinn), and Lenore Zuck (Chicago). Other members of the SC are: Wil van der Aalst (Aachen), Dirk Beyer (Munich), Mikolaj Bojanczyk (Warsaw), Armin Biere (Linz), Luis Caires (Lisbon), Jordi Cabot (Barcelona), Jean Goubault-Larrecq (Cachan), Jurriaan Hage (Utrecht), Rainer Hähnle (Darmstadt), Reiko Heckel (Leicester), Panagiotis Katsaros (Thessaloniki), Barbara König (Duisburg), Kim G. Larsen (Aalborg), Matteo Maffei (Vienna), Tiziana Margaria (Limerick), Peter Müller (Zurich), Flemming Nielson (Copenhagen), Catuscia Palamidessi (Palaiseau), Dave Parker (Birmingham), Andrew M. Pitts (Cambridge), Dave Sands (Gothenburg), Don Sannella (Edinburgh), Alex Simpson (Ljubljana), Gabriele Taentzer (Marburg), Peter Thiemann (Freiburg), Jan Vitek (Prague), Tomas Vojnar (Brno), Heike Wehrheim (Paderborn), Anton Wijs (Eindhoven), and Lijun Zhang (Beijing).

I would like to take this opportunity to thank all speakers, attendants, organizers of the satellite workshops, and Springer for their support. I hope you all enjoy the proceedings of ETAPS 2019. Finally, a big thanks to Jan and Jan and their local organization team for all their enormous efforts enabling a fantastic ETAPS in Prague!

February 2019

Joost-Pieter Katoen
ETAPS SC Chair
ETAPS e.V. President

Preface

This volume contains the papers presented at the 28th European Symposium on Programming (ESOP 2019) held April 8–11, 2019, in Prague, Czech Republic. ESOP is one of the European Joint Conferences on Theory and Practice of Software (ETAPS). It is devoted to fundamental issues in the specification, design, analysis, and implementation of programming languages and systems.

The 28 papers in this volume were selected from 86 submissions based on originality and quality. Each submission was reviewed by at least three Program Committee (PC) members and external reviewers, with an average of 3.2 reviews per paper. Authors were given the opportunity to respond to the reviews of their papers during the rebuttal period, January 11–14, 2019.

Each paper was assigned a guardian in the PC, who was in charge of making sure that additional reviews were solicited if necessary, and for presenting a summary of the reviews, author responses, and decision proposals at the physical PC meeting. All submissions, reviews, and author responses were considered during online discussion, which identified 52 submissions to be further discussed at the physical PC meeting held in Cascais, Portugal, January 19, 2019. All non-conflicted PC members participated in the discussion of each paper's merits.

The PC wrote summaries based on online discussions and on discussions during the physical PC meeting, to help authors understand decisions and improve the final version of their papers. Papers co-authored by members of the PC were held to a higher standard and were discussed first at the physical PC meeting. There were 11 such submissions of which five were accepted. Papers for which the PC chair had a conflict of interest were kindly handled by Shao Zhong.

I would like to thank all who contributed to the success of the conference: the authors who submitted papers for consideration, the external reviewers, who provided expert reviews, and the Program Committee, who worked hard to provide detailed reviews, and engaged in deep discussions about the submissions. I am also grateful to have benefited from the experience of past ESOP PC chairs Amal Ahmed and Jan Vitek, and to the ESOP Steering Committee chairs, Giuseppe Castagna and Peter Thiemann, who provided essential advice for numerous procedural issues. I would like also to thank the ETAPS Steering Committee chair, Joost-Pieter Katoen, for his dedicated work and blazing fast responsiveness.

EasyChair was used to handle submissions, online discussions, and proceedings editing. Finally, I would like to thank the NOVA Laboratory for Computer Science and Informatics and OutSystems SA for supporting the physical PC meeting and Joana Dâmaso for assisting with the organization.

February 2019 Luís Caires

Organization

Program Committee

Nada Amin	Ecole Polytechnique Fédérale de Lausanne, Switzerland
Stephanie Balzer	CMU
Lars Birkedal	Aarhus University, Denmark
Johannes Borgström	Uppsala University, Finland
Luís Caires	Universidade NOVA de Lisboa, Portugal
Ugo Dal Lago	Università di Bologna, Italy, and Inria Sophia Antipolis, France
Constantin Enea	IRIF, University Paris Diderot, France
Deepak Garg	Max Planck Institute for Software Systems, Germany
Simon Gay	University of Glasgow, UK
Alexey Gotsman	IMDEA Software Institute, Spain
Atsushi Igarashi	Kyoto University, Japan
Bart Jacobs	Katholieke Universiteit Leuven, Belgium
Isabella Mastroeni	Università di Verona, Italy
J. Garrett Morris	The University of Kansas, USA
Markus Müller-Olm	Westfälische Wilhelms-Universität Münster, Germany
Tim Nelson	Brown University, USA
Scott Owens	University of Kent, UK
Luca Padovani	Università di Torino, Italy
Brigitte Pientka	McGill University, Canada
Zhong Shao	Yale University, USA
Alexandra Silva	University College London, UK
David Walker	Princeton University, USA

Additional Reviewers

Andersen, Kristoffer Just
Asai, Kenichi
Atkey, Robert
Avanzini, Martin
Berger, Martin
Bernardi, Giovanni
Bocchi, Laura
Bracevac, Oliver
Byrd, William
Cano, Mauricio
Cohen, Liron
Contrastin, Mistral
D'Osualdo, Emanuele
Dahlqvist, Fredrik
Delbianco, Germán Andrés
Dezani, Mariangiola
Docherty, Simon
Fellleisen, Mattthias
Frumin, Dan
Fränzle, Martin
Genestier, Guillaume
Ghyselen, Alexis
Gratzer, Daniel
Gregersen, Simon
Gutsfeld, Jens Oliver
Hackett, Jennifer
Hamza, Jad
Heo, Kihong
Hirai, Yoichi

Hirokawa, Nao
Jung, Ralf
Kammar, Ohad
Kappé, Tobias
Katsumata, Shin-Ya
Kenter, Sebastian
Krebbers, Robbert
Kuchen, Herbert
Laird, James
Lammich, Peter
Lanese, Ivan
Levy, Paul Blain
Liu, Fengyun
Mackie, Ian
Martres, Guillaume
Mazza, Damiano
McLaughlin, Craig
Meyer, Roland
Miltner, Anders
Momigliano, Alberto
Mutluergil, Suha Orhun
Nakazawa, Koji
Norman, Gethin
Novotný, Petr
Ohlenbusch, Marit
Ohrem, Christoph
Pavlogiannis, Andreas
Peressotti, Marco
Rogalewicz, Adam
Sacerdoti Coen, Claudio
Sammartino, Matteo
Scalas, Alceste
Sekiyama, Taro
Sieczkowski, Filip
Sighireanu, Mihaela
Singer, Jeremy
Sjöberg, Vilhelm
Staton, Sam
Stiévenart, Quentin
Sutherland, Julian
Tanter, Éric
Tate, Ross
Thibodeau, David
Timany, Amin
Tsukada, Takeshi
Ulbrich, Mattias
Voorneveld, Niels
Wang, Yuting
Weber, Tjark
Yamada, Akihisa
Zdancewic, Steve
Zinkov, Rob

From Quadcopters to Helicopters: Formal Verification to Eliminate Exploitable Bugs (Abstract of Invited Talk)

Kathleen Fisher

Computer Science Department, Tufts University

For decades, formal methods have offered the promise of software that does not have exploitable bugs. Until recently, however, it has not been possible to verify software of sufficient complexity to be useful. Recently, that situation has changed. SeL4 [1] is an open-source operating system microkernel efficient enough to be used in a wide range of practical applications. It has been proven to be fully functionally correct, ensuring the absence of buffer overflows, null pointer exceptions, use-after-free errors, etc., and to enforce integrity and confidentiality properties.

The CompCert Verifying C Compiler [2] maps source C programs to provably equivalent assembly language, ensuring the absence of exploitable bugs in the compiler. A number of factors have enabled this revolution in the formal methods community, including increased processor speed, better infrastructure like the Isabelle/HOL and Coq theorem provers, specialized logics for reasoning about low-level code, increasing levels of automation afforded by tactic languages and SAT/SMT solvers, and the decision to move away from trying to verify existing artifacts and instead focus on co-developing the code and the correctness proof.

In this talk I will explore the promise and limitations of current formal methods techniques for producing useful software that provably does not contain exploitable bugs. I will discuss these issues in the context of DARPA's HACMS program, which had as its goal the creation of high-assurance software for vehicles, including quad-copters, helicopters, and automobiles. This talk summarizes the goals and results of the HACMS program, which are described in more detail in a recent paper written by the speaker and the two other DARPA program managers who oversaw the HACMS program [3].

References

1. Klein, G., et al.: Comprehensive formal verification of an OS microkernel. ACM Trans. Comput. Syst. **32**(1), 2:1–2:70 (2014). http://doi.acm.org/10.1145/2560537

2. Leroy, X.: Formal certification of a compiler back-end or: programming a compiler with a proof assistant. In: Conference Record of the 33rd ACM SIGPLAN-SIGACT Symposium on Principles of Programming Languages, ser. POPL 2006, pp. 42–54. ACM, New York (2006). http://doi.acm.org/10.1145/1111037.1111042
3. Fisher, K., Launchbury, J., Richards, R.: The HACMS program: using formal methods to eliminate exploitable bugs. Philos. Trans. A **375**(2104) (2017). http://rsta.royalsocietypublishing.org/content/375/2104/20150401

Contents

Program Verification

Time Credits and Time Receipts in Iris

Glen Mével[1], Jacques-Henri Jourdan[2(✉)], and François Pottier[1]

[1] Inria, Paris, France
[2] CNRS, LRI, Univ. Paris Sud, Université Paris Saclay, Orsay, France
jacques-henri.jourdan@lri.fr

Abstract. We present a machine-checked extension of the program logic Iris with time credits and time receipts, two dual means of reasoning about time. Whereas time credits are used to establish an upper bound on a program's execution time, time receipts can be used to establish a lower bound. More strikingly, time receipts can be used to prove that certain undesirable events—such as integer overflows—cannot occur until a very long time has elapsed. We present several machine-checked applications of time credits and time receipts, including an application where both concepts are exploited.

"Alice: How long is forever? White Rabbit: Sometimes, just one second."
— Lewis Carroll, *Alice in Wonderland*

1 Introduction

A program logic, such as Hoare logic or Separation Logic, is a set of deduction rules that can be used to reason about the behavior of a program. To this day, considerable effort has been invested in developing ever-more-powerful program logics that control the *extensional* behavior of programs, that is, logics that guarantee that a program safely computes a valid final result. A lesser effort has been devoted to logics that allow reasoning not just about safety and functional correctness, but also about *intensional* aspects of a program's behavior, such as its time consumption and space usage.

In this paper, we are interested in narrowing the gap between these lines of work. We present a formal study of two mechanisms by which a standard program logic can be extended with means of reasoning about time. As a starting point, we take Iris [11–14], a powerful evolution of Concurrent Separation Logic [3]. We extend Iris with two elementary time-related concepts, namely *time credits* [1, 4,9] and *time receipts*.

Time credits and time receipts are independent concepts: it makes sense to extend a program logic with either of them in isolation or with both of them simultaneously. They are dual concepts: every computation step *consumes one time credit* and *produces one time receipt*. They are purely static: they do not exist at runtime. We view them as Iris assertions. Thus, they can appear in the correctness statements that we formulate about programs and in the proofs of these statements.

L. Caires (Ed.): ESOP 2019, LNCS 11423, pp. 3–29, 2019.
https://doi.org/10.1007/978-3-030-17184-1_1

Time credits can be used to establish an upper bound on the execution time of a program. Dually, time receipts can be used to establish a lower bound, and (as explained shortly) can be used to prove that certain undesirable events cannot occur until a very long time has elapsed.

Until now, time credits have been presented as an ad hoc extension of some fixed flavor of Separation Logic [1,4,9]. In contrast, we propose a construction which in principle allows time credits to be introduced on top of an arbitrary "base logic", provided this base logic is a sufficiently rich variety of Separation Logic. In order to make our definitions and proofs more concrete, we use Iris as the base logic. Our construction involves *composing* the base logic with a program transformation that inserts a *tick*() instruction in front of every computation step. As far as a user of the composite logic is concerned, the *tick*() instruction and the assertion \$1, which represents one time credit, are abstract: the only fact to which the user has access is the Hoare triple $\{\$1\}\ \mathit{tick}()\ \{\mathsf{True}\}$, which states that "*tick*() consumes one time credit".

There are two reasons why we choose Iris [12] as the base logic. First, in the proof of soundness of the composite logic, we must exhibit concrete definitions of *tick* and \$1 such that $\{\$1\}\ \mathit{tick}()\ \{\mathsf{True}\}$ holds. Several features of Iris, such as ghost state and shared invariants, play a key role in this construction. Second, at the user level, the power of Iris can also play a crucial role. To illustrate this, we present the first machine-checked reconstruction of Okasaki's debits [19] in terms of time credits. The construction makes crucial use of both time credits and Iris' ghost monotonic state and shared invariants.

Time receipts are a new concept, a contribution of this paper. To extend a base logic with time receipts, we follow the exact same route as above: we compose the base logic with the *same* program transformation as above, which we refer to as "the tick translation". In the eyes of a user of the composite logic, the *tick*() instruction and the assertion ⧗1, which represents one time receipt, are again abstract: this time, the only published fact about *tick* is the triple $\{\mathsf{True}\}\ \mathit{tick}()\ \{⧗1\}$, which states that "*tick*() produces one time receipt".

Thus far, the symmetry between time credits and time receipts seems perfect: whereas time credits allow establishing an upper bound on the cost of a program fragment, time receipts allow establishing a lower bound. This raises a pragmatic question, though: why invest effort, time and money into a formal proof that a piece of code is slow? What might be the point of such an endeavor? Taking inspiration from Clochard *et al.* [5], we answer this question by turning slowness into a quality. If there is a certain point at which a process might fail, then by showing that this process is slow, we can show that failure is far away into the future. More specifically, Clochard *et al.* propose two abstract types of integer counters, dubbed "one-time" integers and "peano" integers, and provide a paper proof that these counters cannot overflow in a feasible time: that is, it would take infeasible time (say, centuries) for an execution to reach a point where overflow actually occurs. To reflect this idea, we abandon the symmetry between time credits and time receipts and publish a fact about time receipts which has no counterpart on the time-credit side. This fact is an implication: $⧗N \Rrightarrow_{\top} \mathsf{False}$, that is, "$N$ time receipts imply False". The global parameter N can be adjusted so as to represent one's idea of a running time that is infeasible, perhaps due to physical limitations, perhaps due to assumptions about the conditions in which the software is operated. In this paper, we explain what it means for the composite program logic to remain sound in the presence of this axiom, and provide a formal proof that Iris, extended with time receipts, is indeed sound. Furthermore, we verify that Clochard *et al.*'s ad hoc concepts of "one-time" integers and "peano" integers can be reconstructed in terms of time receipts, a more fundamental concept.

Finally, to demonstrate the combined use of time credits and receipts, we present a proof of the Union-Find data structure, where credits are used to express an amortized time complexity bound and receipts are used to prove that a node's integer rank cannot overflow, even if it is stored in very few bits.

In summary, the contributions of this paper are as follows:

1. A way of extending an off-the-shelf program logic with time credits and/or receipts, by composition with a program transformation.
2. Extensions of Iris with time credits and receipts, accompanied with machine-checked proofs of soundness.
3. A machine-checked reconstruction of Okasaki's debits as a library in Iris with time credits.
4. A machine-checked reconstruction of Clochard *et al.*'s "one-time" integers and "peano" integers in Iris with time receipts.
5. A machine-checked verification of Union-Find in Iris with time credits and receipts, offering both an amortized complexity bound and a safety guarantee despite the use of machine integers of very limited width.

All of the results reported in this paper have been checked in Coq [17].

2 A User's Overview of Time Credits and Time Receipts

2.1 Time Credits

A small number of axioms, presented in Fig. 1, govern time credits. The assertion $\$n$ denotes n time credits. The splitting axiom, a logical equivalence, means that *time credits can be split and combined.* Because Iris is an affine logic, it is implicitly understood that *time credits cannot be duplicated, but can be thrown away.*

The axiom timeless($\$n$) means that time credits are independent of Iris' step-indexing. In practice, this allows an Iris invariant that involves time credits to be acquired without causing a "later" modality to appear [12, §5.7]. The reader can safely ignore this detail.

The last axiom, a Hoare triple, means that *every computation step requires and consumes one time credit.* As in Iris, the postconditions of our Hoare triples are λ-abstractions: they take as a parameter the return value of the term. At this point, *tick* () can be thought of as a pseudo-instruction that has no runtime effect and is implicitly inserted in front of every computation step.

$\$: \mathbb{N} \to \mathit{iProp}$	— there is such a thing as "n time credits"
$\mathsf{timeless}(\$n)$	— an Iris technicality
$\mathsf{True} \Rrightarrow_{\top} \$0$	— zero credits can be created out of thin air
$\$(n_1 + n_2) \equiv \$n_1 \ast \$n_2$	— credits can be split and combined
$\mathit{tick} : \mathit{Val}$	— there is a *tick* pseudo-op
$\{\$1\}\ \mathit{tick}\ (v)\ \{\lambda w.\, w = v\}$	— *tick* consumes one credit

Fig. 1. The axiomatic interface *TCIntf* of time credits

$\text{⧗} : \mathbb{N} \to \mathit{iProp}$	— there is such a thing as "n time receipts"
$\mathsf{timeless}(\text{⧗}\, n)$	— an Iris technicality
$\mathsf{True} \Rrightarrow_{\top} \text{⧗}\, 0$	— zero receipts can be created out of thin air
$\text{⧗}(n_1 + n_2) \equiv \text{⧗}\, n_1 \ast \text{⧗}\, n_2$	— receipts can be split and combined
$\mathit{tick} : \mathit{Val}$	— there is a *tick* pseudo-op
$\{\mathsf{True}\}\ \mathit{tick}\ (v)\ \{\lambda w.\, w = v \ast \text{⧗}\, 1\}$	— *tick* produces one receipt
$\text{⧗}\, N \Rrightarrow_{\top} \mathsf{False}$	— no machine runs for N time steps

Fig. 2. The axiomatic interface of exclusive time receipts (further enriched in Fig. 3)

Time credits can be used to express *worst-case time complexity guarantees.* For instance, a sorting algorithm could have the following specification:

$$\begin{gathered}\{\mathit{array}(a, xs) \ast n = |xs| \ast \$(6n \log n)\} \\ \mathit{sort}(a) \\ \{\mathit{array}(a, xs') \wedge xs' = \ldots\}\end{gathered}$$

Here, $\mathit{array}(a, xs)$ asserts the existence and unique ownership of an array at address a, holding the sequence of elements xs. This Hoare triple guarantees not only that the function call $\mathit{sort}(a)$ runs safely and has the effect of sorting the array at address a, but also that $\mathit{sort}(a)$ runs in at most $6n \log n$ time steps, where n is the length of the sequence xs, that is, the length of the array. Indeed, only $6n \log n$ time credits are provided in the precondition, so the algorithm does not have permission to run for a greater number of steps.

2.2 Time Receipts

In contrast with time credits, time receipts are a new concept, a contribution of this paper. We distinguish two forms of time receipts. The most basic form, *exclusive time receipts*, is the dual of time credits, in the sense that *every computation step produces one time receipt.* The second form, *persistent time receipts*, exhibits slightly different properties. Inspired by Clochard *et al.* [5], we show that time receipts can be used to *prove that certain undesirable events, such as integer overflows, cannot occur unless a program is allowed to execute for a very, very long time*—typically centuries. In the following, we explain that exclusive time receipts allow reconstructing Clochard *et al.*'s "one-time" integers [5, §3.2], which are so named because they are not duplicable, whereas persistent time receipts allow reconstructing their "peano" integers [5, §3.2], which are so named because they do not support unrestricted addition.

Exclusive time receipts. The assertion ⧗n denotes n time receipts. Like time credits, these time receipts are "exclusive", by which we mean that they are not duplicable. The basic laws that govern exclusive time receipts appear in Fig. 2. They are the same laws that govern time credits, with two differences. The first difference is that time receipts are the dual of time credits: the specification of *tick*, in this case, states that *every computation step produces one time receipt.*[1] The second difference lies in the last axiom of Fig. 2, which has no analogue in Fig. 1, and which we explain below.

In practice, how do we expect time receipts to be exploited? They can be used to prove lower bounds on the execution time of a program: if the Hoare triple $\{\mathsf{True}\}\ p\ \{⧗ n\}$ holds, then the execution of the program p cannot terminate in less than n steps. Inspired by Clochard *et al.* [5], we note that time receipts can also be used to *prove that certain undesirable events cannot occur in a feasible time.* This is done as follows. Let N be a fixed integer, chosen large enough that a modern processor cannot possibly execute N operations in a feasible time.[2] The last axiom of Fig. 2, $⧗ N \Rrightarrow_\top \mathsf{False}$, states that N time receipts imply a contradiction.[3] This axiom informally means that *we won't compute for N time steps*, because we cannot, or because we promise not to do such a thing. A consequence of this axiom is that ⧗n implies $n < N$: that is, *if we have observed n time steps, then n must be small.*

Adopting this axiom weakens the guarantee offered by the program logic. A Hoare triple $\{\mathsf{True}\}\ p\ \{\mathsf{True}\}$ no longer implies that the program p is forever safe. Instead, it means that p is $(N-1)$-safe: the execution of p cannot go wrong until at least $N-1$ steps have been taken. Because N is very large, for many practical purposes, this is good enough.

How can this axiom be exploited in practice? We hinted above that it can be used to prove the absence of certain integer overflows. Suppose that we wish to use signed w-bit machine integers as a representation of mathematical integers. (For instance, let w be 64.) Whenever we perform an arithmetic operation, such as an addition, we must prove that no overflow can occur. This is reflected in the specification of the addition of two machine integers:

$$\begin{array}{c}\{\iota(x_1) = n_1 \ *\ \iota(x_2) = n_2 \ *\ -2^{w-1} \leq n_1 + n_2 < 2^{w-1}\} \\ add(x_1, x_2) \\ \{\lambda x.\, \iota(x) = n_1 + n_2\}\end{array}$$

Here, the variables x_i denote machine integers, while the auxiliary variables n_i denote mathematical integers, and the function ι is the injection of machine integers into mathematical integers. The conjunct $-2^{w-1} \leq n_1 + n_2 < 2^{w-1}$ in the precondition represents an obligation to prove that no overflow can occur.

[1] For now, we discuss time credits and time receipts separately, which is why we have different specifications for *tick* in either case. They are combined in Sect. 6.

[2] For a specific example, let N be 2^{63}. Clochard *et al.* note that, even at the rate of one billion operations per second, it takes more than 292 years to execute 2^{63} operations. On a 64-bit machine, 2^{63} is also the maximum representable signed integer, plus one.

[3] The connective $\Rrightarrow_\top$ is an Iris view shift, that is, a transition that can involve a side effect on ghost state.

Suppose now that the machine integers x_1 and x_2 represent the lengths of two disjoint linked lists that we wish to concatenate. To construct each of these lists, we must have spent a certain amount of time: as proofs of this work, let us assume that the assertions $\blacktriangleleft n_1$ and $\blacktriangleleft n_2$ are at hand. Let us further assume that the word size w is sufficiently large that it takes a very long time to count up to the largest machine integer. That is, let us make the following assumption:

$$N \leq 2^{w-1} \qquad \text{(large word size assumption)}$$

(E.g., with $N = 2^{63}$ and $w = 64$, this holds.) Then, we can prove that the addition of x_1 and x_2 is permitted. This goes as follows. From the separating conjunction $\blacktriangleleft n_1 * \blacktriangleleft n_2$, we get $\blacktriangleleft(n_1 + n_2)$. The existence of these time receipts allows us to deduce $0 \leq n_1 + n_2 < N$, which implies $0 \leq n_1 + n_2 < 2^{w-1}$. Thus, the precondition of the addition operation $add(x_1, x_2)$ is met.

In summary, we have just verified that the addition of two machine integers satisfies the following alternative specification:

$$\begin{array}{c} \{\iota(x_1) = n_1 * \blacktriangleleft n_1 * \iota(x_2) = n_2 * \blacktriangleleft n_2\} \\ add(x_1, x_2) \\ \{\lambda x.\, \iota(x) = n_1 + n_2 * \blacktriangleleft(n_1 + n_2)\} \end{array}$$

This can be made more readable and more abstract by defining a "clock" to be a machine integer x accompanied with $\iota(x)$ time receipts:

$$clock(x) \triangleq \exists n.(\iota(x) = n * \blacktriangleleft n)$$

Then, the above specification of addition can be reformulated as follows:

$$\begin{array}{c} \{clock(x_1) * clock(x_2)\} \\ add(x_1, x_2) \\ \{\lambda x.\, clock(x) * \iota(x) = \iota(x_1) + \iota(x_2)\} \end{array}$$

In other words, clocks support unrestricted addition, without any risk of overflow. However, because time receipts cannot be duplicated, neither can clocks: $clock(x)$ does not entail $clock(x) * clock(x)$. In other words, a clock is uniquely owned. One can think of a clock x as a *hard-earned integer*: the owner of this clock has spent x units of time to obtain it.

Clocks are a reconstruction of Clochard *et al.*'s "one-time integers" [5], which support unrestricted addition, but cannot be duplicated. Whereas Clochard *et al.* view one-time integers as a primitive concept, and offer a direct paper proof of their soundness, we have just reconstructed them in terms of a more elementary notion, namely time receipts, and in the setting of a more powerful program logic, whose soundness is machine-checked, namely Iris.

Persistent time receipts. In addition to exclusive time receipts, it is useful to introduce a persistent form of time receipts.[4] The axioms that govern both exclusive and persistent time receipts appear in Fig. 3.

[4] Instead of viewing persistent time receipts as a primitive concept, one could define them as a library on top of exclusive time receipts. Unfortunately, this construction leads to slightly weaker laws, which is why we prefer to view them as primitive.

$⧗ : \mathbb{N} \rightarrow iProp$	— there is such a thing as "n exclusive time receipts"
$⧖ : \mathbb{N} \rightarrow iProp$	— and "a persistent receipt for n steps"
$\mathsf{timeless}(⧗ n) \wedge \mathsf{timeless}(⧖ n)$	— an Iris technicality
$\mathsf{persistent}(⧖ n)$	— persistent receipts are persistent
$\mathsf{True} \Rrightarrow_{\top} ⧗ 0$	— zero receipts can be created out of thin air
$⧗(n_1 + n_2) \equiv ⧗ n_1 \ast ⧗ n_2$	— exclusive receipts obey addition
$⧖ \max(n_1, n_2) \equiv ⧖ n_1 \ast ⧖ n_2$	— persistent receipts obey maximum
$⧗ n \Rrightarrow_{\top} ⧗ n \ast ⧖ n$	— taking a snapshot of n exclusive receipts yields a persistent receipt for n steps
$⧖ N \Rrightarrow_{\top} \mathsf{False}$	— no machine runs for N time steps
$tick : Val$	— there is a *tick* pseudo-op
$\{⧖ n\}$ $tick\ (v)$ $\{\lambda w.\, w = v \ast ⧗ 1 \ast ⧖(n+1)\}$	— *tick* produces one exclusive receipt, and can increment an existing persistent receipt

Fig. 3. The axiomatic interface *TRIntf* of time receipts

We write $⧖ n$ for a persistent receipt, a witness that at least n units of time have elapsed. (We avoid the terminology "n persistent time receipts", in the plural form, because persistent time receipts are not additive. We view $⧖ n$ as one receipt whose face value is n.) This assertion is persistent, which in Iris terminology means that once it holds, it holds forever. This implies, in particular, that it is duplicable: $⧖ n \equiv ⧖ n \ast ⧖ n$. It is created just by observing the existence of n exclusive time receipts, as stated by the following axiom, also listed in Fig. 3: $⧗ n \Rrightarrow_{\top} ⧗ n \ast ⧖ n$. Intuitively, someone who has access to the assertion $⧖ n$ is someone who knows that n units of work have been performed, even though they have not necessarily "personally" performed that work. Because this knowledge is not exclusive, the conjunction $⧖ n_1 \ast ⧖ n_2$ does not entail $⧖(n_1 + n_2)$. Instead, we have the following axiom, also listed in Fig. 3: $⧖(\max(n_1, n_2)) \equiv ⧖ n_1 \ast ⧖ n_2$.

More subtly, the specification of *tick* in Fig. 3 is stronger than the one in Fig. 2. According to this strengthened specification, *tick* () does not just produce an exclusive receipt $⧗ 1$. In addition to that, if a persistent time receipt $⧖ n$ is at hand, then *tick* () is able to increment it and to produce a new persistent receipt $⧖(n+1)$, thus reflecting the informal idea that a *new* unit of time has just been spent. A user who does not wish to make use of this feature can pick $n = 0$ and recover the specification of *tick* in Fig. 2 as a special case.

Finally, because $⧖ n$ means that n steps have been taken, and because we promise never to reach N steps, we adopt the axiom $⧖ N \Rrightarrow_{\top} \mathsf{False}$, also listed in Fig. 3. It implies the earlier axiom $⧗ N \Rrightarrow_{\top} \mathsf{False}$, which is therefore not explicitly shown in Fig. 3.

In practice, how are persistent time receipts exploited? By analogy with clocks, let us define a predicate for a machine integer x accompanied with $\iota(x)$ persistent time receipts:

$$snapclock(x) \triangleq \exists n.(\iota(x) = n \ast ⧖ n)$$

By construction, this predicate is persistent, therefore duplicable:

$$\mathit{snapclock}(x) \equiv \mathit{snapclock}(x) \ * \ \mathit{snapclock}(x)$$

We refer to this concept as a "snapclock", as it is not a clock, but can be thought of as a snapshot of some clock. Thanks to the axiom $⧗ k \Rrightarrow_{\top} ⧗ k \ * \ ⧖ k$, we have:

$$\mathit{clock}(x) \Rrightarrow_{\top} \mathit{clock}(x) \ * \ \mathit{snapclock}(x)$$

Furthermore, snapclocks have the valuable property that, by performing just one step of extra work, a snapclock can be incremented, yielding a new snapclock that is greater by one. That is, the following Hoare triple holds:

$$\begin{array}{c}\{\mathit{snapclock}(x)\} \\ \mathit{tick}\ (); \mathit{add}(x, 1) \\ \{\lambda x'.\ \mathit{snapclock}(x') \ * \ \iota(x') = \iota(x) + 1\}\end{array}$$

The proof is not difficult. Unfolding $\mathit{snapclock}(x)$ in the precondition yields $⧖ n$, where $\iota(x) = n$. As per the strengthened specification of *tick*, the execution of *tick* () then yields $⧗ 1 \ * \ ⧖(n+1)$. As in the case of clocks, the assertion $⧖(n+1)$ implies $0 \leq n+1 < 2^{w-1}$, which means that no overflow can occur. Finally, $⧗ 1$ is thrown away and $⧖(n+1)$ is used to justify $\mathit{snapclock}(x')$ in the postcondition.

Adding two arbitrary snapclocks x_1 and x_2 is illegal: from the sole assumption $\mathit{snapclock}(x_1) \ * \ \mathit{snapclock}(x_2)$, one cannot prove that the addition of x_1 and x_2 won't cause an overflow, and one cannot prove that its result is a valid snapclock. However, snapclocks do support a restricted form of addition. The addition of two snapclocks x_1 and x_2 is safe, and produces a valid snapclock x, provided it is known ahead of time that its result is less than some preexisting snapclock y:

$$\begin{array}{c}\{\mathit{snapclock}(x_1) \ * \ \mathit{snapclock}(x_2) \ * \ \iota(x_1 + x_2) \leq \iota(y) \ * \ \mathit{snapclock}(y)\} \\ \mathit{add}(x_1, x_2) \\ \{\lambda x.\ \mathit{snapclock}(x) \ * \ \iota(x) = \iota(x_1) + \iota(x_2)\}\end{array}$$

Snapclocks are a reconstruction of Clochard *et al.*'s "peano integers" [5], which are so named because they do not support unrestricted addition. Clocks and snapclocks represent different compromises: whereas clocks support addition but not duplication, snapclocks support duplication but not addition. They are useful in different scenarios: as a rule of thumb, if an integer counter is involved in the implementation of a mutable data structure, then one should attempt to view it as a clock; if it is involved in the implementation of a persistent data structure, then one should attempt to view it as a snapclock.

3 HeapLang and the Tick Translation

In the next section (Sect. 4), we extend Iris with time credits, yielding a new program logic Iris$^{\$}$. We do this *without modifying* Iris. Instead, we *compose* Iris with a program transformation, the "tick translation", which inserts *tick*()

instructions into the code in front of every computation step. In the construction of Iris$^{⧗}$, our extension of Iris with time receipts, the tick translation is exploited in a similar way (Sect. 5). In this section, we define the tick translation and state some of its properties.

Iris is a generic program logic: it can be instantiated with an arbitrary calculus for which a small-step operational semantics is available [12]. Ideally, our extension of Iris should take place at this generic level, so that it, too, can be instantiated for an arbitrary calculus. Unfortunately, it seems difficult to define the tick translation and to prove it correct in a generic manner. For this reason, we choose to work in the setting of HeapLang [12], an untyped λ-calculus equipped with Booleans, signed machine integers, products, sums, recursive functions, references, and shared-memory concurrency. The three standard operations on mutable references, namely allocation, reading, and writing, are available. A compare-and-set operation $\texttt{CAS}\,(e_1, e_2, e_3)$ and an operation for spawning a new thread are also provided. As the syntax and operational semantics of HeapLang are standard and very much irrelevant in this paper, we omit them. They appear in our online repository [17].

The tick translation transforms a HeapLang expression e to a HeapLang expression $\langle\!\langle e \rangle\!\rangle_{tick}$. It is parameterized by a value *tick*. Its effect is to insert a call to *tick* in front of every operation in the source expression e. The translation of a function application, for instance, is as follows:

$$\langle\!\langle e_1\,(e_2) \rangle\!\rangle_{tick} = tick\,(\langle\!\langle e_1 \rangle\!\rangle_{tick})\,(\langle\!\langle e_2 \rangle\!\rangle_{tick})$$

For convenience, we assume that *tick* can be passed an arbitrary value v as an argument, and returns v. Because evaluation in HeapLang is call-by-value and happens to be right-to-left[5], the above definition means that, after evaluating the argument $\langle\!\langle e_2 \rangle\!\rangle_{tick}$ and the function $\langle\!\langle e_1 \rangle\!\rangle_{tick}$, we invoke *tick*, then carry on with the function call. This translation is syntactically well-behaved: it preserves the property of being a value, and commutes with substitution. This holds for every value *tick*.

$$\begin{aligned} tick_c \triangleq\ & \mathbf{rec}\ self\,(x) = \\ & \quad \mathbf{let}\ k = {!}\,c\ \mathbf{in} \\ & \quad \mathbf{if}\ k = 0\ \mathbf{then}\ oops\,() \\ & \quad \mathbf{else\ if}\ \mathbf{CAS}(c, k, k-1)\ \mathbf{then}\ x\ \mathbf{else}\ self\,(x) \end{aligned}$$

Fig. 4. Implementation of $tick_c$ in HeapLang

As far the end user is concerned, *tick* remains abstract (Sect. 2). Yet, in our constructions of Iris$^{\$}$ and Iris$^{⧗}$, we must provide a concrete implementation of it in HeapLang. This implementation, named $tick_c$, appears in Fig. 4. A global

[5] If HeapLang used left-to-right evaluation, the definition of the translation would be slightly different, but the lemmas that we prove would be the same.

integer counter c stores the number of computation steps that the program is still allowed to take. The call $tick_c\ ()$ decrements a global counter c, if this counter holds a nonzero value, and otherwise invokes *oops* ().

At this point, the memory location c and the value *oops* are parameters.

We stress that $tick_c$ plays a role only in the proofs of soundness of Iris$^{\$}$ and Iris$^{⧗}$. It is never actually executed, nor is it shown to the end user.

Once *tick* is instantiated with $tick_c$, one can prove that the translation is correct in the following sense: the translated code takes the same computation steps as the source code and additionally keeps track of how many steps are taken. More specifically, if the source code can make n computation steps, and if c is initialized with a value m that is sufficiently large (that is, $m \geq n$), then the translated code can make n computation steps as well, and c is decremented from m to $m - n$ in the process.

Lemma 1 (Reduction Preservation). *Assume there is a reduction sequence:*

$$(T_1, \sigma_1) \rightarrow^n_{\mathsf{tp}} (T_2, \sigma_2)$$

Assume c is fresh for this reduction sequence. Let $m \geq n$. Then, there exists a reduction sequence:

$$(\langle\!\langle T_1 \rangle\!\rangle, \langle\!\langle \sigma_1 \rangle\!\rangle\, [c \leftarrow m]) \rightarrow^*_{\mathsf{tp}} (\langle\!\langle T_2 \rangle\!\rangle, \langle\!\langle \sigma_2 \rangle\!\rangle\, [c \leftarrow m - n])$$

In this statement, the metavariable T stands for a thread pool, while σ stands for a heap. The relation $\rightarrow_{\mathsf{tp}}$ is HeapLang's "threadpool reduction". For the sake of brevity, we write just $\langle\!\langle e \rangle\!\rangle$ for $\langle\!\langle e \rangle\!\rangle_{tick_c}$, that is, for the translation of the expression e, where *tick* is instantiated with $tick_c$. This notation is implicitly dependent on the parameters c and *oops*.

The above lemma holds for every choice of *oops*. Indeed, because the counter c initially holds the value m, and because we have $m \geq n$, the counter is never about to fall below zero, so *oops* is never invoked.

The next lemma also holds for every choice of *oops*. It states that if the translated program is safe and if the counter c has not yet reached zero then the source program is not just about to crash.

Lemma 2 (Immediate Safety Preservation). *Assume c is fresh for e. Let $m > 0$. If the configuration $(\langle\!\langle e \rangle\!\rangle, \langle\!\langle \sigma \rangle\!\rangle\, [c \leftarrow m])$ is safe, then either e is a value or the configuration (e, σ) is reducible.*

By combining Lemmas 1 and 2 and by contraposition, we find that safety is preserved backwards, as follows: if, when the counter c is initialized with m, the translated program $\langle\!\langle e \rangle\!\rangle$ is safe, then the source program e is m-safe.

Lemma 3 (Safety Preservation). *If for every location c the configuration $(\langle\!\langle T \rangle\!\rangle, \langle\!\langle \sigma \rangle\!\rangle\, [c \leftarrow m])$ is safe, then the configuration (T, σ) is m-safe.*

4 Iris with Time Credits

The authors of Iris [12] have used Coq both to check that Iris is sound and to offer an implementation of Iris that can be used to carry out proofs of programs. The two are tied: if $\{\mathsf{True}\}\ p\ \{\mathsf{True}\}$ can be established by applying the proof rules of Iris, then one gets a self-contained Coq proof that the program p is safe.

In this section, we temporarily focus on time credits and explain how we extend Iris with time credits, yielding a new program logic Iris$^\$$. The new logic is defined in Coq and still offers an end-to-end guarantee: if $\{\$k\}\ p\ \{\mathsf{True}\}$ can be established in Coq by applying the proof rules of Iris$^\$$, then one has proved in Coq that p is safe and runs in at most k steps.

To define Iris$^\$$, we compose Iris with the tick translation. We are then able to argue that, because this program transformation is operationally correct (that is, it faithfully accounts for the passing of time), and because Iris is sound (that is, it faithfully approximates the behavior of programs), the result of the composition is a sound program logic that is able to reason about time.

In the following, we view the interface *TCIntf* as explicitly parameterized over \$ and *tick*. Thus, we write "*TCIntf* (\$) *tick*" for the separating conjunction of all items in Fig. 1 except the declarations of \$ and *tick*.

We require the end user, who wishes to perform proofs of programs in Iris$^\$$, to work with Iris$^\$$ triples, which are defined as follows:

Definition 1 (Iris$^\$$ triple). *An* Iris$^\$$ triple $\{P\}\ e\ \{\Phi\}_\$$ *is syntactic sugar for:*

$$\forall(\$: \mathbb{N} \to \mathit{iProp}) \quad \forall \mathit{tick} \qquad \mathit{TCIntf}\ (\$)\ \mathit{tick} \;\;-\!\!*\;\; \{P\}\ \langle\!\langle e \rangle\!\rangle_{\mathit{tick}}\ \{\Phi\}$$

Thus, an Iris$^\$$ triple is in reality an Iris triple about the instrumented expression $\langle\!\langle e \rangle\!\rangle_{\mathit{tick}}$. While proving this Iris triple, the end user is given an abstract view of the predicate \$ and the instruction *tick*. He does not have access to their concrete definitions, but does have access to the laws that govern them.

We prove that Iris$^\$$ is sound in the following sense:

Theorem 1 (Soundness of Iris$^\$$). *If* $\{\$n\}\ e\ \{\mathsf{True}\}_\$$ *holds, then the machine configuration* $(e, \varnothing)$*, where* $\varnothing$ *is the empty heap, is safe and terminates in at most* n *steps.*

In other words, a program that is initially granted n time credits cannot run for more than n steps. To establish this theorem, we proceed roughly as follows:

1. we provide a concrete definition of *tick*;
2. we provide a concrete definition of \$ and prove that *TCIntf* (\$) *tick* holds;
3. this yields $\{\$n\}\ \langle\!\langle e \rangle\!\rangle_{\mathit{tick}}\ \{\mathsf{True}\}$; from this and from the correctness of the tick translation, we deduce that e cannot crash or run for more than n steps.

Step 1. Our first step is to provide an implementation of *tick*. As announced earlier (Sect. 3), we use tick_c (Fig. 4). We instantiate the parameter *oops* with *crash*, an arbitrary function whose application is unsafe. (That is, *crash* is chosen so that *crash* () reduces to a stuck term.) For the moment, c remains a parameter.

With these concrete choices of *tick* and *oops*, the translation transforms an out-of-time-budget condition into a hard crash. Because Iris forbids crashes, Iris$^\$$, which is the composition of the translation with Iris, will forbid out-of-time-budget conditions, as desired.

For technical reasons, we need two more lemmas about the translation, whose proofs rely on the fact that *oops* is instantiated with *crash*. They are slightly modified or strengthened variants of Lemmas 2 and 3. First, if the source code can take one step, then the translated code, supplied with zero budget, crashes. Second, if the translated code, supplied with a runtime budget of m, does *not* crash, then the source code terminates in at most m steps.

Lemma 4 (Credit Exhaustion). *Suppose the configuration* (T, σ) *is reducible. Then, for all c, the configuration* $(\langle\!\langle T\rangle\!\rangle, \langle\!\langle \sigma\rangle\!\rangle\,[c \leftarrow 0])$ *is unsafe.*

Lemma 5 (Safety Preservation, Strengthened). *If for every location c the configuration* $(\langle\!\langle T\rangle\!\rangle, \langle\!\langle \sigma\rangle\!\rangle\,[c \leftarrow m])$ *is safe, then* (T, σ) *is safe and terminates in at most m steps.*

Step 2. Our second step, roughly, is to exhibit a definition of $\$: \mathbb{N} \rightarrow \mathit{iProp}$ such that $\mathit{TCIntf}\ (\$)\ \mathit{tick}_c$ is satisfied. That is, we would like to prove something along the lines of: $\exists(\$: \mathbb{N} \rightarrow \mathit{iProp})\quad \mathit{TCIntf}\ (\$)\ \mathit{tick}_c$. However, these informal sentences do not quite make sense. This formula is not an ordinary proposition: it is an Iris assertion, of type *iProp*. Thus, it does not make sense to say that this formula "is true" in an absolute manner. Instead, we prove in Iris that we can *make this assertion true* by performing a view shift, that is, a number of operations that have no runtime effect, such as allocating a ghost location and imposing an invariant that ties this ghost state with the physical state of the counter c. This is stated as follows:

Lemma 6 (Time Credit Initialization). *For every c and n, the following Iris view shift holds:*

$$(c \mapsto n) \quad \Rrightarrow_\top \quad \exists(\$: \mathbb{N} \rightarrow \mathit{iProp}) \quad (\mathit{TCIntf}\ (\$)\ \mathit{tick}_c \ \ast\ \$n)$$

In this statement, on the left-hand side of the view shift symbol, we find the "points-to" assertion $c \mapsto n$, which represents the unique ownership of the memory location c and the assumption that its initial value is n. This assertion no longer appears on the right-hand side of the view shift. This reflects the fact that, when the view shift takes place, it becomes impossible to access c directly; the only way of accessing it is via the operation tick_c.

On the right-hand side of the view shift symbol, beyond the existential quantifier, we find a conjunction of the assertion $\mathit{TCIntf}\ (\$)\ \mathit{tick}_c$, which means that the laws of time credits are satisfied, and $\$n$, which means that there are initially n time credits in existence.

In the interest of space, we provide only a brief summary of the proof of Lemma 6; the reader is referred to the extended version of this paper [18, Appendix A] for more details. In short, the assertion $\$1$ is defined in such a way that it represents an exclusive contribution of one unit to the current value of the global counter c. In other words, we install the following invariant: at every time, the current value of c is (at least) the sum of all time credits in existence. Thus, the assertion $\$1$ guarantees that c is nonzero, and can be viewed as a permission to decrement c by one. This allows us to prove that the specification of *tick* in Fig. 1 is satisfied by our concrete implementation $tick_c$. In particular, $tick_c$ cannot cause a crash: indeed, under the precondition $\$1$, c is not in danger of falling below zero, and *crash* () is not executed—it is in fact dead code.

Step 3. In the last reasoning step, we complete the proof of Theorem 1. The proof is roughly as follows. Suppose the end user has established $\{\$n\}\, e\, \{\mathsf{True}\}_{\$}$. By Safety Preservation, Strengthened (Lemma 5), to prove that $(e, \varnothing)$ is safe and runs in at most n steps, it suffices to show (for an arbitrary location c) that the translated expression $\langle\!\langle e \rangle\!\rangle$, executed in the initial heap $\varnothing\,[c \leftarrow n]$, is safe. To do so, beginning with this initial heap, we perform Time Credit Initialization, that is, we execute the view shift whose statement appears in Lemma 6. This yields an abstract predicate $\$$ as well as the assertions *TCIntf* ($) *tick* and $\$n$. At this point, we unfold the Iris$^{\$}$ triple $\{\$n\}\, e\, \{\mathsf{True}\}_{\$}$, yielding an implication (see Definition 1), and apply it to $, to $tick_c$, and to the hypothesis *TCIntf* ($) *tick*. This yields the Iris triple $\{\$n\}\ \langle\!\langle e \rangle\!\rangle\ \{\mathsf{True}\}$. Because we have $\$n$ at hand and because Iris is sound [12], this implies that $\langle\!\langle e \rangle\!\rangle$ is safe. This concludes the proof.

This last step is, we believe, where the modularity of our approach shines. Iris' soundness theorem is re-used as a black box, without change. In fact, any program logic other than Iris could be used as a basis for our construction, as along as it is expressive enough to prove Time Credit Initialization (Lemma 6). The last ingredient, Safety Preservation, Strengthened (Lemma 5), involves only the operational semantics of HeapLang, and is independent of Iris.

This was just an informal account of our proof. For further details, the reader is referred to the online repository [17].

5 Iris with Time Receipts

In this section, we extend Iris with time receipts and prove the soundness of the new logic, dubbed Iris$^{⧗}$. To do so, we follow the scheme established in the previous section (Sect. 4), and compose Iris with the tick translation.

From here on, let us view the interface of time receipts as parameterized over ⧗, ⧖, and *tick*. Thus, we write "*TRIntf* (⧗) (⧖) *tick*" for the separating conjunction of all items in Fig. 3 except the declarations of ⧗, ⧖, and *tick*.

As in the case of credits, the user is given an abstract view of time receipts:

Definition 2 (Iris$^{⧗}$ triple). *An* Iris$^{⧗}$ triple $\{P\}\, e\, \{\Phi\}_{⧗}$ *is syntactic sugar for:*

$$\forall (⧗, ⧖ : \mathbb{N} \rightarrow iProp) \quad \forall tick \qquad TRIntf\ (⧗)\ (⧖)\ tick \ \ -\!\!* \ \ \{P\}\ \langle\!\langle e \rangle\!\rangle_{tick}\ \{\Phi\}$$

Theorem 2 (Soundness of Iris$^{⧗}$). *If* $\{\mathsf{True}\}\, e\, \{\mathsf{True}\}_{⧗}$ *holds, then the machine configuration* $(e, \varnothing)$ *is* $(N-1)$*-safe.*

As indicated earlier, we assume that the end user is interested in proving that crashes cannot occur until a very long time has elapsed, which is why we state the theorem in this way.[6] Whereas an Iris triple $\{\mathsf{True}\}\, e\, \{\mathsf{True}\}$ guarantees that e is safe, the Iris$^{⧗}$ triple $\{\mathsf{True}\}\, e\, \{\mathsf{True}\}_{⧗}$ guarantees that it takes at least $N-1$ steps of computation for e to crash. In this statement, N is the global parameter that appears in the axiom $⧖ N \Rrightarrow_{\top} \mathsf{False}$ (Fig. 3). Compared with Iris, Iris$^{⧗}$ provides a weaker safety guarantee, but offers additional reasoning principles, leading to increased convenience and modularity.

In order to establish Theorem 2, we again proceed in three steps:

1. provide a concrete definition of *tick*;
2. provide concrete definitions of $⧗, ⧖$ and prove that $\mathit{TRIntf}\ (⧗)\ (⧖)\ \mathit{tick}$ holds;
3. from $\{\mathsf{True}\}\, \langle\!\langle e \rangle\!\rangle_{\mathit{tick}}\, \{\mathsf{True}\}$, deduce that e is $(N-1)$-safe.

Step 1. In this step, we keep our concrete implementation of *tick*, namely tick_c (Fig. 4). One difference with the case of time credits, though, is that we plan to initialize c with $N-1$. Another difference is that, this time, we instantiate the parameter *oops* with *loop*, where *loop* () is an arbitrary divergent term.[7]

Step 2. The next step is to prove that we are able to establish the time receipt interface. We prove the following:

Lemma 7 (Time Receipt Initialization). *For every location c, the following Iris view shift holds:*

$$(c \mapsto N-1) \quad \Rrightarrow_{\top} \ \exists (⧗, ⧖ : \mathbb{N} \to \mathit{iProp}) \quad \mathit{TRIntf}\ (⧗)\ (⧖)\ \mathit{tick}_c$$

We provide only a brief summary of the proof of Lemma 7; for further details, the reader is referred to the extended version of this paper [18, Appendix B]. Roughly speaking, we install the invariant that c holds $N-1-i$, where i is some number that satisfies $0 \leq i < N$. We define $⧗ n$ as an exclusive contribution of n units to the current value of i, and define $⧖ n$ as an observation that i is at least n. (i grows with time, so such an observation is stable.) As part of the proof of the above lemma, we check that the specification of *tick* holds:

$$\{⧖ n\}\ \mathit{tick}\ (v)\ \{\lambda w.\, w = v \ *\ ⧗ 1 \ *\ ⧖ (n+1)\}$$

In contrast with the case of time credits, in this case, the precondition $⧖ n$ does *not* guarantee that c holds a nonzero value. Thus, it *is* possible for *tick*() to be executed when c is zero. This is not a problem, though, because *loop*() is safe to execute in any situation: it satisfies the Hoare triple $\{\mathsf{True}\}\ \mathit{loop}()\ \{\mathsf{False}\}$. In other words, when c is about to fall below zero and therefore the invariant $i < N$ seems about to be broken, *loop* () saves the day by running away and never allowing execution to continue normally.

[6] If the user instead wishes to establish a lower bound on a program's execution time, this is possible as well.

[7] In fact, it is not essential that *loop*() diverges. What matters is that *loop* satisfy the Iris triple $\{\mathsf{True}\}\ \mathit{loop}()\ \{\mathsf{False}\}$. A fatal runtime error that Iris does *not* rule out would work just as well, as it satisfies the same specification.

Step 3. In the last reasoning step, we complete the proof of Theorem 2. Suppose the end user has established $\{\mathsf{True}\}\ e\ \{\mathsf{True}\}_{⧗}$. By Safety Preservation (Lemma 3), to prove that $(e, \varnothing)$ is $(N-1)$-safe, it suffices to show (for an arbitrary location c) that $\langle\!\langle e \rangle\!\rangle$, executed in the initial heap $\varnothing\,[c \leftarrow N-1]$, is safe. To do so, beginning with this initial heap, we perform Time Receipt Initialization, that is, we execute the view shift whose statement appears in Lemma 7. This yields two abstract predicates ⧗ and ⧖ as well as the assertion *TRIntf* (⧗) (⧖) *tick*. At this point, we unfold $\{\mathsf{True}\}\ e\ \{\mathsf{True}\}_{⧗}$ (see Definition 2), yielding an implication, and apply this implication, yielding the Iris triple $\{\mathsf{True}\}\ \langle\!\langle e \rangle\!\rangle\ \{\mathsf{True}\}$. Because Iris is sound [12], this implies that $\langle\!\langle e \rangle\!\rangle$ is safe. This concludes the proof. For further detail, the reader is again referred to our online repository [17].

6 Marrying Time Credits and Time Receipts

It seems desirable to combine time credits and time receipts in a single program logic, Iris$^{\$⧗}$. We have done so [17]. In short, following the scheme of Sects. 4 and 5, the definition of Iris$^{\$⧗}$ involves composing Iris with the tick translation. This time, *tick* serves two purposes: it consumes one time credit *and* produces one exclusive time receipt (and increments a persistent time receipt). Thus, its specification is as follows:

$$\{\$1 \ast ⧖ n\}\ \mathit{tick}\,(v)\ \{\lambda w.\, w = v \ast ⧗1 \ast ⧖(n+1)\}$$

Let us write *TCTRIntf* ($) (⧗) (⧖) *tick* for the combined interface of time credits and time receipts. This interface combines all of the axioms of Figs. 1 and 3, but declares a single *tick* function[8] and proposes a single specification for it, which is the one shown above.

Definition 3 (Iris$^{\$⧗}$ triple). *An* Iris$^{\$⧗}$ triple $\{P\}\ e\ \{\Phi\}_{\$⧗}$ *stands for:*

$$\forall\,(\$)\,(⧗)\,(⧖)\ \mathit{tick} \qquad \mathit{TCTRIntf}\,(\$)\,(⧗)\,(⧖)\ \mathit{tick} \ \twoheadrightarrow\ \{P\}\ \langle\!\langle e \rangle\!\rangle_{\mathit{tick}}\ \{\Phi\}$$

Theorem 3 (Soundness of Iris$^{\$⧗}$). *If* $\{\$n\}\ e\ \{\mathsf{True}\}_{\$⧗}$ *holds then the machine configuration* $(e, \varnothing)$ *is* $(N-1)$*-safe. If furthermore* $n < N$ *holds, then this machine configuration terminates in at most* n *steps.*

Iris$^{\$⧗}$ allows exploiting time credits to prove time complexity bounds and, at the same time, exploiting time receipts to prove the absence of certain integer overflows. Our verification of Union-Find (Sect. 8) illustrates these two aspects.

Guéneau *et al.* [7] use time credits to reason about asymptotic complexity, that is, about the manner in which a program's complexity grows as the size of its input grows towards infinity. Does such asymptotic reasoning make sense in Iris$^{\$⧗}$, where no program is ever executed for N time steps or beyond? It

[8] Even though the interface provides only one *tick* function, it gets instantiated in the soundness theorem with different implementations depending on whether there are more than N time credits or not.

seems to be the case that if a program p satisfies the triple $\{\$n\}\, p\, \{\Phi\}_{\$⧗}$, then it also satisfies the stronger triple $\{\$\min(n, N)\}\, p\, \{\Phi\}_{\$⧗}$, therefore also satisfies $\{\$N\}\, p\, \{\Phi\}_{\$⧗}$. Can one therefore conclude that p has "constant time complexity"? We believe not. Provided N is considered a parameter, as opposed to a constant, one *cannot* claim that "N is $O(1)$", so $\{\$\min(n, N)\}\, p\, \{\Phi\}_{\$⧗}$ does not imply that "p runs in constant time". In other words, a universal quantification on N should come *after* the existential quantifier that is implicit in the O notation. We have not yet attempted to implement this idea; this remains a topic for further investigation.

7 Application: Thunks in Iris$^{\$}$

In this section, we illustrate the power of Iris$^{\$}$ by constructing an implementation of thunks as a library in Iris$^{\$}$. A *thunk*, also known as a *suspension*, is a very simple data structure that represents a suspended computation. There are two operations on thunks, namely *create*, which constructs a new thunk, and *force*, which demands the result of a thunk. A thunk memoizes its result, so that even if it is forced multiple times, the computation only takes place once.

Okasaki [19] proposes a methodology for reasoning about the amortized time complexity of computations that involve shared thunks. For every thunk, he keeps track of a *debit*, which can be thought of as an amount of credit that one must still pay before one is allowed to force this thunk. A ghost operation, *pay*, changes one's view of a thunk, by reducing the debit associated with this thunk. *force* can be applied only to a zero-debit thunk, and has amortized cost $O(1)$. Indeed, if this thunk has been forced already, then *force* really requires constant time; and if this thunk is being forced for the first time, then the cost of performing the suspended computation must have been paid for in advance, possibly in several installments, via *pay*. This discipline is sound even in the presence of sharing, that is, of multiple pointers to a thunk. Indeed, whereas duplicating a credit is unsound, duplicating a debit leads to an over-approximation of the true cost, hence is sound. Danielsson [6] formulates Okasaki's ideas as a type system, which he proves sound in Agda. Pilkiewicz and Pottier [20] reconstruct this type discipline in the setting of a lower-level type system, equipped with basic notions of time credits, hidden state, and monotonic state. Unfortunately, their type system is presented in an informal manner and does not come with a proof of type soundness.

We reproduce Pilkiewicz and Pottier's construction in the formal setting of Iris$^{\$}$. Indeed, Iris$^{\$}$ offers all of the necessary ingredients, namely time credits, hidden state (invariants, in Iris terminology) and monotonic state (a special case of Iris' ghost state). Our reconstruction is carried out inside Coq [17].

7.1 Concurrency and Reentrancy

One new problem that arises here is that Okasaki's analysis, which is valid in a sequential setting, potentially becomes invalid in a concurrent setting. Suppose we wish to allow multiple threads to safely share access to a thunk. A natural, simple-minded approach would be to equip every thunk with a lock and allow competition over this lock. Then, unfortunately, forcing would become a blocking operation: one thread could waste time waiting for another thread to finish forcing. In fact, in the absence of a fairness assumption about the scheduler, an unbounded amount of time could be wasted in this way. This appears to invalidate the property that *force* has amortized cost $O(1)$.

Technically, the manner in which this problem manifests itself in Iris$^\$$ is in the specification of locks. Whereas in Iris a spin lock can be implemented and proved correct with respect to a simple and well-understood specification [2], in Iris$^\$$, it cannot. The *lock*() method contains a potentially infinite loop: therefore, no finite amount of time credits is sufficient to prove that *lock*() is safe. This issue is discussed in greater depth later on (Sect. 9).

A distinct yet related problem is reentrancy. Arguably, an implementation of thunks should guarantee that a suspended computation is evaluated at most once. This guarantee seems particularly useful when the computation has a side effect: the user can then rely on the fact that this side effect occurs at most once. However, this property does not naturally hold: in the presence of heap-allocated mutable state, it is possible to construct an ill-behaved "reentrant" thunk which, when forced, attempts to recursively force itself. Thus, something must be done to dynamically reject or statically prevent reentrancy. In Pilkiewicz and Pottier's code [20], reentrancy is detected at runtime, thanks to a three-color scheme, and causes a fatal runtime failure. In a concurrent system where each thunk is equipped with a lock, reentrancy is also detected at runtime, and turned into deadlock; but we have explained earlier why we wish to avoid locks.

Fortunately, Iris provides us with a static mechanism for forbidding both concurrency and reentrancy. We introduce a unique token $\lightning$, which can be thought of as "permission to use the thunk API", and set things up so that *pay* and *force* require and return $\lightning$. This forbids concurrency: two operations on thunks cannot take place concurrently. Furthermore, when a user-supplied suspended computation is executed, the token $\lightning$ is *not* transmitted to it. This forbids reentrancy.[9] The implementation of this token relies on Iris' "nonatomic invariants" (Sect. 7.4). With these restrictions, we are able to prove that Okasaki's discipline is sound.

7.2 Implementation of Thunks

A simple implementation of thunks in HeapLang appears in Fig. 5. A thunk can be in one of two states: *White f* and *Black v*. A white thunk is unevaluated:

9 Therefore, a suspended computation cannot force *any* thunk. This is admittedly a very severe restriction, which rules out many useful applications of thunks. In fact, we have implemented a more flexible discipline, where thunks can be grouped in multiple "regions" and there is one token per region instead of a single global $\lightning$ token. This discipline allows concurrent or reentrant operations on provably distinct thunks, yet can still be proven sound.

$$
\begin{aligned}
\mathit{create} &\triangleq \lambda f.\, \mathtt{ref}(\mathit{White}\ f) \\
\mathit{force} &\triangleq \lambda t.\, \mathtt{match}\ !t\ \mathtt{with} \\
&\qquad \mathit{White}\ f \Rightarrow \mathtt{let}\ v = f\,()\ \mathtt{in}\ t \leftarrow \mathit{Black}\ v\ ;\ v \\
&\qquad |\ \mathit{Black}\ v \Rightarrow v \\
&\qquad \mathtt{end}
\end{aligned}
$$

Fig. 5. An implementation of thunks

$\mathsf{isThunk} : \mathit{Loc} \to \mathbb{N} \to (\mathit{Val} \to \mathit{iProp}) \to \mathit{iProp}$	— there exist "thunks"
$\mathsf{persistent}(\mathsf{isThunk}\ t\ n\ \Phi)$	— thunks can be shared
$n_1 \le n_2 \twoheadrightarrow$ $\mathsf{isThunk}\ t\ n_1\ \Phi \twoheadrightarrow \mathsf{isThunk}\ t\ n_2\ \Phi$	— it is sound to overestimate a debt
$\lightning : \mathit{iProp}$	— there exist "thunderbolts"
$\lightning$	— the user is handed one
$\{\$3 * \{\$n\}\ \langle\langle f\,()\rangle\rangle\ \{\Phi\}\}$ $\langle\langle \mathit{create}\ (f)\rangle\rangle$ $\{\lambda t.\, \mathsf{isThunk}\ t\ n\ \Phi\}$	— a computation of cost n gives rise to an n-debit thunk; the cost is $O(1)$
$(\forall v.\, \mathsf{duplicable}(\Phi\ v)) \twoheadrightarrow$ $\{\$11 * \mathsf{isThunk}\ t\ 0\ \Phi * \lightning\}$ $\langle\langle \mathit{force}\ (t)\rangle\rangle$ $\{\lambda v.\, \Phi\ v * \lightning\}$	— a 0-debit thunk can be forced; the thunderbolt is required; the cost is $O(1)$
$\mathsf{isThunk}\ t\ n\ \Phi * \$k * \lightning$ $\Rrightarrow_\top \mathsf{isThunk}\ t\ (n-k)\ \Phi * \lightning$	— paying reduces one's debt

Fig. 6. A simple specification of thunks in Iris$^\$$

the function f represents a suspended computation. A black thunk is evaluated: the value v is the result of the computation that has been performed already. Two colors are sufficient: because our static discipline rules out reentrancy, there is no need for a third color, whose purpose would be to dynamically detect an attempt to force a thunk that is already being forced.

7.3 Specification of Thunks in Iris$^\$$

Our specification of thunks appears in Fig. 6. It declares an abstract predicate $\mathsf{isThunk}\ t\ n\ \Phi$, which asserts that t is a valid thunk, that the debt associated with this thunk is n, and that this thunk (once forced) produces a value that satisfies the postcondition Φ. The number n, a *debit*, is the number of credits that remain to be paid before this thunk can be forced. The postcondition Φ is chosen by the user when a thunk is created. It must be duplicable (this is required in the specification of *force*) because *force* can be invoked several times and we must guarantee, every time, that the result v satisfies $\Phi\ v$.

The second axiom states that $\mathsf{isThunk}\ t\ n\ \Phi$ is a persistent assertion. This means that a valid thunk, once created, remains a valid thunk forever. Among other things, it is permitted to create two pointers to a single thunk and to reason independently about each of these pointers.

The third axiom states that isThunk $t\ n\ \Phi$ is covariant in its parameter n. Overestimating a debt still leads to a correct analysis of a program's worst-case time complexity.

Next, the specification declares an abstract assertion $\lightning$, and provides the user with one copy of this assertion. We refer to it as "the thunderbolt".

The next item in Fig. 6 is the specification of *create*. It is higher-order: the precondition of *create* contains a specification of the function f that is passed as an argument to *create*. This axiom states that, if f represents a computation of cost n, then *create* (f) produces an n-debit thunk. The cost of creation itself is 3 credits. This specification is somewhat simplistic, as it does not allow the function f to have a nontrivial precondition. It is possible to offer a richer specification; we eschew it in favor of simplicity.

Next comes the specification of *force*. Only a 0-debit thunk can be forced. The result is a value v that satisfies Φ. The (amortized) cost of forcing is 11 credits. The thunderbolt appears in the pre- and postcondition of *force*, forbidding any concurrent attempts to force a thunk.

The last axiom in Fig. 6 corresponds to *pay*. It is a view shift, a ghost operation. By paying k credits, one turns an n-debit thunk into an $(n-k)$-debit thunk. At runtime, nothing happens: it is the same thunk before and after the payment. Yet, after the view shift, we have a new view of the number of debits associated with this thunk. Here, paying requires the thunderbolt. It should be possible to remove this requirement; we have not yet attempted to do so.

7.4 Proof of Thunks in Iris$^{\$}$

After implementing thunks in HeapLang (Sect. 7.2) and expressing their specification in Iris$^{\$}$ (Sect. 7.3), there remains to prove that this specification can be established. We sketch the key ideas of this proof.

Following Pilkiewicz and Pottier [20], when a new thunk is created, we install a new Iris invariant, which describes this thunk. The invariant is as follows:

$$\begin{aligned} &\mathit{ThunkInv}\ t\ \gamma\ nc\ \Phi \triangleq \\ &\quad \exists ac.\ \left(\boxed{\bullet\, ac}^{\gamma} * \begin{cases} \exists f.\ t \mapsto \mathit{White}\ f\ *\ \{\$nc\}\ f\ ()\ \{\Phi\}\ *\ \$ac \\ \vee\ \exists v.\ t \mapsto \mathit{Black}\ v \end{cases} \right) \end{aligned}$$

γ is a ghost location, which we allocate at the same time as the thunk t. It holds elements of the authoritative monoid $\textsc{Auth}(\mathbb{N}, \max)$ [12]. The variable nc, for "necessary credits", is the cost of the suspended computation: it appears in the precondition of f. The variable ac, for "available credits", is the number of credits that have been paid so far. The disjunction inside the invariant states that:

- either the thunk is white, in which case we have ac credits at hand;
- or the thunk is black, in which case we have no credits at hand, as they have been spent already.

The predicate $\mathsf{isThunk}\ t\ n\ \Phi$ is then defined as follows:

$$\mathsf{isThunk}\ t\ n\ \Phi \triangleq$$
$$\exists \gamma, nc.\ \left(\boxed{\circ\,(nc - n)}^{\gamma} \ast \mathsf{NaInv}(\mathit{ThunkInv}\ t\ \gamma\ nc\ \Phi) \right)$$

The non-authoritative assertion $\boxed{\circ\,(nc - n)}^{\gamma}$ inside $\mathsf{isThunk}\ t\ n\ \Phi$, confronted with the authoritative assertion $\boxed{\bullet\, ac}^{\gamma}$ that can be obtained by acquiring the invariant, implies the inequality $nc - n \leq ac$, therefore $nc \leq ac + n$. That is, the credits paid so far (ac) plus the credits that remain to be paid (n) are sufficient to cover for the actual cost of the computation (nc). In particular, in the proof of *force*, we have a 0-debit thunk, so $nc \leq ac$ holds. In the case where the thunk is white, this means that the ac credits that we have at hand are sufficient to justify the call $f\ ()$, which requires nc credits.

The final aspect that remains to be explained is our use of $\mathsf{NaInv}(\cdots)$, an Iris "nonatomic invariant". Indeed, in this proof, we cannot rely on Iris' primitive invariants. A primitive invariant can be acquired only for the duration of an atomic instruction [12]. In our implementation of thunks (Fig. 5), however, we need a "critical section" that encompasses several instructions. That is, we must acquire the invariant before dereferencing t, and (in the case where this thunk is white) we cannot release it until we have marked this thunk black. Fortunately, Iris provides a library of "nonatomic invariants" for this very purpose. (This library is used in the RustBelt project [10] to implement Rust's type `Cell`.) This library offers separate ghost operations for acquiring and releasing an invariant. Acquiring an invariant consumes a unique token, which is recovered when the invariant is released: this guarantees that an invariant cannot be acquired twice, or in other words, that two threads cannot be in a critical section at the same time. The unique token involved in this protocol is the one that we expose to the end user as "the thunderbolt".

8 Application: Union-Find in Iris$^{\$⧗}$

As an illustration of the use of both time credits and time receipts, we formally verify the functional correctness and time complexity of an implementation of the Union-Find data structure. Our proof [17] is based on Charguéraud and Pottier's work [4]. We port their code from OCaml to HeapLang, and port their proof from Separation Logic with Time Credits to Iris$^{\$⧗}$. At this point, the proof exploits just Iris$^{\$}$, a subset of Iris$^{\$⧗}$. The mathematical analysis of Union-Find, which represents a large part of the proof, is unchanged. Our contribution lies in the fact that we modify the data structure to represent ranks as machine integers instead of unbounded integers, and exploit time receipts in Iris$^{\$⧗}$ to establish the absence of overflow. We equip HeapLang with signed machine integers whose bit width is a parameter w. Under the hypothesis $\log \log N < w - 1$, we are able to prove that, even though the code uses limited-width machine integers, no overflow can occur in a feasible time. If for instance N is 2^{63}, then this condition boils down to $w \geq 7$. Ranks can be stored in just 7 bits without risking overflow.

As in Charguéraud and Pottier's work, the Union-Find library advertises an abstract representation predicate $\mathsf{isUF}\,D\,R\,V$, which describes a well-formed, uniquely-owned Union-Find data structure. The parameter D, a set of nodes, is the domain of the data structure. The parameter R, a function, maps a node to the representative element of its equivalence class. The parameter V, also a function, maps a node to a payload value associated with its equivalence class. We do not show the specification of every operation. Instead, we focus on *union*, which merges two equivalence classes. We establish the following Iris$^{\$⧗}$ triple:

$$\left.\begin{array}{r}\log\log N < w-1\\ x\in D\\ y\in D\end{array}\right\} \Rightarrow \begin{array}{c}\{\mathsf{isUF}\,D\,R\,V \ast \$(44\alpha(|D|)+152)\}\\ \mathit{union}\,(x,y)\\ \left\{\lambda z.\ \begin{array}{c}\mathsf{isUF}\,D\,R'\,V' \ast\\ z=R(x)\lor z=R(y)\end{array}\right\}_{\$⧗}\end{array}$$

where the functions R' and V' are defined as follows:[10]

$$(R'(w),V'(w)) = \begin{cases}(z, \quad V(z)) & \text{if } R(w)=R(x) \text{ or } R(w)=R(y)\\ (R(w),V(w)) & \text{otherwise}\end{cases}$$

The hypotheses $x \in D$ and $y \in D$ and the conjunct $\mathsf{isUF}\,D\,R\,V$ in the precondition require that x and y be two nodes in a valid Union-Find data structure. The postcondition $\lambda z. \ldots$ describes the state of the data structure after the operation and the return value z.

The conjunct $\$(44\alpha(|D|)+152)$ in the precondition indicates that *union* has time complexity $O(\alpha(n))$, where α is an inverse of Ackermann's function and n is the number of nodes in the data structure. This is an amortized bound; the predicate isUF also contains a certain number of time credits, known as the potential of the data structure, which are used to justify *union* operations whose actual cost exceeds the advertised cost. The constants 44 and 152 differ from those found in Charguéraud and Pottier's specification [4] because Iris$^{\$⧗}$ counts every computation step, whereas they count only function calls. Abstracting these constants by using O notation, as proposed by Guéneau *et al.* [7], would be desirable, but we have not attempted to do so yet.

The main novelty, with respect to Charguéraud and Pottier's specification, is the hypothesis $\log\log N < w-1$, which is required to prove that no overflow can occur when the rank of a node is incremented. In our proof, N and w are parameters; once their values are chosen, this hypothesis is easily discharged, once and for all. In the absence of time receipts, we would have to publish the hypothesis $\log\log n < w-1$, where n is the cardinal of D, forcing every (direct and indirect) user of the data structure to keep track of this requirement.

For the proof to go through, we store n time receipts in the data structure: that is, we include the conjunct $⧗\,n$, where n stands for $|D|$, in the definition of the invariant $\mathsf{isUF}\,D\,R\,V$. The operation of creating a new node takes at least one

[10] This definition of R' and V' has free variables x, y, z, therefore in reality must appear inside the postcondition. Here, it is presented separately, for greater readability.

step, therefore produces one new time receipt, which is used to prove that the invariant is preserved by this operation. At any point, then, from the invariant, and from the basic laws of time receipts, we can deduce that $n < N$ holds. Furthermore, it is easy to show that a rank is at most $\log n$. Therefore, a rank is at most $\log N$. In combination with the hypothesis $\log \log N < w - 1$, this suffices to prove that a rank is at most $2^{w-1} - 1$, the largest signed machine integer, and therefore that no overflow can occur in the computation of a rank.

Clochard *et al.* [5, §2] already present Union-Find as a motivating example among several others. They write that "there is obviously no danger of arithmetic overflow here, since [ranks] are only obtained by successive increments by one". This argument would be formalized in their system by representing ranks as either "one-time" or "peano" integers (in our terminology, clocks or snapclocks). This argument could be expressed in Iris$^{\$⧗}$, but would lead to requiring $\log N < w - 1$. In contrast, we use a more refined argument: we note that ranks are logarithmic in n, the number of nodes, and that n itself can never overflow. This leads us to the much weaker requirement $\log \log N < w - 1$, which means that a rank can be stored in very few bits. We believe that this argument cannot be expressed in Clochard *et al.*'s system.

9 Discussion

One feature of Iris and HeapLang that deserves further discussion is concurrency. Iris is an evolution of Concurrent Separation Logic, and HeapLang has shared-memory concurrency. How does this impact our reasoning about time? At a purely formal level, this does not have any impact: Theorems 1, 2, 3 and their proofs are essentially oblivious to the absence or presence of concurrency in the programming language. At a more informal level, though, this impacts our interpretation of the real-world meaning of these theorems. Whereas in a sequential setting a "number of computation steps" can be equated (up to a constant factor) with "time", in a concurrent setting, a "number of computation steps" is referred to as "work", and is related to "time" only up to a factor of p, the number of processors. In short, our system measures work, not time. The number of available processors should be taken into account when choosing a specific value of N: this value must be so large that N computation steps are infeasible even by p processors. With this in mind, we believe that our system can still be used to prove properties that have physical relevance.

In short, our new program logics, Iris$^{\$}$, Iris$^{⧗}$, and Iris$^{\$⧗}$, tolerate concurrency. Yet, is it fair to say that they have "good support" for reasoning about concurrent programs? We believe not yet, and this is an area for future research. The main open issue is that we do not at this time have good support for reasoning about the time complexity of programs that perform busy-waiting on some resource. The root of the difficulty, already mentioned during the presentation of thunks (Sect. 7.1), is that one thread can fail to make progress, due to interference with another thread. A retry is then necessary, wasting time. In a spin lock, for instance, the "compare-and-set" (CAS) instruction that attempts to acquire the lock can fail. There is no bound on the number of attempts that are required until the lock is eventually acquired. Thus, in $\mathrm{Iris}^{\$}$, we are currently unable to assign *any* specification to the *lock* method of a spin lock.

In the future, we wish to take inspiration from Hoffmann, Marmar and Shao [9], who use time credits in Concurrent Separation Logic to establish the lock-freedom of several concurrent data structures. The key idea is to formalize the informal argument that "failure of a thread to make progress is caused by successful progress in another thread". Hoffmann *et al.* set up a "quantitative compensation scheme", that is, a protocol by which successful progress in one thread (say, a successful CAS operation) must transmit a number of time credits to every thread that has encountered a corresponding failure and therefore must retry. Quite interestingly, this protocol is not hardwired into the reasoning rule for CAS. In fact, CAS itself is not primitive; it is encoded in terms of an atomic $\{\ldots\}$ construct. The protocol is set up by the user, by exploiting the basic tools of Concurrent Separation Logic, including shared invariants. Thus, it should be possible in $\mathrm{Iris}^{\$}$ to reproduce Hoffmann *et al.*'s reasoning and to assign useful specifications to certain lock-free data structures. Furthermore, we believe that, under a fairness assumption, it should be possible to assign $\mathrm{Iris}^{\$}$ specifications also to coarse-grained data structures, which involve locks. Roughly speaking, under a fair scheduler, the maximum time spent waiting for a lock is the maximum number of threads that may compete for this lock, multiplied by the maximum cost of a critical section protected by this lock. Whether and how this can be formalized is a topic of future research.

The axiom $\text{⧗} N \Rrightarrow_{\top} \mathsf{False}$ comes with a few caveats that should be mentioned. The same caveats apply to Clochard *et al.*'s system [5], and are known to them.

One caveat is that it is possible in theory to use this axiom to write and justify surprising programs. For instance, in $\mathrm{Iris}^{\text{⧗}}$, the loop "*for* $i = 1$ *to* N *do* () *done*" satisfies the specification $\{\mathsf{True}\} - \{\mathsf{False}\}$: that is, it is possible to prove that this loop "never ends". As a consequence, this loop also satisfies every specification of the form $\{\mathsf{True}\} - \{\Phi\}$. On the face of it, this loop would appear to be a valid solution to every programming assignment! In practice, it is up to the user to exhibit taste and to refrain from exploiting such a paradox. In reality, the situation is no worse than that in plain Iris, a logic of partial correctness, where the infinite loop "*while true do* () *done*" also satisfies $\{\mathsf{True}\} - \{\mathsf{False}\}$.

Another important caveat is that the compiler must in principle be instructed to never optimize ticks away. If, for instance, the compiler was allowed to recognize that the loop "*for* $i = 1$ *to* N *do* () *done*" does nothing, and to replace this loop with a no-op, then this loop, which according to $\mathrm{Iris}^{\text{⧗}}$ "never ends", would in reality end immediately. We would thereby be in danger of proving that a source program cannot crash unless it is allowed to run for centuries, whereas in reality the corresponding compiled program does crash in a short time. In practice, this danger can be avoided by actually instrumenting the source code with *tick*() instructions and by presenting *tick* to the compiler as an unknown external function, which cannot be optimized away. However, this seems a pity, as it disables many compiler optimizations.

We believe that, despite these pitfalls, time receipts can be a useful tool. We hope that, in the future, better ways of avoiding these pitfalls will be discovered.

10 Related Work

Time credits in an affine Separation Logic are not a new concept. Atkey [1] introduces them in the setting of Separation Logic. Pilkiewicz and Pottier [20] exploit them in an informal reconstruction of Danielsson's type discipline for lazy thunks [6], which itself is inspired by Okasaki's work [19]. Several authors subsequently exploit time credits in machine-checked proofs of correctness and time complexity of algorithms and data structures [4,7,22]. Hoffmann, Marmar and Shao [9], whose work was discussed earlier in this paper (Sect. 9), use time credits in Concurrent Separation Logic to prove that several concurrent data structure implementations are lock-free.

At a metatheoretic level, Charguéraud and Pottier [4] provide a machine-checked proof of soundness of a Separation Logic with time credits. Haslbeck and Nipkow [8] compare three program logics that can provide worst-case time complexity guarantees, including Separation Logic with time credits.

To the best of our knowledge, affine (exclusive and persistent) time receipts are new, and the axiom $⧖ N \Rrightarrow_{\top} \mathsf{False}$ is new as well. It is inspired by Clochard *et al.*'s idea that "programs cannot run for centuries" [5], but distills this idea into a simpler form.

Our implementation of thunks and our reconstruction of Okasaki's debits [19] in terms of credits are inspired by earlier work [6,20]. Although Okasaki's analysis assumes a sequential setting, we adapt it to a concurrent setting by explicitly forbidding concurrent operations on thunks; to do so, we rely on Iris nonatomic invariants. In contrast, Danielsson [6] views thunks as a primitive construct in an otherwise pure language. He equips the language with a type discipline, where the type *Thunk*, which is indexed with a debit, forms a monad, and he provides a direct proof of type soundness. The manner in which Danielsson inserts *tick* instructions into programs is a precursor of our tick translation; this idea can in fact be traced at least as far back as Moran and Sands [16]. Pilkiewicz and Pottier [20] sketch an encoding of debits in terms of credits. Because they work in a sequential setting, they are able to install a shared invariant by exploiting the anti-frame rule [21], whereas we use Iris' nonatomic invariants for this purpose. The anti-frame rule does not rule out reentrancy, so they must detect it at runtime, whereas in our case both concurrency and reentrancy are ruled out by our use of nonatomic invariants.

Madhavan *et al.* [15] present an automated system that infers and verifies resource bounds for higher-order functional programs with thunks (and, more generally, with memoization tables). They transform the source program to an instrumented form where the state is explicit and can be described by monotone assertions. For instance, it is possible to assert that a thunk has been forced already (which guarantees that forcing it again has constant cost). This seems analogous in Okasaki's terminology to asserting that a thunk has zero debits, also a monotone assertion. We presently do not know whether Madhavan *et al.*'s system could be encoded into a lower-level program logic such as Iris$^{\$}$; it would be interesting to find out.

11 Conclusion

We have presented two mechanisms, namely time credits and time receipts, by which Iris, a state-of-the-art concurrent program logic, can be extended with means of reasoning about time. We have established soundness theorems that state precisely what guarantees are offered by the extended program logics Iris$^{\$}$, Iris$^{⧗}$, and Iris$^{\$⧗}$. We have defined these new logics modularly, by composing Iris with a program transformation. The three proofs follow a similar pattern: the soundness theorem of Iris is composed with a simulation lemma about the tick translation. We have illustrated the power of the new logics by reconstructing Okasaki's debit-based analysis of thunks, by reconstructing Clochard *et al.*'s technique for proving the absence of certain integer overflows, and by presenting an analysis of Union-Find that exploits both time credits and time receipts.

One limitation of our work is that all of our metatheoretic results are specific to HeapLang, and would have to be reproduced, following the same pattern, if one wished to instantiate Iris$^{\$⧗}$ for another programming language. It would be desirable to make our statements and proofs generic. In future work, we would also like to better understand what can be proved about the time complexity of concurrent programs that involve waiting. Can the time spent waiting be bounded? What specification can one give to a lock, or a thunk that is protected by a lock? A fairness hypothesis about the scheduler seems to be required, but it is not clear yet how to state and exploit such a hypothesis. Hoffmann, Marmar and Shao [9] have carried out pioneering work in this area, but have dealt only with lock-free data structures and only with situations where the number of competing threads is fixed. It would be interesting to transpose their work into Iris$^{\$}$ and to develop it further.

References

1. Atkey, R.: Amortised resource analysis with separation logic. Log. Methods Comput. Sci. **7**(2:17) (2011). http://bentnib.org/amortised-sep-logic-journal.pdf
2. Birkedal, L.: Lecture11: CAS and spin locks, November 2017. https://iris-project.org/tutorial-pdfs/lecture11-cas-spin-lock.pdf
3. Brookes, S., O'Hearn, P.W.: Concurrent separation logic. SIGLOG News **3**(3), 47–65 (2016). http://siglog.hosting.acm.org/wp-content/uploads/2016/07/siglognews9.pdf#page=49
4. Charguéraud, A., Pottier, F.: Verifying the correctness and amortized complexity of a union-find implementation in separation logic with time credits. J. Autom. Reason. (2017). http://gallium.inria.fr/~fpottier/publis/chargueraud-pottier-uf-sltc.pdf

5. Clochard, M., Filliâtre, J.-C., Paskevich, A.: How to avoid proving the absence of integer overflows. In: Gurfinkel, A., Seshia, S.A. (eds.) VSTTE 2015. LNCS, vol. 9593, pp. 94–109. Springer, Cham (2016). https://doi.org/10.1007/978-3-319-29613-5_6. https://hal.inria.fr/al-01162661
6. Danielsson, N.A.: Lightweight semiformal time complexity analysis for purely functional data structures. In: Principles of Programming Languages (POPL) (2008). http://www.cse.chalmers.se/~nad/publications/danielsson-popl2008.pdf
7. Guéneau, A., Charguéraud, A., Pottier, F.: A fistful of dollars: formalizing asymptotic complexity claims via deductive program verification. In: Ahmed, A. (ed.) ESOP 2018. LNCS, vol. 10801, pp. 533–560. Springer, Cham (2018). https://doi.org/10.1007/978-3-319-89884-1_19. http://gallium.inria.fr/~fpottier/publis/gueneau-chargeraud-pottier-esop2018.pdf
8. Haslbeck, M.P.L., Nipkow, T.: Hoare logics for time bounds: a study in meta theory. In: Beyer, D., Huisman, M. (eds.) TACAS 2018. LNCS, vol. 10805, pp. 155–171. Springer, Cham (2018). https://doi.org/10.1007/978-3-319-89960-2_9. https://www21.in.tum.de/~nipkow/pubs/tacas18.pdf
9. Hoffmann, J., Marmar, M., Shao, Z.: Quantitative reasoning for proving lock-freedom. In: Logic in Computer Science (LICS), pp. 124–133 (2013). http://www.cs.cmu.edu/~janh/papers/lockfree2013.pdf
10. Jung, R., Jourdan, J.H., Krebbers, R., Dreyer, D.: RustBelt: securing the foundations of the rust programming language. PACMPL **2**(POPL), 66:1–66:34 (2018). https://people.mpi-sws.org/~dreyer/papers/rustbelt/paper.pdf
11. Jung, R., Krebbers, R., Birkedal, L., Dreyer, D.: Higher-order ghost state. In: International Conference on Functional Programming (ICFP), pp. 256–269 (2016). http://iris-project.org/pdfs/2016-icfp-iris2-final.pdf
12. Jung, R., Krebbers, R., Jourdan, J.H., Bizjak, A., Birkedal, L., Dreyer, D.: Iris from the ground up: a modular foundation for higher-order concurrent separation logic. J. Funct. Program. **28**, e20 (2018). https://people.mpi-sws.org/~dreyer/papers/iris-ground-up/paper.pdf
13. Jung, R., et al.: Iris: monoids and invariants as an orthogonal basis for concurrent reasoning. In: Principles of Programming Languages (POPL), pp. 637–650 (2015). http://plv.mpi-sws.org/iris/paper.pdf
14. Krebbers, R., Jung, R., Bizjak, A., Jourdan, J.-H., Dreyer, D., Birkedal, L.: The essence of higher-order concurrent separation logic. In: Yang, H. (ed.) ESOP 2017. LNCS, vol. 10201, pp. 696–723. Springer, Heidelberg (2017). https://doi.org/10.1007/978-3-662-54434-1_26. http://iris-project.org/pdfs/2017-esop-iris3-final.pdf
15. Madhavan, R., Kulal, S., Kuncak, V.: Contract-based resource verification for higher-order functions with memoization. In: Principles of Programming Languages (POPL), pp. 330–343 (2017). http://lara.epfl.ch/~kandhada/orb-popl17.pdf
16. Moran, A., Sands, D.: Improvement in a lazy context: an operational theory for call-by-need. In: Principles of Programming Languages (POPL), pp. 43–56 (1999). http://www.cse.chalmers.se/~dave/papers/cbneed-theory.pdf
17. Mével, G., Jourdan, J.H., Pottier, F.: Time credits and time receipts in Iris – Coq proofs, October 2018. https://gitlab.inria.fr/gmevel/iris-time-proofs
18. Mével, G., Jourdan, J.H., Pottier, F.: Time credits and time receipts in Iris – extended version (2019). https://jhjourdan.mketjh.fr/pdf/mevel2019time.pdf
19. Okasaki, C.: Purely Functional Data Structures. Cambridge University Press, Cambridge (1999). http://www.cambridge.org/us/catalogue/catalogue.asp?isbn=0521663504

20. Pilkiewicz, A., Pottier, F.: The essence of monotonic state. In: Types in Language Design and Implementation (TLDI) (2011). http://gallium.inria.fr/~fpottier/publis/pilkiewicz-pottier-monotonicity.pdf
21. Pottier, F.: Hiding local state in direct style: a higher-order anti-frame rule. In: Logic in Computer Science (LICS), pp. 331–340 (2008). http://gallium.inria.fr/~fpottier/publis/fpottier-antiframe-2008.pdf
22. Zhan, B., Haslbeck, M.P.L.: Verifying asymptotic time complexity of imperative programs in Isabelle. In: Galmiche, D., Schulz, S., Sebastiani, R. (eds.) IJCAR 2018. LNCS (LNAI), vol. 10900, pp. 532–548. Springer, Cham (2018). https://doi.org/10.1007/978-3-319-94205-6_35. arxiv:1802.01336

Meta-F*: Proof Automation with SMT, Tactics, and Metaprograms

Guido Martínez[1,2(✉)], Danel Ahman[3], Victor Dumitrescu[4], Nick Giannarakis[5], Chris Hawblitzel[6], Cătălin Hriţcu[2], Monal Narasimhamurthy[8], Zoe Paraskevopoulou[5], Clément Pit-Claudel[9], Jonathan Protzenko[6], Tahina Ramananandro[6], Aseem Rastogi[7], and Nikhil Swamy[6]

[1] CIFASIS-CONICET, Rosario, Argentina
martinez@cifasis-conicet.gov.ar
[2] Inria, Paris, France
[3] University of Ljubljana, Ljubljana, Slovenia
[4] MSR-Inria Joint Centre, Paris, France
[5] Princeton University, Princeton, USA
[6] Microsoft Research, Redmond, USA
[7] Microsoft Research, Bangalore, India
[8] University of Colorado Boulder, Boulder, USA
[9] MIT CSAIL, Cambridge, USA

Abstract. We introduce Meta-F*, a tactics and metaprogramming framework for the F* program verifier. The main novelty of Meta-F* is allowing the use of tactics and metaprogramming to discharge assertions not solvable by SMT, or to just simplify them into well-behaved SMT fragments. Plus, Meta-F* can be used to generate verified code automatically.

Meta-F* is implemented as an F* *effect*, which, given the powerful effect system of F*, heavily increases code reuse and even enables the lightweight verification of metaprograms. Metaprograms can be either interpreted, or compiled to efficient native code that can be dynamically loaded into the F* type-checker and can interoperate with interpreted code. Evaluation on realistic case studies shows that Meta-F* provides substantial gains in proof development, efficiency, and robustness.

Keywords: Tactics · Metaprogramming · Program verification · Verification conditions · SMT solvers · Proof assistants

1 Introduction

Scripting proofs using tactics and metaprogramming has a long tradition in interactive theorem provers (ITPs), starting with Milner's Edinburgh LCF [37]. In this lineage, properties of *pure* programs are specified in expressive higher-order (and often dependently typed) logics, and proofs are conducted using various imperative programming languages, starting originally with ML.

Along a different axis, program verifiers like Dafny [47], VCC [23], Why3 [33], and Liquid Haskell [59] target both pure *and effectful* programs, with side-effects

L. Caires (Ed.): ESOP 2019, LNCS 11423, pp. 30–59, 2019.
https://doi.org/10.1007/978-3-030-17184-1_2

ranging from divergence to concurrency, but provide relatively weak logics for specification (e.g., first-order logic with a few selected theories like linear arithmetic). They work primarily by computing verification conditions (VCs) from programs, usually relying on annotations such as pre- and postconditions, and encoding them to automated theorem provers (ATPs) such as satisfiability modulo theories (SMT) solvers, often providing excellent automation.

These two sub-fields have influenced one another, though the situation is somewhat asymmetric. On the one hand, most interactive provers have gained support for exploiting SMT solvers or other ATPs, providing push-button automation for certain kinds of assertions [26,31,43,44,54]. On the other hand, recognizing the importance of interactive proofs, Why3 [33] interfaces with ITPs like Coq. However, working over proof obligations translated from Why3 requires users to be familiar not only with both these systems, but also with the specifics of the translation. And beyond Why3 and the tools based on it [25], no other SMT-based program verifiers have full-fledged support for interactive proving, leading to several downsides:

Limits to expressiveness. The expressiveness of program verifiers can be limited by the ATP used. When dealing with theories that are undecidable and difficult to automate (e.g., non-linear arithmetic or separation logic), proofs in ATP-based systems may become impossible or, at best, extremely tedious.

Boilerplate. To work around this lack of automation, programmers have to construct detailed proofs by hand, often repeating many tedious yet error-prone steps, so as to provide hints to the underlying solver to discover the proof. In contrast, ITPs with metaprogramming facilities excel at expressing domain-specific automation to complete such tedious proofs.

Implicit proof context. In most program verifiers, the logical context of a proof is implicit in the program text and depends on the control flow and the pre- and postconditions of preceding computations. Unlike in interactive proof assistants, programmers have no explicit access, neither visual nor programmatic, to this context, making proof structuring and exploration extremely difficult.

In direct response to these drawbacks, we seek a system that successfully combines the convenience of an automated program verifier for the common case, while seamlessly transitioning to an interactive proving experience for those parts of a proof that are hard to automate. Towards this end, we propose Meta-F*, a tactics and metaprogramming framework for the F* [1,58] program verifier.

Highlights and Contributions of Meta-F*

F* has historically been more deeply rooted as an SMT-based program verifier. Until now, F* discharged VCs exclusively by calling an SMT solver (usually Z3 [28]), providing good automation for many common program verification tasks, but also exhibiting the drawbacks discussed above.

Meta-F* is a framework that allows F* users to manipulate VCs using *tactics*. More generally, it supports *metaprogramming*, allowing programmers to script the construction of programs, by manipulating their syntax and customizing the way they are type-checked. This allows programmers to (1) implement custom procedures for manipulating VCs; (2) eliminate boilerplate in proofs and programs; and (3) to inspect the proof state visually and to manipulate it programmatically, addressing the drawbacks discussed above. SMT still plays a central role in Meta-F*: a typical usage involves implementing tactics to transform VCs, so as to bring them into theories well-supported by SMT, without needing to (re)implement full decision procedures. Further, the generality of Meta-F* allows implementing non-trivial language extensions (e.g., typeclass resolution) entirely as metaprogramming libraries, without changes to the F* type-checker.

The technical **contributions** of our work include the following:

"Meta-" is just an effect (Sect. 3.1). Meta-F* is implemented using F*'s extensible effect system, which keeps programs and metaprograms properly isolated. Being first-class F* programs, metaprograms are typed, call-by-value, direct-style, higher-order functional programs, much like the original ML. Further, metaprograms can be themselves verified (to a degree, see Sect. 3.4) and metaprogrammed.

Reconciling tactics with VC generation (Sect. 4.2). In program verifiers the programmer often guides the solver towards the proof by supplying intermediate assertions. Meta-F* retains this style, but additionally allows assertions to be solved by tactics. To this end, a contribution of our work is extracting, from a VC, a proof state encompassing all relevant hypotheses, including those implicit in the program text.

Executing metaprograms efficiently (Sect. 5). Metaprograms are executed during type-checking. As a baseline, they can be interpreted using F*'s existing (but slow) abstract machine for term normalization, or a faster normalizer based on normalization by evaluation (NbE) [10,16]. For much faster execution speed, metaprograms can also be run natively. This is achieved by combining the existing extraction mechanism of F* to OCaml with a new framework for safely extending the F* type-checker with such native code.

Examples (Sect. 2) and evaluation (Sect. 6). We evaluate Meta-F* on several case studies. First, we present a functional correctness proof for the Poly1305 message authentication code (MAC) [11], using a novel combination of proofs by reflection for dealing with non-linear arithmetic and SMT solving for linear arithmetic. We measure a clear gain in proof robustness: SMT-only proofs succeed only rarely (for reasonable timeouts), whereas our tactic+SMT proof is concise, never fails, and is faster. Next, we demonstrate an improvement in expressiveness, by developing a small library for proofs of heap-manipulating programs in separation logic, which was previously out-of-scope for F*. Finally, we illustrate the ability to automatically construct verified effectful programs, by introducing a library for metaprogramming verified low-level parsers and serializers with applications to network programming, where verification is accelerated by processing the VC with tactics, and by programmatically tweaking the SMT context.

We conclude that tactics and metaprogramming can be prosperously combined with VC generation and SMT solving to build verified programs with better, more scalable, and more robust automation.

The full version of this paper, including appendices, can be found online in https://www.fstar-lang.org/papers/metafstar.

2 Meta-F* by Example

F* is a general-purpose programming language aimed at program verification. It puts together the automation of an SMT-backed deductive verification tool with the expressive power of a language with full-spectrum dependent types. Briefly, it is a functional, higher-order, effectful, dependently typed language, with syntax loosely based on OCaml. F* supports refinement types and Hoare-style specifications, computing VCs of computations via a type-level weakest precondition (WP) calculus packed within *Dijkstra monads* [57]. F*'s effect system is also user-extensible [1]. Using it, one can model or embed imperative programming in styles ranging from ML to C [55] and assembly [35]. After verification, F* programs can be extracted to efficient OCaml or F# code. A first-order fragment of F*, called Low*, can also be extracted to C via the KreMLin compiler [55].

This paper introduces Meta-F*, a metaprogramming framework for F* that allows users to safely customize and extend F* in many ways. For instance, Meta-F* can be used to preprocess or solve proof obligations; synthesize F* expressions; generate top-level definitions; and resolve implicit arguments in user-defined ways, enabling non-trivial extensions. This paper primarily discusses the first two features. Technically, none of these features deeply increase the expressive power of F*, since one could manually program in F* terms that can now be metaprogrammed. However, as we will see shortly, manually programming terms and their proofs can be so prohibitively costly as to be practically infeasible.

Meta-F* is similar to other tactic frameworks, such as Coq's [29] or Lean's [30], in presenting a set of goals to the programmer, providing commands to break them down, allowing to inspect and build abstract syntax, etc. In this paper, we mostly detail the characteristics where Meta-F* *differs* from other engines.

This section presents Meta-F* informally, displaying its usage through case studies. We present any necessary F* background as needed.

2.1 Tactics for Individual Assertions and Partial Canonicalization

Non-linear arithmetic reasoning is crucially needed for the verification of optimized, low-level cryptographic primitives [18,64], an important use case for F* [13] and other verification frameworks, including those that rely on SMT solving alone (e.g., Dafny [47]) as well as those that rely exclusively on tactic-based proofs (e.g., FiatCrypto [32]). While both styles have demonstrated significant successes, we make a case for a middle ground, leveraging the SMT solver for the parts of a VC where it is effective, and using tactics only where it is not.

We focus on Poly1305 [11], a widely-used cryptographic MAC that computes a series of integer multiplications and additions modulo a large prime number $p = 2^{130} - 5$. Implementations of the Poly1305 multiplication and mod operations are carefully hand-optimized to represent 130-bit numbers in terms of smaller 32-bit or 64-bit registers, using clever tricks; proving their correctness requires reasoning about long sequences of additions and multiplications.

Previously: Guiding SMT Solvers by Manually Applying Lemmas. Prior proofs of correctness of Poly1305 and other cryptographic primitives using SMT-based program verifiers, including F* [64] and Dafny [18], use a combination of SMT automation and manual application of lemmas. On the plus side, SMT solvers are excellent at linear arithmetic, so these proofs delegate all associativity-commutativity (AC) reasoning about addition to SMT. Non-linear arithmetic in SMT solvers, even just AC-rewriting and distributivity, are, however, inefficient and unreliable—so much so that the prior efforts above (and other works too [40,41]) simply turn off support for non-linear arithmetic in the solver, in order not to degrade verification performance across the board due to poor interaction of theories. Instead, users need to explicitly invoke lemmas.[1]

For instance, here is a statement and proof of a lemma about Poly1305 in F*. The property and its proof do not really matter; the lines marked "*(∗argh! ∗)*" do. In this particular proof, working around the solver's inability to effectively reason about non-linear arithmetic, the programmer has spelled out basic facts about distributivity of multiplication and addition, by calling the library lemma distributivity_add_right, in order to guide the solver towards the proof. (Below, p44 and p88 represent 2^{44} and 2^{88} respectively)

```
let lemma_carry_limb_unrolled (a0 a1 a2 : nat) : Lemma (ensures (
   a0 % p44 + p44 * ((a1 + a0 / p44) % p44) + p88 * (a2 + ((a1 + a0 / p44) / p44))
   == a0 + p44 * a1 + p88 * a2)) =
  let z = a0 % p44 + p44 * ((a1 + a0 / p44) % p44)
            + p88 * (a2 + ((a1 + a0 / p44) / p44)) in
  distributivity_add_right p88 a2 ((a1 + a0 / p44) / p44); (* argh! *)
  pow2_plus 44 44;
  lemma_div_mod (a1 + a0 / p44) p44;
  distributivity_add_right p44 ((a1 + a0 / p44) % p44)
            (p44 * ((a1 + a0 / p44) / p44)); (* argh! *)
  assert (p44 * ((a1 + a0 / p44) % p44) + p88 * ((a1 + a0 / p44) / p44)
            == p44 * (a1 + a0 / p44) );
  distributivity_add_right p44 a1 (a0 / p44); (* argh! *)
  lemma_div_mod a0 p44
```

Even at this relatively small scale, needing to explicitly instantiate the distributivity lemma is verbose and error prone. Even worse, the user is blind while doing so: the program text does not display the current set of available facts nor

[1] Lemma (requires pre) (ensures post) is F* notation for the type of a computation proving pre $\Longrightarrow$ post—we omit pre when it is trivial. In F*'s standard library, math lemmas are proved using SMT with little or no interactions between problematic theory combinations. These lemmas can then be explicitly invoked in larger contexts, and are deleted during extraction.

the final goal. Proofs at this level of abstraction are painfully detailed in some aspects, yet also heavily reliant on the SMT solver to fill in the aspects of the proof that are missing.

Given enough time, the solver can sometimes find a proof without the additional hints, but this is usually rare and dependent on context, and almost never robust. In this particular example we find by varying Z3's random seed that, in an isolated setting, the lemma is proven automatically about 32% of the time. The numbers are much worse for more complex proofs, and where the context contains many facts, making this style quickly spiral out of control. For example, a proof of one of the main lemmas in Poly1305, poly_multiply, requires 41 steps of rewriting for associativity-commutativity of multiplication, and distributivity of addition and multiplication—making the proof much too long to show here.

SMT and Tactics in Meta-F*. The listing below shows the statement and proof of poly_multiply in Meta-F*, of which the lemma above was previously only a small part. Again, the specific property proven is not particularly relevant to our discussion. But, this time, the proof contains just two steps.

```
let poly_multiply (n p r h r0 r1 h0 h1 h2 s1 d0 d1 d2 h1 h2 hh : int) : Lemma
  (requires p > 0 ∧ r1 ≥ 0 ∧ n > 0 ∧ 4 * (n * n) == p + 5 ∧ r == r1 * n + r0 ∧
          h == h2 * (n * n) + h1 * n + h0 ∧ s1 == r1 + (r1 / 4) ∧ r1 % 4 == 0 ∧
          d0 == h0 * r0 + h1 * s1 ∧ d1 == h0 * r1 + h1 * r0 + h2 * s1 ∧
          d2 == h2 * r0 ∧ hh == d2 * (n * n) + d1 * n + d0)
  (ensures (h * r) % p == hh % p) =
  let r14 = r1 / 4 in
  let h_r_expand = (h2 * (n * n) + h1 * n + h0) * ((r14 * 4) * n + r0) in
  let hh_expand = (h2 * r0) * (n * n) + (h0 * (r14 * 4) + h1 * r0
                                     + h2 * (5 * r14)) * n + (h0 * r0 + h1 * (5 * r14)) in
  let b = (h2 * n + h1) * r14 in
  modulo_addition_lemma hh_expand p b;
  assert (h_r_expand == hh_expand + b * (n * n * 4 + (−5)))
     by (canon_semiring int_csr) (* Proof of this step by Meta-F* tactic *)
```

First, we call a single lemma about modular addition from F*'s standard library. Then, we assert an equality annotated with a tactic (assert..by). Instead of encoding the assertion as-is to the SMT solver, it is preprocessed by the canon_semiring tactic. The tactic is presented with the asserted equality as its goal, in an environment containing not only all variables in scope but also hypotheses for the precondition of poly_multiply and the postcondition of the modulo_addition_lemma call (otherwise, the assertion could not be proven). The tactic will then canonicalize the sides of the equality, but notably only "up to" linear arithmetic conversions. Rather than fully canonicalizing the terms, the tactic just rewrites them into a sum-of-products canonical form, leaving all the remaining work to the SMT solver, which can then easily and robustly discharge the goal using linear arithmetic only.

This tactic works over terms in the commutative semiring of integers (int_csr) using proof-by-reflection [12,20,36,38]. Internally, it is composed of a simpler, also proof-by-reflection based tactic canon_monoid that works over monoids, which is then "stacked" on itself to build canon_semiring. The basic idea of proof-by-reflection is to reduce most of the proof burden to mechanical computation, obtaining much more efficient proofs compared to repeatedly applying lemmas. For canon_monoid, we begin with a type for monoids, a small AST representing monoid values, and a denotation for expressions back into the monoid type.

```
type monoid (a:Type) = { unit : a; mult : (a → a → a); (* + monoid laws ... *) }
type exp (a:Type) = | Unit : exp a | Var : a → exp a | Mult : exp a → exp a → exp a
(* Note on syntax: #a below denotes that a is an implicit argument *)
let rec denote (#a:Type) (m:monoid a) (e:exp a) : a =
  match e with
  | Unit → m.unit | Var x → x | Mult x y → m.mult (denote m x) (denote m y)
```

To canonicalize an exp, it is first converted to a list of operands (flatten) and then reflected back to the monoid (mldenote). The process is proven correct, in the particular case of equalities, by the monoid_reflect lemma.

```
val flatten : #a:Type → exp a → list a
val mldenote : #a:Type → monoid a → list a → a
let monoid_reflect (#a:Type) (m:monoid a) (e1 e2 : exp a)
                  : Lemma (requires (mldenote m (flatten e1) == mldenote m (flatten e2)))
                          (ensures (denote m e1 == denote m e2)) = ...
```

At this stage, if the goal is $t_1 ==$ t_2, we require two monoidal expressions e_1 and e_2 such that $t_1 ==$ denote m e_1 and $t_2 ==$ denote m e_2. They are constructed by the tactic canon_monoid by inspecting the *syntax* of the goal, using Meta-F*'s reflection capabilities (detailed ahead in Sect. 3.3). We have no way to prove once and for all that the expressions built by canon_monoid correctly denote the terms, but this fact can be proven automatically at each application of the tactic, by simple unification. The tactic then applies the lemma monoid_reflect m $e_1 e_2$, and the goal is changed to mldenote m (flatten e_1) $==$ mldenote m (flatten e_2). Finally, by normalization, each side will be canonicalized by running flatten and mldenote.

The canon_semiring tactic follows a similar approach, and is similar to existing reflective tactics for other proof assistants [9,38], except that it only canonicalizes up to linear arithmetic, as explained above. The full VC for poly_multiply contains many other facts, e.g., that p is non-zero so the division is well-defined and that the postcondition does indeed hold. These obligations remain in a "skeleton" VC that is also easily proven by Z3. This proof is much easier for the programmer to write and much more robust, as detailed ahead in Sect. 6.1. The proof of Poly1305's other main lemma, poly_reduce, is also similarly well automated.

Tactic Proofs Without SMT. Of course, one can verify poly_multiply in Coq, following the same conceptual proof used in Meta-F*, but relying on tactics only. Our proof (included in the appendix) is 27 lines long, two of which involve the use of Coq's ring tactic (similar to our canon_semiring tactic) and omega tactic for solving formulas in Presburger arithmetic. The remaining 25 lines include steps to destruct the propositional structure of terms, rewrite by equalities, enriching the context to enable automatic modulo rewriting (Coq does not fully automatically recognize equality modulo p as an equivalence relation compatible with arithmetic operators). While a mature proof assistant like Coq has libraries and tools to ease this kind of manipulation, it can still be verbose.

In contrast, in Meta-F* all of these mundane parts of a proof are simply dispatched to the SMT solver, which decides linear arithmetic efficiently, beyond the quantifier-free Presburger fragment supported by tactics like omega, handles congruence closure natively, etc.

2.2 Tactics for Entire VCs and Separation Logic

A different way to invoke Meta-F* is over an entire VC. While the exact shape of VCs is hard to predict, users with some experience can write tactics that find and solve particular sub-assertions within a VC, or simply massage them into shapes better suited for the SMT solver. We illustrate the idea on proofs for heap-manipulating programs.

One verification method that has eluded F* until now is separation logic, the main reason being that the pervasive "frame rule" requires instantiating existentially quantified heap variables, which is a challenge for SMT solvers, and simply too tedious for users. With Meta-F*, one can do better. We have written a (proof-of-concept) embedding of separation logic and a tactic (sl_auto) that performs heap frame inference automatically.

The approach we follow consists of designing the WP specifications for primitive stateful actions so as to make their footprint syntactically evident. The tactic then descends through VCs until it finds an existential for heaps arising from the frame rule. Then, by solving an equality between heap expressions (which requires canonicalization, for which we use a variant of canon_monoid targeting *commutative* monoids) the tactic finds the frames and instantiates the existentials. Notably, as opposed to other tactic frameworks for separation logic [4,45,49,51], this is *all* our tactic does before dispatching to the SMT solver, which can now be effective over the instantiated VC.

We now provide some detail on the framework. Below, 'emp' represents the empty heap, '•' is the separating conjunction and 'r ↦ v' is the heaplet with the single reference r set to value v.[2] Our development distinguishes between a "heap" and its "memory" for technical reasons, but we will treat the two as equivalent here. Further, defined is a predicate discriminating valid heaps (as in [52]), i.e., those built from separating conjunctions of *actually* disjoint heaps.

We first define the type of WPs and present the WP for the frame rule:

```
let pre = memory → prop (* predicate on initial heaps *)
let post a = a → memory → prop (* predicate on result values and final heaps *)
let wp a = post a → pre (* transformer from postconditions to preconditions *)

let frame_post (#a:Type) (p:post a) (m0:memory) : post a =
  λx m1 → defined (m0 • m1) ∧ p x (m0 • m1)
let frame_wp (#a:Type) (wp:wp a) (post:post a) (m:memory) =
  ∃m0 m1. defined (m0 • m1) ∧ m == (m0 • m1) ∧ wp (frame_post post m1) m0
```

[2] This differs from the usual presentation where these three operators are heap *predicates* instead of heaps.

Intuitively, frame_post p m_0 behaves as the postcondition p "framed" by m_0, i.e., frame_post p m_0 x m_1 holds when the two heaps m_0 and m_1 are disjoint and p holds over the result value x and the conjoined heaps. Then, frame_wp wp takes a postcondition p and initial heap m, and requires that m can be split into disjoint subheaps m_0 (the footprint) and m_1 (the frame), such that the postcondition p, when properly framed, holds over the footprint.

In order to provide specifications for primitive actions we start in small-footprint style. For instance, below is the WP for reading a reference:

```
let read_wp (#a:Type) (r:ref a) = λpost m0 → ∃x. m0 == r ↦ x ∧ post x m0
```

We then insert framing wrappers around such small-footprint WPs when exposing the corresponding stateful actions to the programmer, e.g.,

```
val (!) : #a:Type → r:ref a → STATE a (λ p m → frame_wp (read_wp r) p m)
```

To verify code written in such style, we annotate the corresponding programs to have their VCs processed by sl_auto. For instance, for the swap function below, the tactic successfully finds the frames for the four occurrences of the frame rule and greatly reduces the solver's work. Even in this simple example, not performing such instantiation would cause the solver to fail.

```
let swap_wp (r1 r2 : ref int) =
    λp m → ∃x y. m == (r1 ↦ x • r2 ↦ y) ∧ p () (r1 ↦ y • r2 ↦ x)
let swap (r1 r2 : ref int) : ST unit (swap_wp r1 r2) by (sl_auto ()) =
    let x = !r1 in let y = !r2 in r1 := y; r2 := x
```

The sl_auto tactic: (1) uses syntax inspection to unfold and traverse the goal until it reaches a frame_wp—say, the one for $!r_2$; (2) inspects frame_wp's first explicit argument (here read_wp r_2) to compute the references the current command requires (here r_2); (3) uses unification variables to build a memory expression describing the required framing of input memory (here $r_2 \mapsto ?u_1 \bullet ?u_2$) and instantiates the existentials of frame_wp with these unification variables; (4) builds a goal that equates this memory expression with frame_wp's third argument (here $r_1 \mapsto x \bullet r_2 \mapsto y$); and (5) uses a commutative monoids tactic (similar to Sect. 2.1) with the heap algebra (emp, •) to canonicalize the equality and sort the heaplets. Next, it can solve for the unification variables component-wise, instantiating $?u_1$ to y and $?u_2$ to $r_1 \mapsto x$, and then proceed to the next frame_wp.

In general, after frames are instantiated, the SMT solver can efficiently prove the remaining assertions, such as the obligations about heap definedness. Thus, with relatively little effort, Meta-F* brings an (albeit simple version of a) widely used yet previously out-of-scope program logic (i.e., separation logic) into F*. To the best of our knowledge, the ability to *script* separation logic into an SMT-based program verifier, without any primitive support, is unique.

2.3 Metaprogramming Verified Low-Level Parsers and Serializers

Above, we used Meta-F* to manipulate VCs for user-written code. Here, we focus instead on generating verified code automatically. We loosely refer to the previous setting as using "tactics", and to the current one as "metaprogramming".

In most ITPs, tactics and metaprogramming are not distinguished; however in a program verifier like F*, where some proofs are not materialized at all (Sect. 4.1), proving VCs of existing terms is distinct from generating new terms.

Metaprogramming in F* involves programmatically generating a (potentially effectful) term (e.g., by constructing its syntax and instructing F* how to type-check it) and processing any VCs that arise via tactics. When applicable (e.g., when working in a domain-specific language), metaprogramming verified code can substantially reduce, or even eliminate, the burden of manual proofs.

We illustrate this by automating the generation of parsers and serializers from a type definition. Of course, this is a routine task in many mainstream metaprogramming frameworks (e.g., Template Haskell, camlp4, etc). The novelty here is that we produce imperative parsers and serializers extracted to C, with proofs that they are memory safe, functionally correct, and mutually inverse. This section is slightly simplified, more detail can be found the appendix.

We proceed in several stages. First, we program a library of pure, high-level parser and serializer combinators, proven to be (partial) mutual inverses of each other. A parser for a type t is represented as a function possibly returning a t along with the amount of input bytes consumed. The type of a serializer for a given p:parser t contains a refinement[3] stating that p is an inverse of the serializer. A package is a dependent record of a parser and an associated serializer.

```
let parser t = seq byte → option (t ∗ nat)
let serializer #t (p:parser t) = f:(t → seq byte){∀ x. p (f x) == Some (x, length (f x))}
type package t = { p : parser t ; s : serializer p }
```

Basic combinators in the library include constructs for parsing and serializing base values and pairs, such as the following:

```
val p_u8 : parse u8
val s_u8 : serializer p_u8
val p_pair : parser t1 → parser t2 → parser (t1 ∗ t2)
val s_pair : serializer p1 → serializer p2 → serializer (p_pair p1 p2)
```

Next, we define low-level versions of these combinators, which work over mutable arrays instead of byte sequences. These combinators are coded in the Low* subset of F* (and so can be extracted to C) and are proven to both be memory-safe and respect their high-level variants. The type for low-level parsers, parser_impl (p:parser t), denotes an imperative function that reads from an array of bytes and returns a t, behaving as the specificational parser p. Conversely, a serializer_impl (s:serializer p) writes into an array of bytes, behaving as s.

Given such a library, we would like to build verified, mutually inverse, low-level parsers and serializers for specific data formats. The task is mechanical, yet overwhelmingly tedious by hand, with many auxiliary proof obligations of a predictable structure: a perfect candidate for metaprogramming.

Deriving Specifications from a Type Definition. Consider the following F* type, representing lists of exactly 18 pairs of bytes.

[3] F* syntax for refinements is x:t {ϕ}, denoting the type of all x of type t satisfying ϕ.

```
type sample = nlist 18 (u8 * u8)
```

The first component of our metaprogram is gen_specs, which generates parser and serializer specifications from a type definition.

```
let ps_sample : package sample = _ by (gen_specs (`sample))
```

The syntax _ by τ is the way to call Meta-F* for code generation. Meta-F* will run the metaprogram τ and, if successful, replace the underscore by the result. In this case, the gen_specs (`sample) inspects the syntax of the sample type (Sect. 3.3) and produces the package below (seq_p and seq_s are sequencing combinators):

```
let ps_sample = { p = p_nlist 18 (p_u8 `seq_p` p_u8)
                ; s = s_nlist 18 (s_u8 `seq_s` s_u8) }
```

Deriving Low-Level Implementations that Match Specifications. From this pair of specifications, we can automatically generate Low* implementations for them:

```
let p_low : parser_impl ps_sample.p = _ by gen_parser_impl
let s_low : serializer_impl ps_sample.s = _ by gen_serializer_impl
```

which will produce the following low-level implementations:

```
let p_low = parse_nlist_impl 18ul (parse_u8_impl `seq_pi` parse_u8_impl)
let s_low = serialize_nlist_impl 18ul (serialize_u8_impl `seq_si` serialize_u8_impl)
```

For simple types like the one above, the generated code is fairly simple. However, for more complex types, using the combinator library comes with non-trivial proof obligations. For example, even for a simple enumeration, type color = Red | Green, the parser specification is as follows:

```
parse_synth (parse_bounded_u8 2)
        (λ x2 → mk_if_t (x2 = 0uy) (λ _ → Red) (λ _ → Green))
        (λ x → match x with | Green → 1uy | Red → 0uy)
```

We represent Red with 0uy and Green with 1uy. The parser first parses a "bounded" byte, with only two values. The parse_synth combinator then expects functions between the bounded byte and the datatype being parsed (color), which must be proven to be mutual inverses. This proof is conceptually easy, but for large enumerations nested deep within the structure of other types, it is notoriously hard for SMT solvers. Since the proof is inherently computational, a proof that destructs the inductive type into its cases and then normalizes is much more natural. With our metaprogram, we can produce the term and then discharge these proof obligations with a tactic *on the spot*, eliminating them from the final VC. We also explore simply tweaking the SMT context, again via a tactic, with good results. A quantitative evaluation is provided in Sect. 6.2.

3 The Design of Meta-F*

Having caught a glimpse of the use cases for Meta-F*, we now turn to its design. As usual in proof assistants (such as Coq, Lean and Idris), Meta-F* tactics work over a set of goals and apply primitive actions to transform them, possibly solving some goals and generating new goals in the process. Since this is standard, we will focus the most on describing the aspects where Meta-F* differs from other engines. We first describe how metaprograms are modelled as an effect (Sect. 3.1) and their runtime model (Sect. 3.2). We then detail some of Meta-F*'s syntax inspection and building capabilities (Sect. 3.3). Finally, we show how to perform some (lightweight) verification of metaprograms (Sect. 3.4) within F*.

3.1 An Effect for Metaprogramming

Meta-F* tactics are, at their core, programs that transform the "proof state", i.e. a set of goals needing to be solved. As in Lean [30] and Idris [22], we define a monad combining exceptions and stateful computations over a proof state, along with actions that can access internal components such as the type-checker. For this we first introduce abstract types for the proof state, goals, terms, environments, etc., together with functions to access them, some of them shown below.

```
type proofstate          val goals_of : proofstate → list goal
type goal                val goal_env : goal → env
type term                val goal_type : goal → term
type env                 val goal_solution : goal → term
```

We can now define our metaprogramming monad: tac. It combines F*'s existing effect for potential divergence (Div), with exceptions and stateful computations over a proofstate. The definition of tac, shown below, is straightforward and given in F*'s standard library. Then, we use F*'s effect extension capabilities [1] in order to elevate the tac monad and its actions to an effect, dubbed TAC.

```
type error = exn ∗ proofstate (∗ error and proofstate at the time of failure ∗)
type result a = | Success : a → proofstate → result a | Failed : error → result a
let tac a = proofstate → Div (result a)
let t_return #a (x:a) = λps → Success x ps
let t_bind #a #b (m:tac a) (f:a → tac b) : tac b = λps → ... (∗ omitted, yet simple ∗)
let get () : tac proofstate = λps → Success ps ps
let raise #a (e:exn) : tac a = λps → Failed (e, ps)
new_effect { TAC with repr = tac ; return = t_return ; bind = t_bind
                                 ; get = get ; raise = raise }
```

The new_effect declaration introduces *computation types* of the form TAC t wp, where t is the return type and wp a specification. However, until Sect. 3.4 we shall only use the derived form Tac t, where the specification is trivial. These computation types are distinct from their underlying monadic representation type tac t—users cannot directly access the proof state except via the actions. The simplest actions stem from the tac monad definition: get : unit → Tac proofstate returns the current proof state and raise: exn → Tac α fails with the given exception[4]. Failures can be handled using catch : (unit → Tac α) → Tac (either exn α), which resets the state on failure, including that of unification metavariables.

[4] We use greek letters α, β, ... to abbreviate universally quantified type variables.

We emphasize two points here. First, there is no "set" action. This is to forbid metaprograms from arbitrarily replacing their proof state, which would be unsound. Second, the argument to catch must be thunked, since in F* impure un-suspended computations are evaluated before they are passed into functions.

The only aspect differentiating Tac from other user-defined effects is the existence of effect-specific primitive actions, which give access to the metaprogramming engine proper. We list here but a few:

```
val trivial : unit → Tac unit     val tc : term → Tac term     val dump : string → Tac unit
```

All of these are given an interpretation internally by Meta-F*. For instance, trivial calls into F*'s logical simplifier to check whether the current goal is a trivial proposition and discharges it if so, failing otherwise. The tc primitive queries the type-checker to infer the type of a given term in the current environment (F* types are a kind of terms, hence the codomain of tc is also term). This does not change the proof state; its only purpose is to return useful information to the calling metaprograms. Finally, dump outputs the current proof state to the user in a pretty-printed format, in support of user interaction.

Having introduced the Tac effect and some basic actions, writing metaprograms is as straightforward as writing any other F* code. For instance, here are two metaprogram combinators. The first one repeatedly calls its argument until it fails, returning a list of all the successfully-returned values. The second one behaves similarly, but folds the results with some provided folding function.

```
let rec repeat (τ : unit → Tac α) : Tac (list α) =
  match catch τ with | Inl _ → [] | Inr x → x :: repeat τ

let repeat_fold f e τ = fold_left f e (repeat τ )
```

These two small combinators illustrate a few key points of Meta-F*. As for all other F* effects, metaprograms are written in applicative style, without explicit return, bind, or lift of computations (which are inserted under the hood). This also works across different effects: repeat_fold can seamlessly combine the pure fold_left from F*'s list library with a metaprogram like repeat. Metaprograms are also type- and effect-inferred: while repeat_fold was not at all annotated, F* infers the polymorphic type $(\beta \rightarrow \alpha \rightarrow \beta) \rightarrow \beta \rightarrow (\mathsf{unit} \rightarrow \mathsf{Tac}\ \alpha) \rightarrow \mathsf{Tac}\ \alpha$ for it.

It should be noted that, if lacking an effect extension feature, one could embed metaprograms simply via the (properly abstracted) tac monad instead of the Tac effect. It is just more convenient to use an effect, given we are working within an effectful program verifier already. In what follows, with the exception of Sect. 3.4 where we describe specifications for metaprograms, there is little reliance on using an effect; so, the same ideas could be applied in other settings.

3.2 Executing Meta-F* Metaprograms

Running metaprograms involves three steps. First, they are *reified* [1] into their underlying tac representation, i.e. as state-passing functions. User code cannot reify metaprograms: only F* can do so when about to process a goal.

Second, the reified term is applied to an initial proof state, and then simply evaluated according to F*'s dynamic semantics, for instance using F*'s existing normalizer. For intensive applications, such as proofs by reflection, we provide faster alternatives (Sect. 5). In order to perform this second step, the proof state, which up until this moments exists only internally to F*, must be *embedded* as a term, i.e., as abstract syntax. Here is where its abstraction pays off: since metaprograms cannot interact with a proof state except through a limited interface, it need not be *deeply* embedded as syntax. By simply wrapping the internal proofstate into a new kind of "alien" term, and making the primitives aware of this wrapping, we can readily run the metaprogram that safely carries its alien proof state around. This wrapping of proof states is a constant-time operation.

The third step is interpreting the primitives. They are realized by functions of similar types implemented within the F* type-checker, but over an internal tac monad and the concrete definitions for term, proofstate, etc. Hence, there is a translation involved on every call and return, switching between embedded representations and their concrete variants. Take dump, for example, with type string → Tac unit. Its internal implementation, implemented within the F* type-checker, has type string → proofstate → Div (result unit). When interpreting a call to it, the interpreter must *unembed* the arguments (which are representations of F* terms) into a concrete string and a concrete proofstate to pass to the internal implementation of dump. The situation is symmetric for the return value of the call, which must be *embedded* as a term.

3.3 Syntax Inspection, Generation, and Quotation

If metaprograms are to be reusable over different kinds of goals, they must be able to reflect on the goals they are invoked to solve. Like any metaprogramming system, Meta-F* offers a way to inspect and construct the syntax of F* terms. Our representation of terms as an inductive type, and the variants of quotations, are inspired by the ones in Idris [22] and Lean [30].

Inspecting Syntax. Internally, F* uses a locally-nameless representation [21] with explicit, delayed substitutions. To shield metaprograms from some of this internal bureaucracy, we expose a simplified view [61] of terms. Below we present a few constructors from the term_view type:

```
val inspect : term → Tac term_view    type term_view =
val pack : term_view → term             | Tv_BVar : v:dbvar → term_view
                                        | Tv_Var : v:name → term_view
                                        | Tv_FVar : v:qname → term_view
                                        | Tv_Abs : bv:binder → body:term → term_view
                                        | Tv_App : hd:term → arg:term → term_view
                                        ...
```

The term_view type provides the "one-level-deep" structure of a term: metaprograms must call inspect to reveal the structure of the term, one constructor at a time. The view exposes three kinds of variables: bound variables, Tv_BVar; named local variables Tv_Var; and top-level fully qualified names, Tv_FVar. Bound variables and local variables are distinguished since the internal abstract syntax is locally nameless. For metaprogramming, it is usually simpler to use a fully-named representation, so we provide inspect and pack functions that open and close binders appropriately to maintain this invariant. Since opening binders requires freshness, inspect has effect Tac.[5] As generating large pieces of syntax via the view easily becomes tedious, we also provide some ways of *quoting* terms:

Static Quotations. A static quotation `e is just a shorthand for statically calling the F* parser to convert e into the abstract syntax of F* terms above. For instance, `(f 1 2) is equivalent to the following,

```
pack (Tv_App (pack (Tv_App (pack (Tv_FVar "f"))
                           (pack (Tv_Const (C_Int 1)))))
             (pack (Tv_Const (C_Int 2))))
```

Dynamic Quotations. A second form of quotation is dquote: #a:Type → a → Tac term, an effectful operation that is interpreted by F*'s normalizer during metaprogram evaluation. It returns the syntax of its argument at the time dquote e is evaluated. Evaluating dquote e substitutes all the free variables in e with their current values in the execution environment, suspends further evaluation, and returns the abstract syntax of the resulting term. For instance, evaluating (λx → dquote (x + 1)) 16 produces the abstract syntax of 16 + 1.

Anti-quotations. Static quotations are useful for building big chunks of syntax concisely, but they are of limited use if we cannot combine them with existing bits of syntax. Subterms of a quotation are allowed to "escape" and be substituted by arbitrary expressions. We use the syntax `#t to denote an antiquoted t, where t must be an expression of type term in order for the quotation to be well-typed. For example, `(1 + `#e) creates syntax for an addition where one operand is the integer constant 1 and the other is the term represented by e.

Unquotation. Finally, we provide an effectful operation, unquote: #a:Type → t:term → Tac a, which takes a term representation t and an expected type for it a (usually inferred from the context), and calls the F* type-checker to check and elaborate the term representation into a well-typed term.

3.4 Specifying and Verifying Metaprograms

Since we model metaprograms as a particular kind of effectful program within F*, which is a program verifier, a natural question to ask is whether F* can specify and verify metaprograms. The answer is "yes, to a degree".

To do so, we must use the WP calculus for the TAC effect: TAC-computations are given computation types of the form TAC a wp, where a is the computation's result type and wp is a weakest-precondition transformer of type tacwp a = proofstate → (result a → prop) → prop. However, since WPs tend to not be very

[5] We also provide functions inspect_ln, pack_ln which stay in a locally-nameless representation and are thus pure, total functions.

intuitive, we first define two variants of the TAC effect: TacH in "Hoare-style" with pre- and postconditions and Tac (which we have seen before), which only specifies the return type, but uses trivial pre- and postconditions. The requires and ensures keywords below simply aid readability of pre- and postconditions—they are identity functions.

```
effect TacH (a:Type) (pre : proofstate → prop) (post : proofstate → result a → prop) =
        TAC a (λ ps post' → pre ps ∧ (∀ r. post ps r ⟹ post' r))
effect Tac (a:Type) = TacH a (requires (λ _ → ⊤)) (ensures (λ _ _ → ⊤))
```

Previously, we only showed the simple type for the raise primitive, namely exn → Tac α. In fact, in full detail and Hoare style, its type/specification is:

```
val raise : e:exn→  TacH α (requires (λ _ → ⊤))
                          (ensures (λ ps r → r == Failed (e, ps)))
```

expressing that the primitive has no precondition, always fails with the provided exception, and does not modify the proof state. From the specifications of the primitives, and the automatically obtained Dijkstra monad, F* can already prove interesting properties about metaprograms. We show a few simple examples.

The following metaprogram is accepted by F* as it can conclude, from the type of raise, that the assertion is unreachable, and hence raise_flow can have a trivial precondition (as Tac unit implies).

```
let raise_flow () : Tac unit = raise SomeExn; assert ⊥
```

For cur_goal_safe below, F* verifies that (given the precondition) the pattern match is exhaustive. The postcondition is also asserting that the metaprogram always succeeds without affecting the proof state, returning some unspecified goal. Calls to cur_goal_safe must statically ensure that the goal list is not empty.

```
let cur_goal_safe () : TacH goal (requires (λ ps → ¬(goals_of ps == [])))
                                 (ensures (λ ps r → ∃g. r == Success g ps)) =
   match goals_of (get ()) with | g :: _ → g
```

Finally, the divide combinator below "splits" the goals of a proof state in two at a given index n, and focuses a different metaprogram on each. It includes a runtime check that the given n is non-negative, and raises an exception in the TAC effect otherwise. Afterwards, the call to the (pure) List.splitAt function requires that n be statically known to be non-negative, a fact which can be proven from the specification for raise and the effect definition, which defines the control flow.

```
let divide (n:int) (tl : unit → Tac α) (tr : unit → Tac β) : Tac (α * β) =
   if n < 0 then raise NegativeN;
   let gsl, gsr = List.splitAt n (goals ()) in ...
```

This enables a style of "lightweight" verification of metaprograms, where expressive invariants about their state and control-flow can be encoded. The programmer can exploit dynamic checks (n < 0) and exceptions (raise) or static ones (preconditions), or a mixture of them, as needed.

Due to type abstraction, though, the specifications of most primitives cannot provide complete detail about their behavior, and deeper specifications (such as ensuring a tactic will correctly solve a goal) cannot currently be proven, nor even stated—to do so would require, at least, an internalization of the typing judgment of F*. While this is an exciting possibility [3], we have for now only focused on verifying basic safety properties of metaprograms, which helps users detect errors early, and whose proofs the SMT can handle well. Although in principle, one can also write tactics to discharge the proof obligations of metaprograms.

4 Meta-F*, Formally

We now describe the trust assumptions for Meta-F* (Sect. 4.1) and then how we reconcile tactics within a program verifier, where the exact shape of VCs is not given, nor known a priori by the user (Sect. 4.2).

4.1 Correctness and Trusted Computing Base (TCB)

As in any proof assistant, tactics and metaprogramming would be rather useless if they allowed to "prove" invalid judgments—care must be taken to ensure soundness. We begin with a taste of the specifics of F*'s static semantics, which influence the trust model for Meta-F*, and then provide more detail on the TCB.

Proof Irrelevance in F*. The following two rules for introducing and eliminating refinement types are key in F*, as they form the basis of its proof irrelevance.

$$\textsc{T-Refine}\quad \frac{\Gamma \vdash e : t \quad \Gamma \models \phi[e/x]}{\Gamma \vdash e : x{:}t\{\phi\}} \qquad\qquad \textsc{V-Refine}\quad \frac{\Gamma \vdash e : x{:}t\{\phi\}}{\Gamma \models \phi[e/x]}$$

The $\models$ symbol represents F*'s *validity judgment* [1] which, at a high-level, defines a proof-irrelevant, classical, higher-order logic. These validity hypotheses are usually collected by the type-checker, and then encoded to the SMT solver in bulk. Crucially, the irrelevance of validity is what permits efficient interaction with SMT solvers, since reconstructing F* terms from SMT proofs is unneeded.

As evidenced in the rules, validity and typing are mutually recursive, and therefore Meta-F* must also construct validity derivations. In the implementation, we model these validity goals as holes with a "squash" type [5,53], where $\mathsf{squash}\ \phi = \_{:}\mathsf{unit}\{\phi\}$, i.e., a refinement of unit. Concretely, we model $\Gamma \models \phi$ as $\Gamma \vdash ?\mathsf{u} : \mathsf{squash}\ \phi$ using a unification variable. Meta-F* does not construct deep solutions to squashed goals: if they are proven valid, the variable ?u is simply solved by the unit value '()'. At any point, any such irrelevant goal can be sent to the SMT solver. Relevant goals, on the other hand, cannot be sent to SMT.

Scripting the Typing Judgment. A consequence of validity proofs not being materialized is that type-checking is undecidable in F*. For instance: does the unit value () solve the hole $\Gamma \vdash ?\mathsf{u} : \mathsf{squash}\ \phi$? Well, only if ϕ holds—a condition which no type-checker can effectively decide. This implies that the type-checker cannot, in general, rely on proof terms to reconstruct a proof. Hence, the primitives are designed to provide access to the typing judgment of F* directly, instead of building syntax for proof terms. One can think of F*'s type-checker as implementing one particular algorithmic heuristic of the typing and validity judgments—a heuristic which happens to work well in practice. For convenience, this default type-checking heuristic is also available to metaprograms: this is in fact precisely what the exact primitive does. Having programmatic access to the typing judgment also provides the flexibility to tweak VC generation as needed, instead of leaving it to the default behavior of F*. For instance, the refine_intro primitive implements T-REFINE. When applied, it produces two new goals, including that the refinement actually holds. At that point, a metaprogram can run any arbitrary tactic on it, instead of letting the F* type-checker collect the obligation and send it to the SMT solver in bulk with others.

Trust. There are two common approaches for the correctness of tactic engines: (1) the *de Bruijn criterion* [6], which requires constructing full proofs (or proof terms) and checking them at the end, hence reducing trust to an independent proof-checker; and (2) the LCF style, which applies backwards reasoning while constructing validation functions at every step, reducing trust to primitive, forward-style implementations of the system's inference rules.

As we wish to make use of SMT solvers within F*, the first approach is not easy. Reconstructing the proofs SMT solvers produce, if any, back into a proper derivation remains a significant challenge (even despite recent progress, e.g. [17,31]). Further, the logical encoding from F* to SMT, along with the solver itself, are already part of F*'s TCB: shielding Meta-F* from them would not significantly increase safety of the combined system.

Instead, we roughly follow the LCF approach and implement F*'s typing rules as the basic user-facing metaprogramming actions. However, instead of implementing the rules in forward-style and using them to validate (untrusted) backwards-style tactics, we implement them directly in backwards-style. That is, they run by breaking down goals into subgoals, instead of combining proven facts into new proven facts. Using LCF style makes the primitives part of the TCB. However, given the primitives are sound, any combination of them also is, and any user-provided metaprogram must be safe due to the abstraction imposed by the Tac effect, as discussed next.

Correct Evolutions of the Proof State. For soundness, it is imperative that tactics do not arbitrarily drop goals from the proof state, and only discharge them when they are solved, or when they can be solved by other goals tracked in the proof state. For a concrete example, consider the following program:

```
let f : int → int = _ by (intro (); exact (`42))
```

Here, Meta-F* will create an initial proof state with a single goal of the form $[\emptyset \vdash ?u_1 : \mathsf{int} \to \mathsf{int}]$ and begin executing the metaprogram. When applying the intro primitive, the proof state transitions as shown below.

$$[\emptyset \vdash ?u_1 : \mathsf{int} \to \mathsf{int}] \rightsquigarrow [x{:}\mathsf{int} \vdash ?u_2 : \mathsf{int}]$$

Here, a solution to the original goal has not yet been built, since it *depends* on the solution to the goal on the right hand side. When it is solved with, say, 42, we can solve our original goal with λx → 42. To formalize these dependencies, we say that a proof state ϕ *correctly evolves (via f) to* ψ, denoted $\phi \preceq_f \psi$, when there is a generic transformation f, called a *validation*, from solutions to all of ψ's goals into correct solutions for ϕ's goals. When ϕ has n goals and ψ has m goals, the validation f is a function from term^m into term^n. Validations may be composed, providing the transitivity of correct evolution, and if a proof state ϕ correctly evolves (in any amount of steps) into a state with no more goals, then we have fully defined solutions to all of ϕ's goals. We emphasize that validations are not constructed explicitly during the execution of metaprograms. Instead we exploit unification metavariables to instantiate the solutions automatically.

Note that validations may construct solutions for more than one goal, i.e., their codomain is not a single term. This is required in Meta-F*, where primitive steps may not only decompose goals into subgoals, but actually combine goals as well. Currently, the only primitive providing this behavior is join, which finds a maximal common prefix of the environment of two irrelevant goals, reverts the "extra" binders in both goals and builds their conjunction. Combining goals using join is especially useful for sending multiple goals to the SMT solver in a single call. When there are common obligations within two goals, joining them before calling the SMT solver can result in a significantly faster proof.

We check that every primitive action respects the $\preceq$ preorder. This relies on them modeling F*'s typing rules. For example, and unsurprisingly, the following rule for typing abstractions is what justifies the intro primitive:

$$\textsc{T-Fun}\quad \frac{\Gamma, x : t \vdash e : t'}{\Gamma \vdash \lambda(x : t).e \;:\; (x : t) \to t'}$$

Then, for the proof state evolution above, the validation function f is the (mathematical, meta-level) function taking a term of type *int* (the solution for $?\mathsf{u}_2$) and building syntax for its abstraction over x. Further, the intro primitive respects the correct-evolution preorder, by the very typing rule (T-Fun) from which it is defined. In this manner, every typing rule induces a syntax-building metaprogramming step. Our primitives come from this dual interpretation of typing rules, which ensures that logical consistency is preserved.

Since the $\preceq$ relation is a preorder, and every metaprogramming primitive we provide the user evolves the proof state according $\preceq$, it is trivially the case that the final proof state returned by a (successful) computation is a correct evolution of the initial one. That means that when the metaprogram terminates, one has indeed broken down the proof obligation correctly, and is left with a (hopefully) simpler set of obligations to fulfill. Note that since $\preceq$ is a preorder, Tac provides an interesting example of monotonic state [2].

4.2 Extracting Individual Assertions

As discussed, the logical context of a goal processed by a tactic is not always syntactically evident in the program. And, as shown in the List.splitAt call in divide from Sect. 3.4, some obligations crucially depend on the control-flow of the program. Hence, the proof state must crucially include these assumptions if proving the assertion is to succeed. Below, we describe how Meta-F* finds proper contexts in which to prove the assertions, including control-flow information. Notably, this process is defined over logical formulae and does not depend at all on F*'s WP calculus or VC generator: we believe it should be applicable to any VC generator.

As seen in Sect. 2.1, the basic mechanism by which Meta-F* attaches a tactic to a specific sub-goal is assert ϕ by τ. Our encoding of this expression is built similarly to F*'s existing assert construct, which is simply sugar for a pure function _assert of type ϕ:prop → Lemma (requires ϕ) (ensures ϕ), which essentially introduces a cut in the generated VC. That is, the term (assert ϕ; e) roughly produces the verification condition $\phi \wedge (\phi \Longrightarrow \mathrm{VC}_e)$, requiring a proof of ϕ at this point, and assuming ϕ in the continuation. For Meta-F*, we aim to keep this style while allowing asserted formulae to be decorated with user-provided tactics that are tasked with proving or pre-processing them. We do this in three steps.

First, we define the following "phantom" predicate:

```
let with_tactic (φ : prop) (τ : unit → Tac unit) = φ
```

Here ϕ `with_tactic` τ simply associates the tactic τ with ϕ, and is equivalent to ϕ by its definition. Next, we implement the assert_by_tactic lemma, and desugar assert ϕ by τ into assert_by_tactic ϕ τ. This lemma is trivially provable by F*.

```
let assert_by_tactic (φ : prop) (τ : unit → Tac unit)
                     : Lemma (requires (φ `with_tactic` τ)) (ensures φ) = ()
```

Given this specification, the term (assert ϕ by τ; e) roughly produces the verification condition ϕ `with_tactic` $\tau \wedge (\phi \Longrightarrow \mathrm{VC}_e)$, with a tagged left sub-goal, and ϕ as an hypothesis in the right one. Importantly, F* keeps the with_tactic marker uninterpreted until the VC needs to be discharged. At that point, it may contain several annotated subformulae. For example, suppose the VC is VC0 below, where we distinguish an ambient context of variables and hypotheses Δ:

(VC0) $\Delta \models X \Longrightarrow (\forall$ (x:t). R `with_tactic` $\tau_1 \wedge (R \Longrightarrow S))$

In order to run the τ_1 tactic on R, it must first be "split out". To do so, all logical information "visible" for τ_1 (i.e. the set of premises of the implications traversed and the binders introduced by quantifiers) must be included. As for any program verifier, these hypotheses include the control flow information, postconditions, and any other logical fact that is known to be valid at the program point where the corresponding assert R by τ_1 was called. All of them are collected into Δ as the term is traversed. In this case, the VC for R is:

(VC1) Δ, _:X, x:t $\models$ R

Afterwards, this obligation is removed from the original VC. This is done by replacing it with $\top$, leaving a "skeleton" VC with all remaining facts.

(VC2) $\Delta \models \mathsf{X} \Longrightarrow (\forall\ (\mathsf{x{:}t}).\ \top \land (\mathsf{R} \Longrightarrow \mathsf{S}))$

The validity of VC1 and VC2 implies that of VC0. F* also recursively descends into R and S, in case there are more with_tactic markers in them. Then, tactics are run on the the split VCs (e.g., τ_1 on VC1) to break them down (or solve them). All remaining goals, including the skeleton, are sent to the SMT solver.

Note that while the *obligation* to prove R, in VC1, is preprocessed by the tactic τ_1, the *assumption* R for the continuation of the code, in VC2, is left as-is. This is crucial for tactics such as the canonicalizer from Sect. 2.1: if the skeleton VC2 contained an assumption for the canonicalized equality it would not help the SMT solver show the uncanonicalized postcondition.

However, not all nodes marked with with_tactic are proof obligations. Suppose X in the previous VC was given as (Y `with_tactic` τ_2). In this case, one certainly does not want to attempt to prove Y, since it is an hypothesis. While it would be *sound* to prove it and replace it by $\top$, it is useless at best, and usually irreparably affects the system. Consider asserting the tautology ($\bot$ `with_tactic` τ) $\Longrightarrow \bot$.

Hence, F* splits such obligations only in strictly-positive positions. On all others, F* simply drops the with_tactic marker, e.g., by just unfolding the definition of with_tactic. For regular uses of the assert..by construct, however, all occurrences are strictly-positive. It is only when (expert) users use the with_tactic marker directly that the above discussion might become relevant.

Formally, the soundness of this whole approach is given by the following metatheorem, which justifies the splitting out of sub-assertions, and by the correctness of evolution detailed in Sect. 4.1. The proof of Theorem 1 is straightforward, and included in the appendix. We expect an analogous property to hold in other verifiers as well (in particular, it holds for first-order logic).

Theorem 1. *Let* E *be a context with* $\Gamma \vdash E : prop \Rightarrow prop$*, and* ϕ *a squashed proposition such that* $\Gamma \vdash \phi : prop$*. Then the following holds:*

$$\frac{\Gamma \models E[\top] \quad \Gamma, \gamma(E) \models \phi}{\Gamma \models E[\phi]}$$

where $\gamma(E)$ *is the set of binders* E *introduces. If* E *is strictly-positive, then the reverse implication holds as well.*

5 Executing Metaprograms Efficiently

F* provides three complementary mechanisms for running metaprograms. The first two, F*'s call-by-name (CBN) interpreter and a (newly implemented) call-by-value (CBV) NbE-based evaluator, support strong reduction—henceforth we refer to these as "normalizers". In addition, we design and implement a new *native plugin* mechanism that allows both normalizers to interface with Meta-F* programs extracted to OCaml, reusing F*'s existing extraction pipeline for this purpose. Below we provide a brief overview of the three mechanisms.

5.1 CBN and CBV Strong Reductions

As described in Sect. 3.1, metaprograms, once reified, are simply F* terms of type proofstate → Div (result a). As such, they can be reduced using F*'s existing computation machinery, a CBN interpreter for strong reductions based on the Krivine abstract machine (KAM) [24,46]. Although complete and highly configurable, F*'s KAM interpreter is slow, designed primarily for converting types during dependent type-checking and higher-order unification.

Shifting focus to long-running metaprograms, such as tactics for proofs by reflection, we implemented an NbE-based strong-reduction evaluator for F* computations. The evaluator is implemented in F* and extracted to OCaml (as is the rest of F*), thereby inheriting CBV from OCaml. It is similar to Boespflug et al.'s [16] NbE-based strong-reduction for Coq, although we do not implement their low-level, OCaml-specific tag-elimination optimizations—nevertheless, it is already vastly more efficient than the KAM-based interpreter.

5.2 Native Plugins and Multi-language Interoperability

Since Meta-F* programs are just F* programs, they can also be extracted to OCaml and natively compiled. Further, they can be dynamically linked into F* as "plugins". Plugins can be directly called from the type-checker, as is done for the primitives, which is much more efficient than interpreting them. However, compilation has a cost, and it is not convenient to compile every single invocation. Instead, Meta-F* enables users to choose which metaprograms are to be plugins (presumably those expected to be computation-intensive, e.g. canon_semiring). Users can choose their native plugins, while still quickly scripting their higher-level logic in the interpreter.

This requires (for higher-order metaprograms) a form of multi-language interoperability, converting between representations of terms used in the normalizers and in native code. We designed a small multi-language calculus, with ML-style polymorphism, to model the interaction between normalizers and plugins and conversions between terms. See the appendix for details.

Beyond the notable efficiency gains of running compiled code vs. interpreting it, native metaprograms also require fewer embeddings. Once compiled, metaprograms work over the internal, *concrete* types for proofstate, term, etc., instead of over their F* representations (though still treating them abstractly). Hence, compiled metaprograms can call primitives without needing to embed their arguments or unembed their results. Further, they can call each other directly as well. Indeed, operationally there is little operational difference between a primitive and a compiled metaprogram used as a plugin.

Native plugins, however, are not a replacement for the normalizers, for several reasons. First, the overhead in compilation might not be justified by the execution speed-up. Second, extraction to OCaml erases types and proofs. As a result, the F* *interface* of the native plugins can only contain types that can also be expressed in OCaml, thereby excluding full-dependent types—internally, however, they can be dependently typed. Third, being OCaml programs, native plugins do not support reducing open terms, which is often required. However, when the programs treat their open arguments parametrically, relying on parametric polymorphism, the normalizers can pass such arguments *as-is*, thereby recovering open reductions in some cases. This allows us to use native datastructure implementations (e.g. List), which is much faster than using the normalizers, even for open terms. See the appendix for details.

6 Experimental Evaluation

We now present an experimental evaluation of Meta-F*. First, we provide benchmarks comparing our reflective canonicalizer from Sect. 2.1 to calling the SMT solver directly without any canonicalization. Then, we return to the parsers and serializers from Sect. 2.3 and show how, for VCs that arise, a domain-specific tactic is much more tractable than a SMT-only proof.

6.1 A Reflective Tactic for Partial Canonicalization

In Sect. 2.1, we have described the canon_semiring tactic that rewrites semiring expressions into sums of products. We find that this tactic significantly improves proof robustness. The table below compares the success rates and times for the poly_multiply lemma from Sect. 2.1. To test the robustness of each alternative, we run the tests 200 times while varying the SMT solver's random seed. The `smt`*i*`x` rows represent asking the solver to prove the lemma without any help from tactics, where i represents the resource limit (`rlimit`) multiplier given to the solver. This `rlimit` is memory-allocation based and independent of the particular system or current load. For the interp and native rows, the canon_semiring tactic is used, running it using F*'s KAM normalizer and as a native plugin respectively—both with an `rlimit` of 1. For each setup, we display the success rate of verification, the average (CPU) time taken for the SMT queries (not counting the time for parsing/processing the theory) with its standard deviation, and the average total time (its standard deviation coincides with that of the queries). When applicable, the time for tactic execution (which is independent of the seed) is displayed. The `smt` rows show very poor success rates: even when upping the `rlimit` to a whopping 100x, over three quarters of the attempts fail. Note how the (relative) standard deviation increases with the

	Rate	Queries	Tactic	Total
smt1x	0.5%	0.216 ± 0.001	–	2.937
smt2x	2%	0.265 ± 0.003	–	2.958
smt3x	4%	0.304 ± 0.004	–	3.022
smt6x	10%	0.401 ± 0.008	–	3.155
smt12x	12.5%	0.596 ± 0.031	–	3.321
smt25x	16.5%	1.063 ± 0.079	–	3.790
smt50x	22%	2.319 ± 0.230	–	5.030
smt100x	24%	5.831 ± 0.776	–	8.550
interp	100%	0.141 ± 0.001	1.156	4.003
native	100%	0.139 ± 0.001	0.212	3.071

`rlimit`: this is due to successful runs taking rather random times, and failing ones exhausting their resources in similar times. The setups using the tactic show a clear increase in robustness: canonicalizing the assertion causes this proof to always succeed, even at the default `rlimit`. We recall that the tactic variants still leave goals for SMT solving, namely, the skeleton for the original VC and the canonicalized equality left by the tactic, easily dischargeable by the SMT solver through much more well-behaved linear reasoning. The last column shows that native compilation speeds up this tactic's execution by about 5x.

6.2 Combining SMT and Tactics for the Parser Generator

In Sect. 2.3, we presented a library of combinators and a metaprogramming approach to automate the construction of verified, mutually inverse, low-level parsers and serializers from type descriptions. Beyond generating the code, tactics are used to process and discharge proof obligations that arise when using the combinators.

We present three strategies for discharging these obligations, including those of bijectivity that arise when constructing parsers and serializers for enumerated types. First, we used F*'s default strategy to present all of these proofs directly to the SMT solver. Second, we programmed a ~100 line tactic to discharge these proofs without relying on the SMT solver at all. Finally, we used a hybrid approach where a simple, 5-line tactic is used to prune the context of the proof removing redundant facts before presenting the resulting goals to the SMT solver.

Size	SMT only	Tactic only	Hybrid
4	178	17.3	6.6
7	468	38.3	9.8
10	690	63.0	19.4

The table alongside shows the total time in seconds for verifying metaprogrammed low-level parsers and serializers for enumerations of different sizes. In short, the hybrid approach scales the best; the tactic-only approach is somewhat slower; while the SMT-only approach scales poorly and is an order of magnitude slower. Our hybrid approach is very simple. With some more work, a more sophisticated hybrid strategy could be more performant still, relying on tactic-based normalization proofs for fragments of the VC best handled computationally (where the SMT solver spends most of its time), while using SMT only for integer arithmetic, congruence closure etc. However, with Meta-F*'s ability to manipulate proof contexts programmatically, our simple context-pruning tactic provides a big payoff at a small cost.

7 Related Work

Many SMT-based program verifiers [7,8,19,34,48], rely on user hints, in the form of assertions and lemmas, to complete proofs. This is the predominant style of proving used in tools like Dafny [47], Liquid Haskell [60], Why3 [33], and

F⋆ itself [58]. However, there is a growing trend to augment this style of semi-automated proof with interactive proofs. For example, systems like Why3 [33] allow VCs to be discharged using ITPs such as Coq, Isabelle/HOL, and PVS, but this requires an additional embedding of VCs into the logic of the ITP in question. In recent concurrent work, support for *effectful* reflection proofs was added to Why3 [50], and it would be interesting to investigate if this could also be done in Meta-F⋆. Grov and Tumas [39] present Tacny, a tactic framework for Dafny, which is, however, limited in that it only transforms source code, with the program verifier unchanged. In contrast, Meta-F⋆ combines the benefits of an SMT-based program verifier and those of tactic proofs within a single language.

Moving away from SMT-based verifiers, ITPs have long relied on separate languages for proof scripting, starting with Edinburgh LCF [37] and ML, and continuing with HOL, Isabelle and Coq, which are either extensible via ML, or have dedicated tactic languages [3,29,56,62]. Meta-F⋆ builds instead on a recent idea in the space of dependently typed ITPs [22,30,42,63] of reusing the object-language as the meta-language. This idea first appeared in Mtac, a Coq-based tactics framework for Coq [42,63], and has many generic benefits including reusing the standard library, IDE support, and type checker of the proof assistant. Mtac can additionally check the partial correctness of tactics, which is also sometimes possible in Meta-F⋆ but still rather limited (Sect. 3.4). Meta-F⋆'s design is instead more closely inspired by the metaprogramming frameworks of Idris [22] and Lean [30], which provide a deep embedding of terms that metaprograms can inspect and construct at will without dependent types getting in the way. However, F⋆'s effects, its weakest precondition calculus, and its use of SMT solvers distinguish Meta-F⋆ from these other frameworks, presenting both challenges and opportunities, as discussed in this paper.

Some SMT solvers also include tactic engines [27], which allow to process queries in custom ways. However, using SMT tactics from a program verifier is not very practical. To do so effectively, users must become familiar not only with the solver's language and tactic engine, but also with the translation from the program verifier to the solver. Instead, in Meta-F⋆, everything happens within a single language. Also, to our knowledge, these tactics are usually coarsely-grained, and we do not expect them to enable developments such as Sect. 2.2. Plus, SMT tactics do not enable metaprogramming.

Finally, ITPs are seeing increasing use of "hammers" such as Sledgehammer [14,15,54] in Isabelle/HOL, and similar tools for HOL Light and HOL4 [43], and Mizar [44], to interface with ATPs. This technique is similar to Meta-F⋆, which, given its support for a dependently typed logic is especially related to a recent hammer for Coq [26]. Unlike these hammers, Meta-F⋆ does not aim to reconstruct SMT proofs, gaining efficiency at the cost of trusting the SMT solver. Further, whereas hammers run in the background, lightening the load on a user otherwise tasked with completing the entire proof, Meta-F⋆ relies more heavily on the SMT solver as an end-game tactic in nearly all proofs.

8 Conclusions

A key challenge in program verification is to balance automation and expressiveness. Whereas tactic-based ITPs support highly expressive logics, the tactic author is responsible for all the automation. Conversely, SMT-based program verifiers provide good, scalable automation for comparatively weaker logics, but offer little recourse when verification fails. A design that allows picking the right tool, at the granularity of each verification sub-task, is a worthy area of research. Meta-F* presents a new point in this space: by using hand-written tactics alongside SMT-automation, we have written proofs that were previously impractical in F*, and (to the best of our knowledge) in other SMT-based program verifiers.

Acknowledgements. We thank Leonardo de Moura and the Project Everest team for many useful discussions. The work of Guido Martínez, Nick Giannarakis, Monal Narasimhamurthy, and Zoe Paraskevopoulou was done, in part, while interning at Microsoft Research. Clément Pit-Claudel's work was in part done during an internship at Inria Paris. The work of Danel Ahman, Victor Dumitrescu, and Cătălin Hriţcu is supported by the MSR-Inria Joint Centre and the European Research Council under ERC Starting Grant SECOMP (1-715753).

References

1. Ahman, D., et al.: Dijkstra monads for free. In: POPL (2017). https://doi.org/10.1145/3009837.3009878
2. Ahman, D., Fournet, C., Hriţcu, C., Maillard, K., Rastogi, A., Swamy, N.: Recalling a witness: foundations and applications of monotonic state. PACMPL **2**(POPL), 65:1–65:30 (2018). https://arxiv.org/abs/1707.02466
3. Anand, A., Boulier, S., Cohen, C., Sozeau, M., Tabareau, N.: Towards certified meta-programming with typed Template-Coq. In: Avigad, J., Mahboubi, A. (eds.) ITP 2018. LNCS, vol. 10895, pp. 20–39. Springer, Cham (2018). https://doi.org/10.1007/978-3-319-94821-8_2. https://template-coq.github.io/template-coq/
4. Appel, A.W.: Tactics for separation logic. Early Draft (2006). https://www.cs.princeton.edu/~appel/papers/septacs.pdf
5. Awodey, S., Bauer, A.: Propositions as [Types]. J. Log. Comput. **14**(4), 447–471 (2004). https://doi.org/10.1093/logcom/14.4.447
6. Barendregt, H., Geuvers, H.: Proof-assistants using dependent type systems. In: Handbook of Automated Reasoning, pp. 1149–1238. Elsevier Science Publishers B. V., Amsterdam (2001). http://dl.acm.org/citation.cfm?id=778522.778527
7. Barnett, M., Chang, B.-Y.E., DeLine, R., Jacobs, B., Leino, K.R.M.: Boogie: a modular reusable verifier for object-oriented programs. In: de Boer, F.S., Bonsangue, M.M., Graf, S., de Roever, W.-P. (eds.) FMCO 2005. LNCS, vol. 4111, pp. 364–387. Springer, Heidelberg (2006). https://doi.org/10.1007/11804192_17
8. Barnett, M., et al.: The Spec# programming system: challenges and directions. In: Meyer, B., Woodcock, J. (eds.) VSTTE 2005. LNCS, vol. 4171, pp. 144–152. Springer, Heidelberg (2008). https://doi.org/10.1007/978-3-540-69149-5_16
9. Barras, B., Grégoire, B., Mahboubi, A., Théry, L.: Chap. 25: The ring and field tactic families. Coq reference manual. https://coq.inria.fr/refman/ring.html

10. Berger, U., Schwichtenberg, H.: An inverse of the evaluation functional for typed lambda-calculus. In: LICS (1991). https://doi.org/10.1109/LICS.1991.151645
11. Bernstein, D.J.: The Poly1305-AES message-authentication code. In: Gilbert, H., Handschuh, H. (eds.) FSE 2005. LNCS, vol. 3557, pp. 32–49. Springer, Heidelberg (2005). https://doi.org/10.1007/11502760_3. https://cr.yp.to/mac/poly1305-20050329.pdf
12. Besson, F.: Fast reflexive arithmetic tactics the linear case and beyond. In: Altenkirch, T., McBride, C. (eds.) TYPES 2006. LNCS, vol. 4502, pp. 48–62. Springer, Heidelberg (2007). https://doi.org/10.1007/978-3-540-74464-1_4
13. Bhargavan, K., et al.: Everest: towards a verified, drop-in replacement of HTTPS. In: SNAPL (2017). http://drops.dagstuhl.de/opus/volltexte/2017/7119/pdf/LIPIcs-SNAPL-2017-1.pdf
14. Blanchette, J.C., Popescu, A.: Mechanizing the metatheory of Sledgehammer. In: Fontaine, P., Ringeissen, C., Schmidt, R.A. (eds.) FroCoS 2013. LNCS (LNAI), vol. 8152, pp. 245–260. Springer, Heidelberg (2013). https://doi.org/10.1007/978-3-642-40885-4_17
15. Blanchette, J.C., Böhme, S., Paulson, L.C.: Extending Sledgehammer with SMT solvers. JAR **51**(1), 109–128 (2013). https://doi.org/10.1007/s10817-013-9278-5
16. Boespflug, M., Dénès, M., Grégoire, B.: Full reduction at full throttle. In: Jouannaud, J.-P., Shao, Z. (eds.) CPP 2011. LNCS, vol. 7086, pp. 362–377. Springer, Heidelberg (2011). https://doi.org/10.1007/978-3-642-25379-9_26
17. Böhme, S., Weber, T.: Fast LCF-style proof reconstruction for Z3. In: Kaufmann, M., Paulson, L.C. (eds.) ITP 2010. LNCS, vol. 6172, pp. 179–194. Springer, Heidelberg (2010). https://doi.org/10.1007/978-3-642-14052-5_14
18. Bond, B., et al.: Vale: verifying high-performance cryptographic assembly code. In: USENIX Security (2017). https://www.usenix.org/conference/usenixsecurity17/technical-sessions/presentation/bond
19. Burdy, L., et al.: An overview of JML tools and applications. STTT **7**(3), 212–232 (2005). https://doi.org/10.1007/s10009-004-0167-4
20. Chaieb, A., Nipkow, T.: Proof synthesis and reflection for linear arithmetic. J. Autom. Reason. **41**(1), 33–59 (2008). https://doi.org/10.1007/s10817-008-9101-x
21. Charguéraud, A.: The locally nameless representation. J. Autom. Reason. **49**(3), 363–408 (2012). https://doi.org/10.1007/s10817-011-9225-2
22. Christiansen, D.R., Brady, E.: Elaborator reflection: extending Idris in Idris. In: ICFP (2016). https://doi.org/10.1145/2951913.2951932
23. Cohen, E., Moskal, M., Schulte, W., Tobies, S.: Local verification of global invariants in concurrent programs. In: Touili, T., Cook, B., Jackson, P. (eds.) CAV 2010. LNCS, vol. 6174, pp. 480–494. Springer, Heidelberg (2010). https://doi.org/10.1007/978-3-642-14295-6_42
24. Crégut, P.: Strongly reducing variants of the Krivine abstract machine. HOSC **20**(3), 209–230 (2007). https://doi.org/10.1007/s10990-007-9015-z
25. Cuoq, P., Kirchner, F., Kosmatov, N., Prevosto, V., Signoles, J., Yakobowski, B.: Frama-C: a software analysis perspective. In: Eleftherakis, G., Hinchey, M., Holcombe, M. (eds.) SEFM 2012. LNCS, vol. 7504, pp. 233–247. Springer, Heidelberg (2012). https://doi.org/10.1007/978-3-642-33826-7_16
26. Czajka, Ł., Kaliszyk, C.: Hammer for Coq: automation for dependent type theory. JAR **61**(1–4), 423–453 (2018). https://doi.org/10.1007/s10817-018-9458-4

27. de Moura, L., Passmore, G.O.: The strategy challenge in SMT solving. In: Bonacina, M.P., Stickel, M.E. (eds.) Automated Reasoning and Mathematics. LNCS (LNAI), vol. 7788, pp. 15–44. Springer, Heidelberg (2013). https://doi.org/10.1007/978-3-642-36675-8_2. http://dl.acm.org/citation.cfm?id=2554473.2554475
28. de Moura, L., Bjørner, N.: Z3: an efficient SMT solver. In: Ramakrishnan, C.R., Rehof, J. (eds.) TACAS 2008. LNCS, vol. 4963, pp. 337–340. Springer, Heidelberg (2008). https://doi.org/10.1007/978-3-540-78800-3_24
29. Delahaye, D.: A tactic language for the system Coq. In: Parigot, M., Voronkov, A. (eds.) LPAR 2000. LNAI, vol. 1955, pp. 85–95. Springer, Heidelberg (2000). https://doi.org/10.1007/3-540-44404-1_7
30. Ebner, G., Ullrich, S., Roesch, J., Avigad, J., de Moura, L.: A metaprogramming framework for formal verification. PACMPL **1**(ICFP), 34:1–34:29 (2017). https://doi.org/10.1145/3110278
31. Ekici, B., et al.: SMTCoq: a plug-in for integrating SMT solvers into Coq. In: Majumdar, R., Kunčak, V. (eds.) CAV 2017, Part II. LNCS, vol. 10427, pp. 126–133. Springer, Cham (2017). https://doi.org/10.1007/978-3-319-63390-9_7
32. Erbsen, A., Philipoom, J., Gross, J., Sloan, R., Chlipala, A.: Simple high-level code for cryptographic arithmetic - with proofs, without compromises. In: IEEE S&P (2019). https://doi.org/10.1109/SP.2019.00005
33. Filliâtre, J.-C., Paskevich, A.: Why3 — where programs meet provers. In: Felleisen, M., Gardner, P. (eds.) ESOP 2013. LNCS, vol. 7792, pp. 125–128. Springer, Heidelberg (2013). https://doi.org/10.1007/978-3-642-37036-6_8. https://hal.inria.fr/hal-00789533/document
34. Flanagan, C., Leino, K.R.M., Lillibridge, M., Nelson, G., Saxe, J.B., Stata, R.: PLDI 2002: extended static checking for Java. SIGPLAN Not. **48**(4S), 22–33 (2013). https://doi.org/10.1145/2502508.2502520
35. Fromherz, A., Giannarakis, N., Hawblitzel, C., Parno, B., Rastogi, A., Swamy, N.: A verified, efficient embedding of a verifiable assembly language. PACMPL (POPL) (2019). https://github.com/project-everest/project-everest.github.io/raw/master/assets/vale-popl.pdf
36. Gonthier, G.: Formal proof—the four-color theorem. Not. AMS **55**(11), 1382–1393 (2008). https://www.ams.org/notices/200811/tx081101382p.pdf
37. Gordon, M.J., Milner, A.J., Wadsworth, C.P.: Edinburgh LCF: A Mechanised Logic of Computation. LNCS, vol. 78. Springer, Heidelberg (1979). https://doi.org/10.1007/3-540-09724-4
38. Grégoire, B., Mahboubi, A.: Proving equalities in a commutative ring done right in Coq. In: Hurd, J., Melham, T. (eds.) TPHOLs 2005. LNCS, vol. 3603, pp. 98–113. Springer, Heidelberg (2005). https://doi.org/10.1007/11541868_7
39. Grov, G., Tumas, V.: Tactics for the Dafny program verifier. In: Chechik, M., Raskin, J.-F. (eds.) TACAS 2016. LNCS, vol. 9636, pp. 36–53. Springer, Heidelberg (2016). https://doi.org/10.1007/978-3-662-49674-9_3
40. Hawblitzel, C., et al.: Ironclad apps: end-to-end security via automated full-system verification. In: OSDI (2014). https://www.usenix.org/conference/osdi14/technical-sessions/presentation/hawblitzel
41. Hawblitzel, C., et al.: Ironfleet: proving safety and liveness of practical distributed systems. CACM **60**(7), 83–92 (2017). https://doi.org/10.1145/3068608
42. Kaiser, J., Ziliani, B., Krebbers, R., Régis-Gianas, Y., Dreyer, D.: Mtac2: typed tactics for backward reasoning in Coq. PACMPL **2**(ICFP), 78:1–78:31 (2018). https://doi.org/10.1145/3236773

43. Kaliszyk, C., Urban, J.: Learning-assisted automated reasoning with Flyspeck. JAR **53**(2), 173–213 (2014). https://doi.org/10.1007/s10817-014-9303-3
44. Kaliszyk, C., Urban, J.: MizAR 40 for Mizar 40. JAR **55**(3), 245–256 (2015). https://doi.org/10.1007/s10817-015-9330-8
45. Krebbers, R., Timany, A., Birkedal, L.: Interactive proofs in higher-order concurrent separation logic. In: POPL (2017). http://dl.acm.org/citation.cfm?id=3009855
46. Krivine, J.-L.: A call-by-name lambda-calculus machine. Higher Order Symbol. Comput. **20**(3), 199–207 (2007). https://doi.org/10.1007/s10990-007-9018-9
47. Leino, K.R.M.: Dafny: an automatic program verifier for functional correctness. In: Clarke, E.M., Voronkov, A. (eds.) LPAR 2010. LNCS (LNAI), vol. 6355, pp. 348–370. Springer, Heidelberg (2010). https://doi.org/10.1007/978-3-642-17511-4_20. http://dl.acm.org/citation.cfm?id=1939141.1939161
48. Rustan, K., Leino, M., Nelson, G.: An extended static checker for modula-3. In: Koskimies, K. (ed.) CC 1998. LNCS, vol. 1383, pp. 302–305. Springer, Heidelberg (1998). https://doi.org/10.1007/BFb0026441
49. McCreight, A.: Practical tactics for separation logic. In: Berghofer, S., Nipkow, T., Urban, C., Wenzel, M. (eds.) TPHOLs 2009. LNCS, vol. 5674, pp. 343–358. Springer, Heidelberg (2009). https://doi.org/10.1007/978-3-642-03359-9_24
50. Melquiond, G., Rieu-Helft, R.: A Why3 framework for reflection proofs and its application to GMP's algorithms. In: Galmiche, D., Schulz, S., Sebastiani, R. (eds.) IJCAR 2018. LNCS (LNAI), vol. 10900, pp. 178–193. Springer, Cham (2018). https://doi.org/10.1007/978-3-319-94205-6_13
51. Nanevski, A., Morrisett, J.G., Birkedal, L.: Hoare type theory, polymorphism and separation. JFP **18**(5–6), 865–911 (2008). http://ynot.cs.harvard.edu/papers/jfpsep07.pdf
52. Nanevski, A., Vafeiadis, V., Berdine, J.: Structuring the verification of heap-manipulating programs. In: POPL (2010). https://doi.org/10.1145/1706299.1706331
53. Nogin, A.: Quotient types: a modular approach. In: Carreño, V.A., Muñoz, C.A., Tahar, S. (eds.) TPHOLs 2002. LNCS, vol. 2410, pp. 263–280. Springer, Heidelberg (2002). https://doi.org/10.1007/3-540-45685-6_18
54. Paulson, L.C., Blanchette, J.C.: Three years of experience with Sledgehammer, a practical link between automatic and interactive theorem provers. In: IWIL (2010). https://www21.in.tum.de/~blanchet/iwil2010-sledgehammer.pdf
55. Protzenko, J., et al.: Verified low-level programming embedded in F*. PACMPL **1**(ICFP), 17:1–17:29 (2017). https://doi.org/10.1145/3110261
56. Stampoulis, A., Shao, Z.: VeriML: typed computation of logical terms inside a language with effects. In: ICFP (2010). https://doi.org/10.1145/1863543.1863591
57. Swamy, N., Weinberger, J., Schlesinger, C., Chen, J., Livshits, B.: Verifying higher-order programs with the Dijkstra monad. In: PLDI (2013). https://www.microsoft.com/en-us/research/publication/verifying-higher-order-programs-with-the-dijkstra-monad/
58. Swamy, N., et al.: Dependent types and multi-monadic effects in F*. In: POPL (2016). https://www.fstar-lang.org/papers/mumon/
59. Vazou, N., Seidel, E.L., Jhala, R., Vytiniotis, D., Peyton Jones, S.L.: Refinement types for Haskell. In: ICFP (2014). https://goto.ucsd.edu/~nvazou/refinement_types_for_haskell.pdf
60. Vazou, N., et al.: Refinement reflection: complete verification with SMT. PACMPL **2**(POPL), 53:1–53:31 (2018). https://doi.org/10.1145/3158141

61. Wadler, P.: Views: a way for pattern matching to cohabit with data abstraction. In: POPL (1987). https://dl.acm.org/citation.cfm?doid=41625.41653
62. Wenzel, M.: The Isabelle/Isar reference manual (2017). http://isabelle.in.tum.de/doc/isar-ref.pdf
63. Ziliani, B., Dreyer, D., Krishnaswami, N.R., Nanevski, A., Vafeiadis, V.: Mtac: a monad for typed tactic programming in Coq. JFP **25** (2015). https://doi.org/10.1017/S0956796815000118
64. Zinzindohoué, J.-K., Bhargavan, K., Protzenko, J., Beurdouche, B.: HACL*: a verified modern cryptographic library. In: CCS (2017). http://eprint.iacr.org/2017/536

Semi-automated Reasoning About Non-determinism in C Expressions

Dan Frumin[1(✉)], Léon Gondelman[1], and Robbert Krebbers[2]

[1] Radboud University, Nijmegen, The Netherlands
{dfrumin,lgg}@cs.ru.nl
[2] Delft University of Technology, Delft, The Netherlands
mail@robbertkrebbers.nl

Abstract. Research into C verification often ignores that the C standard leaves the evaluation order of expressions unspecified, and assigns undefined behavior to write-write or read-write conflicts in subexpressions—so called "sequence point violations". These aspects should be accounted for in verification because C compilers exploit them.

We present a verification condition generator (vcgen) that enables one to semi-automatically prove the absence of undefined behavior in a given C program for *any* evaluation order. The key novelty of our approach is a symbolic execution algorithm that computes a *frame* at the same time as a *postcondition*. The frame is used to automatically determine how resources should be distributed among subexpressions.

We prove correctness of our vcgen with respect to a new monadic definitional semantics of a subset of C. This semantics is modular and gives a concise account of non-determinism in C.

We have implemented our vcgen as a tactic in the Coq interactive theorem prover, and have proved correctness of it using a separation logic for the new monadic definitional semantics of a subset of C.

1 Introduction

The ISO C standard [22]—the official specification of the C language—leaves many parts of the language semantics either *unspecified* (*e.g.*, the order of evaluation of expressions), or *undefined* (*e.g.*, dereferencing a NULL pointer or integer overflow). In case of undefined behavior a program may do literally anything, *e.g.*, it may crash, or it may produce an arbitrary result and side-effects. Therefore, to establish the correctness of a C program, one needs to ensure that the program has no undefined behavior for *all* possible choices of non-determinism due to unspecified behavior.

In this paper we focus on the undefined and unspecified behaviors related to C's expression semantics, which have been ignored by most existing verification tools, but are crucial for establishing the correctness of realistic C programs. The C standard does not require subexpressions to be evaluated in a specific order (*e.g.*, from left to right), but rather allows them to be evaluated in *any* order.

L. Caires (Ed.): ESOP 2019, LNCS 11423, pp. 60–87, 2019.
https://doi.org/10.1007/978-3-030-17184-1_3

Moreover, an expression has undefined behavior when there is a conflicting write-write or read-write access to the same location between two *sequence points* [22, 6.5p2] (so called "sequence point violation"). Sequence points occur *e.g.*, at the end of a full expression (;), before and after each function call, and after the first operand of a conditional expression (- ? - : -) has been evaluated [22, Annex C]. Let us illustrate this by means of the following example:

```
int main() {
  int x; int y = (x = 3) + (x = 4);
  printf("%d␣%d\n", x, y);
}
```

Due to the unspecified evaluation order, one would naively expect this program to print either "3 7" or "4 7", depending on which assignment to x was evaluated first. But this program exhibits undefined behavior due to a sequence point violation: there are two conflicting writes to the variable x. Indeed, when compiled with GCC (version 8.2.0), the program in fact prints "4 8", which does not correspond to the expected results of any of the evaluation orders.

One may expect that these programs can be easily ruled out statically using some form of static analysis, but this is not the case. Contrary to the simple program above, one can access the values of arbitrary pointers, making it impossible to statically establish the absence of write-write or read-write conflicts. Besides, one should not merely establish the absence of undefined behavior due to conflicting accesses to the same locations, but one should also establish that there are no other forms of undefined behavior (*e.g.*, that no NULL pointers are dereferenced) for *any evaluation order*.

To deal with this issue, Krebbers [29,30] developed a program logic based on Concurrent Separation Logic (CSL) [46] for establishing the absence of undefined behavior in C programs in the presence of non-determinism. To get an impression of how his logic works, let us consider the rule for the addition operator:

$$\frac{\{P_1\}\ \mathtt{e}_1\ \{\Psi_1\} \qquad \{P_2\}\ \mathtt{e}_2\ \{\Psi_2\} \qquad \forall \mathtt{v}_1\, \mathtt{v}_2.\, \Psi_1\, \mathtt{v}_1 * \Psi_2\, \mathtt{v}_2 \vdash \Phi\, (\mathtt{v}_1 + \mathtt{v}_2)}{\{P_1 * P_2\}\ \mathtt{e}_1 + \mathtt{e}_2\ \{\Phi\}}$$

This rule is much like the rule for parallel composition in CSL—the precondition should be separated into two parts P_1 and P_2 describing the resources needed for proving the Hoare triples of both operands. Crucially, since P_1 and P_2 describe disjoint resources as expressed by the *separating conjunction* $*$, it is guaranteed that $\mathtt{e}_1$ and $\mathtt{e}_2$ do not interfere with each other, and hence cannot cause sequence point violations. The purpose of the rule's last premise is to ensure that for all possible return values $\mathtt{v}_1$ and $\mathtt{v}_2$, the postconditions Ψ_1 and Ψ_2 of both operands can be combined into the postcondition Φ of the whole expression.

Krebbers's logic [29,30] has some limitations that impact its usability:

- The rules are not algorithmic, and hence it is not clear how they could be implemented as part of an automated or interactive tool.
- It is difficult to extend the logic with new features. Soundness was proven with respect to a monolithic and ad-hoc model of separation logic.

In this paper we address both of these problems.

We present a new algorithm for symbolic execution in separation logic. Contrary to ordinary symbolic execution in separation logic [5], our symbolic executor takes an expression and a precondition as its input, and computes not only the postcondition, but also simultaneously computes a *frame* that describes the resources that have *not* been used to prove the postcondition. The frame is used to infer the pre- and postconditions of adjacent subexpressions. For example, in $\mathsf{e}_1 + \mathsf{e}_2$, we use the frame of e_1 to symbolically execute e_2.

In order to enable semi-automated reasoning about C programs, we integrate our symbolic executor into a *verification condition generator (vcgen)*. Our vcgen does not merely turn programs into proof goals, but constructs the proof goals only as long as it can discharge goals automatically using our symbolic executor. When an attempt to use the symbolic executor fails, our vcgen will return a new goal, from which the vcgen can be called back again after the user helped out. This approach is useful when integrated into an interactive theorem prover.

We prove soundness of the symbolic executor and verification condition generator with respect to a refined version of the separation logic by Krebbers [29,30]. Our new logic has been developed on top of the Iris framework [24–26,33], and thereby inherits all advanced features of Iris (like its expressive support for ghost state and invariants), without having to model these explicitly. To make our new logic better suited for proving the correctness of the symbolic executor and verification condition generator, our new logic comes with a weakest precondition connective instead of Hoare triples as in Krebbers's original logic.

To streamline the soundness proof of our new program logic, we give a new *monadic definitional translation* of a subset of C relevant for non-determinism and sequence points into an ML-style functional language with concurrency. Contrary to the direct style operational semantics for a subset of C by Krebbers [29,30], our approach leads to a semantics that is both easier to understand, and easier to extend with additional language features.

We have mechanized our whole development in the Coq interactive theorem prover. The symbolic executor and verification condition generator are defined as computable functions in Coq, and have been integrated into tactics in the Iris Proof Mode/MoSeL framework [32,34]. To obtain end-to-end correctness, we mechanized the proofs of soundness of our symbolic executor and verification condition generator with respect to our new separation logic and new monadic definitional semantics for a subset of C. The Coq development is available at [18].

Contributions. We describe an approach to semi-automatically prove the absence of undefined behavior in a given C program for *any* evaluation order. While doing so, we make the following contributions:

- We define λMC: a small C-style language with a semantics by a monadic translation into an ML-style functional language with concurrency (Sect. 2);
- We present a separation logic with weakest preconditions for λMC based on the separation logic for non-determinism in C by Krebbers [29,30] (Sect. 3);

- We prove soundness of our separation logic with weakest preconditions by giving a modular model using the Iris framework [24–26,33] (Sect. 4);
- We present a new symbolic executor that not only computes the postcondition of a C expression, but also a *frame*, used to determine how resources should be distributed among subexpressions (Sect. 5);
- On top of our symbolic executor, we define a verification condition generator that enables semi-automated proofs using an interactive theorem prover (Sect. 6);
- We demonstrate that our approach can be implemented and proved sound using Coq for a superset of the λMC language considered in this paper (Sect. 7).

2 λMC: A Monadic Definitional Semantics of C

In this section we describe a small C-style language called λMC, which features non-determinism in expressions. We define its semantics by translation into a ML-style functional language with concurrency called HeapLang.

We briefly describe the λMC source language (Sect. 2.1) and the HeapLang target language (Sect. 2.2) of the translation. Then we describe the translation scheme itself (Sect. 2.3). We explain in several steps how to exploit concurrency and monadic programming to give a concise and clear definitional semantics.

2.1 The Source Language λMC

The syntax of our source language called λMC is as follows:

$$
\begin{aligned}
\mathsf{v} \in \mathsf{val} &::= \mathtt{z} \mid \mathtt{f} \mid \mathtt{l} \mid \mathtt{NULL} \mid (\mathtt{v}_1, \mathtt{v}_2) \mid () && (\mathtt{z} \in \mathbb{Z}, \mathtt{l} \in \mathsf{Loc})\\
\mathsf{e} \in \mathsf{expr} &::= \mathtt{v} \mid \mathtt{x} \mid (\mathtt{e}_1, \mathtt{e}_2) \mid \mathtt{e.1} \mid \mathtt{e.2} \mid \mathtt{e}_1 \circledcirc \mathtt{e}_2 \mid && (\circledcirc \in \{+, -, \dots\})\\
&\quad\ \mathtt{x} \leftarrow \mathtt{e}_1 \,;\mathtt{e}_2 \mid \mathtt{if(e_1)\{e_2\}\{e_3\}} \mid \mathtt{while(e_1)\{e_2\}} \mid \mathtt{e_1(e_2)} \mid\\
&\quad\ \mathtt{alloc(e)} \mid \mathtt{*e} \mid \mathtt{e}_1 = \mathtt{e}_2 \mid \mathtt{free(e)}
\end{aligned}
$$

The values include integers, `NULL` pointers, concrete locations `l`, function pointers `f`, structs with two fields (tuples), and the unit value `()` (for functions without return value). There is a global list of function definitions, where each definition is of the form `f(x){e}`. Most of the expression constructs resemble standard C notation, with some exceptions. We do not differentiate between expressions and statements to keep our language uniform. As such, if-then-else and sequencing constructs are not duplicated for both expressions and statements. Moreover, we do not differentiate between *lvalues* and *rvalues* [22, 6.3.2.1]. Hence, there is no address operator `&`, and, similarly to ML, the load (`*e`) and assignment ($\mathtt{e}_1 = \mathtt{e}_2$) operators take a reference as their first argument.

The *sequenced bind* operator $\mathtt{x} \leftarrow \mathtt{e}_1 \,; \mathtt{e}_2$ generalizes the normal sequencing operator $\mathtt{e}_1 \,; \mathtt{e}_2$ of C by binding the result of $\mathtt{e}_1$ to the variable `x` in $\mathtt{e}_2$. As such,

$\mathtt{x} \leftarrow \mathtt{e}_1 \,;\, \mathtt{e}_2$ can be thought of as the declaration of an immutable local variable $\mathtt{x}$. We omit mutable local variables for now, but these can be easily added as an extension to our method, as shown in Sect. 7. We write $\mathtt{e}_1 \,;\, \mathtt{e}_2$ for a sequenced bind $\_ \leftarrow \mathtt{e}_1 \,;\, \mathtt{e}_2$ in which we do not care about the return value of $\mathtt{e}_1$.

To focus on the key topics of the paper—non-determinism and the sequence point restriction—we take a minimalistic approach and omit most other features of C. Notably, we omit non-local control (return, break, continue, and goto). Our memory model is simplified; it only supports structs with two fields (tuples), but no arrays, unions, or machine integers. In Sect. 7 we show that some of these features (arrays, pointer arithmetic, and mutable local variables) can be incorporated.

2.2 The Target Language HeapLang

The target language of our definitional semantics of λMC is an ML-style functional language with concurrency primitives and a call-by-value semantics. This language, called HeapLang, is included as part of the Iris Coq development [21]. The syntax is as follows:

$$
\begin{aligned}
v \in \mathit{Val} &::= z \mid \mathtt{true} \mid \mathtt{false} \mid \mathtt{rec}\, f\, x = e \mid \ell \mid () \mid \ldots \qquad (z \in \mathbb{Z}, \ell \in \mathit{Loc})\\
e \in \mathit{Expr} &::= v \mid x \mid e_1\, e_2 \mid \mathtt{ref}(e) \mid\, !_{\mathsf{HL}}\, e \mid e_1 :=_{\mathsf{HL}} e_2 \mid \mathtt{assert}(e) \mid \\
&\quad\;\; e_1 \,||_{\mathsf{HL}}\, e_2 \mid \mathtt{newmutex} \mid \mathtt{acquire} \mid \mathtt{release} \mid \ldots
\end{aligned}
$$

The language contains some concurrency primitives that we will use to model non-determinism in λMC. Those primitives are $(||_{\mathsf{HL}})$, `newmutex`, `acquire`, and `release`. The first primitive is the parallel composition operator, which executes expressions e_1 and e_2 in parallel, and returns a tuple of their results. The expression `newmutex` () creates a new mutex. If *lk* is a mutex that was created this way, then `acquire` *lk* tries to acquire it and blocks until no other thread is using *lk*. An acquired mutex can be released using `release` *lk*.

2.3 The Monadic Definitional Semantics of λMC

We now give the semantics of λMC by translation into HeapLang. The translation is carried out in several stages, each iteration implementing and illustrating a specific aspect of C. First, we model non-determinism in expressions by concurrency, parallelizing execution of subexpressions (step 1). After that, we add checks for sequence point violations in the translation of the assignment and dereferencing operations (step 2). Finally, we add function calls and demonstrate how the translation can be simplified using a monadic notation (step 3).

Step 1: Non-determinism via Parallel Composition. We model the unspecified evaluation order in binary expressions like $\mathtt{e}_1 + \mathtt{e}_2$ and $\mathtt{e}_1 = \mathtt{e}_2$ by executing the subexpressions in parallel using the $(||_{\mathsf{HL}})$ operator:

$$
\begin{aligned}
[\![\mathtt{e}_1 + \mathtt{e}_2]\!] &\triangleq \mathtt{let}\,(v_1, v_2) = [\![\mathtt{e}_1]\!] \mathbin{||_{\mathsf{HL}}} [\![\mathtt{e}_2]\!]\ \mathtt{in}\ v_1 +_{\mathsf{HL}} v_2 \\
[\![\mathtt{e}_1 = \mathtt{e}_2]\!] &\triangleq \mathtt{let}\,(v_1, v_2) = [\![\mathtt{e}_1]\!] \mathbin{||_{\mathsf{HL}}} [\![\mathtt{e}_2]\!]\ \mathtt{in} \\
&\quad \mathtt{match}\, v_1\, \mathtt{with} \\
&\quad\ \mid \mathtt{None} \rightarrow \mathtt{assert(false)}\quad \mathtt{(*\ NULL\ pointer\ *)} \\
&\quad\ \mid \mathtt{Some}\ l \rightarrow \mathtt{match}\ !_{\mathsf{HL}}\, l\ \mathtt{with} \\
&\qquad\qquad \mid \mathtt{None} \rightarrow \mathtt{assert(false)}\quad \mathtt{(*\ Use\ after\ free\ *)} \\
&\qquad\qquad \mid \mathtt{Some}\ \_ \rightarrow l :=_{\mathsf{HL}} \mathtt{Some}\ v_2;\ v_2
\end{aligned}
$$

Since our memory model is simple, the value interpretation is straightforward:

$$
\begin{aligned}
&[\![\mathtt{z}]\!]_{val} \triangleq \mathtt{z} \quad (\text{if } \mathtt{z} \in \mathbb{Z}) && && [\![\mathtt{NULL}]\!]_{val} \triangleq \mathtt{None} \\
&[\![(\mathtt{v}_1, \mathtt{v}_2)]\!]_{val} \triangleq ([\![\mathtt{v}_1]\!]_{val}, [\![\mathtt{v}_2]\!]_{val}) && [\![()]\!]_{val} \triangleq () && [\![\mathtt{l}]\!]_{val} \triangleq \mathtt{Some\ l}
\end{aligned}
$$

The only interesting case is the translation of locations. Since there is no concept of a `NULL` pointer in HeapLang, we use the option type to distinguish `NULL` pointers from concrete locations (`l`). The interpretation of assignments thus contains a pattern match to check that no `NULL` pointers are dereferenced. A similar check is performed in the interpretation of the load operation (`*e`). Moreover, each location contains an option to distinguish freed from active locations.

Step 2: Sequence Points. So far we have not accounted for undefined behavior due to sequence point violations. For instance, the program `(x = 3) + (x = 4)` gets translated into a HeapLang expression that updates the value of the location `x` non-deterministically to either 3 or 4, and returns 7. However, in C, the behavior of this program is *undefined*, as it exhibits a sequence point violation: there is a write conflict for the location `x`.

To give a semantics for sequence point violations, we follow the approach by Norrish [44], Ellison and Rosu [17], and Krebbers [29,30]. We keep track of a set of locations that have been written to since the last sequence point. We refer to this set as the *environment* of our translation, and represent it using a global variable *env* of the type `mset` *Loc*. Because our target language HeapLang is concurrent, all updates to the environment *env* must be executed *atomically*, *i.e.*, inside a critical section, which we enforce by employing a global mutex *lk*. The interpretation of assignments $\mathtt{e}_1 = \mathtt{e}_2$ now becomes:

$$\begin{aligned}
\texttt{ret}\, e &\triangleq \lambda\,_\,_.\, e\\
e_1 \mid\mid e_2 &\triangleq \lambda\, env\, lk.\, (e_1\ env\ lk) \mid\mid_{\mathsf{HL}} (e_2\ env\ lk)\\
x \leftarrow e_1;\, e_2 &\triangleq \lambda\, env\, lk.\, \texttt{let}\, x = e_1\ env\ lk\ \texttt{in}\, e_2\ env\ lk\\
\texttt{atomic_env}\, e &\triangleq \lambda\, env\, lk.\, \texttt{acquire}\ lk; \texttt{let}\, a = e\ env\ \texttt{in}\,\texttt{release}\ lk; a\\
\texttt{atomic}\, e &\triangleq \lambda\, env\, lk.\, \texttt{acquire}\ lk; \texttt{let}\, a = e\ env\ (\texttt{newmutex}\ ())\ \texttt{in}\,\texttt{release}\ lk; a\\
\texttt{run}(e) &\triangleq e\ (\texttt{mset_create}\ ())\ (\texttt{newmutex}\ ())
\end{aligned}$$

Fig. 1. The monadic combinators.

$$\begin{aligned}
[\![\mathtt{e}_1 = \mathtt{e}_2]\!] \triangleq\ & \texttt{let}\ (v_1, v_2) = [\![\mathtt{e}_1]\!] \mid\mid_{\mathsf{HL}} [\![\mathtt{e}_2]\!]\ \texttt{in}\\
& \texttt{acquire}\ lk;\\
& \texttt{match}\ v_1\ \texttt{with}\\
& \quad \mid \texttt{None} \rightarrow \texttt{assert(false)} \qquad \texttt{(* NULL pointer *)}\\
& \quad \mid \texttt{Some}\ l \rightarrow\\
& \qquad \texttt{assert}(\neg\texttt{mset_member}\ l\ env);\ \texttt{(* Seq. point violation *)}\\
& \qquad \texttt{match}\ !_{\mathsf{HL}}\ l\ \texttt{with}\\
& \qquad\quad \mid \texttt{None} \rightarrow \texttt{assert(false)} \quad \texttt{(* Use after free *)}\\
& \qquad\quad \mid \texttt{Some}\ _ \rightarrow \texttt{mset_add}\ l\ env;\ l :=_{\mathsf{HL}} \texttt{Some}\ v_2;\\
& \texttt{release}\ lk;\ v_2
\end{aligned}$$

Whenever we assign to (or read from) a location l, we check if the location l is not already present in the environment *env*. If the location l is present, then it was already written to since the last sequence point. Hence, accessing the location constitutes undefined behavior (see the `assert` in the interpretation of assignments above). In the interpretation of assignments, we furthermore insert the location l into the environment *env*.

In order to make sure that one can access a variable again after a sequence point, we define the *sequenced bind* operator $\mathtt{x} \leftarrow \mathtt{e}_1 \,;\, \mathtt{e}_2$ as follows:

$$[\![\mathtt{x} \leftarrow \mathtt{e}_1 \,;\, \mathtt{e}_2]\!] \triangleq \texttt{let}\ x = [\![\mathtt{e}_1]\!]\ \texttt{in}\,\texttt{acquire}\ lk;\ \texttt{mset\_clear}\ env;\ \texttt{release}\ lk;\ [\![\mathtt{e}_2]\!]$$

After we finished executing the expression $\mathtt{e}_1$, we clear the environment *env*, so that all locations are accessible in $\mathtt{e}_2$ again.

Step 3: Non-interleaved Function Calls. As the final step, we present the correct translation scheme for function calls. Unlike the other expressions, function calls are not interleaved during the execution of subexpressions [22, 6.5.2.2p10]. For instance, in the program `f() + g()` the possible orders of execution are: either all the instructions in `f()` followed by all the instructions in `g()`, or all the instructions in `g()` followed by all the instructions in `f()`.

```
      ⟦e1 + e2⟧ ≜ (v1, v2) ← ⟦e1⟧ || ⟦e2⟧; ret (v1 +HL v2)
      ⟦e1 = e2⟧ ≜ (v1, v2) ← ⟦e1⟧ || ⟦e2⟧;
                  atomic_env (λ env.
                    match v1 with
                     | None → assert(false)      (* NULL pointer *)
                     | Some l →
                        assert(¬mset_member l env); (* Seq. point violation *)
                        match !HL l with
                         | None → assert(false)  (* Use after free *)
                         | Some _ → mset_add l env; l :=HL Some v2; ret v2)
⟦x ← e1 ; e2⟧ ≜ x ← ⟦e1⟧; _ ← (atomic_env mset_clear); ⟦e2⟧
    ⟦e1(e2)⟧ ≜ (f, a) ← ⟦e1⟧ || ⟦e2⟧; atomic (atomic_env mset_clear; f a)
  ⟦f(x){e}⟧ ≜ let rec f x = v ← ⟦e⟧; _ ← (atomic_env mset_clear); ret v
```

Fig. 2. Selected clauses from the monadic definitional semantics.

To model this, we execute each function call *atomically*. In the previous step we used a global mutex for guarding the access to the environment. We could use that mutex for function calls too. However, reusing a single mutex for entering each critical section would not work because a body of a function may contain invocations of other functions. To that extent, we use multiple mutexes to reflect the hierarchical structure of function calls.

To handle multiple mutexes, each C expression is interpreted as a HeapLang function that receives a mutex and returns its result. That is, each C expression is modeled by a monadic expression in the *reader monad* $M(A) \triangleq \texttt{mset}\ \mathit{Loc} \to \texttt{mutex} \to A$. For consistency's sake, we now also use the monad to thread through the reference to the environment ($\texttt{mset}\ \mathit{Loc}$), instead of using a global variable *env* as we did in the previous step.

We use a small set of monadic combinators, shown in Fig. 1, to build the translation in a more abstract way. The return and bind operators are standard for the reader monad. The parallel operator runs two monadic expressions concurrently, propagating the environment and the mutex. The `atomic` combinator invokes a monadic expression with a fresh mutex. The `atomic_env` combinator atomically executes its body with the current environment as an argument. The `run` function executes the monadic computation by instantiating it with a fresh mutex and a new environment. Selected clauses for the translation are presented in Fig. 2. The translation of the binary operations remains virtually unchanged, except for the usage of monadic parallel composition instead of the standard one. The translation for the assignment and the sequenced bind uses the `atomic_env` combinator for querying and updating the environment. We also have to adapt our translation of values, by wrapping it in `ret` : $[\![\mathtt{v}]\!] \triangleq \texttt{ret}\ [\![\mathtt{v}]\!]_{val}$.

A global function definition `f(x){e}` is translated as a top level let-binding. A function call is then just an atomically executed function invocation in HeapLang, modulo the fact that the function pointer and the arguments are computed in parallel. In addition, sequence points occur at the beginning of each function call and at the end of each function body [22, Annex C], and we reflect that in our translation by clearing the environment at appropriate places.

Our semantics by translation can easily be extended to cover other features of C, *e.g.*, a more advanced memory model (see Sect. 7). However the fragment presented here already illustrates the challenges that non-determinism and sequence point violations pose for verification. In the next section we describe a logic for reasoning about the semantics by translation given in this section.

3 Separation Logic with Weakest Preconditions for λMC

In this section we present a separation logic with weakest precondition propositions for reasoning about λMC programs. The logic tackles the main features of our semantics—non-determinism in expressions evaluation and sequence point violations. We will discuss the high-level rules of the logic pertaining to C connectives by going through a series of small examples.

The logic presented here is similar to the separation logic by Krebbers [29], but it is given in a weakest precondition style, and moreover, it is constructed *synthetically* on top of the separation logic framework Iris [24–26,33], whereas the logic by Krebbers [29] is interpreted directly in a bespoke model.

The following grammar defines the formulas of the logic:

$$\begin{aligned} P, Q \in \mathsf{Prop} ::= \mathsf{True} \mid \mathsf{False} \mid \forall x.\, P \mid \exists x.\, P \mid \mathsf{v}_1 = \mathsf{v}_2 \mid \mathsf{l} \overset{q}{\mapsto}_\xi v \mid \qquad & (q \in (0,1]) \\ P * Q \mid P \mathrel{-\!\!*} Q \mid \mathsf{wp}\, \mathsf{e}\, \{\Phi\} \mid \ldots \qquad & (\xi \in \{L, U\}) \end{aligned}$$

Most of the connectives are commonplace in separation logic, with the exception of the modified points-to connective, which we describe in this section.

As is common, Hoare triples $\{P\}\, \mathsf{e}\, \{\Phi\}$ are syntactic sugar for $P \vdash \mathsf{wp}\, \mathsf{e}\, \{\Phi\}$. The weakest precondition connective $\mathsf{wp}\, \mathsf{e}\, \{\Phi\}$ states that the program e is safe (the program has defined behavior), and if e terminates to a value v, then v satisfies the predicate Φ. We write $\mathsf{wp}\, \mathsf{e}\, \{\mathsf{v}.\, \Phi\, \mathsf{v}\}$ for $\mathsf{wp}\, \mathsf{e}\, \{\lambda \mathsf{v}.\, \Phi\, \mathsf{v}\}$.

Contrary to the paper by Krebbers [29], we use weakest preconditions instead of Hoare triples throughout this paper. There are several reasons for doing so:

1. We do not have to manipulate the preconditions explicitly, *e.g.*, by applying the consequence rule to the precondition.
2. The soundness of our symbolic executor (Theorem 5.1) can be stated more concisely using weakest precondition propositions.
3. It is more convenient to integrate weakest preconditions into the Iris Proof Mode/MoSeL framework in Coq that we use for our implementation (Sect. 7).

A selection of rules is presented in Fig. 3. Each inference rule $\dfrac{P_1 \ \ldots\ P_n}{Q}$ in this paper should be read as the entailment $P_1 * \ldots * P_n \vdash Q$. We now explain and motivate the rules of our logic.

WP-VALUE
$$\frac{\Phi\ \mathtt{v}}{\mathsf{wp}\ \mathtt{v}\ \{\Phi\}}$$

WP-WAND
$$\frac{\mathsf{wp}\ \mathsf{e}\ \{\Phi\} \qquad (\forall \mathtt{v}.\ \Phi\ \mathtt{v} \twoheadrightarrow \Psi\ \mathtt{v})}{\mathsf{wp}\ \mathsf{e}\ \{\Psi\}}$$

WP-SEQ
$$\frac{\mathsf{wp}\ \mathsf{e}_1\ \{\mathtt{v}.\ \mathbb{U}(\mathsf{wp}\ \mathsf{e}_2[\mathtt{v}/\mathtt{x}]\ \{\Phi\})\}}{\mathsf{wp}\ (\mathtt{x} \leftarrow \mathsf{e}_1\ ;\ \mathsf{e}_2)\ \{\Phi\}}$$

WP-BIN-OP
$$\frac{\mathsf{wp}\ \mathsf{e}_1\ \{\Psi_1\} \qquad \mathsf{wp}\ \mathsf{e}_2\ \{\Psi_2\} \qquad (\forall \mathtt{w}_1 \mathtt{w}_2.\ \Psi_1\ \mathtt{w}_1 * \Psi_2\ \mathtt{w}_2 \twoheadrightarrow \Phi(\mathtt{w}_1\ [\![\circledcirc]\!]\ \mathtt{w}_2))}{\mathsf{wp}\ (\mathsf{e}_1 \circledcirc \mathsf{e}_2)\ \{\Phi\}}$$

WP-LOAD
$$\frac{\mathsf{wp}\ \mathsf{e}\left\{\mathtt{l}.\ \exists \mathtt{w}\ q.\ \mathtt{l} \overset{q}{\mapsto}_U \mathtt{w} * (\mathtt{l} \overset{q}{\mapsto}_U \mathtt{w} \twoheadrightarrow \Phi\ \mathtt{w})\right\}}{\mathsf{wp}\ (*\mathsf{e})\ \{\Phi\}}$$

WP-ALLOC
$$\frac{\mathsf{wp}\ \mathsf{e}\ \{\mathtt{v}.\ \forall \mathtt{l}.\ \mathtt{l} \mapsto_U \mathtt{v} \twoheadrightarrow \Phi\ \mathtt{l}\}}{\mathsf{wp}\ \mathtt{alloc(e)}\ \{\Phi\}}$$

WP-STORE
$$\frac{\begin{array}{c}\mathsf{wp}\ \mathsf{e}_1\ \{\Psi_1\} \qquad \mathsf{wp}\ \mathsf{e}_2\ \{\Psi_2\} \\ (\forall \mathtt{l}\,\mathtt{w}.\ \Psi_1\ \mathtt{l} * \Psi_2\ \mathtt{w} \twoheadrightarrow \exists \mathtt{v}.\ \mathtt{l} \mapsto_U \mathtt{v} * (\mathtt{l} \mapsto_L \mathtt{w} \twoheadrightarrow \Phi\ \mathtt{w}))\end{array}}{\mathsf{wp}\ (\mathsf{e}_1 = \mathsf{e}_2)\ \{\Phi\}}$$

WP-FREE
$$\frac{\mathsf{wp}\ \mathsf{e}\ \{\mathtt{l}.\ \exists \mathtt{v}.\ \mathtt{l} \mapsto_U \mathtt{v} * \Phi\ ()\}}{\mathsf{wp}\ \mathtt{free(e)}\ \{\Phi\}}$$

MAPSTO-VALUES-AGREE
$$\frac{\mathtt{l} \overset{q_1}{\mapsto}_{\xi_1} \mathtt{v}_1 \qquad \mathtt{l} \overset{q_2}{\mapsto}_{\xi_2} \mathtt{v}_2}{\mathtt{v}_1 = \mathtt{v}_2}$$

MAPSTO-SPLIT
$$\mathtt{l} \overset{q_1}{\mapsto}_{\xi_1} \mathtt{v} * \mathtt{l} \overset{q_2}{\mapsto}_{\xi_2} \mathtt{v} \dashv\vdash \mathtt{l} \overset{q_1+q_2}{\longmapsto}_{\xi_1 \vee \xi_2} \mathtt{v}$$

U-UNLOCK
$$\frac{\mathtt{l} \overset{q}{\mapsto}_L \mathtt{v}}{\mathbb{U}(\mathtt{l} \overset{q}{\mapsto}_U \mathtt{v})}$$

U-MONO
$$\frac{P \twoheadrightarrow Q}{\mathbb{U}P \twoheadrightarrow \mathbb{U}Q}$$

U-INTRO
$$\frac{P}{\mathbb{U}P}$$

U-SEP
$$\frac{\mathbb{U}P * \mathbb{U}Q}{\mathbb{U}(P * Q)}$$

Fig. 3. Selected rules for weakest preconditions.

Non-determinism. In the introduction (Sect. 1) we have already shown the rule for addition from Krebbers's logic [29], which was written using Hoare triples. Using weakest preconditions, the corresponding rule (WP-BIN-OP) is:

$$\frac{\mathsf{wp}\ \mathsf{e}_1\ \{\Psi_1\} \qquad \mathsf{wp}\ \mathsf{e}_2\ \{\Psi_2\} \qquad (\forall \mathtt{w}_1 \mathtt{w}_2.\ \Psi_1\ \mathtt{w}_1 * \Psi_2\ \mathtt{w}_2 \twoheadrightarrow \Phi(\mathtt{w}_1\ [\![\circledcirc]\!]\ \mathtt{w}_2))}{\mathsf{wp}\ (\mathsf{e}_1 \circledcirc \mathsf{e}_2)\ \{\Phi\}}$$

This rule closely resembles the usual rule for parallel composition in ordinary concurrent separation logic [46]. This should not be surprising, as we have given a definitional semantics to binary operators using the parallel composition operator. It is important to note that the premises WP-BIN-OP are combined using the *separating conjunction* $*$. This ensures that the weakest preconditions $\mathsf{wp}\ \mathsf{e}_1\ \{\Psi_1\}$ and $\mathsf{wp}\ \mathsf{e}_2\ \{\Psi_2\}$ for the subexpressions e_1 and e_2 are verified with respect to disjoint resources. As such they do not interfere with each other, and can be evaluated in parallel without causing sequence point violations.

To see how one can use the rule WP-BIN-OP, let us verify $P \vdash \mathsf{wp}\ (\mathsf{e}_1 + \mathsf{e}_2)\ \{\Phi\}$. That is, we want to show that $(\mathsf{e}_1 + \mathsf{e}_2)$ satisfies the postcondition Φ assuming the precondition P. This goal can be proven by separating the precondition P into disjoint parts $P_1 * P_2 * R \dashv\vdash P$. Then using WP-BIN-OP the goal can be reduced to proving $P_i \vdash \mathsf{wp}\ \mathtt{e}_i\ \{\Psi_i\}$ for $i \in \{0,1\}$, and $R * \Psi_1\ \mathtt{w}_1 * \Psi_2\ \mathtt{w}_2 \vdash \Phi(\mathtt{w}_1\ [\![\circledcirc]\!]\ \mathtt{w}_2)$ for any return values $\mathtt{w}_i$ of the expressions $\mathtt{e}_i$.

Fractional Permissions. Separation logic includes the *points-to connective* $\mathtt{l} \mapsto \mathtt{v}$, which asserts unique ownership of a location $\mathtt{l}$ with value $\mathtt{v}$. This connective is used to specify the behavior of stateful operations, which becomes apparent in the following proposed rule for load:

$$\frac{\mathsf{wp}\ \mathtt{e}\ \{\mathtt{l}.\ \exists \mathtt{w}.\ \mathtt{l} \mapsto \mathtt{w} * (\mathtt{l} \mapsto \mathtt{w} -\!\!* \Phi\ \mathtt{w})\}}{\mathsf{wp}\ (*\mathtt{e})\ \{\Phi\}}$$

In order to verify $*\mathtt{e}$ we first make sure that $\mathtt{e}$ evaluates to a location $\mathtt{l}$, and then we need to provide the points-to connective $\mathtt{l} \mapsto \mathtt{w}$ for some value stored at the location. This rule, together with WP-VALUE, allows for verification of simple programs like $\mathtt{l} \mapsto \mathtt{v} \vdash \mathsf{wp}\ (*\mathtt{l})\ \{\mathtt{w}.\ \mathtt{w} = \mathtt{v} * \mathtt{l} \mapsto \mathtt{v}\}$.

However, the rule above is too weak. Suppose that we wish to verify the program $*\mathtt{l} + *\mathtt{l}$ from the precondition $\mathtt{l} \mapsto \mathtt{v}$. According to WP-BIN-OP, we have to separate the proposition $\mathtt{l} \mapsto \mathtt{v}$ into two disjoint parts, each used to verify the load operation. In order to enable sharing of points-to connectives we use *fractional permissions* [7,8]. In separation logic with fractional permissions each points-to connective is annotated with a fraction $q \in (0,1]$, and the resources can be split in accordance with those fractions:

$$\mathtt{l} \xmapsto{q_1+q_2} \mathtt{v} \dashv\vdash \mathtt{l} \xmapsto{q_1} \mathtt{v} * \mathtt{l} \xmapsto{q_2} \mathtt{v}.$$

A connective $\mathtt{l} \xmapsto{1} \mathtt{v}$ provides a unique ownership of the location, and we refer to it as a *write permission*. A points-to connective with $q \leq 1$ provides shared ownership of the location, referred to as a *read permission*. By convention, we write $\mathtt{l} \mapsto \mathtt{v}$ to denote the write permission $\mathtt{l} \xmapsto{1} \mathtt{v}$.

With fractional permissions at hand, we can relax the proposed load rule, by allowing to dereference a location even if we only have a read permission:

$$\frac{\mathsf{wp}\ \mathtt{e}\ \left\{\mathtt{l}.\ \exists \mathtt{w}\, q.\ \mathtt{l} \xmapsto{q} \mathtt{w} * (\mathtt{l} \xmapsto{q} \mathtt{w} -\!\!* \Phi\ \mathtt{w})\right\}}{\mathsf{wp}\ (*\mathtt{e})\ \{\Phi\}}$$

This corresponds to the intuition that multiple subexpressions can safely dereference the same location, but not write to them.

Using the rule above we can verify $\mathtt{l} \mapsto 1 \vdash \mathsf{wp}\ (*\mathtt{l} + *\mathtt{l})\ \{\mathtt{v}.\ \mathtt{v} = 2 * \mathtt{l} \mapsto 1\}$ by splitting the assumption into $\mathtt{l} \xmapsto{0.5} 1 * \mathtt{l} \xmapsto{0.5} 1$ and first applying WP-BIN-OP with Ψ_1 and Ψ_2 being $\lambda\mathtt{v}.\ (\mathtt{v} = 1) * \mathtt{l} \xmapsto{0.5} 1$. Then we apply WP-LOAD on both subgoals. After that, we can use MAPSTO-SPLIT to prove the remaining formula:

$$(\mathtt{v}_1 = 1) * \mathtt{l} \xmapsto{0.5} 1 * (\mathtt{v}_2 = 1) * \mathtt{l} \xmapsto{0.5} 1 \ \vdash\ (\mathtt{v}_1 + \mathtt{v}_2 = 2) * \mathtt{l} \mapsto 1.$$

The Assignment Operator. The second main operation that accesses the heap is the assignment operator $e_1 = e_2$. The arguments on the both sides of the assignment are evaluated in parallel, and a points-to connective is required to perform an update to the heap. A naive version of the assignment rule can be obtained by combining the binary operation rule and the load rule:

$$\frac{\mathsf{wp}\,\mathsf{e}_1\,\{\Psi_1\} \quad \mathsf{wp}\,\mathsf{e}_2\,\{\Psi_2\} \quad (\forall \mathtt{l}\,\mathtt{w}.\, \Psi_1\,\mathtt{l} * \Psi_2\,\mathtt{w} \mathrel{-\!\!*} \exists \mathtt{v}.\, \mathtt{l} \mapsto \mathtt{v} * (\mathtt{l} \mapsto \mathtt{w} \mathrel{-\!\!*} \Phi\,\mathtt{w}))}{\mathsf{wp}\,(\mathsf{e}_1 = \mathsf{e}_2)\,\{\Phi\}}$$

The write permission $\mathtt{l} \mapsto \mathtt{v}$ can be obtained by combining the resources of both sides of the assignment. This allows us to verify programs like $\mathtt{l} = {*\mathtt{l}} + {*\mathtt{l}}$.

However, the rule above is unsound, because it fails to account for sequence point violations. We could use the rule above to prove safety of undefined programs, *e.g.*, the program $\mathtt{l} = (\mathtt{l} = 3)$.

To account for sequence point violations we decorate the points-to connectives $\mathtt{l} \overset{q}{\mapsto}_\xi \mathtt{v}$ with *access levels* $\xi \in \{L, U\}$. These have the following semantics: we can read from and write to a location that is unlocked (U), and the location becomes locked (L) once someone writes to it. Proposition $\mathtt{l} \overset{q}{\mapsto}_U \mathtt{v}$ (resp. $\mathtt{l} \overset{q}{\mapsto}_L \mathtt{v}$) asserts ownership of the unlocked (resp. locked) location $\mathtt{l}$. We refer to such propositions as *lockable points-to connectives*. Using lockable points-to connectives we can formulate the correct assignment rule:

$$\frac{\mathsf{wp}\,\mathsf{e}_1\,\{\Psi_1\} \quad \mathsf{wp}\,\mathsf{e}_2\,\{\Psi_2\} \quad (\forall \mathtt{l}\,\mathtt{w}.\, \Psi_1\,\mathtt{l} * \Psi_2\,\mathtt{w} \mathrel{-\!\!*} \exists \mathtt{v}.\, \mathtt{l} \mapsto \mathtt{v} * (\mathtt{l} \mapsto_L \mathtt{w} \mathrel{-\!\!*} \Phi\,\mathtt{w}))}{\mathsf{wp}\,(\mathsf{e}_1 = \mathsf{e}_2)\,\{\Phi\}}$$

The set $\{L, U\}$ has a lattice structure with $L \leq U$, and the levels can be combined with a join operation, see MAPSTO-SPLIT. By convention, $\mathtt{l} \overset{q}{\mapsto} \mathtt{v}$ denotes $\mathtt{l} \overset{q}{\mapsto}_U \mathtt{v}$.

The Unlocking Modality. As locations become locked after using the assignment rule, we wish to unlock them in order to perform further heap operations. For instance, in the expression $\mathtt{l} = 4\,; {*\mathtt{l}}$ the location $\mathtt{l}$ becomes unlocked after the sequence point ";" between the store and the dereferencing operations. To reflect this in the logic, we use the rule WP-SEQ which features the *unlocking modality* $\mathbb{U}$ (which is called the unlocking assertion in [29, Definition 5.6]):

$$\frac{\mathsf{wp}\,\mathsf{e}_1\,\{\_.\, \mathbb{U}(\mathsf{wp}\,\mathsf{e}_2\,\{\Phi\})\}}{\mathsf{wp}\,(\mathsf{e}_1\,;\mathsf{e}_2)\,\{\Phi\}}$$

Intuitively, $\mathbb{U}P$ states that P holds, after unlocking all locations. The rules of $\mathbb{U}$ in Fig. 3 allow one to turn $(P_1 * \ldots * P_m) * (\mathtt{l}_1 \mapsto_L \mathtt{v}_1 * \ldots * \mathtt{l}_m \mapsto_L \mathtt{v}_m) \vdash \mathbb{U}Q$ into $(P_1 * \ldots * P_m) * (\mathtt{l}_1 \mapsto_U \mathtt{v}_1 * \ldots * \mathtt{l}_m \mapsto_U \mathtt{v}_m) \vdash Q$. This is done by applying either U-UNLOCK or U-INTRO to each premise; then collecting all premises into one formula under $\mathbb{U}$ by U-SEP; and finally, applying U-MONO to the whole sequent.

4 Soundness of Weakest Preconditions for λMC

In this section we prove adequacy of the separation logic with weakest preconditions for λMC as presented in Sect. 3. We do this by giving a model using the Iris framework that is structured in a similar way as the translation that we gave in Sect. 2. This translation consisted of three layers: the target HeapLang language, the monadic combinators, and the λMC operations themselves. In the model, each corresponding layer abstracts from the details of the previous layer, in such a way that we never have to break the abstraction of a layer. At the end, putting all of this together, we get the following adequacy statement:

Theorem 4.1 (Adequacy of Weakest Preconditions). *If* $\mathsf{wp}\ \mathsf{e}\ \{\Phi\}$ *is derivable, then* e *has no undefined behavior for any evaluation order. In other words,* $\mathtt{run}(\mathsf{e})$ *does not assert false.*

The proof of the adequacy theorem closely follows the layered structure, by combining the correctness of the monadic `run` combinator with adequacy of HeapLang in Iris [25, Theorem 6]. The rest of this section is organized as:

1. Because our translation targets HeapLang, we start by recalling the separation logic with weakest preconditions, for HeapLang part of Iris (Sect. 4.1).
2. On top of the logic for HeapLang, we define a notion of weakest preconditions $\mathsf{wp}_{\mathsf{mon}}\ e\ \{\Phi\}$ for expressions e built from our monadic combinators (Sect. 4.2).
3. Next, we define the lockable points-to connective $\ell \overset{q}{\mapsto}_{\xi} v$ using Iris's machinery for custom ghost state (Sect. 4.3).
4. Finally, we define weakest preconditions for λMC by combining the weakest preconditions for monadic expressions with our translation scheme (Sect. 4.4).

4.1 Weakest Preconditions for HeapLang

We recall the most essential Iris connectives for reasoning about HeapLang programs: $\mathsf{wp}_{\mathsf{HL}}\ e\ \{\Phi\}$ and $\ell \mapsto_{\mathsf{HL}} v$, which are the HeapLang weakest precondition proposition and the HeapLang points-to connective, respectively. Other Iris connectives are described in [6, Section 8.1] or [25,33]. An example rule is the store rule for HeapLang, shown in Fig. 4. The rule requires a points-to connective $\ell \mapsto_{\mathsf{HL}} v$, and the user receives the updated points-to connective $\ell \mapsto_{\mathsf{HL}} w$ back for proving $\Phi\ ()$. Note that the rule is formulated for a concrete location ℓ and a value w, instead of arbitrary expressions. This does not limit the expressive power; since the evaluation order in HeapLang is deterministic[1], arbitrary expressions can be handled using the WP$_{\text{HL}}$-BIND rule. Using this rule, one can bind an expression e in an arbitrary evaluation context K. We can thus use the WP$_{\text{HL}}$-BIND rule twice to derive a more general store rule for HeapLang:

$$\frac{\mathsf{wp}_{\mathsf{HL}}\ e_2\ \{w.\ \mathsf{wp}_{\mathsf{HL}}\ e_1\ \{\ell.\ (\exists v.\ \ell \mapsto_{\mathsf{HL}} v) * (\ell \mapsto_{\mathsf{HL}} w \twoheadrightarrow \Phi\ ())\}\}}{\mathsf{wp}_{\mathsf{HL}}\ (e_1 :=_{\mathsf{HL}} e_2)\ \{\Phi\}}$$

[1] And right-to-left, although our monadic translation does not rely on that.

$$(\ell \mapsto_{\mathsf{HL}} v) * (\ell \mapsto_{\mathsf{HL}} v \twoheadrightarrow \Phi\, v) \vdash \mathsf{wp}_{\mathsf{HL}}\ !_{\mathsf{HL}}\, \ell\, \{\Phi\}$$

$$(\ell \mapsto_{\mathsf{HL}} v) * (\ell \mapsto_{\mathsf{HL}} w \twoheadrightarrow \Phi\, ()) \vdash \mathsf{wp}_{\mathsf{HL}}\ \ell :=_{\mathsf{HL}} w\, \{\Phi\}$$

WPHL-BIND

$$\frac{\mathsf{wp}_{\mathsf{HL}}\, e\, \{v.\, \mathsf{wp}_{\mathsf{HL}}\, K[\, v\,]\, \{\Phi\}\}}{\mathsf{wp}_{\mathsf{HL}}\, K[\, e\,]\, \{\Phi\}}$$

$$R * (\forall \gamma\; lk.\, \mathsf{is\_mutex}(\gamma, lk, R) \twoheadrightarrow \Phi\; lk) \vdash \mathsf{wp}_{\mathsf{HL}}\ \mathtt{newmutex}\ ()\ \{\Phi\}$$

$$\mathsf{is\_mutex}(\gamma, lk, R) * (R * \mathsf{locked}(\gamma) \twoheadrightarrow \Phi\, ()) \vdash \mathsf{wp}_{\mathsf{HL}}\ \mathtt{acquire}\ lk\, \{\Phi\}$$

$$\mathsf{is\_mutex}(\gamma, lk, R) * R * \mathsf{locked}(\gamma) * \Phi\, () \vdash \mathsf{wp}_{\mathsf{HL}}\ \mathtt{release}\ lk\, \{\Phi\}$$

$$\mathsf{is\_mutex}(\gamma, lk, R) * \mathsf{is\_mutex}(\gamma, lk, R) \dashv\vdash \mathsf{is\_mutex}(\gamma, lk, R) \qquad \text{(ISMUTEX-DUPL)}$$

Fig. 4. Selected $\mathsf{wp}_{\mathsf{HL}}$ rules.

To verify the monadic combinators and the translation of $\lambda\mathsf{MC}$ operations in the upcoming Sects. 4.2 and 4.4, we need the specifications for all the functions that we use, including those on mutable sets and mutexes. The rules for mutable sets are standard, and thus omitted. They involve the usual abstract predicate $\mathsf{is\_mset}(s, X)$ stating that the reference s represents a set with contents X. The rules for mutexes are presented in Fig. 4. When a new mutex is created, a user gets access to a proposition $\mathsf{is\_mutex}(\gamma, lk, R)$, which states that the value lk is a mutex containing the resources R. This proposition can be duplicated freely (ISMUTEX-DUPL). A thread can acquire the mutex and receive the resources contained in it. In addition, the thread receives a token $\mathsf{locked}(\gamma)$ meaning that it has entered the critical section. When a thread leaves the critical section and releases the mutex, it has to give up both the token and the resources R.

4.2 Weakest Preconditions for Monadic Expressions

As a next step, we define a weakest precondition proposition $\mathsf{wp}_{\mathsf{mon}}\, e\, \{\Phi\}$ for a monadic expression e. The definition is constructed in the ambient logic, and it encapsulates the monadic operations in a separate layer. Due to that, we are able to carry out proofs of high-level specifications without breaking the abstraction (Sect. 4.4). The specifications for selected monadic operations in terms of $\mathsf{wp}_{\mathsf{mon}}$ are presented in Fig. 5. We define the weakest precondition for a monadic expression e as follows:

$$\mathsf{wp}_{\mathsf{mon}}\, e\, \{\Phi\} \triangleq \mathsf{wp}_{\mathsf{HL}}\, e \left\{ \begin{array}{c} g.\, \forall \gamma\; env\; lk.\, \mathsf{is\_mutex}(\gamma, lk, \mathsf{env\_inv}(env)) \twoheadrightarrow \\ \mathsf{wp}_{\mathsf{HL}}\, (g\; env\; lk)\, \{\Phi\} \end{array} \right\}$$

The idea is that we first reduce e to a monadic value g. To perform this reduction we have the outermost $\mathsf{wp}_{\mathsf{HL}}$ connective in the definition of $\mathsf{wp}_{\mathsf{mon}}$. This monadic value is then evaluated with an arbitrary environment and an arbitrary mutex. Note that we universally quantify over any mutex lk to support nested locking in `atomic`. This definition is parameterized by an *environment invariant* $\mathsf{env\_inv}(env)$, which describes the resources accessible in the critical sections. We show how to define $\mathsf{env\_inv}$ in the next subsection.

WP-RET
$$\frac{\mathsf{wp}_{\mathsf{HL}}\, e\, \{\Phi\}}{\mathsf{wp}_{\mathsf{mon}}\, (\mathtt{ret}\, e)\, \{\Phi\}}$$

WP-BIND
$$\frac{\mathsf{wp}_{\mathsf{mon}}\, e_1\, \{v.\, \mathsf{wp}_{\mathsf{mon}}\, e_2[v/x]\, \{\Phi\}\}}{\mathsf{wp}_{\mathsf{mon}}\, (x \leftarrow e_1;\, e_2)\, \{\Phi\}}$$

WP-PAR
$$\frac{\mathsf{wp}_{\mathsf{mon}}\, e_1\, \{\Psi_1\} \qquad \mathsf{wp}_{\mathsf{mon}}\, e_2\, \{\Psi_2\} \qquad (\forall w_1 w_2.\, \Psi_1\, w_1 * \Psi_2\, w_2 \mathrel{-\!\!*} \Phi\, (w_1, w_2))}{\mathsf{wp}_{\mathsf{mon}}\, (e_1 \mathbin{||} e_2)\, \{\Phi\}}$$

WP-ATOMIC-ENV
$$\frac{\forall env.\, \mathsf{env\_inv}(env) \mathrel{-\!\!*} \mathsf{wp}_{\mathsf{HL}}\, (v\, env)\, \{w.\, \mathsf{env\_inv}(env) * \Phi\, w\}}{\mathsf{wp}_{\mathsf{mon}}\, (\mathtt{atomic\_env}\, v)\, \{\Phi\}}$$

Fig. 5. Selected monadic $\mathsf{wp}_{\mathsf{mon}}$ rules.

Using this definition we derive the monadic rules in Fig. 5. In a monad, the expression evaluation order is made explicit via the bind operation $x \leftarrow e_1; e_2$. To that extent, contrary to HeapLang, we no longer have a rule like WP$_{\text{HL}}$-BIND, which allows to bind an expression in a general evaluation context. Instead, we have the rule WP-BIND, which reflects that the only evaluation context we have is the monadic bind $x \leftarrow [\bullet]; e$.

4.3 Modeling the Heap

The monadic rules in Fig. 5 are expressive enough to derive some of the λMC-level rules, but we are still missing one crucial part: handling of the heap. In order to do that, we need to define lockable points-to connectives $\mathtt{l} \overset{q}{\mapsto}_{\xi} \mathtt{v}$ in such a way that they are linked to the HeapLang points-to connectives $\ell \mapsto_{\mathsf{HL}} v$.

The key idea is the following. The environment invariant env_inv of monadic weakest preconditions will track *all* HeapLang points-to connectives $\ell \mapsto_{\mathsf{HL}} v$ that have ever been allocated at the λMC level. Via Iris ghost state, we then connect this knowledge to the lockable points-to connectives $\mathtt{l} \overset{q}{\mapsto}_{\xi} \mathtt{v}$. We refer to the construction that allows us to carry this out as the *lockable heap*. Note that the description of lockable heap is fairly technical and requires an understanding of the ghost state mechanism in Iris.

A lockable heap is a map $\sigma : Loc \xrightarrow{\text{fin}} \{L, U\} \times Val$ that keeps track of the access levels and values associated with the locations. The connective $\mathsf{full\_heap}(\sigma)$ asserts the ownership of all the locations present in the domain of σ. Specifically, it asserts $\ell \mapsto_{\mathsf{HL}} v$ for each $\{\ell \leftarrow (\xi, v)\} \in \sigma$. The connective $\ell \overset{q}{\mapsto}_{\xi} v$ then states that $\{\ell \leftarrow (\xi, v)\}$ is part of the global lockable heap, and it asserts this with the fractional permission q. We treat the lockable heap as an opaque abstraction, whose exact implementation via Iris ghost state is described in the Coq formalization [18]. The main interface for the locking heap are the rules in Fig. 6. The rule HEAP-ALLOC states that we can turn a HeapLang points-to connective $\ell \mapsto_{\mathsf{HL}} v$ into $\ell \mapsto_{\xi} v$ by changing the lockable heap σ accordingly. The

$$\text{HEAP-ALLOC}\quad \frac{\ell \mapsto_{\mathsf{HL}} v \qquad \mathsf{full\_heap}(\sigma)}{\Rrightarrow \ell \mapsto_U v * \mathsf{full\_heap}(\sigma\,[\ell \leftarrow (U, v)])}$$

$$\text{HEAP-UPD}\quad \frac{\ell \mapsto_U v \qquad \mathsf{full\_heap}(\sigma)}{\Rrightarrow \sigma(\ell) = (U, v) * \ell \mapsto_{\mathsf{HL}} v * (\forall v'\, \xi'.\, \ell \mapsto_{\mathsf{HL}} v' \Rrightarrow\!\!* \; \ell \mapsto_{\xi'} v' * \mathsf{full\_heap}(\sigma\,[\ell \leftarrow (\xi', v')]))}$$

Fig. 6. Selected rules of the lockable heap construction.

rule HEAP-UPD states that given $\ell \mapsto_\xi v$, we can temporarily get a HeapLang points-to connective $\ell \mapsto_{\mathsf{HL}} v$ out of the locking heap and update its value.

The environment invariant $\mathsf{env\_inv}(env)$ in the definition of $\mathsf{wp}_{\mathsf{mon}}$ ties the contents of the lockable heap to the contents of the environment env:

$$\mathsf{env\_inv}(env) \triangleq \exists \sigma\, X.\ \mathsf{is\_set}(env, X) * \mathsf{full\_heap}(\sigma) * (\forall \ell \in X. \exists v.\, \sigma(\ell) = (L, v))$$

The first conjunct states that $X : \wp^{\mathrm{fin}}(Loc)$ is a set of locked locations, according to the environment env. The second conjunct asserts ownership of the global lockable heap σ. Finally, the last conjunct states that the contents of env agrees with the lockable heap: every location that is in X is locked according to σ.

The Unlocking Modality. The unlocking modality is defined in the logic as:

$$\mathbb{U} P \triangleq \exists S.\, (\mathop{\Large *}_{(\mathtt{l},\mathtt{v},q)\in S} \mathtt{l} \overset{q}{\mapsto}_L \mathtt{v}) * ((\mathop{\Large *}_{(\mathtt{l},\mathtt{v},q)\in S} \mathtt{l} \overset{q}{\mapsto}_U \mathtt{v}) \mathrel{-\!\!*} P)$$

Here S is a finite multiset of tuples containing locations, values, and fractions. The update modality accumulates the locked locations, waiting for them to be unlocked at a sequence point.

4.4 Deriving the λMC Rules

To model weakest preconditions for λMC (Fig. 3) we compose the construction we have just defined with the translation of Sect. 2 $\mathsf{wp}\ \mathsf{e}\ \{\Phi\} \triangleq \mathsf{wp}_{\mathsf{mon}}\ [\![\mathsf{e}]\!]\ \{\Phi'\}$. Here, Φ' is the obvious lifting of Φ from λMC values to HeapLang values. Using the rules from Figs. 5 and 6 we derive the high-level λMC rules without unfolding the definition of the monadic $\mathsf{wp}_{\mathsf{mon}}$.

Example 4.2. Consider the rule WP-STORE for assignments $\mathsf{e}_1 = \mathsf{e}_2$. Using WP-BIND and WP-PAR, the soundness of WP-STORE can be reduced to verifying the assignment with e_1 being `l`, e_2 being v', under the assumption $\mathtt{l} \mapsto_U \mathtt{v}$. We use WP-ATOMIC-ENV to turn our goal into a HeapLang weakest precondition proposition and to gain access an environment env, and to the proposition $\mathsf{env\_inv}(env)$, from which we extract the lockable heap σ. We then use HEAP-UPD to get access to the underlying HeapLang location and obtain that `l` is not locked according to σ. Due to the environment invariant, we obtain that `l` is not in *env*, which allows us to prove the `assert` for sequence point violation in the interpretation of the assignment. Finally, we perform the physical update of the location.

5 A Symbolic Executor for λMC

In order to turn our program logic into an automated procedure, it is important to have rules for weakest preconditions that have an algorithmic form. However, the rules for binary operators in our separation logic for λMC do not have such a form. Take for example the rule WP-BIN-OP for binary operators $\mathtt{e}_1 \circledcirc \mathtt{e}_2$. This rule cannot be applied in an algorithmic manner. To use the rule one should supply the postconditions for $\mathtt{e}_1$ and $\mathtt{e}_2$, and frame the resources from the context into two disjoint parts. This is generally impossible to do automatically.

To address this problem, we first describe how the rules for binary operators can be transformed into algorithmic rules by exploiting the notion of *symbolic execution* [5] (Sect. 5.1). We then show how to implement these algorithmic rules as part of an automated symbolic execution procedure (Sect. 5.2).

5.1 Rules for Symbolic Execution

We say that we can *symbolically execute* an expression $\mathtt{e}$ using a *precondition* P, if we can find a *symbolic execution tuple* $(\mathtt{w}, Q, R)$ consisting of a *return value* $\mathtt{w}$, a *postcondition* Q, and a *frame* R satisfying:

$$P \vdash \mathsf{wp}\ \mathtt{e}\ \{\mathtt{v}.\ \mathtt{v} = \mathtt{w} * Q\} * R$$

This specification is much like that of ordinary symbolic execution in separation logic [5], but there is important difference. Apart from computing the postcondition Q and the return value $\mathtt{w}$, there is also the frame R, which describes the resources that are *not used* for proving $\mathtt{e}$. For instance, if the precondition P is $P' * \mathtt{l} \overset{q}{\mapsto} \mathtt{w}$ and $\mathtt{e}$ is a load operation $*\mathtt{l}$, then we can symbolically execute $\mathtt{e}$ with the postcondition Q being $\mathtt{l} \overset{q/2}{\longmapsto} \mathtt{w}$, and the frame R being $P' * \mathtt{l} \overset{q/2}{\longmapsto} \mathtt{w}$. Clearly, P' is not needed for proving the load, so it can be moved into the frame. More interestingly, since loading the contents of $\mathtt{l}$ requires a read permission $\mathtt{l} \overset{p}{\mapsto} \mathtt{w}$, with $p \in (0, 1]$, we can split the hypothesis $\mathtt{l} \overset{q}{\mapsto} \mathtt{w}$ into two halves and move one into the frame. Below we will see why that matters.

If we can symbolically execute one of the operands of a binary expression $\mathtt{e}_1 \circledcirc \mathtt{e}_2$, say $\mathtt{e}_1$ in P, and find a symbolic execution tuple $(\mathtt{w}_1, Q, R)$, then we can use the following admissible rule:

$$\frac{R \vdash \mathsf{wp}\ \mathtt{e}_2\ \{\mathtt{w}_2.\ Q \mathrel{-\!\!*} \Phi\ (\mathtt{w}_1\ [\![\circledcirc]\!]\ \mathtt{w}_2)\}}{P \vdash \mathsf{wp}\ (\mathtt{e}_1 \circledcirc \mathtt{e}_2)\ \{\Phi\}}$$

This rule has a much more algorithmic flavor than the rule WP-BIN-OP. Applying the above rule now boils down to finding such a tuple $(\mathtt{w}, Q, R)$, instead of having to infer postconditions for both operands, as we need to do to apply WP-BIN-OP.

For instance, given an expression (*1) $\circledcirc$ e_2 and a precondition $P' * 1 \overset{q}{\mapsto} v$, we can derive the following rule:

$$\frac{P' * 1 \overset{q/2}{\longmapsto} v \vdash \mathsf{wp}\; e_2 \left\{ w_2.\, 1 \overset{q/2}{\longmapsto} v \mathrel{-\!\!*} \Phi\,(v\,[\![\circledcirc]\!]\,w_2) \right\}}{P' * 1 \overset{q}{\mapsto} v \vdash \mathsf{wp}\,(*1 \circledcirc e_2)\,\{\Phi\}}$$

This rule matches the intuition that only a fraction of the permission $1 \overset{q}{\mapsto} v$ is needed to prove a load *1, so that the remaining half of the permission can be used to prove the correctness of e_2 (which may contain other loads of 1).

5.2 An Algorithm for Symbolic Execution

For an arbitrary expression e and a proposition P, it is unlikely that one can find such a symbolic execution tuple (w, Q, R) automatically. However, for a certain class of C expressions that appear in actual programs we can compute a choice of such a tuple. To illustrate our approach, we will define such an algorithm for a small subset $\overline{\mathsf{expr}}$ of C expressions described by the following grammar:

$$\bar{e} \in \overline{\mathsf{expr}} ::= v \mid *\bar{e} \mid \bar{e}_1 = \bar{e}_2 \mid \bar{e}_1 \circledcirc \bar{e}_2.$$

We keep this subset small to ease presentation. In Sect. 7 we explain how to extend the algorithm to cover the sequenced bind operator $x \leftarrow \bar{e}_1\,;\bar{e}_2$.

Moreover, to implement symbolic execution, we cannot manipulate arbitrary separation logic propositions. We thus restrict to *symbolic heaps* ($m \in \mathsf{sheap}$), which are defined as finite partial functions $\mathsf{Loc} \overset{\text{fin}}{\rightharpoonup} (\{L, U\} \times (0,1] \times \mathsf{val})$ representing a collection of points-to propositions:

$$[\![m]\!] \triangleq \mathop{\Large *}_{\substack{1 \in \mathrm{dom}(m) \\ m(1) = (\xi, q, v)}} 1 \overset{q}{\mapsto}_{\xi} v.$$

We use the following operations on symbolic heaps:

- $m[1 \mapsto (\xi, q, v)]$ sets the entry $m(1)$ to (ξ, q, v);
- $m \setminus \{1 \mapsto \_\}$ removes the entry $m(1)$ from m;
- $m_1 \sqcup m_2$ merges the symbolic heaps m_1 and m_2 in such a way that for each $1 \in \mathrm{dom}(m_1) \cup \mathrm{dom}(m_2)$, we have:

$$(m_1 \sqcup m_2)(1) = \begin{cases} m_i(1) & \text{if } 1 \in \mathrm{dom}(m_i) \text{ and } 1 \notin \mathrm{dom}(m_j) \\ (\xi \vee \xi', q + q', v) & \text{if } m_1(1) = (\xi, q, v) \text{ and } m_2(1) = (\xi', q', \_). \end{cases}$$

With this representation of propositions, we define the symbolic execution algorithm as a partial function $\mathsf{forward} : (\mathsf{sheap} \times \mathsf{expr}) \to (\mathsf{val} \times \mathsf{sheap} \times \mathsf{sheap})$, which satisfies the specification stated in Sect. 5.1, *i.e.*, for which the following holds:

Theorem 5.1. *Given an expression* e *and an symbolic heap* m, *if* $\mathsf{forward}(m, e)$ *returns a tuple* (w, m_1°, m_1), *then* $[\![m]\!] \vdash \mathsf{wp}\; e\, \{v.\, v = w * [\![m_1^{\circ}]\!]\} * [\![m_1]\!]$.

The definition of the algorithm is shown in Fig. 7. Given a tuple $(m, \mathtt{e})$, a call to $\mathsf{forward}(m, \mathtt{e})$ either returns a tuple $(\mathtt{v}, m^o, m')$ or fails, which either happens when $\mathtt{e} \notin \overline{\mathsf{expr}}$ or when one of intermediate steps of computation fails. In the latter cases, we write $\mathsf{forward}(m, \mathtt{e}) = \bot$.

The algorithm proceeds by case analysis on the expression e. In each case, the expected output is described by the equation $\mathsf{forward}(m, \mathtt{e}) = (\mathtt{v}, m^o, m')$. The results of the intermediate computations appear on separate lines under the clause "**where** ...". If one of the corresponding equations does not hold, *e.g.*, a recursive call fails, then the failure is propagated. Let us now explain the case for the assignment operator.

If e is an assignment operator $\mathtt{e}_1 = \mathtt{e}_2$, we first evaluate $\mathtt{e}_1$ and then $\mathtt{e}_2$. Fixing the order of symbolic execution from left to right does not compromise the non-determinism underlying the C semantics of binary operators. Indeed, when $\mathsf{forward}(m, \mathtt{e}_1) = (\mathtt{v}_1, m_1^o, m_1)$, we evaluate the expression $\mathtt{e}_2$, using the frame m_1, *i.e.*, only the resources of m that remain after the execution of $\mathtt{e}_1$. When $\mathsf{forward}(m, \mathtt{e}_1) = (\mathtt{l}, m_1^o, m_1)$, with $\mathtt{l} \in \mathsf{Loc}$, and $\mathsf{forward}(m_1, \mathtt{e}_2) = (\mathtt{v}_2, m_2^o, m_2)$, the function $\mathsf{delete\_full\_2}(\mathtt{l}, m_2, m_1^o \sqcup m_2^o)$ checks whether $(m_2 \sqcup m_1^o \sqcup m_2^o)(\mathtt{l})$

$$\mathsf{forward}(m, \mathtt{v}) \triangleq (\mathtt{v}, \varnothing, m)$$

$$\begin{aligned}
\mathsf{forward}(m, \mathtt{e}_1 \circledcirc \mathtt{e}_2) &\triangleq (\mathtt{v}_1 \, [\![\circledcirc]\!] \, \mathtt{v}_2, m_1^o \sqcup m_2^o, m_2) \\
\textbf{where } (\mathtt{v}_1, m_1^o, m_1) &= \mathsf{forward}(m, \mathtt{e}_1) \\
(\mathtt{v}_2, m_2^o, m_2) &= \mathsf{forward}(m_1, \mathtt{e}_2)
\end{aligned}$$

$$\begin{aligned}
\mathsf{forward}(m, {*}\mathtt{e}_1) &\triangleq (\mathtt{w}, m_2^o \sqcup \{\mathtt{l} \mapsto (U, q, \mathtt{w})\}, m_2) \\
\textbf{where } (\mathtt{l}, m_1^o, m_1) &= \mathsf{forward}(m, \mathtt{e}_1) && \text{provided } \mathtt{l} \in \mathsf{Loc} \\
(m_2, m_2^o, q, \mathtt{w}) &= \mathsf{delete_frac_2}(\mathtt{l}, m_1, m_1^o)
\end{aligned}$$

$$\begin{aligned}
\mathsf{forward}(m, \mathtt{e}_1 = \mathtt{e}_2) &\triangleq (\mathtt{v}_2, m_3^o \sqcup \{\mathtt{l} \mapsto (L, 1, \mathtt{v}_2)\}, m_3) \\
\textbf{where } (\mathtt{l}, m_1^o, m_1) &= \mathsf{forward}(m, \mathtt{e}_1) && \text{provided } \mathtt{l} \in \mathsf{Loc} \\
(\mathtt{v}_2, m_2^o, m_2) &= \mathsf{forward}(m_1, \mathtt{e}_2) \\
(m_3, m_3^o) &= \mathsf{delete_full_2}(\mathtt{l}, m_2, m_1^o \sqcup m_2^o)
\end{aligned}$$

$$\mathsf{forward}(m, \mathtt{e}) \triangleq \bot \qquad \text{if } \mathtt{e} \notin \overline{\mathsf{expr}}$$

Auxiliary functions:

$$\mathsf{delete\_frac\_2}(\mathtt{l}, m_1, m_2) \triangleq \begin{cases} (m_1[\mathtt{l} \mapsto (U, q/2, \mathtt{v})], m_2, q/2, \mathtt{v}) & \text{if } m_1(\mathtt{l}) = (U, q, \mathtt{v}) \\ (m_1, m_2[\mathtt{l} \mapsto (U, q/2, \mathtt{v})], q/2, \mathtt{v}) & \text{if } m_1(\mathtt{l}) \neq (U, \_, \_), \\ & \quad m_2(\mathtt{l}) = (U, q, \mathtt{v}) \\ \bot & \text{otherwise} \end{cases}$$

$$\begin{aligned}
&\mathsf{delete_full_2}(\mathtt{l}, m_1, m_2) \triangleq (m_1 \setminus \{\mathtt{l} \mapsto _\}, m_2 \setminus \{\mathtt{l} \mapsto _\}) \\
&\quad \textbf{where } (U, 1, _) = (m_1 \sqcup m_2)(\mathtt{l})
\end{aligned}$$

Fig. 7. The definition of the symbolic executor.

contains the write permission $\mathtt{l} \mapsto_U \_$. If this holds, it removes the location $\mathtt{l}$, so that the write permission is now consumed. Finally, we merge $\{\mathtt{l} \mapsto (L, 1, \mathrm{v}_2)\}$ with the output heap m_3^o, so that after assignment, the write permission $\mathtt{l} \mapsto_L \mathrm{v}_2$ is given back in a locked state.

6 A Verification Condition Generator for λMC

To establish correctness of programs, we need to prove goals $P \vdash \mathsf{wp}\ \mathsf{e}\ \{\Phi\}$. To prove such a goal, one has to repeatedly apply the rules for weakest preconditions, intertwined with logical reasoning. In this section we will automate this process for λMC by means of a *verification condition generator* (vcgen).

As a first attempt to define a vcgen, one could try to recurse over the expression e and apply the rules in Fig. 3 eagerly. This would turn the goal into a separation logic proposition that subsequently should be solved. However, as we pointed out in Sect. 5.1, the resulting separation logic proposition will be very difficult to prove—either interactively or automatically—due to the existentially quantified postconditions that appear because of uses of the rules for binary operators (*e.g.*, WP-BIN-OP). We then proposed alternative rules that avoid the need for existential quantifiers. These rules look like:

$$\frac{R \vdash \mathsf{wp}\ \mathsf{e}_2\ \{\mathrm{v}_2.\ Q \twoheadrightarrow \Phi\ (\mathrm{v}_1\ [\![\circledcirc]\!]\ \mathrm{v}_2)\}}{P \vdash \mathsf{wp}\ (\mathsf{e}_1 \circledcirc \mathsf{e}_2)\ \{\Phi\}}$$

To use this rule, the crux is to symbolically execute e_1 with precondition P into a symbolic execution triple (v_1, Q, R), which we alluded could be automatically computed by means of the symbolic executor if $\mathsf{e}_1 \in \overline{\mathsf{expr}}$ (Sect. 5.2).

We can only use the symbolic executor if P is of the shape $[\![m]\!]$ for a symbolic heap m. However, in actual program verification, the precondition P is hardly ever of that shape. In addition to a series of points-to connectives (as described by a symbolic heap), we may have arbitrary propositions of separation logic, such as pure facts, abstract predicates, nested Hoare triples, Iris ghost state, *etc.* These propositions may be needed to prove intermediate verification conditions, *e.g.*, for function calls. As such, to effectively apply the above rule, we need to separate our precondition P into two parts: a symbolic heap $[\![m]\!]$ and a remainder P'. Assuming $\mathsf{forward}(m, \mathsf{e}_1) = (\mathrm{v}_1, m_1^o, m_1)$, we may then use the following rule:

$$\frac{P' * [\![m_1]\!] \vdash \mathsf{wp}\ \mathsf{e}_2\ \{\mathrm{v}_2.\ [\![m_1^o]\!] \twoheadrightarrow \Phi\ (\mathrm{v}_1\ [\![\circledcirc]\!]\ \mathrm{v}_2)\}}{P' * [\![m]\!] \vdash \mathsf{wp}\ (\mathsf{e}_1 \circledcirc \mathsf{e}_2)\ \{\Phi\}}$$

It is important to notice that by applying this rule, the remainder P' remains in our precondition as is, but the symbolic heap is changed from $[\![m]\!]$ into $[\![m_1]\!]$, *i.e.*, into the frame that we obtained by symbolically executing e_1.

It should come as no surprise that we can automate this process, by applying rules, such as the one we have given above, recursively, and threading through symbolic heaps. Formally, we do this by defining the vcgen as a total function: $\mathsf{vcg} : (\mathsf{sheap} \times \mathsf{expr} \times (\mathsf{sheap} \to \mathsf{val} \to \mathsf{Prop})) \to \mathsf{Prop}$ where Prop is the type of propositions of our logic. The definition of vcg is given in Fig. 8. Before explaining the details, let us state its correctness theorem:

Theorem 6.1. *Given an expression* e, *a symbolic heap* m, *and a postcondition* Φ, *the following statement holds:*

$$\frac{P' \vdash \mathsf{vcg}\,(m, \mathsf{e}, \lambda m'\, \mathtt{v}.\, [\![m']\!] \mathrel{-\!\!*} \Phi\, \mathtt{v})}{P' * [\![m]\!] \vdash \mathsf{wp}\ \mathsf{e}\ \{\Phi\}}$$

This theorem reflects the general shape of the rules we previously described. We start off with a goal $P' * [\![m]\!] \vdash \mathsf{wp}\ \mathsf{e}\ \{\Phi\}$, and after using the vcgen, we should prove that the generated goal follows from P'. It is important to note that the continuation in the vcgen is not only parameterized by the return value, but also by a symbolic heap corresponding to the resources that remain. To get these resources back, the vcgen is initiated with the continuation $\lambda m'\, \mathtt{v}.\, [\![m']\!] \mathrel{-\!\!*} \Phi\, \mathtt{v}$.

Most clauses of the definition of the vcgen (Fig. 8) follow the approach we described so far. For unary expressions like load we generate a condition that corresponds to the weakest precondition rule. For binary expressions, we symbolically execute either operand, and proceed recursively in the other. There are a number of important bells and whistles that we will discuss now.

Sequencing. In the case of sequenced binds $\mathtt{x} \leftarrow \mathsf{e}_1\, ;\, \mathsf{e}_2$, we recursively compute the verification condition for e_1 with the continuation:

$$\lambda m'\, \mathtt{v}.\, \mathbb{U}\ (\mathsf{vcg}(\mathsf{unlock}(m'), \mathsf{e}_2[\mathtt{v}/\mathtt{x}], \mathcal{K}))\,.$$

Due to a sequence point, all locations modified by e_1 will be in the unlocked state after it is finished executing. Therefore, in the recursive call to e_2 we unlock all locations in the symbolic heap (*c.f.* $\mathsf{unlock}(m')$), and we include a $\mathbb{U}$ modality in the continuation. The $\mathbb{U}$ modality is crucial so that the resources that are not given to the vcgen (the remainder P' in Theorem 6.1) can also be unlocked.

Handling Failure. In the case of binary operators $\mathsf{e}_1 \circledcirc \mathsf{e}_2$, it could be that the symbolic executor fails on both e_1 and e_2, because neither of the arguments were of the right shape (*i.e.*, not an element of $\overline{\mathsf{expr}}$), or the required resources were not present in the symbolic heap. In this case the vcgen generates the goal of the form $[\![m]\!] \mathrel{-\!\!*} \mathsf{wp}\ (\mathsf{e}_1 \circledcirc \mathsf{e}_2)\ \{\mathcal{K}_{\mathtt{ret}}\}$ where $\mathcal{K}_{\mathtt{ret}} \triangleq \lambda \mathtt{w}.\, \exists m'.\, [\![m']\!] * \mathcal{K}\ m'\, \mathtt{w}$. What appears here is that the current symbolic heap $[\![m]\!]$ is given back to the user, which they can use to prove the weakest precondition of $e_1 \circledcirc e_2$ by hand. Through the postcondition $\exists m'.\, [\![m']\!] * \mathcal{K}\ m'\, \mathtt{w}$ the user can resume the vcgen, by choosing a new symbolic heap m' and invoking the continuation $\mathcal{K}\, m'\, \mathtt{w}$.

For assignments $\mathsf{e}_1 = \mathsf{e}_2$ we have a similar situation. Symbolic execution of both e_1 and e_2 may fail, and then we generate a goal similar to the one for binary operators. If the location $\mathtt{l}$ that we wish to assign to is not in the symbolic heap, we use the continuation $[\![m]\!] \mathrel{-\!\!*} \exists \mathtt{w}.\, \mathtt{l} \mapsto_U \mathtt{w} * (\mathtt{l} \mapsto_L \mathtt{v} \mathrel{-\!\!*} \mathcal{K}_{\mathtt{ret}}\ \mathtt{v})$. As before, the user gets back the current symbolic heap $[\![m]\!]$, and could resume the vcgen through the postcondition $\mathcal{K}_{\mathtt{ret}}\ \mathtt{v}$ by picking a new symbolic heap.

$$\mathsf{vcg}(m, \mathtt{v}, \mathcal{K}) \triangleq \mathcal{K}\ m\ \mathtt{v}$$

$$\mathsf{vcg}(m, \mathtt{e}_1 \circledcirc \mathtt{e}_2, \mathcal{K}) \triangleq$$

$$\begin{cases} \mathsf{vcg}(m_2, \mathtt{e}_2, \lambda m'\, \mathtt{v}_2.\, \mathcal{K}\ (m' \sqcup m^o)\, (\mathtt{v}_1 \circledcirc \mathtt{v}_2)) & \text{if } \mathsf{forward}(m, \mathtt{e}_1) = (\mathtt{v}_1, m^o, m_2) \\ \mathsf{vcg}(m_1, \mathtt{e}_1, \lambda m'\, \mathtt{v}_1.\, \mathcal{K}\ (m' \sqcup m^o)\, (\mathtt{v}_1 \circledcirc \mathtt{v}_2)) & \text{if } \mathsf{forward}(m, \mathtt{e}_1) = \bot \text{ and} \\ & \quad \mathsf{forward}(m, \mathtt{e}_2) = (\mathtt{v}_2, m^o, m_1) \\ [\![m]\!] \mathrel{-\!\!*} \mathsf{wp}\ (\mathtt{e}_1 \circledcirc \mathtt{e}_2)\ \{\mathcal{K}_{\mathtt{ret}}\} & \text{otherwise} \end{cases}$$

$$\mathsf{vcg}(m, *\mathtt{e}, \mathcal{K}) \triangleq \mathsf{vcg}(m, \mathtt{e}, \mathcal{K}')$$

$$\textbf{with } \mathcal{K}' \triangleq \lambda m\, \mathtt{l}. \begin{cases} \mathcal{K}\ m\ \mathtt{w} & \text{if } \mathtt{l} \in \mathsf{Loc} \text{ and } m(\mathtt{l}) = (U, q, \mathtt{w}) \\ [\![m]\!] \mathrel{-\!\!*} \exists \mathtt{w}\ q.\, \mathtt{l} \overset{q}{\mapsto}_U \mathtt{w} * (\mathtt{l} \overset{q}{\mapsto}_U \mathtt{w} \mathrel{-\!\!*} \mathcal{K}_{\mathtt{ret}}\ \mathtt{w}) & \text{otherwise} \end{cases}$$

$$\mathsf{vcg}(m, \mathtt{e}_1 = \mathtt{e}_2, \mathcal{K}) \triangleq$$

$$\begin{cases} \mathsf{vcg}(m_2, \mathtt{e}_2, \lambda m'\, \mathtt{v}.\, \mathcal{K}'\ (m' \sqcup m^o)(\mathtt{l}, \mathtt{v})) & \text{if } \mathsf{forward}(m, \mathtt{e}_1) = (\mathtt{l}, m^o, m_2) \\ \mathsf{vcg}(m_1, \mathtt{e}_1, \lambda m'\, \mathtt{l}.\, \mathcal{K}'\ (m' \sqcup m^o)(\mathtt{l}, \mathtt{v})) & \text{if } \mathsf{forward}(m, \mathtt{e}_1) = \bot \text{ and} \\ & \quad \mathsf{forward}(m, \mathtt{e}_2) = (\mathtt{v}, m^o, m_1) \\ [\![m]\!] \mathrel{-\!\!*} \mathsf{wp}\ (\mathtt{e}_1 = \mathtt{e}_2)\ \{\mathcal{K}_{\mathtt{ret}}\} & \text{otherwise} \end{cases}$$

$$\textbf{with } \mathcal{K}' \triangleq \lambda m\, (\mathtt{l}, \mathtt{v}). \begin{cases} \mathcal{K}\ (m' \sqcup \{\mathtt{l} \mapsto (L, 1, \mathtt{v})\})\ \mathtt{v} & \text{if } \mathtt{l} \in \mathsf{Loc} \text{ and } \mathsf{delete\_full}(\mathtt{l}, m) = m' \\ [\![m]\!] \mathrel{-\!\!*} \exists \mathtt{w}.\, \mathtt{l} \mapsto_U \mathtt{w} * (\mathtt{l} \mapsto_L \mathtt{v} \mathrel{-\!\!*} \mathcal{K}_{\mathtt{ret}}\ \mathtt{v}) & \text{otherwise} \end{cases}$$

$$\mathsf{vcg}(m, \mathtt{x} \leftarrow \mathtt{e}_1 \,;\, \mathtt{e}_2, \mathcal{K}) \triangleq \mathsf{vcg}\,(m, \mathtt{e}_1, \lambda m'\, \mathtt{v}.\, \mathbb{U}\ (\mathsf{vcg}(\mathsf{unlock}(m'), \mathtt{e}_2[\mathtt{v}/\mathtt{x}], \mathcal{K})))$$

Auxiliary functions:

$$\mathcal{K}_{\mathtt{ret}} : \mathsf{val} \to \mathsf{Prop} \triangleq \lambda \mathtt{w}.\, (\exists m'.\, [\![m']\!] * \mathcal{K}\ m'\ \mathtt{w}) \qquad \mathsf{unlock}(m) \triangleq \bigsqcup_{\substack{\mathtt{l} \in \mathrm{dom}(m) \\ m(\mathtt{l}) = (\_, q, \mathtt{v})}} \{\mathtt{l} \mapsto (U, q, \mathtt{v})\}$$

Fig. 8. Selected cases of the verification condition generator.

7 Discussion

Extensions of the Language. The memory model that we have presented in this paper was purposely oversimplified. In Coq, the memory model for λMC additionally supports mutable local variables, arrays, and pointer arithmetic. Adding support for these features was relatively easy and required only local changes to the definitional semantics and the separation logic.

For implementing mutable local variables, we tag each location with a Boolean that keeps track of whether it is an allocated or a local variable. That way, we can forbid deallocating local variables using the `free(−)` operator.

Our extended memory model is block/offset-based like CompCert's memory model [38]. Pointers are not simply represented as locations, but as pairs (ℓ, i), where ℓ is a HeapLang reference to a memory block containing a list of values, and i is an offset into that block. The points-to connectives of our separation logic then correspondingly range over block/offset-based pointers.

Symbolic Execution of Sequence Points. We adapt our forward algorithm to handle sequenced bind operators $\mathtt{x} \leftarrow \mathsf{e}_1 \,;\, \mathsf{e}_2$. The subtlety lies in supporting nested sequenced binds. For example, in an expression $(\mathtt{x} \leftarrow \mathsf{e}_1 \,;\, \mathsf{e}_2) + \mathsf{e}_3$ the postcondition of e_1 can be used (along with the frame) for the symbolic execution of e_2, but it cannot be used for the symbolic execution of e_3. In order to solve this, our forward algorithm takes a *stack* of symbolic heaps as an input, and returns a *stack* of symbolic heaps (of the same length) as a frame. All the cases shown in Fig. 7 are easily adapted w.r.t. this modification, and the following definition captures the case for the sequence point bind:

$$\begin{aligned} &\mathsf{forward}(\vec{m}, \mathtt{x} \leftarrow \mathsf{e}_1 \,;\, \mathsf{e}_2) \triangleq (\mathtt{v}_2, m_2^{\circ} \sqcup m', \vec{m}_2) \\ &\quad \textbf{where} \;\; (\mathtt{v}_1, m_1^{\circ}, \vec{m}_1) \qquad\quad\;\; = \mathsf{forward}(\vec{m}, \mathsf{e}_1) \\ &\qquad\qquad\;\; (\mathtt{v}_2, m_2^{\circ}, m' :: \vec{m}_2) = \mathsf{forward}(\mathsf{unlock}(m_1^{\circ}) :: \vec{m}_1, \mathsf{e}_2[\mathtt{v}_1/\mathtt{x}]) \end{aligned}$$

Shared Resource Invariants. As in Krebbers's logic [29], the rules for binary operators in Fig. 3 require the resources to be separated into disjoint parts for the subexpressions. If both sides of a binary operator are function calls, then they can only share read permissions despite that both function calls are executed atomically. Following Krebbers, we address this limitation by adding a shared resource invariant R to our weakest preconditions and add the following rules:

$$\frac{R_1 \qquad \mathsf{wp}_{R_1 * R_2}\, \mathsf{e}\, \{\mathtt{v}.\, R_1 \mathrel{-\!\!*} \Phi\, \mathtt{v}\}}{\mathsf{wp}_{R_2}\, \mathsf{e}\, \{\Phi\}} \qquad \frac{\mathtt{f(x)\{e\}} \text{ defined} \quad R \mathrel{-\!\!*} \mathbb{U}(\mathsf{wp}_{\mathsf{True}}\, \mathsf{e}\,[\mathtt{x}/\mathtt{v}]\; \{\mathtt{w}.\, R * \Phi\, \mathtt{w}\})}{\mathsf{wp}_R\, \mathtt{f(v)}\; \{\Phi\}}$$

To temporarily transfer resources into the invariant, one can use the first rule. Because function calls are not interleaved, one can use the last rule to gain access to the shared resource invariant for the duration of the function call.

Our handling of shared resource invariants generalizes the treatment by Krebbers: using custom ghost state in Iris we can endow the resource invariant with a protocol. This allows us to verify examples that were previously impossible [29]:

```
int f(int *p, int y) { return (*p = y); }
int main() { int x; f(&x, 3) + f(&x, 4); return x; }
```

Krebbers could only prove that `main` returns 0, 3 or 4, whereas we can prove it returns 3 or 4 by combining resource invariants with Iris's ghost state.

Implementation in Coq. In the Coq development [18] we have:

- Defined λMC with the extensions described above, as well as the monadic combinators, as a shallow embedding on top of Iris's HeapLang [21,25].
- Modeled the separation logic for λMC and the monadic combinators as a shallow embedding on top of the Iris's program logic for HeapLang.

- Implemented the symbolic executor and vcgen as computable Coq functions, and proved their soundness w.r.t. our separation logic.
- Turned the verification condition generator into a tactic that integrates into the Iris Proof Mode/MoSeL framework [32,34].

This last point allowed us to leverage the existing machinery for separation logic proofs in Coq. Firstly, we get basic building blocks for implementing the vcgen tactic for free. Secondly, when the vcgen is unable to solve the goal, one can use the Iris Proof Mode/MoSeL tactics to help out in a convenient manner.

To implement the symbolic executor and vcgen, we had to reify the terms and values of λMC. To see why reification is needed, consider the data type for symbolic heaps, which uses locations as keys. In proofs, those locations appear as universally quantified variables. To compute using these, we need to reify them into some symbolic representation. We have implemented the reification mechanism using type classes, following Spitters and van der Weegen [47].

With all the mechanics in place, our vcgen is able to significantly aid us. Consider the following program that copies the contents of one array into another:

```
int arraycopy(int *p, int *q, int n) {
  int pend = p + n;
  while (p < pend) { *(p++) = *(q++); }
}
```

We proved $\{\texttt{p} \mapsto \vec{x} * \texttt{q} \mapsto \vec{y} * (|\vec{x}| = |\vec{y}| = n)\}\texttt{arraycopy(p,q,n)}\{\texttt{p} \mapsto \vec{y} * \texttt{q} \mapsto \vec{y}\}$ in 11 lines of Coq code. The vcgen can automatically process the program up until the while loop. At that point, the user has to manually perform an induction on the array, providing a suitable induction hypothesis. The vcgen is then able to discharge the base case automatically. In the inductive case, it will automatically process the program until the next iteration of the while loop, where the user has to apply the induction hypothesis.

8 Related Work

C Semantics. There has been a considerable body of work on formal semantics for the C language, including several large projects that aimed to formalize substantial subsets of C [17,20,30,37,41,44], and projects that focused on specific aspects like its memory model [10,13,27,28,31,38,40,41], weak memory concurrency [4,36,43], non-local control flow [35], verified compilation [37,48], *etc.*

The focus of this paper—non-determinism in C expressions—has been treated formally a number of times, notably by Norrish [44], Ellison and Rosu [17], Krebbers [31], and Memarian *et al.* [41]. The first three have in common that they model the sequence point restriction by keeping track of the locations that have been written to. The treatment of sequence points in our definitional semantics is closely inspired by the work of Ellison and Rosu [17], which resembles closely what is in the C standard. Krebbers [31] used a more restrictive version of the semantics by Ellison and Rosu—he assigned undefined behavior in some corner cases to ease the soundness theorem of his logic. We directly proved soundness of the logic w.r.t. the more faithful model by Ellison and Rosu.

Memarian *et al.* [41] give a semantics to C by elaboration into a language they call Core. Unspecified evaluation order in Core is modeled using an unseq operation, which is similar to our $||_{\mathsf{HL}}$ operation. Compared to our translation, Core is much closer to C (it has function calls, memory operations, *etc.* as primitives, while we model them with monadic combinators), and supports concurrency.

Reasoning Tools and Program Logics for C. Apart from formalizing the semantics of C, there have been many efforts to create reasoning tools for the C language in one way or another. There are standalone tools, like VeriFast [23], VCC [12], and the Jessie plugin of Frama-C [42], and there are tools built on top of general purpose proof assistants like VST [1,10] in Coq, or AutoCorres [19] in Isabelle/HOL. Although, admittedly, all of these tools cover larger subsets of C than we do, as far as we know, they all ignore non-determinism in expressions.

There are a few exceptions. Norrish proved confluence for a certain class of C expressions [45]. Such a confluence result may be used to justify proofs in a tool that does not have an underlying non-deterministic semantics.

Another exception is the separation logic for non-determinism in C by Krebbers [29]. Our work is inspired by his, but there are several notable differences:

- We have proved soundness with respect to a definitional semantics for a subset of C. We believe that this approach is more modular, since the semantics can be specified at a higher level of abstraction.
- We have built our logic on top of the Iris framework. This makes the development more modular (since we can use all the features as well as the Coq infrastructure of Iris) and more expressive (as shown in Sect. 7).
- There was no automation like our vcgen, so one had to subdivide resources between subexpressions manually all the time. Also, there was not even tactical support for carrying out proofs manually. Our logic is redesigned to get such support from the Iris Proof Mode/MoSeL framework.

To handle missing features of C as part of our vcgen, we plan to explore approaches by other verification projects in proof assistants. A notable example of such a project is VST, which supports machine arithmetic [16] and data types like structs and unions [10] as part of its tactics for symbolic execution.

Separation Logic and Symbolic Execution. In their seminal work, Berdine *et al.* [5] demonstrate the application of symbolic execution to automated reasoning in separation logic. In their setting, frame inference is used to perform symbolic execution of function calls. The frame has to be computed when the call site has more resources than needed to invoke a function. In our setting we compute frames for subexpressions, which, unlike functions, do not have predefined specifications. Due to that, we have to perform frame inference simultaneously with symbolic execution. The symbolic execution algorithm of Berdine *et al.* can handle inductive predicates, and can be extended with shape analysis [15]. We do not support such features, and leave them to future work.

Caper [14] is a tool for automated reasoning in concurrent separation logic, and it also deals with non-determinism, although the nature of non-determinism in Caper is different. Non-determinism in Caper arises due to branching on unknown conditionals and due to multiple possible ways to apply ghost state related rules (rules pertaining to abstract regions and guards). The former cause is tackled by considering sets of symbolic execution traces, and the latter is resolved by employing heuristics based on bi-abduction [9]. Applications of abductive reasoning to our approach to symbolic execution are left for future work.

Recently, Bannister *et al.* [2,3] proposed a new separation logic connective for performing forwards reasoning whilst avoiding frame inference. This approach, however, is aimed at sequential deterministic programs, focusing on a notion of partial correctness that allows for failed executions. Another approach to verification of sequential stateful programs is based on characteristic formulae [11]. A stateful program is transformed into a higher-order logic predicate, implicitly encoding the frame rule. The resulting formula is then proved by a user in Coq.

When implementing a vcgen in a proof assistant (see *e.g.*, [10,39]) it is common to let the vcgen return a new goal when it gets stuck, from which the user can help out and call back the vcgen. The novelty of our work is that this approach is applied to operations that are called in parallel.

Acknowledgments. We are grateful to Gregory Malecha and the anonymous reviewers and for their comments and suggestions. This work was supported by the Netherlands Organisation for Scientific Research (NWO), project numbers STW.14319 (first and second author) and 016.Veni.192.259 (third author).

References

1. Appel, A.W. (ed.): Program Logics for Certified Compilers. Cambridge University Press, New York (2014)
2. Bannister, C., Höfner, P.: False failure: creating failure models for separation logic. In: Desharnais, J., Guttmann, W., Joosten, S. (eds.) RAMiCS 2018. LNCS, vol. 11194, pp. 263–279. Springer, Cham (2018). https://doi.org/10.1007/978-3-030-02149-8_16
3. Bannister, C., Höfner, P., Klein, G.: Backwards and forwards with separation logic. In: Avigad, J., Mahboubi, A. (eds.) ITP 2018. LNCS, vol. 10895, pp. 68–87. Springer, Cham (2018). https://doi.org/10.1007/978-3-319-94821-8_5
4. Batty, M., Owens, S., Sarkar, S., Sewell, P., Weber, T.: Mathematizing C++ concurrency. In: POPL, pp. 55–66 (2011)
5. Berdine, J., Calcagno, C., O'Hearn, P.W.: Symbolic execution with separation logic. In: Yi, K. (ed.) APLAS 2005. LNCS, vol. 3780, pp. 52–68. Springer, Heidelberg (2005). https://doi.org/10.1007/11575467_5
6. Birkedal, L., Bizjak, A.: Lecture Notes on Iris: Higher-Order Concurrent Separation Logic, August 2018. https://iris-project.org/tutorial-material.html
7. Bornat, R., Calcagno, C., O'Hearn, P.W., Parkinson, M.J.: Permission accounting in separation logic. In: POPL, pp. 259–270 (2005)
8. Boyland, J.: Checking interference with fractional permissions. In: Cousot, R. (ed.) SAS 2003. LNCS, vol. 2694, pp. 55–72. Springer, Heidelberg (2003). https://doi.org/10.1007/3-540-44898-5_4
9. Calcagno, C., Distefano, D., O'Hearn, P.W., Yang, H.: Compositional shape analysis by means of bi-abduction. J. ACM **58**(6), 26:1–26:66 (2011)
10. Cao, Q., Beringer, L., Gruetter, S., Dodds, J., Appel, A.W.: VST-Floyd: a separation logic tool to verify correctness of C programs. JAR **61**(1–4), 367–422 (2018)

11. Charguéraud, A.: Characteristic formulae for the verification of imperative programs. SIGPLAN Not. **46**(9), 418–430 (2011)
12. Cohen, E., et al.: VCC: a practical system for verifying concurrent C. In: Berghofer, S., Nipkow, T., Urban, C., Wenzel, M. (eds.) TPHOLs 2009. LNCS, vol. 5674, pp. 23–42. Springer, Heidelberg (2009). https://doi.org/10.1007/978-3-642-03359-9_2
13. Cohen, E., Moskal, M., Tobies, S., Schulte, W.: A precise yet efficient memory model for C. ENTCS **254**, 85–103 (2009)
14. Dinsdale-Young, T., da Rocha Pinto, P., Andersen, K.J., Birkedal, L.: CAPER - automatic verification for fine-grained concurrency. In: Yang, H. (ed.) ESOP 2017. LNCS, vol. 10201, pp. 420–447. Springer, Heidelberg (2017). https://doi.org/10.1007/978-3-662-54434-1_16
15. Distefano, D., O'Hearn, P.W., Yang, H.: A local shape analysis based on separation logic. In: Hermanns, H., Palsberg, J. (eds.) TACAS 2006. LNCS, vol. 3920, pp. 287–302. Springer, Heidelberg (2006). https://doi.org/10.1007/11691372_19
16. Dodds, J., Appel, A.W.: Mostly sound type system improves a foundational program verifier. In: Gonthier, G., Norrish, M. (eds.) CPP 2013. LNCS, vol. 8307, pp. 17–32. Springer, Cham (2013). https://doi.org/10.1007/978-3-319-03545-1_2
17. Ellison, C., Rosu, G.: An executable formal semantics of C with applications. In: POPL, pp. 533–544 (2012)
18. Frumin, D., Gondelman, L., Krebbers, R.: Semi-automated reasoning about non-determinism in C expressions: Coq development, February 2019. https://cs.ru.nl/~dfrumin/wpc/
19. Greenaway, D., Lim, J., Andronick, J., Klein, G.: Don't sweat the small stuff: formal verification of C code without the pain. In: PLDI, pp. 429–439 (2014)
20. Hathhorn, C., Ellison, C., Roşu, G.: Defining the undefinedness of C. In: PLDI, pp. 336–345 (2015)
21. Iris: Iris Project, November 2018. https://iris-project.org/
22. ISO: ISO/IEC 9899–2011: Programming Languages - C. ISO Working Group 14 (2012)
23. Jacobs, B., Smans, J., Piessens, F.: A quick tour of the VeriFast program verifier. In: Ueda, K. (ed.) APLAS 2010. LNCS, vol. 6461, pp. 304–311. Springer, Heidelberg (2010). https://doi.org/10.1007/978-3-642-17164-2_21
24. Jung, R., Krebbers, R., Birkedal, L., Dreyer, D.: Higher-order ghost state. In: ICFP, pp. 256–269 (2016)
25. Jung, R., Krebbers, R., Jourdan, J.H., Bizjak, A., Birkedal, L., Dreyer, D.: Iris from the ground up: a modular foundation for higher-order concurrent separation logic. J. Funct. Program. **28**, e20 (2018). https://doi.org/10.1017/S0956796818000151
26. Jung, R., et al.: Iris: monoids and invariants as an orthogonal basis for concurrent reasoning. In: POPL, pp. 637–650 (2015)
27. Kang, J., Hur, C., Mansky, W., Garbuzov, D., Zdancewic, S., Vafeiadis, V.: A formal C memory model supporting integer-pointer casts. In: POPL, pp. 326–335 (2015)
28. Krebbers, R.: Aliasing restrictions of C11 formalized in Coq. In: Gonthier, G., Norrish, M. (eds.) CPP 2013. LNCS, vol. 8307, pp. 50–65. Springer, Cham (2013). https://doi.org/10.1007/978-3-319-03545-1_4
29. Krebbers, R.: An operational and axiomatic semantics for non-determinism and sequence points in C. In: POPL, pp. 101–112 (2014)
30. Krebbers, R.: The C standard formalized in Coq. Ph.D. thesis, Radboud University Nijmegen (2015)
31. Krebbers, R.: A formal C memory model for separation logic. JAR **57**(4), 319–387 (2016)

32. Krebbers, R., et al.: MoSeL: a general, extensible modal framework for interactive proofs in separation logic. PACMPL **2**(ICFP), 77:1–77:30 (2018)
33. Krebbers, R., Jung, R., Bizjak, A., Jourdan, J.-H., Dreyer, D., Birkedal, L.: The Essence of higher-order concurrent separation logic. In: Yang, H. (ed.) ESOP 2017. LNCS, vol. 10201, pp. 696–723. Springer, Heidelberg (2017). https://doi.org/10.1007/978-3-662-54434-1_26
34. Krebbers, R., Timany, A., Birkedal, L.: Interactive proofs in higher-order concurrent separation logic. In: POPL, pp. 205–217 (2017)
35. Krebbers, R., Wiedijk, F.: Separation logic for non-local control flow and block scope variables. In: Pfenning, F. (ed.) FoSSaCS 2013. LNCS, vol. 7794, pp. 257–272. Springer, Heidelberg (2013). https://doi.org/10.1007/978-3-642-37075-5_17
36. Lahav, O., Vafeiadis, V., Kang, J., Hur, C., Dreyer, D.: Repairing Sequential Consistency in C/C++11. In: PLDI, pp. 618–632 (2017)
37. Leroy, X.: Formal verification of a realistic compiler. CACM **52**(7), 107–115 (2009)
38. Leroy, X., Blazy, S.: Formal verification of a C-like memory model and its uses for verifying program transformations. JAR **41**(1), 1–31 (2008)
39. Malecha, G.: Extensible proof engineering in intensional type theory. Ph.D. thesis, Harvard University (2014)
40. Memarian, K., et al.: Exploring C semantics and pointer provenance. PACMPL **3**(POPL), 67:1–67:32 (2019)
41. Memarian, K., et al.: Into the depths of C: elaborating the De Facto Standards. In: PLDI, pp. 1–15 (2016)
42. Moy, Y., Marché, C.: The Jessie Plugin for Deduction Verification in Frama-C, Tutorial and Reference Manual (2011)
43. Nienhuis, K., Memarian, K., Sewell, P.: An operational semantics for C/C++11 concurrency. In: OOPSLA, pp. 111–128 (2016)
44. Norrish, M.: C Formalised in HOL. Ph.D. thesis, University of Cambridge (1998)
45. Norrish, M.: Deterministic expressions in C. In: Swierstra, S.D. (ed.) ESOP 1999. LNCS, vol. 1576, pp. 147–161. Springer, Heidelberg (1999). https://doi.org/10.1007/3-540-49099-X_10
46. O'Hearn, P.W.: Resources, concurrency, and local reasoning. Theor. Comput. Sci. **375**(1), 271–307 (2007). Festschrift for John C. Reynolds's 70th birthday
47. Spitters, B., Van der Weegen, E.: Type classes for mathematics in type theory. Math. Struct. Comput. Sci. **21**(4), 795–825 (2011)
48. Stewart, G., Beringer, L., Cuellar, S., Appel, A.W.: Compositional CompCert. In: POPL, pp. 275–287 (2015)

Safe Deferred Memory Reclamation with Types

Ismail Kuru([✉]) and Colin S. Gordon

Drexel University, Philadelphia, USA
{ik335,csgordon}@drexel.edu

Abstract. Memory management in lock-free data structures remains a major challenge in concurrent programming. Design techniques including read-copy-update (RCU) and hazard pointers provide workable solutions, and are widely used to great effect. These techniques rely on the concept of a grace period: nodes that should be freed are not deallocated immediately, and all threads obey a protocol to ensure that the deallocating thread can detect when all possible readers have completed their use of the object. This provides an approach to safe deallocation, but only when these subtle protocols are implemented correctly.

We present a static type system to ensure correct use of RCU memory management: that nodes removed from a data structure are always scheduled for subsequent deallocation, and that nodes are scheduled for deallocation at most once. As part of our soundness proof, we give an abstract semantics for RCU memory management primitives which captures the fundamental properties of RCU. Our type system allows us to give the first proofs of memory safety for RCU linked list and binary search tree implementations without requiring full verification.

1 Introduction

For many workloads, lock-based synchronization – even fine-grained locking – has unsatisfactory performance. Often lock-free algorithms yield better performance, at the cost of more complex implementation and additional difficulty reasoning about the code. Much of this complexity is due to memory management: developers must reason about not only other threads violating local assumptions, but whether other threads are *finished accessing* nodes to deallocate. At the time a node is unlinked from a data structure, an unknown number of additional threads may have already been using the node, having read a pointer to it before it was unlinked in the heap.

A key insight for manageable solutions to this challenge is to recognize that just as in traditional garbage collection, the unlinked nodes need not be reclaimed immediately, but can instead be reclaimed later after some protocol finishes running. Hazard pointers [29] are the classic example: all threads actively collaborate on bookkeeping data structures to track who is using a certain reference. For structures with read-biased workloads, Read-Copy-Update (RCU) [23] provides an appealing alternative. The programming style resembles a combination of

L. Caires (Ed.): ESOP 2019, LNCS 11423, pp. 88–116, 2019.
https://doi.org/10.1007/978-3-030-17184-1_4

reader-writer locks and lock-free programming. Multiple concurrent readers perform minimal bookkeeping – often nothing they wouldn't already do. A single writer at a time runs in parallel with readers, performing additional work to track which readers may have observed a node they wish to deallocate. There are now RCU implementations of many common tree data structures [3,5,8,19,24,33], and RCU plays a key role in Linux kernel memory management [27].

However, RCU primitives remain non-trivial to use correctly: developers must ensure they release each node exactly once, from exactly one thread, *after* ensuring other threads are finished with the node in question. Model checking can be used to validate correctness of implementations for a mock client [1,7,17,21], but this does not guarantee correctness of arbitrary client code. Sophisticated verification logics can prove correctness of the RCU primitives and clients [12,15,22,32]. But these techniques require significant verification expertise to apply, and are specialized to individual data structures or implementations. One important reason for the sophistication in these logics stems from the complexity of the underlying memory reclamation model. However, Meyer and Wolff [28] show that a suitable abstraction enables separating verifying *correctness* of concurrent data structures from its underlying reclamation model under the assumption of *memory safety*, and study proofs of correctness assuming memory safety.

We propose a type system to ensure that RCU client code uses the RCU primitives safely, ensuring memory safety for concurrent data structures using RCU memory management. We do this in a general way, not assuming the client implements any specific data structure, only one satisfying some basic properties common to RCU data structures (such as having a *tree* memory footprint). In order to do this, we must also give a formal operational model of the RCU primitives that abstracts many implementations, without assuming a particular implementation of the RCU primitives. We describe our RCU semantics and type system, prove our type system sound against the model (which ensures memory is reclaimed correctly), and show the type system in action on two important RCU data structures.

Our contributions include:

- A general (abstract) operational model for RCU-based memory management
- A type system that ensures code uses RCU memory management correctly, which is significantly simpler than full-blown verification logics
- Demonstration of the type system on two examples: a linked-list based bag and a binary search tree
- A proof that the type system guarantees memory safety when using RCU primitives.

2 Background and Motivation

In this section, we recall the general concepts of read-copy-update concurrency. We use the RCU linked-list-based bag [25] from Fig. 1 as a running example. It includes annotations for our type system, which will be explained in Sect. 4.2.

```
struct BagNode{
  int data;
  BagNode<rcuItr> Next;
}
BagNode<rcuRoot> head;
void add(int toAdd){
WriteBegin;
BagNode nw = new;
{nw: rcuFresh{}}
nw.data = toAdd;
{head: rcuRoot, par: undef, cur: undef}
BagNode<rcuItr> par,cur = head;
{head: rcuRoot, par: rcuItrε{}}
{cur: rcuItrε{}}
cur = par.Next;
{cur: rcuItrNext{}}
{par: rcuItrε{Next ↦ cur}}
while(cur.Next != null){
  {cur: rcuItr(Next)^k.Next{}}
  {par: rcuItr(Next)^k{Next ↦ cur}}
  par = cur;
  cur = par.Next;
  {cur: rcuItr(Next)^k.Next.Next{}}
  {par: rcuItr(Next)^k.Next{Next ↦ cur}}
}
{nw: rcuFresh{}}
{cur: rcuItr(Next)^k.Next{Next ↦ null}}
{par: rcuItr(Next)^k{Next ↦ cur}}
nw.Next= null;
{nw: rcuFresh{Next ↦ null}}
{cur: rcuItr(Next)^k.Next{Next ↦ null}}
cur.Next=nw;
{nw: rcuItr(Next)^k.Next.Next{Next ↦ null}}
{cur: rcuItr(Next)^k.Next{Next ↦ nw}}
WriteEnd;
}
```

```
void remove(int toDel){
WriteBegin;
{head: rcuRoot, par : undef, cur: undef}
BagNode<rcuItr> par,cur = head;
{head: rcuRoot, par: rcuItrε{}, cur: rcuItrε{}}
cur = par.Next;
{cur: rcuItrNext{}}
{par: rcuItrε{Next ↦ cur}}
while(cur.Next != null&&cur.data != toDel)
{
  {cur: rcuItr(Next)^k.Next{}}
  {par: rcuItr(Next)^k{Next ↦ cur}}
  par = cur;
  cur = par.Next;
  {cur: rcuItr(Next)^k.Next.Next{}}
  {par: rcuItr(Next)^k.Next{Next ↦ cur}}
}
{nw: rcuFresh{}}
{par: rcuItr(Next)^k{Next ↦ cur}}
{cur: rcuItr(Next)^k.Next{}}
BagNode<rcuItr> curl = cur.Next;
{cur: rcuItr(Next)^k.Next{Next ↦ curl}}
{curl: rcuItr(Next)^k.Next.Next{}}
par.Next = curl;
{par: rcuItr(Next)^k{Next ↦ curl}}
{cur: unlinked}
{cur: rcuItr(Next)^k.Next{}}
SyncStart;
SyncStop;
{cur: freeable}
Free(cur);
{cur: undef}
WriteEnd;
}
```

Fig. 1. RCU client: singly linked list based bag implementation.

As with concrete RCU implementations, we assume threads operating on a structure are either performing read-only traversals of the structure—*reader threads*—or are performing an update—*writer threads*—similar to the use of many-reader single-writer reader-writer locks.[1] It differs, however, in that readers may execute concurrently with the (single) writer.

This distinction, and some runtime bookkeeping associated with the read- and write-side critical sections, allow this model to determine at modest cost when a node unlinked by the writer can safely be reclaimed.

Figure 1 gives the code for adding and removing nodes from a bag. Type checking for all code, including membership queries for bag, can be found in our technical report [20]. Algorithmically, this code is nearly the same as any sequential implementation. There are only two differences. First, the read-side critical section in `member` is indicated by the use of `ReadBegin` and `ReadEnd`; the write-side critical section is between `WriteBegin` and `WriteEnd`. Second, rather than immediately reclaiming the memory for the unlinked node, `remove` calls

[1] RCU implementations supporting multiple concurrent writers exist [3], but are the minority.

`SyncStart` to begin a *grace period*—a wait for reader threads that may still hold references to unlinked nodes to finish their critical sections. `SyncStop` blocks execution of the writer thread until these readers exit their read critical section (via `ReadEnd`). These are the essential primitives for the implementation of an RCU data structure.

These six primitives together track a critical piece of information: which reader threads' critical sections overlapped the writer's. Implementing them efficiently is challenging [8], but possible. The Linux kernel for example finds ways to reuse existing task switch mechanisms for this tracking, so readers incur no additional overhead. The reader primitives are semantically straightforward – they atomically record the start, or completion, of a read-side critical section.

The more interesting primitives are the write-side primitives and memory reclamation. `WriteBegin` performs a (semantically) standard mutual exclusion with regard to other writers, so only one writer thread may modify the structure *or the writer structures used for grace periods.*

`SyncStart` and `SyncStop` implement *grace periods* [31]: a mechanism to wait for readers to finish with any nodes the writer may have unlinked. A grace period begins when a writer requests one, and finishes when all reader threads active *at the start of the grace period* have finished their current critical section. Any nodes a writer unlinks before a grace period are physically unlinked, but not logically unlinked until after one grace period.

An attentive reader might already realize that our usage of logical/physical unlinking is different than the one used in data-structures literature where typically a *logical deletion* (e.g., marking) is followed by a *physical deletion* (unlinking). Because all threads are forbidden from holding an interior reference into the data structure after leaving their critical sections, waiting for active readers to finish their critical sections ensures they are no longer using any nodes the writer unlinked prior to the grace period. This makes actually freeing an unlinked node after a grace period safe.

`SyncStart` conceptually takes a snapshot of all readers active when it is run. `SyncStop` then blocks until all those threads in the snapshot have finished at least one critical section. `SyncStop` does not wait for *all* readers to finish, and does not wait for all overlapping readers to simultaneously be out of critical sections.

To date, every description of RCU semantics, most centered around the notion of a grace period, has been given algorithmically, as a specific (efficient) implementation. While the implementation aspects are essential to real use, the lack of an abstract characterization makes judging the correctness of these implementations – or clients – difficult in general. In Sect. 3 we give formal *abstract*, *operational* semantics for RCU implementations – inefficient if implemented directly, but correct from a memory-safety and programming model perspective, and not tied to specific low-level RCU implementation details. To use these semantics or a concrete implementation correctly, client code must ensure:

- Reader threads never modify the structure
- No thread holds an interior pointer into the RCU structure across critical sections

- Unlinked nodes are always freed by the unlinking thread *after* the unlinking, *after* a grace period, and *inside* the critical section
- Nodes are freed at most once

In practice, RCU data structures typically ensure additional invariants to simplify the above, e.g.:

- The data structure is always a tree
- A writer thread unlinks or replaces only one node at a time.

and our type system in Sect. 4 guarantees these invariants.

3 Semantics

In this section, we outline the details of an abstract semantics for RCU implementations. It captures the core client-visible semantics of most RCU primitives, but not the implementation details required for efficiency [27]. In our semantics, shown in Fig. 2, an abstract machine state, MState, contains:

- A stack s, of type $\mathsf{Var} \times \mathsf{TID} \rightharpoonup \mathsf{Loc}$
- A heap, h, of type $\mathsf{Loc} \times \mathsf{FName} \rightharpoonup \mathsf{Val}$
- A lock, l, of type $\mathsf{TID} \uplus \{\mathsf{unlocked}\}$
- A root location rt of type Loc
- A read set, R, of type $\mathcal{P}(\mathsf{TID})$ and
- A bounding set, B, of type $\mathcal{P}(\mathsf{TID})$

The lock l enforces mutual exclusion between write-side critical sections. The root location rt is the root of an RCU data structure. We model only a single global RCU data structure; the generalization to multiple structures is straightforward but complicates formal development later in the paper. The reader set R tracks the thread IDs (TIDs) of all threads currently executing a read block. The bounding set B tracks which threads the writer is *actively* waiting for during a grace period—it is empty if the writer is not waiting.

Figure 2 gives operational semantics for *atomic* actions; conditionals, loops, and sequencing all have standard semantics, and parallel composition uses sequentially-consistent interleaving semantics.

The first few atomic actions, for writing and reading fields, assigning among local variables, and allocating new objects, are typical of formal semantics for heaps and mutable local variables. `Free` is similarly standard. A writer thread's critical section is bounded by `WriteBegin` and `WriteEnd`, which acquire and release the lock that enforces mutual exclusion between writers. `WriteBegin` only reduces (acquires) if the lock is unlocked.

Standard RCU APIs include a primitive `synchronize_rcu()` to wait for a grace period for the current readers. We decompose this here into two actions, `SyncStart` and `SyncStop`. `SyncStart` initializes the blocking set to the current set of readers—the threads that may have already observed any nodes the writer has unlinked. `SyncStop` blocks until the blocking set is emptied by completing

$$\alpha ::= \mathsf{skip} \mid \mathsf{x.f} = \mathsf{y} \mid \mathsf{y} = \mathsf{x} \mid \mathsf{y} = \mathsf{x.f} \mid \mathsf{y} = \mathsf{new} \mid \mathsf{Free(x)} \mid \mathsf{Sync} \quad \mathsf{Sync} \triangleq \mathsf{SyncStart};\mathsf{SyncStop}$$

$$\begin{array}{lll}
(\text{RCU-WBEGIN}) & [\![\texttt{WriteBegin}]\!]\ (s, h, \mathsf{unlocked}, rt, R, B) & \Downarrow_{tid}(s, h, l, rt, R, B) \\
(\text{RCU-WEND}) & [\![\texttt{WriteEnd}]\!]\ (s, h, l, rt, R, B) & \Downarrow_{tid}(s, h, \mathsf{unlocked}, rt, R, B) \\
(\text{RCU-RBEGIN}) & [\![\texttt{ReadBegin}]\!]\ (s, h, tid, rt, R, B) & \Downarrow_{tid}(s, h, tid, rt, R \uplus \{tid\}, B) \quad tid \neq l \\
(\text{RCU-REND}) & [\![\texttt{ReadEnd}]\!]\ (s, h, tid, rt, R \uplus \{tid\}, B) & \Downarrow_{tid}(s, h, l, rt, R, B \setminus \{tid\}) \quad tid \neq l \\
(\text{RCU-SSTART}) & [\![\texttt{SyncStart}]\!]\ (s, h, l, rt, R, \emptyset) & \Downarrow_{tid}(s, h, l, rt, R, R) \\
(\text{RCU-SSTOP}) & [\![\texttt{SyncStop}]\!]\ (s, h, l, rt, R, \emptyset) & \Downarrow_{tid}(s, h, l, rt, R, \emptyset) \\
(\text{FREE}) & [\![\texttt{Free}(x)]\!]\ (s, h, l, rt, R, \emptyset) & \Downarrow_{tid}(s, h', l, rt, R, \emptyset)
\end{array}$$

provided $\forall_{f,o'}.\, rt \neq s(x, tid)$ and $o' \neq s(x, tid) \implies h(o', f) = h'(o', f)$ and $\forall_f.\, h'(o, f) = \mathsf{undef}$

$$\begin{array}{ll}
(\text{HUPDT}) & [\![\texttt{x.f=y}]\!]\ (s, h, l, rt, R, B) \Downarrow_{tid}(s, h[s(x, tid), f \mapsto s(y, tid)], l, rt, R, B) \\
(\text{HREAD}) & [\![\texttt{y=x.f}]\!]\ (s, h, l, rt, R, B) \Downarrow_{tid}(s[(y, tid) \mapsto h(s(x, tid), f)], h, l, rt, R, B) \\
(\text{SUPDT}) & [\![\texttt{y=x}]\!]\ (s, h, l, rt, R, B) \Downarrow_{tid}(s[(y, tid) \mapsto (x, tid)], h, l, rt, R, B) \\
(\text{HALLOC}) & [\![\texttt{y=new}]\!]\ (s, h, l, rt, R, B) \Downarrow_{tid}(s, h[\ell \mapsto \mathsf{nullmap}], l, rt, R, B)
\end{array}$$

provided $rt \neq s(y, tid)$ and $s[(y, tid) \mapsto \ell]$, and
$h[\ell \mapsto \mathsf{nullmap}] \stackrel{\text{def}}{=} \lambda(o', f).$ if $o = o'$ then *skip* else $h(o', f)$

Fig. 2. Operational semantics for RCU.

reader threads. However, it does not wait for *all* readers to finish, and does not wait for all overlapping readers to simultaneously be out of critical sections. If two reader threads A and B overlap some `SyncStart`-`SyncStop`'s critical section, it is possible that A may exit and re-enter a read-side critical section before B exits, and vice versa. Implementations must distinguish subsequent read-side critical sections from earlier ones that overlapped the writer's initial request to wait: since `SyncStart` is used *after* a node is physically removed from the data structure and readers may not retain RCU references across critical sections, A re-entering a fresh read-side critical section will not permit it to re-observe the node to be freed.

Reader thread critical sections are bounded by **`ReadBegin`** and **`ReadEnd`**. **`ReadBegin`** simply records the current thread's presence as an active reader. **`ReadEnd`** removes the current thread from the set of active readers, and also removes it (if present) from the blocking set—if a writer was waiting for a certain reader to finish its critical section, this ensures the writer no longer waits once that reader has finished its current read-side critical section.

Grace periods are implemented by the combination of **`ReadBegin`**, **`ReadEnd`**, **`SyncStart`**, and **`SyncStop`**. **`ReadBegin`** ensures the set of active readers is known. When a grace period is required, **`SyncStart;SyncStop;`** will store (in B) the active readers (which may have observed nodes before they were unlinked), and wait for reader threads to record when they have completed their critical section (and implicitly, dropped any references to nodes the writer wants to free) via **`ReadEnd`**.

These semantics do permit a reader in the blocking set to finish its read-side critical section and enter a *new* read-side critical section before the writer wakes. In this case, *the writer waits only for the first critical section of that reader to complete*, since entering the new critical section adds the thread's ID back to R, but not B.

4 Type System and Programming Language

In this section, we present a simple imperative programming language with two block constructs for modeling RCU, and a type system that ensures proper (memory-safe) use of the language. The type system ensures memory safety by enforcing these sufficient conditions:

- A heap node can only be freed if it is no longer accessible from an RCU data structure or from local variables of other threads. To achieve this we ensure the reachability and access which can be suitably restricted. We explain how our types support a delayed ownership transfer for the deallocation.
- Local variables may not point inside an RCU data structure unless they are inside an RCU read or write block.
- Heap mutations are *local*: each unlinks or replaces exactly one node.
- The RCU data structure remains a tree. While not a fundamental constraint of RCU, it is a common constraint across known RCU data structures because it simplifies reasoning (by developers or a type system) about when a node has become unreachable in the heap.

We also demonstrate that the type system is not only sound, but useful: we show how it types Fig. 1's list-based bag implementation [25]. We also give type checked fragments of a binary search tree to motivate advanced features of the type system; the full typing derivation can be found in our technical report [20] Appendix B. The BST requires type narrowing operations that refine a type based on dynamic checks (e.g., determining which of several fields links to a node). In our system, we presume all objects contain all fields, but the number of fields is finite (and in our examples, small). This avoids additional overhead from tracking well-established aspects of the type system—class and field types and presence, for example—and focus on checking correct use of RCU primitives. Essentially, we assume the code our type system applies to is already type-correct for a system like C or Java's type system.

4.1 RCU Type System for Write Critical Section

Section 4.1 introduces RCU types and the need for subtyping. Section 4.2, shows how types describe program states, through code for Fig. 1's list-based bag example. Section 4.3 introduces the type system itself.

RCU Types. There are six types used in Write critical sections

$$\tau ::= \mathsf{rcuItr}\ \rho\ \mathcal{N} \mid \mathsf{rcuFresh}\ \mathcal{N} \mid \mathsf{unlinked} \mid \mathsf{undef} \mid \mathsf{freeable} \mid \mathsf{rcuRoot}$$

rcuItr is the type given to references pointing into a shared RCU data structure. A rcuItr type can be used in either a write region or a read region (without the additional components). It indicates both that the reference points into the shared RCU data structure and that the heap location referenced by rcuItr reference is reachable by following the path ρ from the root. A component $\mathcal{N}$ is a set of field mappings taking the field name to local variable names. Field maps are extended when the referent's fields are read. The field map and path components track reachability from the root, and local reachability between nodes. These are used to ensure the structure remains acyclic, and for the type system to recognize exactly when unlinking can occur.

Read-side critical sections use rcultr without path or field map components. These components are both unnecessary for readers (who perform no updates) and would be invalidated by writer threads anyways. Under the assumption that reader threads do not hold references across critical sections, the read-side rules essentially only ensure the reader performs no writes, so we omit the reader critical section type rules. They can be found in our technical report [20] Appendix E.

unlinked is the type given to references to unlinked heap locations—objects previously part of the structure, but now unreachable via the heap. A heap location referenced by an unlinked reference may still be accessed by reader threads, which may have acquired their own references before the node became unreachable. Newly-arrived readers, however, will be unable to gain access to these referents.

freeable is the type given to references to an unlinked heap location that is safe to reclaim because it is known that no concurrent readers hold references to it. Unlinked references become freeable after a writer has waited for a full grace period.

undef is the type given to references where the content of the referenced location is inaccessible. A local variable of type freeable becomes undef after reclaiming that variable's referent.

rcuFresh is the type given to references to freshly allocated heap locations. Similar to rcultr type, it has field mappings set $\mathcal{N}$. We set the field mappings in the set of an existing rcuFresh reference to be the same as field mappings in the set of rcultr reference when we replace the heap referenced by rcultr with the heap referenced by rcuFresh for memory safe replacement.

rcuRoot is the type given to the fixed reference to the root of the RCU data structure. It may not be overwritten.

Subtyping. It is sometimes necessary to use imprecise types—mostly for control flow joins. Our type system performs these abstractions via subtyping on individual types and full contexts, as in Fig. 3.

Figure 3 includes four judgments for subtyping. The first two—$\vdash \mathcal{N} \prec: \mathcal{N}'$ and $\vdash \rho \prec: \rho'$—describe relaxations of field maps and paths respectively. $\vdash \mathcal{N} \prec: \mathcal{N}'$ is read as "the field map $\mathcal{N}$ is more precise than $\mathcal{N}'$" and similarly for paths. The third judgment $\vdash T \prec: T'$ uses path and field map subtyping to give subtyping among rcultr types—one rcultr is a subtype of another if its paths

$$\mathcal{N} = \{f_0|\dots|f_n \rightharpoonup \{y\} \mid f_i \in \mathsf{FName} \wedge 0 \le i \le n \wedge (y \in \mathsf{Var} \vee y \in \{null\})\} \quad \mathcal{N}_{f,\emptyset} = \mathcal{N} \setminus \{f \rightharpoonup \_\}$$

$$\mathcal{N}_\emptyset = \{\} \quad \mathcal{N}(\cup_{f\rightharpoonup y}) = \mathcal{N} \cup \{f \rightharpoonup y\} \quad \mathcal{N}(\setminus_{f\rightharpoonup y}) = \mathcal{N} - \{f \rightharpoonup y\}$$

$$\mathcal{N}([f \rightharpoonup y]) = \mathcal{N} \text{ where } f \rightharpoonup y \in \mathcal{N} \quad \mathcal{N}(f \rightharpoonup x \setminus y) = \mathcal{N} \setminus \{f \rightharpoonup x\} \cup \{f \rightharpoonup y\}$$

$\boxed{\vdash \mathcal{N} \prec: \mathcal{N}'}$

$$\text{(T-NSub3)}\ \frac{}{\vdash \mathcal{N}_{f,\emptyset} \prec: \mathcal{N}([f \rightharpoonup y])} \qquad \text{(T-NSub4)}\ \frac{}{\vdash \mathcal{N}_\emptyset \prec: \mathcal{N}} \qquad \text{(T-NSub5)}\ \frac{}{\vdash \mathcal{N} \prec: \mathcal{N}}$$

$$\text{(T-NSub2)}\ \frac{}{\vdash \mathcal{N}([f_2 \rightharpoonup y]) \prec: \mathcal{N}([f_1|f_2 \rightharpoonup y])} \qquad \text{(T-NSub1)}\ \frac{}{\vdash \mathcal{N}([f_1 \rightharpoonup y]) \prec: \mathcal{N}([f_1|f_2 \rightharpoonup y])}$$

$\boxed{\vdash \rho \prec: \rho'}$

$$\text{(T-PSub1)}\ \frac{}{\vdash \rho.f_1 \prec: \rho.f_1|f_2} \qquad \text{(T-PSub2)}\ \frac{}{\vdash \rho.f_2 \prec: \rho.f_1|f_2} \qquad \text{(T-PSub3)}\ \frac{}{\vdash \rho \prec: \rho}$$

$\boxed{\vdash T \prec: T'}$

$$\text{(T-TSub2)}\ \frac{}{\vdash \mathsf{rcultr} \prec: \mathsf{rcultr}} \qquad \text{(T-TSub)}\ \frac{}{\vdash \mathsf{rcultr}\ \_ \prec: \mathsf{undef}} \qquad \text{(T-TSub1)}\ \frac{\vdash \rho \prec: \rho' \qquad \vdash \mathcal{N} \prec: \mathcal{N}'}{\vdash \mathsf{rcultr}\ \rho\,\mathcal{N} \prec: \mathsf{rcultr}\ \rho'\,\mathcal{N}'}$$

$\boxed{\vdash \Gamma \prec: \Gamma'}$

$$\text{(T-CSub1)}\ \frac{\vdash \Gamma \prec: \Gamma' \quad \vdash \mathrm{T} \prec: \mathrm{T'}}{\vdash \Gamma, x : \mathrm{T} \prec: \Gamma', x : \mathrm{T'}} \qquad \text{(T-CSub)}\ \frac{}{\vdash \Gamma \prec: \Gamma}$$

Fig. 3. Subtyping rules.

$\boxed{\Gamma \vdash_{M,R} C \dashv \Gamma'}$

$$\text{(T-ReIndex)}\ \frac{}{\Gamma \vdash C_k \dashv \Gamma[\rho.f^k/\rho.f^k.f]} \qquad \text{(T-Loop1)}\ \frac{\Gamma(x) = \mathsf{bool} \qquad \Gamma \vdash C \dashv \Gamma}{\Gamma \vdash \mathsf{while}(x)\{C\} \dashv \Gamma}$$

$$\text{(T-Branch1)}\ \frac{\Gamma, x : \mathsf{rcultr}\ \rho\,\mathcal{N}([f_1 \rightharpoonup z]) \vdash C_1 \dashv \Gamma_4 \qquad \Gamma, x : \mathsf{rcultr}\ \rho\,\mathcal{N}([f_2 \rightharpoonup z]) \vdash C_2 \dashv \Gamma_4}{\Gamma, x : \mathsf{rcultr}\ \rho\,\mathcal{N}([f_1 \mid f_2 \rightharpoonup z]) \vdash \mathsf{if}(x.f_1 == z)\ \mathsf{then}\ C_1\ \mathsf{else}\ C_2 \dashv \Gamma_4}$$

$$\text{(T-Branch3)}\ \frac{\Gamma, x : \mathsf{rcultr}\ \rho\,\mathcal{N}([f \rightharpoonup y \setminus \mathsf{null}]) \vdash C_1 \dashv \Gamma' \qquad \Gamma, x : \mathsf{rcultr}\ \rho\,\mathcal{N}([f \rightharpoonup y]) \vdash C_2 \dashv \Gamma'}{\Gamma, x : \mathsf{rcultr}\ \rho\,\mathcal{N}([f \rightharpoonup y]) \vdash \mathsf{if}(x.f == \mathsf{null})\ \mathsf{then}\ C_1\ \mathsf{else}\ C_2 \dashv \Gamma'}$$

$$\text{(T-Loop2)}\ \frac{\Gamma, x : \mathsf{rcultr}\ \rho\ \mathcal{N}([f \rightharpoonup \_]) \vdash C \dashv \Gamma, x : \mathsf{rcultr}\ \rho'\ \mathcal{N}([f \rightharpoonup \_])}{\Gamma, x : \mathsf{rcultr}\ \rho\ \mathcal{N}([f \rightharpoonup \_]) \vdash \mathsf{while}(x.f \neq \mathsf{null})\{C\} \dashv x : \mathsf{rcultr}\ \rho'\ \mathcal{N}([f \rightharpoonup \mathsf{null}]), \Gamma}$$

$$\text{(T-Branch2)}\ \frac{\Gamma(x) = \mathsf{bool} \qquad \Gamma \vdash C_1 \dashv \Gamma' \qquad \Gamma \vdash C_2 \dashv \Gamma'}{\Gamma \vdash \mathsf{if}(x)\ \mathsf{then}\ C_1\ \mathsf{else}\ C_2 \dashv \Gamma'}$$

Fig. 4. Type rules for control-flow.

and field maps are similarly more precise—and to allow rcultr references to be "forgotten"—this is occasionally needed to satisfy non-interference checks in the type rules. The final judgment $\vdash \Gamma \prec: \Gamma'$ extends subtyping to all assumptions in a type context.

It is often necessary to abstract the contents of field maps or paths, without simply forgetting the contents entirely. In a binary search tree, for example, it may be the case that one node is a child of another, but *which* parent field points to the child depends on which branch was followed in an earlier conditional (consider the lookup in a BST, which alternates between following left and right children). In Fig. 5, we see that `cur` aliases different fields of `par` – either $Left$ or $Right$ – in different branches of the conditional. The types after the conditional must overapproximate this, here as $Left|Right \mapsto cur$ in par's field map, and a similar path disjunction in cur's path. This is reflected in Fig. 3's T-NSUB1-5 and T-PSUB1-2 – within each branch, each type is coerced to a supertype to validate the control flow join.

Another type of control flow join is handling loop invariants – where paths entering the loop meet the back-edge from the end of a loop back to the start for repetition. Because our types include paths describing how they are reachable from the root, some abstraction is required to give loop invariants that work for any number of iterations – in a loop traversing a linked list, the iterator pointer would naïvely have different paths from the root on each iteration, so the exact path is not loop invariant. However, the paths explored by a loop are regular, so we can abstract the paths by permitting (implicitly) existentially quantified indexes on path fragments, which express the existence of *some* path, without saying *which* path. The use of an explicit abstract repetition allows the type system to preserve the fact that different references have common path prefixes, even after a loop.

Assertions for the add function in lines 19 and 20 of Fig. 1 show the *loop*'s effects on paths of iterator references used inside the loop, cur and par. On line 20, par's path contains has $(Next)^k$. The k in the $(Next)^k$ abstracts the number of loop iterations run, implicitly assumed to be non-negative. The trailing $Next$ in cur's path on line 19 – $(Next)^k.Next$ – expresses the relationship between cur and par: par is reachable from the root by following $Next$ k times, and cur is reachable via one additional $Next$. The types of 19 and 20, however, are not the same as lines 23 and 24, so an additional adjustment is needed for the types to become loop-invariant. *Reindexing* (T-REINDEX in Fig. 4) effectively increments an abstract loop counter, contracting $(Next)^k.Next$ to $Next^k$ everywhere in a type environment. This expresses the same relationship between par and cur as before the loop, but the choice of k to make these paths accurate after each iteration would be one larger than the choice before. Reindexing the type environment of lines 23–24 yields the type environment of lines 19–20, making the types loop invariant. The reindexing essentially chooses a new value for the abstract k. This is sound, because the uses of framing in the heap mutation related rules of the type system ensure uses of any indexing variable are never separated – either all are reindexed, or none are.

While abstraction is required to deal with control flow joins, reasoning about whether and which nodes are unlinked or replaced, and whether cycles are created, requires precision. Thus the type system also includes means (Fig. 4) to refine imprecise paths and field maps. In Fig. 5, we see a conditional with the condition $par.Left == cur$. The type system matches this condition to the imprecise types in line 1's typing assertion, and refines the initial type assumptions in each branch accordingly (lines 2 and 7) based on whether execution reflects the truth or falsity of that check. Similarly, it is sometimes required to check – and later remember – whether a field is null, and the type system supports this.

```
{cur : rcultr Left|Right {}, par : rcultr ϵ {Left|Right ↦ cur}}
if(par.Left == cur){
  {cur : rcultr Left {}, par : rcultr ϵ {Left ↦ cur}}
  par = cur;
  cur = par.Left;
  {cur : rcultr Left.Left {}, par : rcultr Left {Left ↦ cur}}
}else{
  {cur : rcultr Right {}, par : rcultr ϵ {Right ↦ cur}}
  par = cur;
  cur = par.Right;
  {cur : rcultr Right.Right {}, par : rcultr Right {Right ↦ cur}}
}
{cur : rcultr Left|Right.Left|Right {}, par : rcultr Left|Right {Left|Right ↦ cur}}
```

Fig. 5. Choosing fields to read.

4.2 Types in Action

The system has three forms of typing judgement: $\Gamma \vdash C$ for standard typing outside RCU critical sections; $\Gamma \vdash_R C \dashv \Gamma'$ for reader critical sections, and $\Gamma \vdash_M C \dashv \Gamma'$ for writer critical sections. The first two are straightforward, essentially preventing mutation of the data structure, and preventing nesting of a writer critical section inside a reader critical section. The last, for writer critical sections, is flow sensitive: the types of variables may differ before and after program statements. This is required in order to reason about local assumptions at different points in the program, such as recognizing that a certain action may unlink a node. Our presentation here focuses exclusively on the judgment for the write-side critical sections.

Below, we explain our types through the list-based bag implementation [25] from Fig. 1, highlighting how the type rules handle different parts of the code. Figure 1 is annotated with "assertions" – local type environments – in the style of a Hoare logic proof outline. As with Hoare proof outlines, these annotations can be used to construct a proper typing derivation.

Reading a Global RCU Root. All RCU data structures have fixed roots, which we characterize with the rcuRoot type. Each operation in Fig. 1 begins by reading the root into a new rcultr reference used to begin traversing the structure. After each initial read (line 12 of `add` and line 4 of `remove`), the path of `cur` reference is the empty path (ϵ) and the field map is empty ($\{\}$), because it is an alias to the root, and none of its field contents are known yet.

Reading an Object Field and a Variable. As expected, we explore the heap of the data structure via reading the objects' fields. Consider line 6 of `remove` and its corresponding pre- and post- type environments. Initially `par`'s field map is empty. After the field read, its field map is updated to reflect that its $Next$ field is aliased in the local variable `cur`. Likewise, after the update, `cur`'s path is $Next$ ($= \epsilon \cdot Next$), extending the par node's path by the field read. This introduces field aliasing information that can subsequently be used to reason about unlinking.

Unlinking Nodes. Line 24 of `remove` in Fig. 1 unlinks a node. The type annotations show that before that line `cur` is in the structure (rcultr), while afterwards its type is unlinked. The type system checks that this unlink disconnects only one node: note how the types of `par`, `cur`, and `curl` just before line 24 completely describe a section of the list.

Grace and Reclamation. After the referent of `cur` is unlinked, concurrent readers traversing the list may still hold references. So it is not safe to actually reclaim the memory until after a grace period. Lines 28–29 of `remove` initiate a grace period and wait for its completion. At the type level, this is reflected by the change of `cur`'s type from unlinked to freeable, reflecting the fact that the grace period extends until any reader critical sections that might have observed the node in the structure have completed. This matches the precondition required by our rules for calling `Free`, which further changes the type of `cur` to undef reflecting that `cur` is no longer a valid reference. The type system also ensures no local (writer) aliases exist to the freed node and understanding this enforcement is twofold. First, the type system requires that only unlinked heap nodes can be freed. Second, framing relations in rules related to the heap mutation ensure no local aliases still consider the node linked.

Fresh Nodes. Some code must also allocate new nodes, and the type system must reason about how they are incorporated into the shared data structure. Line 8 of the add method allocates a new node `nw`, and lines 10 and 29 initialize its fields. The type system gives it a fresh type while tracking its field contents, until line 32 inserts it into the data structure. The type system checks that nodes previously reachable from `cur` remain reachable: note the field maps of `cur` and `nw` in lines 30–31 are equal (trivially, though in general the field need not be null).

4.3 Type Rules

Figure 6 gives the primary type rules used in checking write-side critical section code as in Fig. 1.

T-Root reads a root pointer into an rcultr reference, and T-ReadS copies a local variable into another. In both cases, the free variable condition ensures that updating the modified variable does not invalidate field maps of other variables in Γ. These free variable conditions recur throughout the type system, and we will not comment on them further. T-Alloc and T-Free allocate and reclaim objects. These rules are relatively straightforward. T-ReadH reads a field into a local variable. As suggested earlier, this rule updates the post-environment to reflect that the overwritten variable z holds the same value as $x.f$. T-WriteFH updates a field of a *fresh* (thread-local) object, similarly tracking the update in the fresh object's field map at the type level. The remaining rules are a bit more involved, and form the heart of the type system.

Grace Periods. T-Sync gives pre- and post-environments to the compound statement `SyncStart;SyncStop` implementing grace periods. As mentioned earlier, this updates the environment afterwards to reflect that any nodes unlinked before the wait become freeable afterwards.

$$\boxed{\Gamma \vdash_M \alpha \dashv \Gamma'} \quad (\text{T-Root})\ \frac{y \notin \mathsf{FV}(\Gamma)}{\Gamma, r{:}\mathsf{rcuRoot}, y{:}\mathsf{undef} \vdash y = r \dashv y{:}\mathsf{rcultr}\epsilon\mathcal{N}_{\emptyset}, r{:}\mathsf{rcuRoot}, \Gamma}$$

$$(\text{T-ReadS})\ \frac{z \notin \mathsf{FV}(\Gamma)}{\Gamma, z : \_, x : \mathsf{rcultr}\ \ \rho\ \ \mathcal{N} \vdash z = x \dashv x : \mathsf{rcultr}\ \ \rho\ \ \mathcal{N}, z : \mathsf{rcultr}\ \ \rho\ \ \mathcal{N}, \Gamma}$$

$$(\text{T-Alloc})\ \frac{}{\Gamma, x{:}\mathsf{undef} \vdash x = \mathsf{new} \dashv x{:}\mathsf{rcuFresh}\mathcal{N}_{\emptyset}, \Gamma} \quad (\text{T-Free})\ \frac{}{x{:}\mathsf{freeable} \vdash \mathsf{Free}(x) \dashv x{:}\mathsf{undef}}$$

$$(\text{T-ReadH})\ \frac{\rho.f = \rho' \qquad z \notin \mathsf{FV}(\Gamma)}{\Gamma, z : \_, x{:}\mathsf{rcultr}\rho\mathcal{N} \vdash z = x.f \dashv x{:}\mathsf{rcultr}\rho\mathcal{N}([f \rightharpoonup z]), z{:}\mathsf{rcultr}\rho'\mathcal{N}_{\emptyset}, \Gamma}$$

(T-WriteFH)

$$\frac{z : \mathsf{rcultr}\rho.f\_ \quad \mathcal{N}(f) = z \quad f \notin dom(\mathcal{N}')}{\Gamma, p{:}\mathsf{rcuFresh}\mathcal{N}', x{:}\mathsf{rcultr}\rho\mathcal{N} \vdash_M p.f = z \dashv p{:}\mathsf{rcuFresh}\mathcal{N}'([f \rightharpoonup z]), x{:}\mathsf{rcultr}\rho\mathcal{N}([f \rightharpoonup z]), \Gamma}$$

$$(\text{T-Sync})\ \frac{}{\Gamma \vdash \mathsf{SyncStart}; \mathsf{SyncStop} \dashv \Gamma[\overline{x{:}\mathsf{freeable}/x{:}\mathsf{unlinked}}]}$$

(T-UnlinkH)

$$\frac{\begin{array}{c} \mathcal{N}(f_1) = z \qquad \rho.f_1 = \rho_1 \qquad \rho_1.f_2 = \rho_2 \\ \mathcal{N}' = \mathcal{N}([f_1 \rightharpoonup z \setminus r]) \qquad \forall_{f \in dom(\mathcal{N}_1)}.\ f \neq f_2 \implies (\mathcal{N}_1(f) = \mathsf{null}) \qquad \mathcal{N}(f_1) = z \qquad \mathcal{N}_1(f_2) = r \\ \forall_{n \in \Gamma, m, \mathcal{N}_3, p_3, f}.\ n{:}\mathsf{rcultr}\,\rho_3\,\mathcal{N}_3([f \rightharpoonup m]) \implies \begin{cases} ((\neg\mathsf{MayAlias}(\rho_3, \{\rho, \rho_1, \rho_2\})) \wedge (m \notin \{z, r\})) \\ \wedge(\forall_{\rho_4 \neq \epsilon}.\ \neg\mathsf{MayAlias}(\rho_3, \rho_2.\rho_4)) \end{cases} \end{array}}{\Gamma, x{:}\mathsf{rcultr}\rho\mathcal{N}, z{:}\mathsf{rcultr}\rho_1\mathcal{N}_1, r{:}\mathsf{rcultr}\rho_2\mathcal{N}_2 \vdash x.f_1 = r \dashv z{:}\mathsf{unlinked}, x{:}\mathsf{rcultr}\rho\mathcal{N}', r{:}\mathsf{rcultr}\rho_1\mathcal{N}_2, \Gamma}$$

(T-Replace)

$$\frac{\begin{array}{c} \mathcal{N}(f) = o \qquad \mathcal{N}' = \mathcal{N}([f \rightharpoonup o \setminus n]) \qquad \rho.f = \rho_1 \qquad \mathcal{N}_1 = \mathcal{N}_2 \qquad \mathsf{FV}(\Gamma) \cap \{p, o, n\} = \emptyset \\ \forall_{x \in \Gamma, \mathcal{N}_3, \rho_2, f_1, y}.\ (x{:}\mathsf{rcultr}\,\rho_2\,\mathcal{N}_3([f_1 \rightharpoonup y])) \implies (\neg\mathsf{MayAlias}(\rho_2, \{\rho, \rho_1\}) \wedge (y \neq o)) \end{array}}{\Gamma, p{:}\mathsf{rcultr}\rho\mathcal{N}, o{:}\mathsf{rcultr}\rho_1\mathcal{N}_1, n{:}\mathsf{rcuFresh}\mathcal{N}_2 \vdash p.f = n \dashv p{:}\mathsf{rcultr}\rho\mathcal{N}', n{:}\mathsf{rcultr}\rho_1\mathcal{N}_2, o{:}\mathsf{unlinked}, \Gamma}$$

(T-Insert)

$$\frac{\begin{array}{c} \mathcal{N}' = \mathcal{N}([f \rightharpoonup o \setminus n]) \qquad \rho.f = \rho_1 \qquad \rho_1.f_4 = \rho_2 \\ \mathcal{N}(f) = \mathcal{N}_1(f_4) \qquad \forall_{f_2 \in dom(\mathcal{N}_1)}.\ f_4 \neq f_2 \implies \mathcal{N}_1(f_2) = \mathsf{null} \qquad \mathsf{FV}(\Gamma) \cap \{p, o, n\} = \emptyset \\ \forall_{x \in \Gamma, \mathcal{N}_3, \rho_3, f_1, y}.\ (x : \mathsf{rcultr}\,\rho_3\,\mathcal{N}_3([f_1 \rightharpoonup y])) \implies (\forall_{\rho_4 \neq \epsilon}.\ \neg\mathsf{MayAlias}(\rho_3, \rho.\rho_4)) \end{array}}{\Gamma, p{:}\mathsf{rcultr}\rho\mathcal{N}, o{:}\mathsf{rcultr}\rho_1\mathcal{N}_2, n{:}\mathsf{rcuFresh}\mathcal{N}_1 \vdash p.f = n \dashv p{:}\mathsf{rcultr}\rho\mathcal{N}', n{:}\mathsf{rcultr}\rho_1\mathcal{N}_1, o{:}\mathsf{rcultr}\rho_2\mathcal{N}_2, \Gamma}$$

$$\boxed{\Gamma \vdash_M C \dashv \Gamma'} \quad (\text{ToRCUWrite})\ \frac{\begin{array}{c} \mathsf{NoFresh}(\Gamma') \qquad \mathsf{NoUnlinked}(\Gamma') \qquad \mathsf{NoFreeable}(\Gamma') \\ \Gamma, y{:}\mathsf{rcultr}\_ \vdash_M C \dashv \Gamma' \qquad \mathsf{FType}(f) = \mathsf{RCU} \end{array}}{\Gamma \vdash \mathsf{RCUWrite}\ x.f\ \mathsf{as}\ y\ \mathsf{in}\ \{C\}}$$

Fig. 6. Type rules for write side critical section.

Unlinking. T-UnlinkH type checks heap updates that remove a node from the data structure. The rule assumes three objects x, z, and r, whose identities we will conflate with the local variable names in the type rule. The rule checks the case where $x.f_1 == z$ and $z.f_2 == r$ initially (reflected in the path and field map components, and a write $x.f_1 = r$ removes z from the data structure (we assume, and ensure, the structure is a tree).

The rule must also avoid unlinking multiple nodes: this is the purpose of the first (smaller) implication: it ensures that beyond the reference from z to r, all fields of z are null.

Finally, the rule must ensure that no types in Γ are invalidated. This could happen one of two ways: either a field map in Γ for an alias of x duplicates

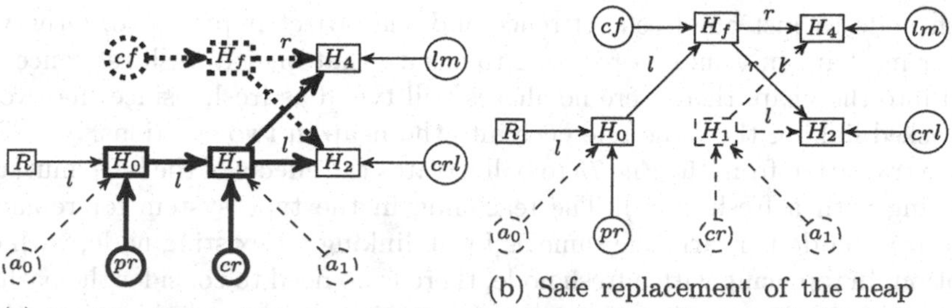

(a) *Freshly* allocated heap node referenced by cf

(b) Safe replacement of the heap node referenced by *cr* with the *fresh* heap node referenced by cf.

Fig. 7. Replacing *existing* heap nodes with *fresh* ones. Type rule T-REPLACE.

the assumption that $x.f_1 == z$ (which is changed by this write), or Γ contains a descendant of r, whose path from the root will change when its ancestor is modified. The final assumption of T-UNLINKH (the implication) checks that for every rcuItr reference n in Γ, it is not a path alias of x, z, or r; no entry of its field map (m) refers to r or z (which would imply n aliased x or z initially); and its path is not an extension of r (i.e., it is not a descendant). MayAlias is a predicate on two paths (or a path and set of paths) which is true if it is possible that any concrete paths the arguments may abstract (e.g., via adding non-determinism through|or abstracting iteration with indexing) *could* be the same. The negation of a MayAlias use is true only when the paths are guaranteed to refer to different locations in the heap.

Replacing with a Fresh Node. Replacing with a rcuFresh reference faces the same aliasing complications as direct unlinking. We illustrate these challenges in Figs. 7a and b. Our technical report [20] also includes Figures 32a and 32b in Appendix D to illustrate complexities in unlinking. The square R nodes are root nodes, and H nodes are general heap nodes. All resources in thick straight lines and dotted lines form the memory foot print of a node replacement. The hollow thick circular nodes – *pr* and *cr* – point to the nodes involved in replacing H_1 (referenced by `cr`) with H_f (referenced by cf) in the structure. We may have a_0 and a_1 which are aliases with *pr* and *cr* respectively. They are *path-aliases* as they share the same path from root to the node that they reference. Edge labels l and r are abbreviations for the $Left$ and $Right$ fields of a binary search tree. The thick dotted H_f denotes the freshly allocated heap node referenced by thick dotted cf. The thick dotted field l is set to point to the referent of *cl* and the thick dotted field r is set to point to the referent of the heap node referenced by lm.

H_f initially (Fig. 7a) is not part of the shared structure. If it was, it would violate the tree shape requirement imposed by the type system. This is why we highlight it separately in thick dots—its static type would be rcuFresh. Note that we cannot duplicate a rcuFresh variable, nor read a field of an object it points to. This restriction localizes our reasoning about the effects of replacing with a fresh node to just one fresh reference and the object it points to. Otherwise another mechanism would be required to ensure that once a fresh reference was linked into the heap, there were no aliases still typed as fresh—since that would have risked linking the same reference into the heap in two locations.

The transition from the Fig. 7a to b illustrates the effects of the heap mutation (replacing with a fresh node). The reasoning in the type system for replacing with a fresh node is nearly the same as for unlinking an existing node, with one exception. In replacing with a fresh node, there is no need to consider the paths of nodes deeper in the tree than the point of mutation. In the unlinking case, those nodes' static paths would become invalid. In the case of replacing with a fresh node, those descendants' paths are preserved. Our type rule for ensuring safe replacement (T-REPLACE) prevents path aliasing (representing the nonexistence of a_0 and a_1 via dashed lines and circles) by negating a MayAlias query and prevents field mapping aliasing (nonexistence of any object field from any other context pointing to cr) via asserting $(y \neq o)$. It is important to note that objects (H_4, H_2) in the field mappings of the cr whose referent is to be unlinked captured by the heap node's field mappings referenced by cf in rcuFresh. This is part of enforcing locality on the heap mutation and captured by assertion $\mathcal{N} = \mathcal{N}'$ in the type rule (T-REPLACE).

Inserting a Fresh Node. T-INSERT type checks heap updates that link a fresh node into a linked data structure. Inserting a rcuFresh reference also faces some of the aliasing complications that we have already discussed for direct unlinking and replacing a node. Unlike the replacement case, the path to the last heap node (the referent of o) from the root is *extended* by f, which risks falsifying the paths for aliases and descendants of o. The final assumption (the implication) of T-INSERT checks for this inconsistency.

There is also another rule, T-LINKF-NULL, not shown in Fig. 6, which handles the case where the fields of the fresh node are not object references, but instead all contain null (e.g., for appending to the end of a linked list or inserting a leaf node in a tree).

Critical Sections (*Referencing inside RCU Blocks*). We introduce the *syntactic sugaring* RCUWrite $x.f$ as y in $\{C\}$ for write-side critical sections where the analogous syntactic sugaring can be found for read-side critical sections in Appendix E of the technical report [20].

The type system ensures unlinked and freeable references are handled linearly, as they cannot be dropped – coerced to undef. The top-level rule TORCUWRITE in Fig. 6 ensures unlinked references have been freed by forbidding them in the critical section's post-type environment. Our technical report [20] also includes the analogous rule TORCUREAD for the read critical section in Figure 33 of Appendix E.

Preventing the reuse of rcuItr references across critical sections is subtler: the non-critical section system is not flow-sensitive, and does not include rcuItr. Therefore, the initial environment lacks rcuItr references, and trailing rcuItr references may not escape.

5 Evaluation

We have used our type system to check correct use of RCU primitives in two RCU data structures representative of the broader space.

Figure 1 gives the type-annotated code for `add` and `remove` operations on a linked list implementation of a bag data structure, following McKenney's example [25]. Our technical report [20] contains code for membership checking.

We have also type checked the most challenging part of an RCU binary search tree, the deletion (which also contains the code for a lookup). Our implementation is a slightly simplified version of the Citrus BST [3]: their code supports fine-grained locking for multiple writers, while ours supports only one writer by virtue of using our single-writer primitives. For lack of space the annotated code is only in Appendix B of the technical report [20], but here we emphasise the important aspects our type system via showing its capabilities of typing BST delete method, which also includes looking up for the node to be deleted.

In Fig. 8, we show the steps for deleting the heap node H_1. To locate the node H_1, as shown in Fig. 8a, we first traverse the subtree T_0 with references *pr* and *cr*, where *pr* is the parent of *cr* during traversal:

$$pr : rcuItr(l|r)^k\{l|r \rightarrow cr\},\ cr : rcuItr(l|r)^k.(l|r)\{\}$$

Traversal of T_0 is summarized as $(l|k)^k$. The most subtle aspect of the deletion is the final step in the case the node H_1 to remove has both children; as shown in Fig. 8b, the code must traverse the subtree T_4 to locate the next element in collection order: the node H_s, the left-most node of H_1's right child (*sc*) and its parent (*lp*):

$$lp : (l|r)^k.(l|r).r.(l|r)^m\{l|r \rightarrow sc\},\ sc : (l|r)^k.(l|r).r.l.(l)^m.l\{\}$$

where the traversal of T_4 is summarized as $(l|m)^m$.

Then H_s is copied into a new *freshly-allocated* node as shown in Fig. 8b, which is then used to *replace* node H_1 as shown in Fig. 8c: the replacement's fields exactly match H_1's except for the data (T-Replace via $\mathcal{N}_1 = \mathcal{N}_2$) as shown in Fig. 8b, and the parent is updated to reference the replacement, unlinking H_1.

At this point, as shown in Figs. 8c and d, there are two nodes with the same value in the tree (the *weak* BST property of the Citrus BST [3]): the replacement node, and what was the left-most node under H_1's right child. This latter (original) node H_s must be unlinked as shown in Fig. 8e, which is simpler because by being left-most the left child is null, avoiding another round of replacement (T-UnlinkH via $\forall_{f \in dom(\mathcal{N}_1)}.\, f \neq f_2 \implies (\mathcal{N}_1(f) = \mathsf{null})$.

Traversing T_4 to find successor complicates the reasoning in an interesting way. After the successor node H_s is found in Fig. 8b, there are *two* local unlinking operations as shown in Figs. 8c and e, at different depths of the tree. This is why the type system must keep separate abstract iteration counts, e.g., k of $(l|r)^k$ or m of $(l|r)^m$, for traversals in loops—these indices act like multiple cursors into the data structure, and allow the types to carry enough information to keep those changes separate and ensure neither introduces a cycle.

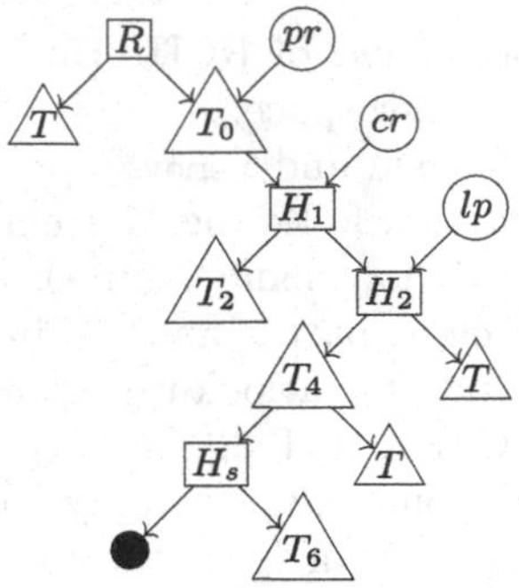

(a) The writer traverses subtree T_0 to find the heap node H_1 with local references *pr* and *cr*. Black-filled node representing the null node.

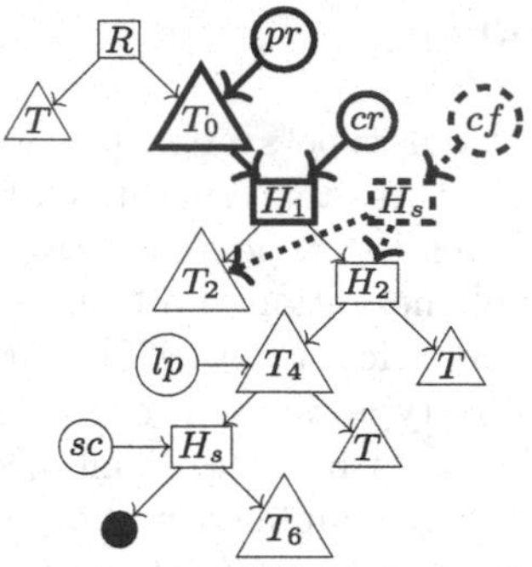

(b) Traverse subtree T_4 starting from H_2 with references *lp* and *sc* to find successor H_s of H_1. Duplicating H_s as a fresh heap node before replacing H_1 with the fresh one.

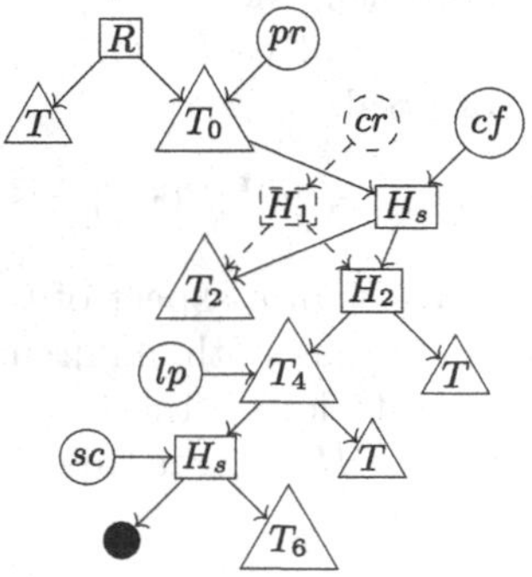

(c) Replace H_1 with fresh successor and synchronize with the readers.

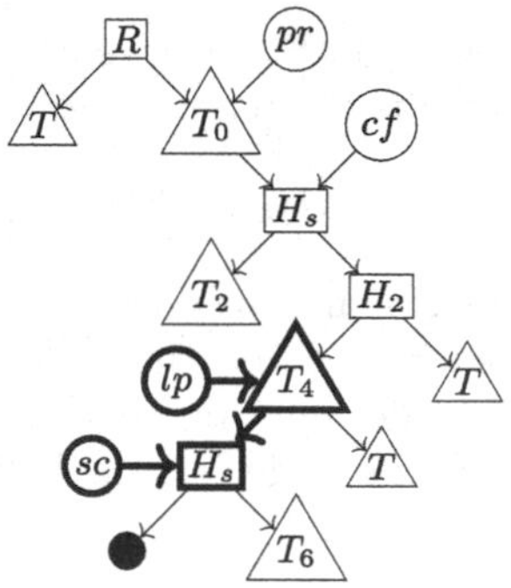

(d) Unlinks old successor referenced by *sc*.

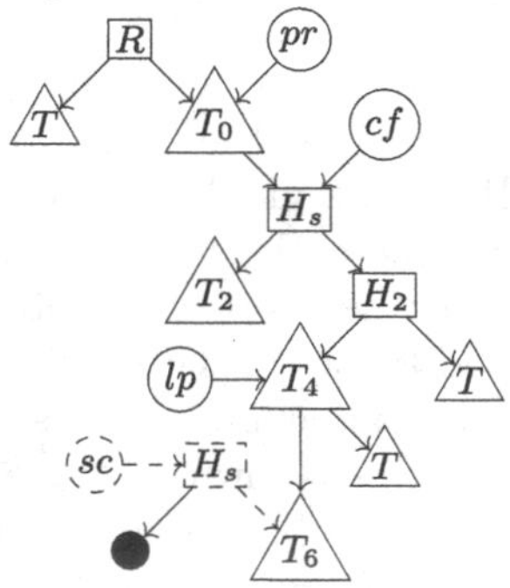

(e) Safe unlinking of the old successor whose left subtree is null.

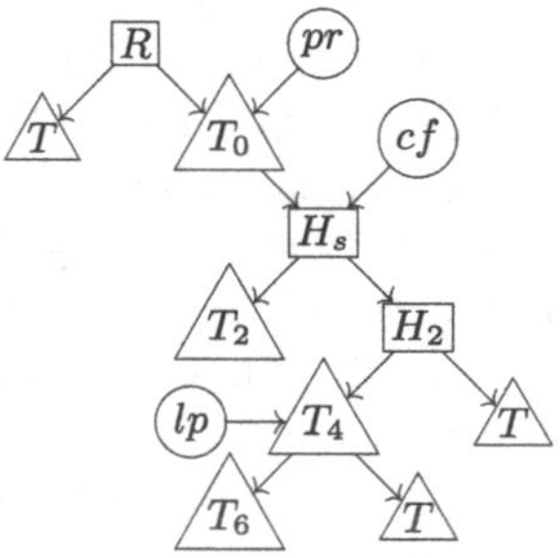

(f) Reclamation of the old successor.

Fig. 8. Delete of a heap node with two children in BST [3].

To the best of our knowledge, we are the first to check such code for memory-safe use of RCU primitives modularly, without appeal to the specific implementation of RCU primitives.

6 Soundness

This section outlines the proof of type soundness – our full proof appears the accompanying technical report [20]. We prove type soundness by embedding the type system into an abstract concurrent separation logic called the Views Framework [9], which when given certain information about proofs for a specific language (primitives and primitive typing) gives back a full program logic including choice and iteration. As with other work taking this approach [13,14], this consists of several key steps explained in the following subsections, but a high-level informal soundness argument is twofold. First, because the parameters given to the Views framework ensure the Views logic's Hoare triples $\{-\}C\{-\}$ are sound, this proves soundness of the type rules with respect to type denotations. Second, as our denotation of types encodes the property that the post-environment of any type rule accurately characterizes which memory is linked vs. unlinked, etc., and the global invariants ensure all allocated heap memory is reachable from the root or from some thread's stack, this entails that our type system prevents memory leaks.

6.1 Proof

This section provides more details on how the Views Framework [9] is used to prove soundness, giving the major parameters to the framework and outlining global invariants and key lemmas.

Logical State. Section 3 defined what Views calls *atomic actions* (the primitive operations) and their semantics on runtime *machine states*. The Views Framework uses a separate notion of instrumented (logical) state over which the logic is built, related by a concretization function $\lfloor - \rfloor$ taking an instrumented state to the machine states of Sect. 3. Most often—including in our proof—the logical state adds useful auxiliary state to the machine state, and the concretization is simply projection. Thus we define our logical states LState as:

- A machine state, $\sigma = (s, h, l, rt, R, B)$
- An observation map, O, of type $\mathsf{Loc} \rightarrow \mathcal{P}(\mathsf{obs})$
- Undefined variable map, U, of type $\mathcal{P}(\mathsf{Var} \times \mathsf{TID})$
- Set of threads, T, of type $\mathcal{P}(\mathsf{TIDS})$
- A to-free map (or free list), F, of type $\mathsf{Loc} \rightharpoonup \mathcal{P}(\mathsf{TID})$

The thread ID set T includes the thread ID of all running threads. The free map F tracks which reader threads may hold references to each location. It is not required for execution of code, and for validating an implementation could be ignored, but we use it later with our type system to help prove that memory deallocation is safe. The (per-thread) variables in the undefined variable map U are those that should not be accessed (e.g., dangling pointers).

The remaining component, the observation map O, requires some further explanation. Each memory allocation/object can be *observed* in one of the following states by a variety of threads, depending on how it was used.

$$\mathsf{obs} := \texttt{iterator}\ \mathsf{tid} \mid \texttt{unlinked} \mid \texttt{fresh} \mid \texttt{freeable} \mid \texttt{root}$$

An object can be observed as part of the structure (iterator), removed but possibly accessible to other threads, freshly allocated, safe to deallocate, or the root of the structure.

Invariants of RCU Views and Denotations of Types. Next, we aim to convey the intuition behind the predicate WellFormed which enforces global invariants on logical states, and how it interacts with the denotations of types (Fig. 9) in key ways.

WellFormed is the conjunction of a number of more specific invariants, which we outline here. For full details, see Appendix A.2 of the technical report [20].

The Invariant for Read Traversal. Reader threads access valid heap locations even during the grace period. The validity of their heap accesses ensured by the observations they make over the heap locations—which can only be iterator as they can only use local rcultr references. To this end, a Readers-Iterators-Only invariant asserts that reader threads can only observe a heap location as iterator.

Invariants on Grace-Period. Our logical state includes a "free list" auxiliary state tracking which readers are still accessing *each* unlinked node during grace periods. This must be consistent with the bounding thread set B in the machine state, and this consistency is asserted by the Readers-In-Free-List invariant. This is essentially tracking which readers are being "shown grace" for each location. The Iterators-Free-List invariant complements this by asserting all readers with such observations on unlinked nodes are in the bounding thread set.

The writer thread can refer to a heap location in the free list with a local reference either in type freeable or unlinked. Once the writer unlinks a heap node, it first observes the heap node as unlinked then freeable. The denotation of freeable is only valid following a grace period: it asserts no readers hold aliases of the freeable reference. The denotation of unlinked permits the either the same (perhaps no readers overlapped) or that it is in the to-free list.

Invariants on Safe Traversal Against Unlinking. The write-side critical section must guarantee that no updates to the heap cause invalid memory accesses. The Writer-Unlink invariant asserts that a heap location observed as iterator by the writer thread cannot be observed differently by other threads. The denotation of the writer thread's rcultr reference, $[\![\mathsf{rcultr}\,\rho\,\mathcal{N}]\!]_{tid}$, asserts that following a path from the root compatible with ρ reaches the referent, and all are observed as iterator.

The denotation of a reader thread's rcultr reference, $[\![\mathsf{rcultr}]\!]_{tid}$ and the invariants Readers-Iterator-Only, Iterators-Free-List and Readers-In-Free-List all together assert that a reader thread (which can also be a bounding thread) can view an unlinked heap location (which can be in the free list) only as iterator. At the same time, it is essential that reader threads arriving after a node is unlinked cannot access it. The invariants Unlinked-Reachability and Free-List-Reachability ensure that any unlinked nodes are reachable only from other unlinked nodes, and never from the root.

$$
\begin{array}{lcl}
[\![x : \mathsf{rcultr}\,\rho\mathcal{N}]\!]_{tid} & = & \left\{ m \in \mathcal{M} \middle| \begin{array}{l} (\mathsf{iterator}\,tid \in O(s(x,tid))) \wedge (x \notin U) \\ \wedge(\forall_{f_i \in dom(\mathcal{N}) x_i \in codom(\mathcal{N})}. \left\{ \begin{array}{l} s(x_i,tid) = h(s(x,tid),f_i) \\ \wedge\mathsf{iterator} \in O(s(x_i,tid))) \end{array} \right. \\ \wedge(\forall_{\rho',\rho''}.\, \rho'.\rho'' = \rho \implies \mathsf{iterator}\,tid \in O(h^*(rt,\rho'))) \\ \wedge h^*(rt,\rho) = s(x,tid) \wedge (l = tid \wedge s(x,\_) \notin dom(F))) \end{array} \right\} \\
[\![x : \mathsf{rcultr}]\!]_{tid} & = & \left\{ m \in \mathcal{M} \middle| \begin{array}{l} (\mathsf{iterator}\,tid \in O(s(x,tid))) \wedge (x \notin U) \wedge \\ (tid \in B) \implies \left\{ \begin{array}{l} (\exists_{T' \subseteq B}.\, \{s(x,tid) \mapsto T'\} \cap F \neq \emptyset) \wedge \\ \wedge(tid \in T') \end{array} \right. \end{array} \right\} \\
[\![x : \mathsf{unlinked}]\!]_{tid} & = & \left\{ m \in \mathcal{M} \middle| \begin{array}{l} (\mathsf{unlinked} \in O(.s(x,tid)) \wedge l = tid \wedge x \notin U) \wedge \\ (\exists_{T' \subseteq T}.\, s(x,tid) \mapsto T' \in F \implies T' \subseteq B \wedge tid \notin T') \end{array} \right\} \\
[\![x : \mathsf{freeable}]\!]_{tid} & = & \left\{ m \in \mathcal{M} \middle| \begin{array}{l} \mathsf{freeable} \in O(s(x,tid)) \wedge l = tid \wedge x \notin U \wedge \\ s(x,tid) \mapsto \{\emptyset\} \in F \end{array} \right\} \\
[\![x : \mathsf{rcuFresh}\,\mathcal{N}]\!]_{tid} & = & \left\{ m \in \mathcal{M} \middle| \begin{array}{l} (\mathsf{fresh} \in O(s(x,tid)) \wedge x \notin U \wedge s(x,tid) \notin dom(F)) \\ (\forall_{f_i \in dom(\mathcal{N}), x_i \in codom(\mathcal{N})}.\, s(x_i,tid) = h(s(x,tid),f_i) \\ \wedge\mathsf{iterator}\,tid \in O(s(x_i,tid)) \wedge s(x_i,tid) \notin dom(F)) \end{array} \right\} \\
[\![x : \mathsf{undef}]\!]_{tid} & = & \left\{ m \in \mathcal{M} \middle| (x,tid) \in U \wedge s(x,tid) \notin dom(F) \right\} \\
[\![x : \mathsf{rcuRoot}]\!]_{tid} & = & \left\{ m \in \mathcal{M} \middle| \begin{array}{l} ((rt \notin U \wedge s(x,tid) = rt \wedge rt \in dom(h) \wedge \\ O(rt) \in \mathsf{root} \wedge s(x,tid) \notin dom(F)) \end{array} \right\}
\end{array}
$$

$$\text{provided } h^* : (\mathsf{Loc} \times \mathsf{Path}) \rightharpoonup \mathsf{Val}$$

Fig. 9. Type environments

Invariants on Safe Traversal Against Inserting/Replacing. A writer replacing an existing node with a fresh one or inserting a single fresh node assumes the fresh (before insertion) node is unreachable to readers before it is published/linked. The Fresh-Writes invariant asserts that a fresh heap location can only be allocated and referenced by the writer thread. The relation between a freshly allocated heap and the rest of the heap is established by the Fresh-Reachable invariant, which requires that there exists no heap node pointing to the freshly allocated one. This invariant supports the preservation of the tree structure. The Fresh-Not-Reader invariant supports the safe traversal of the reader threads via asserting that they cannot observe a heap location as fresh. Moreover, the denotation of the rcuFresh type, $[\![\mathsf{rcuFresh}\,\mathcal{N}]\!]_{tid}$, enforces that fields in $\mathcal{N}$ point to valid heap locations (observed as iterator by the writer thread).

Invariants on Tree Structure. Our invariants enforce the *tree* structure heap layouts for data structures. The Unique-Reachable invariant asserts that every heap location reachable from root can only be reached with following an unique path. To preserve the tree structure, Unique-Root enforces unreachability of the root from any heap location that is reachable from root itself.

Type Environments. Assertions in the Views logic are (almost) sets of the logical states that satisfy a validity predicate WellFormed, outlined above:

$$\mathcal{M} \stackrel{def}{=} \{m \in (\mathsf{MState} \times O \times U \times T \times F) \mid \mathsf{WellFormed}(m)\}$$

Every type environment represents a set of possible views (WellFormed logical states) consistent with the types in the environment. We make this precise with a denotation function

$$[\![-]\!]_{\_} : \mathsf{TypeEnv} \to \mathsf{TID} \to \mathcal{P}(\mathcal{M})$$

$$\bullet \stackrel{\text{def}}{=} (\bullet_\sigma, \bullet_O, \cup, \cup) \quad (F_1 \bullet_F F_2) \stackrel{\text{def}}{=} F_1 \cup F_2 \text{ when } dom(F_1) \cap dom(F_2) = \emptyset$$

$$O_1 \bullet_O O_2(loc) \stackrel{\text{def}}{=} O_1(loc) \cup O_2(loc) \quad (s_1 \bullet_s s_2) \stackrel{\text{def}}{=} s_1 \cup s_2 \text{ when } dom(s_1) \cap dom(s_2) = \emptyset$$

$$(h_1 \bullet_h h_2)(o, f) \stackrel{\text{def}}{=} \begin{cases} \text{undef if } h_1(o,f) = v \wedge h_2(o,f) = v' \wedge v' \neq v \\ v \quad \text{if } h_1(o,f) = v \wedge h_2(o,f) = v \\ v \quad \text{if } h_1(o,f) = \text{undef} \wedge h_2(o,f) = v \\ v \quad \text{if } h_1(o,f) = v \wedge h_2(o,f) = \text{undef} \\ \text{undef if } h_1(o,f) = \text{undef} \wedge h_2(o,f) = \text{undef} \end{cases}$$

$$((s,h,l,rt,R,B),O,U,T,F)\mathcal{R}_0((s',h',l',rt',R',B'),O',U',T',F') \stackrel{\text{def}}{=}$$
$$\bigwedge \left\{ \begin{array}{l} l \in T \to (h = h' \wedge l = l') \\ l \in T \to F = F' \\ \forall tid, o.\ \mathsf{iterator}\ tid \in O(o) \to o \in dom(h) \\ \forall tid, o.\ \mathsf{iterator}\ tid \in O(o) \to o \in dom(h') \\ \forall tid, o.\ \mathsf{root}\ tid \in O(o) \to o \in dom(h) \\ \forall tid, o.\ \mathsf{root}\ tid \in O(o) \to o \in dom(h') \\ O = O' \wedge U = U' \wedge T = T' \wedge R = R' \wedge rt = rt' \\ \forall x, t \in T.\ s(x,t) = s'(x,t) \end{array} \right\}$$

Fig. 10. Composition ($\bullet$) and Thread Interference Relation ($\mathcal{R}_0$)

that yields the set of states corresponding to a given type environment. This is defined as the intersection of individual variables' types as in Fig. 9.

Individual variables' denotations are extended to context denotations slightly differently depending on whether the environment is a reader or writer thread context: writer threads own the global lock, while readers do not:

- For read-side as $[\![x_1 : T_1, \ldots x_n : T_n]\!]_{tid,\mathsf{R}} = [\![x_1 : T_1]\!]_{tid} \cap \ldots \cap [\![x_n : T_n]\!]_{tid} \cap [\![\mathsf{R}]\!]_{tid}$ where $[\![\mathsf{R}]\!]_{tid} = \{(s,h,l,rt,R,B),O,U,T,F \mid tid \in R\}$
- For write-side as $[\![x_1 : T_1, \ldots x_n : T_n]\!]_{tid,\mathsf{M}} = [\![x_1 : T_1]\!]_{tid} \cap \ldots \cap [\![x_n : T_n]\!]_{tid} \cap [\![\mathsf{M}]\!]_{tid}$ where $[\![\mathsf{M}]\!]_{tid} = \{(s,h,l,rt,R,B),O,U,T,F \mid tid = l\}$

Composition and Interference. To support framing (weakening), the Views Framework requires that views form a partial commutative monoid under an operation $\bullet : \mathcal{M} \longrightarrow \mathcal{M} \longrightarrow \mathcal{M}$, provided as a parameter to the framework. The framework also requires an interference relation $\mathcal{R} \subseteq \mathcal{M} \times \mathcal{M}$ between views to reason about local updates to one view preserving validity of adjacent views (akin to the small-footprint property of separation logic). Figure 10 defines our composition operator and the core interference relation $\mathcal{R}_0$—the actual interference between views (between threads, or between a local action and framed-away state) is the reflexive transitive closure of $\mathcal{R}_0$. Composition is mostly straightforward point-wise union (threads' views may overlap) of each component. Interference bounds the interference writers and readers may inflict on each other. Notably, if a view contains the writer thread, other threads may not modify the shared portion of the heap, or release the writer lock. Other aspects of interference are natural restrictions like that threads may not modify each others' local variables. WellFormed states are closed under both composition (with another WellFormed state) and interference ($\mathcal{R}$ relates WellFormed states only to other WellFormed states).

$$\downarrow \mathsf{if}\ (x.f == y)\ C_1\ C_2 \downarrow tid \stackrel{\text{def}}{=} z = x.f; ((\mathsf{assume}(z = y); C_1) + (\mathsf{assume}(z \neq y); C_2))$$

$$[\![\mathsf{assume}(\mathcal{S})]\!](s) \stackrel{\text{def}}{=} \begin{cases} \{s\} & \text{if } s \in \mathcal{S} \\ \emptyset & \text{Otherwise} \end{cases} \quad \downarrow \mathsf{while}\ (e)\ C \downarrow \stackrel{\text{def}}{=} (\mathsf{assume}(e); C)^*; (\mathsf{assume}(\neg e));$$

$$\frac{\{P\} \cap \{\lceil \mathcal{S} \rceil\} \sqsubseteq \{Q\}}{\{P\}\mathsf{assume}\,(\mathcal{S})\,\{Q\}} \quad \text{where } \lceil \mathcal{S} \rceil = \{m \mid \lfloor m \rfloor \cap \mathcal{S} \neq \emptyset\}$$

Fig. 11. Encoding branch conditions with assume(b)

Stable Environment and Views Shift. The framing/weakening type rule will be translated to a use of the frame rule in the Views Framework's logic. There separating conjunction is simply the existence of two composable instrumented states:

$$m \in P * Q \stackrel{def}{=} \exists m'. \exists m''. m' \in P \wedge m'' \in Q \wedge m \in m' \bullet m''$$

In order to validate the frame rule in the Views Framework's logic, the assertions in its logic—sets of well-formed instrumented states—must be restricted to sets of logical states that are *stable* with respect to expected interference from other threads or contexts, and interference must be compatible in some way with separating conjunction. Thus a View—the actual base assertions in the Views logic—are then:

$$\mathsf{View}_{\mathcal{M}} \stackrel{def}{=} \{M \in \mathcal{P}(\mathcal{M}) | \mathcal{R}(M) \subseteq M\}$$

Additionally, interference must distribute over composition:

$$\forall m_1, m_2, m. (m_1 \bullet m_2)\mathcal{R}m \implies \exists m_1' m_2'. m_1 \mathcal{R} m_1' \wedge m_2 \mathcal{R} m_2' \wedge m \in m_1' \bullet m_2'$$

Because we use this induced Views logic to prove soundness of our type system by translation, we must ensure any type environment denotes a valid view:

Lemma 1 (Stable Environment Denotation-M). *For any* closed *environment Γ (i.e., $\forall x \in \mathsf{dom}(\Gamma).,\mathsf{FV}(\Gamma(x)) \subseteq \mathsf{dom}(\Gamma)$): $\mathcal{R}([\![\Gamma]\!]_{\mathsf{M},tid}) \subseteq [\![\Gamma]\!]_{\mathsf{M},tid}$. Alternatively, we say that environment denotation is* stable *(closed under $\mathcal{R}$).*

Proof. In Appendix A.1 Lemma 7 of the technical report [20].

We elide the statement of the analogous result for the read-side critical section, available in Appendix A.1 of the technical report.

With this setup done, we can state the connection between the Views Framework logic induced by earlier parameters, and the type system from Sect. 4. The induced Views logic has a familiar notion of Hoare triple—$\{p\}C\{q\}$ where p and q are elements of $\mathsf{View}_{\mathcal{M}}$—with the usual rules for non-deterministic choice, non-deterministic iteration, sequential composition, and parallel composition, sound given the proof obligations just described above. It is parameterized by a rule for atomic commands that requires a specification of the triples for primitive operations, and their soundness (an obligation we must prove). This can then be used to prove that every typing derivation embeds to a valid derivation in the

Views Logic, roughly $\forall \Gamma, C, \Gamma', tid.\, \Gamma \vdash C \dashv \Gamma' \Rightarrow \{[\![\Gamma]\!]_{tid}\}[\![C]\!]_{tid}\{[\![\Gamma']\!]_{tid}\}$ once for the writer type system, once for the readers.

There are two remaining subtleties to address. First, commands C also require translation: the Views Framework has only non-deterministic branches and loops, so the standard versions from our core language must be encoded. The approach to this is based on a standard idea in verification, which we show here for conditionals as shown in Fig. 11. $\mathsf{assume}(b)$ is a standard idea in verification semantics [4,30], which "does nothing" (freezes) if the condition b is false, so its postcondition in the Views logic can reflect the truth of b. assume in Fig. 11 adapts this for the Views Framework as in other Views-based proofs [13,14], specifying sets of machine states as a predicate. We write boolean expressions as shorthand for the set of machine states making that expression true. With this setup done, the top-level soundness claim then requires proving – once for the reader type system, once for the writer type system – that every valid source typing derivation corresponds to a valid derivation in the Views logic: $\forall \Gamma, C, \Gamma', \Gamma \vdash_M C \dashv \Gamma' \Rightarrow \{[\![\Gamma]\!]\} \downarrow C \downarrow \{[\![\Gamma']\!]\}$.

Second, we have not addressed a way to encode subtyping. One might hope this corresponds to a kind of implication, and therefore subtyping corresponds to consequence. Indeed, this is how we (and prior work [13,14]) address subtyping in a Views-based proof. Views defines the notion of *view shift*[2] ($\sqsubseteq$) as a way to reinterpret a set of instrumented states as a new (compatible) set of instrumented states, offering a kind of logical consequence, used in a rule of consequence in the Views logic:

$$p \sqsubseteq q \stackrel{def}{=} \forall m \in \mathcal{M}.\, \lfloor p * \{m\} \rfloor \subseteq \lfloor q * \mathcal{R}(\{m\}) \rfloor$$

We are now finally ready to prove the key lemmas of the soundness proof, relating subtying to view shifts, proving soundness of the primitive actions, and finally for the full type system. These proofs occur once for the writer type system, and once for the reader; we show here only the (more complex) writer obligations:

Lemma 2 (Axiom of Soundness for Atomic Commands). *For each axiom,* $\Gamma_1 \vdash_M \alpha \dashv \Gamma_2$, *we show* $\forall m.\, [\![\alpha]\!](\lfloor [\![\Gamma_1]\!]_{tid} * \{m\} \rfloor) \subseteq \lfloor [\![\Gamma_2]\!]_{tid} * \mathcal{R}(\{m\}) \rfloor$

Proof. By case analysis on α. Details in Appendix A.1 of the technical report [20].

Lemma 3 (Context-SubTyping-M). $\Gamma \prec: \Gamma' \implies [\![\Gamma]\!]_{M,tid} \sqsubseteq [\![\Gamma']\!]_{M,tid}$

Proof. Induction on the subtyping derivation, then inducting on the single-type subtype relation for the first variable in the non-empty context case.

Lemma 4 (Views Embedding for Write-Side).

$$\forall \Gamma, C, \Gamma', t.\, \Gamma \vdash_M C \dashv \Gamma' \Rightarrow [\![\Gamma]\!]_t \cap [\![M]\!]_t \vdash [\![C]\!]_t \dashv [\![\Gamma']\!]_t \cap [\![M]\!]_t$$

[2] This is the same notion present in later program logics like Iris [18], though more recent variants are more powerful.

Proof. By induction on the typing derivation, appealing to Lemma 2 for primitives, Lemma 3 and consequence for subtyping, and otherwise appealing to structural rules of the Views logic and inductive hypotheses. Full details in Appendix A.1 of the technical report [20].

The corresponding obligations and proofs for the read-side critical section type system are similar in statement and proof approach, just for the read-side type judgments and environment denotations.

7 Discussion and Related Work

Our type system builds on a great deal of related work on RCU implementations and models; and general concurrent program verification. Due to space limit, this section captures only discussions on program logics, modeling RCU and memory models, but our technical report [20] includes detailed discussions on model-checking [8,17,21], language oriented approaches [6,16,16] and realization of our semantics in an implementation as well.

Modeling RCU and Memory Models. Alglave et al. [2] propose a memory model to be assumed by the platform-independent parts of the Linux kernel, regardless of the underlying hardware's memory model. As part of this, they give the first formalization of what it means for an RCU implementation to be correct (previously this was difficult to state, as the guarantees in principle could vary by underlying CPU architecture). Essentially, reader critical sections must not span grace periods. They prove by hand that the Linux kernel RCU implementation [1] satisfies this property. McKenney has defined fundamental requirements of RCU implementations [26]; our model in Sect. 3 is a valid RCU implementation according to those requirements (assuming sequential consistency) aside from one performance optimization, *Read-to-Write Upgrade*, which is important in practice but not memory-safety centric – see the technical report [20] for detailed discussion on satisfying RCU requirements. To the best of our knowledge, ours is the first abstract *operational* model for a Linux kernel-style RCU implementation – others are implementation-specific [22] or axiomatic like Alglave et al.'s.

Tassarotti et al. model a well-known way of implementing RCU synchronization without hurting readers' performance—Quiescent State Based Reclamation (QSBR) [8]—where synchronization between the writer thread and reader threads occurs via per-thread counters. Tassarotti et al. [32] uses a protocol based program logic based on separation and ghost variables called GPS [34] to verify a user-level implementation of RCU with a singly linked list client under *release-acquire* semantics, which is a weaker memory model than sequential-consistency. Despite the weaker model, the protocol that they enforce on their RCU primitives is nearly the same what our type system requires. The reads and writes to per thread QSBR structures are similar to our more abstract updates to reader and bounding sets. Therefore, we anticipate it would be possible to extend our type system in the future for similar weak memory models.

Program Logics. Fu et al. [12] extend Rely-Guarantee and Separation-Logic [10,11,35] with the *past-tense* temporal operator to eliminate the need for using a history variable and lift the standard separation conjunction to assert over on execution histories. Gotsman et al. [15] take assertions from temporal logic to separation logic [35] to capture the essence of epoch-based memory reclamation algorithms and have a simpler proof than what Fu et al. have [12] for Michael's non-blocking stack [29] implementation under a sequentially consistent memory model.

Tassarotti et al. [32] use *abstract-predicates* – e.g. WriterSafe – that are specialized to the singly-linked structure in their evaluation. This means reusing their ideas for another structure, such as a binary search tree, would require revising many of their invariants. By contrast, our types carry similar information (our denotations are similar to their definitions), but are reusable across at least singly-linked and tree data structures (Sect. 5). Their proofs of a linked list also require managing assertions about RCU implementation resources, while these are effectively hidden in the type denotations in our system. On the other hand, their proofs ensure full functional correctness. Meyer and Wolff [28] make a compelling argument that separating memory safety from correctness if profitable, and we provide such a decoupled memory safety argument.

8 Conclusions

We presented the first type system that ensures code uses RCU memory management safely, and which is significantly simpler than full-blown verification logics. To this end, we gave the first general operational model for RCU-based memory management. Based on our suitable abstractions for RCU in the operational semantics we are the first showing that decoupling the *memory-safety* proofs of RCU clients from the underlying reclamation model is possible. Meyer et al. [28] took similar approach for decoupling the *correctness* verification of the data structures from the underlying reclamation model under the assumption of the *memory-safety* for the data structures. We demonstrated the applicability/reusability of our types on two examples: a linked-list based bag [25] and a binary search tree [3]. To our best knowledge, we are the first presenting the *memory-safety* proof for a tree client of RCU. We managed to prove type soundness by embedding the type system into an abstract concurrent separation logic called the Views Framework [9] and encode many RCU properties as either type-denotations or global invariants over abstract RCU state. By doing this, we managed to discharge these invariants once as a part of soundness proof and did not need to prove them for each different client.

Acknowledgements. We are grateful to Matthew Parkinson for guidance and productive discussions on the early phase of this project. We also thank to Nik Sultana and Klaus V. Gleissenthall for their helpful comments and suggestions for improving the paper.

References

1. Alglave, J., Kroening, D., Tautschnig, M.: Partial orders for efficient bounded model checking of concurrent software. In: Sharygina, N., Veith, H. (eds.) CAV 2013. LNCS, vol. 8044, pp. 141–157. Springer, Heidelberg (2013). https://doi.org/10.1007/978-3-642-39799-8_9
2. Alglave, J., Maranget, L., McKenney, P.E., Parri, A., Stern, A.: Frightening small children and disconcerting grown-ups: concurrency in the Linux kernel. In: Proceedings of the Twenty-Third International Conference on Architectural Support for Programming Languages and Operating Systems, ASPLOS 2018, pp. 405–418. ACM, New York (2018). https://doi.org/10.1145/3173162.3177156. http://doi.acm.org/10.1145/3173162.3177156
3. Arbel, M., Attiya, H.: Concurrent updates with RCU: search tree as an example. In: Proceedings of the 2014 ACM Symposium on Principles of Distributed Computing, PODC 2014, pp. 196–205. ACM, New York (2014). https://doi.org/10.1145/2611462.2611471. http://doi.acm.org/10.1145/2611462.2611471
4. Barnett, M., Chang, B.-Y.E., DeLine, R., Jacobs, B., Leino, K.R.M.: Boogie: a modular reusable verifier for object-oriented programs. In: de Boer, F.S., Bonsangue, M.M., Graf, S., de Roever, W.-P. (eds.) FMCO 2005. LNCS, vol. 4111, pp. 364–387. Springer, Heidelberg (2006). https://doi.org/10.1007/11804192_17
5. Clements, A.T., Kaashoek, M.F., Zeldovich, N.: Scalable address spaces using RCU balanced trees. In: Proceedings of the 17th International Conference on Architectural Support for Programming Languages and Operating Systems, ASPLOS 2012, London, UK, 3–7 March 2012, pp. 199–210 (2012). https://doi.org/10.1145/2150976.2150998. http://doi.acm.org/10.1145/2150976.2150998
6. Cooper, T., Walpole, J.: Relativistic programming in Haskell using types to enforce a critical section discipline (2015). http://web.cecs.pdx.edu/~walpole/papers/haskell2015.pdf
7. Desnoyers, M., McKenney, P.E., Dagenais, M.R.: Multi-core systems modeling forformal verification of parallel algorithms. SIGOPS Oper. Syst. Rev. **47**(2), 51–65 (2013). https://doi.org/10.1145/2506164.2506174. http://doi.acm.org/10.1145/2506164.2506174
8. Desnoyers, M., McKenney, P.E., Stern, A., Walpole, J.: User-level implementations of read-copy update. IEEE Trans. Parallel Distrib. Syst. (2009). /static/publications/desnoyers-ieee-urcu-submitted.pdf
9. Dinsdale-Young, T., Birkedal, L., Gardner, P., Parkinson, M.J., Yang, H.: Views: compositional reasoning for concurrent programs. In: The 40th Annual ACM SIGPLAN-SIGACT Symposium on Principles of Programming Languages, POPL 2013, Rome, Italy, 23–25 January, 2013, pp. 287–300 (2013). https://doi.org/10.1145/2429069.2429104. http://doi.acm.org/10.1145/2429069.2429104
10. Feng, X.: Local rely-guarantee reasoning. In: Proceedings of the 36th Annual ACM SIGPLAN-SIGACT Symposium on Principles of Programming Languages, POPL 2009, pp. 315–327. ACM, New York (2009). https://doi.org/10.1145/1480881.1480922. http://doi.acm.org/10.1145/1480881.1480922
11. Feng, X., Ferreira, R., Shao, Z.: On the relationship between concurrent separation logic and assume-guarantee reasoning. In: De Nicola, R. (ed.) ESOP 2007. LNCS, vol. 4421, pp. 173–188. Springer, Heidelberg (2007). https://doi.org/10.1007/978-3-540-71316-6_13

12. Fu, M., Li, Y., Feng, X., Shao, Z., Zhang, Y.: Reasoning about optimistic concurrency using a program logic for history. In: Gastin, P., Laroussinie, F. (eds.) CONCUR 2010. LNCS, vol. 6269, pp. 388–402. Springer, Heidelberg (2010). https://doi.org/10.1007/978-3-642-15375-4_27
13. Gordon, C.S., Ernst, M.D., Grossman, D., Parkinson, M.J.: Verifying invariants of lock-free data structures with rely-guarantee and refinement types. ACM Trans. Program. Lang. Syst. (TOPLAS) **39**(3) (2017). https://doi.org/10.1145/3064850. http://doi.acm.org/10.1145/3064850
14. Gordon, C.S., Parkinson, M.J., Parsons, J., Bromfield, A., Duffy, J.: Uniqueness and reference immutability for safe parallelism. In: Proceedings of the 2012 ACM International Conference on Object Oriented Programming, Systems, Languages, and Applications (OOPSLA 2012), Tucson, AZ, USA, October 2012. https://doi.org/10.1145/2384616.2384619. http://dl.acm.org/citation.cfm?id=2384619
15. Gotsman, A., Rinetzky, N., Yang, H.: Verifying concurrent memory reclamation algorithms with grace. In: Felleisen, M., Gardner, P. (eds.) ESOP 2013. LNCS, vol. 7792, pp. 249–269. Springer, Heidelberg (2013). https://doi.org/10.1007/978-3-642-37036-6_15
16. Howard, P.W., Walpole, J.: A relativistic enhancement to software transactional memory. In: Proceedings of the 3rd USENIX Conference on Hot Topic in Parallelism, HotPar 2011, p. 15. USENIX Association, Berkeley (2011). http://dl.acm.org/citation.cfm?id=2001252.2001267
17. Kokologiannakis, M., Sagonas, K.: Stateless model checking of the Linux kernel's hierarchical read-copy-update (tree RCU). In: Proceedings of the 24th ACM SIGSOFT International SPIN Symposium on Model Checking of Software, SPIN 2017, pp. 172–181. ACM, New York (2017). https://doi.org/10.1145/3092282.3092287. http://doi.acm.org/10.1145/3092282.3092287
18. Krebbers, R., Jung, R., Bizjak, A., Jourdan, J.-H., Dreyer, D., Birkedal, L.: The essence of higher-order concurrent separation logic. In: Yang, H. (ed.) ESOP 2017. LNCS, vol. 10201, pp. 696–723. Springer, Heidelberg (2017). https://doi.org/10.1007/978-3-662-54434-1_26
19. Kung, H.T., Lehman, P.L.: Concurrent manipulation of binary search trees. ACMTrans. Database Syst. **5**(3), 354–382 (1980). https://doi.org/10.1145/320613.320619. http://doi.acm.org/10.1145/320613.320619
20. Kuru, I., Gordon, C.S.: Safe deferred memory reclamation with types. CoRR **abs/1811.11853** (2018). http://arxiv.org/abs/1811.11853
21. Liang, L., McKenney, P.E., Kroening, D., Melham, T.: Verification of the tree-based hierarchical read-copy update in the Linux kernel. CoRR **abs/1610.03052** (2016). http://arxiv.org/abs/1610.03052
22. Mandrykin, M.U., Khoroshilov, A.V.: Towards deductive verification of C programs with shared data. Program. Comput. Softw. **42**(5), 324–332 (2016). https://doi.org/10.1134/S0361768816050054
23. Mckenney, P.E.: Exploiting deferred destruction: an analysis of read-copy-update techniques in operating system kernels. Ph.D. thesis, Oregon Health & Science University (2004). aAI3139819
24. McKenney, P.E.: N4037: non-transactional implementation of atomic tree move, May 2014. http://www.open-std.org/jtc1/sc22/wg21/docs/papers/2014/n4037.pdf
25. McKenney, P.E.: Some examples of kernel-hacker informal correctness reasoning. Technical report paulmck.2015.06.17a (2015). http://www2.rdrop.com/users/paulmck/techreports/IntroRCU.2015.06.17a.pdf

26. Mckenney, P.E.: A tour through RCU's requirements (2017). https://www.kernel.org/doc/Documentation/RCU/Design/Requirements/Requirements.html
27. Mckenney, P.E., et al.: Read-copy update. In: Ottawa Linux Symposium, pp. 338–367 (2001)
28. Meyer, R., Wolff, S.: Decoupling lock-free data structures from memory reclamation for static analysis. PACMPL **3**(POPL), 58:1–58:31 (2019). https://dl.acm.org/citation.cfm?id=3290371
29. Michael, M.M.: Hazard pointers: safe memory reclamation for lock-free objects. IEEE Trans. Parallel Distrib. Syst. **15**(6), 491–504 (2004). https://doi.org/10.1109/TPDS.2004.8
30. Müller, P., Schwerhoff, M., Summers, A.J.: Viper: a verification infrastructure for permission-based reasoning. In: Jobstmann, B., Leino, K.R.M. (eds.) VMCAI 2016. LNCS, vol. 9583, pp. 41–62. Springer, Heidelberg (2016). https://doi.org/10.1007/978-3-662-49122-5_2
31. McKenney, P.E., Mathieu Desnoyers, L.J., Triplett, J.: The RCU-barrier menagerie, November 2016. https://lwn.net/Articles/573497/
32. Tassarotti, J., Dreyer, D., Vafeiadis, V.: Verifying read-copy-update in a logic for weak memory. In: Proceedings of the 36th ACM SIGPLAN Conference on Programming Language Design and Implementation, PLDI 2015, pp. 110–120. ACM, New York (2015). https://doi.org/10.1145/2737924.2737992. http://doi.acm.org/10.1145/2737924.2737992
33. Triplett, J., McKenney, P.E., Walpole, J.: Resizable, scalable, concurrent hash tables via relativistic programming. In: Proceedings of the 2011 USENIX Conference on USENIX Annual Technical Conference, USENIXATC 2011, p. 11. USENIX Association, Berkeley (2011). http://dl.acm.org/citation.cfm?id=2002181.2002192
34. Turon, A., Vafeiadis, V., Dreyer, D.: Gps: Navigating weak memory with ghosts, protocols, and separation. In: Proceedings of the 2014 ACM International Conference on Object Oriented Programming Systems Languages and Applications, OOPSLA 2014, pp. 691–707. ACM, New York (2014). https://doi.org/10.1145/2660193.2660243. http://doi.acm.org/10.1145/2660193.2660243
35. Vafeiadis, V., Parkinson, M.: A marriage of rely/guarantee and separation logic. In: Caires, L., Vasconcelos, V.T. (eds.) CONCUR 2007. LNCS, vol. 4703, pp. 256–271. Springer, Heidelberg (2007). https://doi.org/10.1007/978-3-540-74407-8_18

Language Design

Codata in Action

Paul Downen[1], Zachary Sullivan[1(✉)], Zena M. Ariola[1], and Simon Peyton Jones[2]

[1] University of Oregon, Eugene, USA
{pdownen,zsulliva,ariola}@cs.uoregon.edu
[2] Microsoft Research, Cambridge, UK
simonpj@microsoft.com

Abstract. Computer scientists are well-versed in dealing with data structures. The same cannot be said about their dual: codata. Even though codata is pervasive in category theory, universal algebra, and logic, the use of codata for programming has been mainly relegated to representing infinite objects and processes. Our goal is to demonstrate the benefits of codata as a general-purpose programming abstraction independent of any specific language: eager or lazy, statically or dynamically typed, and functional or object-oriented. While codata is not featured in many programming languages today, we show how codata can be easily adopted and implemented by offering simple inter-compilation techniques between data and codata. We believe codata is a common ground between the functional and object-oriented paradigms; ultimately, we hope to utilize the Curry-Howard isomorphism to further bridge the gap.

Keywords: Codata · Lambda-calculi · Encodings · Curry-Howard · Function programming · Object-oriented programming

1 Introduction

Functional programming enjoys a beautiful connection to logic, known as the Curry-Howard correspondence, or proofs as programs principle [22]; results and notions about a language are translated to those about proofs, and vice-versa [17]. In addition to expressing computation as proof transformations, this connection is also fruitful for education: everybody would understand that the assumption "an x is zero" does not mean "every x is zero," which in turn explains the subtle typing rules for polymorphism in programs. The typing rules for modules are even more cryptic, but knowing that they correspond exactly to the rules for existential quantification certainly gives us more confidence that they are correct! While not everything useful must have a Curry-Howard correspondence, we believe finding these delightful coincidences where the same idea is rediscovered many times in both logic and programming can only be beneficial [42].

P. Downen and Z. M. Ariola—This work is supported by the National Science Foundation under grants CCF-1423617 and CCF-1719158.

L. Caires (Ed.): ESOP 2019, LNCS 11423, pp. 119–146, 2019.
https://doi.org/10.1007/978-3-030-17184-1_5

One such instance involves *codata*. In contrast with the mystique it has as a programming construct, codata is pervasive in mathematics and logic, where it arises through the lens of duality. The most visual way to view the duality is in the categorical diagrams of sums versus products—the defining arrows go *into* a sum and come *out of* a product—and in algebras versus coalgebras [25]. In proof theory, codata has had an impact on theorem proving [5] and on the foundation of computation via *polarity* [29,45]. Polarity recognizes which of two dialogic actors speaks first: the proponent (who seeks to verify or prove a fact) or the opponent (who seeks to refute the fact).

The two-sided, interactive view appears all over the study of programming languages, where data is concerned about how values are constructed and codata is concerned about how they are used [15]. Sometimes, this perspective is readily apparent, like with session types [7] which distinguish internal choice (a provider's decision) versus external choice (a client's decision). But other occurrences are more obscure, like in the semantics of PCF (*i.e.* the call-by-name λ-calculus with numbers and general recursion). In PCF, the result of evaluating a program must be of a ground type in order to respect the laws of functions (namely η) [32]. This is not due to differences between ground types versus "higher types," but to the fact that data types are *directly observable*, whereas codata types are only *indirectly observable* via their interface.

Clearly codata has merit in theoretical pursuits; we think it has merit in practical ones as well. The main application of codata so far has been for representing infinite objects and coinductive proofs in proof assistants [1,39]. However, we believe that codata also makes for an important general-purpose programming feature. Codata is a bridge between the functional and object-oriented paradigms; a common denominator between the two very different approaches to programming. On one hand, functional languages are typically rich in data types—as many as the programmer wants to define via `data` declarations—but has a paucity of codata types (usually just function types). On the other hand, object-oriented languages are rich in codata types—programmer-defined in terms of classes or interfaces—but a paucity of data types (usually just primitives like booleans and numbers). We illustrate this point with a collection of example applications that arise in both styles of programming, including common encodings, demand-driven programming, abstraction, and Hoare-style reasoning.

While codata types can be seen in the shadows behind many examples of programming—often hand-compiled away by the programmer—not many functional languages have native support for them. To this end, we demonstrate a pair of simple compilation techniques between a typical core functional language (with data types) and one with codata. One direction—based on the well-known visitor pattern from object-oriented programming—simultaneously shows how to extend an object-oriented language with data types (as is done by Scala) and how to compile core functional programs to a more object-oriented setting (*e.g.* targeting a backend like JavaScript or the JVM). The other shows how to add native codata types to functional languages by reducing them to commonly-supported data types and how to compile a "pure" object-oriented style of programming to a functional setting. Both of these techniques are macro-expansions that are not specific to any particular language, as they work with both statically and dynamically typed disciplines, and they preserve the well-typed status of programs without increasing the complexity of the types involved.

Our claim is that codata is a universal programming feature that has been thus-far missing or diminished in today's functional programming languages. This is too bad, since codata is not just a feature invented for the convenience of programmers, but a persistent idea that has sprung up over and over from the study of mathematics, logic, and computation. We aim to demystify codata, and en route, bridge the wide gulf between the functional and object-oriented paradigms. Fortunately, it is easy for most mainstream languages to add or bring out codata today without a radical change to their implementation. But ultimately, we believe that the languages of the future should incorporate *both* data and codata outright. To that end, our contributions are to:

- (Section 2) Illustrate the benefits of codata in both theory and practice: (1) a decomposition of well-known λ-calculus encodings by inverting the priority of construction and destruction; (2) a first-class abstraction mechanism; (3) a method of demand-driven programming; and (4) a static type system for representing Hoare-style invariants on resource use.
- (Section 3) Provide simple transformations for compiling data to codata, and vice-versa, which are appropriate for languages with different evaluation strategies (eager or lazy) and type discipline (static or dynamic).
- (Section 4) Demonstrate various implementations of codata for general-purpose programming in two ways: (1) an extension of Haskell with codata; and (2) a prototype language that compiles to several languages of different evaluation strategies, type disciplines, and paradigms.

2 The Many Faces of Codata

Codata can be used to solve other problems in programming besides representing infinite objects and processes like streams and servers [1,39]. We start by presenting codata as a merger between theory and practice, whereby *encodings* of data types in an object-oriented style turn out to be a useful intermediate step in the usual encodings of data in the λ-calculus. *Demand-driven programming* is considered a virtue of lazy languages, but codata is a language-independent tool for capturing this programming idiom. Codata exactly captures the essence of *procedural abstraction*, as achieved with λ-abstractions and objects, with a logically founded formalism [16]. Specifying *pre- and post-conditions* of protocols, which is available in some object systems [14], is straightforward with indexed, recursive codata types, *i.e.* objects with guarded methods [40].

2.1 Church Encodings and Object-Oriented Programming

Crucial information structures, like booleans, numbers, and lists can be encoded in the untyped λ-calculus (*a.k.a.* Church encodings) or in the typed polymorphic

λ-calculus (*a.k.a.* Böhm-Berarducci [9] encodings). It is quite remarkable that data structures can be simulated with just first-class, higher-order functions. The downside is that these encodings can be obtuse at first blush, and have the effect of obscuring the original program when *everything* is written with just λs and application. For example, the λ-representation of the boolean value True, the first projection out of a pair, and the constant function K are all expressed as $\lambda x.\lambda y.x$, which is not that immediately evocative of its multi-purpose nature.

Object-oriented programmers have also been representing data structures in terms of objects. This is especially visible in the Smalltalk lineage of languages like Scala, wherein an objective is that everything that can be an object is. As it turns out, the object-oriented features needed to perform this representation technique are *exactly* those of codata. That is because Church-style encodings and object-oriented representations of data all involve *switching focus from the way values are built (i.e. introduced) to the way they are used (i.e. eliminated).*

Consider the representation of Boolean values as an algebraic data type. There may be many ways to use a `Boolean` value. However, it turns out that there is a *most-general* eliminator of `Booleans`: the expression `if b then x else y`. This basic construct can be used to define all the other uses for `Bools`. Instead of focusing on the constructors `True` and `False` let's then focus on this most-general form of `Bool` elimination; this is the essence of the encodings of booleans in terms of objects. In other words, booleans can be thought of as objects that implement a single method: `If`. So that the expression `if b then x else y` would instead be written as (`b.If x y`). We then define the true and false values in terms of their reaction to `If`:

```
true = {If x y → x}                false = {If x y → y}
```

Or alternatively, we can write the same definition using copatterns, popularized for use in the functional paradigm by Abel *et al.* [1] by generalizing the usual pattern-based definition of functions by multiple clauses, as:

```
true.If x y = x                    false.If x y = y
```

This works just like equational definitions by pattern-matching in functional languages: the expression to the left of the equals sign is the same as the expression to the right (for any binding of `x` and `y`). Either way, the net result is that (`true.If "yes" "no"`) is `"yes"`, whereas (`false.If "yes" "no"`) is `"no"`.

This covers the object-based presentation of booleans in a dynamically typed language, but how do static types come into play? In order to give a type description of the above boolean objects, we can use the following interface, analogous to a Java interface:

```
codata Bool where If : Bool → (forall a. a → a → a)
```

This declaration is dual to a data declaration in a functional language: data declarations define the types of constructors (which produce values of the data type) and codata declarations define the types of destructors (which consume values of the codata type) like `If`. The reason that the `If` observation introduces its own polymorphic type `a` is because an if-then-else might return any type of result (as long as both branches agree on the type). That way, both the two objects `true` and `false` above are values of the codata type `Bool`.

At this point, the representation of booleans as codata looks remarkably close to the encodings of booleans in the λ-calculus! Indeed, the only difference is that in the λ-calculus we "anonymize" booleans. Since they reply to only one request, that request name can be dropped. We then arrive at the familiar encodings in the polymorphic λ-calculus:

$$Bool = \forall a.a \to a \to a \qquad true = \Lambda a.\lambda x{:}a.\lambda y{:}a.x \qquad false = \Lambda a.\lambda x{:}a.\lambda y{:}a.y$$

In addition, the invocation of the `If` method just becomes ordinary function application; `b.If x y` of type a is written as $b\ a\ x\ y$. Otherwise, the definition and behavior of booleans as either codata types or as polymorphic functions are the same.

This style of inverting the definition of data types—either into specific codata types or into polymorphic functions—is also related to another concept in object-oriented programming. First, consider how a functional programmer would represent a binary `Tree` (with integer-labeled leaves) and a `walk` function that traverses a tree by converting the labels on all leaves and combining the results of sub-trees:

```
data Tree where Leaf   : Int → Tree
                Branch : Tree → Tree → Tree

walk : (Int → a) → (a → a → a) → Tree → a
walk b f (Leaf x)     = b x
walk b f (Branch l r) = f (walk b f l) (walk b f r)
```

The above code relies on pattern-matching on values of the `Tree` data type and higher-order functions `b` and `f` for accumulating the result. Now, how might an object-oriented programmer tackle the problem of traversing a tree-like structure? The *visitor pattern*! With this pattern, the programmer specifies a "visitor" object which contains knowledge of what to do at every node of the tree, and tree objects must be able to accept a visitor with a method that will recursively walk down each subcomponent of the tree. In a pure style—which returns an accumulated result directly instead of using mutable state as a side channel for results—the visitor pattern for a simple binary tree interface will look like:

```
codata TreeVisitor a where
  VisitLeaf   : TreeVisitor a → (Int → a)
  VisitBranch : TreeVisitor a → (a → a → a)

codata Tree where
  Walk : Tree → (forall a. TreeVisitor a → a)

leaf         : Int → Tree
leaf     x   = {Walk v → v.VisitLeaf x}

branch       : Tree → Tree → Tree
branch l r = {Walk v → v.VisitBranch (l.Walk v) (r.Walk v)}
```

And again, we can write this same code more elegantly, without the need to break apart the two arguments across the equal sign with a manual abstraction, using copatterns as:

```
(leaf      x).Walk v = v.VisitLeaf x
(branch l r).Walk v = v.VisitBranch (l.Walk v) (r.Walk v)
```

Notice how the above code is just an object-oriented presentation of the following encoding of binary trees into the polymorphic λ-calculus:

$$Tree = \forall a. TreeVisitor\ a \to a \qquad TreeVisitor\ a = (Int \to a) \times (a \to a \to a)$$

$$leaf : Int \to Tree$$

$$leaf\ (x{:}Int) = \Lambda a. \lambda v{:}TreeVisitor\ a.\ (fst\ v)\ x$$

$$branch : \forall a. Tree \to Tree \to Tree$$

$$branch\ (l{:}Tree)\ (r{:}Tree) = \Lambda a. \lambda v{:}TreeVisitor\ a.\ (snd\ v)\ (l\ a\ v)\ (r\ a\ v)$$

The only essential difference between this λ-encoding of trees versus the λ-encoding of booleans above is currying: the representation of the data type *Tree* takes a single product *TreeVisitor a* of the necessary arguments, whereas the data type *Bool* takes the two necessary arguments separately. Besides this easily-converted difference of currying, the usual Böhm-Berarducci encodings shown here correspond to a pure version of the visitor pattern.

2.2 Demand-Driven Programming

In "Why functional programming matters" [23], Hughes motivates the utility of practical functional programming through its excellence in compositionality. When designing programs, one of the goals is to decompose a large problem into several manageable sub-problems, solve each sub-problem in isolation, and then compose the individual parts together into a complete solution. Unfortunately, Hughes identifies some examples of programs which resist this kind of approach.

In particular, numeric algorithms—for computing square roots, derivatives integrals—rely on an infinite sequence of approximations which converge on the true answer only in the limit of the sequence. For these numeric algorithms, the decision on when a particular approximation in the sequence is "close enough" to the real answer lies solely in the eyes of the beholder: only the observer of the answer can say when to stop improving the approximation. As such, standard imperative implementations of these numeric algorithms are expressed as a single, complex loop, which interleaves both the concerns of producing better approximations with the termination decision on when to stop. Even more complex is the branching structure of the classic minimax algorithm from artificial intelligence for searching for reasonable moves in two-player games like chess, which can have an unreasonably large (if not infinite) search space. Here, too, there is difficulty separating generation from selection, and worse there is the intermediate step of pruning out uninteresting sub-trees of the search space (known as alpha-beta pruning). As a result, a standard imperative implementation of minimax is a single, recursive function that combines all the tasks—generation, pruning, estimation, and selection—at once.

Hughes shows how both instances of failed decomposition can be addressed in functional languages through the technique of *demand-driven programming*. In each case, the main obstacle is that the control of how to drive the next step of the algorithm—whether to continue or not—lies with the consumer. The producer of potential approximations and game states, in contrast, should only take over when demanded by the consumer. By giving primary control to the consumer, each of these problems can be decomposed into sensible sub-tasks, and recomposed back together. Hughes uses lazy evaluation, as found in languages like Miranda and Haskell, in order to implement the demand-driven algorithms. However, the downside of relying on lazy evaluation is that it is a whole-language decision: a language is either lazy by default, like Haskell, or not, like OCaml. When working in a strict language, expressing these demand-driven algorithms with manual laziness loses much of their original elegance [33].

In contrast, a language should directly support the capability of yielding control to the consumer independently of the language being strict or lazy; analogously to what happens with lambda abstractions. An abstraction computes on-demand, why is this property relegated to this predefined type only? In fact, the concept of *codata* also has this property. As such, it allows us to describe demand-driven programs in an agnostic way which works just as well in Haskell as in OCaml without any additional modification. For example, we can implement Hughes' demand-driven AI game in terms of codata instead of laziness. To represent the current game state, and all of its potential developments, we can use an arbitrarily-branching tree codata type.

```
codata Tree a where
  Node     : Tree a → a
  Children : Tree a → List (Tree a)
```

The task of generating all potential future boards from the current board state produces one of these tree objects, described as follows (where `moves` of type `Board → List Board` generates a list of possible moves):

```
gameTree : Board → Tree Board
(gameTree b).Node     = b
(gameTree b).Children = map gameTree (moves b)
```

Notice that the tree might be finite, such as in the game of Tic-Tac-Toe. However, it would still be inappropriate to waste resources fully generating all moves before determining which are even worth considering. Fortunately, the fact that the responses of a codata object are only computed when demanded means that the consumer is in full control over how much of the tree is generated, just as in Hughes' algorithm. This fact lets us write the following simplistic `prune` function which cuts off sub-trees at a fixed depth.

```
prune : Int → Tree Board → Tree Board
(prune x t).Node     = t.Node
(prune 0 t).Children = []
(prune x t).Children = map (prune(x-1)) t.Children
```

The more complex alpha-beta pruning algorithm can be written as its own pass, similar to `prune` above. Just like Hughes' original presentation, the evaluation of the best move for the opponent is the composition of a few smaller functions:

```
eval = maximize . maptree score . prune 5 . gameTree
```

What is the difference between this codata version of minimax and the one presented by Hughes that makes use of laziness? They both compute on-demand which makes the game efficient. However, demand-driven code written with codata can be easily ported between strict and lazy languages with only syntactic changes. In other words, codata is a general, portable, programming feature which is the key for compositionality in program design.[1]

2.3 Abstraction Mechanism

In the pursuit of scalable and maintainable program design, the typical followup to composability is abstraction. The basic purpose of abstraction is to hide certain implementation details so that different parts of the code base need not be concerned with them. For example, a large program will usually be organized into several different parts or "modules," some of which may hold general-purpose "library" code and others may be application-specific "clients" of those libraries. Successful abstractions will leverage tools of the programming language in question so that there is a clear interface between libraries and their clients, codifying which details are exposed to the client and which are kept hidden inside the library. A common such detail to hide is the concrete representation of some data type, like strings and collections. Clear abstraction barriers give freedom to both the library implementor (to change hidden details without disrupting any clients) as well as the client (to ignore details not exposed by the interface).

Reynolds [35] identified, and Cook [12] later elaborated on, two different mechanisms to achieve this abstraction: abstract data types and procedural abstraction. Abstract data types are crisply expressed by the Standard ML module system, based on existential types, which serves as a concrete practical touchstone for the notion. Procedural abstraction is pervasively used in object-oriented languages. However, due to the inherent differences among the many languages and the way they express procedural abstraction, it may not be completely clear of what the "essence" is, the way existential types are the essence of modules. *What is the language-agnostic representation of procedural abstraction? Codata!* The combination of observation-based interfaces, message-passing, and dynamic dispatch are exactly the tools needed for procedural abstraction. Other common object-oriented features—like inheritance, subtyping, encapsulation, and mutable state—are orthogonal to this particular abstraction goal. While they may be useful extensions to codata for accomplishing programming tasks, only pure codata itself is needed to represent abstraction.

[1] To see the full code for all the examples of [24] implemented in terms of codata, visit https://github.com/zachsully/codata_examples.

Specifying a codata type is giving an interface—between an implementation and a client—so that instances of the type (implementations) can respond to requests (clients). In fact, method calls are the only way to interact with our objects. As usual, there is no way to "open up" a higher-order function—one example of a codata type—and inspect the way it was implemented. The same intuition applies to all other codata types. For example, Cook's [12] procedural "set" interface can be expressed as a codata type with the following observations:

```
codata Set where
  IsEmpty  : Set → Bool
  Contains : Set → Int → Bool
  Insert   : Set → Int → Set
  Union    : Set → Set → Set
```

Every single object of type `Set` will respond to these observations, which is the only way to interact with it. This abstraction barrier gives us the freedom of defining several different instances of `Set` objects that can all be freely composed with one another. One such instance of `Set` uses a list to keep track of a hidden state of the contained elements (where `elemOf : List Int → Int → Bool` checks if a particular number is an element of the given list, and the operation `fold : (a → b → b) → b → List a → b` is the standard functional fold):

```
finiteSet : List Int → Set
(finiteSet xs).IsEmpty    = xs == []
(finiteSet xs).Contains y = elemOf xs y
(finiteSet xs).Insert   y = finiteSet (y:xs)
(finiteSet xs).Union    s = fold (λx t → t.Insert x) s xs

emptySet = finiteSet []
```

But of course, many other instances of `Set` can also be given. For example, this codata type interface also makes it possible to represent infinite sets like the set `evens` of all even numbers which is defined in terms of the more general `evensUnion` that unions all even numbers with some other set (where the function `isEven : Int → Int` checks if a number is even):

```
evens = evensUnion emptySet

evensUnion : Set → Set
(evensUnion s).IsEmpty    = False
(evensUnion s).Contains y = isEven y || s.Contains y
(evensUnion s).Insert   y = evensUnion (s.Insert y)
(evensUnion s).Union    t = evensUnion (s.Union t)
```

Because of the natural abstraction mechanism provided by codata, different `Set` implementations can interact with each other. For example, we can union a finite set and `evens` together because both definitions of `Union` know nothing of the internal structure of the other `Set`. Therefore, all we can do is apply the observations provided by the `Set` codata type.

While sets of numbers are fairly simplistic, there are many more practical real-world instances of the procedural abstraction provided by codata to be found in object-oriented languages. For example, databases are a good use of abstraction, where basic database queries can be represented as the observations on table objects. A simplified interface to a database table (containing rows of type a) with selection, deletion, and insertion, is given as follows:

```
codata Database a where
  Select : Database a → (a → Bool) → List a
  Delete : Database a → (a → Bool) → Database a
  Insert : Database a → a → Database a
```

On one hand, specific implementations can be given for connecting to and communicating with a variety of different databases—like Postgres, MySQL, or just a simple file system—which are hidden behind this interface. On the other hand, clients can write generic operations independently of any specific database, such as copying rows from one table to another or inserting a row into a list of compatible tables:

```
copy : Database a → Database a → Database a
copy from to = let rows = from.Select(λ_ → True)
               in foldr (λrow db → db.Insert row) to rows

insertAll : List (Database a) → a → List (Database a)
insertAll dbs row = map (λdb → db.Insert row) dbs
```

In addition to abstracting away the details of specific databases, both `copy` and `insertAll` can communicate between completely different databases by just passing in the appropriate object instances, which all have the same generic type. Another use of this generality is for testing. Besides the normal instances of `Database a` which perform permanent operations on actual tables, one can also implement a fictitious *simulation* which records changes only in temporary memory. That way, client code can be seamlessly tested by running and checking the results of simulated database operations that have no external side effects by just passing pure codata objects.

2.4 Representing Pre- and Post-Conditions

The extension of data types with indexes (*a.k.a.* generalized algebraic data types) has proven useful to statically verify a data structure's invariant, like for red-black trees [43]. With indexed data types, the programmer can inform the static type system that a particular value of a data type satisfies some additional conditions by constraining the way in which it was constructed. Unsurprisingly, indexed codata types are dual and allow the creator of an object to constrain the way it is going to be used, thereby adding pre- and post-conditions to the observations of the object. In other words, in a language with type indexes, codata enables the programmer to express more information in its interface.

This additional expressiveness simplifies applications that rely on a type index to guard observations. Thibodeau *et al.* [40] give examples of such programs, including an automaton specification where its transitions correspond to an observation that changes a pre- and post-condition in its index, and a fair resource scheduler where the observation of several resources is controlled by an index tracking the number of times they have been accessed. For concreteness, let's use an indexed codata type to specify safe protocols as in the following example from an object-oriented language with guarded methods:

```
index Raw, Bound, Live

codata Socket i where
  Bind    : Socket Raw   → String → Socket Bound
  Connect : Socket Bound → Socket Live
  Send    : Socket Live  → String → ()
  Receive : Socket Live  → String
  Close   : Socket Live  → ()
```

This example comes from DeLine and Fähndrich [14], where they present an extension to C♯ constraining the pre- and post-conditions for method calls. If we have an instance of this `Socket i` interface, then observing it through the above methods can return new socket objects with a different index. The index thereby governs the order in which clients are allowed to apply these methods. A socket will start with the index `Raw`. The only way to use a `Socket Raw` is to `Bind` it, and the only way to use a `Socket Bound` is to `Connect` it. This forces us to follow a protocol when initializing a `Socket`.

Intermezzo 1. This declaration puts one aspect in the hands of the programmer, though. A client can open a socket and never close it, hogging the resource. We can remedy this problem with linear types, which force us to address any loose ends before finishing the program. With linear types, it would be a type error to have a lingering `Live` socket laying around at the end of the program, and a call to `Close` would use it up. Furthermore, linear types would ensure that outdated copies of `Socket` objects cannot be used again, which is especially appropriate for actions like `Bind` which is meant to *transform* a `Raw` socket into a `Bound` one, and likewise for `Connect` which transforms a `Bound` socket into a `Live` one. Even better, enhancing linear types with a more sophisticated notion of ownership—like in the Rust programming language which differentiates a *permanent* transfer of ownership from *temporarily* borrowing it—makes this resource-sensitive interface especially pleasant. Observations like `Bind`, `Connect`, and `Close` which are meant to fully consume the observed object would involve full ownership of the object itself to the method call and effectively replace the old object with the returned one. In contrast, observations like `Send` and `Receive` which are meant to be repeated on the same object would merely borrow the object for the duration of the action so that it could be used again.

3 Inter-compilation of Core Calculi

We saw previously examples of using codata types to replicate well-known encodings of data types into the λ-calculus. Now, let's dive in and show how data and codata types formally relate to one another. In order to demonstrate the relationship, we will consider two small languages that extend the common polymorphic λ-calculus: λ^{data} extends λ with user-defined algebraic data types, and λ^{codata} extends λ with user-defined codata types. In the end, we will find that both of these foundational languages can be inter-compiled into one another. Data can be represented by codata via the visitor pattern ($\mathfrak{V}$). Codata can be represented by data by tabulating the possible answers of objects ($\mathfrak{T}$).

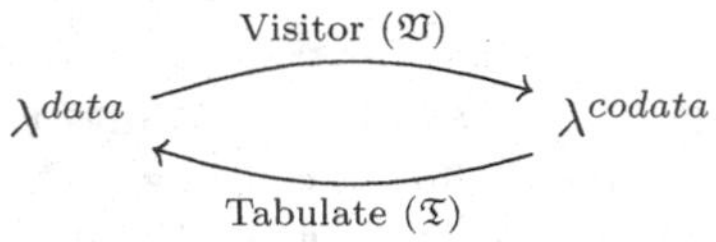

In essence, this demonstrates how to compile programs between the functional and object-oriented paradigms. The $\mathfrak{T}$ direction shows how to extend existing functional languages (like OCaml, Haskell, or Racket) with codata objects without changing their underlying representation. Dually, the $\mathfrak{V}$ direction shows how to compile functional programs with data types into an object-oriented target language (like JavaScript).

Each of the encodings are macro expansions, in the sense that they leave the underlying base λ-calculus constructs of functions, applications, and variables unchanged (as opposed to, for example, continuation-passing style translations). They are defined to operate on untyped terms, but they also preserve typability when given well-typed terms. The naïve encodings preserve the operational semantics of the original term, according to a call-by-name semantics. We also illustrate how the encodings can be modified slightly to correctly simulate the call-by-value operational semantics of the source program. To conclude, we show how the languages and encodings can be generalized to more expressive type systems, which include features like existential types and indexed types (*a.k.a.* generalized algebraic data types and guarded methods).

Notation. We use both an overline $\overline{t}$ and dots $t_1 \ldots$ to indicate a *sequence* of terms t (and likewise for types, variables, *etc.*). The arrow type $\overline{\tau} \to \mathsf{T}$ means $\tau_1 \to \cdots \to \tau_n \to \mathsf{T}$; when n is 0, it is not a function type, *i.e.* just the codomain T. The application $\mathsf{K}\ \overline{t}$ means $(((\mathsf{K}\ t_1)\ \ldots)\ t_n)$; when n is 0, it is not a function application, but the constant K. We write a single step of an operational semantics with the arrow $\mapsto$, and many steps (*i.e.* its reflexive-transitive closure) as $\mapsto\!\!\!\!\to$. Operational steps may occur within an evaluation context E, *i.e.* $t \mapsto t'$ implies that $E[t] \mapsto E[t']$.

3.1 Syntax and Semantics

We present the syntax and semantics of the base language and the two extensions λ^{data} and λ^{codata}. For the sake of simplicity, we keep the languages as minimal as possible to illustrate the main inter-compilations. Therefore, λ^{data} and λ^{codata} do not contain recursion, nested (co)patterns, or indexed types. The extension with recursion is standard, and an explanation of compiling (co)patterns can be found in [11,38,39]. Indexed types are later discussed informally in Sect. 3.6.

Syntax:

$$\text{Type} \ni \quad \tau, \rho ::= a \mid \tau \to \rho \mid \forall a.\, \tau$$
$$\text{Term} \ni t, u, e ::= x \mid t\ u \mid \lambda x.\, e$$

Operational Semantics:

Call-by-name

$$V ::= x \mid \lambda x.\, e \qquad E ::= \square \mid E\ u$$
$$(\lambda x.\, e)\ u \mapsto e[u/x]$$

Call-by-value

$$V ::= x \mid \lambda x.\, e \qquad E ::= \square \mid E\ u \mid V\ E$$
$$(\lambda x.\, e)\ V \mapsto e[V/x]$$

Type System (where $S = t$ for call-by-name and $S = V$ for call-by-value):

$$\frac{x : \tau \in \Gamma}{\Gamma \vdash x : \tau} \qquad \frac{\Gamma \vdash t : \tau \to \rho \quad \Gamma \vdash u : \tau}{\Gamma \vdash t\ u : \rho} \qquad \frac{\Gamma, x : \tau \vdash e : \rho}{\Gamma \vdash \lambda x.\, e : \tau \to \rho}$$
$$\frac{\Gamma, a \vdash S : \tau}{\Gamma \vdash S : \forall a.\, \tau} \qquad \frac{\Gamma \vdash t : \forall a.\tau \quad \Gamma \vdash \rho}{\Gamma \vdash t : \tau[\rho/a]}$$

Fig. 1. Polymorphic λ-calculus: the base language

The Base Language. We will base both our core languages of interest on a common starting point: the polymorphic λ-calculus as shown in Fig. 1.[2] This is the standard simply typed λ-calculus extended with impredicative polymorphism (*a.k.a.* generics). There are only three forms of terms (variables x, applications $t\ u$, and function abstractions $\lambda x.e$) and three forms of types (type variables a, function types $\tau \to \rho$, and polymorphic types $\forall a.\tau$). We keep the type abstraction and instantiation implicit in programs—as opposed to explicit as in System F—for two reasons. First, this more accurately resembles the functional languages in which types are inferred, as opposed to mandatory annotations explicit within the syntax of programs. Second, it more clearly shows how the translations that follow do not rely on first knowing the type of terms, but apply to any untyped term. In other words, the compilation techniques are also appropriate for dynamically typed languages like Scheme and Racket.

Figure 1 reviews both the standard call-by-name and call-by-value operational semantics for the λ-calculus. As usual, the difference between the two is that in call-by-value, the argument of a function call is evaluated prior to substitution, whereas in call-by-name the argument is substituted first. This is implied by the different set of evaluation contexts (E) and the fact that the operational rule uses a more restricted notion of value (V) for substitutable arguments in call-by-value. Note that, there is an interplay between evaluation and typing. In a more general setting where effects are allowed, the typing rule for introducing polymorphism (*i.e.* the rule with $S : \forall a.\tau$ in the conclusion) is only safe for substitutable terms, which imposes the well-known the *value restriction* for call-by-value (limiting S to values), but requires no such restriction in call-by-name where every term is a substitutable value (letting S be any term).

[2] The judgement $\Gamma \vdash \rho$ should be read as: all free type variables in ρ occur in Γ. As usual Γ, a means that a does not occur free in Γ.

Syntax:

$$
\begin{array}{lrl}
\text{Declaration} \ni & d ::= & \mathbf{data}\ \mathsf{T}\ \overline{a}\ \mathbf{where}\ \mathsf{K} : \overline{\tau} \to \mathsf{T}\ \overline{a}\ \ldots \\
\text{Type} \ni & \tau, \rho ::= & a \mid \tau \to \rho \mid \forall a. \tau \mid \mathsf{T}\ \overline{\rho} \\
\text{Term} \ni & t, u, e ::= & x \mid t\ u \mid \lambda x. e \mid \mathsf{K}\ \overline{t} \mid \mathbf{case}\ t\ \{\overline{\mathsf{K}\ \overline{x} \to t}\}
\end{array}
$$

Operational Semantics:

Call-by-name

$$
\begin{array}{l}
V ::= \cdots \mid \mathsf{K}\ \overline{t} \\
E ::= \cdots \mid \mathbf{case}\ E\ \{\overline{\mathsf{K}\ \overline{x} \to e}\}
\end{array}
$$

$$
\mathbf{case}\ (\mathsf{K}\ \overline{t})\ \{\mathsf{K}\ \overline{x} \to e,\ \ldots\} \mapsto e[\overline{t/x}]
$$

Call-by-value

$$
\begin{array}{l}
V ::= \cdots \mid \mathsf{K}\ \overline{V} \\
E ::= \cdots \mid \mathbf{case}\ E\ \{\overline{\mathsf{K}\ \overline{x} \to e}\} \mid \mathsf{K}\ \overline{V}\ E\ \overline{t}
\end{array}
$$

$$
\mathbf{case}\ (\mathsf{K}\ \overline{V})\ \{\mathsf{K}\ \overline{x} \to e,\ \ldots\} \mapsto e[\overline{V/x}]
$$

Type System:

$$
\frac{\mathsf{K} : \forall \overline{a}. \tau_1 \to \cdots \to \mathsf{T}\ \overline{a} \in \Gamma \quad \Gamma \vdash t_1 : \tau_1[\overline{\rho/a}] \quad \ldots}{\Gamma \vdash \mathsf{K}\ t_1 \cdots : \mathsf{T}\ \overline{\rho}}
$$

$$
\frac{\Gamma \vdash t : \mathsf{T}\ \overline{\rho} \quad \mathsf{K}_1 : \forall \overline{a}. \overline{\tau_1} \to \mathsf{T}\ \overline{a} \in \Gamma \quad \Gamma, \overline{x_1 : \tau_1[\overline{\rho/a}]} \vdash e_1 : \tau' \quad \ldots}{\Gamma \vdash \mathbf{case}\ t\ \{\mathsf{K}_1\ \overline{x_1} \to e_1,\ \ldots\} : \tau'}
$$

Fig. 2. λ^{data}: Extending polymorphic λ-calculus with data types

A Language with Data. The first extension of the λ-calculus is with user-defined data types, as shown in Fig. 2; it corresponds to a standard core language for statically typed functional languages. Data declarations introduce a new type constructor (T) as well as some number of associated constructors (K) that build values of that data type. For simplicity, the list of branches in a case expression are considered unordered and non-overlapping (*i.e.* no two branches for the same constructor within a single case expression). The types of constructors are given alongside free variables in Γ, and the typing rule for constructors requires they be fully applied. We also assume an additional side condition to the typing rule for case expressions that the branches are exhaustive (*i.e.* every constructor of the data type in question is covered as a premise).

Figure 2 presents the extension to the operational semantics from Fig. 1, which is also standard. The new evaluation rule for data types reduces a case expression matched with an applied constructor. Note that since the branches are unordered, the one matching the constructor is chosen out of the possibilities and the parameters of the constructor are substituted in the branch's pattern. There is also an additional form of constructed values: in call-by-name any constructor application is a value, whereas in call-by-value only constructors parameterized by other values is a value. As such, call-by-value goes on to evaluate constructor parameters in advance, as shown by the extra evaluation context. In both evaluation strategies, there is a new form of evaluation context that points out the discriminant of a case expression, since it is mandatory to determine which constructor was used before deciding the appropriate branch to take.

Syntax:

$$\begin{array}{lll} \text{Declaration} \ni & d ::= \textbf{codata}\ \mathsf{U}\ \overline{a}\ \textbf{where}\ \overline{\mathsf{H} : \mathsf{U}\ \overline{a} \to \tau} \ldots \\ \text{Type} & \ni \tau, \rho ::= a \mid \tau \to \rho \mid \forall a.\, \tau \mid \mathsf{U}\ \overline{\rho} \\ \text{Term} & \ni t, u, e ::= x \mid t\ u \mid \lambda x.\, e \mid t.\mathsf{H} \mid \{\overline{\mathsf{H} \to e}\} \end{array}$$

Operational Semantics:

Call-by-name

$$V ::= \cdots \mid \{\overline{\mathsf{H} \to e}\} \quad E ::= \cdots \mid E.\mathsf{H}$$

$$\{\mathsf{H} \to e, \ldots\}.\mathsf{H} \mapsto e$$

Call-by-value

$$V ::= \cdots \mid \{\overline{\mathsf{H} \to e}\} \quad E ::= \cdots \mid E.\mathsf{H}$$

$$\{\mathsf{H} \to e, \ldots\}.\mathsf{H} \mapsto e$$

Type System:

$$\frac{\mathsf{H} : \forall \overline{a}.\, \mathsf{U}\ \overline{a} \to \tau \in \Gamma \quad \Gamma \vdash t : \mathsf{U}\ \overline{\rho}}{\Gamma \vdash t.\mathsf{H} : \tau[\overline{\rho}/\overline{a}]} \qquad \frac{\Gamma \vdash \mathsf{H}_1 : \mathsf{U}\ \overline{\rho} \to \tau_1 \quad \Gamma \vdash e_1 : \tau_1 \quad \ldots}{\Gamma \vdash \{\mathsf{H}_1 \to e_1, \ldots\} : \mathsf{U}\ \overline{\rho}}$$

Fig. 3. λ^{codata}: Extending polymorphic λ-calculus with codata types

A Language with Codata. The second extension of the λ-calculus is with user-defined codata types, as shown in Fig. 3. Codata declarations in λ^{codata} define a new type constructor (U) along with some number of associated destructors (H) for projecting responses out of values of a codata type. The type level of λ^{codata} corresponds directly to λ^{data}. However, at the term level, we have codata observations of the form $t.\mathsf{H}$ using "dot notation", which can be thought of as sending the message H to the object t or as a method invocation from object-oriented languages. Values of codata types are introduced in the form $\{\mathsf{H}_1 \to e_1, \ldots, \mathsf{H}_n \to e_n\}$, which lists each response this value gives to all the possible destructors of the type. As with case expressions, we take the branches to be unordered and non-overlapping for simplicity.

Interestingly, the extension of the operational semantics with codata—the values, evaluation contexts, and reduction rules—are identical for both call-by-name and call-by-value evaluation. In either evaluation strategy, a codata object $\{\mathsf{H} \to e, \ldots\}$ is considered a value and the codata observation $t.\mathsf{H}$ *must* evaluate t no matter what to continue, leading to the same form of evaluation context $E.\mathsf{H}$. The additional evaluation rule selects and invokes the matching branch of a codata object and is the same regardless of the evaluation strategy.

Note that the reason that values of codata types are the same in any evaluation strategy is due to the fact that the branches of the object are only ever evaluated on-demand, *i.e.* when they are observed by a destructor, similar to the fact that the body of a function is only ever evaluated when the function is called. This is the semantic difference that separates codata types from records found in many programming languages. Records typically map a collection of labels to a collection of values, which are evaluated in advance in a call-by-value language similar to the constructed values of data types. Whereas with codata objects, labels map to *behavior* which is only invoked when observed.

$$\mathfrak{V}\left[\!\!\left[\begin{array}{l}\textbf{data}\ \mathsf{T}\ \overline{a}\ \textbf{where}\\ \quad \mathsf{K}_1 : \overline{\tau_1} \to \mathsf{T}\ \overline{a}\\ \quad\quad \vdots \\ \quad \mathsf{K}_n : \overline{\tau_n} \to \mathsf{T}\ \overline{a}\end{array}\right]\!\!\right] = \begin{array}{l}\textbf{codata}\ \mathsf{T}_{visit}\ \overline{a}\ b\ \textbf{where}\\ \quad \mathsf{K}_1 : \mathsf{T}_{visit}\ \overline{a}\ b \to \overline{\tau_1} \to b\\ \quad\quad \vdots \\ \quad \mathsf{K}_n : \mathsf{T}_{visit}\ \overline{a}\ b \to \overline{\tau_n} \to b\\ \textbf{codata}\ \mathsf{T}\ \overline{a}\ \textbf{where}\\ \quad \mathsf{Case}_\mathsf{T} : \mathsf{T}\ \overline{a} \to \forall b.\, \mathsf{T}_{visit}\ \overline{a}\ b \to b\end{array}$$

$$\mathfrak{V}[\![\mathsf{K}_i\ \overline{t}]\!] = \{\mathsf{Case}_\mathsf{T} \to \lambda v.\, (v.\mathsf{K}_i)\ \overline{\mathfrak{V}[\![t]\!]}\}$$

$$\mathfrak{V}[\![\textbf{case}\ t\ \{\mathsf{K}_1\ \overline{x_1} \to e_1, \ldots\}]\!] = (\mathfrak{V}[\![t]\!].\mathsf{Case}_\mathsf{T})\ \{\mathsf{K}_1 \to \lambda\overline{x_1}.\, \mathfrak{V}[\![e_1]\!], \ldots\}$$

Fig. 4. $\mathfrak{V} : \lambda^{data} \to \lambda^{codata}$ mapping data to codata via the visitor pattern

The additional typing rules for λ^{codata} are also given in Fig. 3. The rule for typing $t.\mathsf{H}$ is analogous to a combination of type instantiation and application, when viewing H as a function of the given type. The rule for typing a codata object, in contrast, is similar to the rule for typing a case expression of a data type. However, in this comparison, the rule for objects is partially "upside down" in the sense that the primary type in question ($\mathsf{U}\ \overline{\rho}$) appears in the conclusion rather than as a premise. This is the reason why there is one less premise for typing codata objects than there is for typing data case expressions. As with that rule, we assume that the branches are exhaustive, so that every destructor of the codata type appears in the premise.

3.2 Compiling Data to Codata: The Visitor Pattern

In Sect. 2.1, we illustrated how to convert a data type representing trees into a codata type. This encoding corresponds to a rephrasing of the object-oriented visitor pattern to avoid unnecessary side-effects. Now lets look more generally at the pattern, to see how any algebraic data type in λ^{data} can be encoded in terms of codata in λ^{codata}.

The visitor pattern has the net effect of inverting the orientation of a data declaration (wherein construction comes first) into codata declarations (wherein destruction comes first). This reorientation can be used for compiling user-defined data types in λ^{data} to codata types in λ^{codata} as shown in Fig. 4. As with all of the translations we will consider, this is a macro expansion since the syntactic forms from the base λ-calculus are treated homomorphically (*i.e.* $\mathfrak{V}[\![\lambda x.\, e]\!] = \lambda x.\, \mathfrak{V}[\![e]\!]$, $\mathfrak{V}[\![t\ u]\!] = \mathfrak{V}[\![t]\!]\ \mathfrak{V}[\![u]\!]$, and $\mathfrak{V}[\![x]\!] = x$). Furthermore, this translation also perfectly preserves types, since the types of terms are exactly the same after translation (*i.e.* $\mathfrak{V}[\![\tau]\!] = \tau$).

Notice how each data type ($\mathsf{T}\ \overline{a}$) gets represented by *two* codata types: the "visitor" ($\mathsf{T}_{visit}\ \overline{a}\ b$) which says what to do with values made with each constructor, and the type itself ($\mathsf{T}\ \overline{a}$) which has one method which accepts a visitor and returns a value of type b. An object of the codata type, then, must be capable of accepting *any* visitor, no matter what type of result it returns. Also notice that we include no other methods in the codata type representation of $\mathsf{T}\ \overline{a}$.

At the level of terms, first consider how the case expression of the data type is encoded. The branches of the case (contained within the curly braces) are represented as a first-class object of the visitor type: each constructor is mapped to the corresponding destructor of the same name and the variables bound in the pattern are mapped to parameters of the function returned by the object in each case. The whole case expression itself is then implemented by calling the sole method ($\mathsf{Case_T}$) of the codata object and passing the branches of the case as the corresponding visitor object. Shifting focus to the constructors, we can now see that they are compiled as objects that invoke the corresponding destructor on any given visitor, and the terms which were parameters to the constructor are now parameters to a given visitor's destructor. Of course, other uses of the visitor pattern might involve a codata type (T) with more methods implementing additional functionality besides case analysis. However, we only need the one method to represent data types in λ^{data} because case expressions are *the* primitive destructor for values of data types in the language.

For example, consider applying the above visitor pattern to a binary tree data type as follows:

$$\mathfrak{V}\left[\!\!\left[\begin{array}{l}\textbf{data}\ \mathsf{Tree}\ \textbf{where}\\ \quad \mathsf{Leaf} \quad\ : \mathsf{Int} \to \mathsf{Tree}\\ \quad \mathsf{Branch} : \mathsf{Tree} \to \mathsf{Tree} \to \mathsf{Tree}\end{array}\right]\!\!\right] = \begin{array}{l}\textbf{codata}\ \mathsf{Tree}_{visit}\ b\ \textbf{where}\\ \quad \mathsf{Leaf} \quad\ : \mathsf{Int} \to b\\ \quad \mathsf{Branch} : \mathsf{Tree} \to \mathsf{Tree} \to b\\ \\ \textbf{codata}\ \mathsf{Tree}\ \textbf{where}\\ \quad \mathsf{Case_{Tree}} : \mathsf{Tree} \to \forall b.\, \mathsf{Tree}_{visit}\ b \to b\end{array}$$

$$\mathfrak{V}[\![\mathsf{Leaf}\ n]\!] = \{\mathsf{Case_{Tree}} \to \lambda v.\, v.\mathsf{Leaf}\ n\}$$

$$\mathfrak{V}[\![\mathsf{Branch}\ l\ r]\!] = \{\mathsf{Case_{Tree}} \to \lambda v.\, v.\mathsf{Branch}\ l\ r\}$$

$$\mathfrak{V}\left[\!\!\left[\textbf{case}\ t \begin{Bmatrix}\mathsf{Leaf}\ n & \to e_l\\ \mathsf{Branch}\ l\ r & \to e_b\end{Bmatrix}\right]\!\!\right] = \mathfrak{V}[\![t]\!].\mathsf{Case_{Tree}} \begin{Bmatrix}\mathsf{Leaf} & \to & \lambda n.\, \mathfrak{V}[\![e_l]\!]\\ \mathsf{Branch} & \to & \lambda l.\, \lambda r.\, \mathfrak{V}[\![e_b]\!]\end{Bmatrix}$$

Note how this encoding differs from the one that was given in Sect. 2.1 since the $\mathsf{Case_{Tree}}$ method is non-recursive whereas the $\mathsf{Walk_{Tree}}$ method was recursive, in order to model a depth-first search traversal of the tree.

Of course, other operations, like the `walk` function, could be written in terms of case expressions and recursion as usual by an encoding with above method calls. However, it is possible to go one step further and include other primitive destructors—like recursors or iterators in the style of Gödel's system T—by embedding them as other methods of the encoded codata type. For example, we can represent `walk` as a primitive destructor as it was in Sect. 2.1 *in addition* to non-recursive case analysis by adding an alternative visitor Tree_{walk} and one more destructor to the generated Tree codata type like so:

$$\begin{array}{l}\textbf{codata}\ \mathsf{Tree}_{walk}\ b\ \textbf{where}\\ \quad \mathsf{Leaf} \quad\ : \mathsf{Int} \to b\\ \quad \mathsf{Branch} : b \to b \to b\end{array} \qquad \begin{array}{l}\textbf{codata}\ \mathsf{Tree}\ \textbf{where}\\ \quad \mathsf{Case_{Tree}} : \mathsf{Tree} \to \forall b.\, \mathsf{Tree}_{visit}\ b \to b\\ \quad \mathsf{Walk_{Tree}} : \mathsf{Tree} \to \forall b.\, \mathsf{Tree}_{walk}\ b \to b\end{array}$$

$$\mathfrak{V}[\![\mathsf{Leaf}\ n]\!] = \begin{Bmatrix}\mathsf{Case_{Tree}} \to \lambda v.\, v.\mathsf{Leaf}\ n\\ \mathsf{Walk_{Tree}} \to \lambda w.\, w.\mathsf{Leaf}\ n\end{Bmatrix}$$

For codata types with n destructors, where $n \geq 1$:

$$\mathfrak{T}\left[\!\!\left[\begin{array}{l}\textbf{codata}\ \mathsf{U}\ \overline{a}\ \textbf{where}\\ \quad \mathsf{H}_1 : \mathsf{U}\ \overline{a} \to \tau_1\\ \quad\quad \vdots\\ \quad \mathsf{H}_n : \mathsf{U}\ \overline{a} \to \tau_n\end{array}\right]\!\!\right] = \begin{array}{l}\textbf{data}\ \mathsf{U}\ \overline{a}\ \textbf{where}\\ \quad \mathsf{Table_U} : \tau_1 \to \cdots \to \tau_n \to \mathsf{U}\ \overline{a}\end{array}$$

$$\mathfrak{T}[\![t.\mathsf{H}_i]\!] = \textbf{case}\ \mathfrak{T}[\![t]\!]\ \{\mathsf{Table_U}\ y_1 \ldots y_n \to y_i\}$$

$$\mathfrak{T}[\![\{\mathsf{H}_1 \to e_1, \ldots, \mathsf{H}_n \to e_n\}]\!] = \mathsf{Table_U}\ \mathfrak{T}[\![e_1]\!] \ldots \mathfrak{T}[\![e_n]\!]$$

For codata types with 0 destructors (where Unit is the same for every such U):

$$\mathfrak{T}\left[\!\!\left[\begin{array}{l}\textbf{codata}\ \mathsf{U}\ \overline{a}\ \textbf{where}\\ \quad \textit{--no destructors}\end{array}\right]\!\!\right] = \begin{array}{l}\textbf{data}\ \mathsf{Unit}\ \textbf{where}\\ \quad \mathsf{unit} : \mathsf{Unit}\end{array}$$

$$\mathfrak{T}[\![\{\}]\!] = \mathsf{unit}$$

Fig. 5. $\mathfrak{T} : \lambda^{codata} \to \lambda^{data}$ tabulating codata responses with data tuples

$$\mathfrak{V}[\![\mathsf{Branch}\ l\ r]\!] = \left\{\begin{array}{ll}\mathsf{Case_{Tree}} \to \lambda v.\, v.\mathsf{Branch}\ l\ r \\ \mathsf{Walk_{Tree}} \to \lambda w.\, w.\mathsf{Branch}\ (l.\mathsf{Walk_{Tree}})\ (r.\mathsf{Walk_{Tree}})\end{array}\right\}$$

where the definition of Tree_{visit} and the encoding of case expressions is the same. In other words, this compilation technique can generalize to as many primitive observations and recursion schemes as desired.

3.3 Compiling Codata to Data: Tabulation

Having seen how to compile data to codata, how can we go the other way? The reverse compilation would be useful for extending functional languages with user-defined codata types, since many functional languages are compiled to a core representation based on the λ-calculus with data types.

Intuitively, the declared data types in λ^{data} can be thought of as "sums of products." In contrast, the declared codata types in λ^{codata} can be thought of as "products of functions." Since both core languages are based on the λ-calculus, which has higher-order functions, the main challenge is to relate the two notions of "products." The codata sense of products are based on projections out of abstract objects, where the different parts are viewed individually and only when demanded. The data sense of products, instead, are based on tuples, in which all components are laid out in advance in a single concrete structure.

One way to convert codata to data is to *tabulate* an object's potential answers ahead of time into a data structure. This is analogous to the fact that a function of type `Bool` $\to$ `String` can be alternatively represented by a tuple of type `String * String`, where the first and second components are the responses of the original function to `true` and `false`, respectively. This idea can be applied to λ^{codata} in general as shown in the compilation in Fig. 5.

A codata declaration of U becomes a data declaration with a single constructor ($\mathsf{Table}_\mathsf{U}$) representing a tuple containing the response for each of the original destructors of U. At the term level, a codata abstraction is compiled by concretely tabulating each of its responses into a tuple using the $\mathsf{Table}_\mathsf{U}$ constructor. A destructor application returns the specific component of the constructed tuple which corresponds to that projection. Note that, since we assume that each object is exhaustive, the tabulation transformation is relatively straightforward; filling in "missing" method definitions with some error value that can be stored in the tuple at the appropriate index would be done in advance as a separate pre-processing step.

Also notice that there is a special case for non-observable "empty" codata types, which are all collapsed into a single pre-designated Unit data type. The reason for this collapse is to ensure that this compilation preserves typability: if applied to a well-typed term, the result is also well-typed. The complication arises from the fact that when faced with an empty object {}, we have no idea which constructor to use without being given further typing information. So rather than force type checking or annotation in advance for this one degenerate case, we instead collapse them all into a single data type so that there is no need to differentiate based on the type. In contrast, the translation of non-empty objects is straightforward, since we can use the name of any one of the destructors to determine the codata type it is associated with, which then informs us of the correct constructor to use.

3.4 Correctness

For the inter-compilations between λ^{codata} into λ^{data} to be useful in practice, they should preserve the semantics of programs. For now, we focus only on the call-by-name semantics for each of the languages. With the static aspect of the semantics, this means they should preserve the typing of terms.

Proposition 1 (Type Preservation). *For each of the $\mathfrak{V}$ and $\mathfrak{T}$ translations: if $\Gamma \vdash t : \tau$ then $[\![\Gamma]\!] \vdash [\![t]\!] : [\![\tau]\!]$ (in the call-by-name type system).*

Proof (Sketch). By induction on the typing derivation of $\Gamma \vdash t : \tau$.

With the dynamic aspect of the semantics, the translations should preserve the outcome of evaluation (either converging to some value, diverging into an infinite loop, or getting stuck) for both typed and untyped terms. This works because each translation preserves the reduction steps, values, and evaluation contexts of the source calculus' call-by-name operational semantics.

Proposition 2 (Evaluation Preservation). *For each of the $\mathfrak{V}$ and $\mathfrak{T}$ translations: $t \mapsto\!\!\!\!\twoheadrightarrow V$ if and only if $[\![t]\!] \mapsto\!\!\!\!\twoheadrightarrow [\![V]\!]$ (in the call-by-name semantics).*

Proof (Sketch). The forward ("only if") implication is a result of the following facts that hold for each translation in the call-by-name semantics:

- For any redex t in the source, if $t \mapsto t'$ then $[\![t]\!] \mapsto t'' \mapsto\!\!\!\!\to [\![t']\!]$.
- For any value V in the source, $[\![V]\!]$ is a value.
- For any evaluation context E in the source, there is an evaluation context E' in the target such that $[\![E[t]]\!] = E'[[\![t]\!]]$ for all t.

The reverse ("if") implication then follows from the fact that the call-by-name operational semantics of both source and target languages is deterministic.

3.5 Call-by-Value: Correcting the Evaluation Order

The presented inter-compilation techniques are correct for the call-by-name semantics of the calculi. But what about the call-by-value semantics? It turns out that the simple translations seen so far do not correctly preserve the call-by-value semantics of programs, but they can be easily fixed by being more careful about how they treat the values of the source and target calculi. In other words, we need to make sure that values are translated to values, and evaluation contexts to evaluation contexts. For instance, the following translation (up to renaming) does not preserve the call-by-value semantics of the source program:

$$\mathfrak{T}[\![\{\mathsf{Fst} \to \mathit{error}, \mathsf{Snd} \to \mathsf{True}\}]\!] = \mathsf{Pair}\ \mathit{error}\ \mathsf{True}$$

The object $\{\mathsf{Fst} \to \mathit{error}, \mathsf{Snd} \to \mathsf{True}\}$ is a value in call-by-value, and the erroneous response to the Fst will only be evaluated when observed. However, the structure Pair *error* True is not a value in call-by-value, because the field *error* must be evaluated in advance which causes an error immediately. In the other direction, we could also have

$$\mathfrak{V}[\![\mathsf{Pair}\ \mathit{error}\ \mathsf{True}]\!] = \{\mathsf{Case} \to \lambda v.\, v.\mathsf{Pair}\ \mathit{error}\ \mathsf{True}\}$$

Here, the immediate error in Pair *error* True has become incorrectly delayed inside the value $\{\mathsf{Case} \to \lambda v.\, v.\mathsf{Pair}\ \mathit{error}\ \mathsf{True}\}$.

The solution to this problem is straightforward: we must manually delay computations that are lifted out of (object or λ) abstractions, and manually force computations before their results are hidden underneath abstractions. For the visitor pattern, the correction is to only introduce the codata object on constructed values. We can handle other constructed terms by naming their non-value components in the style of administrative-normalization like so:

$$\begin{aligned} \mathfrak{V}[\![\mathsf{K}_i\ \overline{V}]\!] &= \{\mathsf{Case}_\mathsf{T} \to \lambda v.\, v.\mathsf{K}_i\ \overline{V}\} \\ \mathfrak{V}[\![\mathsf{K}_i\ \overline{V}\ u\ \overline{t}]\!] &= \mathbf{let}\ x = u\ \mathbf{in}\ \mathfrak{V}[\![\mathsf{K}_i\ \overline{V}\ x\ \overline{t}]\!] \qquad \text{if } u \text{ is not a value} \end{aligned}$$

Conversely, the tabulating translation $\mathfrak{T}$ will cause the on-demand observations of the object to be converted to preemptive components of a tuple structure. To counter this change in evaluation order, a thunking technique can be employed as follows:

$$\begin{aligned} \mathfrak{T}[\![t.\mathsf{H}_i]\!] &= \mathbf{case}\ \mathfrak{T}[\![t]\!]\ \{\mathsf{Table}_\mathsf{U}\ y_1 \ldots y_n \to \mathbf{force}\, y_i\} \\ \mathfrak{T}[\![\{\mathsf{H}_1 \to e_1, \ldots, \mathsf{H}_n \to e_n\}]\!] &= \mathsf{Table}_\mathsf{U}\ (\mathbf{delay}\, \mathfrak{T}[\![e_1]\!]) \ldots (\mathbf{delay}\, \mathfrak{T}[\![e_n]\!]) \end{aligned}$$

The two operations can be implemented as $\mathbf{delay}\, t = \lambda z.\, t$ and $\mathbf{force}\, t = t\ \mathsf{unit}$ as usual, but can also be implemented as more efficient memoizing operations. With all these corrections, Propositions 1 and 2 also hold for the call-by-value type system and operational semantics.

3.6 Indexed Data and Codata Types: Type Equalities

In the world of types, we have so far only formally addressed inter-compilation between languages with simple and polymorphic types. What about the compilation of indexed data and codata types? It turns out some of the compilation techniques we have discussed so far extend to type indexes without further effort, whereas others need some extra help. In particular, the visitor-pattern-based translation $\mathfrak{V}$ can just be applied straightforwardly to indexed data types:

$$\mathfrak{V}\left[\!\!\left[\begin{array}{l}\mathbf{data}\ \mathsf{T}\ \overline{a}\ \mathbf{where}\\ \quad \mathsf{K}_1 : \overline{\tau_1} \to \mathsf{T}\ \overline{\rho_1}\\ \quad\quad \vdots\\ \quad \mathsf{K}_n : \overline{\tau_n} \to \mathsf{T}\ \overline{\rho_n}\end{array}\right]\!\!\right] = \begin{array}{l}\mathbf{codata}\ \mathsf{T}_{visit}\ \overline{a}\ b\ \mathbf{where}\\ \quad \mathsf{K}_1 : \mathsf{T}_{visit}\ \overline{\rho_1}\ b \to \overline{\tau_1} \to b\\ \quad\quad \vdots\\ \quad \mathsf{K}_n : \mathsf{T}_{visit}\ \overline{\rho_n}\ b \to \overline{\tau_n} \to b\\ \mathbf{codata}\ \mathsf{T}\ \overline{a}\ \mathbf{where}\\ \quad \mathsf{Case}_{\mathsf{T}} : \mathsf{T}\ \overline{a} \to \forall b.\, \mathsf{T}_{visit}\ \overline{a}\ b \to b\end{array}$$

In this case, the notion of an indexed visitor codata type exactly corresponds to the mechanics of case expressions for GADTs. In contrast, the tabulation translation $\mathfrak{T}$ does not correctly capture the semantics of indexed codata types, if applied naïvely.

Thankfully, there is a straightforward way of "simplifying" indexed data types to more conventional data types using some built-in support for *type equalities*. The idea is that a constructor with a more specific return type can be replaced with a conventional constructor that is parameterized by type equalities that *prove* that the normal return type must be the more specific one. The same idea can be applied to indexed codata types as well. A destructor that can only act on a more specific instance of the codata type can instead be replaced by one which works on any instance, but then immediately asks for *proof* that the object's type is the more specific one before completing the observation. These two translations, of replacing type indexes with type equalities, are defined as:

$$\mathfrak{Eq}\left[\!\!\left[\begin{array}{l}\mathbf{data}\ \mathsf{T}\ \overline{a}\ \mathbf{where}\\ \quad \mathsf{K}_1 : \overline{\tau_1} \to \mathsf{T}\ \overline{\rho_1}\\ \quad\quad \vdots\\ \quad \mathsf{K}_n : \overline{\tau_n} \to \mathsf{T}\ \overline{\rho_n}\end{array}\right]\!\!\right] = \begin{array}{l}\mathbf{data}\ \mathsf{T}\ \overline{a}\ \mathbf{where}\\ \quad \mathsf{K}_1 : \overline{a \equiv \rho_1} \to \overline{\tau_1} \to \mathsf{T}\ \overline{a}\\ \quad\quad \vdots\\ \quad \mathsf{K}_n : \overline{a \equiv \rho_n} \to \overline{\tau_n} \to \mathsf{T}\ \overline{a}\end{array}$$

$$\mathfrak{Eq}\left[\!\!\left[\begin{array}{l}\mathbf{codata}\ \mathsf{U}\ \overline{a}\ \mathbf{where}\\ \quad \mathsf{H}_1 : \mathsf{U}\ \overline{\rho_1} \to \overline{\tau_1}\\ \quad\quad \vdots\\ \quad \mathsf{H}_n : \mathsf{U}\ \overline{\rho_n} \to \overline{\tau_n}\end{array}\right]\!\!\right] = \begin{array}{l}\mathbf{codata}\ \mathsf{U}\ \overline{a}\ \mathbf{where}\\ \quad \mathsf{H}_1 : \mathsf{U}\ \overline{a} \to \overline{a \equiv \rho_1} \to \overline{\tau_1}\\ \quad\quad \vdots\\ \quad \mathsf{H}_n : \mathsf{U}\ \overline{a} \to \overline{a \equiv \rho_n} \to \overline{\tau_n}\end{array}$$

This formalizes the intuition that indexed data types can be thought of as *enriching* constructors to carry around additional constraints that were available at their time of construction, whereas indexed codata types can be thought of as *guarding* methods with additional constraints that must be satisfied before an observation can be made. Two of the most basic examples of this simplification are for the type declarations which capture the notion of type equality as an indexed data or indexed codata type, which are defined and simplified like so:

$$\mathfrak{Eq}\left[\!\!\left[\begin{array}{l}\textbf{data}\ \mathsf{Eq}\ a\ b\ \textbf{where}\\ \quad \mathsf{Refl} : \mathsf{Eq}\ a\ a\end{array}\right]\!\!\right] = \begin{array}{l}\textbf{data}\ \mathsf{Eq}\ a\ b\ \textbf{where}\\ \quad \mathsf{Refl} : a \equiv b \to \mathsf{Eq}\ a\ b\end{array}$$

$$\mathfrak{Eq}\left[\!\!\left[\begin{array}{l}\textbf{codata}\ \mathsf{IfEq}\ a\ b\ c\ \textbf{where}\\ \quad \mathsf{AssumeEq} : \mathsf{IfEq}\ a\ a\ c \to c\end{array}\right]\!\!\right] = \begin{array}{l}\textbf{codata}\ \mathsf{IfEq}\ a\ b\ c\ \textbf{where}\\ \quad \mathsf{AssumeEq} : \mathsf{IfEq}\ a\ b\ c \to a \equiv b \to c\end{array}$$

With the above ability to simplify away type indexes, *all* of the presented compilation techniques are easily generalized to indexed data and codata types by composing them with $\mathfrak{Eq}$. For practical programming example, consider the following safe stack codata type indexed by its number of elements.

$$\begin{array}{l}\textbf{codata}\ \mathsf{Stack}\ a\ \textbf{where}\\ \quad \mathsf{Pop}\ \ : \mathsf{Stack}\ (\mathsf{Succ}\ a) \to (\mathbb{Z}, \mathsf{Stack}\ a)\\ \quad \mathsf{Push} : \mathsf{Stack}\ a \to \mathbb{Z} \to \mathsf{Stack}\ (\mathsf{Succ}\ a)\end{array}$$

This stack type is safe in the sense that the Pop operation can only be applied to non-empty Stacks. We cannot compile this to a data type via $\mathfrak{T}$ directly, because that translation does not apply to indexed codata types. However, if we first simplify the Stack type via $\mathfrak{Eq}$, we learn that we can replace the type of the Pop destructor with $\mathsf{Pop} : \mathsf{Stack}\ a \to \forall b. a \equiv \mathsf{Succ}\ b \to (\mathbb{Z}, \mathsf{Stack}\ b)$, whereas the Push destructor is already simple, so it can be left alone. That way, for any object $s : \mathsf{Stack\ Zero}$, even though a client can initiate the observation $s.\mathsf{Pop}$, it will never be completed since there is no way to choose a b and prove that Zero equals $\mathsf{Succ}\ b$. Therefore, the net result of the combined $\mathfrak{T} \circ \mathfrak{Eq}$ translation turns Stack into the following data type, after some further simplification:

$$\begin{array}{l}\textbf{data}\ \mathsf{Stack}\ a\ \textbf{where}\\ \quad \mathsf{MkS} : (\forall b. a \equiv \mathsf{Succ}\ b \to (\mathbb{Z}, \mathsf{Stack}\ b)) \to (\mathbb{Z} \to \mathsf{Stack}\ (\mathsf{Succ}\ a)) \to \mathsf{Stack}\ a\end{array}$$

Notice how the constructor of this type has two fields; one for Pop and one for Push, respectively. However, the Pop operation is guarded by a proof obligation: the client can only receive the top integer and remaining stack if he/she proves that the original stack contains a non-zero number of elements.

4 Compilation in Practice

We have shown how data and codata are related through the use of two different core calculi. To explore how these ideas manifest in practice, we have implemented codata in a couple of settings. First, we extended Haskell with codata

n	Time(s) codata	Time(s) data	Allocs(bytes) codata	Allocs(bytes) data
10000	0.02	0.01	10,143,608	6,877,048
100000	0.39	0.27	495,593,464	463,025,832
1000000	19.64	18.54	44,430,524,144	44,104,487,488

Table 1. Fibonacci scaling tests for the GHC implementation

in order to compare the lazy and codata approaches to demand-driven programming described in Sect. 2.2.[3] Second, we have created a prototype language with indexed (co)data types to further explore the interaction between the compilation and target languages. The prototype language does not commit to a particular evaluation strategy, typing discipline, or paradigm; instead this decision is made when compiling a program to one of several backends. The supported backends include functional ones—Haskell (call-by-need, static types), OCaml (call-by-value, static types), and Racket (call-by-value, dynamic types)—as well as the object-oriented JavaScript.[4] The following issues of complex copattern matching and sharing applies to both implementations; the performance results on efficiency of memoized codata objects are tested with the Haskell extension for the comparison with conventional Haskell code.

Complex Copattern Matching. Our implementations support nested copatterns so that objects can respond to chains of multiple observations, even though λ^{codata} only provides flat copatterns. This extension does not enhance the language expressivity but allows more succinct programs [2]. A flattening step is needed to compile nested copatterns down to a core calculus, which has been explored in previous work by Setzer *et al.* [37] and Thibodeau [39] and implemented in OCaml by Regis-Gianas and Laforgue [33]. Their flattening algorithm requires copatterns to completely cover the object's possible observations because the coverage information is used to drive flattening. This approach was refined and incorporated in a dependently typed setting by Cockx and Abel [11]. With our goal of supporting codata independently of typing discipline and coverage analysis, we have implemented the purely syntax driven approach to flattening found in [38]. For example, the prune function from Sect. 2.2 expands to:

```
prune = λx → λt →
  { Node      → t.Node,
    Children → case x of
                  0 → []
                  _ → map (prune(x-1)) t.Children }
```

Sharing. If codata is to be used instead of laziness for demand-driven programming, then it must have the same performance characteristics, which relies on sharing the results of computations [6]. To test this, we compare the performance of calculating streams of Fibonacci numbers—the poster child for sharing—implemented with both lazy list data types and a stream codata type in Haskell

[3] The GHC fork is at https://github.com/zachsully/ghc/tree/codata-macro.
[4] The prototype compiler is at https://github.com/zachsully/dl/tree/esop2019.

Syntax

$$\text{Values} \ni \quad V ::= \cdots \mid \{\overline{\mathsf{H} \to V}\}$$

$$\text{Terms} \ni t, u, e ::= \cdots \mid t.\mathsf{H} \mid \{\overline{\mathsf{H} \to V}\} \mid \mathbf{let}_{\text{need}}\ \overline{x = t}\ \mathbf{in}\ e$$

Transformation

$$\mathcal{A}[\![t.\mathsf{H}]\!] = \mathcal{A}[\![t]\!].\mathsf{H}$$

$$\mathcal{A}[\![\{\overline{\mathsf{H} \to t}\}]\!] = \mathbf{let}_{\text{need}}\ \overline{x = \mathcal{A}[\![t]\!]}\ \mathbf{in}\ \{\overline{\mathsf{H} \to x}\}$$

Fig. 6. Memoization of λ^{codata}

extended with codata. These tests, presented in Table 1, show the speed of the codata version is always slower in terms of run time and allocations than the lazy list version, but the difference is small and the two versions scale at the same rate. These performance tests are evidence that codata shares the same information when compiled to a call-by-need language; this we get for free because call-by-need data constructors—which codata is compiled into via $\mathfrak{T}$—memoize their fields. In an eager setting, it is enough to use memoized versions of **delay** and **force**, which are introduced by the call-by-value compilation described in Sect. 3.5. This sharing is confirmed by the OCaml and Racket backends of the prototype language which find the 100th Fibonacci in less than a second (a task that takes hours without sharing).

As the object-oriented representative, the JavaScript backend is a compilation from data to codata using the visitor pattern presented in Sect. 3.2. Because codata remains codata (*i.e.* JavaScript objects), an optimization must be performed to ensure the same amount of sharing of codata as the other backends. The solution is to lift out the branches of a codata object, as shown in Fig. 6, where the call-by-need let-bindings can be implemented by **delay** and **force** in strict languages as usual. It turns out that this transformation is also needed in an alternative compilation technique presented by Regis-Gianas and Laforgue [33] where codata is compiled to functions, *i.e.* another form of codata.

5 Related Work

Our work follows in spirit of Amin *et al.*'s [3] desire to provide a minimal theory that can model type parameterization, modules, objects and classes. Another approach to combine type parameterization and modules is also offered by 1ML [36], which is mapped to System F. Amin *et al.*'s work goes one step further by translating System F to a calculus that directly supports objects and classes. Our approach differs in methodology: instead of searching for a logical foundation of a pre-determined notion of objects, we let the logic guide us while exploring what objects are. Even though there is no unanimous consensus that functional and object-oriented paradigms should be combined, there have been several hybrid languages for combining both styles of programming, including Scala, the Common Lisp Object System [8], Objective ML [34], and a proposed but unimplemented object system for Haskell [30].

Arising out of the correspondence between programming languages, category theory, and universal algebras, Hagino [20] first proposed codata as an extension to ML to remedy the asymmetry created by data types. In the same way that data types represent initial F-algebras, codata types represent final F-coalgebras. These structures were implemented in the categorical programming language Charity [10]. On the logical side of the correspondence, codata arises naturally in the sequent calculus [15,28,44] since it provides the right setting to talk about construction of either the provider (*i.e.* the term) or the client (*i.e.* the context) side of a computation, and has roots in classical [13,41] and linear logic [18,19].

In session-typed languages, which also have a foundation in linear logic, external choice can be seen as a codata (product) type dual to the way internal choice corresponds to a data (sum) type. It is interesting that similar problems arise in both settings. Balzer and Pfenning [7] discuss an issue that shows up in choosing between internal and external choice; this corresponds to choosing between data and codata, known as the *expression problem.* They [7] also suggest using the visitor pattern to remedy having external choice (codata) without internal choice (data) as we do in Sect. 3.2. Of course, session types go beyond codata by adding a notion of temporality (via linearity) and multiple processes that communicate over channels.

To explore programming with coinductive types, Ancona and Zucca [4] and Jeannin *et al.* [26] extended Java and OCaml with regular cyclic structures; these have a finite representation that can be eagerly evaluated and fully stored in memory. A less restricted method of programming these structures was introduced by Abel *et al.* [1,2] who popularized the idea of programming by observations, *i.e.* using copatterns. This line of work further developed the functionality of codata types in dependently typed languages by adding indexed codata types [40] and dependent copattern matching [11], which enabled the specification of bisimulation proofs and encodings of productive infinite objects in Agda. We build on these foundations by developing codata in practical languages.

Focusing on implementation, Regis-Gianas and Laforgue [33] added codata with a macro transformation in OCaml. As it turns out, this macro definition corresponds to one of the popular encodings of objects in the λ-calculus [27], where codata/objects are compiled to functions from tagged messages to method bodies. This compilation scheme requires the use of GADTs for static type checking, and is therefore only applicable to dynamically typed languages or the few statically typed languages with expressive enough type systems like Haskell, OCaml, and dependently typed languages. Another popular technique for encoding codata/objects is presented in [31], corresponding to a class-based organization of dynamic dispatch [21], and is presented in this paper. This technique compiles codata/objects to products of methods, which has the advantage of being applicable in a simply-typed setting.

6 Conclusion

We have shown here how codata can be put to use to capture several practical programming idioms and applications, besides just modeling infinite structures.

In order to help incorporate codata in today's programming languages, we have shown how to compile between two core languages: one based on the familiar notion of data types from functional languages such as Haskell and OCaml, and the other one, based on the notion of a structure defined by reactions to observations [1]. This paper works toward the goal of providing common ground between the functional and object-oriented paradigms; as future work, we would like to extend the core with other features of full-fledged functional and object-oriented languages. A better understanding of codata clarifies both the theory and practice of programming languages. Indeed, this work is guiding us in the use of fully-extensional functions for the compilation of Haskell programs. The design is motivated by the desire to improve optimizations, in particular the ones relying on the "arity" of functions, to be more compositional and work between higher-order abstractions. It is interesting that the deepening of our understanding of objects is helping us in better compiling functional languages!

References

1. Abel, A., Pientka, B., Thibodeau, D., Setzer, A.: Copatterns: programming infinite structures by observations. In: Proceedings of the 40th Annual ACM SIGPLAN-SIGACT Symposium on Principles of Programming Languages, POPL 2013, pp. 27–38 (2013)
2. Abel, A.M., Pientka, B.: Wellfounded recursion with copatterns: a unified approach to termination and productivity. In: Proceedings of the 18th ACM SIGPLAN International Conference on Functional Programming, ICFP 2013, pp. 185–196 (2013)
3. Amin, N., Rompf, T., Odersky, M.: Foundations of path-dependent types. In: Proceedings of the 2014 ACM International Conference on Object Oriented Programming Systems Languages & Applications, pp. 233–249 (2014)
4. Ancona, D., Zucca, E.: Corecursive featherweight Java. In: Proceedings of the 14th Workshop on Formal Techniques for Java-Like Programs, FTfJP 2012, Beijing, China, 12 June 2012, pp. 3–10 (2012)
5. Andreoli, J.M.: Logic programming with focusing proofs in linear logic. J. Logic Comput. **2**, 297–347 (1992)
6. Ariola, Z.M., Felleisen, M.: The call-by-need lambda calculus. J. Funct. Program. **7**(3), 265–301 (1997)
7. Balzer, S., Pfenning, F.: Objects as session-typed processes. In: Proceedings of the 5th International Workshop on Programming Based on Actors, Agents, and Decentralized Control, AGERE! 2015, pp. 13–24. ACM, New York (2015)
8. Bobrow, D.G., Kahn, K.M., Kiczales, G., Masinter, L., Stefik, M., Zdybel, F.: Commonloops: merging Lisp and object-oriented programming. In: Conference on Object-Oriented Programming Systems, Languages, and Applications (OOPSLA 1986), Portland, Oregon, USA, Proceedings, pp. 17–29 (1986)
9. Böhm, C., Berarducci, A.: Automatic synthesis of typed lambda-programs on term algebras. Theor. Comput. Sci. **39**, 135–154 (1985)
10. Cockett, R., Fukushima, T.: About charity. Technical report, University of Calgary (1992)
11. Cockx, J., Abel, A.: Elaborating dependent (co)pattern matching. In: Proceedings of the 23rd ACM SIGPLAN International Conference on Functional Programming, ICFP 2018, pp. 75:1–75:30 (2018)

12. Cook, W.R.: On understanding data abstraction, revisited. In: Proceedings of the 24th ACM SIGPLAN Conference on Object Oriented Programming Systems Languages and Applications, pp. 557–572 (2009)
13. Curien, P.L., Herbelin, H.: The duality of computation. In: Proceedings of the Fifth ACM SIGPLAN International Conference on Functional Programming, ICFP 2000, pp. 233–243. ACM, New York (2000)
14. DeLine, R., Fähndrich, M.: Typestates for objects. In: Odersky, M. (ed.) ECOOP 2004. LNCS, vol. 3086, pp. 465–490. Springer, Heidelberg (2004). https://doi.org/10.1007/978-3-540-24851-4_21
15. Downen, P., Ariola, Z.M.: The duality of construction. In: Shao, Z. (ed.) ESOP 2014. LNCS, vol. 8410, pp. 249–269. Springer, Heidelberg (2014). https://doi.org/10.1007/978-3-642-54833-8_14
16. Dummett, M.: The Logical Basis of Methaphysics: The William James Lectures, 1976. Harvard University Press, Cambridge (1991)
17. Gallier, J.: Constructive logics. Part I: a tutorial on proof systems and typed lambda-calculi. Theor. Comput. Sci. **110**(2), 249–339 (1993)
18. Girard, J.Y.: Linear logic. Theor. Comput. Sci. **50**(1), 1–101 (1987)
19. Girard, J.Y.: On the unity of logic. Ann. Pure Appl. Logic **59**(3), 201–217 (1993)
20. Hagino, T.: Codatatypes in ML. J. Symbolic Comput. **8**, 629–650 (1989)
21. Harper, R.: Practical Foundations for Programming Languages, 2nd edn. Cambridge University Press, New York (2016)
22. Howard, W.A.: The formulae-as-types notion of construction. In: Curry, H.B., Hindley, J.R., Seldin, J.P. (eds.) To H.B. Curry Essays on Combinatory Logic, Lambda Calculus and Formalism, pp. 479–490. Academic Press, London (1980). unpublished manuscript of 1969
23. Hughes, J.: Why functional programming matters. Comput. J. **32**(2), 98–107 (1989)
24. Hughes, R.J.M.: Super-combinators: a new implementation method for applicative languages. In: Proceedings of the ACM Symposium on Lisp and Functional Programming, pp. 1–10 (1982)
25. Jacobs, B., Rutten, J.: A tutorial on (co)algebras and (co)induction. EATCS Bull. **62**, 222–259 (1997)
26. Jeannin, J., Kozen, D., Silva, A.: CoCaml: functional programming with regular coinductive types. Fundam. Inform. **150**(3–4), 347–377 (2017)
27. Krishnamurthi, S.: Programming Languages: Application and Interpretation (2007)
28. Munch-Maccagnoni, G.: Focalisation and classical realisability. In: Grädel, E., Kahle, R. (eds.) CSL 2009. LNCS, vol. 5771, pp. 409–423. Springer, Heidelberg (2009). https://doi.org/10.1007/978-3-642-04027-6_30
29. Munch-Maccagnoni, G.: Syntax and models of a non-associative composition of programs and proofs. Ph.D. thesis, Université Paris Diderot (2013)
30. Nordlander, J.: Polymorphic subtyping in O'Haskell. Sci. Comput. Program. **43**(2–3), 93–127 (2002)
31. Pierce, B.C.: Types and Programming Languages. The MIT Press, Cambridge (2002)
32. Plotkin, G.: LCF considered as a programming language. Theor. Comput. Sci. **5**(3), 223–255 (1977)
33. Regis-Gianas, Y., Laforgue, P.: Copattern-matchings and first-class observations in OCaml, with a macro. In: Proceedings of the 19th International Symposium on Principles and Practice of Declarative Programming, PPDP 2017 (2017)

34. Rémy, D., Vouillon, J.: Objective ML: a simple object-oriented extension of ML. In: Proceedings of the 24th ACM SIGPLAN-SIGACT Symposium on Principles of Programming Languages, POPL 1997, pp. 40–53. ACM, New York (1997)
35. Reynolds, J.C.: User-defined types and procedural data structures as complementary approaches to data abstraction. In: Gries, D. (ed.) Programming Methodology. MCS, pp. 309–317. Springer, New York (1978). https://doi.org/10.1007/978-1-4612-6315-9_22
36. Rossberg, A.: 1ML - core and modules united (F-ing first-class modules). In: Proceedings of the 20th ACM SIGPLAN International Conference on Functional Programming, ICFP 2015, pp. 35–47. ACM, New York (2015)
37. Setzer, A., Abel, A., Pientka, B., Thibodeau, D.: Unnesting of copatterns. In: Dowek, G. (ed.) RTA 2014. LNCS, vol. 8560, pp. 31–45. Springer, Cham (2014). https://doi.org/10.1007/978-3-319-08918-8_3
38. Sullivan, Z.: The essence of codata and its implementation. Master's thesis, University of Oregon (2018)
39. Thibodeau, D.: Programming infinite structures using copatterns. Master's thesis, McGill University (2015)
40. Thibodeau, D., Cave, A., Pientka, B.: Indexed codata types. In: Proceedings of the 21st ACM SIGPLAN International Conference on Functional Programming, pp. 351–363 (2016)
41. Wadler, P.: Call-by-value is dual to call-by-name. In: Proceedings of the Eighth ACM SIGPLAN International Conference on Functional Programming, pp. 189–201 (2003)
42. Wadler, P.: Propositions as types. Commun. ACM **58**(12), 75–84 (2015)
43. Weirich, S.: Depending on types. In: Proceedings of the 19th ACM SIGPLAN International Conference on Functional Programming, ICFP 2014 (2014)
44. Zeilberger, N.: On the unity of duality. Ann. Pure Appl. Logic **153**, 66–96 (2008)
45. Zeilberger, N.: The logical basis of evaluation order and pattern-matching. Ph.D. thesis, Carnegie Mellon University (2009)

Composing Bidirectional Programs Monadically

Li-yao Xia[1(✉)], Dominic Orchard[2], and Meng Wang[3]

[1] University of Pennsylvania, Philadelphia, USA
xialiyao@seas.upenn.edu
[2] University of Kent, Canterbury, UK
[3] University of Bristol, Bristol, UK

Abstract. Software frequently converts data from one representation to another and vice versa. Naïvely specifying both conversion directions separately is error prone and introduces conceptual duplication. Instead, *bidirectional programming* techniques allow programs to be written which can be interpreted in both directions. However, these techniques often employ unfamiliar programming idioms via restricted, specialised combinator libraries. Instead, we introduce a framework for composing bidirectional programs monadically, enabling bidirectional programming with familiar abstractions in functional languages such as Haskell. We demonstrate the generality of our approach applied to parsers/printers, lenses, and generators/predicates. We show how to leverage compositionality and equational reasoning for the verification of *round-tripping properties* for such monadic bidirectional programs.

1 Introduction

A *bidirectional transformation* (BX) is a pair of mutually related mappings between source and target data objects. A well-known example solves the *view-update problem* [2] from relational database design. A *view* is a derived database table, computed from concrete *source* tables by a query. The problem is to map an update of the view back to a corresponding update on the source tables. This is captured by a bidirectional transformation. The bidirectional pattern is found in a broad range of applications, including parsing [17,30], refactoring [31], code generation [21,27], and model transformation [32] and XML transformation [25].

When programming a bidirectional transformation, one can separately construct the forwards and backwards functions. However, this approach duplicates effort, is prone to error, and causes subsequent maintenance issues. These problems can be avoided by using specialised programming languages that generate both directions from a single definition [13,16,33], a discipline known as *bidirectional programming*.

The most well-known language family for BX programming is *lenses* [13]. A lens captures transformations between sources S and views V via a pair of functions $\mathsf{get} : S \to V$ and $\mathsf{put} : V \to S \to S$. The get function extracts a view

L. Caires (Ed.): ESOP 2019, LNCS 11423, pp. 147–175, 2019.
https://doi.org/10.1007/978-3-030-17184-1_6

from a source and put takes an updated view and a source as inputs to produce an updated source. The asymmetrical nature of get and put makes it possible for put to recover some of the source data that is not present in the view. In other words, get does not have to be injective to have a corresponding put.

Bidirectional transformations typically respect *round-tripping* laws, capturing the extent to which the transformations preserve information between the two data representations. For example, *well-behaved lenses* [5,13] should satisfy:

$$\mathsf{put}\ (\mathsf{get}\ s)\ s = s \qquad \mathsf{get}\ (\mathsf{put}\ v\ s) = v$$

Lens languages are typically designed to enforce these properties. This focus on unconditional correctness inevitably leads to reduced practicality in programming: lens combinators are often stylised and disconnected from established programming idioms. In this paper, we instead focus on expressing bidirectional programs directly, using monads as an interface for sequential composition.

Monads are a popular pattern [35] (especially in Haskell) which combinator libraries in other domains routinely exploit. Introducing monadic composition to BX programming significantly expands the expressiveness of BX languages and opens up a route for programmers to explore the connection between BX programming and mainstream uni-directional programming. Moreover, it appears that many applications of bidirectional transformations (e.g., parsers and printers [17]) do not share the lens *get*/*put* pattern, and as a result have not been sufficiently explored. However, monadic composition is known to be an effective way to construct at least one direction of such transformations (e.g., parsers).

Contributions. In this paper, we deliberately avoid the well-tried approach of specialised lens languages, instead exploring a novel point in the BX design space based on monadic programming, naturally reusing host language constructs. We revisit lenses, and two more bidirectional patterns, demonstrating how they can be subject to monadic programming. By being uncompromising about the monad interface, we expose the essential ideas behind our framework whilst maximising its utility. The trade off with our approach is that we can no longer enforce correctness in the same way as conventional lenses: our interface does not rule out all non-round-tripping BXs. We tackle this issue by proposing a new compositional reasoning framework that is flexible enough to characterise a variety of round-tripping properties, and simplifies the necessary reasoning.

Specifically, we make the following contributions:

- We describe a method to enable *monadic composition* for bidirectional programs (Sect. 3). Our approach is based on a construction which generates a *monadic profunctor*, parameterised by two application-specific monads which are used to generate the *forward* and *backward* directions.
- To demonstrate the flexibility of our approach, we apply the above method to three different problem domains: parsers/printers (Sects. 3 and 4), lenses (Sect. 5), and generators/predicates for structured data (Sect. 6). While the first two are well-explored areas in the bidirectional programming literature, the third one is a completely new application domain.

- We present a scalable reasoning framework, capturing notions of *compositionality* for bidirectional properties (Sect. 4). We define classes of round-tripping properties inherent to bidirectionalism, which can be verified by following simple criteria. These principles are demonstrated with our three examples. We include some proofs for illustration in the paper. The supplementary material [12] contains machine-checked Coq proofs for the main theorems. An extended version of this manuscript [36] includes additional definitions, proofs, and comparisons in its appendices.
- We have implemented these ideas as Haskell libraries [12], with two wrappers around `attoparsec` for parsers and printers, and `QuickCheck` for generators and predicates, showing the viability of our approach for real programs.

We use Haskell for concrete examples, but the programming patterns can be easily expressed in many functional languages. We use the Haskell notation of assigning type signatures to expressions via an infix double colon "::".

1.1 Further Examples of BX

We introduced lenses briefly above. We now introduce the other two examples used in this paper: *parsers/printers* and *generators/predicates.*

Parsing and printing. Programming language tools (such as interpreters, compilers, and refactoring tools) typically require two intimately linked components: *parsers* and *printers*, respectively mapping from source code to ASTs and back. A simple implementation of these two functions can be given with types:

```
parser :: String → AST          printer :: AST → String
```

Parsers and printers are rarely actual inverses to each other, but instead typically exhibit a variant of round-tripping such as:

```
parser ∘ printer ∘ parser ≡ parser     printer ∘ parser ∘ printer ≡ printer
```

The left equation describes the common situation that parsing discards information about source code, such as whitespace, so that printing the resulting AST does not recover the original source. However, printing retains enough information such that parsing the printed output yields an AST which is equivalent to the AST from parsing the original source. The right equation describes the dual: printing may map different ASTs to the same string. For example, printed code $1 + 2 + 3$ might be produced by left- and right-associated syntax trees.

For particular AST subsets, printing and parsing may actually be left- or right- inverses to each other. Other characterisations are also possible, e.g., with equivalence classes of ASTs (accounting for reassociations). Alternatively, parsers and printers may satisfy properties about the interaction of partially-parsed inputs with the printer and parser, e.g., if `parser :: String → (AST, String)`:

```
(let (x, s') = parser s in parser ((printer x) ++ s'))   ≡  parser s
```

Thus, parsing and printing follows a pattern of inverse-like functions which does not fit the lens paradigm. The pattern resembles lenses between a source (source code) and view (ASTs), but with a compositional notion for the source and partial "gets" which consume some of the source, leaving a remainder.

Writing parsers and printers by hand is often tedious due to the redundancy implied by their inverse-like relation. Thus, various approaches have been proposed for reducing the effort of writing parsers/printers by generating both from a common definition [17,19,30].

Generating and checking. Property-based testing (e.g., QuickCheck) [10] expresses program properties as executable predicates. For instance, the following property checks that an insertion function `insert`, given a sorted list—as checked by the predicate `isSorted :: [Int] → Bool`—produces another sorted list. The combinator $\Longrightarrow$ represents implication for properties.

```
propInsert :: Int → [Int] → Property
propInsert val list = isSorted list ⟹ isSorted (insert val list)
```

To test this property, a testing framework generates random inputs for `val` and `list`. The implementation of $\Longrightarrow$ applied here first checks whether `list` is sorted, and if it is, checks that `insert val list` is sorted as well. This process is repeated with further random inputs until either a counterexample is found or a predetermined number of test cases pass.

However, this naïve method is inefficient: many properties such as `propInsert` have preconditions which are satisfied by an extremely small fraction of inputs. In this case, the ratio of sorted lists among lists of length n is inversely proportional to $n!$, so most generated inputs will be discarded for not satisfying the `isSorted` precondition. Such tests give no information about the validity of the predicate being tested and thus are prohibitively inefficient.

When too many inputs are being discarded, the user must instead supply the framework with *custom generators* of values satisfying the precondition: `genSorted :: Gen [Int]`.

One can expect two complementary properties of such a generator. A generator is *sound* with respect to the predicate `isSorted` if it generates only values satisfying `isSorted`; soundness means that no tests are discarded, hence the tested property is better exercised. A generator is *complete* with respect to `isSorted` if it can generate all satisfying values; completeness ensures the correctness of testing a property with `isSorted` as a precondition, in the sense that if there is a counterexample, it will be eventually generated. In this setting of testing, completeness, which affects the potential adequacy of testing, is arguably more important than soundness, which affects only efficiency.

It is clear that generators and predicates are closely related, forming a pattern similar to that of bidirectional transformations. Given that good generators are usually difficult to construct, the ability to extract both from a common specification with bidirectional programming is a very attractive alternative.

Roadmap. We begin by outlining a concrete example of our monadic approach via parsers and printers (Sect. 2), before explaining the general approach of using *monadic profunctors* to structure bidirectional programs (Sect. 3). Section 4 then presents a compositional reasoning framework for monadic bidirectional programs, with varying degrees of strength adapted to different round-tripping properties. We then replay the developments of the earlier sections to define lenses as well as generators and predicates in Sects. 5 and 6.

2 Monadic Bidirectional Programming

A bidirectional parser, or *biparser*, combines both a parsing direction and printing direction. Our first novelty here is to express biparsers monadically.

In code samples, we use the Haskell pun of naming variables after their types, e.g., a variable of some abstract type `v` will also be called `v`. Similarly, for some type constructor `m`, a variable of type `m v` will be called `mv`. A function `u → m v` (a Kleisli arrow for a monad `m`) will be called `kv`.

Monadic parsers. The following data type provides the standard way to describe parsers of values of type `v` which may consume only part of the input string:

```
data Parser v = Parser { parse :: String → (v, String) }
```

It is well-known that such parsers are monadic [35], i.e., they have a notion of monadic sequential composition embodied by the interface:

```
instance Monad Parser where
  (>>=) :: Parser v → (v → Parser w) → Parser w
  return :: v → Parser v
```

The sequential composition operator `(>>=)`, called *bind*, describes the scheme of constructing a parser by sequentially composing two sub-parsers where the second depends on the output of the first; a parser of `w` values is made up of a parser of `v` and a parser of `w` that depends on the previously parsed `v`. Indeed, this is the implementation given to the monadic interface:

```
pv >>= kw = Parser (λs → let (v, s') = parse pv s in parse (kw v) s')
return v  = Parser (λs → (v, s))
```

Bind first runs the parser `pv` on an input string `s`, resulting in a value `v` which is used to create the parser `kw v`, which is in turn run on the remaining input `s'` to produce parsed values of type `w`. The `return` operation creates a trivial parser for any value `v` which does not consume any input but simply produces `v`.

In practice, parsers composed with `(>>=)` often have a relationship between the output types of the two operands: usually that the former "contains" the latter in some sense. For example, we might parse an expression and compose this with a parser for statements, where statements contain expressions. This relationship will be useful later when we consider printers.

As a shorthand, we can discard the remaining unparsed string of a parser using projection, giving a helper function `parser :: Parser v → (String → v)`.

Monadic printers. Our goal is to augment parsers with their inverse printer, such that we have a monadic type `Biparser` which provides two complementary (bi-directional) transformations:

```
parser  :: Biparser v → (String → v)
printer :: Biparser v → (v → String)
```

However, this type of printer `v → String` (shown also in Sect. 1.1) cannot form a monad because it is *contravariant* in its type parameter `v`. Concretely, we cannot implement the bind (>>=) operator for values with types of this form:

```
-- Failed attempt
bind :: (v → String) → (v → (w → String)) → (w → String)
bind pv kw = λw → let v = (??) in pv v ++ kw v w
```

We are stuck trying to fill the hole (??) as there is no way to get a value of type `v` to pass as an argument to `pv` (first printer) and `kw` (second printer which depends on a `v`). Subsequently, we cannot construct a monadic biparser by simply taking a product of the parser monad and `v → String` and leveraging the result that the product of two monads is a monad.

But what if the type variables of `bind` were related by containment, such that `v` is contained within `w` and thus we have a projection `w → v`? We could use this projection to fill the hole in the failed attempt above, defining a bind-like operator:

```
bind' :: (w → v) → (v → String) → (v → (w → String)) → (w → String)
bind' from pv kw = λw → let v = from w in pv v ++ kw v w
```

This is closer to the monadic form, where `from :: w → v` resolves the difficulty of contravariance by "contextualizing" the printers. Thus, the first printer is no longer just "a printer of `v`", but "a printer of `v` extracted `from` `w`". In the context of constructing a bidirectional parser, having such a function to hand is not an unrealistic expectation: recall that when we compose two parsers, typically the values of the first parser for `v` are contained within the values returned by the second parser for `w`, thus a notion of projection can be defined and used here to recover a `v` in order to build the corresponding printer compositionally.

Of course, this is still not a monad. However, it suggests a way to generate a monadic form by putting the printer and the contextualizing projection together, `(w → v, v → String)` and fusing them into `(w → (v, String))`. This has the advantage of removing the contravariant occurence of `v`, yielding a data type:

```
data Printer w v = Printer { print :: w → (v, String) }
```

If we fix the first parameter type `w`, then the type `Printer w` of printers for `w` values is indeed monadic, combining a *reader monad* (for some global read-only parameter of type `w`) and a *writer monad* (for strings), with implementation:

```
instance Monad (Printer w) where
  return :: v → Printer w v
  return = λv → Printer (λ_ → (v, ""))

  (>>=) :: Printer w v → (v → Printer w t) → Printer w t
  pv >>= kt = Printer (λw → let (v, s) = print pv w
                                (t, s') = print (kt v) w in (t, s ++ s'))
```

The printer `return v` ignores its input and prints nothing. For bind, an input `w` is shared by both printers and the resulting strings are concatenated.

We can adapt the contextualisation of a printer by the following operation which amounts to pre-composition, witnessing the fact that `Printer` is a contravariant functor in its first parameter:

```
comap :: (w → w') → Printer w' v → Printer w v
comap from (Printer f) = Printer (f ∘ from)
```

2.1 Monadic Biparsers

So far so good: we now have a monadic notion of printers. However, our goal is to combine parsers and printers in a single type. Since we have two monads, we use the standard result that a product of monads is a monad, defining *biparsers*:

```
data Biparser u v = Biparser { parse :: String → (v, String)
                             , print :: u      → (v, String) }
```

By pairing parsers and printers we have to unify their covariant parameters. When both the type parameters of `Biparser` are the same it is easy to interpret this type: a biparser `Biparser v v` is a parser from strings to `v` values and printer from `v` values to strings. We refer to biparsers of this type as *aligned* biparsers. What about when the type parameters differ? A biparser of type `Biparser u v` provides a parser from strings to `v` values and a printer from `u` values to strings, but where the printers can compute `v` values from `u` values, i.e., `u` is some common broader representation which contains relevant `v`-typed subcomponents. A biparser `Biparser u v` can be thought of as printing a certain subtree `v` from the broader representation of a syntax tree `u`.

The corresponding monad for `Biparser` is the product of the previous two monad definitions for `Parser` and `Printer`, allowing both to be composed sequentially at the same time. To avoid duplication we elide the definition here which is shown in full in Appendix A of the extended version [36]

We can also lift the previous notion of `comap` from printers to biparsers, which gives us a way to contextualize a printer:

```
comap :: (u → u') → Biparser u' v → Biparser u v
comap f (Biparser parse print) = Biparser parse (print ∘ f)

upon :: Biparser u' v → (u → u') → Biparser u v
upon = flip comap
```

In the rest of this section, we use the alias "upon" for `comap` with flipped parameters where we read ``p `upon` subpart`` as applying the printer of `p :: Biparser u' v` on a subpart of an input of type `u` calculated by `subpart :: u → u'`, thus yielding a biparser of type `Biparser u v`.

An example biparser. Let us write a biparser, `string :: Biparser String String`, for strings which are prefixed by their length and a space. For example, the following unit tests should be true:

```
test1 = parse string "6␣lambda␣calculus" == ("lambda", "␣calculus")
test2 = print string "SKI" == ("SKI", "3␣SKI")
```

We start by defining a primitive biparser of single characters as:

```
char :: Biparser Char Char
char = Biparser (λ (c : s) → (c, s)) (λ c → (c, [c]))
```

A character is parsed by deconstructing the source string into its head and tail. For brevity, we do not handle the failure associated with an empty string. A character `c` is printed as its single-letter string (a singleton list) paired with `c`.

Next, we define a biparser `int` for an integer followed by a single space. An auxiliary biparser `digits` (on the right) parses an integer one digit at a time into a string. Note that in Haskell, the **do**-notation statement "`d ← char ‘upon‘ head`" desugars to "`char ‘upon’ head >>= λ d → ...`" which uses `(>>=)` and a function binding `d` in the scope of the rest of the desugared block.

```
int :: Biparser Int Int
int = do
  ds ← digits ‘upon‘ printedInt
  return (read ds)
  where
    printedInt n = show n ++ "␣"
```

```
digits :: Biparser String String
digits = do
  d ← char ‘upon‘ head
  if isDigit d then do
    igits ← digits ‘upon‘ tail
    return (d : igits)
  else if d == ' ' then return "␣"
  else error "Expected␣digit␣or␣space"
```

On the right, `digits` extracts a `String` consisting of digits followed by a single space. As a parser, it parses a character (`char ‘upon‘ head`); if it is a digit then it continues parsing recursively (`digits ‘upon‘ tail`) appending the first character to the result (`d : igits`). Otherwise, if the parsed character is a space the parser returns `"␣"` . As a printer, `digits` expects a non-empty string of the same format; `‘upon‘ head` extracts the first character of the input, then `char` prints it and returns it back as `d`; if it is a digit, then `‘upon‘ tail` extracts the rest of the input to print recursively. If the character is a space, the printer returns a space and terminates; otherwise (not digit or space) the printer throws an error.

On the left, the biparser `int` uses `read` to convert an input string of digits (parsed by `digits`) into an integer, and `printedInt` to convert an integer to an output string printed by `digits`. A safer implementation could return the `Maybe` type when parsing but we keep things simple here for now.

After parsing an integer `n`, we can parse the string following it by iterating `n` times the biparser `char`. This is captured by the `replicateBiparser` combinator below, defined recursively like `digits` but with the termination condition given by an external parameter. To iterate `n` times a biparser `pv`: if `n == 0` , there is nothing to do and we return the empty list; otherwise for `n > 0`, we run `pv` once to get the head `v`, and recursively iterate `n-1` times to get the tail `vs`.

Note that although not reflected in its type, `replicateBiparser n pv` expects, as a printer, a list `l` of length `n`: if `n == 0` , there is nothing to print; if `n > 0`, `‘upon‘ head` extracts the head of `l` to print it with `pv`, and `‘upon‘ tail` extracts its tail, of length `n-1`, to print it recursively.

```
replicateBiparser :: Int → Biparser u v → Biparser [u] [v]
replicateBiparser 0 pv = return []
replicateBiparser n pv = do
  v  ← pv ‘upon‘ head
  vs ← (replicateBiparser (n - 1) pv) ‘upon‘ tail
  return (v : vs)
```

(akin to replicateM from Haskell's standard library). We can now fulfil our task:

```
string :: Biparser String String
string = int ‘upon‘ length >>= λn → replicateBiparser n char
```

Interestingly, if we erase applications of upon, i.e., we substitute every expression of the form py ‘upon‘ f with py and ignore the second parameter of the types, we obtain what is essentially the definition of a parser in an idiomatic style for monadic parsing. This is because ‘upon‘ f is the identity on the parser component of Biparser. Thus the biparser code closely resembles standard, idiomatic monadic parser code but with "annotations" via upon expressing how to apply the backwards direction of printing to subparts of the parsed string.

Despite its simplicity, the syntax of length-prefixed strings is notably context-sensitive. Thus the example makes crucial use of the monadic interface for bidirectional programming: a value (the length) must first be extracted to dynamically delimit the string that is parsed next. Context-sensitivity is standard for parser combinators in contrast with parser generators, e.g., Yacc, and applicative parsers, which are mostly restricted to context-free languages. By our monadic BX approach, we can now bring this power to bear on *bidirectional* parsing.

3 A Unifying Structure: Monadic Profunctors

The biparser examples of the previous section were enabled by both the monadic structure of Biparser and the comap operation (also called upon, with flipped arguments). We describe a type as being a *monadic profunctor* when it has both a monadic structure and a comap operation (subject to some equations). The notion of a monadic profunctor is general, but it characterises a key class of structures for bidirectional programs, which we explain here. Furthermore, we show a construction of monadic profunctors from pairs of monads which elicits the necessary structure for monadic bidirectional programming in the style of the previous section.

Profunctors. In Sect. 2.1, biparsers were defined by a data type with two type parameters (Biparser u v) which is functorial and monadic in the second parameter and *contravariantly* functorial in the first parameter (provided by the comap operation). In standard terminology, a two-parameter type p which is functorial in both its type parameters is called a *bifunctor*. In Haskell, the term *profunctor* has come to mean any bifunctor which is contravariant in the first type parameter and covariant in the second.[1] This differs slightly from the standard category theory terminology where a profunctor is a bifunctor $\mathsf{F} : \mathcal{D}^{\mathsf{op}} \times \mathcal{C} \rightarrow$

[1] http://hackage.haskell.org//profunctors/docs/Data-Profunctor.html.

Set. This corresponds to the Haskell community's use of the term "profunctor" if we treat Haskell in an idealised way as the category of sets.

We adopt this programming-oriented terminology, capturing the `comap` operation via a class `Profunctor`. In the preceding section, some uses of `comap` involved a partial function, e.g., `comap head`. We make the possibility of partiality explicit via the `Maybe` type, yielding the following definition.

Definition 1. A binary data type is a **profunctor** if it is a contravariant functor in its first parameter and covariant functor in its second, with the operation:

```
class ForallF Functor p ⇒ Profunctor p where
    comap :: (u → Maybe u') → p u' v → p u v
```

which should obey two laws:

```
comap Just = id        comap (f >=> g) = comap f ∘ comap g
```

where `(>=>) :: (a → Maybe b) → (b → Maybe c) → (a → Maybe c)` composes partial functions (left-to-right), captured by Kleisli arrows of the `Maybe` monad.

The constraint `ForallF Functor p` captures a universally quantified constraint [6]: for all types `u` then `p u` has an instance of the `Functor` class.[2]

The requirement for `comap` to take partial functions is in response to the frequent need to restrict the domain of bidirectional transformations. In combinator-based approaches, combinators typically constrain bidirectional programs to be bijections, enforcing domain restrictions by construction. Our more flexible approach requires a way to include such restrictions explicitly, hence `comap`.

Since the contravariant part of the bifunctor applies to functions of type `u → Maybe u'`, the categorical analogy here is more precisely a profunctor $\mathsf{F} : \mathcal{C_T}^{\mathsf{op}} \times \mathcal{C} \to \mathbf{Set}$ where $\mathcal{C}_T$ is the Kleisli category of the partiality (`Maybe`) monad.

Definition 2. A **monadic profunctor** is a profunctor `p` (in the sense of Definition 1) such that `p u` is a monad for all `u`. In terms of type class constraints, this means there is an instance `Profunctor p` and for all `u` there is a `Monad (p u)` instance. Thus, we represent monadic profunctors by the following empty class (which inherits all its methods from its superclasses):

```
class (Profunctor p, ForallF Monad p) ⇒ Profmonad p
```

Monadic profunctors must obey the following laws about the interaction between profunctor and monad operations:

```
comap f (return y)    =   return y
comap f (py >>= kz)   =   comap f py >>= (λ y → comap f (kz y))
```

[2] As of GHC 8.6, the `QuantifiedConstraints` extension allows universal quantification in constraints, written as `forall u. Functor (p u)`, but for simplicity we use the constraint constructor `ForallF` from the `constraints` package: http://hackage.haskell.org/package/constraints.

(for all f :: u → Maybe v, py :: p v y, kz :: y → p v z). These laws are equivalent to saying that comap lifts (partial) functions into monad morphisms. In Haskell, these laws are obtained *for free* by parametricity [34]. This means that every contravariant functor and monad is in fact a monadic profunctor, thus the following universal instance is lawful:

```
instance (Profunctor p, ForallF Monad p) ⇒ Profmonad p
```

Corollary 1. Biparsers form a monadic profunctor as there is an instance of Monad (P u) and Profunctor p satisfying the requisite laws.

Lastly, we introduce a useful piece of terminology (mentioned in the previous section on biparsers) for describing values of a profunctor of a particular form:

Definition 3. A value p :: P u v of a profunctor P is called *aligned* if u = v.

3.1 Constructing Monadic Profunctors

Our examples (parsers/printers, lenses, and generators/predicates) share monadic profunctors as an abstraction, making it possible to write different kinds of bidirectional transformations monadically. Underlying these definitions of monadic profunctors is a common structure, which we explain here using biparsers, and which will be replayed in Sect. 5 for lenses and Sect. 6 for bigenerators.

There are two simple ways in which a covariant functor m (resp. a monad) gives rise to a profunctor (resp. a monadic profunctor). The first is by constructing a profunctor in which the contravariant parameter is discarded, i.e., p u v = m v; the second is as a function type from the contravariant parameter u to m v, i.e., p u v = u → m v. These are standard mathematical constructions, and the latter appears in the Haskell profunctors package with the name Star. Our core construction is based on these two ways of creating a profunctor, which we call Fwd and Bwd respectively:

```
data Fwd m u v = Fwd { unFwd :: m v }       -- ignore contrv. parameter
data Bwd m u v = Bwd { unBwd :: u → m v } -- maps from contrv. parameter
```

The naming reflects the idea that these two constructions will together capture a bidirectional transformation and are related by domain-specific round-tripping properties in our framework. Both Fwd and Bwd map any functor into a profunctor by the following type class instances:

```
instance Functor m ⇒ Functor (Fwd m u) where
  fmap f (Fwd x) = Fwd (fmap f x)
instance Functor m ⇒ Profunctor (Fwd m) where
  comap f (Fwd x) = Fwd x

instance Functor m ⇒ Functor (Bwd m u) where
  fmap f (Bwd x) = Bwd ((fmap f) ∘ x)
instance (Monad m, MonadPartial m) ⇒ Profunctor (Bwd m) where
  comap f (Bwd x) = Bwd ((toFailure ∘ f) >=> x)
```

There is an additional constraint here for Bwd, enforcing that the monad m is a member of the MonadPartial class which we define as:

```
class MonadPartial m  where  toFailure :: Maybe a → m a
```

This provides an interface for monads which can internalise a notion of failure, as captured at the top-level by Maybe in comap.

Furthermore, Fwd and Bwd both map any monad into a monadic profunctor:

```
instance Monad m
    ⇒ Monad (Fwd m u) where
  return x = Fwd (return x)
  Fwd py >>= kz =
    Fwd (py >>= unFwd ∘ kz)
```

```
instance Monad m
    ⇒ Monad (Bwd m u) where
  return x = Bwd (λ_ → return x)
  Bwd my >>= kz = Bwd
    (λu → my u >>= (λy → unBwd (kz y) u))
```

The product of two monadic profunctors is also a monadic profunctor. This follows from the fact that the product of two monads is a monad and the product of two contravariant functors is a contravariant functor.

```
data (:*:) p q u v = (:*:) { pfst :: p u v,  psnd :: q u v }

instance (Monad (p u), Monad (q u)) ⇒ Monad ((p :*: q) u) where
  return y = return y :*: return y
  py :*: qy >>= kz = (py >>= pfst ∘ kz) :*: (qy >>= psnd ∘ kz)

instance (ForallF Functor (p :*: q), Profunctor p, Profunctor q)
      ⇒ Profunctor (p :*: q) where
  comap f (py :*: qy) = comap f py :*: comap f qy
```

3.2 Deriving Biparsers as Monadic Profunctor Pairs

We can redefine biparsers in terms of the above data types, their instances, and two standard monads, the state and writer monads:

```
type State  s a = s → (a, s)
type WriterT w m a = m (a, w)
type Biparser = Fwd (State String) :*: Bwd (WriterT Maybe String)
```

The backward direction composes the writer monad with the Maybe monad using WriterT (the writer monad transformer, equivalent to composing two monads with a distributive law). Thus the backwards component of Biparser corresponds to printers (which may fail) and the forwards component to parsers:

```
Bwd (WriterT Maybe String) u v  ≅  u → Maybe (v, String)
       Fwd (State String) u v  ≅  String → (v, String)
```

For the above code to work in Haskell, the State and WriterT types need to be defined via either a **data** type or **newtype** in order to allow type class instances on partially applied type constructors. We abuse the notation here for simplicity but define smart constructors and deconstructors for the actual implementation:[3]

```
parse :: Biparser u v → (String → (v, String))
print :: Biparser u v → (u → Maybe (v, String))
mkBP  :: (String → (v, String)) → (u → Maybe (v, String)) → Biparser u v
```

The monadic profunctor definition for biparsers now comes for free from the constructions in Sect. 3.1 along with the following instance of `MonadPartial` for the writer monad transformer with the `Maybe` monad:

```
instance Monoid w ⇒ MonadPartial (WriterT w Maybe) where
  toFailure Nothing = WriterT Nothing
  toFailure (Just a) = WriterT (Just (a, mempty))
```

In a similar manner, we will use this monadic profunctor construction to define monadic bidirectional transformations for lenses (Sect. 5) and bigenerators (Sect. 6).

The example biparsers from Sect. 2.1 can be easily redefined using the structure here. For example, the primitive biparser `char` becomes:

```
char :: Biparser Char Char
char = mkBP (λ (c : s) → (c, s)) (λ c → Just (c, [c]))
```

Codec library. The `codec` library [8] provides a general type for bidirectional programming isomorphic to our composite type `Fwd r :*: Bwd w`:

```
data Codec r w c a = Codec { codecIn :: r a, codecOut :: c → w a }
```

Though the original `codec` library was developed independently, its current form is a result of this work. In particular, we contributed to the package by generalising its original type (`codecOut :: c → w ()`) to the one above, and provided `Monad` and `Profunctor` instances to support monadic bidirectional programming with codecs.

4 Reasoning about Bidirectionality

So far we have seen how the monadic profunctor structure provides a way to define biparsers using familiar operations and syntax: monads and **do**-notation. This structuring allows both the forwards and backwards components of a biparser to be defined simultaneously in a single compact definition.

This section studies the interaction of monadic profunctors with the *round-tripping laws* that relate the two components of a bidirectional program. For every bidirectional transformation we can define dual properties: *backward round tripping* (going backwards-then-forwards) and *forward round tripping* (going forwards-then-backwards). In each BX domain, such properties also capture

[3] *Smart constructors* (and dually *smart deconstructors*) are just functions that hide boilerplate code for constructing and deconstructing data types.

additional domain-specific information flow inherent to the transformations. We use biparsers as the running example. We then apply the same principles to our other examples in Sects. 5 and 6. For brevity, we use `Bp` as an alias for `Biparser`.

Definition 4. A biparser `p` :: `Bp u u` is *backward round tripping* if for all `x` :: `u` and `s, s'` :: `String` then (recalling that `print p` :: `u` → `Maybe (v, String)`):

```
fmap snd (print p x) = Just s   ⟹   parse p (s ++ s') = (x, s').
```

That is, if a biparser `p` when used as a printer (going backwards) on an input value `x` produces a string `s`, then using `p` as a parser on a string with prefix `s` and suffix `s'` yields the original input value `x` and the remaining input `s'`.

Note that backward round tripping is defined for *aligned* biparsers (of type `Bp u u`) since the same value `x` is used as both the input of the printer (typed by the first type parameter of `Bp`) and as the expected output of the parser (typed by the second type parameter of `Bp`).

The dual property is *forward* round tripping: a source string `s` is parsed (going forwards) into some value `x` which when printed produces the initial source `s`:

Definition 5. A biparser `p` :: `Bp u u` is *forward round tripping* if for every `x` :: `u` and `s` :: `String` we have that:

```
parse p s = (x, "")   ⟹   fmap snd (print p x) = Just s
```

Proposition 1. The biparser `char` :: `Bp Char Char` (Sect. 3.2) is both backward and forward round tripping. Proof by expanding definitions and algebraic reasoning.

Note, in some applications, forward round tripping is too strong. Here it requires that every printed value corresponds to at most one source string. This is often not the case as ASTs typically discard formatting and comments so that pretty-printed code is lexically different to the original source. However, different notions of equality enable more reasonable forward round-tripping properties.

Although one can check round-tripping properties of biparsers by expanding their definitions and the underlying monadic profunctor operations, a more scalable approach is provided if a round-tripping property is *compositional* with respect to the monadic profunctor operations, i.e., if these operations preserve the property. Compositional properties are easier to enforce and check since only the individual atomic components need round-tripping proofs. Such properties are then guaranteed "by construction" for programs built from those components.

4.1 Compositional Properties of Monadic Bidirectional Programming

Let us first formalize compositionality as follows. A *property* $\mathcal{R}$ over a monadic profunctor `P` is a family of subsets $\mathcal{R}^{\mathtt{u}}_{\mathtt{v}}$ of `P u v` indexed by types `u` and `v`.

Definition 6. A property $\mathcal{R}$ over a monadic profunctor `P` is *compositional* if the monadic profunctor operations are closed over $\mathcal{R}$, i.e., the following conditions hold for all types `u`, `v`, `w`:

1. For all `x :: v`, $\quad$ $(\texttt{return x}) \in \mathcal{R}^{\texttt{u}}_{\texttt{v}}$ $\quad$ (comp-return)
2. For all `p :: P u v` and `k :: v → P u w`,
$$(\texttt{p} \in \mathcal{R}^{\texttt{u}}_{\texttt{v}}) \wedge (\forall \texttt{v}.\ (\texttt{k v}) \in \mathcal{R}^{\texttt{u}}_{\texttt{w}}) \implies (\texttt{p >>= k}) \in \mathcal{R}^{\texttt{u}}_{\texttt{w}} \qquad \text{(comp-bind)}$$
3. For all `p :: P u' v` and `f :: u → Maybe u'`,
$$\texttt{p} \in \mathcal{R}^{\texttt{u'}}_{\texttt{v}} \implies (\texttt{comap f p}) \in \mathcal{R}^{\texttt{u}}_{\texttt{v}} \qquad \text{(comp-comap)}$$

Unfortunately for biparsers, forward and backward round tripping as defined above are *not* compositional: `return` is not backward round tripping and `>>=` does not preserve forward round tripping. Furthermore, these two properties are restricted to biparsers of type `Bp u u` (i.e., aligned biparsers) but compositionality requires that the two type parameters of the monadic profunctor can differ in the case of `comap` and `(>>=)`. This suggests that we need to look for more general properties that capture the full gamut of possible biparsers.

We first focus on backward round tripping. Informally, backward round tripping states that if you print (going backwards) and parse the resulting output (going forwards) then you get back the initial value. However, in a general biparser `p :: Bp u v`, the input type of the printer `u` differs from the output type of the parser `v`, so we cannot compare them. But our intent for printers is that what we actually print is a fragment of `u`, a fragment which is given as the output of the printer. By thus comparing the outputs of both the parser and printer, we obtain the following variant of backward round tripping:

Definition 7. A biparser `p :: Bp u v` is *weak backward round tripping* if for all `x :: u`, `y :: v`, and `s, s' :: String` then:

$$\texttt{print p x = Just (y, s)} \implies \texttt{parse p (s ++ s') = (y, s')}$$

Removing backward round tripping's restriction to aligned biparsers and using the result `y :: v` of the printer gives us a property that *is* compositional:

Proposition 2. Weak backward round tripping of biparsers is compositional.

Proposition 3. The primitive biparser `char` is weak backward round tripping.

Corollary 2. Propositions 2 & 3 imply `string` is weak backward round tripping.

This property is "weak" as it does not constrain the relationship between the input `u` of the printer and its output `v`. In fact, there is no hope for a compositional property to do so: the monadic profunctor combinators do not enforce a relationship between them. However, we can regain compositionality for the stronger backward round-tripping property by combining the weak compositional property with an additional non-compositional property on the relationship between the printer's input and output. This relationship is represented by the function that results from ignoring the printed string, which amounts to removing the main effect of the printer. Thus we call this operation a *purification*:

```
purify :: forall u v. Bp u v → u → Maybe v
purify p u = fmap fst (print p u)
```

Ultimately, when a biparser is aligned (`p :: Bp u u`) we want an input to the printer to be returned in its output, i.e, `purify p` should equal `λx → Just x`. If this is the case, we recover the original backward round tripping property:

Theorem 1. If `p :: P u u` is weak backward round tripping, and for all `x :: u`. `purify p x = Just x`, then `p` is backward round tripping.

Thus, for any biparser `p`, we can get backward round tripping by proving that its atomic subcomponents are weak backward round tripping, and proving that `purify p x = Just x`. The interesting aspect of the purification condition here is that it renders irrelevant the domain-specific effects of the biparser, i.e., those related to manipulating source strings. This considerably simplifies any proof. Furthermore, the definition of `purify` is a *monadic profunctor homomorphism* which provides a set of equations that can be used to expedite the reasoning.

Definition 8. A *monadic profunctor homomorphism* between monadic profunctors `P` and `Q` is a polymorphic function `proj :: P u v → Q u v` such that:

$$\begin{aligned} \texttt{proj (comap}_P\texttt{ f p)} &\equiv \texttt{comap}_Q\texttt{ f (proj p)} \\ \texttt{proj (p >>=}_P\texttt{ k)} &\equiv \texttt{(proj p) >>=}_Q\texttt{ (}\lambda\texttt{x} \rightarrow \texttt{proj (k x))} \\ \texttt{proj (return}_P\texttt{ x)} &\equiv \texttt{return}_Q\texttt{ x} \end{aligned}$$

Proposition 4. The `purify :: Bp u v → u → Maybe v` operation for biparsers (above) is a monadic profunctor homomorphism between `Bp` and the monadic profunctor `PartialFun u v = u → Maybe v`.

Corollary 3. (of Theorem 1 with Corollary 2 and Proposition 4) The biparser `string` is backward round tripping.

Proof First prove (in Appendix B [36]) the following properties of biparsers `char`, `int`, and `replicatedBp :: Int → Bp u v → Bp [u] [v]` (writing `proj` for `purify`):

$$\texttt{proj char n} \equiv \texttt{Just n} \tag{4.1}$$

$$\texttt{proj int n} \equiv \texttt{Just n} \tag{4.2}$$

$$\texttt{proj (replicateBp (length xs) p) xs} \equiv \texttt{mapM (proj p) xs} \tag{4.3}$$

From these and the homomorphism properties we can prove `proj string = Just`:

```
           proj string xs
         ≡ proj (comap length int >>= λn → replicateBp n char) xs
Prop.4   ≡ (comap length (proj int) >>= λn → proj (replicateBp n char)) xs
(4.2)    ≡ (comap length Just >>= λn → proj (replicateBp n char)) xs
Def.2    ≡ proj (replicateBp (length xs) char) xs
(4.3)    ≡ mapM (proj char) xs
(4.1)    ≡ mapM Just xs
{monad}  ≡ Just xs
```

Combining `proj string = Just` with Corollary 2 (`string` is weak backward round tripping) enables Theorem 1, proving that `string` is backward round tripping.

The other two core examples in this paper also permit a definition of `purify`. We capture the general pattern as follows:

Definition 9. A *purifiable monadic profunctor* is a monadic profunctor `P` with a homomorphism `proj` from `P` to the monadic profunctor of partial functions `- → Maybe -`. We say that `proj p` is the *pure projection* of `p`.

Definition 10. A pure projection `proj p :: u → Maybe v` is called the *identity projection* when `proj p x = Just x` for all `x :: u`.

Here and in Sects. 5 and 6, identity projections enable compositional round-tripping properties to be derived from more general non-compositional properties, as seen above for backward round tripping of biparsers.

We have neglected forward round tripping, which is not compositional, not even in a weakened form. However, we can generalise compositionality with conditions related to *injectivity*, enabling a generalisation of forward round tripping. We call the generalised meta-property *quasicompositionality.*

4.2 Quasicompositionality for Monadic Profunctors

An injective function $f : A \to B$ is a function for which there exists a left inverse $f^{-1} : B \to A$, i.e., where $f^{-1} \circ f = id$. We can see this pair of functions as a simple kind of bidirectional program, with a forward round-tripping property (assuming f is the forwards direction). We can lift the notion of injectivity to the monadic profunctor setting and capture forward round-tripping properties that are preserved by the monadic profunctor operations, given some additional injectivity-like restriction. We first formalise the notion of an *injective arrow*.

Informally, an injective arrow `k :: v → m w` produces an output from which the input can be recalculated:

Definition 11. Let m be a monad. A function $k :: v \to m\ w$ is an *injective arrow* if there exists $k' :: w \to v$ (the *left arrow inverse* of k) such that for all $x :: v$:

$$k\ x >>= \lambda y \to \texttt{return}\ (x, y) \equiv k\ x >>= \lambda y \to \texttt{return}\ (k'\ y, y)$$

Next, we define *quasicompositionality* which extends the compositionality meta-property with the requirement for >>= to be applied to injective arrows:

Definition 12. Let P be a monadic profunctor. A property $\mathcal{R}^{u}_{v} \subseteq P\ u\ v$ indexed by types u and v is *quasicompositional* if the following holds

1. For all $x :: v$, $(\texttt{return}\ x) \in \mathcal{R}^{u}_{v}$ (qcomp-return)
2. For all $p :: P\ u\ v$, $k :: v \to P\ u\ w$, **if k is an injective arrow,**
$$(p \in \mathcal{R}^{u}_{v}) \wedge (\forall v. (k\ v) \in \mathcal{R}^{u}_{w}) \implies (p >>= k) \in \mathcal{R}^{u}_{w} \quad \text{(qcomp-bind)}$$
3. For all $p :: P\ u'\ v$, $f :: u \to \texttt{Maybe}\ u'$,
$$p \in \mathcal{R}^{u'}_{v} \wedge \implies (\texttt{comap}\ f\ p) \in \mathcal{R}^{u}_{w} \quad \text{(qcomp-comap)}$$

We now formulate a weakening of forward round tripping. As with weak backward round tripping, we rely on the idea that the printer *outputs* both a string and the value that was printed, so that we need to compare the outputs of both the parser and the printer, as opposed to comparing the output of the parser with the input of the printer as in (strong) forward round tripping. If running the parser component of a biparser on a string s01 yields a value y and a remaining string s1, and the printer outputs that same value y along with a string s0, then s0 is the prefix of s01 that was consumed by the parser, i.e., s01 = s0 ++ s1.

Definition 13. A biparser p : Bp u v is *weak forward round tripping* if for all x :: u, y :: v, and s0, s1, s01 :: String then:

$$\texttt{parse}\ p\ s01 = (y, s1) \wedge \texttt{print}\ p\ x = \texttt{Just}\ (y, s0) \implies s01 = s0\ \texttt{++}\ s1$$

Proposition 5. Weak forward round tripping is quasicompositional.

Proof. We sketch the qcomp-bind case, where p = (m >>= k) for some m and k that are weak forward roundtripping. From parse (m >>= k) s01 = (y, s1), it follows that there exists z, s such that parse m s01 = (z, s) and parse (k z) s = (y, s1). Similarly print (m >>= k) x = Just (y, s0) implies there exists z', s0' such that print m x = Just (z', s0') and print (k z') x = Just (y, s1') and s0 = s0' ++ s1'. Because k is an injective arrow, we have z = z' (see appendix). We then use the assumption that m and k are weak forward roundtripping on m and on k a, and deduce that s01 = s0' ++ s and s = s1' ++ s1 therefore s01 = s0 ++ s1.

Proposition 6. The char biparser is weak forward round tripping.

Corollary 4. Propositions 5 and 6 imply that `string` is weak forward round tripping if we restrict the parser to inputs whose digits do not contain redundant leading zeros.

Proof. All of the right operands of `>>=` in the definition of `string` are injective arrows, apart from `λds → return (read ds)` at the end of the auxiliary `int` biparser. Indeed, the `read` function is not injective since multiple strings may parse to the same integer: `read "0" = read "00" = 0`. But the pre-condition to the proposition (no redundant leading zero digits) restricts the input strings so that `read` is injective. The rest of the proof is a corollary of Propositions 5 and 6.

Thus, quasicompositionality gives us scalable reasoning for weak forward round tripping, which is by construction for biparsers: we just need to prove this property for individual atomic biparsers. Similarly to backward round tripping, we can prove forward round tripping by combining weak forward round tripping with the identity projection property:

Theorem 2. If `p :: P u u` is weak forward round-tripping, and for all `x :: u`, `purify p x = Just x`, then `p` is forward round tripping.

Corollary 5. The biparser `string` is forward round tripping by the above theorem (with identity projection shown in the proof of Corollary 3) and Corollary 4.

In summary, for any BX we can consider two round-tripping properties: forwards-then-backwards and backwards-then-forwards, called just *forward* and *backward* here respectively. Whilst combinator-based approaches can guarantee round-tripping by construction, we have made a trade-off to get greater expressivity in the monadic approach. However, we regain the ability to reason about bidirectional transformations in a manageable, scalable way if round-tripping properties are compositional. Unfortunately, due to the monadic profunctor structuring, this tends not to be the case. Instead, weakened round-tripping properties can be compositional or quasicompositional (adding injectivity). In such cases, we recover the stronger property by proving a simple property on aligned transformations: that the backwards direction faithfully reproduces its input as its output (*identity projection*). Appendix C in our extended manuscript [36] compares this reasoning approach to a proof of backwards round tripping for separately implemented parsers and printers (not using our combined monadic approach).

5 Monadic Bidirectional Programming for Lenses

Lenses are a common object of study in bidirectional programming, comprising a pair of functions (`get` $: S \to V$, `put` $: V \to S \to S$) satisfying *well-behaved lens* laws shown in Sect. 1. Previously, when considering the monadic structure of parsers and printers, the starting point was that parsers already have a well-known monadic structure. The challenge came in finding a reasonable monadic characterisation for printers that was compatible with the parser monad. In the end, this construction was expressed by a product of two monadic profunctors

Fwd m and Bwd n for monads m and n. For lenses we are in the same position: the forwards direction (get) is already a monad—the reader monad. The backwards direction put is not a monad since it is contravariant in its parameter; the same situation as printers. We can apply the same approach of "monadisation" used for parsers and printers, giving the following new data type for lenses:

```
data L s u v = L { get :: s → v, put :: u → s → (v, s) }
```

The result of put is paired with a covariant parameter v (the result type of get) in the same way as monadic printers. Instead of mapping a view and a source to a source, put now maps values of a different type u, which we call a *pre-view*, along with a source s into a pair of a view v and source s. This definition can be structured as a monadic profunctor via a pair of Fwd and Bwd constructions:

```
type L s = (Fwd (Reader s)) :*: (Bwd (State s))
```

Thus by the results of Sect. 3, we now have a monadic profunctor characterisation of lenses that allows us to compose lenses via the monadic interface.

Ideally, get and put should be total, but this is impossible without a way to restrict the domains. In particular, there is the known problem of "duplication" [23], where source data may appear more than once in the view, and a necessary condition for put to be well-behaved is that the duplicates remain equal amid view updates. This problem is inherent to all bidirectional transformations, and bidirectional languages have to rule out inconsistent updates of duplicates either statically [13] or dynamically [23]. To remedy this, we capture both partiality of get and a predicate on sources in put for additional dynamic checking. This is provided by the following Fwd and Bwd monadic profunctors:

```
type ReaderT r m a = r → m a
type StateT s m a  = s → m (a, s)
type WriterT w m a = m (a, w)

type L s = (Fwd (ReaderT s Maybe))
       :*: (Bwd (StateT s (WriterT (s → Bool) Maybe)))

-- Smart deconstructors:
get :: L s u v → (s → Maybe v)
put :: L s u v → (u → s → Maybe ((v, s), s → Bool))
```

Going forwards, *getting* a view v from a source s may fail if there is no view for the current source. Going backwards, *putting* a pre-view u updates some source s (via the state transformer StateT s), but with some further structure returned, provided by WriterT (s → Bool) Maybe (similar to the writer transformer used for biparsers, Sect. 3.2). The Maybe here captures the possibility that put can fail. The WriterT (s → Bool) structure provides a predicate which detects the "duplication" issue mentioned earlier. Informally, the predicate can be used to check that previously modified locations in the source are not modified again. For example, if a lens has a source made up of a bit vector, and a put sets bit i to 1, then the returned predicate will return True for all bit vectors where bit i is

1, and False otherwise. This predicate can then be used to test whether further put operations on the source have modified bit i.

Similarly to biparsers, a pre-view u can be understood as *containing* the view v that is to be merged with the source, and which is returned with the updated source. Ultimately, we wish to form lenses of matching input and output types (i.e. L s v v) satisfying the standard lens well-behavedness laws, modulo explicit management of partiality via Maybe and testing for conflicts via the predicate:

```
put l x s = Just ((_, s'), p') ∧ p' s' ⟹ get l s' = Just x      (L-PutGet)
       get l s = Just x    ⟹    put l x s = Just ((_, s), _)      (L-GetPut)
```

L-PutGet and L-GetPut are backward and forward round tripping respectively. Some lenses, such as the later example, are not defined for all views. In that case we may say that the lens is backward/forward round tripping in some subset P ⊆ u when the above properties only hold when x is an element of P.

For every source type s, the lens type L s is automatically a monadic profunctor by its definition as the pairing of Fwd and Bwd (Sect. 3.1), and the following instance of MonadPartial for handling failure and instance of Monoid to satisfy the requirements of the writer monad:

```
instance MonadPartial (StateT s (WriterT (s → Bool) Maybe)) where
  toFailure Nothing  = StateT (λ_ → WriterT Nothing)
  toFailure (Just x) = StateT (λs → WriterT (Just ((x , s), mempty)))

instance Monoid (s → Bool) where
  mempty     = λ_ → True
  mappend h j = λs0 → h s0 && j s0
```

A simple lens example operates on key-value maps. For keys of type Key and values of type Value, we have the following source type and a simple lens:

```
type Src = Map Key Value
atKey :: Key → L Src Value Value  -- Key-focussed lens
atKey k = mkLens (lookup k)
  (λv → λmap → Just ((v, insert k v map), λm' → lookup k m' == Just v))
```

The get component of the atKey lens does a lookup of the key k in a map, producing Maybe of a Value. The put component inserts a value for key k. When the key already exists, put overwrites its associated value.

Due to our approach, multiple calls to atKey can be composed monadically, giving a lens that gets/sets multiple key-value pairs at once. The list of keys and the list of values are passed separately, and are expected to be the same length.

```
atKeys :: [Key] → L Src [Value] [Value]
atKeys [] = return []
atKeys (k : ks) = do
  x  ← comap headM (atKey k)      -- headM :: [a] → Maybe a
  xs ← comap tailM (atKeys ks)    -- tailM :: [a] → Maybe [a]
  return (x : xs)
```

We refer interested readers to our implementation [12] for more examples, including further examples involving trees.

Round tripping. We apply the reasoning framework of Sect. 4, taking the standard lens laws as the starting point (neither of which are compositional).

We first weaken backward round tripping to be compositional. Informally, the property expresses the idea, that if we `put` some value `x` in a source `s`, resulting in a source `s'`, then what we `get` from `s'` is `x`. However two important changes are needed to adapt to our generalised type of lenses and to ensure compositionality. First, the value `x` that was put is now to be found in the output of `put`, whereas there is no way to constrain the input of `put` because its type `v` is abstract. Second, by sequentially composing lenses such as in `l >>= k`, the output source `s'` of `put l` will be further modified by `put (k x)`, so this round-tripping property must constrain all potential modifications of `s'`. In fact, the predicate `p` ensures exactly that the view `get l` has not changed and is still `x`. It is not even necessary to refer to `s'`, which is just one source for which we expect `p` to be `True`.

Definition 14. A lens `l :: L s u v` is *weak backward round tripping* if for all `x :: u`, `y :: v`, for all sources `s`, `s'`, and for all `p :: s → Bool`, we have:

```
put l x s = Just ((y, _), p) ∧ p s'   ⟹   get l s' = Just y
```

Theorem 3. Weak backward round tripping is a compositional property.

Again, we complement this weakened version of round tripping with the notion of purification.

Proposition 7. Our lens type `L` is a *purifiable* monadic profunctor (Definition 9), with a family of pure projections `proj s` indexed by a source `s`, defined:

```
proj :: s → L s u v → (u → Maybe v)
proj s = λl u → fmap (fst ∘ fst) (put l u s)
```

Theorem 4. If a lens `l :: L s u u` is weak backward round tripping and has identity projections on some subset `P ⊆ u` (i.e., for all `s`, `x` then `x ∈ P ⇒ proj s l x = Just x`) then `l` is also backward round tripping on all `x ∈ P`.

To demonstrate, we apply this result to `atKeys :: [Key] → L Src [Value] [Value]`.

Proposition 8. The lens `atKey k` is weak backward round tripping.

Proposition 9. The lens `atKey k` has identity projection: `proj z (atKey k)=Just`.

Our lens `atKeys ks` is therefore weak backward round tripping by construction. We now interpret/purify `atKeys ks` as a partial function, which is actually the identity function when restricted to lists of the same length as `ks`.

Proposition 10. For all `vs :: [Value]` such that `length vs = length ks`, and for all `s :: Src` then `proj s (atKeys ks) vs = Just vs`.

Corollary 6. By the above results, `atKeys ks :: L Src [Value] [Value]` for all `ks` is backward round tripping on lists of length `length ks`.

The other direction, forward round tripping, follows a similar story. We first restate it as a quasicompositional property.

Definition 15. A lens `l :: L s u v` is *weak forward round tripping* if for all `x :: u`, `y :: v`, for all sources `s`, `s'`, and for all `p :: s → Bool`, we have:

```
get l s = Just y ∧ put l x s = Just ((y, s'), _)   ⟹   s = s'
```

Theorem 5. Weak forward round tripping is a quasicompositional property.

Along with identity projection, this gives the original forward L-GetPut property.

Theorem 6 If a lens `l` is weak forward round tripping and has identity projections on some subset `P` (i.e., for all `s`, `x` then `x ∈ P ⇒ proj s l x = Just x`) then `l` is also forward round tripping on `P`.

We can thus apply this result to our example (details omitted).

Proposition 11. For all `ks`, the lens `atKeys ks :: L Src [Value] [Value]` is forward round tripping on lists of length `length ks`.

6 Monadic Bidirectional Programming for Generators

Lastly, we capture the novel notion of *bidirectional generators* (*bigenerators*) extending random generators in property-based testing frameworks like *QuickCheck* [10] to a bidirectional setting. The forwards direction generates values conforming to a specification; the backwards direction checks whether values conform to a predicate. We capture the two together via our monadic profunctor pair as:

```
type G = (Fwd Gen) :*: (Bwd Maybe)
-- ... with deconstructors and constructors
generate :: G u v → Gen v                          -- forward direction
check    :: G u v → u → Maybe v                    -- backward direction
mkG      :: Gen v → (u → Maybe v) → G u v
```

The forwards direction of a bigenerator is a generator, while the backwards direction is a partial function `u → Maybe v`. A value `G u v` represents a subset of `v`, where `generate` is a generator of values in that subset and `check` maps pre-views `u` to members of the generated subset. In the backwards direction, `check g` defines a predicate on `u`, which is true if and only if `check g u` is `Just` of some value. The function `toPredicate` extracts this predicate from the backward direction:

```
toPredicate :: G u v → u → Bool
toPredicate g x = case check g x of Just _  → True; Nothing → False
```

The bigenerator type `G` is automatically a monadic profunctor due to our construction (Sect. 3). Thus, monad and profunctor instances come for free, modulo (un)wrapping of constructors and given a trivial instance of `MonadPartial`:

```
instance MonadPartial Maybe where toFailure = id
```

Due to space limitations, we refer readers to Appendix E [36] for an example of a compositionally-defined bigenerator that produces binary search trees.

Round tripping. A random generator can be interpreted as the set of values it may generate, while a predicate represents the set of values satisfying it. For a bigenerator `g`, we write `x` ∈ `generate g` when `x` is a possible output of the generator. The generator of a bigenerator `g` should match its predicate `toPredicate g`. This requirement equates to round-tripping properties: a bigenerator is *sound* if every value which it can generate satisfies the predicate (forward round tripping); a bigenerator is *complete* if every value which satisfies the predicate can be generated (backward round tripping). Completeness is often more important than soundness in testing because unsound tests can be filtered out by the predicate, but completeness determines the potential adequacy of testing.

Definition 16. A bigenerator `g :: G u u` is *complete* (backward round tripping) when `toPredicate g x = True` implies `x` ∈ `generate g`.

Definition 17. A bigenerator `g :: G u u` is *sound* (forward round tripping) if for all `x :: u`, `x` ∈ `generate g` implies that `toPredicate g x = True`.

Similarly to backward round tripping of biparsers and lenses, completeness can be split into a compositional weak completeness and a purifiable property.

As before, the compositional weakening of completeness relates the forward and backward components by their outputs, which have the same type.

Definition 18. A bigenerator `g :: G u v` is *weak-complete* when

$$\texttt{check g x = Just y} \implies \texttt{y} \in \texttt{generate g}.$$

Theorem 7. Weak completeness is compositional.

In a separate step, we connect the input of the backward direction, *i.e.*, the checker, by reasoning directly about its pure projection (via a more general form of identity projection) which is defined to be the checker itself:

Theorem 8. A bigenerator `g :: G u u` is complete if it is weak-complete and its checker satisfies a pure projection property: `check g x = Just x'` ⇒ `x = x'`

Thus to prove completeness of a bigenerator `g :: G u u`, we first have weak-completeness by construction, and we can then show that `check g` is a restriction of the identity function, interpreting all bigenerators simply as partial functions.

Considering the other direction, soundness, there is unfortunately no decomposition into a quasicompositional property and a property on pure projections. To see why, let `bool` be a random uniform bigenerator of booleans, then consider for example, `comap isTrue bool` and `comap isTrue (return True)`, where `isTrue True = Just True` and `isTrue False = Nothing`. Both satisfy any quasicompositional property satisfied by `bool`, and both have the same pure projection `isTrue`, and yet the former is unsound—it can generate `False`, which is rejected by `isTrue`—while the latter is sound. This is not a problem in practice, as unsoundness, especially in small scale, is inconsequential in testing. But it does raise an intellectual challenge and an interesting point in the design space, where ease of reasoning has been traded for greater expressivity in the monadic approach.

7 Discussion and Related Work

Bidirectional transformations are a widely applicable technique used in many domains [11]. Among language-based solutions, the lens framework is most influential [3,4,13,14,24,29]. Broadly speaking, combinators are used as programming constructs with which complex lenses are created by combining simpler ones. The combinators preserve round tripping, and therefore the resulting programs are correct by construction. A problem with lens languages is that they tend to be disconnected from more general programming. Lenses can only be constructed by very specialised combinators and are not subject to existing abstraction mechanisms. Our approach allows bidirectional transformations to be built using standard components of functional programming, and gives a reasoning framework for studying compositionality of round-tripping properties.

The framework of *applicative lenses* [18] uses a function representation of lenses to lift the point-free restriction of the combinator-based languages, and enables bidirectional programming with explicit recursion and pattern matching. Note that the use of "applicative" in applicative lenses refers to the transitional sense of programming with λ-abstractions and functional applications, which is not directly related to applicative functors. In a subsequent work, the authors developed a language known as HOBiT [20], which went further in featuring proper binding of variables. Despite the success in supporting λ-abstractions and function applications in programming bidirectional transformations, none of the languages have explored advanced patterns such as monadic programming.

The work on *monadic lenses* [1] investigates lenses with effects. For instance, a "put" could require additional input to resolve conflicts. Representing effects with monads helps reformulate the laws of round-tripping. In contrast, we made the type of lenses itself a monad, and showed how they can be composed monadically. Our method is applicable to monadic lenses, yielding what one might call *monadic monadic lenses*: monadically composable lenses with monadic effects. We conjecture that laws for monadic lenses can be adapted to this setting with similar compositionality properties, reusing our reasoning framework.

Other work leverages profunctors for bidirectionality. Notably, a *Profunctor optic* [26] between a source type `s` and a view type `v` is a function of type `p v v → p s s`, for an abstract profunctor `p`. Profunctor optics and our monadic profunctors offer orthogonal composition patterns: profunctor optics can be composed "vertically" using function composition, whereas monadic profunctor composition is "horizontal" providing sequential composition. In both cases, composition in the other direction can only be obtained by breaking the abstraction.

It is folklore in the Haskell community that profunctors can be combined with applicative functors [22]. The pattern is sometimes called a *monoidal* profunctor. The `codec` library [8] mentioned in Sect. 3 prominently features two applications of this applicative programming style: binary serialisation (a form of parsing/printing) and conversion to and from JSON structures (analogous to lenses above). Opaleye [28], an EDSL of SQL queries for Postgres databases, uses an interface of monoidal profunctors to implement generic operations such as transformations between Haskell datatypes and database queries and responses.

Our framework adapts gracefully to applicative programming, a restricted form of monadic programming. By separating the input type from the output type, we can reuse the existing interface of applicative functors without modification. Besides our generalisation to monads, purification and verifying round-tripping properties via (quasi)compositionality are novel in our framework.

Rendel and Ostermann proposed an interface for programming parsers and printers together [30], but they were unable to reuse the existing structure of `Functor`, `Applicative` and `Alternative` classes (because of the need to handle types that are both covariant and contravariant), and had to reproduce the entire hierarchy separately. In contrast, our approach reuses the standard type class hierarchy, further extending the expressive power of bidirectional programming in Haskell. FliPpr [17,19] is an invertible language that generates a parser from a definition of a pretty printer. In this paper, our biparser definitions are more similar to those of parsers than printers. This makes sense as it has been established that many parsers are monadic. Similar to the case of HOBiT, there is no discussion of monadic programming in the FliPpr work.

Previous approaches to unifying random generators and predicates mostly focused on deriving generators from predicates. One general technique evaluates predicates lazily to drive generation (random or enumerative) [7,9], but one loses control over the resulting distribution of generated values. *Luck* [15] is a domain-specific language blending narrowing and constraint solving to specify generators as predicates with user-provided annotations to control the probability distribution. In contrast, our programs can be viewed as generators annotated with left inverses with which to derive predicates. This reversed perspective comes with trade-offs: high-level properties would be more naturally expressed in a declarative language of predicates, whereas it is *a priori* more convenient to implement complex generation strategies in a specialised framework for random generators.

Conclusions. This paper advances the expressive power of bidirectional programming; we showed that the classic bidirectional patterns of parsers/printers and lenses can be restructured in terms of *monadic profunctors* to provide sequential composition, with associated reasoning techniques. This opens up a new area in the design of embedded domain-specific languages for BX programming, that does not restrict programmers to stylised interfaces. Our example of bigenerators broadened the scope of BX programming from transformations (converting between two data representations) to non-transformational applications.

To demonstrate the applicability of our approach to real code, we have developed two bidirectional libraries [12], one extending the attoparsec monadic parser combinator library to biparsers and one extending QuickCheck to bigenerators. One area for further work is studying biparsers with *lookahead*. Currently lookahead can be expressed in our extended attoparsec, but understanding its interaction with (quasi)compositional round-tripping is further work.

However, this is not the final word on sequentially composable BX programs. In all three applications, round-tripping properties are similarly split into weak round tripping, which is weaker than the original property but compositional, and purifiable, which is equationally friendly. An open question is whether an underlying structure can be formalised, perhaps based on an adjunction model, that captures bidirectionality even more concretely than monadic profunctors.

Acknowledgments. We thank the anonymous reviewers for their helpful comments. The second author was supported partly by EPSRC grant EP/M026124/1.

References

1. Abou-Saleh, F., Cheney, J., Gibbons, J., McKinna, J., Stevens, P.: Reflections on monadic lenses. In: Lindley, S., McBride, C., Trinder, P., Sannella, D. (eds.) A List of Successes That Can Change the World. LNCS, vol. 9600, pp. 1–31. Springer, Cham (2016). https://doi.org/10.1007/978-3-319-30936-1_1
2. Bancilhon, F., Spyratos, N.: Update semantics of relational views. ACM Trans. Database Syst. **6**(4), 557–575 (1981)
3. Barbosa, D.M.J., Cretin, J., Foster, N., Greenberg, M., Pierce, B.C.: Matching lenses: alignment and view update. In: International Conference on Functional Programming (ICFP), pp. 193–204. ACM (2010)
4. Bohannon, A., Foster, J.N., Pierce, B.C., Pilkiewicz, A., Schmitt, A.: Boomerang: resourceful lenses for string data. In: Symposium on Principles of Programming Languages (POPL), pp. 407–419. ACM (2008)
5. Bohannon, A., Pierce, B.C., Vaughan, J.A.: Relational lenses: a language for updatable views. In: Symposium on Principles of Database Systems (PODS), pp. 338–347. ACM (2006)
6. Bottu, G.-J., Karachalias, G., Schrijvers, T., Oliveira, B.C.d.S., Wadler, P.: Quantified class constraints. In: International Symposium on Haskell (Haskell), pp. 148–161. ACM (2017)
7. Boyapati, C., Khurshid, S., Marinov, D.: Korat: automated testing based on Java predicates. In: International Symposium on Software Testing and Analysis (ISSTA), pp. 123–133. ACM (2002)
8. Chilton, P.: Codec library. https://hackage.haskell.org/package/codec
9. Claessen, K., Duregård, J., Palka, M.H.: Generating constrained random data with uniform distribution. J. Funct. Program. **25** (2015). Article e8
10. Claessen, K., Hughes, J.: QuickCheck: a lightweight tool for random testing of Haskell programs. In: International Conference on Functional Programming (ICFP), pp. 268–279. ACM (2000)

11. Czarnecki, K., Foster, J.N., Hu, Z., Lämmel, R., Schürr, A., Terwilliger, J.F.: Bidirectional transformations: a cross-discipline perspective. In: Paige, R.F. (ed.) ICMT 2009. LNCS, vol. 5563, pp. 260–283. Springer, Heidelberg (2009). https://doi.org/10.1007/978-3-642-02408-5_19
12. Xia et al.: Further implementations, November 2018. https://github.com/Lysxia/profunctor-monad
13. Foster, J.N., Greenwald, M.B., Moore, J.T., Pierce, B.C., Schmitt, A.: Combinators for bidirectional tree transformations: a linguistic approach to the view-update problem. ACM Trans. Program. Lang. Syst. **29**(3), 17 (2007)
14. Foster, N., Matsuda, K., Voigtländer, J.: Three complementary approaches to bidirectional programming. In: SSGIP, pp. 1–46 (2010)
15. Lampropoulos, L., Gallois-Wong, D., Hritcu, C., Hughes, J., Pierce, B.C., Xia, L.-y.: Beginner's luck: a language for property-based generators. In: Symposium on Principles of Programming Languages (POPL), pp. 114–129. ACM (2017)
16. Matsuda, K., Hu, Z., Nakano, K., Hamana, M., Takeichi, M.: Bidirectionalization transformation based on automatic derivation of view complement functions. In: International Conference on Functional Programming (ICFP), pp. 47–58. ACM (2007)
17. Matsuda, K., Wang, M.: FliPpr: a prettier invertible printing system. In: Felleisen, M., Gardner, P. (eds.) ESOP 2013. LNCS, vol. 7792, pp. 101–120. Springer, Heidelberg (2013). https://doi.org/10.1007/978-3-642-37036-6_6
18. Matsuda, K., Wang, M.: Applicative bidirectional programming with lenses. In: International Conference on Functional Programming (ICFP), pp. 62–74. ACM (2015)
19. Matsuda, K., Wang, M.: Embedding invertible languages with binders: a case of the FliPpr language. In: International Symposium on Haskell (Haskell), pp. 158–171. ACM (2018)
20. Matsuda, K., Wang, M.: HOBiT: programming lenses without using lens combinators. In: Ahmed, A. (ed.) ESOP 2018. LNCS, vol. 10801, pp. 31–59. Springer, Cham (2018). https://doi.org/10.1007/978-3-319-89884-1_2
21. Mayer, M., Kuncak, V., Chugh, R.: Bidirectional evaluation with direct manipulation. Proc. ACM Program. Lang. **2**(OOPSLA), 127:1–127:28 (2018)
22. McBride, C., Paterson, R.: Applicative programming with effects. J. Funct. Program. **18**(1), 1–13 (2008)
23. Mu, S.-C., Hu, Z., Takeichi, M.: An algebraic approach to bi-directional updating. In: Chin, W.-N. (ed.) APLAS 2004. LNCS, vol. 3302, pp. 2–20. Springer, Heidelberg (2004). https://doi.org/10.1007/978-3-540-30477-7_2
24. Pacheco, H., Hu, Z., Fischer, S.: Monadic combinators for "Putback" style bidirectional programming. In: Workshop on Partial Evaluation and Program Manipulation (PEPM), pp. 39–50. ACM (2014)
25. Pacheco, H., Zan, T., Hu, Z.: BiFluX: a bidirectional functional update language for XML. In: International Symposium on Principles and Practice of Declarative Programming (PPDP). ACM (2014)
26. Pickering, M., Gibbons, J., Wu, N.: Profunctor optics: modular data accessors. Art Sci. Eng. Program. **1**(2) (2017). Article 7
27. Pombrio, J., Krishnamurthi, S.: Resugaring: lifting evaluation sequences through syntactic sugar. In: Programming Language Design and Implementation (PLDI). ACM (2014)
28. Purely Agile. Opaleye library. https://hackage.haskell.org/package/opaleye
29. Rajkumar, R., Lindley, S., Foster, N., Cheney, J.: Lenses for web data. In: International Workshop on Bidirectional Transformations (BX) (2013)

30. Rendel, T., Ostermann, K.: Invertible syntax descriptions: unifying parsing and pretty-printing. In: International Symposium on Haskell (Haskell), pp. 1–12 (2010)
31. Schuster, C., Disney, T., Flanagan, C.: Macrofication: refactoring by reverse macro expansion. In: Thiemann, P. (ed.) ESOP 2016. LNCS, vol. 9632, pp. 644–671. Springer, Heidelberg (2016). https://doi.org/10.1007/978-3-662-49498-1_25
32. Stevens, P.: A landscape of bidirectional model transformations. In: Lämmel, R., Visser, J., Saraiva, J. (eds.) GTTSE 2007. LNCS, vol. 5235, pp. 408–424. Springer, Heidelberg (2008). https://doi.org/10.1007/978-3-540-88643-3_10
33. Voigtländer, J.: Bidirectionalization for free! (Pearl). In: Symposium on Principles of Programming Languages (POPL), pp. 165–176. ACM (2009)
34. Wadler, P.: Theorems for free! In: FPCA, pp. 347–359 (1989)
35. Wadler, P.: Monads for functional programming. In: Jeuring, J., Meijer, E. (eds.) AFP 1995. LNCS, vol. 925, pp. 24–52. Springer, Heidelberg (1995). https://doi.org/10.1007/3-540-59451-5_2
36. Xia, L.-Y., Orchard, D., Wang, M.: Composing bidirectional programs monadically (with appendices) (2019). https://arxiv.org/abs/1902.06950

Counters in Kappa: Semantics, Simulation, and Static Analysis

Pierre Boutillier[1], Ioana Cristescu[2], and Jérôme Feret[3](✉)

[1] Harvard Medical School, Boston, USA
Pierre_Boutillier@hms.harvard.edu
[2] Inria Rennes - Bretagne Atlantique, Rennes, France
ioana-domnina.cristescu@inria.fr
[3] DI-ENS (INRIA/ÉNS/CNRS/PSL*), Paris, France
feret@ens.fr

Abstract. Site-graph rewriting languages, such as Kappa or BNGL, offer parsimonious ways to describe highly combinatorial systems of mechanistic interactions among proteins. These systems may be then simulated efficiently. Yet, the modeling mechanisms that involve counting (a number of phosphorylated sites for instance) require an exponential number of rules in Kappa. In BNGL, updating the set of the potential applications of rules in the current state of the system comes down to the sub-graph isomorphism problem (which is NP-complete).

In this paper, we extend Kappa to deal both parsimoniously and efficiently with counters. We propose a single push-out semantics for Kappa with counters. We show how to compile Kappa with counters into Kappa without counters (without requiring an exponential number of rules). We design a static analysis, based on affine relationships, to identify the meaning of counters and bound their ranges accordingly.

1 Introduction

Site-graph rewriting is a paradigm for modeling mechanistic interactions among proteins. In Kappa [18] and BNGL [3,40], rewriting rules describe how instances of proteins may bind and unbind, and how each protein may activate the interaction sites of each others, by changing their properties. Sophisticated signaling cascades may be described. The long term behavior of such models usually emerges from competition against shared-resources, proteins with multiple-phosphorylation sites, scaffolds, separation of scales, and non-linear feedback loops.

It is often desirable to add more structure to states in order to describe generic mechanisms more compactly. In this paper, we consider extending Kappa with counters with numerical values. As opposed to the properties of classical Kappa sites, which offer no structure, counters allow for expressive preconditions (such as the value of a counter is less than 2), but also for generic update functions (such as incrementing or decrementing the current value of a counter by a given value independently of its current value). Without counters, such

L. Caires (Ed.): ESOP 2019, LNCS 11423, pp. 176–204, 2019.
https://doi.org/10.1007/978-3-030-17184-1_7

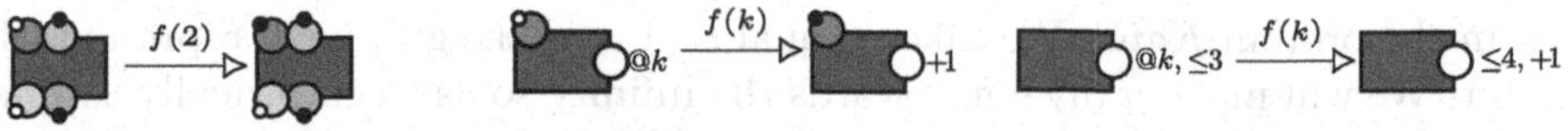

(a) With phosphorylation sites only.

(b) With a counter and phosphorylation sites

(c) With a counter only

Fig. 1. Three representations for the phosphorylation of a site. We assume that the rate of phosphorylation of a site in a protein in which exactly k sites are already phosphorylated, is equal to the value $f(k)$. The function f is left as a parameter of the model. In (a), we do not use counters. In order to get the number of sites that are already phosphorylated, we have to document the state of all the sites of the protein. In this rule, there are exactly 2 sites already phosphorylated, thus the rate of the rule is equal to $f(2)$. In (b), we use a counter to encode the number of sites already phosphorylated. The variable k, that is introduced by the notation $@k$, contains the number of sites that are phosphorylated before the application of the rule. Thus, the rate of the rule is equal to $f(k)$. In the right hand side, the notation $+1$ indicates that the counter is incremented at each application of the rule. The rule in (b) summarizes exactly 8 rules of the kind of the one in (a) (it defines the phosphorylation of the site a regardless of the states of the three other phosphorylation sites). In (c), we abstract away the sites and keep only the counter. The notation $@k$ binds the variable k to the value of the counter. The left hand side also indicates that the rule may be applied only if the value of the counter is less than or equal to 3 (so that at least one site is not already phosphorylated). The right hand side specifies that the value of the counter is incremented at each application of the rule and that after the application of a rule, the value of the counter is always less than or equal to 4. The rule in (c) stands for 32 rules of the kind of the one in (a) (it depends neither on which site is phosphorylated, nor on the state of the three other sites).

update functions would require one rule per potential value of the counter. This raises efficiency issues for the simulation and also blurs any potential reasoning on the causality of the system.

However adding counters cannot be done without consequences. The efficiency of Kappa simulations mainly relies on two ingredients. Firstly, Kappa graphs are rigid [16,39]: an embedding from a connected site-graph into a site-graph, when it exists, is fully determined by the image of one node. Thanks to rigidity, searching for the occurrences of a sub-graph into another graph (up-to isomorphism) may be done without backtracking (once a first node has been placed), and embeddings can be described in memory very concisely. Secondly, the representation of the set of potential applications of rules relies on a categorical construction [6] that optimizes sharing among patterns. Yet this construction cannot cope with the more expressive patterns that involve counters. In order to efficiently simulate models with counters, we need an efficient encoding that preserves rigidity and that use classical site-graph patterns.

Let us consider a case study so as to illustrate the need for counters in Kappa. This example is inspired from the behavior of the protein $KaiC$ that is involved in the synchronization of the proteins in the circadian clock. We consider one kind of protein with n identified sites that can get phosphorylated. Indeed, n is equal to 6 in the protein *KaiC*. We take n equal to 4 to make graphical representation lighter. We will make n diverge towards the infinity so as to empirically estimate the combinatorial complexity of several encoding schemes.

The rate of phosphorylation/dephosphorylation of each site, depends on the number of sites that are already phosphorylated. In Fig. 1(a), we provide the example of a rule that phosphorylates the site a of the protein, assuming that the sites b and c are already phosphorylated and that the site d is not. Proteins are depicted as rectangles. Sites are depicted clockwise from the site a to the site d starting at the top left corner of the protein. Phosphorylation states are depicted with a black mark when the site is phosphorylated, and with a white mark otherwise. To fully encode this model in Kappa, we would require $n \cdot 2^n$ rules. Indeed, we need to decide whether this is a phosphorylation or a dephosphorylation (2 possibilities), then on which site to apply the transformation (n possibilities), then what the state of the other sites is (2^{n-1} possibilities). This combinatorial complexity may be reduced by the means of counters. We consider a fresh site (this site is depicted on the right of the protein) and we assume that this site takes numerical values. Writing each rule carefully, we can enforce that the value of this site is always equal to the number of the sites that are phosphorylated in the protein instance. Thanks to this invariant, describing our model requires $2{\cdot}n$ rules according to whether we describe a phosphorylation or a dephosphorylation (2 possibilities) and to which site the transformation is applied (n possibilities). An example of rule for the phosphorylation of the site a is given in Fig. 1(b). The notation $@k$ assigns the value of the counter before the application of the rule to the variable k. Then the rate of the rule may depend on the value of k. This way, we can make the rate of phosphorylation depend on the number of sites already phosphorylated in the protein. Since there are only n sites that may be phosphorylated, it is straightforward to see that the counter may range only between the values 0 and n.

If only the number of phosphorylated sites matters, we can go even further: we need just one counter and two rules, one for phosphorylating a new site (e. g. see Fig. 1(c)) and one for dephosphorylating it. The value of the counter is no longer related explicitly to a number of phosphorylated sites, thus we need another way to specify that the value of the counter is bounded. We do this, by specifying in the precondition of the rule that the phosphorylation rule may be applied only if the value of the counter is less or equal to $n - 1$, which entails that the value of the counter may range only between the values 0 and n.

Not only parsimonious description of the mechanistic interactions in a model eases the process of writing a model, enhances readability and leads to more efficient simulation, but also it may provide better grain of observation of the system behavior. In Fig. 2, we illustrate this by looking at three causal traces that denote the same execution, but for three different encodings. Intuitively, causal traces [14,15] are inspired by event structures [43]. They describe sets of traces seen up to permutation of concurrent computation steps. The level of representation for the potential configurations of each protein impacts the way causality is defined, because what is tested in rules depends on the representation level. In our case study, the phosphorylation of each site is intuitively causally independent: one site may be phosphorylated whatever the state of the other sites is. Without counters, the only way to specify that the rate of phosphorylation depends on the number of the sites that are already phosphorylated, is to detail the state of every site of the protein in the precondition of the rule. This induces spurious causal relations (e. g. see Fig. 2(a)). Utilizing counters relaxes this constraint. However it is important to equip counters with arithmetic. Without arithmetic, a rule may only set the value of a counter to a constant value. Thus for implementing counter increment, rules have to enumerate the potential values of the counter before their applications, and set the value of this counter accordingly. This induces again spurious causal relations (e. g. see Fig. 2(b)). With arithmetic, incrementing counters becomes a generic operation that may be applied independently of the current value of the counter. As a result the phosphorylation of the four sites can be seen as causally independent (e. g. see Fig. 2(c)). This faithfully represents the fact that the phosphorylation of the four sites may happen in arbitrary order.

Contribution. Now we describe the main contributions of this paper.

In Sect. 2, we formalize a single push-out (SPO) semantics for Kappa with counters. Having a categorical framework dealing with counters, as opposed to implementing counters as syntactic sugar, is important. Firstly, this semantics will serve as a reference for the formal specification of the behavior of counters. Secondly, the categorical setting of Kappa provides efficient ways to define causality [14,15], symmetries [25], and some sound symbolic reasonings on the behavior of the number of occurrences of patterns [1,26] that are used in model reduction. Including counters in the categorical semantics of Kappa allows for extending the definition of these concepts to Kappa with counters for free.

Yet different encodings of counters may be necessary to extend other tools for Kappa. In Sect. 3, we propose a couple of translations from Kappa with counters into Kappa without counters. The goal is to simulate models with counters efficiently without modifying the implementation of the Kappa simulator, KaSim [17]. The first encoding requires counters to be bounded from below and it supports only two kinds of preconditions over counters: a rule may require the value of a counter to be equal to a given value, or to be greater than a given value. Requiring the value of a counter to be less than a given value is not supported. The second encoding supports equality and inequality (in both directions) tests. But it requires the value of each counter to be bounded also from above.

Static analysis is needed not only to prove these requirements, but also to retrieve the meaning of counters. In Sect. 4, we introduce a generic abstract interpretation framework [9] to infer the properties of reachable states of a model. This framework is parametric with respect to a class of properties. In Sect. 5, we instantiate this framework with a relational numerical analysis aiming at relating the value of each counter to its interpretation with respect to the state of the other sites. This is used to detect and prove bounds on the range of counters.

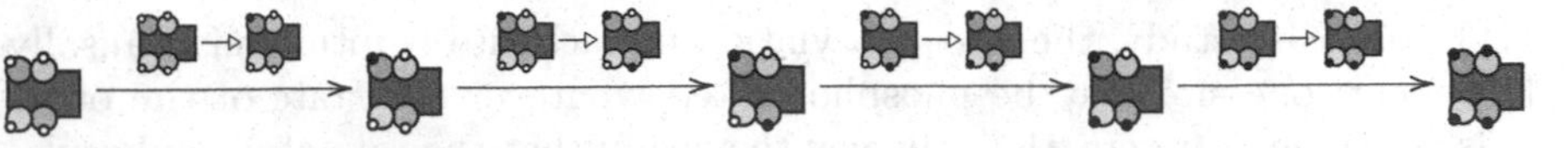

(a) Causal trace for the representation without counters.

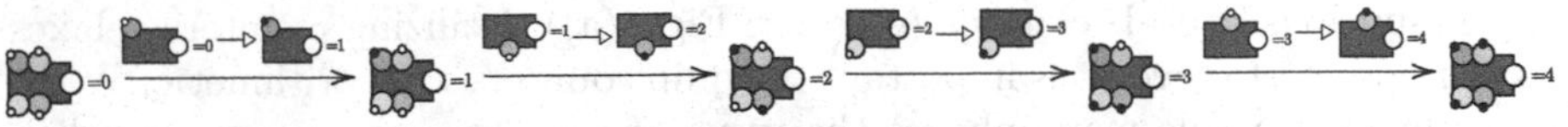

(b) Causal trace for the representation with flat counters.

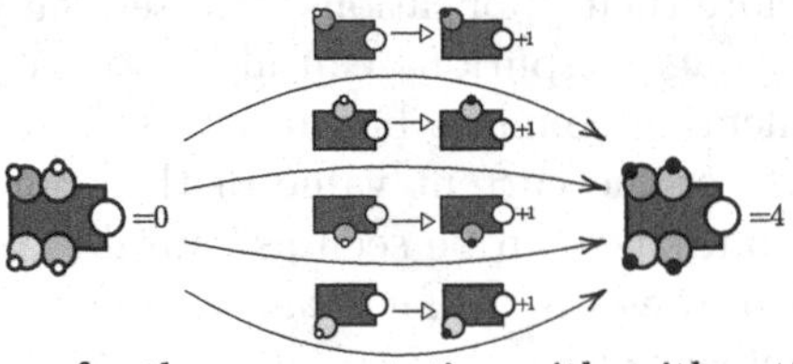

(c) Causal trace for the representation with arithmetical counters.

Fig. 2. Three causal traces. Each causal trace is made of a set of partially ordered computation steps. Roughly speaking, a computation step precedes another one, if the former is necessary to perform the later. Each computation step is denoted as an arrow labeled with the rule that implements it. In (a), counters are not used. Every rule tests the full configuration of the protein. At this level of representation, the k-th phosphorylation causally precedes the $k+1$-th one, whatever the order in which the sites have been phosphorylated. In (b), an additional site is used to record the number of phosphorylated sites in its internal state. With this encoding, the number of phosphorylated sites cannot be incremented without testing explicitly the internal state of the additional site. As a consequence, here again, at this level of representation, each phosphorylation causally depends on the previous one. In (c), we use the expressiveness of arithmetic. We use generic rules to increment the counter regardless of its current value. Hence, at this level of representation, the phosphorylation of the four sites become independent, which flatten the causal trace.

Related Works. Many modeling languages support arbitrary data-types. In Spatial-Kappa [41], counters encode the discrete position of agents. More generally, in Chromar [29] and in colored Petri nets [30,35], agents may be tagged with values in arbitrary auxiliary programming languages. In ML-Rules [28], agents with attributes continuously diffuse within compartments and collide to interact.

We have different motivations. Our goal is to enrich the state of proteins with some redundant information, so as to reduce the number of rules that are necessary to describe their mechanistic interactions. Also we want to avoid too expressive data-types, which could not be integrated within simulation, causality analysis, and static analysis tools, without altering their performance. For instance, analysis of colored Petri nets usually relies on unfolding them into classical ones. Unfolding rule sets into classical ones does not scale because the number of rules would become intractable. Thus we need tools which deal directly with counters.

An encoding of two-counter machines has been proposed to show that most problems in Kappa are undecidable [19,34]. We represent counters the same way in our first encoding, but we provide atomic implementation for more primitives.

The number of isomorphic classes of connected components that may occur in Kappa models during simulation is usually huge (if not infinite), which prevents from using agent-centric approaches [4]. For instance, one of the first non-toy model written in Kappa was involving more than 10^{19} kinds of bio-molecular complexes [16,26]. Kappa follows a rule-centric approach which allows for the description and the execution of models independently from the number of potential complexes. Also, Kappa disallows to describe diffusion of molecules. Instead the state of the system is assumed to satisfy the well-mixed assumption. This provides efficient ways to represent and update the distribution of potential computation steps, along a simulation [6,17].

Equivalent sites [3] or hyperlinks [31] offer promising solutions to extend the decision procedures to extract minimal causal traces in the case of counters, but the rigidity of graphs is lost. Our encodings rely neither on the use of equivalent sites, nor on expanding the rules into more refined and more numerous ones. Hence our encodings preserve the efficiency of the simulation.

Our analysis is based on the use of affine relationships [32]. It relates counter values to the state of the other variables. Such relationships look like the ones that help understanding and proving the correctness of semaphores [20,21]. We use the decision procedure that is described in [23,24] to deduce bounds on the values of counters from the affine relationships. The cost of each atomic computation is cubic with respect to the number of variables. Abstract multi-sets [27,38] may succeed in expressing the properties of interest, but they require a parameter setting a bound on the values that can abstract precisely. In practice, their time-cost is exponential as soon as this bound is not chosen big enough. Our abstraction has an infinite height. It uses widening [11] and reduction [12] to discover the bounds of interest automatically. Octagons [36,37] have a cubic complexity, but they cannot express the properties involving more than two variables which are required in our context. Polyhedra [13] express all the properties needed for an exponential time-cost in practice.

2 Kappa

In this section, we enrich the syntax and the operational semantics of Kappa so as to cope with counters. We focus on the single push-out (SPO) semantics.

2.1 Signature

Firstly we define the signature of a model.

Definition 1 (signature). *The signature of a model is defined as a tuple* $\Sigma = (\Sigma_{ag}, \Sigma_{site}, \Sigma_{int}, \Sigma_{ag\text{-}st}^{int}, \Sigma_{ag\text{-}st}^{lnk}, \Sigma_{ag\text{-}st}^{\$}, Prop_{\$}, Update_{\$})$ *where:*

1. *Σ_{ag} is a finite set of agent types,*
2. *Σ_{site} is a finite set of site identifiers,*
3. *Σ_{int} is a finite set of internal state identifiers,*
4. *$\Sigma^{lnk}_{ag\text{-}st}$, $\Sigma^{int}_{ag\text{-}st}$, and $\Sigma^{\$}_{ag\text{-}st}$ are three site maps (from Σ_{ag} into $\wp(\Sigma_{site})$)*
5. *$Prop_{\$}$ is a potentially infinite set of non-empty subsets of $\mathbb{Z}$,*
6. *$Update_{\$}$ is a potentially infinite set of functions from $\mathbb{Z}$ to $\mathbb{Z}$ containing the identity function.*

For every $G \in Prop_{\$}$, we assume that for every function $f \in Update_{\$}$, the set $\{f(k) \mid k \in G\}$ belongs to the set $Prop_{\$}$, and that for every element $k \in G$, the set $\{k\}$ belongs to the set $Prop_{\$}$ as well.

Agent types in Σ_{ag} denote the agents of interest, the different kinds of proteins for instance. A site identifier in Σ_{site} represents an identified locus for a capability of interaction. Each agent type $A \in \Sigma_{ag}$ is associated with a set of sites $\Sigma^{int}_{ag\text{-}st}(A)$ with an internal state (i.e. a property), a set of sites $\Sigma^{lnk}_{ag\text{-}st}(A)$ which may be linked, and a set of sites $\Sigma^{\$}_{ag\text{-}st}(A)$ with a counter. We assume without any loss of generality that the three sets $\Sigma^{lnk}_{ag\text{-}st}(A)$, $\Sigma^{int}_{ag\text{-}st}(A)$, and $\Sigma^{\$}_{ag\text{-}st}(A)$ are disjoint pairwise. The set $Prop_{\$}$ contains the set of valid conditions that may be checked on the value of counters, whereas the set $Update_{\$}$ contains all the possible update functions for the value of counters. We assume that every singleton that is included in a valid condition is a valid condition as well. In this way, a valid condition may be refined to a fully specified value. Additionally, the image of a valid condition is required to be valid, so that the post-condition obtained by applying an update function to a valid precondition, is valid as well.

Example 1 (running example). We define the signature for our case study as the tuple $(\Sigma_{ag}, \Sigma_{site}, \Sigma_{int}, \Sigma^{int}_{ag\text{-}st}, \Sigma^{lnk}_{ag\text{-}st}, \Sigma^{\$}_{ag\text{-}st}, Prop_{\$}, Update_{\$})$ where:

1. *$\Sigma_{ag} := \{P\}$;*
2. *$\Sigma_{site} := \{a, b, c, d, x\}$;*
3. *$\Sigma_{int} := \{\circ, \bullet\}$;*
4. *$\Sigma^{int}_{ag\text{-}st} := [P \mapsto \{a, b, c, d\}]$;*
5. *$\Sigma^{lnk}_{ag\text{-}st} := [P \mapsto \emptyset]$;*
6. *$\Sigma^{\$}_{ag\text{-}st} := [P \mapsto \{x\}]$;*
7. *$Prop_{\$}$ is the set of all the convex parts of $\mathbb{Z}$;*
8. *$Update_{\$}$ contains the function mapping each integer $n \in \mathbb{Z}$ to its successor, and the function mapping each integer $n \in \mathbb{Z}$ to its predecessor.*

The agent type P denotes the only kind of proteins. It has four sites a, b, c, d carrying an internal state and one site x carrying a counter. □

Until the rest of the paper, we assume given a signature Σ.

2.2 Site-Graphs

Site-graphs describe both patterns and chemical mixtures. Their nodes are typed agents with some sites which may carry internal and binding states, and counters.

(a) G_1. (b) G_2. (c) G_3. (d) G_4.

Fig. 3. Four site-graphs G_1, G_2, G_3, and G_4.

Definition 2 (site-graph). *A site-graph is a tuple* $G = (\mathcal{A}, type, \mathcal{S}, \mathcal{L}, p\kappa, c\kappa)$ *where:*

1. $\mathcal{A}$ *is a finite set of agents,*
2. $type : \mathcal{A} \to \Sigma_{ag}$ *is a function mapping each agent to its type,*
3. $\mathcal{S}$ *is a set of sites satisfying the following property:*

$$\mathcal{S} \subseteq \{(n, i) \mid n \in \mathcal{A}, i \in \Sigma_{ag\text{-}st}(type(n))\},$$

4. $\mathcal{L}$ *maps the set:*

$$\{(n, i) \in \mathcal{S} \mid i \in \Sigma_{ag\text{-}st}^{lnk}(type(n))\}$$

to the set:

$$\{(n, i) \in \mathcal{S} \mid i \in \Sigma_{ag\text{-}st}^{lnk}(type(n))\} \cup \{\dashv, -\},$$

such that:
   (a) *for any site* $(n, i) \in \mathcal{S}$, *we have* $\mathcal{L}(n, i) \neq (n, i)$;
   (b) *for any two sites* $(n, i), (n', i') \in \mathcal{S}$, *we have* $(n', i') = \mathcal{L}(n, i)$ *if and only if* $(n, i) = \mathcal{L}(n', i')$;
5. $p\kappa$ *maps the set* $\{(n, i) \in \mathcal{S} \mid i \in \Sigma_{ag\text{-}st}^{int}(type(n))\}$ *to the set* Σ_{int};
6. $c\kappa$ *maps the set* $\{(n, i) \in \mathcal{S} \mid i \in \Sigma_{ag\text{-}st}^{\$}(type(n))\}$ *to the set* $Prop_{\$}$.

For a site-graph G, we write as $\mathcal{A}_G$ its set of agents, $type_G$ its typing function, $\mathcal{S}_G$ its set of sites, and $\mathcal{L}_G$ its set of links. Given a site-graph G, we write as $\mathcal{S}_G^{lnk}$ (resp. $\mathcal{S}_G^{int}$, resp. $\mathcal{S}_G^{\$}$) its set of binding sites (resp. property sites, resp. counters) that is to say the set of the sites (n, i) such that $i \in \Sigma_{ag\text{-}st}^{lnk}(type_G(n))$ (resp. $i \in \Sigma_{ag\text{-}st}^{int}(type_G(n))$, resp. $i \in \Sigma_{ag\text{-}st}^{\$}(type_G(n))$).

Let us consider a binding site $(n, i) \in \mathcal{S}_G^{lnk}$. Whenever $\mathcal{L}_G(n, i) = \dashv$, the site (n, i) is free. Various levels of information may be given about the sites that are bound. Whenever $\mathcal{L}_G(n, i) = -$, the site (n, i) is bound to an unspecified site. Whenever $\mathcal{L}_G(n, i) = (n', i')$ (and hence $\mathcal{L}_G(n', i') = (n, i)$), the sites (n, i) and (n', i') are bound together.

A *chemical mixture* is a site-graph in which the state of each site is fully specified. Formally, a site-graph G is a chemical mixture, if and only if, the three following properties:

1. the set $\mathcal{S}_G$ is equal to the set $\{(n, i) \mid n \in \mathcal{A}_G,\ i \in \Sigma_{ag\text{-}st}(type_G(n))\}$;
2. every binding site is free or bound to another binding site (i. e. for every $(n, i) \in \mathcal{S}_G \cap \Sigma_{ag\text{-}st}^{lnk}(type_G(n))$, $\mathcal{L}_G(n, i) \neq -$);

3. every counter has a single value (i. e. for every $(n, i) \in \Sigma^{\$}_{ag\text{-}st}$, $c\kappa_G(n, i)$ is a singleton);

are satisfied.

Example 2 (running example). In Fig. 3, we give a graphical representation of the four site-graphs, G_1, G_2, G_3, and G_4 that are defined as follows:

1. (a) $\mathcal{A}_{G_1} = \{1\}$,
   (b) $type_{G_1} = [1 \mapsto P]$,
   (c) $\mathcal{S}_{G_1} = \{(1, a), (1, x)\}$,
   (d) $\mathcal{L}_{G_1} = \emptyset$,
   (e) $p\kappa_{G_1} = [(1, a) \mapsto \circ]$,
   (f) $c\kappa_{G_1} = [(1, x) \mapsto \{k \in \mathbb{Z} \mid k \leq 2\}]$;
2. (a) $\mathcal{A}_{G_2} = \{1\}$,
   (b) $type_{G_2} = [1 \mapsto P]$,
   (c) $\mathcal{S}_{G_2} = \{(1, x)\}$,
   (d) $\mathcal{L}_{G_2} = \emptyset$,
   (e) $p\kappa_{G_2} = []$,
   (f) $c\kappa_{G_2} = [(1, x) \mapsto \{k \in \mathbb{Z} \mid k \leq 2\}]$;
3. (a) $\mathcal{A}_{G_3} = \{1\}$,
   (b) $type_{G_3} = [1 \mapsto P]$,
   (c) $\mathcal{S}_{G_3} = \{(1, a), (1, x)\}$,
   (d) $\mathcal{L}_{G_3} = \emptyset$,
   (e) $p\kappa_{G_3} = [(1, a) \mapsto \bullet]$,
   (f) $c\kappa_{G_3} = [(1, x) \mapsto \{k \in \mathbb{Z} \mid k \leq 3\}]$;
4. (a) $\mathcal{A}_{G_4} = \{1\}$,
   (b) $type_{G_4} = [1 \mapsto P]$,
   (c) $\mathcal{S}_{G_4} = \{(1, a), (1, b), (1, c), (1, d), (1, x)\}$,
   (d) $\mathcal{L}_{G_4} = \emptyset$,
   (e) $p\kappa_{G_4} = [(1, a) \mapsto \circ, (1, b) \mapsto \bullet, (1, c) \mapsto \bullet, (1, d) \mapsto \circ]$,
   (f) $c\kappa_{G_4} = [(1, x) \mapsto \{2\}]$;

The white site on the side of proteins is always the site x. The other sites, starting from the top-left one denote the sites a, b, c, and d clockwise. □

2.3 Sliding Embeddings

In classical Kappa, two site-graphs may be related by structure-preserving injections, which are called embeddings. Here, we extend their definition to cope with counters. There are two main issues: a rule may require the value of a given counter to belong to a non-singleton set; also updating counters may involve arithmetic computations. The smaller the set of the potential values for a counter is, the more information we have. Thus, embeddings may map the potential values of a given counter into a subset. In order to cope with update functions, we equip embeddings with some arithmetic functions which explain how to get from the value of the counter in the source of the embedding to its value in the target. This way, our embeddings not only define instances of site-graphs, but they also contain the information to compute the values of counters.

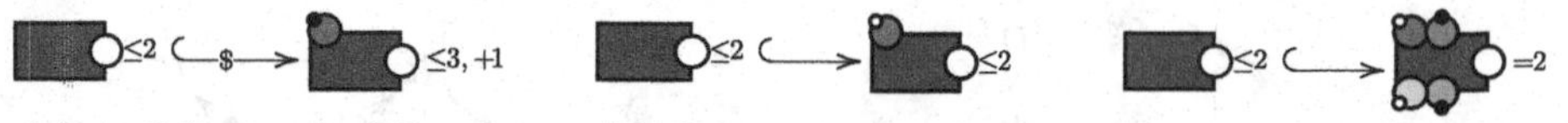

(a) A sliding embedding. (b) A pure embedding. (c) A pure embedding.

Fig. 4. Three sliding embeddings from the G_2 respectively into the site-graphs G_3, G_1, and G_4. Only the second and the third embeddings are pure.

Definition 3 (sliding embedding). *A sliding embedding $h : G \overset{\$}{\hookrightarrow} H$ from a site-graph G into a site-graph H is a pair $(h_e, h_\$)$ where h_e is a function of agents $h_e : \mathcal{A}_G \rightarrow \mathcal{A}_H$ and $h_\$$ is a function mapping the counters of the site-graph G to update functions $h_\$: \mathcal{S}^\$_G \rightarrow Update_\$$ such that for all agent identifiers $m, n, n' \in \mathcal{A}_G$ and for all site identifiers $i \in \Sigma_{ag\text{-}st}(type_G(n))$, $i' \in \Sigma_{ag\text{-}st}(type_G(n'))$, the following properties are satisfied:*

1. *if $m \neq n$, then $h_e(m) \neq h_e(n)$;*
2. *$type_G(n) = type_H(h_e(n))$;*
3. *if $(n, i) \in \mathcal{S}_G$, then $(h_e(n), i) \in \mathcal{S}_H$;*
4. *if $(n, i) \in \mathcal{S}^{lnk}_G$ and $\mathcal{L}_G(n, i) = (n', i')$, then $\mathcal{L}_H(h_e(n), i) = (h_e(n'), i')$;*
5. *if $(n, i) \in \mathcal{S}^{lnk}_G$ and $\mathcal{L}_G(n, i) = \dashv$, then $\mathcal{L}_H(h_e(n), i) = \dashv$;*
6. *if $(n, i) \in \mathcal{S}^{lnk}_G$ and $\mathcal{L}_G(n, i) = -$, then $\mathcal{L}_H(h_e(n), i) \in \{-\} \cup \mathcal{S}_H$;*
7. *if $(n, i) \in \mathcal{S}^{int}_G$ and $p\kappa_G(n, i) = \iota$, then $p\kappa_H(h_e(n), i) = \iota$;*
8. *if $(n, i) \in \mathcal{S}^\$_G$, then $c\kappa_H(h(n), i) \subseteq \{h_\$(k) \mid k \in c\kappa_G(n, i)\}$.*

Two sliding embeddings between site-graphs, from E to F, and from F to G respectively, compose to form a sliding embedding from E to G (functions compose pair-wise). A sliding embedding $(h_e, h_\$)$ such that $h_\$$ maps each counter to the identity function is called a *pure embedding.* A pure embedding from E to F is denoted as $E \hookrightarrow F$. Pure embeddings compose. Two site-graphs E and F are isomorphic if and only if there exist a pure embedding from E to F and a pure embedding from F to E. A pure embedding between two isomorphic site-graphs is called an isomorphism. When it exists, the unique pure embedding $(h_e, h_\$)$ from a site-graph E into the site-graph F such that $\mathcal{A}_E \subseteq \mathcal{A}_F$ and $h_e(n) = n$ for every agent $n \in \mathcal{A}_E$, is called the *inclusion* from E to F and is denoted as $i_{E,F}$ or as $E \overset{\subseteq}{\hookrightarrow} F$. In such a case, we say that the site-graph E is included in the site-graph F. The inclusion from a site-graph into itself always exists and is called an identity embedding.

Example 3 (running example). We show in Fig. 4 three sliding embeddings from the site-graph G_2 respectively into the site-graphs G_3, G_1, and G_4. The first of these three sliding embeddings is assumed to increment the value of the counter of the site x. The last two embeddings are pure. □

Let L, R, and D be three site-graphs, such that R is included in D, and let ϕ be a sliding embedding from L into D. Then there exist a site graph D' that is included in L and a sliding embedding ψ from D' to R such that $i_{R,D}\psi = \phi i_{D',L}$ and such that D' is *maximal* (w.r.t. inclusion among site-graphs) for this property. The pair $(D', i_{D',L}, \psi)$ is called the *pull-pack* of the pair $(\phi, i_{R,D})$.

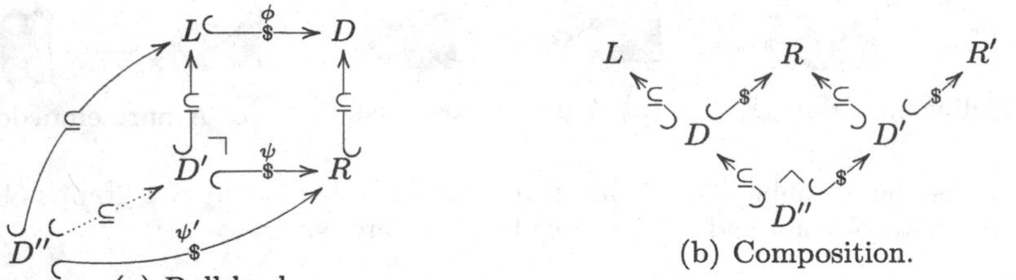

(a) Pull-back. (b) Composition.

Fig. 5. Composition of partial sliding embeddings.

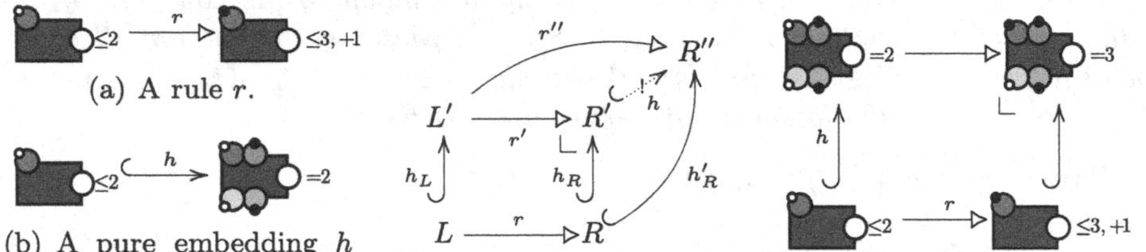

(a) A rule r.

(b) A pure embedding h from the lhs of the rule r to the site-graph G_4.

(c) Universal construction

(d) Application of the rule r on the site-graph G_4.

Fig. 6. Rule application.

Let L, R, and D be three site-graphs such that D is included in L. A *partial sliding embedding* from L into R is defined as a pair made of the inclusion $i_{D,L}$ and a sliding embedding from D to R. Sliding embeddings may be considered as partial sliding embeddings with the inclusion as the identity embedding. Partial sliding embeddings compose by the means of a pull-back (e.g. see Fig. 5(b)).

2.4 Rules

Rules represent transformations between site-graphs. For the sake of simplicity, we only use a fragment of Kappa (we assume here that there are no *side effects*). Rules may break and create bonds between pairs of sites, change the properties of sites, update the value of counters. They may also create and remove agents. When an agent is created, all its sites must be fully specified: binding sites may be either free, or bound to a specific site, and the value of counters must be singletons. So as to ensure that there is no side-effect when an agent is removed, we also assume that the binding sites of removed agents are fully specified. These requirements are formalized as follows:

Definition 4 (rule). *A rule is a partial sliding embedding* $L \hookleftarrow\!\supseteq\, D \xhookrightarrow[\$]{(h_e,h_\$)} R$ *such that:*

1. *(modified agents) for all agents* $n \in \mathcal{A}_D$ *such that* $h_e(n) \in \mathcal{A}_R$ *and for every site identifier* $i \in \Sigma_{site}(type_L(n))$*,*

   (a) *the site* (n,i) *belongs to the set* $\mathcal{S}_L$ *if and only if* $(h_e(n),i)$ *belongs to set* $\mathcal{S}_R$*;*
   (b) *if the site* (n,i) *belongs to the set* $\mathcal{S}_L^{lnk}$*, then either* $\mathcal{L}_L(n,i) = -$ *and* $\mathcal{L}_R(h_e(n),i) = -$*, or* $\mathcal{L}_L(n,i) \in \mathcal{S}_L^{lnk} \cup \{\dashv\}$ *and* $\mathcal{L}_R(h_e(n),i) \in \mathcal{S}_R^{lnk} \cup \{\dashv\}$*;*
   (c) *if the site* (n,i) *belongs to the set* $\mathcal{S}_L^{\$}$*, then the sets* $c\kappa_R(h_e(n),i)$ *and* $\{h_{\$}(v) \mid v \in c\kappa_L(n,i)\}$ *are equal.*
2. *(removed agents) for all agents* $n \in \mathcal{A}_L$ *such that* $n \notin \mathcal{A}_D$*, for every site identifier* $i \in \Sigma_{ag\text{-}st}^{lnk}(type_L(n))$*,* $(n,i) \in \mathcal{S}_L^{lnk}$ *and* $\mathcal{L}_L(n,i) \in \mathcal{S}_L^{lnk} \cup \{\dashv\}$*.*
3. *(created agents) for all agents* $n \in \mathcal{A}_R$ *for which there exists no* $n' \in \mathcal{A}_D$ *such that* $n = h_e(n')$*, and for every site identifier* $i \in \Sigma_{site}(type_R(n))$*,*
   (a) *the site* (n,i) *belongs to the set* $\mathcal{S}_R$*;*
   (b) *if the site* (n,i) *belongs to the set* $\mathcal{S}_R^{lnk}$*, then the binding state* $\mathcal{L}_R(n,i)$ *belong to the set* $\mathcal{S}_R^{lnk} \cup \{\dashv\}$*;*
   (c) *if the site* (n,i) *belongs to the set* $\mathcal{S}_R^{\$}$*, then* $c\kappa_R(n,i)$ *is a singleton.*

In Definition 4, each agent that is *modified* occurs on both hand sides of a rule. Constraint 1a ensures that they document the same sites. Constraint 1b ensures that, if the binding state of a site is modified, then it has to be fully specified (either free, or bound to a specific site) in both hand sides of the rule. Constraint 1c ensures that the post-condition associated to a counter is the direct image of its precondition by its update function. Constraint 2 ensures that the agents that are *removed* have their binding sites fully specified. Constraint 3a ensures that, in the agents that are *created*, all the sites are documented. Beside, constraint 3b requires that the state of their binding site is either free or bound to a specific site. Constraint 3c ensures that their counters have a single value.

An example of a rule is given in Fig. 6(a).

A rule $L \hookleftarrow D \overset{\$}{\hookrightarrow} R$ is usually denoted as $L \twoheadrightarrow R$ (leaving the common region and the sliding embedding implicit). Rules are applied to site-graphs via pure embeddings using the *single push-out* construction [22].

Definition 5 (rule application [14]**).** *Let* r *be a rule* $L \twoheadrightarrow R$*,* L' *be a site-graph, and* h_L *be a pure embedding from* L *to* L'*. Then, there exists a rule* $r' : L' \twoheadrightarrow R'$ *and a pure embedding* $h_R : R \hookrightarrow R'$ *such that the following properties are satisfied (e. g. see Fig. 6(c)):*

1. $h_R r = r' h_L$*;*
2. *for all rules* r'' *between the site-graph* L' *and a site-graph* R'' *and all embeddings* h'_R *from* R *into* R'' *such that* $h'_R r = r'' h_L$*, there exists a unique pure embedding* h *from* R' *into* R'' *such that* $r'' = hr'$ *and* $h'_R = hh_R$*.*

Moreover, whenever the site-graph L' *is a chemical mixture, the site-graph* R' *is a chemical mixture as well.*

We write $L' \xrightarrow{r} R'$ for a transition from the state L' into the state R' via an application of a rule r. Usually transition labels also mention the pure embedding (h_L here), but we omit it since we do not use it in the rest of the paper.

Example 4 (running example). An example of rule application is depicted in Fig. 6. We consider the rule r that takes a protein with the site a unphosphorylated and a counter with a value at least equal to 2, and that phosphorylates the site a while incrementing the counter by 1 (e. g. see Fig. 6(a)). Note that the update function of the counter is written next to its post-condition in the right hand side of the rule. We apply the rule to a protein with the sites b and c phosphorylated, the site d unphosphorylated, and the counter equal to 2 (e. g. see Fig. 6(b)). The result is a protein with the sites a, b, and c phosphorylated, the site d unphosphorylated and the counter equal to 3 (e. g. see Fig. 6(d)). □

A model $\mathcal{M}$ over a given signature Σ is defined as the pair $(G_0, \mathcal{R})$ where G_0 is a chemical mixture, representing the initial state, and $\mathcal{R}$ is a set of rules. Each rule is associated with a functional rate which maps each potential tuple of values for the counters of the left hand side of the rule to a non negative real number. We write $\mathcal{C}(\mathcal{M})$ for the set of states obtained from G_0 by applying a potentially empty sequence of rules in $\mathcal{R}$.

3 Encoding Counters

In this section, we introduce two encodings from Kappa with counters into Kappa without counters. As explained in Sect. 1, our goal is to preserve the rigidity of site-graphs and to avoid the blow-up of the number of rules in the target model. This is mandatory to preserve the good performances of the Kappa simulator. Both encodings rely on syntactic restrictions over the preconditions and the update functions that may be applied to counters and on semantics ones about the potential range of counters. In Sects. 4 and 5, we provide a static analysis to check whether, or not, these semantics assumptions hold.

3.1 Encoding the Value of Counters as Unbounded Chains of Agents

In this encoding, each counter is bound to a chain of fictitious agents the length of which minus 1 denotes the value of the counter (another encoding not requiring the subtraction is possible but it would require side-effects). Encoding counters as chains of agents has already been used in the implementation of two-counter machines in Kappa [19,34]. We slightly extend these works to implement more atomic operations over counters. We assume that the value of counters is bounded from below. For the sake of simplicity, we assume that counters range in $\mathbb{N}$, but arbitrary lower bounds may be considered by shifting each value accordingly. We denote by Ω_1 the set of the site-graphs that have a counter with a negative value. They are considered as erroneous states, since they may not be encoded with chains of agents.

Only two kinds of guards are handled. A rule may require the value of a counter to be equal to a given number or that the value of a counter is greater than a given number. Rules testing whether a value is less than a given number

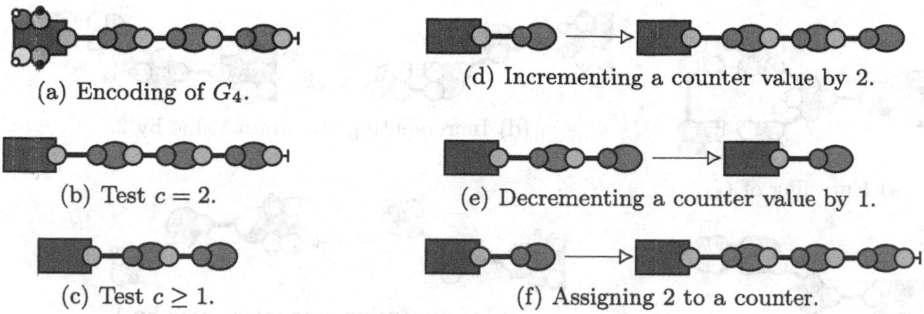

Fig. 7. Encoding the value of counters as unbounded chains of agents.

require unfolding each such rule into several ones (one per potential value). Also when the rate of a rule depends on the value of some counters, we unfold each rule according to the value of these counters, so that the rate of each unfolded rule is a constant (the Kappa simulator requires all the instances of a given rule in a given simulation state to have the same rate, for efficiency concerns). For update functions, we only consider constant functions and the functions that increase/decrease the value of counters by a fixed value. Testing whether the value of a counter is equal to (resp. greater than) n, can be done by requiring the corresponding chain to contain exactly (resp. at least) $n+1$ agents (e. g. see Figs. 7(b) and (c)). Incrementing (resp. decrementing) the value of a counter is modeled by inserting (resp. removing) agents at the beginning its chain (e. g. see Fig. 7(d), resp. Fig. 7(e)). Setting a counter to a fixed value, requires to detach its full chain in order to create a new one of the appropriate length (e. g. see Fig. 7(f)). In such a case, the former chain remains as a junk. Thus the state of the model must be understood up to insertion of junk agents. We introduce the function gc_1 that removes every chain of spurious agents not bound to any counter. We denote as $[\![G]\!]_1^g$ (resp. $[\![r]\!]_1^r$) the encoding of a site-graph G (resp. of a rule r).

3.2 Encoding the Value of Counters as Circular Lists of Agents

In this second encoding, each counter is bound to a ring of agents. Each such agent has three binding sites *zero*, *pred*, and *next*, and a property site *value* which may be activated, or not. In a ring, agents are connected circularly through their site *pred* and *next*. Exactly one agent per ring is bound to a counter and exactly one agent per ring has the site *value* activated. The value of the counter is encoded by the distance between the agent bound to the counter and the agent that is activated, scanning the agents by following the direction given by the site *next* of each agent (clock-wisely in the graphical representation). We have to consider that counter values are bounded from above and below. Without any loss of generality, we assume that the length of each ring is the same, that is to say that counters range from 0 to $n-1$, for a given $n \in \mathbb{N}$. We denote by Ω_2 the set of the site-graphs with at least one counter not satisfying these bounds.

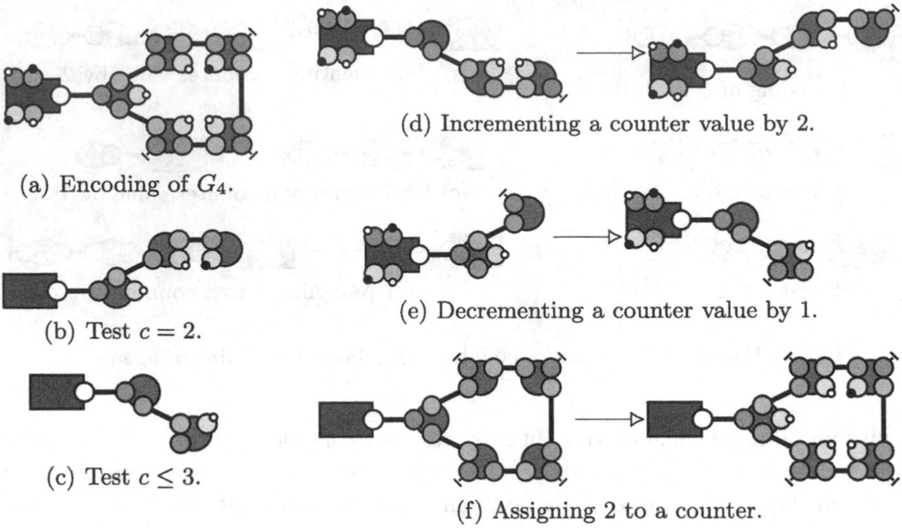

(a) Encoding of G_4.

(b) Test $c = 2$.

(c) Test $c \leq 3$.

(d) Incrementing a counter value by 2.

(e) Decrementing a counter value by 1.

(f) Assigning 2 to a counter.

Fig. 8. Encoding the value of counters as circular lists of agents.

Compared to the first encoding, this one may additionally cope with testing that a counter has a value less than a given constant without having to unfold the rule. Both encodings may deal with the same update functions. Testing whether a counter is equal to a value is done by requiring that the activated agent is at the appropriate distance of the agent that is connected to the counter (e. g. see Fig. 8(b)). It is worth noting that the intermediary agents are required to be not activated. This is not mandatory for the soundness of the encoding, this is an optimization that helps the simulator for detecting early that no embedding may associate a given agent of the left hand side of a rule to a given agent in the current state of the system. Inequalities are handled by checking that enough agents starting from the one that is connected to the counter and in the direction specified by the direction of the inequality, are not activated (e. g. see Fig. 8(c)). Incrementing/decrementing the value of a counter is modeled by making counter glide along the ring (e. g. see Figs. 8(d) and (e)). Special care has to be taken to ensure that the activated agent never crosses the agent linked to the counter (which would cause a numerical wrap-around). Assigning a given value to a counter requires to entirely remove the ring and to replace it with a fresh one (e. g. see Fig. 8(f)). It may be efficiently implemented without memory allocation. As in the first encoding, when the rate of a rule depends on the value of some counters, we unfold each rule according to the value of these counters, so that the rate of each unfolded rule is constant.

We introduce the function gc_2 as the identity function over site-graphs (there are no junk agent in this encoding). We denote as $[\![G]\!]_2^g$ (resp. $[\![r]\!]_2^r$) the encoding without counter of a site-graph G (resp. of a rule r).

3.3 Correspondence

The following theorem states that, whenever there is no numerical overflow and providing that junk agents are neglected, the semantics of Kappa with counters and the semantics of their encodings are in bisimulation.

Theorem 1 (correspondence). *Let i be either 1 or 2. Let G be a fully specified site-graph such that $G \notin \Omega_i$ and r be a rule. Both following properties are satisfied:*

1. *whenever there exists a site-graph G' such that $G \xrightarrow{r} G'$ and $G' \notin \Omega_i$, there exists a site-graph $G'_\$$, such that $[\![G]\!]_i^g \xrightarrow{[\![r]\!]_i^r} G'_\$$ and $[\![G']\!]_i^g = gc_i(G'_\$)$;*
2. *whenever there exists a site-graph $G'_\$$ such that $[\![G]\!]_i^g \xrightarrow{[\![r]\!]_i^r} G'_\$$, there exists a site-graph G' such that $G \xrightarrow{r} G'$, $G' \notin \Omega_i$, and $[\![G']\!]_i^g = gc_i(G'_\$)$.*

3.4 Benchmarks

The experimental evaluation of the impact of both encodings to the performance of the simulator KaSim [6,17] is presented in Fig. 9. We focus on the example that has been presented in Sect. 1. We plot the number of events that are simulated per second of CPU. For the sake of comparison, we also provide the simulation efficiency of the simulator NFSim [40] on the models written in BNGL with equivalent sites (with a linear number of rules only).

We notice that, with KaSim, the direct approach (without counter) is the most efficient when there are less than 9 phosphorylation sites. We explain this overhead, by the fact that each encoding utilizes spurious agents that have to be allocated in memory and relies on rules with bigger left hand sides. Nevertheless this overhead is reasonable if we consider the gain in conciseness in the description of the models. The versions of models with counters rely on a linear number of rules, which make models easier to read, document, and update. For more phosphorylation sites, simulation time for models written without counters blow up very quickly, due to the large number of rules. The simulation of the models with counters scales much better for both encodings.

Models can be concisely described in BNGL without using counters, by the means of equivalent sites. Each version of the model uses n indistinguishable sites and only a linear number of rules is required. However, detecting the potential applications of rules in the case of equivalent sites relies on the sub-graph isomorphism problem on general graphs, which prevent the approach to scale to large value of n. We observe that the efficiency of NFSim on this family of examples is not as good as the ones of KaSim (whatever which of the three modeling methods is used). We also observe a very quick deterioration of the performances starting at n equal to 5.

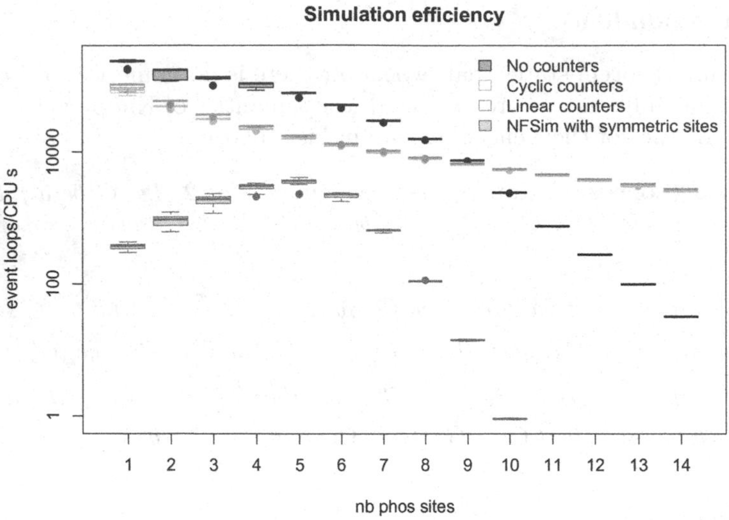

Fig. 9. Efficiency of the simulation for the example in Sect. 1 with n ranging between 1 and 14. We test the simulator KaSim with a version of the models written without counters and versions of the models according to both encodings (including the n phosphorylation sites). For the sake of comparison, we also compare with the efficiency of the simulator NFSim with the same model but written in BNGL by the means of equivalent sites. For each version of the model and each simulation method, we run 15 simulations of 10^5 events on an initial state made of 100 agents and we plot the number of computation steps computed in average per second of CPU on a log scale. Every simulation has been performed on 4 processors: Intel(R) Xeon(R) CPU E5-2609 0 @ 2.40 GHz 126 GB of RAM, running ubuntu 18.04.

4 Generic Abstraction of Reachable States

So far, we have provided two encodings to compile Kappa with counters into Kappa without counters. These encodings are sound under some assumptions over the range of counters. Now we propose a static analysis not only to check that these conditions are satisfied, but also to infer the meaning of the counters (in our case study, that they are equal to the number of phosphorylated sites).

Firstly, we provide a generic abstraction to capture the properties of the states that a Kappa model may potentially take. Our abstraction is parametric with respect to the class of properties. It will be instantiated in Sect. 5. Our analysis is not complete: not all the properties of the program are discovered; nevertheless, the result is sound: all the properties that are captured, are correct.

4.1 Collecting Semantics

Let $\mathcal{Q}$ be the set of all the site-graphs. We are interested in the set $\mathcal{C}(\mathcal{M})$ of all the states that a model $\mathcal{M} = (G_0, \mathcal{R})$ may take in 0, 1, or more computation steps. This is the collecting semantics [7]. By [33], it may be expressed as the least fixpoint of the $\cup$-complete endomorphism $\mathbb{F}$ on the complete lattice $\wp(\mathcal{Q})$ that is defined as $\mathbb{F}(X) = \{G_0\} \cup \{q' \mid \exists q \in X, r \in \mathcal{R} \text{ such that } q \xrightarrow{r} q'\}$. By [42], the collecting semantics is also equal to the meet of all the post-fixpoints of the function $\mathbb{F}$ (i. e. $\mathcal{C}(\mathcal{M}) = \bigcap\{X \in \wp(\mathcal{Q}) \mid \mathbb{F}(X) \subseteq X\}$), that is to say the strongest inductive invariant of our model that is satisfied by the initial state.

4.2 Generic Abstraction

The collecting semantics is usually not decidable. We use the Abstract Interpretation framework [9,10] to compute a sound approximation of it.

Definition 6 (abstraction). *A tuple $\mathcal{A} = (\mathcal{Q}^\sharp, \sqsubseteq, \gamma, \sqcup, \bot, \mathcal{I}^\sharp, t^\sharp, \nabla)$ is called an abstraction when all following conditions are satisfied:*

1. *the pair $(\mathcal{Q}^\sharp, \sqsubseteq)$ is a pre-order of abstract properties;*
2. *the component $\gamma : \mathcal{Q}^\sharp \rightarrow \wp(\mathcal{Q})$ is a monotonic map (i. e. for every two abstract elements $q_1^\sharp$, $q_2^\sharp \in \mathcal{Q}^\sharp$ such that $q_1^\sharp \sqsubseteq q_2^\sharp$, we have $\gamma(q_1^\sharp) \subseteq \gamma(q_2^\sharp)$);*
3. *the component $\sqcup$ maps each finite set of abstract properties $X^\sharp \in \wp_{finite}(\mathcal{Q}^\sharp)$ to an abstract property $\sqcup(X^\sharp) \in \mathcal{Q}^\sharp$ such that for each abstract property $q^\sharp \in X^\sharp$, we have: $q^\sharp \sqsubseteq \sqcup(X^\sharp)$;*
4. *the component $\bot \in \mathcal{Q}^\sharp$ is an abstract property such that $\gamma(\bot) = \emptyset$;*
5. *the component $\mathcal{I}^\sharp$ is an element of the set $\mathcal{Q}^\sharp$ such that $\{G_0\} \subseteq \gamma(\mathcal{I}^\sharp)$;*
6. *the component $t^\sharp$ is a function mapping each pair $(q, r) \in \mathcal{Q}^\sharp \times \mathcal{R}$ to an abstract property $t^\sharp(q, r) \in \mathcal{Q}^\sharp$ such that: $\forall q^\sharp \in \mathcal{Q}^\sharp$, $\forall q \in \gamma(q^\sharp)$, $\forall r \in \mathcal{R}$, $\forall q' \in \mathcal{Q}$, we have $q' \in \gamma(t^\sharp(q^\sharp))$ whenever $q \xrightarrow{r} q'$;*
7. *the component $\nabla : \mathcal{Q}^\sharp \times \mathcal{Q}^\sharp \rightarrow \mathcal{Q}^\sharp$ satisfies both following properties:*
   (a) $\forall q_1^\sharp$, $q_2^\sharp \in \mathcal{Q}^\sharp$, $q_1^\sharp \sqsubseteq q_1^\sharp \nabla q_2^\sharp$ and $q_2^\sharp \sqsubseteq q_1^\sharp \nabla q_2^\sharp$,
   (b) $\forall (q_n^\sharp)_{n\in\mathbb{N}} \in (\mathcal{Q}^\sharp)^{\mathbb{N}}$, the sequence $(q_n^\nabla)_{n\in\mathbb{N}}$ that is defined as $q_0^\nabla = q_0^\sharp$ and $q_{n+1}^\nabla = q_n^\nabla \nabla q_{n+1}^\sharp$ for every integer $n \in \mathbb{N}$, is ultimately stationary.

The set $\mathcal{Q}^\sharp$ is an abstract domain. It captures the properties of interest, and abstracts away the others. Each property $q^\sharp \in \mathcal{Q}^\sharp$ is mapped to the set of the concrete states $\gamma(q^\sharp)$ which satisfy this property by the means of the concretization function γ. The pre-order $\sqsubseteq$ describes the amount of information which is known about the properties that we approximate. We use a pre-order to allow some concrete properties to be described by several unrelated abstract elements. The abstract union $\sqcup$ is used to gather the information described by a finite number of abstract elements. It may not necessarily compute the least upper bound of a finite set of abstract elements (this least bound may not even exist). The abstract element $\bot$ provides the basis for abstract iterations. The concretization function is strict which means that it maps the element $\bot$ to the empty set. The abstract property $\mathcal{I}^\sharp$ is satisfied by the initial state. The function $t^\sharp$ is used to mimic concrete rewriting steps in the abstract. The operator ∇ is called a widening. It ensures the convergence of the analysis in finitely many iterations.

Given an abstraction $(\mathcal{Q}^\sharp, \sqsubseteq, \gamma, \sqcup, \bot, \mathcal{I}^\sharp, t^\sharp, \nabla)$, the abstract counterpart $\mathbb{F}^\sharp$ to $\mathbb{F}$ is defined as $\mathbb{F}^\sharp(q^\sharp) = \sqcup^\sharp\left(\{q^\sharp, \mathcal{I}^\sharp\} \cup \{t^\sharp(q^\sharp, r) \mid r \in \mathcal{R}\}\right)$. The function $\mathbb{F}^\sharp$ satisfies the soundness condition $\forall q^\sharp \in \mathcal{Q}^\sharp$, $[\mathbb{F} \circ \gamma](q^\sharp) \subseteq [\gamma \circ \mathbb{F}^\sharp](q^\sharp)$. Following [7], we compute a sound and decidable approximation of our abstract semantics by using the widening operator ∇. The abstract iteration [10,11] of $\mathbb{F}^\sharp$ is defined by the following induction: $\mathbb{F}_0^\nabla = \bot$ and, for each integer $n \in \mathbb{N}$, $\mathbb{F}_{n+1}^\nabla = \mathbb{F}_n^\nabla$ whenever $\mathbb{F}^\sharp(\mathbb{F}_n^\nabla) \sqsubseteq \mathbb{F}_n^\nabla$, and $\mathbb{F}_{n+1}^\nabla = \mathbb{F}_n^\nabla \nabla \mathbb{F}^\sharp(\mathbb{F}_n^\nabla)$ otherwise.

Theorem 2 (Termination and soundness). *The abstract iteration is ultimately stationary and its limit $\mathbb{F}^\nabla$ satisfies $\mathcal{C}(\mathcal{M}) \subseteq \gamma(\mathbb{F}^\nabla)$.*

Proof. By construction, $\mathbb{F}^\sharp(\mathbb{F}^\nabla) \sqsubseteq \mathbb{F}^\nabla$. Since γ is monotonic, it follows that: $\gamma(\mathbb{F}^\sharp(\mathbb{F}^\nabla)) \subseteq \gamma(\mathbb{F}^\nabla)$. Since, $\mathbb{F} \circ \gamma \,\dot{\subseteq}\, \gamma \circ \mathbb{F}^\sharp$, $\mathbb{F}(\gamma(\mathbb{F}^\nabla)) \subseteq \gamma(\mathbb{F}^\nabla)$. So $\gamma(\mathbb{F}^\nabla)$ is a post-fixpoint of $\mathbb{F}$. By [42], we have *lfp* $\mathbb{F} \subseteq \gamma(\mathbb{F}^\nabla)$. □

4.3 Coalescent Product

Two abstractions may be combined pair-wise to form a new one. The result is a coalescent product that defines a mutual induction over both abstractions.

Definition 7 (coalescent product). *The coalescent product between two abstractions $(\mathcal{Q}_1^\sharp, \sqsubseteq_1, \gamma_1, \sqcup_1, \bot_1, \mathcal{I}_1^\sharp, t_1^\sharp, \nabla_1)$ and $(\mathcal{Q}_2^\sharp, \sqsubseteq_2, \gamma_2, \sqcup_2, \bot_2, \mathcal{I}_2^\sharp, t_2^\sharp, \nabla_2)$ is defined as the tuple $(\mathcal{Q}^\sharp, \sqsubseteq, \gamma, \sqcup, \bot, \mathcal{I}^\sharp, t^\sharp, \nabla)$ where*

1. *$\mathcal{Q}^\sharp = \mathcal{Q}_1^\sharp \times \mathcal{Q}_2^\sharp$;*
2. *$\sqsubseteq$, $\sqcup$, $\bot$, and ∇ are defined pair-wise;*
3. *γ maps every pair $(q_1^\sharp, q_2^\sharp)$ to the meet $\gamma_1(q_1^\sharp) \cap \gamma_2(q_2^\sharp)$ of their respective concretization;*
4. *$\mathcal{I}^\sharp = (\mathcal{I}_1^\sharp, \mathcal{I}_2^\sharp)$;*
5. *$t^\sharp$ maps every pair $((q_1^\sharp, q_2^\sharp), r) \in \mathcal{Q}^\sharp \times \mathcal{R}$ made of a pair of abstract properties and a rule to the abstract property $(t_1^\sharp(q_1^\sharp, r), t_2^\sharp(q_2^\sharp, r))$ whenever $t_1^\sharp(q_1^\sharp, r) \neq \bot_1$ and $t_2^\sharp(q_2^\sharp, r) \neq \bot_2$, and to the pair $(\bot_1, \bot_2)$ otherwise.*

Theorem 3 (Soundness of the coalescent product). *The coalescent product of two abstractions is an abstraction as well.*

We notice that if either of both abstractions proves that the precondition of a rule is not satisfiable, then this rule is discarded in the other abstraction (hence the term coalescent). By mutual induction, the composite abstraction may detect which rules may be safely discarded along the iterations of the analysis.

We may now define an analysis modularly with respect to the class of considered properties. We use the coalescent product to extend the existing static analyzer KaSa [5] with a new abstraction dedicated to the range of counters.

5 Numerical Abstraction

Now we specialize our generic abstraction to detect and prove safe bounds to the range of counters. In general, this requires to relate the value of the counters to the state of others sites. Our approach consists in translating each protein configuration into a vector of relative numbers and in abstracting each rule by its potential effect on these vectors. We obtain an integer linear programming problem that we will solve by choosing an appropriate abstract domain.

The set of convex parts of $\mathbb{Z}$ is written as $\mathcal{I}_{\mathbb{Z}}$. We assume that guards on counters are element of $\mathcal{I}_{\mathbb{Z}}$ and that each update function either set counters to a constant value, or increment/decrement counters by a constant value.

5.1 Encoding States and Preconditions

We propose to translate each agent into a set of numerical constraints. A protein of type A is associated with one variable χ_i^λ for each binding site i and each binding state λ, one variable χ_i^ι for each property site i and each internal state identifier ι, and one variable val_i for each counter in i.

Definition 8 (numerical variables). *Let $A \in \Sigma_{ag}$ be an agent type. We define the set $\mathcal{V}ar_A$ as the set of variables $\mathcal{V}ar_A^{lnk} \cup \mathcal{V}ar_A^{int} \cup \mathcal{V}ar_A^{\$}$ where:*

1. $\mathcal{V}ar_A^{lnk} = \{\chi_i^\lambda \mid i \in \Sigma_{ag\text{-}st}^{lnk}(A), \lambda \in \{\dashv\} \cup \{(A', i') \mid A' \in \Sigma_{ag}, i' \in \Sigma_{ag\text{-}st}^{lnk}(A')\}\}$;
2. $\mathcal{V}ar_A^{int} = \{\chi_i^\iota \mid i \in \Sigma_{ag\text{-}st}^{int}(A), \iota \in \Sigma_{int}\}$;
3. $\mathcal{V}ar_A^{\$} = \{val_i \mid i \in \Sigma_{ag\text{-}st}^{\$}\}$.

Intuitively, variables of the form χ_i^λ (resp. χ_i^ι) take the value 1 if the binding (resp. internal) state of the site i is λ (resp. ι), whereas the variables of the form val_i takes the value of the counter i.

Each agent of type A may be translated into a function mapping each variable in the set $\mathcal{V}ar_A$ into a subset of the set $\mathbb{Z}$. Such a function is called a guard.

Definition 9 (Encoding of agents). *Let G be a site-graph and n be an agent in $\mathcal{A}_G$. We denote by A the type $type_G(n)$. We define as follows the function $guard_G(n)$ from the set $\mathcal{V}ar_A$ into the set $\mathcal{I}_{\mathbb{Z}}$:*

1. *$guard_G(n)(\chi_i^{\dashv})$ is equal to the singleton $\{1\}$ whenever $(n,i) \in \mathcal{S}_G^{lnk}(A)$ and $\mathcal{L}_G(n,i) = \dashv$, to the singleton $\{0\}$ whenever $(n,i) \in \mathcal{S}_G^{lnk}(A)$ and $\mathcal{L}_G(n,i) \neq \dashv$, and to the set $\{0,1\}$ whenever $(n,i) \notin \mathcal{S}_G^{lnk}(A)$;*
2. *$guard_G(n)(\chi_i^{(A',i')})$ is equal to the singleton $\{1\}$ whenever $(n,i) \in \mathcal{S}_G^{lnk}(A)$ and there exists $n' \in \mathcal{A}_G$ such that both conditions $type_G(n') = A'$ and $\mathcal{L}_G(n,i) = (n',i')$ are satisfied, to the singleton $\{0\}$ whenever $(n,i) \in \mathcal{S}_G^{lnk}(A)$ and either $\mathcal{L}_G(n,i) = \dashv$, or there exist an agent identifier $n'' \in \mathcal{A}_G$ and a site name $i'' \in \Sigma_{site}$ such that $(type_G(n''), i'') \neq (A', i')$, and to the set $\{0,1\}$ whenever $(n,i) \notin \mathcal{S}_G^{lnk}(A)$ or $\mathcal{L}_G(n,i) = -$;*
3. *$guard_G(n)(\chi_i^\iota)$ is equal to the singleton $\{1\}$ whenever $(n,i) \in \mathcal{S}_G^{int}(A)$ and $p\kappa_G(n,i) = \iota$; to the singleton $\{0\}$ whenever $(n,i) \in \mathcal{S}_G^{int}(A)$ and $p\kappa_G(n,i) \neq \iota$; and to set $\{0,1\}$ whenever $(n,i) \notin \mathcal{S}_G^{int}(A)$.*

4. *$guard_G(n)(val_i)$ is equal to the set $c\kappa_G(c)$ whenever $(n,i) \in \mathcal{S}_G^{\$}$ and to the set $\mathbb{Z}$ otherwise.*

The variable $\chi_i^{\dashv}$ takes the value $\{1\}$ if we know that the site i is free, the value $\{0\}$ if we know that it is bound, and the value $\{0,1\}$ if we do not know whether the site is free or not. This is the same for binding type, the variable $\chi_i^{(A',i')}$ takes the value $\{1\}$ if we know that the site is bound to the site i' of an agent of type A', the value $\{0\}$ if we know that this is not the case, and the value $\{0,1\}$ otherwise. Property sites work the same way. Lastly, the variable val_i takes as value the set attached to the counter or the value $\mathbb{Z}$ if the site is not mentioned in the agent. We notice that when n is a fully-specified agent of type A, the function $guard_G(n)$ maps every variable in the set $\mathcal{V}ar_A$ to a singleton.

Example 5 (running example). We provide the translation of the unique agent of the site-graph G_1 (e. g. see Fig. 3(a)) and the one of the unique agent of the site-graph G_4 (e. g. see Fig. 3(d)).

The agent of the site-graph G_1 is translated as follows:

$$\left\{\begin{array}{l} \chi_a^{\circ} = \{1\}; \chi_a^{\bullet} = \{0\}; \\ \chi_b^{\circ} = \{0,1\}; \chi_b^{\bullet} = \{0,1\}; \\ \chi_c^{\circ} = \{0,1\}; \chi_c^{\bullet} = \{0,1\}; \\ \chi_d^{\circ} = \{0,1\}; \chi_d^{\bullet} = \{0,1\}; \\ val_x = \{z \in \mathbb{Z} \mid z \leq 2\} \end{array}\right\}.$$

According to the first two constraints, the site a is unphosphorylated. According to the next six ones, the sites b, c, and d have an unspecified state. According to the last constraint, the value of the counter must be less than or equal to 2.

The translation of the agent of the site-graph G_4 is obtained the same way:

$$\left\{\begin{array}{l} \chi_a^{\circ} = \{1\}; \chi_a^{\bullet} = \{0\}; \\ \chi_b^{\circ} = \{0\}; \chi_b^{\bullet} = \{1\}; \\ \chi_c^{\circ} = \{0\}; \chi_c^{\bullet} = \{1\}; \\ \chi_d^{\circ} = \{1\}; \chi_d^{\bullet} = \{0\}; \\ val_x = \{2\} \end{array}\right\}.$$

This means that the sites b and c are phosphorylated while the sites a and d are not. According to the last constraint, the value of the counter is equal to 2.

5.2 Encoding Rules

In Kappa, a rule may be applied only when its precondition is satisfied. Moreover, the application of a rule modifies the state of some sites in agents. We translate each rule into a tuple of guards that encodes its precondition, a set of non-invertible assignments (when a site is given a new state that does not depend on the former one), and a set of invertible assignments (when the new state of a site depends on the previous one). Such a distinction is important as we want to establish relationships among the value of some variables [32]: a non-invertible assignment completely hides the former value of a variable. This is not the case with invertible assignments for which relationships may be propagated more easily. The agents that are created (which have no precondition) and the ones that are removed (which disappear), have a special treatment.

Definition 10 (Encoding of rules). *Each rule* $r : L \leftarrow D \xrightarrow{(h_e,h_\$)} R$ *is associated with the tuple* (pre_r, $not\text{-}invert_r$, $invert_r$, new_r) *where:*

1. pre_r *maps every agent* $n \in \mathcal{A}_L$ *in the left hand side of the rule* r *to its guard* $guard_L(n)$*;*
2. $not\text{-}invert_r$ *maps every agent* $n \in \mathcal{A}_D$ *and every variable* $v \in \mathcal{V}ar_{type_D(n)}$ *such that the set* $guard_R(h_e(n))(v)$ *is a singleton and* $guard_R(h_e(n))(v) \neq guard_L(n)(v)$ *to the unique element of the set* $guard_R(h_e(n))(v)$*.*
3. $invert_r$ *maps every agent* $n \in \mathcal{A}_D$ *and every variable* $v \in \mathcal{V}ar_{type_D(n)}$ *such that the set* $guard_R(h_e(n))(v)$ *is not a singleton and* $h_\$(n,i)$ *is a function of the form* $[z \in \mathbb{Z} \mapsto z + c]$ *with* $c \in \mathbb{Z}$*, to the relative number* c*.*
4. new_r *maps every agent* $n' \in \mathcal{A}_R$ *such that there is no agent* $n \in \mathcal{A}_D$ *satisfying* $h_e(n) = n'$ *to the guard* $guard_R(n')$*.*

Example 6 (running example). The encoding of the rule of Fig. 6(a) is given as follows:

- the function pre_r maps the agent 1 to the following set of constraints:

$$\left\{\begin{array}{l} \chi_a^\circ = \{1\}; \chi_a^\bullet = \{0\}; \\ \chi_b^\circ = \{0,1\}; \chi_b^\bullet = \{0,1\}; \\ \chi_c^\circ = \{0,1\}; \chi_c^\bullet = \{0,1\}; \\ \chi_d^\circ = \{0,1\}; \chi_d^\bullet = \{0,1\}; \\ val_x = \{z \in \mathbb{Z} \mid z \leq 2\} \end{array}\right\};$$

- the function $not\text{-}invert_r$ maps the pair $(1, \chi_a^\circ)$ to the value 0, and the pair $(1, \chi_a^\bullet)$ to the value 1;
- the function $invert_r$ maps the pair $(1, x)$ to the successor function;
- the function new_r is the function with the empty domain.

The guard specifies that the site a must be unphosphorylated and the value of the counter less or equal to 2. Applying the rule modifies the value of three variables. The site a gets phosphorylated. This is a non-invertible modification that sets the variable χ_a° to the constant value 0 and the variable $\chi_a^\bullet$ to the constant value 1. The counter x is incremented. This is an invertible modification that is encoded by incrementing the value of the variable val_x.

5.3 Generic Numerical Abstract Domain

We are now ready to define a generic numerical abstraction.

Definition 11 (Numerical domain). *A numerical abstract domain is a family* $(\mathcal{A}_A^{\mathcal{N}})_{A \in \Sigma_{ag}}$ *of tuples* $(\mathcal{D}_A^{\mathcal{N}}, \sqsubseteq_A^{\mathcal{N}}, \gamma_A, \sqcup_A^{\mathcal{N}}, \bot_A^{\mathcal{N}}, \top_A^{\mathcal{N}}, g_A^{\mathcal{N}}, forget_A^{\mathcal{N}}, \delta_A^{\mathcal{N}}, \nabla_A^{\mathcal{N}})$ *that satisfy the following conditions, for every agent type* $A \in \Sigma_{ag}$*:*

1. *the pair* $(\mathcal{D}^{\mathcal{N}}_A, \sqsubseteq^{\mathcal{N}}_A)$ *is a pre-order;*
2. *the component* $\gamma^{\mathcal{N}}_A : \mathcal{D}^{\mathcal{N}}_A \rightarrow \wp(\mathbb{Z}^{\mathcal{V}ar_A})$ *is a monotonic function;*
3. *the component* $\sqcup^{\mathcal{N}}_A : \wp_{finite}(\mathcal{D}^{\mathcal{N}}_A) \rightarrow \mathcal{D}^{\mathcal{N}}_A$ *is an operator such that* $\forall X^\sharp \in \wp_{finite}(\mathcal{D}^{\mathcal{N}}_A)$, $\forall \rho^\sharp \in X^\sharp$, $\rho^\sharp \sqsubseteq \sqcup(X^\sharp)$;
4. *the component* $\bot^{\mathcal{N}}_A$ *is an element in the set* $\mathcal{D}^{\mathcal{N}}_A$ *such that* $\gamma^{\mathcal{N}}_A(\bot^{\mathcal{N}}_A) = \emptyset$;
5. *the component* $\top^{\mathcal{N}}_A$ *is an element in the set* $\mathcal{D}^{\mathcal{N}}_A$ *such that* $\gamma^{\mathcal{N}}_A(\top^{\mathcal{N}}_A) = \mathbb{Z}^{\mathcal{V}ar_A}$;
6. *the component* $g^{\mathcal{N}}_A$ *is a function mapping each pair* $(g, \rho^\sharp)$ *where* g *is a guard and* $\rho^\sharp$ *an abstract property in* $\mathcal{D}^{\mathcal{N}}_A$ *to an abstract element in* $\mathcal{D}^{\mathcal{N}}_A$ *such that the set* $\gamma^{\mathcal{N}}_A(g^{\mathcal{N}}_A(g, \rho^\sharp))$ *contains at least each function* $\rho \in \gamma^{\mathcal{N}}_A(\rho^\sharp)$ *that verifies the condition* $\rho(v) \in \rho^\sharp(v)$ *for every variable* $v \in \mathcal{V}ar_A$;
7. *the component* $forget^{\mathcal{N}}_A$ *maps each pair* $(V, \rho^\sharp) \in \wp(\mathcal{V}ar_A) \times \mathcal{D}^{\mathcal{N}}_A$ *to an abstract property* $forget^{\mathcal{N}}_A(V, \rho^\sharp) \in \mathcal{D}^{\mathcal{N}}_A$, *the concretization* $\gamma(forget^{\mathcal{N}}_A(V, \rho^\sharp))$ *of which contains at least each function* $\rho \in \mathbb{Z}^{\mathcal{V}ar_A}$ *such that there exists a function* $\rho' \in \gamma^{\mathcal{N}}_A(\rho^\sharp)$ *satisfying* $\rho(v) = \rho'(v)$ *for each variable* $v \in \mathcal{V}ar_A \setminus V$;
8. *the component* $\delta^{\mathcal{N}}_A$ *maps each pair* $(t, \rho^\sharp) \in \mathbb{Z}^{\mathcal{V}ar_A} \times \mathcal{D}^{\mathcal{N}}_A$ *to an abstract property* $\delta^{\mathcal{N}}_A(t, \rho^\sharp) \in \mathcal{D}^{\mathcal{N}}_A$, *such for each function* $\rho \in \gamma^{\mathcal{N}}_A(\rho^\sharp)$, *the function mapping each variable* $v \in \mathcal{V}ar_A$ *to the value* $\rho(v) + t(v)$ *belongs to the set* $\gamma^{\mathcal{N}}_A(\delta^{\mathcal{N}}_A(t, \rho^\sharp))$;
9. *the component* $\nabla^{\mathcal{N}}$ *is a widening operator satisfies both following properties:*
   (a) $\forall \rho^\sharp_1, \rho^\sharp_2 \in \mathcal{D}^{\mathcal{N}}_A$, $\rho^\sharp_1 \sqsubseteq^{\mathcal{N}}_A \rho^\sharp_1 \nabla^{\mathcal{N}} \rho^\sharp_2$ *and* $\rho^\sharp_2 \sqsubseteq^{\mathcal{N}}_A \rho^\sharp_1 \nabla^{\mathcal{N}} \rho^\sharp_2$,
   (b) $\forall (\rho^\sharp_n)_{n\in\mathbb{N}} \in \left(\mathcal{D}^{\mathcal{N}}_A\right)^{\mathbb{N}}$, *the sequence* $(\rho^\nabla_n)_{n\in\mathbb{N}}$ *that is defined as* $\rho^\nabla_0 = \rho^\sharp_0$ *and* $\rho^\nabla_{n+1} = \rho^\nabla_n \nabla^{\mathcal{N}} \rho^\sharp_{n+1}$ *for every integer* $n \in \mathbb{N}$, *is ultimately stationary.*

5.4 Numerical Abstraction

The following theorem explains how to build an abstraction (as defined in Sect. 4) from a numerical abstract domain. We introduce an operator $\uparrow$ to extend the domain of functions with default values. Given a function f, a value v and a super-set X of the domain of f, we write $\uparrow^v_X f$ the extension of the function f that maps each element $x \in X \setminus Dom\ (f)$ to the value v. We also write set_A for the function mapping pairs $(f, X^\sharp)$ where f is a partial function from the set $\mathcal{V}ar_A$ into the set of the convex parts of $\mathbb{Z}$ and $X^\sharp$ an abstract property in $\mathcal{D}^{\mathcal{N}}_A$, to the abstract property: $g^{\mathcal{N}}_A(\uparrow^{\mathbb{Z}}_{\mathcal{V}ar_A} f, forget^{\mathcal{N}}_A(dom(f), X^\sharp))$. The function set_A forgets all the information about the variables in the domain of the function f, and reassign their range to their image by f in the abstract.

Theorem 4. *Let* $(\mathcal{D}^{\mathcal{N}}_A, \sqsubseteq^{\mathcal{N}}_A, \gamma_A, \sqcup^{\mathcal{N}}_A, \bot^{\mathcal{N}}_A, \top^{\mathcal{N}}_A, g^{\mathcal{N}}_A, forget^{\mathcal{N}}_A, \delta^{\mathcal{N}}_A, \nabla^{\mathcal{N}}_A)_{A\in\Sigma_{ag}}$ *be a numerical abstract domain. The tuple* $(\mathcal{Q}^\sharp, \sqsubseteq, \gamma, \sqcup, \bot, \mathcal{I}^\sharp, t^\sharp, \nabla)$ *that is defined by:*

1. *the component* $\mathcal{Q}^\sharp$ *is the set of the functions mapping each agent type* $A \in \Sigma_{ag}$ *to an abstract property in the set* $\mathcal{D}^{\mathcal{N}}_A$;
2. *the component* γ *is the function mapping a function* $X^\sharp \in \mathcal{Q}^\sharp$, *to the set of the fully specified site-graph* G *such that for each agent* $n \in \mathcal{A}_G$, *we have* $guard_G(n) \in \gamma_{type_G(n)}(X^\sharp(type_G(n)))$;
3. *the components* $\sqsubseteq$, $\sqcup$, $\bot$ *are defined component-wise;*

4. *the component* $\mathcal{I}^\sharp$ *maps each agent type* $A \in \Sigma_{ag}$ *to the abstract property* $\sqcup_A^{\mathcal{N}} \{ g_A^{\mathcal{N}}(guard_{G_0}(n), \top_A^{\mathcal{N}}) \mid n \in \mathcal{A}_{G_0} \}$*;*
5. *the component* $t^\sharp$ *is a function mapping each pair* $(X^\sharp, r) \in \mathcal{Q}^\sharp \times \mathcal{R}$ *(we write* $r : L \xleftarrow{\supseteq} D \xhookrightarrow{\$} R$*) to the element* $\bot_A^{\mathcal{N}}$ *whenever there exists an agent* n *in* $\mathcal{A}_L$ *such that* $g_A^{\mathcal{N}}(pre_r(n), X^\sharp(type_L(n))) = \bot_A^{\mathcal{N}}$*, and, otherwise, to the function mapping each agent type* A *to the numerical property:*

$$\sqcup_A^{\mathcal{N}}(\{X^\sharp(A)\} \cup \mathit{fresh}(r, A) \cup \mathit{updated}(r, A, X^\sharp)),$$

with:
   - $\mathit{fresh}(r, A)$ *the set of the numerical abstract elements* $g_A^{\mathcal{N}}(new_r n, \top_A^{\mathcal{N}})$ *for every* $n \in dom(new_r)$ *such that* $type_R(n) = A$*;*
   - *and* $\mathit{updated}(r, A, X^\sharp)$ *the set of the elements:*
     $set_A(not\text{-}invert_r(n), \delta_A^{\mathcal{N}}(\uparrow_A^0 invert_r(n), g_A^{\mathcal{N}}(pre_r(n), X^\sharp(A))))$
     for each agent $n \in \mathcal{A}_D$ *with* $type_D(n) = A$*;*

is a generic abstraction.

Most of the constructions of the abstraction are standard. The expression $g_A^{\mathcal{N}}(pre_r(n), X^\sharp(type_L(n)))$ refines the abstract information about the potential configurations of the n-th agent in the left hand side of the rule, by taking into account its precondition. Whenever a bottom element is obtained for at least one agent, the precondition of the rule is not satisfiable and the rule is discarded at this moment of the iteration. Otherwise, the information about each agent is updated. Starting from the result of the refinement of the abstract element by the precondition, the function $\delta_A^{\mathcal{N}}$ applies the invertible transformations $\uparrow_A^0 invert_r(n)$ (the function $\uparrow_A^0$ extends the domain of the function $invert_r(n)$ by specifying that the variables not in the domain of this function remain unchanged), and the function set_A applies non invertible one $not\text{-}invert_r(n)$.

The domain of intervals [8] and the one of affine relationships [32] provide all the primitives requested by Definition 11. We use a product of them, when all primitives are defined pair-wise, except the guards which refine its output by using the algorithm that is described in [23]. We use widening with thresholds [2] for intervals so as to avoid infinite bounds when possible. This way we obtain a domain, where all operations are cubic with respect to the number of variables.

This is a very good trade-off. A relational domain is required. Other relational domain are either too imprecise [37], or to costly [13], or both [27,38].

5.5 Benchmarks

We run our analysis on the family of models of Sect. 1 for n ranging between 1 and 25. For each version of the model, the protein is made of n phosphorylation sites and a counter. Moreover, our analysis always discover that the counter ranges between 0 and n. CPU time is plot in Fig. 10.

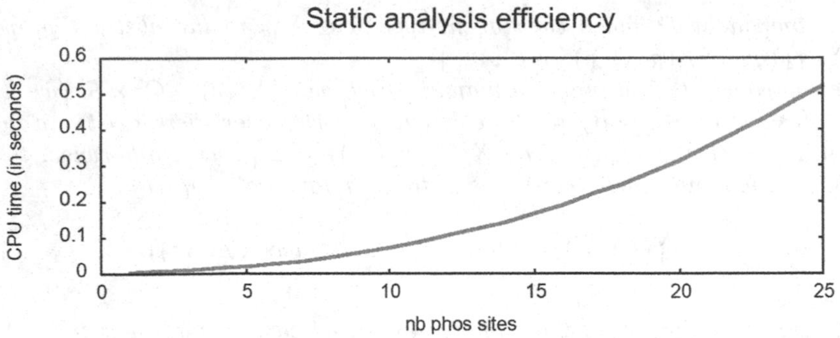

Fig. 10. Efficiency of the static analysis for the example in Sect. 1 with n ranging between 1 and 25. Every analysis has successfully computed the exact range of the counter. The analysis has been performed on a MacBook Pro on a 2.8 GHz intel Core i7, 16 GB of RAM, running under macOS High Sierra version 10.13.6.

6 Conclusion

When potential protein transformations depend on the number of sites satisfying a given property, counters offer a convenient way to describe generic mechanisms while avoiding the explosion in the number of rules. We have extended the semantics of Kappa to deal with counters. We have proposed some encodings to remove counters while preserving the performance of the Kappa simulator. In particular, graphs remain rigid and the number of rules remain the same. Then, we have introduced a static analysis to bound the range of counters.

It is quite common to find proteins with more than 40 phosphorylation sites. Without our contributions, the modeler has no choice but to assume these proteins to be active only when all their sites are phosphorylated. This is a harsh simplification. Modeling simplifications are usually done not only because detailed knowledge is missing, but also because corresponding models cannot be described, executed, or analyzed efficiently. Yet these simplifications are done without any clue of their impact on the behavior of the systems. By providing ways of describing and handling some complex details, we offer the modelers the means to incorporate these details and to test empirically their impact.

Our framework is fully integrated within the Kappa modeling platform which is open-source and usable online (https://kappalanguage.org). It is worth noting that we have taken two radically different approaches to deal with counters in simulation and in static analysis. Encodings are good for simulation, but they tend to obfuscate the properties of interest, hence damaging drastically the capability of the static analysis to infer useful properties about them. The extension of the categorical semantics provides a parsimonious definition of causality between computation steps, as well as means to reason symbolically on the behavior of the number of occurrences of patterns. For further works, we will extend existing decision procedures [14,15] that compute minimal causal traces to cope with counters. It is very likely that a third approach will be required. We suggest to use the traces obtained by simulation, then translate the counters in these traces thanks to equivalent sites, and apply existing decision procedures the traces that will be obtained this way.

References

1. Behr, N., Danos, V., Garnier, I.: Stochastic mechanics of graph rewriting. In: Grohe, M., Koskinen, E., Shankar, N. (eds.) Proceedings of the 31st Annual ACM/IEEE Symposium on Logic in Computer Science (LICS 2016), New York, NY, USA, pp. 46–55. ACM (2016)
2. Blanchet, B., et al.: A static analyzer for large safety-critical software. In: Proceedings of the ACM SIGPLAN 2003 Conference on Programming Language Design and Implementation (PLDI 2003), San Diego, California, USA, 7–14 June 2003, pp. 196–207. ACM Press (2003)
3. Blinov, M.L., Faeder, J.R., Goldstein, B., Hlavacek, W.S.: BioNetGen: software for rule-based modeling of signal transduction based on the interactions of molecular domains. Bioinformatics **20**(17), 3289–3291 (2004)
4. Bortolussi, L., et al.: CARMA: collective adaptive resource-sharing Markovian agents. In: Bertrand, N., Tribastone, M. (eds.) Proceedings of the Thirteenth Workshop on Quantitative Aspects of Programming Languages and Systems (QAPL 2015), London, UK. EPTCS, vol. 194, pp. 16–31 (2015)
5. Boutillier, P., et al.: KaSa: a static analyzer for Kappa. In: Češka, M., Šafránek, D. (eds.) CMSB 2018. LNCS, vol. 11095, pp. 285–291. Springer, Cham (2018). https://doi.org/10.1007/978-3-319-99429-1_17
6. Boutillier, P., Ehrhard, T., Krivine, J.: Incremental update for graph rewriting. In: Yang, H. (ed.) ESOP 2017. LNCS, vol. 10201, pp. 201–228. Springer, Heidelberg (2017). https://doi.org/10.1007/978-3-662-54434-1_8
7. Cousot, P.: Semantic foundations of program analysis. In: Muchnick, S.S., Jones, N.D. (eds.) Program Flow Analysis: Theory and Applications, vol. 10. Prentice-Hall Inc., Englewood Cliffs (1981)
8. Cousot, P., Cousot, R.: Static determination of dynamic properties of programs. In: Proceedings of the Second International Symposium on Programming, pp. 106–130. Dunod, Paris (1976)
9. Cousot, P., Cousot, R.: Abstract interpretation: a unified lattice model for static analysis of programs by construction or approximation of fixpoints. In: Proceedings of POPL 1977. ACM Press (1977)
10. Cousot, P., Cousot, R.: Abstract interpretation frameworks. J. Logic Comput. **2**(4), 511–547 (1992)
11. Cousot, P., Cousot, R.: Comparing the Galois connection and widening/narrowing approaches to abstract interpretation. In: Bruynooghe, M., Wirsing, M. (eds.) PLILP 1992. LNCS, vol. 631, pp. 269–295. Springer, Heidelberg (1992). https://doi.org/10.1007/3-540-55844-6_142
12. Cousot, P., et al.: Combination of abstractions in the Astrée static analyzer. In: Okada, M., Satoh, I. (eds.) ASIAN 2006. LNCS, vol. 4435, pp. 272–300. Springer, Heidelberg (2007). https://doi.org/10.1007/978-3-540-77505-8_23
13. Cousot, P., Halbwachs, N.: Automatic discovery of linear restraints among variables of a program. In: Aho, A.V., Zilles, S.N., Szymanski, T.G. (eds.) Conference Record of the Fifth Annual ACM Symposium on Principles of Programming Languages, Tucson, Arizona, USA, January 1978, pp. 84–96. ACM Press (1978)

14. Danos, V., et al.: Graphs, rewriting and pathway reconstruction for rule-based models. In: D'Souza, D., Kavitha, T., Radhakrishnan, J. (eds.) IARCS Annual Conference on Foundations of Software Technology and Theoretical Computer Science, FSTTCS 2012, Hyderabad, India, 15–17 December 2012. LIPIcs, vol. 18, pp. 276–288. Schloss Dagstuhl - Leibniz-Zentrum fuer Informatik (2012)
15. Danos, V., Feret, J., Fontana, W., Harmer, R., Krivine, J.: Rule-based modelling of cellular signalling. In: Caires, L., Vasconcelos, V.T. (eds.) CONCUR 2007. LNCS, vol. 4703, pp. 17–41. Springer, Heidelberg (2007). https://doi.org/10.1007/978-3-540-74407-8_3
16. Danos, V., Feret, J., Fontana, W., Harmer, R., Krivine, J.: Abstracting the differential semantics of rule-based models: exact and automated model reduction. In: Jouannaud, J.-P. (ed.) Proceedings of the Twenty-Fifth Annual IEEE Symposium on Logic in Computer Science, LICS 2010, Edinburgh, UK, 11–14 July 2010, pp. 362–381. IEEE Computer Society (2010)
17. Danos, V., Feret, J., Fontana, W., Krivine, J.: Scalable simulation of cellular signaling networks. In: Shao, Z. (ed.) APLAS 2007. LNCS, vol. 4807, pp. 139–157. Springer, Heidelberg (2007). https://doi.org/10.1007/978-3-540-76637-7_10
18. Danos, V., Laneve, C.: Formal molecular biology. Theor. Comput. Sci. **325**(1), 69–110 (2004)
19. Delzanno, G., Di Giusto, C., Gabbrielli, M., Laneve, C., Zavattaro, G.: The *kappa*-lattice: decidability boundaries for qualitative analysis in biological languages. In: Degano, P., Gorrieri, R. (eds.) CMSB 2009. LNCS, vol. 5688, pp. 158–172. Springer, Heidelberg (2009). https://doi.org/10.1007/978-3-642-03845-7_11
20. Dijkstra, E.W.: Over de sequentialiteit van procesbeschrijvingen. circulated privately, 1962 or 1963
21. Dijkstra, E.W.: Cooperating sequential processes. Technical report EWD-123 (1965)
22. Ehrig, H., et al.: Algebraic approaches to graph transformation. Part II: single pushout approach and comparison with double pushout approach. In: Handbook of Graph Grammars and Computing by Graph Transformation, pp. 247–312. Springer-Verlag, New York Inc., Secaucus (1997)
23. Feret, J.: Occurrence counting analysis for the pi-calculus. Electron. Notes Theor. Comput. Sci. **39**(2), 1–18 (2001). Workshop on GEometry and Topology in COncurrency theory, PennState, USA, August 21, 2000
24. Feret, J.: Abstract interpretation of mobile systems. J. Log. Algebr. Program. **63**(1), 59–130 (2005)
25. Feret, J.: An algebraic approach for inferring and using symmetries in rule-based models. Electron. Notes Theor. Comput. Sci. **316**, 45–65 (2015)
26. Feret, J., Danos, V., Harmer, R., Fontana, W., Krivine, J.: Internal coarse-graining of molecular systems. PNAS **106**(16), 6453–6458 (2009)
27. Hansen, R.R., Jensen, J.G., Nielson, F., Nielson, H.R.: Abstract interpretation of mobile ambients. In: Cortesi, A., Filé, G. (eds.) SAS 1999. LNCS, vol. 1694, pp. 134–148. Springer, Heidelberg (1999). https://doi.org/10.1007/3-540-48294-6_9
28. Helms, T., Warnke, T., Maus, C., Uhrmacher, A.M.: Semantics and efficient simulation algorithms of an expressive multilevel modeling language. ACM Trans. Model. Comput. Simul. **27**(2), 8:1–8:25 (2017)
29. Honorato-Zimmer, R., Millar, A.J., Plotkin, G.D., Zardilis, A.: Chromar, a language of parameterised agents. Theor. Comput. Sci. (2017)
30. Jensen, K.: Coloured Petri Nets: Basic Concepts, Analysis Methods and Practical Use: Basic Concepts, Analysis Methods and Practical Use. Volume 1. Monographs

in Theoretical Computer Science. An EATCS Series, 2nd edn. Springer, Heidelberg (1996). https://doi.org/10.1007/978-3-662-03241-1
31. John, M., Lhoussaine, C., Niehren, J., Versari, C.: Biochemical reaction rules with constraints. In: Barthe, G. (ed.) ESOP 2011. LNCS, vol. 6602, pp. 338–357. Springer, Heidelberg (2011). https://doi.org/10.1007/978-3-642-19718-5_18
32. Karr, M.: Affine relationships among variables of a program. Acta Informatica **6**(2), 133–151 (1976)
33. Kleene, S.C.: Introduction to Mathematics. ISHI Press International, New York (1952)
34. Kreyßig, P.: Chemical organisation theory beyond classical models: discrete dynamics and rule-based models. Ph.D. thesis, Friedrich-Schiller-University Jena (2015)
35. Liu, F., Blätke, M.A., Heiner, M., Yang, M.: Modelling and simulating reaction-diffusion systems using coloured petri nets. Comput. Biol. Med. **53**, 297–308 (2014)
36. Miné, A.: A new numerical abstract domain based on difference-bound matrices. In: Danvy, O., Filinski, A. (eds.) PADO 2001. LNCS, vol. 2053, pp. 155–172. Springer, Heidelberg (2001). https://doi.org/10.1007/3-540-44978-7_10
37. Miné, A.: The octagon abstract domain. Higher-Order Symbolic Comput. (HOSC) **19**(1), 31–100 (2006)
38. Nielson, H.R., Nielson, F.: Shape analysis for mobile ambients. In: Proceedings of POPL 2000. ACM Press (2000)
39. Petrov, T., Feret, J., Koeppl, H.: Reconstructing species-based dynamics from reduced stochastic rule-based models. In: Laroque, C., Himmelspach, J., Pasupathy, R., Rose, O., Uhrmacher, A.M. (eds.) Winter Simulation Conference, WSC 2012 (2012)
40. Sneddon, M.W., Faeder, J.R., Emonet, T.: Efficient modeling, simulation and coarse-graining of biological complexity with NFsim. Nat. Methods **8**(2), 177–183 (2011)
41. Stewart, D.: Spatial biomodelling. Master thesis, School of Informatics, University of Edinburgh (2010)
42. Tarski, A.: A lattice-theoretical fixpoint theorem and its applications. Pac. J. Math. **5**(2), 285 (1955)
43. Winskel, G.: Event structures. In: Brauer, W., Reisig, W., Rozenberg, G. (eds.) ACPN 1986. LNCS, vol. 255, pp. 325–392. Springer, Heidelberg (1987). https://doi.org/10.1007/3-540-17906-2_31

One Step at a Time

A Functional Derivation of Small-Step Evaluators from Big-Step Counterparts

Ferdinand Vesely[1,2(✉)] and Kathleen Fisher[1]

[1] Tufts University, Medford, USA
{fvesely,kfisher}@eecs.tufts.edu
[2] Swansea University, Swansea, UK
f.vesely@swansea.ac.uk

Abstract. Big-step and small-step are two popular flavors of operational semantics. Big-step is often seen as a more natural transcription of informal descriptions, as well as being more convenient for some applications such as interpreter generation or optimization verification. Small-step allows reasoning about non-terminating computations, concurrency and interactions. It is also generally preferred for reasoning about type systems. Instead of having to manually specify equivalent semantics in both styles for different applications, it would be useful to choose one and derive the other in a systematic or, preferably, automatic way.

Transformations of small-step semantics into big-step have been investigated in various forms by Danvy and others. However, it appears that a corresponding transformation from big-step to small-step semantics has not had the same attention. We present a fully automated transformation that maps big-step evaluators written in direct style to their small-step counterparts. Many of the steps in the transformation, which include CPS-conversion, defunctionalisation, and various continuation manipulations, mirror those used by Danvy and his co-authors. For many standard languages, including those with either call-by-value or call-by-need and those with state, the transformation produces small-step semantics that are close in style to handwritten ones. We evaluate the applicability and correctness of the approach on 20 languages with a range of features.

Keywords: Structural operational semantics · Big-step semantics · Small-step semantics · Interpreters · Transformation · Continuation-passing style · Functional programming

1 Introduction

Operational semantics allow language designers to precisely and concisely specify the meaning of programs. Such semantics support formal type soundness proofs [29], give rise (sometimes automatically) to simple interpreters [15,27] and debuggers [14], and document the correct behavior for compilers. There are

L. Caires (Ed.): ESOP 2019, LNCS 11423, pp. 205–231, 2019.
https://doi.org/10.1007/978-3-030-17184-1_8

two popular approaches for defining operational semantics: big-step and small-step. *Big-step semantics* (also referred to as *natural* or *evaluation* semantics) relate initial program configurations directly to final results in one "big" evaluation step. In contrast, *small-step semantics* relate intermediate configurations consisting of the term currently being evaluated and auxiliary information. The initial configuration corresponds to the entire program, and the final result, if there is one, can be obtained by taking the transitive-reflexive closure of the small-step relation. Thus, computation progresses as a series of "small steps."

The two styles have different strengths and weaknesses, making them suitable for different purposes. For example, big-step semantics naturally correspond to definitional interpreters [23], meaning many big-step semantics can essentially be transliterated into a reasonably efficient interpreter in a functional language. Big-step semantics are also more convenient for verifying program optimizations and compilation – using big-step, semantic preservation can be verified (for terminating programs) by induction on the derivation [20,22].

In contrast, small-step semantics are often better suited for stepping through the evaluation of an example program, and for devising a type system and proving its soundness via the classic syntactic method using progress and preservation proofs [29]. As a result, researchers sometimes develop multiple semantic specifications and then argue for their equivalence [3,20,21]. In an ideal situation, the specifier writes down a single specification and then derives the others.

Approaches to deriving big-step semantics from a small-step variant have been investigated on multiple occasions, starting from semantics specified as either interpreters or rules [4,7,10,12,13]. An obvious question is: what about the reverse direction?

This paper presents a systematic, mechanised transformation from a big-step interpreter into its small-step counterpart. The overall transformation consists of multiple stages performed on an interpreter written in a functional programming language. For the most part, the individual transformations are well known. The key steps in this transformation are to explicitly represent control flow as *continuations*, to defunctionalise these continuations to obtain a datatype of reified continuations, to "tear off" recursive calls to the interpreter, and then to return the reified continuations, which represent the rest of the computation. This process effectively produces a stepping function. The remaining work consists of finding translations from the reified continuations to equivalent terms in the source language. If such a term cannot be found, we introduce a new term constructor. These new constructors correspond to the intermediate auxiliary forms commonly found in handwritten small-step definitions.

We define the transformations on our *evaluator definition language* – an extension of λ-calculus with call-by-value semantics. The language is untyped and, crucially, includes tagged values (variants) and a case analysis construct for building and analysing object language terms. Our algorithm takes as input a big-step interpreter written in this language in the usual style: a main function performing case analysis on a top-level term constructor and recursively calling itself or auxiliary functions. As output, we return the resulting small-step interpreter which we can "pretty-print" as a set of small-step rules in the usual style. Hence our algorithm provides a fully automated path from a restricted class of big-step semantic specifications written as interpreters to corresponding small-step versions.

To evaluate our algorithm, we have applied it to 20 different languages with various features, including languages based on call-by-name and call-by-value λ-calculi, as well as a core imperative language. We extend these base languages with conditionals, loops, and exceptions.

We make the following contributions:

- We present a multi-stage, automated transformation that maps any deterministic big-step evaluator into a small-step counterpart. Section 2 gives an overview of this process. Each stage in the transformation is performed on our *evaluator definition language* – an extended call-by-value λ-calculus. Each stage in the transformation is familiar and principled. Section 4 gives a detailed description.
- We have implemented the transformation process in Haskell and evaluate it on a suite of 20 representative languages in Section 5. We argue that the resulting small-step evaluation rules closely mirror what one would expect from a manually written small-step specification.
- We observe that the same process with minimal modifications can be used to transform a big-step semantics into its *pretty-big-step* [6] counterpart.

2 Overview

In this section, we provide an overview of the transformation steps on a simple example language. The diagram in Fig. 1 shows the transformation pipeline. As the initial step, we first convert the input big-step evaluator into continuation-passing style (CPS). We limit the conversion to the *eval* function itself and leave all other functions in direct style. The resulting continuations take a value as input and advance the computation. In the generalization step, we modify these continuations so that they take an arbitrary term and evaluate it to a value before continuing as before. With this modification, each continuation handles both the general non-value case and the value case itself. The next stage lifts a carefully chosen set of free variables as arguments to continuations, which allows us to define all of them at the same scope level. After generalization and argument lifting, we can invoke continuations directly to switch control, instead of passing them as arguments to the *eval* function. Next we defunctionalize the continuations, converting them into a set of tagged values together with an *apply* function capturing their meaning. This transformation enables the next step, in which we remove recursive tail-calls to *apply*. This allows us to interrupt the interpreter and make it return a continuation or a term: effectively, it yields a stepping function, which is the essence of a small-step semantics. The remainder of the pipeline converts continuations to terms, performs simplifications, and then converts the CPS evaluator back to direct style to obtain the final small-step interpreter. This interpreter can be pretty-printed as a set of small-step rules.

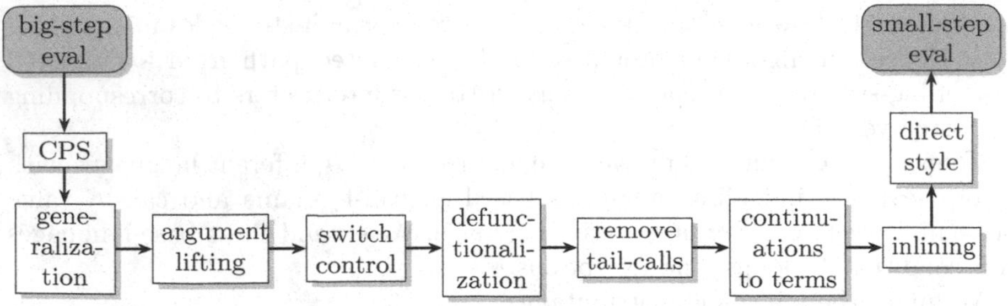

Fig. 1. Transformation overview

Our example language is a λ-calculus with call-by-value semantics. Fig. 2 gives its syntax and big-step rules. We use environments to give meaning to variables. The only values in this language are closures, formed by packaging a λ-abstraction with an environment.

$$x \in \mathit{Var} \qquad \rho \in \mathit{Env} = \mathit{Var} \rightarrow \mathit{Val}$$

$$\begin{aligned} v &::= \mathsf{clo}(x, e, \rho) \\ e &::= \mathsf{var}(x) \\ &\mid \mathsf{val}(v) \\ &\mid \mathsf{lam}(x, e) \\ &\mid \mathsf{app}(e_1, e_2) \end{aligned}$$

$$\frac{}{\rho \vdash \mathsf{val}(v) \Downarrow v} \qquad \frac{\rho(x) = v}{\rho \vdash \mathsf{var}(x) \Downarrow v}$$

$$\frac{}{\rho \vdash \mathsf{lam}(x, e) \Downarrow \mathsf{clo}(x, e, \rho)}$$

$$\frac{\rho \vdash e_1 \Downarrow \mathsf{clo}(x, e, \rho') \qquad \rho \vdash e_2 \Downarrow v_2 \qquad \rho'[x \mapsto v_2] \vdash e \Downarrow v}{\rho \vdash \mathsf{app}(e_1, e_2) \Downarrow v}$$

Fig. 2. Example: Call-by-value λ-calculus, abstract syntax and big-step semantics

We will now give a series of interpreters to illustrate the transformation process. We formally define the syntax of the meta-language in which we write these interpreters in Section 3, but we believe for readers familiar with functional programming the language is intuitive enough to not require a full explanation at this point. Shaded text highlights (often small) changes to subsequent interpreters.

Big-Step Evaluator. We start with an interpreter corresponding directly to the big-step semantics given in Fig. 2. We represent environments as functions – the empty environment returns an error for any variable. The body of the *eval* function consists of a pattern match on the top-level language term. Function abstractions are evaluated to closures by packaging them with the current environment. The only term that requires recursive calls to *eval* is application: both its arguments are evaluated in the current environment, and then its first argument is pattern-matched against a closure, the body of which is then evaluated to a value in an extended environment using a third recursive call to *eval*.

```
let empty = λx. error() in
let update x v ρ = λx'. let xx' = (== x x') in if xx' then v else (ρ x') in
let rec eval e ρ =
  case e of {
    val(v) → v |
    var(x) → let v = (ρ x) in v |
    lam(x, e') → clo(x, e', ρ) |
    app(e1, e2) →
        let v1 = (eval e1 ρ) in
        let v2 = (eval e2 ρ) in
        case v1 of {
          clo(x, e', ρ') →
              let ρ'' = (update x v2 ρ') in
              let v = (eval e' ρ'') in
              v
        }
  }
```

CPS Conversion. Our first transformation introduces a continuation argument to *eval*, capturing the "rest of the computation" [9,26,28]. Instead of returning the resulting value directly, *eval* will pass it to the continuation. For our example we need to introduce three continuations – all of them in the case for **app**. The continuation $kapp_1$ captures what remains to be done after evaluating the first argument of **app**, $kapp_2$ captures the computation remaining after evaluating the second argument, and $kclo_1$ the computation remaining after the closure body is fully evaluated. This final continuation simply applies the top-level continuation to the resulting value and might seem redundant; however, its utility will become apparent in the following step. Note that the CPS conversion is limited to the *eval* function, leaving any other functions in the program intact.

```
let rec eval e ρ k =
  case e of {
    val(v) → (k v) |
    var(x) → let v = (ρ x) in (k v) |
    lam(x, e') → (k clo(x, e', ρ)) |
    app(e1, e2) →
      letcont kapp1 v1 =
          letcont kapp2 v2 =
            case v1 of {
              clo(x, e', ρ') →
                  let ρ'' = (update x v2 ρ') in
                  letcont kclo1 v = (k v) in
                  (eval e' ρ'' (λv. (kclo1 v)))
            } in
            (eval e2 ρ (λv2. (kapp2 v2))) in
      (eval e1 ρ (λv1. (kapp1 v1)))
  }
```

Generalization. Next, we modify the continuation definitions so that they handle both the case when the term is a value (the original case) and the case where it is still a term that needs to be evaluated. To achieve this goal, we introduce a case analysis on the input. If the continuation's argument is a value, the evaluation will proceed as before. Otherwise it will call *eval* with itself as the continuation argument. Intuitively, the latter case will correspond to a congruence rule in the resulting small-step semantics and we refer to these as *congruence cases* in the rest of this paper.

```
let rec eval e ρ k = case e of {
    val(v) → (k val(v)) |
    var(x) → let v = (ρ x) in (k val(v)) |
    lam(x, e') → (k val(clo(x, e', ρ))) |
    app(e1, e2) →
        letcont kapp1 e1 =
          case e1 of {
            val(v1) →
              ...
                            case v1 of {
                              clo(x, e', ρ') →
                                  let ρ'' = (update x v2 ρ') in
                                  letcont kclo1 e =
                                    case e of {
                                      val(v) → (k val(v)) |
                                      ELSE(e) → (eval e ρ'' (λe'. (kclo1 e')))
                                    } in
                                  (eval e' ρ'' (λv. (kclo1 v)))
              ...
            ELSE(e1) → (eval e1 ρ (λe1'. (kapp1 e1')))
          } in
        (eval e1 ρ (λv1. (kapp1 v1)))
}
```

Argument Lifting. The free variables inside each continuation can be divided into those that depend on the top-level term and those that parameterize the evaluation. The former category contains variables dependent on subterms of the top-level term, either by standing for a subterm itself, or by being derived from it. In our example, for $kapp_1$, it is the variable e_2, i.e., the right argument of **app**, for $kapp_2$, the variable v_1 as the value resulting from evaluating the left argument, and for $kclo_1$ it is the environment obtained by extending the closure's environment by binding the closure variable to the operand value (ρ'' derived from v_2). We lift variables that fall into the first category, that is, variables derived from the input term. We leave variables that parametrize the evaluation, such as the input environment or the store, unlifted. The rationale is that, eventually, we want the continuations to act as term constructors and they need to carry information not contained in arguments passed to *eval*.

```
let rec eval e ρ k = case e of {
  ...
  app(e₁, e₂) →
    letcont kapp₁ [e₂] e₁ =
      ...
        letcont kapp₂ [v₁] e₂ =
          ...
              letcont kclo₁ [ρ'] e =
                case e of {
                  val(v) → (k val(v)) |
                  ELSE(e) → (eval e ρ' (λe'. (kclo₁ [ρ'] e')))
                } in
              (eval e' ρ'' (λv. (kclo₁ [ρ''] v)))
          } |
          ELSE(e₂) → (eval e₂ ρ (λe₂'. (kapp₂ [v₁] e₂')))
        } in
        (eval e₂ ρ (λv₂. (kapp₂ [v₁] v₂))) |
      ELSE(e₁) → (eval e₁ ρ (λe₁'. (kapp₁ [e₂] e₁')))
    } in
    (eval e₁ ρ (λv₁. (kapp₁ [e₂] v₁)))
}
```

Continuations Switch Control. Since continuations now handle the full evaluation of their argument themselves, they can be used to switch stages in the evaluation of a term. Observe how in the resulting evaluator below, the evaluation of an **app** term progresses through stages initiated by $kapp_1$, $kapp_2$, and finally $kclo_1$.

```
let rec eval e ρ k = case e of {
  ...
  app(e₁, e₂) →
    letcont kapp₁ e₂ e₁ =
      ...
        letcont kapp₂ v₁ e₂ =
          ...
          letcont kclo₁ ρ' e =
            ...
          in [(kclo₁ ρ'' e')]
          ...
        in [(kapp₂ v₁ e₂)] |
      ...
    in [(kapp₁ e₂ e₁)]
}
```

Defunctionalization. In the next step, we defunctionalize continuations. For each continuation, we introduce a constructor with the corresponding number of arguments. The *apply* function gives the meaning of each defunctionalized continuation.

```
let rec apply eval e_k ρ k = case e_k of {
    kapp1(e2, e1) →
        case e1 of {
          val(v1) → (apply eval kapp2(v1, e2) ρ k) |
          ELSE(e1) → (eval e1 ρ (λe1'. (apply eval kapp1(e2, e1') ρ k)))
        } |
    kapp2(v1, e2) →
        case e2 of {
          val(v2) →
              case v1 of {
                clo(x, e', ρ') →
                    let ρ'' = (update x v2 ρ')
                    in (apply eval kclo1(ρ'', e') ρ k)
              } |
          ELSE(e2) → (eval e2 ρ (λe2'. (apply eval kapp2(v1, e2') ρ k)))
        } |
    kclo1(ρ', e) →
        case e of {
          val(v) → (k val(v)) |
          ELSE(e) → (eval e ρ' (λe'. (apply eval kclo1(ρ', e') ρ k)))
        }
  } in
let rec eval e ρ k = case e of {
    val(v) → (k val(v)) |
    var(x) → let v = (ρ x) in (k val(v)) |
    lam(x, e') → (k val(clo(x, e', ρ))) |
    app(e1, e2) → (apply eval kapp1(e2, e1) ρ k)
  }
```

Remove Tail-Calls. We can now move from a recursive evaluator to a stepping function by modifying the continuation arguments passed to *eval* in congruence cases. Instead of calling *apply* on the defunctionalized continuation, we return the defunctionalized continuation itself. Note, that we leave intact those calls to *apply* that switch control between different continuations (e.g., in the definition of *eval*).

```
let rec apply eval e_k ρ k = case e_k of {
    kapp1(e2, e1) →
        case e1 of {
          val(v1) → (apply eval kapp2(v1, e2) ρ k) |
          ELSE(e1) → (eval e1 ρ (λe1'. (k kapp1(e2, e1'))))
        } |
    kapp2(v1, e2) →
        case e2 of {
          val(v2) → ... (apply eval kclo1(ρ'', e') ρ k) |
          ELSE(e2) → (eval e2 ρ (λe2'. (k kapp2(v1, e2'))))
        } |
    kclo1(ρ', e) →
```

```
    case e of {
      val(v) → (k val(v)) |
      ELSE(e) → (eval e ρ' (λe'. (k kclo1(ρ', e'))))
    }
} in ...
```

Convert Continuations into Terms. At this point, we have a stepping function that returns either a term or a continuation, but we want a function returning only terms. The most straightforward approach to achieving this goal would be to introduce a term constructor for each defunctionalized continuation constructor. However, many of these continuation constructors can be trivially expressed using constructors already present in the object language. We want to avoid introducing redundant terms, so we aim to reuse existing constructors as much as possible. In our example we observe that **kapp1**(e_2, e_1) corresponds to **app**(e_1, e_2), while **kapp2**(v_1, e_2) to **app**(**val**$(v_1), e_2)$. We might also observe that **kclo1**(ρ', e) would correspond to **app**(**clo**$(x, e, \rho), val(v_2))$ if $\rho' =$ update x v_2 ρ. Our current implementation doesn't handle such cases, however, and so we introduce **kclo1** as a new term constructor.

```
let rec apply eval eₖ ρ k = case eₖ of {
  kapp1(e2, e1) →
     case e1 of {
       val(v1) → (apply eval kapp2(v1, e2) ρ k) |
       ELSE(e1) → (eval e1 ρ (λe1'. (k app(e1', e2))))
     } |
  kapp2(v1, e2) →
     case e2 of {
       val(v2) →
          case v1 of {
            clo(x, e', ρ') → let ρ'' = (update x v2 ρ') in kclo1(ρ'', e')
          } |
       ELSE(e2) → (eval e2 ρ (λe2'. (k app(val(v1), e2'))))
     } |
  kclo1(ρ', e) →
     case e of {
       val(v) → (k val(v)) |
       ELSE(e) → (eval e ρ' (λe'. (k kclo1(ρ', e'))))
     }
} in
let rec eval e ρ k = case e of {
  ...
  kclo1(ρ', e') → (apply eval kclo1(ρ', e') ρ k)
}
```

Inlining and Simplification. Next, we eliminate the *apply* function by inlining its applications and simplifying the result. At this point we have obtained a small-step interpreter in continuation-passing style.

```
let rec eval e ρ k = case e of {
  ...
  app(e1, e2) →
      case e1 of {
        val(v1) →
            case e2 of {
              val(v2) →
                  case v1 of {
                    clo(x, e′, ρ′) → let ρ″ = (update x v2 ρ′) in kclo1(ρ″, e′)
                  } |
              ELSE(e2) → (eval e2 ρ (λe′2. (k app(val(v1), e′2))))
            } |
        ELSE(e1) → (eval e1 ρ (λe′1. (k app(e′1, e2))))
      } |
  kclo1(ρ′, e′) →
      case e′ of {
        val(v) → (k val(v)) |
        ELSE(e) → (eval e ρ′ (λe′. (k kclo1(ρ′, e′))))
      }
}
```

Convert to Direct Style and Remove the Value Case. The final transformation is to convert our small-step interpreter back to direct style. Moreover, we also remove the value case **val**$(v) \rightarrow$ **val**(v) as we, usually, do not want values to step.

```
let rec eval e ρ = case e of {
  var(x) → let v = (ρ x) in val(v) |
  lam(x, e′) → val(clo(x, e′, ρ)) |
  app(e1, e2) →
      case e1 of {
        val(v1) →
            case e2 of {
              val(v2) →
                  case v1 of {
                    clo(x, e′, ρ′) → let ρ″ = (update x v2 ρ′) in kclo1(ρ″, e′)
                  } |
              ELSE(e2) → let e′2 = (eval e2 ρ) in app(val(v1), e′2)
            } |
        ELSE(e1) → let e′1 = (eval e1 ρ) in app(e′1, e2)
      } |
  kclo1(ρ′, e′) →
      case e′ of {
        val(v) → val(v) |
        ELSE(e) → let e′ = (eval e ρ′) in kclo1(ρ′, e′)
      }
}
```

Small-Step Evaluator. Fig. 3 shows the small-step rules corresponding to our last interpreter. Barring the introduction of the **kclo1** constructor, the resulting semantics is essentially identical to one we would write manually.

$$1\ \frac{v = \rho\ x}{\rho \vdash \mathsf{var}(x) \to \mathsf{val}(v)} \qquad 2\ \frac{}{\rho \vdash \mathsf{lam}(x, e') \to \mathsf{val}(\mathsf{clo}(x, e', \rho))}$$

$$3\ \frac{\rho'' = \mathsf{update}\ x\ v_2\ \rho'}{\rho \vdash \mathsf{app}(\mathsf{val}(\mathsf{clo}(x, e', \rho')), \mathsf{val}(v_2)) \to \mathsf{kclo1}(\rho'', e')}$$

$$4\ \frac{\rho \vdash e_2 \to e_2'}{\rho \vdash \mathsf{app}(\mathsf{val}(v_1), e_2) \to \mathsf{app}(\mathsf{val}(v_1), e_2')} \qquad 5\ \frac{\rho \vdash e_1 \to e_1'}{\rho \vdash \mathsf{app}(e_1, e_2) \to \mathsf{app}(e_1', e_2)}$$

$$6\ \frac{}{\rho \vdash \mathsf{kclo1}(\rho', \mathsf{val}(v)) \to \mathsf{val}(v)} \qquad 7\ \frac{\rho' \vdash e \to e'}{\rho \vdash \mathsf{kclo1}(\rho', e) \to \mathsf{kclo1}(\rho', e')}$$

Fig. 3. Resulting small-step semantics

3 Big-Step Specifications

We define our transformations on an untyped extended λ-calculus with call-by-value semantics that allows the straightforward definition of big- and small-step interpreters. We call this language an *evaluator definition language* (EDL).

3.1 Evaluator Definition Language

Table 1 gives the syntax of EDL. We choose to restrict ourselves to A-normal form, which greatly simplifies our partial CPS conversion without compromising readability. Our language has the usual call-by-value semantics, with arguments being evaluated left-to-right. All of the examples of the previous section were written in this language.

Our language has 3 forms of let-binding constructs: the usual (optionally recursive) **let**, a let-construct for evaluator definition, and a let-construct for defining continuations. The behavior of all three constructs is the same, however, we treat them differently during the transformations. The **leteval** construct also comes with the additional static restriction that it may appear only once (i.e., there can be only one evaluator). The **leteval** and **letcont** forms are recursive by default, while **let** has an optional **rec** specifier to create a recursive binding. For simplicity, our language does not offer implicit mutual recursion, so mutual recursion has to be made explicit by inserting additional arguments. We do this when we generate the *apply* function during defunctionalization.

Notation and Presentation. We use vector notation to denote syntactic lists belonging to a particular sort. For example, $\vec{e}$ and $\vec{ae}$ are lists of elements of, respectively, *Expr* and *AExpr*, while $\vec{x}$ is a list of variables. Separators can be spaces (e.g., function arguments) or commas (e.g., constructor arguments or configuration components). We expect the actual separator to be clear from the context. Similarly for lists of expressions: $\vec{e}$, $\vec{ae}$, etc. In let bindings, $f\ x_1\ \ldots\ x_n = e$ and $f = \lambda x_1\ \ldots\ x_n.\ e$ are both syntactic sugar for $f = \lambda x_1.\ \ldots\ \lambda x_n.\ e$.

Table 1. Syntax of the evaluator definition language.

$\mathit{Expr} \ni e ::=$	$\textbf{let}\ bn = ce\ \textbf{in}\ e$	(let-binding)
	$\mid \textbf{let rec}\ bn = ce\ \textbf{in}\ e$	(recursive let-binding)
	$\mid \textbf{leteval}\ x = ce\ \textbf{in}\ e$	(evaluator definition)
	$\mid \textbf{letcont}\ k = ce\ \textbf{in}\ e$	(continuation definition)
	$\mid ce$	
$\mathit{CExpr} \ni ce ::=$	$(ae\ ae\ \ldots)$	(application)
	$\mid \textbf{case}\ ae\ \textbf{of}\ \{\ cas \mid \ldots \mid cas\ \}$	(pattern matching)
	$\mid \textbf{if}\ ae\ \textbf{then}\ e\ \textbf{else}\ e$	(conditional)
	$\mid ae$	
$\mathit{AExpr} \ni ae ::=$	$v \mid op$	(value, operator)
	$\mid x \mid k$	(variable, continuation variable)
	$\mid \boldsymbol{\lambda} bn.\ e$	(λ-abstraction)
	$\mid c(ae, \ldots, ae)$	(constructor application)
	$\mid \langle\ ae, \ldots, ae\ \rangle$	(configuration expression)
$\mathit{Binder} \ni bn ::=$	$x \mid \langle\ x, \ldots, x\ \rangle$	(variable, configuration)
$\mathit{Case} \ni cas ::=$	$c(x, \ldots, x) \rightarrow e$	(constructor pattern)
	$\mid \textbf{ELSE}(x) \rightarrow e$	(default pattern)
$\mathit{Value} \ni v ::=$	$n \mid b \mid c(v,\ldots,v) \mid \langle\ v,\ldots,v\ \rangle \mid \textsf{abs}(\boldsymbol{\lambda} x.e, \rho)$	

4 Transformation Steps

In this section, we formally define each of the transformation steps informally described in Section 2. For each transformation function, we list only the most relevant cases; the remaining cases trivially recurse on the A-normal form (ANF) abstract syntax. We annotate functions with E, CE, and AE to indicate the corresponding ANF syntactic classes. We omit annotations when a function only operates on a single syntactic class. For readability, we annotate meta-variables to hint at their intended use – ρ stands for read-only entities (such as environments), whereas σ stands for read-write or "state-like" entities of a configuration (e.g., stores or exception states). These can be mixed with our notation for syntactic lists, so, for example, $\vec{x}^{\sigma}$ is a sequence of variables referring to state-like entities, while $\vec{ae}^{\rho}$ is a sequence of a-expressions corresponding to read-only entities.

4.1 CPS Conversion

The first stage of the process is a *partial* CPS conversion [8,25] to make control flow in the evaluator explicit. We limit this transformation to the main evaluator function, i.e., only the function *eval* will take an additional continuation argument and will pass results to it. Because our input language is already in ANF, the conversion is relatively easy to express. In particular, applications of the evaluator are always **let**-bound to a variable (or appear in a tail position), which makes constructing the current continuation straightforward. Below are the relevant clauses of the conversion. For this transformation we assume the following easily checkable properties:

- The evaluator name is globally unique.
- The evaluator is *never* applied partially.
- All bound variables are distinct.

The conversion is defined as three mutually recursive functions with the following signatures:

$$\begin{aligned}\mathsf{cps}_E &: \mathit{Expr} \to (\mathit{CExpr} \to \mathit{Expr}) \to \mathit{Expr}\\ \mathsf{cps}_{CE} &: \mathit{CExpr} \to (\mathit{CExpr} \to \mathit{Expr}) \to \mathit{Expr}\\ \mathsf{cps}_{AE} &: \mathit{AExpr} \to \mathit{AExpr}\end{aligned}$$

In the equations, $\mathcal{K}$, $\mathcal{I}$, $\mathcal{A}_k : \mathit{CExpr} \to \mathit{Expr}$ are meta-continuations; $\mathcal{I}$ injects a *CExpr* into *Expr*.

$$\begin{aligned}&\mathsf{cps}_E\big[\mathbf{leteval}\ \mathit{eval}\ \vec{bn} = e_1\ \mathbf{in}\ e_2\big]\ \mathcal{K} =\\ &\qquad \mathbf{leteval}\ \mathit{eval}\ \vec{bn}\ k = (\mathsf{cps}_E\,[e_1]\ \mathcal{A}_k)\ \mathbf{in}\ (\mathsf{cps}_E\,[e_2]\ \mathcal{K})\\ &\qquad \text{where } k \text{ is a fresh continuation variable}\end{aligned}$$

$$\begin{aligned}&\mathsf{cps}_E\big[\mathbf{let}\ bn = (\mathit{eval}\ ae_1\ \vec{ae})\ \mathbf{in}\ e\big]\ \mathcal{K} =\\ &\qquad \mathbf{letcont}\ k\ bn = (\mathsf{cps}_E\,[e]\ \mathcal{K})\ \mathbf{in}\ \mathsf{cps}_{CE}\big[(\mathit{eval}\ ae_1\ \vec{ae})\big]\ \mathcal{A}_k\\ &\qquad \text{where } k \text{ is a fresh continuation variable}\end{aligned}$$

$$\begin{aligned}&\mathsf{cps}_E\,\big[\mathbf{let}\ bn = ce\ \mathbf{in}\ e\,\big]\ \mathcal{K} =\\ &\qquad \mathsf{renorm}\big[\mathbf{let'}\ bn = (\mathsf{cps}_{CE}\,[ce]\ \mathcal{I})\ \mathbf{in}\ (\mathsf{cps}_E\,[e]\ \mathcal{K})\big]\end{aligned}$$

$$\begin{aligned}&\mathsf{cps}_{CE}\,\big[(\mathit{eval}\ ae_1\ \vec{ae})\big]\ \mathcal{K} = (\mathit{eval}\ (\mathsf{cps}_{AE}\,[ae_1])\ (\mathsf{cps}_{AE}\,[\vec{ae}])\ (\boldsymbol{\lambda} x.\ \mathcal{K}[x]))\\ &\qquad \text{where } x \text{ is a fresh variable}\end{aligned}$$

$$\mathsf{cps}_{CE}\,[ae]\ \mathcal{K} = \mathcal{K}(\mathsf{cps}_{AE}\,[ae])$$

$$\mathsf{cps}_{AE}\,[\boldsymbol{\lambda} x.e] = \boldsymbol{\lambda} x.\ (\mathsf{cps}_E\,[e]\ \mathcal{I})$$

$$\mathsf{cps}_{AE}\,[ae] = ae$$

where for any k, $\mathcal{A}_k$ is defined as

$$\begin{aligned}\mathcal{A}_k[ae] &= k\ ae\\ \mathcal{A}_k[ce] &= \mathbf{let}\ x = ce\ \mathbf{in}\ k\ x \quad \text{where } x \text{ is fresh}\end{aligned}$$

and

$$\begin{aligned}&\mathsf{renorm}\big[\mathbf{let'}\ x = ce\ \mathbf{in}\ e\big] = \mathbf{let}\ x = ce\ \mathbf{in}\ e\\ &\mathsf{renorm}\big[\mathbf{let'}\ x = (\mathbf{let}\ x' = ce\ \mathbf{in}\ e')\ \mathbf{in}\ e\big] =\\ &\qquad \mathbf{let}\ x' = ce\ \mathbf{in}\ \mathsf{renorm}\big[\mathbf{let'}\ x = e'\ \mathbf{in}\ e\big]\end{aligned}$$

In the above equations, **let**' is a pseudo-construct used to make renormalization more readable. In essence, it is a non-ANF version of **let** where the bound expression is generalized to *Expr*. Note that renorm only works correctly if $x' \notin \mathsf{fv}(e)$, which is implied by our assumption that all bound variables are distinct.

4.2 Generalization of Continuations

The continuations resulting from the above CPS conversion expect to be applied to value terms. The next step is to generalize (or "lift") the continuations so that they recursively call the evaluator to evaluate non-value arguments. In other words, assuming the term type can be factored into values and computations $V + C$, we convert each continuation k with the type $V \to V$ into a continuation $k' : V + C \to V$ using the following schema:

$$\mathbf{let\ rec}\ k'\ t = \mathbf{case}\ t\ \mathbf{of}\ \mathit{inl}\ v \to k\ v \mid \mathit{inr}\ c \to \mathit{eval}\ c\ k'$$

The recursive clauses will correspond to congruence rules in the resulting small-step semantics.

The transformation works by finding the unique application site of the continuation and then inserting the corresponding call to *eval* in the non-value case.

$$\begin{aligned}
\mathsf{gencont}_E\big[\mathbf{letcont}\ k\ \langle\ x,\ \vec{x}^\sigma\ \rangle = e_k\ \mathbf{in}\ e\big] = \\
\mathbf{letcont}\ k\ \langle\ \hat{x}, \vec{x}^\sigma\ \rangle = \\
\mathbf{case}\ \hat{x}\ \mathbf{of}\ \{ \\
\mathsf{val}(x) \to e_k\ ; \\
\mathbf{ELSE}(\hat{x}) \to \mathit{eval}\ \langle\ \hat{x}, \vec{ae}^\sigma\ \rangle\ \vec{ae}^\rho\ ae_k \\
\} \\
\text{if } \mathsf{findApp}\ k\ e = \mathit{eval}\ \langle\ _\,, \vec{ae}^\sigma\ \rangle\ \vec{ae}^\rho\ ae_k
\end{aligned}$$

where

- findApp k e is the unique use site of the continuation k in expression e, that is, the *CExpr* where *eval* is applied with k as its continuation; and
- $\hat{x}$ is a fresh variable associated with x – it stands for "a term corresponding to (the value) x".

Following the CPS conversion, each named continuation is applied exactly once in e, so findApp k e is total and returns the continuation's unique use site. Moreover, because the continuation was originally defined and let-bound at that use site, all free variables in findApp k e are also free in the definition of k.

When performing this generalization transformation, we also modify tail positions in *eval* that return a value so that they wrap their result in the **val** constructor. That is, if the continuation parameter of *eval* is k, then we rewrite all sites applying k to a configuration as follows:

$$k\ \langle\ ae,\ \vec{ae}^\sigma\ \rangle \Rightarrow k\ \langle\ \mathsf{val}(ae),\ \vec{ae}^\sigma\ \rangle$$

4.3 Argument Lifting in Continuations

In the next phase, we partially lift free variables in continuations to make them explicit arguments. We perform a *selective* lifting in that we avoid lifting non-term arguments to the evaluation function. These arguments represent entities that parameterize the evaluation of a term. If an entity is modified during evaluation, the modified entity variable gets lifted. In the running example of Section 2, such a lifting occurred for $kclo_1$.

Function lift specifies the transformation at the continuation definition site:

$$\mathsf{lift}\ \Xi\ \Delta\ [\mathbf{letcont}\ k\ = \boldsymbol{\lambda} x.\, e_k\ \mathbf{in}\ e] =$$
$$\mathbf{letcont}\ k\ =\ \boldsymbol{\lambda}\, x_1\ \ldots\ x_n\ x.\,(\mathsf{lift}\ \Xi'\ \Delta'\ [e_k])\ \mathbf{in}\ (\mathsf{lift}\ \Xi'\ \Delta'\ [e])$$

where

- $\Xi' = \Xi \cup \{k\}$
- $\{x_1, \ldots, x_n\} = \mathsf{fv}\, e_k \cup (\bigcup_{g \in (\mathsf{dom}\,\Delta\ \cap\ \mathsf{fv}\, e_k)} \Delta(g)) - \Xi'$
- $\Delta' = \Delta[k \mapsto (x_1, \ldots, x_n)]$

and at the continuation application site – recall that continuations are always applied fully, but at this point they are only applied to one argument:

$$\mathsf{lift}\ \Xi\ \Delta\ \big[k\ ae\big] =\ k\ x_1\ \ldots\ x_n\ (\mathsf{lift}\ \Xi\ \Delta\ \big[ae'\big])$$

if $k \in \mathsf{dom}\,\Delta$ and $\Delta(k) = (x_1, \ldots, x_n)$.

Our lifting function is a restricted version of a standard argument-lifting algorithm [19]. The first restriction is that we do not lift all free variables, since we do not aim to float and lift the continuations to the top-level of the program, only to the top-level of the evaluation function. The other difference is that we can use a simpler way to compute the set of lifted parameters due to the absence of mutual recursion between continuations. The correctness of this can be proved using the approach of Fischbach [16].

4.4 Continuations Switch Control Directly

At this point, continuations handle the full evaluation of a term themselves. Instead of calling *eval* with the continuation as an argument, we can call the continuation directly to switch control between evaluation stages of a term. We will replace original *eval* call sites with direct applications of the corresponding continuations. The recursive call to *eval* in congruence cases of continuations will be left untouched, as this is where the continuation's argument will be evaluated to a value. Following from the continuation generalization transformation, this call to *eval* is with the same arguments as in the original site (which we are now replacing). In particular, the *eval* is invoked with the same $\vec{ae}^{\rho}$ arguments in the continuation body as in the original call site.

$$\mathsf{directcont}_E\ \big[\mathbf{letcont}\ k = ce\ \mathbf{in}\ e\big] K =$$
$$\mathbf{letcont}\ k =\ \mathsf{directcont}_{CE}\ \big[ce\big] K\ \mathbf{in}\ \mathsf{directcont}_E\ \big[e\big] (K \uplus \{k\})$$

$$\mathsf{directcont}_{CE}\ \big[eval\ \langle\ ae,\ \vec{ae}^{\sigma}\ \rangle\ \vec{ae}^{\rho}\ (\boldsymbol{\lambda} y.\ k\ \vec{x}\ y)\big]\ K = k\ \vec{x}\ \langle\ ae,\ \vec{ae}^{\sigma}\ \rangle \qquad \text{if } k \in K$$

4.5 Defunctionalization

Now we can move towards a first-order representation of continuations which can be further converted into term constructions. We defunctionalize continuations by first collecting all continuations in *eval*, then introducing corresponding constructors (the syntax), and finally generating an *apply* function (the semantics). The collection function accumulates continuation names and their definitions. At the same time it removes the definitions.

$$\mathsf{collect}_E\left[\textbf{letcont}\ k = ce\ \textbf{in}\ e\right] = (\{(k, ce')\} \cup K_{ce} \cup K_e, e')$$
$$\text{where } (K_{ce}, ce') = \mathsf{collect}_{CE}\left[ce\right]$$
$$(K_e, e') = \mathsf{collect}_E\left[e\right]$$

We reuse continuation names for constructors. The *apply* function is generated by simply generating a case analysis on the constructors and reusing the argument names from the continuation function arguments. In addition to the defunctionalized continuations, the generated *apply* function will take the same arguments as *eval*. Because of the absence of mutual recursion in our meta-language, *apply* takes *eval* as an argument.

$$\begin{aligned}
&\mathsf{genApply}\ \vec{x}^\rho\ \vec{x}^\sigma\ k_{top}\ \left\{(k_1, \lambda p_{1,1}\ \ldots p_{1,i}.\ e_1), \ldots, (k_n, \lambda p_{n,1}\ \ldots\ p_{n,j}.\ e_n)\right\} = \\
&\quad \boldsymbol{\lambda} eval\ \langle\ x_k, \vec{x}^\sigma\ \rangle\ \vec{x}^\rho\ k_{top}. \\
&\qquad \textbf{case}\ x_k\ \textbf{of}\ \{ \\
&\qquad\quad k_1(p_{1,1}, \ldots, p_{1,i}) \longrightarrow\ e_1\ ; \\
&\qquad\quad \ldots\ ; \\
&\qquad\quad k_n(p_{n,1}, \ldots, p_{n,j}) \longrightarrow\ e_n \\
&\qquad \}
\end{aligned}$$

Now we need a way to replace calls to continuations with corresponding calls to *apply*. For $\vec{ae}^\rho$ and k_{top} we use the arguments passed to *eval* or *apply* (depending on where we are replacing).

$$\mathsf{replace}_{CE}\left[k\ \vec{ae}_k\ \langle ae, \vec{ae}^\sigma\rangle\right](\vec{x}^\rho, k_{top}) = apply\ eval\ \langle\ k(\vec{ae}_k, ae),\ \vec{ae}^\sigma\ \rangle\ \vec{x}^\rho\ k_{top}$$

Finally, the complete defunctionalization is defined in terms of the above three functions.

4.6 Remove Self-recursive Tail-Calls

This is the transformation which converts a recursive evaluator into a stepping function. The transformation itself is very simple: we simply replace the self-recursive calls to *apply* in congruence cases.

$$\begin{aligned}
&\mathsf{derec}_{CE}\left[eval\ \langle\ ae,\ \vec{ae}^\sigma\ \rangle\ \vec{ae}^\rho\ (\boldsymbol{\lambda}\langle\ x',\ \vec{x}^{\sigma\prime}\ \rangle.\ apply\ eval\ \langle\ c^{\mathrm{K}}(\vec{ae},\ x'),\ \vec{x}^{\sigma\prime}\ \rangle\ \vec{ae}^{\rho\prime}\ k)\right] = \\
&\quad eval\ \langle\ ae,\ \vec{ae}^\sigma\ \rangle\ \vec{ae}^\rho\ (\boldsymbol{\lambda}\langle\ x',\ \vec{x}^{\sigma\prime}\ \rangle.\ k\ \langle\ c^{\mathrm{K}}(\vec{ae},\ x'),\ \vec{x}^{\sigma\prime}\ \rangle)
\end{aligned}$$

Note, that we still leave those invocations of *apply* that serve to switch control through the stages of evaluation. Unless a continuation constructor will become a part of the output language, its application will be inlined in the final phase of our transformation.

4.7 Convert Continuations to Terms

After defunctionalization, we effectively have two sorts of terms: those constructed using the original constructors and those constructed using continuation constructors. Terms in these two sorts are given their semantics by the *eval* and *apply* functions, respectively. To get only one evaluator function at the end of our transformation process, we will join these two sorts, adding extra continuation constructors as new term constructors. We could simply merge *apply* to *eval*, however, this would give us many overlapping constructors. For example, in Section 2, we established that $\mathsf{kapp1}(e_2, e_1) \approx \mathsf{app}(e_1, e_2)$ and $\mathsf{kapp2}(v_1, e_2) \approx \mathsf{app}(\mathsf{val}(v_1), e_2)$. The inference of equivalent term constructors is guided by the following simple principle. For each continuation term $c^{\mathrm{K}}(ae_1, \ldots, ae_n)$ we are looking for a term $c'(ae'_1, \ldots, ae'_m)$, such that, for all $\vec{ae}^{\sigma}$, $\vec{ae}^{\rho}$ and ae_k

$$\begin{aligned} &\mathit{apply}\ \mathit{eval}\ \langle\ c^{\mathrm{K}}(ae_1, \ldots, ae_n), \vec{ae}^{\sigma}\ \rangle\ \vec{ae}^{\rho}\ ae_k \\ &\qquad = \mathit{eval}\ \langle\ c'(ae'_1, \ldots, ae'_m), \vec{ae}^{\sigma}\ \rangle\ \vec{ae}^{\rho}\ ae_k \end{aligned}$$

In our current implementation, we use a conservative approach where, starting from the cases in *eval*, we search for continuations reachable along a control flow path. Variables appearing in the original term are instantiated along the way. Moreover, we collect variables dependent on configuration entities (state). If control flow is split based on information derived from the state, we automatically include any continuation constructors reachable from that point as new constructors in the resulting language and interpreter. This, together with how information flows from the top-level term to subterms in congruence cases, preserves the coupling between state and corresponding subterms between steps.

If, starting from an input term $c(\vec{x})$, an invocation of *apply* on a continuation term $c^{\mathrm{K}}(\vec{ae}_k)$ is reached, and if, after instantiating the variables in the input term $c(\vec{ae})$, the sets of their free variables are equal, then we can introduce a translation from $c^{\mathrm{K}}(\vec{ae}_k)$ into $c(\vec{ae})$. If such a direct path is not found, the c^{K} will become a new term constructor in the language and a case in *eval* is introduced such that the above equation is satisfied.

4.8 Inlining, Simplification and Conversion to Direct Style

To finalize the generation of a small-step interpreter, we inline all invocations of *apply* and simplify the final program. After this, the interpreter will consists of only the *eval* function, still in continuation-passing style. To convert the interpreter to direct style, we simply substitute *eval*'s continuation variable for

($\boldsymbol{\lambda} x.x$) and reduce the new redexes. Then we remove the continuation argument performing rewrites following the scheme:

$$\mathit{eval}\ \vec{ae}\ (\boldsymbol{\lambda} bn.\ e) \ \Rightarrow\ \textbf{let}\ bn\ =\ \mathit{eval}\ \vec{ae}\ \textbf{in}\ e$$

Finally, we remove the reflexive case on values (i.e., $\textsf{val}(v) \longrightarrow \textsf{val}(v)$). At this point we have a small-step interpreter in direct form.

4.9 Removing Vacuous Continuations

After performing the above transformation steps, we may end up with some redundant term constructors, which we call "empty" or vacuous. These are constructors which only have one argument and their semantics is equivalent to the argument itself, save for an extra step which returns the computed value. In other words, they are unary constructs which only have two rules in the resulting small-step semantics matching the following pattern.

$$\frac{}{\vec{\rho} \vdash \langle c(\textsf{val}(v)), \vec{\sigma}\rangle \rightarrow \langle \textsf{val}(v), \vec{\sigma}\rangle} \qquad \frac{\vec{\rho} \vdash \langle e, \vec{\sigma}\rangle \rightarrow \langle e', \vec{\sigma}'\rangle}{\vec{\rho} \vdash \langle c(e), \vec{\sigma}\rangle \rightarrow \langle c(e'), \vec{\sigma}'\rangle}$$

Such a construct will result from a continuation, which, even after generalization and argument lifting, merely evaluates its sole argument and returns the corresponding value:

$\textbf{letcont rec}\ k_i\ e = \textbf{case}\ e\ \textbf{of}\ \{$
$\quad \textsf{val}(v) \longrightarrow k\ v\ |$
$\quad \textsf{ELSE}(e) \longrightarrow \mathit{eval}\ e\ (\boldsymbol{\lambda} e'.\ k_i\ e')$
$\}$

These continuations can be easily identified and removed once argument lifting is performed, or at any point in the transformation pipeline, up until *apply* is absorbed into *eval*.

4.10 Detour: Generating Pretty-Big-Step Semantics

It is interesting to see what kind of semantics we get by rearranging or removing some steps of the above process. If, after CPS conversion, we do not generalize the continuations, but instead just lift their arguments and defunctionalize them,[1] we obtain a *pretty-big-step* [6] interpreter. The distinguishing feature of pretty-big-step semantics is that constructs which would normally have rules with multiple premises are factorized into intermediate constructs. As observed by Charguéraud, each intermediate construct corresponds to an intermediate state of the interpreter, which is why, in turn, they naturally correspond to continuations. Here are the pretty-big-step rules generated from the big-step semantics in Fig. 2 (Section 2).

[1] The complete transformation to pretty-big-step style involves these steps: 1. CPS conversion, 2. argument lifting, 3. removal of vacuous continuations, 4. defunctionalization, 5. merging of apply and eval, and 6. conversion to direct style.

$$\frac{}{\rho \vdash \mathsf{val}(v) \Downarrow_B^P v} \qquad \frac{\rho \vdash e_1 \Downarrow_B^P v_1 \quad \rho \vdash \mathsf{kapp1}(e_2, v_1) \Downarrow_B^P v}{\rho \vdash \mathsf{app}(e_1, e_2) \Downarrow_B^P v}$$

$$\frac{v = \rho\ x}{\rho \vdash \mathsf{var}(x) \Downarrow_B^P v} \qquad \frac{\rho \vdash e_2 \Downarrow_B^P v_2 \quad \rho \vdash \mathsf{kapp2}(v_1, v_2) \Downarrow_B^P v}{\rho \vdash \mathsf{kapp1}(e_2, v_1) \Downarrow_B^P v}$$

$$\frac{}{\rho \vdash \mathsf{lam}(x, e') \Downarrow_B^P \mathsf{clo}(x, e', \rho)} \qquad \frac{\rho'' = \mathsf{update}\ x\ v_2\ \rho' \quad \rho'' \vdash e' \Downarrow_B^P v}{\rho \vdash \mathsf{kapp2}(\mathsf{clo}(x, e', \rho'), v_2) \Downarrow_B^P v}$$

As we can see, the evaluation of **app** now proceeds through two intermediate constructs, **kapp1** and **kapp2**, which correspond to continuations introduced in the CPS conversion. The evaluation of $\mathsf{app}(e_1, e_2)$ starts by evaluating e_1 to v_1. Then **kapp1** is responsible for evaluating e_2 to v_2. Finally, **kapp2** evaluates the closure body just as the third premise of the original rule for **app**. Save for different order of arguments, the resulting intermediate constructs and their rules are identical to Charguéraud's examples.

4.11 Pretty-Printing

For the purpose of presenting and studying the original and transformed semantics, we add a final pretty-printing phase. This amounts to generating inference rules corresponding to the control flow in the interpreter. This pretty-printing stage can be applied to both the big-step and small-step interpreters and was used to generate many of the rules in this paper, as well as for generating the appendix of the full version of this paper [1].

4.12 Correctness

A correctness proof for the full pipeline is not part of our current work. However, several of these steps (partial CPS conversion, partial argument lifting, defunctionalization, conversion to direct style) are instances of well-established techniques. In other cases, such as generalization of continuations (Section 4.2) and removal of self-recursive tail-calls (Section 4.6), we have informal proofs using equational reasoning [1]. The proof for tail-call removal is currently restricted to compositional interpreters.

5 Evaluation

We have evaluated our approach to deriving small-step interpreters on a range of example languages. Table 2 presents an overview of example big-step specifications and their properties, together with their derived small-step counterparts. A full listing of the input and output specifications for these case studies appears in the appendix to the full version of the paper, which is available online [1].

Table 2. Overview of transformed example languages. Input is a given big-step interpreter and our transformations produce a small-step counterpart as output automatically. "Prems" columns only list structural premises: those that check for a big or small step. Unless otherwise stated, environments are used to give meaning to variables and they are represented as functions.

	Big-step		Small-step			
Example	Rules	Prems	Rules	Prems	New	Features
Call-by-value	4	3	7	3	1	
Call-by-value, substitution	4	5	7	4	0	addition
Call-by-value, booleans	13	20	24	11	1	add., conditional, equality
Call-by-value, pairs	7	7	14	7	1	pairs, left/right projection
Call-by-value, dynamic scopes	5	5	10	5	1	add., defunctionalized environments (DEs)
Call-by-value, recursion & iteration	26	44	57	26	6	fixpoint operator, add., sub., let-expressions, applicative for and while loops, cond., strict and "lazy" conjunction, eq., pairs
Call-by-name	5	5	11	5	2	add., DEs
Call-by-name, substitution	4	4	6	3	0	add., DEs
Call-by-name, booleans	13	20	25	11	2	add., cond., eq., DEs
Call-by-name, pairs	7	7	15	7	2	pairs, left/right proj., DEs
Minimal imperative	4	4	6	3	0	add., store without indirection, combined assignment *with* sequencing
While	7	9	14	6	2	add., store w/o indir., assign., seq., while
While, environments	8	10	17	7	3	add., store w/ indir., scoped var. declaration, assign., seq., while
Extended While	17	26	33	15	2	add., subt., mult., seq., store w/o indir., while, cond., "ints as bools", equality, "lazy conj."
Exceptions as state	8	7	11	3	1	add.
Exceptions as values	8	7	10	3	0	add.
Call-by-value, exceptions	21	29	34	12	2	add., div., try block
CBV, exceptions as state	20	26	39	11	8	add., div., handle & try blocks
CBV, non-determinism	7	7	13	5	2	add., choice operator
Store rewinding	8	10	19	8	4	assign., rewinding of the store

For our case studies, we have used call-by-value and call-by-name λ-calculi, and a simple imperative language as base languages and extended them with some common features. Overall, the small-step specifications (as well as the corresponding interpreters) resulting from our transformation are very similar to ones we could find in the literature. The differences are either well justified—for example, by different handling of value terms—or they are due to new term constructors which could be potentially eliminated by a more powerful translation.

We evaluated the correctness of our transformation experimentally, by comparing runs of the original big-step and the transformed small-step interpreters, as well as by inspecting the interpreters themselves. In a few cases, we proved the transformation correct by transcribing the input and output interpreters in Coq (as an evaluation relation coupled with a proof of determinism) and proving them equivalent. From the examples in Table 2, we have done so for "Call-by-value", "Exceptions as state", and a simplified version of "CBV, exceptions as state".

We make a few observations about the resulting semantics here.

New Auxiliary Constructs. In languages that use an environment to look up values bound to variables, new constructs are introduced to keep the updated environment as context. These constructs are simple: they have two arguments – one for the environment (context) and one for the term to be evaluated in that environment. A congruence rule will ensure steps of the term argument in the given context and another rule will return the result. The construct **kclo1** from the λ-calculus based examples is a typical example.

$$\frac{}{\rho \vdash \mathsf{kclo1}(\rho', \mathsf{val}(v)) \to \mathsf{val}(v)} \qquad \frac{\rho' \vdash t \to t'}{\rho \vdash \mathsf{kclo1}(\rho', t) \to \mathsf{kclo1}(\rho', t')}$$

As observed in Section 2, if the environment ρ'' is a result of updating an environment ρ' with a binding of x to v, then the **app** rule

$$\frac{\rho'' = \mathsf{update}\ x\ v\ \rho'}{\rho \vdash \mathsf{app}(\mathsf{clo}(\rho', x, e), v) \to \mathsf{kclo1}(\rho'', e)}$$

and the above two rules can be replaced with the following rules for **app**:

$$\frac{}{\rho \vdash \mathsf{app}(\mathsf{clo}(x, v, \rho'), v_2) \to v} \qquad \frac{\rho'' = \mathsf{update}\ x\ v_2\ \rho' \qquad \rho'' \vdash e \to e'}{\rho \vdash \mathsf{app}(\mathsf{clo}(x, e, \rho'), v_2) \to \mathsf{app}(\mathsf{clo}(x, e', \rho'), v_2)}$$

Another common type of constructs resulting in a recurring pattern of extra auxiliary constructs are loops. For example, the "While" language listed in Table 2 contains a while-loop with the following big-step rules:

$$\frac{\langle e_b, \sigma\rangle \Downarrow \langle \mathsf{false}, \sigma'\rangle}{\langle \mathsf{while}(e_b, c), \sigma\rangle \Downarrow \langle \mathsf{skip}, \sigma'\rangle}$$

$$\frac{\langle e_b, \sigma\rangle \Downarrow \langle \mathsf{true}, \sigma'\rangle \qquad \langle c, \sigma'\rangle \Downarrow \langle \mathsf{skip}, \sigma''\rangle \qquad \langle \mathsf{while}(e_b, c), \sigma''\rangle \Downarrow \langle v, \sigma'''\rangle}{\langle \mathsf{while}(e_b, c), \sigma\rangle \Downarrow \langle v, \sigma'''\rangle}$$

The automatic transformation of these rules introduces two extra constructs, **kwhile1** and **ktrue1**. The former ensures the full evaluation of the condition expression, keeping a copy of it together with the while's body. The latter construct ensures the full evaluation of while's body, keeping a copy of the body together with the condition expression.

$$\frac{}{\langle \textsf{while}(e_b, c),\ \sigma\rangle \longrightarrow \langle \textsf{kwhile1}(c, e_b, e_b),\ \sigma\rangle}$$

$$\frac{}{\langle \textsf{kwhile1}(c, e_b, \textsf{true}),\ \sigma\rangle \longrightarrow \langle \textsf{ktrue1}(e_b, c, c),\ \sigma\rangle}$$

$$\frac{}{\langle \textsf{kwhile1}(c, e_b, \textsf{false}),\ \sigma\rangle \longrightarrow \langle \textsf{skip},\ \sigma\rangle}$$

$$\frac{\langle t,\ \sigma\rangle \longrightarrow \langle t',\ \sigma'\rangle}{\langle \textsf{kwhile1}(c, e_b, t),\ \sigma\rangle \longrightarrow \langle \textsf{kwhile1}(c, e_b, t'),\ \sigma'\rangle}$$

$$\frac{}{\langle \textsf{ktrue1}(e_b, c, \textsf{skip}),\ \sigma\rangle \longrightarrow \langle \textsf{while}(e_b, c),\ \sigma\rangle}$$

$$\frac{\langle t,\ \sigma\rangle \longrightarrow \langle t',\ \sigma'\rangle}{\langle \textsf{ktrue1}(e_b, c, t),\ \sigma\rangle \longrightarrow \langle \textsf{ktrue1}(e_b, c, t'),\ \sigma'\rangle}$$

We observe that in a language with a conditional and a sequencing construct we can find terms corresponding to **kwhile1** and **ktrue1**:

$$\textsf{kwhile1}(c, e_b, e_b') \approx \textsf{if}(e_b', \textsf{seq}(c, \textsf{while}(e_b, c)), \textsf{skip})$$
$$\textsf{ktrue1}(e_b, c, c') \approx \textsf{seq}(c', \textsf{while}(e_b, c))$$

The small-step semantics of **while** could then be simplified to a single rule.

$$\frac{}{\langle \textsf{while}(e_b, c), \sigma\rangle \longrightarrow \langle \textsf{if}(e_b, \textsf{seq}(c, \textsf{while}(e_b, c)), \textsf{skip}), \sigma\rangle}$$

Our current, straightforward way of deriving term–continuation equivalents is not capable of finding these equivalences. In future work, we want to explore external tools, such as SMT solvers, to facilitate searching for translations from continuations to terms. This search could be possibly limited to a specific term depth.

Exceptions as Values. We tested our transformations with two ways of representing exceptions in big-step semantics currently supported by our input language: as values and as state. Representing exceptions as values appears to be more common and is used, for example, in the big-step specification of Standard ML [24], or in [6] in connection with *pretty big-step semantics*. Given a big-step specification (or interpreter) in this style, the generated small-step semantics handles exceptions correctly (based on our experiments). However, since exceptions are just values, propagation to top-level is spread out across multiple steps – depending on the depth of the term which raised the exception. The following example illustrates this behavior.

$$\begin{aligned}\textsf{add}(1, \textsf{add}(2, \textsf{add}(\textsf{raise}(3), \textsf{raise}(4)))) &\longrightarrow \textsf{add}(1, \textsf{add}(2, \textsf{add}(\textsf{exc}(3), \textsf{raise}(4))))\\ &\longrightarrow \textsf{add}(1, \textsf{add}(2, \textsf{exc}(3))) \longrightarrow \textsf{add}(1, \textsf{exc}(3)) \longrightarrow \textsf{exc}(3)\end{aligned}$$

Since we expect the input semantics to be deterministic and the propagation of exceptions in the resulting small-step follows the original big-step semantics, this "slow" propagation is not a problem, even if it does not take advantage of "fast" propagation via labels or state. A possible solution we are considering for future work is to let the user flag values in the big-step semantics and translate such values as labels on arrows or a state change to allow propagating them in a single step.

Exceptions as State. Another approach to specifying exceptions is to use a flag in the configuration. Rules may be specified so that they only apply if the incoming state has no exception indicated. As with the exceptions-as-values approach, propagation rules have to be written to terminate a computation early if a computation of a subterm indicates an exception. Observe the exception propagation rule for **add** and the exception handling rule for **try**.

$$\frac{\langle e_1, \sigma, \textsf{ok}\rangle \Downarrow \langle v_1, \sigma', \textsf{ex}\rangle}{\langle \textsf{app}(e_1, e_2), \sigma, \textsf{ok}\rangle \Downarrow \langle \textsf{skip}, \sigma', \textsf{ex}\rangle}$$

$$\frac{\langle e_1, \sigma, \textsf{ok}\rangle \Downarrow \langle v_1, \sigma', \textsf{ex}\rangle \qquad \langle e_2, \sigma', \textsf{ok}\rangle \Downarrow \langle v_2, \sigma'', \textsf{ok}\rangle}{\langle \textsf{try}(e_1, e_2), \sigma, \textsf{ok}\rangle \Downarrow \langle v_2, \sigma'', \textsf{ok}\rangle}$$

Using state to propagate exceptions is mentioned in connection with small-step SOS in [4]. While this approach has the potential advantage of manifesting the currently raised exception immediately at the top-level, it also poses a problem of locality. If an exception is reinserted into the configuration, it might become decoupled from the original site. This can result, for example, in the wrong handler catching the exception in a following step. Our transformation deals with this style of exceptions naturally by preserving more continuations in the final interpreter. After being raised, an exception is inserted into the state and propagated to top-level by congruence rules. However, it will only be caught after the corresponding subterm has been evaluated, or rather, a value has been propagated upwards to signal a completed computation. This behavior corresponds to exception handling in big-step rules, only it is spread out over multiple steps. Continuations are kept in the final language to correspond to stages of computation and thus, to preserve the locality of a raised exception. A handler will only handle an exception once the raising subterm has become a value. Hence, the exception will be intercepted by the innermost handler – even if the exception is visible at the top-level of a step.

Based on our experiments, the exception-as-state handling in the generated small-step interpreters is a truthful unfolding of the big-step evaluation process. This is further supported by our ad-hoc proofs of equivalence between input and output interpreters. However, the generated semantics suffers from a blowup in the number of rules and moves away from the usual small-step propagation and exception handling in congruence rules. We see this as a shortcoming of the transformation. To overcome this, we briefly experimented with a case-floating stage, which would result in catching exceptions in the congruence cases of continuations. Using such transformation, the resulting interpreter would more closely mirror the standard small-step treatment of exceptions as signals. However, the conditions when this transformations should be triggered need to be considered carefully and we leave this for future work.

Limited Non-determinism. In the present work, our aim was to only consider deterministic semantics implemented as an interpreter in a functional programming language. However, since cases of the interpreter are considered independently in the transformation, some forms of non-determinism in the input semantics get translated correctly. For example, the following internal choice construct (cf. CSP's $\sqcap$ operator [5,17]) gets transformed correctly. The straightforward big-step rules are transformed into small-step rules as expected. Of course, one has to keep in mind that these rules are interpreted as ordered, that is, the first rule in both styles will always apply.

$$\frac{e_1 \Downarrow v_1}{\textsf{choose}(e_1, e_2) \Downarrow v_1} \qquad \frac{}{\textsf{choose}(e_1, e_2) \rightarrow e_1}$$

$$\frac{e_2 \Downarrow v_2}{\textsf{choose}(e_1, e_2) \Downarrow v_2} \qquad \frac{}{\textsf{choose}(e_1, e_2) \rightarrow e_2}$$

6 Related Work

In their short paper [18], the authors propose a direct syntactic way of deriving small-step rules from big-step ones. Unlike our approach, based on manipulating control flow in an interpreter, their transformation applies to a set of inference rules. While axioms are copied over directly, for conditional rules a stack is added to the configuration to keep track of evaluation. For each conditional big-step rule, an auxiliary construct and 4 small-step rules are generated. Results of "premise computations" are accumulated and side-conditions are only discharged at the end of such a computation sequence. For this reason, we can view the resulting semantics more as a "leap" semantics, which makes it less suitable for a semantics-based interpreter or debugger. A further disadvantage is that the resulting semantics is far removed from a typical small-step specification with a higher potential for blow-up as 4 rules are introduced for each conditional rule. On the other hand, the delayed unification of meta-variables and discharging of side-conditions potentially makes the transformation applicable to a wider array of languages, including those where control flow is not as explicit.

In [2], the author explores an approach to constructing abstract machines from big-step (natural) specifications. It applies to a class of big-step specifications called *L-attributed big-step semantics*, which allows for sufficiently interesting languages. The extracted abstract machines use a stack of evaluation contexts to keep track of the stages of computations. In contrast, our transformed interpreters rebuild the context via congruence rules in each step. While this is less efficient as a computation strategy, the intermediate results of the computation are visible in the context of the original program, in line with usual SOS specifications.

A significant body of work has been developed on transformations that take a form of small-step semantics (usually an interpreter) and produce a big-step-style interpreter. The relation between semantic specifications, interpreters and abstract machines has been thoroughly investigated, mainly in the context of reduction semantics [10–13,26]. In particular, our work was inspired by and is based on Danvy's work on refocusing in reduction semantics [13] and on use of CPS conversion and defunctionalization to convert between representations of control in interpreters [11].

A more direct approach to deriving big-step semantics from small-step is taken by authors of [4], where a small-step Modular SOS specification is transformed into a pretty-big-step one. This is done by introducing reflexivity and transitivity rules into a specification, along with a "refocus" rule which effectively compresses a transition sequence into a single step. The original small-step rules are then specialized with respect to these new rules, yielding refocused rules in the style of pretty-big-step semantics [6]. A related approach is by Ciobâcă [7], where big-step rules are generated for a small-step semantics. The big-step rules are, again, close to a pretty-big-step style.

7 Conclusion and Future Work

We have presented a stepwise functional derivation of a small-step interpreter from a big-step one. This derivation proceeds through a sequence of, mostly basic, transformation steps. First, the big-step evaluation function is converted into continuation-passing style to make control-flow explicit. Then, the continuations are generalized (or lifted) to handle non-value inputs. The non-value cases correspond to congruence rules in small-step semantics. After defunctionalization, we remove self-recursive calls, effectively converting the recursive interpreter into a stepping function. The final major step of the transformation is to decide which continuations will have to be introduced as new auxiliary terms into the language. We have evaluated our approach on several languages covering different features. For most of these, the transformation yields small-step semantics which are close to ones we would normally write by hand.

We see this work as an initial exploration of automatic transformations of big-step semantics into small-step counterparts. We identified a few areas where the current process could be significantly improved. These include applying better equational reasoning to identify terms equivalent to continuations, or transforming exceptions as state in a way that would avoid introducing many intermediate terms and would better correspond to usual signal handling in small-step SOS. Another research avenue is to fully verify the transformations in an interactive theorem prover, with the possibility of extracting a correct transformer from the proofs.

Acknowledgements. We would like to thank Jeanne-Marie Musca, Brian LaChance and the anonymous referees for their useful comments and suggestions. This work was supported in part by DARPA award FA8750-15-2-0033.

References

1. https://www.eecs.tufts.edu/~fvesely/esop2019
2. Ager, M.S.: From natural semantics to abstract machines. In: Etalle, S. (ed.) LOPSTR 2004. LNCS, vol. 3573, pp. 245–261. Springer, Heidelberg (2005). https://doi.org/10.1007/11506676_16
3. Amin, N., Rompf, T.: Collapsing towers of interpreters. Proc. ACM Program. Lang. **2**(POPL), 52:1–52:33 (2017). https://doi.org/10.1145/3158140
4. Bach Poulsen, C., Mosses, P.D.: Deriving pretty-big-step semantics from small-step semantics. In: Shao, Z. (ed.) ESOP 2014. LNCS, vol. 8410, pp. 270–289. Springer, Heidelberg (2014). https://doi.org/10.1007/978-3-642-54833-8_15
5. Brookes, S.D., Roscoe, A.W., Walker, D.J.: An operational semantics for CSP. Technical report, Oxford University (1986)
6. Charguéraud, A.: Pretty-big-step semantics. In: Felleisen, M., Gardner, P. (eds.) ESOP 2013. LNCS, vol. 7792, pp. 41–60. Springer, Heidelberg (2013). https://doi.org/10.1007/978-3-642-37036-6_3
7. Ciobâcă, Ş.: From small-step semantics to big-step semantics, automatically. In: Johnsen, E.B., Petre, L. (eds.) IFM 2013. LNCS, vol. 7940, pp. 347–361. Springer, Heidelberg (2013). https://doi.org/10.1007/978-3-642-38613-8_24
8. Danvy, O., Filinski, A.: Representing control: a study of the CPS transformation. Math. Struct. Comput. Sci. **2**(4), 361–391 (1992). https://doi.org/10.1017/S0960129500001535
9. Danvy, O.: On evaluation contexts, continuations, and the rest of computation. In: Thielecke, H. (ed.) Workshop on Continuations, pp. 13–23, Technical report CSR-04-1, Department of Computer Science, Queen Mary's College, Venice, Italy, January 2004
10. Danvy, O.: From reduction-based to reduction-free normalization. Electr. Notes Theor. Comput. Sci. **124**(2), 79–100 (2005). https://doi.org/10.1016/j.entcs.2005.01.007
11. Danvy, O.: Defunctionalized interpreters for programming languages. In: ICFP 2008, pp. 131–142. ACM, New York (2008). https://doi.org/10.1145/1411204.1411206
12. Danvy, O., Johannsen, J., Zerny, I.: A walk in the semantic park. In: PEPM 2011, pp. 1–12. ACM, New York (2011). https://doi.org/10.1145/1929501.1929503
13. Danvy, O., Nielsen, L.R.: Refocusing in reduction semantics. Technical report, BRICS RS-04-26, DAIMI, Department of Computer Science, University of Aarhus, November 2004
14. Ellison, C., Roşu, G.: An executable formal semantics of C with applications. In: POPL 2012, pp. 533–544. ACM, New York (2012). https://doi.org/10.1145/2103656.2103719
15. Felleisen, M., Findler, R.B., Flatt, M.: Semantics Engineering with PLT Redex, 1st edn. The MIT Press, Cambridge (2009)
16. Fischbach, A., Hannan, J.: Specification and correctness of lambda lifting. J. Funct. Program. **13**(3), 509–543 (2003). https://doi.org/10.1017/S0956796802004604
17. Hoare, C.A.R.: Communicating Sequential Processes. Prentice-Hall Inc., Upper Saddle River (1985)

18. Huizing, C., Koymans, R., Kuiper, R.: A small step for mankind. In: Dams, D., Hannemann, U., Steffen, M. (eds.) Concurrency, Compositionality, and Correctness. LNCS, vol. 5930, pp. 66–73. Springer, Heidelberg (2010). https://doi.org/10.1007/978-3-642-11512-7_5
19. Johnsson, T.: Lambda lifting: transforming programs to recursive equations. In: Jouannaud, J.-P. (ed.) FPCA 1985. LNCS, vol. 201, pp. 190–203. Springer, Heidelberg (1985). https://doi.org/10.1007/3-540-15975-4_37
20. Klein, G., Nipkow, T.: A machine-checked model for a Java-like language, virtual machine, and compiler. ACM Trans. Program. Lang. Syst. **28**(4), 619–695 (2006). https://doi.org/10.1145/1146809.1146811
21. Kumar, R., Myreen, M.O., Norrish, M., Owens, S.: CakeML: a verified implementation of ML. In: POPL 2014, pp. 179–191. ACM, New York (2014). https://doi.org/10.1145/2535838.2535841
22. Leroy, X., Grall, H.: Coinductive big-step operational semantics. Inf. Comput. **207**(2), 284–304 (2009). https://doi.org/10.1016/j.ic.2007.12.004
23. Midtgaard, J., Ramsey, N., Larsen, B.: Engineering definitional interpreters. In: PPDP 2013, pp. 121–132. ACM, New York (2013). https://doi.org/10.1145/2505879.2505894
24. Milner, R., Tofte, M., Macqueen, D.: The Definition of Standard ML. MIT Press, Cambridge (1997)
25. Nielsen, L.R.: A selective CPS transformation. Electr. Notes Theor. Comput. Sci. **45**, 311–331 (2001). https://doi.org/10.1016/S1571-0661(04)80969-1
26. Reynolds, J.C.: Definitional interpreters for higher-order programming languages. High. Order Symbolic Comput. **11**(4), 363–397 (1998). https://doi.org/10.1023/A:1010027404223
27. Roşu, G., Şerbănuţă, T.F.: An overview of the K semantic framework. J. Logic Algebraic Program. **79**(6), 397–434 (2010). https://doi.org/10.1016/j.jlap.2010.03.012
28. Strachey, C., Wadsworth, C.P.: Continuations: a mathematical semantics for handling full jumps. High. Order Symbolic Comput. **13**(1), 135–152 (2000). https://doi.org/10.1023/A:1010026413531
29. Wright, A., Felleisen, M.: A syntactic approach to type soundness. Inf. Comput. **115**(1), 38–94 (1994). https://doi.org/10.1006/inco.1994.1093

Program Semantics

Extended Call-by-Push-Value: Reasoning About Effectful Programs and Evaluation Order

Dylan McDermott(✉) and Alan Mycroft

Computer Laboratory, University of Cambridge, Cambridge, UK
{Dylan.McDermott,Alan.Mycroft}@cl.cam.ac.uk

Abstract. Traditionally, reasoning about programs under varying evaluation regimes (call-by-value, call-by-name etc.) was done at the meta-level, treating them as term rewriting systems. Levy's call-by-push-value (CBPV) calculus provides a more powerful approach for reasoning, by treating CBPV terms as a common intermediate language which captures both call-by-value and call-by-name, and by allowing equational reasoning about changes to evaluation order between or within programs.

We extend CBPV to additionally deal with call-by-need, which is non-trivial because of shared reductions. This allows the equational reasoning to also support call-by-need. As an example, we then prove that call-by-need and call-by-name are equivalent if nontermination is the only side-effect in the source language.

We then show how to incorporate an effect system. This enables us to exploit static knowledge of the potential effects of a given expression to augment equational reasoning; thus a program fragment might be invariant under change of evaluation regime only because of knowledge of its effects.

Keywords: Evaluation order · Call-by-need · Call-by-push-value · Logical relations · Effect systems

1 Introduction

Programming languages based on the λ-calculus have different semantics depending on the reduction strategy employed. Three common variants are call-by-value, call-by-name and call-by-need (with the third sometimes also referred to as "lazy evaluation" when data constructors defer evaluation of arguments until the data structure is traversed). Reasoning about such programs and their equivalence under varying reduction strategies can be difficult as we have to reason about meta-level reduction strategies and not merely at the object level.

Levy [17] introduced *call-by-push-value* (CBPV) to improve the situation. CBPV is a calculus with separated notions of value and computation. A characteristic feature is that each CBPV program encodes its own evaluation order. It is

L. Caires (Ed.): ESOP 2019, LNCS 11423, pp. 235–262, 2019.
https://doi.org/10.1007/978-3-030-17184-1_9

best seen as an *intermediate language* into which lambda-calculus-based *source-language* programs can be translated. Moreover, CBPV is powerful enough that programs employing call-by-value or call-by-name (or even a mixture) can be simply translated into it, giving an object-calculus way to reason about the meta-level concept of reduction order.

However, CBPV does not enable us to reason about call-by-need evaluation. An intuitive reason is that call-by-need has "action at a distance" in that reduction of one subterm causes reduction of all other subterms that originated as copies during variable substitution. Indeed call-by-need is often framed using mutable stores (graph reduction [32], or reducing a thunk which is accessed by multiple pointers [16]). CBPV does not allow these to be encoded.

This work presents *extended call-by-push-value* (ECBPV), a calculus similar to CBPV, but which can capture call-by-need reduction in addition to call-by-value and call-by-name. Specifically, ECBPV adds an extra primitive $M \ \mathsf{need} \underline{x}.\, N$ which runs N, with M being evaluated the first time $\underline{x}$ is used. On subsequent uses of $\underline{x}$, the result of the first run is returned immediately. The term M is evaluated at most once. We give the syntax and type system of ECBPV, together with an equational theory that expresses when terms are considered equal.

A key justification for an intermediate language that can express several evaluation orders is that it enables equivalences between the evaluation orders to be proved. If there are no (side-)effects at all in the source language, then call-by-need, call-by-value and call-by-name should be semantically equivalent. If the only effect is nondeterminism, then need and value (but not name) are equivalent. If the only effect is nontermination then need and name (but not value) are equivalent. We show that ECBPV can be used to prove such equivalences by proving the latter using an argument based on *Kripke logical relations of varying arity* [12].

These equivalences rely on the *language* being restricted to particular effects. However, one may wish to switch evaluation order for *subprograms* restricted to particular effects, even if the language itself does not have such a restriction. To allow reasoning to be applied to these cases, we add an *effect system* [20] to ECBPV, which allows the side-effects of subprograms to be statically estimated. This allows us to determine which parts of a program are invariant under changes in evaluation order. As we will see, support for call-by-need (and action at a distance more generally) makes describing an effect system significantly more difficult than for call-by-value.

Contributions. We make the following contributions:

- We describe *extended call-by-push-value*, a version of CBPV containing an extra construct that adds support for call-by-need. We give its syntax, type system, and equational theory (Sect. 2).
- We describe two translations from a lambda-calculus source language into ECBPV: one for call-by-name and one for call-by-need (the first such translation) (Sect. 3). We then show that, if the source language has nontermination as the only effect, call-by-name and call-by-need are equivalent.

- We refine the type system of ECBPV so that its types also carry effect information (Sect. 4). This allows equivalences between evaluation orders to be exploited, both at ECBPV and source level, when subprograms are statically limited to particular effects.

2 Extended Call-by-Push-Value

We describe an extension to call-by-push-value with support for call-by-need. The primary difference between ordinary CBPV and ECBPV is the addition of a primitive that allows computations to be added to the environment, so that they are evaluated only the first time they are used. Before describing this change, we take a closer look at CBPV and how it supports call-by-value and call-by-name.

CBPV stratifies terms into *values*, which do not have side-effects, and *computations*, which might. Evaluation order is irrelevant for values, so we are only concerned with how computations are sequenced. There is exactly one primitive that causes the evaluation of more than one computation, which is the computation $M \, \mathsf{to} \, x.\, N$. This means run the computation M, bind the result to x, and then run the computation N. (It is similar to `M >>= \x -> N` in Haskell.) The evaluation order is fixed: M is always eagerly evaluated. This construct can be used to implement call-by-value: to apply a function, eagerly evaluate the argument and then evaluate the body of the function. No other constructs cause the evaluation of more than one computation.

To allow more control over evaluation order, CBPV allows computations to be thunked. The term $\mathsf{thunk} \, M$ is a value that contains the thunk of the computation M. Thunks can be duplicated (to allow a single computation to be evaluated more than once), and can be converted back into computations with $\mathsf{force} \, V$. This allows call-by-name to be implemented: arguments to functions are thunked computations. Arguments are used by forcing them, so that the computation is evaluated every time the argument is used. Effectively, there is a construct $M \, \mathsf{name} \, \underline{x}.\, N$, which evaluates M each time the variable $\underline{x}$ is used by N, rather than eagerly evaluating. (The variable $\underline{x}$ is underlined here to indicate that it refers to a computation rather than a value: uses of it may have side-effects.)

To support call-by-need, extended call-by-push-value adds another construct $M \, \mathsf{need} \, \underline{x}.\, N$. This term runs the computation N, with the computation M being evaluated the first time $\underline{x}$ is used. On subsequent uses of $\underline{x}$, the result of the first run is returned immediately. The computation M is evaluated at most once. This new construct adds the "action at a distance" missing from ordinary CBPV.

We briefly mention that adding general mutable references to call-by-push-value would allow call-by-need to be encoded. However, reasoning about evaluation order would be difficult, and so we do not take this option.

2.1 Syntax

The syntax of extended call-by-push-value is given in Fig. 1. The highlighted parts are new here. The rest of the syntax is similar to CBPV.[1]

$$\begin{aligned}
V, W &::= c \mid x \mid (V_1, V_2) \mid \mathsf{fst}\, V \mid \mathsf{snd}\, V \mid \mathsf{inl}\, V \mid \mathsf{inr}\, V \\
&\mid \mathsf{case}\, V\, \mathsf{of}\, \{\mathsf{inl}\, x.\, W_1, \mathsf{inr}\, y.\, W_2\} \mid \mathsf{thunk}\, M \\
M, N &::= \underline{x} \mid \mathsf{force}\, V \mid \lambda\{i.\, M_i\}_{i \in I} \mid i`M \mid \lambda x.\, M \mid V`M \mid \mathsf{return}\, V \\
&\mid M\, \mathsf{to}\, x.\, N \mid M\, \mathsf{need}\, \underline{x}.\, N \\
A, B &::= \mathbf{unit} \mid A_1 \times A_2 \mid A_1 + A_2 \mid \mathbf{U}\, \underline{C} \\
\underline{C}, \underline{D} &::= \textstyle\prod_{i \in I} \underline{C}_i \mid A \to \underline{C} \mid \mathbf{Fr}\, A \\
\Gamma &::= \diamond \mid \Gamma, x : A \mid \Gamma, \underline{x} : \mathbf{Fr}\, A
\end{aligned}$$

Fig. 1. Syntax of ECBPV

We assume two sets of variables: *value variables* $x, y, \ldots$ and *computation variables* $\underline{x}, \underline{y}, \ldots$. While ordinary CBPV does not include computation variables, they do not of themselves add any expressive power to the calculus. The ability to use call-by-need in ECBPV comes from the need construct used to bind the variable.[2]

There are two kinds of terms, *value terms* V, W which do not have side-effects (in particular, are strongly normalizing), and *computation terms* M, N which might have side-effects. Value terms include constants c, and specifically the constant $()$ of type **unit**. There are no constant computation terms; value constants suffice (see Sect. 3 for an example). The value term $\mathsf{thunk}\, M$ suspends the computation M; the computation term $\mathsf{force}\, V$ runs the suspended computation V. Computation terms also include I-ary tuples $\lambda\{i.\, M_i\}_{i \in I}$ (where I ranges over *finite* sets); the ith projection of a tuple M is $i`M$. Functions send values to computations, and are computations themselves. Application is written $V`M$, where V is the argument and M is the function to apply. The term $\mathsf{return}\, V$ is a computation that just returns the value V, without causing any side-effects. Eager sequencing of computations is given by $M\, \mathsf{to}\, x.\, N$, which evaluates M until it returns a value, then places the result in x and evaluates N. For example, in $M\, \mathsf{to}\, x.\ \mathsf{return}\, (x, x)$, the term M is evaluated once, and the result is duplicated. In $M\, \mathsf{to}\, x.\ \mathsf{return}\, ()$, the term M is still evaluated once, but its result is never

[1] The only difference is that eliminators of product and sum types are value terms rather than computation terms (which makes value terms slightly more general). Levy [17] calls this CBPV with *complex values.*

[2] Computation variables are not strictly required to support call-by-need (since we can use $x : \mathbf{U}\, (\mathbf{Fr}\, A)$ instead of $\underline{x} : \mathbf{Fr}\, A$), but they simplify reasoning about evaluation order, and therefore we choose to include them.

used. Syntactically, both to and need (explained below) are right-associative (so $M_1 \,\mathsf{to}\, x.\, M_2 \,\mathsf{to}\, y.\, M_3$ means $M_1 \,\mathsf{to}\, x.\, (M_2 \,\mathsf{to}\, y.\, M_3)$).

The primary new construct is $M \,\mathsf{need}\, \underline{x}.\, N$. This term evaluates N. The first time $\underline{x}$ is evaluated (due to a use of $\underline{x}$ inside N) it behaves the same as the computation M. If M returns a value V, then subsequent uses of $\underline{x}$ behave the same as $\mathsf{return}\, V$. Hence only the first use of $\underline{x}$ will evaluate M. If $\underline{x}$ is not used then M is not evaluated at all. The computation variable $\underline{x}$ bound inside the term is primarily used by eagerly sequencing it with other computations. For example,

$$M \,\mathsf{need}\, \underline{x}.\, \underline{x} \,\mathsf{to}\, y.\, \underline{x} \,\mathsf{to}\, z.\ \mathsf{return}\,(y, z)$$

uses $\underline{x}$ twice: once where the result is bound to y, and once where the result is bound to z. Only the first of these uses will evaluate M, so this term has the same semantics as $M \,\mathsf{to}\, x.\ \mathsf{return}(x, x)$. The term $M \,\mathsf{need}\, \underline{x}.\ \mathsf{return}\,()$ does not evaluate M at all, and has the same semantics as $\mathsf{return}\,()$.

With the addition of need it is not in general possible to determine the order in which computations are executed statically. Uses of computation variables are given statically, but not all of these actually evaluate the corresponding computation dynamically. In general, the set of uses of computation variables that actually cause effects depends on run-time behaviour. This will be important when describing the effect system in Sect. 4.

The standard capture-avoiding substitution of value variables in value terms is denoted $V[x \mapsto W]$. We similarly have substitutions of value variables in computation terms, computation variables in value terms, and computation variables in computation terms. Finally, we define the call-by-name construct mentioned above as syntactic sugar for other CBPV primitives:

$$M \,\mathsf{name}\, \underline{x}.\, N \;:=\; \mathsf{thunk}\, M \,\text{`}\, \lambda y.\, N[\underline{x} \mapsto \mathsf{force}\, y]$$

where y is not free in N.

Types are stratified into *value types* A, B and *computation types* $\underline{C}, \underline{D}$. Value types include the unit type, products and sum types. (It is easy to add further base types; we omit Levy's empty types for simplicity.) Value types also include *thunk types* $\mathbf{U}\,\underline{C}$, which are introduced by $\mathsf{thunk}\, M$ and eliminated by $\mathsf{force}\, V$. Computation types include I-ary product types $\prod_{i \in I} \underline{C}_i$ for finite I, function types $A \to \underline{C}$, and *returner types* $\mathbf{Fr}\, A$. The latter are introduced by $\mathsf{return}\, V$, and are the only types of computation that can appear on the left of either to or need (which are the eliminators of returner types). The type constructors $\mathbf{U}$ and $\mathbf{Fr}$ form an *adjunction* in categorical models. Finally, contexts Γ map value variables to value types, and computation variables to computation types of the form $\mathbf{Fr}\, A$. This restriction is due to the fact that the only construct that binds computation variables is need, which only sequences computations of returner type. Allowing computation variables to be associated with other forms of computation type in typing contexts is therefore unnecessary. Typing contexts are ordered lists.

The syntax is parameterized by a *signature*, containing the constants c.

Definition 1 (Signature). *A signature $\mathcal{K}$ consists of a set $\mathcal{K}_A$ of constants of type A for each value type A. All signatures contain $() \in \mathcal{K}_{\mathbf{unit}}$.*

2.2 Type System

The type system of extended call-by-push-value is a minor extension of the type system of ordinary call-by-push-value. Assume a fixed signature $\mathcal{K}$. There are two typing judgements, one for value types and one for computation types. The rules for the value typing judgement $\Gamma \vdash_{\mathrm{v}} V : A$ and the computation typing judgement $\Gamma \vdash M : \underline{C}$ are given in Fig. 2. Rules that add a new variable to the typing context implicitly require that the variable does not already appear in the context. The type system admits the usual weakening and substitution properties for both value and computation variables.

$$\boxed{\Gamma \vdash_{\mathrm{v}} V : A}$$

$$\frac{}{\Gamma \vdash_{\mathrm{v}} x : A}\ \text{if } (x : A) \in \Gamma \qquad \frac{}{\Gamma \vdash_{\mathrm{v}} c : A}\ \text{if } c \in \mathcal{K}_A \qquad \frac{\Gamma \vdash M : \underline{C}}{\Gamma \vdash_{\mathrm{v}} \mathsf{thunk}\, M : \mathbf{U}\,\underline{C}}$$

$$\frac{\Gamma \vdash_{\mathrm{v}} V_1 : A_1 \qquad \Gamma \vdash_{\mathrm{v}} V_2 : A_2}{\Gamma \vdash_{\mathrm{v}} (V_1, V_2) : A_1 \times A_2} \qquad \frac{\Gamma \vdash_{\mathrm{v}} V : A_1 \times A_2}{\Gamma \vdash_{\mathrm{v}} \mathsf{fst}\, V : A_1} \qquad \frac{\Gamma \vdash_{\mathrm{v}} V : A_1 \times A_2}{\Gamma \vdash_{\mathrm{v}} \mathsf{snd}\, V : A_2}$$

$$\frac{\Gamma \vdash_{\mathrm{v}} V : A_1}{\Gamma \vdash_{\mathrm{v}} \mathsf{inl}\, V : A_1 + A_2} \qquad \frac{\Gamma \vdash_{\mathrm{v}} V : A_2}{\Gamma \vdash_{\mathrm{v}} \mathsf{inr}\, V : A_1 + A_2}$$

$$\frac{\Gamma \vdash_{\mathrm{v}} V : A_1 + A_2 \qquad \Gamma, x : A_1 \vdash_{\mathrm{v}} W_1 : B \qquad \Gamma, x : A_2 \vdash_{\mathrm{v}} W_2 : B}{\Gamma \vdash_{\mathrm{v}} \mathsf{case}\, V\, \mathsf{of}\, \{\mathsf{inl}\, x.\, W_1, \mathsf{inr}\, y.\, W_2\} : B}$$

$$\boxed{\Gamma \vdash M : \underline{C}}$$

$$\frac{}{\Gamma \vdash \underline{x} : \mathbf{Fr}\, A}\ \text{if } (\underline{x} : \mathbf{Fr}\, A) \in \Gamma \qquad \frac{\Gamma \vdash_{\mathrm{v}} V : A}{\Gamma \vdash \mathsf{return}\, V : \mathbf{Fr}\, A} \qquad \frac{\Gamma \vdash_{\mathrm{v}} V : \mathbf{U}\,\underline{C}}{\Gamma \vdash \mathsf{force}\, V : \underline{C}}$$

$$\frac{(\Gamma \vdash M_i : \underline{C}_i)_{i \in I}}{\Gamma \vdash \lambda\{i.\, M_i\}_{i \in I} : \prod_{i \in I} \underline{C}_i} \qquad \frac{\Gamma \vdash M : \prod_{i \in I} \underline{C}_i}{\Gamma \vdash i`M : \underline{C}_i}$$

$$\frac{\Gamma, x : A \vdash M : \underline{C}}{\Gamma \vdash \lambda x.\, M : A \to \underline{C}} \qquad \frac{\Gamma \vdash_{\mathrm{v}} V : A \qquad \Gamma \vdash M : A \to \underline{C}}{\Gamma \vdash V`M : \underline{C}}$$

$$\frac{\Gamma \vdash M : \mathbf{Fr}\, A \qquad \Gamma, x : A \vdash N : \underline{C}}{\Gamma \vdash M\, \mathsf{to}\, x.\, N : \underline{C}} \qquad \frac{\Gamma \vdash M : \mathbf{Fr}\, A \qquad \Gamma, \underline{x} : \mathbf{Fr}\, A \vdash N : \underline{C}}{\Gamma \vdash M\, \mathsf{need}\, \underline{x}.\, N : \underline{C}}$$

Fig. 2. Typing rules for ECBPV

It should be clear that ECBPV is actually an extension of call-by-push-value. CBPV terms embed as terms that never use the highlighted forms. We translate call-by-need by encoding call-by-need functions as terms of the form

$$\lambda x'.\,(\mathsf{force}\,x')\ \mathsf{need}\ \underline{x}.\,M$$

where x' is not free in M. This is a call-by-push-value function that accepts a thunk as an argument. The thunk is added to the context, and the body of the function is executed. The first time the argument is used (via $\underline{x}$), the computation inside the thunk is evaluated. Subsequent uses do not run the computation again. A translation based on this idea from a call-by-need source language is given in detail in Sect. 3.2.

2.3 Equational Theory

In this section, we present the *equational theory* of extended call-by-push-value. This is an extension of the equational theory for CBPV given by Levy [17] to support our new constructs. It consists of two judgement forms, one for values and one for computations:

$$\Gamma \vdash_{\mathsf{v}} V \equiv W : A \qquad \Gamma \vdash M \equiv N : \underline{C}$$

These mean both terms are well typed, and are considered equal by the equational theory. We frequently omit the context and type when they are obvious or unimportant.

The definition is given by the axioms in Fig. 3. Note that these axioms only hold when the terms they mention have suitable types, and when suitable constraints on free variables are satisfied. For example, the second sequencing axiom holds only if $\underline{x}$ is not free in N. These conditions are left implicit in the figure. The judgements are additionally reflexive (assuming the typing holds), symmetric and transitive. They are also closed under all possible congruence rules. There are no restrictions on congruence related to evaluation order. None are necessary because ECBPV terms make the evaluation order explicit: all sequencing of computations uses to and need. Finally, note that enriching the signature with additional constants will in general require additional axioms capturing their behaviour; Sect. 3 exemplifies this for constants $\bot_A$ representing nontermination.

For the equational theory to capture call-by-need, we might expect computation terms that are not of the form return V to never be duplicated, since they should not be evaluated more than once. There are two exceptions to this. Such terms can be duplicated in the axioms that duplicate value terms (such as the β laws for sum types). In this case, the syntax ensures such terms are thunked. This is correct because we should allow these terms to be executed once in each separate execution of a computation (and separate executions arise from duplication of thunks). We are only concerned with duplication *within* a single computation. Computation terms can also be duplicated across multiple elements of a tuple $\lambda\{i.\,M_i\}$ of computation terms. This is also correct, because only one component

$$\begin{aligned}
\Gamma \vdash_{\mathsf{v}} \mathsf{fst}\,(V_1, V_2) &\equiv V_1 \;:\; A_1\\
\Gamma \vdash_{\mathsf{v}} \mathsf{snd}\,(V_1, V_2) &\equiv V_2 \;:\; A_2\\
\Gamma \vdash_{\mathsf{v}} \mathsf{case\,inl}\, V\, \mathsf{of}\, \{\mathsf{inl}\, x.\, W_1, \mathsf{inr}\, y.\, W_2\} &\equiv W_1[x \mapsto V] \;:\; B\\
\Gamma \vdash_{\mathsf{v}} \mathsf{case\,inr}\, V\, \mathsf{of}\, \{\mathsf{inl}\, x.\, W_1, \mathsf{inr}\, y.\, W_2\} &\equiv W_2[y \mapsto V] \;:\; B\\
\Gamma \vdash \mathsf{force}(\mathsf{thunk}\, M) &\equiv M \;:\; \underline{C}\\
\Gamma \vdash i\,\text{`}\,\lambda\{i.\, M_i\}_{i \in I} &\equiv M_i \;:\; \underline{C}_i\\
\Gamma \vdash V\,\text{`}\,\lambda x.\, M &\equiv M[x \mapsto V] \;:\; \underline{C}\\
\Gamma \vdash \mathsf{return}\, V\, \mathsf{to}\, x.\, M &\equiv M[x \mapsto V] \;:\; \underline{C}\\
\Gamma \vdash \mathsf{return}\, V\, \mathsf{need}\, \underline{x}.\, M &\equiv M[\underline{x} \mapsto \mathsf{return}\, V] \;:\; \underline{C}
\end{aligned}$$

(a) β laws

$$\begin{aligned}
\Gamma \vdash_{\mathsf{v}} () &\equiv V \;:\; \mathbf{unit}\\
\Gamma \vdash_{\mathsf{v}} (\mathsf{fst}\, V, \mathsf{snd}\, V) &\equiv V \;:\; A_1 \times A_2\\
\Gamma \vdash_{\mathsf{v}} \mathsf{case}\, W\, \mathsf{of}\, \{\mathsf{inl}\, y.\, V[x \mapsto \mathsf{inl}\, y], \mathsf{inr}\, z.\, V[x \mapsto \mathsf{inr}\, z]\} &\equiv V[x \mapsto W] \;:\; B\\
\Gamma \vdash_{\mathsf{v}} \mathsf{thunk}(\mathsf{force}\, M) &\equiv M \;:\; \mathbf{U}\underline{C}\\
\Gamma \vdash \lambda\{i.\, i\,\text{`}\, M\}_{i \in I} &\equiv M \;:\; \textstyle\prod_{i \in I} \underline{C}_i\\
\Gamma \vdash \lambda x.\, x\,\text{`}\, M &\equiv M \;:\; A \to \underline{C}\\
\Gamma \vdash M\, \mathsf{to}\, x.\, \mathsf{return}\, x &\equiv M \;:\; \mathbf{Fr}\, A
\end{aligned}$$

(b) η laws

$$\begin{aligned}
\Gamma \vdash M\, \mathsf{need}\, \underline{x}.\, \underline{x}\, \mathsf{to}\, y.\, N &\equiv M\, \mathsf{to}\, y.\, N[\underline{x} \mapsto \mathsf{return}\, y] \;:\; \underline{C}\\
\Gamma \vdash M\, \mathsf{need}\, \underline{x}.\, N &\equiv N \;:\; \underline{C}
\end{aligned}$$

$$\begin{aligned}
\Gamma \vdash \lambda\{i.\, M\, \mathsf{to}\, x.\, N_i\}_{i \in I} &\equiv M\, \mathsf{to}\, x.\, \lambda\{i.\, N_i\}_{i \in I} \;:\; \textstyle\prod_{i \in I} \underline{C}_i\\
\Gamma \vdash \lambda y.\, M\, \mathsf{to}\, x.\, N &\equiv M\, \mathsf{to}\, x.\, \lambda y.\, N \;:\; A \to \underline{C}\\
\Gamma \vdash \lambda\{i.\, M\, \mathsf{need}\, \underline{x}.\, N_i\}_{i \in I} &\equiv M\, \mathsf{need}\, \underline{x}.\, \lambda\{i.\, N_i\}_{i \in I} \;:\; \textstyle\prod_{i \in I} \underline{C}_i\\
\Gamma \vdash \lambda y.\, M\, \mathsf{need}\, \underline{x}.\, N &\equiv M\, \mathsf{need}\, \underline{x}.\, \lambda y.\, N \;:\; A \to \underline{C}
\end{aligned}$$

$$\begin{aligned}
\Gamma \vdash (M_1\, \mathsf{to}\, x.\, M_2)\, \mathsf{to}\, y.\, M_3 &\equiv M_1\, \mathsf{to}\, x.\, M_2\, \mathsf{to}\, y.\, M_3 \;:\; \underline{C}\\
\Gamma \vdash M_1\, \mathsf{to}\, x.\, M_2\, \mathsf{need}\, \underline{y}.\, M_3 &\equiv M_2\, \mathsf{need}\, \underline{y}.\, M_1\, \mathsf{to}\, x.\, M_3 \;:\; \underline{C}\\
\Gamma \vdash (M_1\, \mathsf{need}\, \underline{x}.\, M_2)\, \mathsf{to}\, y.\, M_3 &\equiv M_1\, \mathsf{need}\, \underline{x}.\, M_2\, \mathsf{to}\, y.\, M_3 \;:\; \underline{C}\\
\Gamma \vdash (M_1\, \mathsf{need}\, \underline{x}.\, M_2)\, \mathsf{need}\, \underline{y}.\, M_3 &\equiv M_1\, \mathsf{need}\, \underline{x}.\, M_2\, \mathsf{need}\, \underline{y}.\, M_3 \;:\; \underline{C}
\end{aligned}$$

(c) Sequencing axioms

Fig. 3. Equational theory of ECBPV

of a tuple can be used within a single computation (without thunking), so the effects still will not happen twice. (There is a similar consideration for functions, which can only be applied once.) The remainder of the axioms never duplicate need-bound terms that might have effects.

The majority of the axioms of the equational theory are standard. Only the axioms involving need are new; these are highlighted. The first new sequencing axiom (in Fig. 3c) is the crucial one. It states that if a computation will next evaluate $\underline{x}$, where $\underline{x}$ is a computation variable bound to M, then this is the same as evaluating M, and then using the result for subsequent uses of $\underline{x}$. In particular, this axiom (together with the η law for $\mathbf{Fr}$) implies that $M \;\mathsf{need}\; \underline{x}.\, \underline{x} \;\equiv\; M$.

The second sequencing axiom does *garbage collection* [22]: if a computation bound by need is not used (because the variable does not appear), then the binding can be dropped. This equation implies, for example, that

$$M_1 \;\mathsf{need}\; \underline{x}_1.\, M_2 \;\mathsf{need}\; \underline{x}_2. \cdots M_n \;\mathsf{need}\; \underline{x}_n.\, \mathsf{return}\,() \;\equiv\; \mathsf{return}\,()$$

The next four sequencing axioms (two from CBPV and two new) state that binding a computation with to or need commutes with the remaining forms of computation terms. These allow to and need to be moved to the outside of other constructs *except* thunks. The final four axioms (one from CBPV and three new) capture associativity and commutativity involving need and to; again these parallel the existing simple associativity axiom for to.

Note that associativity between different evaluation orders is not necessarily valid. In particular, we do not have

$$(M_1 \;\mathsf{to}\; x.\, M_2) \;\mathsf{need}\; \underline{y}.\, M_3 \quad\equiv\quad M_1 \;\mathsf{to}\; x.\, (M_2 \;\mathsf{need}\; \underline{x}.\, M_3)$$

(The first term might not evaluate M_1, the second always does.) This is usually the case when evaluation orders are mixed [26].

These final two groups allow computation terms to be placed in normal forms where bindings of computations are on the outside. (Compare this with the translation of source-language *answers* given in Sect. 3.2.) Finally, the β law for need (in Fig. 3a) parallels the usual β law for to: it gives the behaviour of computation terms that return values without having any effects.

The above equational theory induces a notion of *contextual equivalence* $\cong_{\mathsf{ctx}}$ between ECBPV terms. Two terms are contextually equivalent when they have no observable differences in behaviour. When we discuss *equivalences between evaluation orders* in Sect. 3, $\cong_{\mathsf{ctx}}$ is the notion of *equivalence between terms* that we consider.

Contextual equivalence is defined as follows. The *ground types* G are the value types that do not contain thunks:

$$G ::= \mathbf{unit} \mid G_1 \times G_2 \mid G_1 + G_2$$

A *value-term context* $\mathcal{C}[-]$ is a computation term with a single hole (written $-$), which occurs in a position where a value term is expected. We write $\mathcal{C}[V]$ for the computation term that results from replacing the hole with V. Similarly, *computation-term contexts* $\underline{\mathcal{C}}[-]$ are computation terms with a single hole where a computation term is expected, and $\underline{\mathcal{C}}[M]$ is the term in which the hole is replaced by M. Contextual equivalence says that the terms cannot be distinguished by closed computations that return ground types. (Recall that $\diamond$ is the empty typing context.)

Definition 2 (Contextual equivalence). *There are two judgement forms of* contextual equivalence.

1. *Between value terms:* $\Gamma \vdash_{\mathrm{v}} V \cong_{\mathrm{ctx}} W : A$ *if* $\Gamma \vdash_{\mathrm{v}} V : A$, $\Gamma \vdash_{\mathrm{v}} W : A$, *and for all ground types* G *and value-term contexts* $\mathcal{C}$ *such that* $\diamond \vdash \mathcal{C}[V] : \mathbf{Fr}\, G$ *and* $\diamond \vdash \mathcal{C}[W] : \mathbf{Fr}\, G$ *we have*
$$\diamond \vdash \mathcal{C}[V] \equiv \mathcal{C}[W] : \mathbf{Fr}\, G$$
2. *Between computation terms:* $\Gamma \vdash M \cong_{\mathrm{ctx}} N : \underline{C}$ *if* $\Gamma \vdash M : \underline{C}$, $\Gamma \vdash N : \underline{C}$, *and for all ground types* G *and computation-term contexts* $\underline{\mathcal{C}}[-]$ *such that* $\diamond \vdash \underline{\mathcal{C}}[M] : \mathbf{Fr}\, G$ *and* $\diamond \vdash \underline{\mathcal{C}}[N] : \mathbf{Fr}\, G$ *we have*
$$\diamond \vdash \underline{\mathcal{C}}[M] \equiv \underline{\mathcal{C}}[N] : \mathbf{Fr}\, G$$

3 Call-by-Name and Call-by-Need

Extended call-by-push-value can be used to prove equivalences between evaluation orders. In this section we prove a classic example: if the only effect in the source language is nontermination, then call-by-name is equivalent to call-by-need. We do this in two stages.

First, we show that call-by-name is equivalent to call-by-need *within* ECBPV (Sect. 3.1). Specifically, we show that

$$M \;\mathsf{name}\, \underline{x}.\, N \;\cong_{\mathrm{ctx}}\; M \;\mathsf{need}\, \underline{x}.\, N$$

(Recall that $M \;\mathsf{name}\, \underline{x}.\, N$ is syntactic sugar for $\mathsf{thunk}\, M \;\text{‘}\; \lambda y.\, N[\underline{x} \mapsto \mathsf{force}\, y]$.)

Second, an important corollary is that the meta-level reduction strategies are equivalent (Sect. 3.2). We show this by describing a lambda-calculus-based source language together with a call-by-name and a call-by-need operational semantics and giving sound (see Theorem 2) call-by-name and call-by-need translations into ECBPV. The former is based on the translation into the monadic metalanguage given by Moggi [25] (we expect Levy's translation [17] to work equally well). The call-by-need translation is new here, and its existence shows that ECBPV does indeed subsume call-by-need. We then show that given any source-language expression, the two translations give contextually equivalent ECBPV terms.

To model non-termination being our sole source-language effect, we use the ECBPV signature which contains a constant $\bot_A : \mathbf{U}\,(\mathbf{Fr}\, A)$ for each value type A, representing a thunked diverging computation. It is likely that our proofs still work if we have general fixed-point operators as constants, but for simplicity we do not consider this here. The constants $\bot_A$ enable us to define a diverging computation $\Omega_{\underline{C}}$ for each computation type $\underline{C}$:

$$\Omega_{\mathbf{Fr}A} := \mathsf{force}\,\bot_A \qquad \Omega_{\prod_{i\in I}\underline{C}_i} := \lambda\{i.\,\Omega_{\underline{C}_i}\}_{i\in I} \qquad \Omega_{A\to\underline{C}} := \lambda x.\,\Omega_{\underline{C}}$$

We characterise nontermination by augmenting the equational theory of Sect. 2.3 with the axiom

$$\Gamma \vdash \Omega_{\mathbf{Fr}A}\ \mathsf{to}\ x.\,M \equiv \Omega_{\underline{C}} : \underline{C} \qquad \text{(Omega)}$$

for each context Γ, value type A and computation type $\underline{C}$. In other words, diverging as part of a larger computation causes the entire computation to diverge. This is the only change to the equational theory we need to represent nontermination. In particular, we do not add additional axioms involving need.

3.1 The Equivalence at the Object (Internal) Level

In this section, we show our primary result that

$$M\ \mathsf{name}\ \underline{x}.\,N \ \cong_{\mathrm{ctx}}\ M\ \mathsf{need}\ \underline{x}.\,N$$

As is usually the case for proofs of contextual equivalence, we use *logical relations* to get a strong enough inductive hypothesis for the proof to go through. However, unlike the usual case, it does not suffice to relate *closed* terms. To see why, consider a closed term M of the form

$$\Omega_{\mathbf{Fr}A}\ \mathsf{need}\ \underline{x}.\,N_1\ \mathsf{to}\ y.\,N_2$$

If we relate only closed terms, then we do not learn anything about N_1 itself (since $\underline{x}$ may be free in it). We could attempt to proceed by considering the closed term $\Omega_{\mathbf{Fr}A}\ \mathsf{need}\ \underline{x}.\,N_1$. For example, if this returns a value V then $\underline{x}$ cannot have been evaluated and M should have the same behaviour as $\Omega_{\mathbf{Fr}A}\ \mathsf{need}\ \underline{x}.\,N_2[y \mapsto V]$. However, we get stuck when proving the last step. This is only a problem because $\Omega_{\mathbf{Fr}A}$ is a nonterminating computation: every terminating computation of returner type has the form $\mathsf{return}\,V$ (up to $\equiv$), and when these are bound using need we can eliminate the binding using the equation

$$\mathsf{return}\,V\ \mathsf{need}\ \underline{x}.\,M \equiv M[\underline{x} \mapsto \mathsf{return}\,V]$$

The solution is to relate terms that may have free computation variables (we do not need to consider free value variables). The free computation variables should be thought of as referring to nonterminating computations (because we can remove the bindings of variables that refer to terminating computations). We relate open terms using *Kripke logical relations of varying arity*, which were introduced by Jung and Tiuryn [12] to study lambda definability.

We need a number of definitions first. A context Γ' *weakens* another context Γ, written $\Gamma' \rhd \Gamma$, whenever Γ is a sublist of Γ'. For example, $(\Gamma, \underline{x} : \mathbf{Fr}\,A) \rhd \Gamma$. We define Term_A^{Γ} as the set of equivalence classes (up to the equational theory $\equiv$) of terms of value type A in context Γ, and similarly define $\underline{\text{Term}}^{\Gamma}_{\underline{D}}$ for computation types:

$$\text{Term}^{\Gamma}_{A} := \{[V]_{\equiv} \mid \Gamma \vdash_{\text{v}} V : A\} \qquad \underline{\text{Term}}^{\Gamma}_{\underline{D}} := \{[M]_{\equiv} \mid \Gamma \vdash M : \underline{D}\}$$

Since weakening is admissible for both typing judgements, $\Gamma' \rhd \Gamma$ implies that $\text{Term}^{\Gamma}_{A} \subseteq \text{Term}^{\Gamma'}_{A}$ and $\underline{\text{Term}}^{\Gamma}_{\underline{D}} \subseteq \underline{\text{Term}}^{\Gamma'}_{\underline{D}}$ (note the contravariance).

A *computation context*, ranged over by Δ, is a typing context that maps variables to computation types (i.e. has the form $\underline{x}_1 : \mathbf{Fr}\, A_1, \ldots, \underline{x}_n : \mathbf{Fr}\, A_n$). Variables in computation contexts refer to nonterminating computations for the proof of contextual equivalence. A *Kripke relation* is a family of binary relations indexed by computation contexts that respects weakening of terms:

Definition 3 (Kripke relation). *A* Kripke relation *R over a value type A (respectively a computation type $\underline{D}$) is a family of relations $R^{\Delta} \subseteq \text{Term}^{\Delta}_{A} \times \text{Term}^{\Delta}_{A}$ (respectively $R^{\Delta} \subseteq \underline{\text{Term}}^{\Delta}_{\underline{D}} \times \underline{\text{Term}}^{\Delta}_{\underline{D}}$) indexed by computation contexts Δ such that whenever $\Delta' \rhd \Delta$ we have $R^{\Delta} \subseteq R^{\Delta'}$.*

Note that we consider binary relations on equivalence classes of terms because we want to relate pairs of terms up to $\equiv$ (to prove contextual equivalence). The relations we define are *partial equivalence relations* (i.e. symmetric and transitive), though we do not explicitly use this fact.

We need the Kripke relations we define over computation terms to be closed under sequencing with nonterminating computations. (For the rest of this section, we omit the square brackets around equivalence classes.)

Definition 4. *A Kripke relation R over a computation type $\underline{C}$ is* closed under sequencing *if each of the following holds:*

1. *If $(\underline{x} : \mathbf{Fr}\, A) \in \Delta$ and $M, M' \in \underline{\text{Term}}^{\Delta, y:A}_{\underline{C}}$ then $(\underline{x}\ \mathsf{to}\ y.\, M, \underline{x}\ \mathsf{to}\ y.\, M') \in R^{\Delta}$.*
2. *The pair $(\Omega_{\underline{C}}, \Omega_{\underline{C}})$ is in R^{Δ}.*
3. *For all $(M, M') \in R^{\Delta, \underline{y}:\mathbf{Fr} A}$ and $N \in \{\Omega_{\mathbf{Fr} A}\} \cup \{\underline{x} \mid (\underline{x} : \mathbf{Fr}\, A) \in \Delta\}$, all four of the following pairs are in R^{Δ}:*

$$(N\ \mathsf{need}\ \underline{y}.\, M,\ N\ \mathsf{need}\ \underline{y}.\, M') \qquad (M[\underline{y} \mapsto N],\ M'[\underline{y} \mapsto N])$$
$$(M[\underline{y} \mapsto N],\ N\ \mathsf{need}\ \underline{y}.\, M') \qquad (N\ \mathsf{need}\ \underline{y}.\, M,\ M'[\underline{y} \mapsto N])$$

For the first case of the definition, recall that the computation variables in Δ refer to nonterminating computations. Hence the behaviour of M and M' are irrelevant (they are never evaluated), and we do not need to assume they are related.[3] The second case implies (using axiom Omega) that

$$(\Omega_{\mathbf{Fr} A}\ \mathsf{to}\ y.\, M, \Omega_{\mathbf{Fr} A}\ \mathsf{to}\ y.\, M') \in R^{\Delta}$$

[3] This is why it suffices to consider only computation contexts. If we had to relate M to M' then we would need to consider relations between terms with free value variables.

$$\boxed{R_A^\Delta \subseteq \mathrm{Term}_A^\Delta \times \mathrm{Term}_A^\Delta}$$

$$\begin{aligned}
R_{\mathbf{unit}}^\Delta &:= \{((),())\}\\
R_{A_1\times A_2}^\Delta &:= \{(V,V') \mid (\mathsf{fst}\,V, \mathsf{fst}\,V') \in R_{A_1}^\Delta \wedge (\mathsf{snd}\,V, \mathsf{snd}\,V') \in R_{A_2}^\Delta\}\\
R_{A_1+A_2}^\Delta &:= \{(\mathsf{inl}\,V, \mathsf{inl}\,V') \mid (V,V') \in R_{A_1}^\Delta\} \cup \{(\mathsf{inr}\,V, \mathsf{inr}\,V') \mid (V,V') \in R_{A_2}^\Delta\}\\
R_{\mathrm{U}\underline{C}}^\Delta &:= \{(V,V') \mid (\mathsf{force}\,V, \mathsf{force}\,V') \in R_{\underline{C}}^\Delta\}
\end{aligned}$$

$$\boxed{R_{\underline{C}}^\Delta \subseteq \underline{\mathrm{Term}}_{\underline{C}}^\Delta \times \underline{\mathrm{Term}}_{\underline{C}}^\Delta}$$

$$\begin{aligned}
R_{\mathbf{Fr}A} &:= \text{the smallest closed-under-sequencing Kripke relation such that}\\
&\qquad (V,V') \in R_A^\Delta \;\Rightarrow\; (\mathsf{return}\,V, \mathsf{return}\,V') \in R_{\mathbf{Fr}A}^\Delta\\
R_{\prod_{i\in I}\underline{C}_i}^\Delta &:= \{(M,M') \mid \forall i \in I.\ (i`M, i`M') \in R_{\underline{C}_i}^\Delta\}\\
R_{A\to\underline{C}}^\Delta &:= \{(M,M') \mid \forall \Delta', V, V'.\ \Delta' \rhd \Delta \wedge (V,V') \in R_A^{\Delta'} \;\Rightarrow\; (V`M, V'`M') \in R_{\underline{C}}^{\Delta'}\}
\end{aligned}$$

Fig. 4. Definition of the logical relation

mirroring the first case. The third case is the most important. It is similar to the first (it is there to ensure that the relation is closed under the primitives used to combine computations). However, since we are showing that need is contextually equivalent to substitution, we also want these to be related. We have to consider computation variables in the definition (as possible terms N) only because of our use of Kripke logical relations. For ordinary logical relations, there would be no free variables to consider.

The key part of the proof of contextual equivalence is the definition of the Kripke logical relation, which is a family of relations indexed by value and computation types. It is defined in Fig. 4 by induction on the structure of the types. In the figure, we again omit square brackets around equivalence classes.

The definition of the logical relation on ground types (**unit**, sum types and product types) is standard. Since the only way to use a thunk is to force it, the definition on thunk types just requires the two forced computations to be related.

For returner types, we want any pair of computations that return related values to be related. We also want the relation to be closed under sequencing, in order to show the fundamental lemma (below) for to and need. We therefore define $R_{\mathbf{Fr}A}$ as the smallest such Kripke relation. For products of computation types the definition is similar to products of value types: we require that each of the projections are related. For function types, we require as usual that related arguments are sent to related results. For this to define a Kripke relation, we have to quantify over all computation contexts Δ' that weaken Δ, because of the contravariance of the argument.

The relations we define are Kripke relations. Using the sequencing axioms of the equational theory, and the β and η laws for computation types, we can show that $R_{\underline{C}}$ is closed under sequencing for each computation type $\underline{C}$. These facts are important for the proof of the fundamental lemma.

Substitutions are given by the following grammar:

$$\sigma ::= \diamond \mid \sigma, x \mapsto V \mid \sigma, \underline{x} \mapsto M$$

We have a typing judgement $\Delta \vdash \sigma : \Gamma$ for substitutions, meaning in the context Δ the terms in σ have the types given in Γ. This is defined as follows:

$$\frac{}{\Delta \vdash \diamond : \diamond} \qquad \frac{\Delta \vdash \sigma : \Gamma \qquad \Delta \vdash_{\mathrm{v}} V : A}{\Delta \vdash (\sigma, x \mapsto V) : (\Gamma, x : A)} \qquad \frac{\Delta \vdash \sigma : \Gamma \qquad \Delta \vdash M : \mathbf{Fr}\, A}{\Delta \vdash (\sigma, \underline{x} \mapsto M) : (\Gamma, \underline{x} : \mathbf{Fr}\, A)}$$

We write $V[\sigma]$ and $M[\sigma]$ for the applications of the substitution σ to value terms V and computation terms M. These are defined by induction on the structure of the terms. The key property of the substitution typing judgement is that if $\Delta \vdash \sigma : \Gamma$, then $\Gamma \vdash_{\mathrm{v}} V : A$ implies $\Delta \vdash_{\mathrm{v}} V[\sigma] : A$ and $\Gamma \vdash M : \underline{C}$ implies $\Delta \vdash M[\sigma] : \underline{C}$. The equational theory gives us an obvious pointwise equivalence relation $\equiv$ on well-typed substitutions. We define sets $\mathrm{Subst}_{\Gamma}^{\Delta}$ of equivalence classes of substitutions, and extend the logical relation by defining $R_{\Gamma}^{\Delta} \subseteq \mathrm{Subst}_{\Gamma}^{\Delta} \times \mathrm{Subst}_{\Gamma}^{\Delta}$:

$$\begin{aligned}
\mathrm{Subst}_{\Gamma}^{\Delta} &:= \{[\sigma]_{\equiv} \mid \Delta \vdash \sigma : \Gamma\} \\
R_{\diamond}^{\Delta} &:= \{(\diamond, \diamond)\} \\
R_{\Gamma, x:A}^{\Delta} &:= \{((\sigma, x \mapsto V), (\sigma', x \mapsto V')) \mid (\sigma, \sigma') \in R_{\Gamma}^{\Delta} \wedge (V, V') \in R_{A}^{\Delta}\} \\
R_{\Gamma, \underline{x}:\mathbf{Fr}A}^{\Delta} &:= \{((\sigma, \underline{x} \mapsto M), (\sigma', \underline{x} \mapsto M')) \mid (\sigma, \sigma') \in R_{\Gamma}^{\Delta} \wedge (M, M') \in R_{\mathbf{Fr}A}^{\Delta}\}
\end{aligned}$$

As usual, the logical relations satisfy a *fundamental lemma*.

Lemma 1 (Fundamental)

1. *For all value terms* $\Gamma \vdash_{\mathrm{v}} V : A$,

$$(\sigma, \sigma') \in R_{\Gamma}^{\Delta} \quad \Rightarrow \quad (V[\sigma], V[\sigma']) \in R_{A}^{\Delta}$$

2. *For all computation terms* $\Gamma \vdash M : \underline{C}$,

$$(\sigma, \sigma') \in R_{\Gamma}^{\Delta} \quad \Rightarrow \quad (M[\sigma], M[\sigma']) \in R_{\underline{C}}^{\Delta}$$

The proof is by induction on the structure of the terms. We use the fact that each $R_{\underline{C}}$ is closed under sequencing for the `to` and `need` cases. For the latter, we also use the fact that the relations respect weakening of terms.

We also have the following two facts about the logical relation. The first roughly is that `name` is related to `need` by the logical relation, and is true because of the additional pairs that are related in the definition of closed-under-sequencing (Definition 4).

Lemma 2. *For all computation terms* $\Gamma \vdash M : \mathbf{Fr}\, A$ *and* $\Gamma, \underline{x} : \mathbf{Fr}\, A \vdash N : \underline{C}$ *we have*

$$(\sigma, \sigma') \in R_{\Gamma}^{\Delta} \quad \Rightarrow \quad ((N[\underline{x} \mapsto M])[\sigma], (M \,\mathsf{need}\, \underline{x}.\, N)[\sigma']) \in R_{\underline{C}}^{\Delta}$$

The second fact is that related terms are contextually equivalent.

Lemma 3

1. *For all value terms* $\Gamma \vdash_{\mathrm{v}} V : A$ *and* $\Gamma \vdash_{\mathrm{v}} V' : A$, *if* $(V[\sigma], V'[\sigma']) \in R_A^{\Delta}$ *for all* $(\sigma, \sigma') \in R_{\Gamma}^{\Delta}$ *then*

$$\Gamma \vdash_{\mathrm{v}} V \cong_{\mathrm{ctx}} V' : A$$

2. *For all computation terms* $\Gamma \vdash M : \underline{C}$ *and* $\Gamma \vdash M' : \underline{C}$, *if* $(M[\sigma], M'[\sigma']) \in R_{\underline{C}}^{\Delta}$ *for all* $(\sigma, \sigma') \in R_{\Gamma}^{\Delta}$ *then*

$$\Gamma \vdash M \cong_{\mathrm{ctx}} M' : \underline{C}$$

This gives us enough to achieve the goal of this section.

Theorem 1. *For all computation terms* $\Gamma \vdash M : \mathbf{Fr}\, A$ *and* $\Gamma, \underline{x} : \mathbf{Fr}\, A \vdash N : \underline{C}$, *we have*

$$\Gamma \vdash M \,\mathsf{name}\, \underline{x}.\, N \cong_{\mathrm{ctx}} M \,\mathsf{need}\, \underline{x}.\, N : \underline{C}$$

3.2 The Meta-level Equivalence

In this section, we show that the equivalence between call-by-name and call-by-need also holds on the meta-level; this is a consequence of the object-level theorem, rather than something that is proved from scratch as it would be in a term rewriting system.

To do this, we describe a simple lambda-calculus-based source language with divergence as the only side-effect and give it a call-by-name and a call-by-need operational semantics. We then describe two translations from the source language into ECBPV. The first is a call-by-name translation based on the embedding of call-by-name in Moggi's [25] monadic metalanguage. The second is a call-by-need translation that uses our new constructs. The latter witnesses the fact that ECBPV does actually support call-by-need. Finally, we show that the two translations give contextually equivalent ECBPV terms.

The syntax, type system and operational semantics of the source language are given in Fig. 5. Most of this is standard. We include only booleans and function types for simplicity. In expressions, we include a constant $\mathsf{diverge}_A$ for each type A, representing a diverging computation. (As before, it should not be difficult to replace these with general fixed-point operators.) In typing contexts, we assume that all variables are distinct, and omit the required side-condition from the figure. There is a single set of variables $x, y, \ldots$; we implicitly map these to ECBPV value or computation variables as required.

Types	$A, B ::= \mathbf{bool} \mid A \to B$
Contexts	$\Gamma ::= \diamond \mid \Gamma, x : A$
Expressions	$e ::= x \mid \mathsf{diverge}_A \mid \mathsf{true} \mid \mathsf{false} \mid \mathsf{if}\ e_1\ \mathsf{then}\ e_2\ \mathsf{else}\ e_3 \mid \lambda x.\, e \mid e_1\, e_2$

(a) Syntax

$$\frac{}{\Gamma \vdash x : A}\ \text{if } (x : A) \in \Gamma \qquad \frac{}{\Gamma \vdash \mathsf{diverge}_A : A}$$

$$\frac{}{\Gamma \vdash \mathsf{true} : \mathbf{bool}} \qquad \frac{}{\Gamma \vdash \mathsf{false} : \mathbf{bool}} \qquad \frac{\Gamma \vdash e_1 : \mathbf{bool} \qquad \Gamma \vdash e_2 : A \qquad \Gamma \vdash e_3 : A}{\Gamma \vdash \mathsf{if}\ e_1\ \mathsf{then}\ e_2\ \mathsf{else}\ e_3 : A}$$

$$\frac{\Gamma, x : A \vdash e : B}{\Gamma \vdash \lambda x.\, e : A \to B} \qquad \frac{\Gamma \vdash e_1 : A \to B \qquad \Gamma \vdash e_2 : A}{\Gamma \vdash e_1\, e_2 : B}$$

(b) Typing

$$\mathsf{if\ true\ then}\ e_2\ \mathsf{else}\ e_3 \overset{\text{name}}{\rightsquigarrow} e_2 \qquad \mathsf{diverge}_A \overset{\text{name}}{\rightsquigarrow} \mathsf{diverge}_A$$

$$\mathsf{if\ false\ then}\ e_2\ \mathsf{else}\ e_3 \overset{\text{name}}{\rightsquigarrow} e_3 \qquad \mathsf{if}\ \mathsf{diverge}_{\mathbf{bool}}\ \mathsf{then}\ e_2\ \mathsf{else}\ e_3 \overset{\text{name}}{\rightsquigarrow} \mathsf{diverge}_A$$

$$(\lambda x.\, e)\, e' \overset{\text{name}}{\rightsquigarrow} e[x \mapsto e'] \qquad \mathsf{diverge}_{A \to B}\, e' \overset{\text{name}}{\rightsquigarrow} \mathsf{diverge}_B$$

$$\frac{e_1 \overset{\text{name}}{\rightsquigarrow} e_1'}{\mathsf{if}\ e_1\ \mathsf{then}\ e_2\ \mathsf{else}\ e_3 \overset{\text{name}}{\rightsquigarrow} \mathsf{if}\ e_1'\ \mathsf{then}\ e_2\ \mathsf{else}\ e_3} \qquad \frac{e_1 \overset{\text{name}}{\rightsquigarrow} e_1'}{e_1\, e_2 \overset{\text{name}}{\rightsquigarrow} e_1'\, e_2}$$

(c) Call-by-name operational semantics

Evaluation contexts	$E[-] ::= - \mid \mathsf{if}\ E[-]\ \mathsf{then}\ e_2\ \mathsf{else}\ e_3$
	$\mid E[-]\, e_2 \mid (\lambda x.\, E[x])\, E'[-] \mid (\lambda x.\, E[-])\, e_2$
Values	$v ::= \mathsf{true} \mid \mathsf{false} \mid \lambda x.\, e$
Answers	$a ::= v \mid (\lambda x.\, a)\, e$

$$\mathsf{if\ true\ then}\ e_2\ \mathsf{else}\ e_3 \overset{\text{need}}{\rightsquigarrow} e_2 \qquad \mathsf{diverge}_A \overset{\text{need}}{\rightsquigarrow} \mathsf{diverge}_A$$

$$\mathsf{if\ false\ then}\ e_2\ \mathsf{else}\ e_3 \overset{\text{need}}{\rightsquigarrow} e_3 \qquad E[\mathsf{diverge}_A] \overset{\text{need}}{\rightsquigarrow} \mathsf{diverge}_B$$

$$(\lambda x.\, E[x])\, v \overset{\text{need}}{\rightsquigarrow} (\lambda x.\, E[v])\, v$$

$$(\lambda x.\, a)\, e_1\, e_2 \overset{\text{need}}{\rightsquigarrow} (\lambda x.\, a\, e_2)\, e_1 \qquad \frac{e \overset{\text{need}}{\rightsquigarrow} e'}{E[e] \overset{\text{need}}{\rightsquigarrow} E[e']}$$

$$(\lambda x.\, E[x])\, ((\lambda y.\, a)\, e) \overset{\text{need}}{\rightsquigarrow} (\lambda y.\, (\lambda x.\, E[x])\, a)\, e$$

(d) Call-by-need operational semantics

Fig. 5. The source language

The call-by-name operational semantics is straightforward; its small-step reductions are written $e \overset{\text{name}}{\rightsquigarrow} e'$.

The call-by-need operational semantics is based on Ariola and Felleisen [2]. The only differences between the source language and Ariola and Felleisen's calculus are the addition of booleans, $\mathsf{diverge}_A$, and a type system. It is likely that we can translate other call-by-need calculi, such as those of Launchbury [16] and Maraist et al. [22]. Call-by-need small-step reductions are written $e \overset{\text{need}}{\leadsto} e'$.

The call-by-need semantics needs some auxiliary definitions. An *evaluation context* $E[-]$ is a source-language expression with a single hole, picked from the grammar given in the figure. The hole in an evaluation context indicates where reduction is currently taking place: it says which part of the expression is currently *needed*. We write $E[e]$ for the expression in which the hole is replaced with e. A (source-language) *value* is the result of a computation (the word value should not be confused with the value terms of extended call-by-push-value). An *answer* is a value in some *environment*, which maps variables to expressions. These can be thought of as *closures*. The environment is encoded in an answer using application and lambda abstraction: the answer $(\lambda x.\, a)\, e$ means the answer a where the environment maps x to e. Encoding environments in this way makes the translation slightly simpler than if we had used a Launchbury-style [16] call-by-need language with explicit environments. In the latter case, the translation would need to encode the environments. Here they are already encoded inside expressions. Answers are terminal computations: they do not reduce.

The first two reduction axioms (on the left) of the call-by-need semantics (Fig. 5d) are obvious. The third axiom is the most important: it states that if the subexpression currently being evaluated is a variable x, and the environment maps x to a source-language value v, then that use of x can be replaced with v. Note that $E[v]$ may contain other uses of x; the replacement only occurs when the value is actually needed. This axiom roughly corresponds to the first sequencing axiom of the equational theory of ECBPV (in Fig. 3c). The fourth and fifth axioms of the call-by-need operational semantics rearrange the environment into a standard form. Both use a syntactic restriction to answers so that each expression has at most one reduct (this restriction is not needed to ensure that $\overset{\text{need}}{\leadsto}$ captures call-by-need). The rule on the right of the Fig. 5d states that the reduction relation is a congruence (a needed subexpression can be reduced).

The two translations from the source language to ECBPV are given in Fig. 6. The translation of types (Fig. 6a) is shared between call-by-name and call-by-need. The two translations differ only for contexts and expressions. Types A are translated into value types $(\!|A|\!)$. The type **bool** becomes the two-element sum type **unit** + **unit**. The translation of a function type $A \to B$ is a thunked CBPV function type. The argument is a thunk of a computation that returns an $(\!|A|\!)$, and the result is a computation that returns a $(\!|B|\!)$.

For call-by-name (Fig. 6b), contexts Γ are translated into contexts $(\!|\Gamma|\!)^{\text{name}}$ that contain thunks of computations. We could also have used contexts containing computation variables (omitting the thunks), but choose to use thunks to keep the translation as close as possible to previous translations into call-by-push-value. A well-typed expression $\Gamma \vdash e : A$ is translated into a ECBPV computation term $(\!|e|\!)^{\text{name}}$ that returns $(\!|A|\!)$, in context $(\!|\Gamma|\!)^{\text{name}}$. The translation

$$(\!|\mathbf{bool}|\!) := \mathbf{unit} + \mathbf{unit} \qquad (\!|A \to B|\!) := \mathbf{U}\,(\mathbf{U}\,(\mathbf{Fr}\,(\!|A|\!)) \to \mathbf{Fr}\,(\!|B|\!))$$

(a) Translation $(\!|A|\!)$ of types

Translation $(\!|\Gamma|\!)^{\mathrm{name}}$ of typing contexts

$$(\!|\diamond|\!)^{\mathrm{name}} := \diamond \qquad (\!|\Gamma, x : A|\!)^{\mathrm{name}} := (\!|\Gamma|\!)^{\mathrm{name}}, x : \mathbf{U}\,(\mathbf{Fr}\,(\!|A|\!))$$

Translation $(\!|\Gamma|\!)^{\mathrm{name}} \vdash (\!|e|\!)^{\mathrm{name}} : \mathbf{Fr}\,(\!|A|\!)$ of expressions

$$\begin{aligned}
(\!|x|\!)^{\mathrm{name}} &:= \mathsf{force}\,x & (\!|\mathsf{diverge}_A|\!)^{\mathrm{name}} &:= \mathsf{force}\,\bot_A \\
(\!|\mathsf{true}|\!)^{\mathrm{name}} &:= \mathsf{return}\,\mathsf{inl}\,() & (\!|\mathsf{false}|\!)^{\mathrm{name}} &:= \mathsf{return}\,\mathsf{inr}\,() \\
(\!|\mathsf{if}\ e_1\ \mathsf{then}\ e_2\ \mathsf{else}\ e_3|\!)^{\mathrm{name}} &:= (\!|e_1|\!)^{\mathrm{name}}\ \mathsf{to}\ x.\ \mathsf{force}(\mathsf{case}\,x\,\mathsf{of} \\
&\qquad \{\mathsf{inl}\,z.\ \mathsf{thunk}(\!|e_2|\!)^{\mathrm{name}}, \mathsf{inr}\,z.\ \mathsf{thunk}(\!|e_3|\!)^{\mathrm{name}}\}) \\
(\!|\lambda x.\,e|\!)^{\mathrm{name}} &:= \mathsf{return}\,\mathsf{thunk}(\lambda x.\ (\!|e|\!)^{\mathrm{name}}) \\
(\!|e_1\,e_2|\!)^{\mathrm{name}} &:= (\!|e_1|\!)^{\mathrm{name}}\ \mathsf{to}\ z.\ (\mathsf{thunk}\,(\!|e_2|\!)^{\mathrm{name}})\ \text{`}\ (\mathsf{force}\,z)
\end{aligned}$$

(b) Call-by-name translation

Translation $(\!|\Gamma|\!)^{\mathrm{need}}$ of typing contexts

$$(\!|\diamond|\!)^{\mathrm{need}} := \diamond \qquad (\!|\Gamma, x : A|\!)^{\mathrm{need}} := (\!|\Gamma|\!)^{\mathrm{need}}, \underline{x} : \mathbf{Fr}\,(\!|A|\!)$$

Translation $(\!|\Gamma|\!)^{\mathrm{need}} \vdash (\!|e|\!)^{\mathrm{need}} : \mathbf{Fr}\,(\!|A|\!)$ of expressions

$$\begin{aligned}
(\!|x|\!)^{\mathrm{need}} &:= \underline{x} & (\!|\mathsf{diverge}_A|\!)^{\mathrm{need}} &:= \mathsf{force}\,\bot_A \\
(\!|\mathsf{true}|\!)^{\mathrm{need}} &:= \mathsf{return}\,\mathsf{inl}\,() & (\!|\mathsf{false}|\!)^{\mathrm{need}} &:= \mathsf{return}\,\mathsf{inr}\,() \\
(\!|\mathsf{if}\ e_1\ \mathsf{then}\ e_2\ \mathsf{else}\ e_3|\!)^{\mathrm{need}} &:= (\!|e_1|\!)^{\mathrm{need}}\ \mathsf{to}\ x.\ \mathsf{force}(\mathsf{case}\,x\,\mathsf{of} \\
&\qquad \{\mathsf{inl}\,z.\ \mathsf{thunk}(\!|e_2|\!)^{\mathrm{need}}, \mathsf{inr}\,z.\ \mathsf{thunk}(\!|e_3|\!)^{\mathrm{need}}\}) \\
(\!|\lambda x.\,e|\!)^{\mathrm{need}} &:= \mathsf{return}\,\mathsf{thunk}(\lambda x'.\ (\mathsf{force}\,x')\ \mathsf{need}\ \underline{x}.\ (\!|e|\!)^{\mathrm{need}}) \\
(\!|e_1\,e_2|\!)^{\mathrm{need}} &:= (\!|e_1|\!)^{\mathrm{need}}\ \mathsf{to}\ z.\ (\mathsf{thunk}\,(\!|e_2|\!)^{\mathrm{need}})\ \text{`}\ (\mathsf{force}\,z)
\end{aligned}$$

(c) Call-by-need translation

Fig. 6. Translation from the source language to ECBPV

of variables just forces the relevant variable in the context. The diverging computations $\mathsf{diverge}_A$ just use the diverging constants from our ECBPV signature. The translations of true and false are simple: they are computations that immediately return one of the elements of the sum type **unit** + **unit**. The translation of if e_1 then e_2 else e_3 first evaluates $(\!|e_1|\!)^{\mathrm{name}}$, then uses the result to choose between $(\!|e_2|\!)^{\mathrm{name}}$ and $(\!|e_3|\!)^{\mathrm{name}}$. Lambdas are translated into computations that just return a thunked computation. Finally, application first evaluates the computation that returns a thunk of a function, and then forces this function, passing it a thunk of the argument.

For call-by-need (Fig. 6c), contexts Γ are translated into contexts $(\!|\Gamma|\!)^{\mathsf{need}}$, containing computations that return values. The computations in the context are all bound using need. An expression $\Gamma \vdash e : A$ is translated to a computation $(\!|e|\!)^{\mathsf{need}}$ that returns $(\!|A|\!)$ in the context $(\!|\Gamma|\!)^{\mathsf{need}}$. The typing is therefore similar to call-by-name. The key case is the translation of lambdas. These become computations that immediately return a thunk of a function. The function places the computation given as an argument onto the context using need, so that it is evaluated at most once, before executing the body. The remainder of the cases are similar to call-by-name.

Under the call-by-need translation, the expression $(\lambda x.\, e_1)\, e_2$ is translated into a term that executes the computation $(\!|e_1|\!)^{\mathsf{need}}$, and executes $(\!|e_2|\!)^{\mathsf{need}}$ only when needed. This is the case because, by the β rules for thunks, functions, and returner types:

$$(\!|(\lambda x.\, e_1)\, e_2|\!)^{\mathsf{need}} \equiv (\!|e_2|\!)^{\mathsf{need}}\ \mathsf{need}\ \underline{x}.\ (\!|e_1|\!)^{\mathsf{need}}$$

As a consequence, translations of answers are particularly simple: they have the following form (up to $\equiv$):

$$M_1\ \mathsf{need}\ \underline{x}_1.\ M_2\ \mathsf{need}\ \underline{x}_2.\ \cdots M_n\ \mathsf{need}\ \underline{x}_n.\ \mathsf{return}\ V$$

which intuitively means the value V in the environment mapping each $\underline{x}_i$ to M_i.

It is easy to see that both translations produce terms with the correct types. We prove that both translations are *sound*: if $e \overset{\mathsf{name}}{\rightsquigarrow} e'$ then $(\!|e|\!)^{\mathsf{name}} \equiv (\!|e'|\!)^{\mathsf{name}}$, and if $e \overset{\mathsf{need}}{\rightsquigarrow} e'$ then $(\!|e|\!)^{\mathsf{need}} \equiv (\!|e'|\!)^{\mathsf{need}}$. To do this for call-by-need, we first look at translations of evaluation contexts. The following lemma says the translation captures the idea that the hole in an evaluation context corresponds to the term being evaluated.

Lemma 4. *Define, for each evaluation context $E[-]$, the term $\mathcal{E}_y(\!|E[-]|\!)^{\mathsf{need}}$ by:*

$$\begin{aligned}
\mathcal{E}_y(\!|-|\!)^{\mathsf{need}} &:= \mathsf{return}\ y\\
\mathcal{E}_y(\!|\mathsf{if}\ E[-]\ \mathsf{then}\ e_2\ \mathsf{else}\ e_3|\!)^{\mathsf{need}} &:= \mathcal{E}(\!|E[-]|\!)^{\mathsf{need}}\ \mathsf{to}\ x.\ \mathsf{force}(\mathsf{case}\ x\ \mathsf{of}\\
&\qquad\qquad \{\mathsf{inl}\ z.\ \mathsf{thunk}(\!|e_2|\!)^{\mathsf{need}}\\
&\qquad\qquad ,\mathsf{inr}\ z.\ \mathsf{thunk}(\!|e_3|\!)^{\mathsf{need}}\})\\
\mathcal{E}_y(\!|E[-]\ e_2|\!)^{\mathsf{need}} &:= \mathcal{E}_y(\!|E[-]|\!)^{\mathsf{need}}\ \mathsf{to}\ z.\ \mathsf{thunk}(\!|e_2|\!)^{\mathsf{need}}\ \text{`}\ \mathsf{force}\ z\\
\mathcal{E}_y(\!|(\lambda x.\, E[x])\ E'[-]|\!)^{\mathsf{need}} &:= \mathcal{E}_y(\!|E'[-]|\!)^{\mathsf{need}}\ \mathsf{need}\ \underline{x}.\ (\!|E[x]|\!)^{\mathsf{need}}\\
\mathcal{E}_y(\!|(\lambda x.\, E[-])\ e_2|\!)^{\mathsf{need}} &:= (\!|e_2|\!)^{\mathsf{need}}\ \mathsf{need}\ \underline{x}.\ \mathcal{E}_y(\!|E[-]|\!)^{\mathsf{need}}
\end{aligned}$$

For each expression e we have:

$$(\!|E[e]|\!)^{\mathsf{need}} \equiv (\!|e|\!)^{\mathsf{need}}\ \mathsf{to}\ y.\ \mathcal{E}_y(\!|E[-]|\!)^{\mathsf{need}}$$

This lemma omits the typing of expressions for presentational purposes. It is easy to add suitable constraints on typing. Soundness is now easy to show:

Theorem 2 (Soundness). *For any two well-typed source-language expressions* $\Gamma \vdash e : A$ *and* $\Gamma \vdash e' : A$*:*

1. *If* $e \overset{\text{name}}{\leadsto} e'$ *then* $(\!|e|\!)^{\text{name}} \equiv (\!|e'|\!)^{\text{name}}$.
2. *If* $e \overset{\text{need}}{\leadsto} e'$ *then* $(\!|e|\!)^{\text{need}} \equiv (\!|e'|\!)^{\text{need}}$.

Now that we have sound call-by-name and call-by-need translations, we can state the meta-level equivalence formally. Suppose we are given a possibly open source-language expression $\Gamma \vdash e : B$. Recall that the call-by-need translation uses a context containing computation variables (i.e. $(\!|\Gamma|\!)^{\text{need}}$) and the call-by-name translation uses a context containing value variables, which map to thunks of computations. We have two ECBPV computation terms of type $\mathbf{Fr}\,(\!|B|\!)$ in context $(\!|\Gamma|\!)^{\text{need}}$: one is just $(\!|e|\!)^{\text{need}}$, the other is $(\!|e|\!)^{\text{name}}$ with all of its variables substituted with thunked computations. The theorem then states that these are contextually equivalent.

Theorem 3 (Equivalence between call-by-name and call-by-need). *For all source-language expressions* e *satisfying* $\underline{x}_1 : A_1, \ldots, \underline{x}_n : A_n \vdash e : B$

$$(\!|e|\!)^{\text{name}}[x_1 \mapsto \mathsf{thunk}\,\underline{x}_1, \ldots, x_n \mapsto \mathsf{thunk}\,\underline{x}_n] \quad \cong_{\text{ctx}} \quad (\!|e|\!)^{\text{need}}$$

Proof. The proof of this theorem is by induction on the typing derivation of e. The interesting case is lambda abstraction, where we use the internal equivalence between call-by-name and call-by-need (Theorem 1).

4 An Effect System for Extended Call-by-Push-Value

The equivalence between call-by-name and call-by-need in the previous section is predicated on the only effect in the language being nontermination. However, suppose the primitives of language have various effects (which means that in general the equivalence fails) but a given subprogram may be statically shown to have at most nontermination effects. In this case, we should be allowed to exploit the equivalence on the subprogram, interchanging call-by-need and call-by-name locally, even if the rest of the program uses other effects. In this section, we describe an *effect system* [20] for ECBPV, which statically estimates the side-effects of expressions, allowing us to exploit equivalences which hold only within subprograms. Effect systems can also be used for other purposes, such as proving the correctness of effect-dependent program transformations [7,29]. The ECBPV effect system also allows these.

Call-by-need makes statically estimating effects difficult. Computation variables bound using need might have effects on their first use, but on subsequent uses do not. Hence to precisely determine the effects of a term, we must track which variables have been used. McDermott and Mycroft [23] show how to achieve this for a call-by-need effect system; their technique can be adapted to ECBPV. Here we take a simpler approach. By slightly restricting the *effect algebras* we consider, we remove the need to track variable usage information, while still ensuring the effect information is not an underestimate (an underestimate would enable incorrect transformations). This can reduce the precision of the effect information obtained, but for our use case (determining equivalences between evaluation orders) this is not an issue, since we primarily care about which effects are used (rather than e.g. how many times they are used).

4.1 Effects

The effect system is parameterized by an *effect algebra*, which specifies the information that is tracked. Different effect algebras can be chosen for different applications. There are various forms of effect algebra. We follow Katsumata [15] and use *preordered monoids*, which are the most general.

Definition 5 (Preordered monoid). *A* preordered monoid $(\mathcal{F}, \leq, \cdot, 1)$ *consists of a monoid* $(\mathcal{F}, \cdot, 1)$ *and a preorder* $\leq$ *on* $\mathcal{F}$*, such that the binary operation* $\cdot$ *is monotone in each argument separately.*

Since we do not track variable usage information, we might misestimate the effect of a call-by-need computation variable evaluated for a second time (whose true effect is 1). To ensure this misestimate is an overestimate, we assume that the effect algebra is *pointed* (which is the case for most applications).

Definition 6 (Pointed preordered monoid). *A preordered monoid* $(\mathcal{F}, \leq, \cdot, 1)$ *is* pointed *if for all* $f \in \mathcal{F}$ *we have* $1 \leq f$.

The elements f of the set $\mathcal{F}$ are called *effects*. Each effect abstractly represents some potential side-effecting behaviours. The order $\leq$ provides *approximation* of effects. When $f \leq f'$ this means behaviours represented by f are included in those represented by f'. The binary operation $\cdot$ represents sequencing of effects, and 1 is the effect of a side-effect-free expression.

Traditional (*Gifford-style*) effect systems have some set Σ of *operations* (for example, $\Sigma := \{\mathsf{read}, \mathsf{write}\}$), and use the preordered monoid $(\mathcal{P}\Sigma, \subseteq, \cup, \emptyset)$. In these cases, an effect f is just a set of operations. If a computation has effect f then f contains all of the operations the computation *may* perform. They can therefore be used to enforce that computations do not use particular operations. Another example is the preordered monoid $(\mathbb{N}^{+}, \leq, +, 1)$, which can be used to count the number of possible results a nondeterministic computation can return (or to count the number of times an operation is used).

In our example, where we wish to establish whether the effects of an expression are restricted to nontermination for our main example, we use the two-element preorder $\{\mathsf{diveff} \leq \top\}$ with join for sequencing and diveff as the unit 1. The effect diveff means side-effects restricted to (at most) nontermination, and $\top$ means unrestricted side-effects. Thus we would enable the equivalence between call-by-name and call-by-need when the effect is diveff, and not when it is $\top$. All of these examples are pointed. Others can be found in the literature.

$$\boxed{A <:_{\mathrm{v}} B}$$

$$\frac{}{\textbf{unit} <:_{\mathrm{v}} \textbf{unit}} \qquad \frac{A_1 <:_{\mathrm{v}} B_1 \qquad A_2 <:_{\mathrm{v}} B_2}{A_1 \times A_2 <:_{\mathrm{v}} B_1 \times B_2} \qquad \frac{A_1 <:_{\mathrm{v}} B_1 \qquad A_2 <:_{\mathrm{v}} B_2}{A_1 + A_2 <:_{\mathrm{v}} B_1 + B_2}$$

$$\frac{\underline{C} <: \underline{D}}{\mathbf{U}\,\underline{C} <:_{\mathrm{v}} \mathbf{U}\,\underline{D}}$$

$$\boxed{\underline{C} <: \underline{D}}$$

$$\frac{(\underline{C}_i <: \underline{D}_i)_{i\in I}}{\prod_{i\in I} \underline{C}_i <: \prod_{i\in I} \underline{D}_i} \qquad \frac{A <:_{\mathrm{v}} B \qquad \underline{C} <: \underline{D}}{(B \to \underline{C}) <: (A \to \underline{D})} \qquad \frac{A <:_{\mathrm{v}} B}{\langle f\rangle A <: \langle f'\rangle B}\ \text{if } f \leq f'$$

Fig. 7. Subtyping in the ECBPV effect system

4.2 Effect System and Signature

The effect system includes effects within types. Specifically, each computation of returner type will have some side-effects when it is run, and hence each returner type $\mathbf{Fr}\,A$ is annotated with an element f of $\mathcal{F}$. We write the annotated type as $\langle f\rangle A$. Formally we replace the grammar of ECBPV computation types (and similarly, the grammar of typing contexts) with

$$\underline{C}, \underline{D} ::= \prod_{i\in I} \underline{C}_i \mid A \to \underline{C} \mid \boxed{\langle f\rangle A}$$

$$\Gamma ::= \diamond \mid \Gamma, x : A \mid \boxed{\Gamma, \underline{x} : \langle f\rangle A}$$

(The highlighted parts indicate the differences.) The grammar used for value types is unchanged, except that it uses the new syntax of computation types.

The definition of ECBPV signature is similarly extended to contain the effect algebra as well as the set of constants:

Definition 7 (Signature). *A* signature $(\mathcal{F}, \mathcal{K})$ *consists of a pointed preordered monoid* $(\mathcal{F}, \leq, \cdot, 1)$ *of effects and, for each value type* A*, a set* $\mathcal{K}_A$ *of constants of type* A*, including* $() \in \mathcal{K}_{\mathbf{unit}}$.

We assume a fixed effect system signature for the remainder of this section.

Since types contain effects, which have a notion of subeffecting, there is a natural notion of subtyping. We define (in Fig. 7) two subtyping relations: $A <:_{\mathrm{v}} B$ for value types and $\underline{C} <: \underline{D}$ for computation types.

We treat the type constructor $\langle f\rangle$ as an operation on computation types by defining computation types $\langle f\rangle \underline{C}$.

$$\langle f\rangle\Big(\prod_{i\in I} \underline{C}_i\Big) := \prod_{i\in I} \langle f\rangle \underline{C}_i \qquad \langle f\rangle (A \to \underline{C}) := A \to \langle f\rangle \underline{C} \qquad \langle f\rangle(\langle f'\rangle A) := \langle f \cdot f'\rangle A$$

This is an *action* of the preordered monoid on computation types. Its purpose is to give the typing rule for sequencing of computations. The sequencing of a computation with effect f with a computation of type $\underline{C}$ has type $\langle f\rangle \underline{C}$.

$$\frac{}{\Gamma \vdash \underline{x} : \langle f \rangle A} \text{ if } (\underline{x} : \langle f \rangle A) \in \Gamma \qquad \frac{\Gamma \vdash_{\mathsf{v}} V : A}{\Gamma \vdash \mathsf{return}\, V : \langle 1 \rangle A}$$

$$\frac{\Gamma \vdash M : \langle f \rangle A \qquad \Gamma, x : A \vdash N : \underline{C}}{\Gamma \vdash M\, \mathsf{to}\, x.\, N : \langle f \rangle \underline{C}} \qquad \frac{\Gamma \vdash M : \langle f \rangle A \qquad \Gamma, \underline{x} : \langle f \rangle A \vdash N : \underline{C}}{\Gamma \vdash M\, \mathsf{need}\, \underline{x}.\, N : \underline{C}}$$

$$\frac{\Gamma \vdash_{\mathsf{v}} V : A}{\Gamma \vdash_{\mathsf{v}} V : B} \text{ if } A <:_{\mathsf{v}} B \qquad \frac{\Gamma \vdash_{\mathsf{v}} M : \underline{C}}{\Gamma \vdash_{\mathsf{v}} N : \underline{D}} \text{ if } \underline{C} <: \underline{D}$$

Fig. 8. Effect system modifications to ECBPV

The typing judgements have exactly the same form as before (except for the new syntax of types). The majority of the typing rules, including all of the rules for value terms, are also unchanged. The only rules we change are those for computation variables, return, to and need, which are replaced with the first four rules in Fig. 8. We also add two subtyping rules, one for values and one for computations. These are the last two rules of Fig. 8.

The equational theory does not need to be changed to use it with the new effect system (except that the types appearing in each axiom now include effect information). For each axiom of the equational theory, the two terms still have the same type in the effect system. In particular, for the axiom

$$M\, \mathsf{need}\, \underline{x}.\, \underline{x}\, \mathsf{to}\, y.\, N \;\equiv\; M\, \mathsf{to}\, y.\, N[\underline{x} \mapsto \mathsf{return}\, y]$$

if $\Gamma \vdash M : \langle f \rangle A$ and $\Gamma, \underline{x} : \langle f \rangle A, y : A \vdash N : \underline{C}$ then the left-hand side has type $\langle f \rangle \underline{C}$. For the right-hand-side, we have $\Gamma, y : A \vdash N[\underline{x} \mapsto \mathsf{return}\, y] : \underline{C}$, because of the assumption that the preordered monoid is pointed (which implies $\mathsf{return}\, y$ can have *any* effect by subtyping, not just the unit effect 1). Hence the right-hand-side also has type $\langle f \rangle \underline{C}$. This axiom is the reason for our pointedness requirement. In particular, if we drop need from the language, the pointedness requirement is not required. Thus the rules we give also describe a fully general effect system for CBPV in which the effect algebra can be any preordered monoid.

4.3 Exploiting Effect-Dependent Equivalences

Our primary goal in adding an effect system to ECBPV is to exploit (local, effect-justified) equivalences between evaluation orders even without a whole-language restriction on effects. We sketch how to do this for our example.

When proving the equivalence between call-by-name and call-by-need in Sect. 3 we assumed that the only constants in the language were () and $\bot_A : \mathbf{U}\,(\mathbf{Fr}\, A)$. To relax this restriction, we use the effect algebra with preorder $\{\mathsf{diveff} \leq \top\}$ described above, and change the type of $\bot_A$ from $\mathbf{U}\,(\mathbf{Fr}\, A)$ to $\mathbf{U}\,(\langle \mathsf{diveff} \rangle A)$. We can include other effectful constants, and give them the effect $\top$ (e.g. $\mathsf{write} : \mathbf{U}\,(V \to \langle \top \rangle \mathbf{unit})$).

The statement of the internal (object-level) equivalence becomes:

$$\text{if } \Gamma \vdash M : \langle \mathsf{diveff} \rangle A \text{ and } \Gamma, \underline{x} : \langle \mathsf{diveff} \rangle A \vdash N : \underline{C} \text{ then}$$
$$\Gamma \vdash M \;\mathsf{name}\; \underline{x}.\, N \cong_{\mathrm{ctx}} M \;\mathsf{need}\; \underline{x}.\, N : \underline{C}$$

The premise restricts the effect of M to diveff so that nontermination is its only possible side-effect. To prove this equivalence, we need a logical relation for the effect system, which means we have to define a Kripke relation $R_{\langle f \rangle A}$ for each effect f. For $R_{\langle \mathsf{diveff} \rangle A}$ we use the same definition as before (the definition of $R_{\mathbf{Fr}A}$). The definition of $R_{\langle \top \rangle A}$ depends on the specific other effects included.

To state and prove a meta-level equivalence for a source language that includes other side-effects, we need to define an effect system for the source language. This would use the same effect algebra as the ECBPV effect system, and be such that the translation of source language expressions preserves effects. To do this for the source language of Sect. 3, we replace the syntax of function types with $\langle f \rangle A \xrightarrow{f'} B$, where f is the effect of the argument (required due to lazy evaluation), and f' is the latent effect of the function (the effect it has after application). The translation is then

$$(\!|\langle f \rangle A \xrightarrow{f'} B|\!) := \mathbf{U}\,(\mathbf{U}\,(\langle f \rangle (\!|A|\!)) \to \langle f' \rangle (\!|B|\!))$$

Just as for the object-level equivalence, the statement of the meta-level equivalence similarly requires the source-language expression to have the effect diveff. We omit the details here.

5 Related Work

Metalanguages for Evaluation Order. Call-by-push-value is similar to Moggi's monadic metalanguage [25], except for the distinction between computations and values. Both support several evaluation orders, but neither supports call-by-need. *Polarized* type theories [34] also take the approach of stratifying types into several kinds to capture multiple evaluation orders. Downen and Ariola [10] recently described how to capture call-by-need using polarity. They take a different approach to ours, by splitting up terms according to their evaluation order, rather than whether they might have effects. This means they have three kinds of type, resulting in a more complex language than ours. They also do not apply their language to reasoning about the differences between evaluation orders, which was the primary motivation for ECBPV. It is not clear whether their language can also be used for this purpose.

Multiple evaluation orders can also be captured in a Moggi-style language by using *joinads* instead of monads [28]. It is possible that there is some joinad structure implicit in extended call-by-push-value.

Reasoning About Call-by-Need. The majority of work on reasoning about call-by-need source languages has concentrated on operational semantics based on environments [16], graphs [30,32], and answers [2,3,9,22]. However, these do not compare call-by-need with other evaluation orders. The only type-based analysis of a lazy source language we know of apart from McDermott and Mycroft's effect system [23] is [31,33].

Logical Relations. Kripke logical relations have previously been applied to the problems of lambda definability [12] and normalization [1,11]. Previous proofs of contextual equivalence relate only closed terms. We were forced to relate open terms because of the need construct.

Reasoning about effects using logical relations often runs into a difficulty in ensuring the relations are closed under sequencing of computations. We are able to work around this due to our specific choice of effects. It is possible that considering other effects would require a technique such as Lindley and Stark's *leapfrog method* [18,19].

Effect Systems. Effect systems have a long history, starting with Gifford-style effect systems [20]. We use preordered monoids as effect algebras following Katsumata [15]. Almost all of the previous work on effect systems has concentrated on call-by-value only. Kammar and Plotkin [13,14] describe a Gifford-style call-by-push-value effect system, though their formulation does not generalise to other effect algebras. Our effect system is the first general effect system for a CBPV-like language. The only previous work on call-by-need effects is [23].

There has also been much work on reasoning about program transformations using effect systems, e.g. [4–8,29]. We expect it to be possible to recast much of this in terms of extended call-by-push-value, and therefore apply these transformations for various evaluation orders.

6 Conclusions and Future Work

We have described extended call-by-push-value, a calculus that can be used for reasoning about several evaluation orders. In particular, ECBPV supports call-by-need via the addition of the construct $M \ \mathsf{need}\ \underline{x}.\, N$. This allows us to prove that call-by-name and call-by-need reduction are equivalent if nontermination is the only effect in the source language, both inside the language itself, and on the meta-level. We proved the latter by giving two translations of a source language into ECBPV: one that captures call-by-name reduction, and one that captures call-by-need reduction. We also defined an effect system for ECBPV. The effect system statically bounds the side-effects of terms, allowing equivalences between evaluation orders to be used without restricting the entire language to particular effects. We close with a description of possible future work.

Other Equivalences Between Evaluation Orders. We have proved one example of an equivalence between evaluation orders using ECBPV, but there are others that we might also expect to hold. For example, we would expect call-by-need and call-by-value to be equivalent if the effects are restricted to nondeterminism, allocating state, and reading from state (but not writing). It should be possible to use ECBPV to prove these by defining suitable logical relations. More generally, it might be possible to characterize when particular equivalences hold in terms of the algebraic properties of the effects we restrict to.

Denotational Semantics. Using logical relations to prove contextual equivalence between terms directly is difficult. Adequate denotational semantics would allow us to reduce proofs of contextual equivalence to proofs of equalities in the model. Composing the denotational semantics with the call-by-need translation would also result in a call-by-need denotational semantics for the source language. Some potential approaches to describing the denotational semantics of ECBPV are Maraist et al.'s [21] translation into an affine calculus, combined with a semantics of linear logic [24], and also continuation-passing-style translations [27]. None of these consider side-effects however.

Acknowledgements. We gratefully acknowledge the support of an EPSRC studentship, and thank the anonymous reviewers for helpful comments.

References

1. Altenkirch, T., Hofmann, M., Streicher, T.: Categorical reconstruction of a reduction free normalization proof. In: Pitt, D., Rydeheard, D.E., Johnstone, P. (eds.) CTCS 1995. LNCS, vol. 953, pp. 182–199. Springer, Heidelberg (1995). https://doi.org/10.1007/3-540-60164-3_27
2. Ariola, Z.M., Felleisen, M.: The call-by-need lambda calculus. J. Funct. Program. **7**(3), 265–301 (1997)
3. Ariola, Z.M., Maraist, J., Odersky, M., Felleisen, M., Wadler, P.: A call-by-need lambda calculus. In: Proceedings of the 22nd ACM SIGPLAN-SIGACT Symposium on Principles of Programming Languages, pp. 233–246. ACM (1995). https://doi.org/10.1145/199448.199507
4. Benton, N., Hofmann, M., Nigam, V.: Effect-dependent transformations for concurrent programs. In: Proceedings of the 18th International Symposium on Principles and Practice of Declarative Programming, pp. 188–201. ACM (2016). https://doi.org/10.1145/2967973.2968602
5. Benton, N., Kennedy, A.: Monads, effects and transformations. Electron. Notes Theor. Comput. Sci. **26**, 3–20 (1999). https://doi.org/10.1016/S1571-0661(05)80280-4
6. Benton, N., Kennedy, A., Hofmann, M., Nigam, V.: Counting successes: effects and transformations for non-deterministic programs. In: Lindley, S., McBride, C., Trinder, P., Sannella, D. (eds.) A List of Successes That Can Change the World. LNCS, vol. 9600, pp. 56–72. Springer, Cham (2016). https://doi.org/10.1007/978-3-319-30936-1_3
7. Benton, N., Kennedy, A., Russell, G.: Compiling standard ML to Java bytecodes. In: Proceedings of the Third ACM SIGPLAN International Conference on Functional Programming, pp. 129–140. ACM (1998). https://doi.org/10.1145/289423.289435

8. Birkedal, L., Sieczkowski, F., Thamsborg, J.: A concurrent logical relation. In: Cégielski, P., Durand, A. (eds.) 21st EACSL Annual Conference on Computer Science Logic, CSL 2012. Leibniz International Proceedings in Informatics (LIPIcs), vol. 16, pp. 107–121. Schloss Dagstuhl-Leibniz-Zentrum für Informatik, Dagstuhl (2012). https://doi.org/10.4230/LIPIcs.CSL.2012.107
9. Chang, S., Felleisen, M.: The call-by-need lambda calculus, revisited. In: Seidl, H. (ed.) ESOP 2012. LNCS, vol. 7211, pp. 128–147. Springer, Heidelberg (2012). https://doi.org/10.1007/978-3-642-28869-2_7
10. Downen, P., Ariola, Z.M.: Beyond polarity: towards a multi-discipline intermediate language with sharing. In: 27th EACSL Annual Conference on Computer Science Logic, CSL 2018, pp. 21:1–21:23 (2018). https://doi.org/10.4230/LIPIcs.CSL.2018.21
11. Fiore, M.: Semantic analysis of normalisation by evaluation for typed lambda calculus. In: Proceedings of the 4th ACM SIGPLAN International Conference on Principles and Practice of Declarative Programming, pp. 26–37. ACM (2002). https://doi.org/10.1145/571157.571161
12. Jung, A., Tiuryn, J.: A new characterization of lambda definability. In: Bezem, M., Groote, J.F. (eds.) TLCA 1993. LNCS, vol. 664, pp. 245–257. Springer, Heidelberg (1993). https://doi.org/10.1007/BFb0037110
13. Kammar, O.: Algebraic theory of type-and-effect systems. Ph.D. thesis, University of Edinburgh, UK (2014)
14. Kammar, O., Plotkin, G.D.: Algebraic foundations for effect-dependent optimisations. In: Proceedings of the 39th Annual ACM SIGPLAN-SIGACT Symposium on Principles of Programming Languages, pp. 349–360. ACM (2012). https://doi.org/10.1145/2103656.2103698
15. Katsumata, S.: Parametric effect monads and semantics of effect systems. In: Proceedings of the 41st ACM SIGPLAN-SIGACT Symposium on Principles of Programming Languages, pp. 633–645. ACM (2014). https://doi.org/10.1145/2535838.2535846
16. Launchbury, J.: A natural semantics for lazy evaluation. In: Proceedings of the 20th ACM SIGPLAN-SIGACT Symposium on Principles of Programming Languages, pp. 144–154. ACM (1993). https://doi.org/10.1145/158511.158618
17. Levy, P.B.: Call-by-push-value: a subsuming paradigm. In: Girard, J.-Y. (ed.) TLCA 1999. LNCS, vol. 1581, pp. 228–243. Springer, Heidelberg (1999). https://doi.org/10.1007/3-540-48959-2_17
18. Lindley, S.: Normalisation by evaluation in the compilation of typed functional programming languages. Ph.D. thesis, University of Edinburgh, UK (2005)
19. Lindley, S., Stark, I.: Reducibility and ⊤⊤-lifting for computation types. In: Urzyczyn, P. (ed.) TLCA 2005. LNCS, vol. 3461, pp. 262–277. Springer, Heidelberg (2005). https://doi.org/10.1007/11417170_20
20. Lucassen, J.M., Gifford, D.K.: Polymorphic effect systems. In: Proceedings of the 15th ACM SIGPLAN-SIGACT Symposium on Principles of Programming Languages, pp. 47–57. ACM (1988). https://doi.org/10.1145/73560.73564
21. Maraist, J., Odersky, M., Turner, D.N., Wadler, P.: Call-by-name, call-by-value, call-by-need, and the linear lambda calculus. In: Proceedings of the Eleventh Annual Mathematical Foundations of Programming Semantics Conference, pp. 370–392 (1995). https://doi.org/10.1016/S0304-3975(98)00358-2
22. Maraist, J., Odersky, M., Wadler, P.: The call-by-need lambda calculus. J. Funct. Program. **8**(3), 275–317 (1998). https://doi.org/10.1017/S0956796898003037
23. McDermott, D., Mycroft, A.: Call-by-need effects via coeffects. Open Comput. Sci. **8**, 93–108 (2018). https://doi.org/10.1515/comp-2018-0009

24. Melliès, P.A.: Categorical semantics of linear logic. In: Interactive Models of Computation and Program Behaviour, Panoramas et Synthèses 27, Société Mathématique de France (2009)
25. Moggi, E.: Notions of computation and monads. Inf. Comput. **93**(1), 55–92 (1991). https://doi.org/10.1016/0890-5401(91)90052-4
26. Munch-Maccagnoni, G.: Models of a non-associative composition. In: Muscholl, A. (ed.) FoSSaCS 2014. LNCS, vol. 8412, pp. 396–410. Springer, Heidelberg (2014). https://doi.org/10.1007/978-3-642-54830-7_26
27. Okasaki, C., Lee, P., Tarditi, D.: Call-by-need and continuation-passing style. LISP Symbolic Comput. **7**(1), 57–81 (1994). https://doi.org/10.1007/BF01019945
28. Petricek, T., Syme, D.: Joinads: a retargetable control-flow construct for reactive, parallel and concurrent programming. In: Rocha, R., Launchbury, J. (eds.) PADL 2011. LNCS, vol. 6539, pp. 205–219. Springer, Heidelberg (2011). https://doi.org/10.1007/978-3-642-18378-2_17
29. Tolmach, A.: Optimizing ML using a hierarchy of monadic types. In: Leroy, X., Ohori, A. (eds.) TIC 1998. LNCS, vol. 1473, pp. 97–115. Springer, Heidelberg (1998). https://doi.org/10.1007/BFb0055514
30. Turner, D.A.: A new implementation technique for applicative languages. Softw. Pract. Experience **9**(1), 31–49 (1979). https://doi.org/10.1002/spe.4380090105
31. Turner, D.N., Wadler, P., Mossin, C.: Once upon a type. In: Proceedings of the Seventh International Conference on Functional Programming Languages and Computer Architecture, pp. 1–11. ACM (1995). https://doi.org/10.1145/224164.224168
32. Wadsworth, C.: Semantics and Pragmatics of the Lambda-Calculus. University of Oxford (1971)
33. Wansbrough, K., Peyton Jones, S.: Once upon a polymorphic type. In: Proceedings of the 26th ACM SIGPLAN-SIGACT Symposium on Principles of Programming Languages, pp. 15–28. ACM (1999). https://doi.org/10.1145/292540.292545
34. Zeilberger, N.: The logical basis of evaluation order and pattern-matching. Ph.D. thesis, Carnegie Mellon University, Pittsburgh, PA, USA (2009)

Effectful Normal Form Bisimulation

Ugo Dal Lago[1,2(✉)] and Francesco Gavazzo[1,2(✉)]

[1] University of Bologna, Bologna, Italy
[2] Inria Sophia Antipolis, Sophia Antipolis Cedex, France
ugo.dallago@unibo.it, francesco.gavazzo@gmail.com

Abstract. Normal form bisimulation, also known as *open* bisimulation, is a coinductive technique for higher-order program equivalence in which programs are compared by looking at their essentially infinitary tree-like normal forms, i.e. at their Böhm or Lévy-Longo trees. The technique has been shown to be useful not only when proving metatheorems about λ-calculi and their semantics, but also when looking at concrete examples of terms. In this paper, we show that there is a way to generalise normal form bisimulation to calculi with algebraic effects, *à la* Plotkin and Power. We show that some mild conditions on monads and relators, which have already been shown to guarantee effectful applicative bisimilarity to be a congruence relation, are enough to prove that the obtained notion of bisimilarity, which we call *effectful normal form bisimilarity*, is a congruence relation, and thus sound for contextual equivalence. Additionally, contrary to applicative bisimilarity, normal form bisimilarity allows for enhancements of the bisimulation proof method, hence proving a powerful reasoning principle for effectful programming languages.

1 Introduction

The study of program equivalence has always been one of the central tasks of programming language theory: giving satisfactory definitions and methodologies for it can be fruitful in contexts like program verification and compiler optimisation design, but also helps in understanding the *nature* of the programming language at hand. This is particularly true when dealing with higher-order languages, in which giving satisfactory notions of program equivalence is well-known to be hard. Indeed, the problem has been approached in many different ways. One can define program equivalence through denotational semantics, thus relying on a model. One could also proceed following the route traced by Morris [51], and define programs to be *contextually* equivalent when they behave the same in every context, this way taking program equivalence as the *largest* adequate congruence.

Both these approaches have their drawbacks, the first one relying on the existence of a (not too coarse) denotational model, the latter quantifying over all contexts, and thus making concrete proofs of equivalence hard. Among the

Thanks to the ANR projects 14CE250005 ELICA and 16CE250011 REPAS.

L. Caires (Ed.): ESOP 2019, LNCS 11423, pp. 263–292, 2019.
https://doi.org/10.1007/978-3-030-17184-1_10

many alternative techniques the research community has been proposing along the years, one can cite logical relations and applicative bisimilarity [1,4,8], both based on the idea that equivalent higher-order terms should behave the same when fed with any (pair of related) inputs. This way, terms are compared mimicking any possible action a discriminating context could possibly perform on the tested terms. In other words, the universal quantification on all possible contexts, although not *explicitly* present, is anyway *implicitly* captured by the bisimulation or logical game.

Starting from the pioneering work by Böhm, another way of defining program equivalence has been proved extremely useful not only when giving metatheorems about λ-calculi and programming languages, but also when proving concrete programs to be (contextually) equivalent. What we are referring to, of course, is the notion of a *Böhm tree* of a λ-term e (see [5] for a formal definition), which is a possibly infinite tree representing the *head normal* h form of e, if e has one, but also analyzing the arguments to the head variable of h in a coinductive way. The celebrated Böhm Theorem, also known as Separation Theorem [11], stipulates that two terms are contextually equivalent *if and only if* their respective (appropriately η-equated) Böhm trees are the same.

The notion of equivalence induced by Böhm trees can be characterised without any reference to trees, by means of a suitable bisimilarity relation [37,65]. Additionally, Böhm trees can also be defined when λ-terms are *not* evaluated to their *head* normal form, like in the classical theory of λ-calculus, but to their *weak head* normal form (like in the call-by-name [37,65]), or to their *eager* normal form (like in the call-by-value λ-calculus [38]). In both cases, the notion of program equivalence one obtains by comparing the syntactic structure of trees, admits an elegant coinductive characterisation as a suitable bisimilarity relation. The family of bisimilarity relations thus obtained goes under the generic name of *normal form bisimilarity.*

Real world functional programming languages, however, come equipped not only with higher-order functions, but also with *computational effects*, turning them into *impure* languages in which functions cannot be seen merely as turning an input to an output. This requires switching to a new model, which cannot be the usual, pure, λ-calculus. Indeed, program equivalence in effectful λ-calculi [49,56] have been studied by way of denotational semantics [18,20,31], logical relations [10,14], applicative bisimilarity [13,16,36], and normal form bisimilarity [20,41]. While the denotational semantics, logical relation semantics, and applicative bisimilarity of effectful calculi have been studied in the abstract [15,25,30], the same cannot be said about normal form bisimilarity. Particularly relevant for our purposes is [15], where a notion of applicative bisimilarity for generic algebraic effects, called *effectful applicative bisimilarity*, based on the (standard) notion of a monad, and on the (less standard) notion of a *relator* [71] or *lax extension* [6,26], is introduced.

Intuitively, a relator is an abstraction axiomatising the structural properties of relation lifting operations. This way, relators allow for an abstract description of the possible ways a relation between programs can be lifted to a relation between (the results of) effectful computations, the latter being described throughout monads and algebraic operations. Several concrete notions of program equivalence, such as pure, nondeterministic and probabilistic applicative bisimilarity [1,16,36,52] can be analysed using relators. Additionally, besides their prime role in the study of effectful applicative bisimilarity, relators have also been used to study logic-based equivalences [67] and applicative distances [23] for languages with generic algebraic effects.

The main contribution of [15] consists in devising a set of axioms on monads and relators (summarised in the notions of a *Σ-continuous monad* and a *Σ-continuous relator*) which are both satisfied by many concrete examples, and that abstractly guarantee that the associated notion of applicative bisimilarity is a congruence.

In this paper, we show that an abstract notion of normal form (bi)simulation can indeed be given for calculi with algebraic effects, thus defining a theory analogous to [15]. Remarkably, we show that the defining axioms of Σ-continuous monads and Σ-continuous relators guarantee the resulting notion of normal form (bi)similarity to be a (pre)congruence relation, thus enabling compositional reasoning about program equivalence and refinement. Given that these axioms have already been shown to hold in many relevant examples of calculi with effects, our work shows that there is a way to "cook up" notions of *effectful* normal form bisimulation *without* having to reprove congruence of the obtained notion of program equivalence: this comes somehow for free. Moreover, this holds both when call-by-name and call-by-value program evaluation is considered, although in this paper we will mostly focus on the latter, since the call-by-value reduction strategy is more natural in presence of computational effects[1].

Compared to (effectful) applicative bisimilarity, as well as to other standard operational techniques—such as contextual and CIU equivalence [47,51], or logical relations [55,61]—(effectful) normal form bisimilarity has the major advantage of being an *intensional* program equivalence, equating programs according to the syntactic structure of their (possibly infinitary) normal forms. As a consequence, in order to deem two programs as normal form bisimilar, it is sufficient to test them in isolation, i.e. independently of their interaction with the environment. This way, we obtain easier proofs of equivalence between (effectful) programs. Additionally, normal form bisimilarity allows for enhancements of the bisimulation proof method [60], hence qualifying as a powerful and effective tool for program equivalence.

Intensionality represents a major difference between normal form bisimilarity and applicative bisimilarity, where the environment interacts with the tested programs by passing them arbitrary input arguments (thus making applicative bisimilarity an *extensional* notion of program equivalence). Testing programs in isolation has, however, its drawbacks. In fact, although we prove effectful normal form bisimilarity to be a sound proof technique for (effectful) applicative bisim-

---

[1] Besides, as we will discuss in Sect. 6.4, the formal analysis of call-by-name normal form bisimilarity strictly follows the corresponding (more challenging) analysis of call-by-value normal form bisimilarity.

ilarity (and thus for contextual equivalence), full abstraction fails, as already observed in the case of the pure λ-calculus [3,38] (nonetheless, it is worth mentioning that full abstraction results are known to hold for calculi with a rich expressive power [65,68]).

In light of these observations, we devote some energy to studying some concrete examples which highlight the weaknesses of applicative bisimilarity, on the one hand, and the strengths of normal form bisimilarity, on the other hand.

This paper is structured as follows. In Sect. 2 we informally discuss examples of (pairs of) programs which are operational equivalent, but whose equivalence cannot be readily established using standard operational methods. Throughout this paper, we will show how effectful normal form bisimilarity allows for handy proofs of such equivalences. Section 3 is dedicated to mathematical preliminaries, with a special focus on (selected) examples of monads and algebraic operations. In Sect. 4 we define our vehicle calculus Λ_Σ, an untyped λ-calculus enriched with algebraic operations, to which we give call-by-value monadic operational semantics. Section 5 introduces relators and their main properties. In Sect. 6 we introduce *effectful eager normal form (bi)similarity*, the call-by-value instantiation of effectful normal form (bi)similarity, and its main metatheoretical properties. In particular, we prove effectful eager normal form (bi)similarity to be a (pre)congruence relation (Theorem 2) included in effectful applicative (bi)similarity (Proposition 5). Additionally, we prove soundness of eager normal bisimulation up-to context (Theorem 3), a powerful enhancement of the bisimulation proof method that allows for handy proof of program equivalence. Finally, in Sect. 6.4 we briefly discuss how to modify our theory to deal with call-by-name calculi.

2 From Applicative to Normal Form Bisimilarity

In this section, some examples of (pairs of) programs which can be shown equivalent by effectful normal form bisimilarity will be provided, giving evidence on the flexibility and strength of the proposed technique. We will focus on examples drawn from fixed point theory, simply because these, being infinitary in nature, are quite hard to be dealt with "finitary" techniques like contextual equivalence or applicative bisimilarity.

Example 1. Our first example comes from the ordinary theory of pure, untyped λ-calculus. Let us consider Curry's and Turing's call-by-value fixed point combinators Y and Z:

$$Y \triangleq \lambda y.\Delta\Delta, \quad Z \triangleq \Theta\Theta, \quad \Delta \triangleq \lambda x.y(\lambda z.xxz), \quad \Theta \triangleq \lambda x.\lambda y.y(\lambda z.xxyz).$$

It is well known that Y and Z are contextually equivalent, although proving such an equivalence from first principles is doomed to be hard. For that reason, one usually looks at proof techniques for contextual equivalence. Here we consider applicative bisimilarity [1]. As in the pure λ-calculus applicative bisimilarity coincides with the intersection of applicative similarity and its converse, for the sake of the argument we discuss which difficulties one faces when trying to prove Z to be applicatively similar to Y.

Let us try to construct an applicative simulation $\mathcal{R}$ relating Y and Z. Clearly we need to have $(Y, Z) \in \mathcal{R}$. Since Y evaluates to $\lambda y.\Delta\Delta$, and Z evaluates to $\lambda y.y(\lambda z.\Theta\Theta yz)$, in order for $\mathcal{R}$ to be an applicative simulation, we need to show that for any value v, $(\Delta[v/y]\Delta[v/y], v(\lambda z.\Theta\Theta vz)) \in \mathcal{R}$. Since the result of the evaluation of $\Delta[v/y]\Delta[v/y]$ is the same of $v(\lambda z.\Delta[v/y]\Delta[v/y]z)$, we have reached a point in which we are stuck: in order to ensure $(Y, Z) \in \mathcal{R}$, we need to show that $(v(\lambda z.\Delta[v/y]\Delta[v/y]z), v(\lambda z.\Theta\Theta vz)) \in \mathcal{R}$. However, the value v being provided by the environment, no information on it is available. That is, we have no information on how v tests its input program. In particular, given any context $\mathcal{C}[-]$, we can consider the value $\lambda x.\mathcal{C}[x]$, meaning that proving Y and Z to be applicatively bisimilar is almost as hard as proving them to be contextually equivalent from first principles.

As we will see, proving Z to be normal form similar to Y is straightforward, since in order to test $\lambda y.\Delta\Delta$ and $\lambda y.y(\lambda z.\Theta\Theta yz)$, we simply test their subterms $\Delta\Delta$ and $y(\lambda z.\Theta\Theta yz)$, thus not allowing the environment to influence computations.

Example 2. Our next example is a refinement of Example 1 to a probabilistic setting, as proposed in [66] (but in a call-by-name setting). We consider a variation of Turing's call-by-value fixed point combinator which, at any iteration, can probabilistically decide whether to start another iteration (following the pattern of the standard Turing's fixed point combinator) or to turn for good into Y, where Y and Δ are defined as in Example 1:

$$Z \triangleq \Theta\Theta, \qquad \Theta \triangleq \lambda x.\lambda y.(y(\lambda z.\Delta\Delta z) \,\mathbf{or}\, y(\lambda z.xxyz)).$$

Notice that the constructor **or** behaves as a (fair) probabilistic choice operator, hence acting as an effect producer. It is natural to ask whether these new versions of Y and Z are still equivalent. However, following insights from previous example, it is not hard to see the equivalence between Y and Z cannot be readily proved by means of standard operational methods such as probabilistic contextual equivalence [16], probabilistic CIU equivalence and logical relations [10], and probabilistic applicative bisimilarity [13,16]. All the aforementioned techniques require to test programs in a given environment (such as a whole context or an input argument), and are thus ineffective in handling fixed point combinators such as Y and Z.

We will give an elementary proof of the equivalence between Y and Z in Example 17, and a more elegant proof relying on a suitable *up-to context* technique in Example 18. In [66], the call-by-name counterparts of Y and Z are proved to be equivalent using probabilistic environmental bisimilarity. The notion of an environmental bisimulation [63] involves both an environment storing pairs of terms played during the bisimulation game, and a clause universally quantifying over pairs of terms in the evaluation context closure of such an environment[2], thus making environmental bisimilarity a rather heavy technique to use. Our proof of the equivalence of Y and Z is simpler: in fact, our notion of effectful normal form bisimulation does not involve any universal quantification over all possible closed function arguments (like applicative bisimilarity), or their evaluation context closure (like environmental bisimilarity), or closed instantiation of uses (like CIU equivalence).

Example 3. Our third example concerns call-by-name calculi and shows how our notion of normal form bisimilarity can handle even intricate recursion schemes. We consider the following argument-switching probabilistic fixed point combinators:

$$P \triangleq AA, \qquad A \triangleq \lambda x.\lambda y.\lambda z.(y(xxyz)\ \mathbf{or}\ z(xxzy)),$$
$$Q \triangleq BB, \qquad B \triangleq \lambda x.\lambda y.\lambda z.(y(xxzy)\ \mathbf{or}\ z(xxyz)).$$

We easily see that P and Q satisfy the following (informal) program equations:

$$Pef = e(Pef)\ \mathbf{or}\ f(Pfe), \qquad Qef = e(Qfe)\ \mathbf{or}\ f(Qef).$$

Again, proving the equivalence between P and Q using applicative bisimilarity is problematic. In fact, testing the applicative behaviour of P and Q requires to reason about the behaviour of e.g. $e(Pef)$, which in turn requires to reason about the (arbitrary) term e, on which no information is provided. The (essentially infinitary) normal forms of P and Q, however, can be proved to be essentially the same by reasoning about the syntactical structure of P and Q. Moreover, our *up-to context* technique enables an elegant and concise proof of the equivalence between P and Q (Sect. 6.4).

Example 4. Our last example discusses the use of the cost monad as an *instrument* to facilitate a more intensional analysis of programs. In fact, we can use the ticking operation **tick** to perform cost analysis. For instance, we can consider the following variation of Curry's and Turing's fixed point combinator of Example 1, obtained by adding the operation symbol **tick** after every λ-abstraction.

$$Y \triangleq \lambda y.\mathbf{tick}(\Delta\Delta), \qquad \Delta \triangleq \lambda x.\mathbf{tick}(y(\lambda z.\mathbf{tick}(xxz))),$$
$$Z \triangleq \Theta\Theta, \qquad \Theta \triangleq \lambda x.\mathbf{tick}(\lambda y.\mathbf{tick}(y(\lambda z.\mathbf{tick}(xxyz)))).$$

Every time a β-redex $(\lambda x.\mathbf{tick}(e))v$ is reduced, the ticking operation **tick** increases an imaginary cost counter of a unit. Using ticking, we can provide a more intensional analysis of the relationship between Y and Z, along the lines of Sands' improvement theory [62].

[2] Meaning that two terms e_1, e_2 are tested for their applicative behaviour against all terms of the form $E[e], E[e']$, for any pair of terms (e, e') stored in the environment.

3 Preliminaries: Monads and Algebraic Operations

In this section we recall some basic definitions and results needed in the rest of the paper. Unfortunately, there is no hope to be comprehensive, and thus we assume the reader to be familiar with basic domain theory [2] (in particular with the notions of ω-complete (pointed) partial order—ω-cppo, for short—monotone, and continuous functions), basic order theory [19], and basic category theory [46]. Additionally, we assume the reader to be acquainted with the notion of a Kleisli triple [46] $\mathbb{T} = \langle T, \eta, -^{\dagger}\rangle$. As it is customary, we use the notation $f^{\dagger} : TX \to TY$ for the Kleisli extension of $f : X \to TY$, and reserve the letter η to denote the unit of $\mathbb{T}$. Due to their equivalence, oftentimes we refer to Kleisli triples as monads.

Concerning notation, we try to follow [46] and [2], with the only exception that we use the notation $(x_n)_n$ to denote an ω-chain $x_0 \sqsubseteq \cdots \sqsubseteq x_n \sqsubseteq \cdots$ in a domain $(X, \sqsubseteq, \bot)$. The notation $\mathbb{T} = \langle T, \eta, -^{\dagger}\rangle$ for an arbitrary Kleisli triple is standard, but it is not very handy when dealing with multiple monads at the same time. To fix this issue, we sometimes use the notation $\mathbb{T} = \langle T, \mathrm{T}, -^{\mathrm{T}}\rangle$ to denote a Kleisli triple. Additionally, when unambiguous we omit subscripts. Finally, we denote by Set the category of sets and functions, and by Rel the category of sets and relations. We reserve the symbol 1 to denote the identity function. Unless explicitly stated, we assume functors (and monads) to be functors (and monads) on Set. As a consequence, we write *functors* to refer to endofunctors on Set.

We use monads to give operational semantics to our calculi. Following Moggi [49,50], we model notions of computation as monads, meaning that we use monads as mathematical models of the kind of (side) effects computations may produce. The following are examples of monads modelling relevant notions of computation. Due to space constraints, we omit several interesting examples such as the output, the exception, and the nondeterministic/powerset monad, for which the reader is referred to e.g. [50,73].

Example 5 (Partiality). Partial computations are modelled by the partiality (also called maybe) monad $\mathbb{M} = \langle M, \mathrm{M}, -^{\mathrm{M}}\rangle$. The carrier MX of $\mathbb{M}$ is defined as $\{\mathit{just}\ x \mid x \in X\} \cup \{\bot\}$, where $\bot$ is a special symbol denoting divergence. The unit and Kleisli extension of $\mathbb{M}$ are defined as follows:

$$\mathrm{M}(x) \triangleq \mathit{just}\ x, \qquad f^{\mathrm{M}}(\mathit{just}\ x) \triangleq f(x), \qquad f^{\mathrm{M}}(\bot) \triangleq \bot.$$

Example 6 (Probabilistic Nondeterminism). In this example we assume sets to be countable[3]. The (discrete) distribution monad $\mathbb{D} = \langle D, \mathrm{D}, -^{\mathrm{D}}\rangle$ has carrier $\mathbb{D}X \triangleq \{\mu : X \to [0,1] \mid \sum_x \mu(x) = 1\}$, whereas the maps D and $-^{\mathrm{D}}$ are defined as follows (where $y \neq x$):

$$\mathrm{D}(x)(x) \triangleq 1, \qquad \mathrm{D}(x)(y) \triangleq 0, \qquad f^{\mathrm{D}}(\mu)(y) \triangleq \textstyle\sum_{x \in X} \mu(x) \cdot f(x)(y).$$

[3] Although this is not strictly necessary, for simplicity we work with distributions over countable sets only, as the sets of values and normal forms are countable.

Oftentimes, we write a distribution μ as a weighted formal sum. That is, we write μ as the sum[4] $\sum_{i\in I} p_i \cdot x_i$ such that $\mu(x) = \sum_{x_i = x} p_i$. $\mathbb{D}$ models probabilistic total computations, according to the rationale that a (total) probabilistic program evaluates to a distribution over values, the latter describing the possible results of the evaluation. Finally, we model probabilistic partial computations using the monad $\mathbb{DM} = \langle DM, \mathrm{DM}, -^{\mathbb{DM}}\rangle$. The carrier of $\mathbb{DM}$ is defined as $DMX \triangleq D(MX)$, whereas the unit DM is defined in the obvious way. For $f : X \to DMY$, define:

$$f^{\mathbb{DM}}(\mu)(y) \triangleq \textstyle\sum_{x\in X} \mu(just\ x) \cdot f(x)(y) + \mu(\bot) \cdot \mathrm{D}(\bot)(y).$$

It is easy to see that $\mathbb{DM}$ is isomorphic to the subdistribution monad.

Example 7 (Cost). The cost (also known as ticking or improvement [62]) monad $\mathbb{C} = \langle C, \mathrm{C}, -^{\mathbb{C}}\rangle$ has carrier $CX \triangleq M(\mathbb{N} \times X)$. The unit of $\mathbb{C}$ is defined as $\mathrm{C}(x) \triangleq just\ (0, x)$, whereas Kleisli extension is defined as follows:

$$f^{\mathbb{C}}(\chi) \triangleq \begin{cases} \bot & \text{if } \chi = \bot, \text{ or } \chi = just\ (n, x) \text{ and } f(x) = \bot \\ just\ (n + m, y) & \text{if } \chi = just\ (n, x) \text{ and } f(x) = just\ (m, y). \end{cases}$$

The cost monad is used to model the cost of (partial) computations. An element of the form $just\ (n, x)$ models the result of a computation outputting the value x with cost n (the latter being an abstract notion that can be instantiated to e.g. the number of reduction steps performed). Partiality is modelled as the element $\bot$, according to the rationale that we can assume all divergent computations to have the same cost, so that such information need not be explicitly written (for instance, measuring the number of reduction steps performed, we would have that divergent computations all have cost ∞).

Example 8 (Global states). Let $\mathcal{L}$ be a set of public location names. We assume the content of locations to be encoded as families of values (such as numerals or booleans) and denote the collection of such values as $\mathcal{V}$. A store (or state) is a function $\sigma : \mathcal{L} \to \mathcal{V}$. We write S for the set of stores $\mathcal{V}^{\mathcal{L}}$. The global state monad $\mathbb{G} = \langle G, \mathrm{G}, -^{\mathbb{G}}\rangle$ has carrier $GX \triangleq (X \times S)^S$, whereas G and $-^{\mathbb{G}}$ are defined by:

$$\mathrm{G}(x)(\sigma) \triangleq (x, \sigma), \qquad\qquad f^{\mathbb{G}}(\alpha)(\sigma) \triangleq f(x')(\sigma'),$$

where $\alpha(\sigma) = (x', \sigma')$. It is straightforward to see that we can combine the global state monad with the partiality monad, obtaining the monad $\mathbb{M} \otimes \mathbb{G}$ whose carrier is $(M \otimes G)X \triangleq M(X \times S)^S$. In a similar fashion, we see that we can combine the global state monad with $\mathbb{DM}$ and $\mathbb{C}$, as we are going to see in Remark 1.

Remark 1. The monads $\mathbb{DM}$ and $\mathbb{M} \otimes \mathbb{G}$ of Example 6 and Example 8, respectively, are instances of two general constructions, namely the *sum* and *tensor* of effects [28]. Although these operations are defined on Lawvere theories [29,40], here we can rephrase them in terms of monads as follows.

[4] For simplicity, we write only those p_is such that $p_i > 0$.

Proposition 1. *Given a monad* $\mathbb{T} = \langle T, \mathrm{T}, -^{\mathbb{T}} \rangle$, *define the* sum $\mathbb{T}\mathbb{M}$ *of* $\mathbb{T}$ *and* $\mathbb{M}$ *and the* tensor $\mathbb{T} \otimes \mathbb{G}$ *of* $\mathbb{T}$ *and* $\mathbb{G}$, *as the triples* $\langle TM, \mathrm{TM}, -^{\mathbb{TM}} \rangle$ *and* $\langle T \otimes G, \mathrm{T} \otimes \mathrm{G}, -^{\mathbb{T}\otimes\mathbb{G}} \rangle$, *respectively. The carriers of the triples are defined as* $TMX \triangleq T(MX)$ *and* $(T \otimes G)X \triangleq T(S \times X)^S$, *whereas the maps* TM *and* $\mathrm{T} \otimes \mathrm{G}$ *are defined as* $\mathrm{TM}_X \triangleq \mathrm{T}_{MX} \circ \mathrm{M}_X$ *and* $(\mathrm{T} \otimes \mathrm{G})_X \triangleq \mathsf{curry}\ \mathrm{T}_{S \times X}$, *respectively. Finally, define:*

$$f^{\mathbb{TM}} \triangleq (f_M)^{\mathbb{T}}, \qquad f^{\mathbb{T}\otimes\mathbb{G}}(\alpha)(\sigma) \triangleq (\mathsf{uncurry}\ f)^{\mathbb{T}}(\alpha)(\sigma),$$

where, for a function $f : X \to TMY$ *we define* $f_M : MX \to TMY$ *as* $f_M(\bot) \triangleq \mathrm{T}_{MX}(\bot)$, $f_M(just\ x) \triangleq f(x)$, *and* curry *and* uncurry *are defined as usual. Then* $\mathbb{TM}$ *and* $\mathbb{T} \otimes \mathbb{G}$ *are monads.*

Proving Proposition 1 is a straightforward exercise (the reader can also consult [28]). We notice that tensoring $\mathbb{G}$ with $\mathbb{DM}$ we obtain a monad for probabilistic imperative computations, whereas tensoring $\mathbb{G}$ with $\mathbb{C}$ we obtain a monad for imperative computations with cost.

3.1 Algebraic Operations

Monads provide an elegant way to structure effectful computations. However, they do not offer any actual effect constructor. Following Plotkin and Power [56–58], we use *algebraic operations* as effect producers. From an operational perspective, algebraic operations are those operations whose behaviour is independent of their continuations or, equivalently, of the environment in which they are evaluated. Intuitively, that means that e.g. $E[e_1\ \mathbf{or}\ e_2]$ is operationally equivalent to $E[e_1]$ **or** $E[e_2]$, for any evaluation context E. Examples of algebraic operations are given by (binary) nondeterministic and probabilistic choices as well as primitives for rising exceptions and output operations.

Syntactically, algebraic operations are given via a signature Σ consisting of a set of operation symbols (uninterpreted operations) together with their arity (i.e. their number of operands). Semantically, operation symbols are interpreted as algebraic operations on monads. To any n-ary operation symbol[5] $(\mathbf{op} : n) \in \Sigma$ and any set X we associate a map $[\![\mathbf{op}]\!]_X : (TX)^n \to TX$ (so that we equip TX with a Σ-algebra structure [12]) such that $f^\dagger$ is Σ-algebra morphism, meaning that for any $f : X \to TY$, and elements $\mathfrak{X}_1, \ldots, \mathfrak{X}_n \in TX$ we have $[\![\mathbf{op}]\!]_Y(f^\dagger(\mathfrak{X}_1), \ldots, f^\dagger(\mathfrak{X}_n)) = f^\dagger([\![\mathbf{op}]\!]_X(\mathfrak{X}_1, \ldots, \mathfrak{X}_n))$.

Example 9. The partiality monad $\mathbb{M}$ usually comes with no operation, as the possibility of divergence is an implicit feature of any Turing complete language. However, it is sometimes useful to add an explicit divergence operation (for instance, in strongly normalising calculi). For that, we consider the signature $\Sigma_{\mathbb{M}} \triangleq \{\underline{\Omega} : 0\}$. Having arity zero, the operation $\underline{\Omega}$ acts as a constant, and has semantics $[\![\underline{\Omega}]\!] = \bot$. Since $f^{\mathbb{M}}(\bot) = \bot$, we see that $\underline{\Omega}$ in indeed an algebraic operation on $\mathbb{M}$.

---

[5] Here **op** denotes the operation symbol, whereas $n \geq 0$ denotes its arity.

For the distribution monad $\mathbb{D}$ we define the signature $\Sigma_{\mathbb{D}} \triangleq \{\mathbf{or} : 2\}$. The intended semantics of a program e_1 **or** e_2 is to evaluate to e_i $(i \in \{1, 2\})$ with probability 0.5. The interpretation of **or** is defined by $[\![\mathbf{or}]\!](\mu, \nu)(x) \triangleq 0.5 \cdot \mu(x) + 0.5 \cdot \nu(x)$. It is easy to see that **or** is an algebraic operation on $\mathbb{D}$, and that it trivially extends to $\mathbb{DM}$.

Finally, for the cost monad $\mathbb{C}$ we define the signature $\Sigma_{\mathbb{C}} \triangleq \{\mathbf{tick} : 1\}$. The intended semantics of **tick** is to add a unit to the cost counter:

$$[\![\mathbf{tick}]\!](\bot) \triangleq \bot, \qquad [\![\mathbf{tick}]\!](just\ (n, x)) \triangleq just\ (n + 1, x).$$

The framework we have just described works fine for modelling operations with finite arity, but does not allow to handle operations with infinitary arity. This is witnessed, for instance, by imperative calculi with global stores, where it is natural to have operations of the form $\mathbf{get}_\ell(x.k)$ with the following intended semantics: $\mathbf{get}_\ell(x.k)$ reads the content of the location ℓ, say it is a value v, and continue as $k[v/x]$. In order to take such operations into account, we follow [58] and work with generalised operations.

A *generalised operation* (operation, for short) on a set X is a function $\omega : P \times X^I \to X$. The set P is called the *parameter set* of the operation, whereas the (index) set I is called the *arity* of the operation. A generalised operation $\omega : P \times X^I \to X$ thus takes as arguments a parameter p (such as a location name) and a map $\kappa : I \to X$ giving for each index $i \in I$ the argument $\kappa(i)$ to pass to ω. Syntactically, generalised operations are given via a signature Σ consisting of a set of elements of the form $\mathbf{op} : P \rightsquigarrow I$ (the latter being nothing but a notation denoting that the operation symbols **op** has parameter set P and index set I). Semantically, an interpretation of an operation symbol $\mathbf{op} : P \rightsquigarrow I$ on a monad $\mathbb{T}$ associates to any set X a map $[\![\mathbf{op}]\!]_X : P \times (TX)^I \to TX$ such that for any $f : X \to TY$, $p \in P$, and $\kappa : I \to TX$:

$$f^\dagger([\![\mathbf{op}]\!]_X(p, \kappa)) = [\![\mathbf{op}]\!]_Y(p, f^\dagger \circ \kappa).$$

If $\mathbb{T}$ comes with an interpretation for operation symbols in Σ, we say that $\mathbb{T}$ is *Σ-algebraic.*

It is easy to see by taking the one-element set $1 = \{*\}$ as parameter set and a finite set as arity set, generalised operations subsume finitary operations. For simplicity, we use the notation $\mathbf{op} : n$ in place of $\mathbf{op} : 1 \rightsquigarrow n$, and write $\mathbf{op}(x_1, \ldots, x_n)$ in place of $\mathbf{op}(*, n \mapsto x_n)$.

Example 10. For the global state monad we consider the signature $\Sigma_{\mathbb{G}} \triangleq \{\mathbf{set}_\ell : \mathcal{V} \rightsquigarrow 1, \mathbf{get}_\ell : 1 \rightsquigarrow \mathcal{V} \mid \ell \in \mathcal{L}\}$. From a computational perspective, such operations are used to build programs of the form $\mathbf{set}_\ell(v, e)$ and $\mathbf{get}_\ell(x.e)$. The former stores the value v in the location ℓ and continues as e, whereas the latter reads the content of the location ℓ, say it is v, and continue as $e[v/x]$. Here e is used as the description of a function κ_e from values to terms defined by $\kappa_e(v) \triangleq e[v/x]$. The interpretation of the new operations on $\mathbb{G}$ is standard:

$$[\![\mathbf{set}_\ell]\!](v, \alpha)(\sigma) = \alpha(\sigma[\ell := v]), \qquad [\![\mathbf{get}_\ell]\!](\kappa)(\sigma) = \kappa(\sigma(\ell))(\sigma).$$

Straightforward calculations show that indeed $\mathbf{set}_\ell$ and $\mathbf{get}_\ell$ are algebraic operations on $\mathbb{G}$. Moreover, such operations can be easily extended to the partial global state monad $\mathbb{M} \otimes \mathbb{G}$ as well as to the probabilistic (partial) global store monad $\mathbb{DM} \otimes \mathbb{G}$. These extensions share a common pattern, which is nothing but an instance of the tensor of effects. In fact, given a $\Sigma_\mathbb{T}$-algebraic monad $\mathbb{T}$ we can define the signature $\Sigma_{\mathbb{T}\otimes\mathbb{G}}$ as $\Sigma_\mathbb{T} \cup \Sigma_\mathbb{G}$, and observe that the $\mathbb{T} \otimes \mathbb{G}$ is $\Sigma_{\mathbb{T}\otimes\mathbb{G}}$-algebraic. We refer the reader to [28] for details. Here we simply notice that we can define the interpretation $[\![\mathbf{op}]\!]^{\mathbb{T}\otimes\mathbb{G}}$ of $\mathbf{op} : P \rightsquigarrow \mathcal{V}$ on $\mathbb{T} \otimes \mathbb{G}$ as $[\![\mathbf{op}]\!]^{\mathbb{T}\otimes\mathbb{G}}_X(p,\kappa)(\sigma) \triangleq [\![\mathbf{op}]\!]^{\mathbb{T}}_{S\times X}(p, v \mapsto \kappa(v)(\sigma))$, where $[\![\mathbf{op}]\!]^{\mathbb{T}}$ is the interpretation of $\mathbf{op}$ on $\mathbb{T}$ (the interpretations of $\mathbf{set}_\ell$ and $\mathbf{get}_\ell$ are straightforward).

Monads and algebraic operations provide mathematical abstractions to structure and produce effectful computations. However, in order to give operational semantics to, e.g., probabilistic calculi [17] we need monads to account for infinitary computational behaviours. We thus look at *Σ-continuous monads.*

Definition 1. *A Σ-algebraic monad $\mathbb{T} = \langle T, \eta, -^\dagger\rangle$ is* Σ-continuous *(cf. [24]) if to any set X is associated an order $\sqsubseteq_X$ and an element $\bot_X \in TX$ such that $\langle TX, \sqsubseteq_X, \bot_X\rangle$ is an ω-cppo, and for all $(\mathbf{op} : P \rightsquigarrow I) \in \Sigma$, $f, f_n, g : X \to TY$, $\kappa, \kappa_n, \nu : I \to TX$, $\mathfrak{x}, \mathfrak{x}_n, \mathfrak{y} \in TX$, we have $f^\dagger(\bot) = \bot$ and:*

$$\kappa \sqsubseteq \nu \implies [\![\mathbf{op}]\!](p,\kappa) \sqsubseteq [\![\mathbf{op}]\!](p,\nu) \qquad [\![\mathbf{op}]\!](p, \textstyle\bigsqcup_n \kappa_n) = \textstyle\bigsqcup_n [\![\mathbf{op}]\!](p,\kappa_n)$$
$$f \sqsubseteq g \implies f^\dagger \sqsubseteq g^\dagger \qquad (\textstyle\bigsqcup_n f_n)^\dagger = \textstyle\bigsqcup_n f_n^\dagger$$
$$\mathfrak{x} \sqsubseteq \mathfrak{y} \implies f^\dagger(\mathfrak{x}) \sqsubseteq f^\dagger(\mathfrak{y}) \qquad f^\dagger(\textstyle\bigsqcup_n \mathfrak{x}_n) = \textstyle\bigsqcup_n f^\dagger(\mathfrak{x}_n).$$

When clear from the context, we will omit subscripts in $\bot_X$ and $\sqsubseteq_X$.

Example 11. The monads $\mathbb{M}$, $\mathbb{DM}$, $\mathbb{GM}$, and $\mathbb{C}$ are Σ-continuous. The order on MX and $\mathbb{C}$ is the flat ordering $\sqsubseteq$ defined by $\mathfrak{x} \sqsubseteq \mathfrak{y} \stackrel{\triangle}{\iff} \mathfrak{x} = \bot$ or $\mathfrak{x} = \mathfrak{y}$, whereas the order on DMX is defined by $\mu \sqsubseteq \nu \stackrel{\triangle}{\iff} \forall x \in X.\ \mu(just\ x) \leq \nu(just\ x)$. Finally, the order on GMX is defined pointwise from the flat ordering on $M(X \times S)$.

Having introduced the notion of a Σ-continuous monad, we can now define our vehicle calculus Λ_Σ and its monadic operational semantics.

4 A Computational Call-by-value Calculus with Algebraic Operations

In this section we define the calculus Λ_Σ. Λ_Σ is an untyped λ-calculus parametrised by a signature of operation symbols, and corresponds to the coarse-grain [44] version of the calculus studied in [15]. Formally, terms of Λ_Σ are defined by the following grammar, where x ranges over a countably infinite set of variables and $\mathbf{op}$ is a generalised operation symbol in Σ.

$$e ::= x \;\big|\; \lambda x.e \;\big|\; ee \;\big|\; \mathbf{op}(p, x.e).$$

A value is either a variable or a λ-abstraction. We denote by Λ the collection of terms and by $\mathcal{V}$ the collection of values of Λ_Σ. For an operation symbol $\mathbf{op} : P \rightsquigarrow I$, we assume that set I to be encoded by some subset of $\mathcal{V}$ (using e.g. Church's encoding). In particular, in a term of the form $\mathbf{op}(p, x.e)$, e acts as a function in the variable x that takes as input a value. Notice also how parameters $p \in P$ are part of the syntax. For simplicity, we ignore the specific subset of values used to encode elements of I, and simply write $\mathbf{op} : P \rightsquigarrow \mathcal{V}$ for operation symbols in Σ.

We adopt standard syntactical conventions as in [5] (notably the so-called variable convention). The notion of a free (resp. bound) variable is defined as usual (notice that the variable x is bound in $\mathbf{op}(p, x.e)$). As it is customary, we identify terms up to renaming of bound variables and say that a term is closed if it has no free variables (and that it is open, otherwise). Finally, we write $f[e/x]$ for the capture-free substitution of the term e for all free occurrences of x in f. In particular, $\mathbf{op}(p, x'.f)[e/x]$ is defined as $\mathbf{op}(p, x'.f[e/x])$.

Before giving Λ_Σ call-by-value operational semantics, it is useful to remark a couple of points. First of all, testing terms according to their (possibly infinitary) normal forms obviously requires to work with open terms. Indeed, in order to inspect the *intensional* behaviour of a value $\lambda x.e$, one has to inspect the intensional behaviour of e, which is an open term. As a consequence, contrary to the usual practice, we give operational semantics to both *open* and *closed* terms. Actually, the very distinction between open and closed terms is not that meaningful in this context, and thus we simply speak of terms. Second, we notice that *values* constitute a syntactic category defined independently of the operational semantics of the calculus: values are just variables and λ-abstractions. However, giving operational semantics to arbitrary terms we are interested in richer collections of irreducible expressions, i.e. expressions that cannot be simplified any further. Such collections will be different accordingly to the operational semantics adopted. For instance, in a call-by-name setting it is natural to regard the term $x((\lambda x.x)v)$ as a terminal expression (being it a head normal form), whereas in a call-by-value setting $x((\lambda x.x)v)$ can be further simplified to xv, which in turn should be regarded as a terminal expression.

We now give Λ_Σ a monadic *call-by-value* operational semantics [15], postponing the definition of monadic *call-by-name* operational semantics to Sect. 6.4. Recall that a (call-by-value) evaluation context [22] is a term with a single hole $[-]$ defined by the following grammar, where $e \in \Lambda$ and $v \in \mathcal{V}$:

$$E ::= [-] \mid Ee \mid vE.$$

We write $E[e]$ for the term obtained by substituting the term e for the hole $[-]$ in E.

Following [38], we define a *stuck term* as a term of the form $E[xv]$. Intuitively, a stuck term is an expression whose evaluation is stuck. For instance, the term $e \triangleq y(\lambda x.x)$ is stuck. Obviously, e is not a value, but at the same time it cannot be simplified any further, as y is a variable, and not a λ-abstraction. Following this intuition, we define the collection $\mathcal{E}$ of *eager normal forms* (enfs hereafter) as the collection of values and stuck terms. We let letters $s, t, \ldots$ range over elements in $\mathcal{E}$.

Lemma 1. *Any term e is either a value v, or can be uniquely decomposed as either $E[vw]$ or $E[\mathbf{op}(p, x.f)]$.*

Operational semantics of Λ_Σ is defined with respect to a Σ-continuous monad $\mathbb{T} = \langle T, \eta, -^\dagger \rangle$ relying on Lemma 1. More precisely, we define a *call-by-value* evaluation function $[\![-]\!]$ mapping each term to an element in $T\mathcal{E}$. For instance, evaluating a probabilistic term e we obtain a distribution over eager normal forms (plus bottom), the latter being either values (meaning that the evaluation of e terminates) or stuck terms (meaning that the evaluation of e went stuck at some point).

Definition 2. *Define the $\mathbb{N}$-indexed family of maps $[\![-]\!]_n : \Lambda \to T\mathcal{E}$ as follows:*

$$
\begin{aligned}
[\![e]\!]_0 &\triangleq \bot, \\
[\![v]\!]_{n+1} &\triangleq \eta(v), \\
[\![E[xv]]\!]_{n+1} &\triangleq \eta(E[xv]), \\
[\![E[(\lambda x.e)v]]\!]_{n+1} &\triangleq [\![E[e[v/x]]]\!]_n, \\
[\![E[\mathbf{op}(p, x.e)]]\!]_{n+1} &\triangleq [\![\mathbf{op}]\!]_{\mathcal{E}}(p, v \mapsto [\![E[e[v/x]]]\!]_n).
\end{aligned}
$$

The monad $\mathbb{T}$ being Σ-continuous, we see that the sequence $([\![e]\!]_n)_n$ forms an ω-chain in $T\mathcal{E}$, so that we can define $[\![e]\!]$ as $\bigsqcup_n [\![e]\!]_n$. Moreover, exploiting Σ-continuity of $\mathbb{T}$ we see that $[\![-]\!]$ is continuous.

We compare the behaviour of terms of Λ_Σ relying on the notion of an *effectful eager normal form (bi)simulation*, the extension of eager normal form (bi)simulation [38] to calculi with algebraic effects. In order to account for effectful behaviours, we follow [15] and parametrise our notions of equivalence and refinement by *relators* [6,71].

5 Relators

The notion of a *relator* for a functor T (on Set) [71] (also called *lax extension* of T [6]) is a construction lifting a relation $\mathcal{R}$ between two sets X and Y to a relation $\Gamma\mathcal{R}$ between TX and TY. Besides their applications in categorical topology [6] and coalgebra [71], relators have been recently used to study notions of applicative bisimulation [15], logic-based equivalence [67], and bisimulation-based distances [23] for λ-calculi extended with algebraic effects. Moreover, several forms of monadic lifting [25,32] resembling relators have been used to study abstract notions of logical relations [55,61].

Before defining relators formally, it is useful to recall some background notions on (binary) relations. The reader is referred to [26] for further details. We denote by Rel the category of sets and relations, and use the notation $\mathcal{R} : X \nrightarrow Y$ for a relation $\mathcal{R}$ between sets X and Y. Given relations $\mathcal{R} : X \nrightarrow Y$ and

$\mathcal{S} : Y \nrightarrow Z$, we write $\mathcal{S} \circ \mathcal{R} : X \nrightarrow Z$ for their composition, and $\mathsf{I}_X : X \nrightarrow X$ for the identity relation on X. Finally, we recall that for all sets X, Y, the hom-set $\mathsf{Rel}(X, Y)$ has a complete lattice structure, meaning that we can define relations both inductively and coinductively.

Given a relation $\mathcal{R} : X \nrightarrow Y$, we denote by $\mathcal{R}^\circ : Y \nrightarrow X$ its dual (or opposite) relations and by $-_\circ : \mathsf{Set} \to \mathsf{Rel}$ the graph functor mapping each function $f : X \to Y$ to its graph $f_\circ : X \nrightarrow Y$. The functor $-_\circ$ being faithful, we will often write $f : X \to Y$ in place of $f_\circ : X \nrightarrow Y$. It is useful to keep in mind the pointwise reading of relations of the form $g^\circ \circ \mathcal{S} \circ f$, for a relation $\mathcal{S} : Z \nrightarrow W$ and functions $f : X \to Z$, $g : Y \to W$:

$$(g^\circ \circ \mathcal{S} \circ f)(x, y) = \mathcal{S}(f(x), g(y)).$$

Given $\mathcal{R} : X \nrightarrow Y$, we can thus express a generalised monotonicity condition in a pointfree fashion using the inclusion $\mathcal{R} \subseteq g^\circ \circ \mathcal{S} \circ f$. Finally, since we are interested in preorder and equivalence relations, we recall that a relation $\mathcal{R} : X \nrightarrow X$ is reflexive if $\mathsf{I}_X \subseteq \mathcal{R}$, transitive if $\mathcal{R} \circ \mathcal{R} \subseteq \mathcal{R}$, and symmetric if $\mathcal{R} \subseteq \mathcal{R}^\circ$. We can now define relators formally.

Definition 3. *A* relator *for a functor T (on* Set*) is a set-indexed family of maps $(\mathcal{R} : X \nrightarrow Y) \mapsto (\Gamma\mathcal{R} : TX \nrightarrow TY)$ satisfying conditions* (rel 1)–(rel 4). *We say that Γ is* conversive *if it additionally satisfies condition* (rel 5).

$$\mathsf{I}_{TX} \subseteq \Gamma(\mathsf{I}_X), \tag{rel 1}$$
$$\Gamma\mathcal{S} \circ \Gamma\mathcal{R} \subseteq \Gamma(\mathcal{S} \circ \mathcal{R}), \tag{rel 2}$$
$$Tf \subseteq \Gamma f, \quad (Tf)^\circ \subseteq \Gamma f^\circ, \tag{rel 3}$$
$$\mathcal{R} \subseteq \mathcal{S} \implies \Gamma\mathcal{R} \subseteq \Gamma\mathcal{S}, \tag{rel 4}$$
$$\Gamma(\mathcal{R}^\circ) = (\Gamma\mathcal{R})^\circ. \tag{rel 5}$$

Conditions (rel 1), (rel 2), and (rel 4) are rather standard[6]. As we will see, condition (rel 4) makes the defining functional of (bi)simulation relations monotone, whereas conditions (rel 1) and (rel 2) make notions of (bi)similarity reflexive and transitive. Similarly, condition (rel 5) makes notions of bisimilarity symmetric. Condition (rel 3), which actually consists of two conditions, states that relators behave as expected when acting on (graphs of) functions. In [15,43] a kernel preservation condition is required in place of (rel 3). Such a condition is also known as *stability* in [27]. Stability requires the equality $\Gamma(g^\circ \circ \mathcal{R} \circ f) = (Tg)^\circ \circ \Gamma\mathcal{R} \circ Tf$ to hold. It is easy to see that a relator always satisfies stability (see Corollary III.1.4.4 in [26]).

Relators provide a powerful abstraction of notions of 'relation lifting', as witnessed by the numerous examples of relators we are going to discuss. However, before discussing such examples, we introduce the notion of a *relator for a monad* or *lax extension of a monad.* In fact, since we modelled computational effects as monads, it seems natural to define the notion of a relator for a *monad* (and not just for a functor).

[6] Notice that since $\mathsf{I} = (1)_\circ$ we can derive condition (rel 1) from condition (rel 3).

Definition 4. *Let $\mathbb{T} = \langle T, \eta, -^{\dagger} \rangle$ be a monad, and Γ be a relator for T. We say that Γ is a relator for $\mathbb{T}$ if it satisfies the following conditions:*

$$\mathcal{R} \subseteq \eta_Y^{\circ} \circ \Gamma\mathcal{R} \circ \eta_X, \tag{rel 7}$$

$$\mathcal{R} \subseteq g^{\circ} \circ \Gamma\mathcal{S} \circ f \implies \Gamma\mathcal{R} \subseteq (g^{\dagger})^{\circ} \circ \Gamma\mathcal{S} \circ f^{\dagger}. \tag{rel 8}$$

Finally, we observe that the collection of relators is closed under specific operations (see [43]).

Proposition 2. *Let T, U be functors, and let UT denote their composition. Moreover, let Γ, Δ be relators for T and U, respectively, and $\{\Gamma_i\}_{i\in I}$ be a family of relators for T. Then:*

1. *The map $\Delta\Gamma$ defined by $\Delta\Gamma\mathcal{R} \triangleq \Delta(\Gamma\mathcal{R})$ is a relator for UT.*
2. *The maps $\bigwedge_{i\in I} \Gamma_i$ and Γ° defined by $(\bigwedge_{i\in I} \Gamma_i)\mathcal{R} \triangleq \bigcap_{i\in I} \Gamma_i\mathcal{R}$ and $\Gamma^{\circ}\mathcal{R} \triangleq (\Gamma\mathcal{R}^{\circ})^{\circ}$, respectively, are relators for T.*
3. *Additionally, if Γ is a relator for a monad $\mathbb{T}$, then so are $\bigwedge_{i\in I} \Gamma_i$ and Γ°.*

Example 12. For the partiality monad $\mathbb{M}$ we define the set-indexed family of maps $\hat{\mathbb{M}} : \mathsf{Rel}(X,Y) \to \mathsf{Rel}(MX, MY)$ as:

$$\chi\, \hat{\mathbb{M}}\mathcal{R}\, y \stackrel{\triangle}{\iff} (\chi = \bot) \lor (\exists x \in X.\ \exists y \in Y.\ \chi = just\ x \land y = just\ y \land x \,\mathcal{R}\, y).$$

The mapping $\hat{\mathbb{M}}$ describes the structure of the usual *simulation* clause for partial computations, whereas $\mathbb{M}^{\circ}$ describes the corresponding *co-simulation* clause. It is easy to see that $\hat{\mathbb{M}}$ is a relator for $\mathbb{M}$. By Proposition 2, the map $\hat{\mathbb{M}} \land \hat{\mathbb{M}}^{\circ}$ is a conversive relator for $\mathbb{M}$. It is immediate to see that the latter relator describes the structure of the usual *bisimulation* clause for partial computations.

Example 13. For the distribution monad we define the relator $\hat{\mathbb{D}}$ relying on the notion of a *coupling* and results from optimal transport [72]. Recall that a *coupling* for $\mu \in D(X)$ and $\nu \in D(Y)$ a is a joint distribution $\omega \in D(X \times Y)$ such that: $\mu = \sum_{y\in Y} \omega(-, y)$ and $\nu = \sum_{x\in X} \omega(x, -)$. We denote the set of couplings of μ and ν by $\Omega(\mu, \nu)$. Define the (set-indexed) map $\hat{\mathbb{D}} : \mathsf{Rel}(X,Y) \to \mathsf{Rel}(DX, DY)$ as follows:

$$\mu\, \hat{\mathbb{D}}\mathcal{R}\, \nu \stackrel{\triangle}{\iff} (\exists \omega \in \Omega(\mu, \nu).\ \forall x, y.\ \omega(x, y) > 0 \implies x \,\mathcal{R}\, y).$$

We can show that $\hat{\mathbb{D}}$ is a relator for $\mathbb{D}$ relying on *Strassen's Theorem* [69], which shows that $\hat{\mathbb{D}}$ can be characterised universally (i.e. using an universal quantification).

Theorem 1 (Strassen's Theorem [69]**).** *For all $\mu \in DX$, $\nu \in DY$, and $\mathcal{R} : X \nrightarrow Y$, we have: $\mu\, \hat{\mathbb{D}}\mathcal{R}\, \nu \iff \forall \chi \subseteq X.\ \mu(\chi) \leq \nu(\mathcal{R}[\chi])$.*

As a corollary of Theorem 1, we see that $\hat{\mathbb{D}}$ describes the defining clause of Larsen-Skou bisimulation for Markov chains (based on full distributions) [34]. Finally, we observe that $\mathbb{D}\mathbb{M} \triangleq \hat{\mathbb{D}}\hat{\mathbb{M}}$ is a relator for $\mathbb{D}\mathbb{M}$.

Example 14. For relations $\mathcal{R} : X \nrightarrow Y$, $\mathcal{S} : X' \nrightarrow Y'$, let $\mathcal{R}\times\mathcal{S} : X\times X' \nrightarrow Y\times Y'$ be defined as $(\mathcal{R}\times\mathcal{S})((x,x'),(y,y')) \stackrel{\triangle}{\iff} \mathcal{R}(x,y)\wedge\mathcal{S}(x',y')$. We define the relator $\hat{\mathbb{C}} : \mathsf{Rel}(X,Y) \to \mathsf{Rel}(CX,CY)$ for the cost monad $\mathbb{C}$ as $\hat{\mathbb{C}}\mathcal{R} \triangleq \hat{\mathbb{M}}(\geq \times \mathcal{R})$, where $\geq$ denotes the opposite of the natural ordering on $\mathbb{N}$. It is straightforward to see that $\hat{\mathbb{C}}$ is indeed a relator for $\mathbb{C}$. The use of the opposite of the natural order in the definition of $\hat{\mathbb{C}}$ captures the idea that we use $\hat{\mathbb{C}}$ to measure complexity. Notice that $\hat{\mathbb{C}}$ describes Sands' simulation clause for program improvement [62].

Example 15. For the global state monad $\mathbb{G}$ we define the map $\hat{\mathbb{G}} : \mathsf{Rel}(X,Y) \to \mathsf{Rel}(GX,GY)$ as $\alpha\,\hat{\mathbb{G}}\mathcal{R}\,\beta \stackrel{\triangle}{\iff} \forall\sigma \in S.\ \alpha(\sigma)\ (\mathsf{I}_S \times \mathcal{R})\ \beta(\sigma)$. It is straightforward to see that $\hat{\mathbb{G}}$ is a relator for $\mathbb{G}$.

It is not hard to see that we can extend $\hat{\mathbb{G}}$ to relators for $\mathbb{M}\otimes\mathbb{G}$, $\mathbb{DM}\otimes\mathbb{G}$, and $\mathbb{C}\otimes\mathbb{G}$. In fact, Proposition 1 extends to relators.

Proposition 3. *Given a monad* $\mathbb{T} = \langle T, \tau, -^{\tau}\rangle$ *and a relator* $\hat{\mathbb{T}}$ *for* $\mathbb{T}$*, define the sum* $\hat{\mathbb{TM}}$ *of* $\hat{\mathbb{T}}$ *and* $\hat{\mathbb{M}}$ *as* $\hat{\mathbb{T}}\hat{\mathbb{M}}$*. Additionally, define the tensor* $\widehat{\mathbb{T}\otimes\mathbb{G}}$ *of* $\hat{\mathbb{T}}$ *and* $\hat{\mathbb{G}}$ *by* $\alpha\,(\widehat{\mathbb{T}\otimes\mathbb{G}})\mathcal{R}\,\beta$ *if an only if* $\forall\sigma.\ \alpha(\sigma)\,\hat{\mathbb{T}}(\mathsf{I}_S \times \mathcal{R})\,\beta(\sigma)$*. Then* $\hat{\mathbb{TM}}$ *is a relator for* $\mathbb{TM}$*, and* $(\widehat{\mathbb{T}\otimes\mathbb{G}})$ *is a relator for* $\mathbb{T}\otimes\mathbb{G}$*.*

Finally, we require relators to properly interact with the Σ-continuous structure of monads.

Definition 5. *Let* $\mathbb{T} = \langle T, \eta, -^{\dagger}\rangle$ *be a* Σ*-continuous monad and* Γ *be relator for* $\mathbb{T}$*. We say that* Γ *is* Σ-continuous *if it satisfies the following clauses—called the* inductive conditions*—for any* ω*-chain* $(\chi_n)_n$ *in* TX*, element* $y \in TY$*, elements* $\chi, \chi' \in TX$*, and relation* $\mathcal{R} : X \nrightarrow Y$*.*

$$\bot\,\Gamma\mathcal{R}\,y, \quad \chi \sqsubseteq \chi', \chi'\,\Gamma\mathcal{R}\,y \implies \chi\,\Gamma\mathcal{R}\,y, \quad \forall n.\ \chi_n\,\Gamma\mathcal{R}\,y \implies \bigsqcup_n \chi_n\,\Gamma\mathcal{R}\,y.$$

The relators $\hat{\mathbb{M}}$, $\hat{\mathbb{DM}}$, $\hat{\mathbb{C}}$, $\widehat{\mathbb{M}\otimes\mathbb{G}}$, $\widehat{\mathbb{DM}\otimes\mathbb{G}}$, $\widehat{\mathbb{C}\otimes\mathbb{G}}$ are all Σ-continuous. The reader might have noticed that we have not imposed any condition on how relators should interact with algebraic operations. Nonetheless, it would be quite natural to require a relator Γ to satisfy condition (rel 9) below, for all operation symbol $\mathbf{op} : P \rightsquigarrow I \in \Sigma$, maps $\kappa, \nu : I \to TX$, parameter $p \in P$, and relation $\mathcal{R}$.

$$\forall i \in I.\ \kappa(i)\,\Gamma\mathcal{R}\,\nu(i) \implies [\![\mathbf{op}]\!](p,\kappa)\,\Gamma\mathcal{R}\,[\![\mathbf{op}]\!](p,\nu) \qquad \text{(rel 9)}$$

Remarkably, if $\mathbb{T}$ is Σ-algebraic, then any relator for $\mathbb{T}$ satisfies (rel 9) (cf. [15]).

Proposition 4. *Let* $\mathbb{T} = \langle T, \eta, -^{\dagger}\rangle$ *be a* Σ*-algebraic monad, and let* Γ *be a relator for* $\mathbb{T}$*. Then* Γ *satisfies condition* (rel 9)*.*

Having defined relators and their basic properties, we now introduce the notion of an effectful eager normal form (bi)simulation.

6 Effectful Eager Normal Form (Bi)simulation

In this section we tacitly assume a Σ-continuous monad $\mathbb{T} = \langle T, \eta, -^\dagger \rangle$ and a Σ-continuous relator Γ for it be fixed. Σ-continuity of Γ is not required for defining effectful eager normal form (bi)simulation, but it is crucial to prove that the induced notion of similarity and bisimilarity are precongruence and congruence relations, respectively.

Working with effectful calculi, it is important to distinguish between relations over *terms* and relations over *eager normal forms*. For that reason we will work with pairs of relations of the form $(\mathcal{R}_\Lambda : \Lambda \nrightarrow \Lambda, \mathcal{R}_\mathcal{E} : \mathcal{E} \nrightarrow \mathcal{E})$, which we call λ-term relations (or term relations, for short). We use letters $\mathcal{R}, \mathcal{S}, \ldots$ to denote term relations. The collection of λ-term relations (i.e. $\mathsf{Rel}(\Lambda, \Lambda) \times \mathsf{Rel}(\mathcal{E}, \mathcal{E})$) inherits a complete lattice structure from $\mathsf{Rel}(\Lambda, \Lambda)$ and $\mathsf{Rel}(\mathcal{E}, \mathcal{E})$ pointwise, hence allowing λ-term relations to be defined both inductively and coinductively. We use these properties to define our notion of effectful eager normal form similarity.

Definition 6. *A term relation* $\mathcal{R} = (\mathcal{R}_\Lambda : \Lambda \nrightarrow \Lambda, \mathcal{R}_\mathcal{E} : \mathcal{E} \nrightarrow \mathcal{E})$ *is an* effectful eager normal form simulation *with respect to* Γ *(hereafter enf-simulation, as* Γ *will be clear from the context) if the following conditions hold, where in condition* (enf 4) $z \notin FV(E) \cup FV(E')$.

$$e\, \mathcal{R}_\Lambda\, f \implies [\![e]\!]\, \Gamma\mathcal{R}_\mathcal{E}\, [\![f]\!], \tag{enf 1}$$

$$x\, \mathcal{R}_\mathcal{E}\, s \implies s = x, \tag{enf 2}$$

$$\lambda x.e\, \mathcal{R}_\mathcal{E}\, s \implies \exists f.\ s = \lambda x.f \wedge e\, \mathcal{R}_\Lambda\, f, \tag{enf 3}$$

$$E[xv]\, \mathcal{R}_\mathcal{E}\, s \implies \exists E', v'.\ s = E'[xv'] \wedge v\, \mathcal{R}_\mathcal{E}\, v' \wedge \exists z.\ E[z]\, \mathcal{R}_\Lambda\, E'[z]. \tag{enf 4}$$

We say that relation $\mathcal{R}$ respects enfs *if it satisfies conditions* (enf 2)–(enf 4).

Definition 6 is quite standard. Clause (enf 1) is morally the same clause on terms used to define effectful applicative similarity in [15]. Clauses (enf 2) and (enf 3) state that whenever two enfs are related by $\mathcal{R}_\mathcal{E}$, then they must have the same outermost syntactic structure, and their subterms must be pairwise related. For instance, if $\lambda x.e\, \mathcal{R}_\mathcal{E}\, s$ holds, then s must the a λ-abstraction, i.e. an expression of the form $\lambda x.f$, and e and f must be related by $\mathcal{R}_\Lambda$.

Clause (enf 4) is the most interesting one. It states that whenever $E[xv]\, \mathcal{R}_\mathcal{E}\, s$, then s must be a stuck term $E'[xv']$, for some evaluation context E' and value v'. Notice that $E[xv]$ and s must have the same 'stuck variable' x. Additionally, v and v' must be related by $\mathcal{R}_\mathcal{E}$, and E and E' must be properly related too. The idea is that to see whether E and E' are related, we replace the stuck expressions xv, xv' with a fresh variable z, and test $E[z]$ and $E'[z]$ (thus resuming the evaluation process). We require $E[z]\ \mathcal{R}_\mathcal{E}\ E'[z]$ to hold, for *some* fresh variable z. The choice of the variable does not really matter, provided it is fresh. In fact, as we will see, effectful eager normal form similarity $\preceq^\mathsf{E}$ is substitutive and reflexive. In particular, if $E[z] \preceq^\mathsf{E}_\mathcal{E} E'[z]$ holds, then $E[y] \preceq^\mathsf{E}_\mathcal{E} E'[y]$ holds as well, for any variable $y \notin FV(E) \cup FV(E')$.

Notice that Definition 6 does not involve any universal quantification. In particular, enfs are tested by inspecting their syntactic structure, thus making the definition of an enf-simulation somehow 'local': terms are tested in isolation and not via their interaction with the environment. This is a major difference with e.g. applicative (bi)simulation, where the environment interacts with λ-abstractions by passing them arbitrary (closed) values as arguments.

Definition 6 induces a functional $\mathcal{R} \mapsto [\mathcal{R}]$ on the complete lattice $\mathsf{Rel}(\Lambda, \Lambda) \times \mathsf{Rel}(\mathcal{E}, \mathcal{E})$, where $[\mathcal{R}] = ([\mathcal{R}]_\Lambda, [\mathcal{R}]_\mathcal{E})$ is defined as follows (here $\mathsf{I}_\mathcal{X}$ denotes the identity relation on variables, i.e. the set of pairs of the form (x, x)):

$$
\begin{aligned}
[\mathcal{R}]_\Lambda &\triangleq \{(e, f) \mid [\![e]\!] \,\Gamma\mathcal{R}_\mathcal{E}\, [\![f]\!]\} \\
[\mathcal{R}]_\mathcal{E} &\triangleq \mathsf{I}_\mathcal{X} \cup \{(\lambda x.e, \lambda x.f) \mid e \,\mathcal{R}_\Lambda\, f\}, \\
&\quad \cup \{(E[xv], E'[xv']) \mid v \,\mathcal{R}_\mathcal{E}\, v' \wedge \exists z \notin FV(E) \cup FV(E').\ E[z] \,\mathcal{R}_\Lambda\, E'[z]\}.
\end{aligned}
$$

It is easy to see that a term relation $\mathcal{R}$ is an enf-simulation if and only if $\mathcal{R} \subseteq [\mathcal{R}]$. Notice also that although $[\mathcal{R}]_\mathcal{E}$ always contains the identity relation on variables, $\mathcal{R}_\mathcal{E}$ does not have to: the empty relation $(\emptyset, \emptyset)$ is an enf-simulation. Finally, since relators are monotone (condition (rel 4)), $\mathcal{R} \mapsto [\mathcal{R}]$ is monotone too. As a consequence, by Knaster-Tarski Theorem [70], it has a greatest fixed point which we call *effectful eager normal form similarity* with respect to Γ (hereafter enf-similarity) and denote by $\preceq^{\mathsf{E}} = (\preceq^{\mathsf{E}}_\Lambda, \preceq^{\mathsf{E}}_\mathcal{E})$. Enf-similarity is thus the largest enf-simulation with respect to Γ. Moreover, $\preceq^{\mathsf{E}}$ being defined coinductively, it comes with an associated coinduction proof principle stating that if a term relation $\mathcal{R}$ is an enf-simulation, then it is contained in $\preceq^{\mathsf{E}}$. Symbolically: $\mathcal{R} \subseteq [\mathcal{R}] \implies \mathcal{R} \subseteq \preceq^{\mathsf{E}}$.

Example 16. We use the coinduction proof principle to show that $\preceq^{\mathsf{E}}$ contains the β-rule, viz. $(\lambda x.e)v \preceq^{\mathsf{E}}_\Lambda e[v/x]$. For that, we simply observe that the term relation $(\{((\lambda x.e)v, e[v/x])\}, \mathsf{I}_\mathcal{E})$ is an enf-simulation. Indeed, $[\![(\lambda x.e)v]\!] = [\![e[v/x]]\!]$, so that by (rel 1) we have $[\![(\lambda x.e)v]\!] \,\Gamma\mathsf{I}_\mathcal{E}\, [\![e[v/x]]\!]$.

Finally, we define effectful eager normal form *bisimilarity.*

Definition 7. *A term relation $\mathcal{R}$ is an* effectful eager normal form bisimulation with respect to Γ *(enf-bisimulation, for short) if it is a* symmetric *enf-simulation.* Eager normal bisimilarity with respect to Γ *(enf-bisimilarity, for short)* $\simeq^{\mathsf{E}}$ *is the largest symmetric enf-simulation. In particular, enf-bisimilarity (with respect to Γ) coincides with enf-similarity with respect to $\Gamma \wedge \Gamma^\circ$.*

Example 17. We show that the probabilistic call-by-value fixed point combinators Y and Z of Example 2 are enf-bisimilar. In light of Proposition 5, this allows us to conclude that Y and Z are applicatively bisimilar, and thus contextually equivalent [15]. Let us consider the relator $\hat{\mathbb{D}\mathsf{M}}$ for probabilistic partial computations. We show $Y \simeq^{\mathsf{E}}_{\Lambda} Z$ by coinduction, proving that the symmetric closure of the term relation $\mathcal{R} = (\mathcal{R}_{\Lambda}, \mathcal{R}_{\mathcal{E}})$ defined as follows is an enf-simulation:

$$\mathcal{R}_{\Lambda} \triangleq \{(Y, Z), (\Delta\Delta z, Zyz), (\Delta\Delta, y(\lambda z.\Delta\Delta z) \,\mathbf{or}\, y(\lambda z.Zyz))\} \cup \mathsf{I}_{\Lambda}$$
$$\mathcal{R}_{\mathcal{E}} \triangleq \{(y(\lambda z.\Delta\Delta z), y(\lambda z.Zyz)), (\lambda z.\Delta\Delta z, \lambda z.Zyz),$$
$$(\lambda y.\Delta\Delta, \lambda y.(y(\lambda z.\Delta\Delta z) \,\mathbf{or}\, y(\lambda z.Zyz))), (y(\lambda z.\Delta\Delta z)z, y(\lambda z.Zyz)z)\} \cup \mathsf{I}_{\mathcal{E}}.$$

The term relation $\mathcal{R}$ is obtained from the relation $\{(Y, Z)\}$ by progressively adding terms and enfs according to clauses (enf 1)–(enf 4) in Definition 6. Checking that $\mathcal{R}$ is an enf-simulation is straightforward. As an illustrative example, we prove that $\Delta\Delta z \,\mathcal{R}_{\Lambda}\, Zyz$ implies $[\![\Delta\Delta z]\!] \,\hat{\mathbb{DM}}(\mathcal{R}_{\mathcal{E}})\, [\![Zyz]\!]$. The latter amounts to show:

$$(1 \cdot \mathit{just}\ y(\lambda z.\Delta\Delta z)z) \,\hat{\mathbb{DM}}(\mathcal{R}_{\mathcal{E}})\, (\frac{1}{2} \cdot \mathit{just}\ y(\lambda z.\Delta\Delta z)z + \frac{1}{2} \cdot \mathit{just}\ y(\lambda z.Zyz)z),$$

where, as usual, we write distributions as weighted formal sums. To prove the latter, it is sufficient to find a suitable coupling of $[\![\Delta\Delta z]\!]$ and $[\![Zyz]\!]$. Define the distribution $\omega \in D(M\mathcal{E} \times M\mathcal{E})$ as follows:

$$\omega(\mathit{just}\ y(\lambda z.\Delta\Delta z)z, \mathit{just}\ y(\lambda z.\Delta\Delta z)z) = \frac{1}{2},$$
$$\omega(\mathit{just}\ y(\lambda z.\Delta\Delta z)z, \mathit{just}\ y(\lambda z.Zyz)z) = \frac{1}{2},$$

and assigning zero to all other pairs in $M\mathcal{E} \times M\mathcal{E}$. Obviously ω is a coupling of $[\![\Delta\Delta z]\!]$ and $[\![Zyz]\!]$. Additionally, we see that $\omega(\chi, y)$ implies $\chi \,\hat{\mathbb{M}}\mathcal{R}_{\mathcal{E}}\, y$, since both $y(\lambda z.\Delta\Delta z)z \,\mathcal{R}_{\mathcal{E}}\, y(\lambda z.\Delta\Delta z)z$, and $y(\lambda z.\Delta\Delta z)z \,\mathcal{R}_{\mathcal{E}}\, y(\lambda z.Zyz)z$ hold.

As already discussed in Example 2, the operational equivalence between Y and Z is an example of an equivalence that cannot be readily established using standard operational methods—such as CIU equivalence or applicative bisimilarity—but whose proof is straightforward using enf-bisimilarity. Additionally, Theorem 3 will allow us to reduce the size of $\mathcal{R}$, thus minimising the task of checking that our relation is indeed an enf-bisimulation. To the best of the authors' knowledge, the probabilistic instance of enf-(bi)similarity is the first example of a *probabilistic eager normal form (bi)similarity* in the literature.

6.1 Congruence and Precongruence Theorems

In order for $\preceq^{\mathsf{E}}$ and $\simeq^{\mathsf{E}}$ to qualify as good notions of program refinement and equivalence, respectively, they have to allow for compositional reasoning. Roughly speaking, a term relation $\mathcal{R}$ is compositional if the validity of the relationship $\mathcal{C}[e] \,\mathcal{R}\, \mathcal{C}[e']$ between compound terms $\mathcal{C}[e], \mathcal{C}[e']$ follows from the validity of the relationship $e \,\mathcal{R}\, e'$ between the subterms e, e'. Mathematically, the notion of compositionality is formalised throughout the notion of *compatibility*, which directly leads to the notions of a precongruence and congruence relation. In this section we prove that $\preceq^{\mathsf{E}}$ and $\simeq^{\mathsf{E}}$ are substitutive precongruence and congruence

$$\frac{}{x \,\mathcal{R}^{\mathsf{sc}}_{\mathcal{E}}\, x}\ (\mathsf{sc\text{-}var}) \quad \frac{e \,\mathcal{R}_{\mathsf{x}}\, e'}{e \,\mathcal{R}^{\mathsf{sc}}_{\mathsf{x}}\, e'}\ (\mathsf{sc\text{-}\downarrow}) \quad \frac{s \,\mathcal{R}^{\mathsf{sc}}_{\mathcal{E}}\, s'}{s \,\mathcal{R}^{\mathsf{sc}}_{\Lambda}\, s'}\ (\mathsf{sc\text{-}to\text{-}\lambda})$$

$$\frac{e \,\mathcal{R}^{\mathsf{sc}}_{\Lambda}\, f}{\lambda x.e \,\mathcal{R}^{\mathsf{sc}}_{\mathcal{E}}\, \lambda x.f}\ (\mathsf{sc\text{-}abs}) \quad \frac{e_i \,\mathcal{R}^{\mathsf{sc}}_{\Lambda}\, e'_i}{e_1 e_2 \,\mathcal{R}^{\mathsf{sc}}_{\Lambda}\, e'_1 e'_2}\ (\mathsf{sc\text{-}app}) \quad \frac{e \,\mathcal{R}^{\mathsf{sc}}_{\Lambda}\, f}{\mathbf{op}(p, x.e) \,\mathcal{R}^{\mathsf{sc}}_{\Lambda}\, \mathbf{op}(p, x.f)}\ (\mathsf{sc\text{-}op})$$

$$\frac{v \,\mathcal{R}^{\mathsf{sc}}_{\mathcal{E}}\, v' \quad w \,\mathcal{R}^{\mathsf{sc}}_{\mathcal{E}}\, w'}{v[w/x] \,\mathcal{R}^{\mathsf{sc}}_{\mathcal{E}}\, v'[w'/x]}\ (\mathsf{sc\text{-}subst\text{-}val}) \quad \frac{e \,\mathcal{R}^{\mathsf{sc}}_{\Lambda}\, e' \quad v \,\mathcal{R}^{\mathsf{sc}}_{\mathcal{E}}\, v'}{e[v/x] \,\mathcal{R}^{\mathsf{sc}}_{\Lambda}\, e'[v'/x]}\ (\mathsf{sc\text{-}subst})$$

$$\frac{E[z] \,\mathcal{R}^{\mathsf{sc}}_{\Lambda}\, E'[z] \quad v \,\mathcal{R}^{\mathsf{sc}}_{\mathcal{E}}\, v'}{E[xv] \,\mathcal{R}^{\mathsf{sc}}_{\mathcal{E}}\, E[xv']}\ (\mathsf{sc\text{-}stuck}) \quad \frac{E[z] \,\mathcal{R}^{\mathsf{sc}}_{\Lambda}\, E'[z] \quad e \,\mathcal{R}^{\mathsf{sc}}_{\Lambda}\, e'}{E[e] \,\mathcal{R}^{\mathsf{sc}}_{\Lambda}\, E'[e']}\ (\mathsf{sc\text{-}ectx})$$

Fig. 1. Compatible and substitutive closure construction.

relations, that is preorder and equivalence relations closed under term constructors of Λ_Σ and substitution, respectively. To prove such results, we generalise Lassen's relational construction for the pure call-by-name λ-calculus [37]. Such a construction has been previously adapted to the *pure* call-by-value λ-calculus (and its extension with delimited and abortive control operators) in [9], whereas Lassen has proved compatibility of pure eager normal form bisimilarity via a CPS translation [38]. Both those proofs rely on syntactical properties of the calculus (mostly expressed using suitable small-step semantics), and thus seem to be hardly adaptable to effectful calculi. On the contrary, our proofs rely on the properties of relators, thereby making our results and techniques more modular and thus valid for a large class of effects.

We begin proving precongruence of enf-similarity. The central tool we use to prove the wished precongruence theorem is the so-called *(substitutive) context closure* [37] $\mathcal{R}^{\mathsf{sc}}$ of a term relation $\mathcal{R}$, which is inductively defined by the rules in Fig. 1, where $\mathsf{x} \in \{\Lambda, \mathcal{E}\}$, $i \in \{1, 2\}$, and $z \notin FV(E) \cup FV(E')$.

We easily see that $\mathcal{R}^{\mathsf{sc}}$ is the smallest term relation that contains $\mathcal{R}$, it is closed under language constructors of Λ_Σ (a property known as *compatibility* [5]), and it is closed under the substitution operation (a property known as *substitutivity* [5]). As a consequence, we say that a term relation $\mathcal{R}$ is a *substitutive compatible* relation if $\mathcal{R}^{\mathsf{sc}} \subseteq \mathcal{R}$ (and thus $\mathcal{R} = \mathcal{R}^{\mathsf{sc}}$). If, additionally, $\mathcal{R}$ is a preorder (resp. equivalence) relation, then we say that $\mathcal{R}$ is a *substitutive precongruence* (resp. *substitutive congruence*) relation.

We are now going to prove that if $\mathcal{R}$ is an enf-simulation, then so is $\mathcal{R}^{\mathsf{sc}}$. In particular, we will infer that $(\preceq^{\mathsf{E}})^{\mathsf{sc}}$ is a enf-simulation, and thus it is contained in $\preceq^{\mathsf{E}}$, by coinduction.

Lemma 2 (Main Lemma). *If $\mathcal{R}$ be an enf-simulation, then so is $\mathcal{R}^{\mathsf{sc}}$.*

Proof (sketch). The proof is long and non-trivial. Due to space constraints here we simply give some intuitions behind it. First, a routine proof by induction shows that since $\mathcal{R}$ respects enfs, then so does $\mathcal{R}^{\mathsf{sc}}$. Next, we wish to prove that $e \,\mathcal{R}^{\mathsf{sc}}_{\Lambda}\, f$ implies $[\![e]\!] \,\Gamma\mathcal{R}^{\mathsf{sc}}_{\mathcal{E}}\, [\![f]\!]$. Since Γ is inductive, the latter follows if for any $n \geq 0$, $e\,\mathcal{R}_{\Lambda}^{\mathsf{sc}}\,f$ implies $[\![e]\!]_n\;\Gamma\mathcal{R}_{\mathcal{E}}^{\mathsf{sc}}\;[\![f]\!]$. We prove the latter implication by lexicographic induction on (1) the natural number n and (2) the derivation $e\,\mathcal{R}_{\Lambda}^{\mathsf{sc}}\,f$. The case for $n = 0$ is trivial (since Γ is inductive). The remaining cases are nontrivial, and are handled observing that $[\![E[e]]\!] = (s \mapsto [\![E[s]]\!])^{\dagger}[\![e]\!]$ and $[\![e[v/x]]\!]_n \sqsubseteq [\![-[v/x]]\!]_n^{\dagger}[\![e]\!]_n$. Both these identities allow us to apply condition (rel 8) to simplify proof obligations (usually relying on part (2) of the induction hypothesis as well). This scheme is iterated until we reach either an enf (in which case we are done by condition (rel 7)) or a pair of expressions on which we can apply part (1) of the induction hypothesis.

Theorem 2. *Enf-similarity (resp. bisimilarity) is a substitutive precongruence (resp. congruence) relation.*

Proof. We show that enf-similarity is a substitutive precongruence relation. By Lemma 2, it is sufficient to show that $\preceq^{\mathsf{E}}$ is a preorder. This follows by coinduction, since the term relations I and $\preceq^{\mathsf{E}} \circ \preceq^{\mathsf{E}}$ are enf-simulations (the proofs make use of conditions (rel 1) and (rel 2), as well as of substitutivity of $\preceq^{\mathsf{E}}$).

Finally, we show that enf-bisimilarity is a substitutive congruence relation. Obviously $\simeq^{\mathsf{E}}$ is an equivalence relation, so that it is sufficient to prove $(\simeq^{\mathsf{E}})^{\mathsf{sc}} \subseteq \simeq^{\mathsf{E}}$. That directly follows by coinduction relying on Lemma 2, provided that $(\simeq^{\mathsf{E}})^{\mathsf{sc}}$ is symmetric. An easy inspection of the rules in Fig. 1 reveals that $\mathcal{R}^{\mathsf{sc}}$ is symmetric, whenever $\mathcal{R}$ is.

6.2 Soundness for Effectful Applicative (Bi)similarity

Theorem 2 qualifies enf-bisimilarity and enf-similarity as good candidate notions of program equivalence and refinement for Λ_{Σ}, at least from a structural perspective. However, we gave motivations for such notions looking at specific examples where effectful applicative (bi)similarity is ineffective. It is then natural to ask whether enf-(bi)similarity can be used as a proof technique for effectful applicative (bi)similarity.

Here we give a formal comparison between enf-(bi)similarity and effectful applicative (bi)similarity, as defined in [15]. First of all, we rephrase the notion of an effectful applicative (bi)simulation of [15] to our calculus Λ_{Σ}. For that, we use the following notational convention. Let $\Lambda_0, \mathcal{V}_0$ denote the collections of closed terms and closed values, respectively. We notice that if $e \in \Lambda_0$, then $[\![e]\!] \in T\mathcal{V}_0$. As a consequence, $[\![-]\!]$ induces a closed evaluation function $|-| : \Lambda_0 \to T\mathcal{V}_0$ characterised by the identity $[\![-]\!] \circ \iota = T\iota \circ |-|$, where $\iota : \mathcal{V}_0 \hookrightarrow \mathcal{E}$ is the obvious inclusion map. We can thus phrase the definition of effectful applicative similarity (with respect to a relator Γ) as follows.

Definition 8. *A term relation* $\mathcal{R} = (\mathcal{R}_{\Lambda_0} : \Lambda_0 \nrightarrow \Lambda_0, \mathcal{R}_{\mathcal{V}_0} : \mathcal{V}_0 \nrightarrow \mathcal{V}_0)$ *is an effectful applicative simulation with respect to* Γ *(applicative simulation, for short) if:*

$$e\,\mathcal{R}_{\Lambda_0}\,f \implies |e|\;\Gamma\mathcal{R}_{\mathcal{V}_0}\;|f|, \qquad \text{(app 1)}$$
$$\lambda x.e\,\mathcal{R}_{\mathcal{V}_0}\,\lambda x.f \implies \forall v \in \mathcal{V}_0.\; e[v/x]\,\mathcal{R}_{\Lambda_0}\,f[v/x]. \qquad \text{(app 2)}$$

As usual, we can define effectful applicative similarity with respect to Γ (applicative similarity, for short), denoted by $\preceq^{\mathsf{A}}_0 = (\preceq^{\mathsf{A}}_{\Lambda_0}, \preceq^{\mathsf{A}}_{\mathcal{V}_0})$, coinductively as the largest applicative simulation. Its associated coinduction proof principle states that if a relation is an applicative simulation, then it is contained in applicative similarity. Finally, we extend $\preceq^{\mathsf{A}}_0$ to arbitrary terms by defining the relation $\preceq^{\mathsf{A}} = (\preceq^{\mathsf{A}}_{\Lambda}, \preceq^{\mathsf{A}}_{\mathcal{V}})$ as follows: let e, f, w, u be terms and values with free variables among $\bar{x} = x_1, \ldots, x_n$. We let $\bar{v}$ range over n-ary sequences of closed values $v_1, \ldots, v_n$. Define:

$$e \preceq^{\mathsf{A}}_{\Lambda} f \stackrel{\triangle}{\iff} \forall \bar{v}.\ e[\bar{v}/\bar{x}] \preceq^{\mathsf{A}}_{\Lambda_0} f[\bar{v}/\bar{x}], \qquad w \preceq^{\mathsf{A}}_{\Lambda} u \stackrel{\triangle}{\iff} \forall \bar{v}.\ w[\bar{v}/\bar{x}] \preceq^{\mathsf{A}}_{\Lambda_0} u[\bar{v}/\bar{x}].$$

The following result states that enf-similarity is a sound proof technique for applicative similarity.

Proposition 5. *Enf-similarity $\preceq^{\mathsf{E}}$ is included in applicative similarity $\preceq^{\mathsf{A}}$.*

Proof. Let $\preceq^{\mathsf{C}} = (\preceq^{\mathsf{C}}_{\Lambda}, \preceq^{\mathsf{C}}_{\mathcal{V}})$ denote enf-similarity restricted to closed terms and values. We first show that $\preceq^{\mathsf{C}}$ is an applicative simulation, from which follows, by coinduction, that it is included in $\preceq^{\mathsf{A}}_0$. It is easy to see that $\preceq^{\mathsf{C}}$ satisfies condition (app 2). In order to prove that it also satisfies condition (app 1), we have to show that for all $e, f \in \Lambda_\circ$, $e \preceq^{\mathsf{C}}_{\Lambda} f$ implies $|e|\ \Gamma \preceq^{\mathsf{C}}_{\mathcal{V}} |f|$. Since $e \preceq^{\mathsf{C}}_{\Lambda} f$ obviously implies $\iota(e) \preceq^{\mathsf{E}}_{\Lambda} \iota(f)$, by (enf 1) we infer $[\![\iota(e)]\!]\ \Gamma \preceq^{\mathsf{E}}_{\mathcal{V}} [\![\iota(f)]\!]$, and thus $T\iota|e|\ \Gamma \preceq^{\mathsf{E}}_{\mathcal{V}} T\iota|f|$. By stability of Γ, the latter implies $|e|\ \Gamma(\iota^\circ \circ \preceq_{\mathcal{E}} \circ \iota)\ |f|$, and thus the wished thesis, since $\iota^\circ \circ \preceq_{\mathcal{E}} \circ \iota$ is nothing but $\preceq^{\mathsf{C}}_{\mathcal{V}}$. Finally, we show that for all terms e, f, if $e \preceq^{\mathsf{E}}_{\Lambda} f$, then $e \preceq^{\mathsf{A}}_{\Lambda} f$ (a similar result holds *mutatis mutandis* for values, so that we can conclude $\preceq^{\mathsf{E}} \subseteq \preceq^{\mathsf{A}}$). Indeed, suppose $FV(e) \cup FV(f) \subseteq \bar{x}$, then by substitutivity of $\preceq^{\mathsf{E}}$ we have that $e \preceq^{\mathsf{E}}_{\Lambda} f$ implies $e[\bar{v}/\bar{x}] \preceq^{\mathsf{E}}_{\Lambda} f[\bar{v}/\bar{x}]$, for all closed values $\bar{v}$ (notice that since we are substituting *closed* values, sequential and simultaneous substitution coincide). That essentially means $e[\bar{v}/\bar{x}] \preceq^{\mathsf{C}}_{\Lambda} f[\bar{v}/\bar{x}]$, and thus $e[\bar{v}/\bar{x}] \preceq^{\mathsf{A}}_{\Lambda_0} f[\bar{v}/\bar{x}]$. We thus conclude $e \preceq^{\mathsf{A}}_{\Lambda} f$.

Since in [15] it is shown that effectful applicative similarity (resp. bisimilarity) is contained in effectful contextual approximation (resp. equivalence), Proposition 5 gives the following result.

Corollary 1. *Enf-similarity and enf-bisimilarity are sound proof techniques for contextual approximation and equivalence, respectively.*

Although sound, enf-bisimilarity is *not* fully abstract for applicative bisimilarity. In fact, as already observed in [38], in the pure λ-calculus enf-bisimilarity is strictly finer than applicative bisimilarity (and thus strictly finer than contextual equivalence too). For instance, the terms xv and $(\lambda y.xv)(xv)$ are obviously applicatively bisimilar but not enf-bisimilar.

6.3 Eager Normal Form (Bi)simulation Up-to Context

The up-to context technique [37,60,64] is a refinement of the coinduction proof principle of enf-(bi)similarity that allows for handier proofs of equivalence and refinement between terms. When exhibiting a candidate enf-(bi)simulation relation $\mathcal{R}$, it is desirable for $\mathcal{R}$ to be as small as possible, so to minimise the task of verifying that $\mathcal{R}$ is indeed an enf-(bi)simulation.

The motivation behind such a technique can be easily seen looking at Example 17, where we showed the equivalence between the probabilistic fixed point combinators Y and Z working with relations containing several administrative pairs of terms. The presence of such pairs was forced by Definition 7, although they appear somehow unnecessary in order to convince that Y and Z exhibit the same operational behaviour.

Enf-(bi)simulation up-to context is a refinement of enf-(bi)simulation that allows to check that a relation $\mathcal{R}$ behaves as an enf-(bi)simulation relation up to its substitutive and compatible closure.

Definition 9. *A term relation* $\mathcal{R} = (\mathcal{R}_\Lambda : \Lambda \nrightarrow \Lambda, \mathcal{R}_\mathcal{E} : \mathcal{E} \nrightarrow \mathcal{E})$ *is an* effectful eager normal form simulation up-to context with respect to Γ *(enf-simulation up-to context, hereafter) if satisfies the following conditions, where in condition* (up-to 4) $z \notin FV(E) \cup FV(E')$.

$$e \, \mathcal{R}_\Lambda \, f \implies [\![e]\!] \, \Gamma\mathcal{R}_\mathcal{E}^{\mathsf{sc}} \, [\![f]\!], \quad \text{(up-to 1)}$$

$$x \, \mathcal{R}_\mathcal{E} \, s \implies s = x, \quad \text{(up-to 2)}$$

$$\lambda x.e \, \mathcal{R}_\mathcal{E} \, s \implies \exists f.\ s = \lambda x.f \wedge e \, \mathcal{R}_\Lambda^{\mathsf{sc}} \, f, \quad \text{(up-to 3)}$$

$$E[xv] \, \mathcal{R}_\mathcal{E} \, s \implies \exists E', v'.\ s = E'[xv'] \wedge v \, \mathcal{R}_\mathcal{E}^{\mathsf{sc}} \, v' \wedge \exists z.\ E[z] \, \mathcal{R}_\Lambda^{\mathsf{sc}} \, E'[z]. \quad \text{(up-to 4)}$$

In order for the up-to context technique to be sound, we need to show that every enf-simulation up-to context is contained in enf-similarity. This is a direct consequence of the following variation of Lemma 2.

Lemma 3. *If* $\mathcal{R}$ *is a enf-simulation up-to context, then* $\mathcal{R}^{\mathsf{sc}}$ *is a enf-simulation.*

Proof. The proof is structurally identical to the one of Lemma 2, where we simply observe that wherever we use the assumption that $\mathcal{R}$ is an enf-simulation, we can use the weaker assumption that $\mathcal{R}$ is an enf-simulation up-to context.

In particular, since by Lemma 2 we have that $\preceq^{\mathsf{E}} = (\preceq^{\mathsf{E}})^{\mathsf{sc}}$, we see that enf-similarity is an enf-simulation up-to context. Additionally, by Lemma 3 it is the largest such. Since the same result holds for enf-bisimilarity and enf-bisimilarity up-to context, we have the following theorem.

Theorem 3. *Enf-similarity is the largest enf-simulation up-to context, and enf-bisimilarity is the largest enf-bisimulation up-to context.*

Example 18. We apply Theorem 3 to simplify the proof of the equivalence between Y and Z given in Example 17. In fact, it is sufficient to show that the symmetric closure of term relation $\mathcal{R}$ defined below is an enf-bisimulation up-to context.

$$\mathcal{R}_\Lambda \triangleq \{(Y, Z), (\Delta\Delta z, Zyz), (\Delta\Delta, y(\lambda z.\Delta\Delta z) \textbf{ or } y(\lambda z.Zyz))\}, \qquad \mathcal{R}_\mathcal{E} \triangleq \mathsf{I}_\mathcal{E}.$$

Example 19. Recall the fixed point combinators with ticking operations Y and Z of Example 4. Let us consider the relator $\hat{\mathbb{C}}$. It is not hard to see that Y and Z are not enf-bisimilar (that is because the ticking operation is evaluated at different moments, so to speak). Nonetheless, once we pass them a variable x_0 as argument, we have $Zx_0 \preceq^{\mathsf{E}}_{\Lambda} Yx_0$. For, observe that the term relation $\mathcal{R}$ defined below is an enf-simulation up-context.

$$\mathcal{R}_{\Lambda} \triangleq \{(Yx_0, Zx_0), (\mathbf{tick}(\Delta[x_0/y]\Delta[x_0/y]z), \mathbf{tick}(\Theta\Theta x_0 z))\}, \qquad \mathcal{R}_{\mathcal{E}} = \emptyset.$$

Intuitively, Y executes a tick first, and then proceeds iterating the evaluation of $\Delta[x_0/y]\Delta[x_0/y]$, the latter involving two tickings only. On the contrary, Z proceeds by recursively call itself, hence involving three tickings at any iteration, so to speak. Since $\preceq^{\mathsf{E}}$ is substitutive, for any value v we have $Zv \preceq^{\mathsf{E}} Yv$.

Theorem 3 makes enf-(bi)similarity an extremely powerful proof technique for program equivalence/refinement, especially because it is yet unknown whether there exist *sound* up-to context techniques for applicative (bi)similarity [35].

6.4 Weak Head Normal Form (Bi)simulation

So far we have focused on call-by-value calculi, since in presence of effects the call-by-value evaluation strategy seems the more natural one. Nonetheless, our framework can be easily adapted to deal with call-by-name calculi too. In this last section we spend some words on *effectful weak head normal form (bi)similarity* (whnf-(bi)similarity, for short). The latter is nothing but the call-by-name counterpart of enf-(bi)similarity. The main difference between enf-(bi)similarity and whnf-(bi)similarity relies on the notion of an evaluation context (and thus of a stuck term). In fact, in a call-by-name setting, Λ_{Σ} evaluation contexts are expressions of the form $[-]e_1 \cdots e_n$, which are somehow simpler than their call-by-value counterparts. Such a simplicity is reflected in the definition of whnf-(bi)similarity, which allows to prove *mutatis mutandis* all results proved for enf-(bi)similarity (such results are, without much of a surprise, actually easier to prove).

We briefly expand on that. The collection of weak head normal forms (whnfs, for short) $\mathcal{W}$ is defined as the union of $\mathcal{V}$ and the collection of stuck terms, the latter being expressions of the form $xe_1 \cdots e_n$. The evaluation function of Definition 2 now maps terms to elements in $T\mathcal{W}$, and it is essentially obtained modifying Definition 2 defining $[\![E[xe]]\!]_{n+1} \triangleq \eta(E[xe])$ and $[\![E[(\lambda x.f)e]]\!]_{n+1} \triangleq [\![E[f[e/x]]]\!]_n$. The notion of a whnf-(bi)simulation (and thus the notions of whnf-(bi)similarity) is obtained modifying Definition 6 accordingly. In particular, clauses (enf 2) and (enf 4) are replaced by the following clause, where we use the notation $\mathcal{R} = (\mathcal{R}_{\Lambda} : \Lambda \nrightarrow \Lambda, \mathcal{R}_{\mathcal{W}} : \mathcal{W} \nrightarrow \mathcal{W})$ to denote a (call-by-name) λ-term relation.

$$xe_0 \cdots e_k \, \mathcal{R}_{\mathcal{W}} \, s \implies \exists f_0, \ldots, f_k.\ s = xf_0 \cdots f_k \wedge \forall i.\ e_i \, \mathcal{R}_{\Lambda} \, f_i.$$

A straightforward modifications of the rules in Fig. 1 allows to prove an analogous of Lemma 2 for whnf-simulations, and thus to conclude (pre)congruence properties of whnf-(bi)similarity. Additionally, such results generalise to whnf-(bi)simulation up to-context, the latter being defined according to Definition 9, so that we have an analogous of Theorem 3 as well. The latter allows to infer the equivalence of the argument-switching fixed point combinators of Example 3, simply by noticing that the symmetric closure of the term relation $\mathcal{R} = (\{(P, Q), (Pyz, Qzy), (Pzy, Qyz)\}, \emptyset)$ is a whnf-bisimulation up-to context.

Finally, it is straightforward to observe that whnf-(bi)similarity is included in the call-by-name counterpart of effectful applicative (bi)similarity, but that the inclusion is strict. In fact, the (pure λ-calculus) terms xx and $x(\lambda y.xy)$ are applicatively bisimilar, but not whnf-bisimilar.

7 Related Work

Normal form (bi)similarity has been originally introduced for the call-by-name λ-calculus in [65], where it was called *open bisimilarity*. Open bisimilarity provides a coinductive characterisation of Lévy-Longo tree equivalence [42,45,53], and has been shown to coincide with the equivalence (notably weak bisimilarity) induced by Milner's encoding of the λ-calculus into the π-calculus [48].

In [37] normal form bisimilarity relations characterising both Böhm and Lévy-Longo tree equivalences have been studied by purely operational means, providing new congruence proofs of the aforementioned tree equivalences based on suitable relational constructions. Such results have been extended to the call-by-value λ-calculus in [38], where the so-called *eager normal form bisimilarity* is introduced. The latter is shown to coincide with the Lévy-Longo tree equivalence induced by a suitable CPS translation [54], and thus to be a congruence relation. An elementary proof of congruence properties of eager normal form bisimilarity is given in [9], where Lassen's relational construction [37] is extended to the call-by-value λ-calculus, as well as its extensions with delimited and abortive control operators. Finally, following [65], eager normal form bisimilarity has been recently characterised as the equivalence induced by a suitable encoding of the (call-by-value) λ-calculus in the π-calculus [21].

Concerning effectful extensions of normal form bisimilarity, our work seems to be rather new. In fact, normal form bisimilarity has been studied for *deterministic* extensions of the λ-calculus with specific *non*-algebraic effects, notably control operators [9], as well as control and state [68] (where full abstraction of the obtained notion of normal form bisimilarity is proved). The only extension of normal form bisimilarity to an algebraic effect the authors are aware of, is given in [39], where normal form bisimilarity is studied for a *nondeterministic call-by-name* λ-calculus. However, we should mention that contrary to normal form bisimilarity, both nondeterministic [20] and probabilistic [41] extensions of Böhm tree equivalence have been investigated (although none of them employ, to the best of the authors' knowledge, coinductive techniques).

8 Conclusion

This paper shows that effectful normal form bisimulation is indeed a powerful methodology for program equivalence. Interestingly, the proof of congruence for normal form bisimilarity can be given just once, without the necessity of redoing it for every distinct notion of algebraic effect considered. This relies on the fact that the underlying monad and relator are Σ-continuous, something which has already been proved for many distinct notions of effects [15].

Topics for further work are plentiful. First of all, a natural question is whether the obtained notion of bisimilarity coincides with contextual equivalence. This is known *not* to hold in the deterministic case [37,38], but to hold in presence of control and state [68], which offer the environment the necessary discriminating power. Is there any (sufficient) condition on effects guaranteeing full abstraction of normal form bisimilarity? This is an intriguing question we are currently investigating. In fact, contrary to applicative bisimilarity (which is known to be unsound in presence of non-algebraic effects [33], such as local states), the syntactic nature of normal form bisimilarity seems to be well-suited for languages combining both algebraic and non-algebraic effects.

Another interesting topic for future research, is investigating whether normal form bisimilarity can be extended to languages having both algebraic operations and effect handlers [7,59].

References

1. Abramsky, S.: The lazy lambda calculus. In: Turner, D. (ed.) Research Topics in Functional Programming, pp. 65–117. Addison Wesley, Boston (1990)
2. Abramsky, S., Jung, A.: Domain theory. In: Handbook of Logic in Computer Science, pp. 1–168. Clarendon Press (1994)
3. Abramsky, S., Ong, C.L.: Full abstraction in the lazy lambda calculus. Inf. Comput. **105**(2), 159–267 (1993)
4. Appel, A., McAllester, D.: An indexed model of recursive types for foundational proof-carrying code. ACM Trans. Program. Lang. Syst. **23**(5), 657–683 (2001)
5. Barendregt, H.: The lambda calculus: its syntax and semantics. In: Studies in Logic and the Foundations of Mathematics. North-Holland (1984)
6. Barr, M.: Relational algebras. Lect. Notes Math. **137**, 39–55 (1970)
7. Bauer, A., Pretnar, M.: Programming with algebraic effects and handlers. J. Log. Algebr. Meth. Program. **84**(1), 108–123 (2015)
8. Benton, N., Kennedy, A., Beringer, L., Hofmann, M.: Relational semantics for effect-based program transformations: higher-order store. In: Proceedings of PPDP 2009, pp. 301–312 (2009)
9. Biernacki, D., Lenglet, S., Polesiuk, P.: Proving soundness of extensional normal-form bisimilarities. Electr. Notes Theor. Comput. Sci. **336**, 41–56 (2018)
10. Bizjak, A., Birkedal, L.: Step-indexed logical relations for probability. In: Pitts, A. (ed.) FoSSaCS 2015. LNCS, vol. 9034, pp. 279–294. Springer, Heidelberg (2015). https://doi.org/10.1007/978-3-662-46678-0_18
11. Böhm, C.: Alcune proprietà delle forme $\beta\eta$-normali del λk-calcolo. Pubblicazioni dell'Istituto per le Applicazioni del Calcolo **696** (1968)

12. Burris, S., Sankappanavar, H.: A Course in Universal Algebra. Graduate Texts in Mathematics. Springer, New York (1981)
13. Crubillé, R., Dal Lago, U.: On probabilistic applicative bisimulation and call-by-value λ-Calculi. In: Shao, Z. (ed.) ESOP 2014. LNCS, vol. 8410, pp. 209–228. Springer, Heidelberg (2014). https://doi.org/10.1007/978-3-642-54833-8_12
14. Culpepper, R., Cobb, A.: Contextual equivalence for probabilistic programs with continuous random variables and scoring. In: Yang, H. (ed.) ESOP 2017. LNCS, vol. 10201, pp. 368–392. Springer, Heidelberg (2017). https://doi.org/10.1007/978-3-662-54434-1_14
15. Dal Lago, U., Gavazzo, F., Levy, P.: Effectful applicative bisimilarity: monads, relators, and Howe's method. In: Proceedings of LICS 2017, pp. 1–12 (2017)
16. Dal Lago, U., Sangiorgi, D., Alberti, M.: On coinductive equivalences for higher-order probabilistic functional programs. In: Proceedings of POPL 2014, pp. 297–308 (2014)
17. Dal Lago, U., Zorzi, M.: Probabilistic operational semantics for the lambda calculus. RAIRO - Theor. Inf. Appl. **46**(3), 413–450 (2012)
18. Danos, V., Harmer, R.: Probabilistic game semantics. ACM Trans. Comput. Logic **3**(3), 359–382 (2002)
19. Davey, B., Priestley, H.: Introduction to Lattices and Order. Cambridge University Press, Cambridge (1990)
20. De Liguoro, U., Piperno, A.: Non deterministic extensions of untyped lambda-calculus. Inf. Comput. **122**(2), 149–177 (1995)
21. Durier, A., Hirschkoff, D., Sangiorgi, D.: Eager functions as processes. In: Proceedings of the 33rd Annual ACM/IEEE Symposium on Logic in Computer Science, LICS 2018, pp. 364–373 (2018)
22. Felleisen, M., Hieb, R.: The revised report on the syntactic theories of sequential control and state. Theor. Comput. Sci. **103**(2), 235–271 (1992)
23. Gavazzo, F.: Quantitative behavioural reasoning for higher-order effectful programs: applicative distances. In: Proceedings of the 33rd Annual ACM/IEEE Symposium on Logic in Computer Science, LICS 2018, Oxford, UK, 09–12 July 2018, pp. 452–461 (2018)
24. Goguen, J.A., Thatcher, J.W., Wagner, E.G., Wright, J.B.: Initial algebra semantics and continuous algebras. J. ACM **24**(1), 68–95 (1977)
25. Goubault-Larrecq, J., Lasota, S., Nowak, D.: Logical relations for monadic types. Math. Struct. Comput. Sci. **18**(6), 1169–1217 (2008)
26. Hofmann, D., Seal, G., Tholen, W. (eds.): Monoidal Topology. A Categorical Approach to Order, Metric, and Topology. No. 153 in Encyclopedia of Mathematics and its Applications. Cambridge University Press (2014)
27. Hughes, J., Jacobs, B.: Simulations in coalgebra. Theor. Comput. Sci. **327**(1–2), 71–108 (2004)
28. Hyland, M., Plotkin, G.D., Power, J.: Combining effects: sum and tensor. Theor. Comput. Sci. **357**(1–3), 70–99 (2006)
29. Hyland, M., Power, J.: The category theoretic understanding of universal algebra: Lawvere theories and monads. Electr. Notes Theor. Comput. Sci. **172**, 437–458 (2007)
30. Johann, P., Simpson, A., Voigtländer, J.: A generic operational metatheory for algebraic effects. In: Proceedings of LICS 2010, pp. 209–218. IEEE Computer Society (2010)
31. Jones, C.: Probabilistic non-determinism. Ph.D. thesis, University of Edinburgh, UK (1990)

32. Katsumata, S., Sato, T.: Preorders on monads and coalgebraic simulations. In: Pfenning, F. (ed.) FoSSaCS 2013. LNCS, vol. 7794, pp. 145–160. Springer, Heidelberg (2013). https://doi.org/10.1007/978-3-642-37075-5_10
33. Koutavas, V., Levy, P.B., Sumii, E.: From applicative to environmental bisimulation. Electr. Notes Theor. Comput. Sci. **276**, 215–235 (2011)
34. Larsen, K.G., Skou, A.: Bisimulation through probabilistic testing. In: Proceedings of POPL 1989, pp. 344–352 (1989)
35. Lassen, S.: Relational reasoning about contexts. In: Gordon, A.D., Pitts, A.M. (eds.) Higher Order Operational Techniques in Semantics, pp. 91–136 (1998)
36. Lassen, S.: Relational reasoning about functions and nondeterminism. Ph.D. thesis, Department of Computer Science, University of Aarhus, May 1998
37. Lassen, S.B.: Bisimulation in untyped lambda calculus: Böhm trees and bisimulation up to context. Electr. Notes Theor. Comput. Sci. **20**, 346–374 (1999)
38. Lassen, S.B.: Eager normal form bisimulation. In: Proceedings of LICS 2005, pp. 345–354 (2005)
39. Lassen, S.B.: Normal form simulation for McCarthy's Amb. Electr. Notes Theor. Comput. Sci. **155**, 445–465 (2006)
40. Lawvere, W.F.: Functorial semantics of algebraic theories. Ph.D. thesis (2004)
41. Leventis, T.: Probabilistic Böhm trees and probabilistic separation. In: Proceedings of LICS (2018)
42. Levy, J.-J.: An algebraic interpretation of the $\lambda\beta K$-calculus and a labelled λ-calculus. In: Böhm, C. (ed.) λ-Calculus and Computer Science Theory. LNCS, vol. 37, pp. 147–165. Springer, Heidelberg (1975). https://doi.org/10.1007/BFb0029523
43. Levy, P.B.: Similarity quotients as final coalgebras. In: Hofmann, M. (ed.) FoSSaCS 2011. LNCS, vol. 6604, pp. 27–41. Springer, Heidelberg (2011). https://doi.org/10.1007/978-3-642-19805-2_3
44. Levy, P., Power, J., Thielecke, H.: Modelling environments in call-by-value programming languages. Inf. Comput. **185**(2), 182–210 (2003)
45. Longo, G.: Set-theoretical models of lambda calculus: theories, expansions, isomorphisms. Ann. Pure Appl. Logic **24**, 153–188 (1983)
46. Mac Lane, S.: Categories for the Working Mathematician. GTM, vol. 5. Springer, New York (1971). https://doi.org/10.1007/978-1-4612-9839-7
47. Mason, I.A., Talcott, C.L.: Equivalence in functional languages with effects. J. Funct. Program. **1**(3), 287–327 (1991)
48. Milner, R.: Functions as processes. Math. Struct. Comput. Sci. **2**(2), 119–141 (1992)
49. Moggi, E.: Computational lambda-calculus and monads. In: Proceedings of LICS 1989, pp. 14–23. IEEE Computer Society (1989)
50. Moggi, E.: Notions of computation and monads. Inf. Comput. **93**(1), 55–92 (1991)
51. Morris, J.: Lambda calculus models of programming languages. Ph.D. thesis, MIT (1969)
52. Ong, C.L.: Non-determinism in a functional setting. In: Proceedings of LICS 1993, pp. 275–286. IEEE Computer Society (1993)
53. Ong, C.: The lazy lambda calculus: an investigation into the foundations of functional programming. University of London, Imperial College of Science and Technology (1988)
54. Plotkin, G.: Call-by-name, call-by-value and the lambda-calculus. Theoret. Comput. Sci. **1**(2), 125–159 (1975)
55. Plotkin, G.: Lambda-definability and logical relations. Technical report SAI-RM-4. University of Edinburgh, School of A.I. (1973)

56. Plotkin, G., Power, J.: Adequacy for algebraic effects. In: Honsell, F., Miculan, M. (eds.) FoSSaCS 2001. LNCS, vol. 2030, pp. 1–24. Springer, Heidelberg (2001). https://doi.org/10.1007/3-540-45315-6_1
57. Plotkin, G., Power, J.: Notions of computation determine monads. In: Nielsen, M., Engberg, U. (eds.) FoSSaCS 2002. LNCS, vol. 2303, pp. 342–356. Springer, Heidelberg (2002). https://doi.org/10.1007/3-540-45931-6_24
58. Plotkin, G.D., Power, J.: Algebraic operations and generic effects. Appl. Categorical Struct. **11**(1), 69–94 (2003)
59. Plotkin, G.D., Pretnar, M.: Handling algebraic effects. Logical Methods Comput. Sci. **9**(4), 1–36 (2013)
60. Pous, D., Sangiorgi, D.: Enhancements of the bisimulation proof method. In: Sangiorgi, D., Rutten, J. (eds.) Advanced Topics in Bisimulation and Coinduction. Cambridge University Press, New York (2012)
61. Reynolds, J.: Types, abstraction and parametric polymorphism. In: IFIP Congress, pp. 513–523 (1983)
62. Sands, D.: Improvement theory and its applications. In: Gordon, A.D., Pitts, A.M. (eds.) Higher Order Operational Techniques in Semantics, pp. 275–306. Publications of the Newton Institute, Cambridge University Press (1998)
63. Sangiorgi, D., Kobayashi, N., Sumii, E.: Environmental bisimulations for higher-order languages. ACM Trans. Program. Lang. Syst. **33**(1), 5:1–5:69 (2011)
64. Sangiorgi, D.: A theory of bisimulation for the ϕ-calculus. In: Best, E. (ed.) CONCUR 1993. LNCS, vol. 715, pp. 127–142. Springer, Heidelberg (1993). https://doi.org/10.1007/3-540-57208-2_10
65. Sangiorgi, D.: The lazy lambda calculus in a concurrency scenario. Inf. Comput. **111**(1), 120–153 (1994)
66. Sangiorgi, D., Vignudelli, V.: Environmental bisimulations for probabilistic higher-order languages. In: Proceedings of POPL 2016, pp. 595–607 (2016)
67. Simpson, A., Voorneveld, N.: Behavioural equivalence via modalities for algebraic effects. In: Ahmed, A. (ed.) ESOP 2018. LNCS, vol. 10801, pp. 300–326. Springer, Cham (2018). https://doi.org/10.1007/978-3-319-89884-1_11
68. Støvring, K., Lassen, S.B.: A complete, co-inductive syntactic theory of sequential control and state. In: Proceedings of POPL 2007, pp. 161–172 (2007)
69. Strassen, V.: The existence of probability measures with given marginals. Ann. Math. Statist. **36**(2), 423–439 (1965)
70. Tarski, A.: A lattice-theoretical fixpoint theorem and its applications. Pacific J. Math. **5**(2), 285–309 (1955)
71. Thijs, A.: Simulation and fixpoint semantics. Rijksuniversiteit Groningen (1996)
72. Villani, C.: Optimal Transport: Old and New. Grundlehren der mathematischen Wissenschaften. Springer, Heidelberg (2008). https://doi.org/10.1007/978-3-540-71050-9
73. Wadler, P.: Monads for functional programming. In: Program Design Calculi, Proceedings of the NATO Advanced Study Institute on Program Design Calculi, Marktoberdorf, Germany, 28 July – 9 August 1992, pp. 233–264 (1992)

On the Multi-Language Construction

Samuele Buro(✉) and Isabella Mastroeni(✉)

Department of Computer Science, University of Verona,
Strada le Grazie 15, 37134 Verona, Italy
{samuele.buro,isabella.mastroeni}@univr.it

Abstract. Modern software is no more developed in a single programming language. Instead, programmers tend to exploit *cross-language interoperability mechanisms* to combine code stemming from different languages, and thus yielding fully-fledged *multi-language programs*. Whilst this approach enables developers to benefit from the strengths of each single-language, on the other hand it complicates the semantics of such programs. Indeed, the resulting multi-language does not meet any of the semantics of the combined languages. In this paper, we broaden the *boundary functions*-based approach à la Matthews and Findler to propose an algebraic framework that provides a constructive mathematical notion of *multi-language* able to determine its *semantics*. The aim of this work is to overcome the lack of a formal method (resp., model) to design (resp., represent) a multi-language, regardless of the inherent nature of the underlying languages. We show that our construction ensures the uniqueness of the *semantic function* (i.e., the multi-language semantics induced by the combined languages) by proving the *initiality* of the term model (i.e., the abstract syntax of the multi-language) in its category.

Keywords: Multi-language design · Program semantics · Interoperability

1 Introduction

Two elementary arguments lie at the heart of the *multi-language paradigm*: the large availability of existing programming languages, along with a very high number of already written libraries, and software that, in general, needs to *interoperate*. Although there is consensus in claiming that there is no best programming language regardless of the context [4,8], it is equally true that many of them are conceived and designed in order to excel for specific tasks. Such examples are R for statistical and graphical computation, Perl for data wrangling, Assembly and C for low-level memory management, etc. *"Interoperability between languages has been a problem since the second programming language was invented"* [8], so it is hardly surprising that developers have focused on the design of *cross-language interoperability mechanisms*, enabling programmers to combine code written in different languages. In this sense, we speak of *multi-languages*.

L. Caires (Ed.): ESOP 2019, LNCS 11423, pp. 293–321, 2019.
https://doi.org/10.1007/978-3-030-17184-1_11

The field of cross-language interoperability has been driven more by practical concerns than by theoretical questions. The current scenario sees several engines and frameworks [13,28,29,44,47] (among others) to mix programming languages but only [30] discusses the semantic issues related to the multi-language design from a theoretical perspective. Moreover, the existing interoperability mechanisms differ considerably not only from the viewpoint of the combined languages, but also in terms of the approach used to provide the interoperation. For instance, Nashorn [47] is a JavaScript interpreter written in Java to allow embedding JavaScript in Java applications. Such engineering design works in a similar fashion of *embedded interpreters* [40,41].[1] On the contrary, Java Native Interface (JNI) framework [29] enables the interoperation of Java with native code written in C, C++, or Assembly through external procedure calls between languages, mirroring the widespread mechanism of *foreign function interfaces (FFI)* [14], whereas theoretical papers follow the more elegant approach of *boundary functions* (or, for short, *boundaries*) in the style of Matthews and Findler's multi-language semantics [30]. Simply put, boundaries act as a gate between single-languages. When a value needs to flow on the other language, they perform a conversion so that it complies to the other language specifications.

The major issue concerning this new paradigm is that multi-language programs do not obey any of the semantics of the combined languages. As a consequence, any method of formal reasoning (such as static program analysis or verification) is neutralized by the absence of a semantics specification. In this paper, we propose an algebraic framework based on the mechanism of boundary functions [30] that unambiguously yields the syntax and the semantics of the multi-language regardless the combined languages.

The Lack of a Multi-Language Framework. The notion of *multi-language* is employed naively in several works in literature [2,14,21,30,35–37,49] to indicate the embedding of two programming languages into a new one, with its own syntax and semantics.

The most recurring way to design a multi-language is to exploit a mechanism (like embedded interpreters, FFI, or boundary functions) able to regulate both control flow and value conversion between the underlying languages [30], thus adequate to provide *cross-language interoperability* [8]. The full construction is usually carried out manually by language designers, which define the multi-language by reusing the formal specifications of the single-languages [2,30,36,37] and by applying the selected mechanism for achieving the interoperation. Inevitably, therefore, all these resulting multi-languages notably differ one from another.

These different ways to achieve a cross-language interoperation are all attributable to the lack of a formal description of multi-language that does not provide neither a method for language designers to conceive new multi-languages nor any guarantee on the correctness of such constructions.

[1] Other popular engines that obey the embedded interpreters paradigm are Jython [28], JScript [44], and Rhino [13].

The Proposed Framework: Roadmap and Contributions. Matthews and Findler [30] propose *boundary functions* as a way to regulate the flow of values between languages. They show their approach on different variants of the same multi-language obtained by mixing ML [33] and Scheme [9], representing two "syntactically sugared" versions of the simply-typed and untyped lambda calculi, respectively.

Rather than showing the embedding of two fixed languages, we extend their approach to the much broader class of *order-sorted algebras* [19] with the aim of providing a framework that works regardless of the inherent nature of the combined languages. There are a number of reasons to choose order-sorted algebras as the underlying framework for generalizing the multi-language construction. From the first formulation of *initial algebra semantics* [17], the algebraic approach to program semantics [16] has become a cornerstone in the theory of programming languages [27]. Order-sorted algebras provide a mathematical tool for representing formal systems as algebraic structures through a systematic use of the notion of *sort* and *subsort* to model different forms of polymorphism [18,19], a key aspect when dealing with multi-languages sharing operators among the single-languages. They were initially proposed to ensure a rigorous model-theoretic semantics for error handling, multiple inheritance, retracts, selectors for multiple constructors, polymorphism, and overloading. In the years, several uses [3,6,11,24,25,38,39,52] and different variants [38,43,45, 51] have been proposed for order-sorted algebras, making them a solid starting point for the development of a new framework. In particular, results on *rewriting logic* [32] extend easily to the order-sorted case [31], thus facilitating a future extension of this paper towards the *operational semantics* world. Improvements of the order-sorted algebra framework have also been proposed to model languages together with their type systems [10] and to extend order-sorted specification with high-order functions [38] (see [48] and [18] for detailed surveys).

In this paper, we propose three different multi-language constructions according to the semantic properties of boundary functions. The first one models a general notion of multi-language that do not require any constraints on boundaries (Sect. 3). We argue that when such generality is superfluous, we can achieve a neater approach where boundary functions do not need to be annotated with sorts. Indeed, we show that when the cross-language conversion of a term does not depend on the sort at which the term is considered (i.e., when boundaries are *subsort polymorphic*) the framework is powerful enough to apply the correct conversion (Sect. 4.1). This last construction is an improvement of the original notion of boundaries in [30]. From a practical point of view, it allows programmers to avoid to explicitly deal with sorts when writing code, a non-trivial task that could introduce type cast bugs in real world languages. Finally, we provide a very specific notion of multi-language where no extra operator is added to the syntax (Sect. 4.2). This approach is particularly useful to extend a language in a modular fashion and ensuring the backward compatibility with "old" programs. For each one of these variants we prove an *initiality theorem*, which in turn ensures the uniqueness of the multi-language semantics and thereby legitimating the proposed framework. Moreover, we show that the framework guarantees a fundamental closure property on the construction: The resulting multi-language admits an order-sorted representation, i.e., it falls within the same formal model of the combined languages. Finally, we model the multi-language designed in [30] in order to show an instantiation of the framework (Sect. 6).

2 Background

All the algebraic background of the paper is firstly stated in [15,17,19]. We briefly introduce here the main definitions and results, and we illustrate them on a simple running example.

Given a *set of sorts* S, an *S-sorted set* A is a family of sets indexed by S, i.e., $A = \{ A_s \mid s \in S \}$. Similarly, an *$S$-sorted function* $f: A \to B$ is a family of functions $f = \{ f_s : A_s \to B_s \mid s \in S \}$. We stick to the convention of using s and w as metavariables for sorts in S and S^*, respectively, and we use the $\mathbb{blackboard}$ $\mathbb{bold}$ typeface to indicate a specific sort in S. In addition, if A is an S-sorted set and $w = s_1 \dots s_n \in S^+$, we denote by A_w the cartesian product $A_{s_1} \times \dots \times A_{s_n}$. Likewise, if f is an S-sorted function and $a_i \in A_{s_i}$ for $i = 1, \dots, n$, then the function $f_w : A_w \to B_w$ is such that $f_w(a_1, \dots, a_n) = (f_{s_1}(a_1), \dots, f_{s_n}(a_n))$. Given $P \subseteq S$, the restriction of an S-sorted function f to P is denoted by $f|_P$ and it is the P-sorted function $f|_P = \{ f_s \mid s \in P \}$. Finally, if $g: A \to B$ is a function, we still use the symbol g to denote the *direct image map of* g (also called the *additive lift* of g), i.e., the function $g: \wp(A) \to \wp(B)$ such that $g(X) = \{ g(a) \in B \mid a \in X \}$. Analogously, if $\leq$ is a binary relation on a set A (with elements $a \in A$), we use the same relation symbol to denote its *pointwise extension*, i.e., we write $a_1 \dots a_n \leq a'_1 \dots a'_n$ for $a_1 \leq a'_1, \dots, a_n \leq a'_n$.

The basic notions underpinning the order-sorted algebra framework are the definitions of *signature*, that models symbols forming terms of the language, and *algebra*, that provides an algebraic meaning to symbols.

Definition 1 (Order-Sorted Signature). *An* order-sorted signature *is a triple $\langle S, \leq, \Sigma \rangle$, where S is a set of sorts, $\leq$ is a binary relation on S, and Σ is an $S^* \times S$-sorted set $\Sigma = \{ \Sigma_{w,s} \mid w \in S^* \wedge s \in S \}$, satisfying the following conditions:*

(1os) $\langle S, \leq \rangle$ is a poset; and
(2os) $\sigma \in \Sigma_{w_1,s_1} \cap \Sigma_{w_2,s_2}$ and $w_1 \leq w_2$ imply $s_1 \leq s_2$.

If $\sigma \in \Sigma_{w,s}$ (or, $\sigma : w \to s$ and $\sigma : s$ when $w = \varepsilon$, as shorthands), we call σ an *operator* (*symbol*) or *function symbol*, w the *arity*, s the *sort*, and (w, s) the *rank* of σ; if $w = \varepsilon$, we say that σ is a *constant* (*symbol*). We name $\leq$ the *subsort relation* and Σ a *signature* when $\langle S, \leq \rangle$ is clear from the context. We abuse notation and write $\sigma \in \Sigma$ when $\sigma \in \bigcup_{w,s} \Sigma_{w,s}$.

Definition 2 (Order-Sorted Algebra). *An* order-sorted $\langle S, \leq, \Sigma\rangle$-algebra $\mathcal{A}$ *over an order-sorted signature* $\langle S, \leq, \Sigma\rangle$ *is an* S*-sorted set* A *of* interpretation domains *(or,* carrier sets *or* semantic domains*)* $A = \{ A_s \mid s \in S \}$, *together with* interpretation functions $[\![\sigma]\!]_{\mathcal{A}}^{w,s} : A_w \to A_s$ *(or, if* $w = \varepsilon$, $[\![\sigma]\!]_{\mathcal{A}}^{\varepsilon,s} \in A_s$*)*[2] *for each* $\sigma \in \Sigma_{w,s}$, *such that:*

(1oa) $s \leq s'$ *implies* $A_s \subseteq A_{s'}$*; and*
(2oa) $\sigma \in \Sigma_{w_1,s_1} \cap \Sigma_{w_2,s_2}$ *and* $w_1 \leq w_2$ *imply that* $[\![\sigma]\!]_{\mathcal{A}}^{w_1,s_1}(a) = [\![\sigma]\!]_{\mathcal{A}}^{w_2,s_2}(a)$ *for each* $a \in A_{w_1}$.

An important property of signatures, related to polymorphism, is *regularity*. Its relevance lies in the possibility of linking each term to a unique least sort (see Proposition 2.10 in [19]).

Definition 3 (Regularity of an Order-Sorted Signature). *An order-sorted signature* $\langle S, \leq, \Sigma\rangle$ *is* regular *if for each* $\sigma \in \Sigma_{\tilde{w},\tilde{s}}$ *and for each* lower bound $w_0 \leq \tilde{w}$ *the set* $\{ (w, s) \mid \sigma \in \Sigma_{w,s} \wedge w_0 \leq w \}$ *has minimum. This minimum is called least rank of* σ *with respect to* w_0.

The freely generated algebra $\mathcal{T}_\Sigma$ over a given signature $\mathfrak{S} = \langle S, \leq, \Sigma\rangle$ provides the notion of *term* with respect to $\mathfrak{S}$.

Definition 4 (Order-Sorted Term Algebra). *Let* $\langle S, \leq, \Sigma\rangle$ *be an order-sorted signature. The* order-sorted term $\langle S, \leq, \Sigma\rangle$-algebra $\mathcal{T}_\Sigma$ *is an order-sorted algebra such that:*

- *The* S*-sorted set* $T_\Sigma = \{ T_{\Sigma,s} \mid s \in S \}$ *is inductively defined as the least family satisfying:*
(1ot) $\Sigma_{\varepsilon,s} \subseteq T_{\Sigma,s}$;
(2ot) $s \leq s'$ *implies* $T_{\Sigma,s} \subseteq T_{\Sigma,s'}$*; and*
(3ot) $\sigma \in \Sigma_{w,s}$, $w = s_1 \ldots s_n \in S^+$, *and* $t_i \in T_{\Sigma,s_i}$ *for* $i = 1, \ldots, n$ *imply* $\sigma(t_1 \ldots t_n) \in T_{\Sigma,s}$.
- *For each* $\sigma \in \Sigma_{w,s}$ *the interpretation function* $[\![\sigma]\!]_{\mathcal{T}_\Sigma}^{w,s} : T_{\Sigma,w} \to T_{\Sigma,s}$ *is defined as*
(4ot) $[\![\sigma]\!]_{\mathcal{T}_\Sigma}^{\varepsilon,s} = \sigma$ *if* $\sigma \in \Sigma_{\varepsilon,s}$*; and*
(5ot) $[\![\sigma]\!]_{\mathcal{T}_\Sigma}^{w,s}(t_1, \ldots, t_n) = \sigma(t_1 \ldots t_n)$ *if* $\sigma \in \Sigma_{w,s}$, $w = s_1 \ldots s_n \in S^+$, *and* $t_i \in T_{\Sigma,s_i}$ *for* $i = 1, \ldots, n$.

Homomorphisms between algebras capture the *compositionality* nature of semantics: The meaning of a term is determined by the meanings of its constituents. They are defined as order-sorted functions that preserve the interpretation of operators.

[2] To be pedantic, we should introduce the *one-point domain* $A_\varepsilon = \{ \bullet \}$ and then define $[\![\sigma]\!]_{\mathcal{A}}^{\varepsilon,s}(\bullet) \in A_s$.

$e ::= n \mid e + e \quad \text{where } n \in \mathbb{N}$

(a) The BNF grammar of L_1.

$s ::= - \mid a \mid s + s \quad \text{where } a \in \mathbb{A}$

(b) The BNF grammar of L_2.

Fig. 1. The BNF grammars of the running example languages.

$$\begin{cases} [\![n]\!] = n \\ [\![e + e']\!] = [\![e]\!] + [\![e']\!] \end{cases}$$

(a) The formal semantics of L_1.

$$\begin{cases} [\![-]\!] = \varepsilon \\ [\![a]\!] = a \\ [\![s + -]\!] = [\![- + s]\!] = [\![s]\!] \\ [\![s + - + s']\!] = [\![s + s']\!] \\ [\![a_0 + \ldots + a_n]\!] = a_0 \ldots a_n \quad n > 0 \end{cases}$$

(b) The formal semantics of L_2.

Fig. 2. The two formal semantics of the running example languages.

Definition 5 (Order-Sorted Homomorphism). *Let $\mathcal{A}$ and $\mathcal{B}$ be $\langle S, \leq, \Sigma\rangle$-algebras. An* order-sorted $\langle S, \leq, \Sigma\rangle$-homomorphism *from $\mathcal{A}$ to $\mathcal{B}$, denoted by $h\colon \mathcal{A} \to \mathcal{B}$, is an S-sorted function $h\colon A \to B = \{\, h_s\colon A_s \to B_s \mid s \in S \,\}$ such that:*

(1oh) $h_s([\![\sigma]\!]^{w,s}_{\mathcal{A}}(a)) = [\![\sigma]\!]^{w,s}_{\mathcal{B}}(h_w(a))$ for each $\sigma \in \Sigma_{w,s}$ and $a \in A_w$; and
(2oh) $s \leq s'$ implies $h_s(a) = h_{s'}(a)$ for each $a \in A_s$.

The class of all the order-sorted $\langle S, \leq, \Sigma\rangle$-algebras and the class of all order-sorted $\langle S, \leq, \Sigma\rangle$-homomorphisms form a category denote by $\mathbf{OSAlg}(S, \leq, \Sigma)$. Furthermore, the homomorphism definition determines the property of the term algebra $\mathcal{T}_\Sigma$ of being an *initial object* in its category whenever the signature is *regular*. Since *initiality* is preserved by isomorphisms, it allows to identify $\mathcal{T}_\Sigma$ with the *abstract syntax* of the language. If $\mathcal{T}_\Sigma$ is initial, the homomorphism leaving $\mathcal{T}_\Sigma$ and going to an algebra $\mathcal{A}$ is called the *semantic function* (with respect to $\mathcal{A}$).

Example. Let L_1 and L_2 be two formal languages (see Fig. 1). The former is a language to construct simple mathematical expressions: $n \in \mathbb{N}$ is the metavariable for natural numbers, while e inductively generates all the possible additions (Fig. 1a). The latter is a language to build strings over a finite alphabet of symbols $\mathbb{A} = \{\, \mathsf{a}, \mathsf{b}, \ldots, \mathsf{z} \,\}$: $a \in \mathbb{A}$ is the metavariable for atoms (or, characters), whereas s concatenates them into strings (Fig. 1b). A term in L_1 and L_2 denotes an element in the sets $\mathbb{N}$ and $\mathbb{A}^*$, accordingly to equations in Fig. 2a and b, respectively.

The syntax of the language L_1 can be modeled by an order-sorted signature $\mathfrak{S}_1 = \langle S_1, \leq_1, \Sigma_1\rangle$ defined as follows: $S_1 = \{\, \mathbb{e}, \mathbb{n} \,\}$, a set with sorts $\mathbb{e}$ (stands for *expressions*) and $\mathbb{n}$ (stands for *natural numbers*); $\leq_1$ is the reflexive relation on S_1 plus $\mathbb{n} \leq_1 \mathbb{e}$ (natural numbers are expressions); and the operators in Σ_1 are $0, 1, 2, \ldots : \mathbb{n}$ and $+\colon \mathbb{e}\mathbb{e} \to \mathbb{e}$. Similarly, the signature $\mathfrak{S}_2 = \langle S_2, \leq_2, \Sigma_2\rangle$ models the syntax of the language L_2: the set $S_2 = \{\, \mathbb{s}, \mathbb{a} \,\}$ carries the sort for *strings*

$\mathtt{s}$ and the sort for *atomic symbols* (or, characters) $\mathtt{a}$; the subsort relation $\leq_2$ is the reflexive relation on S_2 plus $\mathtt{a} \leq_2 \mathtt{s}$ (characters are one-symbol strings); and the operator symbols in Σ_2 are $\mathtt{a}, \ldots, \mathtt{z} \colon \mathtt{a}$, $\mathtt{-} \colon \mathtt{s}$, and $\mathtt{+} \colon \mathtt{s}\,\mathtt{s} \to \mathtt{s}$. Semantics of L_1 and L_2 can be embodied by algebras $\mathcal{A}_1$ and $\mathcal{A}_2$ over the signatures $\mathfrak{S}_1$ and $\mathfrak{S}_2$, respectively. We set the interpretation domains of $\mathcal{A}_1$ to $A^1_{\mathtt{n}} = A^1_{\mathtt{e}} = \mathbb{N}$ and those of $\mathcal{A}_2$ to $A^2_{\mathtt{a}} = \mathbb{A} \subseteq \mathbb{A}^* = A^2_{\mathtt{s}}$. Moreover, we define the interpretation functions as follows (the juxtaposition of two or more strings denotes their concatenation, and we use $\hat{a}$ as metavariable ranging over $\mathbb{A}^*$):

$$\begin{cases} [\![n]\!]^{\varepsilon,\mathtt{n}}_{\mathcal{A}_1} = n \\ [\![\mathtt{+}]\!]^{\mathtt{e}\,\mathtt{e},\mathtt{e}}_{\mathcal{A}_1}(n_1, n_2) = n_1 + n_2 \end{cases} \qquad \begin{cases} [\![\mathtt{-}]\!]^{\varepsilon,\mathtt{s}}_{\mathcal{A}_2} = \varepsilon \\ [\![a]\!]^{\varepsilon,\mathtt{a}}_{\mathcal{A}_2} = a \\ [\![\mathtt{+}]\!]^{\mathtt{s}\,\mathtt{s},\mathtt{s}}_{\mathcal{A}_2}(\hat{a}_1, \hat{a}_2) = \hat{a}_1\hat{a}_2 \end{cases}$$

Since $\mathfrak{S}_1$ and $\mathfrak{S}_2$ are regular, then $\mathcal{A}_1$ and $\mathcal{A}_2$ induce the semantic functions $h_1 \colon \mathcal{T}_{\Sigma_1} \to \mathcal{A}_1$ and $h_2 \colon \mathcal{T}_{\Sigma_2} \to \mathcal{A}_2$, providing semantics to the languages.

3 Combining Order-Sorted Theories

The first step towards a multi-language specification is the choice of which terms of one language can be employed in the others [30,35,36]. For instance, a multi-language requirement could demand to use ML expressions in place of Scheme expressions and, possibly, but not necessarily, vice versa (such a multi-language is designed in [30]). A *multi-language signature* is an amenable formalism to specify the compatibility relation between syntactic categories across two languages.

Definition 6 (Multi-Language Signature). *A* multi-language signature *is a triple* $\langle \mathfrak{S}_1, \mathfrak{S}_2, \leq \rangle$, *where* $\mathfrak{S}_1 = \langle S_1, \leq_1, \Sigma_1 \rangle$ *and* $\mathfrak{S}_2 = \langle S_2, \leq_2, \Sigma_2 \rangle$ *are order-sorted signatures, and* $\leq$ *is a binary relation on* $S = S_1 \cup S_2$, *such that satisfies the following condition:*

(1s) $s, s' \in S_i$ *implies* $s \leq s'$ *if and only if* $s \leq_i s'$, *for* $i = 1, 2$.

To make the notation lighter, we introduce the following binary relations on S: $s \ltimes s'$ *if* $s \leq s'$ *but neither* $s \leq_1 s'$ *nor* $s \leq_2 s'$, *and* $s \preccurlyeq s'$ *if* $s \leq s'$ *but not* $s \ltimes s'$.

In the following, we always assume that the sets of sorts S_1 and S_2 of the order-sorted signatures $\mathfrak{S}_1$ and $\mathfrak{S}_2$ are disjoint.[3] Condition (1s) requires the *multi-language subsort relation* $\leq$ to *preserve* the original subsort relations $\leq_1$ and $\leq_2$ (i.e., $\leq \cap\, S_i \times S_i = \leq_i$). The *join relation* $\ltimes$ provides a compatibility relation between sorts[4] in $\mathfrak{S}_1$ and $\mathfrak{S}_2$. More precisely, $S_i \ni s \ltimes s' \in S_j$ suggests that we want to use terms in $\mathcal{T}_{\Sigma_i,s}$ in place of terms in $\mathcal{T}_{\Sigma_j,s'}$, whereas the *intra-language*

---

[3] This hypothesis is non-restrictive: We can always perform a renaming of the sorts.

[4] Sorts may be understood as syntactic categories, in the sense of formal grammars. Given a context-free grammar G, it is possible to define a many-sorted signature Σ_G where non-terminals become sorts and such that each term t in the term algebra $\mathcal{T}_{\Sigma_G}$ is isomorphic to the parse tree of t with respect to G (see [15] for details).

subsort relation $\preccurlyeq$ shifts the standard notion of subsort from the order-sorted to the multi-language world. In a nutshell, the relation $\leq\, = \,\preccurlyeq \cup \ltimes$ can only join (through $\ltimes$) the underlying languages without introducing distortions (indeed, $\preccurlyeq\, = \,\leq_1 \cup \leq_2$).

The role of an algebra is to provide an interpretation domain for each sort, as well as the meaning of every operator symbol in a given signature. When moving towards the multi-language context, the join relation $\ltimes$ may add subsort constraints between sorts belonging to different signatures. Consequently, if $s \ltimes s'$, a multi-language algebra has to specify how values of sort s may be interpreted as values of sort s'. These specifications are called *boundary functions* [30] and provide an algebraic meaning to the subsort constraints added by $\ltimes$. Henceforth, we define $S = S_1 \cup S_2$, $\Sigma = \Sigma_1 \cup \Sigma_2$, and, given $(w, s) \in S_i^* \times S_i$, we denote by $\Sigma^i_{w,s}$ the (w, s)-sorted component in Σ_i.

Definition 7 (Multi-Language Algebra). *Let* $\langle \mathfrak{S}_1, \mathfrak{S}_2, \leq \rangle$ *be a multi-language signature. A* multi-language $\langle \mathfrak{S}_1, \mathfrak{S}_2, \leq \rangle$-algebra $\mathcal{A}$ *is an* S*-sorted set* A *of* interpretation domains *(or,* carrier sets *or* semantic domains*)* $A = \{ A_s \mid s \in S \}$*, together with* interpretation functions $[\![\sigma]\!]^{w,s}_{\mathcal{A}} \colon A_w \to A_s$ *for each* $\sigma \in \Sigma_{w,s}$*, and with a* $\ltimes$*-sorted set* α *of* boundary functions $\alpha = \{ \alpha_{s,s'} \colon A_s \to A_{s'} \mid s \ltimes s' \}$*, such that the following constraint holds:*

(1a) the projected algebra $\mathcal{A}_i$*, where* $i = 1, 2$*, specified by the carrier set* $A_i = \{ A^i_s = A_s \mid s \in S_i \}$ *and interpretation functions* $[\![\sigma]\!]^{w,s}_{\mathcal{A}_i} = [\![\sigma]\!]^{w,s}_{\mathcal{A}}$ *for each* $\sigma \in \Sigma^i_{w,s}$*, must be an order-sorted* $\mathfrak{S}_i$*-algebra.*

If $\mathcal{M}$ is an algebra, we adopt the convention of denoting by M (standard math font) its carrier set and by μ (Greek math font) its boundary functions whenever possible. Condition (1a) is the semantic counterpart of condition (1s): It requires the multi-language to carry (i.e., preserve) the underlying languages order-sorted algebras, whereas the boundary functions model how values can flow between languages.

Given two multi-language $\langle \mathfrak{S}_1, \mathfrak{S}_2, \leq \rangle$-algebras $\mathcal{A}$ and $\mathcal{B}$ we can define morphisms between them that preserve the sorted structure of the underlying projected algebras.

Definition 8 (Multi-Language Homomorphism). *Let* $\mathcal{A}$ *and* $\mathcal{B}$ *be multi-language* $\langle \mathfrak{S}_1, \mathfrak{S}_2, \leq \rangle$*-algebras with sets of boundary functions* α *and* β*, respectively. A* multi-language $\langle \mathfrak{S}_1, \mathfrak{S}_2, \leq \rangle$-homomorphism $h \colon \mathcal{A} \to \mathcal{B}$ *is an* S*-sorted function* $h \colon A \to B$ *such that:*

(1h) the restriction $h|_{S_i}$ *is an order-sorted* $\mathfrak{S}_i$*-homomorphism* $h|_{S_i} \colon \mathcal{A}_i \to \mathcal{B}_i$*, for* $i = 1, 2$*; and*
(2h) $s \ltimes s'$ *implies* $h_{s'} \circ \alpha_{s,s'} = \beta_{s,s'} \circ h_s$.

Conditions (1h) and (2h) are easily intelligible when the domain algebra is the abstract syntax of the language [15]: Simply put, both conditions require the semantics of a term to be a function of the meaning of its subterms, in the sense of [15,46]. In particular, the second condition demands that boundary functions act as operators.[5]

The identity homomorphism on a multi-language algebra $\mathcal{A}$ is denoted by $\mathrm{id}_{\mathcal{A}}$ and it is the set-theoretic identity on the carrier set A of the algebra $\mathcal{A}$. The composition of two homomorphisms $f\colon \mathcal{A} \to \mathcal{B}$ and $g\colon \mathcal{B} \to \mathcal{C}$ is defined as the sorted function composition $g \circ f\colon A \to C$, thus $\mathrm{id}_{\mathcal{A}} \circ f = f = f \circ \mathrm{id}_{\mathcal{B}}$ and associativity follows easily by the definition of $\circ$.

Proposition 1. *Multi-language homomorphisms are closed under composition.*

Hence, as in the many-sorted and order-sorted case [15,19], we have immediately the category of all the multi-language algebras over a multi-language signature:

Theorem 1. *Let $\langle \mathfrak{S}_1, \mathfrak{S}_2, \leq \rangle$ be a multi-language signature. The class of all $\langle \mathfrak{S}_1, \mathfrak{S}_2, \leq \rangle$-algebras and the class of all $\langle \mathfrak{S}_1, \mathfrak{S}_2, \leq \rangle$-homomorphisms form a category denoted by* $\mathbf{Alg}(\mathfrak{S}_1, \mathfrak{S}_2, \leq)$.

3.1 The Initial Term Model

In this section, we introduce the concepts of *(multi-language) term* and *(multi-language) semantics* in order to show how a multi-language algebra yields a unique interpretation for any *regular* (see Definition 11) multi-language specification.

Multi-language terms should comprise all of the underlying languages terms, plus those obtained by the merging of the two languages according to the join relation $\ltimes$. In particular, we aim for a construction where subterms of sort s' may have been replaced by terms of sort s, whenever $s \ltimes s'$ (we recall that s and s' are two syntactic categories of different languages due to Definition 6). Nonetheless, we must be careful not to add ambiguities during this process: A term t may belong to both $\mathfrak{S}_1$ and $\mathfrak{S}_2$ term algebras but with different meanings $[\![t]\!]_{\mathcal{A}_1}$ and $[\![t]\!]_{\mathcal{A}_2}$ (assuming that $\mathcal{A}_1$ and $\mathcal{A}_2$ are algebras over $\mathfrak{S}_1$ and $\mathfrak{S}_2$, respectively). When t is included in the multi-language, we lose the information to determine which one of the two interpretations choose, thus making the (multi-language) semantics of t ambiguous. The same problem arises whenever an operator σ belongs to both languages with different interpretation functions. The simplest solution to avoid such issues is to add syntactical notations to make explicit the context of the language in which we are operating.

Definition 9 (Associated Signature). *The* associated signature *to the multi-language signature $\langle \mathfrak{S}_1, \mathfrak{S}_2, \leq \rangle$ is the ordered triple $\langle S, \preccurlyeq, \Pi \rangle$, where $S = S_1 \cup S_2$, $\preccurlyeq = \leq_1 \cup \leq_2$, and*

$$\begin{aligned} \Pi = &\{\, \sigma_1\colon w \to s \mid \sigma\colon w \to s \in \Sigma_1 \,\} \\ &\cup \{\, \sigma_2\colon w \to s \mid \sigma\colon w \to s \in \Sigma_2 \,\} \\ &\cup \{\, \hookrightarrow_{s,s'}\colon s \to s' \mid s \ltimes s' \,\} \end{aligned}$$

[5] This is essential in order to generalize the concept of syntactical boundary functions of [30] to semantic-only functions in Sect. 4.2.

It is trivial to prove that an associated signature is indeed an order-sorted signature, thus admitting a term algebra $\mathcal{T}_\Pi$. All the symbols forming terms in $\mathcal{T}_\Pi$ carry the source language information as a subscript, and all the new operators $\hookrightarrow_{s,s'}$ specify when a term of sort s is used in place of a term of sort s'. Although $\mathcal{T}_\Pi$ seems a suitable definition for multi-language terms, it is not a multi-language algebra according to Definition 7. However, we can exploit the construction of $\mathcal{T}_\Pi$ in order to provide a fully-fledged multi-language algebra able to generate multi-language terms.

Definition 10 (Multi-Language Term Algebra). *The* multi-language term algebra $\mathcal{T}$ *over a multi-language signature* $\langle \mathfrak{S}_1, \mathfrak{S}_2, \leq \rangle$ *with boundary functions* τ *is defined as follows:*

(1t) $s \in S$ *implies* $T_s = T_{\Pi,s}$*;*
(2t) $\sigma \in \Sigma^i_{w,s}$ *implies* $[\![\sigma]\!]^{w,s}_{\mathcal{T}} = [\![\sigma_i]\!]^{w,s}_{\mathcal{T}_\Pi}$ *for* $i = 1, 2$*; and*
(3t) $s \ltimes s'$ *implies* $\tau_{s,s'} = [\![\hookrightarrow_{s,s'}]\!]^{s,s'}_{\mathcal{T}_\Pi}$.

Proving that $\mathcal{T}$ satisfies Definition 7 is easy and omitted. $\mathcal{T}$ and $\mathcal{T}_\Pi$ share the same carrier sets (condition (1t)), and each single-language operator $\sigma \in \Sigma^i_{w,s}$ is interpreted as its annotated version σ_i in $\mathcal{T}_\Pi$ (condition (2t)). Furthermore, the multi-language operators $\hookrightarrow_{s,s'}$ no longer belong to the signature (they do not belong neither to $\mathfrak{S}_1$ nor to $\mathfrak{S}_2$) but their semantics is inherited by the boundary functions τ (condition (3t)), while their syntactic values are still in the carrier sets of the algebra (this construction is highly technical and very similar to the freely generated $\Sigma(X)$-algebra over a set of variables X, see [15]).

Note that this is exactly the formalization of the ad hoc multi-language specifications in [2,30,36,37]: [2,36,37] exploit distinct colors to disambiguate the source language of the operators, whereas [30] use different font styles for different languages. Moreover, boundary functions in [30] conceptually match the introduced operators $\hookrightarrow_{s,s'}$.

The last step in order to finalize the framework is to provide semantics for each term in $\mathcal{T}$. As with the order-sorted case, we need a notion of *regularity* for proving the initiality of the term algebra in its category, which in turn ensures a single eligible *(initial algebra) semantics.*

Definition 11 (Regularity). *A multi-language signature* $\langle \mathfrak{S}_1, \mathfrak{S}_2, \leq \rangle$ *is* regular *if its associated signature* $\langle S, \preccurlyeq, \Pi \rangle$ *is regular.*

Proposition 2. *The associated signature* $\langle S, \preccurlyeq, \Pi \rangle$ *of a multi-language signature* $\langle \mathfrak{S}_1, \mathfrak{S}_2, \leq \rangle$ *is regular if and only if* $\mathfrak{S}_1$ *and* $\mathfrak{S}_2$ *are regular.*

The last proposition enables to avoid checking the multi-language regularity whenever the regularity of the order-sorted signatures is known.

Theorem 2 (Initiality of $\mathcal{T}$). *The multi-language term algebra* $\mathcal{T}$ *over a regular multi-language signature* $\langle \mathfrak{S}_1, \mathfrak{S}_2, \leq \rangle$ *is initial in the category* $\mathbf{Alg}(\mathfrak{S}_1, \mathfrak{S}_2, \leq)$.

Initiality of $\mathcal{T}$ is essential to assign a unique mathematical meaning to each term, as in the order-sorted case: Given a multi-language algebra $\mathcal{A}$, there is only one way of interpreting each term $t \in \mathcal{T}$ in $\mathcal{A}$ (satisfying the homomorphism conditions).

Definition 12 ((Multi-Language) Semantics). *Let $\mathcal{A}$ be a multi-language algebra over a regular multi-language signature $\langle \mathfrak{S}_1, \mathfrak{S}_2, \leq \rangle$. The* (multi-language) semantics *of a (multi-language) term $t \in \mathcal{T}$ induced by $\mathcal{A}$ is defined as*

$$[\![t]\!]_{\mathcal{A}} = h_{\mathrm{ls}(t)}(t)$$

The last equation is well-defined since h is the unique multi-language homomorphism $h\colon \mathcal{T} \to \mathcal{A}$ and for each $t \in \mathcal{T}$ there exists a least sort $\mathrm{ls}(t) \in S$ such that $t \in T_{\Pi,\mathrm{ls}(t)}$ (see Prop. 2.10 in [19]).

Example. Suppose we are interested in a multi-language over the signatures $\mathfrak{S}_1$ and $\mathfrak{S}_2$ specified in the example given in the background section such that satisfies the following properties:

- Terms denoting natural numbers can be used in place of characters $a \in \mathbb{A}$ according to the function $\mathrm{chr}\colon \mathbb{N} \to \mathbb{A}$ that maps the natural number n to the character symbol $a^{(n \bmod |\mathbb{A}|)}$ (we are assuming a total lexicographical order $a^{(0)}, a^{(1)}, \ldots, a^{(|A|-1)}$ on $\mathbb{A}$);
- Terms denoting strings can be used in place of natural numbers $n \in \mathbb{N}$ according to the function $\mathrm{ord}\colon \mathbb{A} \to \mathbb{N}$, which is the inverse of chr restricted the initial segment on natural numbers $\mathbb{N}_{<|A|}$.

In order to achieve such a multi-language specification, we can simply provide a join relation $\ltimes$ on S and a boundary function $\alpha_{s,s'}$ for each extra-language subsort relation $s \ltimes s'$ introduced by $\ltimes$. We define the join relation and the boundary functions as follows:

$$\mathtt{e} \ltimes \mathtt{a} \quad \wedge \quad \mathtt{n} \ltimes \mathtt{a} \quad \longrightarrow \quad \alpha_{\mathtt{e},\mathtt{a}}(n) = \alpha_{\mathtt{n},\mathtt{a}}(n) = \mathrm{chr}(n)$$

$$\mathtt{s} \ltimes \mathtt{n} \quad \wedge \quad \mathtt{a} \ltimes \mathtt{n} \quad \longrightarrow \quad \begin{cases} \alpha_{\mathtt{a},\mathtt{n}}(a) = \mathrm{ord}(a) \\ \alpha_{\mathtt{s},\mathtt{n}}(a_0 \ldots a_n) = \sum_{k=0}^{n} \alpha_{\mathtt{a},\mathtt{n}}(a_k) \cdot 10^k \end{cases}$$

The multi-language $\langle \mathfrak{S}_1, \mathfrak{S}_2, \leq \rangle$-algebra $\mathcal{A}$ can now be obtained by joining the projected algebras $\mathcal{A}_1$ and $\mathcal{A}_2$ with the set of boundary functions α. The term algebra $\mathcal{T}$ over $\langle \mathfrak{S}_1, \mathfrak{S}_2, \leq \rangle$ provides all the multi-language terms, and Theorem 2 ensures a unique denotation of each $t \in \mathcal{T}$ in $\mathcal{A}$. For instance, the term

$$t = \hookrightarrow_{\mathtt{s},\mathtt{n}}(\underbrace{\mathtt{+}_2(\overbrace{\mathtt{f}_2, \mathtt{+}_2(\mathtt{o}_2, \underbrace{\hookrightarrow_{\mathtt{e},\mathtt{a}}(\overbrace{\mathtt{+}_1(\mathtt{10}_1, \mathtt{5}_1)}^{t_4})}_{t_3})}^{t_2})}_{t_1}) \tag{1}$$

is syntactically equivalent to the following but with a less pedantic notation, where language subscripts are replaced by colors (red for one, and blue for two) and prefix notation is replaced by infix notation

$$\hookrightarrow_{\mathbb{s},\mathbb{n}}(\mathtt{f}\ +\ \mathtt{o}\ +\ \hookrightarrow_{\mathbb{e},\mathbb{a}}(10\ +\ 5))$$

and it denotes the natural numbers 765:

$$\begin{aligned}
[\![t_4]\!]_{\mathcal{A}} &= h_{\mathrm{ls}(t_4)}(t_4) = h_{\mathbb{e}}(t_4) = [\![+]\!]_{\mathcal{A}}^{\mathbb{e}\,\mathbb{e},\mathbb{e}}([\![10]\!]_{\mathcal{A}}, [\![5]\!]_{\mathcal{A}}) = [\![+]\!]_{\mathcal{A}}^{\mathbb{e}\,\mathbb{e},\mathbb{e}}(10, 5) = 15 \\
[\![t_3]\!]_{\mathcal{A}} &= h_{\mathrm{ls}(t_3)}(t_3) = h_{\mathbb{a}}(t_3) = [\![\hookrightarrow_{\mathbb{e},\mathbb{a}}]\!]_{\mathcal{A}}^{\mathbb{e},\mathbb{a}}([\![t_4]\!]_{\mathcal{A}}) = [\![\hookrightarrow_{\mathbb{e},\mathbb{a}}]\!]_{\mathcal{A}}^{\mathbb{e},\mathbb{a}}(15) = \mathtt{o} \\
[\![t_2]\!]_{\mathcal{A}} &= h_{\mathrm{ls}(t_2)}(t_2) = h_{\mathbb{s}}(t_2) = [\![+]\!]_{\mathcal{A}}^{\mathbb{s}\,\mathbb{s},\mathbb{s}}([\![\mathtt{o}]\!]_{\mathcal{A}}, [\![t_3]\!]_{\mathcal{A}}) = [\![+]\!]_{\mathcal{A}}^{\mathbb{s}\,\mathbb{s},\mathbb{s}}(\mathtt{o}, \mathtt{o}) = \mathtt{oo} \\
[\![t_1]\!]_{\mathcal{A}} &= h_{\mathrm{ls}(t_1)}(t_1) = h_{\mathbb{s}}(t_1) = [\![+]\!]_{\mathcal{A}}^{\mathbb{s}\,\mathbb{s},\mathbb{s}}([\![\mathtt{f}]\!]_{\mathcal{A}}, [\![t_2]\!]_{\mathcal{A}}) = [\![+]\!]_{\mathcal{A}}^{\mathbb{s}\,\mathbb{s},\mathbb{s}}(\mathtt{f}, \mathtt{oo}) = \mathtt{foo} \\
[\![t]\!]_{\mathcal{A}} &= h_{\mathrm{ls}(t)}(t) = h_{\mathbb{n}}(t) = [\![\hookrightarrow_{\mathbb{s},\mathbb{n}}]\!]_{\mathcal{A}}^{\mathbb{s},\mathbb{n}}([\![t_1]\!]_{\mathcal{A}}) = [\![\hookrightarrow_{\mathbb{s},\mathbb{n}}]\!]_{\mathcal{A}}^{\mathbb{s},\mathbb{n}}(\mathtt{foo}) = 765
\end{aligned}$$

(see the proof of Prop. 2.10 in [19] to check how to compute the least sort of a term).

4 Refining the Construction

The construction in Sect. 3 does not set any constraint on boundary functions, thus giving a great deal of flexibility to language designers. For instance, they can provide boundary functions that act differently with respect to the intra-language subsort relation $\preccurlyeq$: According to the previous example, it would have been possible to define $\alpha_{\mathbb{n},\mathbb{a}} \neq \alpha_{\mathbb{e},\mathbb{a}}$ to employ different value conversion specifications for terms in $T_{\mathbb{n}}$, based on whether they are used as natural numbers ($\mathbb{n}$) or as expressions ($\mathbb{e}$). However, when this amount of flexibility is not needed, we can refine the previous construction by reducing the amount of syntax introduced by the associated signature. In this section we examine

- the case where boundary functions satisfy the monotonicity conditions of order-sorted algebra operators (Sect. 4.1); and
- the case where boundary functions commutes with the semantics of operator symbols (Sect. 4.2).

In both cases, we prove that the introduced refinements do not affect the initiality of the term algebra, thereby providing unambiguous semantics to the multi-language.

4.1 Subsort Polymorphic Boundary Functions

In Sect. 3, the join relation constraints $s \ltimes s'$ are turned in syntactical operators $\hookrightarrow_{s,s'}$ in the associated signature $\langle S, \preccurlyeq, \Pi\rangle$. We now show how to handle all the syntactical overhead introduced by $\ltimes$ with a single polymorphic operator $\hookrightarrow$ whenever the boundary functions satisfy the monotonicity conditions of the order-sorted algebras [19]. Such conditions require a subsort relation $s_1 \leq s_2$ between the sorts of a polymorphic operator $\sigma \in \Sigma_{w_1,s_1} \cap \Sigma_{w_2,s_2}$, assuming that

$w_1 \leq w_2$. In our case, $\sigma = \hookrightarrow$, and thus we extend Definition 6 with the following ad hoc constraint (2s*):

Definition 6* (SP Multi-Language Signature). *A* subsort polymorphic (SP) multi-language signature *is a multi-language signature* $\langle \mathfrak{S}_1, \mathfrak{S}_2, \leq \rangle$ *such that*

(2s)* $s_1 \ltimes s_1'$, $s_2 \ltimes s_2'$, *and* $s_1 \preccurlyeq s_2$ imply $s_1' \preccurlyeq s_2'$.

Furthermore, order-sorted algebras demand consistency of the interpretation functions of a subsort polymorphic operator on the smaller domain, which results in the following condition (2a*) on boundary functions (that extends Definition 7):

Definition 7* (SP Multi-Language Algebra). *Let* $\langle \mathfrak{S}_1, \mathfrak{S}_2, \leq \rangle$ *be a SP multi-language signature. A* subsort polymorphic (SP) multi-language $\langle \mathfrak{S}_1, \mathfrak{S}_2, \leq \rangle$-algebra *is a multi-language* $\langle \mathfrak{S}_1, \mathfrak{S}_2, \leq \rangle$*-algebra* $\mathcal{A}$ *such that*

(2a)* $s_1 \ltimes s_1'$, $s_2 \ltimes s_2'$, *and* $s_1 \preccurlyeq s_2$ *imply that* $\alpha_{s_1,s_1'}(a) = \alpha_{s_2,s_2'}(a)$ *for each* $a \in A_{s_1}$.

The notion of homomorphism in this new context does not change (an homomorphism between two SP algebras is still an S-sorted function decomposable in two order-sorted homomorphisms that commutes with boundaries), whereas the associated signature to an SP multi-language signature merely differs from Definition 9 for having a unique polymorphic operator $\hookrightarrow$ instead of a family of parametrized symbols $\{ \hookrightarrow_{s,s'} : s \to s' \mid s \ltimes s' \}$.

Definition 9* (SP Associated Signature). *The* subsort polymorphic (SP) associated signature *to the SP multi-language signature* $\langle \mathfrak{S}_1, \mathfrak{S}_2, \leq \rangle$ *is the ordered triple* $\langle S, \preccurlyeq, \Pi \rangle$, *where* $S = S_1 \cup S_2$, $\preccurlyeq \, = \, \leq_1 \cup \leq_2$, *and*

$$\begin{aligned} \Pi = &\{ \sigma_1 : w \to s \mid \sigma : w \to s \in \Sigma_1 \} \\ &\cup \{ \sigma_2 : w \to s \mid \sigma : w \to s \in \Sigma_2 \} \\ &\cup \{ \hookrightarrow : s \to s' \mid s \ltimes s' \} \end{aligned}$$

Since the associated signature is the basis for the term algebra, we need to modify the condition (3t) in Definition 9:

Definition 10* (SP Multi-Language Term Algebra). *The* subsort polymorphic (SP) multi-language term algebra $\mathcal{T}$ *over a SP multi-language signature* $\langle \mathfrak{S}_1, \mathfrak{S}_2, \leq \rangle$ *with boundary functions* τ *is defined as follows:*

(1t) $s \in S$ *implies* $T_s = T_{\Pi,s}$;
(2t) $\sigma \in \Sigma^i_{w,s}$ *implies* $[\![\sigma]\!]^{w,s}_{\mathcal{T}} = [\![\sigma_i]\!]^{w,s}_{\mathcal{T}_\Pi}$ for $i = 1, 2$; *and*
(3t)* $s \ltimes s'$ *implies* $\tau_{s,s'} = [\![\hookrightarrow]\!]^{s,s'}_{\mathcal{T}_\Pi}$.

Signature regularity is still defined as in Definition 11 and Proposition 2 still holds for the extended version developed in this section. As a result, the SP multi-language term $\langle \mathfrak{S}_1, \mathfrak{S}_2, \leq \rangle$-algebra $\mathcal{T}$ is still initial in the category $\mathbf{Alg}^*(\mathfrak{S}_1, \mathfrak{S}_2, \leq)$ of SP multi-language algebras over the SP multi-language signature $\langle \mathfrak{S}_1, \mathfrak{S}_2, \leq \rangle$.

Theorem 3. *Let $\langle\mathfrak{S}_1, \mathfrak{S}_2, \leq\rangle$ be a SP multi-language signature. The class of all SP $\langle\mathfrak{S}_1, \mathfrak{S}_2, \leq\rangle$-algebras and the class of all $\langle\mathfrak{S}_1, \mathfrak{S}_2, \leq\rangle$-homomorphisms form a category denoted by* $\mathbf{Alg}^*(\mathfrak{S}_1, \mathfrak{S}_2, \leq)$.

Theorem 4 (Initiality of $\mathcal{T}$). *The SP multi-language term algebra $\mathcal{T}$ over a regular SP multi-language signature $\langle\mathfrak{S}_1, \mathfrak{S}_2, \leq\rangle$ is initial in the category* $\mathbf{Alg}^*(\mathfrak{S}_1, \mathfrak{S}_2, \leq)$.

The semantics of a term t induced by a SP multi-language algebra $\mathcal{A}$ is defined in the same way of Definition 12, thanks to the initiality result: $[\![t]\!]_{\mathcal{A}} = h_{\mathrm{ls}(t)}(t)$. The main advantage of dealing with SP multi-language terms is that the framework is able to determine the correct interpretation function of the operator $\hookrightarrow$, making the subscript notation developed in the previous section superfluous. This also means that programmers are exempted from explicitly annotating multi-language programs with sorts, a non-trivial task in the general case that could introduce type cast bugs.

Example. The boundary functions of the previous example are subsort polymorphic: $\alpha_{\mathbb{c},\mathbb{n}}(a) = \mathrm{ord}(a) = \alpha_{\mathbb{s},\mathbb{n}}(a)$ for each character $a \in \mathbb{A}$, and $\alpha_{\mathbb{n},\mathbb{c}} = \alpha_{\mathbb{e},\mathbb{c}}$ by definition. Thus, the equivalent of the term t (see Eq. 1) in the SP term algebra is

$$\dot{t} = \hookrightarrow(+_2(\mathtt{f}_2, +_2(\mathtt{o}_2, \hookrightarrow(+_1(10_1, 5_1))))) \tag{2}$$

or, according to the previous notation,

$$\hookrightarrow(\mathtt{f}\ +\ \mathtt{o}\ +\ \hookrightarrow(10\ +\ 5))$$

and denoting the same natural number 765.

4.2 Semantic-Only Boundary Functions

In the previous section, we have shown how to handle the flow of values across different languages with a single polymorphic operator. Now, we present a new multi-language construction where neither extra operators are added to the associated signature, nor single-language operators have to be annotated with subscripts indicating their original language. Thus, the resulting multi-language syntax comprises only symbols in $\Sigma_1 \cup \Sigma_2$. Such a construction is achieved by:

- Imposing commutativity conditions on algebras, making homomorphisms transparently inherit the semantics of boundary functions. The framework is therefore able to apply the correct value conversion function whenever is necessary, without the need for an explicit syntactical operator $\hookrightarrow$.
- Requiring a new form of *cross-language polymorphism* able to cope with shared operators among languages. The initiality of term algebras is preserved by modifying the notion of signature in a way that every operator admits a least sort.

The variant of the framework presented in this section is particularly useful when designing the extension of a language in a modular fashion. For instance, if the signature $\mathfrak{S}_1$ models the syntax of a simple functional language (for an example, see [15, p. 77]) without an explicit encoding for string values, and $\mathfrak{S}_2$ is a language for manipulating strings (similar to the language L_2 of the running example of this paper), we can exploit the construction presented below in order to embed $\mathfrak{S}_2$ into $\mathfrak{S}_1$.

Signature. The main issue that can arise at this stage of multi-language signature is the presence of shared operators in Σ_1 and Σ_2. Contrary to the previous cases where such ambiguity is solved by adding subscripts in the associated signature, the trade off here is requiring ad hoc or subsort polymorphism across signatures.

Definition 6* (SO Multi-Language Signature). *A* semantic-only (SO) multi-language signature *is a multi-language signature $\langle \mathfrak{S}_1, \mathfrak{S}_2, \leq \rangle$ such that*

(2s*) $\langle S, \leq \rangle$ is a poset; and
(3s*) $\sigma \in \Sigma^i_{w_1,s_1} \cap \Sigma^j_{w_2,s_2}$ and $w_1 \ltimes w_2$ imply $s_1 \ltimes s_2$ with $i, j = 1, 2$ and $i \neq j$.

Condition (2s*) forces the subsort relation to be directed, avoiding symmetricity of syntactic categories (this is typical when modeling language extensions), while condition (3s*) shifts the monotonicity condition of order-sorted signature to syntactically equal operators in $\Sigma_1 \cap \Sigma_2$.
The associated signature is defined without adding extra symbols in the signature, i.e., $\Pi = \Sigma_1 \cup \Sigma_2$, and deliberately confounding the relations $\ltimes$ and $\preccurlyeq$ in $\leq$:

Definition 9* (SO Associated Signature). *The* SO associated signature *to the SO multi-language signature $\langle \mathfrak{S}_1, \mathfrak{S}_2, \leq \rangle$ is the ordered triple $\langle S, \leq, \Pi \rangle$, where* $S = S_1 \cup S_2$, $\leq\, = \,\preccurlyeq \cup \ltimes$, and $\Pi = \Sigma_1 \cup \Sigma_2$.

The embedding of $\ltimes$ in $\leq$ (i.e., $\ltimes \subseteq \leq$) in the associated signature enables the order-sorted term algebra construction to automatically build multi-language terms, without the need for an explicit operator $\hookrightarrow$ that acts as a bridge between syntactic categories. It is easy to see that the term algebra over the associated signature is precisely the symbols-free version of multi-language described at the beginning.

Unfortunately, multi-language regularity does not follow anymore from single-languages regularity and vice versa (see Figs. 3 and 4)[6]. More formally, Proposition 2 does not hold in this new context:

[6] An (horizontal) arrow from an arity symbol w to a sort s labelled with an operator symbol σ is an alternative shorthand for $\sigma : w \to s$. A (vertical) single line between two sorts s below s' labelled with a binary relation $\leq$ means that $s \leq s'$ (if the binary relation is the join relation $\ltimes$ the line is doubled). A dotted rectangle around operators is a graphical representation of the set of ranks (w, s) that must have a minimum element (red arrows) in order for the signature to be regular.

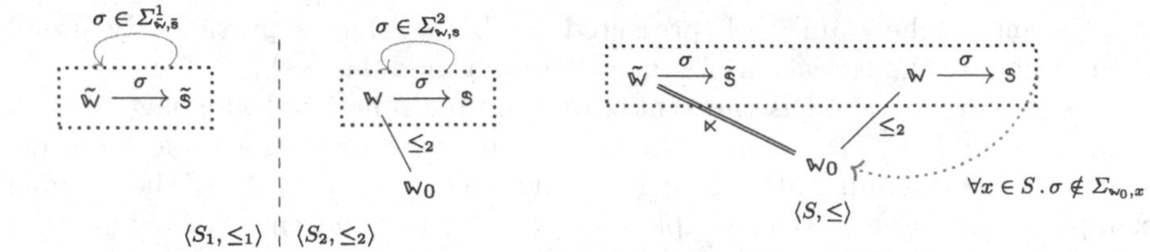

(a) The Hasse-like diagrams of regular signatures $\mathfrak{S}_1$ (left) and $\mathfrak{S}_2$ (right).

(b) The Hasse-like diagram of the non-regular multi-language signature $\langle \mathfrak{S}_1, \mathfrak{S}_2, \leq\rangle$.

Fig. 3. A non-regular multi-language signature comprising two regular order-sorted signatures.

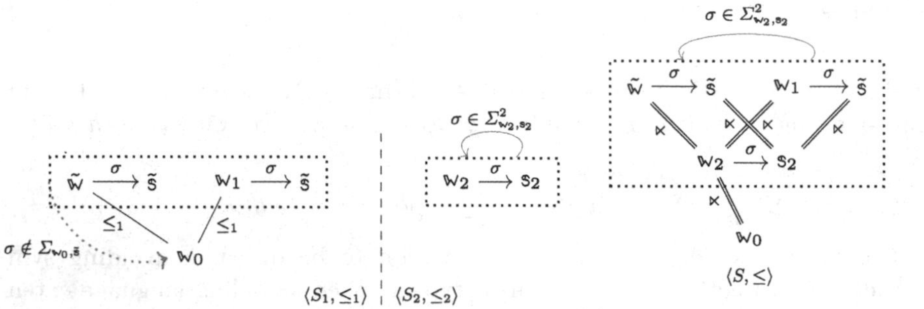

(a) The Hasse-like diagrams of signatures $\mathfrak{S}_1$ (non-regular, left) and $\mathfrak{S}_2$ (regular, right).

(b) The Hasse-like diagram of the regular multi-language signature $\langle \mathfrak{S}_1, \mathfrak{S}_2, \leq\rangle$.

Fig. 4. A regular multi-language signature comprising a non-regular order-sorted signature.

- Suppose $S_1 = \{\tilde{\mathtt{w}}, \tilde{\mathtt{s}}\}$, $S_2 = \{\mathtt{w}_0, \mathtt{w}, \mathtt{s}\}$, $\leq_1$ and $\leq_2$ to be the reflexive relations on S_1 and S_2, respectively, plus $\mathtt{w}_0 \leq_2 \mathtt{w}$, and $\sigma \in \Sigma^1_{\tilde{\mathtt{w}},\tilde{\mathtt{s}}} \cap \Sigma^2_{\mathtt{w},\mathtt{s}}$. If the join relation $\ltimes$ is defined as $\mathtt{w}_0 \ltimes \tilde{\mathtt{w}}$ and $\mathtt{s} \ltimes \tilde{\mathtt{s}}$, the resulting associated signature is no longer regular, although $\mathfrak{S}_1$ and $\mathfrak{S}_2$ are regular (Fig. 3a). In Fig. 3b, it is easy to see that $\sigma \in \Sigma_{\tilde{\mathtt{w}},\tilde{\mathtt{s}}}$ and $\mathtt{w}_0 \leq \mathtt{w}$, but the set $\{(\mathtt{w},\mathtt{s}) \mid \sigma \in \Sigma_{\mathtt{w},\mathtt{s}} \wedge \mathtt{w}_0 \leq \mathtt{w}\} = \{(\tilde{\mathtt{w}},\tilde{\mathtt{s}}), (\mathtt{w},\mathtt{s})\}$ does not have a least element w.r.t. $\mathtt{w}_0$.
- On the other hand, let $S_1 = \{\tilde{\mathtt{w}}, \mathtt{w}_0, \mathtt{w}_1, \tilde{\mathtt{s}}\}$, $S_2 = \{\mathtt{w}_2, \mathtt{s}_2\}$, $\leq_1$ and $\leq_2$ be the reflexive relations on S_1 and S_2, respectively, plus $\mathtt{w}_0 \leq_1 \tilde{\mathtt{w}}$ and $\mathtt{w}_0 \leq_1 \mathtt{w}_1$, and $\sigma \in \Sigma^1_{\tilde{\mathtt{w}},\tilde{\mathtt{s}}} \cap \Sigma^1_{\mathtt{w}_1,\tilde{\mathtt{s}}} \cap \Sigma^2_{\mathtt{w}_2,\mathtt{s}_2}$. If the join relation $\ltimes$ is defined as $\mathtt{w}_2 \ltimes \tilde{\mathtt{w}}$, $\mathtt{w}_2 \ltimes \mathtt{w}_1$, $\mathtt{w}_0 \ltimes \mathtt{w}_2$, and $\mathtt{s}_2 \ltimes \tilde{\mathtt{s}}$, the resulting associated signature is regular (Fig. 4a), although $\mathfrak{S}_1$ is not: given $\sigma \in \Sigma_{\tilde{\mathtt{w}},\tilde{\mathtt{s}}}$ and $\mathtt{w}_0 \leq \tilde{\mathtt{w}}$, the set $\{(\mathtt{w},\mathtt{s}) \mid \sigma \in \Sigma_{\mathtt{w},\mathtt{s}} \wedge \mathtt{w}_0 \leq \mathtt{w}\} = \{(\tilde{\mathtt{w}},\tilde{\mathtt{s}}), (\mathtt{w}_1,\tilde{\mathtt{s}}), (\mathtt{w}_2,\mathtt{s}_2)\}$ has least element $(\mathtt{w}_2,\mathtt{s}_2)$ w.r.t. $\mathtt{w}_0$ (Fig. 4b).

A positive result can be obtained by recalling that regularity is easier to check when $\langle S, \leq \rangle$ satisfies the descending chain condition (DCC):

Lemma 1 (Regularity over DCC poset [19]). *An order-sorted signature Σ over a DCC poset $\langle S, \leq \rangle$ is regular if and only if whenever $\sigma \in \Sigma_{w_1,s_1} \cap \Sigma_{w_2,s_2}$ and there is some $w_0 \leq w_1, w_2$, then there is some $w \leq w_1, w_2$ such that $\sigma \in \Sigma_{w,s}$ and $w_0 \leq w$.*

At this point, we can relate the DCC of the poset $\langle S, \leq \rangle$ in the associated signature of $\langle \mathfrak{S}_1, \mathfrak{S}_2, \leq \rangle$ to the DCC of $\langle S_1, \leq_1 \rangle$ and $\langle S_2, \leq_2 \rangle$:

Proposition 3. *Let $\langle S, \leq, \Sigma \rangle$ be the associated signature of $\langle \mathfrak{S}_1, \mathfrak{S}_2, \leq \rangle$. Then, $\langle S, \leq \rangle$ is DCC if and only if $\langle S_1, \leq_1 \rangle$ and $\langle S_2, \leq_2 \rangle$ are DCC.*

As a result, whenever we know that $\langle S_1, \leq_1 \rangle$ and $\langle S_2, \leq_2 \rangle$ are DCC, we can check the regularity of $\langle \mathfrak{S}_1, \mathfrak{S}_2, \leq \rangle$ by employing the Lemma 1 without checking whether $\langle S, \leq \rangle$ is DCC.

Algebra. In this multi-language construction, the boundary functions behaviour is no more bounded to syntactical operators as in the previous sections, but it is inherited by homomorphisms. A necessary condition to accomplish this aim is the commutativity of interpretation functions with boundary functions:

Definition 7* (SO Multi-Language Algebra). *Let $\langle \mathfrak{S}_1, \mathfrak{S}_2, \leq \rangle$ be an SO multi-language signature. A* semantic-only (SO) multi-language $\langle \mathfrak{S}_1, \mathfrak{S}_2, \leq \rangle$-algebra *is an SP multi-language $\langle \mathfrak{S}_1, \mathfrak{S}_2, \leq \rangle$-algebra $\mathcal{A}$ such that*

(3a*) $\sigma \in \Sigma_{w_1,s_1} \cap \Sigma_{w_2,s_2}$ and *$w_1 \ltimes w_2$* imply that *$\alpha_{s_1,s_2}(\llbracket \sigma \rrbracket_{\mathcal{A}}^{w_1,s_1}(a)) = \llbracket \sigma \rrbracket_{\mathcal{A}}^{w_2,s_2}(\alpha_{w_1,w_2}(a))$* for each *$a \in A_{w_1}$.*

Note that $\sigma \in \Sigma_{w_1,s_1} \cap \Sigma_{w_2,s_2}$ and $w_1 \ltimes w_2$ imply $s_1 \ltimes s_2$ by condition (3s*). The notion of homomorphism remains unchanged from Definition 8 (to understand how the homomorphisms inherit the boundary functions behaviour, see the proof of Theorem 6).

The term algebra is defined similarly to Definition 10, except for boundary functions:

Definition 10* (SO Multi-Language Term Algebra). *The* semantic-only (SO) multi-language term algebra *$\mathcal{T}$ over an SO multi-language signature $\langle \mathfrak{S}_1, \mathfrak{S}_2, \leq \rangle$ with boundary functions τ is defined as follows:*

(1t*) $s \in S$ implies $T_s = T_{\Pi,s}$;
(2t*) $\sigma \in \Sigma_{w,s}$ implies $\llbracket \sigma \rrbracket_{\mathcal{T}}^{w,s} = \llbracket \sigma \rrbracket_{\mathcal{T}_\Pi}^{w,s}$; and
(3t*) $s \ltimes s'$ implies $\tau_{s,s'} = \mathrm{id}_{T_s}$.

Since the subsort relation $\leq$ includes the join relation $\ltimes$, $s \ltimes s'$ implies $T_{\Pi,s} = T_s \subseteq T_{s'} = T_{\Pi,s'}$. Thus, the boundary function $\tau_{s,s'}$ can be defined as the identity on the smaller domain (note that it trivially satisfies the commutativity condition (3a*)).

Proposition 4. *Let* $\langle \mathfrak{S}_1, \mathfrak{S}_2, \leq \rangle$ *be an SO multi-language signature. Then, the SO multi-language term* $\langle \mathfrak{S}_1, \mathfrak{S}_2, \leq \rangle$*-algebra is a proper SO multi-language algebra.*

Theorem 5. *Let* $\langle \mathfrak{S}_1, \mathfrak{S}_2, \leq \rangle$ *be a SO multi-language signature. The class of all SO* $\langle \mathfrak{S}_1, \mathfrak{S}_2, \leq \rangle$*-algebras and the class of all* $\langle \mathfrak{S}_1, \mathfrak{S}_2, \leq \rangle$*-homomorphisms form a category denoted by* $\mathbf{Alg}^\star(\mathfrak{S}_1, \mathfrak{S}_2, \leq)$.

We can now prove the initiality of $\mathcal{T}$ in its category.

Theorem 6 (Initiality of $\mathcal{T}$). *Let* $\langle \mathfrak{S}_1, \mathfrak{S}_2, \leq \rangle$ *be a regular multi-language signature. Then, the term algebra* $\mathcal{T}$ *is an initial object in the category* $\mathbf{Alg}(\mathfrak{S}_1, \mathfrak{S}_2, \leq)$.

Thanks to the initiality of the term algebra, the definition of term semantics is the same of Definition 12.

Example. Let $\mathcal{A}_1$ and $\mathcal{A}_2$ be two order-sorted algebras over the signatures $\mathfrak{S}_1$ and $\mathfrak{S}_2$, respectively, as formalized in the example in Sect. 3. Suppose we are interested in a new multi-language $\mathcal{A}$ over $\mathfrak{S}_1$ and $\mathfrak{S}_2$ such that any string expressions t of sort $\mathbb{s}$ in $\mathfrak{S}_2$ can denote the natural number length($[\![t]\!]_{\mathcal{A}_2}$) when embedded in $\mathfrak{S}_1$ terms. For instance, we require that $[\![\texttt{10 + 5}]\!]_{\mathcal{A}} = [\![\texttt{10 + 5}]\!]_{\mathcal{A}_1} = 15$ and $[\![\texttt{f + o}]\!]_{\mathcal{A}} = [\![\texttt{f + o}]\!]_{\mathcal{A}_2} = \texttt{fo}$, but $[\![\texttt{(f + o) + (10 + 5)}]\!]_{\mathcal{A}} = [\![\texttt{fo + 15}]\!]_{L} = 17$ (parentheses in the last term have only been used to disambiguate the parsing result).

Since the requirements demand to use string expressions in place of natural numbers, the join relation $\ltimes$ shall define $\mathbb{s} \ltimes \mathbb{n}$ and ensure transitivity, hence $\mathbb{s} \ltimes \mathbb{e}$, $\mathbb{a} \ltimes \mathbb{n}$, and $\mathbb{a} \ltimes \mathbb{e}$.

The signatures $\mathfrak{S}_1$ and $\mathfrak{S}_2$ are trivially regular. However, by merging $\mathfrak{S}_1$ and $\mathfrak{S}_2$, we are causing subsort polymorphism on the symbol +, which is used as sum operator in $\mathcal{A}_1$ and as concatenation operator in $\mathcal{A}_2$, and therefore we have to check the regularity: Let $w_1 = \mathbb{e}\mathbb{e}$, $w_2 = \mathbb{s}\mathbb{s}$, $s_1 = \mathbb{e}$, and $s_2 = \mathbb{s}$. Given $+ \in \Sigma_{w_1,s_1} \cap \Sigma_{w_2,s_2}$ and the lower bound $w_0 = \mathbb{a}\mathbb{a} \leq w_1, w_2$, then there exists $w = \mathbb{s}\mathbb{s}$ such that $w \leq w_1, w_2$ and $+ \in \Sigma_{w,s}$, where $s = \mathbb{s} \leq s_1, s_2$ (we have employed Lemma 1 thanks to Proposition 3). Analogously, when $w_0 = w_1, w_2$ the relative least rank is $(\mathbb{s}\mathbb{s}, \mathbb{s})$.

The multi-language $\langle \mathfrak{S}_1, \mathfrak{S}_2, \leq \rangle$-algebra $\mathcal{A}$ is now defined by joining the projected algebras $\mathcal{A}_1$ and $\mathcal{A}_2$ and by defining boundary functions $a_{s,s'}$ for each $s \ltimes s'$ such that convert strings in naturals (their length) when strings are used in place of naturals:

$$a_{\mathbb{a},\mathbb{n}}(a) = a_{\mathbb{a},\mathbb{e}}(a) = 1 \qquad\qquad a_{\mathbb{s},\mathbb{n}}(\hat{a}) = a_{\mathbb{s},\mathbb{e}}(\hat{a}) = \text{length}(\hat{a})$$

The above definition of boundary functions satisfy both conditions (2a*) and (3a*).

The initiality theorem yields the semantic homomorphism from $\mathcal{T}$ to $\mathcal{A}$. For instance, suppose we want to compute the semantics of the term

$$t = \texttt{+}(\underbrace{\texttt{+}(\texttt{f},\texttt{o})}_{t_1}, \overbrace{\texttt{+}(10,5)}^{t_2})$$

The least sorts of t, t_1, and t_2 are $\mathbb{e}$, $\mathbb{s}$, and $\mathbb{e}$, respectively. The operator + belongs to both $\Sigma_{\mathbb{e}\,\mathbb{e},\mathbb{e}}$ and $\Sigma_{\mathbb{s}\,\mathbb{s},\mathbb{s}}$, and its least rank w.r.t. the lower bound $\text{ls}(t_1)\,\text{ls}(t_2) = \mathbb{s}\,\mathbb{e}$ is $(\mathbb{e}\,\mathbb{e}, \mathbb{e})$. By Definition 12 we have

$$[\![t]\!]_{\mathcal{A}} = h_{\mathbb{e}}(t) = [\![\texttt{+}]\!]_{\mathcal{A}}^{\mathbb{e}\,\mathbb{e},\mathbb{e}}(h_{\mathbb{e}}(t_1), h_{\mathbb{e}}(t_2))$$

At this point, since $\text{ls}(t_1) = \mathbb{s}$ and $\text{ls}(\texttt{f}) = \text{ls}(\texttt{o}) = \mathbb{c}$, then the least rank of the root symbol + of t_1 w.r.t. the lower bound $\text{ls}(\texttt{f})\,\text{ls}(\texttt{o}) = \mathbb{c}\,\mathbb{c}$ is $(\mathbb{s}\,\mathbb{s}, \mathbb{s})$, thus

$$h_{\mathbb{e}}(t_1) = a_{\mathbb{s},\mathbb{e}}(h_{\mathbb{s}}(t_1)) = a_{\mathbb{s},\mathbb{e}}([\![\texttt{+}]\!]_{\mathcal{A}}^{\mathbb{s}\,\mathbb{s},\mathbb{s}}(h_{\mathbb{s}}(\texttt{f}), h_{\mathbb{s}}(\texttt{o}))) = a_{\mathbb{s},\mathbb{e}}([\![\texttt{+}]\!]_{\mathcal{A}}^{\mathbb{s}\,\mathbb{s},\mathbb{s}}(\texttt{f},\texttt{o})) = a_{\mathbb{s},\mathbb{e}}(\texttt{fo}) = 2$$

Similarly, $\text{ls}(t_2) = \mathbb{e}$ and $\text{ls}(10) = \text{ls}(5) = \mathbb{n}$. Then, the least rank of the root symbol + of t_2 w.r.t. the lower bound $(\mathbb{n}, \mathbb{n})$ is $(\mathbb{e}\,\mathbb{e}, \mathbb{e})$ and therefore we have

$$h_{\mathbb{e}}(t_2) = [\![\texttt{+}]\!]_{\mathcal{A}}^{\mathbb{e}\,\mathbb{e},\mathbb{e}}(h_{\mathbb{n}}(10), h_{\mathbb{n}}(5)) = [\![\texttt{+}]\!]_{\mathcal{A}}^{\mathbb{e}\,\mathbb{e},\mathbb{e}}(10,5) = 15$$

Finally,

$$[\![t]\!]_{\mathcal{A}} = h_{\mathbb{e}}(t) = [\![\texttt{+}]\!]_{\mathcal{A}}^{\mathbb{e}\,\mathbb{e},\mathbb{e}}(h_{\mathbb{e}}(t_1), h_{\mathbb{e}}(t_2)) = [\![\texttt{+}]\!]_{\mathcal{A}}^{\mathbb{e}\,\mathbb{e},\mathbb{e}}(2,15) = 17$$

as desired.

We can observe that without any syntactical operator the framework is still able to apply the correct boundary functions to move values across languages.

5 Reduction to Order-Sorted Algebra

The constructions in the previous sections beg the question whether a multi-language algebra admits an equivalent order-sorted representation. Conceptually, it would mean that being a multi-language is essentially a matter of perspective: By forgetting how the multi-language has been constructed, what is left is simply an ordinary language. Mathematically speaking, it requires us to exhibit a *reduction functor* F from the multi-language category to an order-sorted one, such that there is an isomorphism ϕ between the carrier sets of the multi-language term $\langle \mathfrak{S}_1, \mathfrak{S}_2, \leq \rangle$-algebra $\mathcal{T}$ and $F(\mathcal{T})$, and such that $[\![t]\!]_{\mathcal{A}} = [\![\phi(t)]\!]_{F(\mathcal{A})}$ for each $t \in \mathcal{T}$ and for each multi-language $\langle \mathfrak{S}_1, \mathfrak{S}_2, \leq \rangle$-algebra $\mathcal{A}$.

In the following, we denote the reduction functor by F, F^*, and $F^\star$ accordingly whether its domain is the category $\mathbf{Alg}(\mathfrak{S}_1, \mathfrak{S}_2, \leq)$, $\mathbf{Alg}^*(\mathfrak{S}_1, \mathfrak{S}_2, \leq)$, and $\mathbf{Alg}^\star(\mathfrak{S}_1, \mathfrak{S}_2, \leq)$, respectively.

In the case of $\mathbf{Alg}(\mathfrak{S}_1, \mathfrak{S}_2, \leq)$ and $\mathbf{Alg}^*(\mathfrak{S}_1, \mathfrak{S}_2, \leq)$ categories, the construction of F and F^* is very simple, and we illustrate it only for the plain multi-language algebras of Sect. 3: Let $\mathcal{A}$ be a multi-language $\langle \mathfrak{S}_1, \mathfrak{S}_2, \leq \rangle$-algebra. Then, we define the order-sorted $\langle S, \preccurlyeq, \Pi \rangle$-algebra $\mathcal{A}_\Pi$ (called the *associated order-sorted algebra* of $\mathcal{A}$) by setting

(1π) $A_{\Pi,s} = A_s$ for each $s \in S$;
(2π) $[\![\sigma_i]\!]^{w,s}_{\mathcal{A}_\Pi} = [\![\sigma]\!]^{w,s}_{\mathcal{A}}$ for each $\sigma \in \Sigma^i_{w,s}$ and $i = 1, 2$; and
(3π) $[\![\hookrightarrow_{s,s'}]\!]^{s,s'}_{\mathcal{A}_\Pi} = \alpha_{s,s'}$ for each $s \ltimes s'$.

If $\mathcal{A}$ and $\mathcal{B}$ are multi-language $\langle \mathfrak{S}_1, \mathfrak{S}_2, \leq \rangle$-algebras, and h is a multi-language $\langle \mathfrak{S}_1, \mathfrak{S}_2, \leq \rangle$-homomorphism from $\mathcal{A}$ to $\mathcal{B}$, the functor F maps $\mathcal{A}$ and $\mathcal{B}$ to their associated order-sorted algebras $\mathcal{A}_\Pi$ and $\mathcal{B}_\Pi$ and the homomorphism h to itself. Since $A_\Pi = A$, the isomorphism ϕ is the identity function.

Theorem 7. *$F\colon$ $\mathbf{Alg}(\mathfrak{S}_1, \mathfrak{S}_2, \leq) \to \mathbf{OSAlg}(\mathfrak{S}_1, \mathfrak{S}_2, \leq)$ is a functor for every multi-language signature $\langle \mathfrak{S}_1, \mathfrak{S}_2, \leq \rangle$. Moreover, $[\![t]\!]_{\mathcal{A}} = [\![t]\!]_{F(\mathcal{A})}$ for each $t \in \mathcal{T}$ and for each multi-language $\langle \mathfrak{S}_1, \mathfrak{S}_2, \leq \rangle$-algebra $\mathcal{A}$.*

If $\mathcal{A}$ is an SP multi-language $\langle \mathfrak{S}_1, \mathfrak{S}_2, \leq \rangle$-algebra, the construction of the reduction functor F^* is similar to the definition of F. The only difference is the equation in the condition (3π) that turns into

(3π^*) $[\![\hookrightarrow]\!]^{s,s'}_{\mathcal{A}_\Pi} = \alpha_{s,s'}$ for each $s \ltimes s'$.

Finally, the definition of $F^\star$ starting from the category $\mathbf{Alg}^\star(\mathfrak{S}_1, \mathfrak{S}_2, \leq)$ of SO multi-language algebras is slightly different. We define $F^\star$ as a map from the multi-language category $\mathbf{Alg}^\star(\mathfrak{S}_1, \mathfrak{S}_2, \leq)$ to the order-sorted category $\mathbf{OSAlg}(S, \preccurlyeq, \Sigma)$. We denote the reduction of a multi-language algebra $\mathcal{A}$ and a homomorphism $h\colon \mathcal{A} \to \mathcal{B}$ as $F(\mathcal{A}) = \mathcal{A}_\downarrow$ and $F(h) = h_\downarrow\colon \mathcal{A}_\downarrow \to \mathcal{B}_\downarrow$. The order-sorted algebra $\mathcal{A}_\downarrow$ has the same carrier sets of the multi-language algebra $\mathcal{A}$, i.e., $A_\downarrow = A$, and interpretation functions $[\![\sigma]\!]^{w,s}_{\mathcal{A}_\downarrow} = [\![\sigma]\!]^{w,s}_{\mathcal{A}}$. Furthermore, we define $h_\downarrow = h$. Intuitively, the algebra $\mathcal{A}_\downarrow$ is formally defined simply by forgetting about the boundary functions, while the homomorphism $h_\downarrow\colon \mathcal{A}_\downarrow \to \mathcal{B}_\downarrow$ inherits their semantics from h. Again, the isomorphism ϕ is the identity.

Theorem 8. *$F^\star\colon$ $\mathbf{Alg}^\star(\mathfrak{S}_1, \mathfrak{S}_2, \leq) \to \mathbf{OSAlg}(S, \preccurlyeq, \Sigma)$ is a functor for every SO multi-language signature $\langle \mathfrak{S}_1, \mathfrak{S}_2, \leq \rangle$. Moreover, $[\![t]\!]_{\mathcal{A}} = [\![t]\!]_{F^\star(\mathcal{A})}$ for each $t \in \mathcal{T}$ and for each SO multi-language $\langle \mathfrak{S}_1, \mathfrak{S}_2, \leq \rangle$-algebra $\mathcal{A}$.*

Unfortunately, even though $\mathcal{T}$ is an initial algebra in its category, $F^\star(\mathcal{T}) = \mathcal{T}_\downarrow$ is not: Given two multi-language algebras $\mathcal{A}$ and $\mathcal{A}'$ that differ only in the boundary functions (we denote by α and α' the families of boundary functions of $\mathcal{A}$ and $\mathcal{A}'$, respectively) they both get mapped by $F^\star$ to the same order-sorted algebra $\mathcal{A}_\downarrow$. Thus, if $h\colon \mathcal{T} \to \mathcal{A}$ and $h'\colon \mathcal{T} \to \mathcal{A}'$ are the unique homomorphisms going from $\mathcal{T}$ to $\mathcal{A}$ and $\mathcal{A}'$, the functor F maps them to two different order-sorted homomorphisms $h_\downarrow\colon \mathcal{T}_\downarrow \to \mathcal{A}_\downarrow$ and $h'_\downarrow\colon \mathcal{T}_\downarrow \to \mathcal{A}_\downarrow$ both leaving $\mathcal{T}_\downarrow$ and going to $\mathcal{A}_\downarrow$, hence losing the uniqueness property. However, this does not pose a problem once fixed a family of boundary functions:

Theorem 9. *Let $\mathcal{T}$ be the multi-language term $\langle \mathfrak{S}_1, \mathfrak{S}_2, \leq \rangle$-algebra and $\mathcal{A}$ be an order-sorted $\langle S, \preccurlyeq, \Sigma \rangle$-algebra. Given a family of boundary functions $\alpha = \{\, \alpha_{s,s'} \mid s \ltimes s' \,\}$ such that satisfies condition (3a*), there exists a unique order-sorted $\langle S, \preccurlyeq, \Sigma \rangle$-homomorphism $h^\alpha\colon \mathcal{T}_\downarrow \to \mathcal{A}$ commuting with α, i.e., if $s \ltimes s'$, then $h^\alpha_{s'}(t) = \alpha_{s,s'}(h^\alpha_s(t))$ for each $t \in T_s$.*

The reduction theorems presented in this section have a strong consequence: all the already known results for the order-sorted algebras can be lifted to the multi-language world.

6 An Example of Multi-Language Construction

The first theoretical paper addressing the problem of multi-language construction is [30]. The authors study the so-called *natural embedding* (a more realistic improvement of the *lump embedding* [7,30,34,40]), in which Scheme terms can be converted to equivalent ML terms, and vice versa.[7] The novelty in their approach is how they succeed to define boundaries in order to translate values from Scheme to ML. Indeed, the latter does not admit an equivalent representation for each Scheme function. Their solution is to *"represent a Scheme procedure in ML at type $\tau_1 \to \tau_2$ by a new procedure that takes an argument of type τ_1, converts it to a Scheme equivalent, runs the original Scheme procedure on that value, and then converts the result back to ML at type τ_2"*.

Our goal here is not to discuss a fully explained presentation of ML and Scheme languages in the form of order-sorted algebras, but rather to show how we can model the natural embedding construction in our framework. Doing so, we provide a sketchy formalization of Scheme and ML syntax and semantics, and we redirect the reader to [30] for all the languages details.

To provide the semantics of Scheme, we follow the same approach of Goguen et al. [15] where the denotational semantics of the *simple applicative language* (SAL) introduced by Reynolds [42] is given by means of an algebra, exploiting the initiality theorem. Such a language is a "syntactically sugared" version of the untyped lambda calculus with the fixpoint operator, which in turn is very similar to Scheme.

Let $X = \{\mathtt{x}_1, \mathtt{x}_2, \dots\}$ be a set of variables and $\mathbb{N}^\diamond$ be the naturals lattice with $\top$ and $\bot$ adjoined. From [46], there exists a complete lattice V such that satisfies the isomorphism $\phi\colon V \cong \mathbb{N}^\diamond + V \diamond\!\!\rightarrow V$, where $+$ is the disjoint union with minimum and maximum elements identified, and $V \diamond\!\!\rightarrow V$ is the complete lattice of Scott-continuous functions from V to V. Given $\xi \in \{\mathbb{N}^\diamond, V \diamond\!\!\rightarrow V\}$, we define the injections $j_\xi\colon \xi \to \mathbb{N}^\diamond + V \diamond\!\!\rightarrow V$ and $i_\xi = \phi^{-1} \circ j_\xi$, and the projection $\pi_\xi\colon V \to \xi$ such that $\pi_\xi(v) = (\!| \phi(v) \in \xi \mathbin{?} \phi(v) \mathbin{⨾} \bot |\!)$. The set of all Scheme environments is the lattice of all total functions $\mathrm{P} = X \to V$ with componentwise ordering $\rho \sqsubseteq \rho'$ if and only if $\rho(x) \sqsubseteq \rho'(x)$ in V for all $x \in X$. Furthermore, we define auxiliary functions (see [15] for a more detailed explanation) in order to provide the semantics of the language (in the following, $x \in X$ and $n \in \mathbb{N}^\diamond$):

- $get_x\colon \mathrm{P} \to V$, $get_x(\rho) = \rho(x)$ (evaluation function);
- $val_n\colon \mathrm{P} \to V$, $val_n(\rho) = n$ (n-constant function);

[7] To be specific, the authors combine *"an extended model of the untyped call-by-value lambda calculus, which is used as a stand-in for Scheme, and an extended model of the simply-typed lambda calculus, which is used as a stand-in for ML"*.

- $put_x\colon \mathrm{P}\times V \to \mathrm{P}$, $put_x(\rho, v) = \rho[v/x]$, where $\rho[v/x](x') = (\!|\, x = x' \mathrel{?} v \mathbin{\S} \rho(x') \,|\!)$ (environment updating);
- $app : V^2 \to V$, $app(v_1, v_2) = (\pi_{V \diamond\!\!\to V}(v_1))(v_2)$ (function application);
- $nat? : V \to V$, $nat?(v) = (\!|\, v \in \mathbb{N}^\diamond \mathrel{?} val_0 \mathbin{\S} val_1 \,|\!)$ (natural predicate);
- $proc? : V \to V$, $proc?(v) = (\!|\, v \in V \diamond\!\!\to V \mathrel{?} val_0 \mathbin{\S} val_1 \,|\!)$ (function predicate);
- given $\hat{e}_i\colon \mathrm{P} \to V$ for $1 \leq i \leq k$, then $\langle\!|\hat{e}_1, \ldots, \hat{e}_k|\!\rangle\colon \mathrm{P} \to V^k$ is defined by $\langle\!|\hat{e}_1, \ldots, \hat{e}_k|\!\rangle(\rho) = (\hat{e}_1(\rho), \ldots, \hat{e}_k(\rho))$ (target-tupling); and
- given D, D' and D'', then abs: $((D \times D') \diamond\!\!\to D'') \to (D \diamond\!\!\to (D' \diamond\!\!\to D''))$ is defined by $((abs(f))(x))(y) = f(x, y)$ (abstraction); and
- $choice : V^3 \to V$ (conditional function), add: $V^2 \to V$ (addition), and sub: $V^2 \to V$ (subtraction)

$$choice(v_1, v_2, v_3) = \begin{cases} \top & \text{if } v_1 = \top \\ v_2 & \text{if } v_1 = 0 \\ v_3 & \text{if } v_1 \neq 0 \\ \bot & \text{otherwise} \end{cases} \qquad add(v_1, v_2) = \begin{cases} \top & \text{if } v_1, v_2 = \top \\ v_1 + v_2 & \text{if } v_1, v_2 \in \mathbb{N} \\ \bot & \text{otherwise} \end{cases}$$

The definition of sub is analogous to the function add, with the only difference that, in the second case, $sub(v_1, v_2) = v_1 -_{\mathbb{N}} v_2$, where $v_1 -_{\mathbb{N}} v_2 = \max\{\, v_1 - v_2, 0 \,\}$ for each $v_1, v_2 \in \mathbb{N}$.

The semantics of the language is obtained by defining an algebra $\mathcal{H}$ over a signature $\mathfrak{H}$,[8] then the initiality yields the unique homomorphism from the term algebra. A Scheme term denotes a continuous function in the semantic domain $H_{\mathbb{e}} = \mathrm{P} \diamond\!\!\to V$. The interpretation functions of the operators are defined by the following equations:

$$\begin{aligned}
&[\![x]\!]^{\varepsilon,\mathbb{e}}_{\mathcal{H}} = get_x &\qquad& [\![\lambda x]\!]^{\mathbb{e},\mathbb{e}}_{\mathcal{H}}(\hat{e}) = \iota_{V \diamond\!\to V} \circ abs_{\mathrm{P},V,V}(\hat{e} \circ put_x) \\
&[\![\blacksquare]\!]^{\mathbb{e}\mathbb{e},\mathbb{e}}_{\mathcal{H}}(\hat{e}_1, \hat{e}_2) = app \circ \langle\!|\hat{e}_1, \hat{e}_2|\!\rangle && [\![\texttt{proc?}]\!]^{\mathbb{e},\mathbb{e}}_{\mathcal{H}}(\hat{e}) = proc? \circ \hat{e} \\
&[\![\overline{n}]\!]^{\varepsilon,\mathbb{e}}_{\mathcal{H}} = val_n && [\![\texttt{if0}]\!]^{\mathbb{e}\mathbb{e}\mathbb{e},\mathbb{e}}_{\mathcal{H}}(\hat{e}_1, \hat{e}_2, \hat{e}_3) = choice \circ \langle\!|\hat{e}_1, \hat{e}_2, \hat{e}_3|\!\rangle \\
&[\![\texttt{+}]\!]^{\mathbb{e}\mathbb{e},\mathbb{e}}_{\mathcal{H}}(\hat{e}_1, \hat{e}_2) = add \circ \langle\!|\hat{e}_1, \hat{e}_2|\!\rangle && [\![\texttt{nat?}]\!]^{\mathbb{e},\mathbb{e}}_{\mathcal{H}}(\hat{e}) = nat? \circ \hat{e} \\
&[\![\texttt{-}]\!]^{\mathbb{e}\mathbb{e},\mathbb{e}}_{\mathcal{H}}(\hat{e}_1, \hat{e}_2) = sub \circ \langle\!|\hat{e}_1, \hat{e}_2|\!\rangle
\end{aligned}$$

For the sake of simplicity, we made a minor change to the language presented in [30]. They have an extra operator `wrong` to print an error message in case of an illegal operation, due to the lack of a type system. For instance, the sum of two functions produces thé error `wrong "non-number"`. To avoid to add cases almost everywhere in the definition of the interpretation functions, we let ill-typed terms to denote the value $\bot$ without an explicit encoding of the error message. Furthermore, we denote by $\blacksquare$ the function application.

[8] We do not define $\mathfrak{H}$ explicitly since it can be inferred by the algebra equations below.

The ML-like language defined in [30] is an extended version of the simply-typed lambda calculus. As before, we provide its semantics by defining an algebra $\mathcal{M}$ over an order-sorted signature $\mathfrak{M} = \langle S_2, \leq_2, \Sigma_2 \rangle$.

Let I (should read 'iota') be a set of *base types* and K a I-sorted set of *base values* $K = \{ K_\iota \mid \iota \in \mathrm{I} \}$. We inductively define the set of *simple types* T: If ι is a base type, then it is a simple type; If τ, τ' are simple types, then $(\tau) \to (\tau')$ is a simple type (henceforth we omit the parentheses). We abuse notation and extend K to the T-sorted set of *simple values* $K = \{ K_\tau \mid \tau \in \mathrm{T} \}$ where $K_{\tau \to \tau'} = K_\tau \to K_{\tau'}$.

The set of all ML environments is defined as the set of all total functions $\Delta = Y \to K$, where $Y = \{ \mathtt{y}_1, \mathtt{y}_2, \dots \}$ is a set of variables disjoint from X (this assumption comes from [30]) and $K = \bigcup_{\tau \in \mathrm{T}} K_\tau$. We instantiate $\mathrm{I} = \{ \mathbb{n} \}$ and $K_{\mathbb{n}} = \mathbb{N}$. The poset $\langle S_2, \leq_2 \rangle$ carries all the simple types (i.e., $\mathrm{T} \subseteq S_2$) and the sort $\mathbb{t}$; $\leq_2$ is the reflexive relation on S_2 plus $\tau \leq_2 \mathbb{t}$ for each $\tau \in \mathrm{T}$. An ML term of type τ denotes a total function in $M_\tau = \Delta \to K_\tau$, and we define $M_{\mathbb{t}} = \Delta \to K$. Due to the Turing-incompleteness of such a language, we do not need all the mathematical machinery of [15,46] to formalize its semantics.

$$[\![y]\!]_{\mathcal{M}}^{\varepsilon,\mathbb{t}} = \delta \mapsto \delta(y) \qquad [\![\lambda y^\tau]\!]_{\mathcal{M}}^{\tau',\tau\to\tau'}(\hat{t}) = \delta \mapsto k_\tau \mapsto \hat{t}(\delta[k_\tau/y])$$

$$[\![\overline{n}]\!]_{\mathcal{M}}^{\varepsilon,\mathbb{n}} = \delta \mapsto n \qquad [\![\blacksquare]\!]_{\mathcal{M}}^{\tau\to\tau'\,\tau,\tau'}(\hat{t}_1, \hat{t}_2) = \delta \mapsto (\hat{t}_1(\delta))(\hat{t}_2(\delta))$$

$$[\![\texttt{+}]\!]_{\mathcal{M}}^{\mathbb{n}\,\mathbb{n},\mathbb{n}}(\hat{n}_1, \hat{n}_2) = \delta \mapsto \hat{n}_1(\delta) + \hat{n}_2(\delta) \qquad [\![\texttt{-}]\!]_{\mathcal{M}}^{\mathbb{n}\,\mathbb{n},\mathbb{n}}(\hat{n}_1, \hat{n}_2) = \delta \mapsto \hat{n}_1(\delta) -_{\mathbb{N}} \hat{n}_2(\delta)$$

$$[\![\texttt{if0}]\!]_{\mathcal{M}}^{\mathbb{n}\,\tau\,\tau,\tau}(\hat{n}, \hat{t}_1, \hat{t}_2) = \delta \mapsto \\ (\!|\, \hat{n}(\delta) = 0 \;?\; \hat{t}_1(\delta) \;:\; \hat{t}_2(\delta) \,|\!)$$

Until now, we have just formalized the single-languages. The multi-language $\mathcal{A}$ that combines Scheme and ML is obtained by requiring $\mathbb{e} \ltimes \tau$ and $\tau \ltimes \mathbb{e}$ in order to use ML terms in place of Scheme terms and vice versa. However, in the simplest version of the natural embedding, *"the system has stuck states, since a boundary might receive a value of an inappropriate shape"* [30]. They restore the type-soundness by first employing dynamic checks, and then by decoupling error-handling from the value conversion through the use of higher-order contracts [12]. We limit ourselves here to describe the first version; the subsequent refinements can be embodied by further complicating the semantics of the boundary functions (we do not have forced any constraints on them).

Since we need a value representing the notion of *stuck state* in ML, we have to extend the algebra $\mathcal{M}$. This is particularly easy by exploiting the underlying framework: We make $\mathcal{M}^\perp$ into an order-sorted $\mathfrak{M}$-algebra by defining $M_\tau^\perp = \Delta^\perp \to K_\tau^\perp$, where $\Delta^\perp = Y \to K^\perp$, $K^\perp = \bigcup_{\tau \in \mathrm{T}} K_\tau^\perp$, and $K_\tau^\perp = K_\tau \cup \{ \perp \}$, and the T-sorted injection ϕ from M_τ to $M_\tau^\perp$ such that $\varphi(\hat{t}) = \hat{t}$. Now, $\mathcal{M}^\perp$ becomes an algebra by letting φ to be an order-sorted $\mathfrak{M}$-homomorphism (this in turn forces $[\![-]\!]_{\mathcal{M}^\perp}^{w,s} = [\![-]\!]_{\mathcal{M}}^{w,s}$) and letting the interpretation functions to denote the value $\perp$ in the remaining non-yet defined cases (namely, they compute the value $\perp$ whenever one of their arguments is $\perp$).

The boundary function $\alpha_{\mathbb{e},\tau}(\hat{e})$ moves the Scheme value $\hat{e}\colon \mathrm{P} \diamond\!\!\rightarrow V$ in M_τ:

$$\alpha_{\mathbb{e},\tau}(\hat{e}) = \begin{cases} \alpha^{\mathbb{N}^\diamond}_{\mathbb{e},\tau}(\hat{e}) & \text{if } \hat{e} = val_n \text{ for some } n \in \mathbb{N}^\diamond \\ \alpha^{V \diamond\!\!\rightarrow V}_{\mathbb{e},\tau}(\hat{e}) & \text{otherwise} \end{cases}$$

where $\alpha^{\mathbb{N}^\diamond}_{\mathbb{e},\tau}(val_n) = (\!|\, \tau = \mathbb{n} \wedge n \in \mathbb{N} \;?\; \delta \mapsto n \,:\, \bot \,|\!)$ and

$$\alpha^{V \diamond\!\!\rightarrow V}_{\mathbb{e},\tau}(\hat{e}) = \begin{cases} \delta \mapsto k'_\tau \mapsto [\![\lambda y^{\tau'}]\!]^{\tau'',\tau' \to \tau''}_{\mathcal{M}^\bot}(\alpha_{\mathbb{e},\tau''}(\hat{e}' \circ put_x(\bot, \alpha_{\tau',\mathbb{e}}(k_{\tau'})))) \\ \quad \text{if } \tau = \tau' \to \tau'' \text{ and } \hat{e} = i_{V \diamond\!\!\rightarrow V} \circ abs_{\mathrm{P},V,V}(\hat{e}' \circ put_x) \\ \quad\quad \text{for some } x \in X \text{ and } \hat{e}' \in V \diamond\!\!\rightarrow V \\ \bot \\ \quad \text{otherwise} \end{cases}$$

Vice versa, $\alpha_{\tau,\mathbb{e}}(\hat{t})$ moves values from ML to Scheme. Its definition is analogous to the previous case: $\alpha_{\mathbb{n},\mathbb{e}}(\hat{n}) = val_n$ where $\hat{n} = \delta \mapsto n$, and

$$\alpha_{\tau \to \tau',\mathbb{e}} = \rho \mapsto v \mapsto [\![\lambda x]\!]^{\mathbb{e},\mathbb{e}}_{\mathcal{H}}(\alpha_{\tau',\mathbb{e}}(\hat{t}(\bot[\alpha_{\mathbb{e},\tau}(v)/y])))$$

These definitions adhere the conversion approach of the natural embedding in [30]: If $\hat{e}$ is the value denoted by a natural number in Scheme, then it is converted—aside from cases deriving from ill-typed terms—by $\alpha^{\mathbb{N}^\diamond}_{\mathbb{e},\mathbb{n}}$ to the corresponding constant function denoting the same natural value in ML. Otherwise, if $\hat{e}$ is the value denoted by a Scheme function, then it is mapped by $\alpha^{V \diamond\!\!\rightarrow V}_{\mathbb{e},\tau \to \tau'}$ to the ML function with variable x at type $\tau \to \tau'$ such that converts its argument of type τ to the Scheme equivalent by its conversion through $\alpha_{\tau,\mathbb{e}}$ to x. Then it runs the original procedure $\hat{e}$ on it and convert back the result by $\alpha_{\mathbb{e},\tau'}$.

Since the given boundary functions are subsort polymorphic, we can improve the construction and handle all the value conversions with a single polymorphic operator as explained in Sect. 4.1.

7 Concluding Remarks

In this paper, we have addressed the problem of providing a formal semantics to the combination of programming languages, the so-called *multi-languages*. We have introduced a new algebraic framework for modeling this new paradigm, and we have constructively shown how to attain a multi-language specification by only stipulate (1) how the syntactic categories of the single-languages have to be combined and (2) how the values may flow from one language to the other. We have proved the suitability of the framework to unambiguously yield the algebraic semantics of each multi-language term, while simultaneously preserving the single-languages semantics. We have also proved that combining languages is a close operation, i.e., that every multi-language admits an equivalent order-sorted representation. In particular, we have focused our study on the semantic properties of boundary functions in order to provide three different notions of multi-language designed to suit both general and specific cases.

To the best of our knowledge, this is the first attempt to provide a formal semantics of a multi-language independently from the combined languages.

Related Works. Cross-language interoperability is a well-researched area both from theoretical and practical points of view. The most related work to our approach is undoubtedly [30], which provides operational semantics to a combined language obtained by embedding a Scheme-like language into an ML-like language. Such an outcome is achieved by introducing *boundaries*, syntactic constructs that model the flow of values from one language to the other. Ours *boundary functions* draw heavily from their work. Nonetheless, we shift them to a semantic level, in order to several variants of multi-language constructions.

[7,21,36,40,53] take a similar line and combine typed and untyped languages (Lua and ML [40], Java and PLT Scheme [21], or Assembly and a typed functional language [36]), focusing on typing issues and values exchanging techniques. Instead of focusing on a particular problem, we adopt a rather general framework to model languages. This choice abstracts away many low-level details, allowing us to reason on semantic concerns in more general terms, without having to fix any particular pair of languages.

A lot of work has been done on multi-language runtime mechanisms: [20] provides a type system for a fragment of Microsoft Intermediate Language (IL) used by the .NET framework, that allows programmers to write components in several languages (C#, Visual Basic, VBScript, ...) which are then translated to IL. [22] proposes a virtual machine that can execute the composition of dynamically typed programming languages (Ruby and JavaScript) and statically typed one (C). [4,5] describes a multi-language runtime mechanism achieved by combining single-language interpreters of (different versions of) Python and Prolog.

Future Works. From our perspective, the research presented in this paper opens up on three directions. Firstly, future works should aim to provide an operational semantics to the formalization of multi-languages. Rewriting logic seems the most reasonable approach to unifying the denotational world, presented in this paper, to the operational one [31]. This line of research is particularly useful in order to move towards an implementation of an automatic tool able to combine languages such that the resulting multi-language guarantees the results proved in the paper.

Secondly, future research applies to use the multi-language model in order to study the problem of analyzing multi-language programs. In particular, we aim at investigating how it is possible to obtain analyses of multi-language programs by merging already existing analyses of the single combined languages.

Finally, further studies should investigate the problem of compiling multi-languages. Current compilers are closed tools, non-parametric on language constructs (for instance, we cannot compile a single `if-then-else` term of a standard language like C or Java unless it is plugged into a valid program). Several works on typing [1,20,26], compiling [2,37], and running [23,50] multi-language programs already exist, but without providing a formal notion of multi-language. It would be beneficial to study how their approaches can be applied to the formal framework developed in this paper.

References

1. Abadi, M., Cardelli, L., Pierce, B.C., Plotkin, G.D.: Dynamic typing in a statically typed language. ACM Trans. Program. Lang. Syst. **13**(2), 237–268 (1991)
2. Ahmed, A., Blume, M.: An equivalence-preserving CPS translation via multi-language semantics. SIGPLAN Not. **46**(9), 431–444 (2011)
3. Alencar, A.J., Goguen, J.A.: Object-oriented specification case studies. In: Lano, K., Haughton, H. (eds.) Specification in OOZE with Examples, pp. 158–183. Prentice Hall International (UK) Ltd., Hertfordshire (1994)
4. Barrett, E., Bolz, C.F., Tratt, L.: Unipycation: a case study in cross-language tracing. In: Proceedings of the 7th ACM Workshop on Virtual Machines and Intermediate Languages, pp. 31–40. ACM, New York (2013)
5. Barrett, E., Bolz, C.F., Tratt, L.: Approaches to interpreter composition. Comput. Lang. Syst. Struct. **44**, 199–217 (2015)
6. Beierle, C., Meyer, G.: Run-time type computations in the Warren abstract machine. J. Log. Program. **18**(2), 123–148 (1994)
7. Benton, N.: Embedded interpreters. J. Funct. Program. **15**(4), 503–542 (2005)
8. Chisnall, D.: The challenge of cross-language interoperability. Commun. ACM **56**(12), 50–56 (2013)
9. Dybvig, R.K.: The Scheme Programming Language, 4th edn. The MIT Press, Cambridge (2009)
10. Erwig, M.: Specifying type systems with multi-level order-sorted algebra. In: Nivat, M., Rattray, C., Rus, T., Scollo, G. (eds.) Algebraic Methodology and Software Technology (AMAST 1993). WORKSHOPS COMP., pp. 177–184. Springer, London (1994). https://doi.org/10.1007/978-1-4471-3227-1_17
11. Erwig, M., Güting, R.H.: Explicit graphs in a functional model for spatial databases. IEEE Trans. Knowl. Data Eng. **6**(5), 787–804 (1994)
12. Findler, R.B., Felleisen, M.: Contracts for higher-order functions. In: Proceedings of the Seventh ACM SIGPLAN International Conference on Functional Programming, ICFP 2002, pp. 48–59. ACM, New York (2002)
13. Flanagan, D.: JavaScript: The Definitive Guide. O'Reilly Media Inc., Sebastopol (2006)
14. Furr, M., Foster, J.S.: Checking type safety of foreign function calls. SIGPLAN Not. **40**(6), 62–72 (2005)
15. Goguen, J.A., Thatcher, J.W., Wagner, E.G., Wright, J.B.: Initial algebra semantics and continuous algebras. J. ACM **24**(1), 68–95 (1977)
16. Goguen, J.: Tossing algebraic flowers down the great divide (1999)
17. Goguen, J.A.: Semantics of computation. In: Manes, E.G. (ed.) Category Theory Applied to Computation and Control. LNCS, vol. 25, pp. 151–163. Springer, Heidelberg (1975). https://doi.org/10.1007/3-540-07142-3_75
18. Goguen, J.A., Diaconescu, R.: An oxford survey of order sorted algebra. Math. Struct. Comput. Sci. **4**(3), 363–392 (1994)
19. Goguen, J.A., Meseguer, J.: Order-sorted algebra I: equational deduction for multiple inheritance, overloading, exceptions and partial operations. Theor. Comput. Sci. **105**(2), 217–273 (1992)

20. Gordon, A.D., Syme, D.: Typing a multi-language intermediate code. In: Conference Record of POPL 2001: The 28th ACM SIGPLAN-SIGACT Symposium on Principles of Programming Languages, London, UK, 17–19 January 2001, pp. 248–260. ACM, New York (2001)
21. Gray, K.E.: Safe cross-language inheritance. In: Vitek, J. (ed.) ECOOP 2008. LNCS, vol. 5142, pp. 52–75. Springer, Heidelberg (2008). https://doi.org/10.1007/978-3-540-70592-5_4
22. Grimmer, M., Schatz, R., Seaton, C., Würthinger, T., Luján, M.: Cross-language interoperability in a multi-language runtime. ACM Trans. Program. Lang. Syst. **40**(2), 8:1–8:43 (2018)
23. Grimmer, M., Seaton, C., Schatz, R., Würthinger, T., Mössenböck, H.: High-performance cross-language interoperability in a multi-language runtime. In: Proceedings of the 11th Symposium on Dynamic Languages, DLS 2015, Part of SPLASH 2015, Pittsburgh, PA, USA, 25–30 October 2015, pp. 78–90. ACM, New York (2015)
24. Haxthausen, A.E.: Order-sorted algebraic specifications with higher-order functions. Theor. Comput. Sci. **183**(2), 157–185 (1997)
25. Hearn, A.C., Schrüfer, E.: A computer algebra system based on order-sorted algebra. J. Symb. Comput. **19**(1), 65–77 (1995)
26. Henglein, F., Rehof, J.: Safe polymorphic type inference for scheme: translating scheme to ML. In: Proceedings of the Seventh International Conference on Functional Programming Languages and Computer Architecture, FPCA 1995, La Jolla, California, USA, 25–28 June 1995, pp. 192–203. ACM, New York (1995)
27. Johann, P., Ghani, N.: Initial algebra semantics is enough!. In: Della Rocca, S.R. (ed.) TLCA 2007. LNCS, vol. 4583, pp. 207–222. Springer, Heidelberg (2007). https://doi.org/10.1007/978-3-540-73228-0_16
28. Juneau, J., Baker, J., Wierzbicki, F., Soto, L., Ng, V.: The Definitive Guide to Jython: Python for the Java Platform, 1st edn. Apress, Berkely (2010)
29. Liang, S.: Java Native Interface: Programmer's Guide and Reference, 1st edn. Addison-Wesley Longman Publishing Co., Inc., Boston (1999)
30. Matthews, J., Findler, R.B.: Operational semantics for multi-language programs. SIGPLAN Not. **42**(1), 3–10 (2007)
31. Meseguer, J., Rosu, G.: The rewriting logic semantics project. Electr. Notes Theor. Comput. Sci. **156**(1), 27–56 (2006)
32. Meseguer, J.: Conditional rewriting logic as a unified model of concurrency. Theor. Comput. Sci. **96**(1), 73–155 (1992)
33. Milner, R., Tofte, M., Macqueen, D.: The Definition of Standard ML. MIT Press, Cambridge (1997)
34. Ohori, A., Kato, K.: Semantics for communication primitives in a polymorphic language. In: Proceedings of the 20th ACM SIGPLAN-SIGACT Symposium on Principles of Programming Languages, POPL 1993, pp. 99–112. ACM, New York (1993)
35. Osera, P.M., Sjöberg, V., Zdancewic, S.: Dependent interoperability. In: Proceedings of the Sixth Workshop on Programming Languages Meets Program Verification, PLPV 2012, pp. 3–14. ACM, New York (2012)
36. Patterson, D., Perconti, J., Dimoulas, C., Ahmed, A.: FunTAL: reasonably mixing a functional language with assembly. SIGPLAN Not. **52**(6), 495–509 (2017)
37. Perconti, J.T., Ahmed, A.: Verifying an open compiler using multi-language semantics. In: Shao, Z. (ed.) ESOP 2014. LNCS, vol. 8410, pp. 128–148. Springer, Heidelberg (2014). https://doi.org/10.1007/978-3-642-54833-8_8

38. Poigné, A.: Parametrization for order-sorted algebraic specification. J. Comput. Syst. Sci. **40**(2), 229–268 (1990)
39. Qian, Z.: Another look at parameterization for order-sorted algebraic specifications. J. Comput. Syst. Sci. **49**(3), 620–666 (1994)
40. Ramsey, N.: Embedding an interpreted language using higher-order functions and types. In: Proceedings of the 2003 Workshop on Interpreters, Virtual Machines and Emulators, IVME 2003, pp. 6–14. ACM, New York (2003)
41. Ramsey, N.: ML module mania: a type-safe, separately compiled, extensible interpreter. Electron. Notes Theor. Comput. Sci. **148**(2), 181–209 (2006)
42. Reynolds, J.C.: Definitional interpreters for higher-order programming languages. In: Proceedings of the ACM Annual Conference - Volume 2, ACM 1972, pp. 717–740. ACM, New York (1972)
43. Robinson, E.: Variations on algebra: monadicity and generalisations of equational therories. Form. Asp. Comput. **13**(3), 308–326 (2002)
44. Rogers, J.: Microsoft JScript.Net Programming. Sams, Indianapolis (2001)
45. Schmidt-Schauß, M. (ed.): Computational Aspects of an Order-Sorted Logic with Term Declarations. LNCS, vol. 395. Springer, Heidelberg (1989). https://doi.org/10.1007/BFb0024065
46. Scott, D.S., Strachey, C.: Toward a Mathematical Semantics for Computer Languages, vol. 1. Oxford University Computing Laboratory, Programming Research Group, Oxford (1971)
47. Sharan, K.: Scripting in Java: Integrating with Groovy and JavaScript, 1st edn. Apress, Berkely (2014)
48. Stell, J.G.: A framework for order-sorted algebra. In: Kirchner, H., Ringeissen, C. (eds.) AMAST 2002. LNCS, vol. 2422, pp. 396–411. Springer, Heidelberg (2002). https://doi.org/10.1007/3-540-45719-4_27
49. Tan, G., Morrisett, G.: Ilea: Inter-language analysis across Java and C. SIGPLAN Not. **42**(10), 39–56 (2007)
50. Trifonov, V., Shao, Z.: Safe and principled language interoperation. In: Swierstra, S.D. (ed.) ESOP 1999. LNCS, vol. 1576, pp. 128–146. Springer, Heidelberg (2002). https://doi.org/10.1007/3-540-49099-X_9
51. Waldmann, U.: Semantics of order-sorted specifications. Theor. Comput. Sci. **94**(1), 1–35 (1992)
52. Wieringa, R.J.: A formalization of objects using equational dynamic logic. In: Delobel, C., Kifer, M., Masunaga, Y. (eds.) DOOD 1991. LNCS, vol. 566, pp. 431–452. Springer, Heidelberg (1991). https://doi.org/10.1007/3-540-55015-1_23
53. Wrigstad, T., Nardelli, F.Z., Lebresne, S., Östlund, J., Vitek, J.: Integrating typed and untyped code in a scripting language. In: Hermenegildo, M.V., Palsberg, J. (eds.) Proceedings of the 37th ACM SIGPLAN-SIGACT Symposium on Principles of Programming Languages, POPL 2010, Madrid, Spain, 17–23 January 2010, pp. 377–388. ACM (2010)

Probabilistic Programming Inference via Intensional Semantics

Simon Castellan[1] and Hugo Paquet[2(✉)]

[1] Imperial College London, London, UK
simon.castellan@phis.me
[2] University of Cambridge, Cambridge, UK
hugo.paquet@cl.cam.ac.uk

Abstract. We define a new denotational semantics for a first-order probabilistic programming language in terms of *probabilistic event structures*. This semantics is *intensional*, meaning that the interpretation of a program contains information about its behaviour throughout execution, rather than a simple distribution on return values. In particular, occurrences of sampling and conditioning are recorded as explicit events, partially ordered according to the data dependencies between the corresponding statements in the program.

This interpretation is *adequate*: we show that the usual measure-theoretic semantics of a program can be recovered from its event structure representation. Moreover it can be leveraged for MCMC inference: we prove correct a version of single-site Metropolis-Hastings with *incremental recomputation*, in which the proposal kernel takes into account the semantic information in order to avoid performing some of the redundant sampling.

Keywords: Probabilistic programming · Denotational semantics · Event structures · Bayesian inference

1 Introduction

Probabilistic programming languages [8] were put forward as promising tools for practitioners of Bayesian statistics. By extending traditional programming languages with primitives for sampling and conditioning, they allow the user to express a wide class of statistical models, and provide a simple interface for encoding inference problems. Although the subject of active research, it is still notoriously difficult to design inference methods for probabilistic programs which perform well for the full class of expressible models.

One popular inference technique, proposed by Wingate et al. [21], involves adapting well-known *Monte-Carlo Markov chain* methods from statistics to probabilistic programs, by manipulating *program traces*. One such method is the Metropolis-Hastings algorithm, which relies on a key *proposal* step: given a program trace x (a sequence $x_1, \ldots, x_n$ of random choices with their likelihood),

L. Caires (Ed.): ESOP 2019, LNCS 11423, pp. 322–349, 2019.
https://doi.org/10.1007/978-3-030-17184-1_12

a proposal for the *next* trace sample is generated by choosing $i \in \{1, \ldots, n\}$ uniformly, resampling x_i, and then continuing to execute the program, only performing additional sampling for those random choices not appearing in x. The variables already present in x are not resampled: only their likelihood is updated according to the new value of x_i. Likewise, some conditioning statements must be re-evaluated in case the corresponding weight is affected by the change to x_i.

Observe that there is some redundancy in this process, since the updating process above will only affect variables and observations when their density directly depends on the value of x_i. This may significantly affect performance: to solve an inference problem one must usually perform a large number of proposal steps. To overcome this problem, some recent implementations, notably [12,25], make use of *incremental recomputation*, whereby some of the redundancy can be avoided via a form of static analysis. However, as pointed out by Kiselyov [13], establishing the correctness of such implementations is tricky.

Here we address this by introducing a theoretical framework in which to reason about data dependencies in probabilistic programs. Specifically, our first contribution is to define a *denotational semantics* for a first-order probabilistic language, in terms of graph-like structures called *event structures* [22]. In event structures, computational events are partially ordered according to the dependencies between them; additionally they can be equipped with quantitative information to represent probabilistic processes [16,23]. This semantics is *intensional*, unlike most existing semantics for probabilistic programs, in which the interpretation of a program resembles a probability distribution on output values. We relate our approach to a measure-theoretic semantics [18] through an *adequacy* result.

Our second contribution is the design of a Metropolis-Hastings algorithm which exploits the event structure representation of the program at hand. Some of the redundancy in the proposal step of the algorithm is avoided by taking into account the extra dependency information given by the semantics. We provide a proof of correctness for this algorithm, and argue that an implementation is realistically achievable: we show in particular that all graph structures involved and the associated quantitative information admit a finite, concrete representation.

Outline of the Paper. In Sect. 2 we give a short introduction to probabilistic programming. We define our main language of study and its measure-theoretic semantics. In Sect. 3.1, we introduce MCMC methods and the Metropolis-Hastings algorithm in the context of probabilistic programming. We then motivate the need for intensional semantics in order to capture data dependency. In Sect. 4 we define our interpretation of programs and prove adequacy. In Sect. 5 we define an updated version of the algorithm, and prove its correctness. We conclude in Sect. 6.

The proofs of the statements are detailed in the technical report [4].

2 Probabilistic Programming

In this section we motivate the need for capturing data dependency in probabilistic programs. Let us start with a brief introduction to probabilistic programming – a more comprehensive account can be found in [8].

2.1 Conditioning and Posterior Distribution

Let us introduce the problem of inference in probabilistic programming from the point of view of programming language theory.

We consider a first-order programming language enriched with a real number type $\mathbb{R}$ and a primitive `sample` for drawing random values from a given family of standard probability distributions. The language is idealised—but it is assumed that an implementation of the language comprises built-in sampling procedures for those standard distributions. Thus, repeatedly running the program `sample Uniform` $(0, 1)$ returns a sequence of values approaching the true uniform distribution on $[0, 1]$.

Via other constructs in the language, standard distributions can be combined, as shown in the following example program of type $\mathbb{R}$:

```
let x = sample Uniform(0, 1) in
let y = sample Gaussian(x, 2) in
x + y
```

Here the output will follow a probability distribution built out of the usual uniform and Gaussian distributions. Many probabilistic programming languages will offer more general programming constructs: conditionals, recursion, higher-order functions, data types, *etc.*, enabling a wide range of distributions to be expressed in this way. Such a program is sometimes called a *generative model.*

Conditioning. The process of conditioning involves rescaling the distribution associated with a generative model, so as to reflect some bias. Going back to the example above, say we have made some external measurement indicating that $y = 0$, but we would like to account for possible noise in the measurement using another Gaussian. To express this we modify the program as follows:

```
let x = sample Uniform (0, 1) in
let y = sample Gaussian (x, 2) in
observe y (Gaussian (0, 0.01));
x + y;
```

The purpose of the `observe` statement is to increase the occurrence of executions in which y is close to 0; the original distribution, known as the **prior**, must be updated accordingly. The probabilistic weight of each execution is multiplied by an appropriate *score*, namely the **likelihood** of the current value of y in the Gaussian distribution with parameters $(0, 0.01)$. (This is known as a *soft constraint.* Conditioning via *hard constraints*, *i.e.* only giving a nonzero score to executions where y is exactly 0, is not practically feasible.)

The language studied here does not have an `observe` construct, but instead an explicit `score` primitive; this appears already in [18,19]. So the third line in the program above would instead be `score(pdf-Gaussian (0, 0.01) (y))` where `pdf-Gaussian (0, 0.01)` is the *density* function of the Gaussian distribution. The resulting distribution is not necessarily normalised. We obtain the **posterior** distribution by computing the normalising constant, following Bayes' rule:

$$\text{posterior} \propto \text{likelihood} \times \text{prior}.$$

This process is known as Bayesian inference and has ubiquitous applications. The difficulty lies in computing the normalising constant, which is usually obtained as an integral. Below we discuss *approximate* methods for sampling from the posterior distribution; they do not rely on this normalising step.

Measure Theory. Because this work makes heavy use of probability theory, we start with a brief account of measure theory. A standard textbook for this is [1]. Recall that a **measurable space** is a set X equipped with a **σ-algebra** Σ_X: a set of subsets of X containing $\emptyset$ and closed under complements and countable unions. Elements of Σ_X are called **measurable sets**. A **measure** on X is a function $\mu : \Sigma_X \to [0, \infty]$, such that $\mu(\emptyset) = 0$ and, for any countable family $\{U_i\}_{i \in I}$ of measurable sets, $\mu(\bigcup_{i \in I} U_i) = \sum_{i \in I} \mu(U_i)$.

An important example is that of the set $\mathbb{R}$ of real numbers, whose σ-algebra $\Sigma_{\mathbb{R}}$ is generated by the intervals $[a, b)$, for $a, b \in \mathbb{R}$ (in other words, it is the smallest σ-algebra containing those intervals). The **Lebesgue measure** on $(\mathbb{R}, \Sigma_{\mathbb{R}})$ is the (unique) measure λ assigning $b - a$ to every interval $[a, b)$ (with $a \leq b$).

Given measurable spaces (X, Σ_X) and (Y, Σ_Y), a function $f : X \to Y$ is **measurable** if for every $U \in \Sigma_Y$, $f^{-1}U \in \Sigma_X$. A measurable function $f : X \to [0, \infty]$ can be *integrated*: given $U \in \Sigma_X$ the **integral** $\int_U f \, d\lambda$ is a well-defined element of $[0, \infty]$; indeed the map $\mu : U \mapsto \int_U f d\lambda$ is a measure on X, and f is said to be a **density** for μ. The precise definition of the integral is standard but slightly more involved; we omit it.

We identify the following important classes of measures: a measure μ on (X, Σ_X) is a **probability measure** if $\mu(X) = 1$. It is **finite** if $\mu(X) < \infty$, and it is **s-finite** if $\mu = \sum_{i \in I} \mu_i$, a pointwise, countable sum of finite measures.

We recall the usual product and coproduct constructions for measurable spaces and measures. If $\{X_i\}_{i \in I}$ is a countable family of measurable spaces, their **product** $\prod_{i \in I} X_i$ and **coproduct** $\coprod_{i \in I} X_i = \bigcup_{i \in I} \{i\} \times X_i$ as sets can be turned into measurable spaces, where:

- $\Sigma_{\prod_{i \in I} X_i}$ is generated by $\{\prod_{i \in I} U_i \mid U_i \in \Sigma_{X_i} \text{ for all } i\}$, and
- $\Sigma_{\coprod_{i \in I} X_i}$ is generated by $\{\{i\} \times U_i \mid i \in I \text{ and } U_i \in \Sigma_{X_i}\}$.

The measurable spaces in this paper all belong to a well-behaved subclass: call (X, Σ_X) a **standard Borel space** if it either countable and discrete (*i.e.* all $U \subseteq X$ are in Σ_X), or measurably isomorphic to $(\mathbb{R}, \Sigma_{\mathbb{R}})$. Note that standard Borel spaces are closed under countable products and coproducts, and that in a standard Borel space all singletons are measurable.

2.2 A First-Order Probabilistic Programming Language

We consider a first-order, call-by-value language $\mathcal{L}$ with types

$$A, B ::= 1 \mid \mathbb{R} \mid \coprod_{i \in I} A_i \mid \prod_{i \in I} A_i$$

where I ranges over nonempty countable sets. The types denote measurable spaces in a natural way: $[\![1]\!]$ is the singleton space, and $[\![\mathbb{R}]\!] = (\mathbb{R}, \Sigma_{\mathbb{R}})$. Products and coproducts are interpreted via the corresponding measure-theoretic constructions: $[\![\prod_{i \in I} A_i]\!] = \prod_{i \in I} [\![A_i]\!]$ and $[\![\coprod_{i \in I} A_i]\!] = \coprod_{i \in I} [\![A_i]\!] = \bigcup_{i \in I} \{i\} \times [\![A_i]\!]$. Moreover, each measurable space $[\![A]\!]$ has a canonical measure $\mu_{[\![A]\!]} : \Sigma_{[\![A]\!]} \to \mathbb{R}$, induced from the Lebesgue measure on $\mathbb{R}$ and the Dirac measure on $[\![1]\!]$ via standard product and coproduct measure constructions.

The terms of $\mathcal{L}$ are given by the following grammar:

$$\begin{aligned} M, N ::= {} & () \mid M; N \mid f \mid \texttt{let } a \texttt{ = } M \texttt{ in } N \mid x \\ & \mid (M_i)_{i \in I} \mid \texttt{case } M \texttt{ of } \{(i, x) \Rightarrow N_i\}_{i \in I} \\ & \mid \texttt{sample } d \texttt{ (} M \texttt{)} \mid \texttt{score } M \end{aligned}$$

and we use standard syntactic sugar to manipulate integers and booleans: $\mathbb{B} = 1 + 1$, $\mathbb{N} = \sum_{i \in \omega} 1$, and constants are given by the appropriate injections. Conditionals and sequencing can be expressed in the usual way: $\texttt{if } M \texttt{ then } N_1 \texttt{ else } N_2 = \texttt{case } M \texttt{ of } \{(i, \_) \Rightarrow N_i\}_{i \in \{1,2\}}$, and $M; N = \texttt{let } a \texttt{ = } M \texttt{ in } N$, where a does not occur in N. In the grammar above:

- f ranges over measurable functions $[\![A]\!] \to [\![B]\!]$, where A and B are types;
- d ranges over a family of *parametric distributions* over the reals, *i.e.* measurable functions $\mathbb{R}^n \times \mathbb{R} \to \mathbb{R}$, for some $n \in \mathbb{N}$, such that for every $\mathbf{r} \in \mathbb{R}^n$, $\int d(\mathbf{r}, -) = 1$. For the purposes of this paper we ignore all issues related to invalid parameters, arising from *e.g.* a call to `gaussian` with standard deviation $\sigma = 0$. (An implementation could, say, choose to behave according to an alternative distribution in this case.)

The typing rules are as follows:

$$\frac{\Gamma \vdash M : A \qquad \Gamma, a : A \vdash N : B}{\Gamma \vdash \texttt{let } a \texttt{ = } M \texttt{ in } N : B} \qquad \frac{\Gamma \vdash M : \mathbb{R}^n \qquad d : \mathbb{R}^n \times \mathbb{R} \to \mathbb{R}}{\Gamma \vdash \texttt{sample } d \texttt{ (} M \texttt{)} : \mathbb{R}}$$

$$\frac{\Gamma \vdash M : \mathbb{R}}{\Gamma \vdash \texttt{score } M : 1} \qquad \frac{}{\Gamma, a : A \vdash a : A} \qquad \frac{}{\Gamma \vdash () : 1}$$

$$\frac{\Gamma \vdash M : \sum_{i \in I} A_i \qquad \Gamma, x : A_i \vdash N_i : C}{\Gamma \vdash \texttt{case } M \texttt{ of } \{(i, x) \Rightarrow N_i\}_{i \in I} : C} \qquad \frac{\Gamma \vdash M_i : A_i}{\Gamma \vdash (M_i)_{i \in I} : \prod_{i \in I} A_i}$$

$$\frac{f : [\![A]\!] \to [\![B]\!] \text{ measurable} \qquad \Gamma \vdash M : A}{\Gamma \vdash f\ M : B}$$

Among the measurable functions f, we point out the following of interest:

- The usual product projections $\pi_i : [\![\prod_{i\in I} A_i]\!] \to [\![A_i]\!]$ and coproduct injections $\iota_i : [\![A_i]\!] \to [\![\coprod_{i\in I} A_i]\!]$;
- The operators $+, \times : \mathbb{R}^2 \to \mathbb{R}$,
- The tests, eg. $\geq 0 : [\![\mathbb{R}]\!] \to [\![\mathbb{B}]\!]$,
- The constant functions $1 \to A$ of the form $() \mapsto a$ for some $a \in [\![A]\!]$.

Examples for d include $\texttt{uniform} : \mathbb{R}^2 \times \mathbb{R} \to \mathbb{R}$, $\texttt{gaussian} : \mathbb{R}^2 \times \mathbb{R} \to \mathbb{R}$, ...

2.3 Measure-Theoretic Semantics of Programs

We now define a semantics of probabilistic programs using the measure-theoretic concept of *kernel*, which we define shortly. The content of this section is not new: using kernels as semantics for probabilistic was originally proposed in [14], while the (more recent) treatment of conditioning (`score`) via *s-finite* kernels is due to Staton [18]. Intuitively, kernels provide a semantics of open terms $\Gamma \vdash M : A$ as measures on $[\![A]\!]$ varying according to the values of variables in Γ.

Formally, a **kernel** from (X, Σ_X) to (Y, Σ_Y) is a function $k : X \times \Sigma_Y \to [0, \infty]$ such that for each $x \in X$, $k(x, -)$ is a measure, and for each $U \in \Sigma_Y$, $k(-, U)$ is measurable. (Here the σ-algebra $\Sigma_{[0,\infty]}$ is the restriction of that of $\mathbb{R}+\{\infty\}$.) We say k is **finite** (resp. **probabilistic**) if each $k(x, -)$ is a finite (resp. probability) measure, and it **s-finite** if it is a countable pointwise sum $\sum_{i\in I} k_i$ of finite kernels. We write $k : X \rightsquigarrow Y$ when k is an s-finite kernel from X to Y.

A term $\Gamma \vdash M : A$ will denote an s-finite kernel $[\![M]\!] : [\![\Gamma]\!] \rightsquigarrow [\![A]\!]$, where the context $\Gamma = x_1 : A_1, \ldots, x_n : A_n$ denotes the product of its components: $[\![\Gamma]\!] = [\![A_1]\!] \times \cdots \times [\![A_n]\!]$.

Notice that any measurable function $f : X \to Y$ can be seen as a *deterministic* kernel $f^\dagger : X \rightsquigarrow Y$. Given two s-finite kernels $k : A \rightsquigarrow B$ and $l : A \times B \rightsquigarrow C$, we define their composition $l \circ k : A \rightsquigarrow C$:

$$(l \circ k)(a, X) = \int_{b\in B} l((a, b), C) \times k(a, \mathrm{d}b).$$

Staton [18] proved that $l \circ k$ is a s-finite kernel.

The interpretation of terms is defined by induction:

- $[\![()]\!]$ is the lifting of $[\![\Gamma]\!] \to 1 : x \mapsto ()$.
- $[\![\texttt{let } a \texttt{ = } M \texttt{ in } N]\!]$ is $[\![N]\!] \circ [\![M]\!]$
- $[\![f\,M]\!] = f^\dagger \circ [\![M]\!]$
- $[\![a]\!](x, X) = \delta_x(X)$, the Dirac distribution $\delta_x(X) = 1$ if $x \in X$ and zero otherwise.
- $[\![\texttt{sample } d \texttt{ (}M\texttt{)}]\!] = \texttt{sam} \circ [\![M]\!]$ where $\texttt{sam}_d : \mathbb{R}^n \rightsquigarrow \mathbb{R}$ is given by $\texttt{sam}_d(\mathbf{r}, X) = \int_{x\in X} d(\mathbf{r}, x)\mathrm{d}x$.
- $[\![\texttt{score } M]\!] = \texttt{sco} \circ [\![M]\!]$ where $\texttt{sco} : [\![R]\!] \to [\![1]\!]$ is $\texttt{sco}(r, X) = r \cdot \delta_{()}(X)$.
- $[\![(M_i)_{i\in I}]\!](\gamma, \prod_{i\in I} X_i) = \prod_{i\in I} [\![M_i]\!](\gamma, X_i)$: this is well-defined since the $\prod X_i$ generate the measurable sets of the product space.

- $[\![\texttt{case}\ M\ \texttt{of}\ \{(i,x) \Rightarrow N_i\}_{i\in I}]\!] = \texttt{coprod} \circ [\![M]\!]$ where $\texttt{coprod} : \Gamma \times [\![\coprod_{i\in I} A_i]\!] \rightsquigarrow [\![B]\!]$ maps $(\gamma, \{i\} \times X)$ to $[\![N_i]\!](\gamma, X)$.

We observe that when M is a program making no use of conditioning (*i.e.* a generative model), the kernel $[\![M]\!]$ is probabilistic:

Lemma 1. *For $\Gamma \vdash M : A$ without scores, $[\![M]\!](\gamma, [\![A]\!]) = 1$ for each $\gamma \in [\![\Gamma]\!]$.*

2.4 Exact Inference

Note that a kernel $1 \rightsquigarrow [\![A]\!]$ is the same as a measure on $[\![A]\!]$. Given a closed program $\vdash M : A$, the measure $[\![M]\!]$ is a combination of the prior (occurrences of `sample`) and the likelihood (`score`). Because `score` can be called on arbitrary arguments, it may be the case that the measure of the total space (that is, the coefficient $[\![M]\!]([\![A]\!])$, often called the *model evidence*) is 0 or ∞.

Whenever this is *not* the case, $[\![M]\!]$ can be normalised to a probability measure, the posterior distribution. For every $U \in \Sigma_{[\![A]\!]}$,

$$\mathrm{norm}[\![M]\!](U) = \frac{[\![M]\!](U)}{[\![M]\!]([\![A]\!])}.$$

However, in many cases, this computation is intractable. Thus the goal of *approximate inference* is to approach $\mathrm{norm}[\![M]\!]$, the *true posterior*, using a well-chosen sequence of samples.

3 Approximate Inference via Intensional Semantics

3.1 An Introduction to Approximate Inference

In this section we describe the Metropolis-Hastings (MH) algorithm for approximate inference in the context of probabilistic programming. Metropolis-Hastings is a generic algorithm to sample from a probability distribution D on a measurable state space $\mathbb{X}$, of which we know the density $d : \mathbb{X} \to \mathbb{R}$ up to some normalising constant.

MH is part of a family of inference algorithms called *Monte-Carlo Markov chain*, in which the posterior distribution is approximated by a series of samples generated using a Markov chain.

Formally, the MH algorithm defines a Markov chain M on the state space $\mathbb{X}$, that is a probabilistic kernel $M : \mathbb{X} \rightsquigarrow \mathbb{X}$. The correctness of the MH algorithm is expressed in terms of convergence. It says that for almost all $x \in \mathbb{X}$, the distribution $M^n(x, \cdot)$ converges to D as n goes to infinity, where M^n is the n-iteration of M: $M \circ \ldots \circ M$. Intuitively, this means that iterated sampling from M gets closer to D with the number of iterations.

The MH algorithm is itself parametrised by a Markov chain, referred to as the **proposal kernel** $P : \mathbb{X} \rightsquigarrow \mathbb{X}$: for each sampled value $x \in \mathbb{X}$, a proposed value for the next sample is drawn according to $P(x, \cdot)$. Note that correctness only holds under certain assumptions on P.

The MH algorithm assumes that we know how to sample from P, and that its density is known, ie. there is a function $p : \mathbb{X}^2 \to \mathbb{R}$ such that $p(x, \cdot)$ is the density of the distribution $P(x, \cdot)$,

The MH Algorithm. On an input state x, the MH algorithm samples from $P(x, \cdot)$ and gets a new sample x'. It then compares the likelihood of x and x' by computing an acceptance ratio $\alpha(x, x')$ which says whether the return state is x' or x. In pseudo-code, for an input state $x \in \mathbb{X}$:

1. Sample a new state x' from the distribution $P(x, \cdot)$
2. Compute the acceptance ratio of x' with respect to x:

$$\alpha(x, x') = \min\left(1, \frac{d(x') \times p(x, x')}{d(x) \times p(x', x)}\right)$$

3. With probability $\alpha(x, x')$, return the new sample x', otherwise return the input state x.

The formula for $\alpha(x, x')$ is known as the Hastings acceptance ratio and is key to the correctness of the algorithm.

Very little is assumed of P, which makes the algorithm very flexible; but of course the convergence rate may vary depending on the choice of P. We give a more formal description of MH in Sect. 5.2.

Single-Site MH and Incremental Recomputation. To apply this algorithm to probabilistic programming, we need a proposal kernel. Given a program M, the execution traces of M form a measurable set $\mathbb{X}_M$. In this setting the proposal is given by a kernel $\mathbb{X}_M \rightsquigarrow \mathbb{X}_M$.

A widely adopted choice of proposal is the *single-site proposal kernel* which, given a trace $x \in \mathbb{X}_M$, generates a new trace x' as follows:

1. Select uniformly one of the random choices s encountered in x.
2. Sample a new value for this instruction.
3. Re-execute the program M from that point onwards and with this new value for s, only ever resampling a variable when the corresponding instruction did not already appear in x.

Observe that there is some redundancy in this process: in the final step, the entire program has to be explored even though only a subset of the random choices will be re-evaluated. Some implementations of Trace MH for probabilistic programming make use of *incremental recomputation.*

We propose in this paper to statically compile a program M to an *event structure* G_M which makes explicit the probabilistic dependences between events, thus avoiding unnecessary sampling.

3.2 Capturing Probabilistic Dependencies Using Event Structures

Consider the program depicted in Fig. 1 in which we are interested in learning the parameters μ and σ of a Gaussian distribution from which we have observed two data points, say v_1 and v_2. For $i = 1, 2$ the function $f_i : \mathbb{R} \to \mathbb{R}$ expresses a soft constraint; it can be understood as indicating how much the sampled value of x*i* matches the observed value v_i.

A *trace* of this program will be of the form

$$\mathsf{Sam}\,\mu \cdot \mathsf{Sam}\,\sigma \cdot \mathsf{Sam}\,x_1 \cdot \mathsf{Sam}\,x_2 \cdot \mathsf{Sco}\,(f_1\,x_1) \cdot \mathsf{Sco}\,(f_2\,x_2) \cdot \mathsf{Rtn}\,(\mu, \sigma),$$

for some μ, σ, x_1, and $x_2 \in \mathbb{R}$ corresponding to sampled values for variables `mu`, `sigma`, `x1` and `x2`.

```
let mu = sample uniform (150, 200) in
let sigma = sample uniform (1, 50) in
let x1 = sample gaussian (mu, sigma) in
let x2 = sample gaussian (mu, sigma) in
score (f1 x1); score (f2 x2);
(mu, sigma)
```

Fig. 1. A simple probabilistic program

A proposal step following the single-site kernel may choose to resample μ; then it must run through the entire trace, checking for potential dependencies to μ, though in this case none of the other variables need to be resampled.

So we argue that viewing a program as tree of traces is not most appropriate in this context: we propose instead to compile a program into a partially ordered structure reflecting the probabilistic dependencies.

With our approach, the example above would yield the partial order displayed below on the right-hand side. The nodes on the first line corresponds to the sample for μ and σ, and those on the second line to x_1 and x_2. This provides an accurate account of the probabilistic dependencies: whenever $e \leq e'$ (where $\leq$ is the reflexive, transitive closure of $\rightarrowtriangle$), it is the case that e' depends on e.

According to this representation of the program, a trace is no longer a linear order, but instead another partial order, similar to the previous one only annotated with a specific value for each variable. This is displayed below, on the left-hand side; note that the order $\leq$ is drawn top to bottom. There is an obvious erasure map from the trace (left) to the graph (right); this will be important later on.

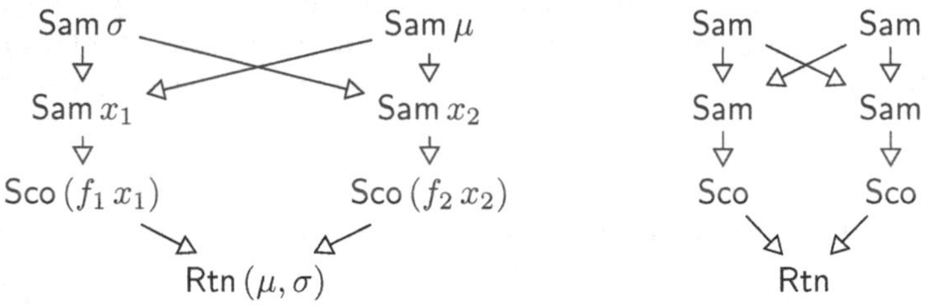

Conflict and Control Flow. We have seen that a partial order can be used to faithfully represent the data dependency in the program; it is however not sufficient to accurately describe the control flow. In particular, computational events may live in different *branches* of a conditional statement, as in the following example:

```
let x = sample uniform (0, 5) in
if x ≥ 2 then sample gaussian (3, 1)
else sample uniform (2, 4)
```

The last two samples are independent, but also *incompatible*: in any given trace only one of them will occur. An example of a trace for this program is $\mathsf{Sam}\,1 \cdot \mathsf{Sam}\,3 \cdot \mathsf{Rtn}\,3$.

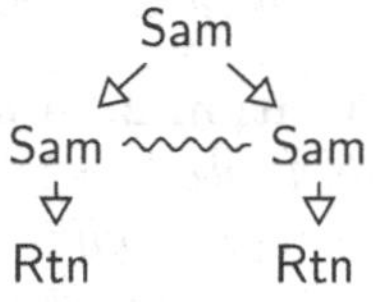

We represent this information by enriching the partial order with a conflict relation, indicating when two actions are in different branches of a conditional statement. The resulting structure is depicted on the right. Combining partial order and conflict in this way can be conveniently formalised using **event structures** [22]:

Definition 1. *An* ***event structure*** *is a tuple* $(E, \leq, \#)$ *where* $(E, \leq)$ *is a partially ordered set and* $\#$ *is an irreflexive, binary relation on* E *such that*

- *for every* $e \in E$*, the set* $[e] = \{e' \in E \mid e' \leq e\}$ *is finite, and*
- *if* $e \# e'$ *and* $e' \leq e''$*, then* $e \# e''$*.*

From the partial order $\leq$, we extract **immediate causality** $\rightarrowtriangle$: $e \rightarrowtriangle e'$ when $e < e'$ with no events in between; and from the conflict relation, we extract **minimal conflict** $\sim\!\sim$: $e \sim\!\sim e'$ when $e \# e'$ and there are no other conflicts in $[e] \cup [e']$. In pictures we draw $\rightarrowtriangle$ and $\sim\!\sim$ rather than $\leq$ and $\#$.

A subset $x \subseteq E$ is a **configuration** of E if it is down-closed (if $e' \leq e \in x$ then $e' \in x$) and conflict-free (if $e, e' \in x$ then $\neg(e \# e')$). So in this framework, configurations correspond to exactly to *partial* executions traces of E.

The configuration $[e]$ is the **causal history** of e; we also write $[e)$ for $[e] \setminus \{e\}$. We write $\mathscr{C}(E)$ for the set of all finite configurations of E, a partial order under inclusion. A configuration x is **maximal** if it is maximal in $\mathscr{C}(E)$: for every $x' \in \mathscr{C}(E)$, if $x \subseteq x'$ then $x = x'$. We use the notation $x \overset{e}{\longrightarrow\!\!\!\!\subset} x'$ when $x' = x \cup \{e\}$, and in that case we say x' **covers** x.

An event structure is **confusion-free** if minimal conflict is transitive, and if any two events e, e' in minimal conflict satisfy $[e) = [e')$.

Compositionality. In order to give semantics to the language in a compositional manner, we must consider arbitrary *open* programs, *i.e.* with free parameters. Therefore we also represent each call to a parameter a as a *read* event, marked $\mathsf{Rd}\,a$. For instance the program $x + y$ with two real parameters will become the event structure

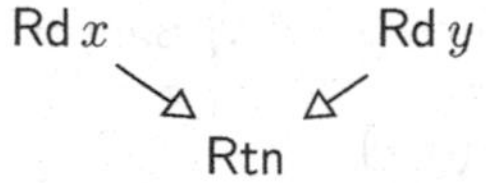

Note that the read actions on x and y are independent in the program (no order is specified), and the event structure respects this independence.

Our dependency graphs are event structures where each event carries information about the syntactic operation it comes from, a **label**, which depends on the typing context of the program:

$$\mathscr{L}^{\mathtt{static}}_{\Gamma \vdash B} ::= \mathsf{Rd}\, a \mid \mathsf{Rtn} \mid \mathsf{Sam} \mid \mathsf{Sco}\,,$$

where a ranges over variables $a : A$ in Γ.

Definition 2. *A* ***dependency graph*** *over $\Gamma \vdash B$ is an event structure G along with a labelling map $\mathsf{lbl} : G \to \mathscr{L}^{static}_{\Gamma \vdash B}$ where any two events $s, s' \in G$ labelled Rtn are in conflict, and all maximal configurations of G are of the form $[r]$ for $r \in G$ a return event.*

The condition on return events ensures that in any configuration of G there is at most one return event. Events of G are called static events.

We use dependency graphs as a causal representation of programs, reflecting the dependency between different parts of the program. In what follows we enrich this representation with runtime information in order to keep track of the dataflow of the program (in Sect. 3.3), and the associated distributions (in Sect. 3.4).

3.3 Runtime Values and Dataflow Graphs

We have seen how data dependency can be captured by representing a program P as a dependency graph G_P. But observe that this graph does not give any runtime information about the data in P; every event $s \in G_P$ only carries a label $\mathsf{lbl}(s)$ indicating the class of action it belongs to. (For an event labelled $\mathsf{Rd}\, a$, G does not specify the value at a; whereas at runtime this will be filled by an element of $[\![A]\!]$ where A is the type of a.)

To each label, we can associate a measurable space of possible runtime values:

$$\mathscr{Q}(\mathsf{Rd}\, b) = [\![\Gamma(b)]\!] \qquad \mathscr{Q}(\mathsf{Rtn}) = [\![A]\!] \qquad \mathscr{Q}(\mathsf{Sam}) = (\mathbb{R}, \Sigma_{\mathbb{R}}) \qquad \mathscr{Q}(\mathsf{Sco}) = (\mathbb{R}, \Sigma_{\mathbb{R}}).$$

Then, in a particular execution, an event $s \in G_P$ has a value in $\mathscr{Q}(\mathsf{lbl}(s))$, and can be instead labelled by the following expanded set:

$$\mathscr{L}^{\mathtt{run}}_{\Gamma \vdash B} ::= \mathsf{Rd}\, a\, v \mid \mathsf{Rtn}\, v \mid \mathsf{Sam}\, r \mid \mathsf{Sco}\, r$$

where r ranges over real numbers; in $\mathsf{Rd}\, a\, v$, $a : A \in \Gamma$ and $v \in [\![A]\!]$; and in $\mathsf{Rtn}\, v$, v ranges over elements of $[\![B]\!]$. Notice that there is an obvious forgetful map $\alpha : \mathscr{L}^{\mathtt{run}}_{\Gamma \vdash A} \to \mathscr{L}^{\mathtt{static}}_{\Gamma \vdash A}$, discarding the runtime value. This runtime value can be extracted from a label in $\mathscr{L}^{\mathtt{run}}_{\Gamma \vdash B}$ as follows:

$$\mathbf{q}(\mathsf{Rd}\, b\, v) = v \qquad \mathbf{q}(\mathsf{Rtn}\, v) = v \qquad \mathbf{q}(\mathsf{Sam}\, r) = r \qquad \mathbf{q}(\mathsf{Sco}\, r) = r.$$

In particular, we have $\mathbf{q}(\ell) \in \mathscr{Q}(\alpha(\ell))$.

Such runtime events organise themselves in an event structure E_P, labelled over $\mathscr{L}^{\mathtt{run}}_{\Gamma\vdash B}$, the **runtime graph** of P. Runtime graphs are in general uncountable, and so difficult to represent pictorially. It can be done in some simple, finite cases: the graph for `if` a `then 2 else 3` is depicted on the right. Recall that in dependency graphs conflict was used to represent conditional branches; here instead conflict is used to keep disjoint the possible outcomes of the same static event. (Necessarily, this static event must be a sample or a read, since other actions (return, score) are deterministic.)

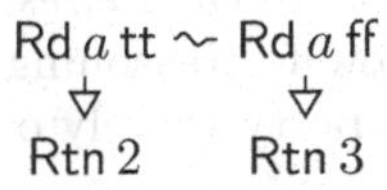

Intuitively one can project runtime events to static events by erasing the runtime information; this suggests the existence of a function $\pi_P : E_P \to G_P$. This function will turn out to satisfy the axioms of a *rigid map of event structures*:

Definition 3. *Given event structures* $(E, \leq_E, \#_E)$ *and* $(G, \leq_G, \#_G)$ *a function* $\pi : E \to G$ *is a* ***rigid map*** *if*

- *it preserves configurations: for every* $x \in \mathscr{C}(E)$, $\pi x \in \mathscr{C}(G)$
- *it is* locally injective*: for every* $x \in \mathscr{C}(E)$ *and* $e, e' \in x$, *if* $\pi(e) = \pi(e')$ *then* $e = e'$.
- *it preserves dependency: if* $e \leq_E e'$ *then* $\pi(e) \leq_G \pi(e')$.

In general π is not injective, since many runtime events may correspond to the same static event – in that case however the axioms will require them to be in conflict. The last condition in the definition ensures that all causal dependencies come from G.

Given $x \in \mathscr{C}(G_P)$ we define the possible runtime values for x as the set $\mathscr{Q}(x)$ of functions mapping $s \in x$ to a runtime value in $\mathscr{Q}(\mathsf{lbl}(s))$; in other words $\mathscr{Q}(x) = \prod_{s\in x} \mathscr{Q}(\mathsf{lbl}(s))$. A configuration x' of E_P can be viewed as a trace over $\pi_P\, x'$; hence $\pi_P^{-1}\{x\} := \{x' \in \mathscr{C}(E_P) \mid \pi_P x' = x\}$ is the set of traces of P over x. We can now define dataflow graphs:

Definition 4. *A* ***dataflow graph*** *on* $\Gamma \vdash B$ *is a triple* $\mathbf{S} = (E_S, G_S, \pi_S : E_S \to G_S)$ *with* G_S *a dependency graph and* E_S *a runtime graph, such that:*

- π_S *is a rigid map and* $\mathit{lbl} \circ \pi_S = \alpha \circ \mathit{lbl} : E_S \to \mathscr{L}^{\mathtt{static}}_{\Gamma\vdash B}$
- *for each* $x \in \mathscr{C}(G_S)$, *the following function is injective*

$$\begin{array}{lll} q_x : \pi_S^{-1}\{x\} & \to \mathscr{Q}(x) \\ \quad x' & \mapsto (s \mapsto \mathbf{q}(\mathit{lbl}(s))) \end{array}$$

- *if* $e, e' \in E_S$ *with* $e \sim e'$ *then* $\pi e = \pi e'$, *and moreover* e *and* e' *are either both sample or both read events.*

As mentioned above, maximal configurations of E_P correspond to total traces of P, and will be the states of the Markov chain in Sect. 5. By the second axiom, they can be seen as pairs $(x \in \mathscr{C}(G_S), q \in \mathscr{Q}(x))$. Because of the third axiom, E_S is always confusion-free.

Measurable Fibres. Rigid maps are convenient in this context because, they allow for reasoning about program traces by organising them as *fibres*. The key property we rely on is the following:

Lemma 2. *If $\pi : E \to G$ is a rigid map of event structures, then the induced map $\pi : \mathscr{C}(E) \to \mathscr{C}(G)$ is a* discrete fibration*: that is, for every $y \in \mathscr{C}(E)$, if $x \subseteq \pi y$ for some $x \in \mathscr{C}(G)$, then there is a unique $y' \in \mathscr{C}(E)$ such that $y' \subseteq y$ and $\pi y' = x$.*

This enables an essential feature of our approach: given a configuration x of the dataflow graph G, the fibre $\pi^{-1}\{x\}$ over it contains all the (possibly partial) program traces over x, *i.e.* those whose path through the program corresponds to that of x. Additionally the lemma implies that every pair of configurations $x, x' \in \mathscr{C}(G)$ such that $x \subseteq x'$ induces a **restriction map** $r_{x,x'} : \pi^{-1}\{x'\} \to \pi^{-1}\{x\}$, whose action on a program trace over x' is to return its *prefix* over x.

Although there is no measure-theoretic structure in the definition of dataflow graphs, we can recover it: for every $x \in \mathscr{C}(G_S)$, the fibre $\pi_S^{-1}\{x\}$ can be equipped with the σ-algebra induced from $\Sigma_{\mathscr{Q}(x)}$ via q_x; it is generated by sets $q_x^{-1}U$ for $U \in \Sigma_{\mathscr{Q}(x)}$.

It is easy to check that this makes the restriction map $r_{x,x'} : \pi_S^{-1}\{x'\} \to \pi_S^{-1}\{x\}$ measurable for each pair x, x' of configurations with $x \subseteq x'$. (Note that this makes $\mathbf{S}$ a *measurable event structure* in the sense of [16].) Moreover, the map $q_{x,s} : \pi_S^{-1}\{x\} \to \mathscr{Q}(\mathsf{lbl}(s))$ for $s \in x \in \mathscr{C}(G_S)$, mapping $x' \in \pi_S^{-1}\{x\}$ to $\mathbf{q}(\mathsf{lbl}(s'))$ for s' the unique antecedent by π_S of s in x', is also measurable.

We will also make use of the following result:

Lemma 3. *Consider a dataflow $\mathbf{S}$ and $x, y, z \in \mathscr{C}(G_S)$ with $x \subseteq y$, $x \subseteq z$, and $y \cup z \in \mathscr{C}(G_S)$. If $y \cap z = x$, then the space $\pi_S^{-1}\{y \cup z\}$ is isomorphic to the set*

$$\{(u_y, u_z) \in \pi_S^{-1}\{y\} \times \pi_S^{-1}\{z\} \mid r_{x,y}(u_y) = r_{x,z}(u_z)\},$$

with σ-algebra generated by sets of the form $\{(u_y, u_z) \in X_y \times X_z \mid X_y \in \Sigma_{\pi_S^{-1}\{y\}}, X_z \in \Sigma_{\pi_S^{-1}\{z\}}$ and $r_{x,y}(u_y) = r_{x,z}(u_z)\}$.

(For the reader with knowledge of category theory, this says exactly that the diagram

$$\begin{array}{ccc} \pi_S^{-1}\{y \cup z\} & \xrightarrow{r_{y,y\cup z}} & \pi_S^{-1}\{y\} \\ {\scriptstyle r_{z,y\cup z}}\downarrow & & \downarrow{\scriptstyle r_{x,y}} \\ \pi_S^{-1}\{z\} & \xrightarrow[r_{x,z}]{} & \pi_S^{-1}\{x\} \end{array}$$

is a pullback in the category of measurable spaces.)

3.4 Quantitative Dataflow Graphs

We can finally introduce the last bit of information we need about programs in order to perform inference: the probabilistic information. So far, in a dataflow graph, we know when the program is sampling, but not from which distribution. This is resolved by adding for each sample event s in the dependency graph a kernel $k_s : \pi^{-1}\{[s)\} \rightsquigarrow \pi^{-1}\{[s]\}$. Given a trace x over $[s)$, k_s specifies a probability distribution according to which x will be extended to a trace over $[s]$. This distribution must of course have support contained in the set $r^{-1}_{[s),[s]}\{x\}$ of traces over $[s]$ of which x is a prefix; this is the meaning of the technical condition in the definition below.

Definition 5. *A* ***quantitative dataflow graph*** *is a tuple* $\mathbf{S} = (E_S, G_S, \pi : E_S \to G_S, (k^S_s))$ *where for each sample event* $s \in G_S$, k^S_s *is a kernel* $\pi^{-1}\{[s)\} \rightsquigarrow \pi^{-1}\{[s]\}$ *satisfying for all* $x \in \pi^{-1}\{[s)\}$,

$$k^S_s(x, \pi^{-1}\{[s]\} \setminus r^{-1}_{[s),[s]}\{x\}) = 0.$$

This axiom stipulates that any extension $x' \in \pi^{-1}_S\{[s]\}$ of $x \in \pi^{-1}_S\{[s)\}$ drawn by k_s must contain x; in effect k_s only samples the runtime value for s.

From Graphs to Kernels. We show how to collapse a quantitative dataflow graph $\mathbf{S}$ on $\Gamma \vdash B$ to a kernel $[\![\Gamma]\!] \rightsquigarrow [\![B]\!]$. First, we extend the kernel family on sampling events $(k^S_s : \pi^{-1}\{[s)\} \rightsquigarrow \pi^{-1}\{[s]\})$ to a family $(k^{S[\gamma]}_s : \pi^{-1}\{[s)\} \rightsquigarrow \pi^{-1}\{[s]\})$ defined on *all* events $s \in S$, parametrised by the value of the environment $\gamma \in [\![\Gamma]\!]$. To define $k^{S[\gamma]}_s(x, \cdot)$ it is enough to specify its value on the generating set for $\Sigma_{\pi^{-1}\{[s]\}}$. As we have seen this contains elements of the form $q^{-1}_{[s]}(U)$ with $U \in \Sigma_{\mathcal{Q}([s])}$. We distinguish the following cases corresponding to the nature of s:

- If s is a sample event, $k^{S[\gamma]}_s = k^S_s$
- If s is a read on $a : A$, any $x \in \pi^{-1}[s)$ has runtime information $q_{[s)}(x)$ in $\mathcal{Q}([s))$ which can be extended to $\mathcal{Q}([s])$ by mapping s to $\gamma(a)$:

$$k^{S[\gamma]}_s(x, q^{-1}_{[s]}U) = \delta_{q_{[s)}(x)[s:=\gamma(a)]}(U)$$

- If s is a return or a score event: any $x \in \pi^{-1}\{[s)\}$ has at most one extension to $o(x) \in \pi^{-1}\{[s]\}$ (because return and score events cannot be involved in a minimal conflict): $k^{S[\gamma]}_s(x, q^{-1}_{[s]}(U)) = \delta_{q_{[s]}(o(x))}(U)$. If $o(x)$ does not exist, we let $k^{S[\gamma]}_s(x, X) = 0$.

We can now define a kernel $k^{S[\gamma]}_{x,s} : \pi^{-1}\{x\} \rightsquigarrow \pi^{-1}\{x'\}$ for every atomic extension $x \stackrel{s}{\longrightarrow\!\!\!\!\subset} x'$ in G_S, ie. when $x' \setminus x = \{s\}$, as follows:

$$k^{S[\gamma]}_{x,s}(y, U) = k_s(r_{[s),x}(y), \{w \in \pi^{-1}_S\{[s]\} \mid (y, w) \in U\}).$$

The second argument to k_s above is always measurable, by a standard measure-theoretic argument based on Lemma 3, as $x \cap [s] = [s)$.

From this definition we derive:

Lemma 4. *If* $x \stackrel{s_1}{\longrightarrow\!\!\!\!\subset} x_1$ *and* $x \stackrel{s_2}{\longrightarrow\!\!\!\!\subset} x_2$ *are concurrent extensions of* x *(*i.e. s_1 *and* s_2 *are not in conflict), then* $k^{S[\gamma]}_{x_1,s_2} \circ k^{S[\gamma]}_{x,s_1} = k^{S[\gamma]}_{x_2,s_1} \circ k^{S[\gamma]}_{x,s_2}$.

Given a configuration $x \in \mathscr{C}(G_S)$ and a covering chain $\emptyset \overset{s_1}{\longrightarrow\!\!\!\subset} x_1 \dots \overset{s_n}{\longrightarrow\!\!\!\subset} x_n = x$, we can finally define a measure on $\pi^{-1}\{x\}$:

$$\mu_x^{S[\gamma]} = k_{x_{n-1},s_n}^{S[\gamma]} \circ \dots \circ k_{\emptyset,s_1}^{S[\gamma]}(*, \cdot),$$

where $*$ is the only trace over $\emptyset$. The particular covering chain used does not matter by the previous lemma. Using this, we can define the kernel of a quantitative dataflow graph $\mathbf{S}$ as follows:

$$\mathsf{kernel}(\mathbf{S})(\gamma, X) = \sum_{r \in G_S, \mathsf{lbl}(r) = \mathsf{Rtn}} \mu_{[r]}^{S[\gamma]}(q_{[r],r}^{-1}(X)),$$

where the measurable map $q_{[r],r} : \pi^{-1}\{r\} \to [\![B]\!]$ looks up the runtime value of r in an element of the fibre over $[r]$ (defined in Sect. 3.3).

Lemma 5. *$\mathsf{kernel}(\mathbf{S})$ is an s-finite kernel $[\![\Gamma]\!] \rightsquigarrow [\![B]\!]$.*

4 Programs as Labelled Event Structures

We now detail our interpretation of programs as quantitative dataflow graphs. Our interpretation is given by induction, similarly to the measure-theoretic interpretation given in Sect. 2.3, in which composition of kernels plays a central role. In Sect. 4.1, we discuss how to compose quantitative dataflow graphs, and in Sect. 4.2, we define our interpretation.

4.1 Composition of Probablistic Event Structures

Consider two quantitative dataflow graphs, S on $\Gamma \vdash A$, and T on $\Gamma, a : A \vdash B$ where a does not occur in Γ. In what follows we show how they can be composed to form a quantitative dataflow graph $T \odot^a S$ on $\Gamma \vdash B$.

Unlike in the kernel model of Sect. 2.3, we will need two notions of composition. The first one is akin to the usual sequential composition: actions in T must wait on S to return before they can proceed. The second is closer to parallel composition: actions on T which do not depend on a read of the variable a can be executed in parallel with S. The latter composition is used to interpret the let construct. In `let` a `=` M `in` N, we want all the probabilistic actions or reads on other variables which do not depend on the value of a to be in parallel with M. However, in a program such as `case` M `of` $\{(i, x) \Rightarrow N_i\}_{i \in I}$ we do not want any actions of N_i to start before the selected branch is known, *i.e.* before the return value of M is known.

By way of illustration, consider the following simple example, in which we only consider runtime graphs, ignoring the rest of the structure for now. Suppose S and T are given by

$S =$ 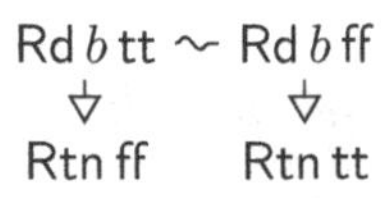
Rd b tt
Rd b ff
Rtn ff
Rtn tt
$T =$ 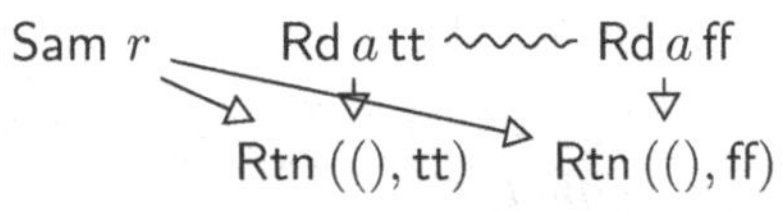
Sam r
Rd a tt
Rd a ff
Rtn ((), tt)
Rtn ((), ff)

The graph S can be seen to correspond to the program `if` b `then ff else tt` and T to the pairing (`sample` d `(0)`, a) for any d. Here S is a runtime graph on $b : \mathbb{B} \vdash \mathbb{B}$ and T on $a : \mathbb{B}, b : \mathbb{B} \vdash \mathbb{B}$.

Both notions of compositions are displayed in the diagram below. The sequential composition (left) corresponds to

$$\texttt{if}\ b\ \texttt{then}\ (\texttt{sample}\ d\ \texttt{(0)}, \mathsf{ff})\ \texttt{else}\ (\texttt{sample}\ d\ \texttt{(0)}, \mathsf{tt})$$

and the parallel composition to (`sample` d `(0)`, `if` b `then ff else tt`):

$$T \odot^a_{\mathrm{seq}} S = \left(\begin{array}{ccc} \mathsf{Rd}\, b\, \mathsf{tt} & \sim & \mathsf{Rd}\, b\, \mathsf{ff} \\ \downarrow & & \downarrow \\ \mathsf{Sam}\ r & & \mathsf{Sam}\ r \\ \downarrow & & \downarrow \\ \mathsf{Rtn}\, \mathsf{ff} & & \mathsf{Rtn}\, \mathsf{tt} \end{array} \right) \qquad T \odot^a_{\mathrm{par}} S = \left(\begin{array}{cccc} \mathsf{Sam}\ r & \mathsf{Rd}\, b\, \mathsf{tt} & \sim & \mathsf{Rd}\, b\, \mathsf{ff} \\ & \downarrow & & \downarrow \\ & \mathsf{Rtn}\, \mathsf{ff} & & \mathsf{Rtn}\, \mathsf{tt} \end{array} \right)$$

Composition of Runtime and Dependency Graphs. Let us now define both composition operators at the level of the event structures. Through the bijection $\mathscr{L}^{\mathtt{static}}_{\Gamma \vdash B} \simeq \mathscr{L}^{\mathtt{run}}_{\Gamma' \vdash 1}$ where $\Gamma'(a) = 1$ for all $a \in \mathrm{dom}(\Gamma)$, we will see dependency graphs and runtime graphs as the same kind of objects, event structures labelled over $\mathscr{L}^{\mathtt{run}}_{\Gamma \vdash A}$.

The two compositions $S \odot^a_{\mathrm{par}} T$ and $S \odot^a_{\mathrm{seq}} T$ are two instances of the same construction, parametrised by a set of labels $D \subseteq \mathscr{L}^{\mathtt{run}}_{\Gamma, a:A \vdash B}$. Informally, D specifies which events of T are to depend on the return value of S in the resulting composition graph. It is natural to assume in particular that D contains all reads on a, and all return events.

Sequential and parallel composition are instances of this construction where D is set to one of the following:

$$D^{\Gamma, a:A \vdash B}_{\mathrm{seq}} = \mathscr{L}^{\mathtt{run}}_{\Gamma, a:A \vdash B} \qquad\qquad D^{\Gamma, a:A \vdash B}_{\mathrm{par}} = \{\mathsf{Rd}\, a\, v, \mathsf{Rtn}\, v \in \mathscr{L}^{\mathtt{run}}_{\Gamma, a:A \vdash B}\}.$$

We proceed to describe the construction for an abstract D. Let T be an event structure labelled by $\mathscr{L}^{\mathtt{run}}_{\Gamma, a:A \vdash B}$ and S labelled by $\mathscr{L}^{\mathtt{run}}_{\Gamma \vdash A}$. A configuration $x \in \mathscr{C}(S)$ is a **justification** of $y \in \mathscr{C}(T)$ when

1. if $\mathsf{lbl}(y)$ intersects D, then x contains a return event
2. for all $t \in y$ with label $\mathsf{Rd}\, a\, v$, there exists an event $s \in x$ labelled $\mathsf{Rtn}\, v$.

In particular if $\mathsf{lbl}(y)$ does not intersect D, then any configuration of S is a justification of y. A **minimal justification** of y is a justification that admits no proper subset which is also a justification of y. We now define the event structure $S \cdot_D T$ as follows:

- *Events*: $S \cup \{(x, t) \mid x \in \mathscr{C}(S), t \in T, x \text{ minimal justification for } [t]\}$;
- *Causality*: $\leq_S \ \cup \{(x, t), (x', t') \mid x \subseteq x' \wedge t \leq t'\} \ \cup \ \{s, (x, t) \mid s \in x\}$;
- *Conflict*: the symmetric closure of

$$\#_S \cup \{(x, t), (x', t') \mid x \cup x' \notin \mathscr{C}(T) \vee t \#_B t'\}$$
$$\cup \{s, (x, t) \mid \{s\} \cup x \notin \mathscr{C}(S)\}.$$

Lemma 6. *$S \cdot_D T$ is an event structure, and the following is an order-isomorphism:*

$$\langle \cdot, \cdot \rangle : \{(x, y) \in \mathscr{C}(S) \times \mathscr{C}(T) \mid x \text{ is a justification of } y\} \cong \mathscr{C}(S \cdot_D T).$$

This event structure is not quite what we want, since it still contains return events from S and reads on a from T. To remove them, we use the following general construction. Given a Σ-labelled event structure E and $V \subseteq E$ a set of visible events, its **projection** $E \downarrow V$ has events V and causality, conflict and labelling inherited from E. Thus the composition of S and T is:

$$S \odot_D^a T := S \cdot_D T \downarrow (\{s \in S \mid s \text{ not a return}\} \cup \{(x, t) \mid t \text{ not a read on } a\}).$$

As a result $S \odot_D^a T$ is labelled over $\mathscr{L}^{\mathtt{run}}_{\Gamma \vdash B}$ as needed.

Dataflow Information. We now explain how this construction lifts to dataflow graphs. Consider dataflow graphs $S = (E_S, G_S, \pi_S : E_S \to G_S)$ on $\Gamma \vdash A$ and $T = (E_T, G_T, \pi_T : E_T \to E_T)$ on $\Gamma, a : A \vdash B$. Given $D \subseteq \mathscr{L}^{\mathtt{static}}_{\Gamma, a:A \vdash B}$ we define

$$E_{S \cdot_D T} = E_S \cdot_{\alpha^{-1} D} E_T \qquad G_{S \cdot_D T} = G_S \cdot_D G_T$$
$$E_{S \odot_D^a T} = E_S \odot^a_{\alpha^{-1} D} E_T \qquad G_{S \odot_D^a T} = G_S \odot_D^a G_T$$

Lemma 7. *The maps π_S and π_T extend to rigid maps*

$$\pi_{S \cdot_D T} : E_{S \cdot_{\alpha^{-1} D} T} \to G_{S \cdot_D T}$$
$$\pi_{S \odot_D^a T} : E_{S \odot^a_{\alpha^{-1} D} T} \to G_{S \odot_D^a T}$$

Moreover, if $\langle x, y \rangle \in \mathscr{C}(E_{S \cdot_D T})$, $\langle \pi_S\, x, \pi_T\, y \rangle$ is a well-defined configuration of $G_{S \cdot_D T}$. As a result, for $\langle x, y \rangle \in \mathscr{C}(G_{S \cdot_D T})$, we have a injection $\varphi_{x,y} : \pi^{-1}\{\langle x, y \rangle\} \to \pi^{-1}\{x\} \times \pi^{-1}\{y\}$ making the following diagram commute:

$$\begin{array}{ccc} \pi^{-1}\{\langle x, y \rangle\} & \xrightarrow{\varphi_{x,y}} & \pi^{-1}\{x\} \times \pi^{-1}\{y\} \\ q_{\langle x, y \rangle} \downarrow & & \downarrow q_x \times q_y \\ \mathscr{Q}(\langle x, y \rangle) & \xrightarrow[\cong]{} & \mathscr{Q}(x) \times \mathscr{Q}(y) \end{array}$$

In particular, $\varphi_{x,y}$ is measurable and induces the σ-algebra on $\pi^{-1}\{\langle x, y \rangle\}$. We write φ_x for the map $\varphi_{x,\emptyset}$, an isomorphism.

Adding Probability. At this point we have defined all the components of dataflow graphs $S \odot_D^a T$ and $S \cdot_D T$. We proceed to make them quantitative.

Observe first that each sampling event of $G_{S \cdot_D T}$ (or equivalently of $G_{S \odot_D^a T}$ – sampling events are never hidden) corresponds either to a sampling event of G_S, or to an event (x, t) where t is a sampling event of G_T. We consider both cases to define a family of kernels $(k_s^{S \cdot_D T})$ between the fibres of $S \cdot_D T$. This will in turn induce a family $(k_s^{S \odot_D^a T})$ on $S \odot_D^a T$.

- If s is a sample event of G_S, we use the isomorphisms $\varphi_{[s)}$ and $\varphi_{[s]}$ of Lemma 7 to define:
$$k_s^{S\odot_D^a T}(v, X) = k_s^S(\varphi_{[s)}^{-1} v, \varphi_{[s]}^{-1} X).$$
- If s corresponds to (x, t) for t a sample event of G_T, then for every $X_x \in \Sigma_{\pi_S^{-1}\{x\}}$ and $X_t \in \Sigma_{\pi_T^{-1}\{[t)\}}$ we define
$$k_{(x,t)}^{S\odot_D^a T}(\langle x', y'\rangle, \varphi_{x,[t]}^{-1}(X_x \times X_t)) = \delta_{x'}(X_x) \times k_t^T(y', X_t).$$
By Lemma 7, the sets $\varphi_{x,[t]}^{-1}(X_x \times X_t)$ form a basis for $\Sigma_{\pi^{-1}\{\langle x,[t)\rangle\}}$, so that this definition determines the entire kernel.

So we have defined a kernel $k_s^{S\cdot_D T}$ for each sample event s of $G_{S\cdot_D T}$. We move to the composition $(S \odot_D^a T)$. Recall that the *causal history* of a configuration $z \in \mathscr{C}(G_{S\odot_D^a T})$ is the set $[z]$, a configuration of $G_{S\cdot_D T}$. We see that hiding does not affect the fibre structure:

Lemma 8. *For any $z \in \mathscr{C}(G_{S\odot_D^a T})$, there is a measurable isomorphism ψ_z : $\pi_{S\odot_D^a T}^{-1}\{z\} \cong \pi_{S\cdot_D T}^{-1}\{[z]\}$.*

Using this result and the fact that $G_{S\odot_D^a T} \subseteq G_{S\cdot_D T}$, we may define for each s:
$$k_s^{S\odot_D^a T}(v, X) = k_s^{S\cdot_D T}(\psi_{[s)}(v), \psi_{[s]}X).$$
We conclude:

Lemma 9. $S \odot_D^a T := (G_{S\odot_D^a T}, E_{S\odot_D^a T}, \pi_{S\odot_D^a T}, (k_s^{S\odot_D^a T}))$ *is a quantitative dataflow graph on $\Gamma \vdash B$.*

Multicomposition. By chaining this composition, we can compose on several variables at once. Given quantitative dataflow graphs S_i on $\Gamma \vdash A_i$ and T on $\Gamma, a_1 : A_1, \ldots, a_n : A_n \vdash A$ we define
$$(S_i) \odot_{\text{par}}^{(a_i)} T := S_1 \odot_{\text{par}}^{a_1} (\ldots \odot_{\text{par}}^{a_n} T)$$
$$(S_i) \odot_{\text{seq}}^{(a_i)} T := S_1 \odot_{\text{seq}}^{a_1} (\ldots \odot_{\text{seq}}^{a_n} T)$$

4.2 Interpretation of Programs

We now describe how to interpret programs of our language using quantitative dataflow graphs. To do so we follow the same pattern as for the measure-theoretical interpretation given in Sect. 2.3.

Interpretation of Functions. Given a measurable function $f : [\![A]\!] \to [\![B]\!]$, we define the quantitative dataflow graph
$$S_f^a = \left(\sum_{v \in [\![A]\!]} \begin{array}{c} \mathsf{Rd}\, a\, v \\ \downarrow \\ \mathsf{Rtn}\,(f\, v) \end{array} \to \begin{array}{c} \mathsf{Rd}\, a \\ \downarrow \\ \mathsf{Rtn} \end{array} \right).$$

We then define $[\![f\, M]\!]_{\mathcal{G}}$ as $[\![M]\!]_{\mathcal{G}} \odot_{\text{par}}^a S_f^a$ where a is chosen so as not to occur free in M.

Probablistic Actions. In order to interpret scoring and sampling primitives, we need the following two quantitative dataflow graphs:

$$\texttt{score} = \left(\sum_{r\in\mathbb{R}} \begin{array}{c} \mathsf{Rd}\,a\,r \\ \downarrow \\ \mathsf{Sco}\,r \\ \downarrow \\ \mathsf{Rtn}\,() \end{array} \to \begin{array}{c} \mathsf{Rd}\,a \\ \downarrow \\ \mathsf{Sco} \\ \downarrow \\ \mathsf{Rtn} \end{array} \right) \qquad \texttt{sample}_d = \left(\sum_{\mathbf{r}\in\mathbb{R}^n} \begin{array}{c} \mathsf{Rd}\,a\,\mathbf{r} \\ \downarrow \\ \mathsf{Sam}\,s \\ \downarrow \\ \mathsf{Rtn}\,() \end{array} \to \begin{array}{c} \mathsf{Rd}\,a \\ \downarrow \\ \mathsf{Sam} \\ \downarrow \\ \mathsf{Rtn} \end{array}, k_{\mathsf{Sam}} \right)$$

and we define k_{Sam} by integrating the density function d; here we identify $\mathscr{Q}(\{\mathsf{Rd}\,a\,,\mathsf{Sam}\})$ and $\pi^{-1}\{\{\mathsf{Rd}\,a\,,\mathsf{Sam}\}\}$:

$$k_{\mathsf{Sam}}(\{\mathsf{Rd}\,a\,\mathbf{r}\}, U) = \int_{q\in U, q(\mathsf{Rd}\,a)=\mathbf{r}} d(\mathbf{r}, q(\mathsf{Sam}))\mathrm{d}\lambda.$$

We can now interpret scoring and sampling constructs:

$$[\![\texttt{score}\ M]\!]_{\mathcal{G}} = [\![M]\!]_{\mathcal{G}} \odot^a_{\text{par}} \texttt{score} \qquad [\![\texttt{sample}\ d\ (M)]\!]_{\mathcal{G}} = [\![M]\!]_{\mathcal{G}} \odot^a_{\text{par}} \texttt{sample}_d.$$

Interpretation of Tuples and Variables. Given a family $(a_i)_{i\in I}$, we define the dataflow graph $\texttt{tuple}_{(a_i:A_i)}$ on $a_1 : A_1, \ldots, a_n : A_n \vdash A_1 \times \ldots \times A_n$ as follows. Its set of events is the disjoint union

$$\bigcup_{i\in I, v\in[\![A_i]\!]} \mathsf{Rd}\,a_i\,v + \bigcup_{\mathbf{v}\in[\![A_1\times\ldots\times A_n]\!]} \mathsf{Rtn}\,\mathbf{v}$$

where the conflict is induced by $\mathsf{Rd}\,a_i\,v \rightsquigarrow \mathsf{Rd}\,a_i\,v'$ for $v \neq v'$; and causality contains all the pairs $\mathsf{Rd}\,a_i\,v \twoheadrightarrow \mathsf{Rtn}\,(v_1, \ldots, v_n)$ where $v_i = v$. Then we form a quantitative dataflow graph $\texttt{Tuple}_{(a_i:A_i)}$, whose dependency graph is $\texttt{tuple}_{(a_i:1)}$ (up to the bijection $\mathscr{L}^{\texttt{run}}_{\Gamma\vdash A} \simeq \mathscr{L}^{\texttt{static}}_{\Gamma'\vdash 1}$ where $\Gamma'(a) = 1$ for $a \in \mathrm{dom}(\Gamma)$); and the runtime graph is $\texttt{tuple}_{(a_i:A_i)}$, along with the obvious rigid map between them.

We then define the semantics of $(M_1, \ldots, M_n)$:

$$[\![(M_1, \ldots, M_n)]\!]_{\mathcal{G}} = ([\![M_i]\!]_{\mathcal{G}})_i \odot^{(a_i)}_{\text{par}} \texttt{Tuple}_{\mathtt{a_i:A_i}},$$

where the a_i are chosen free in all of the M_j. This construction is also useful to interpret variables:

$$[\![a]\!]_{\mathcal{G}} = \texttt{Tuple}_{a:A} \qquad \text{where } \Gamma \vdash a : A.$$

Interpretation of Pattern Matching. Consider now a term of the form $\texttt{case}\ M\ \texttt{of}$ $\{(i, a) \Rightarrow N_i\}_{i\in i}$. By induction, we have that $[\![N_i]\!]_{\mathcal{G}}$ is a quantitative dataflow graph on $\Gamma, a : A_i \vdash B$. Let us write $[\![N_i]\!]^*_{\mathcal{G}}$ for the quantitative dataflow graph on $\Gamma, a : (\sum_{i\in I} A_i) \vdash B$ obtained by relabelling events of the form $\mathsf{Rd}\,a\,v$ to $\mathsf{Rd}\,a\,(i, v)$, and sequentially precomposing with $\texttt{Tuple}_{a:\sum_{i\in I} A_i}$. This ensures that minimal events in $[\![N_i]\!]^*_{\mathcal{G}}$ are reads on a. We then build the quantitative dataflow graph $\sum_{i\in I}[\![N_i]\!]^*_{\mathcal{G}}$ on $\Gamma, a : \sum_{i\in I} A_i \vdash B$. This can be composed with $[\![M]\!]_{\mathcal{G}}$:

$$[\![\texttt{case}\ M\ \texttt{of}\ \{(i,a) \Rightarrow N_i\}_{i\in I}]\!]_{\mathcal{G}} = [\![M]\!]_{\mathcal{G}} \odot^a_{\mathsf{seq}} \left(\sum_{i\in I}[\![N_i]\!]^*_{\mathcal{G}}\right).$$

It is crucial here that one uses *sequential* composition: none of the branches must be evaluated until the outcome of M is known.

Adequacy of Composition. We now prove that our interpretation is adequate with respect to the measure-theoretic semantics described in Sect. 2.3. Given any subset $D \subseteq \mathscr{L}^{\texttt{static}}_{\Gamma,a:A\vdash B}$ containing returns and reads on a, we show that the composition $S \odot^a_D T$ does implement the composition of kernels:

Theorem 1. *For S a quantitative dataflow graph on $\Gamma \vdash A$ and T on $\Gamma, a : A \vdash B$, we have*

$$\mathsf{kernel}(S \odot^a_D T) = \mathsf{kernel}(T) \circ \mathsf{kernel}(S) : [\![\Gamma]\!] \to [\![B]\!].$$

From this result, we can deduce that the semantics in terms of quantitative dataflow graphs is adequate with respect to the measure-theoretic semantics:

Theorem 2. *For every term $\Gamma \vdash M : A$, $\mathsf{kernel}([\![M]\!]_{\mathcal{G}}) = [\![M]\!]$.*

5 An Inference Algorithm

In this section, we exploit the intensional semantics defined above and define a Metropolis-Hastings inference algorithm. We start, in Sect. 5.1, by giving a concrete presentation of those quantitative dataflow graphs arising as the interpretation of probabilistic programs; we argue this makes them well-suited for manipulation by an algorithm. Then, in Sect. 5.2, we give a more formal introduction to the Metropolis-Hastings sampling methods than that given in Sect. 3. Finally, in Sect. 5.3, we build the proposal kernel on which our implementation relies, and conclude.

5.1 A Concrete Presentation of Probabilistic Dataflow Graphs

Quantitative dataflow graphs as presented in the previous sections are not easy to handle inside of an algorithm: among other things, the runtime graph has an uncountable set of events. In this section we show that some dataflow graphs, in particular those needed for modelling programs, admit a finite representation.

Recovering Fibres. Consider a dataflow graph $\mathbf{S} = (E_S, G_S, \pi_S)$ on $\Gamma \vdash B$. It follows from Lemma 3 that the fibre structure of $\mathbf{S}$ is completely determined by the spaces $\pi_S^{-1}\{[s]\}$, for $s \in G_S$, so we focus on trying to give a simplified representation for those spaces.

First, let us notice that if s is a return or score event, given $x \in \pi^{-1}\{x\}$, the value $q_x(s)$ is determined by $q|_{[s)}$. In other words the map $\pi^{-1}\{[s]\} \to \mathscr{Q}([s))$ is an injection. This is due to the fact that minimal conflict in E_S cannot involve return or score events. As a result, E_S induces a partial function $o_s^S : \mathscr{Q}([s)) \rightharpoonup \mathscr{Q}(\mathsf{lbl}(s))$, called the **outcome function**. It is defined as follows:

$$o_s^S(q) = \begin{cases} q_{[s]}(x')(s) & \text{if there exists } x' \in \pi^{-1}\{x'\}, q_{[s]}(x')|_{[s)} = q, \\ \text{undefined} & \text{otherwise.} \end{cases}$$

Note that x' must be unique by the remark above since its projection to $\mathscr{Q}([s))$ is determined by q. The function o^S is partial, because it might be the case that the event s occurs conditionally on the runtime value on $[s)$.

In fact this structure is all we need in order to describe a dataflow graph:

Lemma 10. *Given G_S a dependency graph on $\Gamma \vdash B$, and partial functions $(o_s) : \mathscr{Q}([s)) \rightharpoonup \mathscr{Q}(\mathsf{lbl}(s))$ for score and return events of S. There exists a dataflow graph $(E_S, G_S, \pi_S : E_S \to G_S)$ whose outcome functions coincide with the o_s. Moreover, there is an order-isomorphism*

$$\mathscr{C}(E_S) \cong \{(x, q) \mid x \in \mathscr{C}(G_S), q \in \mathscr{Q}(x), \forall s \in x, o_s(q|_{[s)}) = q(s)\}.$$

Adding Probabilities. To add probabilities, we simply equip each sample event s of G_S with a density function $d_s : \mathscr{Q}([s)) \times \mathbb{R} \rightharpoonup \mathbb{R}$.

Definition 6. *A* ***concrete quantitative dataflow graph*** *is a tuple $(G_S, (o_s : \mathscr{Q}([s)) \rightharpoonup \mathscr{Q}(\mathsf{lbl}(s))), (d_s : \mathscr{Q}([s)) \times \mathbb{R} \rightharpoonup \mathbb{R})_{s \in sample(G_S)})$ where $d_s(x, \cdot)$ is normalised.*

Lemma 11. *Any concrete quantitative dataflow graph $\mathcal{S}$ unfolds to a quantitative dataflow graph* `unfold` *$\mathcal{S}$.*

We see now that the quantitative dataflow graphs arising as the interpretation of a program must be the unfolding of a concrete quantitative dataflow graph:

Lemma 12. *For any concrete quantitative dataflow graphs $\mathcal{S}$ on $\Gamma \vdash A$ and $\mathcal{T}$ on $\Gamma, a : A \vdash B$,* `unfold` *$\mathcal{S} \odot_D^a \mathcal{T}$*`unfold` *$\mathcal{T}$ is the unfolding of a concrete quantitative dataflow graph. It follows that for any program $\Gamma \vdash M : B$, $[\![M]\!]_{\mathcal{G}}$ is the unfolding of a concrete quantitative dataflow graph.*

5.2 Metropolis-Hastings

Recall that the Metropolis-Hastings algorithm is used to sample from a density function $d : \mathbb{A} \to \mathbb{R}$ which may not be normalised. Here $\mathbb{A}$ is a measurable *state space*, equipped with a measure λ. The algorithm works by building a Markov chain whose stationary distribution is D, the probability distribution obtained from d after normalisation:

$$\forall X \in \Sigma_{\mathbb{A}}, D(X) = \frac{\int_{x \in X} d(x)}{\int_{x \in \mathbb{A}} d(x)}.$$

Our presentation and reasoning in the rest of this section are inspired by the work of Borgström et al. [2].

Preliminaries on Markov Chains. A Markov chain on a measurable state space $\mathbb{A}$ is a probability kernel $k : \mathbb{A} \rightsquigarrow \mathbb{A}$, viewed as a transition function: given a state $x \in \mathbb{A}$, the distribution $k(x, \cdot)$ is the distribution from which a next sample state will be drawn. Usually, each $k(x, \cdot)$ comes with a procedure for sampling: we will treat this as a probabilistic program $M(x)$ whose output is the next state. Given an initial state $x \in \mathbb{A}$ and a natural number $n \in \mathbb{N}$, we have a distribution $k^n(x, \cdot)$ on $\mathbb{A}$ obtained by iterating k n times. We say that the Markov chain k has **limit** the distribution μ on $\mathbb{A}$ when

$$\lim_{n\to\infty} ||k^n(x,\cdot) - \mu|| = 0 \qquad \text{where } ||\mu_1 - \mu_2|| = \sup_{A\in\Sigma_{\mathbb{A}}} \mu_1(A) - \mu_2(A).$$

For the purposes of this paper, we call a Markov chain $k : \mathbb{A} \to \mathbb{A}$ **computable** when there exists a type A such that $[\![A]\!] = \mathbb{A}$ (up to iso) and an expression *without scores* $x : A \vdash K : A$ such that $[\![K]\!] = k$. (Recall that programs without conditioning denote probabilistic kernels, and are easily sampled from, since all standard distributions in the language are assumed to come with a built-in sampler.)

We will use terms of our language to describe computable Markov chains language, taking mild liberties with syntax. We assume in particular that programs may call each other as subroutines (this can be done via substitutions), and that manipulating finite structures is computable and thus representable in the language.

The Metropolis-Hastings Algorithm. Recall that we wish to sample from a distribution with un-normalised density $d : \mathbb{A} \to \mathbb{R}$; d is assumed to be computable. The Markov chain defined by the Metropolis-Hastings algorithm has two parameters: a computable Markov chain $x : A \vdash P : A$, the *proposal kernel*, and a measurable, computable function $p : \mathbb{A}^2 \to \mathbb{R}$ representing the kernel $[\![P]\!]$, *i.e.*

$$[\![P]\!](x, X') = \int_{x'\in X'} p(x, x')\, d\lambda(x').$$

The Markov-chain $\mathtt{MH}(P, p, d)$ is defined as

$$\begin{aligned}\mathtt{MH}(P,p,d)(x) := \;& \mathtt{let}\ x' \ \mathtt{=}\ P(x)\ \mathtt{in}\\ & \mathtt{let}\ \alpha\ \mathtt{=}\ \min\left(1, \frac{d(x') \times p(x,x')}{d(x) \times p(x',x)}\right)\ \mathtt{in}\\ & \mathtt{let}\ u\ \mathtt{=}\ \mathtt{sample\ uniform}\ (0,1)\ \mathtt{in}\\ & \mathtt{if}\ u < \alpha\ \mathtt{then}\ x'\ \mathtt{else}\ x\end{aligned}$$

In words, the Markov chain works as follows: given a start state x, it generates a proposal for the next state x' using P. It then computes an *acceptance ratio* α, which is the probability with which the new sample will be *accepted*: the return state will then either be the original x or x', accordingly.

Assuming P and p satisfy a number of conditions, the algorithm is correct:

Theorem 3. *Assume that P and p satisfies the following properties:*

1. ***Strong irreducibility:*** *There exists $n \in \mathbb{N}$ such that for all $x \in \mathbb{A}$ and $X \in \Sigma_{\mathbb{A}}$ such that $D(X) \neq \emptyset$ and $d(x) > 0$, there exists $n \in \mathbb{N}$ such that $[\![P]\!]^n(x, X) > 0$.*
2. *$[\![P]\!](x, X') = \int_{x' \in X'} p(x, x')$.*
3. *If $d(x) > 0$ and $p(x, y) > 0$ then $d(y) > 0$.*
4. *If $d(x) > 0$ and $d(y) > 0$, then $p(x, y) > 0$ iff $p(y, x) > 0$.*

Then, the limit of $\mathtt{MH}(P, p, d)$ for any initial state $x \in \mathbb{A}$ with $d(x) > 0$ is equal to D, the distribution obtained after normalising d.

5.3 Our Proposal Kernel

Consider a closed program $\vdash M : A$ in which every measurable function is a computable one. Then, its interpretation as a concrete quantitative dataflow graph is computable, and we write $\mathcal{S}$ for the quantitative dataflow graph whose unfolding is $[\![M]\!]_{\mathcal{G}}$. Moreover, because M is closed, its measure-theoretic semantics gives a measure $[\![M]\!]$ on $[\![A]\!]$. Assume that $\mathrm{norm}([\![M]\!])$ is well-defined: it is a probability distribution on $[\![A]\!]$. We describe how a Metropolis-Hastings algorithm may be used to sample from it, by reducing this problem to that of sampling from configurations of $E_{\mathcal{S}}$ according to the following density:

$$d_{\mathcal{S}}(x, q) := \left(\prod_{s \in \mathrm{sample}(x)} d_s(q(s)) \right) \left(\prod_{s \in \mathrm{score}(x)} q(s) \right).$$

Lemma 10 induces a natural measure on $\mathscr{C}(E_{\mathcal{S}})$. We have:

Lemma 13. *For all $X \in \Sigma_{\mathscr{C}(E_{\mathcal{S}})}$, $\mu^{\mathcal{S}}(X) = \displaystyle\int_{y \in X} d_{\mathcal{S}}(y) \mathrm{d}y$.*

Note that $d_{\mathcal{S}}(x, q)$ is easy to compute, but it is not normalised. Computing the normalising factor is in general intractable, but the Metropolis-Hastings algorithm does not require the density to be normalised.

Let us write $\mu^{\mathcal{S}}_{\mathrm{norm}}(X) = \frac{\mu^{\mathcal{S}}(X)}{\mu^{\mathcal{S}}(\mathscr{C}(E_{\mathcal{S}}))}$ for the normalised distribution. By adequacy, we have for all $X \in \Sigma_{[\![A]\!]}$:

$$\mathrm{norm}[\![M]\!](X) = \mu^{\mathcal{S}}_{\mathrm{norm}}(\mathtt{result}^{-1}(X)).$$

where $\mathtt{result} : \max \mathscr{C}(E_{\mathcal{S}}) \rightharpoonup [\![A]\!]$ maps a maximal configuration of $E_{\mathcal{S}}$ to its return value, if any. This says that sampling from $\mathrm{norm}[\![M]\!]$ amounts to sampling from $\mu^{\mathcal{S}}_{\mathrm{norm}}$ and only keeping the return value.

Accordingly, we focus on designing a Metropolis-Hastings algorithm for sampling values in $\mathscr{C}(E_{\mathcal{S}})$ following the (unnormalised) density $d_{\mathcal{S}}$. We start by defining a proposal kernel for this algorithm.

To avoid overburdening the notation, we will no longer distinguish between a type and its denotation. Since G_S is finite, it can be represented by a type, and so can $\mathscr{C}(G_S)$. Moreover, $\mathscr{C}(E_S)$ is a subset of $\sum_{x \in \mathscr{C}(G_S)} \mathscr{Q}(x)$ which is also representable as the type of pairs $(x \in \mathscr{C}(G_S), q \in \mathscr{Q}(x))$. Operations on G_S and related objects are all computable and measurable so we can directly use them in the syntax. In particular, we will make use of the function $\texttt{ext} : \mathscr{C}(E_S) \to G_S + 1$ which for each configuration $(x, q) \in \mathscr{C}(E_S)$ returns $(1, \mathfrak{s})$ if there exists $x \stackrel{s}{-\!\!\subset}$ with $o_s(q|_{[s)})$ defined, and $(2, *)$ if (x, q) is maximal.

Informally, for $(x, q) \in \mathscr{C}(E_S)$, the algorithm is:

- Pick a sample event $s \in x$, randomly over the set of sample events of x.
- Construct $x_0 := x \setminus \{s' \in x \mid s' \geq s\} \cup \{s\} \in \mathscr{C}(G_S)$.
- Return a maximal extension (x', q') of $(x_0, q|_{x_0})$ by only resampling the sample events of x' which are not in x.

The last step follows the single-site MH principle: sample events in $x \cap x'$ have already been evaluated in x, and are not updated. However, events which are in $x' \setminus x$ belong to conditional branches not explored in x; they must be sampled.

We start by formalising the last step of the algorithm. We give a probabilistic program `complete` which has three parameters: the original configuration (x, q), the current modification (x_0, q_0) and returns a possible maximal extension:

$$
\begin{aligned}
&\texttt{complete}(x, q, x_0, q_0) = \texttt{case ext}(x_0, q_0) \texttt{ of} \\
&\quad (2, ()) \Rightarrow (x_0, q_0) \\
&\quad (1, s) \Rightarrow \\
&\qquad \texttt{if } s \texttt{ is a return or a score event then} \\
&\qquad\quad \texttt{complete}(x, v, x_0 \cup \{s\}, q_0[s := o_s(q_0)]) \\
&\qquad \texttt{else if } s \in x \\
&\qquad\qquad \texttt{complete}(x, q, x_0 \cup \{s\}, q_0[s := q(s)]) \\
&\qquad \texttt{else} \\
&\qquad\qquad \texttt{complete}(x, q, x_0 \cup \{s\}, q_0[s := \texttt{sample } d \ (q_0)])
\end{aligned}
$$

The program starts by trying to extend (x_0, q_0) by calling `ext`. If (x_0, q_0) is already maximal, we directly return it. Otherwise, we get an event s. To extend the quantitative information, there are three cases:

- if s is not a sample event, ie. since S is closed it must be a return or a score event, we use the function o_s.
- if s is a sample event occurring in x, we use the value in q
- if s is a sample event not occurring in x, we sample a value for it.

This program is recursive, but because G_S is finite, there is a static bound on the number of recursive calls; thus this program can be unfolded to a program expressible in our language. We can now define the proposal kernel:

$P_S(x,q) =$
  $\texttt{let } s \texttt{ = sample uniformly over sample events in } x \texttt{ in}$
  $\texttt{let } r \texttt{ = sample } d_s \; (q_{|}[s]) \texttt{ in}$
  $\texttt{let } x_0 \texttt{ = } x \setminus \{s' \geq s \mid s' \in x\} \texttt{ in}$
  $\texttt{complete}(x, q, x_0, q[s := r])$

We now need to compute the density for P_S to be able to apply Metropolis-Hastings. Given $(x,q),(x',q') \in \mathscr{C}(E_S)$, we define:

$$p_S((x,q),(x',q')) = \sum_{s \in \texttt{sample}(x)} \left(\frac{q_s(v'|_{[s)})}{|\text{sample}(x)|} \times \prod_{s' \in \texttt{sample}(x' \setminus x)} q_{s'}(v|_{[s')}) \right).$$

Theorem 4. *The Markov chain P_S and density p satisfy the hypothesis of Theorem 3, as a result for any $(x,q) \in \mathscr{C}(E_S)$ the distribution $[\![MH(d_S, P_S, p_S)^n]\!]((x,q),\cdot)$ tends to μ^P_{norm} as n goes to infinity.*

One can thus sample from norm($[\![M]\!]$) using the algorithm above, keeping only the return value of the obtained configuration.

Let us re-state the key advantage of our approach: having access to the data dependency information, `complete` requires fewer steps in general, because at each proposal step only a portion of the graph needs exploring.

6 Conclusion

Related Work. There are numerous approaches to the semantics of programs with random choice. Among those concerned with statistical applications of probabilistic programming are Staton et al. [18,19], Ehrhard et al. [7], and Dahlqvist et al. [6]. A game semantics model was announced in [15].

The work of Scibior et al. [17] was influential in suggesting a denotational approach for proving correctness of inference, in the framework of quasi-Borel spaces [9]. It is not clear however how one could reason about data dependencies in this framework, because of the absence of explicit causal information.

Hur et al. [11] gives a proof of correctness for Trace MCMC using new forms of operational semantics for probabilistic programs. This method is extended to higher-order programs with *soft constraints* in Borgström et al. [2]. However, these approaches do not consider incremental recomputation.

To the best of our knowledge, this is the first work addressing formal correctness of incremental recomputation in MCMC. However, methods exist which take advantage of data dependency information to improve the performance of each proposal step in "naive" Trace MCMC. We mention in particular the work on *slicing* by Hur et al. [10]; other approaches include [5,24]. In the present work we claim no immediate improvement in performance over these techniques, but only a mathematical framework for reasoning about the structures involved.

It is worth remarking that our event structure representation is reminiscent of *graphical model* representation made explicit in some languages. Indeed, for a first-order language such as the one of this paper, Bayesian networks can directly be used as a semantics, see [20]. We claim that the alternative view offered by event structures will allow for an easier extension to higher-order programs, using ideas from game semantics.

Perspectives. This is the start of an investigation into intensional semantics for probabilistic programs. Note that the framework of event structures is very flexible and the semantics presented here is by no means the only possible one. Additionally, though the present work only treats the case of a first-order language, we believe that building on recent advances in probabilistic concurrent game semantics [3,16] (from which the present work draws much inspiration), we can extend the techniques of this paper to arbitrary higher-order probabilistic programs with recursion.

Acknowledgements. We thank the anonymous referees for helpful comments and suggestions. We also thank Ohad Kammar for suggesting the idea of using causal structures for reasoning about data dependency in this context. This work has been partially sponsored by: EPSRC EP/K034413/1, EP/K011715/1, EP/L00058X/1, EP/N027833/1, EP/N028201/1, and an EPSRC PhD studentship.

References

1. Billingsley, P.: Probability and Measure. John Wiley & Sons, New York (2008)
2. Borgström, J., Lago, U.D., Gordon, A.D., Szymczak, M.: A lambda-calculus foundation for universal probabilistic programming. In: ACM SIGPLAN Notices, vol. 51, pp. 33–46. ACM (2016)
3. Castellan, S., Clairambault, P., Paquet, H., Winskel, G.: The concurrent game semantics of probabilistic PCF. In: 2018 33rd Annual ACM/IEEE Symposium on Logic in Computer Science (LICS). ACM/IEEE (2018)
4. Castellan, S., Paquet, H.: Probabilistic programming inference via intensional semantics. Technical report (2019). http://iso.mor.phis.me/publis/esop19.pdf
5. Chen, Y., Mansinghka, V., Ghahramani, Z.: Sublinear approximate inference for probabilistic programs. stat, 1050:6 (2014)
6. Dahlqvist, F., Danos, V., Garnier, I., Silva, A.: Borel kernels and their approximation, categorically. arXiv preprint arXiv:1803.02651 (2018)
7. Ehrhard, T., Pagani, M., Tasson, C.: Measurable cones and stable, measurable functions: a model for probabilistic higher-order programming, vol. 2, pp. 59:1–59:28 (2018)
8. Gordon, A.D., Henzinger, T.A., Nori, A.V., Rajamani, S.K.: Probabilistic programming. In: Proceedings of the on Future of Software Engineering, pp. 167–181. ACM (2014)
9. Heunen, C., Kammar, O., Staton, S., Yang, H.: A convenient category for higher-order probability theory. In: LICS 2017, Reykjavik, pp. 1–12 (2017)

10. Hur, C.-K., Nori, A.V., Rajamani, S.K., Samuel, S. Slicing probabilistic programs. In: ACM SIGPLAN Notices, vol. 49, pp. 133–144. ACM (2014)
11. Hur, C.-K., Nori, A.V., Rajamani, S.K., Samuel, S.: A provably correct sampler for probabilistic programs. In: LIPIcs-Leibniz International Proceedings in Informatics, vol. 45. Schloss Dagstuhl-Leibniz-Zentrum fuer Informatik (2015)
12. Kiselyov, O.: Probabilistic programming language and its incremental evaluation. In: Igarashi, A. (ed.) APLAS 2016. LNCS, vol. 10017, pp. 357–376. Springer, Cham (2016). https://doi.org/10.1007/978-3-319-47958-3_19
13. Kiselyov, O.: Problems of the lightweight implementation of probabilistic programming. In: Proceedings of Workshop on Probabilistic Programming Semantics (2016)
14. Kozen, D.: Semantics of probabilistic programs. J. Comput. Syst. Sci. **22**(3), 328–350 (1981)
15. Ong, L., Vákár, M.: S-finite kernels and game semantics for probabilistic programming. In: POPL 2018 Workshop on Probabilistic Programming Semantics (PPS) (2018)
16. Paquet, H., Winskel, G.: Continuous probability distributions in concurrent games. Electr. Notes Theor. Comput. Sci. **341**, 321–344 (2018)
17. Ścibior, A., et al.: Denotational validation of higher-order Bayesian inference. In: Proceedings of the ACM on Programming Languages, vol. 2(POPL), p. 60 (2017)
18. Staton, S.: Commutative semantics for probabilistic programming. In: Yang, H. (ed.) ESOP 2017. LNCS, vol. 10201, pp. 855–879. Springer, Heidelberg (2017). https://doi.org/10.1007/978-3-662-54434-1_32
19. Staton, S., Yang, H., Wood, F.D., Heunen, C., Kammar, O.: Semantics for probabilistic programming: higher-order functions, continuous distributions, and soft constraints. In: Proceedings of LICS 2016, New York, NY, USA, July 5–8, 2016, pp. 525–534 (2016)
20. van de Meent, J.-W., Paige, B., Yang, H., Wood, F.: An introduction to probabilistic programming. arXiv preprint arXiv:1809.10756 (2018)
21. Wingate, D., Stuhlmüller, A., Goodman, N.: Lightweight implementations of probabilistic programming languages via transformational compilation. In: Proceedings of the Fourteenth International Conference on Artificial Intelligence and Statistics, pp. 770–778 (2011)
22. Winskel, G.: Event structures. In: Brauer, W., Reisig, W., Rozenberg, G. (eds.) ACPN 1986. LNCS, vol. 255, pp. 325–392. Springer, Heidelberg (1987). https://doi.org/10.1007/3-540-17906-2_31
23. Winskel, G.: Distributed probabilistic and quantum strategies. Electr. Notes Theor. Comput. Sci. **298**, 403–425 (2013)
24. Wu, Y., Li, L., Russell, S., Bodik, R.: Swift: compiled inference for probabilistic programming languages. arXiv preprint arXiv:1606.09242 (2016)
25. Yang, L., Hanrahan, P., Goodman, N.: Generating efficient MCMC kernels from probabilistic programs. In: Artificial Intelligence and Statistics, pp. 1068–1076 (2014)

Types

Handling Polymorphic Algebraic Effects

Taro Sekiyama[1(✉)] and Atsushi Igarashi[2(✉)]

[1] National Institute of Informatics, Tokyo, Japan
tsekiyama@acm.org
[2] Kyoto University, Kyoto, Japan
igarashi@kuis.kyoto-u.ac.jp

Abstract. Algebraic effects and handlers are a powerful abstraction mechanism to represent and implement control effects. In this work, we study their extension with parametric polymorphism that allows abstracting not only expressions but also effects and handlers. Although polymorphism makes it possible to reuse and reason about effect implementations more effectively, it has long been known that a naive combination of polymorphic effects and let-polymorphism breaks type safety. Although type safety can often be gained by restricting let-bound expressions—e.g., by adopting value restriction or weak polymorphism—we propose a complementary approach that restricts handlers instead of let-bound expressions. Our key observation is that, informally speaking, a handler is safe if resumptions from the handler do not interfere with each other. To formalize our idea, we define a call-by-value lambda calculus $\lambda_{\mathrm{eff}}^{\mathrm{let}}$ that supports let-polymorphism and polymorphic algebraic effects and handlers, design a type system that rejects interfering handlers, and prove type safety of our calculus.

1 Introduction

Algebraic effects [20] and handlers [21] are a powerful abstraction mechanism to represent and implement control effects, such as exceptions, interactive I/O, mutable states, and nondeterminism. They are growing in popularity, thanks to their success in achieving modularity of effects, especially the clear separation between their interfaces and their implementations. An interface of effects is given as a set of *operations*—e.g., an interface of mutable states consists of two operations, namely, put and get—with their signatures. An implementation is given by a *handler* H, which provides a set of interpretations of the operations (called *operation clauses*), and a handle–with expression handle M with H associates effects invoked during the computation of M with handler H. Algebraic effects and handlers work as *resumable exceptions*: when an effect operation is invoked, the run-time system tries to find the nearest handler that handles the invoked operation; if it is found, the corresponding operation clause is evaluated by using the argument to the operation invocation and the continuation up to the handler. The continuation gives the ability to resume the computation from the point where the operation was invoked, using the result from the operation

L. Caires (Ed.): ESOP 2019, LNCS 11423, pp. 353–380, 2019.
https://doi.org/10.1007/978-3-030-17184-1_13

clause. Another modularity that algebraic effects provide is flexible composition: multiple algebraic effects can be combined freely [13].

In this work, we study an extension of algebraic effects and handlers with another type-based abstraction mechanism—parametric polymorphism [22]. In general, parametric polymorphism is a basis of generic programming and enhance code reusability by abstracting expressions over types. This work allows abstracting not only expressions but also effect operations and handlers, which makes it possible to reuse and reason about effect implementations that are independent of concrete type representations. Like in many functional languages, we introduce polymorphism in the form of *let-polymorphism* for its practically desirable properties such as decidable typechecking and type inference.

As is well known, however, a naive combination of polymorphic effects and let-polymorphism breaks type safety [11,23]. Many researchers have attacked this classical problem [1,2,10,12,14,17,23,24], and their common idea is to restrict the form of let-bound expressions. For example, value restriction [23,24], which is the standard way to make ML-like languages with imperative features and let-polymorphism type safe, allows only syntactic values to be polymorphic.

In this work, we propose a new approach to achieving type safety in a language with let-polymorphic and polymorphic effects and handlers: the idea is to restrict handlers instead of let-bound expressions. Since a handler gives an implementation of an effect, our work can be viewed as giving a criterion that suggests what effects can cooperate safely with (unrestricted) let-polymorphism and what effects cannot. Our key observation for type safety is that, informally speaking, an invocation of a polymorphic effect in a let-bound expression is safe if resumptions in the corresponding operation clause do not interfere with each other. We formalize this discipline into a type system and show that typeable programs do not get stuck.

Our contributions are summarized as follows.

- We introduce a call-by-value, statically typed lambda calculus $\lambda_{\mathrm{eff}}^{\mathrm{let}}$ that supports let-polymorphism and polymorphic algebraic effects and handlers. The type system of $\lambda_{\mathrm{eff}}^{\mathrm{let}}$ allows any let-bound expressions involving effects to be polymorphic, but, instead, disallows handlers where resumptions interfere with each other.
- To give the semantics of $\lambda_{\mathrm{eff}}^{\mathrm{let}}$, we formalize an intermediate language $\lambda_{\mathrm{eff}}^{\Lambda}$ wherein type information is made explicit and define a formal elaboration from $\lambda_{\mathrm{eff}}^{\mathrm{let}}$ to $\lambda_{\mathrm{eff}}^{\Lambda}$.
- We prove type safety of $\lambda_{\mathrm{eff}}^{\mathrm{let}}$ by type preservation of the elaboration and type soundness of $\lambda_{\mathrm{eff}}^{\Lambda}$.

We believe that our approach is complementary to the usual approach of restricting let-bound expressions: for handlers that are considered unsafe by our criterion, the value restriction can still be used.

The rest of this paper is organized as follows. Section 2 provides an overview of our work, giving motivating examples of polymorphic effects and handlers, a problem in naive combination of polymorphic effects and let-polymorphism, and our solution to gain type safety with those features. Section 3 defines the surface language $\lambda_{\text{eff}}^{\text{let}}$, and Sect. 4 defines the intermediate language $\lambda_{\text{eff}}^{\Lambda}$ and the elaboration from $\lambda_{\text{eff}}^{\text{let}}$ to $\lambda_{\text{eff}}^{\Lambda}$. We also state that the elaboration is type-preserving and that $\lambda_{\text{eff}}^{\Lambda}$ is type sound in Sect. 4. Finally, we discuss related work in Sect. 5 and conclude in Sect. 6. The proofs of the stated properties and the full definition of the elaboration are given in the full version at https://arxiv.org/abs/1811.07332.

2 Overview

We start with reviewing how monomorphic algebraic effects and handlers work through examples and then extend them to a polymorphic version. We also explain why polymorphic effects are inconsistent with let-polymorphism, if naively combined, and how we resolve it.

2.1 Monomorphic Algebraic Effects and Handlers

Exception. Our first example is exception handling, shown in an ML-like language below.

```
1  effect fail : unit ↪ unit
2
3  let div100 (x:int) : int =
4    if x = 0 then (#fail(); -1)
5    else 100 / x
6
7  let f (y:int) : int option =
8    handle (div_100 y) with
9      return z → Some z
10     fail   z → None
```

`Some` and `None` are constructors of datatype α `option`. Line 1 declares an effect operation `fail`, which signals that an anomaly happens, with its signature `unit` ↪ `unit`, which means that the operation is invoked with the unit value `()`, causes some effect, and may return the unit value. The function `div100`, defined in Lines 3–5, is an example that uses `fail`; it returns the number obtained by dividing 100 by argument `x` if `x` is not zero; otherwise, if `x` is zero, it raises an exception by calling effect operation `fail`.[1] In general, we write `#op(`M`)` for invoking effect operation `op` with argument M. The function `f` (Lines 7–10) calls `div_100` inside a `handle`–`with` expression, which returns `Some` n if `div_100` returns integer n normally and returns `None` if it invokes `fail`.

An expression of the form `handle` M `with` H handles effect operations invoked in M (which we call *handled expression*) according to the effect interpretations given by handler H. A handler H consists of two parts: a single *return*

[1] Here, "`; -1`" is necessary to make the types of both branches the same; it becomes unnecessary when we introduce polymorphic effects.

clause and zero or more *operation clauses*. A return clause `return x` $\rightarrow M'$ will be executed if the evaluation of M results in a value v. Then, the value of M' (where `x` is bound to v) will be the value of the entire `handle–with` expression. For example, in the program above, if a nonzero number n is passed to `f`, the `handle–with` expression would return `Some` $(100/n)$ because `div100` n returns $100/n$. An operation clause `op x` $\rightarrow M'$ defines an implementation of effect `op`: if the evaluation of handled expression M invokes effect `op` with argument v, expression M' will be evaluated after substituting v for `x` and the value of M' will be the value of the entire `handle–with` expression. In the program example above, if zero is given to `f`, then `None` will be returned because `div100 0` invokes `fail`.

As shown above, algebraic effect handling is similar to exception handling. However, a distinctive feature of algebraic effect handling is that it allows *resumption* of the computation from the point where an effect operation was invoked. The next example demonstrates such an ability of algebraic effect handlers.

Choice. The next example is effect `choose`, which returns one of the given two arguments.

```
1  effect choose : int × int ↪ int
2
3  handle (#choose(1,2) + #choose(10,20)) with
4      return x → x
5      choose x → resume (fst x)
```

As usual, $A_1 \times A_2$ is a product type, `(`M_1`,` M_2`)` is a pair expression, and `fst` is the first projection function. The first line declares that effect `choose` is for choosing integers. The handled expression `#choose(1,2) + #choose(10,20)` intuitively suggests that there would be four possible results—11, 21, 12, and 22—depending on which value each invocation of `choose` returns. The handler in this example always chooses the first element of a given pair[2] and returns it by using a `resume` expression, and, as a result, the expression in Lines 3–5 evaluates to 11.

A resumption expression `resume` M in an operation clause makes it possible to return a value of M to the point where an effect operation was invoked. This behavior is realized by constructing a *delimited continuation* from the point of the effect invocation up to the `handle–with` expression that deals with the effect and passing the value of M to the continuation. We illustrate it by using the program above. When the handled expression `#choose(1,2) + #choose(10,20)` is evaluated, continuation $c \stackrel{\text{def}}{=} [\,]$ `+ #choose(10,20)` is constructed. Then, the body `resume (fst x)` of the operation clause is evaluated after binding `x` to the invocation argument `(1,2)`. Receiving the value `1` of `fst (1,2)`, the resumption

[2] We can think of more practical implementations, which choose one of the two arguments by other means, say, random values.

expression passes it to the continuation c and $c[1] =$ `1 + #choose(10,20)` is evaluated under the same handler. Next, `choose` is invoked with argument `(10,20)`. Similarly, continuation $c' \stackrel{\text{def}}{=}$ `1 + [ ]` is constructed and the operation clause for `choose` is executed again. Since `fst (10,20)` evaluates to `10`, $c'[10] =$ `1 + 10` is evaluated under the same handler. Since the `return` clause returns what it receives, the entire expression evaluates to `11`.

Finally, we briefly review how an operation clause involving resumption expressions is typechecked [3,13,16]. Let us consider operation clause `op(x)` $\rightarrow M$ for `op` of type signature $A \hookrightarrow B$. The typechecking is performed as follows. First, argument `x` is assigned the domain type A of the signature as it will be bound to an argument of an effect invocation. Second, for resumption expression `resume` M' in M, (1) M' is required to have the codomain type B of the signature because its value will be passed to the continuation as the result of the invocation and (2) the resumption expression is assigned the same type as the return clause. Third, the type of the body M has to be the same as that of the return clause because the value of M is the result of the entire `handle–with` expression. For example, the above operation clause for `choose` is typechecked as follows: first, argument `x` is assigned type `int` $\times$ `int`; second, it is checked whether the argument `fst x` of the resumption expression has `int`, the codomain type of `choose`; third, it is checked whether the body `resume (fst x)` of the clause has the same type as the return clause, i.e., `int`. If all the requirements are satisfied, the clause is well typed.

2.2 Polymorphic Algebraic Effects and Handlers

This section discusses motivation for polymorphism in algebraic effects and handlers. There are two ways to introduce polymorphism: by *parameterized effects* and by *polymorphic effects*.

The former is used to parameterize the declaration of an effect by types. For example, one might declare:

`effect` α `choose :` $\alpha \times \alpha \hookrightarrow \alpha$

An invocation `#choose` involves a parameterized effect of the form A `choose` (where A denotes a type), according to the type of arguments: For example, `#choose(true,false)` has the effect `bool choose` and `#choose(1,-1)` has `int choose`. Handlers are required for each effect A `choose`.

The latter is used to give a polymorphic type to an effect. For example, one may declare

`effect choose :` $\forall\alpha.\ \alpha \times \alpha \hookrightarrow \alpha$

In this case, the effect can be invoked with different types, but all invocations have the same effect `choose`. One can implement a single operation clause that can handle all invocations of `choose`, regardless of argument types. Koka supports both styles [16] (with the value restriction); we focus, however, on the latter in this paper. A type system for parameterized effects lifting the value restriction is studied by Kammar and Pretnar [14] (see Sect. 5 for comparison).

In what follows, we show a polymorphic version of the examples we have seen, along with brief discussions on how polymorphic effects help with reasoning about effect implementations. Other practical examples of polymorphic effects can be found in Leijen's work [16].

Polymorphic Exception. First, we extend the exception effect `fail` with polymorphism.

```
1 effect fail∀ : ∀α. unit ↪ α
2
3 let div100∀ (x:int) : int =
4   if x = 0 then #fail∀()
5   else 100 / x
```

The polymorphic type signature of effect `fail`$^{\forall}$, given in Line 1, means that the codomain type α can be any. Thus, we do not need to append the dummy value `-1` to the invocation of `fail`$^{\forall}$ by instantiating the bound type variable α with `int` (the shaded part).

Choice. Next, let us make `choose` polymorphic.

```
1  effect choose∀ : ∀α. α × α ↪ α
2
3  let rec random_walk (x:int) : int =
4    let b = #choose∀(true,false) in
5    if b then random_walk (x + #choose∀(1,-1))
6    else x
7
8  let f (s:int) =
9    handle random_walk s with
10     return x   → x
11     choose∀ y → if rand() < 0.0 then resume (fst y)
12                                 else resume (snd y)
```

The function `random_walk` implements random walk; it takes the current coordinate `x`, chooses whether it stops, and, if it decides to continue, recursively calls itself with a new coordinate. In the definition, `choose`$^{\forall}$ is used twice with different types: `bool` and `int`. Lines 11–12 give `choose`$^{\forall}$ an interpretation, which calls `rand` to obtain a random `float`,[3] and returns either the first or the second element of `y`.

Typechecking of operation clauses could be extended in a straightforward manner. That is, an operation clause `op(x)` $\rightarrow M$ for an effect operation of signature $\forall\alpha.A \hookrightarrow B$ would be typechecked as follows: first, α is locally bound in the clause and x is assigned type A; second, an argument of a resumption

[3] One might implement `rand` as another effect operation.

expression must have type B (which may contain type variable α); third, M must have the same type as that of the return clause (its type cannot contain α as α is local) under the assumption that resumption expressions have the same type as the return clause. For example, let us consider typechecking of the above operation clause for $\texttt{choose}^{\forall}$. First, the typechecking algorithm allocates a local type variable α and assigns type $\alpha \times \alpha$ to `y`. The body has two resumption expressions, and it is checked whether the arguments `fst y` and `snd y` have the codomain type α of the signature. Finally, it is checked whether the body is typed at `int` assuming that the resumption expressions have type `int`. The operation clause meets all the requirements, and, therefore, it would be well typed.

An obvious advantage of polymorphic effects is reusability. Without polymorphism, one has to declare many versions of `choose` for different types.

Another pleasant effect of polymorphic effects is that, thanks to parametricity, inappropriate implementations for an effect operation can be excluded. For example, it is not possible for an implementation of $\texttt{choose}^{\forall}$ to resume with values other than the first or second element of `y`. In the monomorphic version, however, it is possible to resume with any integer, as opposed to what the name of the operation suggests. A similar argument applies to $\texttt{fail}^{\forall}$; since the codomain type is α, which does not appear in the domain type, it is not possible to resume! In other words, the signature $\forall\alpha.\ \texttt{unit} \hookrightarrow \alpha$ enforces that no invocation of $\texttt{fail}^{\forall}$ will return.

2.3 Problem in Naive Combination with Let-Polymorphism

Although polymorphic effects and handlers provide an ability to abstract and restrict effect implementations, one may easily expect that their unrestricted use with naive *let-polymorphism*, which allows any let-bound expressions to be polymorphic, breaks type safety. Indeed, it does.

We develop a counterexample, inspired by Harper and Lillibridge [11], below.

```
effect get_id : ∀α. unit ↪ (α → α)

let f () : int =
  let g = #get_id() in (* g : ∀α.α → α *)
  if (g true) then ((g 0) + 1) else 2
```

The function `f` first binds `g` to the invocation result of `op`. The expression `#get_id()` is given type $\alpha \to \alpha$ and the naive let-polymorphism would assign type scheme $\forall\alpha.\alpha \to \alpha$ to `g`, which makes both `g true` and `g 0` (and thus the definition of `f`) well typed.

An intended use of `f` is as follows:

```
handle f () with
  return x → x
  get_id y → resume (λz. z)
```

The operation clause for `get_id` resumes with the identity function `λz.z`. It would be well typed under the typechecking procedure described in Sect. 2.2 and it safely returns `1`.

However, the following strange expression

```
handle f () with
  return x → x
  get_id y → resume (λz1. (resume (λz2. z1)); z1)
```

will get stuck, although this expression would be well typed: both `λz1. ··· ;z1` and `λz2. z1` could be given type $\alpha \rightarrow \alpha$ by assigning both `z1` and `z2` type α, which is the type variable local to this clause. Let us see how the evaluation gets stuck in detail. When the handled expression `f ()` invokes effect `get_id`, the following continuation will be constructed:

$$c \stackrel{\text{def}}{=} \texttt{let g = } [\,] \texttt{ in if (g true) then ((g 0) + 1) else 2}\,.$$

Next, the body of the operation clause `get_id` is evaluated. It immediately resumes and reduces to

$$c'[(\lambda\texttt{z1. } c'[(\lambda\texttt{z2.z1})]\texttt{; z1})]$$

where

$$c' \stackrel{\text{def}}{=} \begin{array}{l}\texttt{handle } c \texttt{ with} \\ \quad \texttt{return x} \rightarrow \texttt{x} \\ \quad \texttt{get\_id y} \rightarrow \texttt{resume (}\lambda\texttt{z1. (resume (}\lambda\texttt{z2.z1)); z1)}\,,\end{array}$$

which is the continuation c under the same handler. The evaluation proceeds as follows (here, $k \stackrel{\text{def}}{=} \lambda\texttt{z1. } c'[(\lambda\texttt{z2.z1})]\texttt{; z1}$):

$$\begin{array}{rl} & c'[(\lambda\texttt{z1. } c'[(\lambda\texttt{z2.z1})]\texttt{; z1})] \\ = & \texttt{handle let g = } k \texttt{ in if (g true) then ((g 0) + 1) else 2 with ...} \\ \longrightarrow & \texttt{handle if (}k\texttt{ true) then ((}k\texttt{ 0) + 1) else 2 with ...} \\ \longrightarrow & \texttt{handle if } c'[(\lambda\texttt{z2.true})]\texttt{; true then ((}k\texttt{ 0) + 1) else 2 with ...} \end{array}$$

Here, the hole in c' is filled by function $(\lambda\texttt{z2.true})$, which returns a Boolean value, *though the hole is supposed to be filled by a function of* $\forall\alpha.\,\alpha \rightarrow \alpha$. This weird gap triggers a run-time error:

$$\begin{array}{rl} & c'[(\lambda\texttt{z2.true})] \\ & \texttt{handle} \\ = & \quad \texttt{let g = } \lambda\texttt{z2.true in if (g true) then ((g 0) + 1) else 2} \\ & \texttt{with ...} \\ \longrightarrow^{*} & \texttt{handle if true then (((}\lambda\texttt{z2.true) 0) + 1) else 2 with ...} \\ \longrightarrow & \texttt{handle ((}\lambda\texttt{z2.true) 0) + 1 with ...} \\ \longrightarrow & \texttt{handle true + 1 with ...} \end{array}$$

We stop here because `true + 1` cannot reduce.

2.4 Our Solution

A standard approach to this problem is to restrict the form of let-bound expressions by some means such as the (relaxed) value restriction [10,23,24] or weak polymorphism [1,12]. This approach amounts to restricting how effect operations can be *used*.

In this paper, we seek for a complementary approach, which is to restrict how effect operations can be *implemented*.[4] More concretely, we develop a type system such that let-bound expressions are polymorphic as long as they invoke only "safe" polymorphic effects and the notion of safe polymorphic effects is formalized in terms of typing rules (for handlers).

To see what are "safe" effects, let us examine the above counterexample to type safety. The crux of the counterexample is that

1. continuation c uses `g` polymorphically, namely, as `bool` $\rightarrow$ `bool` in `g true` and as `int` $\rightarrow$ `int` in `g 1`;
2. c is invoked twice; and
3. the use of `g` as `bool` $\rightarrow$ `bool` in the first invocation of c—where `g` is bound to λ`z1.···; z1`—"alters" the type of λ`z2. z1` (passed to `resume`) from $\alpha \rightarrow \alpha$ to $\alpha \rightarrow$ `bool`, contradicting the second use of `g` as `int` $\rightarrow$ `int` in the second invocation of c.

The last point is crucial—if λ`z2.z1` were, say, λ`z2.z2`, there would be no influence from the first invocation of c and the evaluation would succeed. The problem we see here is that the naive type system mistakenly allows *interference* between the arguments to the two resumptions by assuming that `z1` and `z2` share the same type.

Based on this observation, the typing rule for resumption is revised to disallow interference between different resumptions by separating their types: for each `resume` M in the operation clause for `op` : $\forall \alpha_1 \cdots \alpha_n.A \hookrightarrow B$, M has to have type B' obtained by renaming all type variables α_i in B with *fresh* type variables α'_i. In the case of `get_id`, the two resumptions should be called with $\beta \rightarrow \beta$ and $\gamma \rightarrow \gamma$ for fresh β and γ; for the first `resume` to be well typed, `z1` has to be of type β, although it means that the return type of λ`z2.z1` (given to the second resumption) is β, making the entire clause ill typed, as we expect. If a clause does not have interfering resumptions like

```
get_id y  → resume (λz1.z1)
```

or

```
get_id y  → resume (λz1. (resume (λz2.z2)); z1),
```

it will be well typed.

---

4 We compare our approach with the standard approaches in Sect. 5 in detail.

3 Surface Language: $\lambda_{\text{eff}}^{\text{let}}$

We define a lambda calculus $\lambda_{\text{eff}}^{\text{let}}$ that supports let-polymorphism, polymorphic algebraic effects, and handlers without interfering resumptions. This section introduces the syntax and the type system of $\lambda_{\text{eff}}^{\text{let}}$. The semantics is given by a formal elaboration to intermediate calculus $\lambda_{\text{eff}}^{\Lambda}$, which will be introduced in Sect. 4.

Effect operations	op		**Type variables** α, β, γ
Effects	ϵ	$::=$	sets of effect operations
Base types	ι	$::=$	$\mathsf{bool} \mid \mathsf{int} \mid ...$
Types	A, B, C, D	$::=$	$\alpha \mid \iota \mid A \rightarrow^{\epsilon} B$
Type schemes	σ	$::=$	$A \mid \forall \alpha.\sigma$
Constants	c	$::=$	$\mathsf{true} \mid \mathsf{false} \mid 0 \mid + \mid ...$
Terms	M	$::=$	$x \mid c \mid \lambda x.M \mid M_1\, M_2 \mid \mathsf{let}\, x = M_1 \,\mathsf{in}\, M_2 \mid$ $\#\mathsf{op}(M) \mid \mathsf{handle}\, M \,\mathsf{with}\, H \mid \mathsf{resume}\, M$
Handlers	H	$::=$	$\mathsf{return}\, x \rightarrow M \mid H; \mathsf{op}(x) \rightarrow M$
Typing contexts	Γ	$::=$	$\emptyset \mid \Gamma, x : \sigma \mid \Gamma, \alpha$

Fig. 1. Syntax of $\lambda_{\text{eff}}^{\text{let}}$.

3.1 Syntax

The syntax of $\lambda_{\text{eff}}^{\text{let}}$ is given in Fig. 1. Effect operations are denoted by op and type variables by α, β, and γ. An effect, denoted by ϵ, is a finite set of effect operations. We write $\langle\rangle$ for the empty effect set. A type, denoted by A, B, C, and D, is a type variable; a base type ι, which includes, e.g., bool and int; or a function type $A \rightarrow^{\epsilon} B$, which is given to functions that take an argument of type A and compute a value of type B possibly with effect ϵ. A type scheme σ is obtained by abstracting type variables. Terms, denoted by M, consist of variables; constants (including primitive operations); lambda abstractions $\lambda x.M$, which bind x in M; function applications; let-expressions $\mathsf{let}\, x = M_1 \,\mathsf{in}\, M_2$, which bind x in M_2; effect invocations $\#\mathsf{op}(M)$; handle–with expressions $\mathsf{handle}\, M \,\mathsf{with}\, H$; and resumption expressions $\mathsf{resume}\, M$. All type information in $\lambda_{\text{eff}}^{\text{let}}$ is implicit; thus the terms have no type annotations. A handler H has a single return clause $\mathsf{return}\, x \rightarrow M$, where x is bound in M, and zero or more operation clauses of the form $\mathsf{op}(x) \rightarrow M$, where x is bound in M. A typing context Γ binds a sequence of variable declarations $x : \sigma$ and type variable declarations α.

We introduce the following notations used throughout this paper. We write $\forall \boldsymbol{\alpha}^{i \in I}.A$ for $\forall \alpha_1....\forall \alpha_n.A$ where $I = \{1, ..., n\}$. We often omit indices (i and j) and index sets (I and J) if they are not important: e.g., we often abbreviate $\forall \boldsymbol{\alpha}^{i \in I}.A$ to $\forall \boldsymbol{\alpha}^{I}.A$ or even to $\forall \boldsymbol{\alpha}.A$. Similarly, we use a bold font for other sequences ($\boldsymbol{A}^{i \in I}$ for a sequence of types, $\boldsymbol{v}^{i \in I}$ for a sequence of values, etc.).

We sometimes write $\{\boldsymbol{\alpha}\}$ to view the sequence $\boldsymbol{\alpha}$ as a set by ignoring the order. Free type variables $\mathit{ftv}(\sigma)$ in a type scheme σ and type substitution $B[\boldsymbol{A}/\boldsymbol{\alpha}]$ of $\boldsymbol{A}$ for type variables $\boldsymbol{\alpha}$ in B are defined as usual (with the understanding that the omitted index sets for $\boldsymbol{A}$ and $\boldsymbol{\alpha}$ are the same).

We suppose that each constant c is assigned a first-order closed type $ty(c)$ of the form $\iota_1 \rightarrow_{\langle\rangle} \cdots \rightarrow_{\langle\rangle} \iota_n$ and that each effect operation op is assigned a signature of the form $\forall \boldsymbol{\alpha}.A \hookrightarrow B$, which means that an invocation of op with type instantiation $\boldsymbol{C}$ takes an argument of $A[\boldsymbol{C}/\boldsymbol{\alpha}]$ and returns a value of $B[\boldsymbol{C}/\boldsymbol{\alpha}]$. We also assume that, for $ty(\mathsf{op}) = \forall \boldsymbol{\alpha}.A \hookrightarrow B$, $\mathit{ftv}(A) \subseteq \{\boldsymbol{\alpha}\}$ and $\mathit{ftv}(B) \subseteq \{\boldsymbol{\alpha}\}$.

3.2 Type System

The type system of $\lambda_{\mathrm{eff}}^{\mathrm{let}}$ consists of four judgments: well-formedness of typing contexts $\vdash \Gamma$; well formedness of type schemes $\Gamma \vdash \sigma$; term typing judgment $\Gamma; R \vdash M : A \,|\, \epsilon$, which means that M computes a value of A possibly with effect ϵ under typing context Γ and resumption type R (discussed below); and handler typing judgment $\Gamma; R \vdash H : A \,|\, \epsilon \Rightarrow B \,|\, \epsilon'$, which means that H handles a computation that produces a value of A with effect ϵ and that the clauses in H compute a value of B possibly with effect ϵ' under Γ and R.

A resumption type R contains type information for resumption.

Definition 1 (Resumption type). *Resumption types in $\lambda_{\mathit{eff}}^{\mathit{let}}$, denoted by R, are defined as follows:*

$$R ::= \mathsf{none} \mid (\boldsymbol{\alpha}, A, B \rightarrow_\epsilon C) \qquad (\text{if } \mathit{ftv}(A) \cup \mathit{ftv}(B) \subseteq \{\boldsymbol{\alpha}\} \text{ and } \mathit{ftv}(C) \cap \{\boldsymbol{\alpha}\} = \emptyset)$$

If M is not a subterm of an operation clause, it is typechecked under $R = \mathsf{none}$, which means that M cannot contain resumption expressions. Otherwise, suppose that M is a subterm of an operation clause $\mathsf{op}(x) \rightarrow M'$ that handles effect op of signature $\forall \boldsymbol{\alpha}.A \hookrightarrow B$ and computes a value of C possibly with effect ϵ. Then, M is typechecked under $R = (\boldsymbol{\alpha}, x : A, B \rightarrow_\epsilon C)$, which means that argument x to the operation clause has type A and that resumptions in M are effectful functions from B to C with effect ϵ. Note that type variables $\boldsymbol{\alpha}$ occur free only in A and B but not in C.

Figure 2 shows the inference rules of the judgments (except for $\Gamma \vdash \sigma$, which is defined by: $\Gamma \vdash \sigma$ if and only if all free type variables in σ are bound by Γ). For a sequence of type schemes $\boldsymbol{\sigma}$, we write $\Gamma \vdash \boldsymbol{\sigma}$ if and only if every type scheme in $\boldsymbol{\sigma}$ is well formed under Γ.

Well-formedness rules for typing contexts, shown at the top of Fig. 2, are standard. A typing context is well formed if it is empty (WF_EMPTY) or a variable in the typing context is associated with a type scheme that is well formed in the remaining typing context (WF_VAR) and a type variable in the typing context is not declared (WF_TVAR). For typing context Γ, $\mathit{dom}(\Gamma)$ denotes the set of type and term variables declared in Γ.

Well-formed rules for typing contexts

$\boxed{\vdash \Gamma}$

$$\frac{}{\vdash \emptyset}\ \textsc{WF\_Empty} \qquad \frac{\vdash \Gamma \quad x \notin \mathit{dom}(\Gamma) \quad \Gamma \vdash \sigma}{\vdash \Gamma, x : \sigma}\ \textsc{WF\_Var}$$

$$\frac{\vdash \Gamma \quad \alpha \notin \mathit{dom}(\Gamma)}{\vdash \Gamma, \alpha}\ \textsc{WF\_TyVar}$$

Typing rules

$\boxed{\Gamma; R \vdash M : A \,|\, \epsilon}$

$$\frac{\vdash \Gamma \quad x : \forall \boldsymbol{\alpha}.A \in \Gamma \quad \Gamma \vdash \boldsymbol{B}}{\Gamma; R \vdash x : A[\boldsymbol{B}/\boldsymbol{\alpha}] \,|\, \epsilon}\ \textsc{TS\_Var} \qquad \frac{\vdash \Gamma}{\Gamma; R \vdash c : \mathit{ty}(c) \,|\, \epsilon}\ \textsc{TS\_Const}$$

$$\frac{\Gamma, x : A; R \vdash M : B \,|\, \epsilon'}{\Gamma; R \vdash \lambda x.M : A \rightarrow^{\epsilon'} B \,|\, \epsilon}\ \textsc{TS\_Abs}$$

$$\frac{\Gamma; R \vdash M_1 : A \rightarrow^{\epsilon'} B \,|\, \epsilon \quad \Gamma; R \vdash M_2 : A \,|\, \epsilon \quad \epsilon' \subseteq \epsilon}{\Gamma; R \vdash M_1\, M_2 : B \,|\, \epsilon}\ \textsc{TS\_App}$$

$$\frac{\Gamma, \boldsymbol{\alpha}; R \vdash M_1 : A \,|\, \epsilon \quad \Gamma, x : \forall \boldsymbol{\alpha}.A; R \vdash M_2 : B \,|\, \epsilon}{\Gamma; R \vdash \mathsf{let}\, x = M_1 \,\mathsf{in}\, M_2 : B \,|\, \epsilon}\ \textsc{TS\_Let}$$

$$\frac{\Gamma; R \vdash M : A \,|\, \epsilon' \quad \epsilon' \subseteq \epsilon}{\Gamma; R \vdash M : A \,|\, \epsilon}\ \textsc{TS\_Weak}$$

$$\frac{\mathit{ty}\,(\mathsf{op}) = \forall \boldsymbol{\alpha}.A \hookrightarrow B \quad \mathsf{op} \in \epsilon \quad \Gamma; R \vdash M : A[\boldsymbol{C}/\boldsymbol{\alpha}] \,|\, \epsilon \quad \Gamma \vdash \boldsymbol{C}}{\Gamma; R \vdash \#\mathsf{op}(M) : B[\boldsymbol{C}/\boldsymbol{\alpha}] \,|\, \epsilon}\ \textsc{TS\_Op}$$

$$\frac{\Gamma; R \vdash M : A \,|\, \epsilon \quad \Gamma; R \vdash H : A \,|\, \epsilon \Rightarrow B \,|\, \epsilon'}{\Gamma; R \vdash \mathsf{handle}\, M \,\mathsf{with}\, H : B \,|\, \epsilon'}\ \textsc{TS\_Handle}$$

$$\frac{\begin{array}{c}\vdash \Gamma_1, x : D, \Gamma_2 \quad \boldsymbol{\alpha} \in \Gamma_1 \quad \epsilon \subseteq \epsilon' \\ \Gamma_1, \Gamma_2, \boldsymbol{\beta}, x : A[\boldsymbol{\beta}/\boldsymbol{\alpha}]; (\boldsymbol{\alpha}, x : A, B \rightarrow^{\epsilon} C) \vdash M : B[\boldsymbol{\beta}/\boldsymbol{\alpha}] \,|\, \epsilon'\end{array}}{\Gamma_1, x : D, \Gamma_2; (\boldsymbol{\alpha}, x : A, B \rightarrow^{\epsilon} C) \vdash \mathsf{resume}\, M : C \,|\, \epsilon'}\ \textsc{TS\_Resume}$$

$\boxed{\Gamma; R \vdash H : A \,|\, \epsilon \Rightarrow B \,|\, \epsilon'}$

$$\frac{\Gamma, x : A; R \vdash M : B \,|\, \epsilon' \quad \epsilon \subseteq \epsilon'}{\Gamma; R \vdash \mathsf{return}\, x \rightarrow M : A \,|\, \epsilon \Rightarrow B \,|\, \epsilon'}\ \textsc{THS\_Return}$$

$$\frac{\begin{array}{c}\Gamma; R \vdash H : A \,|\, \epsilon \Rightarrow B \,|\, \epsilon' \\ \mathit{ty}\,(\mathsf{op}) = \forall \boldsymbol{\alpha}.C \hookrightarrow D \quad \Gamma, \boldsymbol{\alpha}, x : C; (\boldsymbol{\alpha}, x : C, D \rightarrow^{\epsilon'} B) \vdash M : B \,|\, \epsilon'\end{array}}{\Gamma; R \vdash H; \mathsf{op}(x) \rightarrow M : A \,|\, \epsilon \uplus \{\mathsf{op}\} \Rightarrow B \,|\, \epsilon'}\ \textsc{THS\_Op}$$

Fig. 2. Typing rules.

Typing rules for terms are given in the middle of Fig. 2. The first six rules are standard for the lambda calculus with let-polymorphism and a type-and-effect system. If a variable x is introduced by a let-expression and has type scheme $\forall \boldsymbol{\alpha}.A$ in Γ, it is given type $A[\boldsymbol{B}/\boldsymbol{\alpha}]$, obtained by instantiating type variables $\boldsymbol{\alpha}$ with well-formed types $\boldsymbol{B}$. If x is bound by other constructors (e.g., a lambda abstraction), x is always bound to a monomorphic type and both $\boldsymbol{\alpha}$ and $\boldsymbol{B}$ are the empty sequence. Note that (TS_VAR) gives any effect ϵ to the typing judgment for x. In general, ϵ in judgment $\Gamma; R \vdash M : A \,|\, \epsilon$ means that the evaluation of M *may* invoke effect operations in ϵ. Since a reference to a variable involves no effect, it is given any effect; for the same reason, value constructors are also given any effect. The rule (TS_CONST) means that the type of a constant is given by (meta-level) function *ty*. The typing rules for lambda abstractions and function applications are standard in the lambda calculus equipped with a type-and-effect system. The rule (TS_ABS) gives lambda abstraction $\lambda x.M$ function type $A \rightarrow_{\epsilon'} B$ if M computes a value of B possibly with effect ϵ' by using x of type A. The rule (TS_APP) requires that (1) the argument type of function part M_1 be equivalent to the type of actual argument M_2 and (2) effect ϵ' invoked by function M_1 be contained in the whole effect ϵ. The rule (TS_WEAK) allows weakening of effects.

The next two rules are mostly standard for algebraic effects and handlers. The rule (TS_OP) is applied to effect invocations. Since $\lambda^{\mathrm{let}}_{\mathrm{eff}}$ supports implicit polymorphism, an invocation $\#\mathsf{op}(M)$ of polymorphic effect op of signature $\forall \boldsymbol{\alpha}.A \hookrightarrow B$ also accompanies implicit type substitution of well-formed types $\boldsymbol{C}$ for $\boldsymbol{\alpha}$. Thus, the type of argument M has to be $A[\boldsymbol{C}/\boldsymbol{\alpha}]$ and the result of the invocation is given type $B[\boldsymbol{C}/\boldsymbol{\alpha}]$. In addition, effect ϵ contains op. The typeability of handle–with expressions depends on the typing of handlers (TS_HANDLE), which will be explained below shortly.

The last typing rule (TS_RESUME) is the key to gaining type safety in this work. Suppose that we are given resumption type $(\boldsymbol{\alpha}, x : A, B \rightarrow_{\epsilon} C)$. Intuitively, $B \rightarrow_{\epsilon} C$ is the type of the continuation for resumption and, therefore, argument M to resume is required to have type B. As we have discussed in Sect. 2, we avoid interference between different resumptions by renaming $\boldsymbol{\alpha}$, the type parameters to the effect operation, to fresh type variables $\boldsymbol{\beta}$, in typechecking M. Freshness of $\boldsymbol{\beta}$ will be ensured when well-formedness of typing contexts $\Gamma_1, \Gamma_2, \boldsymbol{\beta}, \ldots$ is checked at the leaves of the type derivation. The type variables $\boldsymbol{\alpha}$ in the type of x, the parameter to the operation, are also renamed for x to be useful in M. To see why this renaming is useful, let us consider an extension of the calculus with pairs and typechecking of an operation clause for $\mathsf{choose}^{\forall}$ of signature $\forall \alpha.\alpha \times \alpha \hookrightarrow \alpha$:

$$\mathsf{choose}^{\forall}(x) \rightarrow \mathsf{resume}\,(\mathsf{fst}\, x)$$

Variable x is assigned product type $\alpha \times \alpha$ for fresh type variable α and the body $\mathsf{resume}\,(\mathsf{fst}\, x)$ is typechecked under the resumption type $(\alpha, x : \alpha \times \alpha, \alpha \rightarrow_{\epsilon} A)$ for some ϵ and A (see the typing rules for handlers for details). To typecheck $\mathsf{resume}\,(\mathsf{fst}\, x)$, the argument $\mathsf{fst}\, x$ is required to have type β, freshly generated for this resume. Without applying renaming also to x, the clause would not typecheck. Finally, (TS_RESUME) also requires that (1) the typing context contains $\boldsymbol{\alpha}$, which should have been declared at an application of the typing rule for the operation clause that surrounds this resume and (2) effect ϵ, which may be invoked by resumption of a continuation, be contained in the whole effect ϵ'. The binding $x : D$ in the conclusion means that parameter x to the operation clause is declared outside the resumption expression.

The typing rules for handlers are standard [3,13,16]. The rule (THS_RETURN) for a return clause $\mathsf{return}\, x \rightarrow M$ checks that the body M is given a type under the assumption that argument x has type A, which is the type of the handled expression. The effect ϵ stands for effects that are not handled by the operation clauses that follow the return clause and it must be a subset of the effect ϵ' that M may cause.[5] A handler having operation clauses is typechecked by (THS_OP), which checks that the body of the operation clause $\mathsf{op}(x) \rightarrow M$ for op of signature $\forall \boldsymbol{\alpha}. C \hookrightarrow D$ is typed at the result type B, which is the same as the type of the return clause, under the typing context extended with fresh assigned type variables $\boldsymbol{\alpha}$ and argument x of type C, together with the resumption type $(\boldsymbol{\alpha}, x : C, D \rightarrow_{\epsilon'} B)$. The effect $\epsilon \uplus \{\mathsf{op}\}$ in the conclusion means that the effect operation op is handled by this clause and no other clauses (in the present handler) handle it. Our semantics adopts deep handlers [13], i.e., when a handled expression invokes an effect operation, the continuation, which passed to the operation clause, is wrapped by the same handler. Thus, resumption may invoke the same effect ϵ' as the one possibly invoked by the clauses of the handler, hence $D \rightarrow_{\epsilon'} B$ in the resumption type.

Finally, we show how the type system rejects the counterexample given in Sect. 2. The problem is in the following operation clause.

$$\mathsf{op}(y) \rightarrow \mathsf{resume}\, \lambda z_1.(\mathsf{resume}\, \lambda z_2.z_1); z_1$$

where op has effect signature $\forall \alpha.\mathsf{unit} \hookrightarrow (\alpha \rightarrow_{\langle\rangle} \alpha)$. This clause is typechecked under resumption type $(\alpha, y : \mathsf{unit}, \alpha \rightarrow_\epsilon \alpha)$ for some ϵ. By (TS_RESUME), the two resumption expressions are assigned two different type variables γ_1 and γ_2, and the arguments $\lambda z_1.(\mathsf{resume}\, \lambda z_2.z_1); z_1$ and $\lambda z_2.z_1$ are required to have $\gamma_1 \rightarrow_\epsilon \gamma_1$ and $\gamma_2 \rightarrow_\epsilon \gamma_2$, respectively. However, $\lambda z_2.z_1$ cannot because z_1 is associated with γ_1 but not with γ_2.

Remark. The rule (TS_RESUME) allows only the type of the argument to an operation clause to be renamed. Thus, other variables bound by, e.g., lambda abstractions and let-expressions outside the resumption expression cannot be used as such a type. As a result, more care may be required as to where to introduce a new variable. For example, let us consider the following operation clause (which is a variant of the example of $\mathsf{choose}^{\forall}$ above).

$$\mathsf{choose}^{\forall}(x) \rightarrow \mathsf{let}\, y = \mathsf{fst}\, x\, \mathsf{in}\, \mathsf{resume}\, y$$

The variable x is assigned $\alpha \times \alpha$ first and the resumption requires y to be typed at fresh type variable β. This clause would be rejected in the current type system

[5] Thus, handlers in $\lambda_{\mathrm{eff}}^{\mathrm{let}}$ are open [13] in the sense that a handle–with expression does not have to handle *all* effects caused by the handled expression.

because $\mathsf{fst}\, x$ appears outside resume and, therefore, y is given type α, not β. This inconvenience may be addressed by moving down the let-binding in some cases: e.g., $\mathsf{resume}\,(\mathsf{let}\, y = \mathsf{fst}\, x \,\mathsf{in}\, y)$ is well typed.

4 Intermediate Language: $\lambda_{\text{eff}}^{\Lambda}$

The semantics of $\lambda_{\text{eff}}^{\text{let}}$ is given by a formal elaboration to an intermediate language $\lambda_{\text{eff}}^{\Lambda}$, wherein type abstraction and type application appear explicitly. We define the syntax, operational semantics, and type system of $\lambda_{\text{eff}}^{\text{let}}$ and the formal elaboration from $\lambda_{\text{eff}}^{\text{let}}$ to $\lambda_{\text{eff}}^{\Lambda}$. Finally, we show type safety of $\lambda_{\text{eff}}^{\text{let}}$ via type preservation of the elaboration and type soundness of $\lambda_{\text{eff}}^{\Lambda}$.

Values	v	::=	$c \mid \lambda x.e$
Polymorphic values	w	::=	$v \mid \Lambda \alpha.w$
Terms	e	::=	$x\, \boldsymbol{A} \mid c \mid \lambda x.e \mid e_1\, e_2 \mid \mathsf{let}\, x = \Lambda \boldsymbol{\alpha}.e_1 \,\mathsf{in}\, e_2 \mid$ $\#\mathsf{op}(\boldsymbol{A}, e) \mid \#\mathsf{op}(\boldsymbol{\sigma}, w, E) \mid \mathsf{handle}\, e \,\mathsf{with}\, h \mid$ $\mathsf{resume}\, \boldsymbol{\alpha}\, x.e$
Handlers	h	::=	$\mathsf{return}\, x \rightarrow e \mid h; \Lambda \boldsymbol{\alpha}.\mathsf{op}(x) \rightarrow e$
Evaluation contexts	$E^{\boldsymbol{\alpha}^I}$	::=	$[\,]$ (if $\boldsymbol{\alpha}^I = \emptyset$) $\mid E^{\boldsymbol{\alpha}^I}\, e_2 \mid v_1\, E^{\boldsymbol{\alpha}^I} \mid$ $\mathsf{let}\, x = \Lambda \boldsymbol{\beta}^{J_1}.E^{\boldsymbol{\gamma}^{J_2}} \,\mathsf{in}\, e_2$ (if $\boldsymbol{\alpha}^I = \boldsymbol{\beta}^{J_1}, \boldsymbol{\gamma}^{J_2}$) $\mid$ $\#\mathsf{op}(\boldsymbol{A}^J, E^{\boldsymbol{\alpha}^I}) \mid \mathsf{handle}\, E^{\boldsymbol{\alpha}^I} \,\mathsf{with}\, h$

Fig. 3. Syntax of $\lambda_{\text{eff}}^{\Lambda}$.

4.1 Syntax

The syntax of $\lambda_{\text{eff}}^{\Lambda}$ is shown in Fig. 3. Values, denoted by v, consist of constants and lambda abstractions. Polymorphic values, denoted by w, are values abstracted over types. Terms, denoted by e, and handlers, denoted by h, are the same as those of $\lambda_{\text{eff}}^{\text{let}}$ except for the following three points. First, type abstraction and type arguments are explicit in $\lambda_{\text{eff}}^{\Lambda}$: variables and effect invocations are accompanied by a sequence of types and let-bound expressions, resumption expressions, and operation clauses bind type variables. Second, a new term constructor of the form $\#\mathsf{op}(\boldsymbol{\sigma}, w, E)$ is added. It represents an intermediate state in which an effect invocation is capturing the continuation up to the closest handler for op. Here, E is an evaluation context [6] and denotes a continuation to be resumed by an operation clause handling op. In the operational semantics, an operation invocation $\#\mathsf{op}(\boldsymbol{A}, v)$ is first transformed to $\#\mathsf{op}(\boldsymbol{A}, v, [\,])$ (where $[\,]$ denotes the empty context or the identity continuation) and then it bubbles up by capturing its context and pushing it onto the third argument. Note that $\boldsymbol{\sigma}$ and w of $\#\mathsf{op}(\boldsymbol{\sigma}, w, E)$ become polymorphic when it bubbles up from the body of a type abstraction. Third, each resumption expression $\mathsf{resume}\, \boldsymbol{\alpha}\, x.e$ declares distinct (type) variables $\boldsymbol{\alpha}$ and x to denote the (type) argument to an operation

Reduction rules $\boxed{e_1 \rightsquigarrow e_2}$

$$c_1\, c_2 \rightsquigarrow \zeta(c_1, c_2) \quad \text{(R\_Const)} \qquad (\lambda x.e)\, v \rightsquigarrow e[v/x] \quad \text{(R\_Beta)}$$

$$\mathsf{let}\, x = \Lambda \boldsymbol{\alpha}.v \,\mathsf{in}\, e \rightsquigarrow e[\Lambda \boldsymbol{\alpha}.v/x] \quad \text{(R\_Let)} \qquad \mathsf{handle}\, v \,\mathsf{with}\, h \rightsquigarrow e[v/x] \quad \text{(R\_Return)} \quad (\text{where } h^{\mathsf{return}} = \mathsf{return}\, x \rightarrow e)$$

$$\#\mathsf{op}(\boldsymbol{A}, v) \rightsquigarrow \#\mathsf{op}(\boldsymbol{A}, v, [\,]) \quad \text{(R\_Op)}$$

$$\#\mathsf{op}(\boldsymbol{\sigma}, w, E)\, e_2 \rightsquigarrow \#\mathsf{op}(\boldsymbol{\sigma}, w, E\, e_2) \quad \text{(R\_OpApp1)}$$

$$v_1\, \#\mathsf{op}(\boldsymbol{\sigma}, w, E) \rightsquigarrow \#\mathsf{op}(\boldsymbol{\sigma}, w, v_1\, E) \quad \text{(R\_OpApp2)}$$

$$\#\mathsf{op}'(\boldsymbol{A}^I, \#\mathsf{op}(\boldsymbol{\sigma}^J, w, E)) \rightsquigarrow \#\mathsf{op}(\boldsymbol{\sigma}^J, w, \#\mathsf{op}'(\boldsymbol{A}^I, E)) \quad \text{(R\_OpOp)}$$

$$\mathsf{handle}\, \#\mathsf{op}(\boldsymbol{\sigma}, w, E) \,\mathsf{with}\, h \rightsquigarrow \#\mathsf{op}(\boldsymbol{\sigma}, w, \mathsf{handle}\, E \,\mathsf{with}\, h) \quad (\text{where } \mathsf{op} \notin ops(h)) \quad \text{(R\_OpHandle)}$$

$$\mathsf{let}\, x = \Lambda \boldsymbol{\alpha}^I.\#\mathsf{op}(\boldsymbol{\sigma}^J, w, E) \,\mathsf{in}\, e_2 \rightsquigarrow \#\mathsf{op}(\forall \boldsymbol{\alpha}^I.\boldsymbol{\sigma}^J, \Lambda \boldsymbol{\alpha}^I.w, \mathsf{let}\, x = \Lambda \boldsymbol{\alpha}^I.E \,\mathsf{in}\, e_2) \quad \text{(R\_OpLet)}$$

$$\mathsf{handle}\, \#\mathsf{op}(\forall \boldsymbol{\beta}^J.\boldsymbol{A}^I, \Lambda \boldsymbol{\beta}^J.v, E^{\boldsymbol{\beta}^J}) \,\mathsf{with}\, h \rightsquigarrow e[\mathsf{handle}\, E^{\boldsymbol{\beta}^J} \,\mathsf{with}\, h/\mathsf{resume}]^{\forall \boldsymbol{\beta}^J.\boldsymbol{A}^I}_{\Lambda \boldsymbol{\beta}^J.v} [\boldsymbol{A}^I[\bot/\boldsymbol{\beta}^J]/\boldsymbol{\alpha}^I][v[\bot/\boldsymbol{\beta}^J]/x] \quad (\text{where } h^{\mathsf{op}} = \Lambda \boldsymbol{\alpha}^I.\mathsf{op}(x) \rightarrow e) \quad \text{(R\_Handle)}$$

Evaluation rules $\boxed{e_1 \longrightarrow e_2}$

$$\frac{e_1 \rightsquigarrow e_2}{E[e_1] \longrightarrow E[e_2]}\ \text{E\_Eval}$$

Fig. 4. Semantics of $\lambda^{\Lambda}_{\mathrm{eff}}$.

clause, whereas a single variable declared at $\mathsf{op}(x) \rightarrow M$ and implicit type variables are used for the same purpose in $\lambda^{\mathrm{let}}_{\mathrm{eff}}$. For example, the $\lambda^{\mathrm{let}}_{\mathrm{eff}}$ operation clause $\mathsf{choose}^{\forall}(x) \rightarrow \mathsf{resume}\,(\mathsf{fst}\, x)$ is translated to $\Lambda\alpha.\mathsf{choose}^{\forall}(x) \rightarrow \mathsf{resume}\, \beta\, y.(\mathsf{fst}\, y)$. This change simplifies the semantics.

Evaluation contexts, denoted by $E^{\boldsymbol{\alpha}}$, are standard for the lambda calculus with call-by-value, left-to-right evaluation except for two points. First, they contain the form $\mathsf{let}\, x = \Lambda \boldsymbol{\alpha}.E^{\boldsymbol{\beta}} \,\mathsf{in}\, e_2$, which allows the body of a type abstraction to be evaluated. Second, the metavariable E for evaluation contexts is indexed by type variables $\boldsymbol{\alpha}$, meaning that the hole in the context appears under type abstractions binding $\boldsymbol{\alpha}$. For example, $\mathsf{let}\, x = \Lambda\alpha.\mathsf{let}\, y = \Lambda\beta.[\,] \,\mathsf{in}\, e_2 \,\mathsf{in}\, e_1$ is denoted by $E^{\alpha,\beta}$ and, more generally, $\mathsf{let}\, x = \Lambda \boldsymbol{\beta}^{J_1}.E^{\boldsymbol{\gamma}^{J_2}} \,\mathsf{in}\, e$ is denoted by $E^{\boldsymbol{\beta}^{J_1},\boldsymbol{\gamma}^{J_2}}$. (Here, $\boldsymbol{\beta}^{J_1}, \boldsymbol{\gamma}^{J_2}$ stands for the concatenation of the two sequences $\boldsymbol{\beta}^{J_1}$ and $\boldsymbol{\gamma}^{J_2}$.) If $\boldsymbol{\alpha}$ is not important, we simply write E for $E^{\boldsymbol{\alpha}}$. We often use the term "continuation" to mean "evaluation context," especially when it is expected to be resumed.

As usual, substitution $e[w/x]$ of w for x in e is defined in a capture-avoiding manner. Since variables come along with type arguments, the case for variables is defined as follows:

$$(x\,\boldsymbol{A})[\Lambda\boldsymbol{\alpha}.v/x] \stackrel{\text{def}}{=} v[\boldsymbol{A}/\boldsymbol{\alpha}]$$

Application of substitution $[\Lambda\boldsymbol{\alpha}^I.v/x]$ to $x\,\boldsymbol{A}^J$, where $I \neq J$, is undefined. We define free type variables $ftv(e)$ and $ftv(E)$ in e and E, respectively, as usual.

4.2 Semantics

The semantics of $\lambda_{\mathsf{eff}}^{\Lambda}$ is given in the small-step style and consists of two relations: the reduction relation $\rightsquigarrow$, which is for basic computation, and the evaluation relation $\longrightarrow$, which is for top-level execution. Figure 4 shows the rules for these relations. In what follows, we write h^{return} for the return clause of handler h, $ops(h)$ for the set of effect operations handled by h, and h^{op} for the operation clause for op in h.

Most of the reduction rules are standard [13,16]. A constant application $c_1\,c_2$ reduces to $\zeta(c_1, c_2)$ (R_Const), where function ζ maps a pair of constants to another constant. A function application $(\lambda x.e)\,v$ and a let-expression $\mathsf{let}\,x = \Lambda\boldsymbol{\alpha}.v\,\mathsf{in}\,e$ reduce to $e[v/x]$ (R_Beta) and $e[\Lambda\boldsymbol{\alpha}.v/x]$ (R_Let), respectively. If a handled expression is a value v, the handle–with expression reduces to the body of the return clause where v is substituted for the parameter x (R_Return). An effect invocation $\#\mathsf{op}(\boldsymbol{A}, v)$ reduces to $\#\mathsf{op}(\boldsymbol{A}, v, [\,])$ with the identity continuation, as explained above (R_Op); the process of capturing its evaluation context is expressed by the rules (R_OpApp1), (R_OpApp2), (R_OpOp), (R_OpHandle), and (R_OpLet). The rule (R_OpHandle) can be applied only if the handler h does *not* handle op. The rule (R_OpLet) is applied to a let-expression where $\#\mathsf{op}(\boldsymbol{\sigma}^J, w, E)$ appears under a type abstraction with bound type variables $\boldsymbol{\alpha}^I$. Since $\boldsymbol{\sigma}^J$ and w may refer to $\boldsymbol{\alpha}^I$, the reduction result binds $\boldsymbol{\alpha}^I$ in both $\boldsymbol{\sigma}^J$ and w. We write $\forall\,\boldsymbol{\alpha}^I.\boldsymbol{\sigma}^J$ for a sequence $\forall\,\boldsymbol{\alpha}^I.\sigma_{j_1}, \ldots, \forall\,\boldsymbol{\alpha}^I.\sigma_{j_n}$ of type schemes (where $J = \{j_1, \ldots, j_n\}$).

The crux of the semantics is (R_Handle): it is applied when $\#\mathsf{op}(\boldsymbol{\sigma}^I, w, E)$ reaches the handler h that handles op. Since the handled term $\#\mathsf{op}(\boldsymbol{\sigma}^I, w, E)$ is constructed from an effect invocation $\#\mathsf{op}(\boldsymbol{A}^I, v)$, if the captured continuation E binds type variables $\boldsymbol{\beta}^J$, the same type variables $\boldsymbol{\beta}^J$ should have been added to $\boldsymbol{A}^I$ and v along the capture. Thus, the handled expression on the left-hand side of the rule takes the form $\#\mathsf{op}(\forall\,\boldsymbol{\beta}^J.\boldsymbol{A}^I, \Lambda\boldsymbol{\beta}^J.v, E^{\boldsymbol{\beta}^J})$ (with the same type variables $\boldsymbol{\beta}^J$).

The right-hand side of (R_Handle) involves three types of substitution: continuation substitution $[\mathsf{handle}\,E^{\boldsymbol{\beta}^J}\,\mathsf{with}\,h/\mathsf{resume}]^{\forall\boldsymbol{\beta}^J.\boldsymbol{A}^I}_{\Lambda\boldsymbol{\beta}^J.v}$ for resumptions, type substitution for $\boldsymbol{\alpha}^I$, and value substitution for x. We explain them one by one below. In the following, let $h^{\mathsf{op}} = \Lambda\boldsymbol{\alpha}^I.\mathsf{op}(x) \rightarrow e$ and $E'^{\boldsymbol{\beta}^J} = \mathsf{handle}\,E^{\boldsymbol{\beta}^J}\,\mathsf{with}\,h$.

Continuation Substitution. Let us start with a simple case where the sequence $\boldsymbol{\beta}^J$ is empty. Intuitively, continuation substitution $[E'/\mathsf{resume}]^{\boldsymbol{A}^I}_v$ replaces a resumption expression $\mathsf{resume}\,\boldsymbol{\gamma}^I\, z.e'$ in the body e with $E'[v']$, where v' is the value of e', and substitutes $\boldsymbol{A}^I$ and v (arguments to the invocation of op) for $\boldsymbol{\gamma}^I$ and z, respectively. Therefore, assuming resume does not appear in e', we define $(\mathsf{resume}\,\boldsymbol{\gamma}^I\, z.e')[E'/\mathsf{resume}]^{\boldsymbol{A}^I}_v$ to be $\mathsf{let}\, y = e'[\boldsymbol{A}^I/\boldsymbol{\gamma}^I][v/z]\,\mathsf{in}\, E'[y]$ (for fresh y). Note that the evaluation of e' takes place outside of E so that an invocation of an effect in e' is *not* handled by handlers in E. When $\boldsymbol{\beta}^J$ is not empty,

$$(\mathsf{resume}\,\boldsymbol{\gamma}^I\, z.e')[E^{\boldsymbol{\beta}^J}/\mathsf{resume}]^{\forall \boldsymbol{\beta}^J.\boldsymbol{A}^I}_{\Lambda\boldsymbol{\beta}^J.v} \stackrel{\text{def}}{=}$$
$$\mathsf{let}\, y = \Lambda\boldsymbol{\beta}^J.\, e'[\boldsymbol{A}^I/\boldsymbol{\gamma}^I][v/z]\,\mathsf{in}\, E^{\boldsymbol{\beta}^J}[y\,\boldsymbol{\beta}^J]\,.$$

(The differences from the simple case are shaded.) The idea is to bind $\boldsymbol{\beta}^J$ that appear free in $\boldsymbol{A}^I$ and v by type abstraction at let and to instantiate with the same variables at $y\,\boldsymbol{\beta}^J$, where $\boldsymbol{\beta}^J$ are bound by type abstractions in $E^{\boldsymbol{\beta}^J}$.

Continuation substitution is formally defined as follows:

Definition 2 (Continuation substitution). *Substitution of continuation $E^{\boldsymbol{\beta}^J}$ for resumptions in e, written $e[E^{\boldsymbol{\beta}^J}/\mathsf{resume}]^{\forall \boldsymbol{\beta}^J.\boldsymbol{A}^I}_{\Lambda\boldsymbol{\beta}^J.v}$, is defined in a capture-avoiding manner, as follows (we describe only the important cases):*

$$(\mathsf{resume}\,\boldsymbol{\gamma}^I\, z.e)[E^{\boldsymbol{\beta}^J}/\mathsf{resume}]^{\forall \boldsymbol{\beta}^J.\boldsymbol{A}^I}_{\Lambda\boldsymbol{\beta}^J.v} \stackrel{\text{def}}{=}$$
$$\mathsf{let}\, y = \Lambda\boldsymbol{\beta}^J.e[E^{\boldsymbol{\beta}^J}/\mathsf{resume}]^{\forall \boldsymbol{\beta}^J.\boldsymbol{A}^I}_{\Lambda\boldsymbol{\beta}^J.v}[\boldsymbol{A}^I/\boldsymbol{\gamma}^I][v/z]\,\mathsf{in}\, E^{\boldsymbol{\beta}^J}[y\,\boldsymbol{\beta}^J]$$
$$\textit{(if } (\mathit{ftv}(e) \cup \mathit{ftv}(E^{\boldsymbol{\beta}^J})) \cap \{\boldsymbol{\beta}^J\} = \emptyset \textit{ and } y \textit{ is fresh)}$$
$$(\mathsf{return}\, x \rightarrow e)[E/\mathsf{resume}]^{\boldsymbol{\sigma}}_w \stackrel{\text{def}}{=} \mathsf{return}\, x \rightarrow e[E/\mathsf{resume}]^{\boldsymbol{\sigma}}_w$$
$$(h'; \Lambda\boldsymbol{\gamma}^J.\mathsf{op}(x) \rightarrow e)[E/\mathsf{resume}]^{\boldsymbol{\sigma}^I}_w \stackrel{\text{def}}{=} h'[E/\mathsf{resume}]^{\boldsymbol{\sigma}^I}_w; \Lambda\boldsymbol{\gamma}^J.\mathsf{op}(x) \rightarrow e$$

The second and third clauses (for a handler) mean that continuation substitution is applied only to return clauses.

Type and Value Substitution. The type and value substitutions $\boldsymbol{A}^I[\bot^J/\boldsymbol{\beta}^J]$ and $v[\bot^J/\boldsymbol{\beta}^J]$, respectively, in (R_Handle) are for (type) parameters in $h^{\mathsf{op}} = \Lambda\boldsymbol{\alpha}^I.\mathsf{op}(x) \rightarrow e$. The basic idea is to substitute $\boldsymbol{A}^I$ for $\boldsymbol{\beta}^I$ and v for x—similarly to continuation substitution. We erase free type variables $\boldsymbol{\beta}^J$ in $\boldsymbol{A}^I$ and v by substituting the designated base type $\bot$ for all of them. (We write $\boldsymbol{A}^I[\bot^J/\boldsymbol{\beta}^J]$ and $v[\bot^J/\boldsymbol{\beta}^J]$ for the types and value, respectively, after the erasure.)

The evaluation rule is ordinary: Evaluation of a term proceeds by reducing a subterm under an evaluation context.

4.3 Type System

The type system of $\lambda^{\Lambda}_{\mathsf{eff}}$ is similar to that of $\lambda^{\mathsf{let}}_{\mathsf{eff}}$ and has five judgments: well-formedness of typing contexts $\vdash \Gamma$; well formedness of type schemes $\Gamma \vdash \sigma$; term typing judgment $\Gamma; r \vdash e : A \mid \epsilon$; handler typing judgment $\Gamma; r \vdash h : A \mid \epsilon \Rightarrow B \mid \epsilon'$; and continuation typing judgment $\Gamma \vdash E : \forall \boldsymbol{\alpha}.A \multimap B \mid \epsilon$. The first two are defined in the same way as those of $\lambda_{\mathrm{eff}}^{\mathrm{let}}$. The last judgment means that a term obtained by filling the hole of E with a term having A under $\Gamma, \boldsymbol{\alpha}$ is typed at B under Γ and possibly involves effect ϵ. A resumption type r is similar to R but does not contain an argument variable.

Definition 3 (Resumption type). *Resumption types in $\lambda_{\mathrm{eff}}^{\Lambda}$, denoted by r, are defined as follows:*

$$r ::= \mathsf{none} \mid (\boldsymbol{\alpha}, A, B \to^{\epsilon} C) \quad (\text{if } ftv(A) \cup ftv(B) \subseteq \{\boldsymbol{\alpha}\} \text{ and } ftv(C) \cap \{\boldsymbol{\alpha}\} = \emptyset)$$

Typing rules

$\boxed{\Gamma; r \vdash e : A \mid \epsilon}$

$$\frac{\vdash \Gamma \quad x : \forall \boldsymbol{\alpha}.A \in \Gamma \quad \Gamma \vdash \boldsymbol{B}}{\Gamma; r \vdash x\,\boldsymbol{B} : A[\boldsymbol{B}/\boldsymbol{\alpha}] \mid \epsilon}\ \text{T\_VAR} \qquad \frac{\vdash \Gamma}{\Gamma; r \vdash c : ty(c) \mid \epsilon}\ \text{T\_CONST}$$

$$\frac{\Gamma, x : A; r \vdash e : B \mid \epsilon'}{\Gamma; r \vdash \lambda x.e : A \to^{\epsilon'} B \mid \epsilon}\ \text{T\_ABS}$$

$$\frac{\Gamma; r \vdash e_1 : A \to^{\epsilon'} B \mid \epsilon \quad \Gamma; r \vdash e_2 : A \mid \epsilon \quad \epsilon' \subseteq \epsilon}{\Gamma; r \vdash e_1\, e_2 : B \mid \epsilon}\ \text{T\_APP}$$

$$\frac{ty(\mathsf{op}) = \forall \boldsymbol{\alpha}.A \hookrightarrow B \quad \mathsf{op} \in \epsilon \quad \Gamma; r \vdash e : A[\boldsymbol{C}/\boldsymbol{\alpha}] \mid \epsilon \quad \Gamma \vdash \boldsymbol{C}}{\Gamma; r \vdash \#\mathsf{op}(\boldsymbol{C}, e) : B[\boldsymbol{C}/\boldsymbol{\alpha}] \mid \epsilon}\ \text{T\_OP}$$

$$\frac{\begin{array}{c} ty(\mathsf{op}) = \forall \boldsymbol{\alpha}^I.A \hookrightarrow B \quad \mathsf{op} \in \epsilon \quad \Gamma \vdash \forall \boldsymbol{\beta}^J.\boldsymbol{C}^I \\ \Gamma, \boldsymbol{\beta}^J; r \vdash v : A[\boldsymbol{C}^I/\boldsymbol{\alpha}^I] \mid \epsilon \quad \Gamma \vdash E^{\boldsymbol{\beta}^J} : \forall \boldsymbol{\beta}^J.(B[\boldsymbol{C}^I/\boldsymbol{\alpha}^I]) \multimap D \mid \epsilon \end{array}}{\Gamma; r \vdash \#\mathsf{op}(\forall \boldsymbol{\beta}^J.\boldsymbol{C}^I, \Lambda \boldsymbol{\beta}^J.v, E^{\boldsymbol{\beta}^J}) : D \mid \epsilon}\ \text{T\_OPCONT}$$

$$\frac{\Gamma; r \vdash e : A \mid \epsilon' \quad \epsilon' \subseteq \epsilon}{\Gamma; r \vdash e : A \mid \epsilon}\ \text{T\_WEAK}$$

$$\frac{\Gamma; r \vdash e : A \mid \epsilon \quad \Gamma; r \vdash h : A \mid \epsilon \Rightarrow B \mid \epsilon'}{\Gamma; r \vdash \mathsf{handle}\ e\ \mathsf{with}\ h : B \mid \epsilon'}\ \text{T\_HANDLE}$$

$$\frac{\Gamma, \boldsymbol{\alpha}; r \vdash e_1 : A \mid \epsilon \quad \Gamma, x : \forall \boldsymbol{\alpha}.A; r \vdash e_2 : B \mid \epsilon}{\Gamma; r \vdash \mathsf{let}\ x = \Lambda \boldsymbol{\alpha}.e_1\ \mathsf{in}\ e_2 : B \mid \epsilon}\ \text{T\_LET}$$

$$\frac{\boldsymbol{\alpha} \in \Gamma \quad \Gamma, \boldsymbol{\beta}, x : A[\boldsymbol{\beta}/\boldsymbol{\alpha}]; (\boldsymbol{\alpha}, A, B \to^{\epsilon} C) \vdash e : B[\boldsymbol{\beta}/\boldsymbol{\alpha}] \mid \epsilon' \quad \epsilon \subseteq \epsilon'}{\Gamma; (\boldsymbol{\alpha}, A, B \to^{\epsilon} C) \vdash \mathsf{resume}\,\boldsymbol{\beta}\, x.e : C \mid \epsilon'}\ \text{T\_RESUME}$$

Fig. 5. Typing rules for terms in $\lambda_{\mathrm{eff}}^{\Lambda}$.

The typing rules for terms, shown in Fig. 5, and handlers, shown in the upper half of Fig. 6, are similar to those of $\lambda_{\mathsf{eff}}^{\mathrm{let}}$ except for a new rule (T_OpCont), which is applied to an effect invocation $\#\mathsf{op}(\forall\,\boldsymbol{\beta}^J.\boldsymbol{C}^I, \Lambda\boldsymbol{\beta}^J.v, E^{\boldsymbol{\beta}^J})$ with a continuation. Let $ty(\mathsf{op}) = \forall\boldsymbol{\alpha}^I.A \hookrightarrow B$. Since op should have been invoked with $\boldsymbol{C}^I$ and v under type abstractions with bound type variables $\boldsymbol{\beta}^J$, the argument v has type $A[\boldsymbol{C}^I/\boldsymbol{\alpha}^I]$ under the typing context extended with $\boldsymbol{\beta}^J$. Similarly, the hole of $E^{\boldsymbol{\beta}^J}$ expects to be filled with the result of the invocation, i.e., a value of $B[\boldsymbol{C}^I/\boldsymbol{\alpha}^I]$. Since the continuation denotes the context before the evaluation, its result type matches with the type of the whole term.

The typing rules for continuations are shown in the lower half of Fig. 6. They are similar to the corresponding typing rules for terms except that a subterm is replaced with a continuation. In (TE_Let), the continuation $\mathsf{let}\,x = \Lambda\boldsymbol{\alpha}.E\,\mathsf{in}\,e$ has type $\forall\,\boldsymbol{\alpha}.\sigma \multimap B$ because the hole of E appears inside the scope of $\boldsymbol{\alpha}$.

$$\boxed{\Gamma; r \vdash h : A \mid \epsilon \Rightarrow B \mid \epsilon'}$$

$$\frac{\Gamma, x : A; r \vdash e : B \mid \epsilon' \quad \epsilon \subseteq \epsilon'}{\Gamma; r \vdash \mathsf{return}\,x \rightarrow e : A \mid \epsilon \Rightarrow B \mid \epsilon'}\ \text{TH\_Return}$$

$$\frac{\begin{array}{c}\Gamma; r \vdash h : A \mid \epsilon \Rightarrow B \mid \epsilon' \\ ty(\mathsf{op}) = \forall\boldsymbol{\alpha}.C \hookrightarrow D \quad \Gamma, \boldsymbol{\alpha}, x : C; (\boldsymbol{\alpha}, C, D \rightarrow^{\epsilon'} B) \vdash e : B \mid \epsilon'\end{array}}{\Gamma; r \vdash h; \Lambda\boldsymbol{\alpha}.\mathsf{op}(x) \rightarrow e : A \mid \epsilon \uplus \{\mathsf{op}\} \Rightarrow B \mid \epsilon'}\ \text{TH\_Op}$$

$$\boxed{\Gamma \vdash E : \sigma \multimap A \mid \epsilon}$$

$$\frac{}{\Gamma \vdash [\,] : A \multimap A \mid \epsilon}\ \text{TE\_Hole}$$

$$\frac{\Gamma \vdash E : \sigma \multimap (A \rightarrow^{\epsilon'} B) \mid \epsilon \quad \Gamma; \mathsf{none} \vdash e_2 : A \mid \epsilon \quad \epsilon' \subseteq \epsilon}{\Gamma \vdash E\,e_2 : \sigma \multimap B \mid \epsilon}\ \text{TE\_App1}$$

$$\frac{\Gamma; \mathsf{none} \vdash v_1 : (A \rightarrow^{\epsilon'} B) \mid \epsilon \quad \Gamma \vdash E : \sigma \multimap A \mid \epsilon \quad \epsilon' \subseteq \epsilon}{\Gamma \vdash v_1\,E : \sigma \multimap B \mid \epsilon}\ \text{TE\_App2}$$

$$\frac{ty(\mathsf{op}) = \forall\boldsymbol{\alpha}.A \hookrightarrow B \quad \mathsf{op} \in \epsilon \quad \Gamma \vdash E : \sigma \multimap A[\boldsymbol{C}/\boldsymbol{\alpha}] \mid \epsilon \quad \Gamma \vdash \boldsymbol{C}}{\Gamma \vdash \#\mathsf{op}(\boldsymbol{C}, E) : \sigma \multimap B[\boldsymbol{C}/\boldsymbol{\alpha}] \mid \epsilon}\ \text{TE\_Op}$$

$$\frac{\Gamma \vdash E : \sigma \multimap A \mid \epsilon \quad \Gamma; \mathsf{none} \vdash h : A \mid \epsilon \Rightarrow B \mid \epsilon'}{\Gamma \vdash \mathsf{handle}\,E\,\mathsf{with}\,h : \sigma \multimap B \mid \epsilon'}\ \text{TE\_Handle}$$

$$\frac{\Gamma \vdash E : \sigma \multimap A \mid \epsilon' \quad \epsilon' \subseteq \epsilon}{\Gamma \vdash E : \sigma \multimap A \mid \epsilon}\ \text{TE\_Weak}$$

$$\frac{\Gamma, \boldsymbol{\alpha} \vdash E : \sigma \multimap A \mid \epsilon \quad \Gamma, x : \forall\,\boldsymbol{\alpha}.A; \mathsf{none} \vdash e : B \mid \epsilon}{\Gamma \vdash \mathsf{let}\,x = \Lambda\boldsymbol{\alpha}.E\,\mathsf{in}\,e : \forall\,\boldsymbol{\alpha}.\sigma \multimap B \mid \epsilon}\ \text{TE\_Let}$$

Fig. 6. Typing rules for handlers and continuations in $\lambda_{\mathsf{eff}}^{\Lambda}$.

4.4 Elaboration

This section defines the elaboration from $\lambda_{\text{eff}}^{\text{let}}$ to $\lambda_{\text{eff}}^{\Lambda}$. The important difference between the two languages from the viewpoint of elaboration is that, whereas the parameter of an operation clause is referred to by a single variable in $\lambda_{\text{eff}}^{\text{let}}$, it is done by one or more variables in $\lambda_{\text{eff}}^{\Lambda}$. Therefore, one variable in $\lambda_{\text{eff}}^{\text{let}}$ is represented by multiple variables (required for each resume) in $\lambda_{\text{eff}}^{\Lambda}$. We use S, a mapping from variables to variables, to make the correspondence between variable names. We write $S \circ \{x \mapsto y\}$ for the same mapping as S except that x is mapped to y.

Elaboration is defined by two judgments: term elaboration judgment $\Gamma; R \vdash M : A \,|\, \epsilon \rhd^S e$, which denotes elaboration from a typing derivation of judgment $\Gamma; R \vdash M : A \,|\, \epsilon$ to e with S, and handler elaboration judgment $\Gamma; R \vdash H : A \,|\, \epsilon \Rightarrow B \,|\, \epsilon' \rhd^S h$, which denotes elaboration from a typing derivation of judgment $\Gamma; R \vdash H : A \,|\, \epsilon \Rightarrow B \,|\, \epsilon'$ to h with S.

Term elaboration rules $\boxed{\Gamma; R \vdash M : A \,|\, \epsilon \rhd^S e}$

$$\frac{\vdash \Gamma \quad x : \forall \boldsymbol{\alpha}.A \in \Gamma \quad \Gamma \vdash \boldsymbol{B}}{\Gamma; R \vdash x : A[\boldsymbol{B}/\boldsymbol{\alpha}] \,|\, \epsilon \rhd^S S(x)\, \boldsymbol{B}} \text{ Elab\_Var}$$

$$\frac{\Gamma, x : A; R \vdash M : B \,|\, \epsilon' \rhd^{S \circ \{x \mapsto x\}} e}{\Gamma; R \vdash \lambda x.M : A \to^{\epsilon'} B \,|\, \epsilon \rhd^S \lambda x.e} \text{ Elab\_Abs}$$

$$\frac{\Gamma; R \vdash M : A \,|\, \epsilon \rhd^S e \quad \Gamma; R \vdash H : A \,|\, \epsilon \Rightarrow B \,|\, \epsilon' \rhd^S h}{\Gamma; R \vdash \mathsf{handle}\, M\, \mathsf{with}\, H : B \,|\, \epsilon' \rhd^S \mathsf{handle}\, e\, \mathsf{with}\, h} \text{ Elab\_Handle}$$

$$\frac{\begin{array}{c}\Gamma, \boldsymbol{\alpha}; R \vdash M_1 : A \,|\, \epsilon \rhd^S e_1 \quad S' = S \circ \{x \mapsto x\} \\ \Gamma, x : \forall \boldsymbol{\alpha}.A; R \vdash M_2 : B \,|\, \epsilon \rhd^{S'} e_2\end{array}}{\Gamma; R \vdash \mathsf{let}\, x = M_1\, \mathsf{in}\, M_2 : B \,|\, \epsilon \rhd^S \mathsf{let}\, x = \Lambda \boldsymbol{\alpha}.e_1\, \mathsf{in}\, e_2} \text{ Elab\_Let}$$

$$\frac{\begin{array}{c}R = (\boldsymbol{\alpha}, x : A, B \to^{\epsilon} C) \quad \vdash \Gamma_1, x : D, \Gamma_2 \quad \boldsymbol{\alpha} \in \Gamma_1 \quad \epsilon \subseteq \epsilon' \\ y \text{ is fresh} \quad S' = S \circ \{x \mapsto y\} \\ \Gamma_1, \Gamma_2, \boldsymbol{\beta}, x : A[\boldsymbol{\beta}/\boldsymbol{\alpha}]; R \vdash M : B[\boldsymbol{\beta}/\boldsymbol{\alpha}] \,|\, \epsilon' \rhd^{S'} e\end{array}}{\Gamma_1, x : D, \Gamma_2; R \vdash \mathsf{resume}\, M : C \,|\, \epsilon' \rhd^S \mathsf{resume}\, \boldsymbol{\beta}\, y.e} \text{ Elab\_Resume}$$

Handler elaboration rules $\boxed{\Gamma; R \vdash H : A \,|\, \epsilon \Rightarrow B \,|\, \epsilon' \rhd^S h}$

$$\frac{\Gamma, x : A; R \vdash M : B \,|\, \epsilon' \rhd^{S \circ \{x \mapsto x\}} e \quad \epsilon \subseteq \epsilon'}{\Gamma; R \vdash \mathsf{return}\, x \to M : A \,|\, \epsilon \Rightarrow B \,|\, \epsilon' \rhd^S \mathsf{return}\, x \to e} \text{ ElabH\_Return}$$

$$\frac{\begin{array}{c}ty\,(\mathsf{op}) = \forall \boldsymbol{\alpha}.C \hookrightarrow D \quad \Gamma; R \vdash H : A \,|\, \epsilon \Rightarrow B \,|\, \epsilon' \rhd^S h \\ \Gamma, \boldsymbol{\alpha}, x : C; (\boldsymbol{\alpha}, x : C, D \to^{\epsilon'} B) \vdash M : B \,|\, \epsilon' \rhd^{S \circ \{x \mapsto x\}} e\end{array}}{\Gamma; R \vdash H; \mathsf{op}(x) \to M : A \,|\, \epsilon \uplus \{\mathsf{op}\} \Rightarrow B \,|\, \epsilon' \rhd^S h; \Lambda \boldsymbol{\alpha}.\mathsf{op}(x) \to e} \text{ ElabH\_Op}$$

Fig. 7. Elaboration rules (excerpt).

Selected elaboration rules are shown in Fig. 7; the complete set of the rules is found in the full version of the paper. The elaboration rules are straightforward except for the use of S. A variable x is translated to $S(x)$ (ELAB_VAR) and, every time a new variable is introduced, S is extended: see the rules other than (ELAB_VAR) and (ELAB_HANDLE).

4.5 Properties

We show type safety of $\lambda_{\mathsf{eff}}^{\mathsf{let}}$, i.e., a well-typed program in $\lambda_{\mathsf{eff}}^{\mathsf{let}}$ does not get stuck, by proving (1) type preservation of the elaboration from $\lambda_{\mathsf{eff}}^{\mathsf{let}}$ to $\lambda_{\mathsf{eff}}^{\Lambda}$ and (2) type soundness of $\lambda_{\mathsf{eff}}^{\Lambda}$. Term M is a well-typed program of A if and only if $\emptyset; \mathsf{none} \vdash M : A \mid \langle\rangle$.

The first can be shown easily. We write $\emptyset$ also for the identity mapping for variables.

Theorem 1 (Elaboration is type-preserving). *If M is a well-typed program of A, then $\emptyset; \mathsf{none} \vdash M : A \mid \langle\rangle \rhd^{\emptyset} e$ and $\emptyset; \mathsf{none} \vdash e : A \mid \langle\rangle$ for some e.*

We show the second—type soundness of $\lambda_{\mathsf{eff}}^{\Lambda}$—via progress and subject reduction [25]. We write Δ for a typing context that consists only of type variables. Progress can be shown as usual.

Lemma 1 (Progress). *If $\Delta; \mathsf{none} \vdash e : A \mid \epsilon$, then (1) $e \longrightarrow e'$ for some e', (2) e is a value, or (3) $e = \#\mathsf{op}(\boldsymbol{\sigma}, w, E)$ for some $\mathsf{op} \in \epsilon$, $\boldsymbol{\sigma}$, w, and E.*

A key lemma to show subject reduction is type preservation of continuation substitution.

Lemma 2 (Continuation substitution). *Suppose that $\Gamma \vdash \forall \boldsymbol{\beta}^J.\boldsymbol{C}^I$ and $\Gamma \vdash E^{\boldsymbol{\beta}^J} : \forall \boldsymbol{\beta}^J.(B[\boldsymbol{C}^I/\boldsymbol{\alpha}^I]) \multimap D \mid \epsilon$ and $\Gamma, \boldsymbol{\beta}^J \vdash v : A[\boldsymbol{C}^I/\boldsymbol{\alpha}^I]$.*

1. *If $\Gamma; (\boldsymbol{\alpha}^I, A, B \rightarrow_\epsilon D) \vdash e : D' \mid \epsilon'$, then $\Gamma; \mathsf{none} \vdash e[E^{\boldsymbol{\beta}^J}/\mathsf{resume}]^{\forall \boldsymbol{\beta}^J.\boldsymbol{C}^I}_{\Lambda \boldsymbol{\beta}^J.v} : D' \mid \epsilon'$.*
2. *If $\Gamma; (\boldsymbol{\alpha}^I, A, B \rightarrow_\epsilon D) \vdash h : D_1 \mid \epsilon_1 \Rightarrow D_2 \mid \epsilon_2$, then $\Gamma; \mathsf{none} \vdash h[E^{\boldsymbol{\beta}^J}/\mathsf{resume}]^{\forall \boldsymbol{\beta}^J.\boldsymbol{C}^I}_{\Lambda \boldsymbol{\beta}^J.v} : D_1 \mid \epsilon_1 \Rightarrow D_2 \mid \epsilon_2$.*

Using the continuation substitution lemma as well as other lemmas, we show subject reduction.

Lemma 3 (Subject reduction)

1. *If $\Delta; \mathsf{none} \vdash e_1 : A \mid \epsilon$ and $e_1 \rightsquigarrow e_2$, then $\Delta; \mathsf{none} \vdash e_2 : A \mid \epsilon$.*
2. *If $\Delta; \mathsf{none} \vdash e_1 : A \mid \epsilon$ and $e_1 \longrightarrow e_2$, then $\Delta; \mathsf{none} \vdash e_2 : A \mid \epsilon$.*

We write $e \not\longrightarrow$ if and only if e cannot evaluate further. Moreover, $\longrightarrow^*$ denotes the reflexive and transitive closure of the evaluation relation $\longrightarrow$.

Theorem 2 (Type soundness of $\lambda_{\text{eff}}^{\Lambda}$). *If $\Delta; \mathsf{none} \vdash e : A \,|\, \epsilon$ and $e \longrightarrow^* e'$ and $e' \not\longrightarrow$, then (1) e' is a value or (2) $e' = \#\mathsf{op}(\boldsymbol{\sigma}, w, E)$ for some $\mathsf{op} \in \epsilon$, $\boldsymbol{\sigma}$, w, and E.*

Now, type safety of $\lambda_{\text{eff}}^{\text{let}}$ is obtained as a corollary of Theorems 1 and 2.

Corollary 1 (Type safety of $\lambda_{\text{eff}}^{\text{let}}$). *If M is a well-typed program of A, there exists some e such that $\emptyset; \mathsf{none} \vdash M : A \,|\, \langle\rangle \rhd^{\emptyset} e$ and e does not get stuck.*

5 Related Work

5.1 Polymorphic Effects and Let-Polymorphism

Many researchers have attacked the problem of combining effects—not necessarily algebraic—and let-polymorphism so far [1,2,10,12,14,17,23,24]. In particular, most of them have focused on ML-style polymorphic references. The algebraic effect handlers dealt with in this paper seem to be unable to implement general ML-style references—i.e., give an appropriate implementation to a set of effect operations `new` with the signature $\forall\alpha.\alpha \hookrightarrow \alpha\,\mathsf{ref}$, `get` with $\forall\alpha.\alpha\,\mathsf{ref} \hookrightarrow \alpha$, and `put` with $\forall\alpha.\alpha \times \alpha\,\mathsf{ref} \hookrightarrow \mathsf{unit}$ for abstract datatype $\alpha\,\mathsf{ref}$—even without the restriction on handlers because each operation clause in a handler assigns type variables locally and it is impossible to share such type variables between operation clauses.[6] Nevertheless, their approaches would be applicable to algebraic effects and handlers.

A common idea in the literature is to restrict the form of expressions bound by polymorphic let. Thus, they are complementary to our approach in that they restrict how effect operations are used whereas we restrict how effect operations are implemented.

Value restriction [23,24], a standard way adopted in ML-like languages, restricts polymorphic let-bound expressions to syntactic values. Garrigue [10] relaxes the value restriction so that, if a let-bound expression is not a syntactic value, type variables that appear only at positive positions in the type of the expression can be generalized. Although the (relaxed) value restriction is a quite clear criterion that indicates what let-bound expressions can be polymorphic safely and it even accepts interfering handlers, it is too restrictive in some cases. We give an example for such a case below.

```
effect choose∀ : ∀α. α × α ↪ α

let f1 () =
  let g = #choose∀(fst, snd) in
  if g (true,false) then g (-1,1) else g (1,-1)
```

[6] One possible approach to dealing with ML-style references is to extend algebraic effects and handlers so that a handler for *parameterized* effects can be connected with dynamic resources [3].

In the definition of function `f1`, variable `g` is used polymorphically. Execution of this function under an appropriate handler would succeed, and in fact our calculus accepts it. By contrast, the (relaxed) value restriction rejects it because the let-bound expression `#choose`$^{\forall}$`(fst,snd)` is not a syntactic value and the type variable appear in both positive and negative positions, and so `g` is assigned a monomorphic type. A workaround for this problem is to make a function wrapper that calls either of `fst` or `snd` depending on the Boolean value chosen by `choose`$^{\forall}$:

```
let f2 () =
  let b = #choose∀(true,false) in
  let g = λx. if b then (fst x) else (snd x) in
  if g (true,false) then g (-1,1) else g (1,-1)
```

However, this workaround makes the program complicated and incurs additional run-time cost for the branching and an extra call to the wrapper function.

Asai and Kameyama [2] study a combination of let-polymorphism with delimited control operators shift/reset [4]. They allow a let-bound expression to be polymorphic if it invokes no control operation. Thus, the function `f1` above would be rejected in their approach.

Another research line to restrict the use of effects is to allow only type variables unrelated to effect invocations to be generalized. Tofte [23] distinguishes between applicative type variables, which cannot be used for effect invocations, and imperative ones, which can be used, and proposes a type system that enforces restrictions that (1) type variables of imperative operations can be instantiated only with types wherein all type variables are imperative and (2) if a let-bound expression is not a syntactic value, only applicative type variables can be generalized. Leroy and Weis [17] allow generalization only of type variables that do not appear in a parameter type to the reference type in the type of a let-expression. To detect the hidden use of references, their type system gives a term not only a type but also the types of free variables used in the term. Standard ML of New Jersey (before ML97) adopted weak polymorphism [1], which was later formalized and investigated deeply by Hoang et al. [12]. Weak polymorphism equips a type variable with the number of function calls after which a value of a type containing the type variable will be passed to an imperative operation. The type system ensures that type variables with positive numbers are not related to imperative constructs, and so such type variables can be generalized safely. In this line of research, the function `f1` above would not typecheck because generalized type variables are used to instantiate those of the effect signature, although it could be rewritten to an acceptable one by taking care not to involve type variables in effect invocation.

```
let f3 () =
  let g = if #choose∀(true,false) then fst then snd in
  if g (true,false) then g (-1,1) else g (1,-1)
```

More recently, Kammar and Pretnar [14] show that *parameterized* algebraic effects and handlers do not need the value restriction *if* the type variables used in an effect invocation are not generalized. Thus, as the other work that restricts generalized type variables, their approach would reject function `f1` but would accept `f3`.

5.2 Algebraic Effects and Handlers

Algebraic effects [20] are a way to represent the denotation of an effect by giving a set of operations and an equational theory that capture their properties. Algebraic effect handlers, introduced by Plotkin and Pretnar [21], make it possible to provide user-defined effects. Algebraic effect handlers have been gaining popularity owing to their flexibility and have been made available as libraries [13,15,26] or as primitive features of languages, such as Eff [3], Koka [16], Frank [18], and Multicore OCaml [5]. In these languages, let-bound expressions that can be polymorphic are restricted to values or pure expressions.

Recently, Forster et al. [9] investigate the relationships between algebraic effect handlers and other mechanisms for user-defined effects—delimited control shift0 [19] and monadic reflection [7,8]—conjecturing that there would be no type-preserving translation from a language with delimited control or monadic reflection to one with algebraic effect handlers. It would be an interesting direction to export our idea to delimited control and monadic reflection.

6 Conclusion

There has been a long history of collaboration between effects and let-polymorphism. This work focuses on polymorphic algebraic effects and handlers, wherein the type signature of an effect operation can be polymorphic and an operation clause has a type binder, and shows that a naive combination of polymorphic effects and let-polymorphism breaks type safety. Our novel observation to address this problem is that any let-bound expression can be polymorphic safely if resumptions from a handler do not interfere with each other. We formalized this idea by developing a type system that requires the argument of each resumption expression to have a type obtained by renaming the type variables assigned in the operation clause to those assigned in the resumption. We have proven that a well-typed program in our type system does not get stuck via elaboration to an intermediate language wherein type information appears explicitly.

There are many directions for future work. The first is to address the problem, described at the end of Sect. 3, that renaming the type variables assigned in an operation clause to those assigned in a resumption expression is allowed for the argument of the clause but not for variables bound by lambda abstractions and let-expressions outside the resumption expression. Second, we are interested in incorporating other features from the literature on algebraic effect handlers, such as dynamic resources [3] and parameterized algebraic effects, and restriction techniques that have been developed for type-safe imperative programming with let-polymorphism such as (relaxed) value restriction [10,23,24]. For example, we would like to develop a type system that enforces the non-interfering restriction only to handlers implementing effect operations invoked in polymorphic computation. We also expect that it is possible to determine whether implementations of an effect operation have no interfering resumption from the type signature of the operation, as relaxed value restriction makes it possible to find safely generalizable type variables from the type of a let-bound expression [10]. Finally, we are also interested in implementing our idea for a language with effect handlers such as Koka [16] and in applying the idea of analyzing handlers to other settings such as dependent typing.

Acknowledgments. We would like to thank the anonymous reviewers for their valuable comments. This work was supported in part by ERATO HASUO Metamathematics for Systems Design Project (No. JPMJER1603), JST (Sekiyama), and JSPS KAKENHI Grant Number JP15H05706 (Igarashi).

References

1. Appel, A.W., MacQueen, D.B.: Standard ML of New Jersey. In: Maluszyński, J., Wirsing, M. (eds.) PLILP 1991. LNCS, vol. 528, pp. 1–13. Springer, Heidelberg (1991). https://doi.org/10.1007/3-540-54444-5_83
2. Asai, K., Kameyama, Y.: Polymorphic delimited continuations. In: Shao, Z. (ed.) APLAS 2007. LNCS, vol. 4807, pp. 239–254. Springer, Heidelberg (2007). https://doi.org/10.1007/978-3-540-76637-7_16
3. Bauer, A., Pretnar, M.: Programming with algebraic effects and handlers. J. Log. Algebr. Methods Program. **84**(1), 108–123 (2015). https://doi.org/10.1016/j.jlamp.2014.02.001
4. Danvy, O., Filinski, A.: Abstracting control. In: LISP and Functional Programming, pp. 151–160 (1990). https://doi.org/10.1145/91556.91622
5. Dolan, S., Eliopoulos, S., Hillerström, D., Madhavapeddy, A., Sivaramakrishnan, K.C., White, L.: Concurrent system programming with effect handlers. In: Wang, M., Owens, S. (eds.) TFP 2017. LNCS, vol. 10788, pp. 98–117. Springer, Cham (2018). https://doi.org/10.1007/978-3-319-89719-6_6
6. Felleisen, M., Hieb, R.: The revised report on the syntactic theories of sequential control and state. Theor. Comput. Sci. **103**(2), 235–271 (1992). https://doi.org/10.1016/0304-3975(92)90014-7
7. Filinski, A.: Representing monads. In: Proceedings of the 21st ACM SIGPLAN-SIGACT Symposium on Principles of Programming Languages, pp. 446–457 (1994). https://doi.org/10.1145/174675.178047
8. Filinski, A.: Monads in action. In: Proceedings of the 37th ACM SIGPLAN-SIGACT Symposium on Principles of Programming Languages, POPL 2010, pp. 483–494 (2010). https://doi.org/10.1145/1706299.1706354
9. Forster, Y., Kammar, O., Lindley, S., Pretnar, M.: On the expressive power of user-defined effects: effect handlers, monadic reflection, delimited control. PACMPL **1**(ICFP), 13:1–13:29 (2017). https://doi.org/10.1145/3110257
10. Garrigue, J.: Relaxing the value restriction. In: Kameyama, Y., Stuckey, P.J. (eds.) FLOPS 2004. LNCS, vol. 2998, pp. 196–213. Springer, Heidelberg (2004). https://doi.org/10.1007/978-3-540-24754-8_15
11. Harper, R., Lillibridge, M.: Polymorphic type assignment and CPS conversion. Lisp Symb. Comput. **6**(3–4), 361–380 (1993)

12. Hoang, M., Mitchell, J.C., Viswanathan, R.: Standard ML-NJ weak polymorphism and imperative constructs. In: Proceedings of the Eighth Annual Symposium on Logic in Computer Science, LICS 1993 (1993)
13. Kammar, O., Lindley, S., Oury, N.: Handlers in action. In: ACM SIGPLAN International Conference on Functional Programming, ICFP 2013, pp. 145–158 (2013). https://doi.org/10.1145/2500365.2500590
14. Kammar, O., Pretnar, M.: No value restriction is needed for algebraic effects and handlers. J. Funct. Program. **27**, e7 (2017). https://doi.org/10.1017/S0956796816000320
15. Kiselyov, O., Ishii, H.: Freer monads, more extensible effects. In: Proceedings of the 8th ACM SIGPLAN Symposium on Haskell, Haskell 2015, pp. 94–105 (2015). https://doi.org/10.1145/2804302.2804319
16. Leijen, D.: Type directed compilation of row-typed algebraic effects. In: Proceedings of the 44th ACM SIGPLAN Symposium on Principles of Programming Languages, POPL 2017, pp. 486–499 (2017). http://dl.acm.org/citation.cfm?id=3009872
17. Leroy, X., Weis, P.: Polymorphic type inference and assignment. In: Proceedings of the 18th Annual ACM Symposium on Principles of Programming Languages, pp. 291–302 (1991). https://doi.org/10.1145/99583.99622
18. Lindley, S., McBride, C., McLaughlin, C.: Do be do be do. In: Proceedings of the 44th ACM SIGPLAN Symposium on Principles of Programming Languages, POPL 2017, pp. 500–514 (2017). http://dl.acm.org/citation.cfm?id=3009897
19. Materzok, M., Biernacki, D.: A dynamic interpretation of the CPS hierarchy. In: Jhala, R., Igarashi, A. (eds.) APLAS 2012. LNCS, vol. 7705, pp. 296–311. Springer, Heidelberg (2012). https://doi.org/10.1007/978-3-642-35182-2_21
20. Plotkin, G.D., Power, J.: Algebraic operations and generic effects. Appl. Categ. Struct. **11**(1), 69–94 (2003). https://doi.org/10.1023/A:1023064908962
21. Plotkin, G.D., Pretnar, M.: Handlers of algebraic effects. In: Castagna, G. (ed.) ESOP 2009. LNCS, vol. 5502, pp. 80–94. Springer, Heidelberg (2009). https://doi.org/10.1007/978-3-642-00590-9_7
22. Reynolds, J.C.: Types, abstraction and parametric polymorphism. In: IFIP Congress, pp. 513–523 (1983)
23. Tofte, M.: Type inference for polymorphic references. Inf. Comput. **89**(1), 1–34 (1990). https://doi.org/10.1016/0890-5401(90)90018-D
24. Wright, A.K.: Simple imperative polymorphism. Lisp Symb. Comput. **8**(4), 343–355 (1995)
25. Wright, A.K., Felleisen, M.: A syntactic approach to type soundness. Inf. Comput. **115**(1), 38–94 (1994). https://doi.org/10.1006/inco.1994.1093
26. Wu, N., Schrijvers, T., Hinze, R.: Effect handlers in scope. In: Proceedings of the 2014 ACM SIGPLAN Symposium on Haskell, Haskell 2014, pp. 1–12 (2014). https://doi.org/10.1145/2633357.2633358

Distributive Disjoint Polymorphism for Compositional Programming

Xuan Bi[1(✉)], Ningning Xie[1], Bruno C. d. S. Oliveira[1], and Tom Schrijvers[2]

[1] The University of Hong Kong, Hong Kong, China
{xbi,nnxie,bruno}@cs.hku.hk
[2] KU Leuven, Leuven, Belgium
tom.schrijvers@cs.kuleuven.be

Abstract. Popular programming techniques such as *shallow embeddings* of Domain Specific Languages (DSLs), *finally tagless* or *object algebras* are built on the principle of *compositionality*. However, existing programming languages only support simple compositional designs well, and have limited support for more sophisticated ones.

This paper presents the F_i^+ calculus, which supports highly modular and compositional designs that improve on existing techniques. These improvements are due to the combination of three features: *disjoint intersection types* with a *merge operator*; *parametric (disjoint) polymorphism*; and *BCD-style distributive subtyping*. The main technical challenge is F_i^+'s proof of coherence. A naive adaptation of ideas used in System F's *parametricity* to *canonicity* (the logical relation used by F_i^+ to prove coherence) results in an ill-founded logical relation. To solve the problem our canonicity relation employs a different technique based on immediate substitutions and a restriction to predicative instantiations. Besides coherence, we show several other important meta-theoretical results, such as type-safety, sound and complete algorithmic subtyping, and decidability of the type system. Remarkably, unlike $\mathsf{F}_{<:}$'s *bounded polymorphism*, disjoint polymorphism in F_i^+ supports decidable type-checking.

1 Introduction

Compositionality is a desirable property in programming designs. Broadly defined, it is the principle that a system should be built by composing smaller subsystems. For instance, in the area of programming languages, compositionality is a key aspect of *denotational semantics* [48,49], where the denotation of a program is constructed from the denotations of its parts. Compositional definitions have many benefits. One is ease of reasoning: since compositional definitions are recursively defined over smaller elements they can typically be reasoned about using induction. Another benefit is that compositional definitions are easy to extend, without modifying previous definitions.

Programming techniques that support compositional definitions include: *shallow embeddings* of Domain Specific Languages (DSLs) [20], *finally tagless* [11], *polymorphic embeddings* [26] or *object algebras* [35]. These techniques

L. Caires (Ed.): ESOP 2019, LNCS 11423, pp. 381–409, 2019.
https://doi.org/10.1007/978-3-030-17184-1_14

allow us to create compositional definitions, which are easy to extend without modifications. Moreover, when modeling semantics, both finally tagless and object algebras support *multiple interpretations* (or denotations) of syntax, thus offering a solution to the well-known *Expression Problem* [53]. Because of these benefits these techniques have become popular both in the functional and object-oriented programming communities.

However, programming languages often only support simple compositional designs well, while support for more sophisticated compositional designs is lacking. For instance, once we have multiple interpretations of syntax, we may wish to compose them. Particularly useful is a *merge* combinator, which composes two interpretations [35,37,42] to form a new interpretation that, when executed, returns the results of both interpretations.

The merge combinator can be manually defined in existing programming languages, and be used in combination with techniques such as finally tagless or object algebras. Moreover variants of the merge combinator are useful to model more complex combinations of interpretations. A good example are so-called *dependent* interpretations, where an interpretation does not depend *only* on itself, but also on a different interpretation. These definitions with dependencies are quite common in practice, and, although they are not orthogonal to the interpretation they depend on, we would like to model them (and also mutually dependent interpretations) in a modular and compositional style.

Defining the merge combinator in existing programming languages is verbose and cumbersome, requiring code for every new kind of syntax. Yet, that code is essentially mechanical and ought to be automated. While using advanced meta-programming techniques enables automating the merge combinator to a large extent in existing programming languages [37,42], those techniques have several problems: error messages can be problematic, type-unsafe reflection is needed in some approaches [37] and advanced type-level features are required in others [42]. An alternative to the merge combinator that supports modular multiple interpretations and works in OO languages with support for some form of multiple inheritance and covariant type-refinement of fields has also been recently proposed [55]. While this approach is relatively simple, it still requires a lot of manual boilerplate code for composition of interpretations.

This paper presents a calculus and polymorphic type system with *(disjoint) intersection types* [36], called F_i^+. F_i^+ supports our broader notion of compositional designs, and enables the development of highly modular and reusable programs. F_i^+ has a built-in merge operator and a powerful subtyping relation that are used to automate the composition of multiple (possibly dependent) interpretations. In F_i^+ subtyping is coercive and enables the automatic generation of coercions in a *type-directed* fashion. This process is similar to that of other type-directed code generation mechanisms such as *type classes* [52], which eliminate boilerplate code associated to the *dictionary translation* [52].

F_i^+ continues a line of research on disjoint intersection types. Previous work on *disjoint polymorphism* (the F_i calculus) [2] studied the combination of parametric polymorphism and disjoint intersection types, but its subtyping relation does not support BCD-style distributivity rules [3] and the type system also prevents unrestricted intersections [16]. More recently the NeColus calculus (or λ_i^+) [5] introduced a system with *disjoint intersection types* and BCD-style distributivity rules, but did not account for parametric polymorphism. F_i^+ is unique in that it combines all three features in a single calculus: *disjoint intersection types* and a *merge operator*; *parametric (disjoint) polymorphism*; and a BCD-style subtyping relation with *distributivity rules*. The three features together allow us to improve upon the finally tagless and object algebra approaches and support advanced compositional designs. Moreover previous work on disjoint intersection types has shown various other applications that are also possible in F_i^+, including: *first-class traits* and *dynamic inheritance* [4], *extensible records* and *dynamic mixins* [2], and *nested composition* and *family polymorphism* [5].

Unfortunately the combination of the three features has non-trivial complications. The main technical challenge (like for most other calculi with disjoint intersection types) is the proof of coherence for F_i^+. Because of the presence of BCD-style distributivity rules, our coherence proof is based on the recent approach employed in λ_i^+ [5], which uses a *heterogeneous* logical relation called *canonicity*. To account for polymorphism, which λ_i^+'s canonicity does not support, we originally wanted to incorporate the relevant parts of System F's logical relation [43]. However, due to a mismatch between the two relations, this did not work. The parametricity relation has been carefully set up with a delayed type substitution to avoid ill-foundedness due to its impredicative polymorphism. Unfortunately, canonicity is a heterogeneous relation and needs to account for cases that cannot be expressed with the delayed substitution setup of the homogeneous parametricity relation. Therefore, to handle those heterogeneous cases, we resorted to immediate substitutions and *predicative instantiations*. We do not believe that predicativity is a severe restriction in practice, since many source languages (e.g., those based on the Hindley-Milner type system like Haskell and OCaml) are themselves predicative and do not require the full generality of an impredicative core language. Should impredicative instantiation be required, we expect that step-indexing [1] can be used to recover well-foundedness, though at the cost of a much more complicated coherence proof.

The formalization and metatheory of F_i^+ are a significant advance over that of F_i. Besides the support for distributive subtyping, F_i^+ removes several restrictions imposed by the syntactic coherence proof in F_i. In particular F_i^+ supports unrestricted intersections, which are forbidden in F_i. Unrestricted intersections enable, for example, encoding certain forms of bounded quantification [39]. Moreover the new proof method is more robust with respect to language extensions. For instance, F_i^+ supports the bottom type without significant complications in the proofs, while it was a challenging open problem in F_i. A final interesting aspect is that F_i^+'s type-checking is decidable. In the design space of languages with polymorphism and subtyping, similar mechanisms have been known to lead to undecidability. Pierce's seminal paper "*Bounded quantification is undecidable*" [40] shows that the contravariant subtyping rule for bounded quantification in $\mathsf{F}_{<:}$ leads to undecidability of subtyping. In F_i^+ the contravariant rule for disjoint quantification retains decidability. Since with unrestricted intersections F_i^+ can express several use cases of bounded quantification, F_i^+ could be an interesting and decidable alternative to $F_{<:}$.

In summary the contributions of this paper are:

- **The F_i^+ calculus,** which is the first calculus to combine disjoint intersection types, BCD-style distributive subtyping and disjoint polymorphism. We show several meta-theoretical results, such as *type-safety*, *sound and complete algorithmic subtyping*, *coherence* and *decidability* of the type system. F_i^+ includes the *bottom type*, which was considered to be a significant challenge in previous work on disjoint polymorphism [2].
- **An extension of the canonicity relation with polymorphism,** which enables the proof of coherence of F_i^+. We show that the ideas of System F's *parametricity* cannot be ported to F_i^+. To overcome the problem we use a technique based on immediate substitutions and a predicativity restriction.
- **Improved compositional designs:** We show that F_i^+'s combination of features enables improved compositional programming designs and supports automated composition of interpretations in programming techniques like object algebras and finally tagless.
- **Implementation and proofs:** All of the metatheory of this paper, except some manual proofs of decidability, has been mechanically formalized in Coq. Furthermore, F_i^+ is implemented and all code presented in the paper is available. The implementation, Coq proofs and extended version with appendices can be found in https://github.com/bixuanzju/ESOP2019-artifact.

2 Compositional Programming

To demonstrate the compositional properties of F_i^+ we use Gibbons and Wu's shallow embeddings of parallel prefix circuits [20]. By means of several different shallow embeddings, we first illustrate the short-comings of a state-of-the-art compositional approach, popularly known as a *finally tagless* encoding [11], in Haskell. Next we show how parametric polymorphism and distributive intersection types provide a more elegant and compact solution in SEDEL [4], a source language built on top of our F_i^+ calculus.

2.1 A Finally Tagless Encoding in Haskell

The circuit DSL represents networks that map a number of inputs (known as the width) of some type A onto the same number of outputs of the same type. The outputs combine (with repetitions) one or more inputs using a binary associative operator $\oplus : A \times A \to A$. A particularly interesting class of circuits that can be expressed in the DSL are *parallel prefix circuits*. These represent computations that take $n > 0$ inputs $x_1, \ldots, x_n$ and produce n outputs $y_1, \ldots, y_n$, where $y_i = x_1 \oplus x_2 \oplus \ldots \oplus x_i$.

The DSL features 5 language primitives: two basic circuit constructors and three circuit combinators. These are captured in the Haskell type class `Circuit`:

```
data Width = W { width :: Int }
instance Circuit Width where
  identity n    = W n
  fan n         = W n
  beside c1 c2 =
    W (width c1 + width c2)
  above c1 c2  = c1
  stretch ws c = W (sum ws)
```

(a) Width embedding

```
data Depth = D { depth :: Int }
instance Circuit Depth where
  identity n    = D 0
  fan n         = D 1
  beside c1 c2 =
    D (max (depth c1) (depth c2))
  above c1 c2  = D (depth c1 + depth c2)
  stretch ws c = c
```

(b) Depth embedding

Fig. 1. Two finally tagless embeddings of circuits.

```
class Circuit c where
  identity :: Int → c
  fan      :: Int → c
  beside   :: c → c → c
  above    :: c → c → c
  stretch  :: [Int] → c → c
```

An `identity` circuit with n inputs x_i, has n outputs $y_i = x_i$. A `fan` circuit has n inputs x_i and n outputs y_i, where $y_1 = x_1$ and $y_j = x_1 \oplus x_j\,(j > 1)$. The binary `beside` combinator puts two circuits in parallel; the combined circuit takes the inputs of both circuits to the outputs of both circuits. The binary `above` combinator connects the outputs of the first circuit to the inputs of the second; the width of both circuits has to be same. Finally, `stretch ws c` interleaves the wires of circuit `c` with bundles of additional wires that map their input straight on their output. The `ws` parameter specifies the width of the consecutive bundles; the ith wire of `c` is preceded by a bundle of width $ws_i - 1$.

Basic width and depth embeddings. Figure 1 shows two simple shallow embeddings, which represent a circuit respectively in terms of its width and its depth. The former denotes the number of inputs/outputs of a circuit, while the latter is the maximal number of $\oplus$ operators between any input and output. Both definitions follow the same setup: a new Haskell datatype (`Width`/`Depth`) wraps the primitive result value and provides an instance of the `Circuit` type class that interprets the 5 DSL primitives accordingly. The following code creates a so-called Brent-Kung parallel prefix circuit [9]:

```
e1 :: Width
e1 = above (beside (fan 2) (fan 2))
       (above (stretch [2, 2] (fan 2))
          (beside (beside (identity 1) (fan 2)) (identity 1)))
```

Here `e1` evaluates to `W {width = 4}`. If we want to know the depth of the circuit, we have to change type signature to `Depth`.

Interpreting multiple ways. Fortunately, with the help of polymorphism we can define a type of circuits that support multiple interpretations at once.

```
type DCircuit = forall c. Circuit c ⇒ c
```

This way we can provide a single Brent-Kung parallel prefix circuit definition that can be reused for different interpretations.

```
brentKung :: DCircuit
brentKung = above (beside (fan 2) (fan 2))
               (above (stretch [2, 2] (fan 2))
                 (beside (beside (identity 1) (fan 2)) (identity 1)))
```

A type annotation then selects the desired interpretation. For instance, `brentKung :: Width` yields the width and `brentKung :: Depth` the depth.

Composition of embeddings. What is not ideal in the above code is that the same `brentKung` circuit is processed twice, if we want to execute both interpretations. We can do better by processing the circuit only once, computing both interpretations simultaneously. The finally tagless encoding achieves this with a boilerplate instance for tuples of interpretations.

```
instance (Circuit c1, Circuit c2) ⇒ Circuit (c1, c2) where
  identity n     = (identity n, identity n)
  fan n          = (fan n, fan n)
  beside c1 c2   = (beside (fst c1) (fst c2), beside (snd c1) (snd c2))
  above c1 c2    = (above (fst c1) (fst c2), above (snd c1) (snd c2))
  stretch ws c   = (stretch ws (fst c), stretch ws (snd c))
```

Now we can get both embeddings simultaneously as follows:

```
e12 :: (Width, Depth)
e12 = brentKung
```

This evaluates to `(W {width = 4}, D {depth = 2})`.

Composition of dependent interpretations. The composition above is easy because the two embeddings are orthogonal. In contrast, the composition of dependent interpretations is rather cumbersome in the standard finally tagless setup. An example of the latter is the interpretation of circuits as their well-sizedness, which captures whether circuits are well-formed. This interpretation depends on the interpretation of circuits as their width.[1]

```
data WellSized = WS { wS :: Bool, ox :: Width }
instance Circuit WellSized where
 identity n    = WS True (identity n)
 fan n         = WS True (fan n)
 beside c1 c2 = WS (wS c1 && wS c2) (beside (ox c1) (ox c2))
```

---

[1] Dependent recursion schemes are also known as *zygomorphism* [18] after the ancient Greek word ζυγoν for yoke. We have labeled the `Width` field with `ox` because it is pulling the yoke.

```
above c1 c2  = WS (wS c1 && wS c2 && width (ox c1) == width (ox c2))
                  (above (ox c1) (ox c2))
stretch ws c = WS (wS c && length ws==width (ox c)) (stretch ws (ox c))
```

The `WellSized` datatype represents the well-sizedness of a circuit with a Boolean, and also keeps track of the circuit's width. The 5 primitives compute the well-sizedness in terms of both the width and well-sizedness of the subcomponents. What makes the code cumbersome is that it has to explicitly delegate to the `Width` interpretation to collect this additional information.

With the help of a substantially more complicated setup that features a dozen Haskell language extensions, and advanced programming techniques, we can make the explicit delegation implicit (see the appendix). Nevertheless, that approach still requires *a lot of boilerplate* that needs to be repeated for each DSL, as well as explicit projections that need to be written in each interpretation. Another alternative Haskell encoding that also enables multiple dependent interpretations is proposed by Zhang and Oliveira [55], but it does not eliminate the explicit delegation and still requires substantial amounts of boilerplate. A final remark is that adding new primitives (e.g., a "right stretch" `rstretch` combinator [25]) can also be easily achieved [46].

2.2 The SEDEL Encoding

SEDEL is a source language that elaborates to F_i^+, adding a few convenient source level constructs. The SEDEL setup of the circuit DSL is similar to the finally tagless approach. Instead of a `Circuit c` type class, there is a `Circuit[C]` type that gathers the 5 circuit primitives in a record. Like in Haskell, the type parameter `C` expresses that the interpretation of circuits is a parameter.

```
type Circuit[C] = {
  identity : Int → C, fan : Int → C, beside : C → C → C,
  above : C → C → C, stretch : List[Int] → C → C };
```

As a side note if a new constructor (e.g., `rstretch`) is needed, then this is done by means of intersection types (`&` creates an intersection type) in SEDEL:

```
type NCircuit[C] = Circuit[C] & { rstretch : List[Int] → C → C };
```

Figure 2 shows the two basic shallow embeddings for width and depth. In both cases, a named SEDEL definition replaces the corresponding unnamed Haskell type class instance in providing the implementations of the 5 language primitives for a particular interpretation.

The use of the SEDEL embeddings is different from that of their Haskell counterparts. Where Haskell implicitly selects the appropriate type class instance based on the available type information, in SEDEL the programmer explicitly selects the implementation following the style used by object algebras. The following code does this by building a circuit with `l1` (short for `language1`).

```
l1 = language1;
e1 = l1.above (l1.beside (l1.fan 2) (l1.fan 2))
```

```
type Width = { width : Int };
language1 : Circuit[Width] = {
  identity (n : Int) = { width = n },
  fan      (n : Int) = { width = n },
  beside   (c1 : Width) (c2 : Width) = { width = c1.width + c2.width },
  above    (c1 : Width) (c2 : Width) = { width = c1.width },
  stretch  (ws : List[Int]) (c : Width) = { width = sum ws } };
```

```
type Depth = { depth : Int };
language2 : Circuit[Depth] = {
  identity (n : Int) = { depth = 0 },
  fan      (n : Int) = { depth = 1 },
  beside   (c1 : Depth) (c2 : Depth) = { depth = max c1.depth c2.depth},
  above    (c1 : Depth) (c2 : Depth) = { depth = c1.depth + c2.depth},
  stretch  (ws : List[Int]) (c : Depth) = { depth = c.depth } };
```

Fig. 2. Two SEDEL embeddings of circuits.

```
  (l1.above (l1.stretch (cons 2 (cons 2 nil)) (l1.fan 2))
    (l1.beside (l1.beside (l1.identity 1) (l1.fan 2)) (l1.identity 1)));
```

Here `e1` evaluates to `{width = 4}`. If we want to know the depth of the circuit, we have to replicate the code with `language2`.

Dynamically reusable circuits. Just like in Haskell, we can use polymorphism to define a type of circuits that can be interpreted with different languages.

```
type DCircuit = { accept : forall C. Circuit[C] → C };
```

In contrast to the Haskell solution, this implementation explicitly accepts the implementation.

```
brentKung : DCircuit = {
  accept C l = l.above (l.beside (l.fan 2) (l.fan 2))
    (l.above (l.stretch (cons 2 (cons 2 nil)) (l.fan 2))
      (l.beside (l.beside (l.identity 1) (l.fan 2)) (l.identity 1))) };
e1 = brentKung.accept Width language1;
e2 = brentKung.accept Depth language2;
```

Automatic composition of languages. Of course, like in Haskell we can also compute both results simultaneously. However, unlike in Haskell, the composition of the two interpretation requires no boilerplate whatsoever—in particular, there is no SEDEL counterpart of the `Circuit (c1, c2)` instance. Instead, we can just compose the two interpretations with the term-level merge operator (,,) and specify the desired type `Circuit[Width & Depth]`.

```
language3 : Circuit[Width & Depth] = language1 ,, language2;
e3 = brentKung.accept (Width & Depth) language3;
```

Here the use of the merge operator creates a term with the intersection type `Circuit[Width] & Circuit[Depth]`. Implicitly, the SEDEL type system takes care of the details, turning this intersection type into `Circuit[Width & Depth]`. This is possible because intersection (`&`) distributes over function and record types (a distinctive feature of BCD-style subtyping).

Composition of dependent interpretations. In SEDEL the composition scales nicely to dependent interpretations. For instance, the well-sizedness interpretation can be expressed without explicit projections.

```
type WellSized = { wS : Bool };
language4 = {
  identity (n : Int) = { wS = true },
  fan      (n : Int) = { wS = true },
  above (c1 : WellSized & Width) (c2 : WellSized & Width) =
    { wS = c1.wS && c2.wS && c1.width == c2.width },
  beside (c1 : WellSized) (c2 : WellSized) = { wS  = c1.wS && c2.wS  },
  stretch (ws : List[Int]) (c : WellSized & Width) =
    { wS = c.wS && length ws == c.width  } };
```

Here the `WellSized & Width` type in the `above` and `stretch` cases expresses that both the well-sizedness and width of subcircuits must be given, and that the width implementation is left as a dependency—when `language4` is used, then the width implementation must be provided. Again, the distributive properties of `&` in the type system take care of merging the two interpretations.

```
e4   = brentKung.accept (WellSized & Width) (language1 ,, language4);
main = e4.wS -- Output: true
```

Disjoint polymorphism and dynamic merges. While it may seem from the above examples that definitions have to be merged statically, SEDEL in fact supports dynamic merges. For instance, we can encapsulate the merge operator in the `combine` function while abstracting over the two components `x` and `y` that are merged as well as over their types `A` and `B`.

```
combine A [B * A] (x : A) (y : B) = x ,, y;
```

This way the components `x` and `y` are only known at runtime and thus the merge can only happen at that time. The types `A` and `B` cannot be chosen entirely freely. For instance, if both components would contribute an implementation for the same method, which implementation is provided by the combination would be ambiguous. To avoid this problem the two types `A` and `B` have to be *disjoint.* This is expressed in the disjointness constraint `* A` on the quantifier of the type variable `B`. If a quantifier mentions no disjointness constraint, like that of `A`, it defaults to the trivial $* \top$ constraint which implies no restriction.

3 Semantics of the F_i^+ Calculus

This section gives a formal account of F_i^+, the first typed calculus combining disjoint polymorphism [2] (and disjoint intersection types) with BCD subtyping [3].

Types	A, B, C	$::= \mathsf{Int} \mid \top \mid \bot \mid A \to B \mid A \,\&\, B \mid \{l : A\} \mid \alpha \mid \forall(\alpha * A).\, B$
Expressions	E	$::= x \mid i \mid \top \mid \lambda x.\, E \mid E_1\, E_2 \mid E_1 \,,,\, E_2 \mid E : A \mid \{l = E\} \mid E.l$
		$\mid\ \Lambda(\alpha * A).\, E \mid E\, A$
Term contexts Γ		$::= \bullet \mid \Gamma, x : A$
Type contexts Δ		$::= \bullet \mid \Delta, \alpha * A$

Fig. 3. Syntax of F_i^+

The main differences to F_i are in the subtyping, well-formedness and disjointness relations. F_i^+ adds BCD subtyping and unrestricted intersections, and also closes an open problem of F_i by including the bottom type. The dynamic semantics of F_i^+ is given by elaboration to the target calculus F_{co}—a variant of System F extended with products and explicit coercions.

3.1 Syntax and Semantics

Figure 3 shows the syntax of F_i^+. Metavariables A, B, C range over types. Types include standard constructs from prior work [2,36]: integers Int, the top type $\top$, arrows $A \to B$, intersections $A \,\&\, B$, single-field record types $\{l : A\}$ and disjoint quantification $\forall(\alpha * A).\, B$. One novelty in F_i^+ is the addition of the uninhabited bottom type $\bot$. Metavariable E ranges over expressions. Expressions are integer literals i, the top value $\top$, lambda abstractions $\lambda x.\, E$, applications $E_1\, E_2$, merges $E_1 \,,,\, E_2$, annotated terms $E : A$, single-field records $\{l = E\}$, record projections $E.l$, type abstractions $\Lambda(\alpha * A).\, E$ and type applications $E\, A$.

Well-formedness and unrestricted intersections. F_i^+'s well-formedness judgment of types $\Delta \vdash A$ is standard, and only enforces well-scoping. This is one of the key differences from F_i, which uses well-formedness to also ensure that all intersection types are disjoint. In other words, while in F_i all valid intersection types must be disjoint, in F_i^+ unrestricted intersection types such as $\mathsf{Int} \,\&\, \mathsf{Int}$ are allowed. More specifically, the well-formedness of intersection types in F_i^+ and F_i is:

$$\frac{\Delta \vdash A \qquad \Delta \vdash B}{\Delta \vdash A \,\&\, B}\ \textsc{wf-}\mathsf{F}_i^+ \qquad\qquad \frac{\Delta \vdash A \qquad \Delta \vdash B \qquad \Delta \vdash A * B}{\Delta \vdash A \,\&\, B}\ \textsc{wf-}\mathsf{F}_i$$

Notice that F_i has an extra disjointness condition $\Delta \vdash A * B$ in the premise. This is crucial for F_i's syntactic method for proving coherence, but also burdens the calculus with various syntactic restrictions and complicates its metatheory. For example, it requires extra effort to show that F_i only produces disjoint intersection types. As a consequence, F_i features a *weaker* substitution lemma (note the gray part in Proposition 1) than F_i^+ (Lemma 1).

Proposition 1 (Type substitution in F_i). *If $\Delta \vdash A$, $\Delta \vdash B$, $(\alpha * C) \in \Delta$, $\Delta \vdash B * C$ and well-formed context $[B/\alpha]\Delta$, then $[B/\alpha]\Delta \vdash [B/\alpha]A$.*

Lemma 1 (Type substitution in F_i^+). *If $\Delta \vdash A$, $\Delta \vdash B$, $(\alpha * C) \in \Delta$ and well-formed context $[B/\alpha]\Delta$, then $[B/\alpha]\Delta \vdash [B/\alpha]A$.*

$\boxed{A <: B \rightsquigarrow co}$ *(Declarative subtyping)*

$$\frac{}{A <: A \rightsquigarrow \mathsf{id}}\ \textsc{S-refl} \qquad \frac{A_2 <: A_3 \rightsquigarrow co_1 \qquad A_1 <: A_2 \rightsquigarrow co_2}{A_1 <: A_3 \rightsquigarrow co_1 \circ co_2}\ \textsc{S-trans} \qquad \frac{}{A <: \top \rightsquigarrow \mathsf{top}}\ \textsc{S-top}$$

$$\frac{A <: B \rightsquigarrow co}{\{l : A\} <: \{l : B\} \rightsquigarrow co}\ \textsc{S-rcd} \qquad \frac{}{A_1 \,\&\, A_2 <: A_1 \rightsquigarrow \pi_1}\ \textsc{S-andl} \qquad \frac{}{A_1 \,\&\, A_2 <: A_2 \rightsquigarrow \pi_2}\ \textsc{S-andr}$$

$$\frac{B_1 <: A_1 \rightsquigarrow co_1 \qquad A_2 <: B_2 \rightsquigarrow co_2}{A_1 \to A_2 <: B_1 \to B_2 \rightsquigarrow co_1 \to co_2}\ \textsc{S-arr} \qquad \frac{A_1 <: A_2 \rightsquigarrow co_1 \qquad A_1 <: A_3 \rightsquigarrow co_2}{A_1 <: A_2 \,\&\, A_3 \rightsquigarrow \langle co_1, co_2 \rangle}\ \textsc{S-and}$$

$$\frac{}{(A_1 \to A_2) \,\&\, (A_1 \to A_3) <: A_1 \to A_2 \,\&\, A_3 \rightsquigarrow \mathsf{dist}_{\to}}\ \textsc{S-distArr} \qquad \frac{}{\top <: \top \to \top \rightsquigarrow \mathsf{top}_{\to}}\ \textsc{S-topArr}$$

$$\frac{}{\{l : A\} \,\&\, \{l : B\} <: \{l : A \,\&\, B\} \rightsquigarrow \mathsf{id}}\ \textsc{S-distRcd} \qquad \frac{}{\top <: \{l : \top\} \rightsquigarrow \mathsf{id}}\ \textsc{S-topRcd} \qquad \frac{}{\bot <: A \rightsquigarrow \mathsf{bot}}\ \textsc{S-bot}$$

$$\frac{B_1 <: B_2 \rightsquigarrow co \qquad A_2 <: A_1}{\forall (\alpha * A_1).\, B_1 <: \forall (\alpha * A_2).\, B_2 \rightsquigarrow co_{\forall}}\ \textsc{S-forall} \qquad \frac{}{\top <: \forall (\alpha * \top).\, \top \rightsquigarrow \mathsf{top}_{\forall}}\ \textsc{S-topAll}$$

$$\frac{}{(\forall (\alpha * A).\, B_1) \,\&\, (\forall (\alpha * A).\, B_2) <: \forall (\alpha * A).\, B_1 \,\&\, B_2 \rightsquigarrow \mathsf{dist}_{\forall}}\ \textsc{S-distAll}$$

Fig. 4. Declarative subtyping

Declarative subtyping. F_i^+'s subtyping judgment is another major difference to F_i, because it features BCD-style subtyping and a rule for the bottom type. The full set of subtyping rules are shown in Fig. 4. The reader is advised to ignore the gray parts for now. Our subtyping rules extend the BCD-style subtyping rules from λ_i^+ [5] with a rule for parametric (disjoint) polymorphism (rule S-FORALL). Moreover, we have three new rules: rule S-BOT for the bottom type, and rules S-DISTALL and S-TOPALL for distributivity of disjoint quantification. The subtyping relation is a partial order (rules S-REFL and S-TRANS). Most of the rules are quite standard. $\bot$ is a subtype of all types (rule S-BOT). Subtyping of disjoint quantification is covariant in its body, and contravariant in its disjointness constraints (rule S-FORALL). Of particular interest are those so-called "distributivity" rules: rule S-DISTARR says intersections distribute over arrows; rule S-DISTRCD says intersections distribute over records. Similarly, rule S-DISTALL dictates that intersections may distribute over disjoint quantifiers.

$$\boxed{\Delta; \Gamma \vdash E \Rightarrow A \rightsquigarrow e} \qquad \textit{(Inference)}$$

$$\text{T-TOP}\ \frac{\vdash \Delta \qquad \Delta \vdash \Gamma}{\Delta; \Gamma \vdash \top \Rightarrow \top \rightsquigarrow \langle\rangle} \qquad \text{T-NAT}\ \frac{\vdash \Delta \qquad \Delta \vdash \Gamma}{\Delta; \Gamma \vdash i \Rightarrow \mathsf{Int} \rightsquigarrow i} \qquad \text{T-VAR}\ \frac{\vdash \Delta \qquad \Delta \vdash \Gamma \qquad (x : A) \in \Gamma}{\Delta; \Gamma \vdash x \Rightarrow A \rightsquigarrow x}$$

$$\text{T-APP}\ \frac{\Delta; \Gamma \vdash E_1 \Rightarrow A_1 \to A_2 \rightsquigarrow e_1 \qquad \Delta; \Gamma \vdash E_2 \Leftarrow A_1 \rightsquigarrow e_2}{\Delta; \Gamma \vdash E_1\, E_2 \Rightarrow A_2 \rightsquigarrow e_1\, e_2} \qquad \text{T-MERGE}\ \frac{\Delta; \Gamma \vdash E_1 \Rightarrow A_1 \rightsquigarrow e_1 \qquad \Delta; \Gamma \vdash E_2 \Rightarrow A_2 \rightsquigarrow e_2 \qquad \Delta \vdash A_1 * A_2}{\Delta; \Gamma \vdash E_1 \,,,\, E_2 \Rightarrow A_1 \,\&\, A_2 \rightsquigarrow \langle e_1, e_2 \rangle}$$

$$\text{T-ANNO}\ \frac{\Delta; \Gamma \vdash E \Leftarrow A \rightsquigarrow e}{\Delta; \Gamma \vdash E : A \Rightarrow A \rightsquigarrow e} \qquad \text{T-RCD}\ \frac{\Delta; \Gamma \vdash E \Rightarrow A \rightsquigarrow e}{\Delta; \Gamma \vdash \{l = E\} \Rightarrow \{l : A\} \rightsquigarrow e}$$

$$\text{T-PROJ}\ \frac{\Delta; \Gamma \vdash E \Rightarrow \{l : A\} \rightsquigarrow e}{\Delta; \Gamma \vdash E.l \Rightarrow A \rightsquigarrow e} \qquad \text{T-TABS}\ \frac{\Delta, \alpha * A; \Gamma \vdash E \Rightarrow B \rightsquigarrow e \qquad \Delta \vdash A \qquad \Delta \vdash \Gamma}{\Delta; \Gamma \vdash \Lambda(\alpha * A).\, E \Rightarrow \forall(\alpha * A).\, B \rightsquigarrow \Lambda\alpha.\, e}$$

$$\text{T-TAPP}\ \frac{\Delta; \Gamma \vdash E \Rightarrow \forall(\alpha * B).\, C \rightsquigarrow e \qquad \Delta \vdash A * B}{\Delta; \Gamma \vdash E\, A \Rightarrow [A/\alpha]C \rightsquigarrow e\, |A|}$$

$$\boxed{\Delta; \Gamma \vdash E \Leftarrow A \rightsquigarrow e} \qquad \textit{(Checking)}$$

$$\text{T-ABS}\ \frac{\Delta \vdash A \qquad \Delta; \Gamma, x : A \vdash E \Leftarrow B \rightsquigarrow e}{\Delta; \Gamma \vdash \lambda x.\, E \Leftarrow A \to B \rightsquigarrow \lambda x.\, e} \qquad \text{T-SUB}\ \frac{\Delta; \Gamma \vdash E \Rightarrow B \rightsquigarrow e \qquad B <: A \rightsquigarrow co}{\Delta; \Gamma \vdash E \Leftarrow A \rightsquigarrow co\, e}$$

Fig. 5. Bidirectional type system

Typing rules. F_i^+ features a bidirectional type system inherited from F_i. The full set of typing rules are shown in Fig. 5. Again we ignore the gray parts and explain them in Sect. 3.3. The inference judgment $\Delta; \Gamma \vdash E \Rightarrow A$ says that we can synthesize the type A under the contexts Δ and Γ. The checking judgment $\Delta; \Gamma \vdash E \Leftarrow A$ asserts that E checks against the type A under the contexts Δ and Γ. Most of the rules are quite standard in the literature. The merge expression $E_1 \,,,\, E_2$ is well-typed if both sub-expressions are well-typed, and their types are *disjoint* (rule T-MERGE). The disjointness relation will be explained in Sect. 3.2. To infer a type abstraction (rule T-TABS), we add disjointness constraints to the type context. For a type application (rule T-TAPP), we check that the type argument satisfies the disjointness constraints. Rules T-MERGE and T-TAPP are the only rules checking disjointness.

$\boxed{\rceil A \lceil}$ *(Top-like types)*

$$\textsc{TL-top}\ \frac{}{\rceil \top \lceil} \qquad \textsc{TL-and}\ \frac{\rceil A \lceil \quad \rceil B \lceil}{\rceil A \,\&\, B \lceil} \qquad \textsc{TL-arr}\ \frac{\rceil B \lceil}{\rceil A \to B \lceil} \qquad \textsc{TL-rcd}\ \frac{\rceil A \lceil}{\rceil \{l : A\} \lceil} \qquad \textsc{TL-all}\ \frac{\rceil B \lceil}{\rceil \forall(\alpha * A).\, B \lceil}$$

$\boxed{\Delta \vdash A * B}$ *(Disjointness)*

$$\textsc{D-topL}\ \frac{\rceil A \lceil}{\Delta \vdash A * B} \qquad \textsc{D-topR}\ \frac{\rceil B \lceil}{\Delta \vdash A * B} \qquad \textsc{D-arr}\ \frac{\Delta \vdash A_2 * B_2}{\Delta \vdash A_1 \to A_2 * B_1 \to B_2}$$

$$\textsc{D-andL}\ \frac{\Delta \vdash A_1 * B \qquad \Delta \vdash A_2 * B}{\Delta \vdash A_1 \,\&\, A_2 * B} \qquad \textsc{D-andR}\ \frac{\Delta \vdash A * B_1 \qquad \Delta \vdash A * B_2}{\Delta \vdash A * B_1 \,\&\, B_2}$$

$$\textsc{D-rcdEq}\ \frac{\Delta \vdash A * B}{\Delta \vdash \{l : A\} * \{l : B\}} \qquad \textsc{D-rcdNeq}\ \frac{l_1 \neq l_2}{\Delta \vdash \{l_1 : A\} * \{l_2 : B\}} \qquad \textsc{D-tvarL}\ \frac{(\alpha * A) \in \Delta \qquad A <: B}{\Delta \vdash \alpha * B}$$

$$\textsc{D-tvarR}\ \frac{(\alpha * A) \in \Delta \qquad A <: B}{\Delta \vdash B * \alpha} \qquad \textsc{D-forall}\ \frac{\Delta, \alpha * A_1 \,\&\, A_2 \vdash B_1 * B_2}{\Delta \vdash \forall(\alpha * A_1).\, B_1 * \forall(\alpha * A_2).\, B_2} \qquad \textsc{D-ax}\ \frac{A *_{ax} B}{\Delta \vdash A * B}$$

Fig. 6. Selected rules for disjointness

3.2 Disjointness

We now turn to another core judgment of F_i^+—the disjointness relation, shown in Fig. 6. The disjointness rules are mostly inherited from F_i [2], but the new bottom type requires a notable change regarding disjointness with *top-like types.*

Top-like types. Top-like types are all types that are isomorphic to $\top$ (i.e., simultaneously sub- and supertypes of $\top$). Hence, they are inhabited by a single value, isomorphic to the $\top$ value. Figure 6 captures this notion in a syntax-directed fashion in the $\rceil A \lceil$ predicate. As a historical note, the concept of top-like types was already known by Barendregt et al. [3]. The λ_i calculus [36] re-discovered it and coined the term "top-like types"; the F_i calculus [2] extended it with universal quantifiers. Note that in both calculi, top-like types are solely employed for enabling a syntactic method of proving coherence, and due to the lack of BCD subtyping, they do not have a type-theoretic interpretation of top-like types.

Disjointness rules. The disjointness judgment $\Delta \vdash A * B$ is helpful to check whether the merge of two expressions of type A and B preserves coherence. Incoherence arises when both expressions produce distinct values for the same type, either directly when they are both of that same type, or through implicit

Types	τ	$::= \mathsf{Int} \mid \langle\rangle \mid \tau_1 \to \tau_2 \mid \tau_1 \times \tau_2 \mid \alpha \mid \forall \alpha.\, \tau$
Terms	e	$::= x \mid i \mid \langle\rangle \mid \lambda x.\, e \mid e_1\, e_2 \mid \langle e_1, e_2 \rangle \mid \Lambda \alpha.\, e \mid e\, \tau \mid co\, e$
Coercions	co	$::= \mathsf{id} \mid co_1 \circ co_2 \mid \mathsf{top} \mid \mathsf{bot} \mid co_1 \to co_2 \mid \langle co_1, co_2 \rangle \mid \pi_1 \mid \pi_2$
		$\mid\ co_{\forall} \mid \mathsf{dist}_{\to} \mid \mathsf{top}_{\to} \mid \mathsf{top}_{\forall} \mid \mathsf{dist}_{\forall}$
Values	v	$::= i \mid \langle\rangle \mid \lambda x.\, e \mid \langle v_1, v_2 \rangle \mid \Lambda \alpha.\, e \mid (co_1 \to co_2)\, v \mid co_{\forall}\, v$
		$\mid\ \mathsf{dist}_{\to}\, v \mid \mathsf{top}_{\to}\, v \mid \mathsf{top}_{\forall}\, v \mid \mathsf{dist}_{\forall}\, v$
Term contexts	Ψ	$::= \bullet \mid \Psi, x : \tau$
Type contexts	Φ	$::= \bullet \mid \Phi, \alpha$
Evaluation contexts	$\mathcal{E}$	$::= [\cdot] \mid \mathcal{E}\, e \mid v\, \mathcal{E} \mid \langle \mathcal{E}, e \rangle \mid \langle v, \mathcal{E} \rangle \mid co\, \mathcal{E} \mid \mathcal{E}\, \tau$

Fig. 7. Syntax of F_{co}

upcasting to a common supertype. Of course we can safely disregard top-like types in this matter because they do not have two distinct values. In short, it suffices to check that the two types have only top-like supertypes in common.

Because $\bot$ and any another type A always have A as a common supertype, it follows that $\bot$ is only disjoint to A when A is top-like. More generally, if A is a top-like type, then A is disjoint to any type. This is the rationale behind the two rules D-TOPL and D-TOPR, which generalize and subsume $\Delta \vdash \top * A$ and $\Delta \vdash A * \top$ from F_i, and also cater to the bottom type. Two other interesting rules are D-TVARL and D-TVARR, which dictate that a type variable α is disjoint with some type B if its disjointness constraints A is a subtype of B. Disjointness axioms $A *_{ax} B$ (appearing in rule D-AX) take care of two types with different type constructors (e.g., Int and records). Axiom rules can be found in the appendix. Finally we note that the disjointness relation is symmetric.

3.3 Elaboration and Type Safety

The dynamic semantics of F_i^+ is given by elaboration into a target calculus. The target calculus F_{co} is the standard call-by-value System F extended with products and coercions. The syntax of F_{co} is shown in Fig. 7.

Type translation. Definition 1 defines the type translation function $|\cdot|$ from F_i^+ types A to F_{co} types τ. Most cases are straightforward. For example, $\bot$ is mapped to an uninhabited type $\forall \alpha.\, \alpha$; disjoint quantification is mapped to universal quantification, dropping the disjointness constraints. $|\cdot|$ is naturally extended to work on contexts as well.

Definition 1. *Type translation* $|\cdot|$ *is defined as follows:*

$$|\mathsf{Int}| = \mathsf{Int} \qquad |\top| = \langle\rangle \qquad |A \to B| = |A| \to |B|$$
$$|A \,\&\, B| = |A| \times |B| \qquad |\{l : A\}| = |A| \qquad |\alpha| = \alpha$$
$$|\bot| = \forall \alpha.\, \alpha \qquad |\forall (\alpha * A).\, B| = \forall \alpha.\, |B|$$

$\boxed{e \longrightarrow e'}$ *(Single-step reduction)*

$$\text{R-FORALL}\quad \frac{}{(co_{\forall}\ v)\ \tau \longrightarrow co\ (v\ \tau)} \qquad \text{R-TOPALL}\quad \frac{}{(\mathsf{top}_{\forall}\ \langle\rangle)\ \tau \longrightarrow \langle\rangle} \qquad \text{R-DISTALL}\quad \frac{}{(\mathsf{dist}_{\forall}\ \langle v_1, v_2\rangle)\ \tau \longrightarrow \langle v_1\ \tau, v_2\ \tau\rangle}$$

$$\text{R-TAPP}\quad \frac{}{(\Lambda\alpha.\ e)\ \tau \longrightarrow [\tau/\alpha]e} \qquad \text{R-APP}\quad \frac{}{(\lambda x.\ e)\ v \longrightarrow [v/x]e} \qquad \text{R-CTXT}\quad \frac{e \longrightarrow e'}{\mathcal{E}[e] \longrightarrow \mathcal{E}[e']}$$

Fig. 8. Selected reduction rules

Coercions and coercive subtyping. We follow prior work [5,6] by having a syntactic category for coercions [22]. In Fig. 7, we have several new coercions: bot, $co_{\forall}$, $\mathsf{dist}_{\forall}$ and $\mathsf{top}_{\forall}$ due to the addition of polymorphism and bottom type. As seen in Fig. 4 the coercive subtyping judgment has the form $A <: B \rightsquigarrow co$, which says that the subtyping derivation for $A <: B$ produces a coercion co that converts terms of type $|A|$ to $|B|$.

F_{co} *static semantics.* The typing rules of F_{co} are quite standard. We have one rule T-CAPP regarding coercion application, which uses the judgment $co{::}\tau \rhd \tau'$ to type coercions. We show two representative rules CT-FORALL and CT-BOT.

$$\text{T-CAPP}\quad \frac{\Phi; \Psi \vdash e : \tau \qquad co :: \tau \rhd \tau'}{\Phi; \Psi \vdash co\ e : \tau'} \qquad \text{CT-FORALL}\quad \frac{co :: \tau_1 \rhd \tau_2}{co_{\forall} :: \forall\alpha.\ \tau_1 \rhd \forall\alpha.\ \tau_2} \qquad \text{CT-BOT}\quad \frac{}{\mathsf{bot} :: \forall\alpha.\ \alpha \rhd \tau}$$

F_{co} *dynamic semantics.* The dynamic semantics of F_{co} is mostly unremarkable. We write $e \longrightarrow e'$ to mean one-step reduction. Figure 8 shows selected reduction rules. The first line shows three representative rules regarding coercion reductions. They do not contribute to computation but merely rearrange coercions. Our coercion reduction rules are quite standard but not efficient in terms of space. Nevertheless, there is existing work on space-efficient coercions [23,50], which should be applicable to our work as well. Rule R-APP is the usual β-rule that performs actual computation, and rule R-CTXT handles reduction under an evaluation context. As usual, $\longrightarrow^*$ is the reflexive, transitive closure of $\longrightarrow$. Now we can show that F_{co} is type safe:

Theorem 1 (Preservation). *If* $\bullet; \bullet \vdash e : \tau$ *and* $e \longrightarrow e'$, *then* $\bullet; \bullet \vdash e' : \tau$.

Theorem 2 (Progress). *If* $\bullet; \bullet \vdash e : \tau$, *either* e *is a value, or* $\exists e'.\ e \longrightarrow e'$.

Elaboration. Now consider the translation parts in Fig. 5. The key idea of the translation follows the prior work [2,5,16,36]: merges are elaborated to pairs (rule T-MERGE); disjoint quantification and disjoint type applications (rules T-TABS and T-TAPP)) are elaborated to regular universal quantification and type applications, respectively. Finally, the following lemma connects F_i^+ to F_{co}:

Lemma 2 (Elaboration soundness). *We have that:*

- *If* $A <: B \rightsquigarrow co$, *then* $co :: |A| \rhd |B|$.
- *If* $\Delta; \Gamma \vdash E \Rightarrow A \rightsquigarrow e$, *then* $|\Delta|; |\Gamma| \vdash e : |A|$.
- *If* $\Delta; \Gamma \vdash E \Leftarrow A \rightsquigarrow e$, *then* $|\Delta|; |\Gamma| \vdash e : |A|$.

4 Algorithmic System and Decidability

The subtyping relation in Fig. 4 is highly non-algorithmic due to the presence of a transitivity rule. This section presents an alternative algorithmic formulation. Our algorithm extends that of λ_i^+, which itself was inspired by Pierce's decision procedure [38], to handle disjoint quantifiers and the bottom type. We then prove that the algorithm is sound and complete with respect to declarative subtyping.

Additionally we prove that the subtyping and disjointness relations are decidable. Although the proofs of this fact are fairly straightforward, it is nonetheless remarkable since it contrasts with the subtyping relation for (full) $\mathsf{F}_{<:}$ [10], which is undecidable [40]. Thus while bounded quantification is infamous for its undecidability, disjoint quantification has the nicer property of being decidable.

4.1 Algorithmic Subtyping Rules

While Fig. 4 is a fine specification of how subtyping should behave, it cannot be read directly as a subtyping algorithm for two reasons: (1) the conclusions of rules S-REFL and S-TRANS overlap with the other rules, and (2) the premises of rule S-TRANS mention a type that does not appear in the conclusion. Simply dropping the two offending rules from the system is not possible without losing expressivity [29]. Thus we need a different approach. Following λ_i^+, we intend the algorithmic judgment $\mathcal{Q} \vdash A <: B$ to be equivalent to $A <: \mathcal{Q} \Rightarrow B$, where $\mathcal{Q}$ is a queue used to track record labels, domain types and disjointness constraints. The full rules of the algorithmic subtyping of F_i^+ are shown Fig. 9.

Definition 2 ($\mathcal{Q} ::= [] \mid l, \mathcal{Q} \mid B, \mathcal{Q} \mid \alpha * B, \mathcal{Q}$). $\mathcal{Q} \Rightarrow A$ *is defined as follows:*

$$\begin{array}{ll} [] \Rightarrow A = A & (B, \mathcal{Q}) \Rightarrow A = B \rightarrow (\mathcal{Q} \Rightarrow A) \\ (l, \mathcal{Q}) \Rightarrow A = \{l : \mathcal{Q} \Rightarrow A\} & (\alpha * B, \mathcal{Q}) \Rightarrow A = \forall(\alpha * B).\, \mathcal{Q} \Rightarrow A \end{array}$$

For brevity of the algorithm, we use metavariable c to mean type constants:

$$\text{Type Constants} \quad c ::= \mathsf{Int} \mid \bot \mid \alpha$$

The basic idea of $\mathcal{Q} \vdash A <: B$ is to perform a case analysis on B until it reaches type constants. We explain new rules regarding disjoint quantification and the bottom type. When a quantifier is encountered in B, rule A-FORALL pushes the type variables with its disjointness constraints onto $\mathcal{Q}$ and continue with the body. Correspondingly, in rule A-ALLCONST, when a quantifier is encountered in A, and the head of $\mathcal{Q}$ is a type variable, this variable is popped out and we continue with the body. Rule A-BOT is similar to its declarative counterpart. Two meta-functions $[\![\mathcal{Q}]\!]^{\top}$ and $[\![\mathcal{Q}]\!]^{\&}$ are meant to generate correct forms of coercions, and their definitions are shown in the appendix. For other algorithmic rules, we refer to λ_i^+ [5] for detailed explanations.

$\boxed{\mathcal{Q} \vdash A <: B \rightsquigarrow co}$ *(Algorithmic subtyping)*

$$\text{A-TOP}\quad \frac{}{\mathcal{Q} \vdash A <: \top \rightsquigarrow [\![\mathcal{Q}]\!]^{\top} \circ \mathsf{top}} \qquad \text{A-AND}\quad \frac{\mathcal{Q} \vdash A <: B_1 \rightsquigarrow co_1 \qquad \mathcal{Q} \vdash A <: B_2 \rightsquigarrow co_2}{\mathcal{Q} \vdash A <: B_1 \,\&\, B_2 \rightsquigarrow [\![\mathcal{Q}]\!]^{\&} \circ \langle co_1, co_2 \rangle}$$

$$\text{A-ARR}\quad \frac{\mathcal{Q}, B_1 \vdash A <: B_2 \rightsquigarrow co}{\mathcal{Q} \vdash A <: B_1 \to B_2 \rightsquigarrow co} \qquad \text{A-RCD}\quad \frac{\mathcal{Q}, l \vdash A <: B \rightsquigarrow co}{\mathcal{Q} \vdash A <: \{l : B\} \rightsquigarrow co}$$

$$\text{A-FORALL}\quad \frac{\mathcal{Q}, \alpha * B_1 \vdash A <: B_2 \rightsquigarrow co}{\mathcal{Q} \vdash A <: \forall(\alpha * B_1).\, B_2 \rightsquigarrow co} \qquad \text{A-CONST}\quad \frac{}{[\,] \vdash c <: c \rightsquigarrow \mathsf{id}} \qquad \text{A-BOT}\quad \frac{}{\mathcal{Q} \vdash \bot <: c \rightsquigarrow \mathsf{bot}}$$

$$\text{A-ARRCONST}\quad \frac{[\,] \vdash A <: A_1 \rightsquigarrow co_1 \qquad \mathcal{Q} \vdash A_2 <: c \rightsquigarrow co_2}{A, \mathcal{Q} \vdash A_1 \to A_2 <: c \rightsquigarrow co_1 \to co_2} \qquad \text{A-RCDCONST}\quad \frac{\mathcal{Q} \vdash A <: c \rightsquigarrow co}{l, \mathcal{Q} \vdash \{l : A\} <: c \rightsquigarrow co}$$

$$\text{A-ANDCONST}\quad \frac{\mathcal{Q} \vdash A_i <: c \rightsquigarrow co \qquad i \in \{1, 2\}}{\mathcal{Q} \vdash A_1 \,\&\, A_2 <: c \rightsquigarrow co \circ \pi_i} \qquad \text{A-ALLCONST}\quad \frac{[\,] \vdash A <: A_1 \qquad \mathcal{Q} \vdash A_2 <: c \rightsquigarrow co}{(\alpha * A, \mathcal{Q}) \vdash \forall(\alpha * A_1).\, A_2 <: c \rightsquigarrow co_{\forall}}$$

Fig. 9. Algorithmic subtyping

Correctness of the algorithm. We prove that the algorithm is sound and complete with respect to the specification. We refer the reader to our Coq formalization for more details. We only show the two major theorems:

Theorem 3 (Soundness). *If* $\mathcal{Q} \vdash A <: B \rightsquigarrow co$ *then* $A <: \mathcal{Q} \Rightarrow B \rightsquigarrow co$.

Theorem 4 (Completeness). *If* $A <: B \rightsquigarrow co$*, then* $\exists co'.\ [\,] \vdash A <: B \rightsquigarrow co'$.

4.2 Decidability

Moreover, we prove that our algorithmic type system is decidable. To see this, first notice that the bidirectional type system is syntax-directed, so we only need to show decidability of algorithmic subtyping and disjointness. The full (manual) proofs for decidability can be found in the appendix.

Lemma 3 (Decidability of algorithmic subtyping). *Given* $\mathcal{Q}$*,* A *and* B*, it is decidable whether there exists* co*, such that* $\mathcal{Q} \vdash A <: B \rightsquigarrow co$.

Lemma 4 (Decidability of disjointness checking). *Given* Δ*,* A *and* B*, it is decidable whether* $\Delta \vdash A * B$.

One interesting observation here is that although our disjointness quantification has a similar shape to bounded quantification $\forall(\alpha <: A).\, B$ in $\mathsf{F}_{<:}$ [10], subtyping for $\mathsf{F}_{<:}$ is undecidable [40]. In $\mathsf{F}_{<:}$, the subtyping relation between bounded quantification is:

$$\frac{\Delta \vdash A_2 <: A_1 \qquad \Delta, \alpha <: A_2 \vdash B_1 <: B_2}{\Delta \vdash \forall(\alpha <: A_1).\, B_1 <: \forall(\alpha <: A_2).\, B_2} \text{ FSUB-FORALL}$$

Compared with rule S-FORALL, both rules are contravariant on bounded/disjoint types, and covariant on the body. However, with bounded quantification it is fundamental to track the bounds in the environment, which complicates the design of the rules and makes subtyping undecidable with rule FSUB-FORALL. Decidability can be recovered by employing an invariant rule for bounded quantification (that is by forcing A_1 and A_2 to be identical). Disjoint quantification does not require such invariant rule for decidability.

5 Establishing Coherence for F_i^+

In this section, we establish the coherence property for F_i^+. The proof strategy mostly follows that of λ_i^+, but the construction of the heterogeneous logical relation is significantly more complicated. Firstly in Sect. 5.1 we discuss why adding BCD subtyping to disjoint polymorphism introduces significant complications. In Sect. 5.2, we discuss why a natural extension of System F's logical relation to deal with disjoint polymorphism fails. The technical difficulty is *well-foundedness*, stemming from the interaction between impredicativity and disjointness. Finally in Sect. 5.3, we present our (predicative) logical relation that is specially crafted to prove coherence for F_i^+.

5.1 The Challenge

Before we tackle the coherence of F_i^+, let us first consider how F_i (and its predecessor λ_i) enforces coherence. Its essentially syntactic approach is to make sure that there is at most one subtyping derivation for any two types. As an immediate consequence, the produced coercions are uniquely determined and thus the calculus is clearly coherent. Key to this approach is the invariant that the type system only produces *disjoint* intersection types. As we mentioned in Sect. 3, this invariant complicates the calculus and its metatheory, and leads to a weaker substitution lemma. Moreover, the syntactic coherence approach is incompatible with BCD subtyping, which leads to multiple subtyping derivations with different coercions and requires a more general substitution lemma. To accommodate BCD into λ_i, Bi et al. [5] have created the λ_i^+ calculus and developed a semantically-founded proof method based on logical relations. Because λ_i^+ does not feature polymorphism, the problem at hand is to incorporate support for polymorphism in this semantic approach to coherence, which turns out to be more challenging than is apparent.

$$(v_1, v_2) \in \mathcal{V}[\![\mathsf{Int}; \mathsf{Int}]\!] \triangleq \exists i.\, v_1 = v_2 = i$$
$$(v_1, v_2) \in \mathcal{V}[\![\tau_1 \to \tau_2; \tau_1' \to \tau_2']\!] \triangleq \forall (v, v') \in \mathcal{V}[\![\tau_1; \tau_1']\!].\, (v_1\, v, v_2\, v') \in \mathcal{E}[\![\tau_2; \tau_2']\!]$$
$$(\langle v_1, v_2\rangle, v_3) \in \mathcal{V}[\![\tau_1 \times \tau_2; \tau_3]\!] \triangleq (v_1, v_3) \in \mathcal{V}[\![\tau_1; \tau_3]\!] \wedge (v_2, v_3) \in \mathcal{V}[\![\tau_2; \tau_3]\!]$$
$$(v_3, \langle v_1, v_2\rangle) \in \mathcal{V}[\![\tau_3; \tau_1 \times \tau_2]\!] \triangleq (v_3, v_1) \in \mathcal{V}[\![\tau_3; \tau_1]\!] \wedge (v_3, v_2) \in \mathcal{V}[\![\tau_3; \tau_2]\!]$$

Fig. 10. Selected cases from λ_i^+'s canonicity relation

5.2 Impredicativity and Disjointness at Odds

Figure 10 shows selected cases of *canonicity*, which is λ_i^+'s (heterogeneous) logical relation used in the coherence proof. The definition captures that two values v_1 and v_2 of types τ_1 and τ_2 are in $\mathcal{V}[\![\tau_1; \tau_2]\!]$ iff either the types are disjoint or the types are equal and the values are semantically equivalent. Because both alternatives entail coherence, canonicity is key to λ_i^+'s coherence proof.

Well-foundedness issues. For F_i^+, we need to extend canonicity with additional cases to account for universally quantified types. For reasons that will become clear in Sect. 5.3, the type indices become source types (rather than target types as in Fig. 10). A naive formulation of one case rule is:

$$\begin{aligned}&(v_1, v_2) \in \mathcal{V}[\![\forall(\alpha * A_1).\, B_1; \forall(\alpha * A_2).\, B_2]\!] \triangleq \\ &\qquad \forall C_1 * A_1, C_2 * A_2.\, (v_1\, |C_1|, v_2\, |C_2|) \in \mathcal{E}[\![[C_1/\alpha]B_1; [C_2/\alpha]B_2]\!]\end{aligned}$$

This case is problematic because it destroys the well-foundedness of λ_i^+'s logical relation, which is based on structural induction on the type indices. Indeed, the type $[C_1/\alpha]B_1$ may well be larger than $\forall(\alpha * A_1).\, B_1$.

However, System F's well-known parametricity logical relation [43] provides us with a means to avoid this problem. Rather than performing the type substitution immediately as in the above rule, we can defer it to a later point by adding it to an extra parameter ρ of the relation, which accumulates the deferred substitutions. This yields a modified rule where the type indices in the recursive occurrences are indeed smaller:

$$\begin{aligned}&(v_1, v_2) \in \mathcal{V}[\![\forall(\alpha * A_1).\, B_1; \forall(\alpha * A_2).\, B_2]\!]_\rho \triangleq \\ &\qquad \forall C_1 * A_1, C_2 * A_2.(v_1\, |C_1|, v_2\, |C_2|) \in \mathcal{E}[\![B_1; B_2]\!]_{\rho[\alpha \mapsto (C_1, C_2)]}\end{aligned}$$

Of course, the deferred substitution has to be performed eventually, to be precise when the type indices are type variables.

$$(v_1, v_2) \in \mathcal{V}[\![\alpha; \alpha]\!]_\rho \triangleq (v_1, v_2) \in \mathcal{V}[\![\rho_1(\alpha); \rho_2(\alpha)]\!]_\emptyset$$

Unfortunately, this way we have not only moved the type substitution to the type variable case, but also the ill-foundedness problem. Indeed, this problem is also present in System F. The standard solution is to not fix the relation R by which values at type α are related to $\mathcal{V}[\![\rho_1(\alpha); \rho_2(\alpha)]\!]$, but instead to make it a parameter that is tracked by ρ. This yields the following two rules for disjoint quantification and type variables:

$$(v_1, v_2) \in \mathcal{V}[\![\forall(\alpha * A_1).\, B_1; \forall(\alpha * A_2).\, B_2]\!]_\rho \triangleq \forall C_1 * A_1, C_2 * A_2, \mathsf{R} \subseteq C_1 \times C_2.$$
$$(v_1\,|C_1|, v_2\,|C_2|) \in \mathcal{E}[\![B_1; B_2]\!]_{\rho[\alpha \mapsto (C_1, C_2, \mathsf{R})]}$$
$$(v_1, v_2) \in \mathcal{V}[\![\alpha; \alpha]\!]_\rho \triangleq (v_1, v_2) \in \rho_{\mathsf{R}}(\alpha)$$

Now we have finally recovered the well-foundedness of the relation. It is again structurally inductive on the size of the type indexes.

Heterogeneous issues. We have not yet accounted for one major difference between the parametricity relation, from which we have borrowed ideas, and the canonicity relation, to which we have been adding. The former is homogeneous (i.e., the types of the two values is the same) and therefore has one type index, while the latter is heterogeneous (i.e., the two values may have different types) and therefore has two type indices. Thus we must also consider cases like $\mathcal{V}[\![\alpha; \mathsf{Int}]\!]$. A definition that seems to handle this case appropriately is:

$$(v_1, v_2) \in \mathcal{V}[\![\alpha; \mathsf{Int}]\!]_\rho \triangleq (v_1, v_2) \in \mathcal{V}[\![\rho_1(\alpha); \mathsf{Int}]\!]_\emptyset \tag{1}$$

Here is an example to motivate it. Let $E = \Lambda(\alpha * \top).\, ((\lambda x.\, x) : \alpha \,\&\, \mathsf{Int} \rightarrow \alpha \,\&\, \mathsf{Int})$. We expect that $E\,\mathsf{Int}\,1$ evaluates to $\langle 1, 1\rangle$. To prove that, we need to show $(1, 1) \in \mathcal{V}[\![\alpha; \mathsf{Int}]\!]_{[\alpha \mapsto (\mathsf{Int}, \mathsf{Int}, \mathsf{R})]}$. According to Eq. (1), this is indeed the case. However, we run into ill-foundedness issue again, because $\rho_1(\alpha)$ could be larger than α. Alas, this time the parametricity relation has no solution for us.

5.3 The Canonicity Relation for F_i^+

In light of the fact that substitution in the logical relation seems unavoidable in our setting, and that impredicativity is at odds with substitution, we turn to *predicativity*: we change rule T-TAPP to its predicative version:

$$\frac{\Delta; \Gamma \vdash E \Rightarrow \forall(\alpha * B).\, C \rightsquigarrow e \qquad \Delta \vdash t * B}{\Delta; \Gamma \vdash E\, t \Rightarrow [t/\alpha]C \rightsquigarrow e\,|t|}\ \textsc{T-tappMono}$$

where metavariable t ranges over monotypes (types minus disjoint quantification). We do not believe that predicativity is a severe restriction in practice, since many source languages (e.g., those based on the Hindley-Milner type system [24, 32] like Haskell and OCaml) are themselves predicative and do not require the full generality of an impredicative core language.

Luckily, substitution with monotypes does not prevent well-foundedness. Figure 11 defines the *canonicity* relation for F_i^+. The canonicity relation is a family of binary relations over F_{co} values that are *heterogeneous*, i.e., indexed by two F_i^+ types. Two points are worth mentioning. (1) An apparent difference from λ_i^+'s logical relation is that our relation is now indexed by *source types*. The

$$
\begin{aligned}
(v_1, v_2) \in \mathcal{V}[\![\mathsf{Int}; \mathsf{Int}]\!] &\triangleq \exists i.\, v_1 = v_2 = i \\
(v_1, v_2) \in \mathcal{V}[\![\{l : A\}; \{l : B\}]\!] &\triangleq (v_1, v_2) \in \mathcal{V}[\![A; B]\!] \\
(v_1, v_2) \in \mathcal{V}[\![A_1 \to B_1; A_2 \to B_2]\!] &\triangleq \forall (v_2', v_1') \in \mathcal{V}[\![A_2; A_1]\!].\, (v_1\, v_1', v_2\, v_2') \in \mathcal{E}[\![B_1; B_2]\!] \\
(\langle v_1, v_2 \rangle, v_3) \in \mathcal{V}[\![A \,\&\, B; C]\!] &\triangleq (v_1, v_3) \in \mathcal{V}[\![A; C]\!] \wedge (v_2, v_3) \in \mathcal{V}[\![B; C]\!] \\
(v_3, \langle v_1, v_2 \rangle) \in \mathcal{V}[\![C; A \,\&\, B]\!] &\triangleq (v_3, v_1) \in \mathcal{V}[\![C; A]\!] \wedge (v_3, v_2) \in \mathcal{V}[\![C; B]\!] \\
(v_1, v_2) \in \mathcal{V}[\![\forall (\alpha * A_1).\, B_1; \forall (\alpha * A_2).\, B_2]\!] &\triangleq \forall \bullet \vdash t * A_1 \,\&\, A_2.\, (v_1\, |t|, v_2\, |t|) \in \mathcal{E}[\![[t/\alpha]B_1; [t/\alpha]B_2]\!] \\
(v_1, v_2) \in \mathcal{V}[\![A; B]\!] &\triangleq \mathsf{true} \quad \text{otherwise} \\
(e_1, e_2) \in \mathcal{E}[\![A; B]\!] &\triangleq \exists v_1, v_2.\, e_1 \longrightarrow^* v_1 \wedge e_2 \longrightarrow^* v_2 \ \wedge (v_1, v_2) \in \mathcal{V}[\![A; B]\!]
\end{aligned}
$$

$$
\rho \in \mathcal{D}[\![\Delta]\!] \triangleq \frac{}{\emptyset \in \mathcal{D}[\![\bullet]\!]} \qquad \frac{\rho \in \mathcal{D}[\![\Delta]\!] \qquad \bullet \vdash t * \rho(B)}{\rho[\alpha \mapsto t] \in \mathcal{D}[\![\Delta, \alpha * B]\!]}
$$

$$
(\gamma_1, \gamma_2) \in \mathcal{G}[\![\Gamma]\!]_\rho \triangleq \frac{}{(\emptyset, \emptyset) \in \mathcal{G}[\![\bullet]\!]_\rho} \qquad \frac{(\gamma_1, \gamma_2) \in \mathcal{G}[\![\Gamma]\!]_\rho \qquad (v_1, v_2) \in \mathcal{V}[\![\rho(A); \rho(A)]\!]}{(\gamma_1[x \mapsto v_1], \gamma_2[x \mapsto v_2]) \in \mathcal{G}[\![\Gamma, x : A]\!]_\rho}
$$

Fig. 11. The canonicity relation for F_i^+

reason is that the type translation function (Definition 1) discards disjointness constraints, which are crucial in our setting, whereas λ_i^+'s type translation does not have information loss. (2) Heterogeneity allows relating values of different types, and in particular values whose types are disjoint. The rationale behind the canonicity relation is to combine equality checking from traditional (homogeneous) logical relations with disjointness checking. It consists of two relations: the value relation $\mathcal{V}[\![A; B]\!]$ relates *closed* values; and the expression relation $\mathcal{E}[\![A; B]\!]$—defined in terms of the value relation—relates closed expressions.

The relation $\mathcal{V}[\![A; B]\!]$ is defined by induction on the structures of A and B. For integers, it requires the two values to be literally the same. For two records to behave the same, their fields must behave the same. For two functions to behave the same, they are required to produce outputs related at B_1 and B_2 when given related inputs at A_1 and A_2. For the next two cases regarding intersection types, the relation distributes over intersection constructor $\&$. Of particular interest is the case for disjoint quantification. Notice that it *does not* quantify over arbitrary relations, but directly substitutes α with monotype t in B_1 and B_2. This means that our canonicity relation *does not* entail parametricity. However, it suffices for our purposes to prove coherence. Another noticeable thing is that we keep the invariant that A and B are closed types throughout the relation, so we no longer need to consider type variables. This simplifies things a lot. Note that when one type is $\bot$, two values are vacuously related because there simply are no values of type $\bot$. We need to show that the relation is indeed well-founded:

Lemma 5 (Well-foundedness). *The canonicity relation of* F_i^+ *is well-founded.*

Proof. Let $|\cdot|_\forall$ and $|\cdot|_s$ be the number of $\forall$-quantifies and the size of types, respectively. Consider the measure $\langle |\cdot|_\forall, |\cdot|_s \rangle$, where $\langle \dots \rangle$ denotes lexicographic order. For the case of disjoint quantification, the number of $\forall$-quantifiers decreases. For the other cases, the measure of $|\cdot|_\forall$ does not increase, and the measure of $|\cdot|_s$ strictly decreases. □

5.4 Establishing Coherence

Logical equivalence. The canonicity relation can be lifted to open expressions in the standard way, i.e., by considering all possible interpretations of free type and term variables. The logical interpretations of type and term contexts are found in the bottom half of Fig. 11.

Definition 3 (Logical equivalence $\backsimeq_{log}$)

$$\Delta;\Gamma \vdash e_1 \backsimeq_{log} e_2 : A; B \triangleq |\Delta|;|\Gamma| \vdash e_1 : |A| \wedge |\Delta|;|\Gamma| \vdash e_2 : |B| \wedge$$
$$(\forall \rho, \gamma_1, \gamma_2.\ \rho \in \mathcal{D}[\![\Delta]\!] \wedge (\gamma_1, \gamma_2) \in \mathcal{G}[\![\Gamma]\!]_\rho \Longrightarrow (\gamma_1(\rho_1(e_1)), \gamma_2(\rho_2(e_2))) \in \mathcal{E}[\![\rho(A); \rho(B)]\!])$$

For conciseness, we write $\Delta;\Gamma \vdash e_1 \backsimeq_{log} e_2 : A$ to mean $\Delta;\Gamma \vdash e_1 \backsimeq_{log} e_2 : A; A$.

Contextual equivalence. Following λ_i^+, the notion of coherence is based on *contextual equivalence.* The intuition is that two programs are equivalent if we *cannot* tell them apart in any context. As usual, contextual equivalence is expressed using *expression contexts* ($\mathcal{C}$ and $\mathcal{D}$ denote F_i^+ and F_{co} expression contexts, respectively), Due to the bidirectional nature of the type system, the typing judgment of $\mathcal{C}$ features 4 different forms (full rules are in the appendix), e.g., $\mathcal{C} : (\Delta;\Gamma \Rightarrow A) \mapsto (\Delta';\Gamma' \Rightarrow A') \rightsquigarrow \mathcal{D}$ reads if $\Delta;\Gamma \vdash E \Rightarrow A$ then $\Delta';\Gamma' \vdash \mathcal{C}\{E\} \Rightarrow A'$. The judgment also generates a well-typed F_{co} context $\mathcal{D}$. The following two definitions capture the notion of contextual equivalence:

Definition 4 (Kleene Equality $\backsimeq$). *Two complete programs (i.e., closed terms of type* Int*), e and e', are Kleene equal, written $e \backsimeq e'$, iff there exists an integer i such that $e \longrightarrow^* i$ and $e' \longrightarrow^* i$.*

Definition 5 (Contextual Equivalence $\backsimeq_{ctx}$)

$$\Delta;\Gamma \vdash E_1 \backsimeq_{ctx} E_2 : A \triangleq \forall e_1, e_2.\ \Delta;\Gamma \vdash E_1 \Rightarrow A \rightsquigarrow e_1 \wedge \Delta;\Gamma \vdash E_2 \Rightarrow A \rightsquigarrow e_2 \wedge$$
$$(\forall \mathcal{C}, \mathcal{D}.\ \mathcal{C} : (\Delta;\Gamma \Rightarrow A) \mapsto (\bullet;\bullet \Rightarrow \mathsf{Int}) \rightsquigarrow \mathcal{D} \Longrightarrow \mathcal{D}\{e_1\} \backsimeq \mathcal{D}\{e_2\})$$

Coherence. For space reasons, we directly show the coherence statement of F_i^+. We need several technical lemmas such as compatibility lemmas, fundamental property, etc. The interested reader can refer to our Coq formalization.

Theorem 5 (Coherence). *We have that*

- *If $\Delta;\Gamma \vdash E \Rightarrow A$ then $\Delta;\Gamma \vdash E \backsimeq_{ctx} E : A$.*
- *If $\Delta;\Gamma \vdash E \Leftarrow A$ then $\Delta;\Gamma \vdash E \backsimeq_{ctx} E : A$.*

That is, coherence is a special case of Definition 5 where E_1 and E_2 are the same. At first glance, this appears underwhelming: of course E behaves the same as itself! The tricky part is that, if we expand it according to Definition 5, it is not E itself but all its translations e_1 and e_2 that behave the same!

6 Related Work

Coherence. In calculi featuring coercive subtyping, a semantics that interprets the subtyping judgment by introducing explicit coercions is typically defined on typing derivations rather than on typing judgments. A natural question that arises for such systems is whether the semantics is *coherent*, i.e., distinct typing derivations of the same typing judgment possess the same meaning. Since Reynolds [45] proved the coherence of a calculus with intersection types, many researchers have studied the problem of coherence in a variety of typed calculi. Two approaches are commonly found in the literature. The first approach is to find a normal form for a representation of the derivation and show that normal forms are unique for a given typing judgment [8,15,47]. However, this approach cannot be directly applied to Curry-style calculi (where the lambda abstractions are not type annotated). Biernacki and Polesiuk [6] considered the coherence problem of coercion semantics. Their criterion for coherence of the translation is *contextual equivalence* in the target calculus. Inspired by this approach, Bi et al. [5] proposed the canonicity relation to prove coherence for a calculus with disjoint intersection types and BCD subtyping. As we have shown in Sect. 5, constructing a suitable logical relation for F_i^+ is challenging. On the one hand, the original approach by Alpuim et al. [2] in F_i does not work any more due to the addition of BCD subtyping. On the other hand, simply combining System F's logical relation with λ_i^+'s canonicity relation does not work as expected, due to the issue of well-foundedness. To solve the problem, we employ immediate substitutions and a restriction to predicative instantiations.

BCD subtyping and decidability. The BCD type system was first introduced by Barendregt et al. [3] to characterize exactly the strongly normalizing terms. The BCD type system features a powerful subtyping relation, which serves as a base for our subtyping relation. The decidability of BCD subtyping has been shown in several works [27,38,41,51]. Laurent [28] formalized the relation in Coq in order to eliminate transitivity cuts from it, but his formalization does not deliver an algorithm. Only recently, Laurent [30] presented a general way of defining a BCD-like subtyping relation extended with generic contravariant/-covariant type constructors that enjoys the "sub-formula property". Our Coq formalization extends the approach used in λ_i^+, which follows a different idea based on Pierce's decision procedure [38], with parametric (disjoint) polymorphism and corresponding distributivity rules. More recently, Muehlboeck and Tate [34] presented a decidable algorithmic system (proved in Coq) with union and intersection types. Similar to F_i^+, their system also has distributive subtyping rules. They also discussed the addition of polymorphism, but left a Coq formalization for future work. In their work they regard intersections of disjoint types (e.g., $\mathsf{String} \,\&\, \mathsf{Int}$) as uninhabitable, which is different from our interpretation. As a consequence, coherence is a non-issue for them.

Intersection types, the merge operator and polymorphism. Forsythe [44] has intersection types and a merge-like operator. However to ensure coherence, various

	$\lambda_{,,}$ [16]	λ_i [36]	$\lambda_\wedge^\vee$ [7]	λ_i^+ [5]	F_i [2]	F_i^+
Disjointness	○	●	○	●	●	●
Unrestricted intersections	●	○	●	●	○	●
BCD subtyping	○	○	●	●	○	●
Polymorphism	○	○	○	○	●	●
Coherence	○	◑	○	●	◑	●
Bottom type	○	○	●	○	○	●

Fig. 12. Summary of intersection calculi (● = yes, ○ = no, ◑ = syntactic coherence)

restrictions were added to limit the use of merges. In Forsythe merges cannot contain more than one function. Castagna et al. [12] proposed a coherent calculus $\lambda\&$ to study overloaded functions. $\lambda\&$ has a special merge operator that works on functions only. Dunfield proposed a calculus [16] (which we call $\lambda_{,,}$) that shows significant expressiveness of type systems with unrestricted intersection types and an (unrestricted) merge operator. However, because of his unrestricted merge operator (allowing $1\,,,\,2$), his calculus lacks coherence. Blaauwbroek's $\lambda_\wedge^\vee$ [7] enriched $\lambda_{,,}$ with BCD subtyping and computational effects, but he did not address coherence. The coherence issue for a calculus similar to $\lambda_{,,}$ was first addressed in λ_i [36] with the notion of disjointness, but at the cost of dropping unrestricted intersections, and a strict notion of coherence (based on α-equivalence). Later Bi et al. [5] improved calculi with disjoint intersection types by removing several restrictions, adopted BCD subtyping and a semantic notion of coherence (based on contextual equivalence) proved using canonicity. The combination of intersection types, a merge operator and parametric polymorphism, while achieving coherence was first studied in F_i [2], which serves as a foundation for F_i^+. However, F_i suffered the same problems as λ_i. Additionally in F_i a bottom type is problematic due to interactions with disjoint polymorphism and the lack of unrestricted intersections. The issues can be illustrated with the well-typed F_i^+ expression $\Lambda(\alpha * \bot).\, \lambda x : \alpha.\, x\,,,\, x$. In this expression the type of $x\,,,\, x$ is $\alpha \,\&\, \alpha$. Such a merge does not violate disjointness because the only types that α can be instantiated with are top-like, and top-like types do not introduce incoherence. In F_i a type variable α can never be disjoint to another type that contains α, but (as the previous expression shows) the addition of a bottom type allows expressions where such (strict) condition does not hold. In this work, we removed those restrictions, extended BCD subtyping with polymorphism, and proposed a more powerful logical relation for proving coherence. Figure 12 summarizes the main differences between the aforementioned calculi.

There are also several other calculi with intersections and polymorphism. Pierce proposed $\mathsf{F}_\wedge$ [39], a calculus combining intersection types and bounded quantification. Pierce translates $\mathsf{F}_\wedge$ to System F extended with products, but he left coherence as a conjecture. More recently, Castagna et al. [14] proposed a polymorphic calculus with set-theoretic type connectives (intersections, unions, negations). But their calculus does not include a merge operator. Castagna and

Lanvin also proposed a gradual type system [13] with intersection and union types, but also without a merge operator.

Row polymorphism and bounded polymorphism. Row polymorphism was originally proposed by Wand [54] as a mechanism to enable type inference for a simple object-oriented language based on recursive records. These ideas were later adopted into type systems for extensible records [19,21,31]. Our merge operator can be seen as a generalization of record extension/concatenation, and selection is also built-in. In contrast to most record calculi, restriction is not a primitive operation in F_i^+, but can be simulated via subtyping. Disjoint quantification can simulate the *lacks* predicate often present in systems with row polymorphism. Recently Morris and McKinna presented a typed language [33], generalizing and abstracting existing systems of row types and row polymorphism. Alpuim et al. [2] informally studied the relationship between row polymorphism and disjoint polymorphism, but it would be interesting to study such relationship more formally. The work of Morris and McKinna may be interesting for such study in that it gives a general framework for row type systems.

Bounded quantification is currently the dominant mechanism in major mainstream object-oriented languages supporting both subtyping and polymorphism. $\mathsf{F}_{<:}$ [10] provides a simple model for bounded quantification, but type-checking in full $\mathsf{F}_{<:}$ is proved to be undecidable [40]. Pierce's thesis [39] discussed the relationship between calculi with simple polymorphism and intersection types and bounded quantification. He observed that there is a way to "encode" many forms of bounded quantification in a system with intersections and pure (unbounded) second-order polymorphism. That encoding can be easily adapted to F_i^+:

$$\forall (\alpha <: A).\, B \triangleq \forall (\alpha * \top).\, ([A \,\&\, \alpha / \alpha] B)$$

The idea is to replace bounded quantification by (unrestricted) universal quantification and all occurrences of α by $A \,\&\, \alpha$ in the body. Such an encoding seems to indicate that F_i^+ could be used as a decidable alternative to (full) $\mathsf{F}_{<:}$. It is worthwhile to note that this encoding does not work in F_i because $A \,\&\, \alpha$ is not well-formed (α is not disjoint to A). In other words, the encoding requires unrestricted intersections.

7 Conclusion and Future Work

We have proposed F_i^+, a type-safe and coherent calculus with disjoint intersection types, BCD subtyping and parametric polymorphism. F_i^+ improves the state-of-art of compositional designs, and enables the development of highly modular and reusable programs. One interesting and useful further extension would be implicit polymorphism. For that we want to combine Dunfield and Krishnaswami's approach [17] with our bidirectional type system. We would also like to study the parametricity of F_i^+. As we have seen in Sect. 5.2, it is not at all obvious how to extend the standard logical relation of System F to account for disjointness, and avoid potential circularity due to impredicativity. A promising solution is to use step-indexed logical relations [1].

Acknowledgments. We thank the anonymous reviewers and Yaoda Zhou for their helpful comments. This work has been sponsored by the Hong Kong Research Grant Council projects number 17210617 and 17258816, and by the Research Foundation - Flanders.

References

1. Ahmed, A.: Step-indexed syntactic logical relations for recursive and quantified types. In: Sestoft, P. (ed.) ESOP 2006. LNCS, vol. 3924, pp. 69–83. Springer, Heidelberg (2006). https://doi.org/10.1007/11693024_6
2. Alpuim, J., Oliveira, B.C.d.S., Shi, Z.: Disjoint polymorphism. In: Yang, H. (ed.) ESOP 2017. LNCS, vol. 10201, pp. 1–28. Springer, Heidelberg (2017). https://doi.org/10.1007/978-3-662-54434-1_1
3. Barendregt, H., Coppo, M., Dezani-Ciancaglini, M.: A filter lambda model and the completeness of type assignment. J. Symb. Logic **48**(04), 931–940 (1983)
4. Bi, X., Oliveira, B.C.d.S.: Typed first-class traits. In: European Conference on Object-Oriented Programming (ECOOP) (2018)
5. Bi, X., Oliveira, B.C.d.S., Schrijvers, T.: The essence of nested composition. In: European Conference on Object-Oriented Programming (ECOOP) (2018)
6. Biernacki, D., Polesiuk, P.: Logical relations for coherence of effect subtyping. In: International Conference on Typed Lambda Calculi and Applications (TLCA) (2015)
7. Blaauwbroek, L.: On the interaction between unrestricted union and intersection types and computational effects. Master's thesis, Technical University Eindhoven (2017)
8. Breazu-Tannen, V., Coquand, T., Gunter, C.A., Scedrov, A.: Inheritance as implicit coercion. Inf. Comput. **93**(1), 172–221 (1991)
9. Brent, R.P., Kung, H.T.: The chip complexity of binary arithmetic. In: Proceedings of the Twelfth Annual ACM Symposium on Theory of Computing, pp. 190–200 (1980)
10. Cardelli, L., Wegner, P.: On understanding types, data abstraction, and polymorphism. ACM Comput. Surv. **17**(4), 471–523 (1985)
11. Carette, J., Kiselyov, O., Shan, C.C.: Finally tagless, partially evaluated: tagless staged interpreters for simpler typed languages. J. Funct. Program. **19**(05), 509 (2009)
12. Castagna, G., Ghelli, G., Longo, G.: A calculus for overloaded functions with subtyping. In: Conference on LISP and Functional Programming (1992)
13. Castagna, G., Lanvin, V.: Gradual typing with union and intersection types. In: Proceedings of the ACM on Programming Languages, vol. 1, no. (ICFP), pp. 1–28 (2017)
14. Castagna, G., Nguyen, K., Xu, Z., Im, H., Lenglet, S., Padovani, L.: Polymorphic functions with set-theoretic types: part 1: syntax, semantics, and evaluation. In: Principles of Programming Languages (POPL) (2014)
15. Curien, P.L., Ghelli, G.: Coherence of subsumption, minimum typing and type-checking in $f_{\leq}$. Math. Struct. Comput. Sci. (MSCS) **2**(01), 55 (1992)
16. Dunfield, J.: Elaborating intersection and union types. J. Funct. Program. (JFP) **24**(2–3), 133–165 (2014)
17. Dunfield, J., Krishnaswami, N.R.: Complete and easy bidirectional typechecking for higher-rank polymorphism. In: International Conference on Functional Programming (ICFP) (2013)

18. Fokkinga, M.M.: Tupling and mutumorphisms. Squiggolist **1**(4) (1989)
19. Gaster, B.R., Jones, M.P.: A polymorphic type system for extensible records and variants. Technical report, University of Nottingham (1996)
20. Gibbons, J., Wu, N.: Folding domain-specific languages: deep and shallow embeddings (functional pearl). In: ICFP, pp. 339–347. ACM (2014)
21. Harper, R., Pierce, B.: A record calculus based on symmetric concatenation. In: Principles of Programming Languages (POPL) (1991)
22. Henglein, F.: Dynamic typing: syntax and proof theory. Sci. Comput. Program. **22**(3), 197–230 (1994)
23. Herman, D., Tomb, A., Flanagan, C.: Space-efficient gradual typing. High.-Order Symb. Comput. **23**(2), 167 (2010)
24. Hindley, R.: The principal type-scheme of an object in combinatory logic. Trans. Am. Math. Soc. **146**, 29–60 (1969)
25. Hinze, R.: An algebra of scans. In: Kozen, D. (ed.) MPC 2004. LNCS, vol. 3125, pp. 186–210. Springer, Heidelberg (2004). https://doi.org/10.1007/978-3-540-27764-4_11
26. Hofer, C., Ostermann, K., Rendel, T., Moors, A.: Polymorphic embedding of DSLs. In: International Conference on Generative Programming and Component Engineering (GPCE) (2008)
27. Kurata, T., Takahashi, M.: Decidable properties of intersection type systems. In: Dezani-Ciancaglini, M., Plotkin, G. (eds.) TLCA 1995. LNCS, vol. 902, pp. 297–311. Springer, Heidelberg (1995). https://doi.org/10.1007/BFb0014060
28. Laurent, O.: Intersection types with subtyping by means of cut elimination. Fundam. Inf. **121**(1–4), 203–226 (2012)
29. Laurent, O.: A syntactic introduction to intersection types (2012, unpublished note)
30. Laurent, O.: Intersection subtyping with constructors. In: Proceedings of the Ninth Workshop on Intersection Types and Related Systems (2018)
31. Leijen, D.: Extensible records with scoped labels. Trends Funct. Program. **5**, 297–312 (2005)
32. Milner, R.: A theory of type polymorphism in programming. J. Comput. Syst. Sci. **17**(3), 348–375 (1978)
33. Morris, J.G., McKinna, J.: Abstracting extensible data types. In: Principles of Programming Languages (POPL) (2019)
34. Muehlboeck, F., Tate, R.: Empowering union and intersection types with integrated subtyping. In: OOPSLA (2018)
35. Oliveira, B.C.d.S., Cook, W.R.: Extensibility for the masses. In: Noble, J. (ed.) ECOOP 2012. LNCS, vol. 7313, pp. 2–27. Springer, Heidelberg (2012). https://doi.org/10.1007/978-3-642-31057-7_2
36. Oliveira, B.C.d.S., Shi, Z., Alpuim, J.: Disjoint intersection types. In: International Conference on Functional Programming (ICFP) (2016)
37. Oliveira, B.C.d.S., van der Storm, T., Loh, A., Cook, W.R.: Feature-oriented programming with object algebras. In: Castagna, G. (ed.) ECOOP 2013. LNCS, vol. 7920, pp. 27–51. Springer, Heidelberg (2013). https://doi.org/10.1007/978-3-642-39038-8_2
38. Pierce, B.C.: A decision procedure for the subtype relation on intersection types with bounded variables. Technical report, Carnegie Mellon University (1989)
39. Pierce, B.C.: Programming with intersection types and bounded polymorphism. Ph.D. thesis, University of Pennsylvania (1991)
40. Pierce, B.C.: Bounded quantification is undecidable. Inf. Comput. **112**(1), 131–165 (1994)

41. Rehof, J., Urzyczyn, P.: Finite combinatory logic with intersection types. In: Ong, L. (ed.) TLCA 2011. LNCS, vol. 6690, pp. 169–183. Springer, Heidelberg (2011). https://doi.org/10.1007/978-3-642-21691-6_15
42. Rendel, T., Brachthäuser, J.I., Ostermann, K.: From object algebras to attribute grammars. In: Object-Oriented Programming, Systems Languages and Applications (OOPSLA) (2014)
43. Reynolds, J.C.: Types, abstraction and parametric polymorphism. In: Proceedings of the IFIP 9th World Computer Congress (1983)
44. Reynolds, J.C.: Preliminary design of the programming language Forsythe. Technical report, Carnegie Mellon University (1988)
45. Reynolds, J.C.: The coherence of languages with intersection types. In: Ito, T., Meyer, A.R. (eds.) TACS 1991. LNCS, vol. 526, pp. 675–700. Springer, Heidelberg (1991). https://doi.org/10.1007/3-540-54415-1_70
46. Oliveira, B.C.d.S., Hinze, R., Löh, A.: Extensible and modular generics for the masses. In: Revised Selected Papers from the Seventh Symposium on Trends in Functional Programming, TFP 2006, Nottingham, United Kingdom, 19–21 April 2006, pp. 199–216 (2006)
47. Schwinghammer, J.: Coherence of subsumption for monadic types. J. Funct. Program. (JFP) **19**(02), 157 (2008)
48. Scott, D.: Outline of a mathematical theory of computation. Oxford University Computing Laboratory, Programming Research Group (1970)
49. Scott, D.S., Strachey, C.: Toward a Mathematical Semantics for Computer Languages, vol. 1. Oxford University Computing Laboratory, Programming Research Group (1971)
50. Siek, J., Thiemann, P., Wadler, P.: Blame and coercion: together again for the first time. In: Conference on Programming Language Design and Implementation (PLDI) (2015)
51. Statman, R.: A finite model property for intersection types. Electron. Proc. Theor. Comput. Sci. **177**, 1–9 (2015)
52. Wadler, P., Blott, S.: How to make ad-hoc polymorphism less ad hoc. In: Proceedings of the 16th ACM SIGPLAN-SIGACT Symposium on Principles of Programming Languages, POPL 1989 (1989)
53. Wadler, P.: The expression problem. Java-Genericity Mailing List (1998)
54. Wand, M.: Complete type inference for simple objects. In: Symposium on Logic in Computer Science (LICS) (1987)
55. Zhang, W., Oliveira, B.C.d.S: Shallow EDLs and object-oriented programming. Program. J. (2019, to appear)

Types by Need

Beniamino Accattoli[1], Giulio Guerrieri[2(✉)], and Maico Leberle[1]

[1] Inria & LIX, École Polytechnique, UMR 7161, Palaiseau, France
{beniamino.accattoli,maico-carlos.leberle}@inria.fr
[2] Department of Computer Science, University di Bath, Bath, UK
g.guerrieri@bath.ac.uk

Abstract. A cornerstone of the theory of λ-calculus is that intersection types characterise termination properties. They are a flexible tool that can be adapted to various notions of termination, and that also induces adequate denotational models.

Since the seminal work of de Carvalho in 2007, it is known that multi types (*i.e.* non-idempotent intersection types) refine intersection types with quantitative information and a strong connection to linear logic. Typically, type derivations provide bounds for evaluation lengths, and minimal type derivations provide exact bounds.

De Carvalho studied call-by-name evaluation, and Kesner used his system to show the termination equivalence of call-by-need and call-by-name. De Carvalho's system, however, cannot provide exact bounds on call-by-need evaluation lengths.

In this paper we develop a new multi type system for call-by-need. Our system produces exact bounds and induces a denotational model of call-by-need, providing the first tight quantitative semantics of call-by-need.

1 Introduction

Duplications and erasures have always been considered as key phenomena in the λ-calculus—the λI-calculus, where erasures are forbidden, is an example of this. The advent of linear logic [38] gave them a new, prominent logical status. Forbidding erasure and duplication enables single-use resources, i.e. linearity, but limits expressivity, as every computation terminates in linear time. Their controlled reintroduction via the non-linear modality ! recovers the full expressive power of cut-elimination and allows a fine analysis of resource consumption. Duplication and erasure are therefore the key ingredients for logical expressivity, and—via Curry-Howard—for the expressivity of the λ-calculus. They are also essential to understand evaluation strategies.

In a λ-term there can be many β-redexes, that is, places where β-reduction can be applied. In this sense, the λ-calculus is non-deterministic. Non-determinism does not affect the result of evaluation, if any, but it affects whether evaluation terminates, and in how many steps. There are two natural deterministic evaluation strategies, *call-by-name* (shortened to CbN) and *call-by-value* (CbV), which have dual behaviour with respect to duplication and erasure.

L. Caires (Ed.): ESOP 2019, LNCS 11423, pp. 410–439, 2019.
https://doi.org/10.1007/978-3-030-17184-1_15

Call-by-Name = Silly Duplication + Wise Erasure. CbN *never* evaluates arguments of β-redexes before the redexes themselves. As a consequence, it never evaluates in subterms that will be erased. This is wise, and makes CbN a *normalising strategy*, that is, a strategy that reaches a result whenever one exists[1]. A second consequence is that if the argument of the redex is duplicated then it may be evaluated more than once. This is silly, as it repeats work already done.

Call-by-Value = Wise Duplication + Silly Erasure. CbV, on the other hand, *always* evaluates arguments of β-redexes before the redexes themselves. Consequently, arguments are not re-evaluated—this is wise with respect to duplication—but they are also evaluated when they are going to be erased. For instance, on $t := (\lambda x.\lambda y.y)\Omega$, where Ω is the famous looping λ-term, CbV evaluation diverges (it keeps evaluating Ω) while CbN converges in one β-step (simply erasing Ω). This CbV treatment of erasure is clearly as silly as the duplicated work of CbN.

Call-by-Need = Wise Duplication + Wise Erasure. It is natural to try to combine the advantages of both CbN and CbV. The strategy that is wise with respect to both duplications and erasures is usually called *call-by-need* (CbNeed), it was introduced by Wadsworth [57], and dates back to the '70s. Despite being at the core of Haskell, one of the most-used functional programming languages, and—in its strong variant—being at work in the kernel of Coq as designed by Barras [16], the theory of CbNeed is much less developed than that of CbN or CbV.

One of the reasons for this is that it cannot be defined inside the λ-calculus without some hacking. Manageable presentations of CbNeed indeed require first-class sharing and micro-step operational semantics where variable occurrences are replaced one at a time (when needed), and not all at once as in the λ-calculus. Another reason is the less natural logical interpretation.

Linear Logic, Names, Values, and Needs. CbN and CbV have neat interpretations in linear logic. They correspond to two different representations of intuitionistic logic in linear logic, based on two different representations of implication[2].

The logical interpretation of CbNeed—studied by Maraist et al. in [47]—is less neat than those of CbN and CbV. Within linear logic, CbNeed is usually understood as corresponding to the CbV representation where erasures are generalised to all terms, not only those under the scope of a ! modality. So, it is seen as a sort of *affine* CbV. Such an interpretation however is unusual, because it does not match exactly with cut-elimination in linear logic, as for CbN and CbV.

Call-by-Need, Abstractly. The main theorem of the theory of CbNeed is that it is termination equivalent to CbN, that is, on a fixed term, CbNeed evaluation terminates if and only if CbN evaluation terminates, and, moreover, they essentially

1 If a term t admits both converging and diverging evaluation sequences then the diverging sequences occur in erasable subterms of t, which is why CbN avoids them.

2 The CbN translation maps $A \Rightarrow B$ to $(!A^{\text{CbN}}) \multimap B^{\text{CbN}}$, while the CbV maps it to $!A^{\text{CbV}} \multimap !B^{\text{CbV}}$, or equivalently to $!(A^{\text{CbV}} \multimap B^{\text{CbV}})$.

produce the same result (up to some technical details that are irrelevant here). This is due to the fact that both strategies avoid silly divergent sequences such as that of $(\lambda x.\lambda y.y)\Omega$. Termination equivalence is an abstract theorem stating that CbNeed erases as wisely as CbN. Curiously, in the literature there are no abstract theorems reflecting the dual fact that CbNeed duplicates as wisely as CbV—we provide one, as a side contribution of this paper.

Call-by-Need and Denotational Semantics. CbNeed is then usually considered as a CbV optimisation of CbN. In particular, every denotational model of CbN is also a model of CbNeed, and adequacy—that is the fact that the denotation of t is not degenerated if and only if t terminates—transfers from CbN to CbNeed.

Denotational semantics is invariant by evaluation, and so is insensitive to evaluation lengths by definition. It then seems that denotational semantics cannot distinguish between CbN and CbNeed. The aim of this paper is, somewhat counter-intuitively, to separate CbN and CbNeed semantically. We develop a type system whose type judgements induce a model—this is typical of *intersection* type systems—and whose type derivations provide exact bounds for CbNeed evaluation—this is usually obtained via *non-idempotent* intersection types. Unsurprisingly, the design of the type system requires a delicate mix of erasure and duplication and builds on the linear logic understanding of CbN and CbV.

Multi Types. Our typing framework is given by *multi types*, which is an alternative name for *non-idempotent intersection types*[3]. Multi types characterise termination properties exactly as intersection types, having moreover the advantages that they are closely related to (the relational semantics of) linear logic, their type derivations provide quantitative information about evaluation lengths, and the proof techniques are simpler—no need for the reducibility method.

The seminal work of de Carvalho [23] (appeared in 2007 but unpublished until 2018, see also [22]) showed how to use multi types to obtain exact bounds on evaluation lengths in CbN. Ehrhard adapted multi types to CbV [34], and very recently Accattoli and Guerrieri adapted de Carvalho's study of exact bounds to Ehrhard's system and CbV evaluation [8]. Kesner used de Carvalho's CbN multi types to obtain a simple proof that CbNeed is termination equivalent to CbN [40] (first proved with other techniques by Maraist, Odersky, and Wadler [48] and Ariola and Felleisen [11] in the nineties), and then Kesner and coauthors continued exploring the theory of CbNeed via CbN multi types [14,15,42].

Kesner's use of CbN multi types to study CbNeed is *qualitative*, as it deals with termination and not with exact bounds. For a *quantitative* study of CbNeed, de Carvalho's CbN system cannot really be informative: CbN multi types provide bounds for CbNeed which cannot be exact because they already provide exact bounds for CbN, which generally takes more steps than CbNeed.

---

[3] The new terminology is due to the fact that a non-idempotent intersection $A \wedge A \wedge B \wedge C$ can be seen as a multi-set $[A, A, B, C]$.

Multi Types by Need. In this paper we provide the first multi type system characterising CbNeed termination and whose minimal type derivations provide *exact* bounds for CbNeed evaluation lengths. The design of the type system is delicate, as we explain in Sect. 6. One of the key points is that, in contrast to Ehrhard's system for CbV [34], multi types for CbNeed cannot be directly extracted by the relational semantics of linear logic, given that CbNeed does not have a clean representation in it. A by-product of our work is a new denotational semantics of CbNeed, the first one to precisely reflect its quantitative properties.

Beyond the result itself, the paper tries to stress how the key ingredients of our type system are taken from those for CbN and CbV and combined together. To this aim, we first present multi types for CbN and CbV, and only then we proceed to build the CbNeed system and prove its properties.

Along the way, we also prove the missing fundamental property of CbNeed, that is, that it duplicates as efficiently as CbV. The result dualizes the termination equivalence of CbN and CbNeed, which shows that CbNeed erases as wisely as CbN. *Careful*: the CbV system is correct but of course not complete with respect to CbNeed, because CbNeed may normalise when CbV diverges. The proof of the result is straightforward, because of our presentations of CbV and CbNeed. We adopt a liberal, non-deterministic formulation of CbV, and assuming (without loss of generality, see [1]) that garbage collection is always postponed. These two ingredients turn CbNeed into a fragment of CbV, obtaining the new fundamental result as a corollary of correctness of CbV multi types for CbV evaluation.

Technical Development. The paper is extremely uniform, technically speaking. The three evaluations are presented as strategies of Accattoli and Kesner's Linear Substitution Calculus (shortened to LSC) [1,6], a calculus with a simple but expressive form of explicit sharing. The LSC is strongly related to linear logic [2], and provides a neat and manageable presentation of CbNeed, introduced by Accattoli, Barenbaum, and Mazza in [3], and further developed by various authors in [4,5,10,14,15,40,42]. Our type systems count evaluation steps by annotating typing rules in the *exact* same way, and the proofs of correctness and completeness all follow the *exact* same structure. While the results for CbN are very minor variations with respect to those in the literature [7,23], those for CbV are the first ones with respect to a presentation of CbV with sharing.

As it is standard for CbNeed, we restrict our study to closed terms and weak evaluation (that is, out of abstractions). The main consequence of this fact is that normal forms are particularly simple (sometimes called *answers* in the literature). Compared with other recent works dealing with exact bounds such as Accattoli, Graham-Lengrand, and Kesner [7] and Accattoli and Guerrieri [8] the main difference is that the size of normal forms is not taken into account by type derivations. This is because of the simple notions of normal forms in the closed and weak case, and not because the type systems are not accurate.

Related Work About CbNeed. Call-by-need was introduced by Wadsworth [57] in the '70s. In the '90s, it was first reformulated as operational semantics by

Launchbury [46], Maraist, Odersky, and Wadler [48], and Ariola and Felleisen [11,12], and then implemented by Sestoft [55] and further studied by Kutzner and Schmidt-Schauß [45]. More recent papers are Garcia, Lumsdaine, and Sabry [36], Ariola, Herbelin, and Saurin [13], Chang and Felleisen [26], Danvy and Zerny [29], Downen et al. [33], Pédrot and Saurin [53], and Balabonski et al. [14].

Related Work About Multi Types. Intersection types are a standard tool to study λ-calculi—see Coppo and Dezani [27,28], Pottinger [54], and Krivine [44]. Non-idempotent intersection types, *i.e.* multi types, were first considered by Gardner [37], and then by Kfoury [43], Neergaard and Mairson [50], and de Carvalho [23]—a survey is Bucciarelli, Kesner, and Ventura [20].

Many recent works rely on multi types or relational semantics to study properties of programs and proofs. Beyond the cited ones, Diaz-Caro, Manzonetto, and Pagani [32], Carraro and Guerrieri [21], Ehrhard and Guerrieri [35], and Guerrieri [39] deal with CbV, while Bernadet and Lengrand [17], de Carvalho, Pagani, and Tortora de Falco [24] provide exact bounds. Further related work is by Bucciarelli, Ehrhard, and Manzonetto [18], de Carvalho and Tortora de Falco [25], Tsukada and Ong [56], Kesner and Vial [41], Piccolo, Paolini and Ronchi Della Rocca [52], Ong [51], Mazza, Pellissier, and Vial [49], Bucciarelli, Kesner and Ronchi Della Rocca [19]—this list is not exhaustive.

Proofs. Proofs are omitted. They can be found in the technical report [9].

2 Closed λ-Calculi

In this section we define the CbN, CbV, and CbNeed evaluation strategies. We present them in the context of the Accattoli and Kesner's *linear substitution calculus* (LSC) [1,6]. We mainly follow the uniform presentation of these strategies given by Accattoli, Barenbaum, and Mazza [3]. The only difference is that we adopt a non-deterministic presentation of CbV, subsuming both the left-to-right and the right-to-left strategies in [3], that makes our results slightly more general. Such a non-determinism is harmless: not only CbV evaluation is confluent, it even has the diamond property, so that all evaluations have the same length. Moreover, the non-deterministic presentation, together with the postponement of erasing steps discussed below, allows us to see CbNeed as a fragment of CbV, which shall provide a free proof that CbNeed duplicates as wisely as CbV.

Terms and Contexts. The set of terms $\Lambda_{\mathtt{lsc}}$ of the LSC is given by the grammar below, where $t[x{\leftarrow}s]$ is an *explicit substitution* (shortened to ES), that is a more compact notation for $\mathtt{let}\ x = s\ \mathtt{in}\ t$ (intuitively, "t where x will be substituted by s"). Both $\lambda x.t$ and $t[x{\leftarrow}s]$ bind x in t, with the usual notion of α-equivalence.

$$\text{LSC TERMS} \quad t,s,u ::= x \mid v \mid ts \mid t[x{\leftarrow}s] \qquad \text{LSC VALUES} \quad v ::= \lambda x.t$$

The set $\mathtt{fv}(t)$ of *free* variables of a term t is defined as expected, in particular, $\mathtt{fv}(t[x{\leftarrow}s]) := (\mathtt{fv}(t) \setminus \{x\}) \cup \mathtt{fv}(s)$. A term t is *closed* if $\mathtt{fv}(t) = \emptyset$, *open* otherwise. As usual, terms are identified up to α-equivalence.

Contexts are terms with exactly one occurrence of the *hole* $\langle\cdot\rangle$, an additional constant. We shall use many different contexts. The most general ones are *weak contexts* W (i.e. not under abstractions). The (evaluation) contexts C, V and E—used to define CbN, CbV and CbNeed evaluation strategies, respectively—are special cases of weak contexts (in fact, CbV contexts coincide with weak contexts, the consequences of that are discussed on p. 8). To define evaluation strategies, *substitution contexts* (*i.e.* lists of explicit substitutions) also play a role.

WEAK CONTEXTS	$W ::= \langle\cdot\rangle \mid Wt \mid W[x{\leftarrow}t] \mid tW \mid t[x{\leftarrow}W]$
SUBSTITUTION CONTEXTS	$S ::= \langle\cdot\rangle \mid S[x{\leftarrow}t]$
CBN CONTEXTS	$C ::= \langle\cdot\rangle \mid Ct \mid C[x{\leftarrow}t]$
CBV CONTEXTS	$V ::= W$
CBNEED CONTEXTS	$E ::= \langle\cdot\rangle \mid Et \mid E[x{\leftarrow}t] \mid E\langle\!\langle x\rangle\!\rangle[x{\leftarrow}E']$

We write $W\langle t\rangle$ for the term obtained by replacing the hole $\langle\cdot\rangle$ in context W by the term t. This *plugging* operation, as usual with contexts, can capture variables—for instance $((\langle\cdot\rangle t)[x{\leftarrow}s])\langle x\rangle = (xt)[x{\leftarrow}s]$. We write $W\langle\!\langle t\rangle\!\rangle$ when we want to stress that the context W does not capture the free variables of t.

Micro-step Semantics. The rewriting rules decompose the usual small-step semantics for λ-calculi, by *substituting linearly* one variable occurrence at the time, and only when such an occurrence is in evaluation position. We emphasise this fact saying that we adopt a *micro-step semantics.* We now give the definitions, examples of evaluation sequences follow right next.

Formally, a micro-step semantics is defined by first giving its *root-steps* and then taking the closure of root-steps under suitable contexts.

MULTIPLICATIVE ROOT-STEP	$S\langle\lambda x.t\rangle s \mapsto_{\mathtt{m}} S\langle t[x{\leftarrow}s]\rangle$
EXPONENTIAL CBN ROOT-STEP	$C\langle\!\langle x\rangle\!\rangle[x{\leftarrow}t] \mapsto_{\mathsf{e}_{\mathrm{cbn}}} C\langle\!\langle t\rangle\!\rangle[x{\leftarrow}t]$
EXPONENTIAL CBV ROOT-STEP	$V\langle\!\langle x\rangle\!\rangle[x{\leftarrow}S\langle v\rangle] \mapsto_{\mathsf{e}_{\mathrm{cbv}}} S\langle V\langle\!\langle v\rangle\!\rangle[x{\leftarrow}v]\rangle$
EXPONENTIAL CBNEED ROOT-STEP	$E\langle\!\langle x\rangle\!\rangle[x{\leftarrow}S\langle v\rangle] \mapsto_{\mathsf{e}_{\mathrm{need}}} S\langle E\langle\!\langle v\rangle\!\rangle[x{\leftarrow}v]\rangle$

where, in the root-step $\mapsto_{\mathtt{m}}$ (resp. $\mapsto_{\mathsf{e}_{\mathrm{cbv}}}$; $\mapsto_{\mathsf{e}_{\mathrm{need}}}$), if $S := [y_1{\leftarrow}s_1]\ldots[y_n{\leftarrow}s_n]$ for some $n \in \mathbb{N}$, then $\mathtt{fv}(s)$ (resp. $\mathtt{fv}(V\langle\!\langle x\rangle\!\rangle)$; $\mathtt{fv}(E\langle\!\langle x\rangle\!\rangle)$) and $\{y_1,\ldots,y_n\}$ are disjoint. This condition can always be fulfilled by α-equivalence.

The *evaluation strategies* $\rightarrow_{\mathrm{cbn}}$ for CbN, $\rightarrow_{\mathrm{cbv}}$ for CbV, and $\rightarrow_{\mathrm{need}}$ for CbNeed, are defined as the closure of root-steps under CbN, CbV and CbNeed evaluation contexts, respectively (so, all evaluation strategies do not reduce under abstractions, since all such contexts are weak):

CbN	CbV	CbNeed
$\to_{\mathtt{m}_{\text{cbn}}} := C\langle \mapsto_{\mathtt{m}} \rangle$	$\to_{\mathtt{m}_{\text{cbv}}} := V\langle \mapsto_{\mathtt{m}} \rangle$	$\to_{\mathtt{m}_{\text{need}}} := E\langle \mapsto_{\mathtt{m}} \rangle$
$\to_{\mathtt{e}_{\text{cbn}}} := C\langle \mapsto_{\mathtt{e}_{\text{cbn}}} \rangle$	$\to_{\mathtt{e}_{\text{cbv}}} := V\langle \mapsto_{\mathtt{e}_{\text{cbv}}} \rangle$	$\to_{\mathtt{e}_{\text{need}}} := E\langle \mapsto_{\mathtt{e}_{\text{need}}} \rangle$
$\to_{\text{cbn}} := C\langle \mapsto_{\mathtt{m}} \cup \mapsto_{\mathtt{e}_{\text{cbn}}} \rangle$	$\to_{\text{cbv}} := V\langle \mapsto_{\mathtt{m}} \cup \mapsto_{\mathtt{e}_{\text{cbv}}} \rangle$	$\to_{\text{need}} := E\langle \mapsto_{\mathtt{m}} \cup \mapsto_{\mathtt{e}_{\text{need}}} \rangle$

where the notation $\to := W\langle \mapsto \rangle$ means that, given a root-step $\mapsto$, the evaluation $\to$ is defined as follows: $t \to s$ if and only if there are terms t' and s' and a context W such that $t = W\langle t' \rangle$ and $s = W\langle s' \rangle$ and $t' \mapsto s'$.

Note that evaluations $\to_{\text{cbn}}$, $\to_{\text{cbv}}$ and $\to_{\text{need}}$ can equivalently be defined as $\to_{\mathtt{m}_{\text{cbn}}} \cup \to_{\mathtt{e}_{\text{cbn}}}$, $\to_{\mathtt{m}_{\text{cbn}}} \cup \to_{\mathtt{e}_{\text{cbv}}}$ and $\to_{\mathtt{m}_{\text{need}}} \cup \to_{\mathtt{e}_{\text{need}}}$, respectively.

Given an evaluation sequence $d\colon t \to_{\text{cbn}}^* s$ we note with $|d|$ the length of d, and with $|d|_{\mathtt{m}}$ and $|d|_{\mathtt{e}}$ the number of multiplicative and exponential steps in d, respectively—and similarly for $\to_{\text{cbv}}$ and $\to_{\text{need}}$.

Erasing Steps. The reader may be surprised by our evaluation strategies, as none of them includes erasing steps, despite the absolute relevance of erasures pointed out in the introduction. There are no contradictions: in the LSC—in contrast to the λ-calculus—erasing steps can always be postponed (see [1]), and so they are often simply omitted. This is actually close to programming language practice, as the garbage collector acts asynchronously with respect to the evaluation flow. For the sake of clarity let us spell out the erasing rules—they shall nonetheless be ignored in the rest of the paper. In CbN and CbNeed every term is erasable, so the root erasing step takes the following form

$$t[x{\leftarrow}s] \mapsto_{\text{gc}} t \qquad \text{if } x \notin \mathtt{fv}(t)$$

and it is then closed by weak evaluation contexts.

In CbV only values are erasable; so, the root erasing step in CbV is:

$$t[x{\leftarrow}S\langle v \rangle] \mapsto_{\text{gc}} S\langle t \rangle \qquad \text{if } x \notin \mathtt{fv}(t)$$

and it is then closed by weak evaluation contexts.

Example 1. A good example to observe the differences between CbN, CbV, and CbNeed is given by the term $t := ((\lambda x.\lambda y.xx)(II))(II)$ where $I := \lambda z.z$ is the identity combinator. In CbN, it evaluates with 5 multiplicative steps and 5 exponential steps, as follows:

$$\begin{array}{ll}
t \to_{\mathtt{m}_{\text{cbn}}} (\lambda y.xx)[x{\leftarrow}II](II) & \to_{\mathtt{m}_{\text{cbn}}} (xx)[y{\leftarrow}II][x{\leftarrow}II] \\
\to_{\mathtt{e}_{\text{cbn}}} ((II)x)[y{\leftarrow}II][x{\leftarrow}II] & \to_{\mathtt{m}_{\text{cbn}}} (z[z{\leftarrow}I]x)[y{\leftarrow}II][x{\leftarrow}II] \\
\to_{\mathtt{e}_{\text{cbn}}} (I[z{\leftarrow}I]x)[y{\leftarrow}II][x{\leftarrow}II] & \to_{\mathtt{m}_{\text{cbn}}} w[w{\leftarrow}x][z{\leftarrow}I][y{\leftarrow}II][x{\leftarrow}II] \\
\to_{\mathtt{e}_{\text{cbn}}} x[w{\leftarrow}x][z{\leftarrow}I][y{\leftarrow}II][x{\leftarrow}II] & \to_{\mathtt{e}_{\text{cbn}}} (II)[w{\leftarrow}x][z{\leftarrow}I][y{\leftarrow}II][x{\leftarrow}II] \\
\to_{\mathtt{m}_{\text{cbn}}} x'[x'{\leftarrow}I][w{\leftarrow}x][z{\leftarrow}I][y{\leftarrow}II][x{\leftarrow}II] & \to_{\mathtt{e}_{\text{cbn}}} I[x'{\leftarrow}I][w{\leftarrow}x][z{\leftarrow}I][y{\leftarrow}II][x{\leftarrow}II]
\end{array}$$

In CbV, t evaluates with 5 multiplicative steps and 5 exponential steps, for instance from right to left, as follows:

$$\begin{array}{ll} t \to_{\mathtt{m}_{\mathrm{cbv}}} (\lambda x.\lambda y.xx)(II)(z[z{\leftarrow}I]) & \to_{\mathtt{e}_{\mathrm{cbv}}} (\lambda x.\lambda y.xx)(II)(I[z{\leftarrow}I]) \\ \to_{\mathtt{m}_{\mathrm{cbv}}} (\lambda x.\lambda y.xx)(w[w{\leftarrow}I])(I[z{\leftarrow}I]) & \to_{\mathtt{e}_{\mathrm{cbv}}} (\lambda x.\lambda y.xx)(I[w{\leftarrow}I])(I[z{\leftarrow}I]) \\ \to_{\mathtt{m}_{\mathrm{cbv}}} (\lambda y.xx)[x{\leftarrow}I[w{\leftarrow}I]](I[z{\leftarrow}I]) & \to_{\mathtt{m}_{\mathrm{cbv}}} (xx)[y{\leftarrow}I[z{\leftarrow}I]][x{\leftarrow}I[w{\leftarrow}I]] \\ \to_{\mathtt{e}_{\mathrm{cbv}}} (xI)[y{\leftarrow}I[z{\leftarrow}I]][x{\leftarrow}I][w{\leftarrow}I] & \to_{\mathtt{e}_{\mathrm{cbv}}} (II)[y{\leftarrow}I[z{\leftarrow}I]][x{\leftarrow}I][w{\leftarrow}I] \\ \to_{\mathtt{m}_{\mathrm{cbv}}} x'[x'{\leftarrow}I][y{\leftarrow}I[z{\leftarrow}I]][x{\leftarrow}I][w{\leftarrow}I] & \to_{\mathtt{e}_{\mathrm{cbv}}} I[x'{\leftarrow}I][y{\leftarrow}I[z{\leftarrow}I]][x{\leftarrow}I][w{\leftarrow}I] \end{array}$$

Note that the fact that CbN and CbV take the same number of steps is by chance, as they reduce different redexes: CbN never reduce the unneeded redex II associated to y, but it reduces twice the needed II redex associated to x, while CbV reduces both, but each one only once.

In CbNeed, t evaluates in 4 multiplicative steps and 4 exponential steps.

$$\begin{array}{ll} t \to_{\mathtt{m}_{\mathrm{need}}} (\lambda y.xx)[x{\leftarrow}II](II) & \to_{\mathtt{m}_{\mathrm{need}}} (xx)[y{\leftarrow}II][x{\leftarrow}II] \\ \to_{\mathtt{m}_{\mathrm{need}}} (xx)[y{\leftarrow}II][x{\leftarrow}z[z{\leftarrow}I]] & \to_{\mathtt{e}_{\mathrm{need}}} (xx)[y{\leftarrow}II][x{\leftarrow}I[z{\leftarrow}I]] \\ \to_{\mathtt{e}_{\mathrm{need}}} (Ix)[y{\leftarrow}II][x{\leftarrow}I][z{\leftarrow}I] & \to_{\mathtt{m}_{\mathrm{need}}} (w[w{\leftarrow}x])[y{\leftarrow}II][x{\leftarrow}I][z{\leftarrow}I] \\ \to_{\mathtt{e}_{\mathrm{need}}} w[w{\leftarrow}I][y{\leftarrow}II][x{\leftarrow}I][z{\leftarrow}I] & \to_{\mathtt{e}_{\mathrm{need}}} I[w{\leftarrow}I][y{\leftarrow}II][x{\leftarrow}I][z{\leftarrow}I] \end{array}$$

CbV Diamond Property. CbV contexts coincide with weak ones. As a consequence, our presentation of CbV is non-deterministic, as for instance one can have

$$x[x{\leftarrow}I](y[y{\leftarrow}I]) \;{}_{\mathtt{m}_{\mathrm{cbv}}}\!\leftarrow (II)(y[y{\leftarrow}I]) \to_{\mathtt{e}_{\mathrm{cbv}}} (II)(I[y{\leftarrow}I])$$

but it is easily seen that diagrams can be closed in exactly one step (if the two reducts are different). For instance,

$$x[x{\leftarrow}I](y[y{\leftarrow}I]) \to_{\mathtt{e}_{\mathrm{cbv}}} x[x{\leftarrow}I](I[y{\leftarrow}I]) \;{}_{\mathtt{m}_{\mathrm{cbv}}}\!\leftarrow (II)(I[y{\leftarrow}I])$$

Moreover, the kind of steps is preserved, as the example illustrates. This is an instance of the strong form of confluence called *diamond property*. A consequence is that either all evaluation sequences normalise or all diverge, and if they normalise they have all the same length and the same number of steps of each kind. Roughly, the diamond property is a form of relaxed determinism. In particular, it makes sense to talk about the number of multiplicative/exponential steps to normal form, independently of the evaluation sequence. The proof of the property is an omitted routine check of diagrams.

Normal Forms. We use two predicates to characterise normal forms, one for both CbN and CbNeed normal forms, for which ES can contain whatever term, and one for CbV normal forms, where ES can only contain normal terms:

$$\frac{}{\mathsf{normal}(\lambda x.t)} \qquad \frac{\mathsf{normal}(t)}{\mathsf{normal}(t[x{\leftarrow}s])} \qquad \frac{}{\mathsf{normal}_{\mathsf{cbv}}(\lambda x.t)} \qquad \frac{\mathsf{normal}_{\mathsf{cbv}}(t) \quad \mathsf{normal}_{\mathsf{cbv}}(s)}{\mathsf{normal}_{\mathsf{cbv}}(t[x{\leftarrow}s])}$$

Proposition 1 (Syntactic characterization of closed normal forms). *Let t be a closed term.*
1. CbN and CbNeed: *For* $\mathsf{r} \in \{\text{cbn}, \text{need}\}$*,* t *is* r*-normal if and only if* $\mathsf{normal}(t)$.
2. CbV: t *is* cbv*-normal if and only if* $\mathsf{normal_{cbv}}(t)$.

The simple structure of normal forms is the main point where the restriction to closed calculi plays a role in this paper.

From the syntactic characterization of normal forms (Proposition 1) it follows immediately that among closed terms, normal forms for CbN and CbNeed coincide, while normal forms for CbV are a subset of them. Such a subset is proper since the closed term $I[x{\leftarrow}\delta\delta]$ (where $I := \lambda z.z$ and $\delta := \lambda y.yy$) is normal for CbN and CbNeed but not for CbV (and it cannot normalise in CbV).

3 Preliminaries About Multi Types

In this section we define basic notions about multi types, type contexts, and (type) judgements that are shared by the three typing systems of the paper.

Multi-sets. The type systems are based on two layers of types, defined in a mutually recursive way, *linear types* L and finite *multi-sets* M of linear types. The intuition is that a linear type L corresponds to a single use of a term, and that an argument t is typed with a multi-set M of n linear types if it is going to end up (at most) n times in evaluation position, with respect to the strategy associated with the type system. The three systems differ on the definition of linear types, that is therefore not specified here, while all adopt the same notion of finite multi-set M of linear types (named *multi type*), that we now introduce:

$$\text{MULTI TYPES} \qquad M, N ::= [L_i]_{i \in J} \quad \text{(for any finite set } J\text{)}$$

where $[\ldots]$ denotes the multi-set constructor. The empty multi-set $[\,]$ (the multi type obtained for $J = \emptyset$) is called *empty (multi) type* and denoted by the special symbol $\mathbf{0}$. An example of multi-set is $[L, L, L']$, that contains two occurrences of L and one occurrence of L'. Multi-set union is noted $\uplus$.

Type Contexts. A *type context* Γ is a (total) map from variables to multi types such that only finitely many variables are not mapped to $\mathbf{0}$. The *domain* of Γ is the set $\mathtt{dom}(\Gamma) := \{x \mid \Gamma(x) \neq \mathbf{0}\}$. The type context Γ is *empty* if $\mathtt{dom}(\Gamma) = \emptyset$.

Multi-set union $\uplus$ is extended to type contexts point-wise, *i.e.* $(\Gamma \uplus \Pi)(x) := \Gamma(x) \uplus \Pi(x)$ for each variable x. This notion is extended to a finite family of type contexts as expected, so that $\biguplus_{i \in J} \Gamma_i$ denotes a finite union of type contexts—it stands for the empty context when $J = \emptyset$. A type context Γ is denoted by $x_1 : M_1, \ldots, x_n : M_n$ (for some $n \in \mathbb{N}$) if $\mathtt{dom}(\Gamma) \subseteq \{x_1, \ldots, x_n\}$ and $\Gamma(x_i) = M_i$ for all $1 \leq i \leq n$. Given two type contexts Γ and Π such that $\mathtt{dom}(\Gamma) \cap \mathtt{dom}(\Pi) = \emptyset$, the type context Γ, Π is defined by $(\Gamma, \Pi)(x) := \Gamma(x)$ if $x \in \mathtt{dom}(\Gamma)$, $(\Gamma, \Pi)(x) := \Pi(x)$ if $x \in \mathtt{dom}(\Pi)$, and $(\Gamma, \Pi)(x) := \mathbf{0}$ otherwise.

$$\frac{}{x\!:\![L] \vdash^{(0,1)} x\!:\!L}\ \mathsf{ax} \qquad \frac{}{\vdash^{(0,0)} \lambda x.t\!:\!\mathsf{normal}}\ \mathsf{normal}$$

$$\frac{\Gamma, x\!:\!M \vdash^{(m,e)} t\!:\!L}{\Gamma \vdash^{(m,e)} \lambda x.t\!:\!M \multimap L}\ \mathsf{fun} \qquad \frac{(\Pi_i \vdash^{(m_i,e_i)} t\!:\!L_i)_{i\in J}}{\biguplus_{i\in J} \Pi_i \vdash^{(\Sigma_{i\in J} m_i, \Sigma_{i\in J} e_i)} t\!:\![L_i]_{i\in J}}\ \mathsf{many}$$

$$\frac{\Gamma \vdash^{(m,e)} t\!:\!M \multimap L \quad \Pi \vdash^{(m',e')} s\!:\!M}{\Gamma \uplus \Pi \vdash^{(m+m'+1,e+e')} ts\!:\!L}\ \mathsf{app} \qquad \frac{\Gamma, x\!:\!M \vdash^{(m,e)} t\!:\!L \quad \Pi \vdash^{(m',e')} s\!:\!M}{\Gamma \uplus \Pi \vdash^{(m+m',e+e')} t[x\leftarrow s]\!:\!L}\ \mathsf{ES}$$

Fig. 1. Type system for CbN evaluation

Judgements. *Type judgements* are of the form $\Gamma \vdash^{(m,e)} t : L$ or $\Gamma \vdash^{(m,e)} t : M$ (noted also $\vdash^{(m,e)} t : L$ and $\vdash^{(m,e)} t : M$, respectively, when Γ is the empty context), where the *indices* m and e are natural numbers whose intended meaning is that t evaluates to normal form in m multiplicative steps and e exponential steps, with respect to the evaluation strategy associated with the type system.

To make clear in which type systems the judgement is derived, we write $\Phi \triangleright_{\mathrm{cbn}} \Gamma \vdash^{(m,e)} t : L$ if Φ is a derivation in the CbN system ending in the judgement $\Gamma \vdash^{(m,e)} t : L$, and similarly for CbV and CbNeed.

4 Types by Name

In this section we introduce the CbN multi type system, together with intuitions about multi types. We also prove that derivations provide exact bounds on CbN evaluation sequences, and define the induced denotational model.

CbN Types. The system is essentially a reformulation of de Carvalho's system R [23], itself being a type-based presentation of the relational model of the CbN λ-calculus induced by relational model of linear logic via the CbN translation of λ-calculus into linear logic. Definitions:

- CbN *linear types* are given by the following grammar:

  CBN LINEAR TYPES $\qquad L, L' ::= \mathsf{normal} \mid M \multimap L$

  Multi(-sets) types are defined as in Sect. 3, relatively to CbN linear types. Note the linear constant normal (used to type abstractions, which are normal terms): it plays a crucial role in our quantitative analysis of CbN evaluation.
- The CbN *typing rules* are in Fig. 1.
- The many *rule*: it has as many premises as the elements in the (possibly empty) set of indices J. When $J = \emptyset$, the rule has no premises, and it types t with the empty multi type $\mathbf{0}$. The many rule is needed to derive the right premises of the rules app and ES, that have a multi type M on their right-hand side. Essentially, it corresponds to the promotion rule of linear logic, that, in the CbN representation of the λ-calculus, is indeed used for typing the right subterm of applications and the content of explicit substitutions.

– The *size* of a derivation $\Phi \triangleright_{\text{cbn}} \Gamma \vdash^{(m,e)} t : L$ is the sum $m + e$ of the indices. A quick look to the typing rules shows that indices on typing judgements are not needed, as m can be recovered as the number of app rules, and e as the number of ax rules. It is however handy to note them explicitly.

Subtleties and Easy Facts. Let us overview some facts about our presentation of the type system.

1. *Introduction and destruction of multi-sets*: multi-set are introduced on the right by the many rule and on the left by ax. Moreover, on the left they are summed by app and ES.
2. *Vacuous abstractions*: the abstraction rule fun can always abstract a variable x; note that if $M = \mathbf{0}$, then $\Gamma, x : M$ is equal to Γ.
3. *Relevance*: No weakening is allowed in axioms. An easy induction on type derivations shows that

Lemma 1 (Type contexts and variable occurrences for CbN). *Let* $\Phi \triangleright_{\text{cbn}} \Gamma \vdash^{(m,e)} t : L$ *be a derivation. If* $x \notin \mathtt{fv}(t)$ *then* $x \notin \mathtt{dom}(\Gamma)$.

Lemma 1 implies that derivations of closed terms have empty type context. Note that there can be free variables of t not in $\mathtt{dom}(\Gamma)$: the ones only occurring in subterms not touched by the evaluation strategy.

Key Ingredients. Two key points of the CbN system that play a role in the design of the CbNeed one in Sect. 6 are:

1. *Erasable terms and* $\mathbf{0}$: the empty multi type $\mathbf{0}$ is the type of erasable terms. Indeed, abstractions that erase their argument—whose paradigmatic example is $\lambda x.y$—can only be typed with $\mathbf{0} \multimap L$, because of Lemma 1. Note that in CbN every term—even diverging ones—can be typed with $\mathbf{0}$ by rule many (taking 0 premises), because, correctly, in CbN every term can be erased.
2. *Adequacy and linear types*: all CbN typing rules but many assign linear types. And many is used only as right premise of the rules app and ES, to derive M. It is with respect to linear types, in fact, that the adequacy of the system is going to be proved: a term is CbN normalising if and only if it is typable with a linear type, given by Theorems 1 and 2 below.

Tight Derivations. A term may have several derivations, indexed by different pairs (m, e). They always provide upper bounds on CbN evaluation lengths. The interesting aspect of our type systems, however, is that there is a simple description of a class of derivations that provide *exact* bounds for these quantities, as we shall show. Their definition relies on the normal type constant.

Definition 1 (Tight derivations for CbN). *A derivation* $\Phi \triangleright_{\text{cbn}} \Gamma \vdash^{(m,e)} t : L$ *is* tight *(for CbN) if* $L = \mathsf{normal}$ *and* Γ *is empty.*

Example 2. Let us return to the term $t := ((\lambda x.\lambda y.xx)(II))(II)$ used in Example 1 for explaining the difference in reduction lengths among the different strategies. We now give a derivation for it in the CbN type system.

First, let us shorten normal to n. Then, we define Φ as the following derivation for the subterm $\lambda x.\lambda y.xx$ of t:

$$\dfrac{\dfrac{\dfrac{\dfrac{}{x:[[\mathsf{n}]\multimap\mathsf{n}]\vdash^{(0,1)}x:[\mathsf{n}]\multimap\mathsf{n}}\,\mathsf{ax}\qquad\dfrac{\dfrac{}{x:[\mathsf{n}]\vdash^{(0,1)}x:\mathsf{n}}\,\mathsf{ax}}{x:[\mathsf{n}]\vdash^{(0,1)}x:[\mathsf{n}]}\,\mathsf{many}}{x:[\mathsf{n},[\mathsf{n}]\multimap\mathsf{n}]\vdash^{(1,2)}xx:\mathsf{n}}\,\mathsf{app}}{x:[\mathsf{n},[\mathsf{n}]\multimap\mathsf{n}]\vdash^{(1,2)}\lambda y.xx:\mathbf{0}\multimap\mathsf{n}}\,\mathsf{fun}}{\vdash^{(1,2)}\lambda x.\lambda y.xx:[\mathsf{n},[\mathsf{n}]\multimap\mathsf{n}]\multimap(\mathbf{0}\multimap\mathsf{n})}\,\mathsf{fun}$$

Now, we need two derivations for II, one of type n, given by Ψ as follows

$$\dfrac{\dfrac{\dfrac{}{z:[\mathsf{n}]\vdash^{(0,1)}z:\mathsf{n}}\,\mathsf{ax}}{\vdash^{(0,1)}\lambda z.z:[\mathsf{n}]\multimap\mathsf{n}}\,\mathsf{fun}\qquad\dfrac{\dfrac{}{\vdash^{(0,0)}\lambda w.w:\mathsf{n}}\,\mathsf{normal}}{\vdash^{(0,0)}\lambda w.w:[\mathsf{n}]}\,\mathsf{many}}{\vdash^{(1,1)}II:\mathsf{n}}\,\mathsf{app}$$

and one of type $[\mathsf{n}]\multimap\mathsf{n}$, given by Ξ as follows

$$\dfrac{\dfrac{\dfrac{}{z:[[\mathsf{n}]\multimap\mathsf{n}]\vdash^{(0,1)}z:[\mathsf{n}]\multimap\mathsf{n}}\,\mathsf{ax}}{\vdash^{(0,1)}\lambda z.z:[[\mathsf{n}]\multimap\mathsf{n}]\multimap([\mathsf{n}]\multimap\mathsf{n})}\,\mathsf{fun}\qquad\dfrac{\dfrac{\dfrac{}{w:[\mathsf{n}]\vdash^{(0,1)}w:\mathsf{n}}\,\mathsf{ax}}{\vdash^{(0,1)}\lambda w.w:[\mathsf{n}]\multimap\mathsf{n}}\,\mathsf{fun}}{\vdash^{(0,1)}\lambda w.w:[[\mathsf{n}]\multimap\mathsf{n}]}\,\mathsf{many}}{\vdash^{(1,2)}II:[\mathsf{n}]\multimap\mathsf{n}}\,\mathsf{app}$$

Finally, we put Φ, Ψ and Ξ together in the following derivation Θ for $t = (s(II))(II)$, where $s := \lambda x.\lambda y.xx$ and $\mathsf{n}^{[\mathsf{n}]} := [\mathsf{n}]\multimap\mathsf{n}$

$$\dfrac{\dfrac{\dfrac{\vdots\,\Phi}{\vdash^{(1,2)}s:[\mathsf{n},\mathsf{n}^{[\mathsf{n}]}]\multimap(\mathbf{0}\multimap\mathsf{n})}\qquad\dfrac{\dfrac{\vdots\,\Psi}{\vdash^{(1,1)}II:\mathsf{n}}\quad\dfrac{\vdots\,\Xi}{\vdash^{(1,2)}II:\mathsf{n}^{[\mathsf{n}]}}}{\vdash^{(2,3)}II:[\mathsf{n},\mathsf{n}^{[\mathsf{n}]}]}\,\mathsf{many}}{\vdash^{(4,5)}s(II):\mathbf{0}\multimap\mathsf{n}}\,\mathsf{app}\qquad\dfrac{}{\vdash^{(0,0)}II:\mathbf{0}}\,\mathsf{many}}{\vdash^{(5,5)}(s(II))(II):\mathsf{n}}\,\mathsf{app}$$

Note that Θ is a tight derivation and the indices $(5,5)$ correspond to the number of $\mathtt{m}_{\mathrm{cbn}}$-steps and $\mathtt{e}_{\mathrm{cbn}}$-steps, respectively, from t to its cbn-normal form, as shown in Example 1. Theorem 1 below shows that this is not by chance: tight derivations for CbN are minimal and provide exact bounds to evaluation lengths in CbN.

The next two subsections prove the two halves of the properties of the CbN type system, namely correctness and completeness.

4.1 CbN Correctness

Correctness is the fact that *every typable term is CbN normalising*. In our setting it comes with additional quantitative information: the indices m and e of a derivation $\Phi \triangleright_{\text{cbn}} \Gamma \vdash^{(m,e)} t : L$ provide upper bounds on the length of the CbN evaluation of t, that are exact when the derivation is tight.

The proof technique is standard. Moreover, the correctness theorems for CbV and CbNeed in the next sections follow *exactly* the same structure. The proof relies on a quantitative subject reduction property showing that m decreases by *exactly one* at each $\mathtt{m}_{\text{cbn}}$-step, and similarly for e and $\mathtt{e}_{\text{cbn}}$-steps. In turn, subject reduction relies on a linear substitution lemma. Last, correctness for *tight* derivations requires a further property of normal forms.

Let us point out that correctness is stated with respect to closed terms only, but the auxiliary results have to deal with open terms, since they are proved by inductions (over predicates defined by induction) over the structure of terms.

Linear Substitution. The linear substitution lemma states that substituting over a variable occurrence as in the exponential rule consumes exactly one linear type and decreases of one the exponential index e.

Lemma 2 (CbN linear substitution). *If* $\Phi \triangleright_{\text{cbn}} \Gamma, x : M \vdash^{(m,e)} C\langle\langle x\rangle\rangle : L$ *then there is a splitting* $M = [L'] \uplus N$ *such that for every derivation* $\Psi \triangleright_{\text{cbn}} \Pi \vdash^{(m',e')} t : L'$ *there is a derivation* $\Phi' \triangleright_{\text{cbn}} \Gamma \uplus \Pi, x : N \vdash^{(m+m',e+e'-1)} C\langle\langle t\rangle\rangle : L$.

The proof is by induction over CbN evaluation contexts.

Quantitative Subject Reduction. A key point of multi types is that the size of type derivations shrinks after every evaluation step, which is what allows to bound evaluation lengths. Remarkably, the size (defined as the sum of the indices) shrinks by exactly 1 at every evaluation step.

Proposition 2 (Quantitative subject reduction for CbN). *Let* $\Phi \triangleright_{\text{cbn}} \Gamma \vdash^{(m,e)} t : L$ *be a derivation.*

1. Multiplicative*: if* $t \to_{\mathtt{m}_{\text{cbn}}} s$ *then* $m \geq 1$ *and there exists a derivation* $\Psi \triangleright_{\text{cbn}} \Gamma \vdash^{(m-1,e)} s : L$.
2. Exponential*: if* $t \to_{\mathtt{e}_{\text{cbn}}} s$ *then* $e \geq 1$ *and there exists a derivation* $\Psi \triangleright_{\text{cbn}} \Gamma \vdash^{(m,e-1)} s : L$.

The proof is by induction on $t \to_{\mathtt{m}_{\text{cbn}}} s$ and $t \to_{\mathtt{e}_{\text{cbn}}} s$, using the linear substitution lemma for the root exponential step.

Tightness and Normal Forms. Since the indices are always non-negative, quantitative subject reduction (Proposition 2) implies that they bound evaluation lengths. The bound is not necessarily exact, as derivations of normal forms can have strictly positive indices. If they are tight, however, they are indexed by $(0, 0)$, as we now show. The proof of this fact (by induction on the predicate normal) requires a slightly different statement, for the induction to go through.

Proposition 3 (normal **typing of normal forms for CbN).** *Let* t *be such that* normal(t)*, and* $\Phi \triangleright_{\text{cbn}} \Gamma \vdash^{(m,e)} t : \mathsf{normal}$ *be a derivation. Then* Γ *is empty, and so* Φ *is tight, and* $m = e = 0$.

The Tight Correctness Theorem. The theorem is then proved by a straightforward induction on the evaluation length relying on quantitative subject reduction (Proposition 2) for the inductive case, and the properties of tight typings for normal forms (Proposition 3) for the base case.

Theorem 1 (CbN tight correctness). *Let* t *be a closed term. If* $\Phi \triangleright_{\text{cbn}} \vdash^{(m,e)} t : L$ *then there is* s *such that* $d\colon t \to^{*}_{\text{cbn}} s$*, with* normal($s$)*,* $|d|_{\mathtt{m}} \leq m$ *and* $|d|_{\mathtt{e}} \leq e$*. Moreover, if* Φ *is tight then* $|d|_{\mathtt{m}} = m$ *and* $|d|_{\mathtt{e}} = e$.

Note that Theorem 1 implicitly states that tight derivations have *minimal* size among derivations.

4.2 CbN Completeness

Completeness is the fact that *every CbN normalising term has a (tight) type derivation.* As for correctness, the completeness theorem is always obtained via three intermediate steps, dual to those for correctness.

Normal Forms. The first step is to prove (by induction on the predicate normal) that every normal form is typable, and is actually typable with a tight derivation.

Proposition 4 (Normal forms are tightly typable for CbN). *Let* t *be such that* normal(t)*. Then there is tight derivation* $\Phi \triangleright_{\text{cbn}} \vdash^{(0,0)} t : \mathsf{normal}$.

Linear Removal. In order to prove subject expansion, we have to first show that typability can also be pulled back along substitutions, via a linear removal lemma dual to the linear substitution lemma.

Lemma 3 (Linear removal for CbN). *Let* $\Phi \triangleright_{\text{cbn}} \Gamma, x : M \vdash^{(m,e)} C\langle\langle s\rangle\rangle : L$*, where* $x \notin \mathtt{fv}(s)$*. Then there exist*
- *a linear type* L' *and two type contexts* Γ' *and* Π*,*
- *a derivation* $\Phi' \triangleright_{\text{cbn}} \Gamma' \vdash^{(m',e')} s : L'$*, and*
- *a derivation* $\Psi \triangleright_{\text{cbn}} \Pi, x : M \uplus [L'] \vdash^{(m'',e'')} C\langle\langle x\rangle\rangle : L$

such that
- Type contexts*:* $\Gamma = \Gamma' \uplus \Pi$*.*
- Indices*:* $(m, e) = (m' + m'', e' + e'' - 1)$*.*

Quantitative Subject Expansion. This property is the dual of subject reduction.

Proposition 5 (Quantitative subject expansion for CbN). *Let* $\Phi \triangleright_{\text{cbn}} \Gamma \vdash^{(m,e)} s : L$ *be a derivation.*
1. Multiplicative*: if* $t \to_{\mathtt{m}_{\text{cbn}}} s$ *then there is a derivation* $\Psi \triangleright_{\text{cbn}} \Gamma \vdash^{(m+1,e)} t : L$*.*
2. Exponential*: if* $t \to_{\mathtt{e}_{\text{cbn}}} s$ *then there is a derivation* $\Psi \triangleright_{\text{cbn}} \Gamma \vdash^{(m,e+1)} t : L$*.*

The proof is by induction on $t \to_{\mathtt{m}_{\text{cbn}}} s$ and $t \to_{\mathtt{e}_{\text{cbn}}} s$, using the linear removal lemma for the root exponential step.

The Tight Completeness Theorem. The theorem is proved by a straightforward induction on the evaluation length relying on quantitative subject expansion (Proposition 5) in the inductive case, and the existence of tight typings for normal forms (Proposition 4) in the base case.

Theorem 2 (CbN tight completeness). *Let t be a closed term. If $d : t \to^*_{\text{cbn}} s$ and* $\mathsf{normal}(s)$ *then there is a tight derivation* $\Phi \triangleright_{\text{cbn}} \vdash^{(|d|_{\mathtt{m}}, |d|_{\mathtt{e}})} t : \mathsf{normal}$.

Back to Erasing Steps. Our system can be easily adapted to measure also garbage collection steps (the CbN erasing rule is just before Example 1). First, a new, third index g on judgements is necessary. Second, one needs to distinguish the erasing and non-erasing cases of the app and ES rules, discriminated by the $\mathbf{0}$ type. For instance, the ES rules are (the app rules are similar):

$$\frac{\Gamma \vdash^{(m,e,g)} t : L \quad \Gamma(x) = \mathbf{0}}{\Gamma \vdash^{(m,e,g+1)} t[x \leftarrow s] : L}\ \mathsf{ES}_{\text{gc}} \qquad \frac{\Gamma, x : M \vdash^{(m,e,g)} t : L \quad \Pi \vdash^{(m',e',g')} s : M \quad M \neq \mathbf{0}}{\Gamma \uplus \Pi \vdash^{(m+m',e+e',g+g')} t[x \leftarrow s] : L}\ \mathsf{ES}$$

The right premise of rule ES_{gc} has been removed because the only way to introduce $\mathbf{0}$ is via a many rule with no premises. The index g bounds to the number of erasing steps. In the closed case, however, the bound cannot be, in general, exact. Variables typed with $\mathbf{0}$ by Γ do not exactly match variables not appearing in the typed term (that is the condition triggering the erasing step), because a variable typed with $\mathbf{0}$ may appear in the body of abstractions typed with the normal rule, as such bodies are not typed.

It is reasonable to assume that exact bounds for erasing steps can only by provided by a type system characterising strong evaluation, whose typing rules have to inspect abstraction bodies. These erasing typing rules are nonetheless going to play a role in the design of the CbNeed system in Sect. 6.

4.3 CbN Model

The idea to build the denotational model from the multi type system is that the interpretation (or semantics) of a term is simply the set of its type assignments, *i.e.* the set of its derivable types together with their type contexts. More precisely, let t be a term and $x_1, \ldots, x_n$ (with $n \geq 0$) be pairwise distinct variables. If $\mathtt{fv}(t) \subseteq \{x_1, \ldots, x_n\}$, we say that the list $\vec{x} = (x_1, \ldots, x_n)$ is *suitable for t*. If $\vec{x} = (x_1, \ldots, x_n)$ is suitable for t, the *(relational) semantics of t for $\vec{x}$* is

$$[\![t]\!]^{\text{CbN}}_{\vec{x}} := \{((M_1, \ldots, M_n), L) \mid \exists \Phi \triangleright_{\text{cbn}} x_1 : M_1, \ldots, x_n : M_n \vdash^{(m,e)} t : L\}.$$

Subject reduction (Proposition 2) and expansion (Proposition 5) guarantee that the semantics $[\![t]\!]^{\text{CbN}}_{\vec{x}}$ of t (for *any* term t, possibly open) is *invariant* by CbN evaluation. Correctness (Theorem 1) and completeness (Theorem 2) guarantee that, given a *closed* term t, its interpretation $[\![t]\!]^{\text{CbN}}_{\vec{x}}$ is non-empty if and only if t is CbN normalisable, that is, they imply that relational semantics is *adequate*.

$$\frac{}{x : M \vdash^{(0,1)} x : M}\ \mathsf{ax} \qquad \frac{\Gamma \vdash^{(m,e)} t : [N \multimap M] \quad \Pi \vdash^{(m',e')} s : N}{\Gamma \uplus \Pi \vdash^{(m+m'+1,e+e')} ts : M}\ \mathsf{app}$$

$$\frac{\Gamma, x : N \vdash^{(m,e)} t : M}{\Gamma \vdash^{(m,e)} \lambda x.t : N \multimap M}\ \mathsf{fun} \qquad \frac{(\Pi_i \vdash^{(m_i,e_i)} \lambda x.t : L_i)_{i \in J}}{\biguplus_{i \in J} \Pi_i \vdash^{(\sum_{i\in J} m_i, \sum_{i \in J} e_i)} \lambda x.t : [L_i]_{i \in J}}\ \mathsf{many}$$

$$\frac{\Gamma, x : N \vdash^{(m,e)} t : M \quad \Pi \vdash^{(m',e')} s : N}{\Gamma \uplus \Pi \vdash^{(m+m',e+e')} t[x \leftarrow s] : M}\ \mathsf{ES}$$

Fig. 2. Type system for CbV evaluation.

In fact, adequacy also holds with respect to open terms. The issue in that case is that the characterisation of tight derivations is more involved, see Accattoli, Graham-Lengrand and Kesner's [7]. Said differently, weaker correctness and completeness theorems without exact bounds also hold in the open case. The same is true for the CbV and CbNeed systems of the next sections.

5 Types by Value

Here we introduce Ehrhard's CbV multi type system [34] adapted to our presentation of CbV in the LSC, and prove its properties. The system is similar, and yet in many aspects dual, to the CbN one, in particular the grammar of types is different. Linear types for CbV are defined by:

$$\text{CBV LINEAR TYPES} \qquad L, L' ::= M \multimap N$$

Multi(-sets) types are defined as in Sect. 3, relatively to CbV linear types. Note that linear types now have a multi type both as source and as target, and that the normal constant is absent—in CbV, its role is played by **0**.

The typing rules are in Fig. 2. It is a type-based presentation of the relational model of the CbV λ-calculus induced by relational model of linear logic via the CbV translation of λ-calculus into linear logic. Some remarks:

- *Right-hand types*: all rules but fun assign a multi type to the term on the right-hand side, and not a linear type as in CbN.
- *Abstractions and* many: the many rule has a restricted form with respect to the CbN one, it can only be applied to abstractions, that in turn are the only terms that can be typed with a linear type.
- *Indices*: note as the indices are however incremented (on ax and app) and summed (in many and ES) exactly as in the CbN system.

Intuitions: The Empty Type **0**. The empty multi-set type **0** plays a special role in CbV. As in CbN, it is the type of terms that can be erased, but, in contrast to CbN, not every term is erasable in CbV.

In the CbN multi type system every term, even a diverging one, is typable with $\mathbf{0}$. On the one hand, this is correct, because in CbN every term can be erased, and erased terms can also be divergent, because they are never evaluated. On the other hand, adequacy is formulated with respect to non-empty types: a term terminates if and only if it is typable with a non-empty type.

In CbV, instead, terms have to be evaluated before being erased; and, of course, their evaluation has to terminate. Thus, terminating terms and erasable terms coincide. Since the multi type system is meant to characterise terminating terms, in CbV a term is typable if and only if it is typable with $\mathbf{0}$, as we shall prove in this section. Then the empty type is not a degenerate type excluded for adequacy from the interesting types of a term, as in CbN, it rather is *the* type, characterising (adequate) typability altogether. And this is also the reason for the absence of the constant normal—one way to see it is that in CbV $\mathsf{normal} = \mathbf{0}$.

Note that, in particular, in a type judgement $\Gamma \vdash t : M$ the type context Γ may give the empty type to a variable x occurring in t, as for instance in the axiom $x : \mathbf{0} \vdash x : \mathbf{0}$—this may seem very strange to people familiar with CbN multi types. We hope that instead, according to the provided intuition that $\mathbf{0}$ is the type of termination, it would rather seem natural.

Definition 2 (Tight derivation for CbV). *A derivation $\Phi \triangleright_{\text{cbv}} \Gamma \vdash^{(m,e)} t : M$ is* tight *(for CbV) if $M = \mathbf{0}$ and Γ is empty.*

Example 3. Let's consider again the term $t := ((\lambda x.\lambda y.xx)(II))(II)$ of Example 1 (where $I := \lambda z.z$), for which a CbN tight derivation was given in Example 2, and let us type it in the CbV system with a tight derivation.

We define the following derivation Φ_1 for the subterm $s := \lambda x.\lambda y.xx$ of t

$$\dfrac{\dfrac{\dfrac{\dfrac{\dfrac{\dfrac{}{x : [\mathbf{0} \multimap \mathbf{0}] \vdash^{(0,1)} x : [\mathbf{0} \multimap \mathbf{0}]}\,\mathsf{ax} \qquad \dfrac{}{x : \mathbf{0} \vdash^{(0,1)} x : \mathbf{0}}\,\mathsf{ax}}{x : [\mathbf{0} \multimap \mathbf{0}] \vdash^{(1,2)} xx : \mathbf{0}}\,\mathsf{app}}{x : [\mathbf{0} \multimap \mathbf{0}] \vdash^{(1,2)} \lambda y.xx : \mathbf{0} \multimap \mathbf{0}}\,\mathsf{fun}}{x : [\mathbf{0} \multimap \mathbf{0}] \vdash^{(1,2)} \lambda y.xx : [\mathbf{0} \multimap \mathbf{0}]}\,\mathsf{many}}{\vdash^{(1,2)} s : [\mathbf{0} \multimap \mathbf{0}] \multimap [\mathbf{0} \multimap \mathbf{0}]}\,\mathsf{fun}}{\vdash^{(1,2)} s : [[\mathbf{0} \multimap \mathbf{0}] \multimap [\mathbf{0} \multimap \mathbf{0}]]}\,\mathsf{many}$$

Note that $[\mathbf{0} \multimap \mathbf{0}] \uplus \mathbf{0} = [\mathbf{0} \multimap \mathbf{0}]$, which explains the shape of the type context in the conclusion of the app rule. Next, we define the derivation Φ_2 as follows

$$\dfrac{\dfrac{\dfrac{\dfrac{}{z : [\mathbf{0} \multimap \mathbf{0}] \vdash^{(0,1)} z : [\mathbf{0} \multimap \mathbf{0}]}\,\mathsf{ax}}{\vdash^{(0,1)} \lambda z.z : [\mathbf{0} \multimap \mathbf{0}] \multimap [\mathbf{0} \multimap \mathbf{0}]}\,\mathsf{fun}}{\vdash^{(0,1)} \lambda z.z : [[\mathbf{0} \multimap \mathbf{0}] \multimap [\mathbf{0} \multimap \mathbf{0}]]}\,\mathsf{many} \qquad \dfrac{\dfrac{\dfrac{}{w : \mathbf{0} \vdash^{(0,1)} w : \mathbf{0}}\,\mathsf{ax}}{\vdash^{(0,1)} \lambda w.w : \mathbf{0} \multimap \mathbf{0}}\,\mathsf{fun}}{\vdash^{(0,1)} \lambda w.w : [\mathbf{0} \multimap \mathbf{0}]}\,\mathsf{many}}{\vdash^{(1,2)} II : [\mathbf{0} \multimap \mathbf{0}]}\,\mathsf{app}$$

and the derivation Φ_3 as follows

$$\dfrac{\dfrac{\dfrac{\dfrac{}{x' : \mathbf{0} \vdash^{(0,1)} x' : \mathbf{0}}\ \mathsf{ax}}{\vdash^{(0,1)} \lambda x'.x' : \mathbf{0} \multimap \mathbf{0}}\ \mathsf{fun}}{\vdash^{(0,1)} \lambda x'.x' : [\mathbf{0} \multimap \mathbf{0}]}\ \mathsf{many} \qquad \dfrac{}{\vdash^{(0,0)} I : \mathbf{0}}\ \mathsf{many}}{\vdash^{(1,1)} II : \mathbf{0}}\ \mathsf{app}$$

Finally, we put Φ_1, Φ_2 and Φ_3 together in the following derivation Φ for t

$$\dfrac{\dfrac{\overset{\vdots\, \Phi_1}{\vdash^{(1,2)} s : [[\mathbf{0} \multimap \mathbf{0}] \multimap [\mathbf{0} \multimap \mathbf{0}]]} \qquad \overset{\vdots\, \Phi_2}{\vdash^{(1,2)} II : [\mathbf{0} \multimap \mathbf{0}]}}{\vdash^{(3,4)} (\lambda x.\lambda y.xx)(II) : [\mathbf{0} \multimap \mathbf{0}]}\ \mathsf{app} \qquad \overset{\vdots\, \Phi_3}{\vdash^{(1,1)} II : \mathbf{0}}}{\vdash^{(5,5)} ((\lambda x.\lambda y.xx)(II))(II) : \mathbf{0}}\ \mathsf{app}$$

Note that Φ is a tight derivation and the indices $(5, 5)$ correspond to the number of $\mathtt{m}_{\mathrm{cbv}}$-steps and $\mathtt{e}_{\mathrm{cbv}}$-steps, respectively, from t to its cbv-normal form, as shown in Example 1. Theorem 3 below shows that this is not by chance: tight derivations for CbV are minimal and provide exact bounds to evaluation lengths in CbV.

Correctness (*i.e.* typability implies normalisability) and *completeness* (*i.e.* normalisability implies typability) of the CbV type system with respect to CbV evaluation (together with quantitative information about evaluation lengths) follow exactly the same pattern of the CbN case, *mutatis mutandis.*

5.1 CbV Correctness

Lemma 4 (CbV linear substitution). *Let $\Phi \rhd_{\mathrm{cbv}} \Gamma, x : M \vdash^{(m,e)} V\langle\langle x\rangle\rangle : N$ and v be a value. There is a splitting $M = O \uplus P$ such that, for any derivation $\Psi \rhd_{\mathrm{cbv}} \Pi \vdash^{(m',e')} v : O$, there is a derivation $\Phi' \rhd_{\mathrm{cbv}} \Gamma \uplus \Pi, x : P \vdash^{(m+m',e+e'-1)} V\langle\langle v\rangle\rangle : N$.*

Proposition 6 (Quantitative subject reduction for CbV). *Let $\Phi \rhd_{\mathrm{cbv}} \Gamma \vdash^{(m,e)} t : M$ be a derivation.*

1. Multiplicative: *if $t \to_{\mathtt{m}_{\mathrm{cbv}}} t'$ then $m \geq 1$ and there exists a derivation $\Phi' \rhd_{\mathrm{cbv}} \Gamma \vdash^{(m-1,e)} t' : M$.*
2. Exponential: *if $t \to_{\mathtt{e}_{\mathrm{cbv}}} t'$ then $e \geq 1$ and there exists a derivation $\Phi' \rhd_{\mathrm{cbv}} \Gamma \vdash^{(m,e-1)} t' : M$.*

Proposition 7 (Tight typings for normal forms for CbV). *Let $\Phi \rhd_{\mathrm{cbv}} \Gamma \vdash^{(m,e)} t : \mathbf{0}$ be a derivation, with $\mathsf{normal}_{\mathrm{cbv}}(t)$. Then Γ is empty, and so Φ is tight, and $m = e = 0$.*

Theorem 3 (CbV tight correctness). *Let t be a closed term. If $\Phi \rhd_{\mathrm{cbv}} \Gamma \vdash^{(m,e)} t : M$ then there is s such that $d : t \to^*_{\mathrm{cbv}} s$, with $\mathsf{normal}_{\mathrm{cbv}}(s)$, $|d|_{\mathtt{m}} \leq m$ and $|d|_{\mathtt{e}} \leq e$. Moreover, if Φ is tight then $|d|_{\mathtt{m}} = m$ and $|d|_{\mathtt{e}} = e$.*

5.2 CbV Completeness

Proposition 8 (Normal forms are tightly typable for CbV). *Let t be such that* $\mathsf{normal}_{\mathrm{cbv}}(t)$. *Then there exists a tight derivation* $\Phi \triangleright_{\mathrm{cbv}} \vdash^{(0,0)} t : \mathbf{0}$.

Lemma 5 (Linear removal for CbV). *Let* $\Phi \triangleright_{\mathrm{cbv}} \Gamma, x : M \vdash^{(m,e)} V\langle\langle v\rangle\rangle : N$ *and v be a value, where* $x \notin \mathtt{fv}(v)$. *Then, there exist*
- *a multi type M' and two type contexts Γ' and Π,*
- *a derivation* $\Phi' \triangleright_{\mathrm{cbv}} \Gamma' \vdash^{(m',e')} v : M'$ *and*
- *a derivation* $\Psi \triangleright_{\mathrm{cbv}} \Pi, x : M \uplus M' \vdash^{(m'',e'')} V\langle\langle x\rangle\rangle : N$

such that
- Type contexts: $\Gamma = \Gamma' \uplus \Pi$,
- Indices: $(m, e) = (m' + m'', e' + e'' - 1)$.

Proposition 9 (Quantitative subject expansion for CbV). *Let* $\Phi' \triangleright_{\mathrm{cbv}} \Gamma \vdash^{(m,e)} t' : M$ *be a derivation.*
1. Multiplicative*: if* $t \rightarrow_{\mathtt{m}_{\mathrm{cbv}}} t'$ *then there is a derivation* $\Phi \triangleright_{\mathrm{cbv}} \Gamma \vdash^{(m+1,e)} t : M$.
2. Exponential*: if* $t \rightarrow_{\mathtt{e}_{\mathrm{cbv}}} t'$ *then there is a derivation* $\Phi \triangleright_{\mathrm{cbv}} \Gamma \vdash^{(m,e+1)} t : M$.

Theorem 4 (CbV tight completeness). *Let t be a closed term. If* $d : t \rightarrow^*_{\mathrm{cbv}} s$ *with* $\mathsf{normal}_{\mathrm{cbv}}(s)$, *then there is a tight derivation* $\Phi \triangleright_{\mathrm{cbv}} \vdash^{(|d|_{\mathtt{m}},|d|_{\mathtt{e}})} t : \mathbf{0}$.

CbV Model. The interpretation of terms with respect to the CbV system is defined as follows (where $\vec{x} = (x_1, \ldots, x_n)$ is a list of variables suitable for t):

$$[\![t]\!]^{\mathrm{CbV}}_{\vec{x}} := \{((M_1, \ldots, M_n), N) \mid \exists \Phi \triangleright_{\mathrm{cbv}} x_1 : M_1, \ldots, x_n : M_n \vdash^{(m,e)} t : N\}.$$

Note that rule fun assigns a linear type but the interpretation considers only multi types. The *invariance* and the *adequacy* of $[\![t]\!]^{\mathrm{CbV}}_{\vec{x}}$ with respect to CbV evaluation are obtained exactly as for the CbN case.

6 Types by Need

CbNeed as a Blend of CbN and CbV. The multi type system for CbNeed is obtained by carefully blending ingredients from the CbN and CbV ones:
- *Wise erasures from CbN*: in CbN wise erasures are induced by the fact that the empty multi type $\mathbf{0}$ (the type of erasable terms) and the linear type normal (the type of normalisable terms) are distinct and every term is typable with $\mathbf{0}$ by using the many rule with 0 premises. Adequacy is then formulated with respect to (non-empty) linear types.
- *Wise duplications from CbV*: in CbV wise duplications are due to two aspects. First, only abstractions can be collected in multi-sets by rule many. This fact accounts for the evaluation of arguments to normal form—that is, abstractions—before being substituted. Second, terms are typed with multi types instead of linear types. Roughly, this second fact allows the first one to actually work because the argument is reduced once for a whole multi set of types, and not once for each element of the multi set, as in CbN.

$$\frac{}{x : M \vdash^{(0,1)} x : M}\ \mathsf{ax} \qquad \frac{\Gamma \vdash^{(m,e)} t : [N \multimap M] \quad \Pi \vdash^{(m',e')} s : N}{\Gamma \uplus \Pi \vdash^{(m+m'+1,e+e')} ts : M}\ \mathsf{app}$$

$$\frac{}{\vdash^{(0,0)} t : \mathbf{0}}\ \mathsf{many}_0 \qquad \frac{(\Pi_i \vdash^{(m_i,e_i)} \lambda x.t : L_i)_{i \in J} \quad J \neq \emptyset}{\biguplus_{i \in J} \Pi_i \vdash^{(\Sigma_{i \in J} m_i, \Sigma_{i \in J} e_i)} \lambda x.t : [L_i]_{i \in J}}\ \mathsf{many}_{>0}$$

$$\frac{\Gamma, x : N \vdash^{(m,e)} t : M}{\Gamma \vdash^{(m,e)} \lambda x.t : N \multimap M}\ \mathsf{fun} \qquad \frac{\Gamma, x : N \vdash^{(m,e)} t : M \quad \Pi \vdash^{(m',e')} s : N}{\Gamma \uplus \Pi \vdash^{(m+m',e+e')} t[x \leftarrow s] : M}\ \mathsf{ES}$$

$$\frac{}{\vdash^{(0,0)} \lambda x.t : \mathsf{normal}}\ \mathsf{normal}$$

Fig. 3. Naïve type system for CbNeed evaluation.

It seems then that a type system for CbNeed can easily be obtained by basically adopting the CbV system plus

- separating $\mathbf{0}$ and normal, that is, adding normal to the system;
- modifying the many rule by distinguishing two cases: with 0 premises it can assign $\mathbf{0}$ to whatever term—as in CbN—otherwise it is forced to work on abstractions, as in CbV;
- restricting adequacy to non-empty types.

Therefore, the grammar of linear types is:

$$\text{CbNeed linear types} \qquad L, L' ::= \mathsf{normal} \mid M \multimap N$$

Multi(-sets) types are defined as in Sect. 3, relatively to CbNeed linear types. The rules of this *naïve system* for CbNeed are in Fig. 3.

Issue with the Naïve System. Unfortunately, the naïve system does not work: tight derivations—defined as expected: empty type context and the term typed with [normal]—do not provide exact bounds. The problem is that the naïve blend of ingredients allows derivations of $\mathbf{0}$ with strictly positive indices m and e. Instead, derivations of $\mathbf{0}$ should always have 0 in both indices—as is the case when they are derived with a many_0 rule with 0 premises—because they correspond to terms to be erased, that are not evaluated in CbNeed. For any term t, indeed, one can for instance derive the following derivation Φ:

$$\dfrac{\dfrac{\dfrac{\dfrac{}{\vdash^{(0,0)} x : \mathbf{0}}\ \mathsf{many}_0}{\vdash^{(0,0)} \lambda x.x : \mathbf{0} \multimap \mathbf{0}}\ \mathsf{fun}}{\vdash^{(0,0)} \lambda x.x : [\mathbf{0} \multimap \mathbf{0}]}\ \mathsf{many}_{>0} \quad \dfrac{}{\vdash^{(0,0)} t : \mathbf{0}}\ \mathsf{many}_0}{\vdash^{(1,0)} (\lambda x.x)t : \mathbf{0}}\ \mathsf{app}$$

Note that introducing $\vdash^{(0,1)} x:\mathbf{0}$ with rule ax rather than via many_0 (the typing context $x:\mathbf{0}$ is equivalent to the empty type context) would give a derivation with final judgement $\vdash^{(1,1)} (\lambda x.x)t:\mathbf{0}$—thus, the system messes up both indices.

Such bad derivations of $\mathbf{0}$ are not a problem *per se*, because in CbNeed one expects correctness and completeness to hold only for derivations of non-empty multi types. However, they do mess up also derivations of non-empty multi types because they can still appear *inside* tight derivations, as sub-derivations of subterms to be erased; consider for instance:

$$\dfrac{\dfrac{\dfrac{\dfrac{\dfrac{}{\vdash^{(0,0)} I:\mathsf{normal}}\,\mathsf{normal}}{\vdash^{(0,0)} I:[\mathsf{normal}]}\,\mathsf{many}_{>0}}{\vdash^{(0,0)} \lambda y.I:\mathbf{0}\multimap[\mathsf{normal}]}\,\mathsf{fun}}{\vdash^{(0,0)} \lambda y.I:[\mathbf{0}\multimap[\mathsf{normal}]]}\,\mathsf{many}_{>0} \qquad \begin{array}{c}\vdots\,\Phi\\ \vdash^{(1,0)} (\lambda x.x)t:\mathbf{0}\end{array}}{\vdash^{(2,0)} (\lambda y.I)((\lambda x.x)t):[\mathsf{normal}]}\,\mathsf{app}$$

The term normalises in just 1 $\mathtt{m}_{\text{need}}$-step to $I[y{\leftarrow}(\lambda x.x)t]$ but the multiplicative index of the derivation is 2. The mismatch is due to a bad derivation of $\mathbf{0}$ used as right premise of an app rule. Similarly, the induced typing of $I[y{\leftarrow}(\lambda x.x)t]$ is an example of a bad derivation used as right premise of a rule ES:

$$\dfrac{\dfrac{\dfrac{}{\vdash^{(0,0)} I:\mathsf{normal}}\,\mathsf{normal}}{\vdash^{(0,0)} I:[\mathsf{normal}]}\,\mathsf{many}_{>0} \qquad \begin{array}{c}\vdots\,\Phi\\ \vdash^{(1,0)} (\lambda x.x)t:\mathbf{0}\end{array}}{\vdash^{(1,0)} I[y{\leftarrow}(\lambda x.x)t]:[\mathsf{normal}]}\,\mathsf{ES}$$

The Actual Type System. Our solution to such an issue is to modify the system as to avoid derivations of $\mathbf{0}$ to appear as right premises of rules app and ES. We follow the schema of the rules for counting erasing steps given right after Theorem 2.

Therefore, we add two dedicated rules app_{gc} and ES_{gc}, and constrain the right premise of rules app and ES to have a non-empty type. The system is in Fig. 4 and it is based on the same grammar of types of the naïve system. Note that rules many and ax can still introduce $\mathbf{0}$. These $\mathbf{0}$s, however, can no longer mess up the indices of tight derivations, as we are going to show.

Note that the indices m and e are incremented and summed exactly as in the CbN and CbV type systems.

Definition 3 (Tight derivations for CbNeed). *A derivation* $\Phi \rhd_{\text{need}} \Gamma \vdash^{(m,e)} t:M$ *is* tight *(for CbNeed) if* $M = [\mathsf{normal}]$ *and* Γ *is empty.*

Example 4. We return to the term $t := ((\lambda x.\lambda y.xx)(II))(II)$ used in Example 1 and we give it a tight derivation in the CbNeed type system.

Again, we shorten normal to n. Then, we define Ψ as follows

$$\dfrac{}{x:M\vdash^{(0,1)} x:M}\ \mathsf{ax} \qquad \dfrac{}{\vdash^{(0,0)} \lambda x.t:\mathsf{normal}}\ \mathsf{normal}$$

$$\dfrac{\Gamma, x:N\vdash^{(m,e)} t:M}{\Gamma\vdash^{(m,e)} \lambda x.t:N\multimap M}\ \mathsf{fun} \qquad \dfrac{(\Gamma_i\vdash^{(m_i,e_i)} \lambda x.t:L_i)_{i\in J}}{\biguplus_{i\in J}\Gamma_i\vdash^{(\sum_{i\in J}m_i,\sum_{i\in J}e_i)} \lambda x.t:[L_i]_{i\in J}}\ \mathsf{many}$$

$$\dfrac{\Gamma\vdash^{(m,e)} t:[\mathbf{0}\multimap M]}{\Gamma\vdash^{(m+1,e)} ts:M}\ \mathsf{app_{gc}} \qquad \dfrac{\Gamma\vdash^{(m,e)} t:[N\multimap M] \quad \Pi\vdash^{(m',e')} s:N \quad N\neq\mathbf{0}}{\Gamma\uplus\Pi\vdash^{(m+m'+1,e+e')} ts:M}\ \mathsf{app}$$

$$\dfrac{\Gamma\vdash^{(m,e)} t:M \quad \Gamma(x)=\mathbf{0}}{\Gamma\vdash^{(m,e)} t[x{\leftarrow}s]:M}\ \mathsf{ES_{gc}} \qquad \dfrac{\Gamma, x:N\vdash^{(m,e)} t:M \quad \Pi\vdash^{(m',e')} s:N \quad N\neq\mathbf{0}}{\Gamma\uplus\Pi\vdash^{(m+m',e+e')} t[x{\leftarrow}s]:M}\ \mathsf{ES}$$

Fig. 4. Type system for CbNeed evaluation.

$$\dfrac{\dfrac{\dfrac{\dfrac{\dfrac{\dfrac{}{x:[[\mathsf{n}]\multimap[\mathsf{n}]]\vdash^{(0,1)} x:[[\mathsf{n}]\multimap[\mathsf{n}]]}\ \mathsf{ax} \quad \dfrac{}{x:[\mathsf{n}]\vdash^{(0,1)} x:[\mathsf{n}]}\ \mathsf{ax}}{x:[\mathsf{n},[\mathsf{n}]\multimap[\mathsf{n}]]\vdash^{(1,2)} xx:[\mathsf{n}]}\ \mathsf{app}}{x:[\mathsf{n},[\mathsf{n}]\multimap[\mathsf{n}]]\vdash^{(1,2)} \lambda y.xx:\mathbf{0}\multimap[\mathsf{n}]}\ \mathsf{fun}}{x:[\mathsf{n},[\mathsf{n}]\multimap[\mathsf{n}]]\vdash^{(1,2)} \lambda y.xx:[\mathbf{0}\multimap[\mathsf{n}]]}\ \mathsf{many}}{\vdash^{(1,2)} \lambda x.\lambda y.xx:[\mathsf{n},[\mathsf{n}]\multimap[\mathsf{n}]]\multimap[\mathbf{0}\multimap[\mathsf{n}]]}\ \mathsf{fun}}{\vdash^{(1,2)} \lambda x.\lambda y.xx:[[\mathsf{n},[\mathsf{n}]\multimap[\mathsf{n}]]\multimap[\mathbf{0}\multimap[\mathsf{n}]]]}\ \mathsf{many}$$

and, shortening $[\mathsf{n}]\multimap[\mathsf{n}]$ to $[\mathsf{n}]^{[\mathsf{n}]}$, we define Θ as follows

$$\dfrac{\dfrac{\dfrac{\dfrac{}{z:[\mathsf{n},[\mathsf{n}]^{[\mathsf{n}]}]\vdash^{(0,1)} z:[\mathsf{n},[\mathsf{n}]^{[\mathsf{n}]}]}\ \mathsf{ax}}{\vdash^{(0,1)} \lambda z.z:[\mathsf{n},[\mathsf{n}]^{[\mathsf{n}]}]\multimap[\mathsf{n},[\mathsf{n}]^{[\mathsf{n}]}]}\ \mathsf{fun}}{\vdash^{(0,1)} \lambda z.z:[[\mathsf{n},[\mathsf{n}]^{[\mathsf{n}]}]\multimap[\mathsf{n},[\mathsf{n}]^{[\mathsf{n}]}]]}\ \mathsf{many} \quad \dfrac{\dfrac{}{\vdash^{(0,0)} \lambda w.w:\mathsf{n}}\ \mathsf{normal} \quad \dfrac{\dfrac{}{w:[\mathsf{n}]\vdash^{(0,1)} w:[\mathsf{n}]}\ \mathsf{ax}}{\vdash^{(0,1)} \lambda w.w:[\mathsf{n}]^{[\mathsf{n}]}}\ \mathsf{fun}}{\vdash^{(0,1)} \lambda w.w:[\mathsf{n},[\mathsf{n}]^{[\mathsf{n}]}]}\ \mathsf{many}}{\vdash^{(1,2)} II:[\mathsf{n},[\mathsf{n}]^{[\mathsf{n}]}]}\ \mathsf{app}$$

Finally, we put Ψ and Θ together in the following derivation Φ for t

$$\dfrac{\dfrac{\begin{array}{c}\vdots\,\Psi\\ \vdash^{(1,2)} \lambda x.\lambda y.xx:[[\mathsf{n},[\mathsf{n}]^{[\mathsf{n}]}]\multimap[\mathbf{0}\multimap[\mathsf{n}]]]\end{array} \quad \begin{array}{c}\vdots\,\Theta\\ \vdash^{(1,2)} II:[\mathsf{n},[\mathsf{n}]^{[\mathsf{n}]}]\end{array}}{\vdash^{(3,4)} (\lambda x.\lambda y.xx)(II):[\mathbf{0}\multimap[\mathsf{n}]]}\ \mathsf{app}}{\vdash^{(4,4)} ((\lambda x.\lambda y.xx)(II))(II):[\mathsf{n}]}\ \mathsf{app_{gc}}$$

Note that the indices $(4,4)$ correspond exactly to the number of $\mathtt{m}_{\mathrm{need}}$-steps and $\mathtt{e}_{\mathrm{need}}$-steps, respectively, from t to its need-normal form—as shown in Example 1—and that Φ is a *tight* derivation. Forthcoming Theorem 5 shows once again that this is not by chance: tight derivations for CbNeed are minimal and provides exact bounds to evaluation lengths in CbNeed.

Remarkably, the technical development to prove *correctness* and *completeness* of the CbNeed type system with respect to CbNeed evaluation follows smoothly along the same lines of the two other systems, *mutatis mutandis*.

6.1 CbNeed Correctness

Lemma 6 (CbNeed linear substitution). *Let* $\Phi \triangleright_{\mathrm{need}} \Gamma, x{:}M \vdash^{(m,e)} E\langle\langle x\rangle\rangle{:}N$ *and* v *be a value. There is a splitting* $M = O \uplus P$ *such that for any derivation* $\Psi \triangleright_{\mathrm{need}} \Pi \vdash^{(m',e')} v : O$ *there exists* $\Phi' \triangleright_{\mathrm{need}} \Gamma \uplus \Pi, x : P \vdash^{(m+m',e+e'-1)} E\langle\langle v\rangle\rangle : N$.

Proposition 10 (Quantitative subject reduction for CbNeed). *Let* $\Phi \triangleright_{\mathrm{need}} \Gamma \vdash^{(m,e)} t : M$ *be a derivation such that* $M \neq \mathbf{0}$.

- Multiplicative*: if* $t \rightarrow_{\mathtt{m}_{\mathrm{need}}} s$ *then* $m \geq 1$ *and there is a derivation* $\Phi' \triangleright_{\mathrm{need}} \Gamma \vdash^{(m-1,e)} t : M$.
- Exponential*: if* $t \rightarrow_{\mathtt{e}_{\mathrm{need}}} s$ *then* $e \geq 1$ *and there exists a derivation* $\Phi' \triangleright_{\mathrm{need}} \Gamma \vdash^{(m,e-1)} t : M$.

Note the condition $M \neq \mathbf{0}$ in the statement of subject reduction, that is in contrast to the CbV system but akin to the CbN one. It is due to the way multi types are used as arguments, via rules $\mathsf{ES}_{\mathrm{gc}}$ and $\mathsf{app}_{\mathrm{gc}}$. The restriction is necessary: the CbNeed type system derives $\vdash^{(0,1)} x[x\leftarrow\delta\delta] : \mathbf{0}$, but $x[x\leftarrow\delta\delta]$ is not normalising for CbNeed evaluation. And it is expected, as it amounts to the fact that adequacy holds only with respect to non-empty types, as for CbN, and as stressed when introducing the CbNeed type system. The same restriction appears in Theorem 5, Proposition 13 and Theorem 6 below, for the same reason.

Proposition 11 ([normal] typings for normal forms for CbNeed). *Let* $\Phi \triangleright_{\mathrm{need}} \Gamma \vdash^{(m,e)} t : [\mathsf{normal}]$ *be a derivation, with* $\mathsf{normal}(t)$. *Then* Γ *is empty, and so* Φ *is tight, and* $m = e = 0$.

Theorem 5 (CbNeed tight correctness). *Let* t *be a closed term. If* $\Phi \triangleright_{\mathrm{need}} \vdash^{(m,e)} t : M$ *where* $M \neq \mathbf{0}$, *then there is* s *such that* $d\colon t \rightarrow^*_{\mathrm{need}} s$, *with* $\mathsf{normal}(s)$, $|d|_{\mathtt{m}} \leq m$ *and* $|d|_{\mathtt{e}} \leq e$. *Moreover, if* Φ *is tight then* $|d|_{\mathtt{m}} = m$ *and* $|d|_{\mathtt{e}} = e$.

6.2 CbNeed Completeness

Proposition 12 (Normal forms are tightly typable for CbNeed). *Let* t *be such that* $\mathsf{normal}(t)$. *Then there is a tight derivation* $\Phi \triangleright_{\mathrm{need}} \vdash^{(0,0)} t : [\mathsf{normal}]$.

Lemma 7 (Linear removal for CbNeed). *Let* $\Phi \triangleright_{\mathrm{need}} \Gamma, x : M \vdash^{(m,e)} E\langle\langle v\rangle\rangle : N$ *be a derivation and* v *be a value, with* $x \notin \mathtt{fv}(v)$. *Then there exist*

- *a multi type* M' *and two type contexts* Γ' *and* Π,
- *a derivation* $\Phi' \triangleright_{\mathrm{need}} \Gamma' \vdash^{(m',e')} v : M'$, *and*
- *a derivation* $\Psi \triangleright_{\mathrm{need}} \Pi, x : M \uplus M' \vdash^{(m'',e'')} E\langle\langle x\rangle\rangle : N$

such that

- Type contexts*:* $\Gamma = \Pi \uplus \Gamma'$.
- Indices*:* $(m, e) = (m' + m'', e' + e'' - 1)$.

Proposition 13 (Quantitative subject expansion for CbNeed). *Let $\Phi \triangleright_{\text{need}} \Gamma \vdash^{(m,e)} s : M$ be a derivation such that $M \neq \mathbf{0}$. Then,*

- Multiplicative: *if $t \rightarrow_{\mathtt{m}_{\text{need}}} s$ then there is a derivation $\Phi' \triangleright_{\text{need}} \Gamma \vdash^{(m+1,e)} t : M$,*
- Exponential*: if $t \rightarrow_{\mathtt{e}_{\text{need}}} s$ then there is a derivation $\Phi' \triangleright_{\text{need}} \Gamma \vdash^{(m,e+1)} t : M$.*

Theorem 6 (CbNeed tight completeness). *Let t be a closed term. If $d \colon t \rightarrow^{*}_{\text{need}} s$ and* $\mathsf{normal}(s)$ *then there exists a tight derivation $\Phi \triangleright_{\text{need}} \vdash^{(|d|_{\mathtt{m}},|d|_{\mathtt{e}})} t : [\mathsf{normal}]$.*

CbNeed Model. The interpretation $[\![t]\!]^{\text{CbNeed}}_{\vec{x}}$ with respect to the CbNeed system is defined as the set (where $\vec{x} = (x_1, \ldots, x_n)$ is a list of variables suitable for t):

$$\{((M_1, \ldots, M_n), N) \mid \exists \Phi \triangleright_{\text{need}} x_1 : M_1, \ldots, x_n : M_n \vdash^{(m,e)} t : N \text{ and } N \neq \mathbf{0}\}.$$

Note that the right multi type is required to be non-empty. The *invariance* and the *adequacy* of $[\![t]\!]^{\text{CbNeed}}_{\vec{x}}$ with respect to CbNeed evaluation are obtained exactly as for the CbN and CbV cases.

7 A New Fundamental Theorem for Call-by-Need

CbNeed Erases Wisely. In the literature, *the* theorem about CbNeed is the fact that it is operationally equivalent to CbN. This result was first proven independently by two groups, Maraist, Odersky, and Wadler [48], and Ariola and Felleisen [11], in the nineties, using heavy rewriting techniques.

Recently, Kesner gave a much simpler proof via CbN multi types [40]. She uses multi types to first show termination equivalence of CbN and CbNeed, from which she then infers operational equivalence. Termination equivalence means that a given term terminates in CbN if and only if terminates in CbNeed, and it is a consequence of our slogan that *CbN and CbNeed both erase wisely.*

With our terminology and notations, Kesner's result takes the following form.

Theorem 7 (Kesner [40]**).** *Let t be a closed term.*

1. Correctness*: if $\Phi \triangleright_{\text{cbn}} \vdash^{(m,e)} t : L$ then there exists s such that $d \colon t \rightarrow^{*}_{\text{need}} s$,* $\mathsf{normal}(s)$*, $|d|_{\mathtt{m}} \leq m$ and $|d|_{\mathtt{e}} \leq e$.*
2. Completeness*: if $d \colon t \rightarrow^{*}_{\text{need}} s$ and* $\mathsf{normal}(s)$ *then there is $\Phi \triangleright_{\text{cbn}} \vdash^{(m,e)} t{:}\mathsf{normal}$.*

Note that, with respect to the other similar theorems in this paper, the result does not cover tight derivations and it does not provide exact bounds. In fact, the CbN system *cannot* provide exact bounds for CbNeed, because it does provide them for CbN evaluation, that in general is slower than CbNeed. Consider for instance the term t in Example 1 and its CbN tight derivation in Example 2: the derivation provides indices $(5, 5)$ for t (and so t evaluates in 10 CbN steps), but t evaluates in 8 CbNeed steps. Closing such a gap is the main motivation behind this paper, achieved by the CbNeed multi type system in Sect. 6.

CbNeed Duplicates Wisely. Curiously, in the literature there are no dual results showing that CbNeed duplicates as wisely as CbV. One of the reasons is that it is a theorem that does not admit a simple formulation such as operational or termination equivalence, because CbNeed and CbV are not in such relationships. Morally, this is subsumed by the logical interpretation according to which CbNeed corresponds to an affine variant of the linear logic representation of CbV. Yet, it would be nice to have a precise, formal statement establishing that *CbNeed duplicates as wisely as CbV*—we provide it here.

Our result is that the CbV multi type system is correct with respect to CbNeed evaluation. In particular, the indices (m, e) provided by a CbV type derivation provide bounds for CbNeed evaluation lengths. Two important remarks before we proceed with the formal statement:

- *Bounds are not exact*: the indices of a CbV derivation do not generally provide exacts bounds for CbNeed, not even in the case of tight derivations. The reason is that CbNeed does not evaluate unneeded subterms (*i.e.* those typed with $\mathbf{0}$), while CbV does. Consider again the term t of Example 1, for instance, whose CbV tight derivation has indices $(5, 5)$ (and so t evaluates in 10 CbV steps) but it CbNeed evaluates in 8 steps.
- *Completeness cannot hold*: we prove correctness but not completeness simply because the CbV system is not complete with respect to CbNeed evaluation. Consider for instance $(\lambda x.I)\Omega$: it is CbV untypable by Theorem 4, because it is CbV divergent, and yet it is CbNeed normalisable.

CbV Correctness with Respect to CbNeed. Pleasantly, our presentations of CbV and CbNeed make the proof of the result straightforward. It is enough to observe that, since we do not consider garbage collection and we adopt a non-deterministic formulation of CbV, CbNeed is a subsystem of CbV. Formally, if $t \rightarrow_{\mathsf{need}} s$ then $t \rightarrow_{\mathsf{cbv}} s$, as it is easily seen from the definitions (CbNeed reduces only *some* subterms of applications and ES, while CbV reduces *all* such subterms). The result is then a corollary of the correctness theorem for CbV.

Corollary 1 (CbV correctness w.r.t. CbNeed). *Let t be a closed term and $\Phi \triangleright_{\mathsf{cbv}} \;\vdash^{(m,e)} t : M$ be a derivation. Then there exists s such that $d\colon t \rightarrow^*_{\mathsf{need}} s$ and* $\mathsf{normal}(s)$, *with $|d|_{\mathtt{m}} \leq m$ and $|d|_{\mathtt{e}} \leq e$.*

Since the CbNeed system provides exact bounds (Theorem 5), we obtain that CbNeed duplicates as wisely as CbV, when the comparison makes sense, that is, on CbV normalisable terms.

Corollary 2 (CbNeed duplicates as wisely as CbV). *Let $d\colon t \rightarrow^*_{\mathsf{cbv}} u$ with* $\mathsf{normal}_{\mathsf{cbv}}(u)$. *Then there is $d'\colon t \rightarrow^*_{\mathsf{need}} s$ with* $\mathsf{normal}(s)$ *and $|d'|_{\mathtt{m}} \leq |d|_{\mathtt{m}}$ and $|d'|_{\mathtt{e}} \leq |d|_{\mathtt{e}}$.*

8 Conclusions

Contributions. This paper introduces a multi type system for CbNeed evaluation, carefully blending ingredients from multi type systems for CbN and CbV evaluation in the literature. Notably, it is the first type system whose minimal derivations—explicitly characterised—provide exact bounds for evaluation lengths. It also characterises CbNeed termination, and thus its judgements provide an adequate relational semantics.

The technical development is simple, and uniform with respect to those of CbN and CbV multi type systems. The typing rules count evaluation steps following *exactly* the same schema of the CbN and CbV rules. The proofs of correctness and completeness also follow *exactly* the same structure.

A further side contribution of the paper is a new fundamental result of CbNeed, formally stating that it duplicates as wisely as CbV. More precisely, the CbV multi type system is (quantitatively) correct with respect to CbNeed evaluation. Pleasantly, our presentations of CbV and CbNeed provide the result for free. This result dualizes the other fundamental theorem stating that CbNeed erases as wisely as CbN, usually formulated as termination equivalence, and recently re-proved by Kesner using CbN multi types [40].

Future Work. Recently, Barenbaum et al. extended CbNeed to strong evaluation [14], and it is natural to try to extend our type system as well. The definition of the system, in particular the extension of *tight* derivations to that setting, seems however far from being evident. Barembaum, Bonelli, and Mohamed also apply CbN multi types to a CbNeed calculus extended with pattern matching and fixpoints [15], that might be interesting to refine along the lines of our work.

An orthogonal direction is the study of the denotational models of CbNeed. It would be interesting to have a categorical semantics of CbNeed, as well as a categorical way of discriminating our quantitative precise model from the quantitatively lax one given by CbN multi types. It would also be interesting to obtain game semantics of CbNeed, hopefully satisfying a strong correspondence with our multi types in the style of what happens in CbN [30,31,51,56].

A further, unconventional direction is to dualise the inception of the CbNeed type system trying to mix silly duplication from CbN and silly erasure from CbV, obtaining—presumably—a multi types system measuring a perpetual strategy.

Acknowledgements. This work has been partially funded by the ANR JCJC grant COCA HOLA (ANR-16-CE40-004-01) and by the EPSRC grant EP/R029121/1 "Typed Lambda-Calculi with Sharing and Unsharing".

References

1. Accattoli, B.: An abstract factorization theorem for explicit substitutions. In: 23rd International Conference on Rewriting Techniques and Applications (RTA 2012). LIPIcs, vol. 15, pp. 6–21 (2012). https://doi.org/10.4230/LIPIcs.RTA.2012.6
2. Accattoli, B.: Proof nets and the linear substitution calculus. In: Fischer, B., Uustalu, T. (eds.) ICTAC 2018. LNCS, vol. 11187, pp. 37–61. Springer, Cham (2018). https://doi.org/10.1007/978-3-030-02508-3_3
3. Accattoli, B., Barenbaum, P., Mazza, D.: Distilling abstract machines. In: Proceedings of the 19th ACM SIGPLAN International Conference on Functional Programming (ICFP 2014), pp. 363–376 (2014). https://doi.org/10.1145/2628136.2628154

4. Accattoli, B., Barras, B.: Environments and the complexity of abstract machines. In: Proceedings of the 19th International Symposium on Principles and Practice of Declarative Programming (PPDP 2017), pp. 4–16. ACM (2017). https://doi.org/10.1145/3131851.3131855
5. Accattoli, B., Barras, B.: The negligible and yet subtle cost of pattern matching. In: Chang, B.-Y.E. (ed.) APLAS 2017. LNCS, vol. 10695, pp. 426–447. Springer, Cham (2017). https://doi.org/10.1007/978-3-319-71237-6_21
6. Accattoli, B., Bonelli, E., Kesner, D., Lombardi, C.: A nonstandard standardization theorem. In: The 41st Annual Symposium on Principles of Programming Languages (POPL 2014), pp. 659–670. ACM (2014). https://doi.org/10.1145/2535838.2535886
7. Accattoli, B., Graham-Lengrand, S., Kesner, D.: Tight typings and split bounds. PACMPL **2**(ICFP), 94:1–94:30 (2018). https://doi.org/10.1145/3236789
8. Accattoli, B., Guerrieri, G.: Types of fireballs. In: Ryu, S. (ed.) APLAS 2018. LNCS, vol. 11275, pp. 45–66. Springer, Cham (2018). https://doi.org/10.1007/978-3-030-02768-1_3
9. Accattoli, B., Guerrieri, G., Leberle, M.: Types by Need (Extended Version). CoRR abs/1902.05945 (2019)
10. Accattoli, B., Sacerdoti Coen, C.: On the value of variables. Inf. Comput. **255**, 224–242 (2017). https://doi.org/10.1016/j.ic.2017.01.003
11. Ariola, Z.M., Felleisen, M.: The call-by-need lambda calculus. J. Funct. Program. **7**(3), 265–301 (1997)
12. Ariola, Z.M., Felleisen, M., Maraist, J., Odersky, M., Wadler, P.: The call-by-need lambda calculus. In: Conference Record of POPL 1995: 22nd Symposium on Principles of Programming Languages, pp. 233–246. ACM Press (1995). https://doi.org/10.1145/199448.199507
13. Ariola, Z.M., Herbelin, H., Saurin, A.: Classical call-by-need and duality. In: Ong, L. (ed.) TLCA 2011. LNCS, vol. 6690, pp. 27–44. Springer, Heidelberg (2011). https://doi.org/10.1007/978-3-642-21691-6_6
14. Balabonski, T., Barenbaum, P., Bonelli, E., Kesner, D.: Foundations of strong call by need. PACMPL **1**(ICFP), 20:1–20:29 (2017). https://doi.org/10.1145/3110264
15. Barenbaum, P., Bonelli, E., Mohamed, K.: Pattern matching and fixed points: resource types and strong call-by-need: extended abstract. In: Proceedings of the 20th International Symposium on Principles and Practice of Declarative Programming (PPDP 2018), pp. 6:1–6:12. ACM (2018). https://doi.org/10.1145/3236950.3236972
16. Barras, B.: Auto-validation d'un système de preuves avec familles inductives. Ph.D. thesis, Université Paris 7 (1999)
17. Bernadet, A., Graham-Lengrand, S.: Non-idempotent intersection types and strong normalisation. Logical Methods Comput. Sci. **9**(4) (2013). https://doi.org/10.2168/LMCS-9(4:3)2013
18. Bucciarelli, A., Ehrhard, T., Manzonetto, G.: A relational semantics for parallelism and non-determinism in a functional setting. Ann. Pure Appl. Logic **163**(7), 918–934 (2012). https://doi.org/10.1016/j.apal.2011.09.008
19. Bucciarelli, A., Kesner, D., Ronchi Della Rocca, S.: Inhabitation for non-idempotent intersection types. Logical Methods Comput. Sci. **14**(3) (2018). https://doi.org/10.23638/LMCS-14(3:7)2018
20. Bucciarelli, A., Kesner, D., Ventura, D.: Non-idempotent intersection types for the lambda-calculus. Logic J. IGPL **25**(4), 431–464 (2017). https://doi.org/10.1093/jigpal/jzx018

21. Carraro, A., Guerrieri, G.: A semantical and operational account of call-by-value solvability. In: Muscholl, A. (ed.) FoSSaCS 2014. LNCS, vol. 8412, pp. 103–118. Springer, Heidelberg (2014). https://doi.org/10.1007/978-3-642-54830-7_7
22. de Carvalho, D.: Sémantiques de la logique linéaire et temps de calcul. Ph.D. thesis, Université Aix-Marseille II (2007)
23. de Carvalho, D.: Execution time of λ-terms via denotational semantics and intersection types. Math. Struct. Comput. Sci. **28**(7), 1169–1203 (2018). https://doi.org/10.1017/S0960129516000396
24. de Carvalho, D., Pagani, M., Tortora de Falco, L.: A semantic measure of the execution time in linear logic. Theoret. Comput. Sci. **412**(20), 1884–1902 (2011). https://doi.org/10.1016/j.tcs.2010.12.017
25. de Carvalho, D., Tortora de Falco, L.: A semantic account of strong normalization in linear logic. Inf. Comput. **248**, 104–129 (2016). https://doi.org/10.1016/j.ic.2015.12.010
26. Chang, S., Felleisen, M.: The call-by-need lambda calculus, revisited. In: Seidl, H. (ed.) ESOP 2012. LNCS, vol. 7211, pp. 128–147. Springer, Heidelberg (2012). https://doi.org/10.1007/978-3-642-28869-2_7
27. Coppo, M., Dezani-Ciancaglini, M.: A new type assignment for λ-terms. Arch. Math. Log. **19**(1), 139–156 (1978). https://doi.org/10.1007/BF02011875
28. Coppo, M., Dezani-Ciancaglini, M.: An extension of the basic functionality theory for the λ-calculus. Notre Dame J. Formal Logic **21**(4), 685–693 (1980). https://doi.org/10.1305/ndjfl/1093883253
29. Danvy, O., Zerny, I.: A synthetic operational account of call-by-need evaluation. In: 15th International Symposium on Principles and Practice of Declarative Programming (PPDP 2013), pp. 97–108. ACM (2013). https://doi.org/10.1145/2505879.2505898
30. Di Gianantonio, P., Honsell, F., Lenisa, M.: A type assignment system for game semantics. Theor. Comput. Sci. **398**(1–3), 150–169 (2008). https://doi.org/10.1016/j.tcs.2008.01.023
31. Di Gianantonio, P., Lenisa, M.: Innocent game semantics via intersection type assignment systems. In: Computer Science Logic 2013 (CSL 2013). LIPIcs, vol. 23, pp. 231–247 (2013). https://doi.org/10.4230/LIPIcs.CSL.2013.231
32. Díaz-Caro, A., Manzonetto, G., Pagani, M.: Call-by-value non-determinism in a linear logic type discipline. In: Artemov, S., Nerode, A. (eds.) LFCS 2013. LNCS, vol. 7734, pp. 164–178. Springer, Heidelberg (2013). https://doi.org/10.1007/978-3-642-35722-0_12
33. Downen, P., Maurer, L., Ariola, Z.M., Varacca, D.: Continuations, processes, and sharing. In: Proceedings of the 16th International Symposium on Principles and Practice of Declarative Programming (PPDP 2014), pp. 69–80. ACM (2014). https://doi.org/10.1145/2643135.2643155
34. Ehrhard, T.: Collapsing non-idempotent intersection types. In: Computer Science Logic (CSL 2012) - 26th International Workshop/21st Annual Conference of the EACSL. LIPIcs, vol. 16, pp. 259–273 (2012). https://doi.org/10.4230/LIPIcs.CSL.2012.259
35. Ehrhard, T., Guerrieri, G.: The bang calculus: an untyped lambda-calculus generalizing call-by-name and call-by-value. In: Proceedings of the 18th International Symposium on Principles and Practice of Declarative Programming (PPDP 2016), pp. 174–187. ACM (2016). https://doi.org/10.1145/2967973.2968608

36. Garcia, R., Lumsdaine, A., Sabry, A.: Lazy evaluation and delimited control. In: Proceedings of the 36th Symposium on Principles of Programming Languages (POPL 2009), pp. 153–164. ACM (2009). https://doi.org/10.1145/1480881.1480903
37. Gardner, P.: Discovering needed reductions using type theory. In: Hagiya, M., Mitchell, J.C. (eds.) TACS 1994. LNCS, vol. 789, pp. 555–574. Springer, Heidelberg (1994). https://doi.org/10.1007/3-540-57887-0_115
38. Girard, J.Y.: Linear logic. Theoret. Comput. Sci. **50**, 1–102 (1987). https://doi.org/10.1016/0304-3975(87)90045-4
39. Guerrieri, G.: Towards a semantic measure of the execution time in call-by-value lambda-calculus. In: Proceedings of ITRS 2018 (2018, to appear)
40. Kesner, D.: Reasoning about call-by-need by means of types. In: Jacobs, B., Löding, C. (eds.) FoSSaCS 2016. LNCS, vol. 9634, pp. 424–441. Springer, Heidelberg (2016). https://doi.org/10.1007/978-3-662-49630-5_25
41. Kesner, D., Vial, P.: Types as resources for classical natural deduction. In: 2nd International Conference on Formal Structures for Computation and Deduction (FSCD 2017). LIPIcs, vol. 84, pp. 24:1–24:17 (2017). https://doi.org/10.4230/LIPIcs.FSCD.2017.24
42. Kesner, D., Ríos, A., Viso, A.: Call-by-need, neededness and all that. In: Baier, C., Dal Lago, U. (eds.) FoSSaCS 2018. LNCS, vol. 10803, pp. 241–257. Springer, Cham (2018). https://doi.org/10.1007/978-3-319-89366-2_13
43. Kfoury, A.J.: A linearization of the lambda-calculus and consequences. J. Logic Comput. **10**(3), 411–436 (2000). https://doi.org/10.1093/logcom/10.3.411
44. Krivine, J.L.: Lambda-Calculus, Types and Models. Ellis Horwood Series in Computers and Their Applications. Ellis Horwood, Upper Saddle River, NJ, USA (1993)
45. Kutzner, A., Schmidt-Schauß, M.: A non-deterministic call-by-need lambda calculus. In: Proceedings of the Third International Conference on Functional Programming (ICFP 1998), pp. 324–335. ACM (1998). https://doi.org/10.1145/289423.289462
46. Launchbury, J.: A natural semantics for lazy evaluation. In: Conference Record of the Twentieth Annual Symposium on Principles of Programming Languages (POPL 1993), pp. 144–154. ACM Press (1993). https://doi.org/10.1145/158511.158618
47. Maraist, J., Odersky, M., Turner, D.N., Wadler, P.: Call-by-name, call-by-value, call-by-need and the linear lambda calculus. Theor. Comput. Sci. **228**(1–2), 175–210 (1999). https://doi.org/10.1016/S0304-3975(98)00358-2
48. Maraist, J., Odersky, M., Wadler, P.: The call-by-need lambda calculus. J. Funct. Program. **8**(3), 275–317 (1998)
49. Mazza, D., Pellissier, L., Vial, P.: Polyadic approximations, fibrations and intersection types. PACMPL **2**(POPL), 6:1–6:28 (2018). https://doi.org/10.1145/3158094
50. Neergaard, P.M., Mairson, H.G.: Types, potency, and idempotency: why nonlinearity and amnesia make a type system work. In: Proceedings of the Ninth International Conference on Functional Programming (ICFP 2004), pp. 138–149. ACM (2004). https://doi.org/10.1145/1016850.1016871
51. Ong, C.L.: Quantitative semantics of the lambda calculus: some generalisations of the relational model. In: 32nd Annual Symposium on Logic in Computer Science (LICS 2017), pp. 1–12. IEEE Computer Society (2017). https://doi.org/10.1109/LICS.2017.8005064

52. Paolini, L., Piccolo, M., Ronchi Della Rocca, S.: Essential and relational models. Math. Struct. Comput. Sci. **27**(5), 626–650 (2017). https://doi.org/10.1017/S0960129515000316
53. Pédrot, P.-M., Saurin, A.: Classical by-need. In: Thiemann, P. (ed.) ESOP 2016. LNCS, vol. 9632, pp. 616–643. Springer, Heidelberg (2016). https://doi.org/10.1007/978-3-662-49498-1_24
54. Pottinger, G.: A type assignment for the strongly normalizable λ-terms. In: Seldin, J., Hindley, J. (eds.) To H.B. Curry: Essays on Combinatory Logic, Lambda Calculus and Formalism, pp. 561–578. Academic Press, Cambridge (1980)
55. Sestoft, P.: Deriving a lazy abstract machine. J. Funct. Program. **7**(3), 231–264 (1997)
56. Tsukada, T., Ong, C.L.: Plays as resource terms via non-idempotent intersection types. In: Proceedings of the 31st Annual Symposium on Logic in Computer Science (LICS 2016), pp. 237–246. ACM (2016). https://doi.org/10.1145/2933575.2934553
57. Wadsworth, C.P.: Semantics and pragmatics of the lambda-calculus. Ph.D. thesis, University of Oxford (1971). Chapter 4

Verifiable Certificates for Predicate Subtyping

Frederic Gilbert(✉)

Inria, Cachan, France
frederic.a.gilbert@inria.fr

Abstract. Adding *predicate subtyping* to higher-order logic yields a very expressive language in which type-checking is undecidable, making the definition of a system of verifiable certificates challenging. This work presents a solution to this issue with a minimal formalization of predicate subtyping, named PVS-Core, together with a system of verifiable certificates for PVS-Core, named PVS-Cert. PVS-Cert is based on the introduction of proof terms and explicit coercions. Its design is similar to that of PTSs with dependent pairs, with the exception of the definition of conversion, which is based on a specific notion of reduction $\rightarrow_{\beta *}$, corresponding to β-reduction combined with the *erasure of coercions*. The use of this reduction instead of the more standard reduction $\rightarrow_{\beta\sigma}$ allows to establish a simple correspondence between PVS-Core and PVS-Cert. On the other hand, a type-checking algorithm is designed for PVS-Cert, built on proofs of type preservation of $\rightarrow_{\beta\sigma}$ and strong normalization of both $\rightarrow_{\beta\sigma}$ and $\rightarrow_{\beta *}$. Combining these results, PVS-Cert judgements are used as verifiable certificates for predicate subtyping. In addition, the reduction $\rightarrow_{\beta\sigma}$ is used to define a cut elimination procedure for predicate subtyping. This definition provides a new tool to study the properties of predicate subtyping, as illustrated with a proof of consistency.

Keywords: Higher-order logic · Predicate subtyping · Type theory · Proof theory

1 Introduction

Extending higher-order logic with *predicate subtyping* yields a very expressive type system, used notably at the core of the proof system PVS [17]. However, proof judgements and typing judgements become entangled in the presence of predicate subtyping, making type-checking undecidable. As a consequence, defining a language of verifiable proofs for predicate subtyping becomes challenging. In pure higher-order logic, complete judgement derivations are too heavy to be used in practice as certificates, but lighter certificates can be produced by removing typing rules, recording deduction rules only: as this approach requires the decidability of type-checking, it doesn't apply directly to predicate subtyping.

This paper presents a new formal language, PVS-Cert, designed to be used as a language of verifiable certificates for predicate subtyping. PVS-Cert is built

L. Caires (Ed.): ESOP 2019, LNCS 11423, pp. 440–466, 2019.
https://doi.org/10.1007/978-3-030-17184-1_16

starting from a minimal formalization of predicate subtyping named PVS-Core, by adding explicit proofs and coercions. PVS-Cert is also equipped with a notion of *cut elimination*, which can be used directly to study both PVS-Cert and PVS-Core meta-theoretical properties.

1.1 Extending Higher-Order Logic with Predicate Subtyping

Higher-order logic is characterized by the coexistence of *types* and *predicates* as two radically different kinds of attributes to mathematical expressions. For instance, the mathematical expression $1 + 1$ can be assigned a type *Nat* expressing that it is a natural number, or a predicate *Even* expressing that it is divisible by two. The assignment of types remains very simple: in particular, type-checking is decidable in higher-order logic. In return, most attributes of mathematical expressions formulated as predicates cannot be formulated as types: for instance, being a natural number different from 0 is expressible as a predicate, but not as a type.

Predicate subtyping allows to recover a symmetrical situation between the expressivity of types and predicates. It is defined as the addition of new types, referred to as *predicate subtypes*. Given a predicate P defined on a domain A (e.g. *Even*, defined on the domain *Nat*), the predicate subtype $\{x : A \mid P(x)\}$ is defined. An expression t can be assigned this type if and only if it can be assigned the type A and $P(t)$ is provable. For instance, if *Nonzero* is a predicate of domain *Nat* expressing the difference of a natural number from 0, proving $Nonzero(1)$ allows to conclude that 1 admits the type $\{x : Nat \mid Nonzero(x)\}$.

This augmented expressivity of the language of types permits to exclude many unwanted expressions from reasoning. For instance, defining the denominators domain of Euclidean division as $\{x : Nat \mid Nonzero(x)\}$, all divisions in which the denominator is not provably different from zero become ill-typed.

As expressions may have several types, predicate subtyping induces a form of subtyping: for instance, as any expression of type $\{x : Nat|Nonzero(x)\}$ also admits the type *Nat*, the former can be considered as a subtype of the latter.

As previously mentioned, a major counterpart of this extension of higher-order logic is the fact that typing judgements and proof judgements become entangled. For instance, proving the equality $(1/1) = 1$ requires that 1 can be assigned the type $\{x : Nat|Nonzero(x)\}$, which, in turn, requires to prove $Nonzero(1)$. As a direct consequence, type-checking is not decidable in the presence of predicate subtyping.

1.2 Contributions

PVS-Core. Higher-order logic, as well as its extension with predicate subtyping, can be defined in various ways. The first contribution of this paper is the formalization, in Sect. 2, of a minimal system for predicate subtyping, denoted PVS-Core. Besides its minimality, the main design choice for this system is the use of β-equivalence as a conversion relation (or definitional equality).

PVS-Cert and Its Basic Properties. Starting from PVS-Core, the second contribution of this work is the formalization, in Sect. 3, of a language of verifiable proofs for PVS-Core. This new language, denoted PVS-Cert, is designed from PVS-Core with the addition of explicit proof terms, formalized as λ-terms, as well as the addition, at the level of expressions, of explicit coercions based on these proof terms. The addition of explicit proof terms follows the Curry-Howard isomorphism in the sense that PVS-Cert proofs terms are typed by their corresponding formulas.

PVS-Cert is an extension of the Pure Type System (PTS) λ-HOL (see for instance [4], where λ-HOL as well as the general notion of PTS are defined). More precisely, PVS-Cert is designed to extend λ-HOL in the same way that PVS-Core extends higher-order logic (denoted HOL in the following). This situation is illustrated in this diagram, where vertical arrows represent extensions and horizontal arrows represent the introduction of explicit proofs (and, in the case of PVS-Core and PVS-Cert, of explicit coercions).

$$\begin{array}{ccc} \textbf{PVS-Core} & \longrightarrow & \textbf{PVS-Cert} \\ \uparrow & & \uparrow \\ \textbf{HOL} & \longrightarrow & \lambda\textbf{-HOL} \end{array}$$

This choice of a PTS-like system is well-suited to describe reasoning modulo β: all steps of β-reduction or β-expansion are kept implicit in proof terms, which allows to keep them compact. As detailed in Sect. 3.3, PVS-Cert is comparable to the formalism of PTSs with dependent pairs. However, conversion in PVS-Cert is neither defined as $\equiv_{\beta}$ nor as its extension $\equiv_{\beta\sigma}$ (see for instance [16]) used in PTSs with dependent pairs: instead, it uses a new conversion relation $\equiv_{\beta*}$ corresponding to syntactical equality modulo β-reduction *and coercion erasure* (defined in Sect. 3.1). This distinctive definition allows to define a simple correspondence between PVS-Core and PVS-Cert – presented later in Sect. 9.

Basic properties of PVS-Cert are presented in Sect. 4, containing notably the Church-Rosser property for the reduction $\rightarrow_{\beta*}$ underlying the conversion $\equiv_{\beta*}$, as well as the uniqueness of types: contrary to the case of PVS-Core, a well-typed term admits a unique type up to $\equiv_{\beta*}$.

As in λ-HOL, well-typed terms are organized according to a stratification, presented in Sect. 5, which includes a class of *types*, a class of *expressions* (containing notably propositions), and a class of *proof terms*. This stratification is at the core of the correspondence between PVS-Cert and PVS-Core.

Type Preservation and Strong Normalization. In contrast to the case of the reduction $\rightarrow_{\beta\sigma}$ in PTSs with dependent pairs, $\rightarrow_{\beta*}$ is not a type preserving reduction in PVS-Cert. We prove however in Sect. 6 that $\rightarrow_{\beta\sigma}$ is a type preserving reduction in PVS-Cert (Theorem 6).

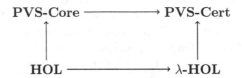

In Sect. 7, we present the main ideas leading to a proof of strong normalization for both $\rightarrow_{\beta*}$ and $\rightarrow_{\beta\sigma}$ (Theorem 7) – the details of the proof can be found in the author's PhD dissertation [1]. Moreover, the strong normalization of the type preserving reduction $\rightarrow_{\beta\sigma}$ defines a *cut elimination theorem* (Theorem 8). This theorem is used in the remainder of this section to prove the consistency of PVS-Cert. This result is used in turn at the very end of this work to conclude the consistency of PVS-Core, illustrating how cut elimination in PVS-Cert can be used to study the meta-theoretical properties of predicate subtyping.

Type-Checking in PVS-Cert. We present in Sect. 8 the design of a type-checking algorithm for PVS-Cert, showing that, contrary to the case of PVS-Core, type-checking is decidable in PVS-Cert. This algorithm is based on the type preservation of $\rightarrow_{\beta\sigma}$ as well as the strong normalization of $\rightarrow_{\beta*}$ and $\rightarrow_{\beta\sigma}$.

Using PVS-Cert as a System of Verifiable Certificates for PVS-Core. The connection between PVS-Core and PVS-Cert is formalized in Sect. 9. On the one hand, a translation from PVS-Cert to PVS-Core is defined through the erasure of coercions. On the other hand, the choice of conversion $\equiv_{\beta*}$ in PVS-Cert allows to define a very simple translation from PVS-Core derivations to PVS-Cert derivable judgements (Definition 7 and Theorem 11).

These translations are used in Sect. 10 together with the PVS-Cert type-checking algorithm to define how to use PVS-Cert judgements as verifiable certificates for PVS-Core, reaching the first purpose of this paper. Such certificates are much lighter than the PVS-Core *derivations* represented through them, as they only require to record one single judgement.

Last, the translations between PVS-Core and PVS-Cert are exploited to transpose the consistency property, established in PVS-Cert using cut elimination, to PVS-Core. This illustrates how the PVS-Cert cut elimination theorem can be used to study both PVS-Cert and PVS-Core meta-theoretical properties.

1.3 Related Works

The most important related work is the author's PhD dissertation [1], which contains detailed versions of all proofs presented in this paper.

The introduction of predicate subtyping can be traced back to the first-order language OBJ2 [9] and its *sort constraints*, allowing to restrict some typing relations to the satisfaction of a predicate. This idea was later refined and combined with higher-order logic in the proof system PVS, which is one of the most important systems based on predicate subtyping. Overviews of the PVS specification language and its use of predicate subtyping are given for instance in [17] and [20].

In the present work, the issue of the undecidability of predicate subtyping is handled with the introduction of an alternative system, PVS-Cert. An alternative approach to this issue is to weaken the definition of predicate subtyping sufficiently to obtain systems in which type-checking remains decidable. This approach has been followed in [13,19]. A intermediary situation is followed in [15], in which predicate subtyping is weakened sufficiently to allow for run-time type-checking verifications. However, contrary to the case of PVS, predicate subtyping is not fully represented in these different systems.

As mentioned in the previous section, PVS-Cert is an adaptation of the formalism of Pure Type Systems (PTSs) – sometimes also referred to as Generalized Type Systems (GTSs) –, presented for instance in [4]. The definition of PTSs is itself the result of several successive works, including notably [3,7,11,24–26]. More specifically, PVS-Cert is derived from the notion of PTSs *with dependent pairs*, which has its roots in the system ECC [16]. A subsystem of PVS-Cert, named PVS-Cert$^-$ and presented in Sect. 3, corresponds directly to a fragment of ECC (PVS-Cert$^-$ is the system obtained from PVS-Cert by replacing $\equiv_{\beta*}$ by the standard conversion $\equiv_{\beta\sigma}$ of PTSs with dependent pairs). PVS-Cert$^-$ is also comparable to the notion of *subset types* in Coq [5]. However, contrary to PVS-Cert, PVS-Cert$^-$ and subset types are not well-suited to reflect predicate subtyping, as conversion in these systems does not reflect conversion in PVS-Core – more precisely, Proposition 5 doesn't hold with $\equiv_{\beta\sigma}$.

Another important related work is [8], in which two systems are presented: ICC_Σ, a type system with *implicit* type constructions, and AICC_Σ, a system obtained from ICC_Σ by adding *explicit* coercions. ICC_Σ contains several advanced features, including a generalization of predicate subtypes. The construction of PVS-Cert from PVS-Core follows the same idea as the construction of AICC_Σ from ICC_Σ: adding the missing information explicitly in the terms of the language to recover the decidability of type-checking. The main difference between the two approaches lies in the complexity of the respective languages. ICC_Σ is a very rich and complex language, making its analysis difficult – in particular, strong normalization in ICC_Σ is kept as a conjecture, on which the decidability of type-checking itself relies. Conversely, PVS-Core is designed as a minimal language including predicate subtyping, making its analysis simpler.

A variant of predicate subtyping was also formalized as an extension of the calculus of constructions in [22]. As in the present work, this presentation contains two systems connected with each other. On the one hand, it includes one system, named Russell, which is comparable to a weakened version of PVS-Core in which a term t of type A admits the type $\{x : A \mid P\}$ even when $P[t/x]$ is not provable. In this variant of predicate subtyping named *subset equivalence*, type-checking is decidable. On the other hand, this work includes a system with explicit coercions which is comparable to PVS-Cert. Contrary to PVS-Core, Russell derivations are not intended to contain all information necessary to build complete terms with explicit coercions: instead, a translation producing incomplete terms in the system with explicit coercions is presented. This system allows to write programs and specifications together in Russell, and to prove their correctness in a second step by filling all proof holes produced through the translation, in a way which is similar to the functioning of PVS.

Contrary to the case of PVS-Core and Russell, PVS-Cert and the counterpart of Russell with explicit coercions have similar characteristics. Although its theoretical properties are not formalized, this latter system is presented as a simple extension of the proof-irrelevant type theory presented in [27]. There exists indeed a tight connection between proof irrelevance and PVS-Cert: if one considers for instance the usual predicate *Even* on natural numbers expressing divisibility by two, the predicate subtype $even = \{x : Nat \mid Even(x)\}$, and two expressions with explicit coercions $\langle 2, p\rangle_{even}$ and $\langle 2, q\rangle_{even}$ of this type with p and q two proofs of $Even(2)$, then the hypothesis of proof irrelevance ensures that the expressions $\langle 2, p\rangle_{even}$ and $\langle 2, q\rangle_{even}$ are convertible, as does the choice of conversion relation $\equiv_{\beta*}$ in PVS-Cert.

This relation between proof irrelevance and predicate subtyping is explored further in [27]. Besides the fact that this work is based on the calculus of constructions and besides some technical differences in the precise definition of conversion between the system presented in this paper and PVS-Cert, analyzing the strong relation between these two systems appears as a very interesting future work. In particular, it would provide a possible strategy for building a proof of strong normalization for this system from the proof of strong normalization presented in Sect. 7. Also following the relation between proof irrelevance and predicate subtyping, the system IITT presented in [2], which is equipped with explicit occurrences of irrelevant terms, also admits some similarities with PVS-Cert. However, it is restricted to predicative type theory, in which higher-order reasoning cannot be expressed.

Another important work carried out on predicate subtyping is the presentation of a *formal semantics* for PVS in [18]. This work defines, for some fragment of the PVS language including predicate subtyping but also other features such as *parametric theories*, set-theoretical interpretations of types and expressions. These interpretations are limited to *standard* interpretations: the interpretation of a function type is the set of all functions from the interpretation of the domain to the interpretation of the co-domain, and the interpretation of the type of propositions is a set containing exactly two elements, distinguishing *true* propositions from *false* ones. Such an approach is complementary to the presented paper, which is only focused on the distinction between *provable* propositions and *unprovable* ones. As a possible future work, it would be interesting to adapt the work presented in [18] to obtain a notion of *standard model* for PVS-Core.

2 PVS-Core: A Minimal Extension of HOL with Predicate Subtyping

This section is dedicated to the first contribution of this work: the formalization of a minimal system for predicate subtyping. This system is named PVS-Core, in reference to PVS [17]. The main distinctive design choice for PVS-Core is the introduction of a conversion relation (or definitional equality), corresponding to β-equivalence.

2.1 Definitions

Variables and Terms. We first define a set of **variables** $\mathcal{V}$ as the disjoint union of two infinite countable sets of symbols $\mathcal{V}_{expressions}$ and $\mathcal{V}_{types}$. We introduce the generic notation v or w to refer to a variable in general, as well as the following specific notations:

- The notation X or Y refers to variables in $\mathcal{V}_{types}$.
- The notation x or y refers to variables in $\mathcal{V}_{expressions}$.

Then, we define a set of **terms** as the disjoint union of the three following sets. The last two are defined together recursively.

- The first set contains a unique symbol: *Type*.
- The second set is the set of **types**. It is given with the following grammar: $A, B := X \mid Prop \mid \Pi x : A.B \mid \{x : A \mid P\}$
- The last set is the set of **expressions**. It is given with the following grammar: $t, u, P, Q := x \mid \forall x : A.P \mid P \Rightarrow Q \mid \lambda x : A.t \mid tu$

Remark 1. There is no formal distinction between the expressions denoted t or u and the expressions denoted P or Q, as all of them refer to expressions in general. Yet, in the following, the notations P and Q will be often used to refer to expressions admitting the type *Prop*, also referred to as *formulas* or *propositions*.

Declarations, Contexts, Judgements. We define:

- Three kinds of **declarations**: $X : Type \mid x : A \mid P$
- **Contexts**, denoted Γ, as lists of declarations: $\Gamma := \varnothing \mid \Gamma, X : Type \mid \Gamma, x : A \mid \Gamma, P$
- Four kinds of **judgements**: $\Gamma \vdash WF \mid \Gamma \vdash A : Type \mid \Gamma \vdash t : A \mid \Gamma \vdash P$

We use the notation $DV(\Gamma)$ to refer to the set of variables declared in a context Γ: for instance, $DV(P, x : A, X : Type) = \{x, X\}$.

Reduction. We equip PVS-Core terms with the usual β-reduction. In the following, we use the notation $\triangleright_\beta$ for the reduction of a β-redex, $\rightarrow_\beta$ for the context closure of $\triangleright_\beta$, $\twoheadrightarrow_\beta$ for the reflexive transitive closure of $\rightarrow_\beta$, and $\equiv_\beta$ for the symmetric closure of $\twoheadrightarrow_\beta$, i.e. β-conversion.

Derivation Rules. The rules of PVS-Core are the following:

Well-formed contexts

$$\frac{}{\varnothing \vdash WF}\ \textsc{Empty} \qquad \frac{\Gamma \vdash WF}{\Gamma, X : Type \vdash WF}\ X \in \mathcal{V}_{types} \backslash DV(\Gamma)\quad \textsc{TypeDecl}$$

$$\frac{\Gamma \vdash P : Prop}{\Gamma, P \vdash WF}\ \textsc{Assumption} \qquad \frac{\Gamma \vdash A : Type}{\Gamma, x : A \vdash WF}\ x \in \mathcal{V}_{expressions} \backslash DV(\Gamma)\quad \textsc{EltDecl}$$

Well-formed types

$$\frac{\Gamma \vdash WF}{\Gamma \vdash X : Type}\ (X : Type) \in \Gamma\quad \textsc{TypeVar} \qquad \frac{\Gamma \vdash WF}{\Gamma \vdash Prop : Type}\ \textsc{Prop}$$

$$\frac{\Gamma, x : A \vdash B : Type}{\Gamma \vdash \Pi x : A.B : Type}\ \textsc{Pi} \qquad \frac{\Gamma, x : A \vdash P : Prop}{\Gamma \vdash \{x : A \mid P\} : Type}\ \textsc{Subtype}$$

Well-typed expressions

$$\frac{\Gamma \vdash WF}{\Gamma \vdash x : A}\ (x : A) \in \Gamma\ \textsc{EltVar} \qquad \frac{\Gamma \vdash t : \{x : A \mid P\}}{\Gamma \vdash t : A}\ \textsc{SubtypeElim1}$$

$$\frac{\Gamma, x : A \vdash t : B}{\Gamma \vdash \lambda x : A.t : \Pi x : A.B}\ \textsc{Lam} \qquad \frac{\Gamma \vdash t : \Pi x : A.B \qquad \Gamma \vdash u : A}{\Gamma \vdash tu : B[u/x]}\ \textsc{App}$$

$$\frac{\Gamma, x : A \vdash P : Prop}{\Gamma \vdash \forall x : A.P : Prop}\ \textsc{Forall} \qquad \frac{\Gamma, P \vdash Q : Prop}{\Gamma \vdash P \Rightarrow Q : Prop}\ \textsc{Imply}$$

$$\frac{\Gamma \vdash t : A \qquad \Gamma \vdash P[t/x] \qquad \Gamma \vdash \{x : A \mid P\} : Type}{\Gamma \vdash t : \{x : A \mid P\}}\ \textsc{SubtypeIntro}$$

$$\frac{\Gamma \vdash t : A \qquad \Gamma \vdash B : Type}{\Gamma \vdash t : B}\ A \equiv_\beta B\ \textsc{TypeConversion}$$

Deductions

$$\frac{\Gamma \vdash WF}{\Gamma \vdash P}\ P \in \Gamma\ \textsc{Axiom} \qquad \frac{\Gamma \vdash P \qquad \Gamma \vdash Q : Prop}{\Gamma \vdash Q}\ P \equiv_\beta Q\ \textsc{PropConversion}$$

$$\frac{\Gamma, P \vdash Q}{\Gamma \vdash P \Rightarrow Q}\ \textsc{ImplyIntro} \qquad \frac{\Gamma \vdash P \Rightarrow Q \qquad \Gamma \vdash P}{\Gamma \vdash Q}\ \textsc{ImplyElim}$$

$$\frac{\Gamma, x : A \vdash P}{\Gamma \vdash \forall x : A.P}\ \textsc{ForallIntro} \qquad \frac{\Gamma \vdash \forall x : A.P \qquad \Gamma \vdash t : A}{\Gamma \vdash P[t/x]}\ \textsc{ForallElim}$$

$$\frac{\Gamma \vdash t : \{x : A \mid P\}}{\Gamma \vdash P[t/x]}\ \textsc{SubtypeElim2}$$

2.2 A Minimal System Expressing Predicate Subtyping

Predicate subtyping is expressed in PVS-Core with the term construction $\{x : A \mid P\}$ and the following rules:

- SUBTYPE, the rule of formation of predicate subtypes.
- SUBTYPEINTRO, which is a rule of introduction.
- SUBTYPEELIM1 and SUBTYPEELIM2, which are rules of elimination.

The system obtained from PVS-Core by removing the construction $\{x : A \mid P\}$ and these four rules is a formulation of constructive higher-order logic. In particular, the types of this subsystem correspond to the expected simple types: for any type of the form $\Pi x : A.B$ in this subsystem, x cannot appear free in B, hence this type is a non-dependent function type. As a consequence, the rule TYPECONVERSION can be safely removed from this subsystem to obtain a simpler but equivalent formulation of higher-order logic.

PVS-Core is a minimal constructive system, which can be extended with classical reasoning or extensionality principles through the addition of axioms.

The rule PROPCONVERSION allows to consider reasoning *modulo* β, which will be useful in the definition of PVS-Core to keep proof terms compact. The rule

TYPECONVERSION is its counterpart at the level of types, allowing to consider typing *modulo* β as well.

3 PVS-Cert: Verifiable Certificates for PVS-Core

This section is dedicated to the presentation of an alternative system, PVS-Cert, which will be used to achieve the purpose of the work: defining a language of verifiable certificates for predicate subtyping.

At first glance, there is no need to introduce any new system to design PVS-Core certificates: the language of PVS-Core derivations itself is a language of verifiable proofs for PVS-Core. However, this language is heavy as many parts of PVS-Core derivations contain unnecessary or redundant information. As a comparison, in higher-order logic, as type-checking is decidable, only the deduction rules need to be recorded.

The main idea in the definition of PVS-Cert as a language of certificates for predicate subtyping is to formalize proofs as new kinds of terms, in addition to the types and expressions which are already present in PVS-Core, and to introduce explicit coercions based on these proof terms in order to ensure the decidability of type-checking. As a consequence, a complete certificate is simply the typing judgement of some proof term with its corresponding theorem. Such certificates are much lighter than PVS-core derivations, as only one single judgement is recorded.

Moreover, PVS-Cert will be equipped (in Sect. 7) with a definition of *cut elimination*, defined as a computation rule on proof terms.

3.1 Definitions

As detailed further in Sect. 3.2, the definition of PVS-Cert is strongly related to the formalism of PTSs, presented for instance in [4].

Terms. We define:

- **Sorts** $\mathcal{S} = \{Prop, Type, Kind\}$
  We use the notation s to refer to a sort.
- **Axioms** $\mathcal{A} = \{(Prop, Type), (Type, Kind)\}$
- **Rules** $\mathcal{R} = \{(Prop, Prop, Prop), (Type, Type, Type), (Type, Prop, Prop)\}$
- **Variables** The set of variables $\mathcal{V}$ is the disjoint union of three infinite countable sets of symbols $\mathcal{V}_{proofs}$, $\mathcal{V}_{expressions}$, and $\mathcal{V}_{types}$. The sets $\mathcal{V}_{expressions}$ and $\mathcal{V}_{types}$ refer to their respective definitions in PVS-Core, while the set $\mathcal{V}_{proofs}$ is new. We use the notation v to refer to a variable and $s(v)$ to refer to the unique sort s such that $v \in \mathcal{V}_s$.
- **Terms** $\mathcal{T}$ is given by the following grammar:
  $M, N, T, U := s \mid v \mid \lambda v : T.M \mid MN \mid \Pi v : T.U \mid \{v : T \mid U\} \mid \langle M, N \rangle_T \mid \pi_1(M) \mid \pi_2(M)$

Contexts, Judgements. We define:

- **Contexts** $\Gamma := \varnothing \mid \Gamma, v : T$
- **Judgements** $\Gamma \vdash WF \mid \Gamma \vdash M : T$

As in PVS-Core, set of variables declared in a context Γ is denoted $DV(\Gamma)$.

Reduction. The main specificity of PVS-Cert is the use of a distinctive notion of reduction and conversion. In addition to the usual β-redex reduction $(\lambda v : T.M)N \rhd_\beta M[N/v]$, we introduce a new reduction relation $\rhd_*$, defined with the following rules:

- $\langle M_1, M_2\rangle_T \rhd_* M_1$
- $\pi_1(M) \rhd_* M$

We denote the union of $\rhd_\beta$ and $\rhd_*$ as $\rhd_{\beta *}$. As in the definition of PVS-Core, we use the notation $\rightarrow_{\beta *}$ for the context closure of $\rhd_{\beta *}$, $\twoheadrightarrow_{\beta *}$ for the reflexive transitive closure of $\rightarrow_{\beta *}$, and $\equiv_{\beta *}$ for the symmetric closure of $\twoheadrightarrow_{\beta *}$.

The new relation $\rhd_*$, which can be interpreted as the elimination of a coercion at the head of a term, allows the expression of predicate subtyping in PVS-Cert. More detailed motivations and justifications for this definition are given in Sect. 3.3.

Derivation Rules. The rules of PVS-Cert are defined as follows:

$$\frac{}{\varnothing \vdash WF}\ \textsc{Empty} \qquad \frac{\Gamma \vdash T : s}{\Gamma, v : T \vdash WF}\ v \in \mathcal{V}_s \backslash DV(\Gamma)\ \textsc{Decl}$$

$$\frac{\Gamma \vdash WF}{\Gamma \vdash v : T}\ (v : T) \in \Gamma\ \textsc{Var} \qquad \frac{\Gamma \vdash M : T \qquad \Gamma \vdash U : s}{\Gamma \vdash M : U}\ T \equiv_{\beta *} U\ \textsc{Conversion}$$

$$\frac{\Gamma \vdash WF}{\Gamma \vdash s_1 : s_2}\ (s_1, s_2) \in \mathcal{A}\ \textsc{Sort}$$

$$\frac{\Gamma \vdash T : s_1 \qquad \Gamma, v : T \vdash U : s_2}{\Gamma \vdash \Pi v : T.U : s_3}\ (s_1, s_2, s_3) \in \mathcal{R}\ \textsc{Prod}$$

$$\frac{\Gamma, v : T \vdash M : U \qquad \Gamma \vdash \Pi v : T.U : s}{\Gamma \vdash \lambda v : T.M : \Pi v : T.U}\ \textsc{Lam}$$

$$\frac{\Gamma \vdash M : \Pi v : T.U \qquad \Gamma \vdash N : T}{\Gamma \vdash MN : U[N/v]}\ \textsc{App}$$

$$\frac{\Gamma \vdash T : Type \qquad \Gamma, v : T \vdash U : Prop}{\Gamma \vdash \{v : T \mid U\} : Type}\ \textsc{Subtype}$$

$$\frac{\Gamma \vdash M : T \qquad \Gamma \vdash N : U[M/v] \qquad \Gamma \vdash \{v : T \mid U\} : Type}{\Gamma \vdash \langle M, N\rangle_{\{v:T \mid U\}} : \{v : T \mid U\}}\ \textsc{Pair}$$

$$\frac{\Gamma \vdash M : \{v : T \mid U\}}{\Gamma \vdash \pi_1(M) : T}\ \textsc{Proj1} \qquad \frac{\Gamma \vdash M : \{v : T \mid U\}}{\Gamma \vdash \pi_2(M) : U[\pi_1(M)/v]}\ \textsc{Proj2}$$

3.2 An Extension of λ-HOL

PVS-Cert is an extension of the PTS λ-HOL (see for instance [4]). More precisely, λ-HOL can be obtained from PVS-Cert by removing the term constructions $\{v : T \mid U\}$, $\pi_i(M)$, and $\langle M, N\rangle_T$, removing the rules SUBTYPE, PAIR, PROJ1, and PROJ2, and replacing $\equiv_{\beta*}$ by $\equiv_\beta$ in the CONVERSION rule.

As PTS-like systems, the formalism of PVS-Cert allows to describe reasoning modulo β: all steps of β-reduction or β-expansion in reasoning are kept implicit, which allows to keep proof terms compact, making PVS-Cert more scalable. Moreover, the choice of formalization of PVS-Cert as a PTS-like system allows to transpose some PTS properties to PVS-Cert, such as the thinning property and the substitution property mentioned in the next section. It also allows to describe this system using a small number of rules in comparison with PVS-Core, making the proof of certain expected properties of PVS-Cert lighter.

The well-typed terms of PVS-Cert are classified into the same classes as in the case of λ-HOL, involving a class of *types*, a class of *expressions*, and a class of *proof terms*. This property is presented in Sect. 5, and referred to as *stratification*.

3.3 Expressing Predicate Subtyping

The expression of predicate subtyping in PVS-Cert is enlightened through the *stratification*: indeed, in any derivable judgement,

- terms of the form $\{v : T \mid U\}$ are *types*, expressing predicate subtypes
- terms of the form $\langle M, N\rangle_T$ or $\pi_1(M)$ are *expressions*, and correspond respectively to explicit coercions going from a type to one of its predicate subtypes and back
- terms of the form $\pi_2(M)$ are *proofs*, expressing the PVS-Core deduction rule SUBTYPEELIM2.

As mentioned in the introduction, this formalism used to express predicate subtyping is very similar to the formalism of dependent pairs, used for instance in the type system ECC [16]. More precisely, the terms $\{v : T \mid U\}$ are comparable with types of dependent pairs (usually denoted $\Sigma v : T.U$), the terms $\langle M, N\rangle_T$ are comparable with dependent pairs, and the terms $\pi_i(M)$ are comparable with projections.

The only difference between PVS-Cert and the formalism of dependent pairs lies in the choice of conversion $\equiv_{\beta*}$: in the case of a system with dependent pairs, $\equiv_{\beta*}$ is replaced by the more standard conversion $\equiv_{\beta\sigma}$. This conversion is defined from the usual reduction $\pi_i\langle M_1, M_2\rangle_T \rhd_\sigma M_i$. We define the relations $\rhd_{\beta\sigma}$, $\rightarrow_{\beta\sigma}$, $\twoheadrightarrow_{\beta\sigma}$, and $\equiv_{\beta\sigma}$ in a similar way to the definitions of $\rhd_{\beta*}$, $\rightarrow_{\beta*}$, $\twoheadrightarrow_{\beta*}$, and $\equiv_{\beta*}$.

Applied to types or expressions, the conversion $\equiv_{\beta*}$ includes the more standard conversion $\equiv_{\beta\sigma}$ (this property is a direct consequence of Theorem 5 together with the Church-Rosser property of $\rightarrow_{\beta\sigma}$). However, this inclusion is strict: for instance, it is not difficult to find two well-typed terms $\langle M, N_1\rangle_T$ and $\langle M, N_2\rangle_T$ which are not convertible using $\equiv_{\beta\sigma}$, although they are convertible using $\equiv_{\beta*}$.

As a direct consequence of this property, PVS-Cert is an extension of the system obtained from it by replacing $\equiv_{\beta*}$ by $\equiv_{\beta\sigma}$, and this extension is strict. In this paper, this subsystem will be referred to as PVS-Cert$^-$. It is a PTS with dependent pairs, and corresponds more precisely to the system obtained from the PTS λ-HOL by adding the single dependent pair rule $(Type, Prop, Type)$. It is strictly included in the type system ECC presented in [16].

An mentioned in the introduction, this choice of a strictly more flexible conversion allows to define a very simple translation from PVS-Core derivations to PVS-Cert derivable judgements. Indeed, using $\equiv_{\beta*}$ ensures that two PVS-Cert types (resp. expressions) are convertible as long as the corresponding types (resp. expressions) in PVS-Core are also convertible, which allows to define a very simple translation from PVS-Core derivations to PVS-Cert derivable judgements (Definition 7 and Theorem 11).

The reduction $\rightarrow_{\beta*}$ underlying conversion does not preserve typing: for instance, the judgement $x : Prop, h : x \vdash \langle x, h\rangle_T : T$ with $T = \{y : Prop \mid y\}$ is derivable, and $\langle x, h\rangle_T \rightarrow_{\beta*} x$, but $x : Prop, h : x \vdash x : T$ is not derivable. However, as presented in Sect. 6, the reduction $\rightarrow_{\beta\sigma}$ is type preserving, and will be used both as a definition of cut elimination for PVS-Cert proofs (Sect. 7) and in the definition of a type checking-algorithm (Sect. 8).

4 Properties of PVS-Cert

One of the most important properties satisfied by PVS-Cert is the Church-Rosser property.

Theorem 1 (Church-Rosser for $\rightarrow_{\beta*}$). *Whenever $M_1 \equiv_{\beta*} M_2$, there exists N such that $M_1 \twoheadrightarrow_{\beta*} N$ and $M_2 \twoheadrightarrow_{\beta*} N$.*

Proof. $\mathcal{T}$ equipped with $\rightarrow_{\beta*}$ is an orthogonal combinatory reduction system (as defined in [14]), as rules are left-linear and non-overlapping. As proved in [14], such a system admits the Church-Rosser property.

In the case of PTSs, the Church-Rosser property of $\rightarrow_\beta$ is at the core of the type preservation of $\rightarrow_\beta$. In the case of PVS-Cert, the situation is different, as $\rightarrow_{\beta*}$ is not a type preserving reduction. However, in a first step, the Church-Rosser property of $\rightarrow_{\beta*}$ will be used to establish the expected stratification theorem, presented in Sect. 5. In a second step, the Church-Rosser property of $\rightarrow_{\beta*}$ will be used again together with the stratification theorem to establish the type preservation of an alternative reduction, $\rightarrow_{\beta\sigma}$, used both as a definition of cut elimination (Sect. 7) and at the core of the definition of a type-checking algorithm (Sect. 8).

Another important property of PVS-Cert used to design a type-checking algorithm is the uniqueness of types modulo conversion. As presented in Sect. 8, this property allows – together with the decidability of $\equiv_{\beta*}$ on well-typed terms – to reduce the problem of *type-checking* to a problem of *type inference*. This property also underlines the fact that, even though PVS-Cert is designed to reflect predicate subtyping, it doesn't admit any subtyping itself. The proof of type uniqueness is standard, and does not involve any specific difficulty.

Theorem 2 (Uniqueness of types). *If two judgements $\Gamma \vdash M : T_0$ and $\Gamma \vdash M : T_1$ are derivable, then $T_0 \equiv_{\beta*} T_1$.*

PVS-Cert also satisfies several other standard properties expected from PTSs and PTSs extended with dependent pairs, among which thinning and substitution, described for instance in [4], as well as context conversion, described for instance in [21], which is based on the extension of conversion to contexts. In these three cases, the corresponding proofs are straightforwardly adapted from the case of PTS.

We end this section with the following important theorem, which also holds in λ-HOL. The proof is adapted from the case of λ-HOL and does not involve any specific difficulty.

Theorem 3. *If $\Gamma \vdash M : T$ is derivable and $T \neq Kind$, there exists a sort s such that $\Gamma \vdash T : s$.*

5 Stratification in PVS-Cert

The stratification of terms in PVS-Cert reveals a strong link between PVS-Cert and PVS-Core (defined in Sect. 9), in the same way that the stratification of terms in λ-HOL reveals its link with higher-order logic. The property of stratification holds for several other systems, such as the injective PTSs presented in [11] – in this paper, PTSs are referred to as GTSs, and this result is referred to as classification.

The main lemma used to establish such a result is the fact that, whenever the rule of conversion is used in some derivation, the two terms involved in the conversion belong to the same class of terms. The simplest way to prove this result is to choose classes of terms that are stable under reduction and to conclude using the Church-Rosser theorem. In the case of injective PTSs, these classes are specific classes of well-typed terms, and the stability under reduction follows from the type preservation of $\rightarrow_\beta$.

However, as mentioned in Sect. 3.3, type preservation does not hold for $\rightarrow_{\beta*}$ in PVS-Cert. For this reason, we will choose a relaxed definition of stratified terms, where the different classes are not restricted to well-typed terms. Using this relaxed definition, it will be possible to prove, even in the absence of type preservation for $\rightarrow_{\beta*}$, that most classes of stratified terms are stable by reduction with $\rightarrow_{\beta*}$.

We first present three classes of terms: **types**, **expressions**, and **proofs**. The expected property of stability by reduction will only be proved for types and expressions (Proposition 1), which is not problematic as the conversion rules are never directly applied to proofs in valid derivations.

Definition 1 (Variables stratification). *We introduce the notations:*

- X, Y, Z *for variables in* $\mathcal{V}_{types}$
- x, y, z *for variables in* $\mathcal{V}_{expressions}$
- h *for variables in* $\mathcal{V}_{proofs}$

Definition 2 (Stratified terms). *We define stratified terms as follows.*

- ***Types*** $A, B := X \mid Prop \mid \Pi x : A.B \mid \{x : A \mid P\}$
- ***Expressions***
  $t, u, P, Q := x \mid \Pi x : A.P \mid \Pi h : P.Q \mid \lambda x : A.t \mid t\ u \mid \langle t, M\rangle_A \mid \pi_1(t)$
- ***Proofs*** $p, q := h \mid \lambda h : P.p \mid \lambda x : A.p \mid p\ q \mid p\ t \mid \pi_2(t)$

Remark 2. As in the case of PVS-Core (Remark 1), there is no formal distinction between the notations t, u, P, and Q although, in the following, the notations of expressions P, Q will be preferred for expressions of type $Prop$.

The most important remark on the definition of stratified terms is the fact that any pair $\langle t, M\rangle_A$ (where t is an expression and A is a type) is accepted as a correct expression: the term M used in it can be arbitrary, and in particular it is not required to be a proof term. This choice is due to the fact that proofs are not stable by $\rightarrow_{\beta *}$: for instance, $(\lambda h : x.h)y$ is a proof, but y is not. Hence, compared to the alternative of restricting pairs to terms of the form $\langle t, p\rangle_A$, the present relaxed definition is necessary to ensure the stability of types and expressions under $\rightarrow_{\beta *}$, which is formalized in the following proposition – the proof does not involve any specific difficulty, as the definitions of types and expressions are designed to satisfy this property.

Proposition 1. *Whenever $M \rightarrow_{\beta *} N$ and M is a type (resp. an expression), so is N.*

Beyond its use in the proof of the stratification theorem (Theorem 4), this stability property is also directly useful in the proof of the strong normalization theorem for $\rightarrow_{\beta *}$ and $\rightarrow_{\beta\sigma}$, as briefly mentioned in Sect. 7.

Finally, we present the expected stratification theorem, based on the following definitions.

Definition 3 (Stratified contexts, stratified judgements). *We define*

- ***stratified contexts*** *as contexts in which all declarations have the form X : $Type$, $x : A$ (for some type A), or $h : P$ (for some expression P).*
- ***stratified judgements*** *as judgements of one of the following forms, in which Γ is a stratified context:*

$\Gamma \vdash WF$	$\Gamma \vdash Type : Kind$
$\Gamma \vdash A : Type$	$\Gamma \vdash t : A$
$\Gamma \vdash p : P$	

Theorem 4 (Stratification). *Any derivable judgement is stratified.*

Proof. The proof is straightforward by induction on the derivation. In the case of CONVERSION, Proposition 1 and the Church-Rosser property of $\rightarrow_{\beta *}$ are used together to conclude that the two convertible terms are either both expressions, both types, both $Type$, or both $Kind$. Basic stability properties of types and expressions under substitution are also involved in the cases PROJ2 and APP. They are proved directly by induction.

6 A Type Preserving Reduction

Contrary to the case of PTSs (resp. PTSs with dependent pairs), in which $\rightarrow_\beta$ (resp. $\rightarrow_{\beta\sigma}$) is a type preserving reduction, $\rightarrow_{\beta*}$ is not a type preserving reduction in PVS-Cert. Instead, we present in this section the type preservation of the reduction $\rightarrow_{\beta\sigma}$ in PVS-Cert. This reduction will be used both as a definition of cut elimination for PVS-Cert proofs (Sect. 7) and in the type-checking algorithm (Sect. 8).

The specificity of this proof of type preservation compared to similar results for PTSs lies in the fact that $M \rightarrow_{\beta\sigma} N$ does not imply $M \equiv_{\beta*} N$ in general. However, this implication always holds if M is either a type or an expression – the corresponding proof involves no particular difficulty.

Theorem 5. *Whenever $M \rightarrow_{\beta\sigma} N$ and M is a type (resp. an expression), so is N, and $M \equiv_{\beta*} N$.*

Finally, the type preservation theorem for $\rightarrow_{\beta\sigma}$ is the following.

Theorem 6. *Given a derivable judgement $\Gamma \vdash M : T$, and N such that $M \rightarrow_{\beta\sigma} N$, the judgement $\Gamma \vdash N : T$ is derivable.*

Proof. The proof is done by induction on the derivation. The situations where $M \not\triangleright_{\beta\sigma} N$ and the cases where $M \triangleright_{\beta\sigma} N$ are separated. We present here one case for each situation – the full proof can be found in the author's PhD dissertation [1].

- We illustrate the situation where $M \not\triangleright_{\beta\sigma} N$ with the case of the rule Prod, which involves Theorem 5. Discarding the notations of the original statement, we describe the last inference step with the following new notations:

$$\frac{\Gamma \vdash T : s_1 \qquad \Gamma, v : T \vdash U : s_2}{\Gamma \vdash \Pi v : T.U : s_3}\ (s_1, s_2, s_3) \in \mathcal{R}\ \textsc{Prod}$$

If the reduction occurs in U, we conclude directly by induction hypothesis. If the reduction occurs in T, we write $T \rightarrow_{\beta\sigma} T'$. By induction hypothesis, $\Gamma \vdash T' : s_1$ is derivable. By the stratification theorem, $v \in \mathcal{V}_{s_1}$, hence $\Gamma, v : T' \vdash WF$ is derivable using the Decl rule. By the stratification theorem and Theorem 5, $T \equiv_{\beta*} T'$. Hence, using the second premise and context conversion (mentioned in Sect. 4), $\Gamma, v : T' \vdash U : s_2$ is derivable. Finally, using Prod, $\Gamma \vdash \Pi v : T'.U : s_3$ is derivable.
- We illustrate the situation where $M \triangleright_{\beta\sigma} N$ with the case of the rule Proj1. As M is a first projection and $M \triangleright_{\beta\sigma} N$, M is a σ-redex. We replace the notation M and T of the original statement by $\pi_1 \langle M, N \rangle_T \triangleright_{\beta\sigma} M$ and T'. In this setting, the last inference step has the following form:

$$\frac{\Gamma \vdash \langle M, N \rangle_T : \{v : T' \mid U'\}}{\Gamma \vdash \pi_1 \langle M, N \rangle_T : T'}\ \textsc{Proj1}$$

Analyzing the derivation of the premise (and more precisely the last rule different from Conversion used in it, which is necessarily Pair), we conclude that T has the form $\{v : T'' \mid U''\}$ where $\{v : T' \mid U'\} \equiv_{\beta*} \{v : T'' \mid U''\}$ and

$\Gamma \vdash \langle M, N \rangle_T : \{v : T'' \mid U''\}$ admits a derivation ending with an inference step of the form

$$\frac{\Gamma \vdash M : T'' \qquad \Gamma \vdash N : U''[M/v] \qquad \Gamma \vdash \{v : T'' \mid U''\} : Type}{\Gamma \vdash \langle M, N \rangle_T : \{v : T'' \mid U''\}} \text{ PAIR}$$

We derive the expected judgement $\Gamma \vdash M : T'$ from the first premise of this latter derivation using conversion. For this, we need to prove $T'' \equiv_{\beta*} T'$ and to derive $\Gamma \vdash T' : s$ for some s. These two requirements are proved as follows. On the one hand, we establish $T'' \equiv_{\beta*} T'$ from $\{v : T'' \mid U''\} \equiv_{\beta*} \{v : T' \mid U'\}$ using the Church-Rosser property (Theorem 1). On the other hand, by the stratification theorem, $T' \neq Kind$, hence we can use Theorem 3 on the original conclusion to establish that $\Gamma \vdash T' : s$ is derivable for some sort s, as expected.

7 Strong Normalization and Cut Elimination

This section is dedicated to the strong normalization of both $\rightarrow_{\beta\sigma}$ and $\rightarrow_{\beta*}$ on well-typed PVS-Cert terms. These two reductions will be used separately in Sect. 8 to define a type-checking algorithm for PVS-Cert: more precisely, the reduction $\rightarrow_{\beta*}$ is used to decide whether two well-typed terms are convertible with $\equiv_{\beta*}$, while the type preserving reduction $\rightarrow_{\beta\sigma}$ will be used in the type-checking of applications. Moreover, the strong normalization of $\rightarrow_{\beta\sigma}$ combined with its type preservation property provides a cut elimination theorem, which is a powerful tool to study properties of both PVS-Cert and PVS-Core. Its use is illustrated in a proof of consistency of PVS-Cert (Theorem 9), used in turn to establish the consistency of PVS-Core (Theorem 12) at the end of this paper.

7.1 Strong Normalization

A direct approach to prove the strong normalization of $\rightarrow_{\beta\sigma}$ and $\rightarrow_{\beta*}$ for well-typed terms would be to prove the strong normalization for well-typed terms of their union, referred to as $\rightarrow_{\beta\sigma*}$. Unfortunately, this reduction is not strongly terminating on well-typed terms, as shown in the following proposition.

Proposition 2. *There exists a well-typed term admitting an infinite reduction using* $\rightarrow_{\beta\sigma*}$.

Proof. We first define two well-typed terms M and N such that MN admits an infinite reduction. It is simple to find two such terms, using the fact that PVS-Cert is an extension of System F [12]. For instance:

- We take $\top = \Pi P : Prop.\Pi h : P.P$ together with $M = \lambda h : \top.h\ \top\ h$ and $N = \lambda h' : \top.\lambda h : \top.h\ \top\ h$
- M admits the type $\Pi h : \top.\top$ and N admits the type $\Pi h' : \top.\Pi h : \top.\top$.
- MN admits an infinite reduction $MN \rightarrow_{\beta\sigma*} N\ \top\ N \rightarrow_{\beta\sigma*} MN \rightarrow_{\beta\sigma*} ...$

Using these terms, we build the expected counter-example of normalization of $\rightarrow_{\beta\sigma*}$ as follows:

- We define $N' = \lambda P : Prop.\lambda h : P.h$, $T = \{x : Prop \mid \Pi h' : \top.\Pi h : \top.\top\}$, and $U = \{y : T \mid \top\}$.
- It is straightforward to show that $M\ \pi_2\langle\langle\top, N\rangle_T, N'\rangle_U$ admits the type $\top$.
- $M\ \pi_2\langle\langle\top, N\rangle_T, N'\rangle_U \twoheadrightarrow_{\beta\sigma*} MN$, hence it admits an infinite reduction.

Because of Proposition 2, we keep the expected strong normalization theorem in PVS-Cert formulated as follows.

Theorem 7 (Strong normalization). *For any derivable judgement $\Gamma \vdash M : T$, M is strongly normalizing under both $\rightarrow_{\beta\sigma}$ and $\rightarrow_{\beta*}$:*

- *any reduction sequence starting from M and using $\rightarrow_{\beta*}$ terminates*
- *any reduction sequence starting from M and using $\rightarrow_{\beta\sigma}$ terminates*

The proof of this theorem is left out of the scope of this paper. It is detailed in the author's PhD dissertation [1]. We simply highlight here some of its specificities, which illustrate the consequences of the choice, in PVS-Cert, of a conversion relation which is not based on a type-preserving reduction.

- The proof uses Tait's approach based on *saturated sets* (see for instance [23]). However, only one single notion of saturated set is used: saturated sets are defined here as specific subsets of the set of terms which are both strongly normalizing under $\rightarrow_{\beta\sigma}$ and strongly normalizing under $\rightarrow_{\beta*}$. As a consequence, compatibility properties for such saturated sets must be proved with respect to both reductions.
- Following Tait's approach, an interpretation function is defined in order to prove that, whenever term M admits a type T, it belongs to the interpretation of T, which is the main theorem established to conclude strong normalization. The definition of this function is inspired from the definitions of Girard in [12] for the strong normalization of F^ω – which corresponds to λ-HOL without type declarations –, but several ideas are also taken from [10], which presents, among other things, a proof of strong normalization of an extension of the calculus of constructions with dependent pairs.
- As the interpretation function is expected to be stable under $\rightarrow_{\beta*}$, its domain cannot be restricted to well-typed terms only, as well-typed terms are not stable under $\rightarrow_{\beta*}$. For this reason, it is chosen to define this interpretation function on the classes of types and expressions, as presented in the definition of stratified terms (Definition 3): indeed, this specific definition, which uses arbitrary terms instead of proof terms in the construction $\langle t, M\rangle_A$, is designed to ensure the stability of types and expressions under $\rightarrow_{\beta*}$.

7.2 Cut Elimination in PVS-Cert

The following cut elimination theorem is a direct corollary of the strong normalization theorem and the type preservation of $\rightarrow_{\beta\sigma}$.

Theorem 8 (Cut elimination). *Whenever some PVS-Cert judgement of the form $\Gamma \vdash p : P$ is derivable for some proposition P and some proof p, p can be reduced using the reduction $\rightarrow_{\beta\sigma}$ to a normal form q such that the judgement $\Gamma \vdash q : P$ is derivable.*

Proof. By the strong normalization theorem, p can be reduced to a normal form q using the reduction $\rightarrow_{\beta\sigma}$. By the type preservation theorem (Theorem 6), the judgement $\Gamma \vdash q : P$ is derivable.

We conclude this section showing how the cut elimination theorem can be used together with the properties of terms in normal form with respect to $\rightarrow_{\beta\sigma}$ as a tool to analyze some meta-theoretical properties of PVS-Cert. As presented at the end of this work, this approach will also allow to use cut elimination in PVS-Cert to analyze some meta-theoretical properties of PVS-Core. This use of cut elimination is illustrated with the following proof of consistency.

Theorem 9. *PVS-Cert is consistent: there exists no proof term p such that* $\vdash p : \Pi x : Prop.x$ *is derivable.*

We use the following notion of *elimination context* in the proof:

Definition 4 (Elimination contexts). *We define the set of elimination contexts* $\mathcal{E}$ *with the grammar* $e := \bullet \mid \pi_i(e) \mid e\, M$.

For any term N we define the instantiation $e[N]$ *by*

$$\bullet[N] = N \qquad \pi_i(e)[N] = \pi_i(e[N]) \qquad (eM)[N] = (e[N])M$$

Proof (Theorem 9). We suppose that there exists a proof p such that the judgement $\vdash p : \Pi x : Prop.x$ admits some derivation, and find a contradiction in the following way. Using the thinning property (mentioned in Sect. 4), $x : Prop \vdash p : \Pi x : Prop.x$ is also derivable. Hence, applying the rule Lam followed by the rule App, $\vdash \lambda x : Prop.(px) : \Pi x : Prop.x$ is derivable.

By the cut elimination Theorem 8, $\lambda x : Prop.(px)$ admits a normal form $\lambda x : Prop.q$ with respect to $\twoheadrightarrow_{\beta\sigma}$, which is such that the judgement $\vdash \lambda x : Prop.q : \Pi x : Prop.x$ is derivable.

Considering the last rule different from Conversion used in such a derivation (which is necessarily Lam), and using the stratification theorem, there exists a derivable judgement $x : Prop \vdash q : t$ for some expression $t \equiv_{\beta*} x$. Hence, using Conversion, $x : Prop \vdash q : x$ is also derivable. We consider D a possible derivation of this judgement.

As q is a proof and is in normal form with respect to $\twoheadrightarrow_{\beta\sigma}$, we conclude from a careful case analysis that q has one of the following forms: $\lambda v : T.M$ or $e[v]$. We discard the first possibility as follows. If $q = \lambda v : T.M$, considering the last rule different from Conversion used in D (which is necessarily Lam), there exists some term of the form $\Pi v' : T'.U'$ such that $\Pi v' : T'.U' \equiv_{\beta*} x$. By the Church-Rosser property (Theorem 1), this conversion cannot hold. As a consequence, q has the form $e[v]$ for some elimination context e and some variable v.

Considering the last rule different from Conversion, Proj1, Proj2, or App used in D (which is necessarily Var), some judgement of the form $x : Prop \vdash v : T$ is derivable, and $v = x$. As q is a proof, $e[x] = q \neq x$. Hence, D admits some subderivation of a judgement of the form $x : Prop \vdash xt' : T'$ or $x : Prop \vdash \pi_i(x) : T'$. Considering the last rule different from Conversion in such a derivation, and using the uniqueness of types (Theorem 2), this implies that there exists a term U

of the form $\Pi v' : T_1.T_2$ or $\{v' : T_1 \mid T_2\}$ such that $U \equiv_{\beta*} Prop$. By the Church-Rosser property (Theorem 1), this conversion cannot hold. As a consequence, there exists no proof term p such that the judgement $\vdash p : \Pi x : Prop.x$ is derivable.

8 Type-Checking in PVS-Cert

The purpose of this section is to present the main ideas leading to the definition of a type-checking algorithm for PVS-Cert. The decidability of type-checking is one of the most important results expected for PVS-Cert. In particular, it will be used in Sect. 10 together with the translation from PVS-Core derivations to PVS-Cert established in Sect. 9 to show that PVS-Cert judgements can be used as verifiable certificates for PVS-Core.

This algorithm is mainly based on the type preservation Theorem 6 and the strong normalization Theorem 7 presented in the previous sections. In this section, we will only focus on the main specificities of the algorithm. Its precise definition, as well as the proofs of its soundness, termination, and completeness can be found in the author's PhD dissertation [1].

The algorithm is comparable to the algorithm presented in [6] for the general case of injective PTSs (which applies to λ-HOL). Besides the fact that our algorithm is extended to handle predicate subtypes, coercions $\langle M, N\rangle_T$ and projections $\pi_i(M)$, the main difference between the two is the use of both reductions $\rightarrow_{\beta*}$ and $\rightarrow_{\beta\sigma}$ in the case of PVS-Cert, while only $\rightarrow_\beta$ is used for injective PTSs.

On the one hand, $\rightarrow_{\beta*}$-normalization is used to check $\equiv_{\beta*}$-conversion on well-typed terms: by the Church-Rosser property and strong normalization, two well-typed terms are $\equiv_{\beta*}$-equivalent if and only if they admit the same normal form, which is unique. As in [6], this decision procedure for conversion on well-typed terms is used in turn together with the uniqueness of types (Theorem 2) to define type-checking from type inference, which is itself defined recursively.

Remark 3. In order to avoid redundant context well-formedness verifications in the multiple recursive calls of the type inference algorithm, we choose here to check the well-formedness of a context Γ beforehand when inferring a type for some term M in Γ. For this reason, type inference and type-checking are defined in two steps. First, we define auxiliary type inference and type-checking algorithms which are only ensured to operate soundly with well-formed contexts. Then, we use these auxiliary functions to define context well-formedness verification as well as complete type inference and type-checking algorithms, which operate soundly with any context.

On the other hand, $\rightarrow_{\beta\sigma}$ is used in type inference to handle applications:

$$\frac{\Gamma \vdash M : \Pi v : T_1.T_2 \qquad \Gamma \vdash N : T_1}{\Gamma \vdash MN : T_2[N/v]}\ \textsc{App}$$

In this situation, the recursive call on the first premise may produce a term U such that $\Gamma \vdash M : U$ is derivable, but U is not ensured to have the form $\Pi v : U_1.U_2$ – counterexamples can be easily found when M is a proof and U is a proposition. The usual solution to this issue, used e.g. in [6], is to reduce U using the reduction underlying conversion (or more specifically its restriction to weak head reduction, which is more economic): indeed, using the uniqueness of types as well as strong normalization, type preservation, and the Church-Rosser property, it can be proved that a term U' will be obtained, that M admits the type U', and that U' has the form $\Pi v : U_1.U_2$ if M admits a type of this form.

However, in the case of PVS-Cert, this approach cannot be followed directly, as the reduction underlying conversion, which is $\rightarrow_{\beta*}$, is not type preserving: U' is not necessary a valid type for M. For this reason, we use instead the type preserving reduction $\rightarrow_{\beta\sigma}$ (again, we use more specifically its restriction to weak head reduction, which is more economic). Using the strong normalization theorem, this operation terminates and yields some term U''. As a direct corollary of type preservation (based on Theorems 3 and 5), M admits the type U''. What is left is to prove that U'' has the form $\Pi v : U_1.U_2$ if M admits a type of this form, which is done as follows. If M admits a type of the form $\Pi v : T_1.T_2$, then $U'' \equiv_{\beta*} \Pi v : T_1.T_2$ by the uniqueness of types. Hence, analyzing the possible forms of the weak head normal form U'' and using the Church-Rosser property, we conclude that U'' has the form $\Pi v : U_1.U_2$, as expected.

Compared to [6], new cases must be added for predicate subtypes, coercions $\langle M, N\rangle_T$, and projections $\pi_i(M)$. These cases are handled in a similar way as in the case of PTSs with dependent pairs (see for instance ECC [16]), and don't involve any specific difficulty. Instead, a more distinctive specificity of the algorithm lies in the case of λ-abstraction:

$$\frac{\Gamma, v : T \vdash M : U \qquad \Gamma \vdash \Pi v : T.U : s}{\Gamma \vdash \lambda v : T.M : \Pi v : T.U}\ \textsc{Lam}$$

As in the case of injective PTSs studied in [6], applying a recursive call on this second premise would be problematic. On the one hand, it would make the algorithm slower. On the other hand, it would break the simplicity of the proof of termination, based on the fact that recursive calls of type inference are done on subterms exclusively.

A general solution for this issue, applicable to any injective PTSs, is presented in [6] using some classification of terms to avoid this unwanted recursive call. The solution selected for PVS-Cert follows the same approach, adapted to the stratified terms of PVS-Cert. It relies on a classifying algorithm $\textsc{Level}(\cdot)$, which ensures that whenever M is either an expression, a type, *Type*, or *Kind*, then $\textsc{Level}(M)$ is either 1, 2, 3, or 4 respectively. As it is specifically suited to PVS-Cert, this definition is simpler than the classification presented in [6], which is intended to be applicable to a wide family of type systems. The algorithm is defined as follows:

Definition 5. *We define the algorithm* $\textsc{Level}(\cdot)$ *by recursion on its argument. The possible cases are the following.*

- $\textsc{Level}(\mathit{Kind}) = 4$, $\textsc{Level}(\mathit{Type}) = 3$, $\textsc{Level}(\mathit{Prop}) = 2$
- $\textsc{Level}(\Pi v : T.U) = \textsc{Level}(U)$, $\textsc{Level}(\{v : T \mid U\}) = 2$, $\textsc{Level}(X) = 2$
- *In all other cases,* $\textsc{Level}(M) = 1$

9 Expressing PVS-Core in PVS-Cert

The final purpose of PVS-Cert is to encode PVS-Core derivations as PVS-Cert judgements, and to use the type-checking algorithm presented in Sect. 8 to use these judgements as verifiable certificates. In this perspective, we define a correspondence between PVS-Core and PVS-Cert. This correspondence reflects the fact that, even though these two systems are very different at the level of terms and judgements, they are almost identical at the level of derivations.

9.1 An Erasing Function from PVS-Cert to PVS-Core

We begin the description of this correspondence with a translation from PVS-Cert to PVS-Core, referred to as *erasing*. This translation mainly consists in the erasure of PVS-Cert explicit coercions $\langle \cdot, M\rangle_A$ and $\pi_1(\cdot)$.

Definition 6. *We define an erasure function* $[\![\cdot]\!]$ *from PVS-Cert expressions, types, and Type to PVS-Core terms recursively as follows.*

$$\begin{array}{lll}
[\![Type]\!] = Type & [\![x]\!] = x & [\![\langle t, M\rangle_A]\!] = [\![t]\!] \\
[\![Prop]\!] = Prop & [\![\lambda x : A.t]\!] = \lambda x : [\![A]\!].[\![t]\!] & [\![\pi_1(t)]\!] = [\![t]\!] \\
[\![X]\!] = X & [\![t\ u]\!] = [\![t]\!]\,[\![u]\!] & \\
[\![\Pi x : A.B]\!] = \Pi x : [\![A]\!].[\![B]\!] & [\![\Pi x : A.P]\!] = \forall x : [\![A]\!].[\![P]\!] & \\
[\![\{x : A \mid P\}]\!] = \{x : [\![A]\!] \mid [\![P]\!]\} & [\![\Pi h : P.Q]\!] = [\![P]\!] \Rightarrow [\![Q]\!] &
\end{array}$$

Then, we extend straightforwardly $[\![\cdot]\!]$ *from PVS-Cert stratified contexts to PVS-Core contexts: for instance,* $[\![P, x : A, X : Type]\!] = [\![P]\!], x : [\![A]\!], X : Type$.

Last, we extend straightforwardly $[\![\cdot]\!]$ *from all PVS-Cert stratified judgements except those of the form* $\Gamma \vdash Type : Kind$ *to PVS-Core judgements. For instance,* $[\![x : A, X : Type \vdash p : P]\!] = x : [\![A]\!], X : Type \vdash [\![P]\!]$. *The PVS-Cert judgements of the form* $\Gamma \vdash Type : Kind$ *are not translated.*

By the stratification theorem in PVS-Cert, all PVS-Cert derivable judgements are stratified judgements. Hence, unless they have the form $\Gamma \vdash Type : Kind$, their erasure in PVS-Core is well-defined. We will prove in Theorem 10 that they are derivable in PVS-Core. This theorem relies in particular on the fact that conversion in PVS-Cert and PVS-Core are related through the erasure function $[\![\cdot]\!]$, established in the following proposition. The corresponding proof does not involve any specific difficulty.

Proposition 3. *For all terms* M *and* N *which are either expressions, types, or Type, whenever* $M \equiv_{\beta *} N$, *then* $[\![M]\!] \equiv_\beta [\![N]\!]$.

Using the two previous propositions and the stratification theorem in PVS-Cert, we conclude the following theorem, which allows to map PVS-Cert derivations to PVS-Core derivations.

Theorem 10. *Every derivable PVS-Cert judgement either has the form* $\Gamma \vdash Type : Kind$ *or admits an image through* $[\![\cdot]\!]$. *In the latter case, this image is derivable in PVS-Core.*

Proof. The first part of the proof is a direct consequence of the stratification theorem. The second part is proved by induction on the height of PVS-Cert derivations. All cases are straightforward, using the stratification theorem when necessary to establish a correspondence between stratified versions of PVS-Cert rules and PVS-Core rules. For instance:

- DECL corresponds either to TYPEDECL, ELTDECL, or ASSUMPTION
- SORT corresponds to PROP only (judgements of the form $\Gamma \vdash Type : Kind$ are not translated)
- PROD corresponds either to PI, FORALL, or IMPLY

9.2 Expressing PVS-Core Derivations as PVS-Cert Judgements

Theorem 10 shows that a PVS-Cert derivable judgement can testify to the PVS-Core derivability of another judgement: its erasure. In this section, we show conversely that, given any PVS-Core derivation, we can build such a PVS-Cert judgement. For this purpose, we first present an algorithm CERTIFICATE, which translates a PVS-Core derivation into a PVS-Cert judgement. In a second step, we will prove that such PVS-Cert judgements are always derivable in PVS-Cert.

Definition 7. *For any PVS-Core derivation* D*, we define recursively the PVS-Cert stratified judgement* CERTIFICATE(D) *such that* $[\![$CERTIFICATE$(D)]\!]$ *corresponds to the conclusion of* D.

In this definition, we use an injective function $h(\cdot)$ *mapping natural numbers to PVS-Cert proof variables, which can be chosen arbitrarily. We present two cases:* ASSUMPTION, *which shows how* $h(\cdot)$ *is used, and* IMPLYELIM. *This latter case (as well as* FORALLELIM*) is more complex than others as it involves the computation of a normal form with respect to* $\triangleright_*$, *i.e. the erasure of coercions at the head of a term. The other cases are detailed in the author's PhD dissertation* [1].

- $$\frac{\Gamma \vdash P : Prop}{\Gamma, P \vdash WF} \text{ ASSUMPTION}$$

  We consider D_1 *the derivation of* $\Gamma \vdash P : Prop$. CERTIFICATE(D_1) *has the form* $\Gamma_1 \vdash P_1 : Prop$. *We consider* n *the number of declarations of the form* $(h : Q)$ *in* Γ_1, *and we define* CERTIFICATE$(D) = \Gamma_1, h(n) : P_1 \vdash WF$.
- $$\frac{\Gamma \vdash P \Rightarrow Q \qquad \Gamma \vdash P}{\Gamma \vdash Q} \text{ IMPLYELIM}$$

  We consider D_1 *and* D_2 *the respective derivations of* $\Gamma \vdash P \Rightarrow Q$ *and* $\Gamma \vdash P$. CERTIFICATE(D_2) *has the form* $\Gamma_2 \vdash p_2 : P_2$ *and* CERTIFICATE(D_1) *has the form* $\Gamma_1 \vdash p_1 : Q_1'$. *As* $[\![Q_1']\!] = (P \Rightarrow Q)$, *its normal form with respect to* $\triangleright_*$ *has the form* $\Pi h : P_1.Q_1$. *We define* CERTIFICATE$(D) = \Gamma_1 \vdash p_1 p_2 : Q_1[p_2/h]$. *As all proof terms are deleted through the erasure function,* $[\![Q_1[p_2/h]]\!] = [\![Q_1]\!]$. *On the other hand, by induction hypothesis,* $[\![Q_1]\!] = Q$, *hence the erasure of this judgement is* $\Gamma \vdash Q$, *as expected.*

9.3 Relating Conversion in PVS-Core and PVS-Cert

In order to prove that the outputs of the algorithm CERTIFICATE are derivable in PVS-Cert (presented in Theorem 11), the main required lemma is the fact that is the converse of Proposition 3: for any terms M and N which are either expressions, types, or *Type* and which verify $[\![M]\!] \equiv_\beta [\![N]\!]$, then $M \equiv_{\beta*} N$. More precisely, this property will be used in the proof of Theorem 11 to handle the cases of conversion rules TYPECONVERSION and PROPCONVERSION.

We first establish a modified version of this expected result, using equality and $\equiv_*$ instead of $\equiv_\beta$ and $\equiv_{\beta*}$ respectively. The proof is straightforward by induction on the two involved terms.

Proposition 4. *For all terms M and N which are either expressions, types, or Type, whenever $[\![M]\!] = [\![N]\!]$, then $M \equiv_* N$.*

Then, we establish the expected converse of Proposition 3 as follows.

Proposition 5. *For all terms M and N which are either expressions, types, or Type, whenever $[\![M]\!] \equiv_\beta [\![N]\!]$, then $M \equiv_{\beta*} N$.*

Proof. We present a proof based on the definition of a simple translation of PVS-Core terms as PVS-Cert expressions, types, or Type, which does not introduce any explicit coercion: for instance,

- $[\Pi x : A.B] = \Pi x : [A].[B]$
- $[P \Rightarrow Q] = \Pi h : [P].[Q]$ for an arbitrary proof variable h

We first show straightforwardly that the respective images through $[\cdot]$ of two terms related by $\equiv_\beta$ are also related by $\equiv_\beta$. As a consequence, $[[\![M]\!]] \equiv_\beta [[\![N]\!]]$.

On the other hand, it is straightforward to show that $[\cdot]$ is a right inverse of the erasure function $[\![\cdot]\!]$. Hence, $[\![[[\![M]\!]]]\!] = [\![M]\!]$. By Proposition 4, we conclude that $[[\![M]\!]] \equiv_* M$. Following the same reasoning, $[[\![N]\!]] \equiv_* N$.

As a consequence, $M \equiv_{\beta*} [[\![M]\!]] \equiv_{\beta*} [[\![N]\!]] \equiv_{\beta*} N$.

9.4 Soundness of the Synthesis of Certificates

The last proposition needed to prove the soundness of the algorithm CERTIFICATE is the following. It shows that the operation of normalization through $\triangleright_*$ (which erases the coercions $\pi_1(\cdot)$ and $\langle \cdot, M \rangle_T$ at the head of a term) is safely used in the definition of CERTIFICATE.

Proposition 6. *For any derivable PVS-Cert judgement of the form $\Gamma \vdash t : \{x_n ... \{x_1 : Prop \mid Q_1\} ... \mid Q_n\}$, if t admits a normal form with respect to $\triangleright_*$ which has the form $\Pi v : M.T$, then $\Gamma \vdash \Pi v : M.T : Prop$ is derivable.*

In fact, only the specific case $n = 0$ is used in the proof of soundness of CERTIFICATE, but this generalization is preferred as it admits a direct proof by induction on t, which does not involve any specific difficulty.

Last, we present the expected soundness property for CERTIFICATE:

Theorem 11. *For any PVS-Core derivation D,* CERTIFICATE(D) *is derivable in PVS-Cert.*

Proof. The proof is done by induction on D. Most cases are proved without any specific difficulty. In particular, the cases of conversion rules TYPECONVERSION and PROPCONVERSION are straightforward using Proposition 5.

The most complex cases correspond to the rules IMPLYELIM and FORALLELIM which involve, by definition of CERTIFICATE, some normalization with respect to $\triangleright_*$. In such cases, Proposition 6 is used to handle the specific difficulties related to this normalization. We present the case IMPLYELIM:

$$\frac{\Gamma \vdash P \Rightarrow Q \qquad \Gamma \vdash P}{\Gamma \vdash Q}\ \text{IMPLYELIM}$$

We consider D_1 and D_2 the respective derivations of $\Gamma \vdash P \Rightarrow Q$ and $\Gamma \vdash P$. CERTIFICATE(D_2) has the form $\Gamma_2 \vdash p_2 : P_2$ and CERTIFICATE(D_1) has the form $\Gamma_1 \vdash p_1 : Q_1'$. As $[\![Q_1']\!] = (P \Rightarrow Q)$, its normal form with respect to $\triangleright_*$ has the form $\Pi h : P_1.Q_1$. In this setting, CERTIFICATE(D) $= \Gamma_1 \vdash p_1 p_2 : Q_1[p_2/h]$. By induction hypothesis, $\Gamma_1 \vdash p_1 : Q_1'$ and $\Gamma_2 \vdash p_2 : P_2$ are derivable in PVS-Cert. By Proposition 3 and the stratification theorem, $\Gamma_1 \vdash Q_1' : Prop$ is derivable in PVS-Cert. Hence, by Proposition 6, $\Gamma_1 \vdash \Pi h : P_1.Q_1 : Prop$ is derivable as well. As $Q_1' \equiv_{\beta *} \Pi h : P_1.Q_1$, we conclude applying the CONVERSION rule that $\Gamma_1 \vdash p_1 : \Pi h : P_1.Q_1$ is derivable.

On the other hand, using Proposition 4, we can conclude from $[\![\Gamma_1]\!] = \Gamma = [\![\Gamma_2]\!]$ that $\Gamma_1 \equiv_* \Gamma_2$ as long as both contexts admit the list of declared proof variables, in the same order. This is the case as, by straightforward induction on PVS-Core derivations, this list is $h(1), h(2), ..., h(n)$, where $h(\cdot)$ is the injective function used in the definition of CERTIFICATE and n is the number of proof variable declarations in Γ_1 and Γ_2. Hence, $\Gamma_1 \equiv_* \Gamma_2$.

As $\Gamma_1 \vdash p_1 : \Pi h : P_1.Q_1$ is derivable, by Theorem 3 and the stratification theorem, $\Gamma_1 \vdash \Pi h : P_1.Q_1 : Prop$ is derivable. Hence, considering the last rule different from CONVERSION used in such a derivation (which is necessarily PROD), and using the stratification theorem, $\Gamma_1 \vdash P_1 : Prop$ is derivable as well. As a consequence, using context conversion (mentioned in Sect. 4), $\Gamma_1 \vdash p_2 : P_1$ is derivable in PVS-Cert. Hence, applying the rule APP, $\Gamma_1 \vdash p_1 p_2 : Q_1[p_2/h]$ is derivable, as expected.

10 Using PVS-Cert as a System of Verifiable Certificates for PVS-Core

This final section shows how to use the different results presented in this paper to answer to the main question addressed in the current work: defining a system of verifiable certificates for PVS-Core.

A PVS-Cert judgement $\Gamma \vdash p : P$ can be used as a certificate for its PVS-Core erasure $[\![\Gamma]\!] \vdash [\![P]\!]$ (Definition 6), which is verifiable using the type-checking algorithm presented in Sect. 8. On the one hand, this approach is sound: whenever the type-checking algorithm succeeds, $\Gamma \vdash p : P$ is derivable in PVS-Cert, hence $[\![\Gamma]\!] \vdash [\![P]\!]$ is derivable in PVS-Core by Theorem 10.

On the other hand, valid certificates can be generated for arbitrary PVS-Core theorems in the following way. Given some PVS-Core judgement $\Delta \vdash Q$ derivable through some derivation D, the PVS-Cert judgement $\textsc{Certificate}(D)$ can be used as a certificate of $\Delta \vdash Q$. Indeed, using the notations $\Gamma \vdash p : P$ for $\textsc{Certificate}(D)$, the following statements hold.

- By definition of $\textsc{Certificate}$, $[\![\Gamma]\!] = \Delta$ and $[\![P]\!] = Q$, hence this judgement is a certificate for $\Delta \vdash Q$.
- By Theorem 11, $\Gamma \vdash p : P$ is derivable, hence the execution of the type-checking algorithm on this judgement succeeds: this certificate is valid.

These PVS-Cert certificates represent PVS-Core derivations in a very compact way. As each of the different constructions of types, expressions, and proofs in PVS-Cert corresponds to some PVS-Core derivation rule, the size of a PVS-Cert certificate is comparable, as a rough estimation, with the size of a corresponding PVS-Core derivation in which all PVS-Core judgements are deleted.

We finally show that, through the construction of certificates, the PVS-Cert cut elimination theorem can be used to study meta-theoretical properties of PVS-Core. This possible use is illustrated with the case of consistency, proved in PVS-Cert in Theorem 9 using cut elimination.

Theorem 12. *The system PVS-Core is consistent: the judgement* $\vdash \forall x : Prop.x$ *is not derivable.*

Proof. If the judgement $\vdash \forall x : Prop.x$ admits a PVS-Core derivation D, we consider $\vdash p : P = \textsc{Certificate}(D)$. By definition, $[\![P]\!] = \forall x : Prop.x = [\![\Pi x : Prop.x]\!]$. Hence, by Proposition 5, $P \equiv_{\beta *} \Pi x : Prop.x$. As $\vdash \Pi x : Prop.x : Prop$ is derivable in PVS-Cert, we can apply the conversion rule to conclude that $\vdash p : \Pi x : Prop.x$ is derivable in PVS-Cert, which is impossible by Theorem 9.

References

1. Gilbert, F.: Extending higher-order logic with predicate subtyping: application to PVS. Ph.D. dissertation, Sorbonne Paris Cité, Inria, CEA LIST (2018)
2. Abel, A., Scherer, G.: On irrelevance and algorithmic equality in predicative type theory. arXiv preprint arXiv:1203.4716 (2012)

3. Barendregt, H.: Introduction to generalized type systems. J. Funct. Program. **1**(2), 125–154 (1991)
4. Barendregt, H.: Lambda calculi with types. In: Abramsky, S., Gabbay, D.M., Maibaum, T.S.E. (eds.) Handbook of Logic in Computer Science, vol. ii. Oxford University Press, Oxford (1992)
5. Barras, B., et al.: The Coq proof assistant reference manual: Version 6.1 (1997)
6. Barthe, G.: Type-checking injective pure type systems. J. Funct. Program. **9**(06), 675–698 (1999)
7. Berardi, S.: Towards a mathematical analysis of the Coquand-Huet calculus of constructions and the other systems in Barendregt's cube. Technical report, Carnegie-Mellon University, USA and Universita di Torino, Italy (1988)
8. Bernardo, B.: An implicit calculus of constructions with dependent sums and decidable type inference. Ph.D. thesis, École polytechnique, October 2015
9. Futatsugi, K., Goguen, J.A., Jouannaud, J.-P., Meseguer, J.: Principles of OBJ2. In: Proceedings of the 12th ACM SIGACT-SIGPLAN Symposium on Principles of Programming Languages, pp. 52–66. ACM (1985)
10. Geuvers, H.: A short and flexible proof of strong normalization for the calculus of constructions. In: Dybjer, P., Nordström, B., Smith, J. (eds.) TYPES 1994. LNCS, vol. 996, pp. 14–38. Springer, Heidelberg (1995). https://doi.org/10.1007/3-540-60579-7_2
11. Geuvers, H., Nederhof, M.-J.: Modular proof of strong normalization for the calculus of constructions. J. Funct. Program. **1**(02), 155–189 (1991)
12. Girard, J.-Y.: Interprétation fonctionelle et élimination des coupures de l'arithmétique d'ordre supérieur. Ph.D. thesis, Université Paris VII (1972)
13. Kent, A.M., Kempe, D., Tobin-Hochstadt, S.: Occurrence typing modulo theories. In: Proceedings of the 37th ACM SIGPLAN Conference on Programming Language Design and Implementation, vol. 51, pp. 296–309. ACM (2016)
14. Klop, J.W., van Oostrom, V., van Raamsdonk, F.: Combinatory reduction systems: introduction and survey. Theoret. Comput. Sci. **121**(1), 279–308 (1993)
15. Knowles, K., Flanagan, C.: Hybrid type checking. ACM Trans. Program. Lang. Syst. (TOPLAS) **32**(2), 6 (2010)
16. Luo, Z.: ECC, an extended calculus of constructions. In: Proceedings of Fourth Annual Symposium on Logic in Computer Science. LICS 1989, pp. 386–395. IEEE (1989)
17. Owre, S., Rushby, J.M., Shankar, N.: PVS: a prototype verification system. In: Kapur, D. (ed.) CADE 1992. LNCS, vol. 607, pp. 748–752. Springer, Heidelberg (1992). https://doi.org/10.1007/3-540-55602-8_217
18. Owre, S., Shankar, N.: The formal semantics of PVS (1999)
19. Rondon, P.M., Kawaguci, M., Jhala, R.: Liquid types. In: ACM SIGPLAN Notices, vol. 43, pp. 159–169. ACM (2008)
20. Rushby, J., Owre, S., Shankar, N.: Subtypes for specifications: predicate subtyping in PVS. IEEE Trans. Softw. Eng. **24**(9), 709–720 (1998)
21. Siles, V., Herbelin, H.: Pure type system conversion is always typable. J. Funct. Program. **22**(2), 153–180 (2012)
22. Sozeau, M.: Subset coercions in Coq. In: Altenkirch, T., McBride, C. (eds.) TYPES 2006. LNCS, vol. 4502, pp. 237–252. Springer, Heidelberg (2007). https://doi.org/10.1007/978-3-540-74464-1_16
23. Tait, W.W.: A realizability interpretation of the theory of species. In: Parikh, R. (ed.) Logic Colloquium, vol. 453, pp. 240–251. Springer, Heidelberg (1975). https://doi.org/10.1007/BFb0064875

24. Terlouw, J.: Een nadere bewijstheoretische analyse van GSTT's. Manuscript (in Dutch) (1989)
25. Terlouw, J.: Sterke normalisatie in C a la Tait. In: Notes of a Talk Held at the Intercity Seminar on Typed Lambda Calculus, Nijmegen, Netherlands (1989)
26. Terlouw, J.: Strong normalization in type systems: a model theoretical approach. Ann. Pure Appl. Logic **73**(1), 53–78 (1995)
27. Werner, B.: On the strength of proof-irrelevant type theories. In: Furbach, U., Shankar, N. (eds.) IJCAR 2006. LNCS (LNAI), vol. 4130, pp. 604–618. Springer, Heidelberg (2006). https://doi.org/10.1007/11814771_49

Security and Incremental Computation

Robustly Safe Compilation

Marco Patrignani[1,2(✉)] and Deepak Garg[3]

[1] Stanford University, Stanford, USA
mp@cs.stanford.edu
[2] CISPA Helmholz Center for Information Security, Saarbrücken, Germany
[3] Max Planck Institute for Software Systems, Saarbrücken, Germany

Abstract. Secure compilers generate compiled code that withstands many target-level attacks such as alteration of control flow, data leaks or memory corruption. Many existing secure compilers are proven to be fully abstract, meaning that they reflect and preserve observational equivalence. Fully abstract compilation is strong and useful but, in certain cases, comes at the cost of requiring expensive runtime constructs in compiled code. These constructs may have no relevance for security, but are needed to accommodate differences between the source and target languages that fully abstract compilation necessarily needs.

As an alternative to fully abstract compilation, this paper explores a different criterion for secure compilation called robustly safe compilation or *RSC*. Briefly, this criterion means that the compiled code preserves relevant safety properties of the source program against all adversarial contexts interacting with the compiled program. We show that *RSC* can be proved more easily than fully abstract compilation and also often results in more efficient code. We also develop two illustrative robustly-safe compilers and, through them, illustrate two different proof techniques for establishing that a compiler attains *RSC*. Based on these, we argue that proving *RSC* can be simpler than proving fully abstraction.

To better explain and clarify notions, this paper uses colours. For a better experience, please print or view this paper in colours.[1]

1 Introduction

Low-level adversaries, such as those written in C or assembly can attack co-linked code written in a high-level language in ways that may not be feasible in the high-level language itself. For example, such an adversary may manipulate or hijack control flow, cause buffer overflows, or directly access private memory,

[1] Specifically, in this paper we use a blue, sans-serif font for source elements, an **orange, bold** font for **target** elements and a *black, italic* font for elements common to both languages (to avoid repeating similar definitions twice). Thus, C is a source-level component, **C** is a target-level component and *C* is generic notation for either a source-level or a target-level component.

L. Caires (Ed.): ESOP 2019, LNCS 11423, pp. 469–498, 2019.
https://doi.org/10.1007/978-3-030-17184-1_17

all in contravention to the abstractions of the high-level language. Specific countermeasures such as Control Flow Integrity [3] or Code Pointer Integrity [41] have been devised to address some of these attacks *individually*. An alternative approach is to devise a *secure compiler*, which seeks to defend against entire *classes* of such attacks. Secure compilers often achieve security by relying on different protection mechanisms, e.g., cryptographic primitives [4,5,22,26], types [10,11], address space layout randomisation [6,37], protected module architectures [9,53,57,59] (also know as enclaves [46]), tagged architectures [7,39], etc. Once designed, the question researchers face is how to formalise that such a compiler is indeed secure, and how to prove this. Basically, we want a criterion that specifies secure compilation. A widely-used criterion for compiler security is fully abstract compilation (*FAC*) [2,35,52], which has been shown to preserve many interesting security properties like confidentiality, integrity, invariant definitions, well-bracketed control flow and hiding of local state [9,37,53,54].

Informally, a compiler is fully abstract if it preserves and reflects observational equivalence of source-level components (i.e., partial programs) in their compiled counterparts. Most existing work instantiates observational equivalence with contextual equivalence: co-divergence of two components in any larger context they interact with. Fully abstract compilation is a very strong property, which preserves *all* source-level abstractions.

Unfortunately, preserving *all* source-level abstractions also has downsides. In fact, while *FAC* preserves many relevant security properties, it also preserves a plethora of other non-security ones, and the latter may force inefficient checks in the compiled code. For example, when the target is assembly, two observationally equivalent components must compile to code of the same size [9,53], else full abstraction is trivially violated. This requirement is security-irrelevant in most cases. Additionally, *FAC* is not well-suited for source languages with undefined behaviour (e.g., `C` and `LLVM`) [39] and, if used naïvely, it can fail to preserve even simple safety properties [60] (though, fortunately, no *existing* work falls prey to this naïvety).

Motivated by this, recent work started investigating alternative secure compilation criteria that overcome these limitations. These security-focussed criteria take the form of preservation of hyperproperties or classes of hyperproperties, such as hypersafety properties or safety properties [8,33]. This paper investigates one of these criteria, namely, *Robustly Safe Compilation* (*RSC*) which has clear security guarantees and can often be attained more efficiently than FAC.

Informally, a compiler attains *RSC* if it is correct and it preserves *robust safety* of source components in the target components it produces. Robust safety is an important security notion that has been widely adopted to formalize security, e.g., of communication protocols [14,17,34]. Before explaining *RSC*, we explain robust safety as a language property.

Robust Safety as a Language Property. Informally, a program property is a safety property if it encodes that "bad" sequences of events do not happen when the program executes [13,63]. A program is *robustly safe* if it has relevant (specified) safety properties *despite* active attacks from adversaries. As the name suggests, robust safety relies on the notions of safety and robustness which we now explain.

Safety. As mentioned, safety asserts that "no bad sequence of events happens", so we can specify a safety property by the set of *finite observations* which characterise all bad sequences of events. A whole program has a safety property if its behaviours exclude these bad observations. Many security properties can be encoded as safety, including integrity, weak secrecy and functional correctness.

Example 1 (Integrity). Integrity ensures that an attacker does not tamper with code invariants on state. For example, consider the function `charge_account(n)` which deducts amount `n` from an account as part of an electronic card payment. A card PIN is required if `n` is larger than 10 euros. So the function checks whether `n` > 10, requests the PIN if this is the case, and then changes the account balance. We expect this function to have a safety (integrity) property in the account balance: A reduction of more than 10 euros in the account balance must be preceded by a call to `request_pin()`. Here, the relevant observation is a trace (sequence) of account balances and calls to `request_pin()`. Bad observations for this safety property are those where an account balance is at least 10 euros less than the previous one, without a call to `request_pin()` in between. Note that this function seems to have this safety property, but it may not have the safety property *robustly*: a target-level adversary may transfer control directly to the "else" branch of the check `n` > 10 after setting `n` to more than 10, to violate the safety property. ⊡

Example 2 (Weak Secrecy). Weak secrecy asserts that a program secret never flows *explicitly* to the attacker. For example, consider code that manages `network_h`, a handler (socket descriptor) for a sensitive network interface. This code does not expose `network_h` directly to external code but it provides an API to use it. This API makes some security checks internally. If the handler is directly accessible to outer code, then it can be misused in insecure ways (since the security checks may not be made). If the code has weak secrecy wrt `network_h` then we know that the handler is never passed to an attacker. In this case we can define bad observations as those where `network_h` is passed to external code (e.g., as a parameter, as a return value on or on the heap). ⊡

Example 3 (Correctness). Program correctness can also be formalized as a safety property. Consider a program that computes the `n`th Fibonacci number. The program reads `n` from an input source and writes its output to an output source. Correctness of this program is a safety property. Our observations are pairs of an input (read by the program) and the corresponding output. A bad observation is one where the input is `n` (for some `n`) but the output is different from the `n`th Fibonacci number. ⊡

These examples not only illustrate the expressiveness of safety properties, but also show that safety properties are quite *coarse-grained*: they are only concerned with (sequences of) relevant events like calls to specific functions, changes to specific heap variables, inputs, and outputs. They do not specify or constrain how the program computes between these events, leaving the programmer and the compiler considerable flexibility in optimizations. However, safety properties are not a panacea for security, and there are security properties that are not safety. For example, noninterference [70,72], the standard information flow property, is not safety. Nonetheless, many interesting security properties are safety. In fact, many non-safety properties including noninterference can be conservatively approximated as safety properties [20]. Hence, safety properties are a meaningful goal to pursue for secure compilation.

Robustness. We often want to reason about properties of a component of interest that hold irrespective of any other components the component interacts with. These other components may be the libraries the component is linked against, or the language runtime. Often, these surrounding components are modelled as the *program context* whose hole the component of interest fills. From a security perspective the context represents the attacker in the threat model. When the component of interest links to a context, we have a whole program that can run. A property holds *robustly* for a component if it holds in *any* context that the component of interest can be linked to.

Robust Safety Preservation as a Compiler Property. A compiler attains robustly safe compilation or *RSC* if it maps any source component that has a safety property *robustly* to a compiled component that has the *same* safety property robustly. Thus, safety has to hold robustly in the target language, which often does not have the powerful abstractions (e.g., typing) that the source language has. Hence, the compiler must insert enough defensive runtime checks into the compiled code to prevent the more powerful target contexts from launching attacks (violations of safety properties) that source contexts could not launch. This is unlike correct compilation, which either considers only those target contexts that behave like source contexts [40,49,65] or considers only whole programs [43].

As mentioned, safety properties are usually quite coarse-grained. This means that *RSC* still allows the compiler to optimise code internally, as long as the sequence of observable events is not affected. For example, when compiling the `fibonacci` function of Example 3, the compiler can do any internal optimisation such as caching intermediate results, as long as the end result is correct. Crucially, however, these intermediate results must be protected from tampering by a (target-level) attacker, else the output can be incorrect, breaking *RSC*.

A *RSC*-attaining compiler focuses only on preserving security (as captured by robust safety) instead of contextual equivalence (typically captured by full abstraction). So, such a compiler can produce code that is more efficient than code compiled with a fully abstract compiler as it does not have to preserve *all* source abstractions (we illustrate this later).

Finally, robust safety scales naturally to thread-based concurrency [1,34,58]. Thus *RSC* also scales naturally to thread-based concurrency (we demonstrate this too). This is unlike *FAC*, where thread-based concurrency can introduce additional undesired abstractions that also need to be preserved.

RSC is a very recently proposed criterion for secure compilers. Recent work [8,33] define *RSC* abstractly in terms of preservation of program behaviours, but their development is limited to the definition only. Our goal in this paper is to examine how *RSC* can be realized and established, and to show that in certain cases it leads to compiled code that is more efficient than what *FAC* leads to. To this end, we consider a specific setting where observations are values in specific (sensitive) heap locations at cross-component calls. We define robust safety and *RSC* for this specific setting (Sect. 2). Unlike previous work [8,33] which assumed that the domain of traces (behaviours) is the same in the source and target languages, our *RSC* definition allows for different trace domains in the source and target languages, as long as they can be suitably related. The second contribution of our paper is two proof techniques to establish *RSC*.

- The first technique is an adaption of trace-based backtranslation, an existing technique for proving *FAC* [7,9,59]. To illustrate this technique, we build a compiler from an untyped source language to an untyped target language with support for fine-grained memory protection via so-called capabilities [23,71] (Sect. 3). Here, we guarantee that if a source program is robustly safe, then so is its compilation.
- The second proof technique shows that if source programs are *verified* for robust safety, then one can simplify the proof of *RSC* so that no backtranslation is needed. In this case, we develop a compiler from a *typed* source language where the types already enforce robust safety, to a target language similar to that of the first compiler (Sect. 4). In this instance, both languages also support shared-memory concurrency. Here, we guarantee that all compiled target programs are robustly safe.

To argue that *RSC* is general and is not limited to compilation targets based on capabilities, we also develop a third compiler. This compiler starts from the same source language as our second compiler but targets an untyped concurrent language with support for *coarse-grained memory isolation*, modelling recent hardware extensions such as Intel's SGX [46]. Due to space constraints, we report this result only in the companion technical report [61].

The final contribution of this paper is a comparison between *RSC* and *FAC*. For this, we describe changes that would be needed to attain *FAC* for the first compiler and argue that these changes make generated code inefficient and also complicate the backtranslation proof significantly (Sect. 5).

Due to space constraints, we elide some technical details and limit proofs to sketches. These are fully resolved in the companion technical report [61].

2 Robustly Safe Compilation

This section first discusses robust safety as a language (not a compiler) property (Sect. 2.1) and then presents *RSC* as a compiler property along with an informal discussion of techniques to prove it (Sect. 2.2).

2.1 Safety and Robust Safety

To explain robust safety, we first describe a general *imperative* programming model that we use. Programmers write *components* on which they want to enforce safety properties robustly. A component is a list of function definitions that can be linked with other components (the context) in order to have a runnable whole program (functions in "other" components are like `extern` functions in C). Additionally, every component declares a set of "sensitive" locations that contain all the data that is safety-relevant. For instance, in Example 1 this set may contain the account balance and in Example 3 it may contain the I/O buffers. We explain the relevance of this set after we define safety properties.

We want safety properties to specify that a component never executes a "bad" sequence of events. For this, we first need to fix a notion of events. We have several choices here, e.g., our events could be inputs and outputs, all syscalls, all changes to the heap (as in CompCert [44]), etc. Here, we make a specific choice motivated by our interest in robustness: We define events as calls/returns that cross a component boundary, together with the state of the heap at that point. Consequently, our safety properties can constrain the contents of the heap at component boundaries. This choice of component boundaries as the point of observation is meaningful because, in our programming model, control transfers to/from an adversary happen only at component boundaries (more precisely, they happen at cross-component function call and returns). This allows the compiler complete flexibility in optimizing code within a component, while not reducing the ability of safety properties to constrain observations of the adversary.

Concretely, a component behaviour is a *trace*, i.e., a sequence of *actions* recording component boundary interactions and, in particular, the heap at these points. *Actions*, the items on a trace, have the following grammar:

$$\textit{Actions}\ \alpha ::= \texttt{call}\ f\ v\ H? \mid \texttt{call}\ f\ v\ H! \mid \texttt{ret}\ H! \mid \texttt{ret}\ H?$$

These actions respectively capture call and callback to a function f with parameter v when the heap is H as well as return and returnback with a certain heap H.[2] We use ? and ! decorations to indicate whether the control flow of the action goes from the context to the component (?) or from the component to the context (!). Well-formed traces have alternations of ? and ! decorated actions,

[2] A callback is a call from the component to the context, so it generates label $\texttt{call}\ f\ v\ H!$. A returnback is a return from such a callback, i.e., the context returning to the component, and it generates the label $\texttt{ret}\ H?$.

starting with ? since execution starts in the context. For a sequence of actions $\overline{\alpha}$, $\texttt{relevant}(\overline{\alpha})$ is the list of heaps $\overline{H}$ mentioned in the actions of $\overline{\alpha}$.

Next, we need a representation of safety properties. Generally, properties are sets of traces, but safety properties specifically can be specified as automata (or monitors in the sequel) [63]. We choose this representation since monitors are less abstract than sets of traces and they are closer to enforcement mechanisms used for safety properties, e.g., runtime monitors. Briefly, a safety property is a monitor that transitions states in response to events of the program trace. At any point, the monitor may refuse to transition (it gets *stuck*), which encodes property violation. While a monitor can transition, the property has not been violated. Schneider [63] argues that all properties codable this way are safety properties and that all enforceable safety properties can be coded this way.

Formally, a monitor M in our setting consists of a set of abstract states $\{\sigma\cdots\}$, the transition relation $\rightsquigarrow$, an initial state σ_0, the set of heap locations that matter for the monitor, $\{l\cdots\}$, and the current state σ_c (we indicate a set of elements of class e as $\{e\cdots\}$). The transition relation $\rightsquigarrow$ is a set of triples of the form (σ_s, H, σ_f) consisting of a starting state σ_s, a final state σ_f and a heap H. The transition (σ_s, H, σ_f) is interpreted as "*state σ_s transitions to σ_f when the heap is H*". When determining the monitor transition in response to a program action, we restrict the program's heap to the location set $\{l\cdots\}$, i.e., to the set of locations the monitor cares about. This heap restriction is written $H\big|_{\{l\cdots\}}$. We assume determinism of the transition relation: for any σ_s and (restricted heap) H, there is at most one σ_f such that $(\sigma_s, H, \sigma_f) \in \rightsquigarrow$.

Given the behaviour of a program as a trace $\overline{\alpha}$ and a monitor M specifying a safety property, $M \vdash \overline{\alpha}$ denotes that the trace satisfies the safety property. Intuitively, to satisfy a safety property, the sequence of heaps in the actions of a trace must never get the monitor stuck (Rule Valid trace). Every single heap must allow the monitor to step according to its transition relation (Rule Monitor Step). Note that we overload the $\rightsquigarrow$ notation here to also denote an auxiliary relation, the *monitor small-step semantics* (Rule Monitor Step-base and Rule Monitor Step-ind).

(Valid trace)
$$\frac{M; \texttt{relevant}(\overline{\alpha}) \rightsquigarrow M'}{M \vdash \overline{\alpha}}$$

(Monitor Step-base)
$$\frac{}{M; \varnothing \rightsquigarrow M}$$

(Monitor Step-ind)
$$\frac{M; \overline{H} \rightsquigarrow M'' \qquad M''; H \rightsquigarrow M'}{M; \overline{H} \cdot H \rightsquigarrow M'}$$

(Monitor Step)
$$\frac{(\sigma_c, H\big|_{\{l\cdots\}}, \sigma_f) \in \rightsquigarrow}{(\{\sigma\cdots\}, \rightsquigarrow, \sigma_0, \{l\cdots\}, \sigma_c); H \rightsquigarrow (\{\sigma\cdots\}, \rightsquigarrow, \sigma_0, \{l\cdots\}, \sigma_f)}$$

With this setup in place, we can formalise safety, attackers and robust safety. In defining (robust) safety for a component, we only admit monitors (safety properties) whose $\{l\cdots\}$ agrees with the sensitive locations declared by the component. Making the set of safety-relevant locations explicit in the component and the monitor gives the compiler more flexibility by telling it precisely which locations need to be protected against target-level attacks (the compiler may choose to not protect the rest). At the same time, it allows for expressive modelling. For instance, in Example 3 the safety-relevant locations could be the

I/O buffers from which the program performs inputs and outputs, and the safety property can constrain the input and output buffers at corresponding call and return actions involving the Fibonacci function.

Definition 1 (Safety, attacker and robust safety).

$$M \vdash C : \textit{safe} \stackrel{\text{def}}{=} \textit{if} \vdash C : \textit{whole then if } \Omega_0(C) \xrightarrow{\overline{\alpha}} \_ \textit{ then } M \vdash \overline{\alpha}$$

$$C \vdash A : \textit{atk} \stackrel{\text{def}}{=} C = \{l \cdots\}, \overline{F} \text{ and } \{l \cdots\} \cap \mathtt{fn}(A) = \varnothing$$

$$M \vdash C : \textit{rs} \stackrel{\text{def}}{=} \forall A. \textit{ if } M \frown C \textit{ and } C \vdash A : \textit{atk then } M \vdash A[C] : \textit{safe}$$

A whole program C is safe for a monitor M, written $M \vdash C : \textit{safe}$, if the monitor accepts any trace the program generates from its initial state ($\Omega_0(C)$).

An attacker A is valid for a component C, written $C \vdash A : \textit{atk}$, if A's free names (denoted $\mathtt{fn}(A)$) do not refer to the locations that the component cares about. This is a basic sanity check: if we allow an attacker to mention heap locations that the component cares about, the attacker will be able to modify those locations, causing all but trivial safety properties to not hold robustly.

A component C is robustly safe wrt monitor M, written $M \vdash C : \textit{rs}$, if C composed with *any* attacker is safe wrt M. As mentioned, for this setup to make sense, the monitor and the component must agree on the locations that are safety-relevant. This agreement is denoted $M \frown C$.

2.2 Robustly Safe Compilation

Robustly-safe compilation ensures that robust safety properties *and their meanings* are preserved across compilation. But what does it means to preserve meanings across languages? If a source safety property says never write 3 to a location, and we compile to an assembly language by mapping numbers to binary, the corresponding target property should say never write 0x11 to an address.

In order to relate properties across languages, we assume a relation $\approx$: $\mathsf{v} \times \mathrm{v}$ between source and target values that is *total*, so it maps any source value v to a target value v : $\forall \mathsf{v}. \exists \mathrm{v}. \mathsf{v} \approx \mathrm{v}$. This value relation is used to define a relation between heaps: $\mathsf{H} \approx \mathrm{H}$, which intuitively holds when related locations point to related values. This is then used to define a relation between actions: $\alpha \approx \alpha$, which holds when the two actions are the "same" modulo this relation, i.e., $\mathtt{call} \cdots ?$ only relates to $\mathtt{call} \cdots ?$ and the arguments of the action (values and heap) are related. Next, we require a relation $\mathsf{M} \approx \mathrm{M}$ between source and target monitors, which means that the source monitor M and the target monitor M code the same safety property, modulo the relation $\approx$ on values assumed above. The precise definition of this relation depends on the source and target languages; specific instances are shown in Sects. 3.3 and 4.3.[3]

[3] Accounting for the difference in the representation of safety properties sets us apart from recent work [8,33], which assumes that the source and target languages have the same trace alphabet. The latter works only in some settings.

We denote a compiler from language S to language $\mathbf{T}$ by $[\![\cdot]\!]^{\mathsf{S}}_{\mathbf{T}}$. A compiler $[\![\cdot]\!]^{\mathsf{S}}_{\mathbf{T}}$ attains *RSC*, if it maps any component C that is robustly safe wrt M to a component $\mathbf{C}$ that is robustly safe wrt $\mathbf{M}$, provided that $\mathsf{M} \approx \mathbf{M}$.

Definition 2 (Robustly Safe Compilation).

$$\vdash [\![\cdot]\!]^{\mathsf{S}}_{\mathbf{T}} : \mathit{RSC} \stackrel{\mathsf{def}}{=} \forall \mathsf{C}, \mathsf{M}, \mathbf{M}.\ \mathit{if}\ \mathsf{M} \vdash \mathsf{C} : \mathsf{rs}\ \mathit{and}\ \mathsf{M} \approx \mathbf{M}\ \mathit{then}\ \mathbf{M} \vdash [\![\mathsf{C}]\!]^{\mathsf{S}}_{\mathbf{T}} : \mathbf{rs}$$

A consequence of the universal quantification over monitors here is that the compiler cannot be property-sensitive. A robustly-safe compiler preserves all robust safety properties, not just a specific one, e.g., it does not just enforce that `fibonacci` is correct. This seemingly strong goal is sensible as compiler writers will likely not know what safety properties individual programmers will want to preserve.

Remark. Some readers may wonder why we do not follow existing work and specify safety as "programmer-written assertions never fail" [31,34,45,68]. Unfortunately, this approach does not yield a meaningful criterion for specifying a compiler, since assertions in the compiled program (if any) are generated by the compiler itself. Thus a compiler could just erase all assertions and the compiled code it generates would be trivially (robustly) safe – no assertion can fail if there are no assertions in the first place!

Proving *RSC*. Proving that a compiler attains *RSC* can be done either by proving that a compiler satisfies Definition 2 or by proving something *equivalent*. To this end, Definition 3 below presents an alternative, equivalent formulation of *RSC*. We call this characterisation *property-free* as it does not mention monitors explicitly (it mentions the `relevant(·)` function for reasons we explain below).

Definition 3 (Property-Free *RSC*).

$$\begin{aligned}
&\vdash [\![\cdot]\!]^{\mathsf{S}}_{\mathbf{T}} : \mathit{PF\text{-}RSC} \stackrel{\mathsf{def}}{=} \forall \mathsf{C}, \mathbf{A}, \overline{\alpha}.\\
&\qquad \mathit{if}\ [\![\mathsf{C}]\!]^{\mathsf{S}}_{\mathbf{T}} \vdash \mathbf{A} : \mathbf{atk}\ \mathit{and} \vdash \mathbf{A}\left[[\![\mathsf{C}]\!]^{\mathsf{S}}_{\mathbf{T}}\right] : \mathbf{whole}\ \mathit{and}\ \Omega_0\left(\mathbf{A}\left[[\![\mathsf{C}]\!]^{\mathsf{S}}_{\mathbf{T}}\right]\right) \stackrel{\overline{\alpha}}{\Longrightarrow} _\\
&\quad \mathit{then}\ \exists \mathsf{A}, \overline{\alpha}.\ \mathsf{C} \vdash \mathsf{A} : \mathsf{atk}\ \mathit{and} \vdash \mathsf{A}\,[\mathsf{C}] : \mathsf{whole}\ \mathit{and}\ \Omega_0\,(\mathsf{A}\,[\mathsf{C}]) \stackrel{\overline{\alpha}}{\Longrightarrow} _\\
&\qquad \mathit{and}\ \mathtt{relevant}(\overline{\alpha}) \approx \mathtt{relevant}(\overline{\alpha})
\end{aligned}$$

Specifically, *PF-RSC* states that the compiled code produces behaviours that *refine* source level behaviours *robustly* (taking contexts into account).

PF-RSC and *RSC* should, in general, be equivalent (Proposition 1).

Proposition 1 (*PF-RSC* and *RSC* are equivalent).

$$\forall [\![\cdot]\!]^{\mathsf{S}}_{\mathbf{T}}, \vdash [\![\cdot]\!]^{\mathsf{S}}_{\mathbf{T}} : \mathit{PF\text{-}RSC} \iff \vdash [\![\cdot]\!]^{\mathsf{S}}_{\mathbf{T}} : \mathit{RSC}$$

Informally, a property is safety if and only if it implies programs not having any trace prefix from a given set of bad prefixes (i.e., finite traces). Hence, *not* having a safety property robustly amounts to some context being able to induce a bad prefix. Consequently, preserving *all* robust safety properties (*RSC*) amounts to ensuring that all target prefixes can be generated (by some context) in the source too (*PF-RSC*). Formally, since Definition 2 relies on the monitor relation, we can prove Proposition 1 only after such a relation is finalised. We give such a monitor relation and proof in Sect. 3.3 (see Theorem 3). However, in general this result should hold for any cross-language monitor relation that correctly relates safety properties. If the proposition does not hold, then the relation does not capture how safety in one language is represented in the other.

Assuming Proposition 1, we can prove *PF-RSC* for a compiler in place of *RSC*. *PF-RSC* can be proved with a *backtranslation* technique. This technique has been often used to prove full abstraction [7–9,33,39,50,53,54,59] and it aims at building a source context starting from a target one. In fact *PF-RSC*, leads directly to a backtranslation-based proof technique since it can be rewritten (eliding irrelevant details) as:

$$\text{If } \exists \mathbf{A}, \overline{\alpha}.\Omega_0\left(\mathbf{A}\left[[\![\mathsf{C}]\!]_{\mathrm{T}}^{\mathsf{S}}\right]\right) \xrightarrow{\overline{\alpha}} \_$$
$$\text{then } \exists \mathsf{A}, \overline{\alpha}.\Omega_0\left(\mathsf{A}\left[\mathsf{C}\right]\right) \xrightarrow{\overline{\alpha}} \_ \text{ and } \texttt{relevant}(\overline{\alpha}) \approx \texttt{relevant}(\overline{\alpha})$$

Essentially, given a target context $\mathbf{A}$, a compiled program $[\![\mathsf{C}]\!]_{\mathrm{T}}^{\mathsf{S}}$ and a target trace $\overline{\alpha}$ that $\mathbf{A}$ causes $[\![\mathsf{C}]\!]_{\mathrm{T}}^{\mathsf{S}}$ to have, we need to construct, or *backtranslate* to, a source context A that will cause the source program C to simulate $\overline{\alpha}$. Such backtranslation based proofs can be quite difficult, depending on the features of the languages and the compiler. However, backtranslation for *RSC* (as we show in Sect. 3.3) is not as complex as backtranslation for *FAC* (Sect. 5.2).

A simpler proof strategy is also viable for *RSC* when we compile only those source programs that have been *verified* to be robustly safe (e.g., using a type system). The idea is this: from the verification of the source program, we can find an invariant which is always maintained by the target code, and which, in turn, implies the robust safety of the target code. For example, if the safety property is that values in the heap always have their expected types, then the invariant can simply be that values in the target heap are always related to the source ones (which have their expected types). This is tantamount to proving type preservation in the target in the presence of an active adversary. This is harder than standard type preservation (because of the active adversary) but is still much easier than backtranslation as there is no need to map target constructs to source contexts syntactically. We illustrate this proof technique in Sect. 4.

***RSC* Implies Compiler Correctness.** As stated in Sect. 1, *RSC* implies (a form of) compiler correctness. While this may not be apparent from Definition 2, it is more apparent from its equivalent characterization in Definition 3. We elaborate this here.

Whether concerned with whole programs or partial programs, compiler correctness states that the behaviour of compiled programs *refines* the behaviour of source programs [18,36,40,44,49,65]. So, if $\{\overline{\alpha}\cdots\}$ and $\{\overline{\alpha}\cdots\}$ are the sets of compiled and source behaviours, then a compiler should force $\{\overline{\alpha}\cdots\} \lessapprox \{\overline{\alpha}\cdots\}$, where $\lessapprox$ is the composition of $\subseteq$ and of the relation $\approx^{-1}$.

If we consider a source component C that is whole, then it can only link against empty contexts, both in the source and in the target. Hence, in this special case, *PF-RSC* simplifies to standard refinement of traces, i.e., whole program compiler correctness. Hence, assuming that the correctness criterion for a compiler is concerned with the same observations as safety properties (values in safety-relevant heap locations at component crossings in our illustrative setting), *PF-RSC* implies whole program compiler correctness.

However, *PF-RSC* (or, equivalently, *RSC*) does not imply, nor is implied by, any form of *compositional compiler correctness* (CCC) [40,49,65]. CCC requires that the behaviours produced by a compiled component linked against a target context that is related (in behaviour) to a source context can also be produced by the source component linked against the *related* source context. In contrast, *PF-RSC* allows picking *any* source context to simulate the behaviours. Hence, *PF-RSC* does not imply CCC. On the other hand, *PF-RSC* universally quantifies over all target contexts, while CCC only quantifies over target contexts related to a source context, so CCC does not imply *PF-RSC* either. Hence, compositional compiler correctness, if desirable, must be imposed in addition to *PF-RSC*. Note that this lack of implications is unsurprising: *PF-RSC* and CCC capture two very different aspects of compilation: security (against all contexts) and compositional preservation of behaviour (against well-behaved contexts).

3 *RSC* via Trace-Based Backtranslation

This section illustrates how to prove that a compiler attains *RSC* by means of a trace-based backtranslation technique [7,53,59]. To present such a proof, we first introduce our source language $\mathsf{L^U}$, an untyped, first-order imperative language with abstract references and hidden local state (Sect. 3.1). Then, we present our target language $\mathbf{L^P}$, an untyped imperative target language with a concrete heap, whose locations are natural numbers that the context can compute. $\mathbf{L^P}$ provides hidden local state via a fine-grained capability mechanism on heap accesses (Sect. 3.2). Finally, we present the compiler $[\![\cdot]\!]^{\mathsf{L^U}}_{\mathbf{L^P}}$ and prove that it attains *RSC* (Sect. 3.3) by means of a trace-based backtranslation. The section conclude with an example detailing why *RSC* preserves security (Example 4).

To avoid focussing on mundane details, we deliberately use source and target languages that are fairly similar. However, they differ substantially in one key point: the heap model. This affords the target-level adversary attacks like guessing private locations and writing to them that do not obviously exist in the source (and makes our proofs nontrivial). We believe that (with due effort) the ideas here will generalize to languages with larger gaps and more features.

3.1 The Source Language $\mathsf{L^U}$

$\mathsf{L^U}$ is an untyped imperative while language [51]. Components C are triples of function definitions, interfaces and a special location written ℓ_{root}, so C ::=

$\ell_{\mathsf{root}}; \overline{\mathsf{F}}; \overline{\mathsf{I}}$. Each function definition maps a function name and a formal argument to a body s: $\mathsf{F} ::= \ \mathsf{f(x)} \mapsto \mathsf{s}; \mathsf{return};$. An interface is a list of functions that the component relies on the context to provide (similar to C's `extern` declarations). The special location ℓ_{root} defines the locations that are monitored for safety, as explained below. Attackers A (program contexts) are function definitions that represent untrusted code that a component interacts with. A function's body is a statement, s. Statements are rather standard, so we omit a formal syntax. Briefly, they can manipulate the heap (location creation $\mathsf{let\ x = new\ e\ in\ s}$, assignment $\mathsf{x := e}$), do recursive function calls ($\mathsf{call\ f\ e}$), condition (if-then-else), define local variables (let-in) and loop. Statements use effect-free expressions, e, which contain standard boolean expressions ($\mathsf{e} \otimes \mathsf{e}$), arithmetic expressions ($\mathsf{e} \oplus \mathsf{e}$), pairing ($\langle \mathsf{e}, \mathsf{e} \rangle$) and projections, and location dereference ($!\mathsf{e}$). Heaps H are maps from abstract locations ℓ to values v.

As explained in Sect. 2.1, safety properties are specified by monitors. L^{U}'s monitors have the form: $\mathsf{M} ::= \ (\{\sigma \cdots\}, \rightsquigarrow, \sigma_0, \ell_{\mathsf{root}}, \sigma_{\mathsf{c}})$. Note that in place of the set $\{l \cdots\}$ of safety-relevant locations, the description of a monitor here (as well as a component above) contains a *single* location ℓ_{root}. The interpretation is that any location *reachable* in the heap starting from ℓ_{root} is relevant for safety. This set of locations can change as the program executes, and hence this is more flexible than statically specifying all of $\{l \cdots\}$ upfront. This representation of the set by a single location is made explicit in the following monitor rule:

$$\frac{\begin{array}{cc} \mathsf{M} = (\{\sigma \cdots\}, \rightsquigarrow, \sigma_0, \ell_{\mathsf{root}}, \sigma_{\mathsf{c}}) & \mathsf{M}' = (\{\sigma \cdots\}, \rightsquigarrow, \sigma_0, \ell_{\mathsf{root}}, \sigma_{\mathsf{f}}) \\ (\sigma_{\mathsf{c}}, \mathsf{H}', \sigma_{\mathsf{f}}) \in \rightsquigarrow \qquad \mathsf{H}' \subseteq \mathsf{H} & \mathtt{dom}(\mathsf{H}') = \mathtt{reach}(\ell_{\mathsf{root}}, \mathsf{H}) \end{array}}{\mathsf{M}; \mathsf{H} \rightsquigarrow \mathsf{M}'} \ (\mathsf{L}^{\mathsf{U}}\text{-Monitor Step})$$

Other than this small point, monitors, safety, robust safety and *RSC* are defined as in Sect. 2. In particular, a monitor and a component agree if they mention the same ℓ_{root}: $\mathsf{M} \frown \mathsf{C} \stackrel{\mathsf{def}}{=} (\mathsf{M} = (\{\sigma \cdots\}, \rightsquigarrow, \sigma_0, \ell_{\mathsf{root}}, \sigma_{\mathsf{c}}))$ and $(\mathsf{C} = (\ell_{\mathsf{root}}; \overline{\mathsf{F}}; \overline{\mathsf{I}}))$

A program state $\mathsf{C}, \mathsf{H} \triangleright (\mathsf{s})_{\overline{\mathsf{f}}}$ (denoted with Ω) includes the function bodies C, the heap H, a statement s being executed and a stack of function calls $\overline{\mathsf{f}}$ (often omitted in the rules for simplicity). The latter is used to populate judgements of the form $\overline{\mathsf{I}} \vdash \mathsf{f}, \mathsf{f}' : \mathsf{internal/in/out}$. These determine whether calls and returns are $\mathsf{internal}$ (within the attacker or within the component), directed from the attacker to the component (in) or directed from the component to the attacker (out). This information is used to determine whether the semantics should generate a label, as in Rules EL^{U}-return to EL^{U}-retback, or no label, as in Rules EL^{U}-ret-internal and EL^{U}-call-internal since internal calls should not be observable. L^{U} has a big-step semantics for expressions ($\mathsf{H} \triangleright \mathsf{e} \hookrightarrow\!\!\!\!\rightarrow \mathsf{v}$) that relies on evaluation contexts, a small-step semantics for statements ($\Omega \xrightarrow{\lambda} \Omega'$) that has labels $\lambda ::= \epsilon \mid \alpha$ and a semantics that accumulates labels in traces ($\Omega \xRightarrow{\overline{\alpha}} \Omega'$) by omitting silent actions ϵ and concatenating the rest. Unlike existing work on compositional compiler correctness which only rely on having the component [40], the semantics relies on having both the component and the context.

$$\frac{\mathsf{H} \triangleright \mathsf{e} \hookrightarrow\!\!\!\!\rightarrow \mathsf{v} \qquad \ell \notin \mathtt{dom}(\mathsf{H})}{\mathsf{C}, \mathsf{H} \triangleright \mathsf{let}\ \mathsf{x} = \mathsf{new}\ \mathsf{e}\ \mathsf{in}\ \mathsf{s} \longrightarrow \mathsf{C}, \mathsf{H}; \ell \mapsto \mathsf{v} \triangleright \mathsf{s}[\ell \,/\, \mathsf{x}]}\ (\mathsf{EL^U\text{-}alloc})$$

$$\frac{\overline{\mathsf{f}'} = \overline{\mathsf{f}''}; \mathsf{f}' \qquad \overline{\mathsf{C}}.\mathtt{intfs} \vdash \mathsf{f}, \mathsf{f}' : \mathsf{out}}{\mathsf{C}, \mathsf{H} \triangleright (\mathsf{return};)_{\overline{\mathsf{f}'};\mathsf{f}} \xrightarrow{\mathtt{ret\ H!}} \mathsf{C}, \mathsf{H} \triangleright (\mathsf{skip})_{\overline{\mathsf{f}'}}}\ (\mathsf{EL^U\text{-}return})$$

$$\frac{\overline{\mathsf{f}'} = \overline{\mathsf{f}''}; \mathsf{f}' \qquad \mathsf{f}(\mathsf{x}) \mapsto \mathsf{s}; \mathsf{return}; \in \mathsf{C}.\mathtt{funs} \qquad \overline{\mathsf{C}}.\mathtt{intfs} \vdash \mathsf{f}', \mathsf{f} : \mathsf{in} \qquad \mathsf{H} \triangleright \mathsf{e} \hookrightarrow\!\!\!\!\rightarrow \mathsf{v}}{\mathsf{C}, \mathsf{H} \triangleright (\mathsf{call}\ \mathsf{f}\ \mathsf{e})_{\overline{\mathsf{f}'}} \xrightarrow{\mathtt{call\ f\ v\ H?}} \mathsf{C}, \mathsf{H} \triangleright (\mathsf{s}; \mathsf{return}; [\mathsf{v} \,/\, \mathsf{x}])_{\overline{\mathsf{f}'};\mathsf{f}}}\ (\mathsf{EL^U\text{-}call})$$

$$\frac{\overline{\mathsf{f}'} = \overline{\mathsf{f}''}; \mathsf{f}' \qquad \mathsf{f}(\mathsf{x}) \mapsto \mathsf{s}; \mathsf{return}; \in \overline{\mathsf{F}} \qquad \overline{\mathsf{C}}.\mathtt{intfs} \vdash \mathsf{f}', \mathsf{f} : \mathsf{out} \qquad \mathsf{H} \triangleright \mathsf{e} \hookrightarrow\!\!\!\!\rightarrow \mathsf{v}}{\mathsf{C}, \mathsf{H} \triangleright (\mathsf{call}\ \mathsf{f}\ \mathsf{e})_{\overline{\mathsf{f}'}} \xrightarrow{\mathtt{call\ f\ v\ H!}} \mathsf{C}, \mathsf{H} \triangleright (\mathsf{s}; \mathsf{return}; [\mathsf{v} \,/\, \mathsf{x}])_{\overline{\mathsf{f}'};\mathsf{f}}}\ (\mathsf{EL^U\text{-}callback})$$

$$\frac{\overline{\mathsf{f}'} = \overline{\mathsf{f}''}; \mathsf{f}' \qquad \overline{\mathsf{C}}.\mathtt{intfs} \vdash \mathsf{f}, \mathsf{f}' : \mathsf{in}}{\mathsf{C}, \mathsf{H} \triangleright (\mathsf{return};)_{\overline{\mathsf{f}'};\mathsf{f}} \xrightarrow{\mathtt{ret\ H?}} \mathsf{C}, \mathsf{H} \triangleright (\mathsf{skip})_{\overline{\mathsf{f}'}}}\ (\mathsf{EL^U\text{-}retback})$$

$$\frac{\overline{\mathsf{f}'} = \overline{\mathsf{f}''}; \mathsf{f}' \qquad \overline{\mathsf{C}}.\mathtt{intfs} \vdash \mathsf{f}, \mathsf{f}' : \mathsf{internal}}{\mathsf{C}, \mathsf{H} \triangleright (\mathsf{return};)_{\overline{\mathsf{f}'};\mathsf{f}} \xrightarrow{\epsilon} \mathsf{C}, \mathsf{H} \triangleright (\mathsf{skip})_{\overline{\mathsf{f}'}}}\ (\mathsf{EL^U\text{-}ret\text{-}internal})$$

$$\frac{\overline{\mathsf{C}}.\mathtt{intfs} \vdash \mathsf{f}, \mathsf{f}' : \mathsf{internal} \qquad \overline{\mathsf{f}'} = \overline{\mathsf{f}''}; \mathsf{f}' \qquad \mathsf{f}(\mathsf{x}) \mapsto \mathsf{s}; \mathsf{return}; \in \mathsf{C}.\mathtt{funs} \qquad \mathsf{H} \triangleright \mathsf{e} \hookrightarrow\!\!\!\!\rightarrow \mathsf{v}}{\mathsf{C}, \mathsf{H} \triangleright (\mathsf{call}\ \mathsf{f}\ \mathsf{e})_{\overline{\mathsf{f}'}} \xrightarrow{\epsilon} \mathsf{C}, \mathsf{H} \triangleright (\mathsf{s}; \mathsf{return}; [\mathsf{v} \,/\, \mathsf{x}])_{\overline{\mathsf{f}'};\mathsf{f}}}\ (\mathsf{EL^U\text{-}call\text{-}internal})$$

3.2 The Target Language $\mathbf{L^P}$

$\mathbf{L^P}$ is an untyped, imperative language that follows the structure of $\mathsf{L^U}$ and it has similar expressions and statements. However, there are critical differences (that make the compiler interesting). The main difference is that heap locations in $\mathbf{L^P}$ are concrete natural numbers. Upfront, an adversarial context can guess locations used as private state by a component and clobber them. To support hidden local state, a location can be "hidden" explicitly via the statement $\mathbf{let\ x = hide\ e\ in\ s}$, which allocates a new capability $\mathbf{k}$, an abstract token that grants access to the location $\mathbf{n}$ to which $\mathbf{e}$ points [64]. Subsequently, all reads and writes to $\mathbf{n}$ must be authenticated with the capability, so reading and writing a location take another parameter as follows: $\mathbf{!e\ with\ e}$ and $\mathbf{x := e\ with\ e}$. In both cases, the $\mathbf{e}$ after the $\mathbf{with}$ is the capability. Unlike locations, capabilities cannot be guessed. To make a location private, the compiler can make the capability of the location private. To bootstrap this hiding process, we assume that a component has one location that can only be accessed by it, a priori in the semantics (in our formalization, we always focus on only one component and we assume that, for this component, this special location is at address $\mathbf{0}$).

In detail, $\mathbf{L^P}$ heaps $\mathbf{H}$ are maps from natural numbers (locations) $\mathbf{n}$ to values $\mathbf{v}$ and a tag η as well as capabilities, so $\mathbf{H} ::= \varnothing \mid \mathbf{H}; \mathbf{n} \mapsto \mathbf{v} : \eta \mid \mathbf{H}; \mathbf{k}$. The tag η can be $\bot$, which means that $\mathbf{n}$ is globally available (not protected) or a capability $\mathbf{k}$, which protects $\mathbf{n}$. A globally available location can be freely read and written but one that is protected by a capability requires the capability to be supplied at the time of read/write (Rule $\mathbf{EL^P}$-assign, Rule $\mathbf{EL^P}$-deref).

$\mathbf{L^P}$ also has a big-step semantics for expressions, a labelled small-step semantics and a semantics that accumulates traces analogous to that of $\mathsf{L^U}$.

$$\frac{n \mapsto v : \eta \in H \quad (\eta = \bot) \text{ or } (\eta = k \text{ and } v' = k)}{H \triangleright !n \text{ with } v' \hookrightarrow\!\!\!\rightarrow H \triangleright v} \ (\mathsf{EL^P\text{-deref}})$$

$$\frac{H = H_1; n \mapsto (v, \eta) \quad H \triangleright e \hookrightarrow\!\!\!\rightarrow v \quad H' = H; n+1 \mapsto v : \bot}{C, H \triangleright \text{let } x = \text{new } e \text{ in } s \longrightarrow C, H' \triangleright s[n+1 / x]} \ (\mathsf{EL^P\text{-new}})$$

$$\frac{H \triangleright e \hookrightarrow\!\!\!\rightarrow n \quad k \notin \mathtt{dom}(H) \quad H = H_1; n \mapsto v : \bot; H_2 \quad H' = H_1; n \mapsto v : k; H_2; k}{C, H \triangleright \text{let } x = \text{hide } e \text{ in } s \longrightarrow C, H' \triangleright s[k / x]} \ (\mathsf{EL^P\text{-hide}})$$

$$\frac{\begin{array}{c} H \triangleright e \hookrightarrow\!\!\!\rightarrow v \quad H = H_1; n \mapsto \_ : \eta; H_2 \quad H' = H_1; n \mapsto v : \eta; H_2 \\ (\eta = \bot) \text{ or } (\eta = k \text{ and } v' = k) \end{array}}{C, H \triangleright n := e \text{ with } v' \longrightarrow C, H' \triangleright \text{skip}} \ (\mathsf{EL^P\text{-assign}})$$

A second difference between L^P and $\mathsf{L^U}$ is that L^P has no booleans, while $\mathsf{L^U}$ has them. This makes the compiler and the related proofs interesting, as discussed in the proof of Theorem 1.

In L^P, the locations of interest to a monitor are all those that can be reached from the address 0. 0 itself is protected with a capability k_{root} that is assumed to occur only in the code of the component in focus, so a component is defined as $C ::= k_{root}; \overline{F}; \overline{I}$. We can now give a precise definition of component-monitor agreement for L^P as well as a precise definition of attacker, which must care about the k_{root} capability.

$$M \frown C \overset{\mathsf{def}}{=} (M = (\{\sigma \cdots\}, \rightsquigarrow, \sigma_0, k_{root}, \sigma_c)) \text{ and } (C = (k_{root}; \overline{F}; \overline{I}))$$

$$C \vdash A : atk \overset{\mathsf{def}}{=} C = (k_{root}; \overline{F}; \overline{I}), A = \overline{F'}, k_{root} \notin \mathtt{fn}(\overline{F'})$$

3.3 Compiler from $\mathsf{L^U}$ to L^P

We now present $[\![\cdot]\!]^{\mathsf{L^U}}_{L^P}$, the compiler from $\mathsf{L^U}$ to L^P, detailing how it uses the capabilities of L^P to achieve *RSC*. Then, we prove that $[\![\cdot]\!]^{\mathsf{L^U}}_{L^P}$ attains *RSC*.

Compiler $[\![\cdot]\!]^{\mathsf{L^U}}_{L^P}$ takes as input a $\mathsf{L^U}$ component C and returns a L^P component (excerpts of the translation are shown below). The compiler performs a simple pass on the structure of functions, expressions and statements. Each $\mathsf{L^U}$ location is encoded as a pair of a L^P location and the capability to access the location; location update and dereference are compiled accordingly. The compiler codes source booleans true to 0 and false to 1, and the source number n to the target counterpart n.

$$[\![\ell_{root}; \overline{\mathsf{F}}; \overline{\mathsf{I}}]\!]^{\mathsf{L^U}}_{L^P} = k_{root}; [\![\overline{\mathsf{F}}]\!]^{\mathsf{L^U}}_{L^P}; [\![\overline{\mathsf{I}}]\!]^{\mathsf{L^U}}_{L^P}$$

$$[\![!\mathsf{e}]\!]^{\mathsf{L^U}}_{L^P} = ![\![\mathsf{e}]\!]^{\mathsf{L^U}}_{L^P}.1 \text{ with } [\![\mathsf{e}]\!]^{\mathsf{L^U}}_{L^P}.2$$

$$\left[\!\!\left[\begin{array}{l}\mathsf{let\ x = new\ e} \\ \mathsf{in\ s}\end{array}\right]\!\!\right]^{\mathsf{L^U}}_{L^P} = \begin{array}{l} \text{let } x_{loc} = \text{new } [\![\mathsf{e}]\!]^{\mathsf{L^U}}_{L^P} \text{ in let } x_{cap} = \text{hide } x_{loc} \text{ in} \\ \quad \text{let } x = \langle x_{loc}, x_{cap} \rangle \text{ in } [\![\mathsf{s}]\!]^{\mathsf{L^U}}_{L^P} \end{array}$$

$$[\![\mathsf{x := e'}]\!]^{\mathsf{L^U}}_{L^P} = \text{let } x_{loc} = x.1 \text{ in let } x_{cap} = x.2 \text{ in } x_{loc} := [\![\mathsf{e'}]\!]^{\mathsf{L^U}}_{L^P} \text{ with } x_{cap}$$

This compiler solely relies on the capability abstraction of the target language as a defence mechanism to attain *RSC*. Unlike existing secure compilers, $[\![\cdot]\!]^{\mathsf{L^U}}_{\mathrm{L^P}}$ needs neither dynamic checks nor other constructs that introduce runtime overhead to attain *RSC* [9,32,39,53,59].

Proof of *RSC*. Compiler $[\![\cdot]\!]^{\mathsf{L^U}}_{\mathrm{L^P}}$ attains *RSC* (Theorem 1). In order to set up this theorem, we need to instantiate the cross-language relation for values, which we write as $\approx_\beta$ here. The relation is parametrised by a partial bijection $\beta : \ell \times \mathrm{n} \times \eta$ from source heap locations to target heap locations which determines when a source location and a target location (and its capability) are related. On values, $\approx_\beta$ is defined as follows: $\mathsf{true} \approx_\beta 0$; $\mathsf{false} \approx_\beta \mathrm{n}$ when $\mathrm{n} \neq 0$; $\mathsf{n} \approx_\beta \mathrm{n}$; $\ell \approx_\beta \langle \mathrm{n}, \mathrm{k} \rangle$ if $(\ell, \mathrm{n}, \mathrm{k}) \in \beta$; $\ell \approx_\beta \langle \mathrm{n}, \_ \rangle$ if $(\ell, \mathrm{n}, \bot) \in \beta$; $\langle \mathsf{v_1}, \mathsf{v_2} \rangle \approx_\beta \langle \mathrm{v_1}, \mathrm{v_2} \rangle$ if $\mathsf{v_1} \approx_\beta \mathrm{v_1}$ and $\mathsf{v_2} \approx_\beta \mathrm{v_2}$. This relation is then used to define the heap, monitor state and action relations. Heaps are related, written $\mathsf{H} \approx_\beta \mathrm{H}$, when locations related in β point to related values. States are related, written $\Omega \approx_\beta \Omega$, when they have related heaps. The action relation $(\alpha \approx_\beta \alpha)$ is defined as in Sect. 2.2.

Monitor Relation. In Sect. 2.2, we left the monitor relation abstract. Here, we define it for our two languages. Two monitors are related when they can *simulate* each other on related heaps. Given a monitor-specific relation $\sigma \approx \sigma$ on monitor states, we say that a relation $\mathcal{R}$ on source and target monitors is a *bisimulation* if the following hold whenever $\mathsf{M} = (\{\sigma \cdots\}, \rightsquigarrow, \sigma_0, \ell_{\mathsf{root}}, \sigma_{\mathsf{c}})$ and $\mathrm{M} = (\{\sigma \cdots\}, \rightsquigarrow, \sigma_0, \mathrm{k_{root}}, \sigma_{\mathrm{c}})$ are related by $\mathcal{R}$:

1. $\sigma_0 \approx \sigma_0$, and $\sigma_{\mathsf{c}} \approx \sigma_{\mathrm{c}}$, and
2. For all β containing $(\ell_{\mathsf{root}}, 0, \mathrm{k_{root}})$ and all H, H with $\mathsf{H} \approx_\beta \mathrm{H}$:
   (a) $(\sigma_{\mathsf{c}}, \mathsf{H}, \_) \in \rightsquigarrow$ iff $(\sigma_{\mathrm{c}}, \mathrm{H}, \_) \in \rightsquigarrow$, and
   (b) $(\sigma_{\mathsf{c}}, \mathsf{H}, \sigma') \in \rightsquigarrow$ and $(\sigma_{\mathrm{c}}, \mathrm{H}, \sigma') \in \rightsquigarrow$ imply
   $(\{\sigma \cdots\}, \rightsquigarrow, \sigma_0, \ell_{\mathsf{root}}, \sigma')\mathcal{R}(\{\sigma \cdots\}, \rightsquigarrow, \sigma_0, \mathrm{k_{root}}, \sigma')$.

In words, $\mathcal{R}$ is a bisimulation only if $\mathsf{M}\mathcal{R}\mathrm{M}$ implies that M and M simulate each other on heaps related by *any* β that relates ℓ_{root} to 0. In particular, this means that neither M nor M can be sensitive to the *specific* addresses allocated during the run of the program. However, they can be sensitive to the "shape" of the heap or the values stored in the heap. Note that the union of any two bisimulations is a bisimulation. Hence, there is a largest bisimulation, which we denote as $\approx$. Intuitively, $\mathsf{M} \approx \mathrm{M}$ implies that M and M encode the same safety property (up to the aforementioned relation on values $\approx_\beta$). With all the boilerplate for *RSC* in place, we state our main theorem.

Theorem 1 (**$[\![\cdot]\!]^{\mathsf{L^U}}_{\mathrm{L^P}}$ attains *RSC***). $\vdash [\![\cdot]\!]^{\mathsf{L^U}}_{\mathrm{L^P}} : RSC$

We outline our proof of Theorem 1, which relies on a backtranslation $\langle\!\langle\cdot\rangle\!\rangle^{\mathrm{L^P}}_{\mathsf{L^U}}$. Intuitively, $\langle\!\langle\cdot\rangle\!\rangle^{\mathrm{L^P}}_{\mathsf{L^U}}$ takes a target trace $\overline{\alpha}$ and builds a *set* of source contexts such that *one* of them when linked with C, produces a related trace $\overline{\alpha}$ in the source (Theorem 2). In prior work, backtranslations return a single context [10,11,21,

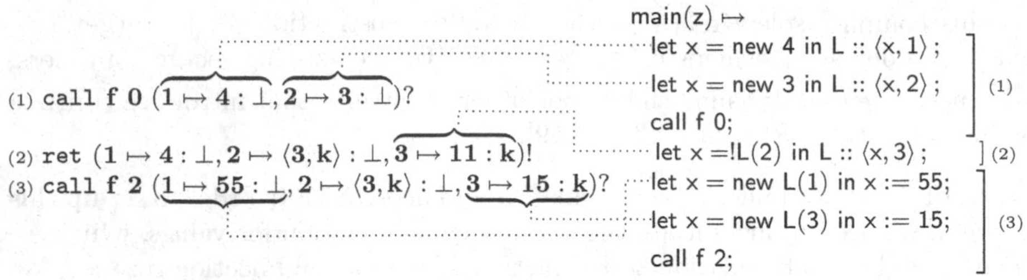

(1) call f 0 (1 ↦ 4 : ⊥, 2 ↦ 3 : ⊥)?
(2) ret (1 ↦ 4 : ⊥, 2 ↦ ⟨3, k⟩ : ⊥, 3 ↦ 11 : k)!
(3) call f 2 (1 ↦ 55 : ⊥, 2 ↦ ⟨3, k⟩ : ⊥, 3 ↦ 15 : k)?
main(z) ↦
let x = new 4 in L :: ⟨x, 1⟩ ;
let x = new 3 in L :: ⟨x, 2⟩ ;
call f 0;
let x = !L(2) in L :: ⟨x, 3⟩ ;
let x = new L(1) in x := 55;
let x = new L(3) in x := 15;
call f 2;
(1)
(2)
(3)

Fig. 1. Example of a trace and its backtranslated code.

28, 50, 53, 59]. This is because they all, explicitly or implicitly, assume that $\approx$ is injective from source to target. Under this assumption, the backtranslation is unique: a target value v will be related to at most one source value v. We do away with this assumption (e.g., the target value 0 is related to both source values 0 and true) and thus there can be multiple source values related to any given target value. This results in a set of backtranslated contexts, of which at least one will reproduce the trace as we need it.

We bypass the lengthy technical setup for this proof and provide an informal description of why the backtranslation achieves what it is supposed to. As an example, Fig. 1 contains a trace $\overline{\alpha}$ and the the output of $\langle\!\langle\overline{\alpha}\rangle\!\rangle^{\mathrm{L^P}}_{\mathsf{L^U}}$.

$\langle\!\langle\cdot\rangle\!\rangle^{\mathrm{L^P}}_{\mathsf{L^U}}$ first generates empty method bodies for all context methods called by the compiled component. Then it backtranslates each *action* on the given trace, generating code blocks that mimic that action and places that code inside the appropriate method body. Figure 1 shows the code blocks generated for each action. Backtranslated code maintains a support data structure at runtime, a list of locations denoted L where locations are added (::) and they are looked up (L(n)) based on their second field n, which is their target-level address. In order to backtranslate the first call, we need to set up the heap with the right values and then perform the call. In the diagram, dotted lines describe which source statement generates which part of the heap. The return only generates code that will update the list L to ensure that the context has access to all the locations it knows in the target too. In order to backtranslate the last call we lookup the locations to be updated in L so we can ensure that when the call f 2 statement is executed, the heap is in the right state.

For the backtranslation to be used in the proof we need to prove its correctness, i.e., that $\langle\!\langle\overline{\alpha}\rangle\!\rangle^{\mathrm{L^P}}_{\mathsf{L^U}}$ generates a context A that, together with C, generates a trace $\overline{\alpha}$ related to the given target trace $\overline{\alpha}$.

Theorem 2 **($\langle\!\langle\cdot\rangle\!\rangle^{\mathrm{L^P}}_{\mathsf{L^U}}$ is correct)**

$$\textit{if } \mathrm{A}\left[\llbracket \mathsf{C} \rrbracket^{\mathsf{L^U}}_{\mathrm{L^P}}\right] \stackrel{\overline{\alpha}}{\Longrightarrow} \Omega \textit{ then } \exists \mathsf{A} \in \langle\!\langle\overline{\alpha}\rangle\!\rangle^{\mathrm{L^P}}_{\mathsf{L^U}} .\, \mathsf{A}\left[\mathsf{C}\right] \stackrel{\overline{\alpha}}{\Longrightarrow} \Omega \textit{ and } \overline{\alpha} \approx_\beta \overline{\alpha} \textit{ and } \Omega \approx_\beta \Omega.$$

This theorem immediately implies that $\vdash [\![\cdot]\!]^{\mathsf{L^U}}_{\mathrm{L^P}} : \mathit{PF\text{-}RSC}$, which, by Theorem 3 below, implies that $\vdash [\![\cdot]\!]^{\mathsf{L^U}}_{\mathrm{L^P}} : \mathit{RSC}$.

Theorem 3 (*PF-RSC* **and** *RSC* **are equivalent for** $[\![\cdot]\!]^{\mathsf{L^U}}_{\mathrm{L^P}}$**).**

$$\vdash [\![\cdot]\!]^{\mathsf{L^U}}_{\mathrm{L^P}} : \mathit{PF\text{-}RSC} \iff \vdash [\![\cdot]\!]^{\mathsf{L^U}}_{\mathrm{L^P}} : \mathit{RSC}$$

Example 4 (Compiling a secure program). To illustrate *RSC* at work, let us consider the following source component $\mathsf{C_a}$, which manages an account whose balance is security-relevant. Accordingly, the balance is stored in a location (ℓ_{root} that is tracked by the monitor. $\mathsf{C_a}$ provides functions to deposit to the account as well as to print the account balance.

$$\begin{aligned}&\mathsf{deposit(x)} \mapsto \mathsf{let\ q{=}abs(x)\ in\ let\ amt} = !\ell_{\mathsf{root}}\ \mathsf{in}\ \ell_{\mathsf{root}} := \mathsf{amt} + \mathsf{q}\\ &\mathsf{balance()} \mapsto !\ell_{\mathsf{root}}\end{aligned}$$

$\mathsf{C_a}$ never leaks any sensitive location (ℓ_{root}) to an attacker. Additionally, an attacker has no way to decrement the amount of the balance since deposit only adds the absolute value $\mathsf{abs(x)}$ of its input x to the existing balance.

By compiling $\mathsf{C_a}$ with $[\![\cdot]\!]^{\mathsf{L^U}}_{\mathrm{L^P}}$, we obtain the following target program.

$$\begin{aligned}&\mathbf{deposit(x)} \mapsto \mathbf{let\ q{=}abs(x)\ in}\\ &\qquad\qquad \mathbf{let\ amt{=}!0\ with\ k_{root}\ in\ 0 := amt + q\ with\ k_{root}}\\ &\mathbf{balance()} \mapsto \mathbf{!0\ with\ k_{root}}\end{aligned}$$

Recall that location ℓ_{root} is mapped to location $\mathbf{0}$ and protected by the $\mathbf{k_{root}}$ capability. In the compiled code, while location $\mathbf{0}$ is freely computable by a target attacker, capability $\mathbf{k_{root}}$ is not. Since that capability is not leaked to an attacker, an attacker will not be able to tamper with the balance stored in location $\mathbf{0}$. ⊡

4 *RSC* via Bisimulation

If the source language has a verification system that enforces robust safety, proving that a compiler attains *RSC* can be simpler than that of Sect. 3—it may not require a back translation. To demonstrate this, we consider a specific class of monitors, namely those that enforce type invariants on a specific set of locations. Our source language, $\mathsf{L^\tau}$, is similar to $\mathsf{L^U}$ but it has a type system that accepts only those source programs whose traces the source monitor never rejects. Our compiler $[\![\cdot]\!]^{\mathsf{L^\tau}}_{\mathrm{L^\pi}}$ is directed by typing derivations, and its proof of *RSC* establishes a specific cross-language invariant on program execution, rather than a backtranslation. A second, independent goal of this section is to show that *RSC* is compatible with concurrency. Consequently, our source and target languages include constructs for forking threads.

4.1 The Source Language L^τ

L^τ extends L^U with concurrency, so it has a fork statement ($\parallel$ s), processes and process soups [19]. Components define a set of safety-relevant locations Δ, so $\mathsf{C} ::= \Delta; \overline{\mathsf{F}}; \overline{\mathsf{I}}$ and heaps carry type information, so $\mathsf{H} ::= \varnothing \mid \mathsf{H}; \ell \mapsto \mathsf{v} : \tau$. Δ also specifies a type for each safety-relevant location, so $\Delta ::= \varnothing \mid \Delta; (\ell : \tau)$.

L^τ has an unconventional type system that enforces *robust type safety* [1,14, 31,34,45,58], which means that no context can cause the static types of sensitive heap locations to be violated at runtime. Using a special type UN that is described below, a program component statically partitions heap locations it deals with into those it cares about (sensitive or "trusted" locations) and those it does not care about ("untrusted" locations). Call a value *shareable* if only untrusted locations can be extracted from it using the language's elimination constructs. The type system then ensures that a program component only ever shares shareable values with the context. This ensures that the context cannot violate any invariants (including static types) of the trusted locations, since it can never gets direct access to them.

Technically, the type system considers the types $\tau ::= \mathsf{Bool} \mid \mathsf{Nat} \mid \tau \times \tau \mid \mathsf{Ref}\ \tau \mid \mathsf{UN}$ and the following typing judgements (Γ maps variables to types).

$\vdash \mathsf{C} : \mathsf{UN}$	Component C is well-typed.	$\Delta, \Gamma \vdash \mathsf{e} : \tau$	Expression e has type τ.
$\tau \vdash \circ$	Type τ is shareable.	$\mathsf{C}, \Delta, \Gamma \vdash \mathsf{s}$	Statement s is well-typed.

$$\frac{}{\mathsf{Bool} \vdash \circ}\ (\mathsf{TL}^\tau\text{-bool-pub}) \qquad \frac{}{\mathsf{Nat} \vdash \circ}\ (\mathsf{TL}^\tau\text{-nat-pub}) \qquad \frac{\tau \vdash \circ \quad \tau' \vdash \circ}{\tau \times \tau' \vdash \circ}\ (\mathsf{TL}^\tau\text{-pair-pub}) \qquad \frac{}{\mathsf{UN} \vdash \circ}\ (\mathsf{TL}^\tau\text{-un-pub}) \qquad \frac{}{\mathsf{Ref}\ \mathsf{UN} \vdash \circ}\ (\mathsf{TL}^\tau\text{-references-pub})$$

Type UN stands for "untrusted" or "shareable" and contains all values that can be passed to the context. Every type that is not a subtype of UN is implicitly trusted and cannot be passed to the context. Untrusted locations are explicitly marked UN at their allocation points in the program. Other types are deemed shareable via subtyping. Intuitively, a type is safe if values in it can only yield locations of type UN by the language elimination constructs. For example, $\mathsf{UN} \times \mathsf{UN}$ is a subtype of UN. We write $\tau \vdash \circ$ to mean that τ is a subtype of UN.

Further, L^τ contains an *endorsement* statement ($\mathsf{endorse\ x = e\ as}\ \varphi\ \mathsf{in\ s}$) that dynamically checks the top-level constructor of a value of type UN and gives it a more precise superficial type $\varphi ::= \mathsf{Bool} \mid \mathsf{Nat} \mid \mathsf{UN} \times \mathsf{UN} \mid \mathsf{Ref\ UN}$ [24]. This allows a program to safely inspect values coming from the context. It is similar to existing type casts [48] but it only inspects one structural layer of the value (this simplifies the compilation).

The operational semantics of L^τ updates that of L^U to deal with concurrency and endorsement. The latter performs a runtime check on the endorsed value [62].

Monitors $\mathsf{M} ::= (\{\sigma \cdots\}, \rightsquigarrow, \sigma_0, \Delta, \sigma_\mathsf{c})$ check at runtime that the set of trusted heap locations Δ have values of their intended static types. Accordingly, the description of the monitor includes a list of trusted locations and their expected types (in the form of an environment Δ). The type τ of any location in Δ must be trusted, so $\tau \nvdash \circ$. To facilitate checks of the monitor, every heap location carries a type at runtime (in addition to a value). The monitor transitions should therefore be of the form (σ, Δ, σ), but since Δ never changes, we write the transitions as (σ, σ).

A monitor and a component agree if they have the same Δ: $\mathsf{M} \frown \mathsf{C} \stackrel{\mathsf{def}}{=} (\{\sigma \cdots\}, \rightsquigarrow, \sigma_0, \Delta, \sigma_c) \frown (\Delta; \overline{\mathsf{F}}; \overline{\mathsf{I}})$. Other definitions (safety, robust safety and actions) are as in Sect. 2. Importantly, a well-typed component generates traces that are always accepted, so every component typed at UN is robustly safe.

Theorem 4 (Typability Implies Robust Safety in L^τ)

$$\textit{If } \vdash \mathsf{C} : \mathsf{UN} \textit{ and } \mathsf{C} \frown \mathsf{M} \textit{ then } \mathsf{M} \vdash \mathsf{C} : \mathsf{rs}$$

Richer Source Monitors. In L^τ, source language monitors only enforce the property of type safety on specific memory locations (robustly). This can be generalized substantially to enforce arbitrary invariants other than types on locations. The only requirement is to find a type system (e.g., based on refinements or Hoare logics) that can enforce robust safety in the source (cf. [68]). Our compilation and proof strategy should work with little modification. Another easy generalization is allowing the set of locations considered by the monitor to grow over time, as in Sect. 3.

4.2 The Target Language $\mathbf{L}^\pi$

Our target language, $\mathbf{L}^\pi$, extends the previous target language $\mathbf{L}^\mathbf{P}$, with support for concurrency (forking, processes and process soups), atomic co-creation of a protected location and its protecting capability ($\mathbf{let\ x = newhide\ e\ in\ s}$) and for examining the top-level construct of a value ($\mathbf{destruct\ x = e\ as\ B\ in\ s\ or\ s'}$) according to a pattern ($\mathbf{B} ::= \mathbf{nat} \mid \mathbf{pair}$).

$$\frac{\mathbf{H} \triangleright \mathbf{e} \hookrightarrow\!\!\!\!\rightarrow \mathbf{n}}{\mathbf{C}, \mathbf{H} \triangleright \mathbf{destruct\ x = e\ as\ nat\ in\ s\ or\ s'} \longrightarrow \mathbf{C}, \mathbf{H} \triangleright \mathbf{s}[\mathbf{n} / \mathbf{x}]}\ (\mathsf{EL}^\pi\text{-destruct-nat})$$

$$\frac{\mathbf{H} = \mathbf{H_1}; \mathbf{n} \mapsto (\mathbf{v}, \eta) \quad \mathbf{H} \triangleright \mathbf{e} \hookrightarrow\!\!\!\!\rightarrow \mathbf{v} \quad \mathbf{k} \notin \mathtt{dom}(\mathbf{H}) \quad \mathbf{s}' = \mathbf{s}[\langle \mathbf{n}+1, \mathbf{k}\rangle / \mathbf{x}]}{\mathbf{C}, \mathbf{H} \triangleright \mathbf{let\ x = newhide\ e\ in\ s} \longrightarrow \mathbf{C}, \mathbf{H}; \mathbf{n}+1 \mapsto \mathbf{v} : \mathbf{k}; \mathbf{k} \triangleright \mathbf{s}'}\ (\mathsf{EL}^\pi\text{-new})$$

Monitors are also updated to consider a fixed set of locations (a heap $\mathbf{H_0}$), so $\mathbf{M} ::= (\{\sigma \cdots\}, \rightsquigarrow, \sigma_0, \mathbf{H_0}, \sigma_c)$. The atomic creation of capabilities is provided to match modern security architectures such as Cheri [71] (which implement capabilities at the hardware level). This atomicity is not strictly necessary and we prove that *RSC* is attained both by a compiler relying on it and by one that allocates a location and then protects it non-atomically. The former compiler (with this atomicity in the target) is a bit easier to describe, so for space reasons, we only describe that here and defer the other one to the companion report [61].

4.3 Compiler from L^τ to L^π

The high-level structure of the compiler, $[\![\cdot]\!]^{\mathsf{L}^\tau}_{\mathrm{L}^\pi}$, is similar to that of our earlier compiler $[\![\cdot]\!]^{\mathsf{L}^U}_{\mathrm{L}^P}$ (Sect. 3.3). However, $[\![\cdot]\!]^{\mathsf{L}^\tau}_{\mathrm{L}^\pi}$ is defined by induction on the type derivation of the component to be compiled. The case for allocation (presented below) explicitly uses type information to achieve security efficiently, protecting only those locations whose type is not UN.

$$\left[\!\!\left[\frac{\begin{array}{c}\Delta,\Gamma\vdash \mathsf{e}:\tau\\ \mathsf{C},\Delta,\Gamma;\mathsf{x}:\mathsf{Ref}\ \tau\vdash \mathsf{s}\end{array}}{\begin{array}{l}\mathsf{C},\Delta,\Gamma\vdash\\ \quad\mathsf{let\ x = new_\tau\ e\ in\ s}\end{array}}\right]\!\!\right]^{\mathsf{L}^\tau}_{\mathrm{L}^\pi} = \begin{cases}\begin{array}{l}\mathrm{let\ xo\ = new}\ [\![\Delta,\Gamma\vdash \mathsf{e}:\tau]\!]^{\mathsf{L}^\tau}_{\mathrm{L}^\pi}\\ \quad\mathrm{in\ let\ x} = \langle \mathrm{xo}, 0\rangle\\ \quad\mathrm{in}\ [\![\mathsf{C},\Delta,\Gamma;\mathsf{x}:\mathsf{Ref}\ \tau\vdash \mathsf{s}]\!]^{\mathsf{L}^\tau}_{\mathrm{L}^\pi}\end{array} & \text{if } \tau=\mathsf{UN}\\[2em] \begin{array}{l}\mathrm{let\ x\ = newhide}\ [\![\Delta,\Gamma\vdash \mathsf{e}:\tau]\!]^{\mathsf{L}^\tau}_{\mathrm{L}^\pi}\\ \quad\mathrm{in}\ [\![\mathsf{C},\Delta,\Gamma;\mathsf{x}:\mathsf{Ref}\ \tau\vdash \mathsf{s}]\!]^{\mathsf{L}^\tau}_{\mathrm{L}^\pi}\end{array} & \text{otherwise}\end{cases}$$

New Monitor Relation. As monitors have changed, we also need a new monitor relation $\mathsf{M}\approx\mathrm{M}$. Informally, a source and a target monitor are related if the target monitor can always step whenever the target heap satisfies the types specified in the source monitor (up to renaming by the partial bijection β).

We write $\vdash \mathsf{H}:\Delta$ to mean that for each location $\ell\in\Delta$, $\vdash \mathsf{H}(\ell):\Delta(\ell)$. Given a partial bijection β from source to target locations, we say that a target monitor $\mathrm{M} = (\{\sigma\cdots\}, \rightsquigarrow, \sigma_0, \mathrm{H}_0, \sigma_c)$ is good, written $\vdash \mathrm{M}:\beta,\Delta$, if for all $\sigma\in\{\sigma\cdots\}$ and all $\mathsf{H}\approx_\beta \mathrm{H}$ such that $\vdash \mathsf{H}:\Delta$, there is a σ' such that $(\sigma,\mathrm{H},\sigma')\in\rightsquigarrow$. For a fixed partial bijection β_0 between the domains of Δ and H_0, we say that the source monitor M and the target monitor M are related, written $\mathsf{M}\approx\mathrm{M}$, if $\vdash \mathrm{M}:\beta_0,\Delta$ for the Δ in M. With this setup, we define *RSC* as in Sect. 2.

Theorem 5 (Compiler $[\![\cdot]\!]^{\mathsf{L}^\tau}_{\mathrm{L}^\pi}$ attains *RSC*). $\vdash [\![\cdot]\!]^{\mathsf{L}^\tau}_{\mathrm{L}^\pi}$: *RSC*

To prove that $[\![\cdot]\!]^{\mathsf{L}^\tau}_{\mathrm{L}^\pi}$ attains *RSC* we do not rely on a backtranslation. Here, we know statically which locations can be monitor-sensitive: they must all be trusted, i.e., must have a type τ satisfying $\tau\nvdash\circ$. Using this, we set up a simple cross-language relation and show it to be an invariant on runs of source and compiled target components. The relation captures the following:

- Heaps (both source and target) can be partitioned into two parts, a *trusted* part and an *untrusted* part;
- The trusted source heap contains only locations whose type is trusted ($\tau\nvdash\circ$);
- The trusted target heap contains only locations related to trusted source locations and these point to related values; more importantly, every trusted target location is protected by a capability;
- In the target, any capability protecting a trusted location does not occur in attacker code, nor is it stored in an untrusted heap location.

We need to prove that this relation is preserved by reductions both in compiled and in attacker code. The former follows from source robust safety (Theorem 4). The latter is simple since all trusted locations are protected with capabilities, attackers have no access to trusted locations, and capabilities are unforgeable and unguessable (by the semantics of $\mathbf{L}^{\pi}$). At this point, knowing that monitors are related, and that source traces are always accepted by source monitors, we can conclude that target traces are always accepted by target monitors too. Note that this kind of an argument requires all compilable source programs to be robustly safe and is, therefore, impossible for our first compiler $[\![\cdot]\!]^{\mathsf{L^U}}_{\mathrm{L^P}}$. Avoiding the backtranslation results in a proof much simpler than that of Sect. 3.

5 Fully Abstract Compilation

Our next goal is to compare *RSC* to *FAC* at an intuitive level. We first define fully abstract compilation or *FAC* (Sect. 5.1). Then, we present an example of how *FAC* may result in inefficient compiled code and use that to present in Sect. 5.2 what would be needed to write a fully abstract compiler from $\mathsf{L^U}$ to $\mathrm{L^P}$ (the languages of our first compiler). We use this example to compare *RSC* and *FAC* concretely, showing that, at least on this example, *RSC* permits more efficient code and affords simpler proofs that *FAC*.

However, this does not imply that one should always prefer *RSC* to *FAC* blindly. In some cases, one may want to establish full abstraction for reasons other than security. Also, when the target language is typed [10,11,21,50] or has abstractions similar to those of the source, full abstraction may have no downsides (in terms of efficiency of compiled code and simplicity of proofs) relative to *RSC*. However, in many settings, including those we consider, target languages are not typed, and often differ significantly from the source in their abstractions. In such cases, *RSC* is a worthy alternative.

5.1 Formalising Fully Abstract Compilation

As stated in Sect. 1, *FAC* requires the preservation and reflection of observational equivalence, and most existing work instantiates observational equivalence with contextual equivalence ($\simeq_{ctx}$). Contextual equivalence and *FAC* are defined below. Informally, two components C_1 and C_2 are contextually equivalent if no context A interacting with them can tell them apart, i.e., they are *indistinguishable.* Contextual equivalence can encode security properties such as confidentiality, integrity, invariant maintenance and non-interference [6,9,53,60]. We do not explain this well-known observation here, but refer the interested reader to the survey of Patrignani *et al.* [54]. Informally, a compiler $[\![\cdot]\!]^{\mathsf{S}}_{\mathrm{T}}$ is fully abstract if it translates (only) contextually-equivalent source components into contextually-equivalent target ones.

Definition 4 (Contextual equivalence and fully abstract compilation).

$$C_1 \simeq_{ctx} C_2 \stackrel{\mathsf{def}}{=} \forall A. A\,[C_1]\Uparrow \iff A\,[C_2]\Uparrow, \text{ where } \Uparrow \text{ means execution divergence}$$

$$\vdash [\![\cdot]\!]^{\mathsf{S}}_{\mathrm{T}} : FAC \stackrel{\mathsf{def}}{=} \forall \mathsf{C}_1, \mathsf{C}_2.\, \mathsf{C}_1 \simeq_{ctx} \mathsf{C}_2 \iff [\![\mathsf{C}_1]\!]^{\mathsf{S}}_{\mathrm{T}} \simeq_{ctx} [\![\mathsf{C}_2]\!]^{\mathsf{S}}_{\mathrm{T}}$$

The security-relevant part of *FAC* is the $\Rightarrow$ implication [29]. This part is security-relevant because the proof thesis concerns target contextual equivalence ($\simeq_{ctx}$). Unfolding the definition of $\simeq_{ctx}$ on the right of the implication yields a universal quantification over all possible target contexts $\mathbf{A}$, which captures malicious attackers. In fact, there may be target contexts $\mathbf{A}$ that can interact with compiled code in ways that are impossible in the source language. Compilers that attain *FAC* with untyped target languages often insert checks in compiled code that detect such interactions and respond to them securely [60], often by halting the execution [6,9,29,37,39,42,53,54]. These checks are often inefficient, but must be performed even if the interactions are not security-relevant. We now present an example of this.

Example 5 (Wrappers for heap resources). Consider a password manager written in an object-oriented language that is compiled to an assembly-like language. The password manager defines a `private List` object where it stores the passwords locally. Shown below are two implementations of the `newList` method inside `List` which we call $\mathsf{C_{one}}$ and $\mathsf{C_{two}}$. The only difference between $\mathsf{C_{one}}$ and $\mathsf{C_{two}}$ is that $\mathsf{C_{two}}$ allocates two lists internally; one of these (`shadow`) is used for internal purposes only.

```
public newList(): List{

  ell = new List();
  return ell;
}
```

```
public newList(): List{
  shadow = new List(); // diff
  ell = new List();
  return ell;
}
```

$\mathsf{C_{one}}$ and $\mathsf{C_{two}}$ are equivalent in a source language that does not allow pointer comparison (like our source languages). To attain *FAC* when the target allows pointer comparisons (as in our target languages), the pointers returned by `newList` in the two implementations must be the same, but this is very difficult to ensure since the second implementation does more allocations. A simple solution to this problem is to wrap `ell` in a proxy object and return the proxy [9,47,53,59]. Compiled code needs to maintain a lookup table mapping the proxy to the original object and proxies must have allocation-independent addresses. Proxies work but they are inefficient due to the need to look up the table on every object access. ⊡

In this example, *FAC* forces all privately allocated locations to be wrapped in proxies. However, *RSC* does not require this. Our target languages $\mathbf{L^P}$ and $\mathbf{L^\pi}$ support address comparison (addresses are natural numbers in their heaps) but $[\![\cdot]\!]^{\mathsf{L^U}}_{\mathbf{L^P}}$ and $[\![\cdot]\!]^{\mathsf{L^\tau}}_{\mathbf{L^\pi}}$ just use capabilities to attain security efficiently while $[\![\cdot]\!]^{\mathsf{L^\tau}}_{\mathbf{L^I}}$ relies on memory isolation. On the other hand, for attaining *FAC*, capabilities alone would be insufficient since they do not hide addresses. We explain this in detail in the next subsection.

Remarks. Our technical report lists many other cases of *FAC* forcing security-irrelevant inefficiency in compiled code [61]. All of these can be avoided by just replacing contextual equivalence with a different notion of equivalence in the statement of *FAC*. However, it is not clear how this can be done generally for any given kind of inefficiency, and what the security consequences of such instantiations of the statement of *FAC* are. On the other hand, *RSC* is *uniform* and it does not induce any of these inefficiencies.

A security issue that cannot be addressed just by tweaking equivalences is information leaks on side channels, as side channels are, by definition, not expressible in the language. Neither *FAC* nor *RSC* deals with side channels.

5.2 Towards a Fully Abstract Compiler from $\mathsf{L^U}$ to $\mathrm{L^P}$

To further compare *FAC* and *RSC*, we now sketch what *would* be needed to construct a fully abstract compiler from $\mathsf{L^U}$ to $\mathrm{L^P}$. In particular, this compiler should not suffer from the "attack" described in Example 5.

Inefficiency. We denote with $[\![\boxed{\cdot}]\!]^{\mathsf{L^U}}_{\mathrm{L^P}}$ a (hypothetical) new compiler from $\mathsf{L^U}$ to $\mathrm{L^P}$ that attains *FAC*. We describe informally what code generated by this compiler would have to do. We know that fully abstract compilation preserves *all* source abstractions in the target language. One abstraction that distinguishes $\mathrm{L^P}$ from $\mathsf{L^U}$ is that locations are abstract in $\mathrm{L^P}$, but concrete natural numbers in $\mathsf{L^U}$. Thus, locations allocated by compiled code must not be passed directly to the context as this would reveal the allocation order. Instead of passing the location $\langle \mathrm{n}, \mathrm{k} \rangle$ to the context, the compiler arranges for an opaque handle $\langle \mathrm{n}', \mathrm{k_{com}} \rangle$ (that cannot be used to access any location directly) to be passed. Such an opaque handle is often called a *mask* or *seal* in the literature [66].

To ensure that masking is done properly, $[\![\boxed{\cdot}]\!]^{\mathsf{L^U}}_{\mathrm{L^P}}$ can insert code at entry and exit points of compiled code, *wrapping* the compiled code in a way that enforces masking [32,59]. The wrapper keeps a list $\overline{\mathrm{L}}$ of component-allocated locations that are shared with the context in order to know their masks. When a component-allocated location is shared, it is added to the list $\overline{\mathrm{L}}$. The mask of a location is its index in this list. If the same location is shared again it is not added again but its previous index is used. To implement lookup in $\overline{\mathrm{L}}$ we must compare capabilities too, so we need to add that expression to the target language. To ensure capabilities do not leak to the context, the second field of the pair is a constant capability $\mathrm{k_{com}}$ which compiled code does not use otherwise. Clearly, this wrapping can increase the cost of all cross-component calls and returns.

However, this wrapping is not sufficient to attain *FAC*. A component-allocated location could be passed to the context on the heap, so before passing control to the context the compiled code needs to *scan the whole heap* where a location can be passed and mask all found component-allocated locations. Dually, when receiving control the compiled code must scan the heap to unmask any masked location so it can use the location. The problem now is determining what parts of the heap to scan and how. Specifically, the compiled code needs to keep track of all the locations (and related capabilities) that are shared, i.e., (i) passed from the context to the component and (ii) passed from the component to the context. Both keeping track of these locations as well as scanning them on every cross-component control transfer is likely to be *very* expensive.

Finally, masked locations cannot be used directly by the context to be read and written. Thus, compiled code must provide a read and a write function that implement reading and writing to masked locations. The additional unmasking in these functions (as opposed to native reads and writes) adds to the inefficiency.

It should be clear as opposed to the *RSC* compiler $[\![\cdot]\!]^{\mathsf{L^U}}_{\mathrm{L^P}}$ (Sect. 3), the *FAC* compiler $[\![\boxed{\cdot}]\!]^{\mathsf{L^U}}_{\mathrm{L^P}}$ just sketched is likely to generate far more inefficient code.

Proof Difficulty. Proving that $[\![\boxed{\cdot}]\!]^{\mathsf{L^U}}_{\mathrm{L^P}}$ attains *FAC* can only be done by backtranslating *traces*, not contexts alone, since the newly-added target expressions cannot be directly backtranslated to valid source ones [7,9,59]. For this, we need a trace semantics that captures all information available to the context. This is often called a fully abstract trace semantics [38,55,56]. However, the trace semantics we defined for $\mathrm{L^P}$ is not fully abstract, as its actions record the entire heap in every action, including private parts of the heap. Hence, we cannot use this trace semantics for proving *FAC* and so we design a new one. Building a fully abstract trace semantics for $\mathrm{L^P}$ is challenging because we have to keep track of locations that have been shared with the context in the past. This substantially complicates both the definition of traces and the proofs that build on the definition.

Finally, the source context that the backtranslation constructs from a target trace must simulate the shared part of the heap at every context switch. Since locations in the target may be masked, the source context has to maintain a map from the source locations to the corresponding masked target ones, which complicates the backtranslation and the proof substantially.

To summarize, it should be clear that the proof of *FAC* for $[\![\boxed{\cdot}]\!]^{\mathsf{L^U}}_{\mathrm{L^P}}$ would be much harder than the proof of *RSC* for $[\![\cdot]\!]^{\mathsf{L^U}}_{\mathrm{L^P}}$, even though the source and target languages are the same and so is the broad proof technique (backtranslation).

6 Related Work

Recent work [8,33] presents new criteria for secure compilation that ensure preservation of subclasses of hyperproperties. Hyperproperties [25] are a formal representation of predicates on programs, i.e., they are predicates on sets of traces. Hyperproperties capture many security-relevant properties including not just conventional safety and liveness, which are predicates on traces, but also properties like non-interference, which is a predicate on pairs of traces. Modulo technical differences, our definition of *RSC* coincides with the criterion of "robust safety property preservation" in [8,33]. We show, through concrete instances, that this criterion can be easily realized by compilers, and develop two proof techniques for establishing it. We further show that the criterion leads to more efficient compiled code than does *FAC*. Additionally, the criteria in [8,33] assume that behaviours in the source and target are represented using the same alphabet. Hence, the definitions (somewhat unrealistically or ideally) do not require a translation of source properties to target properties. In contrast, we consider differences in the representation of behaviour in the source and in the target and this is accounted for in our monitor relation $\mathsf{M} \approx \mathrm{M}$. A slightly different account of this difference is presented by Patrignani and Garg [60] in the context of reactive black-box programs.

Abate *et al.* [7] define a variant of robustly-safe compilation called RSCC specifically tailored to the case where (source) components can perform undefined behaviour. RSCC does not consider attacks from arbitrary target contexts but from compiled components that can become compromised and behave in arbitrary ways. To demonstrate RSCC, Abate *et al.* [7] rely on two backends for their compiler: software fault isolation and tag-based monitors. On the other hand, we rely on capability machines and memory isolation (the latter in the companion report). RSCC also preserves (a form of) safety properties and can be achieved by relying on a trace-based backtranslation; it is unclear whether proofs can be simplified when the source is verified and concurrent, as in our second compiler.

ASLR [6,37], protected module architectures [9,42,53,59], tagged architectures [39], capability machines [69] and cryptographic primitives [4,5,22,26] have been used as targets for *FAC*. We believe all of these can also be used as targets of *RSC*-attaining compilers. In fact, some targets such as capability machines seem to be better suited to *RSC* than *FAC*, as we demonstrated.

Ahmed *et al.* prove full abstraction for several compilers between typed languages [10,11,50]. As compiler intermediate languages are often typed, and as these types often serve as the basis for complex static analyses, full abstraction seems like a reasonable goal for (fully typed) intermediate compilation steps. In the last few steps of compilation, where the target languages are unlikely to be typed, one could establish robust safety preservation and combine the two properties (vertically) to get an end-to-end security guarantee.

There are three other criteria for secure compilation that we would like to mention: securely compartmentalised compilation (SCC) [39], trace-preserving compilation (TPC) [60] and non-interference-preserving compilation (NIPC) [12, 15,16,27]. SCC is a re-statement of the "hard" part of full abstraction (the forward implication), but adapted to languages with undefined behaviour and a strict notion of components. Thus, SCC suffers from much of the same efficiency drawbacks as *FAC*. TPC is a stronger criterion than *FAC*, that most existing fully abstract compilers also attain. Again, compilers attaining TPC also suffer from the drawbacks of compilers attaining *FAC*.

NIPC preserves a single property: noninterference (NI). However, this line of work does not consider active target-level adversaries yet. Instead, the focus is on compiling whole programs. Since noninterference is not a safety property, it is difficult to compare NIPC to *RSC* directly. However, noninterference can also be approximated as a safety property [20]. So, in principle, *RSC* (with adequate massaging of observations) can be applied to stronger end-goals than NIPC.

Swamy *et al.* [67] embed an F* model of a gradually and robustly typed variant of JavaScript into an F* model of JavaScript. Gradual typing supports constructs similar to our endorsement construct in L^{τ}. Their type-directed compiler is proven to attain memory isolation as well as static and dynamic memory safety. However, they do not consider general safety properties, nor a specific, general criterion for compiler security.

Two of our target languages rely on capabilities for restricting access to sensitive locations from the context. Although capabilities are not mainstream in any processor, fully functional research prototypes such as Cheri exist [71]. Capability machines have previously been advocated as a target for efficient secure compilation [30] and preliminary work on compiling C-like languages to them exists, but the criterion applied is *FAC* [69].

7 Conclusion

This paper has examined robustly safe compilation (*RSC*), a soundness criterion for compilers with direct relevance to security. We have shown that the criterion is easily realizable and may lead to more efficient code than does fully abstract compilation wrt contextual equivalence. We have also presented two techniques for establishing that a compiler attains *RSC*. One is an adaptation of an existing technique, backtranslation, and the other is based on inductive invariants.

Acknowledgements. The authors would like to thank Dominique Devriese, Akram El-Korashy, Cătălin Hriţcu, Frank Piessens, David Swasey and the anonymous reviewers for useful feedback and discussions on an earlier draft.

This work was partially supported by the German Federal Ministry of Education and Research (BMBF) through funding for the CISPA-Stanford Center for Cybersecurity (FKZ: 13N1S0762).

References

1. Abadi, M.: Secrecy by typing in security protocols. In: Abadi, M., Ito, T. (eds.) TACS 1997. LNCS, vol. 1281, pp. 611–638. Springer, Heidelberg (1997). https://doi.org/10.1007/BFb0014571
2. Abadi, M.: Protection in programming-language translations. In: Vitek, J., Jensen, C.D. (eds.) Secure Internet Programming. LNCS, vol. 1603, pp. 19–34. Springer, Heidelberg (1999). https://doi.org/10.1007/3-540-48749-2_2
3. Abadi, M., Budiu, M., Erlingsson, Ú., Ligatti, J.: Control-flow integrity principles, implementations, and applications. ACM Trans. Inf. Syst. Secur. **13**(1), 4:1–4:40 (2009)
4. Abadi, M., Fournet, C., Gonthier, G.: Authentication primitives and their compilation. In: Proceedings of the 27th ACM SIGPLAN-SIGACT Symposium on Principles of Programming Languages, POPL 2000, pp. 302–315. ACM, New York (2000)

5. Abadi, M., Fournet, C., Gonthier, G.: Secure implementation of channel abstractions. Inf. Comput. **174**, 37–83 (2002)
6. Abadi, M., Plotkin, G.D.: On protection by layout randomization. ACM Trans. Inf. Syst. Secur. **15**, 8:1–8:29 (2012)
7. Abate, C., et al.: When good components go bad: formally secure compilation despite dynamic compromise. In: CCS 2018 (2018)
8. Abate, C., Blanco, R., Garg, D., Hriţcu, C., Patrignani, M., Thibault, J.: Journey beyond full abstraction: exploring robust property preservation for secure compilation. arXiv:1807.04603, July 2018
9. Agten, P., Strackx, R., Jacobs, B., Piessens, F.: Secure compilation to modern processors. In: 2012 IEEE 25th Computer Security Foundations Symposium, CSF 2012, pp. 171–185. IEEE (2012)
10. Ahmed, A., Blume, M.: Typed closure conversion preserves observational equivalence. In: Proceedings of the 13th ACM SIGPLAN International Conference on Functional Programming, ICFP 2008, pp. 157–168. ACM, New York (2008)
11. Ahmed, A., Blume, M.: An equivalence-preserving CPS translation via multi-language semantics. In: Proceedings of the 16th ACM SIGPLAN International Conference on Functional Programming, ICFP 2011, pp. 431–444. ACM, New York (2011)
12. Almeida, J.B., et al.: Jasmin: high-assurance and high-speed cryptography. In: ACM Conference on Computer and Communications Security, pp. 1807–1823. ACM (2017)
13. Alpern, B., Schneider, F.B.: Defining liveness. Inf. Process. Lett. **21**(4), 181–185 (1985)
14. Backes, M., Hritcu, C., Maffei, M.: Union, intersection and refinement types and reasoning about type disjointness for secure protocol implementations. J. Comput. Secur. **22**(2), 301–353 (2014)
15. Barthe, G., Grégoire, B., Laporte, V.: Secure compilation of side-channel countermeasures: the case of cryptographic "constant-time". In: CSF 2018 (2018)
16. Barthe, G., Rezk, T., Basu, A.: Security types preserving compilation. Comput. Lang. Syst. Struct. **33**, 35–59 (2007)
17. Bengtson, J., Bhargavan, K., Fournet, C., Gordon, A.D., Maffeis, S.: Refinement types for secure implementations. ACM Trans. Program. Lang. Syst. **33**(2), 8:1–8:45 (2011)
18. Benton, N., Hur, C.-K.: Realizability and compositional compiler correctness for a polymorphic language. Technical report, MSR (2010)
19. Berry, G., Boudol, G.: The chemical abstract machine. Theor. Comput. Sci. **96**(1), 217–248 (1992)
20. Boudol, G.: Secure information flow as a safety property. In: Degano, P., Guttman, J., Martinelli, F. (eds.) FAST 2008. LNCS, vol. 5491, pp. 20–34. Springer, Heidelberg (2009). https://doi.org/10.1007/978-3-642-01465-9_2
21. Bowman, W.J., Ahmed, A.: Noninterference for free. In: Proceedings of the 20th ACM SIGPLAN International Conference on Functional Programming, ICFP 2015. ACM, New York (2015)
22. Bugliesi, M., Giunti, M.: Secure implementations of typed channel abstractions. In: Proceedings of the 34th Annual ACM SIGPLAN-SIGACT Symposium on Principles of Programming Languages, POPL 2007, pp. 251–262. ACM, New York (2007)
23. Carter, N.P., Keckler, S.W., Dally, W.J.: Hardware support for fast capability-based addressing. SIGPLAN Not. **29**, 319–327 (1994)
24. Chong, S.: Expressive and enforceable information security policies. Ph.D. thesis, Cornell University, August 2008

25. Clarkson, M.R., Schneider, F.B.: Hyperproperties. J. Comput. Secur. **18**(6), 1157–1210 (2010)
26. Corin, R., Deniélou, P.-M., Fournet, C., Bhargavan, K., Leifer, J.: A secure compiler for session abstractions. J. Comput. Secur. **16**, 573–636 (2008)
27. Costanzo, D., Shao, Z., Gu, R.: End-to-end verification of information-flow security for C and assembly programs. In: PLDI, pp. 648–664. ACM (2016)
28. Devriese, D., Patrignani, M., Keuchel, S., Piessens, F.: Modular, fully-abstract compilation by approximate back-translation. Log. Methods Comput. Sci. **13**(4) (2017). https://lmcs.episciences.org/4011
29. Devriese, D., Patrignani, M., Piessens, F.: Secure compilation by approximate back-translation. In: POPL 2016 (2016)
30. El-Korashy, A.: A formal model for capability machines - an illustrative case study towards secure compilation to CHERI. Master's thesis, Universitat des Saarlandes (2016)
31. Fournet, C., Gordon, A.D., Maffeis, S.: A type discipline for authorization policies. ACM Trans. Program. Lang. Syst. **29**(5), 141–156 (2007)
32. Fournet, C., Swamy, N., Chen, J., Dagand, P.-E., Strub, P.-Y., Livshits, B.: Fully abstract compilation to JavaScript. In: Proceedings of the 40th Annual ACM SIGPLAN-SIGACT Symposium on Principles of Programming Languages, POPL 2013, pp. 371–384. ACM, New York (2013)
33. Garg, D., Hritcu, C., Patrignani, M., Stronati, M., Swasey, D.: Robust hyperproperty preservation for secure compilation (extended abstract). ArXiv e-prints, October 2017
34. Gordon, A.D., Jeffrey, A.: Authenticity by typing for security protocols. J. Comput. Secur. **11**(4), 451–519 (2003)
35. Gorla, D., Nestman, U.: Full abstraction for expressiveness: history, myths and facts. Math. Struct. Comput. Sci. **26**(4), 639–654 (2016)
36. Hur, C.-K., Dreyer, D.: A Kripke logical relation between ML and assembly. SIGPLAN Not. **46**, 133–146 (2011)
37. Jagadeesan, R., Pitcher, C., Rathke, J., Riely, J.: Local memory via layout randomization. In: Proceedings of the 2011 IEEE 24th Computer Security Foundations Symposium, CSF 2011, Washington, DC, USA, pp. 161–174. IEEE Computer Society (2011)
38. Jeffrey, A., Rathke, J.: Java JR: fully abstract trace semantics for a core Java language. In: Sagiv, M. (ed.) ESOP 2005. LNCS, vol. 3444, pp. 423–438. Springer, Heidelberg (2005). https://doi.org/10.1007/978-3-540-31987-0_29
39. Juglaret, Y., Hriţcu, C., de Amorim, A.A., Pierce, B.C.: Beyond good and evil: formalizing the security guarantees of compartmentalizing compilation. In: 29th IEEE Symposium on Computer Security Foundations (CSF). IEEE Computer Society Press, July 2016. To appear
40. Kang, J., Kim, Y., Hur, C.-K., Dreyer, D., Vafeiadis, V.: Lightweight verification of separate compilation. In: POPL 2016, pp. 178–190 (2016)
41. Kuznetsov, V., Szekeres, L., Payer, M., Candea, G., Sekar, R., Song, D.: Code-pointer integrity. In: Proceedings of the 11th USENIX Conference on Operating Systems Design and Implementation, OSDI 2014, Berkeley, CA, USA, pp. 147–163. USENIX Association (2014)
42. Larmuseau, A., Patrignani, M., Clarke, D.: A secure compiler for ML modules. In: Feng, X., Park, S. (eds.) APLAS 2015. LNCS, vol. 9458, pp. 29–48. Springer, Cham (2015). https://doi.org/10.1007/978-3-319-26529-2_3
43. Leroy, X.: Formal certification of a compiler back-end or: programming a compiler with a proof assistant. In: POPL, pp. 42–54 (2006)

44. Leroy, X.: A formally verified compiler back-end. J. Autom. Reason. **43**(4), 363–446 (2009)
45. Maffeis, S., Abadi, M., Fournet, C., Gordon, A.D.: Code-carrying authorization. In: Jajodia, S., Lopez, J. (eds.) ESORICS 2008. LNCS, vol. 5283, pp. 563–579. Springer, Heidelberg (2008). https://doi.org/10.1007/978-3-540-88313-5_36
46. McKeen, F., et al.: Innovative instructions and software model for isolated execution. In: HASP 2013, pp. 10:1–10:1. ACM (2013)
47. Morris Jr., J.H.: Protection in programming languages. Commun. ACM **16**, 15–21 (1973)
48. Neis, G., Dreyer, D., Rossberg, A.: Non-parametric parametricity. SIGPLAN Not. **44**(9), 135–148 (2009)
49. Neis, G., Hur, C.-K., Kaiser, J.-O., McLaughlin, C., Dreyer, D., Vafeiadis, V.: Pilsner: a compositionally verified compiler for a higher-order imperative language. In: Proceedings of the 20th ACM SIGPLAN International Conference on Functional Programming, ICFP 2015, pp. 166–178. ACM (2015)
50. New, M.S., Bowman, W.J., Ahmed, A.: Fully abstract compilation via universal embedding. In: Proceedings of the 21st ACM SIGPLAN International Conference on Functional Programming, ICFP 2016, pp. 103–116. ACM, New York (2016)
51. Nielson, F., Nielson, H.R., Hankin, C.: Principles of Program Analysis. Springer, New York (1999). https://doi.org/10.1007/978-3-662-03811-6
52. Parrow, J.: General conditions for full abstraction. Math. Struct. Comput. Sci. **26**(4), 655–657 (2014)
53. Patrignani, M., Agten, P., Strackx, R., Jacobs, B., Clarke, D., Piessens, F.: Secure compilation to protected module architectures. ACM Trans. Program. Lang. Syst. **37**, 6:1–6:50 (2015)
54. Patrignani, M., Ahmed, A., Clarke, D.: Formal approaches to secure compilation a survey of fully abstract compilation and related work. ACM Comput. Surv. **51**(6), 125:1–125:36 (2019)
55. Patrignani, M., Clarke, D.: Fully abstract trace semantics of low-level isolation mechanisms. In: Proceedings of the 29th Annual ACM Symposium on Applied Computing, SAC 2014, pp. 1562–1569. ACM (2014)
56. Patrignani, M., Clarke, D.: Fully abstract trace semantics for protected module architectures. Comput. Lang. Syst. Struct. **42**(0), 22–45 (2015)
57. Patrignani, M., Clarke, D., Piessens, F.: Secure compilation of object-oriented components to protected module architectures. In: Shan, C. (ed.) APLAS 2013. LNCS, vol. 8301, pp. 176–191. Springer, Cham (2013). https://doi.org/10.1007/978-3-319-03542-0_13
58. Patrignani, M., Clarke, D., Sangiorgi, D.: Ownership types for the join calculus. In: Bruni, R., Dingel, J. (eds.) FMOODS/FORTE -2011. LNCS, vol. 6722, pp. 289–303. Springer, Heidelberg (2011). https://doi.org/10.1007/978-3-642-21461-5_19
59. Patrignani, M., Devriese, D., Piessens, F.: On modular and fully abstract compilation. In: Proceedings of the 29th IEEE Computer Security Foundations Symposium, CSF 2016 (2016)
60. Patrignani, M., Garg, D.: Secure compilation and hyperproperties preservation. In: Proceedings of the 30th IEEE Computer Security Foundations Symposium, CSF 2017, Santa Barbara, USA (2017)
61. Patrignani, M., Garg, D.: Robustly safe compilation or, efficient, provably secure compilation. CoRR, abs/1804.00489 (2018)
62. Sabelfeld, A., Sands, D.: Declassification: dimensions and principles. J. Comput. Secur. **17**(5), 517–548 (2009)

63. Schneider, F.B.: Enforceable security policies. ACM Trans. Inf. Syst. Secur. **3**(1), 30–50 (2000)
64. Stark, I.: Names and higher-order functions. Ph.D. thesis, University of Cambridge, December 1994. Also available as Technical Report 363, University of Cambridge Computer Laboratory
65. Stewart, G., Beringer, L., Cuellar, S., Appel, A.W.: Compositional compcert. In: Proceedings of the 42nd Annual ACM SIGPLAN-SIGACT Symposium on Principles of Programming Languages, POPL 2015, pp. 275–287. ACM, New York (2015)
66. Sumii, E., Pierce, B.C.: A bisimulation for dynamic sealing. In: Principles of Programming Languages, pp. 161–172 (2004)
67. Swamy, N., Fournet, C., Rastogi, A., Bhargavan, K., Chen, J., Strub, P.-Y., Bierman, G.: Gradual typing embedded securely in Javascript. SIGPLAN Not. **49**(1), 425–437 (2014)
68. Swasey, D., Garg, D., Dreyer, D.: Robust and compositional verification of object capability patterns. In: Proceedings of the 2017 ACM SIGPLAN International Conference on Object-Oriented Programming, Systems, Languages, and Applications, OOPSLA 2017, 22–27 October 2017 (2017)
69. Tsampas, S., El-Korashy, A., Patrignani, M., Devriese, D., Garg, D., Piessens, F.: Towards automatic compartmentalization of C programs on capability machines. In: 2017 Workshop on Foundations of Computer Security, FCS 2017, 21 August 2017 (2017)
70. Volpano, D., Irvine, C., Smith, G.: A sound type system for secure flow analysis. J. Comput. Secur. **4**, 167–187 (1996)
71. Woodruff, J., et al.: The CHERI capability model: revisiting RISC in an age of risk. In: Proceeding of the 41st Annual International Symposium on Computer Architecuture, ISCA 2014, Piscataway, NJ, USA, pp. 457–468. IEEE Press (2014)
72. Zdancewic, S.A.: Programming languages for information security. Ph.D. thesis, Cornell University (2002)

Compiling Sandboxes: Formally Verified Software Fault Isolation

Frédéric Besson[1(✉)], Sandrine Blazy[1], Alexandre Dang[1], Thomas Jensen[1], and Pierre Wilke[2]

[1] Inria, Univ Rennes, CNRS, IRISA, Rennes, France
frederic.besson@inria.fr
[2] CentraleSupélec, Inria, Univ Rennes, CNRS, IRISA, Rennes, France

Abstract. Software Fault Isolation (SFI) is a security-enhancing program transformation for instrumenting an untrusted binary module so that it runs inside a dedicated isolated address space, called a sandbox. To ensure that the untrusted module cannot escape its sandbox, existing approaches such as Google's Native Client rely on a binary verifier to check that all memory accesses are within the sandbox. Instead of relying on *a posteriori* verification, we design, implement and prove correct a program instrumentation phase as part of the formally verified compiler CompCert that enforces a sandboxing security property *a priori*. This eliminates the need for a binary verifier and, instead, leverages the soundness proof of the compiler to prove the security of the sandboxing transformation. The technical contributions are a novel sandboxing transformation that has a well-defined C semantics and which supports arbitrary function pointers, and a formally verified C compiler that implements SFI. Experiments show that our formally verified technique is a competitive way of implementing SFI.

1 Introduction

Isolating programs with various levels of trustworthiness is a fundamental security concern, be it on a cloud computing platform running untrusted code provided by customers, or in a web browser running untrusted code coming from different origins. In these contexts, it is of the utmost importance to provide adequate isolation mechanisms so that a faulty or malicious computation cannot compromise the host or neighbouring computations.

There exists a number of mechanisms for enforcing isolation that intervene at various levels, from the hardware up to the operating system. Hypervisors [10], virtual machines [2] but also system processes [17] can ensure strong isolation properties, at the expense of costly context switches and limited flexibility in the interaction between components. Language-based techniques such as strong typing offer alternative techniques for ensuring memory safety, upon which access control policies and isolation can be implemented. This approach is implemented e.g. by the Java language for which it provides isolation guarantees, as proved by Leroy and Rouaix [21]. The isolation is fined-grained and very flexible but

L. Caires (Ed.): ESOP 2019, LNCS 11423, pp. 499–524, 2019.
https://doi.org/10.1007/978-3-030-17184-1_18

the security mechanisms, e.g. stack inspection, may be hard to reason about [7]. In the web browser realm, JavaScript is dynamically typed and also ensures memory safety upon which access control can be implemented [29].

1.1 Software Fault Isolation

Software Fault Isolation (SFI) is an alternative for unsafe languages, e.g. C, where memory safety is not granted but needs to be enforced at runtime by program instrumentation. Pioneered by Wahbe *et al.* [35] and popularised by Google's Native Client [30,37,38], SFI is a program transformation which confines a software component to a memory sandbox. This is done by pre-fixing every memory access with a carefully designed code sequence which efficiently ensures that the memory access occurs within the sandbox. In practice, the sandbox is aligned and the sandbox addresses are thus of the form $0xYZ$ where Y is a fixed bit-pattern and Z is an arbitrary bit-pattern *i.e.*, $Z \in [0x0 \ldots 0, 0xF \ldots F]$. Hence, enforcing that memory accesses are within the sandbox range of addresses can be efficiently implemented by a *masking* operation which exploits the binary representation of pointers: it retains the lowest bits Z and sets the highest bits to the bit-pattern Y.

Traditionally, the SFI transformation is performed at the binary level and is followed by an *a posteriori* verification by a trusted SFI verifier [23,31,35]. Because the verifier can assume that the code has undergone the SFI transformation, it can be kept simple (almost syntactic), thereby reducing both verification time and the Trusted Computing Base (TCB). This approach to SFI can be viewed as a simple instance of Proof Carrying Code [25] where the compiler is untrusted and the binary verifier is either trusted or verified.

Traditional SFI is well suited for executing binary code from an untrusted origin that must, for an adequate user experience, start running as soon as possible. Google's Native Client [30,37] is a state-of-the-art SFI implementation which has been deployed in the Chrome web browser for isolating binary code in untrusted pages. ARMor [39] features the first fully verified SFI implementation where the TCB is reduced to the formal ARM semantics in the HOL proof-assistant [9]. RockSalt [24] is a formally verified implementation of an SFI verifier for the x86 architecture, demonstrating that an efficient binary verifier can be obtained from a machine-checked specification.

1.2 Software Fault Isolation Through Compilation

A downside of the traditional SFI approach is that it hinders most compiler optimisations because the optimised code no longer respects the simple properties that the SFI verifier is capable of checking. For example, the SFI verifier expects that every memory access is immediately preceded by a specific syntactic code pattern that implements the sandboxing operation. A semantically equivalent but syntactically different code sequence would be rejected. An alternative to the *a posteriori* binary verifier approach is Portable Software Fault Isolation (PSFI), proposed by Kroll *et al.* [16]. In this methodology, there is no verifier to trust. Instead isolation is obtained by compilation with a machine-checked compiler, such as CompCert [18]. Portability comes from the fact that PSFI can reuse existing compiler back-ends and therefore target all the architectures supported by the compiler without additional effort.

PSFI is applicable in scenarios where the source code is available or the binary code is provided by a trusted third-party that controls the build process. For example, the original motivation for Proof Carrying Code [25] was to provide safe kernel extensions [26] as binary code to replace scripts written in an interpreted language. This falls within the scope of PSFI. Another PSFI scenario is when the binary code is produced in a controlled environment and/or by a trusted party. In this case, the primary goal is not to protect against an attacker trying to insert malicious code but to prevent honest parties from exposing a host platform to exploitable bugs. This is the case *e.g.* in the avionics industry, where software from different third-parties is integrated on the same host that needs to ensure strong isolation properties between tasks whose levels of criticality differ. In those cases, PSFI can deliver both security and a performance advantage. In Sect. 8, we provide experimental evidence that PSFI is competitive and sometimes outperforms SFI in terms of efficiency of the binary code.

1.3 Challenges in Formally Verified SFI

PSFI inserts the masking operations during compilation and does away with the *a posteriori* SFI verifier. The challenge is then to ensure that the security, enforced at an intermediate representation of the code, still holds for the running code. Indeed, compiler optimisation often breaks such security [33]. The insight of Kroll *et al.* is that a safety theorem of the compiled code (i.e., that its behaviour is well-defined) can be exploited to obtain a security theorem for that same compiled code, guaranteeing that it makes no memory accesses outside its sandbox. We explain this in more detail in Sect. 2.2.

One challenge we face with this approach is that it is far from evident that the sandboxing operations and hence the transformed program have well-defined behaviour. An unsafe language such as C admits undefined behaviours (e.g. bitwise operations on pointers), which means that it is possible for the observational behaviour of a program to differ depending on the level of optimisation. This is not a compiler bug: compilers only guarantee semantics preservation *if* the code to compile has a well-defined semantics [36]. Therefore, our SFI transformation must turn any program into a program with a well-defined semantics.

The seminal paper of Kroll *et al.* emphasises that the absence of undefined behaviour is a prerequisite but they do not provide a transformation that enforces this property. More precisely, their transformation may produce a program with undefined behaviours (*e.g.* because the input program had undefined behaviours). This fact was one of the motivation for the present work, and explains the need for a new PSFI technique. One difficulty is to remove undefined behaviours due to restrictions on pointer arithmetic. For example, bitwise operators on pointers have undefined C semantics, but traditional masking operations of SFI rely heavily on these operators. Another difficulty is to deal with indirect function calls and ensure that, as prescribed by the C standard, they are resolved to valid function pointers. To tackle these problems, we propose an original sandboxing transformation which unlike previous proposals is compliant with the C standard [13] and therefore has well-defined behaviour.

1.4 Contributions

We have developed and proved correct CompCertSfi, the first full-fledged, fully verified implementation of SFI inside a C compiler. The SFI transformation is performed early in the compilation chain, thereby permitting the generated code to benefit from existing optimisations that are performed by the back-end. The technical contributions behind CompCertSfi can be summarised as follows.

- An original design and implementation of the SFI transformation based on well-defined pointer arithmetic and which supports function pointers. This novel design of the SFI transformation is necessary for the safety proof.
- A machine-checked proof of the **security** and **safety** of the SFI transformation. Our formal development is available online [1].
- A small, lightweight runtime system for managing the sandbox, built using a standard program loader and configured by compiler-generated information.
- Experimental evidence demonstrating that the portable SFI approach is competitive and sometimes even outperforms traditional SFI, in particular state-of-the-art implementations of (P)Native Client.

The rest of the paper is organised as follows. In Sect. 2, we present background information about the CompCert compiler (Sect. 2.1) and the PSFI approach (Sect. 2.2). Section 3 provides an overview of the layout of the sandbox and the masking operations implementing our SFI. In Sect. 4 we explain how to overcome the problem with undefined pointer arithmetic and define masking operations with a well-defined C semantics. Section 5 describes how control-flow integrity in the presence of function pointers can be achieved by a sligthly more flexible SFI policy which allows reads in well-defined areas outside the sandbox. Section 6 specifies the SFI policy in more detail, and describes the formal Coq proofs of safety and security. Section 7 presents the design of our runtime library and how it exploits compiler support. Experimental results are detailed in Sect. 8. Section 9 presents related work and Sect. 10 concludes.

2 Background

This section presents background information about the CompCert compiler [18] and the Portable Software Fault Isolation proposed by Kroll *et al.* [16].

2.1 CompCert

The CompCert compiler [18] is a machine-checked compiler programmed and proved correct using the Coq proof-assistant [22]. It compiles C programs down

$$
\begin{array}{rl}
\textit{constant} \ni c ::= & i32 \mid i64 \mid f32 \mid f64 \mid \&gl \mid \&stk \\
\textit{chunk} \ni \kappa ::= & is_8 \mid iu_8 \mid is_{16} \mid iu_{16} \mid i_{32} \mid i_{64} \mid f_{32} \mid f_{64} \\
\textit{expr} \ni e ::= & x \mid c \mid \rhd e \mid e_1 \Box e_2 \mid [e]_\kappa \\
\textit{stmt} \ni s ::= & \textbf{skip} \mid x := e \mid [e_1]_\kappa := e_2 \mid \textbf{return}\ e \mid x := e(e_1 \ldots, e_n)_\sigma \\
& \mid \textbf{if}\ e\ \textbf{then}\ s_1\ \textbf{else}\ s_2 \mid s_1; s_2 \mid \textbf{loop}\ s \mid \{s\} \mid \textbf{exit}\ n \mid \textbf{goto}\ lb
\end{array}
$$

Fig. 1. CMINOR syntax

to assembly code through a succession of compiler passes which are shown to be semantics preserving. COMPCERT features an architecture independent front-end. The back-end supports four main architectures: x86, ARM, PowerPC and RiscV. To target all the back-ends without additional effort, our secure transformation is performed in the compiler front-end, at the level of the CMINOR language that is the last architecture-independent language of the COMPCERT compiler chain. Our transformation can obviously be applied on C programs by first compiling them into CMINOR, and then applying the transformation itself.

The CMINOR language is a minimal imperative language with explicit stack allocation of certain local variables [19]. Its syntax is given in Fig. 1. Constants range over 32-bit and 64-bit integers but also IEEE floating-point numbers. It is possible to get the address of a global variable *gl* or the address of the stack allocated local variables (i.e., *stk* denotes the address of the current stack frame). In COMPCERT parlance, a memory chunk κ specifies how many bytes need to be read (resp. written) from (resp. to) memory and whether the result should be interpreted as a signed or unsigned quantity. For instance, the memory chunk is_{16} denotes a 16-bit signed integer and f_{64} denotes a 64-bit floating-point number. In CMINOR, memory accesses, written $[e]_\kappa$, are annotated with the relevant memory chunk κ. Expressions are built from pseudo-registers, constants, unary ($\rhd$) and binary ($\Box$) operators. COMPCERT features the relevant unary and binary operators needed to encode the semantics of C. Expressions are side-effect free but may contain memory reads.

Instructions are fairly standard. Similarly to a memory read, a memory store $[e_1]_\kappa = e_2$ is annotated by a memory chunk κ. In CMINOR, a function call such as $e(e_1 \ldots, e_n)_\sigma$ represents an indirect function call through a function pointer denoted by the expression e, σ is the signature of the function and $e_1 \ldots, e_n$ are the arguments. A direct call is a special case where the expression e is a constant (function) pointer. CMINOR is a structured language and features a conditional, a block construct $\{s\}$ and an infinite loop **loop** s. Exiting the nth enclosing loop or block can be done using an **exit** n instruction. CMINOR is structured but **goto**s towards a symbolic label *lb* are also possible. Returning from a function is done by a return instruction. CMINOR is equipped with a small-step operational semantics. The intra-procedural and inter-procedural control flows are modelled using an explicit continuation which therefore contains a call stack.

CompCert Soundness Theorem. Each compiler pass is proved to be semantics preserving using a simulation argument. Theorem 1 states semantics preservation.

Theorem 1 (Semantics Preservation). *If the compilation of program p succeeds and generates a target program tp, then for any behaviour beh of program tp there exists a behaviour of p, beh′, such that beh* improves *beh′.*

In this statement, a behaviour is a trace of observable events that are typically generated when performing external function calls. CompCert classifies behaviours depending on whether the program terminates normally, diverges or goes wrong. A *goes wrong* behaviour corresponds to a situation where the program semantics gets stuck (i.e., has an undefined behaviour). In this situation, the compiler has the liberty to generate a program with an *improved* behaviour i.e., the semantics of the transformed program may be more defined (i.e., it may not get stuck at all or may get stuck later on).

The consequence is that Theorem 1 is not sufficient to preserve a safety property because the target program *tp* may have behaviours that are not accounted for in the program *p* and could therefore violate the property. Corollary 1 states that in the absence of going-wrong behaviour, the behaviours of the target program are a subset of the behaviours of the source program.

Corollary 1 (Safety preservation). *Let p be a program and tp be a target program. Consider that none of the behaviours of p is a going-wrong behaviour. If the compilation of p succeeds and generates a target program tp, then any behaviour of program tp is a behaviour of p.*

As a consequence, any (safety) property of the behaviours of *p* is preserved by the target program *tp*. In Sect. 2.2, we show how the PSFI approach leverages Corollary 1 to transfer an isolation property obtained at the Cminor level to the assembly code.

Going-wrong behaviours in CompCert. As safety is an essential property of our PSFI transformation, we give below a detailed account of the going-wrong behaviours of the CompCert languages with a focus on Cminor.

Undefined evaluation of expressions. CompCert's runtime values are dynamically typed and defined below:

$$values \ni v ::= \mathbf{undef} \mid \mathbf{int}(i_{32}) \mid \mathbf{long}(i_{64}) \mid \mathbf{single}(f_{32}) \mid \mathbf{float}(f_{64}) \mid \mathbf{ptr}(b, o)$$

Values are built from numeric values (32-bit and 64-bit integers and floating point numbers), the **undef** value representing an indeterminate value, and pointer values made of a pair (b, o) where b is a memory block identifier and o is an offset which, depending on the architecture, is either a 32-bit or a 64-bit integer.

For Cminor, like all languages of CompCert, the unary ($\triangleright$) and binary ($\Box$) operators are not total. They may directly produce going-wrong behaviours *e.g.* in case of division by $\mathbf{int}(0)$. They may also return **undef** if (i) the arguments are not in the right range *e.g.* the left-shift $\mathbf{int}(i) << \mathbf{int}(32)$; or (ii) the arguments are not well-typed *e.g.* $\mathbf{int}(i) +_{int} \mathbf{float}(f)$. Pointer arithmetic is strictly conforming to the C standard [13] and any pointer operation that is implementation-defined according to the standard returns **undef**.

$$
\begin{array}{lll}
\mathbf{ptr}(b,o) \pm \mathbf{long}(l) & = \mathbf{ptr}(b, o \pm l) & \\
\mathbf{ptr}(b,o) - \mathbf{ptr}(b,o') & = \mathbf{long}(o - o') & \\
\mathbf{ptr}(b,o)\,\texttt{!=}\mathbf{long}(0) & = \mathbf{tt} & \text{if } W(b,o) \\
\mathbf{ptr}(b,o) == \mathbf{long}(0) & = \mathbf{ff} & \text{if } W(b,o) \\
\mathbf{ptr}(b,o) \star \mathbf{ptr}(b,o') & = o \star o' & \text{if } W(b,o) \wedge W(b,o') \\
\mathbf{ptr}(b,o) == \mathbf{ptr}(b',o') & = \mathbf{ff} & \text{if } b \neq b' \wedge V(b,o) \wedge V(b',o') \\
\mathbf{ptr}(b,o)\,\texttt{!=}\mathbf{ptr}(b',o') & = \mathbf{tt} & \text{if } b \neq b' \wedge V(b,o) \wedge V(b',o') \\
\multicolumn{3}{c}{\text{where } \star \in \{<, \leq, ==, \geq, >, \texttt{!=}\}}
\end{array}
$$

Fig. 2. Pointer arithmetic in CompCert

The precise semantics of pointer operations is given in Fig. 2. For simplicity, we provide the semantics for a 64-bit architecture. Pointer operations are often only defined provided that the pointers are valid, written V, or weakly valid, written W. This validity condition requires that the offset o of a pointer $\mathbf{ptr}(b, o)$ is strictly within the bounds of the block b. The weakly valid condition refers to a pointer whose offset is either valid or one-past-the-end of the block b. Any pointer arithmetic operation that is not listed in Fig. 2 returns **undef**. This is in particular the case for bitwise operations which are typically used for the masking operation needed to implement SFI.

The indeterminate value **undef** is not *per se* a going-wrong behaviour. Yet, branching over a test evaluating to **undef**, performing a memory access over an **undef** address and returning **undef** from the `main` function are going-wrong behaviours.

Memory accesses are ruled by a unified memory model [20] that is used throughout the whole compiler. The memory is made of a collection of separated blocks. For a given block, each offset o below the block size is given a permission $p \in \{\mathbf{r}, \mathbf{w}, \dots\}$ and contains a memory value

$$mval \ni mv ::= \mathbf{undef} \mid \mathbf{byte}(b) \mid [\mathbf{ptr}(b,o)]_n$$

where b is a concrete byte value and $[\mathbf{ptr}(b,o)]_n$ represents the nth byte of the pointer $\mathbf{ptr}(b,o)$ for $n \in \{1 \dots 8\}$. A memory write $storev(\kappa, m, a, v)$ is only defined if the address a is a pointer $\mathbf{ptr}(b, o)$ to an existing block b such that the memory locations $(b, o), \dots, (b, o+ \mid \kappa \mid -1)$ have the permission $\mathbf{w}$ and the offset o satisfies the alignment constraint of κ. A memory read $loadv(\kappa, m, a)$ is only defined under similar conditions with the additional restriction that not reading all the consecutive fragments of a pointer returns **undef**.

Control-flow transfers may go-wrong if the target of the control-flow transfer is not well-defined. Hence, a **goto** *lb* instruction goes wrong if, in the current function, there is no statement labelled by *lb*; and an **exit** n instruction goes wrong if there are less than n enclosing blocks around the statement containing the exit instruction. A conditional **if** e **then** s_1 **else** s_2 goes wrong if the expression e does not evaluate to $\mathbf{int}(i)$ for some i. Also, the execution goes wrong if the last statement of a function is not a **return** instruction. Last but not least, a function call $x := e(e_1 \ldots, e_n)_\sigma$ goes wrong if the expression e does not evaluate to a pointer $\mathbf{ptr}(b, 0)$ where b is a function pointer with signature σ.

We show in Sect. 4 how our transformation ensures that pointer arithmetic and memory accesses are always well-defined. Section 5 shows how we make sure indirect calls are always correctly resolved. Section 6 shows that, together with other statically checkable verifications, our PSFI transformation rules out all possible going-wrong behaviours.

2.2 Portable Software Fault Isolation

Kroll, Stewart and Appel have pioneered the concept of Portable Software Fault Isolation (PSFI) [16] whereby SFI is enforced by a pass of the compiler front-end that is architecture independent. The main expected advantage is that isolation is implemented, once and for all, for any target architecture. Moreover, the generated code is optimised by the back-end passes of the compiler. Compared to traditional SFI, there is no architecture-specific binary verifier but instead the compiler enters the TCB. The key insight of Kroll *et al.* is to leverage a formally verified compiler, namely CompCert, to transfer a security proof of isolation obtained at the Cminor level through the compiler back-end, with minimal proof effort. In the following, we recall the only basic properties that a Cminor SFI transformation needs to satisfy so that isolation holds at assembly level.

In CompCert's terms, the sandbox is identified by a dedicated memory block *sb*. A Cminor program is secure (Property 1) under the condition that all its memory accesses are performed within the sandbox.

Property 1 (Program security). A Cminor program p is secure if all its memory accesses are within the sandbox block *sb*.

After compilation, the assembly code is secure if its observable behaviours are the same as the observable behaviours of the Cminor program. In order to apply CompCert's semantics preservation theorem (more precisely Corollary 1), it remains to ensure that the Cminor program has a well-defined semantics (Property 2).

Property 2 (Program safety). A Cminor program p is safe if all its behaviours are well-defined, i.e., not wrong.

Kroll *et al.* state Property 1 by means of an instrumented Cminor semantics which gets stuck in case of memory accesses outside the sandbox. They prove formally that the additional semantic safeguards are never triggered for a transformed program.

Kroll *et al.* also sketch some necessary steps to prove the Property 2 of safety but do not propose a formal proof. This leaves open a number of challenging issues such as whether it is feasible to define a masking operation that has a defined Cminor semantics and how to deal with indirect function calls through function pointers, More generally, the work leaves open whether a formal proof of Property 2 on safety is possible given the restrictions of CompCert's semantics (notably pointer arithmetic) and without relying on axioms asserting properties of an external masking primitive. One of the central contributions of this work is to provide a positive answer to this question and propose solutions to these issues where neither the sandboxing of memory accesses nor the sandboxing of function pointers is part of a TCB. The transformation that circumvents the limitations imposed by pointer arithmetic is original and, we surmise, is a necessary component to transfer security down to assembly. For a precise comparison with Kroll *et al.* see Sect. 9).

3 A Thread-Aware Sandbox

The memory address space of a C program is partitioned into a runtime stack of frames, a heap and a dedicated space for global variables. The address space of a sandboxed program is re-organised to fit into a single global variable, *sb*, where the global variables, the heap and the stack frames are relocated. Figure 3a depicts the memory layout of the program after our SFI transformation. Each global variable is relocated and allocated in the sandbox at a given offset, and each global memory access of the program is translated into a memory access in the sandbox. For managing the heap it suffices to use a sandbox-aware `malloc` implementation that allocates memory inside the sandbox.

To prevent buffer overflows, a standard approach consists in introducing a so-called *shadow stack* that is used to store the function stack frames. Our implementation supports multi-threaded applications and therefore there are as many shadow stacks as there are threads. Upon thread creation, we allocate a novel shadow stack in the sandbox. The shadow-stack pointer is passed as an additional argument to each function call. This is efficient when arguments are passed by register, with the only drawback of reserving an additional register. Frames are allocated by incrementing the shadow-stack pointer at function entry. All accesses to the original stack are then translated into accesses to the sandbox shadow stack. The following Example 1 and the code snippet in Fig. 3 illustrate the essence of the transformation.

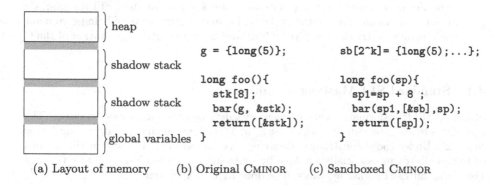

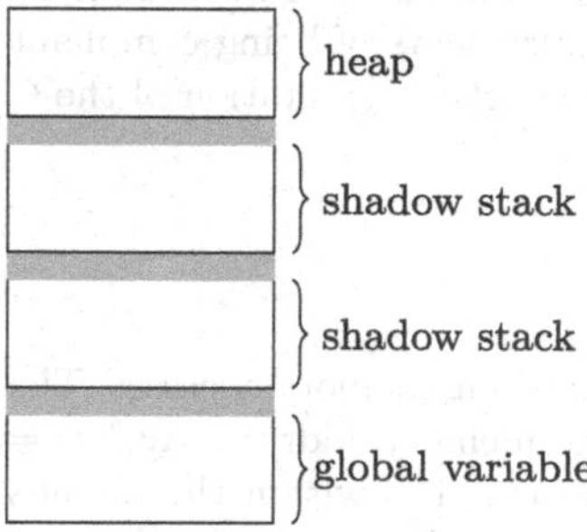

(a) Layout of memory

```
g = {long(5)};

long foo(){
  stk[8];
  bar(g, &stk);
  return([&stk]);
}
```

(b) Original CMINOR

```
sb[2^k]= {long(5);...};

long foo(sp){
  sp1=sp + 8 ;
  bar(sp1,[&sb],sp);
  return([sp]);
}
```

(c) Sandboxed CMINOR

Fig. 3. Sandbox transformation

Example 1. The CMINOR program of Fig. 3b declares a global variable `g` initialised to the 64-bit integer 5. The function `foo` allocates a stack frame of 8 bytes that will be used to store a 64-bit local variable. By convention, the current stack frame is called `stk`. The function `foo` calls the function `bar` with as arguments the value of `g` and the address of the local variable `stk`; and returns the value, presumably updated by `bar`, of the local variable.

Syntactically, the program of Fig. 3c only performs memory accesses on the global sandbox `sb` variable. The size of `sb` variable is 2^k for some predefined k. At thread creation, a shadow stack is allocated by our sandbox-aware `malloc` in the sandbox after the statically allocated global variables. For our program, the unique global variable `g` is stored at offset 0 and spans over 8 bytes. Therefore, the initial value of the shadow-stack pointer `sp` is 8. After the transformation, the function `foo` reserves the space for the local variable `stk` by incrementing the pseudo-register `sp`. The function `bar` is called with the incremented shadow-stack pointer `sp1`, the value stored at offset 0 in the sandbox (i.e., the value of the global variable `g`) and the address of the local variable `stk` which is given by the value of the stack pointer `sp`. At function exit, the value of the local variable `stk` is returned by dereferencing the shadow-stack pointer `sp`.

Our SFI transformation enforces the isolation security policy stipulating that all memory accesses are performed within the sandbox *sb*—at the CMINOR level. However, this holds because the semantics gets stuck (i.e., the semantics *goes wrong*) whenever the program performs an access outside the bounds of the sandbox. As explained earlier, the compiler is free to translate this into an insecure program that would escape the sandbox at runtime. To get a formal security guarantee, it is necessary to transform further the CMINOR program to rule out any behaviour that *goes wrong* i.e., ensure Property 2. Given the numerous undefined behaviours of the C language, ruling out any *going-wrong* behaviour may seem a daunting task. In general, this requires to ensure both memory safety and control-flow integrity. The following two sections describe how we can exploit the SFI transformation and the knowledge that all memory accesses are inside the sandbox to ensure both memory safety and control-flow integrity.

4 Memory-Safe Masking

For SFI, memory safety is obtained by making sure that every memory access is performed inside the sandbox. Starting from an analysis of the standard SFI solution, we present our own design which satisfies the additional requirements of being compliant with the semantic restrictions of COMPCERT and with a strict interpretation of the C standard.

4.1 Standard SFI Masking of Addresses

Standard SFI transformations ensure memory safety by masking memory accesses. The gist of it is to allocate a sandbox *sb* of size 2^k at a 2^k aligned memory address, say $\&sb = tag \times 2^k$. Under those constraints, enforcing that an address A is within the bounds of the sandbox can essentially be done by replacing the high-address bits by those of *tag*. Using bitwise operations, this can be done by the expression $(A\&(2^k-1))|tag \times 2^k$, where & is the bitwise *and* and | is the bitwise *or*. More visually, this can be written $(A\&\underbrace{1\cdots1}_{k})|tag\underbrace{0\cdots0}_{k}$.

At binary level, this masking transformation is defined and the cost is modest: two bitwise operations. However, this masking operation has no well-defined C semantics. This is also the case for the semantics of CompCert and in particular for the Cminor language. The reason is twofold: bitwise operations over pointer values return **undef** and concrete addresses (e.g. $tag \times 2^k$) are not pointers for CompCert where they are represented by a block and an offset (see Fig. 2).

4.2 Specialised Masking for 32-Bit Sandboxes

For 32-bit sandboxes, there exists a variant of the sandboxing primitive which has the advantages (1) that the sandbox address does not need to be aligned; (2) that the cost of masking may be reduced to a single instruction. In its simplest form, the masking primitive is defined by

$$\&sb + (A - \&sb)_{64 \to 32 \to 64}$$

where $\&sb$ is the symbolic address of the sandbox. The subtraction of $\&sb$ extracts the offset of the pointer and the double (unsigned) cast $64 \to 32 \to 64$ has the effect of truncating the offset to a 32-bit quantity that is therefore within the bounds of a 32-bit sandbox. At first sight, this masking is less efficient than the standard masking but it is efficient for typical address computations which require both displacement and scaling (e.g. $A = t + k + k' * i_{32 \to 64}$ where t is a 64-bit address, k and k' are constants and i is a 32-bit integer). Assuming that each cast or arithmetic operation is mapped to a single instruction[1], the masked address A can be computed using 8 instructions: 4 instructions for computing the address A and 4 more for the sandboxing primitive. Using simple properties of modular arithmetic, it is possible to distribute the $64 \to 32$ cast over addition and multiplication to obtain the following equivalent formulation of the sandboxed address:

$$\&sb + A'_{32 \to 64} \quad with \quad A' = t_{64 \to 32} + c_1 + c_2 * i$$

where c_1 and c_2 are compile-time constants: $c_1 = (k - \&sb)_{64 \to 32}$ and $c_2 = k'_{64 \to 32}$. Using this formulation, the address A' still requires 4 instructions but the cost of the sandboxing is reduced to 2 instructions making it on par with the standard sandboxing. On x86, 32-bit registers are just zero-extended 64-bit registers. Therefore, the cast $A'_{32 \to 64}$ is actually redundant and the overhead induced by the sandboxing is reduced to a single instruction. Our experiments (see Sect. 8.2) validate the practical advantage of this encoding.

Still, as for the standard sandboxing, this sanboxing primitive has no semantics in CompCert due to the limitations of pointer arithmetic. As a consequence, the solution of Kroll *et al.* [16] does not give actual code for the masking primitive, but rather axiomatise its behaviour as an external function. This prevents optimisations such as common subexpression elimination or function inlining from happening and induces the cost of a function call for each memory access.

4.3 Towards Well-Defined Pointer Arithmetic

To illustrate the limitations of pointer arithmetic, we examine the semantic behaviour of the standard sandboxing primitive (the specialised sandboxing primitive has similar

[1] Some architecture have rich addressing modes allowing for more compact encodings.

issues). The standard sandboxing primitive can be written $(A\&(2^k-1))\,|\,\&sb$ where $\&sb$ is the address of the sandbox variable. If sb is allocated at runtime at address $tag \times 2^k$ for some tag, this formulation is equivalent at binary level. Again, this heavily relies on pointer arithmetic that is undefined and on information about where the sandbox is linked at runtime.

Consider the alternative formulation $(A\&(2^k-1)) + \&sb$ where the bitwise $|$ is replaced by a $+$. This formulation has the advantage that incrementing a pointer, here sb, is well-defined (see Fig. 2). As on modern hardware, both addition and bitwise operations take a single cycle, the difference in efficiency should be negligible. Moreover, at least for x86, the addition can be compiled into the addressing mode.

Still, this does not solve our issue. To understand this, suppose that A is a pointer. In this case, the bitwise &, whose purpose is to extract the pointer offset, is still undefined. Therefore, the whole expression $(A\&(2^k-1)) + \&sb$ is undefined. Because dereferencing an undefined expression is a *going-wrong* behaviour, the compiled program may have an arbitrary runtime behaviour and escape the sandbox. A prerequisite for our masking primitive is therefore to ensure that the evaluation is defined i.e., different from **undef**. As all the semantic operators of CompCert are strict in **undef** (if any argument is **undef**, so is the result), a necessary condition is that A is not **undef**. As A can be obtained from any expression, a challenge is to ensure that every expression evaluates to a defined value. A particular difficulty is that the many undefined pointer operations (see Fig. 2) cannot be detected by runtime checks.

4.4 Arithmetisation of the Heap

To tackle this challenge and ensure that every computation is defined, we propose an original and radical approach which ensures syntactically that pointers are neither stored in memory nor in local variables. As a result, the program is only manipulating integer values and memory addresses are only constructed by the sandboxing primitives. This approach implies, as a side-effect, that our previously undefined masking primitives are defined. Let asb be the runtime address of the symbolic address $\&sb$ of the sandbox. The masking of an address A can be written

$$A' + \&sb$$

where A' is either defined by $A' = A\&(2^k-1)$ or $A' = (A - asb)_{64\to 32\to 64}$. As A is necessarily an integer, A' is necessarily a defined integer and therefore $A' + \&sb$ returns a defined pointer $\mathbf{ptr}(sb, o)$ that is necessarily inside the sandbox.

An additional subtlety is that memory accesses are indexed by a memory chunk κ which mandates an alignment constraint (e.g. the chunk i_{64} mandates an 8-byte aligned address). As a result, the masking primitive is parameterised by the chunk κ and the masking primitive for i_{64} is $A'\&msk_{i_{64}} + \&sb$ where $msk_{i_{64}} = (2^{k-3}-1) \times 2^3$.

Only computing over numeric values is facilitated by the fact that the sandboxed program is only manipulating pointers relative to a single object, the sandbox. Therefore, a solution could be to only compute with pointer offsets. This is not totally satisfactory because the null pointer (i.e., 0) would be undistinguishable from the base pointer $\mathbf{ptr}(sb, 0)$. Instead, we use the integer asb that is the integer runtime address of the sandbox (i.e., we have $asb = \&sb$) and perform the following transformation t over program expressions.

$$
\begin{aligned}
t(\&sb) &= asb\\
t(c) &= c \text{ for } c \in \{i32, i64, f32, f64\}\\
t(\triangleright e) &= \blacktriangleright t(e)\\
t(e_1 \square e_2) &= t(e_1) \blacksquare t(e_2)\\
t([e]_\kappa) &= [msk_\kappa(t(e))]
\end{aligned}
$$

The operators $\blacktriangleright$ and $\blacksquare$ ensure that, if the expressions are well-typed, they never return the **undef** value. Typical examples include division, modulus, and bitwise shifts. We transform expressions so that they evaluate to an arbitrary value when their original semantics is undefined. For example, we transform the left-shift operations on 32-bit integers so that the resulting expression always has a shift amount less than 32:

```
a≪b   ⇝   a ≪ (b & 31).
```

Similarly, we transform divisions and modulus in the following way, to rule out the undefined cases of division by zero and signed division of `MIN_SIGNED` by `-1`:

```
a/b ⇝ (a+(a==MIN_SIGNED & b==-1))/(b+(b==0)).
```

We can prove that the resulting division expression is always defined. Most of the other expressions are always defined and do not need further transformations.

5 Enforcement of Control-Flow Integrity

Correct sandboxing of code requires some degree of control-flow integrity. Existing SFI implementations enforce a weak form of control-flow integrity which only ensures that jumps are aligned and within a sandbox of code. This is achieved by inserting a masking operation before indirect jumps, that will mask the target address to ensure that the jump is within the sandbox. Additional padding with no-ops is inserted to ensure that all the instructions are indeed aligned [30,37,38]. We enforce a stronger, more traditional, form of control-flow integrity where any control-flow transfer has a well-defined Cminor semantics.

5.1 Relaxation of the Cminor SFI Property

Intraprocedural control-flow integrity is ensured by simple syntactic checks. For instance, they ensure that a **goto** *lb* has a corresponding label *lb* and that an **exit** n has at least n enclosing blocks. The semantics of Cminor prescribes that function calls and returns necessarily match. For this to still hold at the assembly level where the return address is explicitly stored in the stack frame, it is sufficient to prove that the Cminor program has no *going-wrong* behaviour. To ensure control-flow integrity, the only remaining issue is due to indirect calls through function pointers. Our control-flow integrity counter-measure implements software trampolines and ensures that an indirect call with signature σ can only be resolved by a function pointer towards a function with signature σ.

For this purpose, the existing Cminor SFI security policy i.e., Property 1, which rules out any memory access outside the sandbox is too restrictive. As we shall see, the implementation of trampolines necessitates controlled memory reads, outside the sandbox, within compiler-generated variables. To accommodate for this extension, we propose a slightly relaxed SFI security property which, in addition to memory accesses inside the sandbox, authorises other memory reads in read-only regions.

Property 3. A CMINOR program is secure if all its memory accesses are within either the sandbox block *sb* or some read-only memory.

This relaxed property still ensures the integrity of the runtime because all memory writes are confined to the sandbox. Note that Property 3 and Property 1 are equivalent if the trusted runtime library has no read-only memory. This can be achieved at modest cost by modifying slightly the source code and remove the C type qualifier `const` which instructs the compiler that the memory is read-only.

5.2 Control-Flow Integrity of Indirect Calls

In Sect. 4, we have eluded the presence of function pointers. They actually perfectly fit our strategy of encoding pointers by integers. In this case, each function pointer is encoded as an index and the trampoline code translates the index into a valid function pointer.

Consider a function f of signature σ and suppose that the function pointer $\&f$ is compiled into the index i. The reverse mapping from indexes to function pointers is obtained from a compiler-generated array variable A_σ such that $A_\sigma[i] = \&f$. The array variable A_σ is made of all the function pointers with signature σ. The array variable is also padded with a default function pointer such that its length is a power of two. At the call site, the instruction $e(e_1 \ldots, e_n)_\sigma$ is transformed into $[te\&msk_\sigma + \&A_\sigma](te_1, \ldots, te_n)_\sigma$ where $te, te_1 \ldots, te_n$ are transformed expressions such that all memory accesses are masked and msk_σ is the binary mask ensuring that the index te is within the bounds of the variable A_σ. In our actual implementation, we optimise direct calls and in this case bypass the trampoline. Therefore, when the expression e is a constant pointer $\&f$ to an existing function with signature σ, we generate directly $(\&f)(te_1 \ldots,\ te_n)$. As a result, only C code using indirect calls goes through the trampoline code.

Though our implementation only exploits the relaxation of Property 3 for the sake of trampolines, a more aggressive implementation could sometimes avoid to relocate read-only memory inside the sandbox. This could have a positive impact on optimisations which exploit the immutability of read-only memory.

6 Safety and Security Proofs

We next give an overview of our fully verified Coq proof of security and safety.

6.1 Security Proof

Property 3 is an informal formulation of our security property that is formally stated as a CMINOR instrumented semantics. This semantics mimics the CMINOR semantics with the exception that memory accesses are restricted: a memory read is either performed within the sandbox or in a read-only memory region; a memory write is necessarily performed within the sandbox.

The goal of the security proof is to show that all the memory accesses abide by the restrictions of the instrumented semantics. This is stated by Theorem 2 which establishes that for a transformed program *tp*, no behaviour of the standard CMINOR semantics gets stuck for the instrumented CMINOR semantics.

Theorem 2 (Security). *For any transformed program tp, every behaviour of tp in the standard semantics of* CMINOR *is also a behaviour of tp in the instrumented semantics.*

The proof is based on the standard technique of forward simulation that is used in COMPCERT to ensure the preservation of semantics by compiler passes. Here, the forward simulation has the distinctive feature of relating the same (transformed) program equipped with a standard and an instrumented semantics. Since the only difference between the two semantics is that memory accesses must be secure, the crux of the proof lies in the correctness of the masking primitive, as stated in the following lemma.

Lemma 1. *For any masked expression e, if e evaluates to some pointer* $\mathbf{ptr}(b, o)$*, then b is the block of the sandbox i.e., sb.*

The proof relies on the definition of the masking primitive: a masked expression e is of the form $e' + \&sb$. Since $\&sb$ evaluates to the pointer $\mathbf{ptr}(sb, 0)$, then if the whole expression evaluates to a pointer $\mathbf{ptr}(b, o)$, necessarily $b = sb$.

6.2 Safety Proof

In order to benefit from COMPCERT's semantic preservation theorem and transport our security proof to the compiled assembly program, we must also prove that the sandboxed program is safe, i.e., it never gets *stuck*. We address all the going-wrong behaviours that we enumerated in Sect. 2.1. The well-formedness properties of a program (calling only defined functions, accessing only defined variables, jumping only to defined labels, exiting from no more blocks than currently enclosed in) are checked statically and make the transformation fail if they are violated. Next, the memory accesses require the addresses to be valid and adequately aligned: our masking operation ensures that this is always the case. Then, the evaluation of expressions must always be defined: this has mostly been dealt with the arithmetisation of the memory (Sect. 4.4). Finally, function calls should always be performed with the appropriate number of well-typed arguments. This is easy to check statically for direct function calls, but requires trampolines (as described in Sect. 5.2) for indirect function calls. The following sandbox invariant encapsulates all these conditions.

Definition 1 (Sandbox Invariant). *A state S of program P satisfies the sandbox invariant if the following conditions are satisfied:*

1. *indirect control-flow transfers are well-defined in P (e.g.* `goto` *instructions in the functions of P only jump to defined labels);*
2. *every function of P ends with an explicit return;*
3. *every function of P is well-typed;*
4. *every function of P starts by explicitly initialising its local variables;*
5. *the global array* A_σ *for signature* σ *contains function pointers to functions of signature* σ*;*
6. *the environment for local variables and the memory in S only contain properly initialised, numerical values.*

Properties 1, 2, 3 are ensured by a set of syntactic checks over the bodies of all the functions of the program. Property 4 is enforced by our function transformation which inserts assignments that explicitly initialise all declared local variables. Property 5 is ensured by construction of the arrays for function pointers. All these properties can be established solely on the program body and do not change during the execution of the program. By contrast, Property 6 cannot be checked statically and depends on the state of the program at each point.

Safe Evaluation of Expressions. A necessary condition for the safe evaluation of expressions is that the program is well typed. CompCert does not generate these type guarantees so we have integrated a verified (simple) type-inference algorithm for Cminor programs. Type-checking alone is not sufficient to rule out undefined behaviours of C operators, but together with the transformations explained in Sect. 4.4, we prove the following lemma about the evaluation of transformed expressions.

Lemma 2 (Safe evaluation of expressions). *In a memory state and a well-typed environment for local variables containing only defined numerical values, the transformation of any well-typed expression e evaluates to a defined numerical value.*

Lemma 2 follows directly from the properties of our expression transformation.

Safety of Calls through Trampolines. As mentioned in Sect. 5, we implement software trampolines to secure function calls through function pointers. To ensure the safety of indirect function calls, we maintain a map *smap* from function signatures to the corresponding array identifier and the length of this array. The proof of safety relies on the fact that for every function f of signature σ present in a program, we have $smap(\sigma) = (A_\sigma, l_\sigma)$ such that all offsets lower than l_σ in A_σ contain a pointer to a function of signature σ. The safety proof of indirect calls itself is not hard, but we need to set up this signature map and establish invariants relating it to the global environment of the program.

Safety Theorem. Considering the invariants defined in Definition 1, we prove Lemma 3 which is our main technical result.

Lemma 3 (Safety). *For any* Cminor *program state S that satisfies the invariants, either S is a final state or there exists a sequence of steps from S to some S' such that S' also satisfies the invariants.*

A subtlety of the proof is that at function entry, the local variables carry the value **undef** and therefore the sandbox invariant only holds after they have been initialised by a sequence of assignments (see Property 4 of Definition 1).

Using Lemma 3, we can show Property 2, in the form of Theorem 3.

Theorem 3 (Safety of the transformation). *All behaviours of the transformed program are well-defined, i.e., not wrong.*

Proof. A going-wrong behaviour occurs precisely when a state is reached, from which no further step can be taken, though it is not a final state. Lemma 3, together with a proof that the initial state of the transformed prorgam satisfies the invariants, tells us that no such reachable state exists, concluding the proof. □

As a result, we benefit from CompCert's semantic preservation theorem and can transport the security proof down to the assembly program.

Theorem 4 (Security of the compiled program). *Let p be a transformed* Cminor *program. If p compiles into the assembly program tp, then tp is secure.*

The proof uses Corollary 1 and Theorem 2 to conclude that the behaviours of *tp* are the same as those of *p*, and hence secure.

7 SFI Runtime and Library

Our modified CompCert compiler, CompCertSfi, takes as input a C program unit in the form of a list of C files. Each C file is first compiled down to the Cminor language using the existing passes of the CompCert compiler. Then, all the Cminor programs are syntactically linked [14] together to form the program unit to be isolated inside the sandbox. CompCertSfi comes with a lightweight runtime and a generic support for interfacing with a trusted library (e.g. a libC). An originality of our approach is that the runtime is using a standard program loader. Moreover, the runtime gets some of its configuration through compiler-generated variables.

7.1 Loading the SFI Application

The sandboxed code is linked with our runtime library by a linker script which specifies where to load at runtime the *sb* variable, viewed as the data segment. The compiler also emits a sandbox configuration map which contains the symbolic address of the sandbox, its numeric value at runtime, the total size of the sandbox and the range of addresses reserved for global variables.

Our runtime code is executed before starting the sandboxed `main` function. It first checks that the sandbox is properly linked according to the sandbox configuration map, sets the shadow-stack pointer and initialises the sandbox heap using our sandbox-aware implementation of `malloc` based on `ptmalloc3`[2].

By construction, our runtime stack is free of buffer overruns. Yet, if the recursion is too deep, the stack may overflow. Therefore, the runtime inserts an unmapped page guard at the bottom of the stack and intercepts the segmentation fault. This protection suffices provided that the size of each function stack frame does not exceed a page; which can be checked at compile-time. Eventually, after copying its arguments inside the sandbox, the runtime calls the `main` function of the sandboxed application.

7.2 Monitoring Calls to the Runtime Library

The runtime library is trusted and therefore part of the TCB. To ensure isolation, each call towards the runtime library is monitored to check the validity of the arguments. For this purpose, a call to a library function, say `foo`, is renamed in the object file into a call to a function `sb_foo` which sanitises its arguments before really calling the function `foo`. The verifications are library specific but usually straightforward to implement. For `stdio`, the `FILE` structures are allocated by the runtime outside of the sandbox. Hence, the returned `FILE*` cannot be dereferenced to corrupt the `FILE` structure. To prevent the sandboxed program to forge `FILE*` pointers, the runtime maintains at all time the set of valid `FILE*`. For variadic functions *e.g.*, `printf`, we statically compile the format into a sequence of safe primitive calls. (We reject programs using formats computed at runtime). For functions in `string`, we check beforehand that the range of memory accesses is within the range of the sandbox. We also allow callbacks and therefore a runtime function may take a function pointer as argument. To ensure that the function is valid, the runtime is using the trampoline programming pattern presented in Sect. 5.2.

[2] http://www.malloc.de/malloc/ptmalloc3-current.tar.gz.

7.3 Communication via Global Variables

Programs may not only communicate *via* function calls but also directly *via* global variables. For the libC, this includes e.g. `stdout` or `errno`. To ensure isolation, CompCertSfi relocates those variables inside the sandbox but also generates a global variable map which is an array variable of the form

$$\{\&n_1, o_1, \ldots, \&n_i, o_i, \ldots, \&n_m, o_m\}$$

where $\&n_i$ is the symbolic address of a global variable and o_i is its offset in the sandbox. Using this information, the runtime has the ability to synchronise the values of the variables inside and outside the sandbox. For example, at program startup, the value of `stdout` (a `stream` pointer) is copied inside the sandbox at the relevant offset. This allows the sandboxed program to call `stdio` functions but protects the integrity of the stream. For `errno`, it is the responsibility of each runtime library call to synchronise the value of `errno` in the sandbox.

8 Experiments

We have evaluated our PSFI approach over the CompCert benchmark suite and a port of Quake. All the experiments have been carried over a quad-core Intel 6600U laptop at 2.6 GHz with 16 GB of RAM running Linux Fedora 27. For Quake, we explain how to adapt the code to our runtime library and verify the absence of noticeable slowdown. For the other benchmarks, we make a more detailed performance evaluation and compare CompCertSfi with CompCert, gcc, clang but also the state-of-the-art (P)NaCl implementation of SFI. In our experiments, all the benchmarks are ordered by increasing running time. Moreover, for computing a runtime overhead, the running time is obtained by taking the harmonic mean of 3 consecutive runs.

8.1 Porting Quake

Quake engines come in various flavours and we use the tyr-quake[3] implementation linking with Xlib. The port requires the addition of several functions to our runtime library from Xlib and the libC. Most of them are not problematic and require no or little modification. For instance, the `getopt` function which is used to parse command-line options is using the global variables `optarg`, `optind`, `opterr`, and `optopt`. As explained in Sect. 7.3, the runtime library copies the values of these variables at reserved places inside the sandbox.

Other functions, *e.g.* `gethostbyname`, allocate memory on their own and return a pointer to this piece of data which is therefore not accessible to the sandboxed code. For the specific case of `gethostbyname`, the library provides the function `gethostbyname_r` which, instead of allocating memory, takes as argument a data-structure that is filled by the function. In our case, we pass as argument a sandbox allocated piece of memory. This does not solve our problem entirely as inner pointers may still point outside the sandbox. To cope with this issue, we perform a deep copy of the relevant piece of data inside the sandbox.

A last issue is that the video memory is shared between the application and the X server using the system call `shmat`. Fortunately, the libC provides the relevant flags to

[3] https://disenchant.net/git/tyrquake.git.

bind shared memory at a specific address. Hence, we were able to allocate it inside the sandbox thus allowing a seamless communication with the X server. After these modifications, the sandboxed QUAKE runs without noticeable slowdown which is encouraging and an indication of the good overall performance of our sandboxing technique. In the following, we complement this with a more precise runtime evaluation for the COMPCERT benchmarks.

8.2 PSFI Overhead: Impact of Sandboxing Primitives

Next, we compare the efficiency of a standard masking primitive (Sect. 4.1) with a specialised version for 32-bit sandboxes (Sect. 4.2).

Figure 4 shows the overhead of the standard sandboxing primitive with respect to the specialised sandboxing primitive. There are 6 benchmarks for which the overhead incurred by the standard sandboxing is above 10% reaching 40% for 2 benchmarks. These cases illustrate the significant performance advantage that is sometime obtained by the specialised sandboxing. For some benchmarks, the standard sandboxing outperforms our optimised sandboxing. Yet when it does it is by a very small margin (below 3%). Overall, for the vast majority of our benchmarks, the specialised sandboxing primitive is very competitive.

In Sect. 4.1, we gave theoretical arguments for the advantage of the specialised sandboxing. Another argument comes from the fact that the specialised sandboxing is easier to optimise. First, note that the standard and the specialised sandboxing primitives are both using a bitwise mask but for different purposes. For the standard primitive, it is used to enforce that the pointer is within the sandbox bounds but also to enforce alignment constraints. For the specialised primitive, it is only used to enforce alignment constraints. Using the existing COMPCERT dataflow framework, we have implemented an alignment analysis that is quite effective at removing redundant alignment masks. To enable more optimisations, we explicit alignment constraints in the CMINOR code program (e.g. by specifying that function arguments of a pointer type are necessarily aligned). Thus, our experimental results are explained by both the theoretical advantages given in Sect. 4.2 and the effectiveness of our alignment analysis.

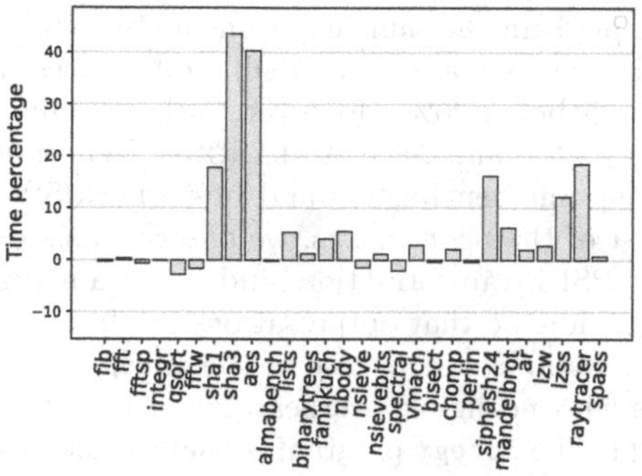

Fig. 4. Overhead of standard w.r.t specialised sandboxing

8.3 PSFI Overhead: Impact of Compiler Back-End

As a second experiment, we evaluate the overhead of our PSFI transformation for various compilers: CompCert, gcc and clang. CompCert is a *moderately optimising compiler* and the benchmarks run significantly faster using gcc and clang. In Fig. 5, the baseline is given by the minimum of the execution times of the three compilers without PSFI instrumentation. The black bar is the overhead of a compiler (e.g. CompCert), with respect to the baseline and the grey bar is the overhead of the same compiler but with the PSFI transformation (e.g. CompCertSfi). In order to use gcc and clang, we implement a trusted decompiler from our secured Cminor programs to Clight, a subset of C in CompCert. These Clight programs are then compiled with gcc or clang.

For a fair comparison, we should compare programs for which we actually have a reasonable security guarantee. We have a formal proof of security and safety (see Sect. 6) for the sandboxed Cminor program, and we are confident that our syntax-directed decompiler preserves this property. For CompCert, this would suffice to preserve the security of the compiled Clight code, but this is not the case for gcc and clang because of semantic discrepancies between the compilers. To limit this risk, we have set the compiler flags to instruct gcc and clang to adhere to the specificity of CompCert semantics: signed integer arithmetic is defined and so are wraps around (flag `-fwrapv`), strict aliasing is irrelevant (flag `-fno-strict-aliasing`), and floating-point arithmetic is strictly IEEE 754 compliant (flags `-frounding-math` and `-fsignaling-nans`). We also instruct the compilers to ignore any knowledge about the C library (`-fno-builtin`).

Our experimental results are shown in Fig. 5. In Fig. 5a, we have the overhead of CompCert and CompCertSfi. The overhead of CompCert over gcc and clang is expected and corroborates existing results[4]. For 10% of the benchmarks, the overhead CompCertSfi over CompCert is negligible and sometimes the PSFI transformation even improves performance. Those are programs for which the PSFI transformation introduces few masking operations, if any. For 41% of the benchmarks, the overhead is below 10% and can be considered, for most applications, a reasonable efficiency/security trade-off. For all the other benchmarks except `binarytrees` and `vmach`, the overhead is below 25%. The two remaining benchmarks have a significant overhead reaching 82% for `binarytrees`. This corresponds to programs which are memory intensive and where sandboxing cannot be optimised.

In Fig. 5b and c, we perform the same experiments but with gcc and clang. The results have some similarities but also have visible differences. For about 60% of the benchmarks the overhead is below 20%. Moreover, for both compilers, the average overhead is similar: 22% for gccSfi and 24% for clangSfi. Yet, on average gccSfi makes a better job at optimising our benchmarks and best clangSfi for about 75% of the benchmarks. For the rest of the benchmarks, we observe a significant overhead, up to 20%, indicating that the PSFI transformation hinders certain aggressive optimisations. The results also seem to indicate that optimisations are fragile as the overhead is not always consistent across compilers. The case of the `integr` benchmark is particularly striking because it runs with negligible overhead for clangSfi but exhibits the worst case overhead for gccSfi. The `integr` program is using a function pointer inside a loop and we suspect that gccSfi, unlike clangSfi, fails to optimise the program due to the inserted trampoline code. Though less striking, the benchmarks `fftw` and `raytracer` follow the opposite trend; these are programs where the overhead of clangSfi is much higher than gccSfi.

[4] http://compcert.inria.fr/compcert-C.html#perfs.

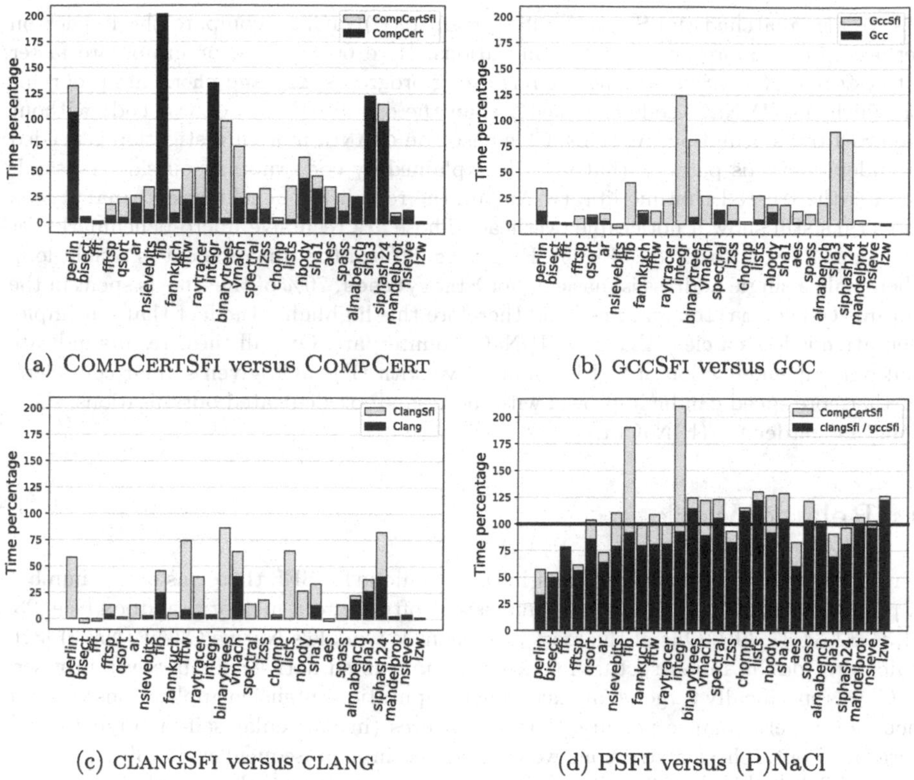

(a) CompCertSfi versus CompCert

(b) gccSfi versus gcc

(c) clangSfi versus clang

(d) PSFI versus (P)NaCl

Fig. 5. Overhead of PSFI:CompCert, clang, gcc, (P)NaCl

8.4 PSFI Versus (P)NaCl

We also compare our compiler-based SFI approach with (P)NaCl [30], which to our knowledge is one of the most mature implementations of SFI. Figure 5d shows the overhead of CompCertSfi, gccSfi, clangSfi with respect to (P)NaCl. The baseline is given by the best among NaCl and PNaCl. The best of clangSfi and gccSfi is given in dark gray and CompCertSfi is given in light grey.

We first analyse the results of CompCertSfi. Our benchmarks are ordered by increasing runtime. The first 5 benchmarks have a runtime below one second. They are not representative of the performance of both approaches but only illustrate the fact that (P)NaCl has a startup penalty due to the verification of the binary and the setup of the sandbox. The overhead peaks above 75% for two programs (i.e., `fib` and `integr`). As the PSFI transformation keeps `fib` unmodified and only inserts a trampoline call in `integr`, these programs only highlight the limited optimisations performed by CompCert. Of the remaining benchmarks, 40% of them run faster or have similar speed with CompCertSfi. For those benchmarks, the average overhead of CompCertSfi w.r.t (P)NaCl is around 9%. Except for a few programs whose overhead skyrockets due to CompCert not being specialised for speed, we can say that CompCertSfi performance is comparable to (P)NaCl, having programs with better speed in both sides and a large number having similar results.

We also matched GCCSFI/CLANGSFI against (P)NaCl to compare the impact on performance of more aggressive optimisations. Here 60% of the programs are faster with GCCSFI/CLANGSFI. Among the remaining programs, `lzw` and `chomp` are programs for which the (P)NaCl code runs faster than the optimised GCC CLANG code without the PSFI transformation. As (P)NaCl is based on CLANG, more investigation is needed to understand this paradox that may be explained by code running outside the sandbox *i.e.* the trusted runtime library. Among the remaining benchmarks, `binarytrees` and `lists` still show a noticeable overhead. Those are recursive micro-benchmarks for which our PSFI is costly (see Fig. 5). For `lists`, 99% of the time is spent in a tight loop where only a single address is masked. For `binarytrees`, 70% of the time is spent in the runtime code of `malloc` and `free` and therefore this highlights the fact that our implementation is less efficient than the (P)NaCl counterpart. Overall these results indicate that our implementation of SFI is competitive with (P)NaCl, given similar compilers. Furthermore speed can be improved with more sandbox-dedicated optimisations; these would be harder for (P)NaCl to check.

9 Related Work

Since Wahbe *et al.* [35] proposed their initial technique for SFI, there has been a number of proposals for efficiently confining untrusted software to a memory sandbox (see [23, 24,31,32,34,37,39]). One of the most prominent is Google's Native Client (NaCl) [37], which provides an infrastructure for executing untrusted native code in a web browser. NaCl was specifically targeted at executing computation-intensive applications without incurring a performance penalty. Certain features (in particular self-modifying code) were ruled out. These restrictions were addressed in a subsequent work [3].

RockSalt [24] is an SFI verifier for x86 code which has been developed and formally verified with the proof assistant Coq. The major contribution of RockSalt is to provide a formal model of the x86 architecture, from which it is possible to extract a decoder for a subset of the very rich set of x86 instructions, and build a verifier for the NaCl sandbox policy. Their experiments show that the formally verified checker performs marginally better than the NaCl verifier. In comparison, our approach avoids the complexities of the x86 instruction set by relying on the COMPCERT compiler back-end to produce binaries whose adherence to the sandbox policy is guaranteed by a combination of a sandbox verification at a higher level (CMINOR) and the COMPCERT's correctness theorem.

ARMor [39] is using the binary rewriter Diablo [28] to implement SFI for ARM processors. Using an untrusted program analysis, a proof of SFI safety is automatically constructed using the HOL theorem prover. ARMor was tested with some programs of the MiBench benchmark [11], namely BitCount and StringSearch. These programs required 2.5 and 8 h respectively to prove the memory safety and control-flow integrity of the executables, which means that the approach is not practically viable as it is.

Kroll *et al.* [16] proposed PSFI as an alternative methodology to the standard, verification-based SFI. In PSFI, the sandbox is built by inserting the necessary masking instructions during compilation. This means that the correctness of the transformation can be argued at an intermediate stage in the compilation where the program representation retains a high-level structure. Our work extends the seminal proposal in a number of ways that we detail below. Unlike Kroll *et al.*, we exclude from the TCB the masking primitive and the trampoline mechanism for calling external functions. In our implementation, these crucial components are written entirely in CMINOR and proved correct without introducing trusted, unproved, code. Kroll *et al.* sketch a proof of safety but do not identify the issue of pointer arithmetic. To sidestep the semantics limitation of pointer arithmetic, we introduce a compile-time encoding of pointer as integers. This transformation is instrumental for our Coq verified proof of safety, which itself is mandatory to transfer security down to assembly.

Since the seminal work of Norrish [27], several works propose formal semantics of the C language [8, 12, 15]. All these share the limitations of CompCert with respect to pointer arithmetic. Recent works specifically aim at providing a more defined semantics for pointers. The proposal of Besson *et al.* [4] is able to cope with most existing low-level pointer manipulations and has been ported to CompCert [5, 6]. Yet, it has nonetheless limitations and the design of our PSFI transformation would not benefit from the increased expressiveness. The semantics of Kang *et al.* [14] is more permissive because, after a cast, a pointer is indistinguishable from an integer value. To our knowledge, their semantics has not been ported to the CompCert compiler. Our SFI transformation has the advantage of being compatible with the existing semantics of CompCert with the caveat that pointers needs to be explicitly compiled into integers.

10 Conclusion

We have presented CompCertSfi, a formally verified implementation of Software Fault Isolation based on the CompCert compiler. Our approach provides security guarantees at runtime when the source code may be malicious or has security vulnerabilities but the build process is trusted. This is typically the case when a final product is built using code originating from multiple third parties. Our work shows that it is possible to perform security-enhancing compilation that is both formally verified and competitive with existing approaches in terms of efficiency. CompCertSfi does not rely on *a posteriori* binary verification for guaranteeing security, and hence has a reduced TCB compared to traditional SFI solutions. The reduction in TCB is obtained through a formal, machine-checked proof of the fact that the security guaranteed by our SFI transformation in the compiler front-end, still holds at the assembly level. Key to achieving this property has been to fine-tune the transformation (and in particular its pointer manipulations) to ensure that the secured program has a well-defined semantics.

The impact of SFI has been evaluated on a series of benchmarks, showing that the transformed code can in a few cases be more efficient, and that the average runtime overhead incurred is about 9%. We have evaluated the impact of back-end optimisation on the transformed code on three different compilers. The gains vary, with clang being more efficient than CompCert and gcc, and CompCert being slightly more efficient than gcc. The experiments show that CompCertSfi combined with an aggressive back-end optimiser can sometimes achieve performances superior to Native Client implementations. In addition, there is still room for further optimisation of the generated code. We have observed that existing optimisations are sometimes hindered by our SFI transformation, so we gain by having more optimisation before the SFI transformation. We also intend to investigate optimisations for removing redundant sandboxing operations and in particular hoisting sandboxing outside loops.

References

1. Supplementary material. https://www.irisa.fr/celtique/ext/compcertsfi
2. Andronick, J., Chetali, B., Ly, O.: Using Coq to verify Java Card^{TM} applet isolation properties. In: Basin, D., Wolff, B. (eds.) TPHOLs 2003. LNCS, vol. 2758, pp. 335–351. Springer, Heidelberg (2003). https://doi.org/10.1007/10930755_22
3. Ansel, J., et al.: Language-independent sandboxing of just-in-time compilation and self-modifying code. In: PLDI, pp. 355–366 (2011)
4. Besson, F., Blazy, S., Wilke, P.: A precise and abstract memory model for C using symbolic values. In: Garrigue, J. (ed.) APLAS 2014. LNCS, vol. 8858, pp. 449–468. Springer, Cham (2014). https://doi.org/10.1007/978-3-319-12736-1_24
5. Besson, F., Blazy, S., Wilke, P.: CompCertS: a memory-aware verified C compiler using pointer as integer semantics. In: Ayala-Rincón, M., Muñoz, C.A. (eds.) ITP 2017. LNCS, vol. 10499, pp. 81–97. Springer, Cham (2017). https://doi.org/10.1007/978-3-319-66107-0_6
6. Besson, F., Blazy, S., Wilke, P.: A verified CompCert front-end for a memory model supporting pointer arithmetic and uninitialised data. J. Autom. Reasoning (2018, accepted for publication)
7. Besson, F., de Grenier de Latour, T., Jensen, T.P.: Interfaces for stack inspection. J. Funct. Program. **15**(2), 179–217 (2005)
8. Ellison, C., Roşu, G.: An executable formal semantics of C with applications. In: POPL. ACM (2012)
9. Fox, A., Myreen, M.O.: A trustworthy monadic formalization of the ARMv7 instruction set architecture. In: Kaufmann, M., Paulson, L.C. (eds.) ITP 2010. LNCS, vol. 6172, pp. 243–258. Springer, Heidelberg (2010). https://doi.org/10.1007/978-3-642-14052-5_18
10. Guanciale, R., Nemati, H., Dam, M., Baumann, C.: Provably secure memory isolation for Linux on ARM. J. Comput. Secur. **24**(6), 793–837 (2016)
11. Guthaus, M., Ringenberg, J., Ernst, D., Austin, T., Mudge, T., Brown, R.: MiBench: a free, commercially representative embedded benchmark suite, pp. 3–14. Institute of Electrical and Electronics Engineers Inc., United States (2001)
12. Hathhorn, C., Ellison, C., Roşu, G.: Defining the undefinedness of C. In: PLDI, pp. 336–345. ACM, June 2015
13. ISO: ISO C Standard 1999. Technical report (1999)
14. Kang, J., Kim, Y., Hur, C., Dreyer, D., Vafeiadis, V.: Lightweight verification of separate compilation. In: POPL, pp. 178–190. ACM (2016)
15. Krebbers, R.: An operational and axiomatic semantics for non-determinism and sequence points in C. In: POPL. ACM (2014)
16. Kroll, J.A., Stewart, G., Appel, A.W.: Portable software fault isolation. In: CSF, pp. 18–32. IEEE (2014)
17. Larus, J.R., Hunt, G.C.: The singularity system. Commun. ACM **53**(8), 72–79 (2010)
18. Leroy, X.: Formal verification of a realistic compiler. Commun. ACM **52**(7), 107–115 (2009)
19. Leroy, X.: A formally verified compiler back-end. J. Autom. Reason. **43**(4), 363–446 (2009)
20. Leroy, X., Appel, A.W., Blazy, S., Stewart, G.: The CompCert memory model. In: Program Logics for Certified Compilers. Cambridge University Press (2014)

21. Leroy, X., Rouaix, F.: Security properties of typed applets. In: Vitek, J., Jensen, C.D. (eds.) Secure Internet Programming, Security Issues for Mobile and Distributed Objects. LNCS, vol. 1603, pp. 147–182. Springer, Heidelberg (1999). https://doi.org/10.1007/3-540-48749-2_7
22. The Coq development team: The Coq proof assistant reference manual (2017). http://coq.inria.fr, version 8.7
23. McCamant, S., Morrisett, G.: Evaluating SFI for a CISC architecture. In: Proceedings of the 15th Conference on USENIX Security Symposium, USENIX-SS 2006, vol. 15. USENIX Association (2006)
24. Morrisett, G., Tan, G., Tassarotti, J., Tristan, J.B., Gan, E.: RockSalt: better, faster, stronger SFI for the x86. In: PLDI, pp. 395–404. ACM (2012)
25. Necula, G.C.: Proof-carrying code. In: POPL, pp. 106–119. ACM Press (1997)
26. Necula, G.C., Lee, P.: Safe kernel extensions without run-time checking. In: OSDI, pp. 229–243. ACM (1996)
27. Norrish, M.: C formalised in HOL. Ph.D. thesis, University of Cambridge (1998)
28. Put, L.V., Chanet, D., Bus, B.D., Sutter, B.D., Bosschere, K.D.: DIABLO: a reliable, retargetable and extensible link-time rewriting framework. In: In IEEE International Symposium On Signal Processing And Information Technology (2005)
29. Richards, G., Hammer, C., Nardelli, F.Z., Jagannathan, S., Vitek, J.: Flexible access control for JavaScript. In: OOPSLA, pp. 305–322. ACM (2013)
30. Sehr, D., et al.: Adapting software fault isolation to contemporary CPU architectures. In: 19th USENIX Security Symposium, pp. 1–12. USENIX Association (2010)
31. Sehr, D., et al.: Adapting software fault isolation to contemporary CPU architectures. In: Proceedings of the 19th USENIX Conference on Security, USENIX Security 2010, p. 1. USENIX Association (2010)
32. Shu, R., et al.: A study of security isolation techniques. ACM Comput. Surv. **49**(3), 50:1–50:37 (2016)
33. Simon, L., Chisnall, D., Anderson, R.J.: What you get is what you C: controlling side effects in mainstream C compilers. In: EuroS&P, pp. 1–15. IEEE (2018)
34. Sinha, R., et al.: A design and verification methodology for secure isolated regions. In: PLDI, pp. 665–681. ACM (2016)
35. Wahbe, R., Lucco, S., Anderson, T.E., Graham, S.L.: Efficient software-based fault isolation. In: SOSP, pp. 203–216. ACM (1993)
36. Wang, X., Chen, H., Cheung, A., Jia, Z., Zeldovich, N., Kaashoek, M.: Undefined behavior: what happened to my code? In: APSYS (2012)
37. Yee, B., et al.: Native client: a sandbox for portable, untrusted x86 native code. In: S&P, pp. 79–93. IEEE (2009)
38. Yee, B., et al.: Native client: a sandbox for portable, untrusted x86 native code. Commun. ACM **53**(1), 91–99 (2010)
39. Zhao, L., Li, G., Sutter, B.D., Regehr, J.: ARMor: fully verified software fault isolation. In: EMSOFT, pp. 289–298. ACM (2011)

Fixing Incremental Computation

Derivatives of Fixpoints, and the Recursive Semantics of Datalog

Mario Alvarez-Picallo[1(✉)], Alex Eyers-Taylor[2], Michael Peyton Jones[2(✉)], and C.-H. Luke Ong[1]

[1] University of Oxford, Oxford, UK
{mario.alvarez-picallo,luke.ong}@cs.ox.ac.uk
[2] Semmle Ltd., Oxford, UK
alexet@semmle.com, me@michaelpj.com

Abstract. Incremental computation has recently been studied using the concepts of *change structures* and *derivatives* of programs, where the derivative of a function allows updating the output of the function based on a change to its input. We generalise change structures to *change actions*, and study their algebraic properties. We develop change actions for common structures in computer science, including directed-complete partial orders and Boolean algebras. We then show how to compute derivatives of fixpoints. This allows us to perform incremental evaluation and maintenance of recursively defined functions with particular application generalised Datalog programs. Moreover, unlike previous results, our techniques are *modular* in that they are easy to apply both to variants of Datalog and to other programming languages.

Keywords: Incremental computation · Datalog · Semantics · Fixpoints

1 Introduction

Consider the following classic Datalog program[1], which computes the transitive closure of an edge relation e:

$$tc(x, y) \leftarrow e(x, y)$$
$$tc(x, y) \leftarrow e(x, z) \wedge tc(z, y)$$

The semantics of Datalog tells us that the denotation of this program is the least fixpoint of the rule tc. Kleene's fixpoint Theorem tells us that we can compute this fixpoint by repeatedly applying the rule until the output stops changing, starting from the empty relation. For example, supposing that $e = \{(1, 2), (2, 3), (3, 4)\}$, we get the following evaluation trace:

[1] See [1, part D] for an introduction to Datalog.

L. Caires (Ed.): ESOP 2019, LNCS 11423, pp. 525–552, 2019.
https://doi.org/10.1007/978-3-030-17184-1_19

Iteration	Newly deduced facts	Accumulated data in tc
0	$\{\}$	$\{\}$
1	$\{(1,2),(2,3),(3,4)\}$	$\{(1,2),(2,3),(3,4)\}$
2	$\{(1,2),(2,3),(3,4),$ $(1,3),(2,4)\}$	$\{(1,2),(2,3),(3,4),$ $(1,3),(2,4)\}$
3	$\{(1,2),(2,3),(3,4),$ $(1,3),(2,4),(1,4),(1,4)\}$	$\{(1,2),(2,3),(3,4),$ $(1,3),(2,4),(1,4)\}$
4	(as above)	(as above)

At this point we have reached a fixpoint, and so we are done.

However, this process is quite wasteful. We deduced the fact $(1,2)$ at every iteration, even though we had already deduced it in the first iteration. Indeed, for a chain of n such edges we will deduce $O(n^2)$ facts along the way.

The standard improvement to this evaluation strategy is known as "semi-naive" evaluation (see [1, section 13.1]), where we transform the program into a *delta* program with two parts:

- A *delta* rule that computes the *new* facts at each iteration.
- An *accumulator* rule that accumulates the delta at each iteration to compute the final result.

In this case our delta rule is simple: we only get new transitive edges at iteration $n+1$ if we can deduce them from transitive edges we deduced at iteration n.

$$\begin{aligned}
\Delta tc_0(x,y) &\leftarrow e(x,y)\\
\Delta tc_{i+1}(x,y) &\leftarrow e(x,z) \wedge \Delta tc_i(z,y)\\
tc_0(x,y) &\leftarrow \Delta tc_0(x,y)\\
tc_{i+1}(x,y) &\leftarrow tc_i(x,y) \vee \Delta tc_{i+1}(x,y)
\end{aligned}$$

Iteration	Δtc_i	tc_i
0	$\{(1,2),(2,3),(3,4)\}$	$\{(1,2),(2,3),(3,4)\}$
1	$\{(1,3),(2,4)\}$	$\{(1,2),(2,3),(3,4),$ $(1,3),(2,4)\}$
2	$\{(1,4)\}$	$\{(1,2),(2,3),(3,4),$ $(1,3),(2,4),(1,4)\}$
3	$\{\}$	(as above)

This is much better—we have turned a quadratic computation into a linear one. The delta transformation is a kind of *incremental computation*: at each stage we compute the changes in the rule given the previous changes to its inputs.

But the delta rule translation works only for traditional Datalog. It is common to liberalise the formula syntax with additional features, such as disjunction, existential quantification, negation, and aggregation.[2] This allows us to

[2] See, for example, LogiQL [26,32], Datomic [18], Souffle [38,42], and DES [36], which between them have all of these features and more. We do not here explore supporting extensions to the syntax of rule *heads*, although as long as this can be given a denotational semantics in a similar style our techniques should be applicable.

write programs like the following, where we compute whether all the nodes in a subtree given by *child* have some property *p*:

$$treeP(x) \leftarrow p(x) \wedge \neg\exists y.(child(x,y) \wedge \neg treeP(y))$$

The body of this predicate amounts to recursion through an *universal* quantifier (encoded as $\neg\exists\neg$). We would like to be able to use semi-naive evaluation for this rule too, but the standard definition of semi-naive transformation is not well defined for the extended program syntax, and it is unclear how to extend it (and the correctness proof) to handle such cases.

It is possible, however, to write a delta program for *treeP* by hand; indeed, here is a definition for the delta predicate (the accumulator is as before):[3]

$$\begin{aligned} \Delta_{i+1}treeP(x) \leftarrow & p(x) \\ & \wedge \exists y.(child(x,y) \wedge \Delta_i treeP(y)) \\ & \wedge \neg\exists y.(child(x,y) \wedge \neg treeP_i(y)) \end{aligned}$$

This is a *correct* delta program (in that using it to iteratively compute *treeP* gives the right answer), but it is not *precise* because it derives some facts repeatedly. We will show how to construct correct delta programs generally using a program transformation, and show how we have some freedom to optimize within a range of possible alternatives to improve precision or ease evaluation.

Handling extended Datalog is of more than theoretical interest—the research in this paper was carried out at Semmle, which makes heavy use of a commercial Datalog implementation to implement large-scale static program analysis [7,37, 39,40]. Semmle's implementation includes parity-stratified negation[4], recursive aggregates [34], and other non-standard features, so we are faced with a dilemma: either abandon the new language features, or abandon incremental computation.

We can tell a similar story about *maintenance* of Datalog programs. Maintenance means updating the results of the program when its inputs change, for example, updating the value of *tc* given a change to *e*. Again, this is a kind of incremental computation, and there are known solutions for traditional Datalog [25], but these break down when the language is extended.

There is a piece of folkloric knowledge in the Datalog community that hints at a solution: the semi-naive translation of a rule corresponds to the *derivative* of that rule [8,9, section 3.2.2]. The idea of performing incremental computation using derivatives has been studied recently by Cai et al. [14], who give an account using *change structures*. They use this to provide a framework for incrementally evaluating lambda calculus programs.

---

[3] This rule should be read as: we can newly deduce that x is in *treeP* if x satisfies the predicate, and we have newly deduced that one of its children is in *treeP*, and we currently believe that all of its children are in *treeP*.

[4] Parity-stratified negation means that recursive calls must appear under an even number of negations. This ensures that the rule remains monotone, so the least fixpoint still exists.

However, Cai et al.'s work isn't directly applicable to Datalog: the tricky part of Datalog's semantics are recursive definitions and the need for the *fixpoints*, so we need some additional theory to tell us how to handle incremental evaluation and maintenance of fixpoint computations.

This paper aims to bridge that gap by providing a solid semantic foundation for the incremental computation of Datalog, and other recursive programs, in terms of changes and differentiable functions.

Contributions. We start by generalizing change structures to *change actions* (Sect. 2). Change actions are simpler and weaker than change structures, while still providing enough structure to handle incremental computation, and have fruitful interactions with a variety of structures (Sects. 3 and 6.1).

We then show how change actions can be used to perform incremental evaluation and maintenance of non-recursive program semantics, using the formula semantics of generalized Datalog as our primary example (Sect. 4). Moreover, the structure of the approach is modular, and can accommodate arbitrary additional formula constructs (Sect. 4.3).

We also provide a method of incrementally computing and maintaining fixpoints (Sect. 6.2). We use this to perform incremental evaluation and maintenance of *recursive* program semantics, including generalized recursive Datalog (Sect. 7). This provides, to the best of our knowledge, the world's first incremental evaluation and maintenance mechanism for Datalog that can handle negation, disjunction, and existential quantification.

We have omitted the proofs from this paper. Most of the results have routine proofs, but the proofs of the more substantial results (especially those in Sect. 6.2) are included in an extended report [3], along with some extended worked examples, and additional material on the precision of derivatives.

2 Change Actions and Derivatives

Incremental computation requires understanding how values *change*. For example, we can change an integer by adding a natural to it. Abstractly, we have a set of values (the integers), and a set of changes (the naturals) which we can "apply" to a value (by addition) to get a new value.

This kind of structure is well-known—it is a set action. It is also very natural to want to combine changes sequentially, and if we do this then we find ourselves with a monoid action.

Using monoid actions for changes gives us a reason to think that change actions are an adequate representation of changes: any subset of $A \to A$ which is closed under composition can be represented as a monoid action on A, so we are able to capture all of these as change actions.

2.1 Change Actions

Definition 1. *A* change action *is a tuple:*

$$\hat{A} := (A, \Delta A, \oplus_A)$$

where A is a set, ΔA is a monoid, and $\oplus_A : A \times \Delta A \to A$ is a monoid action on A.[5]

We will call A the base set, and ΔA the change set *of the change action. We will use $\cdot$ for the monoid operation of ΔA, and $\mathbf{0}$ for its identity element. When there is no risk of confusion, we will simply write $\oplus$ for $\oplus_A$.*

Examples. A typical example of a change action is $(A^*, A^*, +\!\!+)$ where A^* is the set of finite words (or lists) of A. Here we represent changes to a word made by concatenating another word onto it. The changes themselves can be combined using $+\!\!+$ as the monoid operation with the empty word as the identity, and this is a monoid action: $(a +\!\!+ b) +\!\!+ c = a +\!\!+ (b +\!\!+ c)$.

This is a very common case: any monoid $(A, \cdot, \mathbf{0})$ can be seen as a change action $(A, (A, \cdot, \mathbf{0}), \cdot)$. Many practical change actions can be constructed in this way. In particular, for any change action $(A, \Delta A, \oplus)$, $(\Delta A, \Delta A, \cdot)$ is also a change action. This means that we do not have to do any extra work to talk about changes to changes—we can always take $\Delta\Delta A = \Delta A$ (although there may be other change actions available).

Three examples of change actions are of particular interest to us. First, whenever L is a Boolean algebra, we can give it the change actions $(L, L, \vee)$ and $(L, L, \wedge)$, as well as a combination of these (see Sect. 3.2). Second, the natural numbers with addition have a change action $\hat{\mathbb{N}} := (\mathbb{N}, \mathbb{N}, +)$, which will prove useful during inductive proofs.

Another interesting example of change actions is *semiautomata*. A semiautomaton is a triple (Q, Σ, T), where Q is a set of states, Σ is a (non-empty) finite input alphabet and $T : Q \times \Sigma \to Q$ is a transition function. Every semiautomaton corresponds to a change action (Q, Σ^*, T^*) on the free monoid over Σ^*, with T^* being the free extension of T. Conversely, every change action $\hat{A}$ whose change set ΔA is freely generated by a finite set corresponds to a semiautomaton.

Other recurring examples of change actions are:

- $\hat{A}_\bot := (A, M, \lambda(a, \delta a).a)$, where M is any monoid, which we call the *empty* change action on any base set, since it induces no changes at all.
- $\hat{A}_\top := (A, A \to A, \mathrm{ev})$, where A is an arbitrary set, $A \to A$ denotes the set of all functions from A into itself, considered as a monoid under composition and ev is the usual evaluation map. We will call this the "full" change action on A since it contains every possible non-redundant change.

These are particularly relevant because they are, in a sense, the "smallest" and "largest" change actions that can be imposed on an arbitrary set A.

Many other notions in computer science can be understood naturally in terms of change actions, *e.g.* databases and database updates, files and diffs, Git repositories and commits, even video compression algorithms that encode a frame as a series of changes to the previous frame.

[5] Why not just work with monoid actions? The reason is that while the category of monoid actions and the category of change actions have the same objects, they have different morphisms. See Sect. 8.1 for further discussion.

2.2 Derivatives

When we do incremental computation we are usually trying to save ourselves some work. We have an expensive function $f : A \to B$, which we've evaluated at some point a. Now we are interested in evaluating f after some change δa to a, but ideally we want to avoid actually computing $f(a \oplus \delta a)$ directly.

A solution to this problem is a function $f' : A \times \Delta A \to \Delta B$, which given a and δa tells us how to change $f(a)$ to $f(a \oplus \delta a)$. We call this a *derivative* of a function.

Definition 2. *Let $\hat{A}$ and $\hat{B}$ be change actions. A* derivative *of a function $f : A \to B$ is a function $f' : A \times \Delta A \to \Delta B$ such that*

$$f(a \oplus_A \delta a) = f(a) \oplus_B f'(a, \delta a)$$

A function which has a derivative is differentiable, *and we will write $\hat{A} \to \hat{B}$ for the set of differentiable functions between A and B.*[6]

Derivatives need not be unique in general, so we will speak of "a" derivative. Functions into "thin" change actions—where $a \oplus \delta a = a \oplus \delta b$ implies $\delta a = \delta b$—have unique derivatives, but many change actions are not thin. For example, $(\mathcal{P}(\mathbb{N}), \mathcal{P}(\mathbb{N}), \cap)$ is not thin because $\{0\} \cap \{1\} = \{0\} \cap \{2\}$.

Derivatives capture the structure of incremental computation, but there are important operational considerations that affect whether using them for computation actually saves us any work. As we will see in a moment (Proposition 1), for many change actions we will have the option of picking the "worst" derivative, which merely computes $f(a \oplus \delta a)$ directly and then works out the change that maps $f(a)$ to this new value. While this is formally a derivative, using it certainly does not save us any work! We will be concerned with both the possibility of constructing correct derivatives (Sects. 3.2 and 6.2 in particular), and also in giving ourselves a range of derivatives to choose from so that we can soundly optimize for operational value.

For our Datalog case study, we aim to cash out the folkloric idea that incremental computation functions via a derivative. We will construct a derivative of the semantics of Datalog in stages: first the non-recursive formula semantics (Sect. 4); and later the full, recursive, semantics (Sect. 7).

2.3 Useful Facts About Change Actions and Derivatives

The Chain Rule. The derivative of a function can be computed compositionally, because derivatives satisfy the standard chain rule.

---

[6] Note that we do not require that $f'(a, \delta a \cdot \delta b) = f'(a, \delta a) \cdot f'(a \oplus \delta a, \delta b)$ nor that $f'(a, \mathbf{0}) = \mathbf{0}$. These are natural conditions, and all the derivatives we have studied also satisfy them, but none of the results on this paper require them to hold.

Theorem 1 (The Chain Rule). *Let $f : \hat{A} \to \hat{B}$, $g : \hat{B} \to \hat{C}$ be differentiable functions. Then $g \circ f$ is also differentiable, with a derivative given by*

$$(g \circ f)'(x, \delta x) = g'\left(f(x), f'(x, \delta x)\right)$$

or, in curried form

$$(g \circ f)'(x) = g'(f(x)) \circ f'(x)$$

Complete change actions and minus operators. Complete change actions are an important class of change actions, because they have changes between *any* two values in the base set.

Definition 3. *A change action is* complete *if for any $a, b \in A$, there is a change $\delta a \in \Delta A$ such that $a \oplus \delta a = b$.*

Complete change actions have convenient "minus operators" that allow us to compute the difference between two values.

Definition 4. *A* minus operator *is a function $\ominus : A \times A \to \Delta A$ such that $a \oplus (b \ominus a) = b$ for all $a, b \in A$.*

Proposition 1. *Given a minus operator $\ominus$, and a function f, let*

$$f'_{\ominus}(a, \delta a) := f(a \oplus \delta a) \ominus f(a)$$

Then $f'_{\ominus}$ is a derivative for f.

Proposition 2. *Let $\hat{A}$ be a change action. Then the following are equivalent:*

- *$\hat{A}$ is complete.*
- *There is a minus operator on $\hat{A}$.*
- *For any change action $\hat{B}$ all functions $f : B \to A$ are differentiable.*

This last property is of the utmost importance, since we are often concerned with the differentiability of functions.

Products and sums. Given change actions on sets A and B, the question immediately arises of whether there are change actions on their Cartesian product $A \times B$ or disjoint union $A + B$. While there are many candidates, there is a clear "natural" choice for both.

Proposition 3 (Products). *Let $\hat{A} = (A, \Delta A, \oplus_A)$ and $\hat{B} = (B, \Delta B, \oplus_B)$ be change actions.*

Then $\hat{A} \times \hat{B} := (A \times B, \Delta A \times \Delta B, \oplus_\times)$ is a change action, where $\oplus_\times$ is defined by:

$$(a, b) \oplus_{A \times B} (\delta a, \delta b) := (a \oplus_A \delta a, b \oplus_B \delta b)$$

The projection maps π_1,π_2 are differentiable with respect to it. Furthermore, a function $f : A \times B \to C$ is differentiable from $\hat{A} \times \hat{B}$ into $\hat{C}$ if and only if, for every fixed $a \in A$ and $b \in B$, the partially applied functions

$$f(a, \cdot) : B \to C$$
$$f(\cdot, b) : A \to C$$

are differentiable.

Whenever $f : A \times B \to C$ is differentiable, we will sometimes use $\partial_1 f$ and $\partial_2 f$ to refer to derivatives of the partially applied versions, i.e. if $f'_a : B \times \Delta B \to \Delta C$ and $f'_b : A \times \Delta A \to \Delta C$ refer to derivatives for $f(a, \cdot)$, $f(\cdot, b)$ respectively, then

$$\partial_1 f : A \times \Delta A \times B \to \Delta C$$
$$\partial_1 f(a, \delta a, b) := f'_b(a, \delta a)$$
$$\partial_2 f : A \times B \times \Delta B \to \Delta C$$
$$\partial_2 f(a, b, \delta b) := f'_a(b, \delta b)$$

Proposition 4 (Disjoint unions). *Let $\hat{A} = (A, \Delta A, \oplus_A)$ and $\hat{B} = (B, \Delta B, \oplus_B)$ be change actions.*

Then $\hat{A} + \hat{B} := (A + B, \Delta A \times \Delta B, \oplus_+)$ is a change action, where $\oplus_+$ is defined as:

$$\iota_1 a \oplus_+ (\delta a, \delta b) := \iota_1(a \oplus_A \delta a)$$
$$\iota_2 b \oplus_+ (\delta a, \delta b) := \iota_2(b \oplus_B \delta b)$$

The injection maps ι_1, ι_2 are differentiable with respect to $\hat{A}+\hat{B}$. Furthermore, whenever $\hat{C}$ is a change action and $f : A \to C, g : B \to C$ are differentiable, then so is $[f, g]$.

2.4 Comparing Change Actions

Much like topological spaces, we can compare change actions on the same base set according to coarseness. This is useful since differentiability of functions between change actions is characterized entirely by the coarseness of the actions.

Definition 5. *Let $\hat{A}_1$ and $\hat{A}_2$ be change actions on A. We say that $\hat{A}_1$ is* coarser *than $\hat{A}_2$ (or that $\hat{A}_2$ is* finer *than $\hat{A}_1$) whenever for every $x \in A$ and change $\delta a_1 \in \Delta A_1$, there is a change $\delta a_2 \in \Delta A_2$ such that $x \oplus_{A_1} \delta a_1 = x \oplus_{A_2} \delta a_2$.*

We will write $\hat{A}_1 \leq \hat{A}_2$ whenever $\hat{A}_1$ is coarser than $\hat{A}_2$. If $\hat{A}_1$ is both finer and coarser than $\hat{A}_2$, we will say that $\hat{A}_1$ and $\hat{A}_2$ are equivalent.

The relation $\leq$ defines a preorder (but not a partial order) on the set of all change actions over a fixed set A. Least and greatest elements do exist up to equivalence, and correspond respectively to the empty change action $\hat{A}_\bot$ and any complete change action, such as the full change action $\hat{A}_\top$, defined in Sect. 2.1.

Proposition 5. *Let $\hat{A}_2 \leq \hat{A}_1$, $\hat{B}_1 \leq \hat{B}_2$ be change actions, and suppose the function $f : A \to B$ is differentiable as a function from $\hat{A}_1$ into $\hat{B}_1$. Then f is differentiable as a function from $\hat{A}_2$ into $\hat{B}_2$.*

A consequence of this fact is that whenever two change actions are equivalent they can be used interchangeably without affecting which functions are differentiable. One last parallel with topology is the following result, which establishes a simple criterion for when a change action is coarser than another:

Proposition 6. *Let $\hat{A}_1, \hat{A}_2$ be change actions on A. Then $\hat{A}_1$ is coarser than $\hat{A}_2$ if and only if the identity function* id $: A \to A$ *is differentiable from $\hat{A}_1$ to $\hat{A}_2$.*

3 Posets and Boolean Algebras

The semantic domain of Datalog is a complete Boolean algebra, and so our next step is to construct a good change action for Boolean algebras. Along the way, we will consider change actions over posets, which give us the ability to *approximate* derivatives, which will turn out to be very important in practice.

3.1 Posets

Ordered sets give us a constrained class of functions: monotone functions. We can define *ordered* change actions, which are those that are well-behaved with respect to the order on the underlying set.[7]

Definition 6. *A change action $\hat{A}$ is* ordered *if*

- *A and ΔA are posets.*
- *$\oplus$ is monotone as a map from $A \times \Delta A \to A$*
- *$\cdot$ is monotone as a map from $\Delta A \times \Delta A \to \Delta A$*

In fact, any change action whose base set is a poset induces a partial order on the corresponding change set:

Definition 7. *$\delta a \leq_\Delta \delta b$ iff for all $a \in A$ it is the case that $a \oplus \delta a \leq a \oplus \delta b$.*

Proposition 7. *Let $\hat{A}$ be a change action on a set A equipped with a partial order $\leq$ such that $\oplus$ is monotone in its first argument. Then $\hat{A}$ is an ordered change action when ΔA is equipped with the partial order $\leq_\Delta$.*

In what follows, we will extend the partial order $\leq_\Delta$ on some change set ΔB pointwise to functions from some A into ΔB. This pointwise order interacts nicely with derivatives, in that it gives us the following lemma:

[7] If we were giving a presentation that was generic in the base category, then this would simply be the definition of being a change action in the category of posets and monotone maps.

Theorem 2 (Sandwich lemma). *Let $\hat{A}$ be a change action, and $\hat{B}$ be an ordered change action, and let $f : A \to B$ and $g : A \times \Delta A \to \Delta B$ be function. If $f_\uparrow$ and $f_\downarrow$ are derivatives for f such that*

$$f_\downarrow \leq_\Delta g \leq_\Delta f_\uparrow$$

then g is a derivative for f.

If unique minimal and maximal derivatives exist, then this gives us a characterisation of all the derivatives for a function.

Theorem 3. *Let $\hat{A}$ and $\hat{B}$ be change actions, with $\hat{B}$ ordered, and let $f : A \to B$ be a function. If there exist $f_{\downarrow\downarrow}$ and $f_{\uparrow\uparrow}$ which are unique minimal and maximal derivatives of f, respectively, then the derivatives of f are precisely the functions f' such that*

$$f_{\downarrow\downarrow} \leq_\Delta f' \leq_\Delta f_{\uparrow\uparrow}$$

This theorem gives us the leeway that we need when trying to pick a derivative: we can pick out the bounds, and that tells us how much "wiggle room" we have above and below.

3.2 Boolean Algebras

Complete Boolean algebras are a particularly nice domain for change actions because they have a negation operator. This is very helpful for computing differences, and indeed Boolean algebras have a complete change action.

Proposition 8 (Boolean algebra change actions). *Let L be a complete Boolean algebra. Define*

$$\hat{L}_{\bowtie} := (L, L \bowtie L, \oplus_{\bowtie})$$

where

$$L \bowtie L := \{(a, b) \in L \times L \mid a \wedge b = \bot\}$$
$$a \oplus_{\bowtie} (p, q) := (a \vee p) \wedge \neg q$$

$$(p, q) \cdot (r, s) := ((p \wedge \neg s) \vee r, (q \wedge \neg r) \vee s)$$

with identity element $(\bot, \bot)$.

Then $\hat{L}_{\bowtie}$ is a complete change action on L.

We can think of $\hat{L}_{\bowtie}$ as tracking changes as pairs of "upwards" and "downwards" changes, where the monoid action simply applies one after the other, with an adjustment to make sure that the components remain disjoint.[8] For example,

[8] The intuition that $\hat{L}_{\bowtie}$ is made up of an "upwards" and a "downwards" change action glued together can in fact be made precise, but the specifics are outside the scope of this paper.

in the powerset Boolean algebra $\mathcal{P}(\mathbb{N})$, a change to $\{1,2\}$ might consist of *adding* $\{3\}$ and *removing* $\{1\}$, producing $\{2,3\}$. In $\mathcal{P}(\mathbb{N})_{\bowtie}$ this would be represented as $(\{1,2\}) \oplus (\{3\},\{1\}) = \{2,3\}$.

Boolean algebras also have unique maximal and minimal derivatives, under the usual partial order based on implication. The change set is, as usual, given the change partial order, which in this case corresponds to the natural order on $L \times L^{\mathrm{op}}$.

Proposition 9. *Let L be a complete Boolean algebra with the $\hat{L}_{\bowtie}$ change action, and $f : A \to L$ be a function. Then, the following are minus operators:*

$$a \ominus_{\bot} b = (a \wedge \neg b, \neg a)$$
$$a \ominus_{\top} b = (a, b \wedge \neg a)$$

Additionally, $f'_{\ominus_\bot}$ and $f'_{\ominus_\top}$ define unique least and greatest derivatives for f.

Theorem 3 then gives us bounds for all the derivatives on Boolean algebras:

Corollary 1. *Let L be a complete Boolean algebra with the corresponding change action $\hat{L}_{\bowtie}$, $\hat{A}$ be an arbitrary change action, and $f : A \to L$ be a function. Then the derivatives of f are precisely those functions $f' : A \times \Delta A \to \Delta A$ such that*

$$f'_{\ominus_\bot} \leq_{\Delta} f' \leq_{\Delta} f'_{\ominus_\top}$$

This makes Theorem 3 actually usable in practice, since we have concrete definitions for our bounds (which we will make use of in Sect. 4.2).

4 Derivatives for Non-recursive Datalog

We now want to apply the theory we have developed to the specific case of the semantics of Datalog. Giving a differentiable semantics for Datalog will lead us to a strategy for performing incremental evaluation and maintenance of Datalog programs. To begin with, we will restrict ourselves to the non-recursive fragment of the language—the formulae that make up the right hand sides of Datalog rules. We will tackle the full program semantics in a later section, once we know how to handle fixpoints.

Although the techniques we are using should work for any language, Datalog provides a non-trivial case study where the need for incremental computation is real and pressing, as we saw in Sect. 1.

4.1 Semantics of Datalog Formulae

Datalog is usually given a logical semantics where formulae are interpreted as first-order logic predicates and the semantics of a program is the set of models of its constituent predicates. We will instead give a simple denotational semantics (as is typical when working with fixpoints, see e.g. [17]) that treats a Datalog formula as directly denoting a relation, i.e. a set of named tuples, with variables ranging over a finite schema.

Definition 8. *A* schema Γ *is a finite set of names. A* named tuple *over* Γ *is an assignment of a value* v_i *for each name* x_i *in* Γ*. Given disjoint schemata* $\Gamma = \{x_1, \ldots, x_n\}$ *and* $\Sigma = \{y_1, \ldots, y_m\}$*, the* selection function σ_Γ *is defined as*

$$\sigma_\Gamma(\{x_1 \mapsto v_1, \ldots, x_n \mapsto v_n, y_1 \mapsto w_1, \ldots, y_m \mapsto w_m\}) := \{x_1 \mapsto v_1, \ldots, x_n \mapsto v_n\}$$

i.e. σ_Γ *restricts a named tuple over* $\Gamma \cup \Sigma$ *into a tuple over* Γ *with the same values for the names in* Γ*. We denote the elementwise extension of* σ_Γ *to sets of tuples also as* σ_Γ*.*

We will adopt the usual closed-world assumption to give a denotation to negation.

Definition 9. *For any schema* Γ*, there exists a universal relation* $\mathcal{U}_\Gamma$*. Negation on relations can then be defined as*

$$\neg R := \mathcal{U}_\Gamma \setminus R$$

This makes $\mathbf{Rel}_\Gamma$, the set of all subsets of $\mathcal{U}_\Gamma$, a complete Boolean algebra.

Definition 10. *A Datalog formula* T *whose free term variables are contained in* Γ *denotes a function from* $\mathbf{Rel}_\Gamma^n$ *to* $\mathbf{Rel}_\Gamma$*.*

$$[\![\_]\!]_\Gamma : \text{Formula} \to \mathbf{Rel}_\Gamma^n \to \mathbf{Rel}_\Gamma$$

If $\mathcal{R} = (\mathcal{R}_1, \ldots, \mathcal{R}_n)$ *is a choice of a relation* $\mathcal{R}_i$ *for each of the variables* R_i*,* $[\![T]\!](\mathcal{R})$ *is inductively defined according to the rules in Fig. 1.*

$$\begin{aligned} [\![\top]\!]_\Gamma(\mathcal{R}) &:= \mathcal{U}_\Gamma & [\![T \wedge U]\!]_\Gamma(\mathcal{R}) &:= [\![T]\!]_\Gamma(\mathcal{R}) \cap [\![U]\!]_\Gamma(\mathcal{R}) \\ [\![\bot]\!]_\Gamma(\mathcal{R}) &:= \emptyset & [\![T \vee U]\!]_\Gamma(\mathcal{R}) &:= [\![T]\!]_\Gamma(\mathcal{R}) \cup [\![U]\!]_\Gamma(\mathcal{R}) \\ [\![R_j]\!]_\Gamma(\mathcal{R}) &:= \mathcal{R}_j & [\![\neg T]\!]_\Gamma(\mathcal{R}) &:= \neg [\![T]\!]_\Gamma(\mathcal{R}) \end{aligned}$$

$$[\![\exists x.T]\!]_\Gamma(\mathcal{R}) := \sigma_\Gamma([\![T]\!]_{\Gamma \cup \{x\}}(\mathcal{R}))$$

Fig. 1. Formula semantics for Datalog

Since $\mathbf{Rel}_\Gamma$ is a complete Boolean algebra, and so is $\mathbf{Rel}_\Gamma^n$, $[\![T]\!]_\Gamma$ is a function between complete Boolean algebras. For brevity, we will often leave the schema implicit, as it is clear from the context.

4.2 Differentiability of Datalog Formula Semantics

In order to actually perform our incremental computation, we first need to provide a concrete derivative for the semantics of Datalog formulae. Of course, since $[\![T]\!]_\Gamma$ is a function between the complete Boolean algebras $\mathbf{Rel}_\Gamma^n$ and $\mathbf{Rel}_\Gamma$, and

$$
\begin{aligned}
\Delta(\bot) &:= \bot & \nabla(\bot) &:= \bot \\
\Delta(\top) &:= \bot & \nabla(\top) &:= \bot \\
\Delta(R_j) &:= \Delta R_j & \nabla(R_j) &:= \nabla R_j \\
\Delta(T \vee U) &:= \Delta(T) \vee \Delta(U) & \nabla(T \vee U) &:= (\nabla(T) \wedge \neg \mathsf{X}(U)) \\
\Delta(T \wedge U) &:= (\Delta(T) \wedge \mathsf{X}(U)) & &\quad \vee (\nabla(U) \wedge \neg \mathsf{X}(T)) \\
&\quad \vee (\Delta(U) \wedge \mathsf{X}(T)) & \nabla(T \wedge U) &:= (\nabla(T) \wedge U) \vee (T \wedge \nabla(U)) \\
\Delta(\neg T) &:= \nabla(T) & \nabla(\neg T) &:= \Delta(T) \\
\Delta(\exists x.T) &:= \exists x.\Delta(T) & \nabla(\exists x.T) &:= \exists x.\nabla(T) \wedge \neg \exists x.\mathsf{X}(T)
\end{aligned}
$$

$$
\mathsf{X}(R) := (R \vee \Delta(R)) \wedge \neg \nabla(R)
$$

Fig. 2. Upwards and downwards formula derivatives for Datalog

we know that the corresponding change actions $\widehat{\mathbf{Rel}^n_{\Gamma\bowtie}}$ and $\widehat{\mathbf{Rel}_{\Gamma\bowtie}}$ are complete, this guarantees the existence of a derivative for $[\![T]\!]$.

Unfortunately, this does not necessarily provide us with an *efficient* derivative for $[\![T]\!]$. The derivatives that we know how to compute (Corollary 1) rely on computing $f(a \oplus \delta a)$ itself, which is the very thing we were trying to avoid computing!

Of course, given a concrete definition of a derivative we can simplify this expression and hopefully make it easier to compute. But we also know from Corollary 1 that *any* function bounded by $f'_{\ominus\bot}$ and $f'_{\ominus\top}$ is a valid derivative, and we can therefore optimize anywhere within that range to make a trade-off between ease of computation and precision.[9]

There is also the question of how to compute the derivative. Since the change set for $\widehat{\mathbf{Rel}_{\bowtie}}$ is a subset of $\mathbf{Rel} \times \mathbf{Rel}$, it is possible and indeed very natural to compute the two components via a pair of Datalog formulae, which allows us to reuse an existing Datalog formula evaluator. Indeed, if this process is occurring in an optimizing compiler, the derivative formulae can themselves be optimized. This is very beneficial in practice, since the initial formulae may be quite complex.

This does give us additional constraints that the derivative formulae must satisfy: for example, we need to be able to evaluate them; and we may wish to pick formulae that will be easy or cheap for our evaluation engine to compute, even if they compute a less precise derivative.

The upshot of these considerations is that the optimal choice of derivatives is likely to be quite dependent on the precise variant of Datalog being evaluated, and the specifics of the evaluation engine. Here is one possibility, which is the one used at Semmle.

9 The idea of using an approximation to the precise derivative, and a soundness condition, appears in Bancilhon [9].

A concrete Datalog formula derivative. In Fig. 2, we define a "symbolic" derivative operator as a pair of mutually recursive functions, Δ and ∇, which turn a Datalog formula T into new formulae that compute the upwards and downwards parts of the derivative, respectively. Our definition uses an auxiliary function, X, which computes the "neXt" value of a term by applying the upwards and downwards derivatives. As is typical for a derivative, the new formulae will have additional free relation variables for the upwards and downwards derivatives of the free relation variables of T, denoted as ΔR and ∇R respectively. Evaluating the formula as a derivative means evaluating it as a normal Datalog formula with the new relation variables set to the input relation changes.

While the definitions mostly exhibit the dualities we would expect between corresponding operators, there are a few asymmetries to explain.

The asymmetry between the cases for $\Delta(T \vee U)$ and $\nabla(T \wedge U)$ is for operational reasons. The symmetrical version of $\Delta(T \vee U)$ is $(\Delta(T) \wedge \neg U) \vee (\Delta(U) \wedge \neg T)$ (which is also precise). The reason we omit the negated conjuncts is simply that they are costly to compute and not especially helpful to our evaluation engine.

The asymmetry between the cases for $\exists$ is because our dialect of Datalog does not have a primitive universal quantifier. If we did have one, the cases for $\exists$ would be dual to the corresponding cases for $\forall$.

Theorem 4 (Concrete Datalog formula derivatives). *Let* Δ, ∇, X : Formula $\rightarrow$ Formula *be mutually recursive functions defined by structural induction as in Fig. 2.*

Then $\Delta(T)$ *and* $\nabla(T)$ *are disjoint, and for any schema* Γ *and any Datalog formula* T *whose free term variables are contained in* Γ, $[\![T]\!]'_\Gamma := ([\![\Delta(T)]\!]_\Gamma, [\![\nabla(T)]\!]_\Gamma)$ *is a derivative for* $[\![T]\!]_\Gamma$.

We can give a derivative for our *treeP* predicate by mechanically applying the recursive functions defined in Fig. 2.

$$\begin{aligned}&\Delta(\mathit{treeP}(x))\\&= p(x) \wedge \exists y.(\mathit{child}(x,y) \wedge \Delta(\mathit{treeP}(y))) \wedge \neg\exists y.(\mathit{child}(x,y) \wedge \neg\mathsf{X}(\mathit{treeP}(y)))\end{aligned}$$

$$\begin{aligned}&\nabla(\mathit{treeP}(x))\\&= p(x) \wedge \exists y.(\mathit{child}(x,y) \wedge \nabla(\mathit{treeP}(y)))\end{aligned}$$

The upwards difference in particular is not especially easy to compute. If we naively compute it, the third conjunct requires us to recompute the whole of the recursive part. However, the second conjunct gives us a guard: if it is empty we then the whole formula will be, so we only need to evaluate the third conjunct if the second conjunct is non-empty, i.e if there is *some* change in the body of the existential.

This shows that our derivatives aren't a panacea: it is simply *hard* to compute downwards differences for $\exists$ (and, equivalently, upwards differences for $\forall$) because we must check that there is no other way of deriving the same facts.[10] However,

[10] The "support" data structures introduced by [25] are an attempt to avoid this issue by tracking the number of derivations of each tuple.

we can still avoid the re-evaluation in many cases, and the inefficiency is local to this subformula.

4.3 Extensions to Datalog

Our formulation of Datalog formula semantics and derivatives is generic and modular, so it is easy to extend the language with new formula constructs: all we need to do is add cases for Δ and ∇.

In fact, because we are using a complete change action, we can *always* do this by using the maximal or minimal derivative. This justifies our claim that we can support *arbitrary* additional formula constructs: although the maximal and minimal derivatives are likely to be impractical, having them available as options means that we will never be completely stymied.

This is important in practice: here is a real example from Semmle's variant of Datalog. This includes a kind of aggregates which have well-defined recursive semantics. Aggregates have the form

$$r = \mathrm{agg}(p)(vs \mid T \mid U)$$

where agg refers to an aggregation function (such as "sum" or "min"), vs is a sequence of variables, p and r are variables, T is a formula possibly mentioning vs, and U is a formula possibly mentioning vs and p. The full details can been found in Moor and Baars [34], but for example this allows us to write

$$\begin{aligned} \mathit{height}(n,h) \leftarrow & \neg\exists c.(\mathit{child}(n,c)) \wedge h = 0 \\ & \vee \exists h'.(h' = \max(p)(c \mid \mathit{child}(n,c) \mid \mathit{height}(c,p)) \wedge h = h' + 1) \end{aligned}$$

which recursively computes the height of a node in a tree.

Here is an upwards derivative for an aggregate formula:

$$\Delta(r = \mathrm{agg}(p)(vs \mid T \mid U)) := \exists vs.(T \wedge \Delta U) \wedge r = \mathrm{agg}(p)(vs \mid T \mid U)$$

While this isn't a precise derivative, it is still substantially cheaper than re-evaluating the whole subformula, as the first conjunct acts as a guard, allowing us to skip the second conjunct when U has not changed.

5 Changes on Functions

So far we have defined change actions for the kinds of things that typically make up *data*, but we would also like to have change actions on *functions*. This would allow us to define derivatives for higher-order languages (where functions are first-class); and for semantic operators like fixpoint operators $\mathbf{fix} : (A \to A) \to A$, which also operate on functions.

Function spaces, however, differ from products and disjoint unions in that there is no obvious "best" change action on $A \to B$. Therefore instead of trying to define a single choice of change action, we will instead pick out subsets of function spaces which have "well-behaved" change actions.

Definition 11 (Functional Change Action). *Given change actions $\hat{A}$ and $\hat{B}$ and a set $U \subseteq A \to B$, a change action $\hat{U} = (U, \Delta U, \oplus_U)$ is* functional *whenever the evaluation map* $\mathrm{ev} : U \times A \to B$ *is differentiable, that is to say, whenever there exists a function* $\mathrm{ev}' : (U \times A) \times (\Delta U \times \Delta A) \to \Delta B$ *such that:*

$$(f \oplus_U \delta f)(a \oplus_A \delta a) = f(a) \oplus_B \mathrm{ev}'((f, a), (\delta f, \delta a))$$

We will write $\hat{U} \subseteq \hat{A} \Rightarrow \hat{B}$ whenever $U \subseteq A \to B$ and $\hat{U}$ is functional.

There are two reasons why functional change actions are usually associated with a *subset* of $U \subseteq A \to B$. Firstly, it allows us to restrict ourselves to spaces of monotone or continuous functions. But more importantly, functional change actions are necessarily made up of differentiable functions, and thus a functional change action may not exist for the entire function space $A \to B$.

Proposition 10. *Let $\hat{U} \subseteq \hat{A} \Rightarrow \hat{B}$ be a functional change action. Then every $f \in U$ is differentiable, with a derivative f' given by:*

$$f'(x, \delta x) = \mathrm{ev}'((f, x), (\mathbf{0}, \delta x))$$

5.1 Pointwise Functional Change Actions

Even if we restrict ourselves to the differentiable functions between $\hat{A}$ and $\hat{B}$ it is hard to find a concrete functional change action for this set. Fortunately, in many important cases there is a simple change action on the set of differentiable functions.

Definition 12 (Pointwise functional change action). *Let $\hat{A}$ and $\hat{B}$ be change actions. The* pointwise functional change action $\hat{A} \Rightarrow_{pt} \hat{B}$, *when it is defined, is given by $(\hat{A} \to \hat{B}, A \to \Delta B, \oplus_{\to})$, with the monoid structure $(A \to \Delta B, \cdot_{\to}, \mathbf{0}_{\to})$ and the action $\oplus_{\to}$ defined by:*

$$(f \oplus_{\to} \delta f)(x) := f(x) \oplus_B \delta f(x)$$
$$(\delta f \cdot_{\to} \delta g)(x) := \delta f(x) \cdot_B \delta g(x)$$
$$\mathbf{0}_{\to}(x) := \mathbf{0}_B$$

That is, a change is given pointwise, mapping each point in the domain to a change in the codomain.

The above definition is not always well-typed, since given $f : \hat{A} \to \hat{B}$ and $\delta f : A \to \Delta B$ there is no guarantee that $f \oplus_{\to} \delta f$ is differentiable. We present two sufficient criteria that guarantee this.

Theorem 5. *Let $\hat{A}$ and $\hat{B}$ be change actions, and suppose that $\hat{B}$ satisfies one of the following conditions:*

- *$\hat{B}$ is a complete change action.*
- *The change action $\widehat{\Delta B} := (\Delta B, \Delta B, \cdot_B)$ is complete and $\oplus_B : B \times \Delta B \to B$ is differentiable.*

Then the pointwise functional change action $(\hat{A} \to \hat{B}, A \to \Delta B, \oplus_{\to})$ *is well defined.*[11]

As a direct consequence of this, it follows that whenever L is a Boolean algebra (and hence has a complete change action), the pointwise functional change action $\hat{A} \Rightarrow_{pt} \hat{L}_{\bowtie}$ is well-defined.

Pointwise functional change actions are functional in the sense of Definition 11. Moreover, the derivative of the evaluation map is quite easy to compute.

Proposition 11 (Derivatives of the evaluation map). *Let* $\hat{A}$ *and* $\hat{B}$ *be change actions such that the pointwise functional change action* $\hat{A} \Rightarrow_{pt} \hat{B}$ *is well defined, and let* $f : \hat{A} \to \hat{B}$, $a \in A$, $\delta a \in \Delta A$, $\delta f \in A \to \Delta B$.

Then the following are both derivatives of the evaluation map:

$$\mathrm{ev}'_1((f, a), (\delta f, \delta a)) := f'(a, \delta a) \cdot \delta f(a \oplus \delta a)$$
$$\mathrm{ev}'_2((f, a), (\delta f, \delta a)) := \delta f(a) \cdot (f \oplus \delta f)'(a, \delta a)$$

A functional change action merely tells us that a derivative of the evaluation map exists—a pointwise change action actually gives us a definition of it. In practice, this means that we will only be able to use the results in Sect. 6.2 (incremental computation and derivatives of fixpoints) when we have pointwise change actions, or where we have some other way of computing a derivative of the evaluation map.

6 Directed-Complete Partial Orders and Fixpoints

Directed-complete partial orders (dcpos) equipped with a least element, are an important class of posets. They allow us to take *fixpoints* of (Scott-)continuous maps, which is important for interpreting recursion in program semantics.

6.1 Dcpos

As before, we can define change actions on dcpos, rather than sets, as change actions whose base and change sets are endowed with a dcpo structure, and where the monoid operation and action are (Scott-)continuous.

Definition 13. *A change action* $\hat{A}$ *is* continuous *if*

- A *and* ΔA *are dcpos.*
- $\oplus$ *is Scott-continuous as a map from* $A \times \Delta A \to A$.
- $\cdot$ *is Scott-continuous as a map from* $\Delta A \times \Delta A \to \Delta A$.

[11] Either of these conditions is enough to guarantee that the pointwise functional change action is well defined, but it can be the case that $\hat{B}$ satisfies neither and yet pointwise change actions into $\hat{B}$ do exist. A precise account of when pointwise functional change actions exist is outside the scope of this paper.

Unlike posets, the change order $\leq_\Delta$ does *not*, in general, induce a dcpo on ΔA. As a counterexample, consider the change action $(\overline{\mathbb{N}}, \mathbb{N}, +)$, where $\overline{\mathbb{N}}$ denotes the dcpo of natural numbers extended with positive infinity.

A key example of a continuous change action is the $\hat{L}_{\bowtie}$ change action on Boolean algebras.

Proposition 12 (Boolean algebra continuity). *Let L be a Boolean algebra. Then $\hat{L}_{\bowtie}$ is a continuous change action.*

For a general overview of results in domain theory and dcpos, we refer the reader to an introductory work such as [2], but we state here some specific results that we shall be using, such as the following, whose proof can be found in [2, Lemma 3.2.6]:

Proposition 13. *A function $f : A \times B \to C$ is continuous iff it is continuous in each variable separately.*

It is a well-known result in standard calculus that the limit of an absolutely convergent sequence of differentiable functions $\{f_i\}$ is itself differentiable, and its derivative is equal to the limit of the derivatives of the f_i. A consequence of Proposition 13 is the following analogous result:

Corollary 2. *Let $\hat{A}$ and $\hat{B}$ be change actions, with $\hat{B}$ continuous and let $\{f_i\}$ and $\{f_i'\}$ be I-indexed directed sets of functions in $A \to B$ and $A \times \Delta A \to \Delta B$ respectively.*

Then, if for every $i \in I$ it is the case that f_i' is a derivative of f_i, then $\bigsqcup_{i \in I} f_i'$ is a derivative of $\bigsqcup_{i \in I} f_i$.

6.2 Fixpoints

Fixpoints appear frequently in the semantics of languages with recursion. If we can give a generic account of how to compute fixpoints using change actions, then this gives us a compositional way of extending a derivative for the non-recursive semantics of a language to a derivative that can also handle recursion. We will later apply this technique to create a derivative for the semantics of full recursive Datalog (Sect. 7.2).

Iteration functions. Over directed-complete partial orders we can define a least fixpoint operator **lfp** in terms of the iteration function **iter**:

$$\begin{aligned}
&\mathbf{iter} : (A \to A) \times \mathbb{N} \to A \\
&\mathbf{iter}(f, 0) := \bot \\
&\mathbf{iter}(f, n) := f^n(\bot) \\
&\mathbf{lfp} : (A \to A) \to A \\
&\mathbf{lfp}(f) := \bigsqcup_{n \in \mathbb{N}} \mathbf{iter}(f, n) && \text{(where } f \text{ is continuous)}
\end{aligned}$$

The iteration function is the basis for all the results in this section: we can take a partial derivative with respect to n, and this will give us a way to get to the next iteration incrementally; and we can take the partial derivative with respect to f, and this will give us a way to get from iterating f to iterating $f \oplus \delta f$.

Incremental computation of fixpoints. The following theorems provide a generalization of semi-naive evaluation to any differentiable function over a continuous change action. Throughout this section we will assume that we have a continuous change action $\hat{A}$, and any reference to the change action $\hat{\mathbb{N}}$ will refer to the monoidal change action on the naturals defined in Sect. 2.1.

Since we are trying to incrementalize the iterative step, we start by taking the partial derivative of **iter** with respect to n.

Proposition 14 (Derivative of the iteration map with respect to n). *Let $\hat{A}$ be a complete change action and let $f : A \to A$ be a differentiable function. Then* **iter** *is differentiable with respect to its second argument, and a partial derivative is given by:*

$$\begin{aligned}
&\partial_2\mathbf{iter} : (A \to A) \times \mathbb{N} \times \Delta\mathbb{N} \to \Delta A\\
&\partial_2\mathbf{iter}(f, \mathbf{0}, m) := \mathbf{iter}(f, m) \ominus \mathbf{iter}(f, 0)\\
&\partial_2\mathbf{iter}(f, n+1, m) := f'(\mathbf{iter}(f, n), \partial_2\mathbf{iter}(f, n, m))
\end{aligned}$$

By using the following recurrence relation, we can then compute $\partial_2\mathbf{iter}$ along with **iter** simultaneously:

$$\begin{aligned}
&\mathbf{recur}_f : A \times \Delta A \to A \times \Delta A\\
&\mathbf{recur}_f(\bot, \bot) := (\bot, f(\bot) \ominus \bot)\\
&\mathbf{recur}_f(a, \delta a) := (a \oplus \delta a, f'(a, \delta a))
\end{aligned}$$

Which has the property that

$$\mathbf{recur}_f^n(\bot, \bot) = (\mathbf{iter}(f, n), \partial_2\mathbf{iter}(f, n, 1))$$

This gives us a way to compute a fixpoint incrementally, by adding successive changes to an accumulator until we reach it. This is exactly how semi-naive evaluation works: you compute the delta relation and the accumulator simultaneously, adding the delta into the accumulator at each stage until it becomes the final output.

Theorem 6 (Incremental computation of least fixpoints). *Let $\hat{A}$ be a complete, continuous change action, $f : \hat{A} \to \hat{A}$ be continuous and differentiable. Then* $\mathbf{lfp}(f) = \bigsqcup_{n\in\mathbb{N}}(\pi_1(\mathbf{recur}_f^n(\bot, \bot)))$.[12]

[12] Note that we have *not* taken the fixpoint of $\mathbf{recur}_f$, since it is not continuous.

Derivatives of fixpoints. In the previous section we have shown how to use derivatives to compute fixpoints more efficiently, but we also want to take the derivative of the fixpoint operator itself. A typical use case for this is where we have calculated some fixpoint

$$F_E := \mathbf{fix}(\lambda X.F(E, X))$$

then update the parameter E with some change δE and wish to compute the new value of the fixpoint, i.e.

$$F_{E \oplus \delta E} := \mathbf{fix}(\lambda X.F(E \oplus \delta E, X))$$

This can be seen as applying a change to the *function* whose fixpoint we are taking. We go from computing the fixpoint of $F(E, \_)$ to computing the fixpoint of $F(E \oplus \delta E, \_)$. If we have a pointwise functional change action then we can express this change as a function giving the change at each point, that is:

$$\lambda X.F(E \oplus \delta E, X) \ominus F(E, X)$$

In Datalog this would allow us to update a recursively defined relation given an update to one of its non-recursive dependencies, or the extensional database. For example, we might want to take the transitive closure relation and update it by changing the edge relation e.

However, to compute these examples would requires us to provide a derivative for the fixpoint operator **fix**: we want to know how the resulting fixpoint changes given a change to its input function.

Definition 14 (Derivatives of fixpoints). *Let $\hat{A}$ be a change action, let $\hat{U} \subseteq \hat{A} \Rightarrow \hat{A}$ be a functional change action (not necessarily pointwise) and suppose $\mathbf{fix}_U$ and $\mathbf{fix}_{\Delta A}$ are fixpoint operators for endofunctions on U and ΔA respectively.*

Then we define

$$\begin{aligned}
&\mathbf{adjust} : U \times \Delta U \to (\Delta A \to \Delta A)\\
&\mathbf{adjust}(f, \delta f) := \lambda\ \delta a.\, \mathrm{ev}'((f, \mathbf{fix}_U(f)), (\delta f, \delta a))\\
&\mathbf{fix}'_U : U \times \Delta U \to \Delta A\\
&\mathbf{fix}'_U(f, \delta f) := \mathbf{fix}_{\Delta A}(\mathbf{adjust}(f, \delta f))
\end{aligned}$$

The suggestively named $\mathbf{fix}'_U$ will in fact turn out to be a derivative—for *least* fixpoints. The appearance of ev′, a derivative of the evaluation map, in the definition of **adjust** is also no coincidence: as evaluating a fixpoint consists of many steps of applying the evaluation map, so computing the derivative of a fixpoint consists of many steps of applying the derivative of the evaluation map.[13]

[13] Perhaps surprisingly, the authors first discovered an expanded version of this formula, and it was only later that we realised the remarkable connection to ev′.

Since **lfp** is characterized as the limit of a chain of functions, Corollary 2 suggests a way to compute its derivative. It suffices to find a derivative $\mathbf{iter}'_n$ of each iteration map such that the resulting set $\{\mathbf{iter}'_n \mid n \in \mathbb{N}\}$ is directed, which will entail that $\bigsqcup_{n\in\mathbb{N}} \mathbf{iter}'_n$ is a derivative of **lfp**.

These correspond to the first partial derivative of **iter**—this time with respect to f. While we are differentiating with respect to f, we are still going to need to define our derivatives inductively in terms of n.

Proposition 15 (Derivative of the iteration map with respect to f). **iter** *is differentiable with respect to its first argument and a derivative is given by:*

$$\begin{aligned}
&\partial_1\mathbf{iter} : (A \to A) \times \Delta(A \to A) \times \mathbb{N} \to \Delta A\\
&\partial_1\mathbf{iter}(f, \delta f, \mathbf{0}) := \bot_{\Delta A}\\
&\partial_1\mathbf{iter}(f, \delta f, n+1) := \mathrm{ev}'((f, \mathbf{iter}(f, n)), (\delta f, \partial_1\mathbf{iter}(f, \delta f, n)))
\end{aligned}$$

As before, we can now compute $\partial_1\mathbf{iter}$ together with **iter** by mutual recursion.[14]

$$\begin{aligned}
&\mathbf{recur}_{f,\delta f} : A \times \Delta A \to A \times \Delta A\\
&\mathbf{recur}_{f,\delta f}(a, \delta a) := (f(a), \mathrm{ev}'((f, a), (\delta f, \delta a)))
\end{aligned}$$

Which has the property that

$$\mathbf{recur}^n_{f,\delta f}(\bot, \bot) = (\mathbf{iter}(f, n), \partial_1\mathbf{iter}(f, \delta f, n)).$$

This indeed provides us with a function whose limit we can take. If we do so we will discover that it is exactly $\mathbf{lfp}'$ (defined as in Definition 14), showing that $\mathbf{lfp}'$ is a true derivative.

Theorem 7 (Derivatives of least fixpoint operators). *Let*

- $\hat{A}$ *be a continuous change action*
- U *be the set of continuous functions* $f : A \to A$, *with a functional change action* $\hat{U} \subseteq \hat{A} \Rightarrow \hat{A}$
- $f \in U$ *be a continuous, differentiable function*
- $\delta f \in \Delta U$ *be a function change*
- ev' *be a derivative of the evaluation map which is continuous with respect to* a *and* δa.

Then $\mathbf{lfp}'$ *is a derivative of* **lfp**.

Computing this derivative still requires computing a fixpoint—over the change lattice—but this may still be significantly less expensive than recomputing the full new fixpoint.

[14] In fact, the recursion here is not *mutual*: the first component does not depend on the second. However, writing it in this way makes it amenable to computation by fixpoint, and we will in fact be able to avoid the recomputation of $\mathbf{iter}_n$ when we show that it is equivalent to $\mathbf{lfp}'$.

7 Derivatives for Recursive Datalog

Given the non-recursive semantics for a language, we can extend it to handle recursive definitions using fixpoints. Section 6.2 lets us extend our derivative for the non-recursive semantics to a derivative for the recursive semantics, as well as letting us compute the fixpoints themselves incrementally.

Again, we will demonstrate the technique with Datalog, although the approach is generic.

7.1 Semantics of Datalog Programs

First of all, we define the usual "immediate consequence operator" which computes "one step" of our program semantics.

Definition 15. *Given a program $\mathbb{P} = (P_1, \ldots, P_n)$, where P_i is a predicate, with schema Γ_i, the* immediate consequence operator $\mathcal{I} : \mathbf{Rel}^n \to \mathbf{Rel}^n$ *is defined as follows:*

$$\mathcal{I}(\mathcal{R}_1, \ldots, \mathcal{R}_n) = (\llbracket P_1 \rrbracket_{\Gamma_1}(\mathcal{R}_1, \ldots, \mathcal{R}_n), \ldots, \llbracket P_n \rrbracket_{\Gamma_n}(\mathcal{R}_1, \ldots, \mathcal{R}_n))$$

That is, given a value for the program, we pass in all the relations to the denotation of each predicate, to get a new tuple of relations.

Definition 16. *The semantics of a program $\mathbb{P}$ is defined to be*

$$\llbracket \mathbb{P} \rrbracket := \mathbf{lfp}_{\mathbf{Rel}^n}(\mathcal{I})$$

and may be calculated by iterative application of $\mathcal{I}$ to $\bot$ until fixpoint is reached.

Whether or not this program semantics exists will depend on whether the fixpoint exists. Typically this is ensured by constraining the program such that $\mathcal{I}$ is monotone (or, in the context of a dcpo, continuous). We do not require monotonicity to apply Theorem 6 (and hence we can incrementally compute fixpoints that happen to exist even though the generating function is not monotonic), but it is required to apply Theorem 7.

7.2 Incremental Evaluation of Datalog

We can easily extend a derivative for the formula semantics to a derivative for the immediate consequence operator $\mathcal{I}$. Putting this together with the results from Sect. 6.2, we have now created *modular* proofs for the two main results, which allows us to preserve them in the face of changes to the underlying language.

Corollary 3. *Datalog program semantics can be evaluated incrementally.*

Corollary 4. *Datalog program semantics can be incrementally maintained with changes to relations.*

Note that our approach makes no particular distinction between changes to the *extensional* relations (adding or removing facts), and changes to the *intensional* relations (changing the definition). The latter simply amounts to a change to the denotation of that relation, which can be incrementally propagated in exactly the same way as we would propagate a change to the extensional relations.

8 Related Work

8.1 Change Actions and Incremental Computation

Change structures. The seminal paper in this area is Cai et al. [14]. We deviate from that excellent paper in three regards: the inclusion of minus operators, the nature of function changes, and the use of dependent types.

We have omitted minus operators from our definition because there are many interesting change actions that are not complete and so cannot have a minus operator. Where we can find a change structure with a minus operator, often we are forced to use unwieldy representations for change sets, and Cai et al. cite this as their reason for using a dependent type of changes. For example, the monoidal change actions on sets and lists are clearly useful for incremental computation on streams, yet they do not admit minus operators—instead, one would be forced to work with e.g. multisets admitting negative arities, as Cai et al. do.

Our function changes (when well behaved) correspond to what Cai et al. call *pointwise differences* (see [14, section 2.2]). As they point out, you can reconstruct their function changes from pointwise changes and derivatives, so the two formulations are equivalent.

The equivalence of our presentations means that our work should be compatible with their Incremental Lambda Calculus (see [14, section 3]). The derivatives we give in Sect. 4.2 are more or less a "change semantics" for Datalog (see [14, section 3.5]).

S-acts. S-acts (i.e the category of monoid actions on sets) and their categorical structure have received a fair amount of attention over the years (Kilp, Knauer, and Mikhalev [30] is a good overview). However, there is a key difference between change actions considered as a category (**CAct**) and the category of S-acts (**SAct**): the objects of **SAct** all maintain the same monoid structure, whereas we are interested in changing both the base set *and* the structure of the action.

Derivatives of fixpoints. Arntzenius [5] gives a derivative operator for fixpoints based on the framework in Cai et al. [14]. However, since we have different notions of function changes, the result is inapplicable as stated. In addition, we require a somewhat different set of conditions; in particular, we do not require our changes to always be increasing.

8.2 Datalog

Incremental evaluation. The earliest interpretation of semi-naive evaluation as a derivative appears in Bancilhon [8]. The idea of using an approximate derivative and the requisite soundness condition appears as a throwaway comment in Bancilhon and Ramakrishnan [9, section 3.2.2], and it would appear that nobody has since developed that approach.

As far as we know, traditional semi-naive is the state of the art in incremental, bottom-up, Datalog evaluation, and there are no strategies that accommodate additional language features such as parity-stratified negation and aggregates.

Incremental maintenance. There is existing literature on incremental maintenance of relational algebra expressions.

Griffin, Libkin, and Trickey [24] following Qian and Wiederhold [35] compute differences with both an "upwards" and a "downwards" component, and produce a set of rules that look quite similar to those we derive in Theorem 4. However, our presentation is significantly more generic, handles recursive expressions, and works on set semantics rather than bag semantics.[15]

Several approaches [25,27]—most notably DReD—remove facts until one can start applying the rules again to reach the new fixpoint. Given a good way of deciding what facts to remove this can be quite efficient. However, such techniques tend to be tightly coupled to the domain. Although we know of no theoretical reason why either approach should give superior performance when both are applicable, an empirical investigation of this could prove interesting.

Other approaches [19,43] consider only restricted subsets of Datalog, or incur other substantial constraints.

Embedding Datalog. Datafun (Arntzenius and Krishnaswami [6]) is a functional programming language that embeds Datalog, allowing significant improvements in genericity, such as the use of higher-order functions. Since we have directly defined a change action and derivative operator for Datalog, our work could be used as a "plugin" in the sense of Cai et al., allowing Datafun to compute its internal fixpoints incrementally, but also allowing Datafun expressions to be fully incrementally maintained.

In a different direction, Cathcart Burn, Ong, and Ramsay [15] have proposed *higher-order constrained Horn clauses* (HoCHC), a new class of constraints for the automatic verification of higher-order programs. HoCHC may be viewed as a higher-order extension of Datalog. Change actions can be readily applied to organise an efficient semi-naive method for solving HoCHC systems.

8.3 Differential λ-calculus

Another setting where derivatives of arbitrary higher-order programs have been studied is the *differential λ-calculus* [20,21]. This is a higher-order, simply-typed

[15] The same approach of finding derivatives would work with bag semantics, although unfortunately the Boolean algebra structure is missing.

λ-calculus which allows for computing the derivative of a function, in a similar way to the notion of derivative in Cai's work and the present paper.

While there are clear similarities between the two systems, the most important difference is the properties of the derivatives themselves: in the differential λ-calculus, derivatives are guaranteed to be linear in their second argument, whereas in our approach derivatives do not have this restriction but are instead required to satisfy a strong relation to the function that is being differentiated (see Definition 2).

Families of denotational models for the differential λ-calculus have been studied in depth [12,13,16,29], and the relationship between these and change actions is the subject of ongoing work.

8.4 Higher-Order Automatic Differentiation

Automatic differentiation [23] is a technique that allows for efficiently computing the derivative of arbitrary programs, with applications in probabilistic modeling [31] and machine learning [10] among other areas. In recent times, this technique has been successfully applied to higher-order languages [11,41]. While some approaches have been suggested [28,33], a general theoretical framework for this technique is still a matter of open research.

To this purpose, some authors have proposed the incremental λ-calculus as a foundational framework on which models of automatic differentiation can be based [28]. We believe our change actions are better suited to this purpose than the incremental λ-calculus, since one can easily give them a synthetic differential geometric reading (by interpreting $\hat{A}$ as an Euclidean module and ΔA as its corresponding spectrum, for example).

9 Conclusions and Future Work

We have presented change actions and their properties, and used them to provide novel, compositional, strategies for incrementally evaluating and maintaining recursive functions, in particular the semantics of Datalog.

The main avenue for future theoretical work is the categorical structure of change actions. This has begun to be explored by the authors in [4], where change actions are generalized to arbitrary Cartesian base categories and a construction is provided to obtain "canonical" Cartesian closed categories of change actions and differentiable maps.

We hope that these generalizations would allow us to extend the theory of change actions towards other classes of models, such as synthetic differential geometry and domain theory. Some early results in [4] also indicate a connection between 2-categories and change actions which has yet to be fully mapped.

The compositional nature of these techniques suggest that an approach like that used in [22] could be used for an even more generic approach to automatic differentiation.

In addition, there is plenty of scope for practical application of the techniques given here to languages other than Datalog.

References

1. Abiteboul, S., Hull, R., Vianu, V.: Foundations of Databases: The Logical Level. Addison-Wesley Longman Publishing Co., Inc., Boston (1995)
2. Abramsky, S., Jung, A.: Domain theory. In: Handbook of Logic in Computer Science. Oxford University Press, New York (1994)
3. Alvarez-Picallo, M., Eyers-Taylor, A., Jones, M.P., Ong, C.L.: Fixing incremental computation: derivatives of fixpoints, and the recursive semantics of datalog. CoRR abs/1811.06069 (2018). http://arxiv.org/abs/1811.06069
4. Alvarez-Picallo, M., Ong, C.H.L.: Change actions: models of generalised differentiation. In: International Conference on Foundations of Software Science and Computation Structures. Springer (2019, in press)
5. Arntzenius, M.: Static differentiation of monotone fixpoints (2017). http://www.rntz.net/files/fixderiv.pdf
6. Arntzenius, M., Krishnaswami, N.R.: Datafun: a functional datalog. In: Proceedings of the 21st ACM SIGPLAN International Conference on Functional Programming, pp. 214–227. ACM (2016)
7. Avgustinov, P., de Moor, O., Jones, M.P., Schäfer, M.: QL: object-oriented queries on relational data. In: LIPIcs-Leibniz International Proceedings in Informatics, vol. 56. Schloss Dagstuhl-Leibniz-Zentrum fuer Informatik (2016)
8. Bancilhon, F.: Naive evaluation of recursively defined relations. In: Brodie, M.L., Mylopoulos, J. (eds.) On Knowledge Base Management Systems. TINF, pp. 165–178. Springer, New York (1986). https://doi.org/10.1007/978-1-4612-4980-1_17
9. Bancilhon, F., Ramakrishnan, R.: An amateur's introduction to recursive query processing strategies, vol. 15. ACM (1986)
10. Baydin, A.G., Pearlmutter, B.A.: Automatic differentiation of algorithms for machine learning. arXiv preprint arXiv:1404.7456 (2014)
11. Baydin, A.G., Pearlmutter, B.A., Siskind, J.M.: DiffSharp: an AD library for .NET languages. arXiv preprint arXiv:1611.03423 (2016)
12. Blute, R., Ehrhard, T., Tasson, C.: A convenient differential category. arXiv preprint arXiv:1006.3140 (2010)
13. Bucciarelli, A., Ehrhard, T., Manzonetto, G.: Categorical models for simply typed resource calculi. Electron. Notes Theor. Comput. Sci. **265**, 213–230 (2010)
14. Cai, Y., Giarrusso, P.G., Rendel, T., Ostermann, K.: A theory of changes for higher-order languages: incrementalizing λ-calculi by static differentiation. In: ACM SIGPLAN Notices, vol. 49, pp. 145–155. ACM (2014)
15. Cathcart Burn, T., Ong, C.L., Ramsay, S.J.: Higher-order constrained horn clauses for verification. PACMPL **2**(POPL), 11:1–11:28 (2018). https://doi.org/10.1145/3158099
16. Cockett, J.R.B., Gallagher, J.: Categorical models of the differential λ-calculus revisited. Electron. Notes Theor. Comput. Sci. **325**, 63–83 (2016)
17. Compton, K.J.: Stratified least fixpoint logic. Theor. Comput. Sci. **131**(1), 95–120 (1994)
18. Datomic website (2018). https://www.datomic.com. Accessed 01 Jan 2018
19. Dong, G., Su, J.: Incremental maintenance of recursive views using relational calculus/SQL. ACM SIGMOD Rec. **29**(1), 44–51 (2000)
20. Ehrhard, T.: An introduction to differential linear logic: proof-nets, models and antiderivatives. Math. Struct. Comput. Sci. 1–66 (2017)
21. Ehrhard, T., Regnier, L.: The differential lambda-calculus. Theor. Comput. Sci. **309**(1–3), 1–41 (2003)

22. Elliott, C.: The simple essence of automatic differentiation. Proc. ACM Program. Lang. **2**(ICFP), 70 (2018)
23. Griewank, A., Walther, A.: Evaluating Derivatives: Principles and Techniques of Algorithmic Differentiation, vol. 105. SIAM, Philadelphia (2008)
24. Griffin, T., Libkin, L., Trickey, H.: An improved algorithm for the incremental recomputation of active relational expressions. IEEE Trans. Knowl. Data Eng. **3**, 508–511 (1997)
25. Gupta, A., Mumick, I.S., Subrahmanian, V.S.: Maintaining views incrementally. ACM SIGMOD Rec. **22**(2), 157–166 (1993)
26. Halpin, T., Rugaber, S.: LogiQL: A Query Language for Smart Databases. CRC Press, Boca Raton (2014)
27. Harrison, J.V., Dietrich, S.W.: Maintenance of materialized views in a deductive database: an update propagation approach. In: Workshop on Deductive Databases, JICSLP, pp. 56–65 (1992)
28. Kelly, R., Pearlmutter, B.A., Siskind, J.M.: Evolving the incremental λ calculus into a model of forward automatic differentiation (AD). arXiv preprint arXiv:1611.03429 (2016)
29. Kerjean, M., Tasson, C.: Mackey-complete spaces and power series-a topological model of differential linear logic. Math. Struct. Comput. Sci. 1–36 (2016)
30. Kilp, M., Knauer, U., Mikhalev, A.V.: Monoids, Acts and Categories: With Applications to Wreath Products and Graphs. A Handbook for Students and Researchers, vol. 29. Walter de Gruyter, Berlin (2000)
31. Kucukelbir, A., Tran, D., Ranganath, R., Gelman, A., Blei, D.M.: Automatic differentiation variational inference. J. Mach. Learn. Res. **18**(1), 430–474 (2017)
32. LogicBlox Inc. website (2018). http://www.logicblox.com. Accessed 01 Jan 2018
33. Manzyuk, O.: A simply typed λ-calculus of forward automatic differentiation. Electron. Notes Theor. Comput. Sci. **286**, 257–272 (2012)
34. de Moor, O., Baars, A.: Doing a doaitse: simple recursive aggregates in datalog. In: Liber Amicorum for Doaitse Swierstra, pp. 207–216 (2013). http://www.staff.science.uu.nl/~hage0101/liberdoaitseswierstra.pdf. Accessed 01 Jan 2018
35. Qian, X., Wiederhold, G.: Incremental recomputation of active relational expressions. IEEE Trans. Knowl. Data Eng. **3**(3), 337–341 (1991)
36. Sáenz-Pérez, F.: DES: a deductive database system. Electron. Notes Theor. Comput. Sci. **271**, 63–78 (2011)
37. Schäfer, M., de Moor, O.: Type inference for datalog with complex type hierarchies. In: ACM SIGPLAN Notices, vol. 45, pp. 145–156. ACM (2010)
38. Scholz, B., Jordan, H., Subotić, P., Westmann, T.: On fast large-scale program analysis in datalog. In: Proceedings of the 25th International Conference on Compiler Construction, pp. 196–206. ACM (2016)
39. Semmle Ltd. website (2018). https://semmle.com. Accessed 01 Jan 2018
40. Sereni, D., Avgustinov, P., de Moor, O.: Adding magic to an optimising datalog compiler. In: Proceedings of the 2008 ACM SIGMOD International Conference on Management of Data, pp. 553–566. ACM (2008)
41. Siskind, J.M., Pearlmutter, B.A.: Nesting forward-mode AD in a functional framework. High.-Order Symb. Comput. **21**(4), 361–376 (2008)
42. Souffle language website (2018). http://souffle-lang.org. Accessed 01 Jan 2018
43. Urpi, T., Olive, A.: A method for change computation in deductive databases. In: VLDB, vol. 92, pp. 225–237 (1992)

Incremental λ-Calculus in Cache-Transfer Style
Static Memoization by Program Transformation

Paolo G. Giarrusso[1(✉)], Yann Régis-Gianas[2], and Philipp Schuster[3]

[1] LAMP—EPFL, Lausanne, Switzerland
[2] IRIF, University of Paris Diderot, Inria, Paris, France
[3] University of Tübingen, Tübingen, Germany

Abstract. Incremental computation requires propagating changes and reusing intermediate results of base computations. Derivatives, as produced by static differentiation [7], propagate changes but do not reuse intermediate results, leading to wasteful recomputation. As a solution, we introduce conversion to *Cache-Transfer-Style*, an additional program transformations producing purely incremental functional programs that create and maintain nested tuples of intermediate results. To prove CTS conversion correct, we extend the correctness proof of static differentiation from STLC to untyped λ-calculus via *step-indexed logical relations*, and prove sound the additional transformation via simulation theorems.

To show ILC-based languages can improve performance relative to from-scratch recomputation, and that CTS conversion can extend its applicability, we perform an initial performance case study. We provide derivatives of primitives for operations on collections and incrementalize selected example programs using those primitives, confirming expected asymptotic speedups.

1 Introduction

After computing a base output from some base input, we often need to produce updated outputs corresponding to updated inputs. Instead of rerunning the same *base program* on the updated input, incremental computation transforms the input change to an output change, potentially reducing asymptotic time complexity and significantly improving efficiency, especially for computations running on large data sets.

Incremental λ-Calculus (ILC) [7] is a recent framework for *higher-order* incremental computation. ILC represents changes from a base value v_1 to an updated value v_2 as a first-class *change value* dv. Since functions are first-class values, change values include *function changes*.

ILC also statically transforms *base programs* to *incremental programs* or *derivatives*, that are functions mapping input changes to output changes. Incremental language designers can then provide their language with (higher-order) primitives (with their derivatives) that efficiently encapsulate incrementalizable

L. Caires (Ed.): ESOP 2019, LNCS 11423, pp. 553–580, 2019.
https://doi.org/10.1007/978-3-030-17184-1_20

computation skeletons (such as tree-shaped folds), and ILC will incrementalize higher-order programs written in terms of these primitives.

Alas, ILC only incrementalizes efficiently *self-maintainable computations* [7, Sect. 4.3], that is, computations whose output changes can be computed using only input changes, but not the inputs themselves [11]. Few computations are self-maintainable: for instance, mapping self-maintainable functions on a sequence is self-maintainable, but dividing numbers is not! We elaborate on this problem in Sect. 2.1. In this paper, we extend ILC to non-self-maintainable computations. To this end, we must enable derivatives to reuse intermediate results created by the base computation.

Many incrementalization approaches remember intermediate results through dynamic memoization: they typically use hashtables to memoize function results, or dynamic dependence graphs [1] to remember a computation trace. However, looking up intermediate results in such dynamic data structure has a runtime cost that is hard to optimize; and reasoning on dynamic dependence graphs and computation traces is often complex. Instead, ILC produces purely functional programs, suitable for further optimizations and equational reasoning.

To that end, we replace dynamic memoization with *static memoization*: following Liu and Teitelbaum [20], we transform programs to *cache-transfer style (CTS)*. A CTS function outputs their primary result along with *caches* of intermediate results. These caches are just nested tuples whose structure is derived from code, and accessing them does not involve looking up keys depending on inputs. Instead, intermediate results can be fetched from these tuples using statically known locations. To integrate CTS with ILC, we extend differentiation to produce *CTS derivatives*: these can extract from caches any intermediate results they need, and produce updated caches for the next computation step.

The correctness proof of static differentiation in CTS is challenging. First, we must show a forward simulation relation between two triples of reduction traces (the first triple being made of the source base evaluation, the source updated evaluation and the source derivative evaluation; the second triple being made of the corresponding CTS-translated evaluations). Dealing with six distinct evaluation environments at the same time was error prone on paper and for this reason, we conducted the proof using Coq [26]. Second, the simulation relation must not only track values but also caches, which are only partially updated while in the middle of the evaluation of derivatives. Finally, we study the translation for an untyped λ-calculus, while previous ILC correctness proofs were restricted to simply-typed λ-calculus. Hence, we define which changes are valid via a *logical relation* and show its *fundamental property*. Being in an untyped setting, our logical relation is not indexed by types, but *step-indexed*. We study an untyped language, but our work also applies to the erasure of typed languages. Formalizing a type-preserving translation is left for future work because giving a type to CTS programs is challenging, as we shall explain.

In addition to the correctness proof, we present preliminary experimental results from three case studies. We obtain efficient incremental programs even on non self-maintainable functions.

We present our contributions as follows. First, we summarize ILC and illustrate the need to extend it to remember intermediate results via CTS (Sect. 2). Second, in our mechanized formalization (Sect. 3), we give a novel proof of correctness for ILC differentiation for untyped λ-calculus, based on step-indexed logical relations (Sect. 3.4). Third, building on top of ILC differentiation, we show how to transform untyped higher-order programs to CTS (Sect. 3.5) and we show that CTS functions and derivatives *simulate* correctly their non-CTS counterparts (Sect. 3.7). Finally, in our case studies (Sect. 4), we compare the performance of the generated code to the base programs. Section 4.4 discusses limitations and future work. Section 5 discusses related work and Sect. 6 concludes. Our mechanized proof in Coq, the case study material, and the extended version of this paper with appendixes are available online at https://github.com/yurug/cts.

2 ILC and CTS Primer

In this section we exemplify ILC by applying it on an average function, show why the resulting incremental program is asymptotically inefficient, and use CTS conversion and differentiation to incrementalize our example efficiently and speed it up asymptotically (as confirmed by benchmarks in Sect. 4.1). Further examples in Sect. 4 apply CTS to higher-order programs and suggest that CTS enables incrementalizing efficiently some core database primitives such as joins.

2.1 Incrementalizing *average* via ILC

Our example computes the average of a bag of numbers. After computing the *base output* y_1 of the average function on the *base input* bag xs_1, we want to update the output in response to a stream of updates to the input bag. Here and throughout the paper, we contrast *base* vs *updated* inputs, outputs, values, computations, and so on. For simplicity, we assume we have two *updated inputs* xs_2 and xs_3 and want to compute two *updated outputs* y_2 and y_3. We express this program in Haskell as follows:

$$\begin{aligned}
&\mathit{average} && :: \mathit{Bag}\ \mathbb{Z} \to \mathbb{Z}\\
&\mathit{average}\ xs && = \mathbf{let}\ s = \mathit{sum}\ xs; n = \mathit{length}\ xs; r = \mathit{div}\ s\ n\ \mathbf{in}\ r\\
&\mathit{average}_3 && = \mathbf{let}\ y_1 = \mathit{average}\ xs_1; y_2 = \mathit{average}\ xs_2; y_3 = \mathit{average}\ xs_3\\
& && \quad\ \mathbf{in}\ (y_1, y_2, y_3)
\end{aligned}$$

To compute the updated outputs y_2 and y_3 in $\mathit{average}_3$ faster, we try using ILC. For that, we assume that we receive not only updated inputs xs_2 and xs_3 but also *input change* dxs_1 from xs_1 to xs_2 and input change dxs_2 from xs_2 to xs_3. A change dx from x_1 to x_2 describes the changes from base value x_1 to updated value x_2, so that x_2 can be computed via the *update operator* $\oplus$ as $x_1 \oplus dx$. A nil change $\mathbf{0}_x$ is a change from base value x to updated value x itself.

ILC differentiation automatically transforms the *average* function to its derivative $daverage :: Bag\ \mathbb{Z} \to \Delta(Bag\ \mathbb{Z}) \to \Delta\mathbb{Z}$. A derivative maps input changes to output changes: here, $dy_1 = daverage\ xs_1\ dxs_1$ is a change from base output $y_1 = average\ xs_1$ to updated output $y_2 = average\ xs_2$, hence $y_2 = y_1 \oplus dy_1$.

Thanks to *daverage*'s correctness, we can rewrite $average_3$ to avoid expensive calls to *average* on updated inputs and use *daverage* instead:

$$
\begin{array}{l}
incrementalAverage_3 :: (\mathbb{Z}, \mathbb{Z}, \mathbb{Z}) \\
incrementalAverage_3 = \\
\quad \textbf{let}\ y_1 = average\ xs_1; dy_1 = daverage\ xs_1\ dxs_1 \\
\qquad\quad y_2 = y_1 \oplus dy_1; dy_2 = daverage\ xs_2\ dxs_2 \\
\qquad\quad y_3 = y_2 \oplus dy_2 \\
\quad \textbf{in}\ \ (y_1, y_2, y_3)
\end{array}
$$

In general, also the value of a function $f :: A \to B$ can change from a base value f_1 to an updated value f_2, mainly when f is a closure over changing data. In that case, the change from base output $f_1\ x_1$ to updated output $f_2\ x_2$ is given by $df\ x_1\ dx$, where $df :: A \to \Delta A \to \Delta B$ is now a *function change* from f_1 to f_2. Above, *average* exemplifies the special case where $f_1 = f_2 = f$: then the function change df is a nil change, and $df\ x_1\ dx$ is a change from $f_1\ x_1 = f\ x_1$ and $f_2\ x_2 = f\ x_2$. That is, a nil function change for f is a derivative of f.

2.2 Self-maintainability and Efficiency of Derivatives

Alas, derivatives are efficient only if they are *self-maintainable*, and *daverage* is not, so $incrementalAverage_3$ is no faster than $average_3$! Consider the result of differentiating *average*:

$$
\begin{array}{l}
daverage :: Bag\ \mathbb{Z} \to \Delta(Bag\ \mathbb{Z}) \to \Delta\mathbb{Z} \\
daverage\ xs\ dxs = \textbf{let}\ s = sum\ xs; ds = dsum\ xs\ dxs; \\
\qquad\qquad\qquad\qquad\quad n = length\ xs; dn = dlength\ xs\ dxs; \\
\qquad\qquad\qquad\qquad\quad r = div\ s\ n; dr = ddiv\ s\ ds\ n\ dn \\
\qquad\qquad\qquad\quad \textbf{in}\ dr
\end{array}
$$

Just like *average* combines *sum*, *length*, and *div*, its derivative *daverage* combines those functions and their derivatives. *daverage* recomputes base intermediate results s, n and r exactly as done in *average*, because they might be needed as base inputs of derivatives. Since r is unused, its recomputation can be dropped during later optimizations, but expensive intermediate results s and n are used by *ddiv*:

$$
\begin{array}{l}
ddiv :: \mathbb{Z} \to \Delta\mathbb{Z} \to \mathbb{Z} \to \Delta\mathbb{Z} \to \Delta\mathbb{Z} \\
ddiv\ a\ da\ b\ db = div\ (a \oplus da)\ (b \oplus db) - div\ a\ b
\end{array}
$$

Function *ddiv* computes the difference between the updated and the original result, so it needs its base inputs a and b. Hence, *daverage* must recompute s and n and will be slower than *average*!

Typically, ILC derivatives are only efficient if they are *self-maintainable*: a self-maintainable derivative does not inspect its base inputs, but only its change inputs, so recomputation of its base inputs can be elided. Cai et al. [7] leave efficient support for non-self-maintainable derivatives for future work.

But this problem is fixable: executing *daverage xs dxs* will compute exactly the same s and n as executing *average xs*, so to avoid recomputation we must simply save s and n and reuse them. Hence, we CTS-convert each function f to a *CTS function fC* and a *CTS derivative dfC*: CTS function *fC* produces, together with its final result, a *cache* containing intermediate results, that the caller must pass to CTS derivative *dfC*.

CTS-converting our example produces the following code, which requires no wasteful recomputation.

$$
\begin{array}{l}
\textbf{type}\ \mathit{AverageC} = (\mathbb{Z}, \mathit{SumC}, \mathbb{Z}, \mathit{LengthC}, \mathbb{Z}, \mathit{DivC}) \\
\mathit{averageC} :: \mathit{Bag}\ \mathbb{Z} \rightarrow (\mathbb{Z}, \mathit{AverageC}) \\
\mathit{averageC}\ \mathit{xs} = \\
\quad \textbf{let}\ (s, cs_1) = \mathit{sumC}\ \mathit{xs}; (n, cn_1) = \mathit{lengthC}\ \mathit{xs}; (r, cr_1) = \mathit{divC}\ s\ n \\
\quad \textbf{in}\ \ (r, (s, cs_1, n, cn_1, r, cr_1)) \\
\mathit{daverageC} :: \mathit{Bag}\ \mathbb{Z} \rightarrow \Delta(\mathit{Bag}\ \mathbb{Z}) \rightarrow \mathit{AverageC} \rightarrow (\Delta\mathbb{Z}, \mathit{AverageC}) \\
\mathit{daverageC}\ \mathit{xs}\ \mathit{dxs}\ (s, cs_1, n, cn_1, r, cr_1) = \\
\quad \textbf{let}\ (ds, cs_2)\ \ = \mathit{dsumC}\ \mathit{xs}\ \mathit{dxs}\ cs_1 \\
\qquad\ \ (dn, cn_2) = \mathit{dlengthC}\ \mathit{xs}\ \mathit{dxs}\ cn_1 \\
\qquad\ \ (dr, cr_2)\ \ = \mathit{ddivC}\ s\ ds\ n\ dn\ cr_1 \\
\quad \textbf{in}\ \ (dr, ((s \oplus ds), cs_2, (n \oplus dn), cn_2, (r \oplus dr), cr_2))
\end{array}
$$

For each function f, we introduce a type *FC* for its cache, such that a CTS function *fC* has type $A \rightarrow (B, FC)$ and CTS derivative *dfC* has type $A \rightarrow \Delta A \rightarrow FC \rightarrow (\Delta B, FC)$. Crucially, CTS derivatives like *daverageC* must return an updated cache to ensure correct incrementalization, so that application of further changes works correctly. In general, if $(y_1, c_1) = fC\ x_1$ and $(dy, c_2) = dfC\ x_1\ dx\ c_1$, then $(y_1 \oplus dy, c_2)$ must equal the result of the base function *fC* applied to the updated input $x_1 \oplus dx$, that is $(y_1 \oplus dy, c_2) = fC\ (x_1 \oplus dx)$.

For CTS-converted functions, the cache type *FC* is a tuple of intermediate results and caches of subcalls. For primitive functions like *div*, the cache type *DivC* could contain information needed for efficient computation of output changes. In the case of *div*, no additional information is needed. The definition of *divC* uses *div* and produces an empty cache, and the definition of *ddivC* follows the earlier definition for *ddiv*, except that we now pass along an empty cache.

$$
\begin{array}{l}
\textbf{data}\ \mathit{DivC} = \mathit{DivC} \\
\mathit{divC} :: \mathbb{Z} \rightarrow \mathbb{Z} \rightarrow (\mathbb{Z}, \mathit{DivC}) \\
\mathit{divC}\ a\ b = (\mathit{div}\ a\ b, \mathit{DivC}) \\
\mathit{ddivC} :: \mathbb{Z} \rightarrow \Delta\mathbb{Z} \rightarrow \mathbb{Z} \rightarrow \Delta\mathbb{Z} \rightarrow \mathit{DivC} \rightarrow (\Delta\mathbb{Z}, \mathit{DivC}) \\
\mathit{ddivC}\ a\ da\ b\ db\ \mathit{DivC} = (\mathit{div}\ (a \oplus da)\ (b \oplus db) - \mathit{div}\ a\ b, \mathit{DivC})
\end{array}
$$

Finally, we can rewrite $average_3$ to incrementally compute y_2 and y_3:

$$\begin{array}{l}
\mathit{ctsIncrementalAverage}_3 :: (\mathbb{Z}, \mathbb{Z}, \mathbb{Z}) \\
\mathit{ctsIncrementalAverage}_3 = \\
\quad \mathbf{let}\ (y_1, c_1) = \mathit{averageC}\ xs_1; (dy_1, c_2) = \mathit{daverageC}\ xs_1\ dxs_1\ c_1 \\
\quad\quad\quad y_2 = y_1 \oplus dy_1; (dy_2, c_3) = \mathit{daverageC}\ xs_2\ dxs_2\ c_2 \\
\quad\quad\quad y_3 = y_2 \oplus dy_2 \\
\quad \mathbf{in}\ (y_1, y_2, y_3)
\end{array}$$

Since functions of the same type translate to CTS functions of different types, in a higher-order language CTS translation is not always type-preserving; however, this is not a problem for our case studies (Sect. 4); Sect. 4.1 shows how to map such functions, and we return to this problem in Sect. 4.4.

3 Formalization

We now formalize CTS-differentiation for an untyped Turing-complete λ-calculus, and formally prove it sound with respect to differentiation. We also give a novel proof of correctness for differentiation itself, since we cannot simply adapt Cai et al. [7]'s proof to the new syntax: Our language is untyped and Turing-complete, while Cai et al. [7]'s proof assumed a strongly normalizing simply-typed λ-calculus and relied on its naive set-theoretic denotational semantics. Our entire formalization is mechanized using Coq [26]. For reasons of space, some details are deferred to the appendix.

	Terms		***Closed values***
$a_t ::= \mathbf{let}\, a_p = a_t\, \mathbf{in}\, a_t$	*Let*	$a_v ::= a_E[\lambda \overline{a_p}.\, a_t]$	*Closure*
$\mid\ a_T$	*Tuple*	$\mid\ (\overline{a_v})$	*Tuple*
$\mid\ f\, \overline{x}$	*Application*	$\mid\ \ell$	*Literal*
	Nested tuples	$\mid\ \mathbf{p}$	*Primitive*
$a_T ::= x$	*Variable*	$\mid\ 0_{\mathbf{p}}$	*Nil change for primitive*
$\mid\ x \oplus dx$	*Update*	$\mid\ !a_v$	*Replacement change*
$\mid\ (\overline{a_T})$	*Tuple*		***Value environments***
	Patterns	$a_E ::= \bullet$	*Empty*
$a_p ::= x$	*Variable*	$\mid\ a_E; x = a_v$	*Value binding*
$\mid\ (\overline{a_p})$	*Tuple*	$j, k, n \in \mathbb{N}$	***Step indexes***

Fig. 1. Our language λ_L of lambda-lifted programs. Tuples can be nullary.

Transformations. We introduce and prove sound three term transformations, namely differentiation, CTS translation and CTS differentiation, that take a function to its corresponding (non-CTS) derivative, CTS function and CTS derivative. Each CTS function produces a base output and a cache from a base input, while each CTS derivative produces an output change and an updated cache from an input, an input change and a base cache.

Proof technique. To show soundness, we prove that CTS functions and derivatives simulate respectively non-CTS functions and derivatives. In turn, we formalize (non-CTS) differentiation as well, and we prove differentiation sound with respect to non-incremental evaluation. Overall, this shows that CTS functions and derivatives are sound relatively to non-incremental evaluation. Our presentation proceeds in the converse order: first, we present differentiation, formulated as a variant of Cai et al. [7]'s definition; then, we study CTS differentiation.

By using logical relations, we simplify significantly the setup of Cai et al. [7]. To handle an untyped language, we employ *step-indexed* logical relations. Besides, we conduct our development with big-step operational semantics because that choice simplifies the correctness proof for CTS conversion. Using big-step semantics for a Turing complete language restricts us to terminating computations. But that is not a problem: to show incrementalization is correct, we need only consider computations that terminate on both old and new inputs, following Acar et al. [3] (compared with in Sect. 5).

Structure of the formalization. Section 3.1 introduces the syntax of the language λ_L we consider in this development, and introduces its four sublanguages λ_{AL}, λ_{IAL}, λ_{CAL} and λ_{ICAL}. Section 3.2 presents the syntax and the semantics of λ_{AL}, the source language for our transformations. Section 3.3 defines differentiation and its target language λ_{IAL}, and Sect. 3.4 proves differentiation correct. Section 3.5 defines CTS conversion, comprising CTS translation and CTS differentiation, and their target languages λ_{CAL} and λ_{ICAL}. Section 3.6 presents the semantics of λ_{CAL}. Finally, Sect. 3.7 proves CTS conversion correct.

Notations. We write $\overline{X}$ for a sequence of X of some unspecified length $X_1, \ldots, X_m$.

3.1 Syntax for λ_L

A superlanguage. To simplify our transformations, we require input programs to have been lambda-lifted [15] and converted to A'-normal form (A'NF). Lambda-lifted programs are convenient because they allow us to avoid a specific treatment for free variables in transformations. A'NF is a minor variant of ANF [24], where every result is bound to a variable before use; unlike ANF, we also bind the result of the tail call. Thus, every result can thus be stored in a cache by CTS conversion and reused later (as described in Sect. 2). This requirement is not onerous: A'NF is a minimal variant of ANF, and lambda-lifting and ANF conversion are routine in compilers for functional languages. Most examples we show are in this form.

In contrast, our transformation's outputs are lambda-lifted but not in A'NF. For instance, we restrict base functions to take exactly one argument—a base input. As shown in Sect. 2.1, CTS functions take instead two arguments—a base input and a cache—and CTS derivatives take three arguments—an input, an input change, and a cache. We could normalize transformation outputs to inhabit the source language and follow the same invariants, but this would complicate our proofs for little benefit. Hence, we do not *prescribe* transformation outputs to satisfy the same invariants, and we rather *describe* transformation outputs through separate grammars.

As a result of this design choice, we consider languages for base programs, derivatives, CTS programs and CTS derivatives. In our Coq mechanization, we formalize those as four separate languages, saving us many proof steps to check the validity of required structural invariants. For simplicity, in this paper we define a single language called λ_L (for λ-Lifted). This language satisfies invariants common to all these languages (including some of the A'NF invariants). Then, we define *sublanguages* of λ_L. We describe the semantics of λ_L informally, and we only formalize the semantics of its sublanguages.

Syntax for terms. The λ_L language is a relatively conventional lambda-lifted λ-calculus with a limited form of pattern matching on tuples. The syntax for terms and values is presented in Fig. 1. We separate terms and values in two distinct syntactic classes because we use big-step operational semantics. Our **let**-bindings are non-recursive as usual, and support shadowing. Terms cannot contain λ-expressions directly, but only refer to closures through the environment, and similarly for literals and primitives; we elaborate on this in Sect. 3.2. We do not introduce case expressions, but only bindings that destructure tuples, both in **let**-bindings and λ-expressions of closures. Our semantics does not assign meaning to match failures, but pattern-matchings are only used in generated programs and our correctness proofs ensure that the matches always succeed. We allow tuples to contain terms of form $x \oplus dx$, which update base values x with changes in dx, because A'NF-converting these updates is not necessary to the transformations. We often inspect the result of a function call "$f\ x$", which is not a valid term in our syntax. Hence, we write "$@(f, x)$" as a syntactic sugar for "$\textbf{let}\ y = f\ x\ \textbf{in}\ y$" with y chosen fresh.

Syntax for closed values. A closed value is either a closure, a tuple of values, a literal, a primitive, a nil change for a primitive or a replacement change. A closure is a pair of an evaluation environment E and a λ-abstraction closed with respect to E. The set of available literals ℓ is left abstract. It may contain usual first-order literals like integers. We also leave abstract the primitives $\mathbf{p}$ like `if-then-else` or projections of tuple components. Each primitive $\mathbf{p}$ comes with a nil change, which is its derivative as explained in Sect. 2. A change value can also represent a replacement by some closed value a_v. Replacement changes are not produced by static differentiation but are useful for clients of derivatives: we include them in the formalization to make sure that they are not incompatible with our system. As usual, environments E map variables to closed values.

Sublanguages of λ_L. The source language for all our transformations is a sublanguage of λ_L named λ_{AL}, where A stands for A'NF. To each transformation we associate a target language, which matches the transformation image. The target language for CTS conversion is named λ_{CAL}, where "C" stands for CTS. The target languages of differentiation and CTS differentiation are called, respectively, λ_{IAL} and λ_{ICAL}, where the "I" stands for incremental.

3.2 The Source Language λ_{AL}

We show the syntax of λ_{AL} in Fig. 2. As said above, λ_{AL} is a sublanguage of λ_L denoting lambda-lifted base terms in A'NF. With no loss of generality, we assume that all bound variables in λ_{AL} programs and closures are distinct. The step-indexed big-step semantics (Fig. 3) for base terms is defined by the judgment written $E \vdash t \Downarrow_n v$ (where n can be omitted) and pronounced "Under environment E, base term t evaluates to closed value v in n steps." Intuitively, our step-indexes count the number of "nodes" of a big-step derivation.[1] As they are relatively standard, we defer the explanations of these rules to Appendix B.

Term differentiation $\boxed{dt = \mathcal{D}^\iota(t)}$

$$\begin{aligned}
\mathcal{D}^\iota(x) &= dx \\
\mathcal{D}^\iota(\textbf{let}\ y = f\ x\ \textbf{in}\ t) &= \\
&\textbf{let}\ y = f\ x, dy = df\ x\ dx\ \textbf{in}\ \mathcal{D}^\iota(t) \\
\mathcal{D}^\iota(\textbf{let}\ y = (\overline{x})\ \textbf{in}\ t) &= \\
&\textbf{let}\ y = (\overline{x}), dy = (\overline{dx})\ \textbf{in}\ \mathcal{D}^\iota(t)
\end{aligned}$$

Value differentiation $\boxed{dv = \mathcal{D}^\iota(v)}$

$$\begin{aligned}
\mathcal{D}^\iota((\overline{v})) &= (\overline{\mathcal{D}^\iota(v)}) \\
\mathcal{D}^\iota(E_f[\lambda x.\, t]) &= \mathcal{D}^\iota(E_f)[\lambda x\ dx.\, \mathcal{D}^\iota(t)] \\
\mathcal{D}^\iota(\ell) &= \textbf{nil}\,\ell \\
\mathcal{D}^\iota(\mathbf{p}) &= 0_{\mathbf{p}}
\end{aligned}$$

Environment differentiation $\boxed{dE = \mathcal{D}^\iota(E)}$

$$\begin{aligned}
\mathcal{D}^\iota(\bullet) &= \bullet \\
\mathcal{D}^\iota(E; x = v) &= \mathcal{D}^\iota(E); x = v; dx = \mathcal{D}^\iota(v)
\end{aligned}$$

Base/updated environment $\boxed{E = \lfloor dE \rfloor_i}$

$$\begin{aligned}
\lfloor \bullet \rfloor_i &= \bullet \qquad i = 1, 2 \\
\lfloor dE; x = v; dx = dv \rfloor_i &= \lfloor dE \rfloor_i; x = v' \\
&\quad v' = v \text{ if } i = 1 \text{ or} \\
&\quad v' = v \oplus dv \text{ if } i = 2
\end{aligned}$$

λ_{IAL} change terms

$$\begin{aligned}
dt ::=\ & dx \\
\mid\ & \textbf{let}\ y = f\ x, dy = df\ x\ dx \\
& \textbf{in}\ dt \\
\mid\ & \textbf{let}\ y = (\overline{x}), dy = (\overline{dx}) \\
& \textbf{in}\ dt
\end{aligned}$$

λ_{IAL} change values

$$\begin{aligned}
dv ::=\ & (\overline{dv}) \mid dE[\lambda x\ dx.\, dt] \mid \\
& d\ell \mid 0_{\mathbf{p}} \mid !v
\end{aligned}$$

λ_{IAL} change environments

$$dE ::= \bullet \mid dE; x = v; dx = dv$$

λ_{AL} base terms

$$\begin{aligned}
t ::=\ & x \mid \textbf{let}\ y = f\ x\ \textbf{in}\ t \mid \\
& \textbf{let}\ y = (\overline{x})\ \textbf{in}\ t
\end{aligned}$$

λ_{AL} closed values

$$v ::= (\overline{v}) \mid E[\lambda x.\, t] \mid \ell \mid \mathbf{p}$$

λ_{AL} value environments

$$E ::= \bullet \mid E; x = v$$

Fig. 2. Static differentiation $\mathcal{D}^\iota(-)$; syntax of its target language λ_{IAL}, tailored to the output of differentiation; syntax of its source language λ_{AL}. We assume that in λ_{IAL} the same **let** binds both y and dy and that α-renaming preserves this invariant. We also define the *base environment* $\lfloor dE \rfloor_1$ and the *updated environment* $\lfloor dE \rfloor_2$ of a change environment dE.

Expressiveness. A closure in the base environment can be used to represent a top-level definition. Since environment entries can point to primitives, we need no syntax to directly represent calls of primitives in the syntax of base terms. To encode in our syntax a program with top-level definitions and a term to be evaluated representing the entry point, one can produce a term t representing the

[1] It is more common to count instead small-step evaluation steps [3,4], but our choice simplifies some proofs and makes a minor difference in others.

$$\text{[SVAR]}\ \frac{}{E \vdash x \Downarrow_1 E(x)} \qquad \text{[STUPLE]}\ \frac{E; y = (E(\overline{x})) \vdash t \Downarrow_n v}{E \vdash \mathbf{let}\, y = (\overline{x})\, \mathbf{in}\, t \Downarrow_{n+1} v} \qquad \text{[SPRIMITIVECALL]}\ \frac{E(f) = \mathbf{p} \quad E; y = \delta_{\mathbf{p}}(E(x)) \vdash t \Downarrow_n v}{E \vdash \mathbf{let}\, y = f\, x\, \mathbf{in}\, t \Downarrow_{n+1} v}$$

$$\text{[SCLOSURECALL]}\ \frac{E(f) = E_f[\lambda x.\, t_f] \qquad E_f; x = E(x) \vdash t_f \Downarrow_m v_y \qquad E; y = v_y \vdash t \Downarrow_n v}{E \vdash \mathbf{let}\, y = f\, x\, \mathbf{in}\, t \Downarrow_{m+n+1} v}$$

Fig. 3. Step-indexed big-step semantics for base terms of source language λ_{AL}.

entry point together with an environment E containing as values any top-level definitions, primitives and literals used in the program. Semi-formally, given an environment E_0 mentioning needed primitives and literals, and a list of top-level function definitions $D = \overline{f = \lambda x.\, t}$ defined in terms of E_0, we can produce a base environment $E = \mathcal{L}(D)$, with $\mathcal{L}$ defined by:

$$\mathcal{L}(\bullet) = E_0 \text{ and } \mathcal{L}(D, f = \lambda x.\, t) = E, f = E[\lambda x.\, t] \text{ where } \mathcal{L}(D) = E$$

Correspondingly, we extend all our term transformations to values and environments to transform such encoded top-level definitions.

Our mechanization can encode n-ary functions "$\lambda(x_1, x_2, \ldots, x_n).\, t$" through unary functions that accept tuples; we encode partial application using a **curry** primitive such that, essentially, $\mathbf{curry}\, f\, x\, y = f\,(x, y)$; suspended partial applications are represented as closures. This encoding does not support currying efficiently, we further discuss this limitation in Sect. 4.4.

Control operators, like recursion combinators or branching, can be introduced as primitive operations as well. If the branching condition changes, expressing the output change in general requires replacement changes. Similarly to branching we can add tagged unions.

To check the assertions of the last two paragraphs, the Coq development contains the definition of a **curry** primitive as well as a primitive for a fixpoint combinator, allowing general recursion and recursive data structures as well.

3.3 Static Differentiation from λ_{AL} to λ_{IAL}

Previous work [7] defines static differentiation for simply-typed λ-calculus terms. Figure 2 transposes differentiation as a transformation from λ_{AL} to λ_{IAL} and defines λ_{IAL}'s syntax.

Differentiating a base term t produces a change term $\mathcal{D}^{\iota}(t)$, its *derivative*. Differentiating final result variable x produces its change variable dx. Differentiation copies each binding of an intermediate result y to the output and adds a new binding for its change dy. If y is bound to tuple $(\overline{x})$, then dy will be bound to the change tuple $(\overline{dx})$. If y is bound to function application "$f\ x$", then dy will be bound to the application of function change df to input x and its change dx. We explain differentiation of environments $\mathcal{D}^{\iota}(E)$ later in this section.

$$\text{[SDVar]}\quad \frac{}{dE \vdash dx \Downarrow_1 dE(dx)}$$

$$\text{[SDTuple]}\quad \frac{dE(\overline{x}, \overline{dx}) = \overline{v}_x, \overline{dv}_x \qquad dE; y = (\overline{v}_x); dy = (\overline{dv}_x) \vdash dt \Downarrow_n dv}{dE \vdash \textbf{let}\ y = (\overline{x}), dy = (\overline{dx})\ \textbf{in}\ dt \Downarrow_{n+1} dv}$$

$$\text{[SDReplaceCall]}\quad \frac{\lfloor dE \rfloor_1 \vdash @(f, x) \Downarrow_m v_y \qquad \lfloor dE \rfloor_2 \vdash @(f, x) \Downarrow_n v_y{}' \qquad dE(df) = !v_f \qquad dE; y = v_y; dy = !v_y{}' \vdash dt \Downarrow_p dv}{dE \vdash \textbf{let}\ y = f\ x, dy = df\ x\ dx\ \textbf{in}\ dt \Downarrow_{m+n+p+1} dv}$$

$$\text{[SDPrimitiveNil]}\quad \frac{dE(f, df) = \mathbf{p}, 0_{\mathbf{p}} \qquad dE(x, dx) = v_x, dv_x \qquad dE; y = \delta_{\mathbf{p}}(v_x); dy = \Delta_{\mathbf{p}}(v_x, dv_x) \vdash dt \Downarrow_n dv}{dE \vdash \textbf{let}\ y = f\ x, dy = df\ x\ dx\ \textbf{in}\ dt \Downarrow_{n+1} dv}$$

$$\text{[SDClosureChange]}\quad \frac{\begin{array}{c} dE(f, df) = E_f[\lambda x.\, t_f], dE_f[\lambda x\ dx.\, dt_f] \\ dE(x, dx) = v_x, dv_x \qquad E_f; x = v_x \vdash t_f \Downarrow_m v_y \\ dE_f; x = v_x; dx = dv_x \vdash dt_f \Downarrow_n dv_y \qquad dE; y = v_y; dy = dv_y \vdash dt \Downarrow_p dv \end{array}}{dE \vdash \textbf{let}\ y = f\ x, dy = df\ x\ dx\ \textbf{in}\ dt \Downarrow_{m+n+p+1} dv}$$

Fig. 4. Step-indexed big-step semantics for the change terms of λ_{IAL}.

Evaluating $\mathcal{D}^\iota(t)$ recomputes all intermediate results computed by t. This recomputation will be avoided through cache-transfer style in Sect. 3.5. A comparison with the original static differentiation [7] can be found in Appendix A.

Semantics for λ_{IAL}. We move on to define how λ_{IAL} change terms evaluate to change values. We start by defining necessary definitions and operations on changes, such as define *change values* dv, *change environments* dE, and the *update operator* $\oplus$.

Closed change values dv are particular λ_L values a_v. They are either a closure change, a tuple change, a literal change, a replacement change or a primitive nil change. A closure change is a closure containing a change environment dE and a λ-abstraction expecting a value and a change value as arguments to evaluate a change term into an output change value. An evaluation environment dE follows the same structure as **let**-bindings of change terms: it binds variables to closed values and each variable x is immediately followed by a binding for its associated change variable dx. As with **let**-bindings of change terms, α-renamings in an environment dE must rename dx into dy if x is renamed into y. We define the *update operator* $\oplus$ to update a value with a change. This operator is a partial function written "$v \oplus dv$", defined as follows:

$$
\begin{aligned}
v_1 \oplus\, !v_2 &= v_2 \\
\ell \oplus d\ell &= \delta_{\oplus}(\ell, d\ell) \\
E[\lambda x.\, t] \oplus dE[\lambda x\; dx.\, dt] &= (E \oplus dE)[\lambda x.\, t] \\
(v_1, \ldots, v_n) \oplus (dv_1, \ldots, dv_n) &= (v_1 \oplus dv_1, \ldots, v_n \oplus dv_n) \\
\mathbf{p} \oplus 0_{\mathbf{p}} &= \mathbf{p}
\end{aligned}
$$

where $(E; x = v) \oplus (dE; x = v; dx = dv) = ((E \oplus dE); x = (v \oplus dv))$.

Replacement changes can be used to update all values (literals, tuples, primitives and closures), while tuple changes can only update tuples, literal changes can only update literals, primitive nil can only update primitives and closure changes can only update closures. A replacement change overrides the current value v with a new one v'. On literals, $\oplus$ is defined via some interpretation function $\delta_{\oplus}$, which takes a literal and a literal change to produce an updated literal. Change update for a closure ignores dt instead of computing something like $dE[t \oplus dt]$. This may seem surprising, but we only need $\oplus$ to behave well for valid changes (as shown by Theorem 3.1): for valid closure changes, dt must behave anyway similarly to $\mathcal{D}^{\iota}(t)$, which Cai et al. [7] show to be a nil change. Hence, $t \oplus \mathcal{D}^{\iota}(t)$ and $t \oplus dt$ both behave like t, so $\oplus$ can ignore dt and only consider environment updates. This definition also avoids having to modify terms at runtime, which would be difficult to implement safely. We could also implement $f \oplus df$ as a function that invokes both f and df on its argument, as done by Cai et al. [7], but we believe that would be less efficient when $\oplus$ is used at runtime. As we discuss in Sect. 3.4, we restrict validity to avoid this runtime overhead.

Having given these definitions, we show in Fig. 4 a step-indexed big-step semantics for change terms, defined through judgment $dE \vdash dt \Downarrow_n dv$ (where n can be omitted). This judgment is pronounced "Under the environment dE, the change term dt evaluates into the closed change value dv in n steps." Rules [SDVar] and [SDTuple] are unsurprising. To evaluate function calls in **let**-bindings "**let** $y = f\ x, dy = df\ x\ dx$ **in** dt" we have three rules, depending on the shape of $dE(df)$. These rules all recompute the value v_y of y in the original environment, but compute differently the change dy to y. If $dE(df)$ replaces the value of f, [SDReplaceCall] recomputes $v'_y = f\ x$ from scratch in the new environment, and bind dy to $!v'_y$ when evaluating the **let** body. If $dE(df)$ is the nil change for primitive $\mathbf{p}$, [SDPrimitiveNil] computes dy by running $\mathbf{p}$'s derivative through function $\Delta_{\mathbf{p}}(-)$. If $dE(df)$ is a closure change, [SDClosureChange] invokes it normally to compute its change dv_y. As we show, if the closure change is valid, its body behaves like f's derivative, hence incrementalizes f correctly.

Closure changes with non-nil environment changes represent partial application of derivatives to non-nil changes; for instance, if f takes a pair and dx is a non-nil change, $0_{\mathbf{curry}}\ f\ df\ x\ dx$ constructs a closure change containing dx, using the derivative of **curry** mentioned in Sect. 3.2. In general, such closure changes do not arise from the rules we show, only from derivatives of primitives.

3.4 A New Soundness Proof for Static Differentiation

In this section, we show that static differentiation is sound (Theorem 3.3) and that Eq. (1) holds:

$$f\ a_2 = f\ a_1 \oplus \mathcal{D}^{\iota}(f)\ a_1\ da \tag{1}$$

whenever da is a valid change from a_1 to a_2 (as defined later). One might want to prove this equation assuming only that $a_1 \oplus da = a_2$, but this is false in general. A direct proof by induction on terms fails in the case for application (ultimately because $f_1 \oplus df = f_2$ and $a_1 \oplus da = a_2$ do not imply that $f_1\ a_1 \oplus df\ a_1\ da = f_2\ a_2$). As usual, this can be fixed by introducing a logical relation. We call ours *validity*: a function change is valid if it turns valid input changes into valid output changes.

- $d\ell \rhd_n \ell \hookrightarrow \delta_{\oplus}(\ell, d\ell)$ • $!v_2 \rhd_n v_1 \hookrightarrow v_2$ • $0_{\mathbf{p}} \rhd_n \mathbf{p} \hookrightarrow \mathbf{p}$
- $(dv_1, \ldots, dv_m) \rhd_n (v_1, \ldots, v_m) \hookrightarrow (v_1', \ldots, v_m')$
  if and only if $(v_1, \ldots, v_m) \oplus (dv_1, \ldots, dv_m) = (v_1', \ldots, v_m')$
  and $\forall k < n,\ \forall i \in [1 \ldots m],\ dv_i \rhd_k v_i \hookrightarrow v_i'$
- $dE[\lambda x\ dx.\ dt] \rhd_n E_1[\lambda x.\ t] \hookrightarrow E_2[\lambda x.\ t]$
  if and only if $E_2 = E_1 \oplus dE$ and
  $\forall k < n, v_1, dv, v_2,$
  if $dv \rhd_k v_1 \hookrightarrow v_2$ then
  $(dE; x = v_1; dx = dv \vdash dt) \blacktriangleright_k (E_1; x = v_1 \vdash t) \hookrightarrow (E_2; x = v_2 \vdash t)$
- $(dE \vdash dt) \blacktriangleright_n (E_1 \vdash t_1) \hookrightarrow (E_2 \vdash t_2)$
  if and only if $\forall k < n, v_1, v_2,$
  $E_1 \vdash t_1 \Downarrow_k v_1$ and $E_2 \vdash t_2 \Downarrow v_2$ implies that
  $\exists dv, dE \vdash dt \Downarrow dv \wedge dv \rhd_{n-k} v_1 \hookrightarrow v_2$

Fig. 5. Step-indexed validity, through judgments for values and for terms.

Static differentiation is only sound on input changes that are *valid*. Cai et al. [7] show soundness for a strongly normalizing simply-typed λ-calculus using denotational semantics. Using an operational semantics, we generalize this result to an untyped and Turing-complete language, so we must turn to a *step-indexed* logical relation [3,4].

Validity as a step-indexed logical relation. We say that "dv is a valid change from v_1 to v_2, up to k steps" and write

$$dv \rhd_k v_1 \hookrightarrow v_2$$

to mean that dv is a change from v_1 to v_2 and that dv is a *valid* description of the differences between v_1 and v_2, with validity tested with up to k steps. This relation *approximates* validity; if a change dv is valid at all approximations, it is simply valid (between v_1 and v_2); we write then $dv \rhd v_1 \hookrightarrow v_2$ (omitting the step-index k) to mean that validity holds at all step-indexes. We similarly omit step-indexes k from other step-indexed relations when they hold for all k.

To justify this intuition of validity, we show that a valid change from v_1 to v_2 goes indeed from v_1 to v_2 (Theorem 3.1), and that if a change is valid up to k steps, it is also valid up to fewer steps (Lemma 3.2).

Theorem 3.1 ($\oplus$ agrees with validity)
If $dv \rhd_k v_1 \hookrightarrow v_2$ holds for all $k > 0$, then $v_1 \oplus dv = v_2$.

Lemma 3.2 (Downward-closure)
If $N \geq n$, then $dv \rhd_N v_1 \hookrightarrow v_2$ implies $dv \rhd_n v_1 \hookrightarrow v_2$.

Crucially, Theorem 3.1 enables (a) computing v_2 from a valid change and its source, and (b) showing Eq. (1) through validity. As discussed, $\oplus$ ignores changes to closure bodies to be faster, which is only sound if those changes are nil; to ensure Theorem 3.1 still holds, validity on closure changes must be adapted accordingly and forbid non-nil changes to closure bodies. This choice, while unusual, does not affect our results: if input changes do not modify closure bodies, intermediate changes will not modify closure bodies either. Logical relation experts might regard this as a domain-specific invariant we add to our relation. Alternatives are discussed by Giarrusso [10, Appendix C].

As usual with step-indexing, validity is defined by well-founded induction over naturals ordered by $<$; to show well-foundedness we observe that evaluation always takes at least one step.

Validity for values, terms and environments is formally defined by cases in Fig. 5. First, a literal change $d\ell$ is a valid change from ℓ to $\ell \oplus d\ell = \delta_{\oplus}(\ell, d\ell)$. Since the function $\delta_{\oplus}$ is partial, the relation only holds for the literal changes $d\ell$ which are valid changes for ℓ. Second, a replacement change $!v_2$ is always a valid change from any value v_1 to v_2. Third, a primitive nil change is a valid change between any primitive and itself. Fourth, a tuple change is valid up to step n, if each of its components is valid up to any step strictly less than n. Fifth, we define validity for closure changes. Roughly speaking, this statement means that a closure change is valid if (i) its environment change dE is valid for the original closure environment E_1 and for the new closure environment E_2; and (ii) when applied to related values, the closure *bodies* t are related by dt, as defined by the auxiliary judgment $(dE \vdash dt) \blacktriangleright_n (E_1 \vdash t_1) \hookrightarrow (E_2 \vdash t_2)$ for validity between terms under related environments (defined in Appendix C). As usual with step-indexed logical relations, in the definition for this judgment about terms, the number k of steps required to evaluate the term t_1 is subtracted from the number of steps n that can be used to relate the outcomes of the term evaluations.

Soundness of differentiation. We can state a soundness theorem for differentiation without mentioning step-indexes; thanks to this theorem, we can compute the updated result v_2 not by rerunning a computation, but by updating the base result v_1 with the result change dv that we compute through a derivative on the input change. A corollary shows Eq. (1).

Theorem 3.3 (Soundness of differentiation in λ_{AL}). *If dE is a valid change environment from base environment E_1 to updated environment E_2, that is $dE \rhd E_1 \hookrightarrow E_2$, and if t converges both in the base and updated environment, that is $E_1 \vdash t \Downarrow v_1$ and $E_2 \vdash t \Downarrow v_2$, then $\mathcal{D}^{\iota}(t)$ evaluates under the change environment dE to a valid change dv between base result v_1 and updated result v_2, that is $dE \vdash \mathcal{D}^{\iota}(t) \Downarrow dv$, $dv \rhd v_1 \hookrightarrow v_2$ and $v_1 \oplus dv = v_2$.*

We must first show that derivatives map input changes valid up to k steps to output changes valid up to k steps, that is, the *fundamental property* of our step-indexed logical relation:

Lemma 3.4 (Fundamental Property)
For each n, if $dE \rhd_n E_1 \hookrightarrow E_2$ then $(dE \vdash \mathcal{D}^{\iota}(t)) \blacktriangleright_n (E_1 \vdash t) \hookrightarrow (E_2 \vdash t)$.

Translation of terms $\boxed{M = \mathcal{T}_t(t')}$

$$\mathcal{T}_t(\textbf{let}\, y = f\, x\, \textbf{in}\, t') = \textbf{let}\, y, c^y_{fx} = f\, x\, \textbf{in}\, \mathcal{T}_t(t')$$
$$\mathcal{T}_t(\textbf{let}\, y = (\overline{x})\, \textbf{in}\, t') = \textbf{let}\, y = (\overline{x})\, \textbf{in}\, \mathcal{T}_t(t')$$
$$\mathcal{T}_t(x) = (x, \mathcal{C}(t))$$

Cache of a term $\boxed{C = \mathcal{C}(t)}$

$$\mathcal{C}(\textbf{let}\, y = f\, x\, \textbf{in}\, t) = ((\mathcal{C}(t), y), c^y_{fx})$$
$$\mathcal{C}(\textbf{let}\, y = (\overline{x})\, \textbf{in}\, t) = (\mathcal{C}(t), y)$$
$$\mathcal{C}(x) = ()$$

Translation of values $\boxed{V = \mathcal{T}(v)}$

$$\mathcal{T}((\overline{v})) = (\overline{\mathcal{T}(v)})$$
$$\mathcal{T}(E[\lambda x.\, t]) = \mathcal{T}(E)[\lambda x.\, \mathcal{T}_t(t)]$$
$$\mathcal{T}(\ell) = \ell$$
$$\mathcal{T}(\mathbf{p}) = \mathbf{p}$$

Base terms

$$M ::= \textbf{let}\, y, c^y_{fx} = f\, x\, \textbf{in}\, M \mid \textbf{let}\, y = (\overline{x})\, \textbf{in}\, M \mid (x, C)$$

Cache terms/patterns

$$C ::= (C, c^y_{fx}) \mid (C, x) \mid ()$$

Closed values

$$V ::= (\overline{V}) \mid F[\lambda x.\, M] \mid \ell \mid \mathbf{p}$$

Cache values

$$V_c ::= () \mid (V_c, V_c) \mid (V_c, V)$$

Evaluation environments

$$F ::= \bullet \mid F; D_v$$

Base environment entries

$$D_v ::= x = V \mid c^y_{fx} = V_c$$

Fig. 6. Cache-Transfer Style translation and syntax of its target language λ_{CAL}.

3.5 CTS Conversion

Figures 6 and 7 define both the syntax of λ_{CAL} and λ_{ICAL} and CTS conversion. The latter comprises CTS differentiation $\mathcal{D}(-)$, from λ_{AL} to λ_{ICAL}, and CTS translation $\mathcal{T}(-)$, from λ_{AL} to λ_{CAL}.

Syntax definitions for the target languages λ_{CAL} and λ_{ICAL}. Terms of λ_{CAL} follow again λ-lifted A'NF, like λ_{AL}, except that a **let**-binding for a function application "$f\, x$" now binds an extra *cache identifier* c^y_{fx} besides output y. Cache identifiers have non-standard syntax: it can be seen as a triple that refers to the value identifiers f, x and y. Hence, an α-renaming of one of these three identifiers must refresh the cache identifier accordingly. Result terms explicitly return cache C through syntax (x, C). Caches are encoded through nested tuples, but they are in fact a tree-like data structure that is isomorphic to an execution trace. This trace contains both immediate values and the execution traces of nested function calls.

The syntax for λ_{ICAL} matches the image of the CTS derivative and witnesses the CTS discipline followed by the derivatives: to determine dy, the derivative of f evaluated at point x with change dx expects the cache produced by evaluating y in the base term. The derivative returns the updated cache which contains the intermediate results that would be gathered by the evaluation of $f\ (x \oplus dx)$. The result term of every change term returns the computed change and a cache update dC, where each value identifier x of the input cache is updated with its corresponding change dx.

Differentiation of terms $\boxed{dM = \mathcal{D}_t(t')}$

$$\mathcal{D}_t(\textbf{let}\ y = f\ x\ \textbf{in}\ t') = \textbf{let}\ dy, c^y_{fx} = df\ x\ dx\ c^y_{fx}\ \textbf{in}\ \mathcal{D}_t(t')$$
$$\mathcal{D}_t(\textbf{let}\ y = (\overline{x})\ \textbf{in}\ t') = \textbf{let}\ dy = (\overline{dx})\ \textbf{in}\ \mathcal{D}_t(M')$$
$$\mathcal{D}_t(x) = (dx, \mathcal{U}(t))$$

Cache update of a term $\boxed{dC = \mathcal{U}(t)}$

$$\mathcal{U}(\textbf{let}\ y = f\ x\ \textbf{in}\ t) = ((\mathcal{U}(t), y \oplus dy), c^y_{fx})$$
$$\mathcal{U}(\textbf{let}\ y = (\overline{x})\ \textbf{in}\ t) = (\mathcal{U}(t), y \oplus dy)$$
$$\mathcal{U}(x) = ()$$

Differentiation of change values $\boxed{dV = \mathcal{T}(dv)}$

$$\mathcal{T}((\overline{dv})) = (\overline{\mathcal{T}(dv)})$$
$$\mathcal{T}(dE[\lambda x\ dx. \mathcal{D}^{\iota}(t)]) = \mathcal{T}(dE)[\lambda x\ dx\ (\mathcal{C}(t)). \mathcal{D}_t(t)]$$
$$\mathcal{T}(!v) = !\mathcal{T}(v)$$
$$\mathcal{T}(d\ell) = d\ell$$
$$\mathcal{T}(0_{\mathbf{p}}) = 0_{\mathbf{p}}$$

Change terms

$$dM ::= \textbf{let}\ dy, c^y_{fx} = df\ x\ dx\ c^y_{fx}\ \textbf{in}\ dM \mid \textbf{let}\ dy = (\overline{dx})\ \textbf{in}\ dM \mid (dx, dC)$$

Cache updates

$$dC ::= (dC, c^y_{fx}) \mid (dC, x \oplus dx) \mid ()$$

Change values

$$dV ::= (\overline{dV}) \mid dF[\lambda x\ dx\ C.\ dM] \mid d\ell \mid 0_{\mathbf{p}} \mid !V$$

Change environments

$$dF ::= \bullet \mid dF; dD_v$$

Change environment entries

$$dD_v ::= D_v \mid dx = dV$$

Fig. 7. CTS differentiation and syntax of its target language λ_{ICAL}. Beware $\mathcal{T}(dE[\lambda x\ dx. \mathcal{D}^{\iota}(t)])$ applies a left-inverse of $\mathcal{D}^{\iota}(t)$ during pattern matching.

CTS conversion and differentiation. These translations use two auxiliary functions: $\mathcal{C}(t)$ which computes the cache term of a λ_{AL} term t, and $\mathcal{U}(t)$, which computes the cache update of t's derivative.

CTS translation on terms, $\mathcal{T}_t(t')$, accepts as inputs a *global* term t and a subterm t' of t. In tail position ($t' = x$), the translation generates code to return both the result x and the cache $\mathcal{C}(t)$ of the global term t. When the transformation visits **let**-bindings, it outputs extra bindings for caches c^y_{fx} on function calls and visits the **let**-body.

Similarly to $\mathcal{T}_t(t')$, CTS derivation $\mathcal{D}_t(t')$ accepts a global term t and a subterm t' of t. In tail position, the translation returns both the result change dx and the cache update $\mathcal{U}(t)$. On **let**-bindings, it *does not* output bindings for y but for dy, it outputs extra bindings for c^y_{fx} as in the previous case and visits the **let**-body.

To handle function definitions, we transform the base environment E through $\mathcal{T}(E)$ and $\mathcal{T}(\mathcal{D}^{\iota}(E))$ (translations of environments are done pointwise, see Appendix D). Since $\mathcal{D}^{\iota}(E)$ includes E, we describe $\mathcal{T}(\mathcal{D}^{\iota}(E))$ to also cover $\mathcal{T}(E)$. Overall, $\mathcal{T}(\mathcal{D}^{\iota}(E))$ CTS-converts each source closure $f = E[\lambda x. t]$ to a CTS-translated function, with body $\mathcal{T}_t(t)$, and to the CTS derivative df of f. This CTS derivative pattern matches on its input cache using cache pattern $\mathcal{C}(t)$. That way, we make sure that the shape of the cache expected by df is consistent with the shape of the cache produced by f. The body of derivative df is computed by CTS-deriving f's body via $\mathcal{D}_t(t)$.

3.6 Semantics of λ_{CAL} and λ_{ICAL}

An evaluation environment F of λ_{CAL} contains both values and cache values. Values V resemble λ_{AL} values v, cache values V_c match cache terms C and change values dV match λ_{IAL} change values dv. Evaluation environments dF for change terms must also bind change values, so functions in change closures take not just a base input x and an input change dx, like in λ_{IAL}, but also an input cache C. By abuse of notation, we reuse the same syntax C to both deconstruct and construct caches.

Base terms of the language are evaluated using a conventional big-step semantics, consisting of two judgments. Judgment "$F \vdash M \Downarrow (V, V_c)$" is read "Under evaluation environment F, base term M evaluates to value V and cache V_c". The semantics follows the one of λ_{AL}; since terms include extra code to produce and carry caches along the computation, the semantics evaluates that code as well. For space reasons, we defer semantic rules to Appendix E. Auxiliary judgment "$F \vdash C \Downarrow V_c$" evaluates cache terms into cache values: It traverses a cache term and looks up the environment for the values to be cached.

Change terms of λ_{ICAL} are also evaluated using a big-step semantics, which resembles the semantics of λ_{IAL} and λ_{CAL}. Unlike those semantics, evaluating cache updates $(dC, x \oplus dx)$ is evaluated using the $\oplus$ operator (overloaded on λ_{CAL} values and λ_{ICAL} changes). By lack of space, its rules are deferred to Appendix E. This semantics relies on three judgments. Judgment "$dF \vdash dM \Downarrow (dV, V_c)$" is read "Under evaluation environment F, change term dM evaluates to change value dV and updated cache V_c". The first auxiliary judgment "$dF \vdash dC \Downarrow V_c$" defines evaluation of cache update terms. The final auxiliary judgment "$V_c \sim C \rightarrow dF$" describes a limited form of pattern matching used by CTS derivatives: namely, how a cache pattern C matches a cache value V_c to produce a change environment dF.

3.7 Soundness of CTS Conversion

The proof is based on a simulation in lock-step, but two subtle points emerge. First, we must relate λ_{AL} environments that do not contain caches, with λ_{CAL} environments that do. Second, while evaluating CTS derivatives, the evaluation environment mixes caches from the base computation and updated caches computed by the derivatives.

Theorem 3.7 follows because differentiation is sound (Theorem 3.3) and evaluation commutes with CTS conversion; this last point requires two lemmas. First, CTS translation of base terms commutes with our semantics:

Lemma 3.5 (Commutation for base evaluations)
For all E, t *and* v, *if* $E \vdash t \Downarrow v$, *there exists* V_c, $\mathcal{T}(E) \vdash \mathcal{T}_t(t) \Downarrow (\mathcal{T}(v), V_c)$.

Second, we need a corresponding lemma for CTS translation of differentiation results: intuitively, evaluating a derivative and CTS translating the resulting change value must give the same result as evaluating the CTS derivative. But to formalize this, we must specify which environments are used for evaluation, and this requires two technicalities.

Assume derivative $\mathcal{D}^{\iota}(t)$ evaluates correctly in some environment dE. Evaluating CTS derivative $\mathcal{D}_t(t)$ requires cache values from the base computation, but they are not in $\mathcal{T}(dE)$! Therefore, we must introduce a judgment to complete a CTS-translated environment with the appropriate caches (see Appendix F).

Next, consider evaluating a change term of the form $dM = \mathbb{C}[dM']$, where $\mathbb{C}$ is a standard single-hole change-term context—that is, for λ_{ICAL}, a sequence of **let**-bindings. When evaluating dM, we eventually evaluate dM' in a change environment dF updated by $\mathbb{C}$: the change environment dF contains both the updated caches coming from the evaluation of $\mathbb{C}$ and the caches coming from the base computation (which will be updated by the evaluation of dM). Again, a new judgment, given in Appendix F, is required to model this process.

With these two judgments, the second key Lemma stating the commutation between evaluation of derivatives and evaluation of CTS derivatives can be stated. We give here an informal version of this Lemma, the actual formal version can be found in Appendix F.

Lemma 3.6 (Commutation for derivatives evaluation)
If the evaluation of $\mathcal{D}^{\iota}(t)$ *leads to an environment* dE_0 *when it reaches the differentiated context* $\mathcal{D}^{\iota}(\mathbb{C})$ *where* $t = \mathbb{C}[t']$, *and if the CTS conversion of* t *under this environment completed with base (resp. changed) caches evaluates into a base value* $\mathcal{T}(v)$ *(resp. a changed value* $\mathcal{T}(v')$*) and a base cache value* V_c *(resp. an updated cache value* V_c'*), then under an environment containing the caches already updated by the evaluation of* $\mathcal{D}^{\iota}(\mathbb{C})$ *and the base caches to be updated, the CTS derivative of* t' *evaluates to* $\mathcal{T}(dv)$ *such that* $v \oplus dv = v'$ *and to the updated cache* V_c'.

Finally, we can state soundness of CTS differentiation. This theorem says that CTS derivatives not only produce valid changes for incrementalization but that they also correctly consume and update caches.

Theorem 3.7 (Soundness of CTS differentiation)
If the following hypotheses hold:

1. $dE \triangleright E \hookrightarrow E'$
2. $E \vdash t \Downarrow v$
3. $E' \vdash t \Downarrow v'$

then there exists dv, V_c, V_c' *and* F_0 *such that:*

1. $\mathcal{T}(E) \vdash \mathcal{T}(t) \Downarrow (\mathcal{T}(v), V_c)$
2. $\mathcal{T}(E') \vdash \mathcal{T}(t) \Downarrow (\mathcal{T}(v'), V_c')$
3. $\mathcal{C}(t) \sim V_c \rightarrow F_0$
4. $\mathcal{T}(dE); F_0 \vdash \mathcal{D}_t(t) \Downarrow (\mathcal{T}(dv), V_c')$
5. $v \oplus dv = v'$

4 Incrementalization Case Studies

In this section, we investigate two questions: whether our transformations can target a typed language like Haskell and whether automatically transformed programs can perform well. We implement by hand primitives on sequences, bags and maps in Haskell. The input terms in all case studies are written in a deep embedding of λ_{AL} into Haskell. The transformations generate Haskell code that uses our primitives and their derivatives.

We run the transformations on three case studies: a computation of the average value of a bag of integers, a nested loop over two sequences and a more involved example inspired by Koch et al. [17]'s work on incrementalizing database queries. For each case study, we make sure that results are consistent between from scratch recomputation and incremental evaluation; we measure the execution time for from scratch recomputation and incremental computation as well as the space consumption of caches. We obtain efficient incremental programs, that is ones for which incremental computation is faster than from scratch recomputation. The measurements indicate that we do get the expected asymptotic improvement in time of incremental computation over from scratch recomputation by a linear factor while the caches grows in a similar linear factor.

Our benchmarks were compiled by GHC 8.2.2 and run on a 2.20 GHz hexa core Intel(R) Xeon(R) CPU E5-2420 v2 with 32 GB of RAM running Ubuntu 14.04. We use the *criterion* [21] benchmarking library.

4.1 Averaging Bags of Integers

Section 2.1 motivates our transformation with a running example of computing the average over a bag of integers. We represent bags as maps from elements to (possibly negative) multiplicities. Earlier work [7,17] represents bag changes as bags of removed and added elements. We use a different representation of bag changes that takes advantage of the changes to elements and provide primitives on bags and their derivatives. The CTS variant of *map*, that we call *mapC*, takes a function *fC* in CTS and a bag *as* and produces a bag and a cache. The cache stores for each invocation of *fC*, and therefore for each distinct element in *as*, the result of *fC* of type *b* and the cache of type *c*.

Inspired by Rossberg et al. [23], all higher-order functions (and typically, also their caches) are parametric over cache types of their function arguments. Here, functions *mapC* and *dmapC* and cache type *MapC* are parametric over the cache type *c* of *fC* and *dfC*.

$$map :: (a \to b) \to Bag\ a \to Bag\ b$$
$$\mathbf{data}\ MapC\ a\ b\ c = MapC\ (Map\ a\ (b, c))$$
$$mapC :: (a \to (b, c)) \to Bag\ a \to (Bag\ b, MapC\ a\ b\ c)$$
$$dmapC :: (a \to (b, c)) \to (a \to \Delta a \to c \to (\Delta b, c)) \to Bag\ a \to \Delta(Bag\ a) \to MapC\ a\ b\ c \to (\Delta(Bag\ b), MapC\ a\ b\ c)$$

We wrote the *length* and *sum* functions used in our benchmarks in terms of primitives *map* and *foldGroup* and had their CTS function and CTS derivative generated automatically.

We evaluate whether we can produce an updated result with *daverageC* shown in Sect. 2.1 faster than by from scratch recomputation with *average*. We expect the speedup of *daverageC* to depend on the size of the input bag n. We fix an input bag of size n as the bag containing the numbers from 1 to n. We define a change that inserts the integer 1 into the bag. To measure execution time of from scratch recomputation, we apply *average* to the input bag updated with the change. To measure execution time of the CTS function *averageC*, we apply *averageC* to the input bag updated with the change. To measure execution time of the CTS derivative *daverageC*, we apply *daverageC* to the input bag, the change and the cache produced by *averageC* when applied to the input bag. In all three cases we ensure that all results and caches are fully forced so as to not hide any computational cost behind laziness.

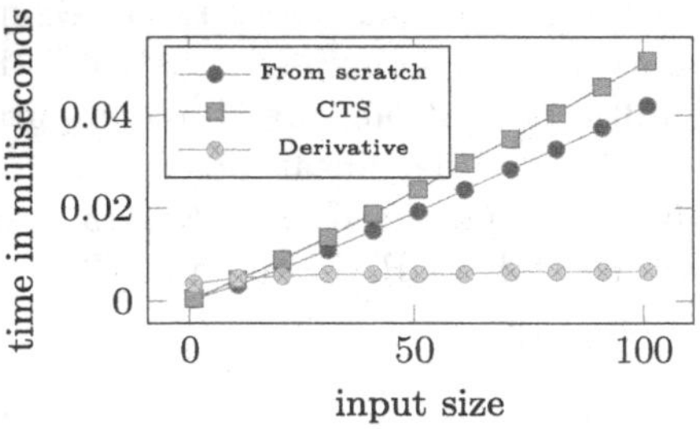

(a) Benchmark results for *average*

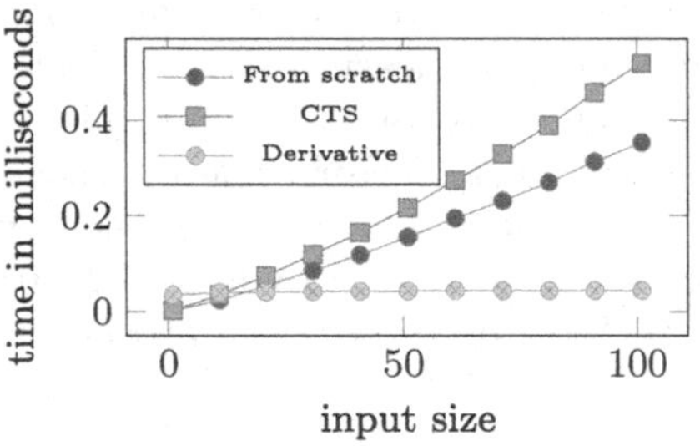

(b) Benchmark results for *totalPrice*

Fig. 8. Benchmark results for *average* and *totalPrice*

The plot in Fig. 8a shows execution time versus the size n of the base input. To produce the base result and cache, the CTS transformed function *averageC* takes longer than the original *average* function takes to produce just the result. Producing the updated result incrementally is slower than from scratch recomputation for small input sizes, but because of the difference in time complexity becomes faster as the input size grows. The size of the cache grows linearly with the size of the input, which is not optimal for this example. We leave optimizing the space usage of examples like this to future work.

4.2 Nested Loops over Two Sequences

Next, we consider CTS differentiation on a higher-order example. To incrementalize this example efficiently, we have to enable detecting nil function changes at runtime by representing function changes as closures that can be inspected by incremental programs. Our example here is the Cartesian product of two sequences computed in terms of functions *map* and *concat*.

$$\begin{aligned}&\mathit{cartesianProduct} :: \mathit{Sequence}\ a \to \mathit{Sequence}\ b \to \mathit{Sequence}\ (a, b)\\&\mathit{cartesianProduct}\ \mathit{xs}\ \mathit{ys} = \mathit{concatMap}\ (\lambda x \to \mathit{map}\ (\lambda y \to (x, y))\ \mathit{ys})\ \mathit{xs}\end{aligned}$$

$$\begin{aligned}&\mathit{concatMap} :: (a \to \mathit{Sequence}\ b) \to \mathit{Sequence}\ a \to \mathit{Sequence}\ b\\&\mathit{concatMap}\ f\ \mathit{xs} = \mathit{concat}\ (\mathit{map}\ f\ \mathit{xs})\end{aligned}$$

We implemented incremental sequences and related primitives following Firsov and Jeltsch [9]: our change operations and first-order operations (such as *concat*) reuse their implementation. On the other hand, we must extend higher-order operations such as *map* to handle non-nil function changes and caching. A correct and efficient CTS derivative *dmapC* has to work differently depending on whether the given function change is nil or not: For a non-nil function change it has to go over the input sequence; for a nil function change it has to avoid that.

Cai et al. [7] use static analysis to conservatively approximate nil function changes as changes to terms that are closed in the original program. But in this example the function argument $(\lambda y \to (x, y))$ to *map* in *cartesianProduct* is not a closed term. It is, however, crucial for the asymptotic improvement that we avoid looping over the inner sequence when the change to the free variable x in the change environment is $\mathbf{0}_x$.

To enable runtime nil change detection, we apply closure conversion to the original program and explicitly construct closures and changes to closures. While the only valid change for closed functions is their nil change, for closures we can have non-nil function changes. A function change *df*, represented as a closure change, is nil exactly when all changes it closes over are nil.

We represent closed functions and closures as variants of the same type. Correspondingly we represent changes to a closed function and changes to a closure as variants of the same type of function changes. We inspect this representation at runtime to find out if a function change is a nil change.

$$\begin{aligned}&\mathbf{data}\ \mathit{Fun}\ a\ b\ c\ \mathbf{where}\\&\quad \mathit{Closed} :: (a \to (b, c)) \to \mathit{Fun}\ a\ b\ c\\&\quad \mathit{Closure} :: (e \to a \to (b, c)) \to e \to \mathit{Fun}\ a\ b\ c\\&\mathbf{data}\ \Delta(\mathit{Fun}\ a\ b\ c)\ \mathbf{where}\\&\quad \mathit{DClosed} :: (a \to \Delta a \to c \to (\Delta b, c)) \to \Delta(\mathit{Fun}\ a\ b\ c)\\&\quad \mathit{DClosure} :: (e \to \Delta e \to a \to \Delta a \to c \to (\Delta b, c)) \to e \to \Delta e \to \Delta(\mathit{Fun}\ a\ b\ c)\end{aligned}$$

We use the same benchmark setup as in the benchmark for the average computation on bags. The input of size n is a pair of sequences $(\mathit{xs}, \mathit{ys})$. Each sequence initially contains the integers from 1 to n. Updating the result in reaction to a change dxs to the outer sequence xs takes less time than updating the result in reaction to a change dys to the inner sequence ys. While a change to the outer sequence xs results in an easily located change in the output sequence, a change for the inner sequence ys results in a change that needs a lot more calculation to find the elements it affects. We benchmark changes to the outer sequence xs and the inner sequence ys separately where the change to one sequence is the insertion of a single integer 1 at position 1 and the change for the other one is the nil change.

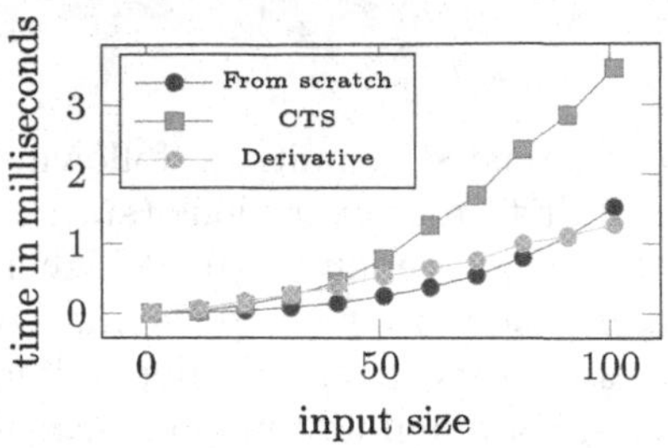

(a) Benchmark results for Cartesian product changing *inner* sequence.

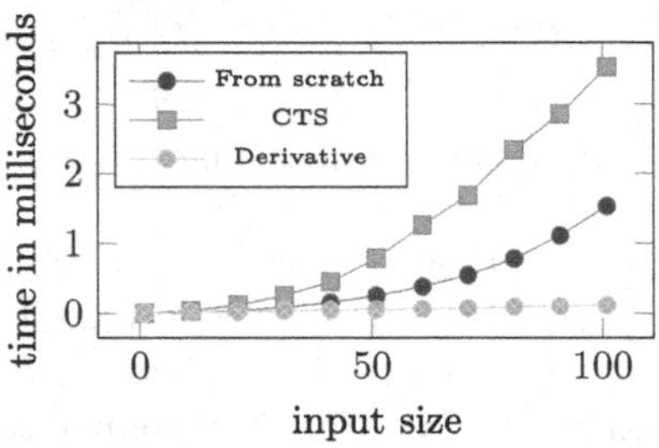

(b) Benchmark results for Cartesian product changing *outer* sequence.

Fig. 9. Benchmark results for *cartesianProduct*

Figure 9 shows execution time versus input size. In this example again preparing the cache takes longer than from scratch recomputation alone. The speedup of incremental computation over from scratch recomputation increases with the size of the base input sequences because of the difference in time complexity. Eventually we do get speedups for both kinds of changes (to the inner and to the outer sequence), but for changes to the outer sequence we get a speedup earlier, at a smaller input size. The size of the cache grows super linearly in this example.

4.3 Indexed Joins of Two Bags

Our goal is to show that we can compose primitive functions into larger and more complex programs and apply CTS differentiation to get a fast incremental program. We use an example inspired from the DBToaster literature [17]. In this example we have a bag of orders and a bag of line items. An order is a pair of an order key and an exchange rate. A line item is a pair of an order key and a price. We build an index mapping each order key to the sum of all exchange rates of the orders with this key and an index from order key to the sum of the prices of all line items with this key. We then merge the two maps by key, multiplying corresponding sums of exchange rates and sums of prices. We compute the total price of the orders and line items as the sum of those products.

$$
\begin{array}{l}
\textbf{type}\ \mathit{Order} = (\mathbb{Z}, \mathbb{Z}) \\
\textbf{type}\ \mathit{LineItem} = (\mathbb{Z}, \mathbb{Z}) \\
\mathit{totalPrice} :: \mathit{Bag}\ \mathit{Order} \rightarrow \mathit{Bag}\ \mathit{LineItem} \rightarrow \mathbb{Z} \\
\mathit{totalPrice}\ \mathit{orders}\ \mathit{lineItems} = \textbf{let} \\
\quad \mathit{orderIndex} = \mathit{groupBy}\ \mathit{fst}\ \mathit{orders} \\
\quad \mathit{orderSumIndex} = \mathit{Map.map}\ (\mathit{Bag.foldMapGroup}\ \mathit{snd})\ \mathit{orderIndex} \\
\quad \mathit{lineItemIndex} = \mathit{groupBy}\ \mathit{fst}\ \mathit{lineItems} \\
\quad \mathit{lineItemSumIndex} = \mathit{Map.map}\ (\mathit{Bag.foldMapGroup}\ \mathit{snd})\ \mathit{lineItemIndex} \\
\quad \mathit{merged} = \mathit{Map.merge}\ \mathit{orderSumIndex}\ \mathit{lineItemSumIndex} \\
\quad \mathit{total} = \mathit{Map.foldMapGroup}\ \mathit{multiply}\ \mathit{merged} \\
\quad \textbf{in}\ \mathit{total} \\
\mathit{groupBy} :: (a \rightarrow k) \rightarrow \mathit{Bag}\ a \rightarrow \mathit{Map}\ k\ (\mathit{Bag}\ a) \\
\mathit{groupBy}\ \mathit{keyOf}\ \mathit{bag} = \\
\quad \mathit{Bag.foldMapGroup}\ (\lambda a \rightarrow \mathit{Map.singleton}\ (\mathit{keyOf}\ a)\ (\mathit{Bag.singleton}\ a))\ \mathit{bag}
\end{array}
$$

Unlike DBToaster, we assume our program is already transformed to explicitly use indexes, as above. Because our indexes are maps, we implemented a change structure, CTS primitives and their CTS derivatives for maps.

To build the indexes, we use a *groupBy* function built from primitive functions *foldMapGroup* on bags and *singleton* for bags and maps respectively. The CTS function *groupByC* and the CTS derivative *dgroupByC* are automatically generated. While computing the indexes with *groupBy* is self-maintainable, merging them is not. We need to cache and incrementally update the intermediately created indexes to avoid recomputing them.

We evaluate the performance in the same way we did in the other case studies. The input of size n is a pair of bags where both contain the pairs (i, i) for i between 1 and n. The change is an insertion of the order $(1, 1)$ into the orders bag. For sufficiently large inputs, our CTS derivative of the original program produces updated results much faster than from scratch recomputation, again because of a difference in time complexity as indicated by Fig. 8b. The size of the cache grows linearly with the size of the input in this example. This is unavoidable, because we need to keep the indexes.

4.4 Limitations and Future Work

Typing of CTS programs. Functions of the same type $f_1, f_2 :: A \rightarrow B$ can be transformed to CTS functions $f_1 :: A \rightarrow (B, C_1), f_2 :: A \rightarrow (B, C_2)$ with different cache types C_1, C_2, since cache types depend on the implementation. This heterogeneous typing of translated functions poses difficult typing issues, e.g. what is the translated type of a *list* $(A \rightarrow B)$? We cannot hide cache types behind existential quantifiers because they would be too abstract for derivatives, which only work on very specific cache types. We can fix this problem with some runtime overhead by using a single type *Cache*, defined as a tagged union of all cache types or, maybe with more sophisticated type systems—like first-class translucent sums, open existentials or Typed Adapton's refinement types [12]—that could be able to correctly track down cache types properly.

In any case, we believe that these machineries would add a lot of complexity without helping much with the proof of correctness. Indeed, the simulation relation is more handy here because it maintains a global invariant about the whole evaluations (typically the consistency of cache types between base computations and derivatives), not many local invariants about values as types would.

One might wonder why caches could not be totally hidden from the programmer by embedding them in the derivatives themselves; or in other words, why we did not simply translate functions of type $A \to B$ into functions of type $A \to B \times (\Delta A \to \Delta B)$. We tried this as well; but unlike automatic differentiation, we must remember and update caches according to input changes (especially when receiving a sequence of such changes as in Sect. 2.1). Returning the updated cache to the caller works; we tried closing over the caches in the derivative, but this ultimately fails (because we could receive function changes to the original function, but those would need access to such caches).

Comprehensive performance evaluation. This paper focuses on theory and we leave benchmarking in comparison to other implementations of incremental computation to future work. The examples in our case study were rather simple (except perhaps for the indexed join). Nevertheless, the results were encouraging and we expect them to carry over to more complex examples, but not to all programs. A comparison to other work would also include a comparison of space usage for auxiliary data structure, in our case the caches.

Cache pruning via absence analysis. To reduce memory usage and runtime overhead, it should be possible to automatically remove from transformed programs any caches or cache fragments that are not used (directly or indirectly) to compute outputs. Liu [19] performs this transformation on CTS programs by using *absence analysis*, which was later extended to higher-order languages by Sergey et al. [25]. In lazy languages, absence analysis removes thunks that are not needed to compute the output. We conjecture that the analysis could remove unused caches or inputs, if it is extended to *not* treat caches as part of the output.

Unary vs n-ary abstraction. We only show our transformation correct for unary functions and tuples. But many languages provide efficient support for applying curried functions such as $div :: \mathbb{Z} \to \mathbb{Z} \to \mathbb{Z}$. Naively transforming such a curried function to CTS would produce a function $divC$ of type $\mathbb{Z} \to (\mathbb{Z} \to (\mathbb{Z}, DivC_2)), DivC_1$ with $DivC_1 = ()$, which adds excessive overhead. In Sect. 2 and our evaluation we use curried functions and never need to use this naive encoding, but only because we always invoke functions of known arity.

5 Related Work

Cache-transfer-style. Liu [19]'s work has been the fundamental inspiration to this work, but her approach has no correctness proof and is restricted to a first-order untyped language. Moreover, while the idea of cache-transfer-style is similar, it's unclear if her approach to incrementalization would extend to higher-order programs. Firsov and Jeltsch [9] also approach incrementalization by code transformation, but their approach does not deal with changes to functions. Instead of transforming functions written in terms of primitives, they provide combinators to write CTS functions and derivatives together. On the other hand, they extend their approach to support mutable caches, while restricting to immutable ones as we do might lead to a logarithmic slowdown.

Finite differencing. Incremental computation on collections or databases by finite differencing has a long tradition [6,22]. The most recent and impressive line of work is the one on DBToaster [16,17], which is a highly efficient approach to incrementalize queries over bags by combining iterated finite differencing with other program transformations. They show asymptotic speedups both in theory and through experimental evaluations. Changes are only allowed for datatypes that form groups (such as bags or certain maps), but not for instance for lists or sets. Similar ideas were recently extended to higher-order and nested computation [18], though only for datatypes that can be turned into groups. Koch et al. [18] emphasize that iterated differentiation is necessary to obtain efficient derivatives; however, ANF conversion and remembering intermediate results appear to address the same problem, similarly to the field of automatic differentiation [27].

Logical relations. To study correctness of incremental programs we use a logical relation among base values v_1, updated values v_2 and changes dv. To define a logical relation for an untyped λ-calculus we use a *step-indexed* logical relation, following Ahmed [4], Appel and McAllester [5]; in particular, our definitions are closest to the ones by Acar et al. [3], who also work with an untyped language, big-step semantics and (a different form of) incremental computation. However, they do not consider first-class changes. Technically, we use environments rather than substitution, and index our big-step semantics differently.

Dynamic incrementalization. The approaches to incremental computation with the widest applicability are in the family of self-adjusting computation [1,2], including its descendant Adapton [14]. These approaches incrementalize programs by combining memoization and change propagation: after creating a trace of base computations, updated inputs are compared with old ones in $O(1)$ to find corresponding outputs, which are updated to account for input modifications. Compared to self-adjusting computation, Adapton only updates results that are demanded. As usual, incrementalization is not efficient on arbitrary programs, but only on programs designed so that input changes produce small changes to the computation trace; refinement type systems have been designed to assist in this task [8,12]. To identify matching inputs, Nominal Adapton [13] replaces input comparisons by pointer equality with first-class labels, enabling more reuse.

6 Conclusion

We have presented a program transformation which turns a functional program into its derivative and efficiently shares redundant computations between them thanks to a statically computed cache.

Although our first practical case studies show promising results, this paper focused on putting CTS differentiation on solid theoretical ground. For the moment, we only have scratched the surface of the incrementalization opportunities opened by CTS primitives and their CTS derivatives: in our opinion, exploring the design space for cache data structures will lead to interesting new results in purely functional incremental programming.

Acknowledgments. We are grateful to anonymous reviewers: they made important suggestions to help us improve our technical presentation. We also thank Cai Yufei, Tillmann Rendel, Lourdes del Carmen González Huesca, Klaus Ostermann, Sebastian Erdweg for helpful discussions on this project. This work was partially supported by DFG project 282458149 and by SNF grant No. 200021_166154.

References

1. Acar, U.A.: Self-adjusting computation. Ph.D. thesis, Carnegie Mellon University (2005)
2. Acar, U.A.: Self-adjusting computation: (an overview). In: PEPM, pp. 1–6. ACM (2009)
3. Acar, U.A., Ahmed, A., Blume, M.: Imperative self-adjusting computation. In: Proceedings of the 35th Annual ACM SIGPLAN-SIGACT Symposium on Principles of Programming Languages, POPL 2008, pp. 309–322. ACM, New York (2008). https://doi.acm.org/10.1145/1328438.1328476
4. Ahmed, A.: Step-indexed syntactic logical relations for recursive and quantified types. In: Sestoft, P. (ed.) ESOP 2006. LNCS, vol. 3924, pp. 69–83. Springer, Heidelberg (2006). https://doi.org/10.1007/11693024_6
5. Appel, A.W., McAllester, D.: An indexed model of recursive types for foundational proof-carrying code. ACM Trans. Program. Lang. Syst. **23**(5), 657–683 (2001). https://doi.acm.org/10.1145/504709.504712
6. Blakeley, J.A., Larson, P.A., Tompa, F.W.: Efficiently updating materialized views. In: SIGMOD, pp. 61–71. ACM (1986)
7. Cai, Y., Giarrusso, P.G., Rendel, T., Ostermann, K.: A theory of changes for higher-order languages—incrementalizing λ-calculi by static differentiation. In: Proceedings of the 35th ACM SIGPLAN Conference on Programming Language Design and Implementation, PLDI 2014, pp. 145–155. ACM, New York (2014). https://doi.acm.org/10.1145/2594291.2594304
8. Çiçek, E., Paraskevopoulou, Z., Garg, D.: A type theory for incremental computational complexity with control flow changes. In: Proceedings of the 21st ACM SIGPLAN International Conference on Functional Programming, ICFP 2016, pp. 132–145. ACM, New York (2016)

9. Firsov, D., Jeltsch, W.: Purely functional incremental computing. In: Castor, F., Liu, Y.D. (eds.) SBLP 2016. LNCS, vol. 9889, pp. 62–77. Springer, Cham (2016). https://doi.org/10.1007/978-3-319-45279-1_5
10. Giarrusso, P.G.: Optimizing and incrementalizing higher-order collection queries by AST transformation. Ph.D. thesis, University of Tübingen (2018). Defended. http://inc-lc.github.io/
11. Gupta, A., Mumick, I.S.: Maintenance of materialized views: problems, techniques, and applications. In: Gupta, A., Mumick, I.S. (eds.) Materialized Views, pp. 145–157. MIT Press (1999)
12. Hammer, M.A., Dunfield, J., Economou, D.J., Narasimhamurthy, M.: Typed adapton: refinement types for incremental computations with precise names. October 2016 arXiv:1610.00097 [cs]
13. Hammer, M.A., et al.: Incremental computation with names. In: Proceedings of the 2015 ACM SIGPLAN International Conference on Object-Oriented Programming, Systems, Languages, and Applications, OOPSLA 2015, pp. 748–766. ACM, New York (2015). https://doi.acm.org/10.1145/2814270.2814305
14. Hammer, M.A., Phang, K.Y., Hicks, M., Foster, J.S.: Adapton: composable, demand-driven incremental computation. In: Proceedings of the 35th ACM SIGPLAN Conference on Programming Language Design and Implementation, PLDI 2014, pp. 156–166. ACM, New York (2014)
15. Johnsson, T.: Lambda lifting: transforming programs to recursive equations. In: Jouannaud, J.-P. (ed.) FPCA 1985. LNCS, vol. 201, pp. 190–203. Springer, Heidelberg (1985). https://doi.org/10.1007/3-540-15975-4_37
16. Koch, C.: Incremental query evaluation in a ring of databases. In: Symposium Principles of Database Systems (PODS), pp. 87–98. ACM (2010)
17. Koch, C., et al.: DBToaster: higher-order delta processing for dynamic, frequently fresh views. VLDB J. **23**(2), 253–278 (2014). https://doi.org/10.1007/s00778-013-0348-4
18. Koch, C., Lupei, D., Tannen, V.: Incremental view maintenance for collection programming. In: Proceedings of the 35th ACM SIGMOD-SIGACT-SIGAI Symposium on Principles of Database Systems, PODS 2016, pp. 75–90. ACM, New York (2016)
19. Liu, Y.A.: Efficiency by incrementalization: an introduction. HOSC **13**(4), 289–313 (2000)
20. Liu, Y.A., Teitelbaum, T.: Caching intermediate results for program improvement. In: Proceedings of the 1995 ACM SIGPLAN Symposium on Partial Evaluation and Semantics-based Program Manipulation, PEPM 1995, pp. 190–201. ACM, New York (1995). https://doi.acm.org/10.1145/215465.215590
21. O'Sullivan, B.: criterion: a Haskell microbenchmarking library (2014). http://www.serpentine.com/criterion/
22. Paige, R., Koenig, S.: Finite differencing of computable expressions. TOPLAS **4**(3), 402–454 (1982)
23. Rossberg, A., Russo, C.V., Dreyer, D.: F-ing modules. In: Proceedings of the 5th ACM SIGPLAN Workshop on Types in Language Design and Implementation, TLDI 2010, pp. 89–102. ACM, New York (2010)
24. Sabry, A., Felleisen, M.: Reasoning about programs in continuation-passing style. LISP Symb. Comput. **6**(3–4), 289–360 (1993)
25. Sergey, I., Vytiniotis, D., Peyton Jones, S.: Modular, higher-order cardinality analysis in theory and practice. In: Proceedings of the 41st ACM SIGPLAN-SIGACT Symposium on Principles of Programming Languages, POPL 2014, pp. 335–347. ACM, New York (2014)

26. The Coq Development Team: The Coq proof assistant reference manual, version 8.8 (2018). http://coq.inria.fr
27. Wang, F., Wu, X., Essertel, G., Decker, J., Rompf, T.: Demystifying differentiable programming: shift/reset the penultimate backpropagator. Technical report (2018). https://arxiv.org/abs/1803.10228

Concurrency and Distribution

Asynchronous Timed Session Types
From Duality to Time-Sensitive Processes

Laura Bocchi[1(✉)], Maurizio Murgia[1,4], Vasco Thudichum Vasconcelos[2], and Nobuko Yoshida[3]

[1] University of Kent, Canterbury, UK
l.bocchi@kent.ac.uk
[2] LASIGE, Faculty of Sciences, University of Lisbon, Lisbon, Portugal
[3] Imperial College London, London, UK
[4] University of Cagliari, Cagliari, Italy

Abstract. We present a behavioural typing system for a higher-order timed calculus using session types to model timed protocols. Behavioural typing ensures that processes in the calculus perform actions in the time-windows prescribed by their protocols. We introduce duality and subtyping for timed asynchronous session types. Our notion of duality allows typing a larger class of processes with respect to previous proposals. Subtyping is critical for the precision of our typing system, especially in the presence of session delegation. The composition of dual (timed asynchronous) types enjoys progress when using an urgent receive semantics, in which receive actions are executed as soon as the expected message is available. Our calculus increases the modelling power of extant calculi on timed sessions, adding a blocking receive primitive with timeout and a primitive that consumes an arbitrary amount of time in a given range.

Keywords: Session types · Timers · Duality · π-calculus

1 Introduction

Time is at the basis of many real-life protocols. These include common client-server interactions as for example, *"An SMTP server SHOULD have a timeout of at least 5 minutes while it is awaiting the next command from the sender"* [22]. By protocol, we intend application-level specifications of interaction patterns (via message passing) among distributed applications. An extensive literature offers theories and tools for formal analysis of timed protocols, modelled for instance as timed automata [3,26,34] or Message Sequence Charts [2]. These works allow to reason on the properties of *protocols*, defined as formal models. Recent work,

This work has been partially supported by EPSRC EP/N035372/1, EP/K011715/1, EP/N027833/1, EP/K034413/1, EP/L00058X/1, EP/N028201/1, Aut. Reg. of Sardinia projects *Sardcoin* and *Smart collaborative engineering*, FCT through project Confident PTDC/EEI-CTP/4503/2014 and the LASIGE Research Unit UID/CEC/00408/2019. We thank Julien Lange for his advise and comments.

L. Caires (Ed.): ESOP 2019, LNCS 11423, pp. 583–610, 2019.
https://doi.org/10.1007/978-3-030-17184-1_21

based on session types, focus on the relationship between time-sensitive protocols, modelled as timed extensions of session types, and their implementations abstracted as *processes* in some timed calculus. The relationship between protocols and processes is given in terms of static behavioural typing [12,15] or run-time monitoring [6,7,30] of processes against types. Existing work on timed session types [7,12,15,30] is based on simple abstractions for processes which do not capture time sensitive primitives such as blocking (as well as non-blocking) receive primitives with timeout and time consuming actions with variable, yet bound, duration. This paper provides a theory of asynchronous timed session types for a calculus that features these two primitives. We focus on the asynchronous scenario, as modern distributed systems (e.g., web) are often based on asynchronous communications via FIFO channels [4,33]. The link between protocols and processes is given in terms of static behavioural typing, checking for punctuality of interactions with respect to protocols prescriptions. Unlike previous work on asynchronous timed session types [12], our type system can check processes against protocols that are *not wait-free*. In wait-free protocols, the time-windows for corresponding send and receive actions have an empty intersection. We illustrate wait-freedom using a protocol modelled as two timed session types, each owning a set of clocks (with no shared clocks between types).

$$S_{\mathtt{C}} = !\mathtt{Command}(x < 5, \{x\}).S'_{\mathtt{C}} \qquad S_{\mathtt{S}} = ?\mathtt{Command}(\mathtt{y} < 5, \{y\}).S'_{\mathtt{S}} \tag{1}$$

The protocol in (1) involves a client $S_{\mathtt{C}}$ with a clock x, and a server $S_{\mathtt{S}}$ with a clock y (with both x and y initially set to 0). Following the protocol, the client must send a message of type `Command` within 5 min, reset x, and continue as $S'_{\mathtt{C}}$. Dually, the server must be ready to receive a command with a timeout of 5 min, reset y, and continue as $S'_{\mathtt{S}}$. The model in (1) is *not wait-free*: the intersection of the time-windows for the send and receive actions is non-empty (the time-windows actually coincide). The protocol in (2), where the server must wait until after the client's deadline to read the message, is wait-free.

$$!\mathtt{Command}(x < 5, \{x\}).S''_{\mathtt{C}} \qquad ?\mathtt{Command}(\mathtt{y} = 5, \{y\}).S''_{\mathtt{S}} \tag{2}$$

Patterns like the one in (1) are common (e.g., the SMPT fragment mentioned at the beginning of this introduction) but, unfortunately, they are *not wait-free*, hence ruled out in previous work [12]. Arguably, (2) is an unpractical wait-free variant of (1): the client must always wait for at least 5 min to have the message read, no matter how early this message was sent. The definition of protocols for our typing system (which allows for *not wait-free* protocols) is based on a notion of *asynchronous timed duality*, and on a subtyping relation that provides accuracy of typing, especially in the case of channel passing.

Asynchronous timed duality. In the untimed scenario, each session type has one unique *dual* that is obtained by changing the polarities of the actions (send vs. receive, and selection vs. branching). For example, the dual of a session type S

that sends an integer and then receives a string is a session type $\overline{S}$ that receives an integer and then sends a string.

$$S = !\texttt{Int}.?\texttt{String} \qquad \overline{S} = ?\texttt{Int}.!\texttt{String}$$

Duality characterises well-behaved systems: the behaviour described by the composition of dual types has no communication mismatches (e.g., unexpected messages, or messages with values of unexpected types) nor deadlocks. In the timed scenario, this is no longer true. Consider a timed extension of session types (using the model of time in timed automata [3]), and of (untimed) duality so that dual send/receive actions have equivalent time constraints and resets. The example below shows a timed type S with its dual $\overline{S}$, where S owns clock x, and $\overline{S}$ owns clock y (with x and y initially set to 0):

$$S = !\texttt{Int}(x \leqslant 1, x).?\texttt{String}(x \leqslant 2) \qquad \overline{S} = ?\texttt{Int}(y \leqslant 1, y).!\texttt{String}(y \leqslant 2)$$

Here S sends an integer at any time satisfying $x \leqslant 1$, and then resets x. After that, S receives a string at any time satisfying $x \leqslant 2$. The timed dual of S is obtained by keeping the same time constraints (and renaming the clock—to make it clear that clocks are not shared). To illustrate our point, we use the semantics from timed session types [12], borrowed from Communicating Timed automata [23]. This semantics is *separated*, in the sense that only time actions may 'take time', while all other actions (e.g., communications) are instantaneous.[1] The aforementioned semantics allows for the following execution of $S \mid \overline{S}$:

$$\begin{array}{lll} S \mid \overline{S} \xrightarrow{0.4}\xrightarrow{\texttt{Int}} & ?\texttt{String}(x \leqslant 2) \mid \overline{S} & (\text{clocks values: } x = 0,\ y = 0.4) \\ \xrightarrow{0.6}\xrightarrow{\texttt{Int}} & ?\texttt{String}(x \leqslant 2) \mid !\texttt{String}(x \leqslant 2) & (\text{clocks values: } x = 0.6,\ y = 0) \\ \xrightarrow{2}\xrightarrow{!\texttt{String}} & ?\texttt{String}(x \leqslant 2) & (\text{clocks values: } x = 2.6,\ y = 2) \end{array}$$

where: (i) the system makes a time step of 0.4, then S sends the integer and resets x, yielding a state where $x = 0$ and $y = 0.4$; (ii) the system makes a time step of 0.6, then $\overline{S}$ receives the integer and resets y, yielding a state where $x = 0.6$ and $y = 0$; (iii) the system makes a time step of 2, then the continuation of $\overline{S}$ sends the string, when $y = 2$ and $x = 2.6$. In (iii), the string was sent too late: constraint $x \leqslant 2$ of the receiving endpoint is now unsatisfiable. The system cannot do any further legal step, and is stuck.

Urgent receive semantics. The example above shows that, in the timed asynchronous scenario, the straightforward extension of duality to the timed scenario does not necessarily characterise well-behaved communications. We argue, however, that the execution of $S \mid \overline{S}$, in particular the time reduction with label 0.6, does not reflect the semantics of most common receive primitives. In fact, most mainstream programming languages implement *urgent receive* semantics

[1] Separated semantics can describe situations where actions have an associated duration.

for receive actions. We call a semantics *urgent receive* when receive actions are executed as soon as the expected message is available, given that the guard of that action is satisfied. Conversely, *non-urgent receive* semantics allows receive actions to fire at any time satisfying the time constraint, as long as the message is in the queue. The aforementioned reduction with label 0.6 is permitted by non-urgent receive semantics such as the one in [23], since it defers the reception of the integer despite the integer being ready for reception and the guard ($y \leqslant 2$) being satisfied, but not by urgent receive semantics. Urgent receive semantics allows, instead, the following execution for $S \mid \overline{S}$:

$$
\begin{array}{lll}
S \mid \overline{S} \xrightarrow{0.4} \xrightarrow{!\mathtt{int}} & ?\mathtt{String}(x \leqslant 2) \mid \overline{S} & \text{(clocks values: } x = 0,\ y = 0.4) \\
\xrightarrow{?\mathtt{int}} & ?\mathtt{String}(x \leqslant 2) \mid !\mathtt{String}(x \leqslant 2) & \text{(clocks values: } x = 0,\ y = 0) \\
\xrightarrow{2} \xrightarrow{!\mathtt{String}} & ?\mathtt{String}(x \leqslant 2) & \text{(clocks values: } x = 2,\ y = 2)
\end{array}
$$

If S sends the integer when $x = 0.4$, then $\overline{S}$ must receive the integer immediately, when $y = 0.4$. At this point, both endpoints reset their respective clocks, and the communication will continue in sync. Urgent receive primitives are common; some examples are the non-blocking `WaitFreeReadQueue.read()` and blocking `WaitFreeReadQueue.waitForData()` of Real-Time Java [13], and the receive primitives in Erlang and Golang. *Urgent receive semantics make interactions "more synchronous" but still as asynchronous as real-life programs.*

A calculus for timed asynchronous processes. Our calculus features two time-sensitive primitives. The first is a parametric receive operation $a^n(b).P$ on a channel a, with a timeout n that can be ∞ or any number in $\mathbf{R}_{\geqslant 0}$. The parametric receive captures a range of receive primitives: non-blocking ($n = 0$), blocking without timeout ($n = \infty$), or blocking with timeout ($n \in \mathbf{R}_{>0}$). The second primitive is a time-consuming action, $\mathtt{delay}(\delta).P$, where δ is a constraint expressing the time-window for the time consumed by that action. Delay processes model primitives like `Thread.sleep(n)` in real-time Java [13] or, more generally, any time-consuming action, with δ being an estimation of the delay of computation.

Processes in our calculus abstract implementations of protocols given as pairs of dual types. Consider the processes below.

$$P_C = \mathtt{delay}(x < 3).\,\overline{a}\,\mathtt{HELO}.P'_C \quad P_S = \mathtt{delay}(x = 5).\,a^0(b).P'_S \quad Q_S = a^5(b).Q'_S$$

Processes abiding the protocols in (2) could be as follows: P_C for the client S_C, and P_S for the server S_S. The client process P_C performs a time consuming action for up to 3 min, then sends command HELO to the server, and continues as P'_C. The server process P_S sleeps for exactly 5 min, receives the message immediately (without blocking), and continues as P'_S. A process for the protocol in (1) could, instead be the parallel composition of P_C, again for the client, and Q_S for the server. Process Q_S uses a blocking primitive with timeout; the server now blocks on the receive action with a timeout of 5 min, and continues as Q'_S as soon as a message is received. The blocking receive primitive with timeout is crucial to model processes typed against protocols one can express with asynchronous timed duality, in particular those that are not wait-free.

A type system for timed asynchronous processes. The relationship between types and processes in our calculus is given as a typing system. Well-typed processes are ensured to communicate at the times prescribed by their types. This result is given via Subject Reduction (Theorem 4), establishing that well-typedness is preserved by reduction. In our timed scenario, Subject Reduction holds under *receive liveness*, an assumption on the interaction structure of processes. This assumption is orthogonal to time. To characterise the interaction structures of a timed process we erase timing information from that processes (*time erasure*). Receive liveness requires that, whenever a time-erased processes is waiting for a message, the corresponding message is eventually provided by the rest of the system. While receive liveness is not needed for Subject Reduction in untimed systems [21], it is required for timed processes. This reflects the natural intuition that if an untimed-process violates progress, then its timed counterpart may miss deadlines. Notably, we can rely on existing behavioural checking techniques from the untimed setting to ensure receive liveness [17].

Receive liveness is not required for Subject Reduction in a related work on asynchronous timed session types [12]. The dissimilarity in the assumptions is only apparent; it derives from differences in the two semantics for processes. When our processes cannot proceed correctly (e.g., in case of missed deadlines) they reduce to a failed state, whereas the processes in [12] become stuck (indicating violation of progress).

Synopsis. In Sect. 2 we introduce the syntax and the formation rules for asynchronous timed session types. In Sect. 3, we give a modular Labelled Transition System (LTS) for types in isolation (Sect. 3.1) and for compositions of types (Sect. 3.3). The subtyping relation is given in Sect. 3.2 and motivated in Example 8, after introducing the typing rules. We introduce timed asynchronous duality and its properties in Sect. 4. Remarkably, the composition of dual timed asynchronous types enjoys progress when using an urgent receive semantics (Theorem 1). Section 5 presents a calculus for timed processes and Sect. 6 introduces its typing system. The properties of our typing system—Subject Reduction (Theorem 4) and Time Safety (Theorem 5)—are introduced in Sect. 7. Conclusions and related works are in Sect. 8. Proofs and additional material can be found in the online report [11].

2 Asynchronous Timed Session Types

Clocks and predicates. We use the model of time from timed automata [3]. Let $\mathbb{X}$ be a finite set of clocks, let $x_1, \ldots, x_n$ range over clocks, and let each clock take values in $\mathbf{R}_{\geqslant 0}$. Let $t_1, \ldots, t_n$ range over non-negative real numbers and $n_1, \ldots, n_n$ range over non-negative rationals. The set $\mathcal{G}(\mathbb{X})$ of predicates over $\mathbb{X}$ is defined by the following grammar.

$$\delta ::= \texttt{true} \mid x > n \mid x = n \mid x - y > n \mid x - y = n \mid \neg\delta \mid \delta_1 \wedge \delta_2 \quad \text{where } x, y \in \mathbb{X}$$

We derive `false`, $<$, $\geqslant$, $\leqslant$ in the standard way. Predicates in the form $x - y > n$ and $x - y = n$ are called *diagonal* predicates; in these cases we assume $x \neq y$. Notation $cn(\delta)$ stands for the set of clocks in δ.

Clock valuation and resets. A clock valuation $\nu : \mathbb{X} \mapsto \mathbf{R}_{\geqslant 0}$ returns the time of the clocks in $\mathbb{X}$. We write $\nu + t$ for the valuation mapping all $x \in \mathbb{X}$ to $\nu(x) + t$, ν_0 for the initial valuation (mapping all clocks to 0), and, more generally, ν_t for the valuation mapping all clocks to t. Let $\nu \models \delta$ denote that δ is satisfied by ν. A reset predicate λ over $\mathbb{X}$ is a subset of $\mathbb{X}$. When λ is $\varnothing$ then no reset occurs, otherwise the assignment for each $x \in \lambda$ is set to 0. We write $\nu\,[\lambda \mapsto 0]$ for the clock assignment that is like ν everywhere except that its assigns 0 to all clocks in λ.

Types. Timed session types, hereafter just types, have the following syntax:

$$T \; ::= \; (\delta, S) \mid \mathtt{Nat} \mid \mathtt{Bool} \mid \ldots$$

$$S \; ::= \; !T(\delta,\lambda).S \;\mid\; ?T(\delta,\lambda).S \;\mid\; \oplus\,\{\mathrm{l_i}(\delta_i,\lambda_i) : S_i\}_{i\in I} \;\mid\; \&\{\mathrm{l_i}(\delta_i,\lambda_i) : S_i\}_{i\in I} \;\mid\; \mu\alpha.S \;\mid\; \alpha \;\mid\; \mathtt{end}$$

Sorts T include base types (`Nat`, `Bool`, etc.), and sessions (δ, S). Messages of type (δ, S) allow a participant involved in a session to delegate the remaining behaviour S; upon delegation the sender will no longer participate in the delegated session and receiver will execute the protocol described by S under any clock assignment satisfying δ. We denote the set of types with $\mathbb{T}$.

Type $!T(\delta, \lambda).S$ models a *send action* of a payload with sort T. The sending action is allowed at any time that satisfies the guard δ. The clocks in λ are reset upon sending. Type $?T(\delta, \lambda).S$ models the dual *receive action* of a payload with sort T. The receiving types require the endpoint to be ready to receive the message in the precise time window specified by the guard.

Type $\oplus\{\mathrm{l_i}(\delta_i, \lambda_i) : S_i\}_{i\in I}$ is a *select action*: the party chooses a branch $i \in I$, where I is a finite set of indices, selects the label l_i, and continues as prescribed by S_i. Each branch is annotated with a guard δ and reset λ. A branch j can be selected at any time allowed by δ_j. The dual type is $\&\{\mathrm{l_i}(\delta_i, \lambda_i) : S_i\}_{i\in I}$ for *branching actions*. Each branch is annotated with a guard and a reset. The endpoint must be ready to receive the label for j at any time allowed by δ_j (or until another branch is selected).

Recursive type $\mu\alpha.S$ associates a *type variable* α to a recursion body S. We assume that type variables are guarded in the standard way (i.e., they only occur under actions or branches). We let $\mathcal{A}$ denote the set of type variables.

Type `end` models successful termination.

2.1 Type Formation

The grammar for types allow to generate types that are not implementable in practice, as the one shown in Example 1.

Example 1 (Junk-types). Consider S in (3) under initial clock valuation ν_0.

$$S = ?T(x < 5, \varnothing).!T(x < 2, \varnothing).\mathtt{end} \tag{3}$$

The specified endpoint must be ready to receive a message in the time-window between 0 and 5 time units, as we evaluate $x < 5$ in ν_0. Assume that this receive action happens when $x = 3$, yielding a new state in which: (i) the clock valuation maps x to 3, and (ii) the endpoint must perform a send action while $x < 2$. Evidently, (ii) is no longer possible in the new clock valuation, as the $x < 2$ is now unsatisfiable. We could amend (3) in several ways: (a) by resetting x after the receive action; (b) by restricting the guard of the receive action (e.g., $x < 2$ instead of $x < 5$); or (c) by relaxing the guard of the send action. All these amendments would, however, yield a different type.

In the remainder of this section we introduce formation rules to rule out junk types as the one in Example 1 and characterise types that are well-formed. Intuitively, well-formed types allow, at any point, to perform some action in the present time or at some point in the future, unless the type is $\mathtt{end}$.

Judgments. The formation rules for types are defined on judgments of the form

$$A;\ \delta \vdash S$$

where A is an environment assigning type variables to guards, and δ is a guard in $\mathcal{G}(\mathbb{X})$. A is used as an invariant to form recursive types. Guard δ collects the possible 'pasts' from which the next action in S could be executed (unless S is $\mathtt{end}$). We use notation $\downarrow \delta$ (the past of δ) for a guard δ' such that $\nu \models \delta'$ if and only if $\exists t : \nu + t \models \delta$. For example, $\downarrow (1 \leqslant x \leqslant 2) = x \leqslant 2$ and $\downarrow (x \geqslant 3) = \mathtt{true}$. Similarly, we use the notation $\delta[\lambda \mapsto 0]$ to denote a guard in which all clocks in λ are reset. For example, $(x \leqslant 3 \wedge y \leqslant 2)[x \mapsto 0] = (x = 0 \wedge y \leqslant 2)$. We use the notation $\delta_1 \sqsubseteq \delta_2$ whenever, for all ν, $\nu \models \delta_1 \implies \nu \models \delta_2$. The past and reset of a guard can be inferred algorithmically, and $\sqsubseteq$ is decidable [8].

$$\frac{}{A;\ \mathtt{true} \vdash \mathtt{end}}\ [\mathtt{end}]$$

$$\frac{\Box \in \{!, ?\} \qquad A;\ \gamma \vdash S \qquad \delta[\lambda \mapsto 0] \sqsubseteq \gamma \qquad T \text{ base type}}{A;\ \downarrow \delta \vdash\ \Box\, T(\delta, \lambda).S}\ [\mathtt{interact}]$$

$$\frac{\begin{array}{c}\Box \in \{!, ?\} \qquad A;\ \gamma \vdash S \qquad \delta[\lambda \mapsto 0] \sqsubseteq \gamma \quad T = (\delta', S') \\ \varnothing;\ \gamma' \vdash S' \quad \delta' \sqsubseteq \gamma'\end{array}}{A;\ \downarrow \delta \vdash\ \Box\, T(\delta, \lambda).S}\ [\mathtt{delegate}]$$

$$\frac{\Box \in \{\oplus, \&\} \qquad \forall i \in I \quad A;\ \gamma_i \vdash S_i \quad \delta_i[\lambda_i \mapsto 0] \sqsubseteq \gamma_i}{A;\ \downarrow \bigvee_{i \in I} \delta_i \vdash\ \Box\, \{\mathrm{l_i}(\delta_i, \lambda_i) : S_i\}_{i \in I}}\ [\mathtt{choice}]$$

$$\frac{A, \alpha : \delta;\ \delta \vdash S}{A;\ \delta \vdash \mu\alpha.S}\ [\mathtt{rec}] \qquad \frac{}{A, \alpha : \delta;\ \delta \vdash \alpha}\ [\mathtt{var}]$$

Rule [end] states that the terminated type is well-formed against any A. The guard of the judgement is true since end is a final state (as end has no continuation, morally, the constraint of its continuation is always satisfiable). Rule [interact] ensures that the past of the current action δ entails the past of the subsequent action γ (considering resets if necessary): this rules out types in which the subsequent action can only be performed in the past. Rules [end] and [interact] are illustrated by the three examples below.

Example 2. The judgment below shows a type being *discarded* after an application of rule [interact] :

$$\emptyset;\ x \leqslant 3 \nvdash\ ?\mathtt{Nat}(1 \leqslant x \leqslant 3, \emptyset).!\mathtt{Nat}(1 \leqslant x \leqslant 2, \emptyset).\mathtt{end} \tag{4}$$

The premise of [interact] would be $\delta \not\subseteq\ \downarrow \gamma$, which does not hold for $\delta = 1 \leqslant x \leqslant 3$ and $\downarrow \gamma = x \leqslant 2$. This means that guard $(1 \leqslant x \leqslant 3, \emptyset)$ of the first action may lead to a state in which guard $1 \leqslant x \leqslant 2$ for the subsequent action is unsatisfiable. If we amend the type in (4) by adding a reset in the first action, we obtain a well-formed type. We show its formation below, where for simplicity we omit obvious preconditions like Nat base type, etc.

$$\dfrac{\dfrac{\dfrac{}{\emptyset;\ \mathtt{true} \vdash \mathtt{end}}\,[\mathtt{end}] \qquad 1 \leqslant x \leqslant 2 \subseteq \mathtt{true}}{\emptyset;\ x \leqslant 2 \vdash !\mathtt{Nat}(1 \leqslant x \leqslant 2, \emptyset).\mathtt{end} \qquad x = 0 \subseteq x \leqslant 2}\,[\mathtt{interact}]}{\emptyset;\ x \leqslant 3 \vdash ?\mathtt{Nat}(1 \leqslant x \leqslant 3, \{x\}).!\mathtt{Nat}(1 \leqslant x \leqslant 2, \emptyset).\mathtt{end}}\,[\mathtt{interact}]$$

Rule [delegate] behaves as [interact] , with two additional premises on the delegated session: (1) S' needs to be well-formed, and (2) the guard of the next action in S' needs to be satisfiable with respect to δ'. Guard δ' is used to ensure a correspondence between the state of the delegating endpoint and that of the receiving endpoint. Rule [choice] is similar to [interact] but requires that there is at least one viable branch (this is accomplished by considering the weaker past $\downarrow \bigvee_{i \in I} \delta_i$) and checking each branch for formation. Rules [rec] and [var] are for recursive types and variables, respectively. In [rec] the guard δ can be easily computed by taking the past of the next action of the in S (or the disjunction if S is a branching or selection). An algorithm for deciding type formation can be found in [11].

Definition 1 (Well-formed types). *We say that S is well-formed against clock valuation ν if $\emptyset;\ \delta \vdash S$ and $\nu \models \delta$, for some guard δ. We say that S is well-formed if it is well formed against ν_0.*

We will tacitly assume types are well-formed, unless otherwise specified. The intuition of well-formedness is that if $A;\ \delta \vdash S$ then S can be run (using the types semantics given in Sect. 3) under any clock valuation ν such that $\nu \models \delta$. In the sequel, we take (well-formed) types equi-recursively [31].

3 Asynchronous Session Types Semantics and Subtyping

We give a compositional semantics of types. First, we focus on types in isolation from their environment and from their queues, which we call *simple type configurations*. Next we define subtyping for simple type configurations. Finally, we consider systems (i.e., composition of types communicating via queues).

$$\frac{\nu \models \delta}{(\nu, !T(\delta,\lambda)).S \xrightarrow{!T} (\nu\,[\lambda \mapsto 0], S)}\ [\text{snd}] \qquad \frac{\nu \models \delta}{(\nu, ?T(\delta,\lambda).S) \xrightarrow{?T} (\nu\,[\lambda \mapsto 0], S)}\ [\text{rcv}]$$

$$\frac{\nu \models \delta_j \qquad j \in I}{(\nu, \oplus\{\text{l}_\text{i}(\delta_i,\lambda_i) : S_i\}_{i\in I}) \xrightarrow{!\text{l}_\text{j}} (\nu\,[\lambda_j \mapsto 0], S_j)}\ [\text{sel}]$$

$$\frac{\nu \models \delta_j \qquad j \in I}{(\nu, \&\{\text{l}_\text{i}(\delta,\lambda_i) : S_i\}_{i\in I}) \xrightarrow{?\text{l}_\text{j}} (\nu\,[\lambda_j \mapsto 0], S_j)}\ [\text{bra}]$$

$$\frac{(\nu, S[\mu\text{t}.S/\text{t}]) \xrightarrow{\ell} (\nu',\ S')}{(\nu, \mu\text{t}.S) \xrightarrow{\ell} (\nu', S')}\ [\text{rec}] \qquad (\nu, S) \xrightarrow{t} (\nu + t, S)\ [\text{time}]$$

Fig. 1. LTS for simple type configurations

3.1 Types in Isolation

The behaviour of *simple type configurations* is described by the Labelled Transition System (LTS) on pairs (ν, S) over $(\mathbb{V} \times \mathcal{S})$, where clock valuation ν gives the values of clocks in a specific state. The LTS is defined over the following labels

$$\ell ::= !m \mid ?m \mid t \mid \tau \qquad\qquad m ::= d \mid \text{l}$$

Label $!m$ denotes an output action of message m and $?m$ an input action of m. A message m can be a sort T (that can be either a higher order message (δ, S) or base type), or a branching label l. The LTS for single types is defined as the least relation satisfying the rules in Fig. 1. Rules [snd], [rcv], [sel], and [bra] can only happen if the constraint of the next action is satisfied in the current clock valuation. Rule [rec] unfolds recursive types, and [time] always lets time elapse.

Let $\mathbf{s}$, $\mathbf{s}'$, $\mathbf{s}_i$ $(i \in \mathbb{N})$ range over simple type configurations (ν, S). We write $\mathbf{s} \xrightarrow{\ell}$ when there exists $\mathbf{s}'$ such that $\mathbf{s} \xrightarrow{\ell} \mathbf{s}'$, and write $\mathbf{s} \xrightarrow{t\,\ell}$ for $\mathbf{s} \xrightarrow{t}\xrightarrow{\ell}$.

3.2 Asynchronous Timed Subtyping

We define subtyping as a partial relation on simple type configurations. As in other subtyping relations for session types we consider send and receive actions dually [14,16,19]. Our subtyping relation is covariant on output actions and contra-variant on input actions, similarly to that of [14]. In this way, our subtyping $S <: S'$ captures the intuition that a process well-typed against S can be safely substituted with a process well-typed against S'. Definition 2, introduces a notation that is useful in the rest of this section.

Definition 2 (Future enabled send/receive). *Action ℓ is future enabled in* $\mathbf{s}$ *if* $\exists t : \mathbf{s} \xrightarrow{t\,\ell}$. *We write* $\mathbf{s} \overset{!}{\Rightarrow}$ *(resp.* $\mathbf{s} \overset{?}{\Rightarrow}$*) if there exists a sending action* $!m$ *(resp. a receiving action* $?m$*) that is future enabled in* $\mathbf{s}$.

As common in session types, the communication structure does not allow for mixed choices: the grammar of types enforces choices to be either all input (branching actions), or output (selection actions). From this fact it follows that, given $\mathbf{s}$, reductions $\mathbf{s} \overset{!}{\Rightarrow}$ and $\mathbf{s} \overset{?}{\Rightarrow}$ cannot hold simultaneously.

Definition 3 (Timed Type Simulation). *Fix* $\mathbf{s}_1 = (\nu_1, S_1)$ *and* $\mathbf{s}_2 = (\nu_2, S_2)$. *A relation* $\mathcal{R} \in (\mathbb{V} \times \mathcal{S})^2$ *is a* timed type simulation *if* $(\mathbf{s}_1, \mathbf{s}_2) \in \mathcal{R}$ *implies the following conditions:*

1. $S_1 = \mathtt{end}$ *implies* $S_2 = \mathtt{end}$
2. $\mathbf{s}_1 \xrightarrow{t\,!m_1} \mathbf{s}_1'$ *implies* $\exists \mathbf{s}_2', m_2 : \mathbf{s}_2 \xrightarrow{t\,!m_2} \mathbf{s}_2'$, $(m_2, m_1) \in \mathcal{S}, (\mathbf{s}_1', \mathbf{s}_2') \in \mathcal{R}$
3. $\mathbf{s}_2 \xrightarrow{t\,?m_2} \mathbf{s}_2'$ *implies* $\exists \mathbf{s}_1', m_1 : \mathbf{s}_1 \xrightarrow{t\,?m_1} \mathbf{s}_1'$, $(m_1, m_2) \in \mathcal{S}$, $(\mathbf{s}_1', \mathbf{s}_2') \in \mathcal{R}$
4. $\mathbf{s}_1 \overset{?}{\Rightarrow}$ *implies* $\mathbf{s}_2 \overset{?}{\Rightarrow}$ *and* $\mathbf{s}_2 \overset{!}{\Rightarrow}$ *implies* $\mathbf{s}_1 \overset{!}{\Rightarrow}$

where $\mathcal{S}$ *is the following extension of* $\mathcal{R}$ *to messages: (1)* $(T, T') \in \mathcal{S}$ *if* T *and* T' *are base types, and* T' *is a subtype of* T *by sorts subtyping, e.g.,* $(\mathtt{int}, \mathtt{nat}) \in \mathcal{S}$*; (2)* $(\mathrm{l}, \mathrm{l}) \in \mathcal{S}$*; (3)* $((\delta_1, S_1), (\delta_2, S_2)) \in \mathcal{S}$*, if* $\forall \nu_1 \models \delta_1 \, \exists \nu_2 \models \delta_2 : ((\nu_1, S_1), (\nu_2, S_2)) \in \mathcal{R}$ *and* $\forall \nu_2 \models \delta_2 \, \exists \nu_1 \models \delta_1 : ((\nu_1, S_1), (\nu_2, S_2)) \in \mathcal{R}$.

Intuitively, if $(\mathbf{s}_1, \mathbf{s}_2) \in \mathcal{R}$ then any environment that can safely interact with $\mathbf{s}_2$, can do so with $\mathbf{s}_1$. We write that $\mathbf{s}_2$ simulates $\mathbf{s}_1$ whenever $\mathbf{s}_1$ and $\mathbf{s}_2$ are in a timed type simulation. Below, $\mathbf{s}_2$ simulates $\mathbf{s}_1$:

$$\mathbf{s}_1 = (\nu_0, !\mathtt{nat}(x < 5, \varnothing).\mathtt{end}) \;\; \mathbf{s}_2 = (\nu_0, !\mathtt{int}(x \leqslant 10, \varnothing).\mathtt{end})$$

Conversely, $\mathbf{s}_1$ does not simulate $\mathbf{s}_2$ because of condition (2). Precisely, $\mathbf{s}_2$ can make a transition $\mathbf{s}_2 \xrightarrow{10\,!\mathtt{int}}$ that cannot be matched by $\mathbf{s}_1$ for two reasons: guard $x < 5$ is no longer satisfiable when $x = 10$, and $(\mathtt{nat}, \mathtt{int}) \notin \mathcal{S}$ since $\mathtt{int}$ is not a subtype of $\mathtt{nat}$. For receive actions, instead, we could substitute $\mathbf{s}$ with $\mathbf{s}'$ if $\mathbf{s}'$ had at least the receiving capabilities of $\mathbf{s}$. Condition (4) in Definition 3 rules out relations that include, e.g., $((\nu, ?T(\mathtt{true}, \varnothing).\mathtt{end}), (\nu, !T(\mathtt{true}, \varnothing).\mathtt{end}))$.

Live simple type configurations. In our subtyping definition we are interested in simple type configurations that are not stuck. Consider the example below:

$$(\nu, !\mathtt{Int}(x \leqslant 10, \varnothing).\mathtt{end}) \tag{5}$$

The simple type configuration in (5) would not be stuck if $\nu = \nu_0$, but would be stuck for any $\nu = \nu'[x \mapsto 10]$. Definition 4 gives a formal definition of simple type configurations that are not stuck, i.e., that are *live*.

Definition 4 (Live simple type configuration). *A simple configuration* (ν, S) *is said* live *if:*

$$S = \mathtt{end} \quad or \; \exists t, \ell : (\nu, S) \xrightarrow{t \circ m} \qquad (\circ \in \{!, ?\})$$

Observe that for all well-formed S, (ν_0, S) is live.

Subtyping for simple type configurations. We can now define subtyping for simple type configurations and state its decidability.

Definition 5 (Subtyping). *$\mathbf{s}_1$ is a subtype of $\mathbf{s}_2$, written $\mathbf{s}_1 <: \mathbf{s}_2$, if there exists a timed type simulation $\mathcal{R}$* on live simple type configurations *such that $(\mathbf{s}_1, \mathbf{s}_2) \in \mathcal{R}$. We write $S_1 <: S_2$ when $(\nu_0, S_1) <: (\nu_0, S_2)$. Abusing the notation, we write $m <: m'$ iff there exists $\mathcal{S}$ such that $(m, m') \in \mathcal{S}$.*

Subtyping has been shown to be decidable in the untimed setting [19] and in the timed first order setting [6]. In [6], decidability is shown through a reduction to model checking of timed automata networks. The result in [6] can be extended to higher-order messages using the techniques in [3], based on finite representations (called regions) of possibly infinite sets of clock valuations.

Proposition 1 (Decidability of subtyping). *Checking if $(\delta_1, S_1) <: (\delta_2, S_2)$ is decidable.*

3.3 Types with Queues, and Their Composition

As interactions are asynchronous, the behaviour of types must capture the states in which messages are in transit. To do this, we extend simple type configurations with queues. A *configuration* $\mathbf{S}$ is a triple $(\nu, S, \mathtt{M})$ where ν is clock valuation, S is a type and $\mathtt{M}$ a FIFO unbounded queue of the following form:

$$\mathtt{M} ::= \varnothing \mid m; \mathtt{M}$$

$\mathtt{M}$ contains the messages sent by the co-party of S and not yet received by S. We write $\mathtt{M}$ for $\mathtt{M}; \varnothing$, and call $(\nu, S, \mathtt{M})$ *initial* if $\nu = \nu_0$ and $\mathtt{M} = \varnothing$.

Composing types. Configurations are composed into *systems.* We denote $\mathbf{S} \mid \mathbf{S}'$ as the parallel composition of the two configurations $\mathbf{S}$ and $\mathbf{S}'$.

The labelled transition rules for systems are given in Fig. 2. Rule (snd) is for send actions. A send action can occur only if the time constraint of S is satisfied (by the premise, which uses either rule [snd] or [sel] in Fig. 1). Rule (que) models actions on queues. A queue is always ready to receive any message m. Rule (rcv) is for receive actions, where a message is read from the queue. A receiving action can only occur if the time constraint of S is satisfied (by the premise, which uses either rule [rcv] or [bra] in Fig. 1). The message is removed from the head of the queue of the receiving configuration. The third clause in the premise uses the notion of subtyping (Definition 3) for basic sorts, labels, and higher order messages. Rule (crcv) is the action of a configuration pulling a message of its queue. Rule (com) is for communication between a sending configuration and a buffer. Rule (ctime) lets time elapse in the same way for all configurations in a system. Rule (time) models time passing for single configurations. Time passing is subject to two constrains, expressed by the second and third conditions in the premise. Condition $(\nu, S) \overset{!}{\Rightarrow}$ requires the time action t to preserve the satisfiability of some send action. For example, in configuration

$$\frac{(\nu,S) \xrightarrow{!m} (\nu',S')}{(\nu,S,\mathtt{M}) \xrightarrow{!m} (\nu',S',\mathtt{M})} \text{ (snd)} \qquad (\nu,S,\mathtt{M}) \xrightarrow{?m} (\nu,S,\mathtt{M};m) \text{ (que)}$$

$$\frac{(\nu,S) \xrightarrow{?m'} (\nu',S') \quad m' <: m}{(\nu,S,m;\mathtt{M}) \xrightarrow{\tau} (\nu',S',\mathtt{M})} \text{ (rcv)} \qquad \frac{\mathbf{S}_1 \xrightarrow{\tau} \mathbf{S}_1'}{\mathbf{S}_1 \mid \mathbf{S}_2 \xrightarrow{\tau} \mathbf{S}_1' \mid \mathbf{S}_2} \text{ (crcv)}$$

$$\frac{\mathbf{S}_1 \xrightarrow{!m} \mathbf{S}_1' \quad \mathbf{S}_2 \xrightarrow{?m} \mathbf{S}_2'}{\mathbf{S}_1 \mid \mathbf{S}_2 \xrightarrow{\tau} \mathbf{S}_1' \mid \mathbf{S}_2'} \text{ (com)} \qquad \frac{\mathbf{S}_1 \xrightarrow{t} \mathbf{S}_1' \quad \mathbf{S}_2 \xrightarrow{t} \mathbf{S}_2'}{\mathbf{S}_1 \mid \mathbf{S}_2 \xrightarrow{t} \mathbf{S}_1' \mid \mathbf{S}_2'} \text{ (ctime)}$$

$$\frac{(\nu,S) \xrightarrow{t} (\nu',S) \qquad (\nu,S) \stackrel{!}{\Rightarrow} \text{ implies } (\nu',S) \stackrel{!}{\Rightarrow} \qquad \forall t' < t : (\nu+t',S,\mathtt{M}) \stackrel{\tau}{\not\rightarrow}}{(\nu,S,\mathtt{M}) \xrightarrow{t} (\nu',S,\mathtt{M})} \text{ (time)}$$

Fig. 2. LTS for systems. We omit the symmetric rules of (crcv), and (csnd).

$(\nu_0, !T(x < 2, \varnothing).S, \varnothing)$, a transition with label 2 would *not* preserve any send action (hence would not be allowed), while a transition with label 1.8 would be allowed by condition $(\nu, S) \stackrel{!}{\Rightarrow}$. Condition $\forall t' < t : (\nu + t', S, \mathtt{M}) \stackrel{\tau}{\not\rightarrow}$ in the premise of rule (time) checks that there is no ready message to be received in the queue. This is to model urgency: when a configuration is in a receiving state and a message is in the queue then the receiving action must happen without delay. For example, $(\nu_0, ?T(x < 2, \varnothing).S, \varnothing)$ can make a transition with label 1, but $(\nu_0, ?T(x < 2, \varnothing).S, m)$ cannot make any time transition. Below we show two examples of system executions. Example 3 illustrates a good communication, thanks to urgency. We also illustrate in Example 4 that without an urgent semantics the system in Example 3 gets stuck.

Example 3 (A good communication). Consider the following types:

$$S_1 = !T(x \leqslant 1, x).?T(x \leqslant 2).\mathtt{end} \qquad S_2 = ?T(y \leqslant 1, y).!T(y \leqslant 2).\mathtt{end}$$

System $(\nu[x \mapsto 0], S_1, \varnothing) \mid (\nu[x \mapsto 0], S_2, \varnothing)$ can make a time step with label 0.5 by (ctime), yielding the system in (6)

$$(\nu[x \mapsto 0.5], S_1, \varnothing) \mid (\nu[x \mapsto 0.5], S_2, \varnothing) \tag{6}$$

The system in (6) can move by a τ step thanks to (com): the left-hand side configuration makes a step with label $!T$ by (snd) while the right-hand side configuration makes a step $?T$ by (que), yielding system (7) below.

$$(\nu[x \mapsto 0], ?T(x \leqslant 2).\mathtt{end}, \varnothing) \mid (\nu[y \mapsto 0.5], S_2, T) \tag{7}$$

The right-hand side configuration in the system in (7) must *urgently* receive message T due to the third clause in the premise of rule (time). Hence, the only possible step forward for (7) is by (crcv) yielding the system in (8).

$$(\nu[x \mapsto 0], ?T(x \leqslant 2).\mathtt{end}, \varnothing) \mid (\nu[y \mapsto 0], !T(y \leqslant 2).\mathtt{end}, \varnothing) \tag{8}$$

Example 4 (In absence of urgency). Without urgency, the system in (7) from Example 3 may get stuck. Assume the third clause of rule (time) was removed: this would allow (7) to make a time step with label 0.5, followed by a step by (rcv) yielding the system in (9), where clock y is reset after the receive action.

$$(\nu[x \mapsto 0.5], ?T(x \leqslant 2).\mathtt{end}, \varnothing) \mid (\nu[y \mapsto 0], !T(y \leqslant 2).\mathtt{end}, \varnothing) \tag{9}$$

followed by a τ step by (com) reaching the following state:

$$(\nu[x \mapsto 2.5], ?T(x \leqslant 2).\mathtt{end}, T) \mid (\nu[y \mapsto 0], \mathtt{end}, \varnothing) \tag{10}$$

The message in the queue in (10) will never be received as the guard $x \leqslant 2$ is not satisfiable now or at any point in the future. This system is stuck. Instead, thanks to urgency, the clocks of the configurations of system (8) have been 'synchronised' after the receive action, preventing the system from getting stuck.

4 Timed Asynchronous Duality

We introduce a timed extension of duality. As in untimed duality, we let each send/select action be complemented by a corresponding receive/branching action. Moreover, we require time constraints and resets to match.

Definition 6 (Timed duality). *The dual type $\overline{S}$ of S is defined as follows:*

$$\overline{!T(\delta,\lambda).S} = ?T(\delta,\lambda).\overline{S} \qquad \overline{?T(\delta,\lambda).S} = !T(\delta,\lambda).\overline{S} \qquad \overline{\mu\alpha.S} = \mu\alpha.\overline{S}$$
$$\overline{\oplus\{\mathrm{l}_i(\delta_i,\lambda_i) : S_i\}_{i\in I}} = \&\{\mathrm{l}_i(\delta_i,\lambda_i) : \overline{S_i}\}_{i\in I} \qquad \overline{\alpha} = \alpha$$
$$\overline{\&\{\mathrm{l}_i(\delta_i,\lambda_i) : S_i\}_{i\in I}} = \oplus\{\mathrm{l}_i(\delta_i,\lambda_i) : \overline{S_i}\}_{i\in I} \qquad \overline{\mathtt{end}} = \mathtt{end}$$

Duality with urgent receive semantics enjoys the following properties: systems with dual types fulfil progress (Theorem 1); behaviour (resp. progress) of a system is preserved by the substitution of a type with a subtype (Theorem 2) (resp. Theorem 3). A system enjoys progress if it reaches states that are either final or that allow further communications, possibly after a delay. Recall that we assume types to be well-formed (cf. Definition 1): Theorems 1, 2, and 3 rely on this assumption.

Definition 7 (Type progress). *We say that a system $(\nu, S, \mathtt{M})$ is a* success *if $S = \mathtt{end}$ and $\mathtt{M} = \varnothing$. We say that $\mathbf{S}_1 \mid \mathbf{S}_2$ satisfies* progress *if:*

$$\mathbf{S}_1 \mid \mathbf{S}_2 \longrightarrow^* \mathbf{S}_1' \mid \mathbf{S}_2' \quad \Longrightarrow \quad \mathbf{S}_1' \text{ and } \mathbf{S}_2' \text{ are success or } \exists t : \mathbf{S}_1' \mid \mathbf{S}_2' \xrightarrow{t\,\tau}$$

Theorem 1 (Duality progress). *System $(\nu_0, S, \varnothing) \mid (\nu_0, \overline{S}, \varnothing)$ enjoys progress.*

We show that subtyping does not introduce new behaviour, via the usual notion of timed simulation [1]. Let $\mathbf{c}, \mathbf{c}_1, \mathbf{c}_2$ range over systems. Fix $\mathbf{c}_1 = (\nu_1^1, S_1^1, \mathtt{M}_1^1) \mid (\nu_2^1, S_2^1, \mathtt{M}_2^1)$, and $\mathbf{c}_2 = (\nu_1^2, S_1^2, \mathtt{M}_1^2) \mid (\nu_2^2, S_2^2, \mathtt{M}_2^2)$. We say that a binary relation over systems preserves $\mathtt{end}$ if: $S_1^i = \mathtt{end} \wedge \mathtt{M}_1^i = \varnothing$ iff $S_2^i = \mathtt{end} \wedge \mathtt{M}_2^i = \varnothing$ for all $i \in \{1,2\}$. Write $\mathbf{c}_1 \lesssim \mathbf{c}_2$ if $(\mathbf{c}_1, \mathbf{c}_2)$ are in a timed simulation that preserves $\mathtt{end}$.

Theorem 2 (Safe substitution). *If* $S' <: \overline{S}$, *then* $(\nu_0, S, \varnothing) \mid (\nu_0, S', \varnothing) \lesssim (\nu_0, S, \varnothing) \mid (\nu_0, \overline{S}, \varnothing)$.

Theorem 3 (Progressing substitution). *If* $S' <: \overline{S}$, *then* $(\nu_0, S, \varnothing) \mid (\nu_0, S', \varnothing)$ *satisfies progress.*

5 A Calculus for Asynchronous Timed Processes

We introduce our asynchronous calculus for timed processes. The calculus abstracts implementations that execute one or more sessions. We let $P, P', Q, \ldots$ range over processes, X range over process variables, and define $n \in \mathbb{R}_{\geqslant 0} \cup \{\infty\}$. We use the notation $\boldsymbol{a}$ for ordered sequences of channels or variables.

$$
\begin{array}{rlll}
P ::= & \overline{a}\, v.P & \mid\ \mathtt{delay}(\delta).\, P & \text{(time-consuming)} \\
\mid & a \triangleleft \mathrm{l}.\, P & \mid\ a^n(b).\, P & \\
\mid & \mathtt{if}\ v\ \mathtt{then}\ P\ \mathtt{else}\ P & \mid\ a^n \rhd \{\mathrm{l}_i : P_i\}_{i \in I} & \\
\mid & P \mid P & \mid\ \mathtt{failed} & \text{(run-time)} \\
\mid & 0 & \mid\ \mathtt{delay}(t).\, P & \\
\mid & \mathtt{def}\ D\ \mathtt{in}\ P & & \\
\mid & X\langle \boldsymbol{a}\,;\,\boldsymbol{a}\rangle & D ::= X(\boldsymbol{a}\,;\,\boldsymbol{a}) = P & \\
\mid & (\nu ab)P & & \\
\mid & ab : h & h ::= \varnothing \mid h \cdot v \mid h \cdot a &
\end{array}
$$

$\overline{a}\, v.P$ sends a value v on channel a and continues as P. Similarly, $a \triangleleft \mathrm{l}.\, P$ sends a label l on channel a and continue as P. Process $\mathtt{if}\ v\ \mathtt{then}\ P\ \mathtt{else}\ Q$ behaves as either P or Q depending on the boolean value v. Process $P \mid Q$ is for parallel composition of P and Q, and 0 is the idle process. $\mathtt{def}\ D\ \mathtt{in}\ P$ is the standard recursive process: D is a declaration, and P is a process that may contain recursive calls. In recursive calls $X\langle \boldsymbol{a}\,;\,\boldsymbol{a}\rangle$ the first list of parameters has to be instantiated with values of ground types, while the second with channels. Recursive calls are instantiated with equations $X(\boldsymbol{a}\,;\,\boldsymbol{a})$ in D. Process $(\nu ab)P$ is for scope restriction of endpoints a and b. Process $ab : h$ is a queue with name ab (colloquially used to indicate that it contains messages in transit from a to b) and content h. (νab) binds endpoints a and b, and queues ab and ba in P.

There are two kind of time-consuming processes: those performing a time-consuming action (e.g., method invocation, sleep), and those waiting to receive a message. We model the first kind of processes with $\mathtt{delay}(\delta).\, P$, and the second kind of processes with $a^n(b).\, P$ (receive) and $a^n \rhd \{\mathrm{l}_i : P_i\}_{i \in I}$ (branching). In $\mathtt{delay}(\delta).\, P$, δ is a constraints as those defined for types, but on one single clock x. The name of the clock here is immaterial: clock x is used as a syntactic tool to define intervals for the time-consuming (delay) action. In this sense, assume x is bound in $\mathtt{delay}(\delta).\, P$. Process $\mathtt{delay}(\delta).\, P$ consumes any amount of time t such that t is a solution of δ. For example $\mathtt{delay}(x \leqslant 3).\, P$ consumes any value between 0 to 3 time units, then behaves as P. Process $a^n(b).\, P$ receive a message on channel a, instantiates b and continue as P. Parameter n models different receive primitives: non-blocking ($n = 0$), blocking ($n = \infty$), and blocking with timeout ($n \in \mathbb{R}^{\geqslant 0}$). If $n \in \mathbb{R}^{\geqslant 0}$ and no message is in the queue, the process waits n time units before moving into a failed state. If n is set to ∞ the process models a blocking primitive without timeout. Branching process $a^n \rhd \{l_i : P_i\}_{i \in I}$ is similar, but receives a label l_i and continues as P_i.

Run-time processes are not written by programmers and only appear upon execution. Process **failed** is the process that has violated a time constraint. We say that P is a *failed state* if it has **failed** as a syntactic sub-term. Process $\mathtt{delay}(t).P$ delays for exactly t time units.

Well-formed processes. Sessions are modelled as processes of the following form

$$(\nu ab)(P \mid ab : h \mid ba : h')$$

where P is the process for endpoints a and b, ab is the queue for messages from a to b, and ba is the queues for messages from b to a. A process can have more than one ongoing session. For each, we expect that all necessary queues are present and well-placed. We ensure that queues are well-placed via a well-formedness property for processes (see [11] for an inductive definition). Well-formedness rules out processes of the following form:

$$(\nu ab)\ (a^n(c).(ba : h' \mid P) \mid Q \mid ab : h) \tag{11}$$

The process in (11) in not well-formed since queue ba for communications to endpoint a is not usable as it is in the continuation of the receive action. Well-formedness of processes is necessary to our safety results. We check well-formedness orthogonally to the typing system for the sake of simpler typing rules. While well-formedness ensures the absence of misplaced queues, the presence of an appropriate pair of queues for every session is ensured by the typing rules.

Session creation. Usually well-formedness is ensured by construction, as sessions are created by a specific (synchronous) reduction rule [10,21]. This kind of session creation is cumbersome in the timed setting as it allows delays that are not captured by protocols, hence well-typed processes may miss deadlines. Other work on timed session types [12] avoids this problem by requiring that all session creations occur before any delay action. Our calculus allows session to be created at any point, even after delays. In (12) a session with endpoints c and d is created after a send action (assume P includes the queues for this new session).

$$(\nu ab)\ (\overline{a}\, v.\mathtt{delay}(x \leqslant 3).(\nu cd)(P) \mid Q \mid ab : h \mid ba : h') \tag{12}$$

A process like the one in (12) may be thought as a dynamic session creation that happens synchronously (as in [10,21]), but assuming that all participants are ready to engage without delays. Our approach yields a simplification to the calculus (syntax and reduction rules) and, yet, a more general treatment of session initiation than the work in [12].

$$\frac{P \rightharpoonup P'}{P \longrightarrow P'} \qquad \frac{P \rightsquigarrow P'}{P \longrightarrow P'} \qquad \texttt{[Red1/Red2]}$$

$$\bar{a}\, v.P \mid ab : h \;\rightharpoonup\; P \mid ab : h \cdot v \qquad \texttt{[Send]}$$

$$a^n(c).\, P \mid ba : v \cdot h \;\rightharpoonup\; P[v/c] \mid ba : h \qquad \texttt{[Rcv]}$$

$$a \lhd \mathrm{l}.\, P \mid ab : h \;\rightharpoonup\; P \mid ab : h \cdot \mathtt{l} \qquad \texttt{[Sel]}$$

$$a^n \rhd \{\mathrm{l}_i : P_i\}_{i \in I} \mid ba : \mathtt{l}_j \cdot h \;\rightharpoonup\; P_j \mid ba : h \qquad (j \in I) \qquad \texttt{[Bra]}$$

$$\frac{\models \delta[t/x]}{\mathtt{delay}(\delta).\, P \;\rightharpoonup\; \mathtt{delay}(t).\, P} \qquad \texttt{[Det]}$$

$$\mathtt{if\ true\ then}\ P\ \mathtt{else}\ Q \;\rightharpoonup\; P \qquad \texttt{[IfT]}$$

$$\frac{P \rightharpoonup P'}{P \mid Q \rightharpoonup P' \mid Q} \qquad \frac{P \rightharpoonup P'}{\mathtt{def}\ D\ \mathtt{in}\ P \rightharpoonup \mathtt{def}\ D\ \mathtt{in}\ P'} \qquad \texttt{[Par/Def]}$$

$$\mathtt{def}\ X(\boldsymbol{a}' \,;\, \boldsymbol{b}') = P'\ \mathtt{in}\ X\langle \boldsymbol{v} \,;\, \boldsymbol{b}\rangle \mid Q \;\rightharpoonup\; \mathtt{def}\ X(\boldsymbol{a}' \,;\, \boldsymbol{b}') = P'\ \mathtt{in}\ P'[\boldsymbol{v}, \boldsymbol{b}/\boldsymbol{a}', \boldsymbol{b}'] \mid Q \qquad \texttt{[Rec]}$$

$$\frac{P \equiv P' \quad P' \rightharpoonup Q' \quad Q' \equiv Q}{P \rightharpoonup Q} \qquad \frac{P \rightharpoonup P'}{(\nu ab)P \rightharpoonup (\nu ab)P'} \qquad \texttt{[AStr/AScope]}$$

$$\frac{P \equiv P' \quad P' \rightsquigarrow Q' \quad Q' \equiv Q}{P \rightsquigarrow Q} \qquad P \rightsquigarrow \Phi_t(P) \qquad \texttt{[TStr/Delay]}$$

Fig. 3. Reduction for processes (rule [IfF], symmetric for [IfT] is omitted).

$$\Phi_t(0) = 0 \qquad \Phi_t(ab : h) = ab : h \qquad \Phi_t(\mathtt{failed}) = \mathtt{failed}$$

$$\Phi_t(P_1 \mid P_2) = \Phi_t(P_1) \mid \Phi_t(P_2), \text{ if } \mathtt{Wait}(P_i) \cap \mathtt{NEQueue}(P_j) = \varnothing,\ i \neq j \in \{1, 2\}$$

$$\Phi_t(\mathtt{delay}(t').\, P) = \mathtt{delay}(t' - t).\, P \quad \text{if } t' \geqslant t$$

$$\Phi_t(a^{t'}(a').\, P) = \begin{cases} a^{t'-t}(a').\, P & \text{if } t' \geqslant t \\ \mathtt{failed} & \text{otherwise} \end{cases}$$

$$\Phi_t(a^{\infty}(a').\, P) = a^{\infty}(a').\, P$$

$$\Phi_t((\nu ab)P) = (\nu ab)\Phi_t(P)$$

$$\Phi_t(\mathtt{def}\ D\ \mathtt{in}\ P) = \mathtt{def}\ D\ \mathtt{in}\ \Phi_t(P)$$

Fig. 4. Time-passing function $\Phi_t(P)$. Rule for $a^{t'} \rhd \{\mathrm{l}_i : P_i\}_{i \in I}$ is omitted for brevity. $\phi_t(P)$ is undefined in the remaining cases.

Reduction for processes. Processes are considered modulo structural equivalence, denoted by $\equiv$, and defined by adding the following rule for delays to the standard ones [28]: $\texttt{delay}(0).\, P \equiv P$. Reduction rules for processes are given in Fig. 3. A reduction step $\longrightarrow$ can happen because of either an instantaneous step $\rightharpoonup$ by [Red1] or time-consuming step $\rightsquigarrow$ by [Red2]. Rules [Send], [Rcv], [Sel], and [Bra] are the usual asynchronous communication rules. Rule [Det] models the random occurrence of a precise delay t, with t being a solution of δ. The other untimed rules, [IfT], [Par], [Def], [Rec], [AStr], and [AScope] are standard. Note that rule [Par] does not allow time passing, which is handled by rule [Delay]. Rule [TStr] is the timed version of [AStr]. Rule [Delay] applies a *time-passing* function Φ_t (defined in Fig. 4) which distributes the delay t across all the parts of a process. $\Phi_t(P)$ is a partial function: it is undefined if P can immediately make an urgent action, such as evaluation of expressions or output actions. If $\Phi_t(P)$ is defined, it returns the process resulting from letting t time units elapse in P. $\Phi_t(P)$ may return a failed state, if delay t makes a deadline in P expire. The definition of $\Phi_t(P_1 \mid P_2)$ relies on two auxiliary functions: $\texttt{Wait}(P)$ and $\texttt{NEQueue}(P)$ (see [11] for the full definition). $\texttt{Wait}(P)$ returns the set of channels on which P (or some syntactic sub-term of P) is waiting to receive a message/label. $\texttt{NEQueue}(P)$ returns the set of endpoints with a non-empty inbound queue. For example, $\texttt{Wait}(a^t(b).\, Q) = \texttt{Wait}(a^t \rhd \{l_i : P_i\}_{i \in I}) = \{a\}$ and $\texttt{NEQueue}(ba : h) = \{a\}$ given that $h \neq \varnothing$. $\Phi_t(P_1 \mid P_2)$ is defined only if no urgent action could immediately happen in $P_1 \mid P_2$. For example, $\Phi_t(P_1 \mid P_2)$ is undefined for $P_1 = a^t(b).\, Q$ and $P_2 = ba : v$.

In the rest of this section we show the reductions of two processes: one with urgent actions (Example 5), and one to a failed state (Example 6). We omit processes that are immaterial for the illustration (e.g., unused queues).

Example 5 (Urgency and undefined Φ_t). We show the reduction of process $P = (\nu ab)(\overline{a}\,\text{`Hi'}.Q \mid ab : \varnothing \mid b^{10}(c).\, P')$ that has an urgent action. Process P can make the following reduction by [Send]:

$$P \;\rightharpoonup\; (\nu ab)(Q \mid ab : \text{`Hi'} \mid b^{10}(c).\, P')$$

At this point, to apply rule [Delay], say with $t = 5$, we need to apply the time-passing function as shown below:

$$\Phi_5((\nu ab)(\overline{a}\,\text{`Hi'}.Q \mid ab : \text{`Hi'} \mid b^{10}(c).\, P')) = (\nu ab)(\overline{a}\,\text{`Hi'}.Q \mid \Phi_5(ab : \text{`Hi'} \mid b^{10}(c).\, P'))$$

which is undefined. $\Phi_5(ab : \varnothing \mid b^{10}(c).\, P')$ is undefined because $\texttt{Wait}(b^{10}(c).\, P) \cap \texttt{NEQueue}(ab : \text{`Hi'}) = \{b\} \neq \varnothing$. Since $\Phi_5(P')$ is undefined. Instead, the message in queue ab can be received by rule [Rcv]:

$$(\nu ab)(Q \mid ab : \text{`Hi'} \mid b^{10}(c).\, P') \;\rightharpoonup\; (\nu ab)(Q \mid ab : \varnothing \mid P[\text{`Hi'}/c])$$

Example 6 (An execution with failure). We show a reduction to a failing state of a process with a non-blocking receive action (expecting a message immediately) composed with another process that sends a message after a delay.

$$\begin{array}{lll} & \texttt{delay}(x=3).\,\overline{a}\,\text{`Hi'}.Q \mid ab:\varnothing \mid b^0(c).\,P & \text{apply [Det]} \\ \rightharpoonup & \texttt{delay}(3).\,\overline{a}\,\text{`Hi'}.Q \mid ab:\varnothing \mid b^0(c).\,P = P' & \text{apply [Delay] with } t=3 \\ \rightharpoonup & \Phi_3(P') & \end{array}$$

The application of the time-passing function to P' yields a failing state (a message is not received in time) as shown below, where the second equality holds since $\texttt{Wait}(b^0(c).\,P) \cap \texttt{NEQueue}(ab:\varnothing) = \varnothing$:

$$\begin{array}{l} \Phi_3(\texttt{delay}(3).\,\overline{a}\,\text{`Hi'}.Q \mid b^0(c).\,P \mid ab:\varnothing) = \\ \Phi_3(\texttt{delay}(3).\,\overline{a}\,\text{`Hi'}.Q) \mid \Phi_3(b^0(c).\,P \mid \Phi_3(ab:\varnothing)) = \\ \texttt{delay}(0).\,\overline{a}\,\text{`Hi'}.Q \mid \texttt{failed} \mid ab:\varnothing \end{array}$$

6 Typing for Asynchronous Timed Processes

We validate programs against specifications using judgements of the form $\Gamma \vdash P \rhd \Delta$. Environments are defined as follows:

$$\begin{array}{ll} \Delta ::= \varnothing \mid \Delta, a:(\nu, S) \mid \Delta, ab:\mathtt{M} \qquad & \Theta ::= \varnothing \mid \Theta \cup \{\Delta\} \\ \Gamma ::= \varnothing \mid \Gamma, a:T \mid \Gamma, X:(\boldsymbol{T};\Theta) & \end{array}$$

Environment Δ is a session environment, used to keep track of the ongoing sessions. When $\Delta(a) = (\nu, S)$ it means that the process being validated is acting as a role in session a specified by S, and ν is the clock valuation describing a (virtual) time in which the next action in S may be executed. We write $\mathrm{dom}(\Delta)$ for the set of variables and channels in Δ. Environment Γ maps variables a to sorts T and process variables X to pairs $(\boldsymbol{T};\Theta)$, where $\boldsymbol{T}$ is a vector of sorts and Θ is a set of session environments. The mapping of process variable is used to type recursive processes: $\boldsymbol{T}$ is used to ensure well-typed instantiation of the recursion parameters, and Θ is used to model the set of possible scenarios when a new iteration begins.

Notation, assumptions, and auxiliary definitions. We write $\Delta + t$ for the session environment obtained by incrementing all clock valuations in the codomain of Δ by t.

Definition 8. *We define the disjoint union $A \uplus B$ of sets of clocks A and B as:*

$$A \uplus B = \{in_l(x) \mid x \in A\} \cup \{in_r(x) \mid x \in B\}$$

where in_l and in_r are one to one endofunctions on clocks and, for all $x \in A$ and $y \in B$, $in_l(x) \neq in_r(y)$. With an abuse of notation, we define the disjoint union of clock valuations ν_1, ν_2, in symbols $\nu_1 \uplus \nu_2$, as a clock valuation satisfying:

$$\nu_1 \uplus \nu_2(in_l(x)) = \nu_1(x) \qquad \nu_1 \uplus \nu_2(in_r(x)) = \nu_2(x)$$

We use the symbol $\biguplus$ for the iterate disjoint union.

For a configuration (ν, S) we define $\mathtt{val}((\nu,\mathtt{S})) = \nu$, and $\mathtt{type}((\nu,\mathtt{S})) = S$. We overload function val to session environments Δ as follows:

$$\mathtt{val}(\Delta) = \biguplus_{a \in \mathrm{dom}(\Delta)} \mathtt{val}(\Delta(a))$$

We require Θ to satisfy the following three conditions:

1. If $\Delta \in \Theta$ and $\Delta(a) = (\nu, S)$, then S is well-formed (Definition 1) against ν;
2. For all $\Delta_1 \in \Theta$, $\Delta_2 \in \Theta$: $\mathtt{type}(\Delta_1(a)) = S$ iff $\mathtt{type}(\Delta_2(a)) = S$;
3. There is guard δ such that:

$$\{\nu \mid \nu \models \delta\} = \bigcup_{\Delta \in \Theta} \mathtt{val}(\Delta).$$

The last condition ensures that Θ is finitely representable, and is key for decidability of type checking.

Example 7. We show some examples of Θ that do or do not satisfy the last requirement above. Let $S_1 = !T(x \leqslant 2).\mathbf{end}$ and $S_2 = !T(y \leqslant 2).\mathbf{end}$, and let:

$$\begin{aligned}
\Theta_1 &= \{\Delta \mid \Delta(a) = (\nu_1, S_1) \wedge \Delta(b) = (\nu_2, S_2) \wedge \nu_1(x) \leqslant 2 \wedge \nu_1(x) = \nu_2(y)\};\\
\Theta_2 &= \{\Delta \mid \Delta(a) = (\nu_1, S_1) \wedge \Delta(b) = (\nu_2, S_2) \wedge \nu_1(x) \leqslant \sqrt{2} \wedge \nu_1(x) = \nu_2(y)\};\\
\Theta_3 &= \{\Delta \mid \Delta(a) = (\nu_1, S_1) \wedge \Delta(b) = (\nu_2, S_2) \wedge \nu_1(x) + \nu_2(y) = 2\}.
\end{aligned}$$

We have that Θ_1 satisfies condition (3): let $\delta_1 = x \leqslant 2 \wedge y - x = 0$. It is easy to see that $\{\nu \mid \nu \models \delta_1\} = \bigcup_{\Delta \in \Theta} \mathtt{val}(\Delta)$. For Θ_2, a candidate proposition would be $\delta_2 = x \leqslant \sqrt{2} \wedge y - x = 0$. However, δ_2 can not be derived with the syntax of propositions, as $\sqrt{2}$ is irrational. Indeed, Θ_2 does not satisfy the condition. For Θ_3, let $\delta_3 = x + y = 2$. Again, δ_3 is not a guard, as additive constraints in the form $x + y = n$ are not allowed. Indeed, also Θ_3 does not satisfy the condition.

In the following, we write $\boldsymbol{a} : \boldsymbol{T}$ for $a_1 : T_1, \ldots, a_n : T_n$ when $\boldsymbol{a} = a_1, \ldots, a_n$ and $\boldsymbol{T} = T_1, \ldots, T_n$ (assuming $\boldsymbol{a}$ and $\boldsymbol{T}$ have the same number of elements). Similarly for $\boldsymbol{b} : (\boldsymbol{\nu}, \boldsymbol{S})$. In the typing rules, we use a few auxiliary definitions: Definition 9 (t-reading Δ) checks if any ongoing sessions in a Δ can perform an input action within a given timespan, and Definition 10 (Compatibility of configurations) extends the notion of duality to systems that are not in an initial state.

Definition 9 (t-reading Δ). *Session environment Δ is t-reading if there exist some $a \in \mathrm{dom}(\Delta)$, $t' < t$ and m such that: $\Delta(a) = (\nu, S) \wedge (\nu + t', S) \xrightarrow{?m}$.*

Namely, Δ is t-reading if any of the open sessions in the mapping prescribe a read action within the time-frame between ν and $\nu + t$. Definition 9 is used in the typing rules for time-consuming processes – [Vrcv], [Drcv], and [Del*t*] – to 'disallow' derivations when a (urgent) receive may happen.

Definition 10 (Compatibility of configurations). *Configuration $(\nu_1, S_1, \mathtt{M}_1)$ is compatible with $(\nu_2, S_2, \mathtt{M}_2)$, written $(\nu_1, S_1, \mathtt{M}_1) \perp (\nu_2, S_2, \mathtt{M}_2)$, if:*

1. $\mathtt{M}_1 = \varnothing \vee \mathtt{M}_2 = \varnothing$,
2. $\forall i \neq j \in \{1,2\} : \mathtt{M}_i = m;\mathtt{M}'_i \Rightarrow \exists \nu'_i, S'_i, m' : (\nu_i, S_i) \xrightarrow{?m'} (\nu'_i, S'_i) \wedge m <: m' \wedge (\nu'_i, S'_i, \mathtt{M}'_i) \bot (\nu_j, S_j, \mathtt{M}_j)$,
3. $\mathtt{M}_1 = \varnothing \wedge \mathtt{M}_2 = \varnothing \Rightarrow \nu_1 = \nu_2 \wedge S_1 = \overline{S_2}$.

By condition (3) initial configurations are compatible when they include dual types, i.e., $(\nu_0, S, \varnothing) \bot (\nu_0, \overline{S}, \varnothing)$. By condition (2) two configurations may temporarily misalign as execution proceeds: one may have read a message from its queue, while the other has not, as long as the former is ready to receive it immediately. Thanks to the particular shape of type's interactions, initial configurations – of the form $(\nu_0, S, \varnothing) \bot (\nu_0, \overline{S}, \varnothing)$ – will only reach systems, say $(\nu_1, S_1, \mathtt{M}_1) \bot (\nu_2, S_2, \mathtt{M}_2)$, in which at least one between $\mathtt{M}_1$ and $\mathtt{M}_2$ is empty. Condition (1) requires compatible configurations to satisfy this basic property.

Typing rules. The typing rules are given in Fig. 5. Rule [Vrcv] is for input processes. The first premise consists of two conditions requiring the time-span $[\nu, \nu + n]$ in which the process can receive the message to *coincide* with δ:

- $\nu + t \models \delta \Rightarrow t \leqslant n$ rules out processes that are not ready to receive a message when prescribed by the type.
- $t \leqslant n \Rightarrow \nu + t \models \delta$ requires that $a^n(b).P$ can read only at times that satisfy the type prescription δ.[2]

The second premise of [Vrcv] requires the continuation P to be well-typed against the continuation of the type, for all possible session environments where the virtual time is somewhere between $[\nu, \nu + n]$, where the virtual valuation ν in the mapping of session a is reset according to λ. Rule [Drcv], for processes receiving delegated sessions, is like [Vrcv] except: (a) the continuation P is typed against a session environment *extended with the received session* S', and (b) the clock valuation ν' of the receiving session must satisfy δ'. Recall that by formation rules (Sect. 2.1) S' is well-formed against all ν' that satisfy δ'.

Rule [Vsend] is for output processes. Send actions are instantaneous, hence the type current ν needs to satisfy δ. As customary, the continuation of the process needs to be well-typed against the continuation of the type (with ν being reset according to λ, and Γ extended with information on the sort of b). [Dsend] for delegation is similar but: (a) the delegated session is removed from the session environment (the process can no longer engage in the delegated session), and (b) valuation ν' of the delegated session must satisfy guard δ'.

Rule [Delδ] checks that P is well-typed against all possible solutions of δ. Rule [Del$t$] shifts the virtual valuations in the session environment of t. This is as the corresponding rule in [12] but with the addition of the check that Δ is not t-reading, needed because of urgent semantics.

Rule [Res] is for processes with scopes.

[2] While not necessary for our safety results, this constraint simplifies our theory. Timing variations between types and programs are all handled in one place: rule [Subt].

Rule [Rec] is for recursive processes. The rule is as usual [21] except that we use a set of session environments Θ (instead of a single Δ) to capture a set of possible scenarios in which a recursion instance may start, which may have different clock valuations. Rule [Var] is also as expected except for the use of Θ.

Rules [Par] and [Subt] straightforward.

Example 8 (Typing with subtyping). Subtyping substantially increases the power of our type system, in particular in the presence of channel passing. Intuitively, without subtyping, the type of any higher-order send action should be an equality constraint (e.g., $x = 1$) rather than more general timeout (e.g., $x < 1$). We illustrate our point using P defined below:

$$P = (\nu a_1 b_1)(\nu a_2 b_2)(P_1 \mid P_2 \mid P_3 \mid Q) \qquad P_1 = \mathtt{delay}(x \leqslant 1).\, \overline{a_1}\, a_2$$
$$P_2 = b_1^1(c).\, c^2(d) \qquad P_3 = \mathtt{delay}(1 \leqslant x \wedge x \leqslant 2).\, \overline{b_2}\, \mathtt{true}$$

where Q contains empty queues of the involved endpoints. Intuitively, P proceeds as follows: (1) P_1 sends channel a_2 to P_2 within one time unit, and terminates; (2) P_2 reads the message as soon as it arrives, and listens for a message across the received channel (a_2) for two time units; (3) P_3 sends value true through channel b_2 at a time in between 1 and 2, unaware that now she is communicating with P_2, and then terminates; (4) P_2 reads the message immediately and terminates. See below for one possible reduction:

$$\begin{aligned} P &\longrightarrow^* (\nu a_1 b_1)(\nu a_2 b_2)(\overline{a_1}\, a_2 \mid b_1^0(c).\, c^2(d) \mid \mathtt{delay}(0 \leqslant x \wedge x \leqslant 1).\, \overline{b_2}\, \mathtt{true}) \mid Q) \\ &\longrightarrow^* (\nu a_1 b_1)(\nu a_2 b_2)(0 \mid a_2^2(d) \mid \mathtt{delay}(0.5).\, \overline{b_2}\, \mathtt{true} \mid Q) \\ &\longrightarrow (\nu a_1 b_1)(\nu a_2 b_2)(0 \mid a_2^{1.5}(d) \mid \overline{b_2}\, \mathtt{true} \mid Q) \\ &\longrightarrow^* (\nu a_1 b_1)(\nu a_2 b_2)(0 \mid 0 \mid 0 \mid Q) \end{aligned}$$

Although P executes correctly, the involved processes are well-typed against types that are not dual:

$$\vdash\; P_1 \rhd a_1 : (\nu_0, S_1), a_2 : (\nu_0, S_2) \qquad \vdash\; P_2 \rhd b_1 : (\nu_0, S_1') \qquad \vdash\; P_3 \rhd b_2 : (\nu_0, \overline{S_2})$$

for $S_1 = !(y \leqslant 1, S_2)(x \leqslant 1)$, $S_2 = ?\mathtt{Bool}(1 \leqslant y \wedge y \leqslant 2)$, $S_1' = ?(y = 0, S_2')(x \leqslant 1)$. In order to type-check P, we need to apply rule [Res], requiring endpoints of the same session to have dual types. But clearly: $S_1' \neq \overline{S_1}$. Without subtyping, P would not be well-typed. By subtyping, however, $(y \leqslant 1, S_2) <: (y = 0, S_2')$ with $S_2' = ?\mathtt{Bool}(y \leqslant 2).\mathtt{end}$, and then $S_1' <: \overline{S_1}$. Thanks to the subtyping rule [subt] we can derive $\vdash\; P_2 \rhd b_1 :\; (\nu_0, \overline{S_1})$ and, in turn, $\vdash\; P \rhd \varnothing$.

7 Subject Reduction and Time Safety

The main properties of our typing system are Subject Reduction and Time Safety. Time Safety ensures that the execution of well-typed processes will only

$$\frac{\begin{array}{c}\forall t: \quad \nu + t \models \delta \iff t \leqslant n \\ \forall t \leqslant n: \quad \Gamma, b : T \vdash P \rhd \Delta + t, a : (\nu + t[\lambda \mapsto 0],\ S) \quad \Delta \text{ not } t\text{-reading}\end{array}}{\Gamma \vdash a^n(b).P \rhd \Delta, a : (\nu,\ ?T(\delta,\lambda).S)} \text{[Vrcv]}$$

$$\frac{\begin{array}{c}\forall t: \ \nu + t \models \delta \iff t \leqslant n \quad T = (\delta', S') \quad \nu' \models \delta' \\ \forall t \leqslant n: \ \Gamma \vdash P \rhd \Delta + t, a : (\nu + t[\lambda \mapsto 0],\ S), b : (\nu',\ S') \quad \Delta \text{ not } t\text{-reading}\end{array}}{\Gamma \vdash a^n(b).P \rhd \Delta, a : (\nu,\ ?T(\delta,\lambda).S)}$$

[Drcv]

$$\frac{\Gamma \vdash b : T \quad \nu \models \delta \quad \Gamma \vdash P \rhd \Delta, a : (\nu[\lambda \mapsto 0],\ S)}{\Gamma \vdash \overline{a}\, b.P \rhd \Delta, a : (\nu,\ !T(\delta,\lambda).S)} \text{[Vsend]}$$

$$\frac{T = (\delta', S') \quad \nu' \models \delta' \quad \nu \models \delta \quad \Gamma \vdash P \rhd \Delta, a : (\nu[\lambda \mapsto 0],\ S)}{\Gamma \vdash \overline{a}\, b.P \rhd \Delta, a : (\nu,\ !T(\delta,\lambda).S), b : (\nu',\ S')} \text{[Dsend]}$$

$$\frac{\forall t \in \delta : \Gamma \vdash \mathtt{delay}(t).P \rhd \Delta}{\Gamma \vdash \mathtt{delay}(\delta).P \rhd \Delta} \quad \frac{\Gamma \vdash P \rhd \Delta + t \quad \Delta \text{ not } t\text{-reading}}{\Gamma \vdash \mathtt{delay}(t).P \rhd \Delta} \text{[Del}\delta\text{/Del}t\text{]}$$

$$\frac{(\nu_1, S_1, \mathtt{M}_1) \bot (\nu_2, S_2, \mathtt{M}_2) \quad \Gamma \vdash P \rhd \Delta,\ a : (\nu_1,\ S_1),\ b : (\nu_2,\ S_2),\ ba : \mathtt{M}_1,\ ab : \mathtt{M}_2}{\Gamma \vdash (\nu ab)P \rhd \Delta}$$

[Res]

$$\frac{\Delta \in \Theta \quad \forall i: \ \Gamma \vdash \boldsymbol{v}_i : \boldsymbol{T}_i}{\Gamma, X : \boldsymbol{T}; \Theta \vdash X\langle \boldsymbol{v}\ ;\ \boldsymbol{b}\rangle \rhd \Delta} \quad \frac{\Gamma \vdash P \rhd \Delta_1 \quad \Gamma \vdash Q \rhd \Delta_2}{\Gamma \vdash P \mid Q \rhd \Delta_1, \Delta_2} \text{[Var/Par]}$$

$$\frac{\forall (\boldsymbol{\nu}, \boldsymbol{S}) \in \Theta: \ \Gamma, \boldsymbol{a} : \boldsymbol{T}, X : \boldsymbol{T}; \Theta \vdash P \rhd \boldsymbol{b} : (\boldsymbol{\nu}, \boldsymbol{S}) \quad \Gamma, X : \boldsymbol{T}; \Theta \vdash Q \rhd \Delta}{\Gamma \vdash \mathtt{def}\ X(\boldsymbol{a}\ ;\ \boldsymbol{b}) = P\ \mathtt{in}\ Q \rhd \Delta} \text{[Rec]}$$

$$\frac{\Gamma \vdash P \rhd \Delta' \quad \Delta' <: \Delta}{\Gamma \vdash P \rhd \Delta} \quad \frac{\Gamma \vdash P \rhd \Delta}{\Gamma \vdash P \rhd \Delta, a : (\nu,\ \mathtt{end})} \text{[Subt/Weak]}$$

Fig. 5. Selected typing rules for processes

reach *fail-free* states. Recall, P is fail-free when none of its sub-terms is the process `failed`. Time Safety builds on a condition that is not related with time, but with the structure of the process interactions. If an untimed process gets stuck due to mismatches in its communication structure, a timed process with the same communication structure may move to a failed state. Consider P below:

$$\begin{array}{ll} P = (\nu ab)(\nu cd)\, Q & R = ab : \varnothing \mid ba : \varnothing \mid cd : \varnothing \mid dc : \varnothing \\ Q = a^5(e).\,\overline{d}\, e.0 \mid c^5(e).\,\overline{b}\, e.0 \mid R & \end{array} \tag{13}$$

P is well-typed: $\varnothing \vdash P \rhd a : (\nu_0, S), b : (\nu_0, \overline{S}), c : (\nu_0, S), d : (\nu_0, \overline{S})$ with $S = ?\mathtt{Int}(x \leqslant 5, \varnothing).\mathtt{end}$. However, P can only make time steps, and when, overall, more than 5 time units elapse (e.g., 6 in the reduction below) P reaches a failed state due to a circular dependency between actions of sessions (νab) and (νcd):

$$P \quad \longrightarrow \quad \Phi_6(Q) = (\nu ab)(\nu cd)\,(\mathtt{failed} \mid \mathtt{failed} \mid R)$$

Our typing system does not check against such circularities across different interleaved sessions. This is common in work on untimed [21] and timed [12] session types. However, in the untimed scenario, progress for interleaved sessions can be guaranteed by means of additional checks on processes [17]. Time Safety builds on the results in [17] by using an assumption (receive liveness) on the underneath structure of the timed processes. This assumptions is formally captured in Definition 11, which is based on an untimed variant of our calculus.

The untimed calculus. We define untimed processes, denoted by $\hat{P}$, as processes obtained from the grammar given for timed processes (Sect. 5) without delays and failed processes. In untimed processes, time annotations of branching/receive processes are immaterial, hence omitted in the rest of the paper.

Given a (timed) process P, one can obtain its untimed counter-part by *erasing* delays and failed processes; we denoted the result of such erasure on P by $\texttt{erase}(P)$. The semantics of untimed processes is defined as the one for timed processes (Sect. 5) except that reduction rules [Delay], [TStr], and [Red2], are removed. Abusing the notation, we write $\hat{P} \longrightarrow \hat{P}'$ when an untimed process $\hat{P}$ moves to a state $\hat{P}'$ using the semantics for untimed processes. The definitions of $\texttt{Wait}(\hat{P})$ and $\texttt{NEQueue}(\hat{P})$ can be derived from the definitions for timed processes in the straightforward way.

Definition 11 (receive liveness) formalises our assumption on the interaction structures of a process.

Definition 11 (Receive liveness). *$\hat{P}$ is said to satisfy receive liveness (or is* live*, for short) if, for all $\hat{P}'$ such that $\hat{P} \longrightarrow^* \hat{P}'$:*

$$\hat{P}' \equiv (\nu ab)\hat{Q} \wedge a \in \texttt{Wait}(\hat{Q}) \implies \exists \hat{Q}' : \hat{Q} \longrightarrow^* \hat{Q}' \wedge a \in \texttt{NEQueue}(\hat{Q}')$$

In any reachable state $\hat{P}'$ of a live untimed process $\hat{P}$, if any endpoint a in $\hat{P}'$ is waiting to receive a message ($a \in \texttt{Wait}(\hat{Q})$), then the overall process is able to reach a state $\hat{Q}'$ where a can perform the receive action ($a \in \texttt{NEQueue}(\hat{Q}')$).

Consider process P in (13). The untimed process $\texttt{erase}(P)$ is not live because $\texttt{Wait}(\texttt{erase}(P)) = \{a, c\}$ and $a, c \notin \texttt{NEQueue}(\texttt{erase}(P))$, since $\texttt{NEQueue}(\texttt{erase}(P))$ is the empty set. Syntactically, $\texttt{erase}(P)$ is as P, but it does not have the same behaviour. P can only make time steps, reaching a failed process, while $\texttt{erase}(P)$ is stuck, as untimed processes only make communication steps.

Properties. Time safety relies on Subject Reduction Theorem 4, which establishes a relation (preserved by reduction) of well-typed processes and their types.

Theorem 4 (Subject reduction for closed systems). *Let $\texttt{erase}(P)$ be live. If $\emptyset \vdash P \rhd \emptyset$ and $P \longrightarrow P'$ then $\emptyset \vdash P' \rhd \emptyset$.*

Note that Subject Reduction assumes $\texttt{erase}(P)$ to be live. For instance, the example of P in (13) is well-typed, but $\texttt{erase}(P)$ is not live. The process can reduce to a failed state (as illustrated earlier in this section) that cannot be typed (failed processes are not well-typed). Time Safety establishes that well-typed processes only reduce to fail-free states.

Theorem 5 (Time safety). *If* $\texttt{erase}(P)$ *is live,* $\vdash P \rhd \emptyset$ *and* $P \longrightarrow^* P'$, *then* P' *is fail-free.*

Typing is decidable if one uses processes annotated with the following information: (1) scope restrictions $(\nu ab : S)P$ are annotated with the type S of the session for endpoint a (the type of b is implicitly assumed to be $\overline{S}$ and both endpoints are type checked in the initial clock valuation ν_0); (2) receive actions $a^n(b : T).\,P$ are annotated with the type T of the received message; (3) recursion $X(\boldsymbol{a} : \boldsymbol{T}\ ;\ \boldsymbol{a} : \boldsymbol{S}, \delta) = P$ are annotated with types for each parameter, and a guard modelling the state of the clocks. We call annotated programs those annotated processes derived without using productions marked as run-time (i.e., $\texttt{failed}$ and $\texttt{delay}(t).\,P$), and where n in $a^n(b : T).\,P$ ranges over $\mathbb{Q}_{\geqslant 0} \cup \{\infty\}$.

Proposition 2. *Type checking for annotated programs is decidable.*

8 Conclusion and Related Work

We introduced duality and subtyping relations for asynchronous timed session types. Unlike for untimed and timed synchronous [6] dualities, the composition of dual types does not enjoy progress in general. Compositions of asynchronous timed dual types enjoy progress *when using an urgent receive semantics*. We propose a behavioural typing system for a timed calculus that features non-blocking and blocking receive primitives (with and without timeout), and time consuming primitives of arbitrary but constrained delays. The main properties of the typing system are Subject Reduction and Time Safety; both results rely on an assumption (receive liveness) of the underneath interaction structure of processes. In related work on timed session types [12], receive liveness is not required for Subject Reduction; this is because the processes in [12] block (rather than reaching a failed state) whenever they cannot progress correctly, hence e.g., missed deadline are regarded as progress violations. By explicitly capturing failures, our calculus paves the way for future work on combining static checking with run-time instrumentation to prevent or handle failures.

Asynchronous timed session types have been introduced in [12], in a multiparty setting, together with a timed π-calculus, and a type system. The direct extension of session types with time introduces unfeasible executions (i.e., types may get stuck), as we have shown in Example 1. [12] features a notion of feasibility for choreographies, which ensures that types enjoy progress. We ensure progress of types by formation and duality. The semantics of types in [12] is different from ours in that receive actions are not urgent. The work in [12] gives one extra condition on types (wait-freedom), because feasible types may still yield undesirable executions in well-typed processes. Thanks to our duality, subtyping, and calculus (in particular the blocking receive primitive with timeout) this condition is unnecessary in this work. As a result, our typing system allows for types that are *not wait-free*. By dropping wait-freedom, we can type a class of common real-world protocols in which processes may be ready to receive messages even before the final deadline of the corresponding senders. Remarkably,

SMTP mentioned in the introduction is *not wait-free*. For some other aspects, our work is less general than the one in [12], as we consider binary sessions rather than multiparty sessions. A theory of timed multiparty asynchronous protocols that encompasses the protocols in [12] and those considered here is an interesting future direction. The work in [6] introduces a theory of synchronous timed session types, based on a decidable notion of compatibility, called *compliance*, that ensures progress of types, and is equivalent to synchronous timed duality and subtyping in a precise sense [6]. Our duality and subtyping are similar to those in [6], but apply to the asynchronous scenario. The work in [15] introduces a typed calculus based on temporal session types. The temporal modalities in [15] can be used as a discrete model of time. Timed session types, thanks to clocks and resets, are able to model complex timed dependencies that temporal session types do not seem able to capture. Other work studies models for asynchronous timed interactions, e.g., Communicating Timed Automata [23] (CTA), timed Message Sequence Charts [2], but not their relationships with processes. The work in [5] introduces a refinement for CTA, and presents a notion of urgency similar to the one used in this paper, preliminary studied also in [29].

Several timed calculi have been introduced outside the context of behavioural types. The work in [32] extends the π- calculus with time primitives inspired in CTA and is closer, in principle, to our types than our processes. Another timed extension of the π-calculus with time-consuming actions has been applied to the analysis the active times of processes [18]. Some works focus on specific aspects of timed behaviour, such as timeouts [9], transactions [24,27], and services [25]. Our calculus does not feature exception handlers, nor timed transactions. Our focus in on detecting time violations via static typing, so that a process only moves to fail-free states.

The calculi in [7,12,15] have been used in combination with session types. The calculus in [12] features a non-blocking receive primitive similar to our $a^0(b).\,P$, but that never fails (i.e., time is not allowed to flow if a process tries to read from an empty buffer—possibly leading to a stuck process rather than a failed state). The calculus in [7] features a blocking receive primitive without timeout, equivalent to our $a^\infty(b).\,P$. The calculus in [15], seems able to encode a non-blocking receive primitive like the one of [12] and a blocking receive primitive without timeout like our $a^\infty(b).\,P$. None of these works features blocking receive primitives with timeouts. Furthermore, existing works feature [7,12] or can encode [15] only precise delays, equivalent to $\texttt{delay}(x = n).\,P$. Such punctual predictions are often difficult to achieve. Arbitrary but constrained delays are closer abstractions of time-consuming programming primitives (and possibly, of predictions one can derive by cost analysis, e.g., [20]).

As to applications, timed session types have been used for run-time monitoring [7,30] and static checking [12]. A promising future direction is that of integrating static typing with run-time verification and enforcement, towards a theory of hybrid timed session types. In this context, extending our calculus with exception handlers [9,24,27] could allow an extension of the typing system, that introduces run-time instrumentation to handle unexpected time failures.

References

1. Aceto, L., Ingólfsdóttir, A., Larsen, K.G., Srba, J.: Reactive Systems: Modelling, Specification and Verification. Cambridge University Press, Cambridge (2007). https://doi.org/10.1017/CBO9780511814105
2. Akshay, S., Gastin, P., Mukund, M., Kumar, K.N.: Model checking time-constrained scenario-based specifications. In: FSTTCS. LIPIcs, vol. 8, pp. 204–215. Schloss Dagstuhl - Leibniz-Zentrum fuer Informatik (2010). https://doi.org/10.4230/LIPIcs.FSTTCS.2010.204
3. Alur, R., Dill, D.L.: A theory of timed automata. TCS **126**, 183–235 (1994)
4. Advanced Message Queuing Protocols (AMQP). https://www.amqp.org/
5. Bartoletti, M., Bocchi, L., Murgia, M.: Progress-preserving refinements of CTA. In: CONCUR. LIPIcs, vol. 118, pp. 40:1–40:19. Schloss Dagstuhl-Leibniz-Zentrum fuer Informatik (2018). https://doi.org/10.4230/LIPIcs.CONCUR.2018.40
6. Bartoletti, M., Cimoli, T., Murgia, M.: Timed session types. Log. Methods Comput. Sci. **13**(4) (2017). https://doi.org/10.23638/LMCS-13(4:25)2017
7. Bartoletti, M., Cimoli, T., Murgia, M., Podda, A.S., Pompianu, L.: A contract-oriented middleware. In: Braga, C., Ölveczky, P.C. (eds.) FACS 2015. LNCS, vol. 9539, pp. 86–104. Springer, Cham (2016). https://doi.org/10.1007/978-3-319-28934-2_5
8. Bengtsson, J., Yi, W.: Timed automata: semantics, algorithms and tools. In: Desel, J., Reisig, W., Rozenberg, G. (eds.) ACPN 2003. LNCS, vol. 3098, pp. 87–124. Springer, Heidelberg (2004). https://doi.org/10.1007/978-3-540-27755-2_3
9. Berger, M., Yoshida, N.: Timed, distributed, probabilistic, typed processes. In: Shao, Z. (ed.) APLAS 2007. LNCS, vol. 4807, pp. 158–174. Springer, Heidelberg (2007). https://doi.org/10.1007/978-3-540-76637-7_11
10. Bettini, L., Coppo, M., D'Antoni, L., De Luca, M., Dezani-Ciancaglini, M., Yoshida, N.: Global progress in dynamically interleaved multiparty sessions. In: van Breugel, F., Chechik, M. (eds.) CONCUR 2008. LNCS, vol. 5201, pp. 418–433. Springer, Heidelberg (2008). https://doi.org/10.1007/978-3-540-85361-9_33
11. Bocchi, L., Murgia, M., Vasconcelos, V., Yoshida, N.: Asynchronous timed session types: from duality to time-sensitive processes (2018). https://www.cs.kent.ac.uk/people/staff/lb514/tstp.html
12. Bocchi, L., Yang, W., Yoshida, N.: Timed multiparty session types. In: Baldan, P., Gorla, D. (eds.) CONCUR 2014. LNCS, vol. 8704, pp. 419–434. Springer, Heidelberg (2014). https://doi.org/10.1007/978-3-662-44584-6_29
13. Bruno, E.J., Bollella, G.: Real-Time Java Programming: With Java RTS, 1st edn. Prentice Hall PTR, Upper Saddle River (2009)
14. Chen, T.C., Dezani-Ciancaglini, M., Yoshida, N.: On the preciseness of subtyping in session types. In: PPDP, pp. 135–146. ACM (2014). https://doi.org/10.1145/2643135.2643138
15. Das, A., Hoffmann, J., Pfenning, F.: Parallel complexity analysis with temporal session types. Proc. ACM Program. Lang. **2**(ICFP), 91:1–91:30 (2018). https://doi.org/10.1145/3236786
16. Demangeon, R., Honda, K.: Full abstraction in a subtyped pi-calculus with linear types. In: Katoen, J.-P., König, B. (eds.) CONCUR 2011. LNCS, vol. 6901, pp. 280–296. Springer, Heidelberg (2011). https://doi.org/10.1007/978-3-642-23217-6_19

17. Dezani-Ciancaglini, M., de'Liguoro, U., Yoshida, N.: On progress for structured communications. In: Barthe, G., Fournet, C. (eds.) TGC 2007. LNCS, vol. 4912, pp. 257–275. Springer, Heidelberg (2008). https://doi.org/10.1007/978-3-540-78663-4_18
18. Fischer, M., Förster, S., Windisch, A., Monjau, D., Balser, B.: A new time extension to π-calculus based on time consuming transition semanticss. In: Grimm, C. (ed.) Languages for System Specification, pp. 271–283. Springer, Boston (2004). https://doi.org/10.1007/1-4020-7991-5_17
19. Gay, S.J., Hole, M.: Subtyping for session types in the pi calculus. Acta Inf. **42**(2–3), 191–225 (2005). https://doi.org/10.1007/s00236-005-0177-z
20. Hoffmann, J., Shao, Z.: Automatic static cost analysis for parallel programs. In: Vitek, J. (ed.) ESOP 2015. LNCS, vol. 9032, pp. 132–157. Springer, Heidelberg (2015). https://doi.org/10.1007/978-3-662-46669-8_6
21. Honda, K., Yoshida, N., Carbone, M.: Multiparty asynchronous session types. In: POPL, pp. 273–284. ACM (2008)
22. Klensin, J.: Simple mail transfer protocol. RFC 5321, October 2008. https://tools.ietf.org/html/rfc5321
23. Krcal, P., Yi, W.: Communicating timed automata: the more synchronous, the more difficult to verify. In: Ball, T., Jones, R.B. (eds.) CAV 2006. LNCS, vol. 4144, pp. 249–262. Springer, Heidelberg (2006). https://doi.org/10.1007/11817963_24
24. Laneve, C., Zavattaro, G.: Foundations of web transactions. In: Sassone, V. (ed.) FoSSaCS 2005. LNCS, vol. 3441, pp. 282–298. Springer, Heidelberg (2005). https://doi.org/10.1007/978-3-540-31982-5_18
25. Lapadula, A., Pugliese, R., Tiezzi, F.: CWS: a timed service-oriented calculus. In: Jones, C.B., Liu, Z., Woodcock, J. (eds.) ICTAC 2007. LNCS, vol. 4711, pp. 275–290. Springer, Heidelberg (2007). https://doi.org/10.1007/978-3-540-75292-9_19
26. Larsen, K.G., Pettersson, P., Yi, W.: Uppaal in a nutshell. Int. J. Softw. Tools Technolo. Transf. **1**, 134–152 (1997)
27. López, H.A., Pérez, J.A.: Time and exceptional behavior in multiparty structured interactions. In: Carbone, M., Petit, J.-M. (eds.) WS-FM 2011. LNCS, vol. 7176, pp. 48–63. Springer, Heidelberg (2012). https://doi.org/10.1007/978-3-642-29834-9_5
28. Milner, R.: Communicating and Mobile Systems: The π-calculus. Cambridge University Press, New York (1999)
29. Murgia, M.: On urgency in asynchronous timed session types. In: ICE. EPTCS, vol. 279, pp. 85–94 (2018). https://doi.org/10.4204/EPTCS.279.9
30. Neykova, R., Bocchi, L., Yoshida, N.: Timed runtime monitoring for multiparty conversations. Formal Asp. Comput. **29**(5), 877–910 (2017). https://doi.org/10.1007/s00165-017-0420-8
31. Pierce, B.C.: Types and Programming Languages. MIT Press, Cambridge (2002)
32. Saeedloei, N., Gupta, G.: Timed π-calculus. In: Abadi, M., Lluch Lafuente, A. (eds.) TGC 2013. LNCS, vol. 8358, pp. 119–135. Springer, Cham (2014). https://doi.org/10.1007/978-3-319-05119-2_8
33. Vinoski, S.: Advanced message queuing protocol. IEEE Internet Comput. **10**(6), 87–89 (2006). https://doi.org/10.1109/MIC.2006.116
34. Yovine, S.: Kronos: a verification tool for real-time systems. (Kronos user's manual release 2.2). Int. J. Softw. Tools Technol. Transf. **1**, 123–133 (1997)

Manifest Deadlock-Freedom for Shared Session Types

Stephanie Balzer[1(✉)], Bernardo Toninho[2(✉)], and Frank Pfenning[1]

[1] Carnegie Mellon University, Pittsburgh, USA
balzers@cs.cmu.edu
[2] NOVA LINCS, Universidade Nova de Lisboa, Lisbon, Portugal
btoninho@fct.unl.pt

Abstract. Shared session types generalize the Curry-Howard correspondence between intuitionistic linear logic and the session-typed π-calculus with adjoint modalities that mediate between linear and shared session types, giving rise to a programming model where shared channels must be used according to a locking discipline of acquire-release. While this generalization greatly increases the range of programs that can be written, the gain in expressiveness comes at the cost of deadlock-freedom, a property which holds for many linear session type systems. In this paper, we develop a type system for logically-shared sessions in which types capture not only the interactive behavior of processes but also constrain the order of resources (i.e., shared processes) they may acquire. This type-level information is then used to rule out cyclic dependencies among acquires and synchronization points, resulting in a system that ensures *deadlock-free communication* for well-typed processes in the presence of shared sessions, higher-order channel passing, and recursive processes. We illustrate our approach on a series of examples, showing that it rules out deadlocks in circular networks of both shared and linear recursive processes, while still being permissive enough to type concurrent implementations of shared imperative data structures as processes.

Keywords: Linear and shared session types · Deadlock-freedom

1 Introduction

Session types [25–27] naturally describe the interaction protocols that arise amongst concurrent processes that communicate via message-passing. This typing discipline has been integrated (with varying static safety guarantees) into several mainstream language such as Java [28,29], F# [43], Scala [49,50], Go [11] and Rust [33]. Session types moreover enjoy a logical correspondence between *linear logic* and the *session-typed π-calculus* [8,9,51,55]. Languages building on this correspondence [24,52,55] not only guarantee *session*

Supported by NSF Grant No. CCF-1718267: "Enriching Session Types for Practical Concurrent Programming" and NOVA LINCS (Ref. UID/CEC/04516/2019).

L. Caires (Ed.): ESOP 2019, LNCS 11423, pp. 611–639, 2019.
https://doi.org/10.1007/978-3-030-17184-1_22

fidelity (i.e., type preservation) but also *deadlock-freedom* (i.e., global progress). The latter is guaranteed even in the presence of interleaved sessions, which are often excluded from the deadlock-free fragments of traditional session-typed frameworks [20,26,27,53]. These logical session types, however, exclude programming scenarios that demand *sharing* of mutable resources (e.g., shared databases or shared output devices) instead of functional resource replication.

To increase their practicality, logical session types have been extended with *manifest sharing* [2]. In the resulting language, linear and shared sessions coexist, but the type system enforces that clients of shared sessions run in mutual exclusion of each other. This separation is achieved by enforcing an *acquire-release* policy, where a client of a shared session must first acquire the session before it can participate in it along a private linear channel. Conversely, when a client releases a session, it gives up its linear channel and only retains a shared reference to the session. Thus, sessions in the presence of manifest sharing can change, or *shift*, between shared and linear execution modes. At the type-level, the acquire-release policy manifests in a stratification of session types into linear and shared with adjoint modalities [5,47,48], connecting the two strata. Operationally, the modality shifting *up* from the linear to the shared layer translates into an *acquire* and the one shifting *down* from shared to linear into a *release*.

Manifest sharing greatly increases the range of programs that can be written because it recovers the expressiveness of the untyped asynchronous π-calculus [3] while maintaining session fidelity. As in the π-calculus, however, the gain in expressiveness comes at the cost of *deadlock-freedom*. An illustrative example is an implementation of the classical dining philosophers problem, shown in Fig. 1, using the language $\mathsf{SILL_S}$ [2] that supports manifest sharing (in this setting we often equate a process with the session it offers along a distinguished channel). The code shows the process *fork_proc*, implementing a session of type sfork, and the processes *thinking* and *eating*, implementing sessions of type philosopher. We defer the details of the typing and the definition of the session types sfork and philosopher to Sect. 2 and focus on the programmatic working of the processes for now. For ease of reading, we typeset shared session types and variables denoting shared channel references in red.

A *fork_proc* process represents a fork that can be perpetually acquired and released. The actions accept and detach are the duals of acquire and release, respectively, allowing a process to accept an acquire by a client and to initiate a release by a client, respectively. Process thinking has two shared channel references as arguments, for the forks to the left and right of the philosopher, which the process tries to acquire. If the acquire succeeds, the process recurs as an eating philosopher with two (now) linear channel references of type lfork. Once a philosopher is done eating, it releases both forks and recurs as a thinking philosopher. Let's set a table for three philosopher that share three forks, all spawned as processes executing in parallel:

$$f_0 \leftarrow \textit{fork\_proc} \; ; \; f_1 \leftarrow \textit{fork\_proc} \; ; \; f_2 \leftarrow \textit{fork\_proc} \; ;$$
$$p_0 \leftarrow \textit{thinking} \leftarrow f_0, f_1 \; ; \; p_1 \leftarrow \textit{thinking} \leftarrow f_1, f_2 \; ; \; p_2 \leftarrow \textit{thinking} \leftarrow f_2, f_0 \; ;$$

$$
\begin{array}{lll}
\mathit{fork\_proc} : \{\mathsf{sfork}\} & \mathit{thinking} : \{\mathsf{phil} \leftarrow \mathsf{sfork}, \mathsf{sfork}\} & \mathit{eating} : \{\mathsf{phil} \leftarrow \mathsf{lfork}, \mathsf{lfork}\} \\
c \leftarrow \mathit{fork\_proc} = & c \leftarrow \mathit{thinking} \leftarrow \mathit{left}, \mathit{right} = & c \leftarrow \mathit{eating} \leftarrow \mathit{left}', \mathit{right}' = \\
\quad c' \leftarrow \mathsf{accept}\ c\ ; & \quad \mathit{left}' \leftarrow \mathsf{acquire}\ \mathit{left}\ ; & \quad \mathit{right} \leftarrow \mathsf{release}\ \mathit{right}'\ ; \\
\quad c \leftarrow \mathsf{detach}\ c'\ ; & \quad \mathit{right}' \leftarrow \mathsf{acquire}\ \mathit{right}\ ; & \quad \mathit{left} \leftarrow \mathsf{release}\ \mathit{left}'\ ; \\
\quad c \leftarrow \mathit{fork\_proc} & \quad c \leftarrow \mathit{eating} \leftarrow \mathit{left}', \mathit{right}'\ ; & \quad c \leftarrow \mathit{thinking} \leftarrow \mathit{left}, \mathit{right}
\end{array}
$$

Fig. 1. Dining philosophers in $\mathsf{SILL_S}$ [2].

Infamously, this configuration may deadlock because of the *circular* dependency between the acquires. We can break this cycle by changing the last line to $p_2 \leftarrow \mathit{thinking} \leftarrow f_0, f_2$, ensuring that forks are acquired in increasing order.

Perhaps surprisingly, cyclic dependencies between acquire requests are not the only source of deadlocks. Fig. 2 gives an example, defining the processes *owner* and *contester*, which both have a shared channel reference to a common resource that can be perpetually acquired and released. Both processes acquire the shared resource, but additionally exchange the message ping. More precisely, process *owner* spawns the process *contester*, acquires the shared resource, and only releases the resource after having received the message ping from the *contester*. Process *contester*, on the other hand, first attempts to acquire the resource and then sends the message *ping* to the owner. The program deadlocks if process *owner* acquires the resource first. In that case, process *owner* waits for process *contester* to send the message ping while process *contester* waits to acquire the resource held by process *owner*. We note that this deadlock arises in both synchronous and asynchronous semantics.

$$
\begin{array}{ll}
\mathit{owner} : \{\mathbf{1} \leftarrow \mathsf{sres}\} & \mathit{contester} : \{\oplus\{\mathsf{ping} : \mathbf{1}\} \leftarrow \mathsf{sres}\} \\
o \leftarrow \mathit{owner} \leftarrow \mathit{sr} = & c \leftarrow \mathit{contester} \leftarrow \mathit{sr} = \\
\quad c \leftarrow \mathit{contester} \leftarrow \mathit{sr}\ ; & \quad \mathit{lr} \leftarrow \mathsf{acquire}\ \mathit{sr}\ ; \\
\quad \mathit{lr} \leftarrow \mathsf{acquire}\ \mathit{sr}\ ; & \quad c.\mathsf{ping}\ ; \\
\quad \mathsf{case}\ c\ \mathsf{of} & \quad \mathit{sr} \leftarrow \mathsf{release}\ \mathit{lr}\ ; \\
\quad \mid \mathsf{ping} \rightarrow \mathsf{wait}\ c\ ; & \quad \mathsf{close}\ c \\
\qquad\qquad \mathit{sr} \leftarrow \mathsf{release}\ \mathit{lr}\ ;\ \mathsf{close}\ o &
\end{array}
$$

Fig. 2. Circular dependencies among acquire and synchronization actions.

In this paper, we develop a type system for manifest sharing that rules out cycles between acquire requests and interdependencies between acquire requests and synchronization actions, detecting the two kinds of deadlocks explained above. In our type system, session types not only prescribe *when* resources must be acquired and released, but also the *range* of resources that may be acquired. To this end, we equip the type system with the notion of a *world*, an abstract value at which a process resides, and type processes relative to an acyclic *ordering* on worlds, akin to the partial-order based approaches of [34,37]. The contributions of this paper are:

- a characterization of the possible forms of deadlocks that can arise in shared session types;
- the introduction of manifest deadlock-freedom, where resource dependencies are manifest in the type structure via world modalities;
- its elaboration in the programming language $\mathsf{SILL}_{\mathsf{S}^+}$, resulting in a type system, a synchronous operational semantics, and proofs of session fidelity (preservation) and a strong form of progress that excludes all deadlocks;
- the novel abstraction of green and red arrows to reason about the interdependencies between processes;
- an illustration of the concepts on various examples, including an extensive comparison with related work.

This paper is structured as follows: Sect. 2 provides a short introduction to manifest sharing. Sect. 3 develops the type system and dynamics of the language $\mathsf{SILL}_{\mathsf{S}^+}$. Sect. 4 illustrates the introduced concepts on an extended example. Sect. 5 discusses the meta-theoretical properties of $\mathsf{SILL}_{\mathsf{S}^+}$, emphasizing progress. Sect. 6 compares with examples of related work and identifies future work. Sect. 7 discusses related work, and Sect. 8 concludes this paper.

2 Manifest Sharing

In the previous section, we have already explored the programmatic workings of *manifest sharing* [2], which enforces an *acquire-release* policy on shared channel references. In this section, we clarify the typing of shared processes.

A key contribution of manifest sharing is not only to support acquire-release as a programming primitive but also to make it *manifest* in the type system. Generalizing the idea of type *stratification* [5,47,48], session types are partitioned into a linear and shared layer with two *adjoint modalities* connecting the layers:

$$\begin{array}{ll} A_{\mathsf{S}} & \triangleq \uparrow_{\mathsf{L}}^{\mathsf{S}} A_{\mathsf{L}} \\ A_{\mathsf{L}}, B_{\mathsf{L}} & \triangleq A_{\mathsf{L}} \otimes B_{\mathsf{L}} \mid \oplus\{\overline{l : A_{\mathsf{L}}}\} \mid \&\{\overline{l : A_{\mathsf{L}}}\} \mid A_{\mathsf{L}} \multimap B_{\mathsf{L}} \mid \exists x{:}A_{\mathsf{S}}.B_{\mathsf{L}} \mid \Pi x{:}A_{\mathsf{S}}.B_{\mathsf{L}} \mid \mathbf{1} \mid \downarrow_{\mathsf{L}}^{\mathsf{S}} A_{\mathsf{S}} \end{array}$$

In the linear layer, we get the standard connectives of intuitionistic linear logic ($A_{\mathsf{L}} \otimes B_{\mathsf{L}}$, $A_{\mathsf{L}} \multimap B_{\mathsf{L}}$, $\oplus\{\overline{l : A_{\mathsf{L}}}\}$, $\&\{\overline{l : A_{\mathsf{L}}}\}$, and $\mathbf{1}$). These connectives are extended with the modal operator $\downarrow_{\mathsf{L}}^{\mathsf{S}} A_{\mathsf{S}}$, shifting *down* from the shared to the linear layer. Similarly, in the shared layer, we have the operator $\uparrow_{\mathsf{L}}^{\mathsf{S}} A_{\mathsf{L}}$, shifting *up* from the linear to the shared layer. The former translates into a *release* (and, dually, detach), the latter into an *acquire* (and, dually, accept). As a result, we obtain a system in which session types prescribe all forms of communication, including the acquisition and release of shared processes.

Table 1 provides an overview of $\mathsf{SILL}_{\mathsf{S}}$'s session types and their operational reading. Since $\mathsf{SILL}_{\mathsf{S}}$ is based on an intuitionistic interpretation of linear logic session types [8], types are expressed from the point of view of the *providing process* with the channel along which the process provides the session behavior being characterized by its session type. This choice avoids the explicit duality operation present in original presentations of session types [25,26] and in those based

Table 1. Session types in $\mathsf{SILL_S}$ and their operational meaning.

Session type		**Process term**		
current	**cont**	**current**	**cont**	**Description**
$c_\mathsf{L} : \oplus\{\overline{l : A_\mathsf{L}}\}$	$c_\mathsf{L} : A_{\mathsf{L}_h}$	$c_\mathsf{L}.l_h \,; P$	P	sends label l_h along c_L
		$\mathsf{case}\ c_\mathsf{L}\ \mathsf{of}\ \overline{l \Rightarrow Q}$	Q_h	receives label l_h along c_L
$c_\mathsf{L} : \&\{\overline{l : A_\mathsf{L}}\}$	$c_\mathsf{L} : A_{\mathsf{L}_h}$	$\mathsf{case}\ c_\mathsf{L}\ \mathsf{of}\ \overline{l \Rightarrow P}$	P_h	receives label l_h along c
		$c_\mathsf{L}.l_h \,; Q$	Q	sends label l_h along c_L
$c_\mathsf{L} : A_\mathsf{L} \otimes B_\mathsf{L}$	$c_\mathsf{L} : B_\mathsf{L}$	$\mathsf{send}\ c_\mathsf{L}\ d_\mathsf{L} \,; P$	P	sends channel $d_\mathsf{L} : A_\mathsf{L}$ along c_L
		$y_\mathsf{L} \leftarrow \mathsf{recv}\ c_\mathsf{L} \,; Q_{y_\mathsf{L}}$	$[d_\mathsf{L}/y_\mathsf{L}]\, Q_{y_\mathsf{L}}$	receives channel $d_\mathsf{L} : A_\mathsf{L}$ along c_L
$c_\mathsf{L} : A_\mathsf{L} \multimap B_\mathsf{L}$	$c_\mathsf{L} : B_\mathsf{L}$	$y_\mathsf{L} \leftarrow \mathsf{recv}\ c_\mathsf{L} \,; P_{y_\mathsf{L}}$	$[d_\mathsf{L}/y_\mathsf{L}]\, P_{y_\mathsf{L}}$	receives channel $d_\mathsf{L} : A_\mathsf{L}$ along c_L
		$\mathsf{send}\ c_\mathsf{L}\ d_\mathsf{L} \,; Q$	Q	sends channel $d_\mathsf{L} : A_\mathsf{L}$ along c_L
$c_\mathsf{L} : \Pi x{:}A_\mathsf{S}.B_\mathsf{L}$	$c_\mathsf{L} : B_\mathsf{L}$	$\mathsf{send}\ c_\mathsf{L}\ d_\mathsf{S} \,; P$	P	sends channel $d_\mathsf{S} : A_\mathsf{S}$ along c_L
		$y_\mathsf{S} \leftarrow \mathsf{recv}\ c_\mathsf{L} \,; Q_{y_\mathsf{S}}$	$[d_\mathsf{S}/y_\mathsf{S}]\, Q_{y_\mathsf{S}}$	receives channel $d_\mathsf{S} : A_\mathsf{S}$ along c_L
$c_\mathsf{L} : \exists x{:}A_\mathsf{S}.B_\mathsf{L}$	$c_\mathsf{L} : B_\mathsf{L}$	$y_\mathsf{S} \leftarrow \mathsf{recv}\ c_\mathsf{L} \,; P_{y_\mathsf{S}}$	$[d_\mathsf{S}/y_\mathsf{S}]\, P_{y_\mathsf{S}}$	receives channel $d_\mathsf{S} : A_\mathsf{S}$ along c_L
		$\mathsf{send}\ c_\mathsf{L}\ d_\mathsf{S} \,; Q$	Q	sends channel $d_\mathsf{S} : A_\mathsf{S}$ along c_L
$c_\mathsf{L} : \mathbf{1}$	-	$\mathsf{close}\ c_\mathsf{L}$	-	sends "end" along c_L
		$\mathsf{wait}\ c_\mathsf{L} \,; Q$	Q	receives "end" along c_L
$c_\mathsf{L} : \downarrow^\mathsf{S}_\mathsf{L} A_\mathsf{S}$	$c_\mathsf{S} : A_\mathsf{S}$	$c_\mathsf{S} \leftarrow \mathsf{detach}\ c_\mathsf{L} \,; P_{x_\mathsf{S}}$	$[c_\mathsf{S}/x_\mathsf{S}]\, P_{x_\mathsf{S}}$	sends "detach c_S" along c_L
		$x_\mathsf{S} \leftarrow \mathsf{release}\ c_\mathsf{L} \,; Q_{x_\mathsf{S}}$	$[c_\mathsf{S}/x_\mathsf{S}]\, Q_{x_\mathsf{S}}$	receives "detach c_S" along c_L
$c_\mathsf{S} : \uparrow^\mathsf{S}_\mathsf{L} A_\mathsf{L}$	$c_\mathsf{L} : A_\mathsf{L}$	$c_\mathsf{L} \leftarrow \mathsf{acquire}\ c_\mathsf{S} \,; Q_{x_\mathsf{L}}$	$[c_\mathsf{L}/x_\mathsf{L}]\, Q_{x_\mathsf{L}}$	sends "acquire c_L" along c_S
		$x_\mathsf{L} \leftarrow \mathsf{accept}\ c_\mathsf{S} \,; P_{x_\mathsf{L}}$	$[c_\mathsf{L}/x_\mathsf{L}]\, P_{x_\mathsf{L}}$	receives "acquire c_L" along c_S

on classical linear logic [55]. Table 1 lists the points of view of the *provider* and *client* of a given connective in the first and second lines, respectively. Moreover, Table 1 gives for each connective its session type before and after the message exchange, along with their respective process terms. We can see that the process terms of a provider and a client for a given connective come in matching pairs, indicating that the participants' views of the session change consistently. We use the subscripts L and S to distinguish between linear and shared channels, respectively.

We are now able to give the session types of the processes *fork_proc*, *thinking*, and *eating* defined in the previous section:

$$\begin{aligned}&\mathsf{lfork} = \downarrow^\mathsf{S}_\mathsf{L} \mathsf{sfork}\\ &\mathsf{sfork} = \uparrow^\mathsf{S}_\mathsf{L} \mathsf{lfork}\\ &\mathsf{phil} = \mathbf{1}\end{aligned}$$

The mutually recursive session types lfork and sfork represent a fork that can perpetually be acquired and released. We adopt an *equi-recursive* [14] interpretation for recursive session types, silently equating a recursive type with its unfolding and requiring types to be *contractive* [19].

We briefly discuss the typing and the dynamics of acquire-release. The typing and the dynamics of the residual linear connectives are standard, and we detail them in the context of $\mathsf{SILL_{S+}}$ (see Sect. 3). As is usual for an intuitionistic interpretation, each connective gives rise to a left and a right rule, denoting the use and provision, respectively, of a session of the given type:

$$(\text{T-}\uparrow_{\mathsf{L}}^{\mathsf{S}}\text{R})\quad \frac{\Gamma; \cdot \vdash P_{x_{\mathsf{L}}} :: (x_{\mathsf{L}} : A_{\mathsf{L}})}{\Gamma \vdash x_{\mathsf{L}} \leftarrow \mathsf{accept}\, x_{\mathsf{S}}; P_{x_{\mathsf{L}}} :: (x_{\mathsf{S}} : \uparrow_{\mathsf{L}}^{\mathsf{S}} A_{\mathsf{L}})} \qquad (\text{T-}\uparrow_{\mathsf{L}}^{\mathsf{S}}\text{L})\quad \frac{\Gamma, x_{\mathsf{S}} : \uparrow_{\mathsf{L}}^{\mathsf{S}} A_{\mathsf{L}}; \Delta, x_{\mathsf{L}} : A_{\mathsf{L}} \vdash Q_{x_{\mathsf{L}}} :: (z_{\mathsf{L}} : C_{\mathsf{L}})}{\Gamma, x_{\mathsf{S}} : \uparrow_{\mathsf{L}}^{\mathsf{S}} A_{\mathsf{L}}; \Delta \vdash x_{\mathsf{L}} \leftarrow \mathsf{acquire}\, x_{\mathsf{S}}; Q_{x_{\mathsf{L}}} :: (z_{\mathsf{L}} : C_{\mathsf{L}})}$$

$$(\text{T-}\downarrow_{\mathsf{L}}^{\mathsf{S}}\text{R})\quad \frac{\Gamma \vdash P_{x_{\mathsf{S}}} :: (x_{\mathsf{S}} : A_{\mathsf{S}})}{\Gamma; \cdot \vdash x_{\mathsf{S}} \leftarrow \mathsf{detach}\, x_{\mathsf{L}}; P_{x_{\mathsf{S}}} :: (x_{\mathsf{L}} : \downarrow_{\mathsf{L}}^{\mathsf{S}} A_{\mathsf{S}})} \qquad (\text{T-}\downarrow_{\mathsf{L}}^{\mathsf{S}}\text{L})\quad \frac{\Gamma, x_{\mathsf{S}} : A_{\mathsf{S}}; \Delta \vdash Q_{x_{\mathsf{S}}} :: (z_{\mathsf{L}} : C_{\mathsf{L}})}{\Gamma; \Delta, x_{\mathsf{L}} : \downarrow_{\mathsf{L}}^{\mathsf{S}} A_{\mathsf{S}} \vdash x_{\mathsf{S}} \leftarrow \mathsf{release}\, x_{\mathsf{L}}; Q_{x_{\mathsf{S}}} :: (z_{\mathsf{L}} : C_{\mathsf{L}})}$$

The typing judgments $\Gamma \vdash P :: (x_{\mathsf{S}} : A_{\mathsf{S}})$ and $\Gamma; \Delta \vdash P :: (x_{\mathsf{L}} : A_{\mathsf{L}})$ indicate that process P provides a session of type A along channel x, given the typing of the channels specified in typing contexts Γ (and Δ). Γ and Δ consist of hypotheses on the typing of shared and linear channels, respectively, where Γ is a structural and Δ a linear context. To allow for recursive process definitions, the typing judgment depends on a signature Σ that is populated with all process definitions prior to type-checking. The adjoint formulation precludes shared processes from depending on linear channel references [2,47], a restriction motivated from logic referred to as the independence principle [47]. Thus, when a shared session accepts an acquire and shifts to linear, it starts with an empty linear context.

Operationally, the dynamics of $\mathsf{SILL}_{\mathsf{S}}$ is captured by *multiset rewriting rules* [12], which denote computation in terms of state transitions between configurations of processes. Multiset rewriting rules are local in that they only mention the parts of a configuration they rewrite. For acquire-release we have the following:

$(\text{D-}\uparrow_{\mathsf{L}}^{\mathsf{S}})$
$\mathsf{proc}(a_{\mathsf{S}},\, x_{\mathsf{L}} \leftarrow \mathsf{accept}\, a_{\mathsf{S}}\,;\, P_{x_{\mathsf{L}}}),\ \mathsf{proc}(c_{\mathsf{L}},\, x_{\mathsf{L}} \leftarrow \mathsf{acquire}\, a_{\mathsf{S}}\,;\, Q_{x_{\mathsf{L}}})$
$\longrightarrow \mathsf{proc}(a_{\mathsf{L}},\, [a_{\mathsf{L}}/x_{\mathsf{L}}]\, P_{x_{\mathsf{L}}}),\ \mathsf{proc}(c_{\mathsf{L}},\, [a_{\mathsf{L}}/x_{\mathsf{L}}]\, Q_{x_{\mathsf{L}}}),\ \mathsf{unavail}(a_{\mathsf{S}})$

$(\text{D-}\downarrow_{\mathsf{L}}^{\mathsf{S}})$
$\mathsf{proc}(a_{\mathsf{L}},\, x_{\mathsf{S}} \leftarrow \mathsf{detach}\, a_{\mathsf{L}}\,;\, P_{x_{\mathsf{S}}}),\ \mathsf{proc}(c_{\mathsf{L}},\, x_{\mathsf{S}} \leftarrow \mathsf{release}\, a_{\mathsf{L}}\,;\, Q_{x_{\mathsf{S}}}),\ \mathsf{unavail}(a_{\mathsf{S}})$
$\longrightarrow \mathsf{proc}(a_{\mathsf{S}},\, [a_{\mathsf{S}}/x_{\mathsf{S}}]\, P_{x_{\mathsf{S}}}),\ \mathsf{proc}(c_{\mathsf{L}},\, [a_{\mathsf{S}}/x_{\mathsf{S}}]\, Q_{x_{\mathsf{S}}})$

Configuration states are defined by the predicates $\mathsf{proc}(c_m,\, P)$ and $\mathsf{unavail}(a_{\mathsf{S}})$. The former denotes a running process with process term P providing along channel c_m, the latter acts as a placeholder for a shared process providing along channel a_{S} that is currently not available. The above rule exploits the invariant that a process' providing channel a can appear at one of two modes, a linear one, a_{L}, and a shared one, a_{S}. While the process (i.e. the session) is linear, it provides along a_{L}, while it is shared, along a_{S}. When a process shifts between modes, it switches between the two modes of its offering channel. The channel at the appropriate mode is substituted for the variables occurring in process terms.

3 Manifest Deadlock-Freedom

In this section, we introduce our language $\mathsf{SILL}_{\mathsf{S}^+}$, a session-typed language that supports sharing without deadlock. We focus on $\mathsf{SILL}_{\mathsf{S}^+}$'s type system and dynamics in this section and discuss its meta-theoretical properties in Sect. 5.

3.1 Competition and Collaboration

The introduction of acquire-release, to ensure that the multiple clients of a shared process interact with the process in mutual exclusion from each other, gives rise to an obvious source of deadlocks, as acquire-release effectively amounts to a locking discipline. The typical approach to prevent deadlocks in that case is to impose a partial order on the resources and to *"lock-up"*, i.e., to lock the resources in ascending order. We adopted this strategy in Sect. 1 (Fig. 1) to break the cyclic dependencies among the acquires in the dining philosophers.

In Sect. 1, however, we also considered another example (Fig. 2) and discovered that *cyclic acquisitions* are not the only source of deadlocks, but deadlocks can also arise from *interdependent acquisitions and synchronizations.* In that example, we can prevent the deadlock by moving the acquire past the synchronization, in either of the two processes. Whereas in a purely linear session-typed system the sequencing of actions within a process do not affect other processes, the relative placement of acquire requests and synchronizations become relevant in a shared session-typed system.

Based on this observation, we can divide the processes in a shared-session discipline into *competitors* and *collaborators.* The former compete for a set of resources, whereas the latter do not overlap in the set of resources they acquire. For example, in the dining philosophers (Fig. 1), the philosophers p_0, p_1, and p_2 compete with each other for the set of forks f_0, f_1, and f_2, whereas the process that spawns the philosophers and the forks collaborates with either of them.

Transferring this idea to the process graph that emerges at run-time, we note that competitors are siblings whereas collaborators stand in a parent-descendant relationship. We illustrate this outcome on Fig. 3 that shows a possible run-time process graph for the dining philosophers. Linear processes are depicted as solid black circles with a white identifier and shared processes are depicted as dotted filled violet circles with a black identifier. Linear channels are depicted as black lines, shared channel references as dotted violet lines with the arrow head pointing to the shared process being acquired[1]. The identifiers P_0, P_1, and P_2 stand for the three philosophers, F_0, F_1, and F_2 for the three forks, and T for the process that sets the table. The current run-time graph depicts the scenario in which P_1 is eating, while the other two philosophers are still thinking.

Embedded in the graph is a *tree* that arises from the linear processes and the linear channels connecting them. For any two nodes in this tree, the *parent* node denotes the *client* process and the *child* node the *providing* process. We note that the *independence principle* (see Sect. 2), which precludes shared processes from depending on linear channel references, guarantees that there exists exactly one tree in the process graph, with the linear main process as its root. The shape of the tree changes when new processes are spawned, linear channels exchanged (through $\otimes$ and $\multimap$), or shared processes acquired. For example, process P_2 could acquire the shared fork F_0, which then becomes a linear child process of P_2, should the acquire succeed. As indicated by the shared channel references, the

[1] We have made sure to make the different concepts distinguishable in greyscale mode.

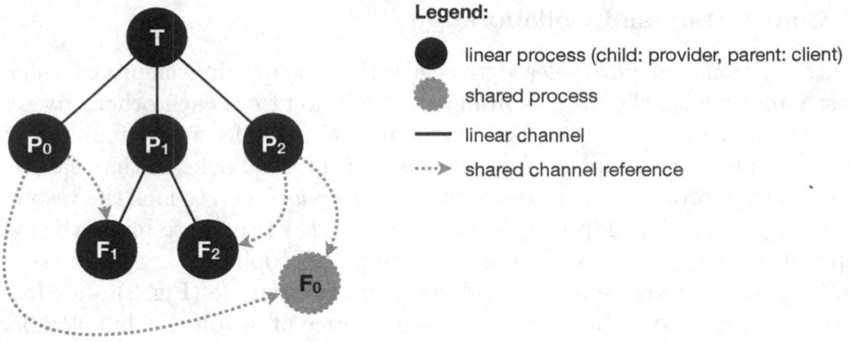

Fig. 3. Run-time process graph for dining philosophers (see Fig. 1).

sibling nodes P_0, P_1, and P_2 compete with each other for the nodes F_0, F_1, and F_2, whereas the node T does not compete for any of the resources acquired by its *descendants* (including F_1 and F_2). Our type system enforces this paradigm, as we discuss in the next section.

3.2 Type System

Invariants. Having identified the notions of *collaborators* and *competitors*, our type system must guarantee: *(i)* that collaborators acquire mutually disjoint sets of resources; *(ii)* that competitors employ a locking-up strategy for the resources they share; and, *(iii)* that competitors have released all acquired resources when synchronizing with other competitors. Invariant *(ii)* rules out cyclic acquisitions and invariants *(i)* and *(iii)* combined rule out interdependent acquisitions and synchronizations.

To express the high-level invariants above in our type system, we introduce the notion of a *world* – an abstract value that is equipped with a partial order – and associate such a world with every process. Programmers can *create* worlds, indicate the world at which a process resides at spawn time, and define an *order* on worlds. Moreover, we associate with each process a *range of worlds* that indicates the worlds of resources that the process may acquire. As a result, we obtain the following typing judgments:

$$\Psi; \Gamma \vdash P :: (x_{\mathsf{S}} : A_{\mathsf{S}}[\omega_k \updownarrow^{\omega_n}_{\omega_l}]) \quad \text{(where } \Psi^+ \text{ irreflexive)}$$

$$\Psi; \Gamma; \Phi; \Delta \vdash P :: (x_{\mathsf{L}} : A_{\mathsf{L}}[\omega_k \updownarrow^{\omega_n}_{\omega_l}]) \quad \text{(where } \Psi^+ \text{ irreflexive)}$$

The typing judgments reveal that we impose worlds at the *judgmental level*, resulting in a *hybrid system*, in which the adjoint modalities for acquire-release are complemented with world modalities that occur as *syntactic objects* in propositions [7]. We use the notation $x_m : A_m[\omega_k \updownarrow^{\omega_n}_{\omega_l}]$ (where m stands for S or L) to associate worlds ω_k, ω_l, and ω_n with a process that offers a session of type A_m along channel x. World ω_k denotes the world at which the process resides.

We refer to this world as the *self* world. Worlds ω_l and ω_n indicate the range of worlds of resources that the process may acquire, with ω_l denoting the *minimal (min)* world in this range and ω_n the *maximal (max)* one.

Process terms are typed relative to the order specified in Ψ and the contexts Γ, Φ, and Δ. As in Sect. 2, Γ is a structural context consisting of hypotheses on the typing of variables bound to shared channel references, augmented with world annotations. We find it necessary to split the linear context "Δ" from Sect. 2 into the two disjoint contexts Φ and Δ, allowing us to separate channels that are possibly aliased (due to sharing) from those that are not, respectively. Both Φ and Δ consist of hypotheses on the typing of variables that are bound to linear channels, augmented with world annotations. Ψ is presupposed to be *acyclic* and defined as: $\Psi \triangleq \cdot \mid \Psi',\ \omega_k < \omega_l \mid \Psi',\ \omega_o$, where ω stands for a concrete *world* w or a *world variable* δ. We allow Ψ to contain single worlds, to support singletons as well as to accommodate world creation prior to order declaration. We define the transitive closure Ψ^+, yielding a *strict partial order*, and the reflexive transitive closure Ψ^*, yielding a *partial order*.

The high-level invariants *(i)*, *(ii)*, and *(iii)* identified earlier naturally transcribe into the following invariants, which we impose on the typing judgments above. We use the notation $\_\langle x_m \rangle; P$ to denote a process term that currently executes an action along channel x_m.

1. $\mathsf{min(parent)} \leq \mathsf{self(acquired\_child)} \leq \mathsf{max(parent)}$:
   $\forall y_{\mathsf{L}} : B_{\mathsf{L}}[\omega_o \updownarrow^{\omega_r}_{\omega_p}] \in \Phi : \Psi^* \vdash \omega_l \leq \omega_o \leq \omega_n$
2. $\mathsf{max(parent)} < \mathsf{min(child)}$:
   $\forall y_{\mathsf{L}} : B_{\mathsf{L}}[\omega_o \updownarrow^{\omega_r}_{\omega_p}] \in \Delta \cup \Phi : \Psi^+ \vdash \omega_n < \omega_p$
3. If $\Psi;\ \Gamma, x_{\mathsf{S}} : A[\omega_t \updownarrow^{\omega_v}_{\omega_u}];\ \Phi;\ \Delta \vdash x_{\mathsf{L}} \leftarrow \mathsf{acquire}\ x_{\mathsf{S}};\ Q_{x_{\mathsf{S}}} :: (z_{\mathsf{L}} : C_{\mathsf{L}}[\omega_k \updownarrow^{\omega_n}_{\omega_l}])$, then
   $\forall y_{\mathsf{L}} : B_{\mathsf{L}}[\omega_o \updownarrow^{\omega_r}_{\omega_p}] \in \Phi : \Psi^+ \vdash \omega_o < \omega_t$.
4. If $\Psi;\ \Gamma;\ \Phi;\ \Delta \vdash \_\langle x_m \rangle; P :: (x_{\mathsf{L}} : A_{\mathsf{L}}[\omega_k \updownarrow^{\omega_n}_{\omega_l}])$, then $\Phi = (\cdot)$.

Invariants 1 and 2 ensure that, for any node in the tree, the acquired resources reside at smaller worlds than those acquired by any descendant. As a result, the two invariants guarantee high-level invariant *(i)*. Invariant 3, on the other hand, imposes a lock-up strategy on acquires and thus guarantees high-level invariant *(ii)*. To guarantee high-level invariant *(iii)*, we impose Invariant 4, which forces a process to release any acquired resources before communicating along its offering channel. Since sibling nodes cannot be directly connected by a linear channel, the only way for them to synchronize is through a common parent. Finally, to guarantee that world annotations are internally consistent, we require for each annotation $[\omega_k \updownarrow^{\omega_n}_{\omega_l}]$ that $\omega_k < \omega_l \leq \omega_n$.

Rules. We now present select process typing rules, a complete listing is provided in the companion technical report [4]. The only new rules with respect to the language $\mathsf{SILL}_{\mathsf{S}}$ [2] are those pertaining to world creation and order determination. These are extra-logical judgmental rules. We allow both linear and shared processes to create and relate worlds. Rules (T-New$_{\mathsf{L}}$) and (T-New$_{\mathsf{S}}$) create a new world w and make it available to the continuation Q_{w}. Rules (T-Ord$_{\mathsf{L}}$) and (T-Ord$_{\mathsf{S}}$) relate two existing worlds, while preserving acyclicity of the order.

$$\frac{\Psi, \mathsf{w};\ \Gamma;\ \Phi;\ \Delta \vdash Q_{\mathsf{w}} :: (x_{\mathsf{L}} : A_{\mathsf{L}}[\omega_m \updownarrow^{\omega_v}_{\omega_u}])}{\Psi;\ \Gamma;\ \Phi;\ \Delta \vdash \mathsf{w} \leftarrow \mathsf{new\_world};\ Q_{\mathsf{w}} :: (x_{\mathsf{L}} : A_{\mathsf{L}}[\omega_m \updownarrow^{\omega_v}_{\omega_u}])}\ (\text{T-New}_{\mathsf{L}})$$

$$\frac{\Psi, \mathsf{w};\ \Gamma \vdash Q_{\mathsf{w}} :: (x_{\mathsf{S}} : A_{\mathsf{S}}[\omega_m \updownarrow^{\omega_v}_{\omega_u}])}{\Psi;\ \Gamma \vdash \mathsf{w} \leftarrow \mathsf{new\_world};\ Q_{\mathsf{w}} :: (x_{\mathsf{S}} : A_{\mathsf{S}}[\omega_m \updownarrow^{\omega_v}_{\omega_u}])}\ (\text{T-New}_{\mathsf{S}})$$

$$\frac{\omega_p, \omega_r \in \Psi \qquad (\Psi, \omega_p < \omega_r)^+ \text{ irreflexive} \qquad \Psi, \omega_p < \omega_r;\ \Gamma;\ \Phi;\ \Delta \vdash Q :: (x_{\mathsf{L}} : A_{\mathsf{L}}[\omega_m \updownarrow^{\omega_v}_{\omega_u}])}{\Psi;\ \Gamma;\ \Phi;\ \Delta \vdash \omega_p < \omega_r;\ Q :: (x_{\mathsf{L}} : A_{\mathsf{L}}[\omega_m \updownarrow^{\omega_v}_{\omega_u}])}\ (\text{T-Ord}_{\mathsf{L}})$$

$$\frac{\omega_p, \omega_r \in \Psi \qquad (\Psi, \omega_p < \omega_r)^+ \text{ irreflexive} \qquad \Psi, \omega_p < \omega_r;\ \Gamma \vdash Q :: (x_{\mathsf{S}} : A_{\mathsf{S}}[\omega_m \updownarrow^{\omega_v}_{\omega_u}])}{\Psi;\ \Gamma \vdash \omega_p < \omega_r;\ Q :: (x_{\mathsf{S}} : A_{\mathsf{S}}[\omega_m \updownarrow^{\omega_v}_{\omega_u}])}\ (\text{T-Ord}_{\mathsf{S}})$$

We now consider the typing rule for acquire, which must explicitly enforce the various low-level invariants above. Since an acquire results in the addition of a new child node to the executing process, the rule can interfere with Invariants 1 and 2. The first two premises of the rule ensure that the two invariants are preserved. Moreover, the rule has to ensure that the acquiring process is locking-up (Invariant 3), which is achieved by the third premise.

$$\frac{\Psi^* \vdash \omega_k \leq \omega_m \leq \omega_n \qquad \Psi^+ \vdash \omega_n < \omega_u \qquad \forall y_{\mathsf{L}} : B_{\mathsf{L}}[\omega_l \updownarrow^{\omega_r}_{\omega_p}] \in \Phi : \omega_l < \omega_m \qquad \Psi;\ \Gamma, x_{\mathsf{S}} : \uparrow^{\mathsf{S}}_{\mathsf{L}} A_{\mathsf{L}}[\omega_m \updownarrow^{\omega_v}_{\omega_u}];\ \Phi, x_{\mathsf{L}} : A_{\mathsf{L}}[\omega_m \updownarrow^{\omega_v}_{\omega_u}];\ \Delta \vdash Q_{x_{\mathsf{L}}} :: (z_{\mathsf{L}} : C_{\mathsf{L}}[\omega_j \updownarrow^{\omega_n}_{\omega_k}])}{\Psi;\ \Gamma, x_{\mathsf{S}} : \uparrow^{\mathsf{S}}_{\mathsf{L}} A_{\mathsf{L}}[\omega_m \updownarrow^{\omega_v}_{\omega_u}];\ \Phi;\ \Delta \vdash x_{\mathsf{L}} \leftarrow \mathsf{acquire}\, x_{\mathsf{S}}\, ;\ Q_{x_{\mathsf{L}}} :: (z_{\mathsf{L}} : C_{\mathsf{L}}[\omega_j \updownarrow^{\omega_n}_{\omega_k}])}\ (\text{T-}{\uparrow^{\mathsf{S}}_{\mathsf{L}}}\text{L})$$

The remaining shift rules are actually *unchanged* with respect to $\mathsf{SILL_S}$, modulo the world annotations. In particular, low-level Invariant 4 is already satisfied because the conclusion of rule (T-$\uparrow^{\mathsf{S}}_{\mathsf{L}}$R) does not have a context Φ and because the independence principle forces Φ to be empty in rule (T-$\downarrow^{\mathsf{S}}_{\mathsf{L}}$R).

$$\frac{\Psi;\ \Gamma;\ \cdot;\ \cdot \vdash P_{x_{\mathsf{L}}} :: (x_{\mathsf{L}} : A_{\mathsf{L}}[\omega_m \updownarrow^{\omega_v}_{\omega_u}])}{\Psi;\ \Gamma \vdash x_{\mathsf{L}} \leftarrow \mathsf{accept}\, x_{\mathsf{S}}\, ;\ P_{x_{\mathsf{L}}} :: (x_{\mathsf{S}} : \uparrow^{\mathsf{S}}_{\mathsf{L}} A_{\mathsf{L}}[\omega_m \updownarrow^{\omega_v}_{\omega_u}])}\ (\text{T-}{\uparrow^{\mathsf{S}}_{\mathsf{L}}}\text{R})$$

$$\frac{\Psi;\ \Gamma, x_{\mathsf{S}} : A_{\mathsf{S}}[\omega_m \updownarrow^{\omega_v}_{\omega_u}];\ \Phi;\ \Delta \vdash Q_{x_{\mathsf{S}}} :: (z_{\mathsf{L}} : C_{\mathsf{L}}[\omega_j \updownarrow^{\omega_n}_{\omega_k}])}{\Psi;\ \Gamma;\ \Phi, x_{\mathsf{L}} : \downarrow^{\mathsf{S}}_{\mathsf{L}} A_{\mathsf{S}}[\omega_m \updownarrow^{\omega_v}_{\omega_u}];\ \Delta \vdash x_{\mathsf{S}} \leftarrow \mathsf{release}\, x_{\mathsf{L}}\, ;\ Q_{x_{\mathsf{S}}} :: (z_{\mathsf{L}} : C_{\mathsf{L}}[\omega_j \updownarrow^{\omega_n}_{\omega_k}])}\ (\text{T-}{\downarrow^{\mathsf{S}}_{\mathsf{L}}}\text{L})$$

$$\frac{\Psi;\ \Gamma \vdash P_{x_{\mathsf{S}}} :: (x_{\mathsf{S}} : A_{\mathsf{S}}[\omega_m \updownarrow^{\omega_v}_{\omega_u}])}{\Psi;\ \Gamma;\ \cdot;\ \cdot \vdash x_{\mathsf{S}} \leftarrow \mathsf{detach}\, x_{\mathsf{L}}\, ;\ P_{x_{\mathsf{S}}} :: (x_{\mathsf{L}} : \downarrow^{\mathsf{S}}_{\mathsf{L}} A_{\mathsf{S}}[\omega_m \updownarrow^{\omega_v}_{\omega_u}])}\ (\text{T-}{\downarrow^{\mathsf{S}}_{\mathsf{L}}}\text{R})$$

We now consider the linear connectives, starting with **1**. Rule (T-$\mathbf{1}_{\mathrm{L}}$) reveals that only processes that have never been acquired may be terminated. This restriction is important to guarantee progress because existing clients of a shared process may wait indefinitely otherwise. We impose the restriction as a well-formedness condition on a session type, giving rise to a *strictly equi-synchronizing* session type. The notion of an *equi-synchronizing* session type [2] has been defined for $\mathsf{SILL_S}$ and guarantees that a process that has been acquired at a type A_{S} is released back to the type A_{S}, should it ever be released. A *strictly* equi-synchronizing session type additionally requires that an acquired resource *must* be released. The corresponding rules can be found in [4]. Linearity enforces Invariant 4 in rule (T-$\mathbf{1}_{\mathrm{R}}$), making sure that no linear channels are left behind.

$$\frac{\Psi;\ \Gamma;\ \Phi;\ \Delta \vdash Q :: (z_{\mathsf{L}} : C_{\mathsf{L}}[\omega_j \updownarrow^{\omega_n}_{\omega_k}])}{\Psi;\ \Gamma;\ \Phi;\ \Delta, x_{\mathsf{L}} : \mathbf{1}[\omega_m \updownarrow^{\omega_v}_{\omega_u}] \vdash \mathsf{wait}\, x_{\mathsf{L}} \,; Q :: (z_{\mathsf{L}} : C_{\mathsf{L}}[\omega_j \updownarrow^{\omega_n}_{\omega_k}])}\ (\text{T-}\mathbf{1}_{\text{L}})$$

$$\frac{}{\Psi;\ \Gamma;\ \cdot;\ \cdot \vdash \mathsf{close}\, x_{\mathsf{L}} :: (x_{\mathsf{L}} : \mathbf{1}[\omega_m \updownarrow^{\omega_v}_{\omega_u}])}\ (\text{T-}\mathbf{1}_{\text{R}})$$

Next, we consider internal and external choice. Since internal and external choice cannot alter the linear process tree of a process graph, the rules are very similar to the ones in $\mathsf{SILL_S}$. The only differences are that we get two left rules for each connective and that the Φ-context of each right rule must be empty to satisfy Invariant 4. The former is merely due to the tracking of possibly aliased sessions in the Φ context. We only list rules for internal choice, those for external choice are dual and can be found in [4].

$$\frac{(\forall i)\ \Psi;\ \Gamma;\ \Phi;\ \Delta, x_{\mathsf{L}} : A_{\mathsf{L}_i}[\omega_m \updownarrow^{\omega_v}_{\omega_u}] \vdash Q_i :: (z_{\mathsf{L}} : C_{\mathsf{L}}[\omega_j \updownarrow^{\omega_n}_{\omega_k}])}{\Psi;\ \Gamma;\ \Phi;\ \Delta, x_{\mathsf{L}} : \oplus\{\overline{l : A_{\mathsf{L}}}\}[\omega_m \updownarrow^{\omega_v}_{\omega_u}] \vdash \mathsf{case}\ x_{\mathsf{L}}\ \mathsf{of}\ \overline{l \Rightarrow Q} :: (z_{\mathsf{L}} : C_{\mathsf{L}}[\omega_j \updownarrow^{\omega_n}_{\omega_k}])}\ (\text{T-}\oplus_{\text{L}_1})$$

$$\frac{(\forall i)\ \Psi;\ \Gamma;\ \Phi, x_{\mathsf{L}} : A_{\mathsf{L}_i}[\omega_m \updownarrow^{\omega_v}_{\omega_u}];\ \Delta \vdash Q_i :: (z_{\mathsf{L}} : C_{\mathsf{L}}[\omega_j \updownarrow^{\omega_n}_{\omega_k}])}{\Psi;\ \Gamma;\ \Phi, x_{\mathsf{L}} : \oplus\{\overline{l : A_{\mathsf{L}}}\}[\omega_m \updownarrow^{\omega_v}_{\omega_u}];\ \Delta \vdash \mathsf{case}\ x_{\mathsf{L}}\ \mathsf{of}\ \overline{l \Rightarrow Q} :: (z_{\mathsf{L}} : C_{\mathsf{L}}[\omega_j \updownarrow^{\omega_n}_{\omega_k}])}\ (\text{T-}\oplus_{\text{L}_2})$$

$$\frac{\Psi;\ \Gamma;\ \cdot;\ \Delta \vdash P :: (x_{\mathsf{L}} : A_{\mathsf{L}\,h}[\omega_m \updownarrow^{\omega_v}_{\omega_u}])}{\Psi;\ \Gamma;\ \cdot;\ \Delta \vdash x_{\mathsf{L}}.l_h \,; P :: (x_{\mathsf{L}} : \oplus\{\overline{l : A_{\mathsf{L}}}\}[\omega_m \updownarrow^{\omega_v}_{\omega_u}])}\ (\text{T-}\oplus_{\text{R}})$$

More interesting are linear channel output and input, since these alter the linear process tree of a process graph. Moreover, additional world annotations are needed to indicate the worlds of the channel that is exchanged. For the latter we use the notation $@\omega_l \updownarrow^{\omega_r}_{\omega_p}$, indicating that the exchanged channel has the worlds ω_l, ω_p, and ω_r for self, min, and max, respectively. To account for induced changes in the process graph, the rules that type an input of a linear channel must guard against any disturbance of Invariants 1 and 2. Because the two invariants guarantee that parents do not overlap with their descendants in terms of acquired resources, they prevent any exchange of acquired channels. We thus restrict $\otimes$ and $\multimap$ to the exchange of channels that have not yet been acquired. This is not a limitation since, as we will see below, shared channel output and input are unrestricted.

Even with the above restriction in place, we still have to make sure that a received channel satisfies Invariant 2. If we were to state a corresponding premise on the receiving rules, invertibility of the rules would be disturbed. To uphold invertibility, we impose a well-formedness condition on session types that ensures for a session of type $A_{\mathsf{L}}@\omega_l \updownarrow^{\omega_r}_{\omega_p} \otimes B_{\mathsf{L}}[\omega_m \updownarrow^{\omega_v}_{\omega_u}]$ that $\omega_v < \omega_p$ and, analogously, for a session of type $A_{\mathsf{L}}@\omega_l \updownarrow^{\omega_r}_{\omega_p} \multimap B_{\mathsf{L}}[\omega_m \updownarrow^{\omega_v}_{\omega_u}]$ that $\omega_v < \omega_p$. Session types are checked to be well-formed upon process definition. Given type well-formedness, we obtain the following rules for $\multimap$, noting that the right rule enforces Invariant 4 by requiring an empty Φ-context. The rules for $\otimes$ are dual.

$$\frac{\Psi;\ \Gamma;\ \Phi;\ \Delta, x_{\mathsf{L}} : B_{\mathsf{L}}[\omega_m \updownarrow_{\omega_u}^{\omega_v}] \vdash Q :: (z_{\mathsf{L}} : C_{\mathsf{L}}[\omega_j \updownarrow_{\omega_k}^{\omega_n}])}{\Psi;\ \Gamma;\ \Phi;\ \Delta, x_{\mathsf{L}} : A_{\mathsf{L}}@\omega_l \updownarrow_{\omega_p}^{\omega_r} \multimap B_{\mathsf{L}}[\omega_m \updownarrow_{\omega_u}^{\omega_v}], y_{\mathsf{L}} : A_{\mathsf{L}}[\omega_l \updownarrow_{\omega_p}^{\omega_r}] \vdash \mathsf{send}\ x_{\mathsf{L}}\ y_{\mathsf{L}}\ ;Q :: (z_{\mathsf{L}} : C_{\mathsf{L}}[\omega_j \updownarrow_{\omega_k}^{\omega_n}])}\ (\text{T-}{\multimap}\text{L}_1)$$

$$\frac{\Psi;\ \Gamma;\ \Phi, x_{\mathsf{L}} : B_{\mathsf{L}}[\omega_m \updownarrow_{\omega_u}^{\omega_v}];\ \Delta \vdash Q :: (z_{\mathsf{L}} : C_{\mathsf{L}}[\omega_j \updownarrow_{\omega_k}^{\omega_n}])}{\Psi;\ \Gamma;\ \Phi, x_{\mathsf{L}} : A_{\mathsf{L}}@\omega_l \updownarrow_{\omega_p}^{\omega_r} \multimap B_{\mathsf{L}}[\omega_m \updownarrow_{\omega_u}^{\omega_v}];\ \Delta, y_{\mathsf{L}} : A_{\mathsf{L}}[\omega_l \updownarrow_{\omega_p}^{\omega_r}] \vdash \mathsf{send}\ x_{\mathsf{L}}\ y_{\mathsf{L}}\ ;Q :: (z_{\mathsf{L}} : C_{\mathsf{L}}[\omega_j \updownarrow_{\omega_k}^{\omega_n}])}\ (\text{T-}{\multimap}\text{L}_2)$$

$$\frac{\Psi;\ \Gamma;\ \cdot\ ;\ \Delta, y_{\mathsf{L}} : A_{\mathsf{L}}[\omega_l \updownarrow_{\omega_p}^{\omega_r}] \vdash P_{y_{\mathsf{L}}} :: (x_{\mathsf{L}} : B_{\mathsf{L}}[\omega_m \updownarrow_{\omega_u}^{\omega_v}])}{\Psi;\ \Gamma;\ \cdot\ ;\ \Delta \vdash y_{\mathsf{L}} \leftarrow \mathsf{recv}\ x_{\mathsf{L}}\ ; P_{y_{\mathsf{L}}} :: (x_{\mathsf{L}} : A_{\mathsf{L}}@\omega_l \updownarrow_{\omega_p}^{\omega_r} \multimap B_{\mathsf{L}}[\omega_m \updownarrow_{\omega_u}^{\omega_v}])}\ (\text{T-}{\multimap}\text{R})$$

Since there are no invariants imposed on the shared context Γ, the rules for shared channel output and input are identical to those in $\mathsf{SILL_S}$. The only differences are that we have two left rules and that the Φ-context of the right rule must be empty to satisfy Invariant 4. The former is merely due to the tracking of possibly aliased sessions in the Φ context.

$$\frac{\Psi;\ \Gamma, y_{\mathsf{S}} : A_{\mathsf{S}}[\omega_l \updownarrow_{\omega_p}^{\omega_r}];\Phi;\ \Delta, x_{\mathsf{L}} : B_{\mathsf{L}}[\omega_m \updownarrow_{\omega_u}^{\omega_v}] \vdash Q_{y_{\mathsf{S}}} :: (z_{\mathsf{L}} : C_{\mathsf{L}}[\omega_j \updownarrow_{\omega_k}^{\omega_n}])}{\Psi;\ \Gamma;\Phi;\ \Delta, x_{\mathsf{L}} : \exists x{:}A_{\mathsf{S}}@\omega_l \updownarrow_{\omega_p}^{\omega_r}\ .\ B_{\mathsf{L}}[\omega_m \updownarrow_{\omega_u}^{\omega_v}] \vdash y_{\mathsf{S}} \leftarrow \mathsf{recv}\ x_{\mathsf{L}}\ ;Q_{y_{\mathsf{S}}} :: (z_{\mathsf{L}} : C_{\mathsf{L}}[\omega_j \updownarrow_{\omega_k}^{\omega_n}])}\ (\text{T-}\exists\text{L}_1)$$

$$\frac{\Psi;\ \Gamma, y_{\mathsf{S}} : A_{\mathsf{S}}[\omega_l \updownarrow_{\omega_p}^{\omega_r}];\Phi, x_{\mathsf{L}} : B_{\mathsf{L}}[\omega_m \updownarrow_{\omega_u}^{\omega_v}];\ \Delta \vdash Q_{y_{\mathsf{S}}} :: (z_{\mathsf{L}} : C_{\mathsf{L}}[\omega_j \updownarrow_{\omega_k}^{\omega_n}])}{\Psi;\ \Gamma;\Phi, x_{\mathsf{L}} : \exists x{:}A_{\mathsf{S}}@\omega_l \updownarrow_{\omega_p}^{\omega_r}\ .\ B_{\mathsf{L}}[\omega_m \updownarrow_{\omega_u}^{\omega_v}];\ \Delta \vdash y_{\mathsf{S}} \leftarrow \mathsf{recv}\ x_{\mathsf{L}}\ ;Q_{y_{\mathsf{S}}} :: (z_{\mathsf{L}} : C_{\mathsf{L}}[\omega_j \updownarrow_{\omega_k}^{\omega_n}])}\ (\text{T-}\exists\text{L}_2)$$

$$\frac{\Psi;\ \Gamma, y_{\mathsf{S}} : A_{\mathsf{S}}[\omega_l \updownarrow_{\omega_p}^{\omega_r}];\cdot\ ;\ \Delta \vdash P :: (x_{\mathsf{L}} : B_{\mathsf{L}}[\omega_m \updownarrow_{\omega_u}^{\omega_v}])}{\Psi;\ \Gamma, y_{\mathsf{S}} : A_{\mathsf{S}}[\omega_l \updownarrow_{\omega_p}^{\omega_r}];\cdot\ ;\ \Delta \vdash \mathsf{send}\ x_{\mathsf{L}}\ y_{\mathsf{S}}\ ;P :: (x_{\mathsf{L}} : \exists x{:}A_{\mathsf{S}}@\omega_l \updownarrow_{\omega_p}^{\omega_r}\ .\ B_{\mathsf{L}}[\omega_m \updownarrow_{\omega_u}^{\omega_v}])}\ (\text{T-}\exists\text{R})$$

We finally consider the rules for forwarding and spawning. We allow a shared forward between processes that offer the same session at the same worlds. Because forwards have to be *world-invariant*, however, no well-typed program could ever have a linear forward. The process being forwarded to must be in either of the contexts Φ or Δ, and thus satisfies Invariant 2, making it impossible for the world annotations of the forwarder and forwardee to match. We omit linear forwarding and discuss possible future extensions in Sect. 6.

$$\frac{}{\Psi;\ \Gamma, y_{\mathsf{S}} : A_{\mathsf{S}}[\omega_j \updownarrow_{\omega_k}^{\omega_n}] \vdash \mathsf{fwd}\ x_{\mathsf{S}}\ y_{\mathsf{S}} :: (x_{\mathsf{S}} : A_{\mathsf{S}}[\omega_j \updownarrow_{\omega_k}^{\omega_n}])}\ (\text{T-ID}_{\mathsf{S}})$$

The rules for spawning depend on the possible modes of the spawning and spawned processes: (T-SPAWN$_{\mathsf{LL}}$) specifies how a linear process can spawn another linear process; (T-SPAWN$_{\mathsf{SS}}$) specifies how a shared processes can spawn another shared process. The rules are checked relative to a process definition found in the signature Σ and to a world substitution mapping $\gamma : |\Psi| \rightarrow |\Psi'|$, such that for each $\delta \in \Psi'$ we have $\Psi \vdash \gamma(\delta)$, where $|\Psi|$ denotes the *field* of Ψ (i.e., the union of its domain and range). As usual, we lift substitution to types $\hat{\gamma}(A_m)$, contexts $\hat{\gamma}(\Gamma)$, and orders $\hat{\gamma}(\Psi)$. Both rules ensure that, given the mapping γ, the order Ψ of the spawning process entails the one of the process definition ($\Psi \vdash \hat{\gamma}(\Psi')$). The linear spawn rule (T-SPAWN$_{\mathsf{LL}}$) further enforces Invariant 2 for the spawned child. We note that the spawned child enters the linear context Δ in the spawning process' continuation since no aliases to such a process can exist at this point.

$$\dfrac{\begin{array}{c}\Delta_1 = \overline{y_{\mathsf{L}} : B_{\mathsf{L}}[\omega_m \updownarrow^{\omega_v}_{\omega_u}]} \qquad \Phi_1 = \overline{\tilde{y}_{\mathsf{L}} : \tilde{B}_{\mathsf{L}}[\tilde{\omega}_m \updownarrow^{\tilde{\omega}_v}_{\tilde{\omega}_u}]} \qquad \Gamma_1 = \overline{z_{\mathsf{S}} : C_{\mathsf{S}}[\omega_l \updownarrow^{\omega_r}_{\omega_p}]} \\ (\Psi' \vdash x'_{\mathsf{L}} : A'_{\mathsf{L}}[\delta_j \updownarrow^{\delta_n}_{\delta_k}] \leftarrow X_{\mathsf{L}} \leftarrow \Delta', \Phi', \Gamma' = P_{x'_{\mathsf{L}}, \mathsf{dom}(\Delta'), \mathsf{dom}(\Phi'), \mathsf{dom}(\Gamma'), \Psi''}) \in \Sigma \\ \hat{\gamma}(A'_{\mathsf{L}}[\delta_j \updownarrow^{\delta_n}_{\delta_k}]) = A_{\mathsf{L}}[\omega_j \updownarrow^{\omega_n}_{\omega_k}] \qquad \hat{\gamma}(\Delta') = \Delta_1 \qquad \hat{\gamma}(\Phi') = \Phi_1 \qquad \hat{\gamma}(\Gamma') = \Gamma_1 \qquad \Psi \vdash \hat{\gamma}(\Psi') \\ \Psi^+ \vdash \omega_t < \omega_k \\ \Psi;\, \Gamma_1, \Gamma_2;\, \Phi_2;\, \Delta_2, x_{\mathsf{L}} : A_{\mathsf{L}}[\omega_j \updownarrow^{\omega_n}_{\omega_k}] \vdash Q_{x_{\mathsf{L}}} :: (z''_{\mathsf{L}} : D_{\mathsf{L}}[\omega_i \updownarrow^{\omega_t}_{\omega_q}])\end{array}}{\Psi;\, \Gamma_1, \Gamma_2;\, \Phi_1, \Phi_2;\, \Delta_1, \Delta_2 \vdash x_{\mathsf{L}} : A_{\mathsf{L}}[\omega_j \updownarrow^{\omega_n}_{\omega_k}] \leftarrow X_{\mathsf{L}} \leftarrow \overline{y_{\mathsf{L}}}, \overline{\tilde{y}_{\mathsf{L}}}, \overline{z_{\mathsf{S}}};\; Q_{x_{\mathsf{L}}} :: (z''_{\mathsf{L}} : D_{\mathsf{L}}[\omega_i \updownarrow^{\omega_t}_{\omega_q}])} \;(\text{T-S}{\scriptstyle\text{PAWN}}_{\mathsf{LL}})$$

$$\dfrac{\begin{array}{c}\Gamma_1 = \overline{z_{\mathsf{S}} : C_{\mathsf{S}}[\omega_l \updownarrow^{\omega_r}_{\omega_p}]} \qquad (\Psi' \vdash x'_{\mathsf{S}} : A'_{\mathsf{S}}[\delta_j \updownarrow^{\delta_n}_{\delta_k}] \leftarrow X_{\mathsf{S}} \leftarrow \Gamma' = P_{x'_{\mathsf{S}}, \mathsf{dom}(\Gamma'), \Psi''}) \in \Sigma \\ \hat{\gamma}(A'_{\mathsf{S}}[\delta_j \updownarrow^{\delta_n}_{\delta_k}]) = A_{\mathsf{S}}[\omega_j \updownarrow^{\omega_n}_{\omega_k}] \qquad \hat{\gamma}(\Gamma') = \Gamma_1 \qquad \Psi \vdash \hat{\gamma}(\Psi') \\ \Psi;\, \Gamma_1, \Gamma_2, x_{\mathsf{S}} : A_{\mathsf{S}}[\omega_j \updownarrow^{\omega_n}_{\omega_k}] \vdash Q_{x_{\mathsf{S}}} :: (z''_{\mathsf{S}} : D_{\mathsf{S}}[\omega_i \updownarrow^{\omega_t}_{\omega_q}])\end{array}}{\Psi;\, \Gamma_1, \Gamma_2 \vdash x_{\mathsf{S}} : A_{\mathsf{S}}[\omega_j \updownarrow^{\omega_n}_{\omega_k}] \leftarrow X_{\mathsf{S}} \leftarrow \overline{z_{\mathsf{S}}};\; Q_{x_{\mathsf{S}}} :: (z''_{\mathsf{S}} : D_{\mathsf{S}}[\omega_i \updownarrow^{\omega_t}_{\omega_q}])} \;(\text{T-S}{\scriptstyle\text{PAWN}}_{\mathsf{SS}})$$

In the companion technical report [4], we provide a variant of rule (T-SPAWN$_{\mathsf{LL}}$) for the case of a linear recursive tail call. Without linear forwarding, a linear tail call can no longer be implicitly "de-sugared" into a spawn and a linear forward [2,22,52], but must be accounted for explicitly. In the report, we also provide the rules for checking process definitions. Those rules make sure that the process' world order is acyclic, that the types of the providing session and argument sessions are well-formed, and that the process satisfies Invariants 1 and 2.

3.3 Dining Philosophers in $\mathsf{SILL}_{\mathsf{S}+}$

Having introduced our type system, we revisit the dining philosophers from Sect. 1 and show how to program the example in $\mathsf{SILL}_{\mathsf{S}+}$, ensuring that the program will run without deadlocks. The code is given in Fig. 4. We note the world annotations in the signature of the process definitions. For instance,

$$\textit{thinking} : \{\delta_0 < \delta_1, \delta_1 < \delta_2, \delta_2 < \delta_3 \vdash \mathsf{phil}[\delta_0 \updownarrow^{\delta_2}_{\delta_1}] \leftarrow \mathsf{sfork}[\delta_1 \updownarrow^{\delta_3}_{\delta_3}], \mathsf{sfork}[\delta_2 \updownarrow^{\delta_3}_{\delta_3}]; \cdot; \cdot\}$$

indicates that, given the order $\delta_0 < \delta_1 < \delta_2 < \delta_3$, process *thinking* provides a session of type $\mathsf{phil}[\delta_0 \updownarrow^{\delta_2}_{\delta_1}]$ and uses two shared channel references of type $\mathsf{sfork}[\delta_1 \updownarrow^{\delta_3}_{\delta_3}]$ and $\mathsf{sfork}[\delta_2 \updownarrow^{\delta_3}_{\delta_3}]$. The two $\cdot$ signify that neither acquired nor linear channel references are given as arguments. The signature indicates that the two shared fork references reside at different worlds, such that the world of the first one is smaller than the one of the second.

Let's briefly convince ourselves that the two acquires in process *thinking* in Fig. 4 are type-correct. For each acquire we have to show that: the world of the resource to be acquired is within the acquiring process' range; the max of the acquiring process is smaller than the min of the acquired resource; and, that the self of the acquired resource is larger than those of all already acquired resources. We can convince ourselves that all those conditions are readily met.

$\mathit{thinking} : \{\delta_0 < \delta_1, \delta_1 < \delta_2, \delta_2 < \delta_3 \vdash$
$\quad \mathsf{phil}[\delta_0 \updownarrow^{\delta_2}_{\delta_1}] \leftarrow \mathsf{sfork}[\delta_1 \updownarrow^{\delta_3}_{\delta_3}], \mathsf{sfork}[\delta_2 \updownarrow^{\delta_3}_{\delta_3}]; \cdot; \cdot\}$
$c[\delta_0 \updownarrow^{\delta_2}_{\delta_1}] \leftarrow \mathit{thinking} \leftarrow \mathit{left}[\delta_1 \updownarrow^{\delta_3}_{\delta_3}], \mathit{right}[\delta_2 \updownarrow^{\delta_3}_{\delta_3}] =$
$\quad \mathit{left}' \leftarrow \mathsf{acquire}\ \mathit{left}$;
$\quad \mathit{right}' \leftarrow \mathsf{acquire}\ \mathit{right}$;
$\quad c \leftarrow \mathit{eating} \leftarrow \mathit{left}', \mathit{right}'$;

$\mathit{eating} : \{\delta_0 < \delta_1, \delta_1 < \delta_2, \delta_2 < \delta_3 \vdash$
$\quad \mathsf{phil}[\delta_0 \updownarrow^{\delta_2}_{\delta_1}] \leftarrow \cdot; \mathsf{lfork}[\delta_1 \updownarrow^{\delta_3}_{\delta_3}], \mathsf{lfork}[\delta_2 \updownarrow^{\delta_3}_{\delta_3}]; \cdot\}$
$c[\delta_0 \updownarrow^{\delta_2}_{\delta_1}] \leftarrow \mathit{eating} \leftarrow \mathit{left}'[\delta_1 \updownarrow^{\delta_3}_{\delta_3}], \mathit{right}'[\delta_2 \updownarrow^{\delta_3}_{\delta_3}] =$
$\quad \mathit{right} \leftarrow \mathsf{release}\ \mathit{right}'$;
$\quad \mathit{left} \leftarrow \mathsf{release}\ \mathit{left}'$;
$\quad c \leftarrow \mathit{thinking} \leftarrow \mathit{left}, \mathit{right}$

$\mathsf{lfork} = \downarrow^{\mathsf{S}}_{\mathsf{L}} \mathsf{sfork}$
$\mathsf{sfork} = \uparrow^{\mathsf{S}}_{\mathsf{L}} \mathsf{lfork}$
$\mathsf{phil} = \mathbf{1}$

$\mathit{fork\_proc} : \{\delta_0 < \delta_1 \vdash \mathsf{sfork}[\delta_0 \updownarrow^{\delta_1}_{\delta_1}]\}$
$c[\delta_0 \updownarrow^{\delta_1}_{\delta_1}] \leftarrow \mathit{fork\_proc} =$
$\quad c' \leftarrow \mathsf{accept}\ c$;
$\quad c \leftarrow \mathsf{detach}\ c'$;
$\quad c'' : \mathsf{sfork}[\delta_0 \updownarrow^{\delta_1}_{\delta_1}] \leftarrow \mathit{fork\_proc}$;
$\quad \mathsf{fwd}\ c\ c''$

Fig. 4. Deadlock-free version of dining philosophers in $\mathsf{SILL}_{\mathsf{S}+}$.

We note, however, that if we were to swap the two acquires, the program would not type-check.

Let us once more set the table for three philosophers and three forks. We execute this code in a process with world annotations $[\delta_a \updownarrow^{\delta_b}_{\delta_b}]$ such that $\delta_a < \delta_b$. We first create new worlds and define their order:

$\mathsf{w}_1 \leftarrow \mathsf{new\_world}; \mathsf{w}_2 \leftarrow \mathsf{new\_world}; \mathsf{w}_3 \leftarrow \mathsf{new\_world}; \mathsf{w}_4 \leftarrow \mathsf{new\_world};$
$\delta_a < \mathsf{w}_1; \delta_a < \mathsf{w}_2; \delta_b < \mathsf{w}_1; \mathsf{w}_1 < \mathsf{w}_2; \mathsf{w}_1 < \mathsf{w}_3; \mathsf{w}_1 < \mathsf{w}_4; \mathsf{w}_2 < \mathsf{w}_3; \mathsf{w}_2 < \mathsf{w}_4; \mathsf{w}_3 < \mathsf{w}_4;$

We then spawn the forks, each residing at a different world, such that the max world of a fork is higher than the self of the highest fork, ensuring Invariant 2 for the philosopher processes that we spawn afterwards:

$f_1 : \mathsf{sfork}[\mathsf{w}_1 \updownarrow^{\mathsf{w}_4}_{\mathsf{w}_4}] \leftarrow \mathit{fork\_proc}$; $f_2 : \mathsf{sfork}[\mathsf{w}_2 \updownarrow^{\mathsf{w}_4}_{\mathsf{w}_4}] \leftarrow \mathit{fork\_proc}$;
$f_3 : \mathsf{sfork}[\mathsf{w}_3 \updownarrow^{\mathsf{w}_4}_{\mathsf{w}_4}] \leftarrow \mathit{fork\_proc}$;

When we spawn the philosophers, we ensure that P_0 is going to pick up fork F_1 and then F_2, P_1 is going to pick up F_2 and then F_3, and P_2 is going to pick up F_1 and then F_3.

$p_0 : \mathsf{phil}[\delta_a \updownarrow^{\mathsf{w}_2}_{\mathsf{w}_1}] \leftarrow \mathit{thinking} \leftarrow \cdot; \cdot; f_1, f_2$; $p_1 : \mathsf{phil}[\delta_a \updownarrow^{\mathsf{w}_3}_{\mathsf{w}_2}] \leftarrow \mathit{thinking} \leftarrow \cdot; \cdot; f_2, f_3$;
$p_2 : \mathsf{phil}[\delta_a \updownarrow^{\mathsf{w}_3}_{\mathsf{w}_1}] \leftarrow \mathit{thinking} \leftarrow \cdot; \cdot; f_1, f_3$;

We note that the deadlocking spawn

$p_2 : \mathsf{phil}[\delta_a \updownarrow^{\mathsf{w}_3}_{\mathsf{w}_1}] \leftarrow \mathit{thinking} \leftarrow \cdot; \cdot; f_3, f_1$;

is type-incorrect since we would substitute both w_1 and w_3 for δ_1 and w_3 and w_1 for δ_2, which violates the ordering constraints put in place by typing.

3.4 Dynamics

We now give the *dynamics* of $\mathsf{SILL_{S^+}}$. Our current system is based on a *synchronous* dynamics. While this choice is more conservative, it allows us to narrow the complexity of the problem at hand.

As in $\mathsf{SILL_S}$, we use *multiset rewriting rules* [12] to capture the dynamics of $\mathsf{SILL_{S^+}}$ (see Sect. 2). Multiset rewriting rules represent computation in terms of local state transitions between configurations of processes, only mentioning the parts of a configuration they rewrite. We use the predicates $\mathsf{proc}(a_m, \mathsf{w}_{\mathsf{a}_1} \updownarrow^{\mathsf{w}_{\mathsf{a}_3}}_{\mathsf{w}_{\mathsf{a}_2}}, P_{a_m})$ and $\mathsf{unavail}(a_\mathsf{S}, \mathsf{w}_{\mathsf{a}_1} \updownarrow^{\mathsf{w}_{\mathsf{a}_3}}_{\mathsf{w}_{\mathsf{a}_2}})$ to define the states of a configuration (see Sect. 5.1). The former denotes a process executing term P that provides along channel a_m at mode m with worlds $\mathsf{w}_{\mathsf{a}_1}$, $\mathsf{w}_{\mathsf{a}_2}$, and $\mathsf{w}_{\mathsf{a}_3}$ for self, min, and max, respectively. The latter acts as a placeholder for a shared process providing along channel a_s with worlds $\mathsf{w}_{\mathsf{a}_1}$, $\mathsf{w}_{\mathsf{a}_2}$, and $\mathsf{w}_{\mathsf{a}_3}$ for self, min, and max, respectively, that is currently unavailable. We note that since worlds are also run-time artifacts, they must occur as part of the state-defining predicates.

Fig. 5 lists selected rules of the dynamics. Since the rules remain largely the same as those of $\mathsf{SILL_S}$, apart from the world annotations that are "threaded through" unchanged, we only discuss the rules that actually differ from the $\mathsf{SILL_S}$ rules. The interested reader can find the remaining rules in the companion technical report [4].

(D-SPAWN$_{\mathsf{LL}}$)

$$\begin{array}{l}
\mathsf{proc}(a_\mathsf{L}, \mathsf{w}_{\mathsf{a}_1} \updownarrow^{\mathsf{w}_{\mathsf{a}_3}}_{\mathsf{w}_{\mathsf{a}_2}}, x_\mathsf{L} : A_\mathsf{L}[\mathsf{w}_{\mathsf{b}_1} \updownarrow^{\mathsf{w}_{\mathsf{b}_3}}_{\mathsf{w}_{\mathsf{b}_2}}] \leftarrow X_\mathsf{L} \leftarrow \overline{c_\mathsf{L}}, \overline{\tilde{c}_\mathsf{L}}, \overline{d_\mathsf{S}};\ Q_{x_\mathsf{L}}),\\
!\mathsf{def}(\Psi' \vdash x'_\mathsf{L} : A'_\mathsf{L}[\delta_j \updownarrow^{\delta_n}_{\delta_k}] \leftarrow X_\mathsf{L} \leftarrow \Delta', \Phi', \Gamma' = P_{x'_\mathsf{L}, \mathsf{dom}(\Delta'), \mathsf{dom}(\Phi'), \mathsf{dom}(\Gamma'), \Psi''})\\
\longrightarrow \mathsf{proc}(b_\mathsf{L}, \mathsf{w}_{\mathsf{b}_1} \updownarrow^{\mathsf{w}_{\mathsf{b}_3}}_{\mathsf{w}_{\mathsf{b}_2}}, [b_\mathsf{L}/x'_\mathsf{L}, \overline{c_\mathsf{L}}/\mathsf{dom}(\Delta'), \overline{\tilde{c}_\mathsf{L}}/\mathsf{dom}(\Phi'), \overline{d_\mathsf{S}}/\mathsf{dom}(\Gamma')]\hat{\gamma}(P_{x'_\mathsf{L}, \mathsf{dom}(\Delta'), \mathsf{dom}(\Phi'), \mathsf{dom}(\Gamma'), \Psi''})),\\
\qquad \mathsf{proc}(a_\mathsf{L}, \mathsf{w}_{\mathsf{a}_1} \updownarrow^{\mathsf{w}_{\mathsf{a}_3}}_{\mathsf{w}_{\mathsf{a}_2}}, [b_\mathsf{L}/x_\mathsf{L}] Q_{x_\mathsf{L}}),\\
\qquad \mathsf{unavail}(b_\mathsf{S}, \mathsf{w}_{\mathsf{b}_1} \updownarrow^{\mathsf{w}_{\mathsf{b}_3}}_{\mathsf{w}_{\mathsf{b}_2}}) \quad (b\ \textit{fresh})
\end{array}$$

(D-NEW)

$$\mathsf{proc}(a, \mathsf{w}_{\mathsf{a}_1} \updownarrow^{\mathsf{w}_{\mathsf{a}_3}}_{\mathsf{w}_{\mathsf{a}_2}}, \mathsf{w} \leftarrow \mathsf{new\_world};\ Q_\mathsf{w}) \longrightarrow \mathsf{proc}(a, \mathsf{w}_{\mathsf{a}_1} \updownarrow^{\mathsf{w}_{\mathsf{a}_3}}_{\mathsf{w}_{\mathsf{a}_2}}, Q_\mathsf{w}) \quad (\mathsf{w}\ \textit{fresh})$$

(D-ORD)

$$\mathsf{proc}(a, \mathsf{w}_{\mathsf{a}_1} \updownarrow^{\mathsf{w}_{\mathsf{a}_3}}_{\mathsf{w}_{\mathsf{a}_2}}, \mathsf{w} < \mathsf{w}';\ Q) \longrightarrow \mathsf{proc}(a, \mathsf{w}_{\mathsf{a}_1} \updownarrow^{\mathsf{w}_{\mathsf{a}_3}}_{\mathsf{w}_{\mathsf{a}_2}}, Q)$$

Fig. 5. Selected multiset rewriting rules of $\mathsf{SILL_{S^+}}$.

Noteworthy are the rules D-NEW and D-ORD for creating and relating worlds, respectively. Rule D-NEW creates a fresh world, which will be globally available in the configuration. Rule D-ORD, on the other hand, updates the configuration's order with the pair $\mathsf{w} < \mathsf{w}'$. Rule D-SPAWN$_{\mathsf{LL}}$, lastly, substitutes actual worlds for world variables in the body of the spawned process, using the substitution mapping γ defined earlier. It relies on the existence of a corresponding definition predicate for each process definition contained in the signature Σ. We note that the substitution γ in rule D-SPAWN$_{\mathsf{LL}}$ instantiates the appropriate world variables in the spawned process P.

4 Extended Example: An Imperative Shared Queue

We now develop a typical imperative-style implementation of a queue that uses a list data structure internally to store the queue's elements and has shared references to the front and the back of the list for concurrent dequeueing and enqueueing, respectively. The session types for the queue and the list are[2]

$$\begin{array}{rl}\mathsf{queue}\ A_{\mathsf{S}} = \uparrow_{\mathsf{L}}^{\mathsf{S}}\&\{ & \mathsf{enq} : \Pi x{:}A_{\mathsf{S}}.\, \downarrow_{\mathsf{L}}^{\mathsf{S}}\mathsf{queue}\ A_{\mathsf{S}}, \\ & \mathsf{deq} : \oplus\{\mathsf{none} : \downarrow_{\mathsf{L}}^{\mathsf{S}}\mathsf{queue}\ A_{\mathsf{S}}, \mathsf{some} : \exists x{:}A_{\mathsf{S}}.\, \downarrow_{\mathsf{L}}^{\mathsf{S}}\mathsf{queue}\ A_{\mathsf{S}}\}\}\end{array}$$

$$\begin{array}{rl}\mathsf{list}\ A_{\mathsf{S}} = \uparrow_{\mathsf{L}}^{\mathsf{S}}\&\{ & \mathsf{ins} : \Pi x{:}A_{\mathsf{S}}.\, \exists y{:}\mathsf{list}\ A_{\mathsf{S}}.\, \downarrow_{\mathsf{L}}^{\mathsf{S}}\mathsf{list}\ A_{\mathsf{S}}, \\ & \mathsf{del} : \oplus\{\mathsf{none} : \downarrow_{\mathsf{L}}^{\mathsf{S}}\mathsf{list}\ A_{\mathsf{S}}, \mathsf{some} : \exists x{:}A_{\mathsf{S}}.\, \downarrow_{\mathsf{L}}^{\mathsf{S}}\mathsf{list}\ A_{\mathsf{S}}\}\end{array}$$

The list is implemented in terms of processes *empty* and *elem*, denoting the empty list and a cons cell, respectively. We show the more interesting case of a cons cell (Fig. 6). The queue is defined by processes *head* (Fig. 7) and *queue_proc* (Fig. 8), the latter being the queue's interface to its clients.

$$\begin{array}{l}
\mathit{elem} : \{\delta_1 < \delta_2, \delta_2 < \delta_3, \delta_3 < \delta_4 \vdash \mathsf{list}[\delta_1 \updownarrow^{\delta_2}_{\delta_2}] A_{\mathsf{S}}[\delta_3 \updownarrow^{\delta_4}_{\delta_4}] \leftarrow A_{\mathsf{S}}[\delta_3 \updownarrow^{\delta_4}_{\delta_4}], \mathsf{list}[\delta_1 \updownarrow^{\delta_2}_{\delta_2}] A_{\mathsf{S}}[\delta_3 \updownarrow^{\delta_4}_{\delta_4}]\} \\
c[\delta_1 \updownarrow^{\delta_2}_{\delta_2}][\delta_3 \updownarrow^{\delta_4}_{\delta_4}] \leftarrow \mathit{elem} \leftarrow x[\delta_3 \updownarrow^{\delta_4}_{\delta_4}], \mathit{next}[\delta_1 \updownarrow^{\delta_2}_{\delta_2}][\delta_3 \updownarrow^{\delta_4}_{\delta_4}] = \\
\quad c' \leftarrow \mathsf{accept}\ c\ ; \\
\quad \mathsf{case}\ c'\ \mathsf{of} \\
\quad \mid \mathsf{ins} \rightarrow y \leftarrow \mathsf{recv}\ c'\ ;\ n \leftarrow \mathit{elem} \leftarrow y,\ \mathit{next}\ ;\ \mathsf{send}\ c'\ n\ ; \\
\qquad\qquad c \leftarrow \mathsf{detach}\ c'\ ; \\
\qquad\qquad c'' : \mathsf{list}[\delta_1 \updownarrow^{\delta_2}_{\delta_2}] A_{\mathsf{S}}[\delta_3 \updownarrow^{\delta_4}_{\delta_4}] \leftarrow \mathit{elem} \leftarrow x,\ n\ ;\ \mathsf{fwd}\ c\ c'' \\
\quad \mid \mathsf{del} \rightarrow c'.\mathsf{some}\ ;\ \mathsf{send}\ c'\ x\ ; \\
\qquad\qquad c \leftarrow \mathsf{detach}\ c'\ ;\ \mathsf{fwd}\ c\ \mathit{next}
\end{array}$$

Fig. 6. Imperative queue – *elem* process.

We can now define a client (Fig. 8) for the queue, assuming existence of a corresponding shared session type item and a process *item_proc* offering a session of type $\mathsf{item}[\delta_3 \updownarrow^{\delta_4}_{\delta_4}]$. The client instantiates the queue at world δ_b, allowing it to acquire resources at world w_1, which is exactly the world at which process *queue_proc* instantiates the list. Given that the client itself resides at world δ_a, which is smaller than the queue's world δ_b, the client is allowed to acquire the queue, which in turn will acquire the list to satisfy any requests by the client.

The example showcases a paradigmatic use of several collaborators, where collaborators can hold resources while they "talk down" in the tree. In particular, as illustrated in Fig. 9, the clients C_1, C_2, and C_3 compete for resources at world δ_b, i.e., the queue Q. On the other hand, a client C_i collaborates with the queue Q, the list elements L_i, and the items I_i, since they do not overlap in

[2] We adopt polymorphism for the example without formal treatment since it is orthogonal and has been studied for session types in [23,46].

$$head : \{\delta_0 < \delta_1, \delta_1 < \delta_2, \delta_2 < \delta_3, \delta_3 < \delta_4 \vdash \mathsf{queue}[\delta_0 \updownarrow^{\delta_1}_{\delta_1}] A_{\mathsf{S}}[\delta_3 \updownarrow^{\delta_4}_{\delta_4}] \leftarrow \mathsf{list}[\delta_1 \updownarrow^{\delta_2}_{\delta_2}] A_{\mathsf{S}}[\delta_3 \updownarrow^{\delta_4}_{\delta_4}], \mathsf{list}[\delta_1 \updownarrow^{\delta_2}_{\delta_2}] A_{\mathsf{S}}[\delta_3 \updownarrow^{\delta_4}_{\delta_4}]\}$$

$c[\delta_0 \updownarrow^{\delta_1}_{\delta_1}][\delta_3 \updownarrow^{\delta_4}_{\delta_4}] \leftarrow head \leftarrow front[\delta_1 \updownarrow^{\delta_2}_{\delta_2}][\delta_3 \updownarrow^{\delta_4}_{\delta_4}],\ back[\delta_1 \updownarrow^{\delta_2}_{\delta_2}][\delta_3 \updownarrow^{\delta_4}_{\delta_4}] =$
  $c' \leftarrow \mathsf{accept}\ c$;
  case c' of
  | enq $\rightarrow x \leftarrow \mathsf{recv}\ c'$;
      $back' \leftarrow \mathsf{acquire}\ back$;
      $back'$.ins ; send $back'\ x$; $e \leftarrow \mathsf{recv}\ back'$;
      $back \leftarrow \mathsf{release}\ back'$;
      $c \leftarrow \mathsf{detach}\ c'$; $c'' : \mathsf{queue}[\delta_0 \updownarrow^{\delta_1}_{\delta_1}] A_{\mathsf{S}}[\delta_3 \updownarrow^{\delta_4}_{\delta_4}] \leftarrow head \leftarrow front,\ e$; fwd $c\ c''$
  | deq $\rightarrow front' \leftarrow \mathsf{acquire}\ front$;
      $front'$.del ;
      (case $front'$ of
      | none $\rightarrow front \leftarrow \mathsf{release}\ front'$; c'.none ; $c \leftarrow \mathsf{detach}\ c'$;
          $c'' : \mathsf{queue}[\delta_0 \updownarrow^{\delta_1}_{\delta_1}] A_{\mathsf{S}}[\delta_3 \updownarrow^{\delta_4}_{\delta_4}] \leftarrow head \leftarrow front,\ back$; fwd $c\ c''$
      | some $\rightarrow x \leftarrow \mathsf{recv}\ front'$;
          $front \leftarrow \mathsf{release}\ front'$;
          c'.some ; send $c'\ x$; $c \leftarrow \mathsf{detach}\ c'$;
          $c'' : \mathsf{queue}[\delta_0 \updownarrow^{\delta_1}_{\delta_1}] A_{\mathsf{S}}[\delta_3 \updownarrow^{\delta_4}_{\delta_4}] \leftarrow head \leftarrow front,\ back$; fwd $c\ c''$)

Fig. 7. Imperative queue – *head* process.

$queue\_proc : \{\delta_0 < \delta_1, \delta_1 < \delta_3, \delta_3 < \delta_4 \vdash \mathsf{queue}[\delta_0 \updownarrow^{\delta_1}_{\delta_1}] A_{\mathsf{S}}[\delta_3 \updownarrow^{\delta_4}_{\delta_4}]\}$

$c[\delta_0 \updownarrow^{\delta_1}_{\delta_1}][\delta_3 \updownarrow^{\delta_4}_{\delta_4}] \leftarrow queue\_proc =$
  $\mathsf{w}_2 \leftarrow \mathsf{new\_world}$;
  $\delta_1 < \mathsf{w}_2$; $\mathsf{w}_2 < \delta_3$;
  $e : \mathsf{list}[\delta_1 \updownarrow^{\mathsf{w}_2}_{\mathsf{w}_2}] A_{\mathsf{S}}[\delta_3 \updownarrow^{\delta_4}_{\delta_4}] \leftarrow empty$;
  $c'' : \mathsf{queue}[\delta_0 \updownarrow^{\delta_1}_{\delta_1}] A_{\mathsf{S}}[\delta_3 \updownarrow^{\delta_4}_{\delta_4}] \leftarrow head \leftarrow e, e$;
  fwd $c\ c''$

$client : \{\delta_a < \delta_b \vdash \mathbf{1}[\delta_a \updownarrow^{\delta_b}_{\delta_b}]\}$

$c[\delta_a \updownarrow^{\delta_b}_{\delta_b}] \leftarrow client =$
  $\mathsf{w}_1 \leftarrow \mathsf{new\_world}$; $\mathsf{w}_3 \leftarrow \mathsf{new\_world}$;
  $\mathsf{w}_4 \leftarrow \mathsf{new\_world}$;
  $\delta_b < \mathsf{w}_1$; $\mathsf{w}_1 < \mathsf{w}_3$; $\mathsf{w}_3 < \mathsf{w}_4$;
  $i_0 : \mathsf{item}[\mathsf{w}_3 \updownarrow^{\mathsf{w}_4}_{\mathsf{w}_4}] \leftarrow item\_proc$;
  $q : \mathsf{queue}[\delta_b \updownarrow^{\mathsf{w}_1}_{\mathsf{w}_1}] A_{\mathsf{S}}[\mathsf{w}_3 \updownarrow^{\mathsf{w}_4}_{\mathsf{w}_4}] \leftarrow queue\_proc$;
  $q' \leftarrow \mathsf{acquire}\ q$; q'.enq ; send $q'\ i_0$;
  $q \leftarrow \mathsf{release}\ q'$; close c

Fig. 8. Imperative queue – *queue_proc* process and *client* process.

the set of resources they may acquire: a client acquires resources at δ_b, a queue resources at w_1, a list resources at w_2, and an item resources at w_4, and we have $\delta_a < \delta_b < \mathsf{w}_1 < \mathsf{w}_2 < \mathsf{w}_3 < \mathsf{w}_4$. We note in particular that the setup prevents a list element from acquiring its successor, forcing linear access through the queue.

5 Semantics

In this section, we discuss the meta-theoretical properties of $\mathsf{SILL}_{\mathsf{S}^+}$, focusing on deadlock-freedom. The companion technical report [4] provides further details.

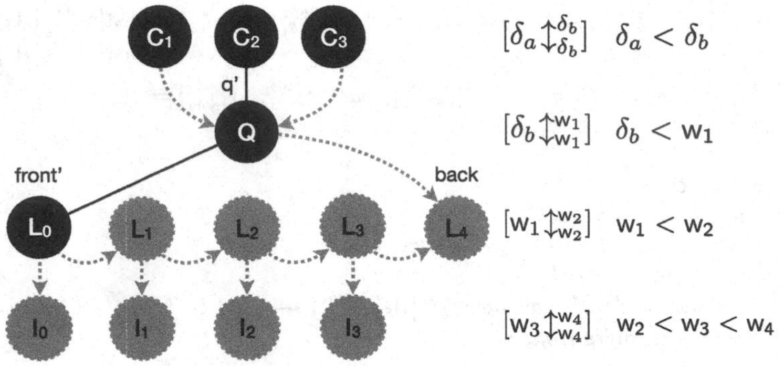

Fig. 9. Run-time process graph for imperative queue (see Fig. 3 for legend).

5.1 Configuration Typing and Preservation

Given the hierarchy between mode S and L and the fact that shared processes cannot depend on linear processes, we divide a configuration into a *shared* part Λ and a linear part Θ. We use the typing judgment $\Psi; \Gamma \models \Lambda; \Theta :: \Gamma; \Phi, \Delta$ to type configurations. The judgment expresses that a well-formed configuration $\Lambda; \Theta$ provides the shared channels in Γ and the linear channels in Φ and Δ. A configuration is type-checked relative to all shared channel references and a global order Ψ. While type-checking is compositional insofar as each process definition can be type-checked separately, solely relying on the process' local Ψ (and Γ), at run-time, the entire order that a configuration relies upon is considered. We give the configuration typing rules in Fig. 10.

Our progress theorem crucially depends on the guarantee that the Invariants 1 and 2 from Sect. 3 hold for every linear process in a configuration's tree. This is expressed by the premises $\mathsf{Inv}_1(\mathsf{proc}(a_{\mathsf{L}}, \mathsf{w}_{a_1} \updownarrow^{\mathsf{w}_{a_3}}_{\mathsf{w}_{a_2}}, P_{a_{\mathsf{L}}}))$ and $\mathsf{Inv}_2(\mathsf{proc}(a_{\mathsf{L}}, \mathsf{w}_{a_1} \updownarrow^{\mathsf{w}_{a_3}}_{\mathsf{w}_{a_2}}, P_{a_{\mathsf{L}}}))$ in rule (T-Θ_2), based on the Definitions 1 and 2 below that restate Invariants 1 and 2 for an entire configuration. We note that Invariant 2 is based on the set of all transitive children (i.e., *descendants*) of a process. We formally define the notion of a descendant inductively over a well-typed linear configuration. The interested reader can find the definition in the companion technical report [4].

Invariant 1 ($\mathsf{min(parent)} \leq \mathsf{self(acquired\_child)} \leq \mathsf{max(parent)}$). *If* $\Psi; \Gamma \models \Theta :: \Phi, \Delta$ *and for any* $\mathsf{proc}(a_{\mathsf{L}}, \mathsf{w}_{a_1} \updownarrow^{\mathsf{w}_{a_3}}_{\mathsf{w}_{a_2}}, P_{a_{\mathsf{L}}}) \in \Theta$ *such that* $\Psi; \Gamma; \Phi_1; \Delta_1 \vdash P_{a_{\mathsf{L}}} :: (a_{\mathsf{L}} : A_{\mathsf{L}}[\mathsf{w}_{a_1} \updownarrow^{\mathsf{w}_{a_3}}_{\mathsf{w}_{a_2}}])$, $\mathsf{Inv}_1(\mathsf{proc}(a_{\mathsf{L}}, \mathsf{w}_{a_1} \updownarrow^{\mathsf{w}_{a_3}}_{\mathsf{w}_{a_2}}, P_{a_{\mathsf{L}}}))$ *holds if an only if for every acquired resource* $b_{\mathsf{L}} : B_{\mathsf{L}}[\mathsf{w}_{b_1} \updownarrow^{\mathsf{w}_{b_3}}_{\mathsf{w}_{b_2}}] \in \Phi_1$ *it holds that* $\Psi^* \vdash \mathsf{w}_{a_2} \leq \mathsf{w}_{b_1} \leq \mathsf{w}_{a_3}$. *Moreover, if* $P_{a_{\mathsf{L}}} = x_{\mathsf{L}} \leftarrow \mathsf{acquire}\, c_{\mathsf{S}} ; Q_{x_{\mathsf{L}}}$, *for a* $(c_{\mathsf{S}} : \uparrow^{\mathsf{S}}_{\mathsf{L}} C_{\mathsf{L}}[\mathsf{w}_{c_1} \updownarrow^{\mathsf{w}_{c_3}}_{\mathsf{w}_{c_2}}]) \in \Gamma$, *then, for every acquired resource* $b_{\mathsf{L}} : B_{\mathsf{L}}[\mathsf{w}_{b_1} \updownarrow^{\mathsf{w}_{b_3}}_{\mathsf{w}_{b_2}}] \in \Phi_1$, *it holds that* $\Psi^+ \vdash \mathsf{w}_{b_1} < \mathsf{w}_{c_1}$ *and that* $\Psi^* \vdash \mathsf{w}_{a_2} \leq \mathsf{w}_{c_1} \leq \mathsf{w}_{a_3}$.

$$\frac{}{\Psi; \Gamma \vDash (\cdot) :: (\cdot)}\ (\text{T-}\Theta_1)$$

$$\frac{\begin{array}{c}(a_{\mathsf{S}} : \hat{B}[\mathsf{w}_{a_1} \updownarrow^{\mathsf{w}_{a_3}}_{\mathsf{w}_{a_2}}]) \in \Gamma \qquad \vdash (A_{\mathsf{L}}, \hat{B})\ \mathsf{sesync} \qquad \Psi \vdash A_{\mathsf{L}}[\mathsf{w}_{a_1} \updownarrow^{\mathsf{w}_{a_3}}_{\mathsf{w}_{a_2}}]\ \mathsf{type} \\ \Psi^* \vdash \mathsf{w}_{a_2} \leq \mathsf{w}_{a_3} \qquad \mathsf{Inv}_1(\mathsf{proc}(a_{\mathsf{L}}, \mathsf{w}_{a_1} \updownarrow^{\mathsf{w}_{a_3}}_{\mathsf{w}_{a_2}}, P_{a_{\mathsf{L}}})) \qquad \mathsf{Inv}_2(\mathsf{proc}(a_{\mathsf{L}}, \mathsf{w}_{a_1} \updownarrow^{\mathsf{w}_{a_3}}_{\mathsf{w}_{a_2}}, P_{a_{\mathsf{L}}})) \\ \Psi; \Gamma \vDash \Theta :: \Phi, \Phi_1, \Delta, \Delta_1 \qquad \Psi; \Gamma; \Phi_1; \Delta_1 \vdash P_{a_{\mathsf{L}}} :: (a_{\mathsf{L}} : A_{\mathsf{L}}[\mathsf{w}_{a_1} \updownarrow^{\mathsf{w}_{a_3}}_{\mathsf{w}_{a_2}}])\end{array}}{\Psi; \Gamma \vDash \Theta, \mathsf{proc}(a_{\mathsf{L}}, \mathsf{w}_{a_1} \updownarrow^{\mathsf{w}_{a_3}}_{\mathsf{w}_{a_2}}, P_{a_{\mathsf{L}}}) :: (\Phi, \Delta, a_{\mathsf{L}} : A_{\mathsf{L}}[\mathsf{w}_{a_1} \updownarrow^{\mathsf{w}_{a_3}}_{\mathsf{w}_{a_2}}])}\ (\text{T-}\Theta_2)$$

$$\frac{}{\Psi; \Gamma \vDash (\cdot) :: (\cdot)}\ (\text{T-}\Lambda_1) \qquad \frac{\begin{array}{c}\vdash (\uparrow^{\mathsf{S}}_{\mathsf{L}} A_{\mathsf{L}}, \uparrow^{\mathsf{S}}_{\mathsf{L}} A_{\mathsf{L}})\ \mathsf{sesync} \qquad \Psi \vdash \uparrow^{\mathsf{S}}_{\mathsf{L}} A_{\mathsf{L}}[\mathsf{w}_{a_1} \updownarrow^{\mathsf{w}_{a_3}}_{\mathsf{w}_{a_2}}]\ \mathsf{type} \\ \Psi^* \vdash \mathsf{w}_{a_2} \leq \mathsf{w}_{a_3} \qquad \Psi; \Gamma \vdash P_{a_{\mathsf{S}}} :: (a_{\mathsf{S}} : \uparrow^{\mathsf{S}}_{\mathsf{L}} A_{\mathsf{L}}[\mathsf{w}_{a_1} \updownarrow^{\mathsf{w}_{a_3}}_{\mathsf{w}_{a_2}}])\end{array}}{\Psi; \Gamma \vDash \mathsf{proc}(a_{\mathsf{S}}, \mathsf{w}_{a_1} \updownarrow^{\mathsf{w}_{a_3}}_{\mathsf{w}_{a_2}}, P_{a_{\mathsf{S}}}) :: (a_{\mathsf{S}} : \uparrow^{\mathsf{S}}_{\mathsf{L}} A_{\mathsf{L}}[\mathsf{w}_{a_1} \updownarrow^{\mathsf{w}_{a_3}}_{\mathsf{w}_{a_2}}])}\ (\text{T-}\Lambda_2)$$

$$\frac{}{\Psi; \Gamma \vDash \mathsf{unavail}(a_{\mathsf{S}}, \mathsf{w}_{a_1} \updownarrow^{\mathsf{w}_{a_3}}_{\mathsf{w}_{a_2}}) :: (a_{\mathsf{S}} : \hat{A}[\mathsf{w}_{a_1} \updownarrow^{\mathsf{w}_{a_3}}_{\mathsf{w}_{a_2}}])}\ (\text{T-}\Lambda_3) \qquad \frac{\Psi; \Gamma \vDash \Lambda :: \Gamma_1 \qquad \Psi; \Gamma \vDash \Lambda' :: \Gamma_2}{\Psi; \Gamma \vDash \Lambda, \Lambda' :: \Gamma_1, \Gamma_2}\ (\text{T-}\Lambda_4)$$

$$\frac{\Psi; \Gamma \vDash \Lambda :: \Gamma \qquad \Psi; \Gamma \vDash \Theta :: \Phi, \Delta}{\Psi; \Gamma \vDash \Lambda; \Theta :: \Gamma; \Phi, \Delta}\ (\text{T-}\Omega)$$

Fig. 10. Configuration typing

Invariant 2 (max(parent) < minima(descendants)). *If* $\Psi; \Gamma \vDash \Theta :: \Phi, \Delta$ *and for any* $\mathsf{proc}(a_{\mathsf{L}}, \mathsf{w}_{a_1} \updownarrow^{\mathsf{w}_{a_3}}_{\mathsf{w}_{a_2}}, P_{a_{\mathsf{L}}}) \in \Theta$ *and that process' descendants* $(\Psi; \Gamma \vDash \Theta :: \Phi, \Delta) \rhd a_{\mathsf{L}} = (\Phi', \Delta')$, $\mathsf{Inv}_2(\mathsf{proc}(a_{\mathsf{L}}, \mathsf{w}_{a_1} \updownarrow^{\mathsf{w}_{a_3}}_{\mathsf{w}_{a_2}}, P_{a_{\mathsf{L}}}))$ *holds iff for every descendant* $b_{\mathsf{L}} : B_{\mathsf{L}}[\mathsf{w}_{b_1} \updownarrow^{\mathsf{w}_{b_3}}_{\mathsf{w}_{b_2}}] \in (\Phi', \Delta')$ *it holds that* $\Psi^+ \vdash \mathsf{w}_{a_3} < \mathsf{w}_{b_2}$.

Our preservation theorem states that Invariants 1 and 2 are preserved for every linear process in the configuration along transitions. Moreover, the theorem expresses that the types of the providing linear channels Φ and Δ are maintained along transitions and that new shared channels and worlds may be allocated. The proof relies, in particular, on session types being strictly equi-synchronizing, on a process' type well-formedness and assurance that the process' min world is less than or equal to its max world.

Theorem 5.1 (Preservation). *If* $\Psi; \Gamma \vDash \Lambda; \Theta :: \Gamma; \Phi, \Delta$ *and* $\Lambda; \Theta \longrightarrow \Lambda'; \Theta'$, *then* $\Psi'; \Gamma' \vDash \Lambda'; \Theta' :: \Gamma'; \Phi, \Delta$, *for some* Λ', Θ', Ψ', *and* Γ'.

5.2 Progress

In our development so far we have distilled the two scenarios of interdependencies between processes that can lead to deadlocks: *cyclic acquisitions* and *interdependent acquisitions and synchronizations*. This has lead to the development of a type system that ingrains the notions of *competitors* and *collaborators*, such that the former compete for a set of resources whereas the latter do not overlap in the set of resources they acquire. Our type system then ties these notions to a configuration's linear process tree such that collaborators stand in a parent-descendant relationship to each other and competitors in a sibling/cousin relationship. In this section, we prove that this orchestration is sufficient to rule out any of the aforementioned interdependencies.

To this end we introduce the notions of *red* and *green arrows* that allow us to reason about process interdependencies in a configuration's tree. A red arrow points from a linear $\mathsf{proc}(a_{\mathsf{L}}, \mathsf{w}_{\mathsf{a}_1} \updownarrow^{\mathsf{w}_{\mathsf{a}_3}}_{\mathsf{w}_{\mathsf{a}_2}}, Q)$ to a linear $\mathsf{proc}(b_{\mathsf{L}}, \mathsf{w}_{\mathsf{b}_1} \updownarrow^{\mathsf{w}_{\mathsf{b}_3}}_{\mathsf{w}_{\mathsf{b}_2}}, P)$, if the former is attempting to acquire a resource held by the latter and, consequently, is waiting for the latter to release that resource. A green arrow points from a linear $\mathsf{proc}(a_{\mathsf{L}}, \mathsf{w}_{\mathsf{a}_1} \updownarrow^{\mathsf{w}_{\mathsf{a}_3}}_{\mathsf{w}_{\mathsf{a}_2}}, Q)$ to a linear $\mathsf{proc}(b_{\mathsf{L}}, \mathsf{w}_{\mathsf{b}_1} \updownarrow^{\mathsf{w}_{\mathsf{b}_3}}_{\mathsf{w}_{\mathsf{b}_2}}, P)$, if the former is waiting to synchronize with the latter. We define these arrows formally as follows:

Definition 5.2 (Acquire Dependency — "Red Arrow"). *Given a well-formed and well-typed configuration* $\Psi; \Gamma \vDash \Lambda; \Theta :: \Gamma; \Phi, \Delta$*, there exists a waiting-due-to-acquire relation* $\mathcal{A}(\Theta)$ *among linear processes in* Θ *at run-time such that*

$$\mathsf{proc}(a_{\mathsf{L}}, \mathsf{w}_{\mathsf{a}_1} \updownarrow^{\mathsf{w}_{\mathsf{a}_3}}_{\mathsf{w}_{\mathsf{a}_2}}, x_{\mathsf{L}} \leftarrow \mathsf{acquire}\ c_{\mathsf{S}};\ Q_{x_{\mathsf{L}}}) <_{\mathcal{A}} \mathsf{proc}(b_{\mathsf{L}}, \mathsf{w}_{\mathsf{b}_1} \updownarrow^{\mathsf{w}_{\mathsf{b}_3}}_{\mathsf{w}_{\mathsf{b}_2}}, P\langle c_{\mathsf{L}}\rangle)$$

where $P\langle c_{\mathsf{L}}\rangle$ *denotes a process term with an occurrence of channel* c_{L}*.*

Definition 5.3 (Synchronization Dependency — "Green Arrow"). *Given a well-formed and well-typed configuration* $\Psi; \Gamma \vDash \Lambda; \Theta :: \Gamma; \Phi, \Delta$*, there exists a waiting-due-to-synchronization relation* $\mathcal{S}(\Theta)$ *among linear processes in* Θ *at run-time such that*

$$\mathsf{proc}(a_{\mathsf{L}}, \mathsf{w}_{\mathsf{a}_1} \updownarrow^{\mathsf{w}_{\mathsf{a}_3}}_{\mathsf{w}_{\mathsf{a}_2}}, \_\langle b_{\mathsf{L}}\rangle; Q) <_{\mathcal{S}} \mathsf{proc}(b_{\mathsf{L}}, \mathsf{w}_{\mathsf{b}_1} \updownarrow^{\mathsf{w}_{\mathsf{b}_3}}_{\mathsf{w}_{\mathsf{b}_2}}, \_\langle \neg b_{\mathsf{L}}\rangle; P)$$
$$\mathsf{proc}(b_{\mathsf{L}}, \mathsf{w}_{\mathsf{b}_1} \updownarrow^{\mathsf{w}_{\mathsf{b}_3}}_{\mathsf{w}_{\mathsf{b}_2}}, \_\langle b_{\mathsf{L}}\rangle; P) <_{\mathcal{S}} \mathsf{proc}(a_{\mathsf{L}}, \mathsf{w}_{\mathsf{a}_1} \updownarrow^{\mathsf{w}_{\mathsf{a}_3}}_{\mathsf{w}_{\mathsf{a}_2}}, \_\langle \neg b_{\mathsf{L}}\rangle; Q\langle b_{\mathsf{L}}\rangle)$$

where $P\langle a_{\mathsf{L}}\rangle$ *denotes a process term with an occurrence of channel* b_{L}*,* $\_\langle a\rangle; P$ *a process term that currently executes an action along channel* a*, and* $\_\langle \neg a\rangle; P$ *a process term whose currently executing action does not involve the channel* a*.*

It may be helpful to consult Fig. 3 at this point and note the semantic difference between the violet arrows in that figure and the red arrows discussed here. Whereas violet arrows point from the acquiring process to the resource being acquired, red arrows point from the acquiring process to the process that is holding the resource. Thus, violet arrows can go out of the tree, while red arrows stay within. Given the definitions of red and green arrows, we can define the relation $\mathcal{W}(\Theta)$ on the configuration's tree, which contains all process pairs that are in some way waiting for each other:

Definition 5.4 (Waiting Dependency). *Given a well-formed and well-typed configuration* $\Psi; \Gamma \vDash \Lambda; \Theta :: \Gamma; \Phi, \Delta$*, there exists a waiting relation* $\mathcal{W}(\Theta)$ *among processes in* Θ *at run-time such that* $\mathsf{proc}(a_{\mathsf{L}}, \mathsf{w}_{\mathsf{a}_1} \updownarrow^{\mathsf{w}_{\mathsf{a}_3}}_{\mathsf{w}_{\mathsf{a}_2}}, P) <_{\mathcal{W}} \mathsf{proc}(b_{\mathsf{L}}, \mathsf{w}_{\mathsf{b}_1} \updownarrow^{\mathsf{w}_{\mathsf{b}_3}}_{\mathsf{w}_{\mathsf{b}_2}}, Q)$*,*

- *if* $\mathsf{proc}(a_{\mathsf{L}}, \mathsf{w}_{\mathsf{a}_1} \updownarrow^{\mathsf{w}_{\mathsf{a}_3}}_{\mathsf{w}_{\mathsf{a}_2}}, P) <_{\mathcal{A}} \mathsf{proc}(b_{\mathsf{L}}, \mathsf{w}_{\mathsf{b}_1} \updownarrow^{\mathsf{w}_{\mathsf{b}_3}}_{\mathsf{w}_{\mathsf{b}_2}}, Q)$*, or*
- *if* $\mathsf{proc}(a_{\mathsf{L}}, \mathsf{w}_{\mathsf{a}_1} \updownarrow^{\mathsf{w}_{\mathsf{a}_3}}_{\mathsf{w}_{\mathsf{a}_2}}, P) <_{\mathcal{S}} \mathsf{proc}(b_{\mathsf{L}}, \mathsf{w}_{\mathsf{b}_1} \updownarrow^{\mathsf{w}_{\mathsf{b}_3}}_{\mathsf{w}_{\mathsf{b}_2}}, Q)$*.*

Having defined the relation $\mathcal{W}(\Theta)$, we can now state the key lemma underlying our progress theorem, indicating that $\mathcal{W}(\Theta)$ is acyclic in a well-formed and well-typed configuration.

Lemma 5.5 (Acyclicity of $\mathcal{W}(\Theta)$). *If $\Psi; \Gamma \models \Lambda; \Theta :: \Gamma; \Phi, \Delta$, then $\mathcal{W}(\Theta)$ is acyclic.*

We focus on explaining the main idea of the proof here. The proof proceeds by induction on $\Psi;\Gamma \models \Theta :: \Phi, \Delta$, assuming for the non-empty case $\Psi;\Gamma \models \Theta, \mathsf{proc}(a_{\mathsf{L}}, \mathsf{w}_{a_1} \updownarrow^{\mathsf{w}_{a_3}}_{\mathsf{w}_{a_2}}, P_{a_{\mathsf{L}}}) :: (\Phi, \Delta, a_{\mathsf{L}} : A_{\mathsf{L}}[\mathsf{w}_{a_1} \updownarrow^{\mathsf{w}_{a_3}}_{\mathsf{w}_{a_2}}])$ that $\mathcal{W}(\Theta)$ is acyclic, by the inductive hypothesis. We then know that there cannot exist any paths of green and red arrows in Θ that form a cycle, and we have to show that there is no way of introducing such a cyclic path by adding node $\mathsf{proc}(a_{\mathsf{L}}, \mathsf{w}_{a_1} \updownarrow^{\mathsf{w}_{a_3}}_{\mathsf{w}_{a_2}}, P_{a_{\mathsf{L}}})$ to the configuration Θ. In particular, the proof considers all possible new arrows that may be introduced by adding the node and that are necessary for creating a cycle, showing that such arrows cannot come about in a well-typed configuration.

We illustrate the reasoning for the two selected cases shown in Fig. 11. Case **(a)** represents a case in which process $P_{a_{\mathsf{L}}}$ is waiting to synchronize with its child $P_{b_{\mathsf{L}}}$ while holding a resource a descendant of $P_{b_{\mathsf{L}}}$ or $P_{b_{\mathsf{L}}}$ itself wants to acquire. However, this scenario cannot come about in a well-typed configuration because $P_{a_{\mathsf{L}}}$ and $P_{b_{\mathsf{L}}}$ are collaborators and thus cannot overlap in resources they acquire. Case **(b)** represents a case in which process $P_{a_{\mathsf{L}}}$ is waiting to synchronize with its child $P_{b_{\mathsf{L}}}$ while another child, process $P_{c_{\mathsf{L}}}$, is waiting to synchronize with $P_{a_{\mathsf{L}}}$. Given acyclicity of $\mathcal{W}(\Theta)$, a necessary condition for a cycle to form is that there already must exist a red arrow **C** in the configuration that connects the subtrees in which the siblings $P_{b_{\mathsf{L}}}$ and $P_{c_{\mathsf{L}}}$ reside. However, this scenario cannot come about in a well-typed configuration because $P_{b_{\mathsf{L}}}$ and $P_{c_{\mathsf{L}}}$ are competitors, forcing $P_{c_{\mathsf{L}}}$ or any of its descendant to release a resource before synchronizing with $P_{a_{\mathsf{L}}}$. These arguments are made precise in various lemmas in [4].

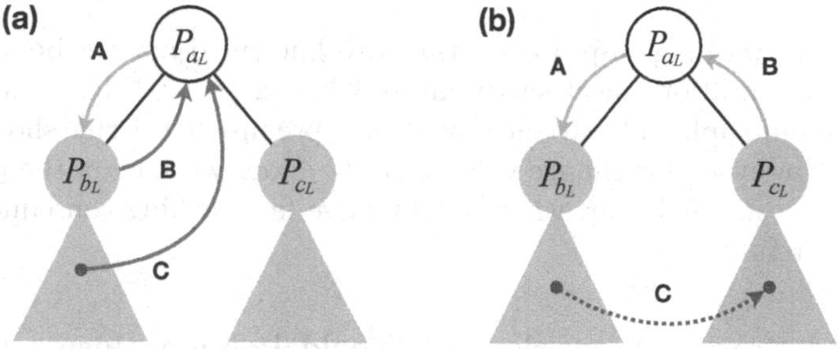

Fig. 11. Two prototypical cases in proof of acyclicty of $\mathcal{W}(\Theta)$.

Given acyclicity of $\mathcal{W}(\Theta)$, we can state and prove the following strong progress theorem. The theorem relies on the notion of a *poised* process, a process currently executing an action along its offering channel, and distinguishes a configuration only consisting of the top-level, linear "main" process from one that consists of several linear processes. We use $|\Theta|$ to denote the cardinality of Θ:

Theorem 5.6 (Progress). *If* $\Psi; \Gamma \vDash \Lambda; \Theta :: (\Gamma; c_{\mathsf{L}} : \mathbf{1}[\mathsf{w}_{c_1} \updownarrow^{\mathsf{w}_{c_3}}_{\mathsf{w}_{c_2}}])$*, then either*

- $\Lambda \longrightarrow \Lambda'$*, for some* Λ'*, or*
- Λ *is poised and*
  - *if* $|\Theta| = 1$*, then either* $\Lambda; \Theta \longrightarrow \Lambda'; \Theta'$*, for some* Λ' *and* Θ'*, or* Θ *is poised, or*
  - *if* $|\Theta| > 1$*, then* $\Lambda; \Theta \longrightarrow \Lambda'; \Theta'$*, for some* Λ' *and* Θ'*.*

The theorem indicates that, as long as there exist at least two linear processes in the configuration, the configuration can always step. If the configuration only consists of the main process, then this process will become poised (i.e., ready to close), once all sub-computations are finished. The proof of the theorem relies on the acyclicity of $\mathcal{W}(\Theta)$ and the fact that all sessions must be strictly equi-synchronizing.

6 Additional Discussion

Linear Forwarding. Our current formalization does not include linear forwarding because a forward changes the process tree and thus endangers the invariants imposed on it. This means that certain programs from the purely linear fragment may not type-check in our system. However, the correspondingly η-expanded versions of these programs should be expressible and type-checkable in $\mathsf{SILL}_{\mathsf{S}^+}$. As part of future work, we want to explore the addition of the linear forward

$$\frac{\Psi^+ \vdash \omega_n < \omega_u}{\Psi;\, \Gamma;\, \cdot;\, y_{\mathsf{L}} : A_{\mathsf{L}}[\omega_m \updownarrow^{\omega_v}_{\omega_u}] \vdash \mathsf{fwd}\ x_{\mathsf{L}}\ y_{\mathsf{L}} :: (x_{\mathsf{L}} : A_{\mathsf{L}}[\omega_j \updownarrow^{\omega_n}_{\omega_k}])}\ (\text{T-ID}_{\mathsf{L}})$$

which allows forwarding to processes that are known to not yet be aliased and whose world annotations meet the premise $\Psi^+ \vdash \omega_n < \omega_u$. Restricting to processes in Δ should uphold Invariant 1, while the premise of the rule should uphold Invariant 2. However, this change will affect the inner working of the proofs, the use of inversion in particular, which might have far-reaching consequences that need to be carefully explored.

Unbounded Process Networks and World Polymorphism. The typing discipline presented in the previous sections, while rich enough to account for a wide range of interesting programs, cannot type programs that spawn a statically undetermined number of shared sessions that are then to be used. For instance, while we can easily type a configuration of any given number of dining philosophers (Sect. 3.3), we cannot type a recursive process in which the number of philosophers (and forks) is potentially unbounded (as done in [21,38]), due to the way worlds are created and propagated across processes.

The general issue lies in implementing a statically unbounded network of processes that interact with each other. These interactions require the processes to be spawned at different worlds which must be generated dynamically as needed.

To interact with such a statically unknown number of processes uniformly, their offering channels must be stored in a list-like structure for later use. However, in our system, recursive types have to be invariant with respect to worlds. For instance, in a recursive type such as $T = A_{\mathsf{L}}@\omega_l \updownarrow_{\omega_p}^{\omega_r} \otimes T$, the worlds ω_l, ω_p, ω_r are fixed in the unfoldings of T. Thus, we cannot type a world-heterogeneous list and cannot form such process networks.

Given that the issues preventing us from typing such unbounded networks lie in problems of world invariance, the natural solution is to explore some form of *world polymorphism*, where types can be parameterized by worlds which are instantiated at a later stage. Such techniques have been studied in the context of hybrid logical processes in [7] by considering session types of the form $\forall\delta.A$ and $\exists\delta.A$, sessions that are parametric in the world variable δ, that is instantiated by a concrete reachable world at runtime. While their development cannot be mapped directly to our setting, it is a promising avenue of future work.

7 Related Work

Behavioral Type Analysis of Deadlocks. The addition of channel usage information to types in a concurrent, message-passing setting was pioneered by Kobayashi and Igarashi [30,34], who applied the idea to deadlock prevention in the π-calculus and later to more general properties [31,32], giving rise to a generic system that can be instantiated to produce a variety of concrete typing disciplines for the π-calculus (e.g., race detection, deadlock detection, etc.).

This line of work types π-calculus processes with a simplified form of *process* (akin to CCS [42] terms without name restriction) that characterizes the input/output behavior of processes. These types are augmented with abstract data that pertain to the relative ordering of channel actions, with the type system ensuring that the transitive closure of such orderings forms a strict partial order, ensuring deadlock-freedom (i.e., communication succeeds unless a process diverges). Building on this, Kobayashi et al. proposed type systems that ensure a stronger property dubbed lock-freedom [35] (i.e., communication always succeeds), and variants that are amenable to type inference [36,39]. Kobayashi [37] extended this latter system to more accurately account for recursive processes while preserving the existence of a type inference algorithm.

Our system draws significant inspiration from this line of work, insofar as we also equip types with abstract ordering data on certain communication actions, which is then statically enforced to form a strict partial order. We note that our $\mathsf{SILL}_{\mathsf{S}+}$ language differs sufficiently from the pure π-calculus in terms of its constructs and semantics to make the formulation of a direct comparison or an immediate application of their work unclear (e.g., [37] uses replication to encode recursive processes). Moreover, we integrate this style of order-based reasoning with both linear and shared session typing, which interact in non-trivial ways (especially in the presence of recursive types and recursive process definitions).

In terms of typability, enforcing session fidelity can be a double-edged sword: some examples of the works above can be transposed to $\mathsf{SILL}_{\mathsf{S}+}$ with mostly cosmetic changes and without making use of shared sessions (e.g., a parallel implementation of factorial that recurses via replication but always answers on a private channel); others are incompatible with linear sessions and require the use of shared sessions via the acquire-release discipline, which entails a more indirect but still arguably faithful modelling of the original π-calculus behavior; some examples, however, cannot be easily adapted to the shared session discipline (e.g., $*c?(x, y).x?(z).y?(z) \mid *c?(x, y).y?(z).x?(z)$ is typable in [37], where $x?(z)$ denotes input on x and $*c?(x, y)$ denotes replicated input) and their transcription, while possible, would be too far removed from the original term to be deemed a faithful representation. Recursive processes are known to produce patterns that can be challenging to analyze using such order-based techniques. The work of [21,38] specializes Kobayashi's system to account for potentially unbounded process networks with non-trivial forms of sharing. Such systems are not typable in our work (see Sect. 6 for additional discussion on this topic).

The work of Padovani [44] develops techniques inspired by [35,37] to develop a typing system for deadlock (and lock) freedom for the linear π-calculus where (linear) channels must be used exactly once. By enforcing this form of linearity, the resulting system uses only one piece of ordering data per channel usage and can easily integrate a form of channel polymorphism that accounts for intricate cyclic interleavings of recursive processes. The combination of manifest sharing and linear session typing does not seem possible without the use of additional ordering data, and the lack of single-use linear channels make the robust channel polymorphism of [44] not feasible in our setting.

Dardha and Gay [15] recently integrated a system of Kobayashi-style orderings in a logical session π-calculus based on classical linear logic, extended with the ability to form *cyclic dependencies* of actions on *linear* session channels (Atkey et al. [1] study similar cycles but do not consider deadlock-freedom), without the need for new process constructs or an acquire-release discipline. Their work considers only a restricted form of replication common in linear logic-based works, not including recursive types nor recursive process definitions. This reduces the complexity of their system, at the cost of expressiveness. We also note that the cycles enabled by their system are produced by processes sharing multiple *linear* names. Since linearity is still enforced, they cannot represent the more general form of cycles that exploit shared channels, as we do.

A comparative study of session typing and Kobayashi-style systems in terms of sharing was developed by Dardha and Pérez [16], showing that such order-based techniques can account for sharing in ways that are out of reach of both classical session typing and pure logic-based session typing. Our system (and that of [15]) aims to combine the heightened power of Kobayashi-style systems with the benefits of session typing, which seems to be better suited as a typing discipline for a high-level programming language [18].

Progress and Session Typing. To address limitations of classical binary session types, Honda et al. [27] introduced *multiparty* session types, where sessions are described by so-called global types that capture the interactions between an arbitrary number of session participants. Under some well-formedness constraints, global types can be used to ensure that a collection of processes correctly implements the global behavior in a deadlock-free way. However, these global type-based approaches do not ensure deadlock freedom in the presence of higher-order channel passing or interleaved multiparty sessions. Coppo et al. [13] and Bettini et al. [6] develop systems that track usage orders among interleaved multiparty sessions, ruling out cyclic dependencies that can lead to deadlocks. The resulting system is quite intricate, since it combines the full multiparty session theory with the order tracking mechanism, interacts negatively with recursion (essentially disallowing interleaving with recursion) and, by tracking order at the multiparty session-level, ends up rejecting various benign configurations that can be accounted for by our more fine-grained analysis. We also highlight the analyses of Vieira and Vasconcelos [54] and Padovani et al. [45] that are more powerful than the approaches above, at the cost of a more complex analysis based on conversation types [10] (themselves a partial-order based technique).

Static Analysis of Concurrent Programs. Lange et al. [40,41] develop a deadlock detection framework applied to the Go programming language. Their work distills CCS processes from programs which are then checked for deadlocks by a form of symbolic execution [40] and *model-checked* against modal μ-calculus formulae [41] which encode deadlock-freedom of the abstracted process (among other properties of interest). Their abstraction introduces some distance between the original program and the analysed process and so the analysis is sound only for certain restricted program fragments, excluding any combination of recursion and process spawning. Our direct approach does not suffer from this limitation.

de'Liguoro and Padovani [17] develop a typing discipline for deadlock-freedom in a setting where processes exchange messages via unordered mailboxes. Their calculus subsumes the actor model and their analysis combines both so-called mailbox types and specialized dependency graphs to track potential cycles between mailboxes in actor-based systems. The unordered nature of actor-based communication introduces significant differences wrt our work, which crucially exploits the ordering of exchanged messages.

8 Concluding Remarks

In this paper we have developed the concept of manifest deadlock-freedom in the context of the language $\mathsf{SILL}_{\mathsf{S}^+}$, a shared session-typed language, showcasing both the programming methodology and the expressiveness of our framework with a series of examples. Deadlock-freedom of well-typed programs is established by a novel abstraction of so-called green and red arrows to reason about the interdependencies between processes in terms of linear and shared channel references.

In future work, we plan to address some of the limitations of the interactions of deadlock-free shared sessions with recursion, by considering promising notions of world polymorphism and world communication. We also plan to study the problem of world inference and the inclusion of a linear forwarding construct.

References

1. Atkey, R., Lindley, S., Morris, J.G.: Conflation confers concurrency. In: Lindley, S., McBride, C., Trinder, P., Sannella, D. (eds.) A List of Successes That Can Change the World. LNCS, vol. 9600, pp. 32–55. Springer, Cham (2016). https://doi.org/10.1007/978-3-319-30936-1_2
2. Balzer, S., Pfenning, F.: Manifest sharing with session types. Proc. ACM Program. Lang. (PACMPL) **1**(ICEP), 37:1–37:29 (2017)
3. Balzer, S., Pfenning, F., Toninho, B.: A universal session type for untyped asynchronous communication. In: 29th International Conference on Concurrency Theory (CONCUR). LIPIcs, pp. 30:1–30:18. Schloss Dagstuhl - Leibniz-Zentrum fuer Informatik (2018)
4. Balzer, S., Toninho, B., Pfenning, F.: Manifest deadlock-freedom for shared session types. Technical report CMU-CS-19-102, Carnegie Mellon University (2019)
5. Benton, P.N.: A mixed linear and non-linear logic: proofs, terms and models. In: Pacholski, L., Tiuryn, J. (eds.) CSL 1994. LNCS, vol. 933, pp. 121–135. Springer, Heidelberg (1995). https://doi.org/10.1007/BFb0022251
6. Bettini, L., Coppo, M., D'Antoni, L., Luca, M.D., Dezani-Ciancaglini, M., Yoshida, N.: Global progress in dynamically interleaved multiparty sessions. In: van Breugel, F., Chechik, M. (eds.) CONCUR 2008. LNCS, vol. 5201, pp. 418–433. Springer, Heidelberg (2008). https://doi.org/10.1007/978-3-540-85361-9_33
7. Caires, L., Pérez, J.A., Pfenning, F., Toninho, B.: Logic-based domain-aware session types, unpublished draft
8. Caires, L., Pfenning, F.: Session types as intuitionistic linear propositions. In: Gastin, P., Laroussinie, F. (eds.) CONCUR 2010. LNCS, vol. 6269, pp. 222–236. Springer, Heidelberg (2010). https://doi.org/10.1007/978-3-642-15375-4_16
9. Caires, L., Pfenning, F., Toninho, B.: Linear logic propositions as session types. Math. Struct. Comput. Sci. **26**(3), 367–423 (2016)
10. Caires, L., Vieira, H.T.: Conversation types. Theor. Comput. Sci. **411**(51–52), 4399–4440 (2010)
11. Castro, D., Hu, R., Jongmans, S., Ng, N., Yoshida, N.: Distributed programming using role-parametric session types in go: statically-typed endpoint APIs for dynamically-instantiated communication structures. PACMPL **3**(POPL), 29:1–29:30 (2019)
12. Cervesato, I., Scedrov, A.: Relating state-based and process-based concurrency through linear logic. Inf. Comput. **207**(10), 1044–1077 (2009)
13. Coppo, M., Dezani-Ciancaglini, M., Yoshida, N., Padovani, L.: Global progress for dynamically interleaved multiparty sessions. Math. Struct. Comput. Sci. **26**(2), 238–302 (2016)
14. Crary, K., Harper, R., Puri, S.: What is a recursive module? In: ACM SIGPLAN Conference on Programming Language Design and Implementation (PLDI), pp. 50–63 (1999)
15. Dardha, O., Gay, S.J.: A new linear logic for deadlock-free session-typed processes. In: Baier, C., Dal Lago, U. (eds.) FoSSaCS 2018. LNCS, vol. 10803, pp. 91–109. Springer, Cham (2018). https://doi.org/10.1007/978-3-319-89366-2_5
16. Dardha, O., Pérez, J.A.: Comparing deadlock-free session typed processes. In: EXPRESS/SOS, pp. 1–15 (2015)
17. de'Liguoro, U., Padovani, L.: Mailbox types for unordered interactions. In: 32nd European Conference on Object-Oriented Programming, ECOOP 2018, pp. 15:1–15:28 (2018)

18. Gay, S.J., Gesbert, N., Ravara, A.: Session types as generic process types. In: 21st International Workshop on Expressiveness in Concurrency and 11th Workshop on Structural Operational Semantics, EXPRESS/SOS 2014, pp. 94–110 (2014)
19. Gay, S.J., Hole, M.: Subtyping for session types in the π-calculus. Acta Informatica **42**(2–3), 191–225 (2005)
20. Gay, S.J., Vasconcelos, V.T., Ravara, A., Gesbert, N., Caldeira, A.Z.: Modular session types for distributed object-oriented programming. In: 37th ACM SIGPLAN-SIGACT Symposium on Principles of Programming Languages (POPL), pp. 299–312 (2010)
21. Giachino, E., Kobayashi, N., Laneve, C.: Deadlock analysis of unbounded process networks. In: Baldan, P., Gorla, D. (eds.) CONCUR 2014. LNCS, vol. 8704, pp. 63–77. Springer, Heidelberg (2014). https://doi.org/10.1007/978-3-662-44584-6_6
22. Gommerstadt, H., Jia, L., Pfenning, F.: Session-typed concurrent contracts. In: Ahmed, A. (ed.) ESOP 2018. LNCS, vol. 10801, pp. 771–798. Springer, Cham (2018). https://doi.org/10.1007/978-3-319-89884-1_27
23. Griffith, D.: Polarized substructural session types. Ph.D. thesis, University of Illinois at Urbana-Champaign (2016)
24. Griffith, D., Pfenning, F.: SILL (2015). https://github.com/ISANobody/sill
25. Honda, K.: Types for dyadic interaction. In: Best, E. (ed.) CONCUR 1993. LNCS, vol. 715, pp. 509–523. Springer, Heidelberg (1993). https://doi.org/10.1007/3-540-57208-2_35
26. Honda, K., Vasconcelos, V.T., Kubo, M.: Language primitives and type discipline for structured communication-based programming. In: Hankin, C. (ed.) ESOP 1998. LNCS, vol. 1381, pp. 122–138. Springer, Heidelberg (1998). https://doi.org/10.1007/BFb0053567
27. Honda, K., Yoshida, N., Carbone, M.: Multiparty asynchronous session types. In: 35th ACM SIGPLAN-SIGACT Symposium on Principles of Programming Languages (POPL), pp. 273–284. ACM (2008)
28. Hu, R., Yoshida, N.: Hybrid session verification through endpoint API generation. In: Stevens, P., Wąsowski, A. (eds.) FASE 2016. LNCS, vol. 9633, pp. 401–418. Springer, Heidelberg (2016). https://doi.org/10.1007/978-3-662-49665-7_24
29. Hu, R., Yoshida, N.: Explicit connection actions in multiparty session types. In: Huisman, M., Rubin, J. (eds.) FASE 2017. LNCS, vol. 10202, pp. 116–133. Springer, Heidelberg (2017). https://doi.org/10.1007/978-3-662-54494-5_7
30. Igarashi, A., Kobayashi, N.: Type-based analysis of communication for concurrent programming languages. In: Van Hentenryck, P. (ed.) SAS 1997. LNCS, vol. 1302, pp. 187–201. Springer, Heidelberg (1997). https://doi.org/10.1007/BFb0032742
31. Igarashi, A., Kobayashi, N.: A generic type system for the Pi-calculus. In: Conference Record of POPL 2001: The 28th ACM SIGPLAN-SIGACT Symposium on Principles of Programming Languages, pp. 128–141 (2001)
32. Igarashi, A., Kobayashi, N.: A generic type system for the Pi-calculus. Theor. Comput. Sci. **311**(1–3), 121–163 (2004)
33. Jespersen, T.B.L., Munksgaard, P., Larsen, K.F.: Session types for rust. In: 11th ACM SIGPLAN Workshop on Generic Programming, WGP 2015, pp. 13–22 (2015)
34. Kobayashi, N.: A partially deadlock-free typed process calculus. In: Proceedings of the 12th Annual IEEE Symposium on Logic in Computer Science, pp. 128–139 (1997)
35. Kobayashi, N.: A type system for lock-free processes. Inf. Comput. **177**(2), 122–159 (2002)
36. Kobayashi, N.: Type-based information flow analysis for the π-calculus. Acta Inf. **42**(4–5), 291–347 (2005)

37. Kobayashi, N.: A new type system for deadlock-free processes. In: Baier, C., Hermanns, H. (eds.) CONCUR 2006. LNCS, vol. 4137, pp. 233–247. Springer, Heidelberg (2006). https://doi.org/10.1007/11817949_16
38. Kobayashi, N., Laneve, C.: Deadlock analysis of unbounded process networks. Inf. Comput. **252**, 48–70 (2017)
39. Kobayashi, N., Saito, S., Sumii, E.: An implicitly-typed deadlock-free process calculus. In: Palamidessi, C. (ed.) CONCUR 2000. LNCS, vol. 1877, pp. 489–504. Springer, Heidelberg (2000). https://doi.org/10.1007/3-540-44618-4_35
40. Lange, J., Ng, N., Toninho, B., Yoshida, N.: Fencing off go: liveness and safety for channel-based programming. In: 44th ACM SIGPLAN-SIGACT Symposium on Principles of Programming Languages (POPL), pp. 748–761. ACM (2017)
41. Lange, J., Ng, N., Toninho, B., Yoshida, N.: A static verification framework for message passing in go using behavioural types. In: Proceedings of the 40th International Conference on Software Engineering, ICSE 2018, Gothenburg, Sweden, 27 May–03 June 2018, pp. 1137–1148 (2018)
42. Milner, R.: A Calculus of Communicating Systems. LNCS, vol. 92. Springer, Heidelberg (1980). https://doi.org/10.1007/3-540-10235-3
43. Neykova, R., Hu, R., Yoshida, N., Abdeljallal, F.: A session type provider: compile-time API generation of distributed protocols with refinements in F#. In: Proceedings of the 27th International Conference on Compiler Construction, CC 2018, pp. 128–138 (2018)
44. Padovani, L.: Deadlock and lock freedom in the linear π-calculus. In: Computer Science Logic - Logic in Computer Science (CSL-LICS), pp. 72:1–72:10 (2014)
45. Padovani, L., Vasconcelos, V.T., Vieira, H.T.: Typing liveness in multiparty communicating systems. In: Kühn, E., Pugliese, R. (eds.) COORDINATION 2014. LNCS, vol. 8459, pp. 147–162. Springer, Heidelberg (2014). https://doi.org/10.1007/978-3-662-43376-8_10
46. Pérez, J.A., Caires, L., Pfenning, F., Toninho, B.: Linear logical relations and observational equivalences for session-based concurrency. Inf. Comput. **239**, 254–302 (2014)
47. Pfenning, F., Griffith, D.: Polarized substructural session types. In: Pitts, A. (ed.) FoSSaCS 2015. LNCS, vol. 9034, pp. 3–22. Springer, Heidelberg (2015). https://doi.org/10.1007/978-3-662-46678-0_1
48. Reed, J.: A judgmental deconstruction of modal logic, January 2009. http://www.cs.cmu.edu/~jcreed/papers/jdml.pdf, unpublished manuscript
49. Scalas, A., Dardha, O., Hu, R., Yoshida, N.: A linear decomposition of multiparty sessions for safe distributed programming. In: 31st European Conference on Object-Oriented Programming, ECOOP 2017, pp. 24:1–24:31 (2017)
50. Scalas, A., Yoshida, N.: Lightweight session programming in scala. In: 30th European Conference on Object-Oriented Programming, ECOOP 2016, pp. 21:1–21:28 (2016)
51. Toninho, B.: A logical foundation for session-based concurrent computation. Ph.D. thesis, Carnegie Mellon University and New University of Lisbon (2015)
52. Toninho, B., Caires, L., Pfenning, F.: Higher-order processes, functions, and sessions: a monadic integration. In: Felleisen, M., Gardner, P. (eds.) ESOP 2013. LNCS, vol. 7792, pp. 350–369. Springer, Heidelberg (2013). https://doi.org/10.1007/978-3-642-37036-6_20

53. Vasconcelos, V.T.: Fundamentals of session types. Inf. Comput. **217**, 52–70 (2012)
54. Vieira, H.T., Vasconcelos, V.T.: Typing progress in communication-centred systems. In: De Nicola, R., Julien, C. (eds.) COORDINATION 2013. LNCS, vol. 7890, pp. 236–250. Springer, Heidelberg (2013). https://doi.org/10.1007/978-3-642-38493-6_17
55. Wadler, P.: Propositions as sessions. In: 17th ACM SIGPLAN International Conference on Functional Programming (ICFP), pp. 273–286. ACM (2012)

A Categorical Model of an i/o-typed π-calculus

Ken Sakayori(✉) and Takeshi Tsukada

The University of Tokyo, Tokyo, Japan
sakayori@kb.is.s.u-tokyo.ac.jp

Abstract. This paper introduces a new categorical structure that is a model of a variant of the **i**/**o**-typed π-calculus, in the same way that a cartesian closed category is a model of the λ-calculus. To the best of our knowledge, no categorical model has been given for the **i**/**o**-typed π-calculus, in contrast to session-typed calculi, to which corresponding logic and categorical structure were given. The categorical structure introduced in this paper has a simple definition, combining two well-known structures, namely, closed Freyd category and compact closed category. The former is a model of effectful computation in a general setting, and the latter describes connections via channels, which cause the effect we focus on in this paper. To demonstrate the relevance of the categorical model, we show by a semantic consideration that the π-calculus is equivalent to a core calculus of Concurrent ML.

Keywords: π-calculus · Categorical type theory · Compact closed category · Closed Freyd category

1 Introduction

The Curry-Howard-Lambek correspondence reveals the trinity of the simply-typed λ-calculus, propositional intuitionistic logic and cartesian closed category. Via the correspondence, a type of the calculus can be seen as a formula of the logic, and as an object of a category; a term can be seen as a proof and as a morphism (see, e.g., [23]). Since its discovery, a number of variations have been proposed and studied.

In concurrency theory, a correspondence between a process calculus and logic was established by Caires, Pfenning and Toninho [8,9] and later by Wadler [48]. What they found is that session types [18,20] can be seen as formulas of linear logic [14], and processes as proofs. This remarkable result has inspired lots of work (e.g. [3,4,10,25,45,46]).

This correspondence is, however, not completely satisfactory as pointed out in [3,26], as well as by Wadler himself [48]. The session-typed calculi in [9,48] corresponding to linear logic have only well-behaved processes, because the session type systems guarantee deadlock-freedom and race-freedom of well-typed processes. This strong guarantee is often useful for programmers writing processes

L. Caires (Ed.): ESOP 2019, LNCS 11423, pp. 640–667, 2019.
https://doi.org/10.1007/978-3-030-17184-1_23

in the typed calculus, but can be seen as a significant limitation of expressive power. For example, it prevents us from modelling wild concurrent systems or programs that might fall into deadlocks or race conditions.

This paper describes an approach to a Curry-Howard-Lambek correspondence for concurrency in the presence of deadlocks and race conditions, from the viewpoint of categorical type theory.

What Is the Categorical Model of the π-calculus? We focus on the π-calculus [30,31] in this paper. This is not only because the π-calculus is widely used and powerful, but also because of a classical result by Sangiorgi [39,42], which is the starting point of our development.

Sangiorgi, in the early 90s, gave translations between the conventional, first-order π-calculus and its higher-order variant [39,42]. This translation allows us to regard the π-calculus as a higher-order programming language.

Let us review the observation by Sangiorgi, using a core of the asynchronous π-calculus: $P ::= \mathbf{0} \mid (P|Q) \mid \bar{a}\langle x\rangle \mid a(x).P$.[1] The idea is to decompose the input-prefixing $a(x).P$ into a and $(x).P$. Let us write $a[(x).P]$ for $a(x).P$ to emphasise the decomposition. Then a reduction can also be decomposed as

$$\bar{a}\langle x\rangle \mid a[(y).P] \mid Q \longrightarrow [(y).P]\langle x\rangle \mid Q \longrightarrow P\{x/y\} \mid Q,$$

where the first step is the communication and the second step is the β-reduction (i.e. $(\lambda y.P)\,x \longrightarrow P\{x/y\}$ in the λ-calculus notation). Hence we regard

- an output $\bar{a}\langle x\rangle$ as an application of a function $\bar{a}$ to x, and
- an input $a(x).P$ as an abstraction $(x).P$ (or $\lambda x.P$) "located" at $a[-]$.

Now, ignoring the mysterious operator $a[-]$, what we had are the core operations of functional programming languages (i.e. abstraction and application). This functional programming language is effectful; in fact, communication via channels is a side effect.

This observation leads us to base our categorical model for the π-calculus on a model for effectful functional programs. Among several models, we choose *closed Freyd category* [37] for modelling the functional part.

Then what is the categorical counterpart of $a[-]$? As this operation seems responsible for communication, this question can be rephrased as: what is the categorical structure for communication? An observation by Abramsky et al. [2] answered this question. They pointed out the importance of *compact closed category* [21] in concurrency theory, which nicely describes CCS-like processes interconnected via ports.

By combining the two structures described above, this paper introduces a categorical structure, which we call *compact closed Freyd category*, as a categorical model of the π-calculus.[2] Despite its simplicity, compact closed Freyd

[1] This calculus slightly differs from the calculus we shall introduce in Sect. 2, but the differences are not important here.

[2] Here is the reason why we do not use a monad for modelling the effect: it is unclear for us how to integrate a monad with the compact closed structure. On the contrary, a Freyd category has a (pre)monoidal category as its component; we can simply require that it is compact closed.

category captures the strong expressive power of the π-calculus. The compact closed structure allows us to connect ports in an arbitrary way, in return for the possibility of deadlocks; the Freyd structure allows us to duplicate objects, and duplication of input channels introduces the possibility of race conditions.

Reconstructing Calculi. This paper introduces two calculi that are sound and complete with respect to the compact closed Freyd category model. One is a variant of the π-calculus, named π_F; the design of π_F is based on the observations described above. The other is a higher-order programming language λ_{ch} defined as an instance of the computational λ-calculus [33]. Designing λ_{ch} is not so difficult because we can make use of the correspondence between computational λ-calculus and closed Freyd category (see Sect. 4). The λ_{ch}-calculus have operations for creating a channel and for sending a value via the channel and, therefore, can be seen as a core calculus of *Concurrent ML* (or *CML*) [38].

Since the higher-order calculus λ_{ch} and π_F correspond to the same categorical model, we can obtain translations between these calculi by simple semantic computations. These translations are "correct by definition" and, interestingly, coincide with those between higher-order and first-order π-calculus [39,42].

On β- vs. $\beta\eta$-theories. The categorical analysis of this paper reveals that many conventional behavioural equivalences for the π-calculus are problematic from a viewpoint of categorical type theory. The problem is that they induce only *semicategories*, which may not have identities for some objects. This is a reminiscent of the β-theory of the λ-calculus, of which categorical model is given by semi-categorical notions [16].

Adding a single rule (which we call the *η-rule*) resolves the problem. Our categorical type theory deals with only equivalences that admits the η-rule, and the simplicity of the theory of this paper essentially relies on the η-rule.

Interestingly the η-rule seems to explain some phenomenon in the literature. For example, Sangiorgi observed that a syntactic constraint called *locality* [28,49] is essential for his translation [39,42]. The correctness of the translation can be proved without using the η-rule, when one restricts the calculus local; we expect that Sangiorgi's observation can be related to this phenomenon.

Contributions. This paper introduces a new variant of the **i**/**o**-typed π-calculus, which we call π_F. A remarkable feature of π_F is that it has a categorical counterpart, called compact closed Freyd category. The correspondence is fairly firm; the categorical semantics is sound and complete, and the term model is the classifying category. The relevance of the model is demonstrated by a semantic reconstruction of Sangiorgi's translation [39,42]. These results open a new frontier in the Curry-Howard-Lambek correspondence for concurrency; session-type is not the only base for a Curry-Howard-Lambek correspondence for π-calculi.

Organisation of this Paper. Section 2 introduces the calculus π_F and discuss equivalences on processes. Section 3 gives the categorical semantics of π_F and shows soundness and completeness. A connection to a higher-order programming language with channels is studied in Sect. 4. In Sect. 5, we (1) discuss how our work relates to linear logic and (2) present some ideas for how to extend the application range of our model. We discuss related work in Sect. 6 and conclude in Sect. 7. Omitted proofs, as well as detailed definitions, are available in the full version.

2 A Polyadic, Asynchronous π-calculus with i/o-types

This section introduces a variant of π-calculus, named π_F. It is based on a fairly standard calculus, namely polyadic and asynchronous π-calculus with **i**/**o**-types, but the details are carefully designed so that π_F has a categorical model.

2.1 The π_F-calculus

This subsection defines the calculus π_F, which is based on an asynchronous variant of the polyadic π-calculus with **i**/**o**-types in [35]. The aim of this subsection is to explain what are the differences from the conventional π-calculus. Although π_F has some uncommon features, each of them was studied in the literature; see Related Work (Sect. 6) for related ideas and calculi.

Types. The set of *types*, ranged over by S and T, is given by

$$S, T ::= \mathbf{ch}^o[T_1, \ldots, T_n] \mid \mathbf{ch}^i[T_1, \ldots, T_n] \qquad (n \geq 0).$$

The type $\mathbf{ch}^o[T_1, \ldots, T_n]$ is for output channels sending n arguments of types $T_1, \ldots, T_n$. The type $\mathbf{ch}^i[T_1, \ldots, T_n]$ is for input channels. The *dual* $T^\perp$ of type T is defined by $\mathbf{ch}^o[\vec{T}]^\perp \stackrel{\text{def}}{=} \mathbf{ch}^i[\vec{T}]$ and $\mathbf{ch}^i[\vec{T}]^\perp \stackrel{\text{def}}{=} \mathbf{ch}^o[\vec{T}]$. For a sequence $\vec{T} \stackrel{\text{def}}{=} T_1, \ldots, T_n$ of types, we write $\vec{T}^\perp$ for $T_1^\perp, \ldots, T_n^\perp$.

An important difference from [35] is that no channel allows both input and output operations. We will refer this feature of π_F as **i**/**o**-*separation.*

Processes. Let $\mathcal{N}$ be a denumerable set of *names*, ranged over by x, y and z. Each name is either input-only or output-only, because of **i**/**o**-separation.

The set of *processes*, ranged over by P, Q and R, is defined by

$$P, Q, R ::= \mathbf{0} \mid (P|Q) \mid (\boldsymbol{\nu}_{\mathbf{ch}^o[\vec{T}]}\, xy)P \mid x\langle\vec{y}\rangle \mid !x(\vec{y}).P.$$

The notion of *free names*, as well as *bound names*, is defined as usual. The set of free names (resp. bound names) of P is written as $\mathbf{fn}(P)$ (resp. $\mathbf{bn}(P)$). We allow tacit renaming of bound names, and identify α-equivalent processes.

The meaning of the constructs should be clear, except for $(\boldsymbol{\nu}_T\, xy)P$ which is less common. The process $\mathbf{0}$ is the inaction; $P \mid Q$ is a parallel composition; $x\langle\vec{y}\rangle$ is an output; and $!x(\vec{x}).P$ is a replicated input. The restriction $(\boldsymbol{\nu}_T\, xy)P$ hides the names x and y of type T and $T^\perp$ and, at the same time, establishes a connection between x and y. Communication takes place only over bound names explicitly connected by $\boldsymbol{\nu}$. This is in contrast to the conventional π-calculus, in which input-output correspondence is *a priori* (i.e. $\bar{a}$ is the output to a).

$$\frac{}{\Gamma \vdash \mathbf{0} : \diamond} \qquad \frac{\Gamma \vdash P : \diamond \qquad \Gamma \vdash Q : \diamond}{\Gamma \vdash P \mid Q : \diamond} \qquad \frac{\Gamma, x : \mathbf{ch}^o[\vec{T}], y : \mathbf{ch}^i[\vec{T}] \vdash P : \diamond}{\Gamma \vdash (\boldsymbol{\nu}_{\mathbf{ch}^o[\vec{T}]}\, xy)P : \diamond}$$

$$\frac{(x : \mathbf{ch}^i[\vec{T}]) \in \Gamma \qquad \Gamma, \vec{y} : \vec{T} \vdash P : \diamond}{\Gamma \vdash !x(\vec{y}).P : \diamond} \qquad \frac{(x : \mathbf{ch}^o[\vec{T}]) \in \Gamma \qquad \vec{y} : \vec{T} \subseteq \Gamma}{\Gamma \vdash x\langle \vec{y} \rangle : \diamond}$$

Fig. 1. Typing rules for processes

The π_F-calculus does not have non-replicated input $x(\vec{y}).P$.

Typing Rules. A *type environment* Γ is a finite sequence of type bindings of the form $x\colon T$. We assume the names in Γ are pairwise distinct. If $\vec{x} = x_1, \ldots, x_n$ and $\vec{T} = T_1, \ldots, T_n$, we write $\vec{x}\colon \vec{T}$ for $x_1\colon T_1, \ldots, x_n\colon T_n$. We write $(\vec{x}\colon \vec{T}) \subseteq \Gamma$ to mean $x_i\colon T_i \in \Gamma$ for every i.

A *type judgement* is of the form $\Gamma \vdash P : \diamond$, meaning that P is a well-typed process under Γ. The typing rules are listed in Fig. 1.

Notation 1. We define $(\boldsymbol{\nu}_{\mathbf{ch}^i[\vec{T}]}\, xy)P$ as $(\boldsymbol{\nu}_{\mathbf{ch}^o[\vec{T}]}\, yx)P$; then $(\boldsymbol{\nu}_T\, xy)P$ is defined for every T. We abbreviate $(\boldsymbol{\nu}_{T_1}\, x_1 y_1) \ldots (\boldsymbol{\nu}_{T_n}\, x_n y_n)P$ as $(\boldsymbol{\nu}_{\vec{T}}\, \vec{x}\vec{y})P$. We often omit type annotations and write $(\boldsymbol{\nu} xy)$ for $(\boldsymbol{\nu}_T\, xy)$ and $(\boldsymbol{\nu} \vec{x}\vec{y})$ for $(\boldsymbol{\nu}_{\vec{T}}\, \vec{x}\vec{y})$. We use a and b for names of input channel types and $\bar{a}$ and $\bar{b}$ for output. Note that a and $\bar{a}$ are connected only if they are bound by the same occurrence of $\boldsymbol{\nu}$. $\square$

Operational Semantics. *Structural congruence*, written $\equiv$, is the smallest congruence relation on processes that satisfies the following rules:

$$P \mid \mathbf{0} \equiv P \qquad P \mid Q \equiv Q \mid P \qquad (P \mid Q) \mid R \equiv P \mid (Q \mid R)$$
$$(\boldsymbol{\nu} xy)(P \mid Q) \equiv ((\boldsymbol{\nu} xy)P) \mid Q \qquad (\boldsymbol{\nu} wx)(\boldsymbol{\nu} yz)P \equiv (\boldsymbol{\nu} yz)(\boldsymbol{\nu} wx)P$$

where $x, y \notin \mathbf{fn}(Q)$ in the fourth rule and w, x, y, z are distinct in the fifth rule.

The *reduction relation* on processes, written $\longrightarrow$, is defined by the base rule

$$(\boldsymbol{\nu} \vec{w}\vec{z})(\boldsymbol{\nu} \bar{a}a)(!a(\vec{x}).P \mid \bar{a}\langle \vec{y} \rangle \mid Q) \longrightarrow (\boldsymbol{\nu} \vec{w}\vec{z})(\boldsymbol{\nu} \bar{a}a)(!a(\vec{x}).P \mid P\{\vec{y}/\vec{x}\} \mid Q)$$

(where $P\{\vec{x}/\vec{y}\}$ is the capture-avoiding substitution) and the structural rule which concludes $P \longrightarrow Q$ from $\exists P'\, Q'.\, P \equiv P' \longrightarrow Q' \equiv Q$. Note that, unlike conventional π-calculi, communication only occurs over bound names connected by ν. We write $\longrightarrow^*$ for the reflexive and transitive closure of $\longrightarrow$.

It should be clear that deadlocks and racy communications can be expressed in π_F. An example of race is $(\boldsymbol{\nu} \bar{a}a)(\bar{a}\langle \vec{y} \rangle \mid !a(\vec{x}).P \mid !a(\vec{x}).Q)$, where two input actions are trying to consume the output regarded as a resource. A similar process $(\boldsymbol{\nu} \bar{a}a)(!a(\vec{x}).P \mid \bar{a}\langle \vec{y} \rangle \mid \bar{a}\langle \vec{z} \rangle)$ does not have a race since the receiver $!a(\vec{x}).P$ is replicated. In general, race conditions on output actions do not occur in π_F.

2.2 Equivalences on Processes

To establish a Curry-Howard-Lambek correspondence is to find a nice algebraic or categorical structure of terms. For example, the original Curry-Howard-Lambek correspondence reveals the cartesian closed structure of λ-terms.

Such a nice structure would become visible only when appropriate notions of composition and of equivalence could be identified, such as substitution and $\beta\eta$-equivalence for the λ-calculus.

As for process calculi, so-called "parallel composition + hiding" paradigm [17] has been used to compose processes. Given typed processes

$$\vec{x} : \vec{T},\ \vec{y} : \vec{S} \vdash P : \diamond \quad \text{and} \quad \vec{w} : \vec{S}^{\perp},\ \vec{u} : \vec{U} \vdash Q : \diamond,$$

their composite via $(\vec{y}, \vec{w})$ is defined as

$$\vec{x} : \vec{T},\ \vec{u} : \vec{U} \vdash (\boldsymbol{\nu}_{\vec{S}}\, \vec{y}\vec{w})(P \mid Q) : \diamond.$$

This kind of composition appears quite often in logical studies of π-calculi [1, 5, 19]. It also plays a central role in *interaction category paradigm* proposed by Abramsky, Gay and Nagarajan [2].

So it remains to determine an equivalence on π-calculus processes, appropriate for our purpose. This subsection approaches the problem from two directions:

- Examining behavioural equivalences proposed and studied in the literature
- Developing a new equivalence based on categorical considerations

Let us clarify the notion of equivalence discussed below. An *equation-in-context* is a judgement of the form $\Gamma \vdash P = Q$, where $\Gamma \vdash P : \diamond$ and $\Gamma \vdash Q : \diamond$. An *equivalence* $\mathcal{E}$ is a set of equations-in-context that is reflexive, transitive and symmetric (e.g. $(\Gamma \vdash P = P) \in \mathcal{E}$ for every $\Gamma \vdash P : \diamond$).

Behavioural Equivalences. As mentioned above, we are interested in the structure of π_F-processes modulo existing behavioural equivalences. Among the various behavioural equivalence, we start with studying *barbed congruence* [32], which is one of the most widely used equivalences.

We define (asynchronous and weak) barbed congruence for π_F. For each name $\bar{a}$, we write $P{\downarrow_{\bar{a}}}$ if $P \equiv (\boldsymbol{\nu}\vec{x}\vec{y})(\bar{a}\langle\vec{z}\rangle \mid Q)$ and $\bar{a}$ is free, and $P{\Downarrow_{\bar{a}}}$ if $\exists Q.\, P \longrightarrow^* Q{\downarrow_{\bar{a}}}$. A (Γ/Δ)-*context* is a context C such that $\Gamma \vdash C[P] : \diamond$ for every $\Delta \vdash P : \diamond$.

Definition 1. *A* barbed bisimulation *is a symmetric relation $\mathcal{R}$ on processes such that, whenever $P \mathrel{\mathcal{R}} Q$, (1) $P{\downarrow_{\bar{a}}}$ implies $Q{\Downarrow_{\bar{a}}}$ and (2) $P \longrightarrow P'$ implies* $\exists Q'.\, (Q \longrightarrow^* Q') \wedge (P' \mathrel{\mathcal{R}} Q')$. Barbed bisimilarity $\overset{\bullet}{\approx}$ *is the largest barbed bisimulation. Typed processes $\Delta \vdash P : \diamond$ and $\Delta \vdash Q : \diamond$ are* barbed congruent at Δ, *written $\Delta \vdash P \approx^c Q$, if $C[P] \overset{\bullet}{\approx} C[Q]$ for every (Γ/Δ)-context C.* □

Let us consider a category-like structure $\mathcal{C}$ in which an object is a type and a morphism is an equivalence class of π_F-processes modulo barbed congruence. More precisely, a morphism from T to S is a process $x{:}\ T,\ y{:}\ S^{\perp} \vdash P{:}\ \diamond$ modulo barbed congruence (and renaming of free names x and y). Then the composition (i.e. "parallel composition + hiding") is well-defined on equivalence classes, because barbed congruence is a congruence. This is a fairly natural setting.

We have a strikingly negative result.

Theorem 1. *$\mathcal{C}$ is not a category.*

Proof. In every category, if $f : A \longrightarrow A$ is a left-identity on A (i.e. $f \circ g = g$ for every $g : A \longrightarrow A$), then f is the identity on A. The process $a : \mathbf{ch}^o[], \bar{b} : \mathbf{ch}^i[] \vdash\ !a().\bar{b}\langle\rangle : \diamond$ seen as a morphism $(\mathbf{ch}^o[]) \longrightarrow (\mathbf{ch}^o[])$ is a left-identity but not the identity. The former means that $c\colon \mathbf{ch}^o[], \bar{b}\colon \mathbf{ch}^i[] \vdash ((\boldsymbol{\nu}\bar{a}a)(!a().\bar{b}\langle\rangle \mid P)) \approx^c P\{\bar{b}/\bar{a}\}$ for every $c\colon \mathbf{ch}^o[], \bar{a}\colon \mathbf{ch}^i[] \vdash P\colon \diamond$, which is a consequence of the *replicator theorems* [35]. To prove the latter, observe that $(\boldsymbol{\nu}\bar{b}b)(!a().\bar{b}\langle\rangle \mid \mathbf{0})$ and $\mathbf{0}$ are not barbed congruent. Indeed the context $C \stackrel{\text{def}}{=} (\boldsymbol{\nu}\bar{a}a)(\bar{a}\langle\rangle \mid !a().\bar{o}\langle\rangle \mid [])$ distinguishes the processes, where $\bar{o}$ is the observable. □

Note that race condition is essential for the proof, specifically, for the part proving that the process $!a().\bar{b}\langle\rangle$ is not the identity. A race condition occurs in $C[(\boldsymbol{\nu}\bar{b}b)(!a().\bar{b}\langle\rangle \mid \mathbf{0})]$, where $\bar{a}$ in C has two receivers.

The process $!a().\bar{b}\langle\rangle$ is called *forwarder*, and forwarders will play a central role in this paper. Its general form is $a \hookrightarrow \bar{b} \stackrel{\text{def}}{=}\ !a(\vec{x}).\bar{b}\langle\vec{x}\rangle$. When $x : T$ and $y : T^{\perp}$, we write $x \leftrightharpoons y$ to mean $x \hookrightarrow y$ if $T = \mathbf{ch}^i[\vec{S}]$ and otherwise $y \hookrightarrow x$.

Remark 1. The argument in the proof of Theorem 1 is widely applicable to **i**/**o**-typed calculi, not specific to π_F. In particular, **i**/**o**-separation (i.e. absence of $\mathbf{ch}^{i/o}[\vec{T}]$) is not the cause, but the existence of $\mathbf{ch}^o[\vec{T}]$ or $\mathbf{ch}^i[\vec{T}]$ is. □

Remark 2. Session-typed calculi in Caires, Pfenning and Toninho [8,9], which correspond to linear logic, do not seem to suffer from this problem. In our understanding, this is because of race-freedom of their calculi. □

To obtain a category, we should think of a coarser equivalence that identifies $(\boldsymbol{\nu}\bar{b}b)(!a().\bar{b}\langle\rangle \mid \mathbf{0})$ with $\mathbf{0}$. Such an equivalence should be very coarse; even *must-testing equivalence* [11] fails to equate them. As long as we have checked, only *may-testing equivalence* [11] defined below satisfies the requirement.

Definition 2. *Typed processes $\Delta \vdash P : \diamond$ and $\Delta \vdash Q : \diamond$ are* may-testing equivalent *at Δ, written $\Delta \vdash P =_{may} Q$, if $C[P]\Downarrow_{\bar{a}} \Leftrightarrow C[Q]\Downarrow_{\bar{a}}$ for every (Γ/Δ)-context C and name $\bar{a}$.* □

As we shall see, π_F-processes modulo may-testing equivalence behaves well. May-testing equivalence is, however, often too coarse.

Category-Driven Approach. In this approach, we first guess an appropriate categorical structure sufficient for interpreting π_F, based on intuitions discussed in Introduction (see also Sect. 3.1), and then design an equivalence so that it is sound and complete with respect to the categorical semantics.

Figure 2 defines the equivalence, described as a set of rules. A π_F*-theory* is an equivalence that behaves well from the categorical perspective.

$$\frac{a \notin \mathbf{fn}(P, C) \qquad \bar{a} \notin \mathbf{bn}(C)}{\Gamma \vdash (\boldsymbol{\nu}\bar{a}a)(!a(\vec{x}).P \mid C[\bar{a}\langle\vec{y}\rangle]) = (\boldsymbol{\nu}\bar{a}a)(!a(\vec{x}).P \mid C[P\{\vec{y}/\vec{x}\}])} \text{(E-BETA)}$$

$$\frac{a, \bar{a} \notin \mathbf{fn}(P)}{\Gamma \vdash (\boldsymbol{\nu}\bar{a}a)!a(\vec{y}).P = \mathbf{0}} \text{(E-GC)} \qquad \frac{\bar{a}, a \notin \mathbf{fn}(\bar{c}\langle\vec{x}\rangle)}{\Gamma \vdash \bar{c}\langle\vec{x}\rangle = (\boldsymbol{\nu}\bar{a}a)(a \hookrightarrow \bar{b} \mid \bar{c}\langle\vec{x}\{\bar{a}/\bar{b}\}\rangle)} \text{(E-FOUT)}$$

$$\frac{b, \bar{a} \notin \mathbf{fn}(P)}{\Gamma \vdash (\boldsymbol{\nu}\bar{a}a)(b \hookrightarrow \bar{a} \mid P) = P\{b/a\}} \text{(E-ETA)}$$

$$\frac{P \equiv Q}{\Gamma \vdash P = Q} \text{(E-SCONG)} \qquad \frac{\Delta \vdash P = Q \qquad C\colon \Gamma/\Delta\text{-context}}{\Gamma \vdash C[P] = C[Q]} \text{(E-CTX)}$$

Fig. 2. Inference rules of equations-in-context. Each rule has implicit assumptions that the both sides of the equation are well-typed processes.

Definition 3. *An equivalence* $\mathcal{E}$ *is a* π_F-theory *if it is closed under the rules in Fig. 2. Any set* Ax *of equations-in-context has the minimum theory* $Th(Ax)$ *that contains* Ax*. We write* $Ax \rhd \Gamma \vdash P = Q$ *if* $(\Gamma \vdash P = Q) \in Th(Ax)$*.* □

Let us examine each rule in Fig. 2.

The rule (E-BETA) should be compared with the reduction relation. When $C = ([\,] \mid Q)$, then (E-BETA) claims

$$(\boldsymbol{\nu}\bar{a}a)(!a(\vec{x}).P \mid \bar{a}\langle\vec{y}\rangle \mid Q) = (\boldsymbol{\nu}\bar{a}a)(!a(\vec{x}).P \mid P\{\vec{y}/\vec{x}\} \mid Q)$$

provided that $a \notin \mathbf{fn}(P, Q)$, which is indeed an instance of the reduction.

A significant difference from reduction is the side condition. It is essential in the presence of race conditions. Without the side condition, every π_F-theory would be forced to contain the symmetric and transitive closure of the reduction relation; thus it would identify $P \mid (\boldsymbol{\nu}\bar{a}a)(!a().P \mid !a().Q)$ with $Q \mid (\boldsymbol{\nu}\bar{a}a)(!a().P \mid !a().Q)$ for every processes P and Q (where $\bar{a}, a$ are fresh), because

$$\begin{aligned} (\boldsymbol{\nu}\bar{a}a)(\bar{a}\langle\rangle \mid !a().P \mid !a().Q) &\longrightarrow P \mid (\boldsymbol{\nu}\bar{a}a)(!a().P \mid !a().Q) \\ (\boldsymbol{\nu}\bar{a}a)(\bar{a}\langle\rangle \mid !a().P \mid !a().Q) &\longrightarrow Q \mid (\boldsymbol{\nu}\bar{a}a)(!a().P \mid !a().Q). \end{aligned}$$

The side condition prevents π_F-theories from collapsing.

Another, relatively minor, difference is that application of (E-BETA) is not limited to the contexts of the form $[\,] \mid Q$. This kind of extension can be found in, for example, work by Honda and Laurent [19] studying π-calculus from a logical perspective.

The rule (E-GC) runs "garbage-collection". Because no one can send a message to the hidden name a, the process $!a(\vec{x}).P$ will never be invoked and thus is safely discarded. This rule is sound with respect to many behavioural equivalences, including barbed congruence. Rules of this kind often appear in the literature studying logical aspects of concurrent calculi (as in Honda and Laurent [19] and Wadler [48]). There is, however, a subtle difference in the side condition: (E-GC) requires that a and $\bar{a}$ do not appear at all in P.

The rule (E-FOut) can be seen as the η-rule of abstractions, as in the λ-calculus and in the higher-order π-calculus [39]. In the latter, an output name $\bar{b}$ can be identified with an abstraction $(\vec{y}).\bar{b}\langle\vec{y}\rangle$. Then we have, for example,

$$(\boldsymbol{\nu}\bar{a}a)(a \hookrightarrow \bar{b} \mid \bar{c}\langle\bar{a}\rangle) \;=\; (\boldsymbol{\nu}\bar{a}a)(a \hookrightarrow \bar{b} \mid \bar{c}\langle\,(\vec{y}).\bar{a}\langle\vec{y}\rangle\,\rangle) \;=\; \bar{c}\langle\,(\vec{y}).\bar{b}\langle\vec{y}\rangle\,\rangle \;=\; \bar{c}\langle\bar{b}\rangle$$

where we use (E-Beta) and (E-GC) in the second step. An important usage of (E-FOut) is to replace an output of free names with that of bound names. This kind of operation has been studied in [7,28] as a part of translations from the π-calculus to its local/internal fragments.[3]

The rule (E-Eta) requires the forwarders are left-identities, directly describing the requirement discussed above.[4]

The rules (E-SCong) and (E-Ctx) are easy to understand. The former requires that structurally congruent processes should be identified; the latter says that a π_F-theory is a congruence.

These rules can be justified from the operational viewpoint, as well. A well-known result on the **i**/**o**-typed π-calculus (see, e.g., [35,43]) shows the following propositions.

Proposition 1. *Barbed congruence is closed under all rules but* (E-Eta). □

Proposition 2. *May-testing equivalence is a* π_F*-theory.* □

In particular, the latter means that may-testing equivalence is in the scope of the categorical framework of this paper; see Theorem 5.

3 Categorical Semantics

This section introduces the class of *compact closed Freyd categories* and discusses the interpretation of the π_F-calculus in the categories. We show that the categorical semantics is sound and complete with respect to the equational theory given in Sect. 2.2, and that the syntax of the π_F-calculus induces a model.

This section, by its nature, is slightly theoretical compared with other sections. Section 3.1 explains the ideas of this section without heavily using categorical notions; the subsequent subsections require familiarity with categorical type theory.

3.1 Overview

As mentioned in Sect. 1, the categorical model of π_F is *compact closed Freyd category*, which has both closed Freyd and compact closed structures. Here we

[3] Free outputs can be eliminated from π_F-processes by using the rules (E-FOut) and (E-Eta), i.e. external mobility can be encoded by internal mobility [7,40]. If the calculus is local [28,49], then we do not need (E-Eta) to eliminate free outputs.

[4] A forwarder behaves as a right-identity with respect to every π_F-theory. This is a consequence of rules (E-Beta), (E-GC) and (E-FOut).

informally discuss what is a compact closed Freyd category and how to interpret π_F by using syntactic representation.

A *closed Freyd category* is a model of higher-order programs with side effects. It has, among others, the structures to interpret the function type $A \Rightarrow B$ and its constructor and destructor, namely, abstraction $\lambda x.t$ and application $t\,u$. It also has a mechanism for unrestricted duplication of variables; in terms of logic, contraction is admissible.

A *compact closed category* can be seen as MLL [14] with the left rule:

$$\frac{\Gamma, A^*, A \vdash I}{\Gamma \vdash I} \qquad \left[\frac{\Gamma \vdash A^* \qquad \Delta \vdash A}{\Gamma, \Delta \vdash I}\right].$$

(The right rule is the companion, which itself is derivable in MLL.)

A *compact closed Freyd category* has all the constructs. It has the structures corresponding to the following type constructors:

$$\text{(closed Freyd)} \quad I, A \otimes B, A \Rightarrow B \qquad \text{(compact closed)} \quad I, A \otimes B, A^*.$$

Note that the pair type $A \otimes B$ (as well as the unit I) coming from the closed Freyd structure is identified with that from the compact closed structure. Inference rules for a compact closed Freyd category is those for functional languages and the above rules of the compact closed structure.

Interpreting π_F in a compact closed Freyd category is to interpret it by using these constructs. As mentioned in Sect. 1, following Sangiorgi [39], we regard

- an output $\bar{a}\langle\vec{x}\rangle$ as an application of a function $\bar{a}$ to a tuple $\langle\vec{x}\rangle$, and
- an input $!a(\vec{x}).P$ as an abstraction $(\vec{x}).P$ (or $\lambda\vec{x}.P$) located at a.

We interpret the output action by using the function application. Hence the type $\mathbf{ch}^o[T]$ is regarded as a function type $T \Rightarrow I$ (where the unit type I is the type for processes i.e. $\diamond$); then the typing rule for output actions becomes

$$\frac{\Gamma, \bar{a}\colon (T \Rightarrow I), x\colon T \vdash \bar{a} : T \Rightarrow I \qquad \Gamma, \bar{a}\colon (T \Rightarrow I), x\colon T \vdash x : T}{\Gamma, \bar{a}\colon (T \Rightarrow I), x\colon T \vdash \bar{a}\langle x\rangle : I}$$

The type $\mathbf{ch}^i[T]$ is understood as $(T \Rightarrow I)^*$; the input-prefixing rule becomes

$$\frac{\dfrac{}{\Gamma, a\colon (T \Rightarrow I)^* \vdash a : (T \Rightarrow I)^*} \qquad \dfrac{\Gamma, a\colon (T \Rightarrow I)^*, x\colon T \vdash P : I}{\Gamma, a\colon (T \Rightarrow I)^* \vdash (x).P : T \Rightarrow I}}{\Gamma, a\colon (T \Rightarrow I)^* \vdash !a(x).P : I}$$

This derivation directly expresses the intuition that an input-prefixing is abstraction followed by allocation; here allocation is interpreted by using the compact closed structure, i.e. connection of ports. The name restriction also has a natural derivation:

$$\frac{\Gamma, a\colon (T \Rightarrow I)^*, \bar{a}\colon (T \Rightarrow I) \vdash P : I}{\Gamma \vdash (\boldsymbol{\nu}\bar{a}a)P : I}$$

3.2 Compact Closed Freyd Category

Let us formalise the ideas given in Sect. 3.1. Hereafter in this section, we assume basic knowledge of category theory and of categorical type theory.

We recall the definitions of compact closed category and closed Freyd category. For simplicity, the structures below are strict and chosen; a functor is required to preserve the chosen structures on the nose.

Definition 4 (Compact closed category [21]**).** *Let* $(\mathcal{C}, \otimes, I)$ *be a symmetric strict monoidal category. The* dual *of an object* A *in* $\mathcal{C}$ *is an object* A^* *equipped with* unit $\eta_A \colon I \longrightarrow A \otimes A^*$ *and* counit $\epsilon_A \colon A^* \otimes A \longrightarrow I$ *that satisfy the "triangle identities"* $(\eta_A \otimes \mathrm{id}_A); (\mathrm{id}_A \otimes \epsilon_A) = \mathrm{id}_A$ *and* $(\mathrm{id}_{A^*} \otimes \eta_A); (\epsilon_A \otimes \mathrm{id}_{A^*}) = \mathrm{id}_{A^*}$*. The category* $\mathcal{C}$ *is* compact closed *if each object is equipped with a chosen dual.* □

Definition 5 (Closed Freyd category [37]**).** *A* Freyd category *is given by (1) a category with chosen finite products* $(\mathcal{C}, \otimes, I)$*, called* value category*, (2) a symmetric strict monoidal category* $(\mathcal{K}, \otimes, I, \mathbf{symm})$*, called* producer category*, and (3) an identity-on-object strict symmetric monoidal functor* $J \colon \mathcal{C} \to \mathcal{K}$*. A Freyd category is a* closed Freyd category *if the functor* $J(-) \otimes A \colon \mathcal{C} \to \mathcal{K}$ *has the (chosen) right adjoint* $A \Rightarrow - \colon \mathcal{K} \to \mathcal{C}$ *for every object* A*. We write* $\Lambda_{A,B,C}$ *for the natural bijection* $\mathcal{K}(J(A) \otimes B, C) \longrightarrow \mathcal{C}(A, B \Rightarrow C)$ *and* $\mathbf{eval}_{A,B}$ *for* $\Lambda^{-1}(\mathrm{id}_{A \Rightarrow B}) \colon (A \Rightarrow B) \otimes A \longrightarrow B$ *in* $\mathcal{K}$*.* □

Remark 3. The above definition is a restriction of the original one [37], in which $\mathcal{K}$ is a *premonoidal* [36] category. This change reflects concurrency of the calculus. In fact, it validates the following law, expressed by the syntax of the computational λ-calculus [33],

$$\mathbf{let}\, x = M \,\mathbf{in}\, \mathbf{let}\, y = N \,\mathbf{in}\, L \quad = \quad \mathbf{let}\, y = N \,\mathbf{in}\, \mathbf{let}\, x = M \,\mathbf{in}\, L.$$

Then one can evaluate M by using the left form and N by using the right form. This law allows us to evaluate M and N in arbitrary order, or concurrently. □

We now introduce the categorical structure corresponding to the π_F-calculus.

Definition 6 (Compact closed Freyd category). *A* compact closed Freyd category *is a Freyd category* $J : \mathcal{C} \longrightarrow \mathcal{K}$ *such that (1)* $\mathcal{K}$ *is compact closed, and (2)* J *has the (chosen) right adjoint* $I \Rightarrow - \colon \mathcal{K} \to \mathcal{C}$*.* □

We shall often write J for a compact closed Freyd category $J \colon \mathcal{C} \rightleftarrows \mathcal{K}$ (with $\perp$).

A compact closed Freyd category is a closed Freyd category:

$$\mathcal{K}(J(A) \otimes B, C) \;\cong\; \mathcal{K}(J(A), B^* \otimes C) \;\cong\; \mathcal{C}(A, I \Rightarrow (B^* \otimes C)).$$

Example 1. The most basic example of a compact closed Freyd category is (the strict monoidal version of) $J \colon \mathbf{Sets} \rightleftarrows \mathbf{Rel} \colon \mathcal{P}$ (with $\perp$). Here J is the identity-on-object functor that maps a function to its graph and $\mathcal{P}$ is the "power set functor"

$$\begin{aligned}
[\![\mathbf{ch}^i[T_1,\dots,T_n]]\!] &\stackrel{\text{def}}{=} (([\![T_1]\!] \otimes \dots \otimes [\![T_n]\!]) \Rightarrow I)^* \\
[\![\mathbf{ch}^o[T_1,\dots,T_n]]\!] &\stackrel{\text{def}}{=} ([\![T_1]\!] \otimes \dots \otimes [\![T_n]\!]) \Rightarrow I \\
[\![\Gamma \vdash \mathbf{0} : \diamond]\!] &\stackrel{\text{def}}{=} J(!_\Gamma) \\
[\![\Gamma \vdash !a(\vec{x}).P : \diamond]\!] &\stackrel{\text{def}}{=} J(\langle \pi^\Gamma_a, \Lambda_{\Gamma,\vec{T},I}([\![\Gamma,\vec{x}:\vec{T} \vdash P : \diamond]\!])\rangle); \epsilon_{\mathbf{ch}[\vec{T}]} \\
[\![\Gamma \vdash \bar{a}\langle\vec{x}\rangle : \diamond]\!] &\stackrel{\text{def}}{=} J(\langle \pi^\Gamma_{\bar{a}}, \pi^\Gamma_{x_1}, \dots, \pi^\Gamma_{x_n}\rangle); \mathbf{eval}_{\vec{T},I} \\
[\![\Gamma \vdash P \mid Q : \diamond]\!] &\stackrel{\text{def}}{=} J(\Delta_\Gamma); ([\![\Gamma \vdash P : \diamond]\!] \otimes [\![\Gamma \vdash Q : \diamond]\!]) \\
[\![\Gamma \vdash (\boldsymbol{\nu} xy)P : \diamond]\!] &\stackrel{\text{def}}{=} (\mathrm{id}_\Gamma \otimes \eta_T); [\![\Gamma, x:T, y:T^\perp \vdash P : \diamond]\!]
\end{aligned}$$

Fig. 3. Interpretation of types and processes. Here $!_\Gamma$, Δ_Γ and π^Γ_y are maps in $\mathcal{C}$ induced by the cartesian structure, namely, $!_\Gamma\colon [\![\Gamma]\!] \longrightarrow I$ is the terminal map, $\Delta_\Gamma\colon [\![\Gamma]\!] \longrightarrow [\![\Gamma]\!] \otimes [\![\Gamma]\!]$ is the diagonal map and, when $\Gamma = (y_1\colon T_1,\dots,y_n\colon T_n)$ and $x = y_j$, the morphism $\pi^\Gamma_x : [\![\Gamma]\!] \longrightarrow [\![T_j]\!]$ is the j-th projection. The interpretation of a type environment $x_1\colon T_1,\dots,x_n\colon T_n$ is $[\![T_1]\!] \otimes \dots \otimes [\![T_n]\!]$.

that maps a relation $\mathcal{R} \subseteq A \times B$ to a function $\mathcal{P}(\mathcal{R}) \stackrel{\text{def}}{=} \{(S_A, S_B) \mid S_B = \{b \mid a \in S_A, a \mathrel{\mathcal{R}} b\}\}$. Another example is obtained by replacing sets with posets, functions with monotone functions and relations with downward closed relations. □

Example 2. A more sophisticated example is taken from Laird's game-semantic model of π-calculus [22]. Precisely speaking, the model in [22] itself is not compact closed Freyd, but its variant (with non-negative arenas) is. This model is important since it is fully abstract w.r.t. may-testing equivalence [22, Theorem 1]; hence our framework has a model that captures the may-testing equivalence. □

3.3 Interpretation

Given a compact closed Freyd category $J\colon \mathcal{C} \rightleftarrows_\perp \mathcal{K}$, this section defines the interpretation $[\![-]\!]_J$. It maps types and type environments to objects as usual, and a well-typed process $\Gamma \vdash P : \diamond$ to a morphism $[\![P]\!]\colon [\![\Gamma]\!] \to I$ in $\mathcal{K}$ (recall that the tensor unit I is the interpretation of the type for processes).

Figure 3 defines the interpretation of types and processes. It simply formalises the ideas presented in Sect. 3.1: for example, the interpretation of $!a(\vec{x}).P$ is the abstraction Λ (from the closed Freyd structure) followed by location ϵ (from the compact closed structure). There are some points worth noting.

- $(A \Rightarrow I)^*$ is *not* isomorphic to $A^* \Rightarrow I$, $A \Rightarrow I$ nor $I \Rightarrow A$. Indeed $(A \Rightarrow I)^*$ cannot be simplified. Do not confuse it with a valid law $I \Rightarrow (A^*) \cong A \Rightarrow I$.
- A parallel composition is interpreted as a pair. Recall that two components of a pair are evaluated in parallel in this setting (cf. Remark 3).
- All but the last rule use the cartesian structure of $\mathcal{C}$ in order to duplicate or discard the environment.

Example 3. Let us consider $y : T \vdash (\boldsymbol{\nu}\bar{a}a)(\bar{a}\langle y\rangle \mid !a(x).P) : \diamond$, where $\bar{a}, a, y \notin \mathbf{fn}(P)$ and $a \colon \mathbf{ch}^{i}[T]$. By (E-Beta) and (E-GC), this process is equal to $P\{y/x\}$. It is natural to expect that the interpretations of the two processes coincide; indeed it is. As the following calculation indicates, our semantics factorises the reduction into two steps: (1) the "transmission" of the closure $\lambda\vec{x}.P$ by the triangle identity of the compact closed structure, and (2) the β-reduction modelled by **eval** of the closed Freyd structure:

$$
\begin{aligned}
&[\![y : T \vdash (\boldsymbol{\nu}\bar{a}a)(\bar{a}\langle y\rangle \mid !a(x).P) : \diamond]\!]\\
&= (\mathrm{id}_T \otimes \eta_{\mathbf{ch}^o[T]}); [\![y : T, \bar{a} : \mathbf{ch}^o[T], a : \mathbf{ch}^i[T] \vdash \bar{a}\langle y\rangle \mid !a(x).P : \diamond]\!]\\
&= (\mathrm{id} \otimes \eta); ([\![y : T, \bar{a} : \mathbf{ch}^o[T] \vdash \bar{a}\langle y\rangle : \diamond]\!] \otimes [\![a : \mathbf{ch}^i[T] \vdash !a(x).P : \diamond]\!])\\
&= (\mathrm{id} \otimes \eta); ((\mathbf{symm}_{T,\mathbf{ch}^o[T]}; \mathbf{eval}_{T,I}) \otimes (\mathrm{id}_{\mathbf{ch}[T]^*} \otimes J(\Lambda([\![x : T \vdash P : \diamond]\!])))); \epsilon_{T \Rightarrow I}\\
&= (\mathrm{id}_T \otimes J(\Lambda([\![x : T \vdash P : \diamond]\!]))); \mathbf{symm}_{T,\mathbf{ch}^o[T]}; \mathbf{eval}_{T,I} \quad \text{(By triangle identity)}\\
&= (J(\Lambda([\![x : T \vdash P : \diamond]\!])) \otimes \mathrm{id}_T); \mathbf{eval}_{T,I}\\
&= [\![x : T \vdash P]\!] \qquad \text{(By the universality of } \mathbf{eval}\text{)}\\
&= [\![y : T \vdash P\{y/x\} : \diamond]\!].
\end{aligned}
$$

(Here we implicitly use derived rules for weakening and exchange.) □

Example 4. The interpretation of a forwarder $a : \mathbf{ch}^i[\vec{T}], \bar{b} : \mathbf{ch}^o[\vec{T}] \vdash a \hookrightarrow \bar{b} : \diamond$ is the counit $\epsilon_{\mathbf{ch}^o[\vec{T}]} : [\![\mathbf{ch}^o[\vec{T}]]\!]^* \otimes [\![\mathbf{ch}^o[\vec{T}]]\!] \longrightarrow I$ in $\mathcal{K}$, which is the one-sided form of the identity. Recall that a forwarder is the identity in every π_F-theory. □

The semantics is sound and complete. That means, a judgement $Ax \rhd \Gamma \vdash P = Q$ is provable if and only if $\Gamma \vdash P = Q$ is valid in all models J of Ax.

Here we define the related notions and prove soundness; completeness is the topic of the next subsection.

Definition 7. *An equational judgement $\Gamma \vdash P = Q$ is* valid in J *if $[\![\Gamma \vdash P : \diamond]\!]_J = [\![\Gamma \vdash Q : \diamond]\!]_J$. Given a set Ax of non-logical axioms, J is a* model of Ax, *written $J \models Ax$, if it validates all judgements in Ax. We write $Ax \rhd \Gamma \Vdash P = Q$ if $\Gamma \vdash P = Q$ is valid in every J such that $J \models Ax$.* □

Theorem 2 (Soundness). *If $Ax \rhd \Gamma \vdash P = Q$, then $Ax \rhd \Gamma \Vdash P = Q$.* □

3.4 Term Model

A *term model* is a category whose objects are type environments and whose morphisms are terms (i.e. processes in this setting). This section gives a construction of the term model, by which we show completeness. This subsection basically follows the standard arguments in categorical type theory; we mainly focus on the features unique to our model, giving a sketch to the common part.

Given a set Ax of axioms, we define the term model $J_{Ax} \colon \mathcal{C}_{Ax} \rightleftarrows_{\perp} \mathcal{K}_{Ax}$, which we also write as $Cl(Ax)$.

The definition of the producer category $\mathcal{K}_{Ax}$ follows the standard recipe. As usual, its objects are finite lists of types. The monoidal product $\vec{T} \otimes \vec{S}$ is the concatenation of the lists and the dual $\vec{T}^*$ is $\vec{T}^\perp$. Given objects $\vec{T}$ and $\vec{S}$, a morphism from $\vec{T}$ to $\vec{S}$ is a process $\vec{x}\colon \vec{T},\ \vec{y}\colon \vec{S}^\perp \vdash P : \diamond$ (modulo renaming of variables $\vec{x}$ and $\vec{y}$). If $Ax \rhd \vec{x}\colon \vec{T},\ \vec{y}\colon \vec{S}^\perp \vdash P = Q$ is provable, then P and Q are regarded as the same morphism. Composition of morphisms is defined as "parallel composition plus hiding": For morphisms $P : \vec{T} \longrightarrow \vec{S}$ and $Q : \vec{S} \longrightarrow \vec{U}$, i.e. processes such that $\vec{x}\colon \vec{T},\ \vec{y}\colon \vec{S}^\perp \vdash P : \diamond$ and $\vec{z}\colon \vec{S},\ \vec{w}\colon \vec{U}^\perp \vdash Q : \diamond$, their composite is $\vec{x}\colon \vec{T}, \vec{w}\colon \vec{U}^\perp \vdash (\boldsymbol{\nu}\vec{y}\vec{z})(P \mid Q) : \diamond$. The monoidal product $P \otimes Q$ of morphisms is the parallel composition $P \mid Q$. The identity, as well as the symmetry of the monoidal product and the unit and counit of the compact closed structure, is a parallel composition of forwarders: for example, the identity on $\vec{S}$ is $\vec{x} : \vec{S}, \vec{y} : \vec{S}^\perp \vdash x_1 \leftrightharpoons y_1 \mid \cdots \mid x_n \leftrightharpoons y_n : \diamond$ where n is the length of $\vec{S}$. The facts that most structural morphisms are forwarders and that forwarders compose are the keys to show that $\mathcal{K}_{Ax}$ is a compact closed category.

We then see the definition of $\mathcal{C}_{Ax}$, of which the definition of morphisms has a subtle point. The objects of $\mathcal{C}_{Ax}$ are by definition the same as $\mathcal{K}_{Ax}$, i.e. lists of types. The definition of morphisms relies on the notion of *values*. The values are defined by the grammar $V ::= x \mid (\vec{x}).P$, where P is a process and $(\vec{x}).P$ is called an *abstraction*. Typing rules for values are as follows:

$$\frac{x : T \in \Gamma}{\Gamma \vdash x : T} \qquad \frac{\Gamma, \vec{x}\colon \vec{T} \vdash P}{\Gamma \vdash (\vec{x}).P : \mathbf{ch}^o[\vec{T}]}.$$

(To understand the right rule, recall that $[\![\mathbf{ch}^o[\vec{T}]]\!] = [\![\vec{T}]\!] \Rightarrow I$.) A morphism from $\vec{T}$ to $\vec{S} = (S_1, \ldots, S_n)$ is an n-tuple $(V_1, \ldots, V_n)$ of values of type $\vec{x}\colon \vec{T} \vdash V_i\colon S_i$ for each i (modulo renaming of $\vec{x}$). Composition is intuitively defined by "substitution followed by β-reduction" whose definition is omitted here.[5]

The functor J_{Ax} places the values to the channels. For example, let $\vec{T} = (\mathbf{ch}^i[U_1], \mathbf{ch}^o[U_2])$ and consider the morphism in $\mathcal{C}_{Ax}$ given by

$$a\colon \mathbf{ch}^i[T_1], \bar{b}\colon \mathbf{ch}^o[T_2] \vdash (a, \bar{b}, (\vec{x}).P) : (\mathbf{ch}^i[T_1], \mathbf{ch}^o[T_2], \mathbf{ch}^o[\vec{S}])$$

where $\vec{S}$ is the type for $\vec{x}$. The image of this morphism by the functor J_{Ax} is

$$a\colon \mathbf{ch}^i[T_1], \bar{b}\colon \mathbf{ch}^o[T_2], \bar{c}\colon \mathbf{ch}^o[T_1], d\colon \mathbf{ch}^i[T_2], e\colon \mathbf{ch}^i[\vec{S}] \vdash a \hookrightarrow \bar{c} \mid d \hookrightarrow \bar{b} \mid !e(\vec{x}).P : \diamond.$$

This example contains all the three ways to place a value to a given channel.

Theorem 3. *Cl*(Ax) *is a compact closed Freyd category for every* Ax. □

In the model *Cl*(Ax), the interpretation of a process $\Gamma \vdash P : \diamond$ is the equivalence class that P belongs to. This fact leads to completeness.

[5] Here is a subtle technical issue that we shall not address in this paper; see the long version for the formal definition. We think, however, that this paragraph conveys a precise intuition.

Theorem 4 (Completeness). *If* $Ax \rhd \Gamma \Vdash P = Q$*, then* $Ax \rhd \Gamma \vdash P = Q$*.* □

Theorem 5. *There exists a compact closed Freyd category* J *that is fully abstract w.r.t. may-testing equivalence, i.e.* $\Gamma \vdash P =_{may} Q$ *iff* $[\![P]\!]_J = [\![Q]\!]_J$*.*

Proof. Let J be the term model $Cl(=_{may})$ and use Proposition 2. □

3.5 Theory/Model Correspondence

It is natural to expect that $Cl(Ax)$ is the *classifying category* as in the standard categorical type theory. This means, to give a model of Ax in J is equivalent to give a structure-preserving functor $Cl(Ax) \longrightarrow J$. This subsection clarifies and studies this claim.

The set $\mathrm{Mod}(Ax, J)$ of models of Ax in J is defined as follows. If $J \models Ax$, then $\mathrm{Mod}(Ax, J)$ is a singleton set[6]; otherwise $\mathrm{Mod}(Ax, J)$ is the empty set.

We then define the notion of structure-preserving functors.

Definition 8. *A* strict compact closed Freyd functor *from* $J : \mathcal{C} \underset{\perp}{\rightleftarrows} \mathcal{K} : I \Rightarrow (-)$ *to* $J' : \mathcal{C}' \underset{\perp}{\rightleftarrows} \mathcal{K}' : I \Rightarrow' (-)$ *is a pair of functor* (Φ, Ψ) *such that*

- Φ *is a strict finite product preserving functor from* $\mathcal{C}$ *to* $\mathcal{C}'$*,*
- Ψ *is a strict symmetric monoidal functor from* $\mathcal{K}$ *to* $\mathcal{K}'$ *that preserves the chosen compact closed structures (i.e. units and counits) on the nose, and*
- (Φ, Ψ) *is a map of adjoints between* $J \dashv I \Rightarrow (-)$ *and* $J' \dashv I \Rightarrow' (-)$*.*

□

The collection of (small) compact closed Freyd categories and strict compact closed Freyd functors form a 1-category, which we write as $CCFC$.

Now the question is whether $\mathrm{Mod}(Ax, J) \overset{?}{\cong} CCFC(Cl(Ax), J)$ in **Set**.

Unfortunately this does not hold. More precisely, the left-to-right inclusion does not hold in general. This means that the term model satisfies some additional axioms reflecting some aspects of the π_F-calculus.

The additional axioms reflect the definition of the dual $\vec{T}^*$ in the term model; we have $\vec{T}^* \overset{\mathrm{def}}{=} \vec{T}^\perp$ by definition, and thus $\vec{T}^{**} = \vec{T}$ and $(\vec{T} \otimes \vec{S})^* = \vec{T}^* \otimes \vec{S}^*$. It might be surprising that these equations are harmful because isomorphisms $A^{**} \cong A$ and $(A \otimes B)^* \cong A^* \otimes B^*$ exist in every compact closed category. The point is that the equations also require $\mathcal{C}$ to have isomorphisms $A^{**} \cong A$ and $(A \otimes B)^* \cong A^* \otimes B^*$ (witnessed by the respective identities).

We formally define the additional axioms, which we call **(I)** and **(D)**:

(I) The canonical isomorphism $A^{**} \longrightarrow A$ in $\mathcal{K}$ is the identity.
(D) The canonical isomorphism $(A \otimes B)^* \longrightarrow A^* \otimes B^*$ in $\mathcal{K}$ is the identity.

Theorem 6. $\mathrm{Mod}(Ax, J) \cong CCFC(Cl(Ax), J)$ *if* J *satisfies **(I)** and **(D)**.* □

[6] Because we consider only the empty signature, the set of valuations is singleton.

$$\sigma ::= \tau \rightarrow \tau' \qquad \xi ::= \sigma \qquad \tau ::= (\xi_1, \ldots, \xi_n)$$
$$V ::= x \mid \lambda\langle\vec{x}\rangle.M$$
$$M ::= \langle\vec{V}\rangle \mid V\,\langle\vec{V}\rangle \mid \mathbf{let}\,\langle\vec{x}\rangle = M\,\mathbf{in}\,M'$$

(a) λ_c

$$\xi ::= \cdots \mid \sigma^*$$
$$V ::= \cdots \mid \mathbf{channel}_\sigma \mid \mathbf{send}_\sigma$$

(b) λ_{ch} (difference from λ_c)

Fig. 4. Syntax of types and terms of the λ_c- and λ_{ch}-calculi. The syntax of λ_c is adapted to the setting of this paper.

4 A Concurrent λ-calculus and (de)compilation

In order to demonstrate the relevance of our semantic framework, this section tries to give a semantic reconstruction of fully-abstract compilation and decompilation from a higher-order calculus to the (first-order) π-calculus, such as [39,42]. We first design an instance of the computational λ-calculus [33], named λ_{ch}, that is sound and complete with respect to compact closed Freyd categories. It is obtained by a straightforward extension of the coincidence between the computational λ-calculus and closed Freyd categories (Sect. 4.1). There are translations between π_F and λ_{ch} since both are sound and complete with respect to compact closed Freyd categories. Section 4.2 actually calculates the translations, and compare them with those in [39,42].

4.1 The λ_{ch}-calculus

The λ_{ch}-calculus is a computational λ-calculus with additional constructors dealing with channels. This section introduces and explains the calculus.

The situation is nicely expressed by the following intuitive equation:

$$\frac{\lambda_{ch}}{\lambda_c} \approx \frac{(\text{compact closed Freyd category} + \mathbf{I} + \mathbf{D})}{(\text{closed Freyd category})}.$$

The base calculus λ_c is the *computational λ-calculus*, which corresponds to closed Freyd category [33,37]. It is a call-by-value higher-order programming language, given in Fig. 4(a). Our calculus λ_{ch} is obtained by adding type and term constructors originating from the compact closed structure, which λ_c does not have.

Syntax. As for types, λ_{ch} has a new constructor coming from the dual object A^*. Normalising occurrences of the dual A^* using the axioms **(I)** $A^{**} = A$ and **(D)** $(A \otimes B)^* = A^* \otimes B^*$, we obtain the following grammar of types:

$$\sigma ::= \tau \rightarrow \tau' \qquad \xi ::= \sigma \mid \sigma^* \qquad \tau ::= (\xi_1, \ldots, \xi_n)$$

where $n \geq 0$ and $(\xi_1, \ldots, \xi_n)$ is an alternative notation for $\xi_1 \otimes \cdots \otimes \xi_n$. Compared with λ_c, the only new type is the dual type σ^* of a function type σ.

As for terms, λ_{ch} has constructors corresponding to the unit and counit

$$\eta_A : I \longrightarrow A \otimes A^* \qquad \epsilon_A : A^* \otimes A \longrightarrow I \qquad \text{(for each object } A)$$

of the compact closed structure. We simply add these morphisms as constants:

$$\frac{}{\Gamma \vdash \mathbf{channel}_\sigma : () \to (\sigma, \sigma^*)} \quad \text{and} \quad \frac{}{\Gamma \vdash \mathbf{send}_\sigma : (\sigma^*, \sigma) \to ()}.$$

We shall often omit the subscript σ.

In summary, we obtain the syntax of λ_{ch} shown in Fig. 4. Interestingly, λ_{ch} can be seen as a very core of Concurrent ML [38], a practical higher-order concurrent language, although λ_{ch} is developed from purely semantic considerations.

Semantics. Let us first discuss the intuitive meanings of the new constructors. The type σ^* is for *output channels*; **channel** $\langle\rangle$ creates and returns a pair of an input channel and an output channel that are connected; and **send** $\langle\alpha, V\rangle$ sends the value V via the output channel α. The following points are worth noting.

- λ_{ch} has no type constructor for *input channels*. The type system does not distinguish between input channels for type σ and values of type σ.
- λ_{ch} has no *receive* constructor. Receiving operation is implicit and on demand, delayed as much as possible.
- The send operator broadcasts a value via a channel. Several receivers may receive the same value from the same channel.

The first two points reflect the asynchrony of π_F, and the last point reflects the absence of non-replicated input (cf. Sect. 4.2).

Based on this intuition, we develop the operational, axiomatic and categorical semantics of λ_{ch}. We shall use the following abbreviations:

$$(\nu xy)M \stackrel{\text{def}}{=} \mathbf{let}\,\langle x, y\rangle = \mathbf{channel}\,\langle\rangle\,\mathbf{in}\,M \qquad M \parallel N \stackrel{\text{def}}{=} \mathbf{let}\,\langle\rangle = M\,\mathbf{in}\,N.$$

Operational Semantics. Assume an infinite set $\mathcal{X}$ of *channels*, ranged over by α and β. For each channel α, we write α for the input name and $\bar{\alpha}$ for the output name, both of which are values. A *configuration* is a tuple $(M, \vec{\alpha}, \mu)$ of a term M, a sequence $\vec{\alpha}$ of generated channels and a sequence μ of performed send operations, i.e. $\mu = (\mathbf{send}\,\langle\bar{\beta}_1, V_1\rangle, \ldots, \mathbf{send}\,\langle\bar{\beta}_k, V_k\rangle)$. The *reduction relation* is defined by the following rules for channels

$$\begin{aligned}
(E[\mathbf{channel}\,\langle\rangle],\ \vec{\alpha},\ \mu) &\longrightarrow (E[\langle\beta, \bar{\beta}\rangle],\ \vec{\alpha}\cdot\beta,\ \mu) && (\beta \notin \vec{\alpha})\\
(E[\mathbf{send}\,\langle\bar{\beta}, V\rangle],\ \vec{\alpha},\ \mu) &\longrightarrow (E[\langle\rangle],\ \vec{\alpha},\ \mu\cdot\mathbf{send}\,\langle\bar{\beta}, V\rangle)\\
(E[\beta\, V],\ \vec{\alpha},\ \mu) &\longrightarrow (E[W\,V],\ \vec{\alpha},\ \mu) && (\mathbf{send}\,\langle\bar{\beta}, W\rangle \in \mu).
\end{aligned}$$

in addition to the standard rules for λ-abstractions and let-expressions, which change only M. Here the set of *evaluation contexts* is given by the grammar:

$$E ::= [\,] \mid \mathbf{let}\,\langle\vec{x}\rangle = E\,\mathbf{in}\,M \mid \mathbf{let}\,\langle\vec{x}\rangle = M\,\mathbf{in}\,E.$$

Note that M and N in $\mathbf{let}\,\langle\vec{x}\rangle = M\,\mathbf{in}\,N$ are evaluated in parallel (cf. Remark 3). This justifies the notation $M \parallel N$, an abbreviation for $\mathbf{let}\,\langle\rangle = M\,\mathbf{in}\,N$.

Axiomatic Semantics. The inference rules of the equational logic for λ_{ch} are those for λ_c with the rule of concurrent evaluation

$$\mathbf{let}\,\langle\vec{x}\rangle = M\,\mathbf{in}\,\mathbf{let}\,\langle\vec{y}\rangle = N\,\mathbf{in}\,L \quad = \quad \mathbf{let}\,\langle\vec{y}\rangle = N\,\mathbf{in}\,\mathbf{let}\,\langle\vec{x}\rangle = M\,\mathbf{in}\,L;$$

the β- and η-rules for channels

$$\begin{aligned}(\boldsymbol{\nu} x\bar{x})(\mathbf{send}\,\langle\bar{x}, V\rangle \parallel M) &= (\boldsymbol{\nu} x\bar{x})(\mathbf{send}\,\langle\bar{x}, V\rangle \parallel M\{V/x\}) \\ (\boldsymbol{\nu} y\bar{y})(\mathbf{send}\,\langle\bar{z}, y\rangle \parallel N) &= N\{\bar{z}/\bar{y}\}\end{aligned}$$

where $\bar{x} \notin \mathbf{Fv}(V) \cup \mathbf{Fv}(M)$, $y \notin \mathbf{Fv}(N)$ and $\bar{z} \neq \bar{y}$; and a GC rule.

Categorical Semantics. One can interpret λ_{ch}-terms in a compact closed Freyd category with **(I)** and **(D)**. The interpretation of the λ_c-calculus part is standard [24,37]; the constant $\mathbf{channel}_\sigma$ (resp. $\mathbf{send}_\sigma$) is interpreted as the "closure" whose body is η_σ (resp. ϵ_σ) as expected.

$$\begin{aligned}[\![\Gamma \vdash \mathbf{channel}_\sigma : () \to (\sigma, \sigma^*)]\!] &\stackrel{\text{def}}{=} J(!_\Gamma; \Lambda_{I,I,\sigma\otimes\sigma^*}(\eta_\sigma)) \\ [\![\Gamma \vdash \mathbf{send}_\sigma : (\sigma^*, \sigma) \to ()]\!] &\stackrel{\text{def}}{=} J(!_\Gamma; \Lambda_{I,\sigma\otimes\sigma^*,I}(\epsilon_\sigma)).\end{aligned}$$

The categorical semantics is sound and complete with respect to the equational theory of the λ_{ch}-calculus. The proofs are basically straightforward but there is a subtle issue in the definition of the term model: we have different definitions of the right adjoint $I \Rightarrow (-)$, which are of course equivalent but do not coincide on the nose. Our choice here is $I \Rightarrow \langle\vec{\xi}\rangle \stackrel{\text{def}}{=} (\vec{\xi}^{\perp}) \to ()$.

4.2 Translations Between λ_{ch} and π_F

The higher-order calculus λ_{ch} is equivalent to π_F. This is because both calculi correspond to the same class of categories, namely, the class of compact closed Freyd categories with **(I)** and **(D)**, i.e.,

$$(\lambda_{ch}) \approx (\text{compact closed Freyd category} + \mathbf{I} + \mathbf{D}) \approx (\pi_F).$$

This subsection studies translations derived from this semantic correspondence.

The translations are defined by the interpretations in the term models. For example, the translation $(\!|-|\!)$ from λ_{ch} to π_F is induced by the interpretation of λ_{ch}-terms in the term model $Cl(\emptyset)$. The interpretation $[\![M]\!]_{Cl(\emptyset)}$ of a λ_{ch}-term M is an equivalence class of π_F-processes, since a morphism in $Cl(\emptyset)$ is an equivalence class of π_F-processes. The translation $(\!|M|\!)$ is defined by choosing a representative of the equivalence class. The other direction $[\![-]\!]$ is obtained by the interpretation of π_F in the term model of λ_{ch}.

Figures 5 and 6 are concrete definitions of the translations for a natural choice of representatives. Let us discuss the translations in more details.

The translation from π_F to λ_{ch} (Fig. 5) is easy to understand. It directly expresses the higher-order view of the first-order π-calculus. For example, an

$$[\![\mathbf{ch}^o[\vec{T}]]\!] \stackrel{\mathrm{def}}{=} [\![\vec{T}]\!] \to () \qquad [\![\mathbf{ch}^i[\vec{T}]]\!] \stackrel{\mathrm{def}}{=} ([\![\vec{T}]\!] \to ())^* \qquad [\![(T_1, \ldots, T_n)]\!] \stackrel{\mathrm{def}}{=} ([\![T_1]\!], \ldots, [\![T_n]\!])$$

$$[\![\mathbf{0}]\!] \stackrel{\mathrm{def}}{=} \langle\rangle \qquad [\![P \mid Q]\!] \stackrel{\mathrm{def}}{=} [\![P]\!] \parallel [\![Q]\!] \qquad [\![(\boldsymbol{\nu} xy)P]\!] \stackrel{\mathrm{def}}{=} (\boldsymbol{\nu} xy)[\![P]\!]$$

$$[\![\bar{a}\langle\vec{x}\rangle]\!] \stackrel{\mathrm{def}}{=} \bar{a}\,\langle\vec{x}\rangle \qquad [\![!a(\vec{x}).P]\!] \stackrel{\mathrm{def}}{=} \mathbf{send}\,\langle a, \lambda(\vec{x}).[\![P]\!]\rangle$$

Fig. 5. Translation from π_F to λ_{ch}

$$(\!|\tau_1 \to \tau_2|\!) \stackrel{\mathrm{def}}{=} \mathbf{ch}^o[(\!|\tau_1|\!), (\!|\tau_2|\!)^\perp] \qquad (\!|\sigma^*|\!) \stackrel{\mathrm{def}}{=} (\!|\sigma|\!)^\perp \qquad (\!|(\tau_1, \ldots, \tau_n)|\!) \stackrel{\mathrm{def}}{=} ((\!|\tau_1|\!), \ldots, (\!|\tau_n|\!))$$

$$(\!|x|\!)_p \stackrel{\mathrm{def}}{=} (p \leftrightharpoons x) \qquad (\!|\lambda\vec{x}.M|\!)_p \stackrel{\mathrm{def}}{=} !p(\vec{x}, \vec{q}).(\!|M|\!)_{\vec{q}} \qquad (\!|\langle\vec{V}\rangle|\!)_{\vec{p}} \stackrel{\mathrm{def}}{=} (\!|V_1|\!)_{p_1} \mid \cdots \mid (\!|V_n|\!)_{p_n}$$

$$(\!|V\,\langle\vec{W}\rangle|\!)_{\vec{p}} \stackrel{\mathrm{def}}{=} (\boldsymbol{\nu} a\bar{a})(\boldsymbol{\nu}\vec{r}\vec{s})((\!|V|\!)_a \mid (\!|\langle\vec{W}\rangle|\!)_{\vec{s}} \mid \bar{a}\langle\vec{r}, \vec{p}\rangle)$$

$$(\!|\mathbf{let}\,\langle\vec{x}\rangle = M\,\mathbf{in}\,N|\!)_{\vec{p}} \stackrel{\mathrm{def}}{=} (\boldsymbol{\nu}\vec{x}\vec{q})((\!|M|\!)_{\vec{q}} \mid (\!|N|\!)_{\vec{p}})$$

$$(\!|\mathbf{channel}|\!)_p \stackrel{\mathrm{def}}{=} !p(x, y).x \hookrightarrow y \qquad (\!|\mathbf{send}|\!)_p \stackrel{\mathrm{def}}{=} !p(x, y).x \hookrightarrow y$$

Fig. 6. Translation from λ_{ch} to π_F

output action is mapped to an application and an input-prefixing $!a(\vec{x}).P$ to a send operation of the value $\lambda\langle\vec{x}\rangle.P$ via the channel a.

An interesting (and perhaps confusing) phenomenon is that an input channel in π_F is mapped to an output channel in λ_{ch}. This can be explained as follows. In the name-passing viewpoint, the reduction

$$(\boldsymbol{\nu} xy)(!y(\vec{z}).P \mid x\langle\vec{u}\rangle) \quad \longrightarrow \quad (\boldsymbol{\nu} xy)(!y(\vec{z}).P \mid P\{\vec{u}/\vec{z}\})$$

sends $\vec{u}$ to the process $!y(\vec{z}).P$, and thus x is output and y is input. In the process-passing viewpoint, the abstraction $(\vec{z}).P$ is sent to the location of x, and thus y is the output and x is the input.

Next, we explain the translation from λ_{ch} to π_F (Fig. 6).

Let us first examine the translation of types. The most non-trivial part is the translation of a function type $\tau_1 \to \tau_2$. A key to understand the translation is the isomorphism $\tau_1 \to \tau_2 \cong \tau_1 \otimes \tau_2^\perp \to ()$. The latter form of function type corresponds to an output channel type in π_F. Hence a function is understood as a process additionally taking channels to which the return values are passed.

The translation $(\!|M|\!)_{\vec{p}}$ of a λ_{ch}-term $\Gamma \vdash M : (\xi_1, \ldots, \xi_n)$ takes extra parameters $\vec{p} = p_1, \ldots, p_n$ to which the values should be placed. This is a consequence of the definition in the π_F-term model that a morphism $\vec{T} \longrightarrow \vec{S}$ is a process $\vec{x}\colon \vec{T}, \vec{y}\colon \vec{S}^\perp \vdash P : \diamond$. Here $\vec{p}$ corresponds to $\vec{y}$, Γ to $\vec{x}\colon \vec{T}$ and $\vec{\xi}$ to $\vec{S}$.

Now it is not so difficult to understand the interpretations of constructs in the λ_c-calculus. For example, the abstraction $(\!|\lambda\langle\vec{x}\rangle.M|\!)_p$ is mapped to an abstraction $(\vec{x}, \vec{q}).(\!|M|\!)_{\vec{q}}$ placed at p, which takes additional channels $\vec{q}$ to which the results of the evaluation of M should be sent.

It might be surprising that the interpretations of **channel** and **send** coincide. This is because of the one-sided formulation of π_F. In the two-sided formulation, the unit η and counit ϵ of the compact closed structure, corresponding to **channel** and **send**, can be written as logical inference rules

$$(\!|\mathbf{0}|\!) \stackrel{\text{def}}{=} \mathbf{0} \qquad (\!|P \mid Q|\!) \stackrel{\text{def}}{=} (\!|P|\!) \mid (\!|Q|\!) \qquad (\!|(\boldsymbol{\nu} xy)P|\!) \stackrel{\text{def}}{=} (\boldsymbol{\nu} xy)(\!|P|\!) \qquad (\!|\,!x\, v|\!) \stackrel{\text{def}}{=} (\!|v|\!)_x$$

$$(\!|v\langle w_1,\ldots,w_n\rangle|\!) \stackrel{\text{def}}{=} (\boldsymbol{\nu}\bar{a}a)(\boldsymbol{\nu}\bar{b}_1 b_1)\ldots(\boldsymbol{\nu}\bar{b}_n b_n)((\!|v|\!)_a \mid (\!|w_1|\!)_{b_1} \mid \cdots \mid (\!|w_n|\!)_{b_n} \mid \bar{a}\langle \bar{b}_1,\ldots,\bar{b}_n\rangle)$$

$$(\!|x|\!)_a \stackrel{\text{def}}{=} (a \hookrightarrow x) \qquad (\!|(\vec{x}).P|\!)_a \stackrel{\text{def}}{=} !a(\vec{x}).(\!|P|\!)$$

Fig. 7. Translation from AHOπ to π_F

$$\frac{\Gamma, A, A^{\perp} \vdash \Delta}{\Gamma \vdash \Delta} \quad \text{and} \quad \frac{\Gamma \vdash A^{\perp}, A, \Delta}{\Gamma \vdash \Delta},$$

which are different. In the one-sided formulation, however, they become

$$\frac{\Gamma, A, A^{\perp}, \Delta^{\perp} \vdash}{\Gamma, \Delta^{\perp} \vdash}.$$

Hence η and ϵ (or **channel** and **send**) cannot be distinguished in π_F.

The translation $(\!|-|\!)$ must be the inverse of $[\![-]\!]$ because both the term models are the initial compact closed Freyd category with **(I)** and **(D)**. That means, $\emptyset \rhd \Gamma \vdash P = (\!|[\![P]\!]|\!)$ and $\emptyset \rhd \Gamma \vdash M = [\![(\!|M|\!)]\!]$ are provable for every P and M. This result is independent of the choice of representatives.

4.3 Relation to Other Calculi and Translations

A number of higher-order concurrent calculi, as well as their translations to the first-order π-calculus, have been proposed and studied (e.g. [29,39,40,42,45,47]). The calculus λ_{ch} and the translations have a lot of ideas in common with those calculi and translations; see Sect. 6.

This subsection mainly discusses the relationship to the translations by Sangiorgi [42] (see also [43]) between *asynchronous higher-order π-calculus* (*AHOπ* for short) and *asynchronous local π-calculus* (*Lπ* for short). Here we focus on this work because it is closest to ours. We shall see that our semantic or categorical development provides us with a semantic reconstruction of Sangiorgi's translations, as well as an extension.

A variant of AHOπ can be seen as a fragment of λ_{ch}. The syntax of processes of AHOπ and representation by λ_{ch}-terms are given as follow:

$$\begin{array}{llllllll} v, w ::= x \mid (\vec{x}).P & P, Q ::= \mathbf{0} \mid (P \mid Q) \mid (\boldsymbol{\nu} xy)P \mid & !x\, v & \mid v\langle\vec{w}\rangle \\ \quad\; x \quad \lambda\langle\vec{x}\rangle.P & \qquad\quad \langle\rangle \quad P \parallel Q \quad (\boldsymbol{\nu} xy)P & \mathbf{send}\,\langle x, v\rangle & v\,\langle\vec{w}\rangle. \end{array}$$

(It slightly differs from the original syntax, as $\boldsymbol{\nu}$ binds a pair of names.)

This fragment is nicely described as the limitation on types:

$$\sigma ::= (\vec{\sigma}) \to () \qquad \xi ::= \sigma \mid \sigma^* \qquad \tau ::= ().$$

Recall that σ is a type for abstractions, ξ is a type for variables, and τ is a type for terms. This limitation means that (1) an abstraction cannot take a channel as an argument, and (2) a term M must be of the unit type, i.e. a process.

Once regarding AHOπ as a fragment of λ_{ch}, the translation from AHOπ to π_F is obtained by restricting $(\!|-|\!)$ to AHOπ. The resulting translation is in Fig. 7. As mentioned, the translation is the same as that of Sangiorgi [42] except for minor differences due to the slight change of the syntax.

Sangiorgi also gave a translation in the opposite direction, from Lπ to AHOπ in the same paper. The calculus Lπ is a fragment of the π-calculus in which only output channels can be passed. The **i/o**-separation of π_F allows us to characterise the local version of π_F by a limitation on types. In the local variant, the output channel type is restricted to $T ::= \mathbf{ch}^o[\vec{T}]$, expressing that only output channels can be passed via an output channel. Then the definition of type environment should be changed accordingly: $\Gamma ::= \cdot \mid x : T \mid x : T^{\perp}$ (since the syntactic class represented by T is not closed under the dual $(-)^{\perp}$ in the local setting).

Interestingly the limitation on types in AHOπ coincides with that in Lπ, when one identify $\mathbf{ch}^o[\vec{T}]$ with $(\vec{T}) \to ()$ (as we have done in many places). In other words, the syntactic restrictions of AHOπ and Lπ are the same semantic conditions described in different syntax. As a consequence, the image of Lπ by $[\![-]\!]$ is indeed in AHOπ.

Remark 4. There is, however, a notable difference from Sangiorgi's work [42]. Sangiorgi proved that the translation is fully-abstract with respect to barbed congruence; in contrast, we only show that $\vdash M = N$ iff $\vdash (\!|M|\!) = (\!|N|\!)$. In particular, the η-rule is inevitable for our argument. The presence of the η-rules significantly simplifies the argument, at the cost of operational justification (recall that the η-rule is not sound with respect to barbed congruence).

It is natural to ask how one can reconstruct the full-abstraction result with respect to barbed congruence. An interesting observation is that, if M and N are AHOπ processes, then $\vdash^{\ominus} M = N$ iff $\vdash^{\ominus} (\!|M|\!) = (\!|N|\!)$, where $\vdash^{\ominus}$ means provability without using η-rules. We expect that this semantic observation explains why locality is essential as noted in [42]; we leave the details for future work. □

5 Discussions

Connection to Logics. We have so far studied a connection between compact closed Freyd category and π-calculus. Here we briefly discuss the missing piece of the Curry-Howard-Lambek correspondence, namely logic.

The model of this paper is closely related to linear logic. Actually, every compact closed Freyd category is a model of linear logic (more precisely, MELL), as an instance of linear-non-linear model [6] (see, e.g., [27] for categorical models of linear logic). The interpretation of formulas is shown in Table 1. It differs from the translations by Abramsky [1] and Bellin and Scott [5] and from the Curry-Howard correspondence for session types by Caires and Pfenning [8], but resembles the connection between a variant of local π-calculus and a polarised linear logic by Honda and Laurent [19]; a detailed analysis of the translation is left for future work.

The logic corresponding to compact closed Freyd category should be a proper extension of linear logic, since compact closed Freyd categories form a proper

Table 1. The categorical and π_F-calculus interpretations of MELL formulas

linear logic (formula)	compact closed Freyd category (object)	π_F-calculus (type environment)
$A \otimes B$ $A \parr B$	$A \otimes B$	$x : A, y : B$
$!A$	$I \Rightarrow A$	$x : \mathbf{ch}^o[A^\perp]$
$?A$	$(A \Rightarrow I)^*$	$x : \mathbf{ch}^i[A]$

subclass of linear-non-linear models. For example, the following rules are invalid in linear logic but admissible in compact closed Freyd categories:

$$\frac{\vdash \Gamma \qquad \vdash \Delta}{\vdash \Gamma, \Delta} \qquad \frac{\vdash \Gamma, A, B \qquad \vdash \Delta, A^\perp, B^\perp}{\vdash \Gamma, \Delta} \qquad \frac{\vdash \Gamma, A, A^\perp}{\vdash \Gamma}.$$

These rules, especially the second rule called *multicut*, were often studied in concurrency theory; see Abramsky et al. [2] for their relevance to concurrency.

Do the above rules fill the gap between linear logic and compact closed Freyd category? Recent work by Hasegawa [15] suggests that MELL with above rules is still weaker than compact closed Freyd category. First observe that the above rules can be interpreted in any linear-non-linear model of which the monoidal category is compact closed. Hasegawa showed that a linear-non-linear model whose monoidal category is compact closed induces a closed Freyd category of which the monoidal category is *traced* (and vice versa) but the induced Freyd category is not necessarily compact closed. Hence the logic corresponding to compact closed Freyd category has further axioms or rules in addition to the above ones. A reasonable candidate for the additional axiom is $! \cong ?$; interestingly, Atkey et al. [3] reached a similar rule from a different perspective. Further investigation is left for future work.

Non-empty Signature. The categorical type theory for the λ-calculus considers a family parameterised by *signatures*, consisting of atomic types and constants. It covers, for example, the λ-calculus with natural number type and arithmetic constants (such as addition and multiplication), as well as a calculus with integer reference type and read and update functions.

Although this paper only considers the calculus with the empty signature, which has no additional type nor constant, extending our theory to handle non-empty signatures is, in a sense, not difficult. The easiest way is to apply the established theory of the computational λ-calculus [33,37]. As we have seen in Sect. 4, the π_F-calculus can be seen as a computational λ-calculus λ_{ch} having constants for manipulating channels; hence the π_F-calculus with additional constants is λ_{ch} with the additional constants, which is still in the family of computational λ-calculus.

The π_F-calculus with non-empty signature has several applications. We shall briefly discuss some of them.

An important example of π_F with non-empty signature is the calculus with non-replicated input, which we regard as a calculus with additional "process constants" but without any additional type. A key observation is that every non-replicated input process $a(\vec{x}).P$ can be expressed as

$$a(\vec{x}).P \approx^c (\boldsymbol{\nu}\bar{b}b)(a(\vec{x}).\bar{b}\langle\vec{x}\rangle \mid !b(\vec{x}).P) \qquad (\approx^c \text{ is weak barbed congruence})$$

and thus it suffices to deal with non-replicated input processes in special form, namely $a : \mathbf{ch}^i[\vec{T}],\ \bar{b} : \mathbf{ch}^o[\vec{T}] \vdash a(\vec{x}).\bar{b}\langle\vec{x}\rangle : \diamond$. Adding these processes as constants and the computational rules of $a(\vec{x}).\bar{b}\langle\vec{x}\rangle$ as equational axioms results in a calculus with non-replicated inputs. The categorical model is a compact closed Freyd category with distinguished morphisms $(A \Rightarrow I) \longrightarrow (A \Rightarrow I)$ for each object A which satisfy certain axioms.

This technique is applicable to synchronous output as well. Because

$$\bar{a}\langle\vec{x}\rangle.P \approx^c (\boldsymbol{\nu}\bar{b}b)(\bar{a}\langle\vec{x}\rangle.\bar{b}\langle\rangle \mid !b().P),$$

it suffices to consider constants representing $\bar{a}:\mathbf{ch}^o[\vec{T}], \vec{x}:\vec{T}, \bar{b}:\mathbf{ch}^o[] \vdash \bar{a}\langle\vec{x}\rangle.\bar{b}\langle\rangle:\diamond$.

6 Related Work

Logical Studies of π-calculi. There is a considerable amount of studies on connections between process calculi and linear logic. Here we divide these studies into two classes. These classes are substantially different; for example, one regards the formula $A \otimes B$ as a type for processes with two "ports" of type A and B, whereas the other as the session-type $!A.B$. Our work is more closely related to the former than the latter, but some interesting coincidence to the latter kind of studies can also be found.

The former class of research dates back to the work by Abramsky [1] and Bellin and Scott [5], where they discovered that π-calculus processes can encode proof-nets of classical linear logic. Later, Abramsky et al. [2] introduced the *interaction categories* to give a semantic description of a CCS-like process calculus. In their work, they observed that the compact closed structure is important to capture the strong expressive power of process calculi.

A tighter connection between π-calculus and proof-nets was recently presented by Honda and Laurent [19]. They showed that an $\mathbf{i}/\mathbf{o}$-typed π-calculus corresponds to *polarised proof-nets*, and introduced the notion of *extended reduction* for the π-calculus to simulate cut-elimination. The π-calculus used in this work is very similar to π_F in terms of syntax and reduction. Their calculus is asynchronous, does not allow non-replicated inputs, and requires $\mathbf{i}/\mathbf{o}$-separation. Furthermore, the extended reduction is almost the same as the rules (E-Beta) and (E-GC) except for the side conditions. A significant difference compared to our work is that their calculus is *local* [28,49], reflecting the fact that the corresponding logic is polarised.

Our work is inspired by these studies. The idea of $\mathbf{i}/\mathbf{o}$-separation can already be found in the work by Bellin and Scott and the use of compact closed category is motivated by the study of interaction category. It is worth mentioning here that the design of π_F is also influenced by the calculus introduced by Laird [22], although it is not a logical study but categorical (see below).

The latter approach started with the Curry-Howard correspondences between session-typed π-calculi and linear logic established by Caires, Pfenning and Toninho [8,9] and subsequently by Wadler [48]. These correspondences are exact in the sense that every process has a corresponding proof, and vice versa. As a consequence, processes of the calculi inherit good properties of linear logic proofs such as termination and confluence of cut-elimination. In terms of process calculi, process of these calculi do not fall into deadlock or race condition. This can be seen as a serious restriction of expressive power [3,26,48].

Several extensions to increase the expressiveness of these calculi have been proposed and studied. Interestingly, ideas behind some of these extensions are related to our work, in particular to Sect. 5 discussing the multicut rule [2] and the axiom $! \cong ?$. Atkey et al. [3] studied *CP* [48] with the multicut rule and $! \cong ?$ and discussed how these extensions increase the expressiveness of the calculus, at the cost of losing some good properties of CP. Dardha and Gay [10] studied another extension of CP with multicut, keeping the calculus deadlock-free by an elaborated type system.

Balzer and Pfenning [4] proposed a session-typed calculus with shared (mutable) resources, inspired by linear-non-linear adjunction [6].

Categorical Semantics of π-calculi. The idea of using a closed Freyd category to model the π-calculus is strongly inspired by Laird [22]. He introduced the *distributive-closed Freyd category* to describe abstract properties of a game-semantic model of the asynchronous π-calculus and showed that distributive-closed Freyd categories with some additional structures suffice to interpret the asynchronous π-calculus. The additional structures are specific to his game model and not completely axiomatised.[7] Our notion of compact closed Freyd category might be seen as a reformulation of his idea, obtained by filtering out some structures difficult to axiomatise and by strengthening some others to make axioms simpler. A significant difference is that our categorical model does not deal with non-replicated inputs, which we think is essential for a simple axiomatisation.

Another approach for categorical semantics of the π-calculus has been the presheaf based approach [12,44]. These studies gave particular categories that nicely handles the nominal aspects of the π-calculus; these studies, however, do not aim for a correspondence between a categorical structure and the π-calculus.

Higher-Order Calculi with Channels. Besides the λ_{ch}-calculus, there are numbers of functional languages augmented by communication channels, from theoretical ones [13,25,46,48] to practical languages [34,38].

On the practical side, Concurrent ML (CML) [38], among others, is a well-developed higher-order concurrent language. CML has primitives to create channels and threads, and primitives to send and accept values through channels.

[7] A list of properties in [22] does not seem to be complete. We could not prove some claims in the paper only from these properties, but with ones specific to his model.

Since our λ_{ch}-calculus can create (non-linear) channels and send values via channels, the λ_{ch}-calculus can be seen as a core calculus of CML despite its origin in categorical semantics. The major difference between CML and the λ_{ch}-calculus is that communications in CML are synchronous whereas communications in the λ_{ch}-calculus are asynchronous.

On the theoretical side, session-typed functional languages have been actively studied [13,25,46,48]. Notably, some of these languages [25,46,48] are built upon the Curry-Howard foundation between linear logic and session-typed processes. It might be interesting to investigate whether we can relate these languages and the λ_{ch}-calculus through the lens of Curry-Howard-Lambek correspondence.

Higher-Order vs. First-Order π-calculus. A number of translations from higher-order languages to the π-calculus have been developed [39,40,42,45,47] since Milner [29] presented the encodings of the λ-calculus into the π-calculus. The basic idea shared by these studies is to transform $\lambda x.M$ to a process $!a(x,p).P$ that receives the argument x together with a name p where the rest of the computation will be transmitted. In our framework, this idea is described as the isomorphism $A \Rightarrow B \cong A \otimes B^* \Rightarrow I$.

Among others, the translation from AHOπ to Lπ [42] is the closest to our translation from the λ_{ch}-calculus to the π_F-calculus. Sangiorgi [41] observed that Milner's translation can be established via the translation of AHOπ by applying the CPS transformation to the λ-calculus. This observation also applies to our translation. That is, we can obtain Milner's translation by combining CPS transformation and the compilation of the λ_{ch}-calculus.

7 Conclusion and Future Work

We have introduced an **i**/**o**-typed π-calculus (π_F-calculus) as well as the categorical counterpart of π_F-calculus (compact closed Freyd category) and showed the categorical type theory correspondence between them. The correspondence was established by regarding the π-calculus as a higher-order programming language, introducing the **i**/**o**-separation, and introducing the η-rule, a rule that explains the mismatch between behavioural equivalences and categorical models.

As an application of our semantic framework we introduced a higher-order calculus λ_{ch}-calculus "equivalent" to the π_F-calculus. We have demonstrated that translations between λ_{ch}-calculus and π_F-calculus can be derived by a simple semantic argument, and showed that the translation from λ_{ch} to π_F is a generalisation of the translation from AHOπ to Lπ given by Sangiorgi [42].

There are three main directions for future work. First, further investigation on the η-rule is indispensable. We plan to construct a categorical model of the π_F-calculus with an additional constant that captures barbed congruence. Revealing the relationship between locality and the η-rule is another important problem. Second, the operational properties of the λ_{ch}-calculus and its relation to the equational theory needs a further investigation. Third, finding the logical counterpart of compact closed Freyd category to establish a proper Curry-Howard-Lambek correspondence is an interesting future work.

Acknowledgement. We would like to thank Naoki Kobayashi, Masahito Hasegawa and James Laird for discussions, and anonymous referees for valuable comments. This work was supported by JSPS KAKENHI Grant Number 15H05706 and 16K16004.

References

1. Abramsky, S.: Proofs as processes. Theor. Comput. Sci. **135**(1), 5–9 (1994)
2. Abramsky, S., Gay, S.J., Nagarajan, R.: Interaction categories and the foundations of typed concurrent programming. In: Proceedings of the NATO Advanced Study Institute on Deductive Program Design, Marktoberdorf, Germany, pp. 35–113 (1996)
3. Atkey, R., Lindley, S., Morris, J.G.: Conflation confers concurrency. In: A List of Successes That Can Change the World - Essays Dedicated to Philip Wadler on the Occasion of His 60th Birthday, pp. 32–55 (2016)
4. Balzer, S., Pfenning, F.: Manifest sharing with session types. PACMPL **1**(ICFP), 37:1–37:29 (2017)
5. Bellin, G., Scott, P.J.: On the π-calculus and linear logic. Theor. Comput. Sci. **135**(1), 11–65 (1994)
6. Benton, P.N.: A mixed linear and non-linear logic: proofs, terms and models. In: Pacholski, L., Tiuryn, J. (eds.) CSL 1994. LNCS, vol. 933, pp. 121–135. Springer, Heidelberg (1995). https://doi.org/10.1007/BFb0022251
7. Boreale, M.: On the expressiveness of internal mobility in name-passing calculi. Theor. Comput. Sci. **195**(2), 205–226 (1998)
8. Caires, L., Pfenning, F.: Session types as intuitionistic linear propositions. In: Gastin, P., Laroussinie, F. (eds.) CONCUR 2010. LNCS, vol. 6269, pp. 222–236. Springer, Heidelberg (2010). https://doi.org/10.1007/978-3-642-15375-4_16
9. Caires, L., Pfenning, F., Toninho, B.: Linear logic propositions as session types. Math. Struct. Comput. Sci. **26**(3), 367–423 (2016)
10. Dardha, O., Gay, S.J.: A new linear logic for deadlock-free session-typed processes. In: Baier, C., Dal Lago, U. (eds.) FoSSaCS 2018. LNCS, vol. 10803, pp. 91–109. Springer, Cham (2018). https://doi.org/10.1007/978-3-319-89366-2_5
11. de Nicola, R., Hennessy, M.C.B.: Testing equivalences for processes. In: Diaz, J. (ed.) ICALP 1983. LNCS, vol. 154, pp. 548–560. Springer, Heidelberg (1983). https://doi.org/10.1007/BFb0036936
12. Fiore, M.P., Moggi, E., Sangiorgi, D.: A fully abstract model for the π-calculus. Inf. Comput. **179**(1), 76–117 (2002)
13. Gay, S.J., Vasconcelos, V.T.: Linear type theory for asynchronous session types. J. Funct. Program. **20**(1), 19–50 (2010)
14. Girard, J.: Linear logic. Theor. Comput. Sci. **50**, 1–102 (1987)
15. Hasegawa, M.: From linear logic to cyclic sharing. Lecture slides, Linearity (2018)
16. Hayashi, S.: Adjunction of semifunctors: categorical structures in nonextensional lambda calculus. Theor. Comput. Sci. **41**, 95–104 (1985)
17. Hoare, C.A.R.: Communicating Sequential Processes. Prentice-Hall, Upper Saddle River (1985)
18. Honda, K.: Types for dyadic interaction. In: Best, E. (ed.) CONCUR 1993. LNCS, vol. 715, pp. 509–523. Springer, Heidelberg (1993). https://doi.org/10.1007/3-540-57208-2_35
19. Honda, K., Laurent, O.: An exact correspondence between a typed pi-calculus and polarised proof-nets. Theor. Comput. Sci. **411**(22–24), 2223–2238 (2010)

20. Honda, K., Vasconcelos, V.T., Kubo, M.: Language primitives and type discipline for structured communication-based programming. In: Hankin, C. (ed.) ESOP 1998. LNCS, vol. 1381, pp. 122–138. Springer, Heidelberg (1998). https://doi.org/10.1007/BFb0053567
21. Kelly, G.M., Laplaza, M.L.: Coherence for compact closed categories. J. Pure Appl. Algebra **19**, 193–213 (1980)
22. Laird, J.: A game semantics of the asynchronous π-calculus. In: Abadi, M., de Alfaro, L. (eds.) CONCUR 2005. LNCS, vol. 3653, pp. 51–65. Springer, Heidelberg (2005). https://doi.org/10.1007/11539452_8
23. Lambek, J., Scott, P.J.: Introduction to Higher-Order Categorical Logic, vol. 7. Cambridge University Press, New York (1988)
24. Levy, P.B., Power, J., Thielecke, H.: Modelling environments in call-by-value programming languages. Inf. Comput. **185**(2), 182–210 (2003)
25. Lindley, S., Morris, J.G.: A semantics for propositions as sessions. In: Vitek, J. (ed.) ESOP 2015. LNCS, vol. 9032, pp. 560–584. Springer, Heidelberg (2015). https://doi.org/10.1007/978-3-662-46669-8_23
26. Mazza, D.: The true concurrency of differential interaction nets. Math. Struct. Comput. Sci. **28**(7), 1097–1125 (2018)
27. Melliès, P.A.: Categorical semantics of linear logic. Panoramas et syntheses **27**, 15–215 (2009)
28. Merro, M.: Locality in the π-calculus and applications to distributed objects. Ph.D. thesis, École Nationale Supérieure des Mines de Paris (2000)
29. Milner, R.: Functions as processes. Math. Struct. Comput. Sci. **2**(2), 119–141 (1992)
30. Milner, R., Parrow, J., Walker, D.: A calculus of mobile processes, I. Inf. Comput. **100**(1), 1–40 (1992)
31. Milner, R., Parrow, J., Walker, D.: A calculus of mobile processes, II. Inf. Comput. **100**(1), 41–77 (1992)
32. Milner, R., Sangiorgi, D.: Barbed bisimulation. In: Kuich, W. (ed.) ICALP 1992. LNCS, vol. 623, pp. 685–695. Springer, Heidelberg (1992). https://doi.org/10.1007/3-540-55719-9_114
33. Moggi, E.: Computational lambda-calculus and monads. In: Proceedings of the Fourth Annual Symposium on Logic in Computer Science (LICS 1989), Pacific Grove, California, USA, 5–8 June 1989, pp. 14–23 (1989)
34. Peyton Jones, S.L., Gordon, A.D., Finne, S.: Concurrent Haskell. In: Conference Record of POPL 1996: The 23rd ACM SIGPLAN-SIGACT Symposium on Principles of Programming Languages, Papers Presented at the Symposium, St. Petersburg Beach, Florida, USA, 21–24 January 1996, pp. 295–308 (1996)
35. Pierce, B.C., Sangiorgi, D.: Typing and subtyping for mobile processes. Math. Struct. Comput. Sci. **6**(5), 409–453 (1996)
36. Power, J., Robinson, E.: Premonoidal categories and notions of computation. Math. Struct. Comput. Sci. **7**(5), 453–468 (1997)
37. Power, J., Thielecke, H.: Closed Freyd- and κ-categories. In: Wiedermann, J., van Emde Boas, P., Nielsen, M. (eds.) ICALP 1999. LNCS, vol. 1644, pp. 625–634. Springer, Heidelberg (1999). https://doi.org/10.1007/3-540-48523-6_59
38. Reppy, J.H.: CML: a higher-order concurrent language. In: Proceedings of the ACM SIGPLAN 1991 Conference on Programming Language Design and Implementation (PLDI), Toronto, Ontario, Canada, 26–28 June 1991, pp. 293–305 (1991)
39. Sangiorgi, D.: Expressing mobility in process algebras: first-order and higher-order paradigms. Ph.D. thesis, University of Edinburgh, UK (1993)

40. Sangiorgi, D.: π-Calculus, internal mobility, and agent-passing calculi. Theor. Comput. Sci. **167**(1&2), 235–274 (1996)
41. Sangiorgi, D.: From λ to π; or, rediscovering continuations. Math. Struct. Comput. Sci. **9**(4), 367–401 (1999)
42. Sangiorgi, D.: Asynchronous process calculi: the first- and higher-order paradigms. Theor. Comput. Sci. **253**(2), 311–350 (2001)
43. Sangiorgi, D., Walker, D.: The π-calculus—A Theory of Mobile Processes. Cambridge University Press, New York (2001)
44. Stark, I.: A fully abstract domain model for the π-calculus. In: Proceedings, 11th Annual IEEE Symposium on Logic in Computer Science, New Brunswick, New Jersey, USA, 27–30 July 1996, pp. 36–42 (1996)
45. Toninho, B., Caires, L., Pfenning, F.: Functions as session-typed processes. In: Birkedal, L. (ed.) FoSSaCS 2012. LNCS, vol. 7213, pp. 346–360. Springer, Heidelberg (2012). https://doi.org/10.1007/978-3-642-28729-9_23
46. Toninho, B., Caires, L., Pfenning, F.: Higher-order processes, functions, and sessions: a monadic integration. In: Felleisen, M., Gardner, P. (eds.) ESOP 2013. LNCS, vol. 7792, pp. 350–369. Springer, Heidelberg (2013). https://doi.org/10.1007/978-3-642-37036-6_20
47. Turner, D.N.: The polymorphic Pi-calculus: theory and implementation. Ph.D. thesis, University of Edinburgh, UK (1996)
48. Wadler, P.: Propositions as sessions. J. Funct. Program. **24**(2–3), 384–418 (2014)
49. Yoshida, N.: Minimality and separation results on asynchronous mobile processes - representability theorems by concurrent combinators. Theor. Comput. Sci. **274**(1–2), 231–276 (2002)

A Process Algebra for Link Layer Protocols

Rob van Glabbeek[1,2(✉)], Peter Höfner[1,2], and Michael Markl[1,3]

[1] Data61, CSIRO, Sydney, Australia
rvg@cs.stanford.edu
[2] Computer Science and Engineering, University of New South Wales, Sydney, Australia
[3] Institut für Informatik, Universität Augsburg, Augsburg, Germany

Abstract. We propose a process algebra for link layer protocols, featuring a unique mechanism for modelling frame collisions. We also formalise suitable liveness properties for link layer protocols specified in this framework. To show applicability we model and analyse two versions of the Carrier-Sense Multiple Access with Collision Avoidance (CSMA/CA) protocol. Our analysis confirms the hidden station problem for the version without virtual carrier sensing. However, we show that the version with virtual carrier sensing not only overcomes this problem, but also the exposed station problem with probability 1. Yet the protocol cannot guarantee packet delivery, not even with probability 1.

1 Introduction

The (data) link layer is the 2nd layer of the ISO/OSI model of computer networking [18]. Amongst others, it is responsible for the transfer of data between adjacent nodes in Wide Area Networks (WANs) and Local Area Networks (LANs).

Examples of link layer protocols are Ethernet for LANs [16], the Point-to-Point Protocol [24] and the High-Level Data Link Control protocol (e.g. [14]). Part of this layer are also multiple access protocols such as the Carrier-Sense Multiple Access with Collision Detection (CSMA/CD) protocol for re-transmission in Ethernet bus networks and hub networks, or the Carrier-Sense Multiple Access with Collision Avoidance (CSMA/CA) protocol [17,19] in wireless networks.

One of the unique characteristics of the link layer is that when devices attempt to use a medium simultaneously, *collisions of messages* occur. So, any modelling language and formal analysis of layer-2 protocols has to support such collisions. Moreover, some protocols are of probabilistic nature: CSMA/CA for example chooses time slots probabilistically with discrete uniform distribution.

As we are not aware of any formal framework with primitives for modelling data collisions, this paper introduces a process algebra for modelling and analysing link layer protocols. In Sect. 2 we present an algebra featuring a unique mechanism for modelling collisions, 'hard-wired' in the semantics. It is the non-probabilistic fragment of the Algebra for Link Layer protocols (ALL), which we

L. Caires (Ed.): ESOP 2019, LNCS 11423, pp. 668–693, 2019.
https://doi.org/10.1007/978-3-030-17184-1_24

introduce in Sect. 3. In Sect. 4 we formulate *packet delivery*, a liveness property that ideally ought to hold for link layer protocols, either outright, or with a high probability. In Sect. 5 we use this framework to formally model and analyse the CSMA/CA protocol.

Our analysis confirms the hidden station problem for the version of CSMA/CA without virtual carrier sensing (Sect. 5.2). However, we also show that the version with virtual carrier sensing overcomes not only this problem, but also the exposed station problem with probability 1. Yet the protocol cannot guarantee packet delivery, not even with probability 1.

2 A Non-probabilistic Subalgebra

In this section we propose a timed process algebra that can model the collision of link layer messages, called *frames*.[1] It can be used for link layer protocols that do not feature probabilistic choice, and is inspired by the (Timed) Algebra for Wireless Networks ((T-)AWN) [2,12,13], a process algebra suitable for modelling and analysing protocols on layers 3 (network) and 4 (transport) of the OSI model.

The process algebra models a (wired or wireless) network as an encapsulated parallel composition of network nodes. Due to the nature of the protocols under consideration, on each node exactly one sequential process is running. The algebra features a discrete model of time, where each sequential process maintains a local variable `now` holding its local clock value—an integer. We employ only one clock for each sequential process. All sequential processes in a network synchronise in taking time steps, and at each time step all local clocks advance by one unit. Since this means that all clocks are in sync and do not run at different speeds it is clear that we do not consider the problem of clock shift. For the rest, the variable `now` behaves like any other variable maintained by a process: its value can be read when evaluating guards, thereby making progress time-dependant, and any value can be assigned to it, thereby resetting the local clock. Network nodes communicate with their direct neighbours—those nodes that are in transmission range. The algebra provides a mobility option that allows nodes to move in or out of transmission range. The encapsulation of the entire network inhibits communications between network nodes and the outside world, with the exception of the receipt and delivery of data packets from or to clients (the higher OSI layers).

2.1 A Language for Sequential Processes

The internal state of a process is determined, in part, by the values of certain data variables that are maintained by that process. To this end, we assume a data structure with several types, variables ranging over these types, operators and predicates. Predicate logic yields terms (or *data expressions*) and formulas

[1] As it is the nonprobabilistic fragment of a forthcoming algebra we do not name it.

to denote data values and statements about them. Our data structure always contains the types TIME, DATA, MSG, CHUNK, ID and $\mathscr{P}(\texttt{ID})$ of discrete *time values*, which we take to be integers, *network layer data*, *messages*, *chunks* of messages that take one time unit to transmit, *node identifiers* and *sets of node identifiers*. We further assume that there are variables now of type TIME and rfr of type CHUNK. In addition, we assume a set of *process names*. Each process name X comes with a *defining equation*

$$X(\texttt{var}_1, \ldots, \texttt{var}_n) \stackrel{def}{=} P\,,$$

in which $n \in \mathbb{N}$, $\texttt{var}_i$ are variables and P is a *sequential process expression* defined by the grammar below. It may contain the variables $\texttt{var}_i$ as well as X. However, all occurrences of data variables in P have to be *bound*.[2] The choice of the underlying data structure and the process names with their defining equations can be tailored to any particular application of our language.

The *sequential process expressions* are given by the following grammar:

$$P ::= X(exp_1, \ldots, exp_n) \mid [\varphi]P \mid [\![\texttt{var} := exp]\!]P \mid \alpha.P \mid P + P$$
$$\alpha ::= \textbf{transmit}(ms) \mid \textbf{newpkt}(\texttt{data}, \texttt{dest}) \mid \textbf{deliver}(\texttt{data})$$

Here X is a process name, exp_i a data expression of the same type as $\texttt{var}_i$, φ a data formula, $\texttt{var} := exp$ an assignment of a data expression exp to a variable var of the same type, ms a data expression of type MSG, and data, dest data variables of types DATA, ID respectively.

Given a valuation of the data variables by concrete data values, the sequential process $[\varphi]P$ acts as P if φ evaluates to true, and deadlocks if φ evaluates to false. In case φ contains free variables that are not yet interpreted as data values, values are assigned to these variables in any way that satisfies φ, if possible. The process $[\![\texttt{var} := exp]\!]P$ acts as P, but under an updated valuation of the data variable var. The process $P+Q$ may act either as P or as Q, depending on which of the two processes is able to act at all. In a context where both are able to act, it is not specified how the choice is made. The process $\alpha.P$ first performs the action α and subsequently acts as P. The above behaviour is identical to AWN, and many other standard process algebras. The action **transmit**(ms) transmits (the data value bound to the expression) ms to all other network nodes within transmission range. The action **newpkt**(data, dest) models the injection by the network layer of a data packet data to be transmitted to a destination dest. Technically, data and dest are variables that will be bound to the obtained values upon receipt of a **newpkt**. Data is delivered to the network layer by **deliver**(data). In contrast to AWN, we do not have a primitive for

[2] An occurrence of a data variable in P is *bound* if it is one of the variables $\texttt{var}_i$, one of the two special variables now or rfr, a variable var occurring in a subexpression $[\![\texttt{var} := exp]\!]Q$, an occurrence in a subexpression $[\varphi]Q$ of a variable occurring free in φ, or a variable data or dest occurring in a subexpression **newpkt**(data, dest)$.Q$. Here Q is an arbitrary sequential process expression.

receiving messages from neighbouring nodes, because our processes are *always* listening to neighbouring nodes, in parallel with anything else they do.

As in AWN, the internal state of a sequential process described by an expression P is determined by P, together with a *valuation* ξ associating values $\xi(\mathtt{var})$ to variables var maintained by this process. Valuations naturally extend to ξ-*closed* expressions—those in which all variables are either bound or in the domain of ξ. We denote the valuation that assigns the value v to the variable var, and agrees with ξ on all other variables, by $\xi[\mathtt{var} := v]$. The valuation $\xi_{|S}$ agrees with ξ on all variables var $\in S$ and is undefined otherwise. Moreover we use $\xi[\mathtt{var}\,\texttt{++}]$ as an abbreviation for $\xi[\mathtt{var} := \xi(\mathtt{var}) + 1]$, for suitable types.

To capture the durational nature of transmitting a message between network nodes, we model a message as a sequence of *chunks*, each of which takes one time unit to transmit. The function $\mathtt{dur} : \mathtt{MSG} \to \mathtt{TIME}_{>0}$ calculates the amount of time steps needed for a sending a message, i.e. it calculates the number of chunks. We employ the internal data type $\mathtt{CHUNK} := \{m{:}c \mid m \in \mathtt{MSG}, 1 \leq c \leq \mathtt{dur}(m)\} \cup \{\underline{\mathtt{conflict}}, \underline{\mathtt{idle}}\}$. The chunk $m{:}c$ indicates the cth fragment of a message m. Data conflicts—junk transmitted via the medium—is modelled by the special chunk $\underline{\mathtt{conflict}}$, and the absence of an incoming chunk is modelled by $\underline{\mathtt{idle}}$.

Our process algebra maintains a variable rfr of type CHUNK, storing the fragment of the current message received so far.

As a value of this variable, $m{:}c$ indicates that the first c chunks of message m have been received in order; $\underline{\mathtt{conflict}}$ indicates that the last incoming chunk was not the expected (next) part of a message in progress, and $\underline{\mathtt{idle}}$ indicates that the channel was idle during the last time step. The table on the right, with $*$ a wild card, shows how the value of rfr evolves upon receiving a new chunk *ch*.

rfr	*ch*	rfr $\star$ *ch*
$*$	$\underline{\mathtt{conflict}}$	$\underline{\mathtt{conflict}}$
$*$	$\underline{\mathtt{idle}}$	$\underline{\mathtt{idle}}$
$*$	$m{:}1$	$m{:}1$
$m{:}c$	$m{:}c{+}1$	$m{:}c{+}1$
rfr	$m{:}c{+}1$	$\underline{\mathtt{conflict}}$ if $rfr \neq m{:}c$

Specifications may refer to the data type CHUNK only through the Boolean functions NEW—having a single argument *msg* of type MSG—and IDLE, defined by $\text{NEW}(msg) := (\mathtt{rfr} = (msg : \mathtt{dur}(msg))$ and $\text{IDLE} := (\mathtt{rfr} = \underline{\mathtt{idle}})$. A guard $[\text{NEW}(msg)]$ evaluates to true iff a new message *msg* has just been received; $[\text{IDLE}]$ evaluates to true iff in the last time slice the medium was idle.

The structural operational semantics of Table 1 describes how one internal state can evolve into another by performing an *action*. The set Act of actions consists of **transmit**$(m{:}c, ch)$, **wait**(ch), **newpkt**$(d, dest)$, **deliver**(d), and internal actions τ, for each choice of $m \in \mathtt{MSG}$, $c \in \{1, \ldots, \mathtt{dur}(m)\}$, $ch \in \mathtt{CHUNK}$, $d \in \mathtt{DATA}$ and $dest \in \mathtt{ID}$, where the first two actions are time consuming. On every time-consuming action, each process receives a chunk *ch* and updates the variable rfr accordingly; moreover, the variable now is incremented on all process expressions in a (complete) network synchronously.

Besides the special variables now and rfr, the formal semantics employs an internal variable $\mathtt{cntr} \in \mathbb{N}$ that enumerates the chunks of split messages and is

Table 1. Structural operational semantics for sequential process expressions

(1)
$$\xi, \textbf{transmit}(ms).P \xrightarrow{\textbf{transmit}(\xi(ms):\mathtt{c+},ch)} \xi\begin{bmatrix}\mathtt{cntr}\,\mathtt{++}\\ \mathtt{rfr} := \mathtt{rfr} \star ch\\ \mathtt{now}\,\mathtt{++}\end{bmatrix}, \textbf{transmit}(\xi(ms)).P \qquad \begin{array}{r}(\text{if } \mathtt{c+} < \mathtt{dur}(\xi(ms)))\\ (\forall ch \in \mathtt{CHUNK})\end{array}$$

(2)
$$\xi, \textbf{transmit}(ms).P \xrightarrow{\textbf{transmit}(\xi(ms):\mathtt{c+},ch)} \xi\begin{bmatrix}\mathtt{cntr} := 0\\ \mathtt{rfr} := \mathtt{rfr} \star ch\\ \mathtt{now}\,\mathtt{++}\end{bmatrix}, P \qquad \begin{array}{r}(\text{if } \mathtt{c+} = \mathtt{dur}(\xi(ms)))\\ (\forall ch \in \mathtt{CHUNK})\end{array}$$

(3)
$$\xi, \textbf{newpkt}(\mathtt{data}, \mathtt{dest}).P \xrightarrow{\textbf{newpkt}(d,dest)} \xi\begin{bmatrix}\mathtt{data} := d\\ \mathtt{dest} := dest\end{bmatrix}, P \qquad (\forall d \in \mathtt{DATA},\ dest \in \mathtt{ID})$$

(4)
$$\xi, \textbf{newpkt}(\mathtt{data}, \mathtt{dest}).P \xrightarrow{\textbf{wait}(ch)} \xi\begin{bmatrix}\mathtt{rfr} := \mathtt{rfr} \star ch\\ \mathtt{now}\,\mathtt{++}\end{bmatrix}, \textbf{newpkt}(\mathtt{data}, \mathtt{dest}).P \qquad (\forall ch \in \mathtt{CHUNK})$$

(5)
$$\xi, \textbf{deliver}(\mathtt{data}).P \xrightarrow{\textbf{deliver}(\xi(\mathtt{data}))} \xi, P$$

(6)
$$\xi, [\![\mathtt{var} := exp]\!]P \xrightarrow{\tau} \xi[\mathtt{var} := \xi(exp)], P$$

(7)
$$\frac{\xi_{|\mathtt{RO}}[\mathtt{var}_i := \xi(exp_i)]_{i=1}^{n}, P \xrightarrow{a} \zeta, P'}{\xi, X(exp_1, \ldots, exp_n) \xrightarrow{a} \zeta, P'}\ (X(\mathtt{var}_1, \ldots, \mathtt{var}_n) \stackrel{def}{=} P) \qquad (\forall a \in \mathrm{Act} - \{\textbf{wait}(ch) \mid ch \in \mathtt{CHUNK}\})$$

(8)
$$\frac{\xi_{|\mathtt{RO}}[\mathtt{var}_i := \xi(exp_i)]_{i=1}^{n}, P \xrightarrow{\textbf{wait}(ch)} \zeta, P'}{\xi, X(exp_1, \ldots, exp_n) \xrightarrow{\textbf{wait}(ch)} \xi\begin{bmatrix}\mathtt{rfr} := \mathtt{rfr} \star ch\\ \mathtt{now}\,\mathtt{++}\end{bmatrix}, X(exp_1, \ldots, exp_n)}\ (X(\mathtt{var}_1, \ldots, \mathtt{var}_n) \stackrel{def}{=} P) \qquad (\forall ch \in \mathtt{CHUNK})$$

(9)
$$\xi, P \xrightarrow{\textbf{wait}(ch)} \xi\begin{bmatrix}\mathtt{rfr} := \mathtt{rfr} \star ch\\ \mathtt{now}\,\mathtt{++}\end{bmatrix}, P \qquad \begin{array}{r}(\text{if } \xi(P)\uparrow)\\ (\forall ch \in \mathtt{CHUNK})\end{array}$$

(10)
$$\frac{\xi, P \xrightarrow{a} \zeta, P'}{\xi, P + Q \xrightarrow{a} \zeta, P'} \quad \frac{\xi, Q \xrightarrow{a} \zeta, Q'}{\xi, P + Q \xrightarrow{a} \zeta, Q'} \qquad (\forall a \in \mathrm{Act} - \{\textbf{wait}(ch) \mid ch \in \mathtt{CHUNK}\})$$

(11)
$$\frac{\xi, P \xrightarrow{\textbf{wait}(ch)} \zeta, P' \quad \xi, Q \xrightarrow{\textbf{wait}(ch)} \zeta', Q'}{\xi, P + Q \xrightarrow{\textbf{wait}(ch)} \zeta, P' + Q'} \qquad (\forall ch \in \mathtt{CHUNK})$$

(12)
$$\frac{\xi \xrightarrow{\varphi} \zeta}{\xi, [\varphi]P \xrightarrow{\tau} \zeta, P} \quad \frac{\xi \not\xrightarrow{\varphi}}{\xi, [\varphi]P \xrightarrow{\textbf{wait}(ch)} \xi\begin{bmatrix}\mathtt{rfr} := \mathtt{rfr} \star ch\\ \mathtt{now}\,\mathtt{++}\end{bmatrix}, [\varphi]P} \qquad (\forall ch \in \mathtt{CHUNK})$$

used to identify which chunk needs to be sent next. The variables `now`, `rfr` and `cntr` are not meant to be changed by ALL specifications, e.g. by using assignments. We call them read-only and collect them in the set $\mathtt{RO} = \{\mathtt{now}, \mathtt{rfr}, \mathtt{cntr}\}$.

Let us have a closer look at the rules of Table 1.

The first two rules describe the sending of a message *ms*. Remember that $\mathtt{dur}(ms)$ calculates the time needed to send *ms*. The counter `cntr` keeps track of the time passed already. The action $\mathbf{transmit}(m{:}c, ch)$ occurs when the node transmits the fragment $m{:}c$; simultaneously, it receives the fragment *ch*.[3] The counter `cntr` is 0 before a message is sent, and is incremented before the transmission of each chunk. So, each chunk sent has the form $\xi(ms){:}\xi(\mathtt{cntr}){+}1$. To ease readability we abbreviate $\xi(\mathtt{cntr}){+}1$ by `c+`. In case the (already incremented) counter `c+` is strictly smaller than the number of chunks needed to send $\xi(ms)$, another **transmit**-action is needed (Rule 1); if the last fragment has been sent ($\mathtt{c+} = \mathtt{dur}(\xi(ms))$) the process can continue to act as P (Rule 2).

The actions $\mathbf{newpkt}(d, dest)$ and $\mathbf{deliver}(d)$ are instantaneous and model the submission of data d from the network layer, destined for *dest*, and the delivery of data d to the network layer, respectively. The process $\mathbf{newpkt}(d, dest).P$ has also the possibility to wait, namely if no network layer instruction arrives.

Rule 6 defines a rule for assignment in a straightforward fashion; only the valuation of the variable `var` is updated.

In Rules 7 and 8, which define recursion, $\xi_{|\mathtt{RO}}[\mathtt{var}_i := \xi(exp_i)]_{i=1}^{n}$ is the valuation that *only* assigns the values $\xi(exp_i)$ to the variables $\mathtt{var}_i$, for $i = 1, \ldots, n$, and maintains the values of the variables `now`, `rfr` and `cntr`. These rules state that a defined process X has the same transitions as the body p of its defining equation. In case of a **wait**-transition, the sequential process does not progress, and accordingly the recursion is not yet unfolded.

Most transition rules so far feature statements of the form $\xi(exp)$ where *exp* is a data expression. The application of the rule depends on $\xi(exp)$ being defined. Rule 9 covers all cases where the above rules cannot be applied since at least one data expression in an action α is not defined. A state ξ, P is *unvalued*, denoted by $\xi(p)\!\uparrow$, if P has the form $\mathbf{transmit}(ms).P$, $\mathbf{deliver}(\mathtt{data}).P$, $[\![\mathtt{var} := exp]\!]P$ or $X(exp_1, \ldots, exp_n)$ with either $\xi(ms)$ or $\xi(\mathtt{data})$ or $\xi(exp)$ or some $\xi(exp_i)$ undefined. From such a state the process can merely wait.

A process $P + Q$ can wait *only* if both P and Q can do the same; if either P or Q can achieve 'proper' progress, the choice process $P + Q$ always chooses progress over waiting. A simple induction shows that if $\xi, P \xrightarrow{\mathbf{wait}(ch)} \zeta, P'$ and $\xi, Q \xrightarrow{\mathbf{wait}(ch)} \zeta', Q'$ then $P = P'$, $Q = Q'$ and $\zeta = \zeta'$.

The first rule of (12), describing the semantics of guards $[\varphi]$, is taken from AWN. Here $\xi \xrightarrow{\varphi} \zeta$ says that ζ is an extension of ξ, i.e. a valuation that agrees with ξ on all variables on which ξ is defined, and evaluates other variables occurring free in φ, such that the formula φ holds under ζ. All variables not free in φ and not evaluated by ξ are also not evaluated by ζ. Its negation $\xi \not\xrightarrow{\varphi}$ says

[3] Normally, a node is in its own transmission range. In that case the received chunk *ch* will be either the chunk $m{:}c$ it is transmitting itself, or <u>`conflict`</u> in case some other node within transmission range is transmitting as well.

that no such extension exists, and thus, that φ is false in the current state, no matter how we interpret the variables whose values are still undefined. If that is the case, the process $[\varphi]p$ will idle by performing the action $\textbf{wait}(ch)$.

2.2 A Language for Node Expressions

We model network nodes in the context of a (wireless) network by *node expressions* of the form

$$id\colon(\xi, P)\colon R\,.$$

Here $id \in \texttt{ID}$ is the *address* of the node, P is a sequential process expression with a valuation ξ, and $R \in \mathscr{P}(\texttt{ID})$ is the *range* of the node, defined as the set of nodes within transmission range of id. Unlike AWN, the process algebra does not offer a parallel operator for combining sequential processes; such an operator is not needed due to the nature of link layer protocols.

In the semantics of this layer it is crucial to handle frame collisions. The idea is that all chunks sent are recorded, together with the respective recipient. In case a node receives more than one chunk at a time, a conflict is raised, as it is impossible to send two or more messages via the same medium at the same time.

The formal semantics for node expressions, presented in Table 2, uses transition labels $\textbf{traffic}(\mathcal{T}, \mathcal{R})$, $id\colon\textbf{deliver}(d)$, $id\colon\textbf{newpkt}(d, id')$, $\textbf{connect}(id, id')$, $\textbf{disconnect}(id, id')$ and τ, with partial functions $\mathcal{T}, \mathcal{R}\colon \texttt{ID} \rightharpoonup \texttt{CHUNK}$, $id, id' \in \texttt{ID}$, and $d \in \texttt{DATA}$.

Table 2. Structural operational semantics for node expressions

$$\frac{P \xrightarrow{\textbf{wait}(\texttt{idle})} P'}{id\colon P\colon R \xrightarrow{\textbf{traffic}(\emptyset,\emptyset)} id\colon P'\colon R} \qquad \frac{P \xrightarrow{\textbf{transmit}(m:c,\texttt{idle})} P'}{id\colon P\colon R \xrightarrow{\textbf{traffic}(\{(r,\,m:c)\,|\,r\in R\},\emptyset)} id\colon P'\colon R}$$

$$\frac{P \xrightarrow{\textbf{wait}(ch)} P' \quad (ch \neq \texttt{idle})}{id\colon P\colon R \xrightarrow{\textbf{traffic}(\emptyset,\{(id,\,ch)\})} id\colon P'\colon R} \qquad \frac{P \xrightarrow{\textbf{transmit}(m:c,ch)} P' \quad (ch \neq \texttt{idle})}{id\colon P\colon R \xrightarrow{\textbf{traffic}(\{(r,\,m:c)\,|\,r\in R\},\{(id,\,ch)\})} id\colon P'\colon R}$$

$$\frac{P \xrightarrow{\textbf{deliver}(d)} P'}{id\colon P\colon R \xrightarrow{id\,:\,\textbf{deliver}(d)} id\colon P'\colon R} \qquad \frac{P \xrightarrow{\textbf{newpkt}(d,dest)} P'}{id\colon P\colon R \xrightarrow{id\,:\,\textbf{newpkt}(d,dest)} id\colon P'\colon R} \qquad \frac{P \xrightarrow{\tau} P'}{id\colon P\colon R \xrightarrow{\tau} id\colon P'\colon R}$$

$$id\colon P\colon R \xrightarrow{\textbf{connect}(id,id')} id\colon P\colon R \cup \{id'\} \qquad id\colon P\colon R \xrightarrow{\textbf{disconnect}(id,id')} id\colon P\colon R - \{id'\}$$

$$id\colon P\colon R \xrightarrow{\textbf{connect}(id',id)} id\colon P\colon R \cup \{id'\} \qquad id\colon P\colon R \xrightarrow{\textbf{disconnect}(id',id)} id\colon P\colon R - \{id'\}$$

$$\frac{id \notin \{id', id''\}}{id\colon P\colon R \xrightarrow{\textbf{connect}(id',id'')} id\colon P\colon R} \qquad \frac{id \notin \{id', id''\}}{id\colon P\colon R \xrightarrow{\textbf{disconnect}(id',id'')} id\colon P\colon R}$$

All time-consuming actions on process level ($\textbf{transmit}(m{:}c, ch)$ and $\textbf{wait}(ch)$) are transformed into an action $\textbf{traffic}(\mathcal{T}, \mathcal{R})$ on node level: the first argument

Table 3. Structural operational semantics for network expressions

$$\frac{M \xrightarrow{a} M'}{M\|N \xrightarrow{a} M'\|N} \qquad \frac{N \xrightarrow{a} N'}{M\|N \xrightarrow{a} M\|N'} \qquad \frac{M \xrightarrow{a} M'}{[M] \xrightarrow{a} [M']} \qquad \left(\forall a \in \left\{\begin{matrix}\tau,\, id\!:\!\mathbf{deliver}(d),\\ id\!:\!\mathbf{newpkt}(d, id),\end{matrix}\right\}\right)$$

$$\frac{M \xrightarrow{a} M' \quad N \xrightarrow{a} N'}{M\|N \xrightarrow{a} M'\|N'} \qquad \frac{M \xrightarrow{a} M'}{[M] \xrightarrow{a} [M']} \qquad \left(\forall a \in \left\{\begin{matrix}\mathbf{connect}(id, id'),\\ \mathbf{disconnect}(id, id')\end{matrix}\right\}\right)$$

$$\frac{M \xrightarrow{\mathbf{traffic}(\mathcal{T}_1,\mathcal{R}_1)} M' \quad N \xrightarrow{\mathbf{traffic}(\mathcal{T}_2,\mathcal{R}_2)} N'}{M\|N \xrightarrow{\mathbf{traffic}(\mathcal{T}_1 \uplus \mathcal{T}_2,\mathcal{R}_1 \uplus \mathcal{R}_2)} M'\|N'} \qquad \frac{M \xrightarrow{\mathbf{traffic}(\mathcal{R},\mathcal{R})} M'}{[M] \xrightarrow{\mathbf{tick}} [M']}$$

$\mathcal{T}$ maps *dest* to $m{:}c$ if and only if the chunk $m{:}c$ is transmitted to *dest*. The second argument $\mathcal{R}$ maps *id* to $m{:}c$ if and only if the chunk $m{:}c$ is received on process level at node *id*. For the sos-rules of Table 2 we use the set-theoretic presentation of partial functions. The two rules for **wait** set $\mathcal{T} := \emptyset$, as no chunks are transmitted; the rules for **transmit** allow a transmitted chunk $m{:}c$ to travel to all nodes within transmission range: $\mathcal{T} := \{(r, m{:}c) \mid r \in R\}$. In case that during the transmission or waiting no chunk is received ($ch = \underline{\texttt{idle}}$) we set $\mathcal{R} = \emptyset$; otherwise $\mathcal{R} = \{(id, ch)\}$, indicating that chunk *ch* is received by node *id*.

The actions id: **newpkt**$(d, dest)$ and id: **deliver**(d) as well as the internal actions τ are simply inherited by node expressions from the processes that run on these nodes.

The remaining rules of Table 2 model the mobility aspect of wireless networks; the rules are taken straight from AWN [12,13]. We allow actions **connect**(id, id') and **disconnect**(id, id') for $id, id' \in \texttt{ID}$ modelling a change in network topology. These actions can be thought of as occurring nondeterministically, or as actions instigated by the environment of the modelled network protocol. In this formalisation node *id'* is in the range of node *id*, meaning that *id'* can receive messages sent by *id*, if and only if *id* is in the range of *id'*. To break this symmetry, one just skips the last four rules of Table 2 and replaces the synchronisation rules for **connect** and **disconnect** in Table 3 by interleaving rules (like the ones for **deliver**, **newpkt** and τ) [12]. For some applications a wired or non-mobile network need to be considered. In such cases the last six rules of Table 2 are dropped.

Whether a node $id{:}P{:}R$ receives its own transmissions depends on whether $id \in R$. Only if $id \in R$ our process algebra will disallow the transmission from and to a single node *id* at the same time, yielding a $\underline{\texttt{conflict}}$.

2.3 A Language for Networks

A *partial network* is modelled by a *parallel composition* $\|$ of node expressions, one for every node in the network. A *complete network* is a partial network within an *encapsulation operator* $[\_]$, which limits the communication between network nodes and the outside world to the receipt and delivery of data packets to and from the network layer.

The syntax of networks is described by the following grammar:

$$N ::= [M^T_T] \qquad M^T_{S_1 \cup S_2} ::= M^T_{S_1} \| M^T_{S_2} \qquad M^T_{\{id\}} ::= id\!:\!(\xi, P)\!:\!R \ ,$$

with $\{id\} \cup R \subseteq T \subseteq \texttt{ID}$. Here M^T_S models a partial network describing the behaviour of all nodes $id \in S$. The set T contains the identifiers of all nodes that are part of the complete network. This grammar guarantees that node identifiers of node expressions—the first component of $id\!:\!P\!:\!R$—are unique.

The operational semantics of network expressions is given in Table 3. Internal actions τ as well as the actions id:**deliver**(d) and id:**newpkt**(d,id) are interleaved in the parallel composition of nodes that makes up a network, and then lifted to encapsulated networks (Line 1 of Table 3).

Actions **traffic** and (**dis**)**connect** are synchronised. The rule for synchronising the action **traffic** (Line 3), the only action that consumes time on the network layer, uses the union $\uplus$ of partial functions. It is formally defined as

$$(\mathcal{R}_1 \uplus \mathcal{R}_2)(id) := \begin{cases} \underline{\texttt{conflict}} & \text{if } id \in \texttt{dom}(\mathcal{R}_1) \cap \texttt{dom}(\mathcal{R}_2) \\ \mathcal{R}_1(id) & \text{if } id \in \texttt{dom}(\mathcal{R}_1) - \texttt{dom}(\mathcal{R}_2) \\ \mathcal{R}_2(id) & \text{if } id \in \texttt{dom}(\mathcal{R}_2) - \texttt{dom}(\mathcal{R}_1) \ . \end{cases}$$

The synchronisation of the sets $\mathcal{R}_i$ and $\mathcal{T}_i$ has the following intuition: if a node identifier $id \in \texttt{ID}$ is in both $\texttt{dom}(\mathcal{T}_1)$ and $\texttt{dom}(\mathcal{T}_2)$ then there exist two nodes that transmit to node id at the same time, and therefore a frame collision occurs. In our algebra this is modelled by the special chunk $\underline{\texttt{conflict}}$. The sos rules of Tables 2 and 3 guarantee that there cannot be collisions within the set of received chunks $\mathcal{R}$. The reason is that each node merely contributes to $\mathcal{R}$ a chunk for itself; it can be the chunk $\underline{\texttt{conflict}}$ though. Therefore we could have written $\mathcal{R}_1 \cup \mathcal{R}_2$ instead of $\mathcal{R}_1 \uplus \mathcal{R}_2$ in the sixth rule of Table 3.

The last rule propagates a **traffic**$(\mathcal{T}, \mathcal{R})$-action of a partial network M to a complete network $[M]$. By then $\mathcal{T}$ consists of all chunks (after collision detection) that are being transmitted by any member in the network, and $\mathcal{R}$ consists of all chunks that are received. The condition $\mathcal{R} = \mathcal{T}$ determines the content of the messages in $\mathcal{R}$. The **traffic**$(\mathcal{T}, \mathcal{R})$-actions become internal at this level, as they cannot be steered by the outside world; all that is left is a time-step **tick**.

2.4 Results on the Process Algebra

As for the process algebra T-AWN [2], but with a slightly simplified proof, one can show that our processes have no *time deadlocks*:

Theorem 2.1. *A complete network N in our process algebra always admits a transition, independently of the outside environment, i.e. $\forall N, \exists a$ such that $N \xrightarrow{a}$ and $a \notin \{$**connect**(id, id'), **disconnect**(id, id'), id:$\texttt{newpkt}(d, dest)\}$.*
More precisely, either $N \xrightarrow{\textbf{tick}}$, or $N \xrightarrow{id:\,\textbf{deliver}(d)}$ or $N \xrightarrow{\tau}$.

The following results (statements and proofs) are very similar to the results about the process algebra AWN, as presented in [13]. A rich body of foundational meta theory of process algebra allows the transfer of the results to our setting, without too much overhead work.

Identical to AWN and its timed version T-AWN, our process algebra admits a translation into one without data structures (although we cannot describe the target algebra without using data structures). The idea is to replace any variable by all possible values it can take. The target algebra differs from the original only on the level of sequential processes; the subsequent layers are unchanged. The construction closely follows the one given in the appendix of [2]. The inductive definition contains the rules

$\mathscr{T}_\xi(\textbf{deliver}(\mathit{data}).P) = \textbf{deliver}(\xi(\mathit{data})).\mathscr{T}_\xi(P)$ and

$\mathscr{T}_\xi([\![\mathtt{var} := \mathit{exp}]\!]P) = \tau.\mathscr{T}_{\xi[\mathtt{var} := \xi(\mathit{exp})]}(P)$.

Most other rules require extra operators that keep track of the passage of time and the evolution of other internal variables. The resulting process algebra has a structural operational semantics in the (infinitary) *de Simone* format, generating the same transition system—up to strong bisimilarity, $\leftrightarrows$—as the original. It follows that $\leftrightarrows$, and many other semantic equivalences, are congruences on our language [23].

Theorem 2.2. *Strong bisimilarity is a congruence for all operators of our language.*

This is a deep result that usually takes many pages to establish (e.g. [25]). Here we get it directly from the existing theory on structural operational semantics, as a result of carefully designing our language within the disciplined framework described by de Simone [23]. □

Theorem 2.3. *The operator* $\|$ *is associative and commutative, up to* $\leftrightarrows$.

Proof. The operational rules for this operator fits a format presented in [6], guaranteeing associativity up to $\leftrightarrows$. The *ASSOC*-de Simone format of [6] applies to all transition system specifications (TSSs) in de Simone format, and allows 7 different types of rules (named 1–7) for the operators in question. Our TSS is in de Simone format; the four rules for $\|$ of Table 3 are of types 1, 2 and 7, respectively. To be precise, it has rules 1_a and 2_a for $a \in \{\tau, \mathit{id}\colon \textbf{deliver}(d), \mathit{id}\colon \textbf{newpkt}(d, \mathit{dest})\}$, rules $7_{(a,b)}$ for

$$(a,b) \in \{(\textbf{traffic}(\mathcal{T}_1,\mathcal{R}_1), \textbf{traffic}(\mathcal{T}_2,\mathcal{R}_2)) \mid \mathcal{R}_1,\mathcal{R}_2,\mathcal{T}_1,\mathcal{T}_2 \in \mathtt{ID} \rightharpoonup \mathtt{CHUNK}\}$$

and rules $7_{(c,c)}$ for $c \in \{\textbf{connect}(\mathit{id},\mathit{id}'), \textbf{disconnect}(\mathit{id},\mathit{id}') \mid \mathit{id},\mathit{id}' \in \mathtt{ID}\}$. Moreover, the partial *communication function* $\gamma : \mathrm{Act} \times \mathrm{Act} \rightharpoonup \mathrm{Act}$ is given by $\gamma(\textbf{traffic}(\mathcal{T}_1,\mathcal{R}_1), \textbf{traffic}(\mathcal{T}_2,\mathcal{R}_2)) = \textbf{traffic}(\mathcal{T}_1 \uplus \mathcal{T}_2, \mathcal{R}_1 \uplus \mathcal{R}_2)$ and $\gamma(c,c) = c$. The main result of [6] is that an operator is guaranteed to be associative, provided that γ is associative and six conditions are fulfilled. In the absence of rules of types 3, 4, 5 and 6, five of these conditions are trivially fulfilled, and the remaining one reduces to

$$7_{(a,b)} \Rightarrow (1_a \Leftrightarrow 2_b) \wedge (2_a \Leftrightarrow 2_{\gamma(a,b)}) \wedge (1_b \Leftrightarrow 1_{\gamma(a,b)}).$$

Here 1_a says that rule 1_a is present, etc. This condition is trivially met for $\|$ as there neither exists a rule of the form $1_{\mathbf{traffic}(\mathcal{T},\mathcal{R})}$ nor of the form $2_{\mathbf{traffic}(\mathcal{T},\mathcal{R})}$, or 1_c, 2_c with c as above. As on **traffic** actions γ is basically the union of partial functions ($\uplus$), where a collision in domains is indicated by an error $\underline{\texttt{conflict}}$, it is straightforward to prove associativity of γ.

Commutativity of $\|$ follows by symmetry of the sos rules. □

3 An Algebra for Link Layer Protocols

We now introduce ALL, the *Algebra for Link Layer protocols.* It is obtained from the process algebra presented in the previous section by the addition of a probabilistic choice operator $\bigoplus_0^n$. As a consequence, the semantics of the algebra is no longer a labelled transition system, but a *probabilistic labelled transition system* (pLTS) [8]. This is a triple $(S, \mathrm{Act}, \rightarrow)$, where

(i) S is a set of states
(ii) Act is a set of actions
(iii) $\rightarrow \subseteq S \times \mathrm{Act} \times \mathcal{D}(S)$, where $\mathcal{D}(S)$ is the set of all (discrete) probability distributions over S: functions $\Delta : S \rightarrow [0,1]$ with $\sum_{s\in S} \Delta(s) = 1$.

As with LTSs, we usually write $s \xrightarrow{\alpha} \Delta$ instead of $(s, \alpha, \Delta) \in \rightarrow$. The *point distribution* δ_s, for $s \in S$, is the distribution with $\delta_s(s) = 1$. We simply write $s \xrightarrow{\alpha} t$ for $s \xrightarrow{\alpha} \delta_t$. An LTS may be viewed as a degenerate pLTS, in which only point distributions occur. For a uniform distribution over $s_0, \ldots, s_n \in S$ we write $\mathcal{U}_{i=0}^n s_i$. The pLTS associated to ALL takes S to be the disjoint union of the pairs ξ, P, with P a sequential process expression, and the network expressions. Act is the collection of transition labels, and $\rightarrow$ consists of the transitions derivable from the structural operational semantics of the language.

Rules (1)–(6), (9), (11) and (12) of Table 1 are adopted to ALL unchanged, whereas in Rules (7), (8) and (10) the state ζ, P' (or ζ, Q') is replaced by an arbitrary distribution Δ. Add to those the following rule for the probabilistic choice operator:

$$\xi, \bigoplus_{\mathtt{i}=0}^{n} P \xrightarrow{\tau} \mathcal{U}_{i=0}^{\xi(n)}\ \xi[\mathtt{i} := i]\ , P$$

Here the data variable i may occur in P. The rules of Tables 2 and 3 are adapted to ALL unchanged, except that P', M' and N' are now replaced by arbitrary distributions over sequential processes and network expressions, respectively. Here we adapt the convention that a unary or binary operation on states lifts to distributions in the standard manner. For example, if Δ is a distribution over sequential processes, $id \in \mathtt{ID}$ and $R \subseteq \mathtt{ID}$, then $id{:}\Delta{:}R$ describes the distribution over node expressions that only has probability mass on nodes with address id and range R, and for which the probability of $id{:}P{:}R$ is $\Delta(P)$. Likewise, if Δ and Θ are distributions over network expressions, then $\Delta\|\Theta$ is the distribution over network expressions of the form $M\|N$, where $(\Delta\|\Theta)(M\|N) = \Delta(M)\cdot\Theta(N)$.

4 Formalising Liveness Properties of Link Layer Protocols

Link layer protocols communicate with the network layer through the actions $id{:}\,\mathbf{newpkt}(d, dest)$ and $id{:}\,\mathbf{deliver}(d)$. The typical liveness property expected of a link layer protocol is that if the network layer at node *id* injects a data packet *d* for delivery at destination *dest* then this packet is delivered eventually. In terms of our process algebra, this says that every execution of the action $id{:}\,\mathbf{newpkt}(d, dest)$ ought to be followed by the action $dest{:}\,\mathbf{deliver}(d)$. This property can be formalised in Linear-time Temporal Logic [22] as

$$\mathbf{G}\big(id{:}\,\mathbf{newpkt}(d, dest) \Rightarrow \mathbf{F}(dest{:}\,\mathbf{deliver}(d))\big) \tag{1}$$

for any $id, dest \in \mathtt{ID}$ and $d \in \mathtt{DATA}$. This formula has the shape $\mathbf{G}\big(\phi^{pre} \Rightarrow \mathbf{F}\phi^{post}\big)$, and is called an *eventuality property* in [22]. It says that whenever we reach a state in which the precondition ϕ^{pre} is satisfied, this state will surely be followed by a state were the postcondition ϕ^{post} holds. In [7,13] it is explained how action occurrences can be seen or encoded as state-based conditions. Here we will not define how to interpret general LTL-formula in pLTSs, but below we do this for eventuality properties with specific choices of ϕ^{pre} and ϕ^{post}.

Formula (1) is too strong and does not hold in general: in case the nodes *id* and *dest* are not within transmission range of each other, the delivery of messages from *id* to *dest* is doomed to fail. We need to postulate two side conditions to make this liveness property plausible. Firstly, when the request to deliver the message comes in, *id* needs to be connected to *dest*. We introduce the predicate $\mathbf{cntd}(id, dest)$ to express this, and hence take ϕ^{pre} to be $\mathbf{cntd}(id, dest) \wedge id{:}\,\mathbf{newpkt}(d, dest)$. Secondly, we assume that the link between *id* and *dest* does not break until the message is delivered. As remarked in [13], such a side condition can be formalised by taking ϕ^{post} to be $dest{:}\,\mathbf{deliver}(d) \vee \mathbf{disconnect}(id, dest)$. Thus the liveness property we are after is

$$\begin{array}{c}\mathbf{G}\big(\mathbf{cntd}(id, dest) \wedge id{:}\,\mathbf{newpkt}(d, dest) \Rightarrow \\ \mathbf{F}(dest{:}\,\mathbf{deliver}(d) \vee \mathbf{disconnect}(id, dest) \vee \mathbf{disconnect}(dest, id))\big)\end{array} \tag{2}$$

We now define the validity of eventuality properties $\mathbf{G}\big(\phi^{pre} \Rightarrow \mathbf{F}\phi^{post}\big)$. Here ϕ^{pre} and ϕ^{post} denote sets of transitions and actions, respectively, and hold if one of the transitions or actions in the set occurs. In (2), ϕ^{pre} denotes the transitions with label $id{:}\,\mathbf{newpkt}(d, dest)$ that occur when the side condition $\mathbf{cntd}(id, dest)$ is met, whereas $\phi^{post} = \{dest{:}\,\mathbf{deliver}(d), \mathbf{disconnect}(id, dest), \mathbf{disconnect}(dest, id)\}$ is a set of actions.

A *path* in a pLTS $(S, \mathrm{Act}, \rightarrow)$ is an alternating sequence $s_0, \alpha_1, s_1, \alpha_2, \ldots$ of states and actions, starting with a state and either being infinite or ending with a state, such that there is a transition $s_i \xrightarrow{\alpha_{i+1}} \Delta_{i+1}$ with $\Delta_{i+1}(s_{i+1}) > 0$ for each i. The path is *rooted* if it starts with a state marked as 'initial', and *complete* if either it is infinite, or there is no transition starting from its last state. A state or transition is *reachable* if it occurs in a rooted path.

In a pLTS with an initial state, an eventually formula $\mathbf{G}(\phi^{pre} \Rightarrow \mathbf{F}\phi^{post})$, with ϕ^{pre} and ϕ^{post} denoting sets of transitions and actions, *holds outright* if all complete paths starting with a reachable transition from ϕ^{pre} contain a transition with a label from ϕ^{post}.

Definitions 3 and 5 in [9] define the set of probabilities that a pLTS with an initial state will ever execute the action ω. One obtains a set of probabilities rather than a single probability due to the possibility of nondeterministic choice. This definition generalises to *sets* of actions ϕ^{post} (seen as disjunctions) by first renaming all actions in such a set into ω. It also generalises trivially to pLTSs with an *initial transition*. For t a transition in a pLTS, let $Prob(t, \phi^{post})$ be the infimum of the set of probabilities that the pLTS in which t is taken to be the initial transition will ever execute ϕ^{post}. Now in a pLTS with an initial state, an eventually formula $\mathbf{G}(\phi^{pre} \Rightarrow \mathbf{F}\phi^{post})$ *holds with probability at least* p if for all reachable transitions t in ϕ^{pre} we have $Prob(t, \phi^{post}) \geq p$.

Possible correctness criteria for link layer protocols are that the liveness property (2) either holds outright, holds with probability 1, or at least holds with probability p for a sufficiently high value of p.

Sometimes we are content to establish that (2) holds under the additional assumptions that the network is stable until our packet is delivered, meaning that no links between any nodes are broken or established, and/or that the network layer refrains from injecting more packets. This is modelled by taking

$$\phi^{post} = \{dest\colon \mathbf{deliver}(d), \mathbf{disconnect}(*,*), \mathbf{connect}(*,*), \mathbf{newpkt}(*,*)\}. \quad (3)$$

We will refer to this version of (2) as the *weak packet delivery* property. *Packet delivery* is the strengthening without **newpkt**$(*,*)$ in (3), i.e. not assuming that the network layer refrains from injecting more packets.

5 Modelling and Analysing the CSMA/CA Protocol

In this section we model two versions of the CSMA/CA protocol, using the process algebra ALL. Moreover, we briefly discuss some results we obtained while analysing these protocols.

The *Carrier-Sense Multiple Access* (CSMA) protocol is a media access control (MAC) protocol in which a node verifies the absence of other traffic before transmitting on a shared transmission medium. If a carrier is sensed, the node waits for the transmission in progress to end before initiating its own transmission. Using CSMA, multiple nodes may, in turn, send and receive on the same medium. Transmissions by one node are generally received by all other nodes connected to the medium.

The CSMA protocol with Collision Avoidance (CSMA/CA) [17,19][4] improves the performance of CSMA. If the transmission medium is sensed busy

[4] The primary medium access control (MAC) technique of IEEE 802.11 [19] is called *distributed coordination function* (DCF), which is a CSMA/CA protocol.

before transmission then the transmission is deferred for a *random* time interval. This interval reduces the likelihood that two or more nodes waiting to transmit will simultaneously begin transmission upon termination of the detected transmission. CSMA/CA is used, for example, in Wi-Fi.

It is well known that CSMA/CA suffers from the *hidden station problem* (see Sect. 5.2). To overcome this problem, CSMA/CA is often supplemented by the request-to-send/clear-to-send (RTS/CTS) handshaking [19]. This mechanism is known as the IEEE 802.11 RTS/CTS exchange, or *virtual carrier sensing.* While this extension reduces the amount of collisions, wireless 802.11 implementations do not typically implement RTS/CTS for all transmissions because the transmission overhead is too great for small data transfers.

We use the process algebra ALL to model both the CSMA/CA without and with virtual carrier sensing.

5.1 A Formal Model for CSMA/CA

Our formal specification of CSMA/CA consists of four short processes written in ALL. It is precise and free of ambiguities—one of the many advantages formal methods provide, in contrast to specifications written in English prose.

The syntax of ALL is intended to look like pseudo code, and it is our belief that the specification can easily be read and understood by software engineers, who may or may not have experience with process algebra.

As the underlying data structure of our model is straightforward, we do not present it explicitly, but introduce it while describing the different processes.

The basic process CSMA, depicted in Process 1, is the protocol's entry point.

Process 1. The Basic Routine

```
CSMA(id) ≝
1. newpkt(data,dest). INIT(id,0,dataframe(data,id,dest))
2. + [NEW(dataframe(data,src,id))] deliver(data) .
3.   (
4.     ⟦timeout := now + sifs⟧ [now ≥ timeout]
5.     transmit(ackframe(src)) . CSMA(id)
6.   )
```

This process maintains a single data variable `id` in which it stores its own identity. It waits until either it receives a request from the network layer to transmit a packet `data` to destination `dest`, or it receives from another node in the network a CSMA message (data frame) destined for itself.

In case of a newly injected data packet (Line 1), the process `INIT` is called; this process (described below) initiates the sending of the message via the medium. When passing the message on to `INIT` we use a function `dataframe` : $\mathtt{DATA} \times \mathtt{ID} \times \mathtt{ID} \rightarrow \mathtt{MSG}$ that generates a message in a format used by the protocol: next to the header fields (from which we abstract) it contains the injected `data` as well as the designated receiver `dest` and the sender `id`—the current node.

In case of an incoming dataframe destined for this node (the third argument carrying the destination is id) (Line 2)—any other incoming message is ignored by this process—the data is handed over to the network layer (**deliver**(data)) followed by the transmission of an acknowledgement back to the sender of the message (src). CSMA/CA requires a short period of idling medium before sending the acknowledgement: in [19] this interval is called *short interframe space* (sifs). The process waits until the time of the interframe spacing has passed, and then transmits the acknowledgement. The acknowledgement sent is not always received by src, e.g. due to data collision; therefore src could send the same message again (see Process 4) and id could deliver the same data to the network layer again.

Process 2. Protocol Initialisation

```
INIT(id,tries,dframe) ≝
 1. [tries ≤ max_retransmit]
 2.    ⟦cw := cwmin × 2^tries⟧
 3.    ⊕_{b=0}^{cw−1} CCA(id,b,tries,dframe)     /* choose a backoff from {0,...,cw−1} */
 4. + [tries > max_retransmit]
 5.    deliver(channel_access_failure) . CSMA(id)
```

The process INIT (Process 2) initiates the sending of a message via the medium. Next to the variable id, which is maintained by all processes, it maintains the variable tries and dframe: tries stores the number of attempts already made to send message dframe. When the process is called the first time for a message dframe (Line 1 of Process 1) the value of tries is 0.

The constant max_retransmit specifies the maximum number of attempts the protocol is allowed to retransmit the same message. If the limit is not yet reached (Line 1) the message dframe is sent. As mentioned above, CSMA/CA defers messages for a *random* time interval to avoid collision. The node must start transmission within the contention window cw, a.k.a. backoff time. cw is calculated in Line 2; it increases exponentially.[5] After cw is determined, the process CCA is called, which performs the actual **transmit**-action. In case the maximum number of retransmits is reached (Line 4), the process notifies the network layer and restarts the protocol, awaiting new instructions from the application layer, or a new incoming message.

Process 3 takes care of the actual transmission of dframe. However, the protocol has a complicated procedure when to send this message.

First, the process senses the medium and awaits the point in time when it is idle (Line 6). In case, before this happens, it receives from another node in the network a CSMA message destined for itself (Line 1), this message is handled just as in Process 1, except that after acknowledging this message the protocol returns to Process 3.

[5] A typical value for cwmin is 16; it must satisfy cwmin > 0.

Process 3. Clear Channel Assessment With Physical Carrier Sense

```
CCA(id,b,tries,dframe) ≝
 1. [NEW(dataframe(data,src,id))] deliver(data) .
 2.   (
 3.     ⟦timeout := now + sifs⟧ [now ≥ timeout]
 4.     transmit(ackframe(src)) . CCA(id,b,tries,dframe)
 5.   )
 6. + [IDLE]
 7.   ⟦timeout:=now+difs⟧        /* start wait for duration difs */
 8.   (
 9.     [¬IDLE] CCA(id,b,tries,dframe)
10.     + [IDLE ∧ now ≥ timeout]
11.       ⟦timeout := now + b⟧
12.       (
13.         [¬IDLE]      /* busy during backoff time */
14.           ⟦b := timeout − now⟧ CCA(id,b,tries,dframe)
15.         + [IDLE ∧ now ≥ timeout]      /* idle for backoff time */
16.           transmit(dframe) .
17.           ACKRECV(id,tries,now+max_ack_wait,dframe)
18.       )
19.   )
```

To guarantee a gap between messages sent via the medium, CSMA/CA (as well as other protocols) specifies the *distributed (coordination function) interframe space* (**difs** ∈ TIME), which is usually small,[6] but larger than **sifs**, so that acknowledgements get priority over new data frames. When the medium becomes busy during the interframe space, another node started transmitting and the process goes back to listening to the medium (Line 9). In case nothing happens on the medium and the end of the interframe space is reached (Line 10), the process determines the actual time to start transmitting the message, taking the backoff time b into account (Line 11). If the medium is idle for the entire backoff period (Line 15), the message is transmitted (Line 16), and the process calls the process ACKRECV that will await an acknowledgement from the recipient of dframe (Line 17); the third argument specifies the maximum time the process should wait for such an acknowledgement. (As mentioned before an acknowledgement may never arrive.) If another node transmits on the medium during the backoff period, the protocol restarts the routine (Lines 13 and 14), with an adjusted backoff value b—the process already started waiting and should not be punished when the waiting is restarted; this update guarantees fairness of the protocol.

The process awaiting an acknowledgement (Process 4) is straightforward. It waits until either it receives a CSMA message destined for itself (Line 1), or it receives an acknowledgement (Line 6), or it has waited for this acknowledgement as long as it is going to (Line 8).

[6] Recommended values for the constant **difs** are given in [19].

In the first case, the message is handled just as in Process 1, except that after acknowledging this message the protocol returns to Process 4. In the second case the network layer is informed that the sending of `dframe` was successful and the process loops back to Process 1 (Line 7). Line 8 describes the situation where no acknowledgement message arrives and the process times out. Here CSMA/CA retries to send the message; the counter `tries` is incremented.

Process 4. Receiving an ACK

```
ACKRECV(id,tries,acktimeout,dframe) ≝
1. [NEW(dataframe(data,src,id))] deliver(data) .
2.   (
3.      ⟦timeout := now + sifs⟧ [now ≥ timeout]
4.      transmit(ackframe(src)) . ACKRECV(id,tries,acktimeout,dframe)
5.   )
6. + [NEW(ackframe(id))]      /* acknowledgement received */
7.   deliver(success) . CSMA(id)
8. + [now ≥ acktimeout] INIT(id,tries+1,dframe)
```

5.2 The Hidden Station Problem

As mentioned in the introduction to this section, CSMA/CA suffers from the hidden station problem. This refers to the situation where two nodes A and C are not within transmission range of each other, while a node B is in range of both. In this situation C may be transmitting to B, but A is not able to sense this, and thus may start a transmission to B at roughly the same time, leading to data collisions at B.

While CSMA/CA is not able to avoid such collisions as a whole—it is always possible that two (or more) nodes hidden from each other happen to (randomly) choose the same backoff time to send messages—it is the exponential growth of the backoff slots that makes the problem less pressing in the long run, as the following theorem shows.

Theorem 5.1. If max_retransmit$=\infty$ then weak packet delivery holds with probability 1.

Proof sketch. Since the number of messages that nodes transmit is bounded, and all nodes select random times to start transmitting out of an increasing longer time span, with probability 1 each message will eventually go through. □

In practice, max_retransmit is set to a value that is not high enough to approximate the idea behind the above proof. In fact, the transmission time of a single message may be larger than the maximal backoff period allowed. For this reason the hidden station problem does occur when running the CSMA/CA protocol, as studies have shown [5]. Nevertheless, the above analysis still shows that link layer protocols can be formally analysed by process algebra in general, and ALL in particular.

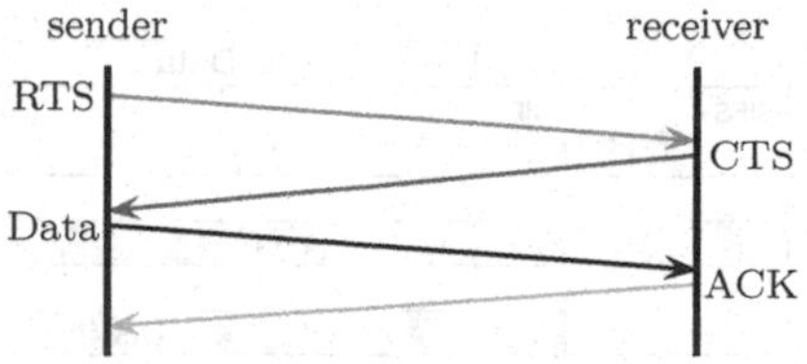

Fig. 1. RTS/CTS exchange

5.3 A Formal Model for CSMA/CA with Virtual Carrier Sensing

To overcome the hidden station problem the usage of a request-to-send/clear-to-send (RTS/CTS) handshaking [19] mechanism is available. This mechanism is also known as *virtual carrier sensing.* The exchange of RTS/CTS messages happens just before the actual data is sent, see Fig. 1. The mechanism serves two purposes: (a) As the RTS and CTS messages are very short—they only contain two node identifiers as well as a natural number indicating the time it will take to send the actual `data` (plus overhead)—the likelihood of a collision is reduced. (b) While the handshaking does not help with solving the hidden station problem for the RTS message itself, it avoids the problem for the sending of `data`. The reason is that a hidden node, which could interfere with the sending of `data` will receive the CTS message from the designated recipient of `data`, and the hidden node will remain silent until the `data` has been sent.

As for the CSMA/CA protocol we have modelled this extension in ALL, based on the model of CSMA/CA we presented earlier.

Our extended model uses two functions to generate `rts` and `cts` messages, respectively. The signature of both is $\mathtt{ID} \times \mathtt{ID} \times \mathtt{TIME} \rightarrow \mathtt{MSG}$. The first argument carries the sender (source) of the message, the second the indented destination, and the third argument a duration (time period) of silence that is requested/granted. For example, before the message `rts(src,dest,d)` is transmitted, the time period `d` is calculated by
The calculation is straightforward as it follows the protocol logic and determines the amount of time needed until the acknowledgement would be received (see Fig. 2). After the `rts` message has been received the medium should be idle for the interframe space $\underline{\mathtt{sifs}}$; then a `cts` message is sent back, which takes time $\underline{\mathtt{dur\_cts}}$; then another interframe space is needed, followed by the actual transmission of the message—the sending will take `dur(dataframe(data,id,dest))` time units; after the message is received (hopefully) another interframe space is required before the acknowledgement is sent back.

$$[\![\mathtt{d} := \underline{\mathtt{sifs}} + \underline{\mathtt{dur\_cts}} + \underline{\mathtt{sifs}} + \mathtt{dur(dataframe(data,id,dest))} + \underline{\mathtt{sifs}} + \underline{\mathtt{dur\_ack}}]\!] \,.$$

Process 2 remains essentially unchanged; it is merely equipped with the destination `dest` of the message that needs to be transmitted, and an additional timed variable $\mathtt{nav} \in \mathtt{TIME}$. These variables are not used in this process, but required later on. Variable `nav` holds the point in time until the process should

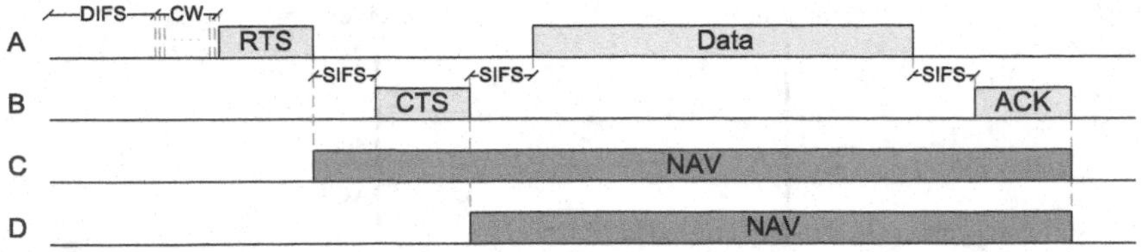

Fig. 2. The use of virtual channel sensing using CSMA/CA [3]

not transmit any `rts` or `cts` message. This period of silence is necessary as the node figures out that until time `nav` another node will transmit message(s).[7]

Process 5 is the modified version of Process 1. Identical to Process 1 it awaits an instruction from the network layer, or an incoming CSMA message destined for itself. Lines 1–3 are identical to Process 1. Lines 4–11 handle the two new message types. In case an `rts` message `rts(src,dest,d)` is received that is intended for another recipient ($\texttt{dest} \neq \texttt{id}$) the node concludes that another node wants to use the medium for the amount of `d` time units; the process updates the variable `nav` if needed, indicating the period the node should remain silent, by taking the maximum of the current value of `nav`, and `now+d`, the point in time until the sender `src` of the `rts` message requires the medium. The same behaviour occurs if a `cts` message is received that is not intended for the node itself (Line 4). If the incoming message is an `rts` message intended for the node itself (Line 6) by default the node answers with a clear-to-send message back to the sender (Line 9). However, when the receiver of the `rts` has knowledge about other nodes requiring the medium ($\texttt{now} \leq \texttt{nav}$), a clear-to-send cannot be granted, and the request is dropped (Line 6). Similar to the sending of an acknowledgement (Line 2), the process waits for the short interframe space ($\underline{\texttt{sifs}}$) before sending the CTS (Line 6). Line 8 handles the case where the medium becomes busy ($\neg$IDLE) during this period; also here a clear-to-send cannot be granted, and the request is dropped.[8] Only when the medium stays idle during the entire interframe space the node `id` can inform the source of the `rts` message that the medium is clear to send; the `cts` is transmitted in Line 9. The time a receiver of this message has to be silent is adjusted by deducting the time elapsed before this happens. In Line 10 the process resets `nav` to remind itself not to issue any `rts` message until the present exchange has been completed.[9]

[7] After a successful RTS/CTS exchange, communicating nodes proceed with transmitting the data and an acknowledgement regardless of the value of `nav`.

[8] The condition $\texttt{now} > \texttt{timeout}-\underline{\texttt{sifs}}$ prevents the process from dropping the request in the very first time slice that `CSMA` is running. Here the medium counts as busy, but only because we have just received an `rts` message.

[9] A case NEW(`cts(src,dest,d)`) $\wedge$ $\texttt{dest} = \texttt{id}$ is not required as a `cts` message is only expected in case an `rts` was sent, and hence handled in process `RTSREACT`.

Process 5. The Basic Routine (RTS/CTS)

```
CSMA(id,nav) ≝
newpkt(data,dest). INIT(id,dest,0,dataframe(data,id,dest),nav)
+ [NEW(dataframe(data,src,id))] deliver(data) . ⟦timeout := now + sifs⟧
  [now ≥ timeout] transmit(ackframe(src)) . CSMA(id,nav)
+ [(NEW(rts(src,dest,d)) ∨ NEW(cts(src,dest,d))) ∧ dest ≠ id ∧ nav < now+d]
  ⟦nav := now+d⟧ CSMA(id, nav)
+ [NEW(rts(src,id,d)) ∧ now > nav] ⟦timeout := now + sifs⟧
  (
    [¬IDLE ∧ now > timeout−sifs] CSMA(id,nav)
    + [IDLE ∧ now ≥ timeout] transmit(cts(id,src,d−dur_cts−sifs)) .
      ⟦nav := now+d−dur_cts−sifs⟧ CSMA(id, nav)
  )
```

Process 6. Clear Channel Assessment With Virtual Carrier Sense

```
CCA(id,dest,b,tries,dframe,nav) ≝
1.  [NEW(dataframe(data,src,id))] deliver(data) . ⟦timeout := now + sifs⟧
2.    [now ≥ timeout] transmit(ackframe(src)) . CCA(id,dest,b,tries,dframe,nav)
3.  + [(NEW(rts(src,dest,d)) ∨ NEW(cts(src,dest,d))) ∧ dest ≠ id ∧ nav < now+d]
4.    ⟦nav := now+d⟧ CCA(id,dest,b,tries,dframe,nav)
5.  + [NEW(rts(src,id,d)) ∧ now > nav] ⟦timeout := now + sifs⟧
6.    (
7.      [¬IDLE ∧ now > timeout−sifs] CCA(id,dest,b,tries,dframe,nav)
8.      + [IDLE ∧ now ≥ timeout] transmit(cts(id,src,d−dur_cts−sifs)) .
9.        ⟦nav := now+d−dur_cts−sifs⟧ CCA(id,dest,b,tries,dframe,nav)
10.   )
11. + [IDLE ∧ now > nav]
12.   ⟦timeout:=now+difs⟧
13.   (
14.     [¬IDLE] CCA(id,dest,b,tries,dframe,nav)
15.     + [IDLE ∧ now ≥ timeout]
16.       ⟦timeout := now + b⟧
17.       (
18.         [¬IDLE]      /* busy during backoff time */
19.           ⟦b := timeout − now⟧ CCA(id,dest,b,tries,dframe,nav)
20.         + [IDLE ∧ now ≥ timeout]      /* idle for backoff time */
21.           ⟦d := sifs + dur_cts + sifs + dur(dframe) + sifs + dur_ack⟧
22.           transmit(rts(id,dest,d)) .
23.           CTSRECV(id,dest,tries,now + max_cts_wait,dframe,nav)
24.       )
25.   )
```

Process 6 is the modified version of Process 3. The goal of this process is to send an **rts** message (Line 22). Before it can start its work, it waits until the medium is idle, and any time it is required to be silent has elapsed (Line 11).

Until this happens incoming data frames, rts or cts messages are treated just as in Process 5: Lines 1–10 copy Lines 2–11 of Process 5, except that afterwards the process returns to itself. Then Lines 12–20 are copied from Lines 7–15 from Process 3. Line 21 calculates the time other nodes ought to keep silent when receiving the rts message, and Line 23 passes control to the process CTSRECV, which awaits a cts response to the rts message transmitted in Line 22. The fourth argument of CTSRECV specifies the maximum time that process should wait for such a response; a good value for max_cts_wait is sifs + dur_cts.

Process CTSRECV listens for this time to a cts message with source dest and destination id. In case the expected cts message arrives in time (Line 1), the node waits for a time sifs (Line 2) and then transmits the data frame and proceeds to await an acknowledgement (Line 3). The fourth argument of ACKRECV specifies the maximum time the process should wait for such an acknowledgement; a good value for max_ack_wait is sifs + dur_ack. If the cts message does not arrive in time (Line 6), the process returns to INIT to send another rts message, while incrementing the counter tries (Line 7). While waiting for the cts message, any incoming rts or cts message destined for another node is treated exactly as in Process 5 (Lines 4–5). Incoming data frames cannot arrive when this process is running, and incoming rts messages to id are ignored.

Process 7. Receiving a CTS

```
CTSRECV(id,dest,tries,ctstimeout,dframe,nav) ≝
1. [NEW(cts(dest,id,d))]
2.    ⟦timeout := now + sifs⟧ [now ≥ timeout]
3.    transmit(dframe) . ACKRECV(id,dest,tries,now + max_ack_wait,dframe,nav)
4. + [(NEW(rts(src,dest,d)) ∨ NEW(cts(src,dest,d))) ∧ dest ≠ id ∧ nav < now+d]
5.    ⟦nav := now+d⟧ CTSRECV(id,dest,tries,ctstimeout,dframe,nav)
6. + [now ≥ ctstimeout]
7.    INIT(id,dest,tries+1,dframe,nav)
```

Process 8. Receiving an ACK

```
ACKRECV(id,dest,tries,acktimeout,dframe,nav) ≝
1. [NEW(ackframe(id))]
2.    deliver(success) . CSMA(id,nav)
3. + [(NEW(rts(src,dest,d)) ∨ NEW(cts(src,dest,d))) ∧ dest ≠ id ∧ nav < now+d]
4.    ⟦nav := now+d⟧ ACKRECV(id,dest,tries,acktimeout,dframe,nav)
5. + [now ≥ timeout]      /* nothing received */
6.    INIT(id,dest,tries+1,dframe,nav)
```

Process 8 handles the receipt of an acknowledgement in response to a successful data transmission. If an acknowledgement arrives, it must be from the node to which id has transmitted a data frame. In that case (Line 1), the network layer is informed that the sending of dframe was successful and the process loops back to Process 5 (Line 2). Line 5 describes the situation where no acknowledgement message arrives and the process times out. Also here CSMA/CA retries to send the message; the counter `tries` is incremented. Lines 3–4 describe the usual handling of incoming `rts` or `cts` messages destined for another node.

5.4 The Exposed Station Problem

Another source of collisions in CSMA/CA is the well-known *exposed station problem*. This refers to a linear topology $A - B - C - D$, where an unending stream of messages between C and D interferes with attempts by A to get a message across to B. In the default CSMA/CA protocol as formalised in Sect. 5.1, transmissions from A to B may perpetually collide at B with transmissions from C destined for D. CSMA/CA with virtual carrier sensing mitigates this problem, for a `cts` sent by B in response to an `rts` sent by A will tell C to keep silent for the required duration. In fact, we can show that in the above topology, if <u>`max_retransmit`</u>$=\infty$ then packet delivery holds with probability 1. A non-probabilistic guarantee cannot be given since nodes A and C could behave in the same way, meaning if one node is sending out a message the other does the same at the very same moment, and if one is silent the other remains silent as well. In this scenario all messages to be sent are doomed.

Based on our formalisation, we can prove that once the RTS/CTS handshake has been successfully concluded, meaning that all nodes within range of the intended recipient have received the `cts`, then packet delivery holds outright. So the only problem left is to achieve a successful RTS/CTS handshake. Since `rts` and `cts` messages are rather short, even by modest values of <u>`max_retransmit`</u> it becomes likely that such messages do not collide.

In spite of this, CSMA/CA with (or without) virtual channel sensing cannot achieve packet delivery with probability 1 for general topologies. Assume the following network topology

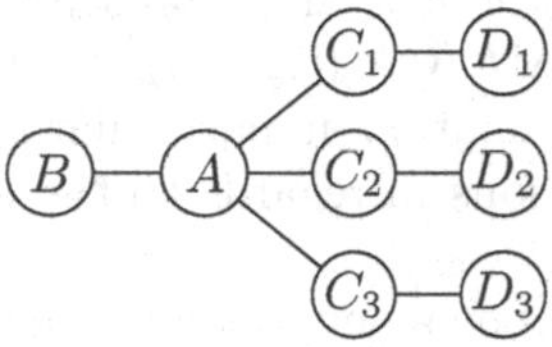

Here it may happen that one of the C_is is always busy transmitting a large message to D_i; any given C_i is occasionally silent (not sending any message), but then one of the others is transmitting. As C_i is disconnected from C_j, for $j \neq i$, coordination between the nodes is impossible. As a consequence, the medium at A will always be busy, so that A cannot send an `rts` message from B.

6 Related Work

The CSMA protocol in its different variants has been analysed with different formalisms in the past.

Multiple analyses were performed for the CSMA/CD protocol (CSMA with collision detection), a predecessor of CSMA/CA that has a constant backoff, i.e.

the backoff time is not increased exponentially, see [10,11,20,21,26]. In all these approaches frame collisions have to be modelled explicitly, as part of the protocol description. In contrast, our approach handles collisions in the semantics; thereby achieving a clear separation between protocol specifications and link layer behaviour.

Duflot et al. [10,11] use probabilistic timed automata (PTAs) to model the protocol, and use probabilistic model checking (PRISM) and approximate model checking (APMC) for their analysis. The model explained in [26] is based on PTAs as well, but uses the model checker UPPAAL as verification tool. These approaches, although formal, have very little in common with our approach. On the one hand it is not easy to change the model from CSMA/CD to CSMA/CA, as the latter requires unbounded data structures (or alike) to model the exponential backoff. On the other hand, as usual, model checking suffers from state space explosion and only small networks (usually fewer than ten nodes) can be analysed. This is sufficient and convenient when it comes to finding counter examples, but these approaches cannot provide guarantees for arbitrary network topologies, as ours does.

Jensen et al. [20] use models of CSMA/CD to compare the tools SPIN and UPPAAL. Their models are much more abstract than ours. It is proven that no collisions will ever occur, without stating the exact conditions under which this statement holds.

To the best of our knowledge, Parrow [21] is the only one who used process algebra (CCS) to model and analyse CSMA. His untimed model of CSMA/CD is extremely abstract and the analysis performed is limited to two nodes only, avoiding scenarios such as the hidden station problem.

There are far fewer formal analyses techniques available when it comes to CSMA/CA (with and without virtual medium sensing). Traditional approaches to the analysis of network protocols are simulation and test-bed experiments. This is also the case for CSMA/CA (e.g. [4]). While these are important and valid methods for protocol evaluation, in particular for quantitative performance evaluation, they have limitations in regards to the evaluation of basic protocol correctness properties.

Following the spirit of the above-mentioned research of model checking CSMA, Fruth [15] analyses CSMA/CA using PTAs and PRISM. He considers properties such as the minimum probability of two nodes successfully completing their transmissions, and maximum expected number of collisions until two nodes have successfully completed their transmissions. As before, this analysis technique does not scale; in [15] the experiments are limited to two contending nodes only.

Beyond model checking, simulation and test-bed experiments, we are only aware of two other formal approaches. In [1] Markov chains are used to derive an accurate, analytical model to compute the throughput of CSMA/CA. Calculating throughput is an orthogonal task to our vision of proving (functional) correctness.

An approach aiming at proving the correctness of CSMA/CA with virtual carrier sensing (RTS/CTS), and hence related to ours, is presented in [3]. Based on stochastic bigraphs with sharing it uses rewrite rules to analyse quantitative properties. Although it is an approach that is capable to analyse arbitrary topologies, to apply the rewrite rules a particular topology needs to be modelled by a directed acyclic graph structure, which is part of the bigraph.

7 Conclusion

In this paper we have proposed a novel process algebra, called ALL, that can be used to model, verify and analyse link layer protocols. Since we aimed at a process algebra featuring aspects of the link layer such as frame collisions, as well as arbitrary data structures (to model a rich class of protocols), we could not use any of the existing algebras. The design of ALL is layered. The first layer allows modelling protocols in some sort of pseudo code, which hopefully makes our approach accessible for network and software researchers/engineers. The other layers are mainly for giving a formal semantics to the language. The layer of partial network expressions, the third layer, provides a unique and sophisticated mechanism for modelling the collision of frames. As it is hard-wired in the semantics there is no need to model collisions manually when modelling a protocol, as it was done before [21]. Next to primitives needed for modelling link layer protocols (e.g. **transmit**) and standard operators of process algebra (e.g. nondeterministic choice), ALL provides an operator for probabilistic choice.

This operator is needed to model aspects of link layer protocols such as the exponential backoff for the Carrier-Sense Multiple Access with Collision Avoidance protocol, the case study we have chosen to demonstrate the applicability of ALL. We have modelled and analysed two versions of CSMA/CA, without and with virtual carrier sensing. Our analysis has confirmed the hidden station problem for the version without virtual carrier sensing. However, we have also shown that the version with virtual carrier sensing overcomes not only this problem, but also the exposed station problem with probability 1. Yet the protocol cannot guarantee packet delivery, not even with probability 1.

To perform this analysis we had to formalise suitable liveness properties for link layer protocols specified in our framework.

Acknowledgement. We thank Tran Ngoc Ma for her involvement in this project in a very early phase. We also like to thank the German Academic Exchange Service (DAAD) that funded an internship of the third author at Data61, CSIRO.

References

1. Bianchi, G.: Performance analysis of the IEEE 802.11 distributed coordination function. IEEE J. Sel. Areas Commun. **18**(3), 535–547 (2000). https://doi.org/10.1109/49.840210
2. Bres, E., van Glabbeek, R.J., Höfner, P.: A timed process algebra for wireless networks with an application in routing. In: Thiemann, P. (ed.) ESOP 2016. LNCS, vol. 9632, pp. 95–122. Springer, Heidelberg (2016). https://doi.org/10.1007/978-3-662-49498-1_5

3. Calder, M., Sevegnani, M.: Modelling IEEE 802.11 CSMA/CA RTS/CTS with stochastic bigraphs with sharing. Formal Aspects Comput. **26**(3), 537–561 (2014). https://doi.org/10.1007/s00165-012-0270-3
4. Chhaya, H.S., Gupta, S.: Performance modeling of asynchronous data transfer methods of IEEE 802.11 MAC Protocol. Wirel. Netw. **3**, 217–234 (1997). https://doi.org/10.1023/A:1019109301754
5. Comer, D.: Computer Networks and Internets. Pearson Education Inc., UpperSaddle River (2009)
6. Cranen, S., Mousavi, M.R., Reniers, M.A.: A rule format for associativity. In: van Breugel, F., Chechik, M. (eds.) CONCUR 2008. LNCS, vol. 5201, pp. 447–461. Springer, Heidelberg (2008). https://doi.org/10.1007/978-3-540-85361-9_35
7. De Nicola, R., Vaandrager, F.W.: Three logics for branching bisimulation. J. ACM **42**(2), 458–487 (1995). https://doi.org/10.1145/201019.201032
8. Deng, Y., van Glabbeek, R.J., Hennessy, M., Morgan, C.C., Zhang, C.: Remarks on testing probabilistic processes. In: Cardelli, L., Fiore, M., Winskel, G. (eds.) Computation, Meaning, and Logic: Articles Dedicated to Gordon Plotkin, Electronic Notes in Theoretical Computer Science, vol. 172, pp. 359–397. Elsevier (2007). https://doi.org/10.1016/j.entcs.2007.02.013
9. Deng, Y., van Glabbeek, R.J., Morgan, C.C., Zhang, C.: Scalar outcomes suffice for finitary probabilistic testing. In: De Nicola, R. (ed.) ESOP 2007. LNCS, vol. 4421, pp. 363–378. Springer, Heidelberg (2007). https://doi.org/10.1007/978-3-540-71316-6_25
10. Duflot, M., et al.: Probabilistic model checking of the CSMA/CD, protocol using PRISM and APMC. In: Automated Verification of Critical Systems (AVoCS 2004). Electronic Notes in Theoretical Computer Science Series, vol. 128, pp. 195–214 (2004). https://doi.org/10.1016/j.entcs.2005.04.012
11. Duflot, M., et al.: Practical applications of probabilistic model checking to communication protocols. In: Gnesi, S., Margaria, T. (eds.) Formal Methods for Industrial Critical Systems: A Survey of Applications, pp. 133–150. IEEE (2013). https://doi.org/10.1002/9781118459898.ch7
12. Fehnker, A., van Glabbeek, R.J., Höfner, P., McIver, A.K., Portmann, M., Tan, W.L.: A process algebra for wireless mesh networks. In: Seidl, H. (ed.) ESOP 2012. LNCS, vol. 7211, pp. 295–315. Springer, Heidelberg (2012). https://doi.org/10.1007/978-3-642-28869-2_15
13. Fehnker, A., van Glabbeek, R.J., Höfner, P., McIver, A.K., Portmann, M., Tan, W.L.: A process algebra for wireless mesh networks used for modelling, verifying and analysing AODV. Technical report 5513, NICTA (2013). http://arxiv.org/abs/1312.7645
14. Friend, G.E., Fike, J.L., Baker, H.C., Bellamy, J.C.: Understanding Data Communications, 2nd edn. Howard W. Sams & Company, Indianapolis (1988)
15. Fruth, M.: Probabilistic model checking of contention resolution in the IEEE 802.15.4 low-rate wireless personal area network protocol. In: Leveraging Applications of Formal Methods, Second International Symposium (ISoLA 2006), pp. 290–297. IEEE Computer Society (2006). https://doi.org/10.1109/ISoLA.2006.34
16. IEEE: IEEE standard for ethernet (2016). https://doi.org/10.1109/IEEESTD.2016.7428776
17. IEEE: IEEE standard for low-rate wireless networks (2016). https://doi.org/10.1109/IEEESTD.2016.7460875
18. ISO/IEC 7498–1: Information technology—open systems interconnection—basic reference model: The basic model (1994). https://www.iso.org/standard/20269.html

19. ISO/IEC/IEEE 8802–11: Information technology—telecommunications and information exchange between systems—local and metropolitan area networks—specific requirements—part 11: Wireless LAN medium access control (MAC) and physical layer (PHY) specifications (2018). https://www.iso.org/standard/73367.html
20. Jensen, H.E., Larsen, K.G., Skou, A.: Modelling and analysis of a collision avoidance protocol using Spin and Uppaal. In: The Spin Verification System. Discrete Mathematics and Theoretical Computer Science, vol. 32, pp. 33–50. DIMACS/AMS (1996). https://doi.org/10.7146/brics.v3i24.20005
21. Parrow, J.: Verifying a CSMA/CD-protocol with CCS. In: Aggarwal, S. (eds.) IFIP Symposium on Protocol Specification, Testing and Verification (PSTV 1988), North-Holland, pp. 373–384 (1988)
22. Pnueli, A.: The temporal logic of programs. In: Foundations of Computer Science (FOCS 1977), pp. 46–57. IEEE (1977). https://doi.org/10.1109/SFCS.1977.32
23. de Simone, R.: Higher-level synchronising devices in Meije-SCCS. TCS **37**, 245–267 (1985). https://doi.org/10.1016/0304-3975(85)90093-3
24. Simpson, W.: The point-to-point protocol (PPP). RFC 1661 Internet Standard (1994). http://www.ietf.org/rfc/rfc1661.txt
25. Singh, A., Ramakrishnan, C.R., Smolka, S.A.: A process calculus for mobile ad hoc networks. Sci. Comput. Program. **75**, 440–469 (2010). https://doi.org/10.1016/j.scico.2009.07.008
26. Zhao, J., Li, X., Zheng, T., Zheng, G.: Removing irrelevant atomic formulas for checking timed automata efficiently. In: Larsen, K.G., Niebert, P. (eds.) FORMATS 2003. LNCS, vol. 2791, pp. 34–45. Springer, Heidelberg (2004). https://doi.org/10.1007/978-3-540-40903-8_4

Program Analysis and Automated Verification

Data Races and Static Analysis for Interrupt-Driven Kernels

Nikita Chopra, Rekha Pai(✉), and Deepak D'Souza

Indian Institute of Science, Bangalore, India
{nikita,rekhapai,deepakd}@iisc.ac.in

Abstract. We consider a class of interrupt-driven programs that model the kernel API libraries of some popular real-time embedded operating systems and the synchronization mechanisms they use. We define a natural notion of data races and a happens-before ordering for such programs. The key insight is the notion of *disjoint blocks* to define the synchronizes-with relation. This notion also suggests an efficient and effective lockset based analysis for race detection. It also enables us to define efficient "sync-CFG" based static analyses for such programs, which exploit data race freedom. We use this theory to carry out static analysis on the FreeRTOS kernel library to detect races and to infer simple relational invariants on key kernel variables and data-structures.

Keywords: Static analysis · Interrupt-driven programs · Data races

1 Introduction

Embedded software is widespread and increasingly employed in safety-critical applications in medical, automobile, and aerospace domains. These programs are typically multi-threaded applications, running on uni-processor systems, that are compiled along with a kernel library that provides priority-based scheduling, and other task management and communication functionality. The applications themselves are similar to classical multi-threaded programs (using lock, semaphore, or queue based synchronization) although they are distinguished by their priority-based execution semantics. The kernel on the other hand typically makes use of non-standard low-level synchronization mechanisms (like disabling-enabling interrupts, suspending the scheduler, and flag-based synchronization) to ensure thread-safe access to its data-structures. In the literature such software (both applications and kernels) are referred to as *interrupt-driven* programs. Our interest in this paper is in the subclass of interrupt-driven programs corresponding to kernel libraries.

Efficient static analysis of concurrent programs is a challenging problem. One could carry out a precise analysis by considering the *product* of the control flow graphs (CFGs) of the threads, however this is prohibitively expensive due to the exponential number of program points in the product graph. A promising direction is to focus on the subclass of *race-free* programs. This is an important class

L. Caires (Ed.): ESOP 2019, LNCS 11423, pp. 697–723, 2019.
https://doi.org/10.1007/978-3-030-17184-1_25

of programs, as most developers aim to write race-free code, and one could try to exploit this property to give an efficient way of analyzing programs that fall in this class. In recent years there have been many techniques [7,11,12,18,21] that exploit the race-freedom property to perform sound and efficient static analysis. In particular [11,21] create an appealing structure called a "sync-CFG" which is the *union* of the control flow graphs of the threads augmented with possible "synchronization" edges, and essentially perform sequential analysis on this graph to obtain sound facts about the concurrent program. However these techniques are all for classical lock-based concurrent programs. A natural question asks if we can analyze interrupt-driven programs in a similar way.

There are several challenges in doing this. Firstly one needs to define *what* constitutes a data race in a generalized setting that includes these programs. Secondly, how does one define the happens-before order, and in particular the *synchronizes-with* relation that many of the race-free analysis techniques rely on, given the ad-hoc synchronization mechanisms used in these programs.

A natural route that suggests itself is to translate a given interrupt-driven program into one that uses classical locks, and faithfully captures the interleaved executions of the original program. One could then use existing techniques for lock-based concurrency to analyze these programs. However, this route is fraught with many challenges. To begin with, it is not clear how one would handle flag-based synchronization which is one of the main synchronization mechanisms used in these programs. Even if one could handle this, such a translation *may not* preserve data races, in that the original program might have had a race but the translated program does not. Finally, some of the synchronizes-with edges in the translated program are clearly unnecessary, leading to imprecise data-flow facts in the analyses.

In this paper, we show that it is possible to take a more organic route and address these challenges in a principled way that could apply to other non-standard classes of concurrent systems as well. Firstly, we propose a general definition of a data race that is not based on a happens-before order, but on the operational semantics of the class of programs under consideration. The definition essentially says that two statements s and t can race, if two notional "blocks" around them can *overlap* in time during an execution. We believe that this definition accurately captures what it is that a programmer tries to avoid while dealing with shared variables whose values matter. Secondly we propose a way of defining the *synchronizes-with* relation, based on the notion of *disjoint blocks*. These are statically identifiable pairs of path segments in the CFGs of different threads that are guaranteed to never overlap (in time) during an execution of the program, much like blocks of code that lie between an acquire and release of the same lock. This relation now suggests a natural sync-CFG structure on which we can perform analyses like value-set (including interval, null-deference, and points-to analysis), and region-based relational invariant analysis, in a sound and efficient manner. We also use the notion of disjoint blocks to define an efficient and precise lock-set-based analysis for detecting races in interrupt-driven programs.

We implement some of these analyses on the FreeRTOS kernel library [3] which is one of the most widely used open-source real-time kernels for embedded systems, comprising about 3,500 lines of C code. Our race-detection analysis reports a total of 64 races in kernel methods, of which 18 turn out to be true positives. We also carry out a region-based relational analysis using an implementation based on CIL [22]/Apron [15], to prove several relational invariants on the kernel variables and abstracted data-structures.

2 Overview

We give an overview of our contributions via an illustrative example modelled on a portion of the FreeRTOS kernel library. Figure 1 shows an interrupt-driven program that contains a main thread that first initializes the kernel variables. The variables represent components of a message queue, like `msgw` (the number of messages waiting in the queue), `len` (max length of the queue), `wtosend` (the number of tasks waiting to send to the queue), `wtorec` (the number of tasks waiting to receive from the queue), and `RxLock` (a counter which also acts as a synchronization flag that mediates access to the waiting queues). The main thread then creates (or spawns) two threads: *qsend* which models the kernel API method for sending a message to the queue, and *qrec_ISR* which models a method for receiving a message, and which is meant to be called from an interrupt-service routine. The basic semantics of this program is that the ISR thread can interrupt *qsend* at any time (provided interrupts are not disabled), but always runs to completion itself. The threads use `disableint`/`enableint` to disable and enable interrupts, `suspendsch`/`resumesch` to suspend/resume the scheduler (thereby preventing preemption by another non-ISR thread), and finally flag-based synchronization (using the `RxLock` variable), as different means to ensure mutual exclusion.

Our first contribution is a general notion of data races which is applicable to such programs. We say that two conflicting statements s and t in two different threads are involved in a data race if assuming s and t were enclosed in a notional "block" of skip statements, there is an execution in which the two blocks "overlap" in time. The given program can be seen to be free of races. However if we were to remove the `disableint` statement of line 10, then the statements accessing `msgw` in lines 12 and 42 would be racy, since soon after the access of `msgw` in *qsend* at line 12, there could be preemption by *qrec_ISR* which goes on to execute line 42.

Next we illustrate the notion of "disjoint blocks" which is the key to defining synchronizes-with edges, which we need in our sync-CFG analysis as well as to define an appropriate happens-before relation. Disjoint blocks are also used in our race-detection algorithm. A pair of blocks of code (for example any of the like-shaded blocks of code in the figure) are *disjoint* if they can never overlap during an execution. For example, the block comprising lines 11–14 in *qsend* and the whole of *qrec_ISR*, form a pair of disjoint blocks.

Next we give an analysis for checking race-freedom, by adapting the standard lockset analysis [24] for classical concurrent programs. We associate a unique

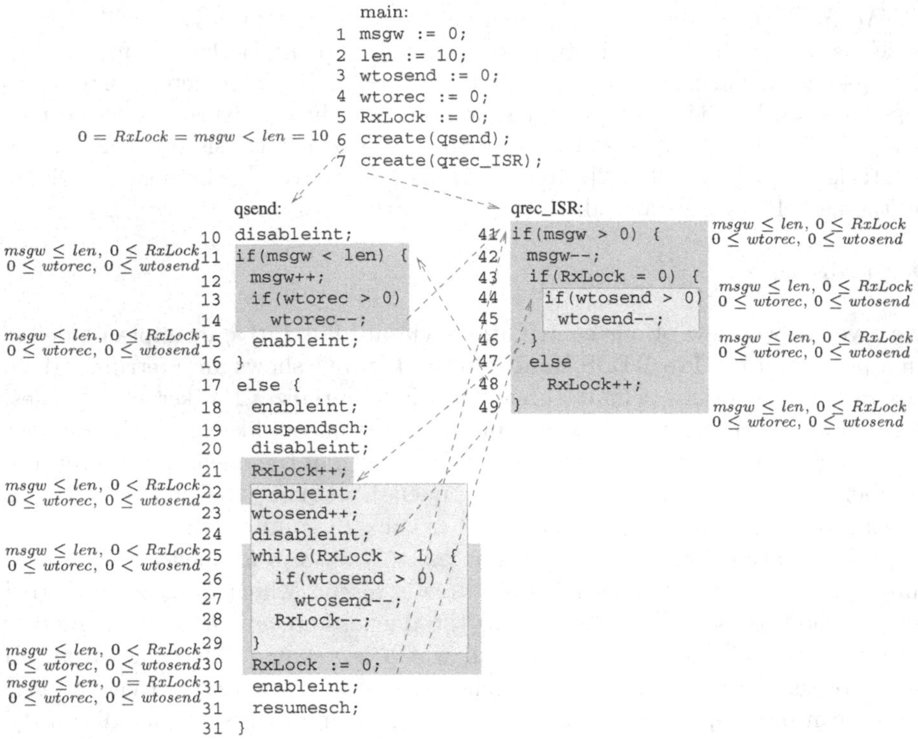

Fig. 1. An interrupt-driven program modelled on the FreeRTOS kernel library. Similarly shaded blocks denote disjoint blocks. Some of the sync-with edges are shown in dashed lines. Some edges like $22 \rightarrow 41$ and $49 \rightarrow 20$ have been omitted for clarity.

lock with each pair of disjoint blocks, and add notional acquires and releases of this lock at the beginning and end (respectively) of these blocks. We now do the standard lockset analysis on this version of the program, and declare two accesses to be non-racy if they hold sets of locks with a non-empty intersection.

Finally, we show how to do data-flow analysis for such programs in a sound and efficient way. The basic idea is to construct a "sync-CFG" for the program by unioning the control-flow graphs of the threads, and adding *sync* edges that capture the synchronizes-with edges (going from the end of a block to the beginning of its paired block), for example line 14 to line 41 and line 49 to line 11. The sync-edges are shown by dashed arrows in the figure. We now do a standard "value-set" analysis (for example interval analysis) on this graph, keeping track of a set of values each variable can take. The resulting facts about a variable are guaranteed to be sound at points where the variable is accessed (or even "owned" in the sense that a notional read of the variable at that point is non-racy). For example an interval analysis on this program would give us that $0 <$ `msgw` at line 14. Finally, we could do a region-based value-set analysis, by identifying regions of variables that are accessed as a unit – for example `msgw` and `len` could be in one region, while `wtosend` and `wtorec` could be in another. The figure shows some facts inferred by a polyhedral analysis based on these regions, for the given program.

3 Interrupt-Driven Programs

The programs we consider have a finite number of (static) threads, with a designated "main" thread in which execution begins. The threads access a set of shared global variables, some of which are used as "synchronization flags", using a standard set of commands like assignment statements of the form `x := e`, conditional statements (`if-then-else`), loop statements (`while`), etc. In addition, the threads can use commands like `disableint`, `enableint` (to disable and enable interrupts, respectively), `suspendsch`, `resumesch` (to suspend and resume the scheduler, respectively), while the main thread can also `create` a thread (enable it for execution). Table 1 shows the set of basic statements $cmd_{V,T}$ over a set of variables V and a set of threads T.

We allow standard integer and Boolean expressions over a set of variables V. For an integer expression e over V, and an environment ϕ for V, we denote by $[\![e]\!]_\phi$ the integer value that e evaluates to in ϕ. Similarly for a Boolean expression b, we denote the Boolean value (*true* or *false*) that b evaluates to in ϕ by $[\![b]\!]_\phi$. For a set of environments Φ for a set of variables V, we define the set of integer values that e can evaluate to in an environment in Φ, by $[\![e]\!]_\Phi = \{[\![e]\!]_\phi \mid \phi \in \Phi\}$. Similarly, for a boolean expression b, we define the set of environments in Φ that satisfy b to be $[\![b]\!]_\Phi = \{\phi \in \Phi \mid [\![b]\!]_\phi = true\}$.

Each thread is of one of two *types*: "task" threads that are like standard threads, and "ISR" threads that represent threads that run as interrupt service routines. The *main* thread is a task thread, which is the only task thread enabled initially. The *main* thread can enable other threads (both task and ISR) for execution using the `create` command. Task threads can be preempted by other task threads (whenever interrupts are not disabled, and the scheduler is not suspended) or by ISR threads (whenever interrupts are not disabled). On the other hand ISR threads cannot be preempted and are assumed to run to completion.

Only task threads are allowed to use `disableint`, `enableint`, `suspendsch` and `resumesch` commands. Similarly, if flag-based synchronization is used, only task threads can modify the flag variable, while an ISR can only check whether the flag is set or not, and perform some actions accordingly.

Formally we represent an interrupt-driven program P as a tuple (V, T) where V is a finite set of integer variables, and T is a finite set of named threads. Each thread $t \in T$ has a *type* which is one of *task* or *ISR*, and an associated control-flow graph of the form $G_t = (L_t, s_t, inst_t)$ where L_t is a finite set of *locations* of thread t, $s_t \in L_t$ is the *start* location of thread t, $inst_t \subseteq L_t \times cmd_{V,T} \times L_t$ is a finite set of *instructions* of thread t.

Some definitions related to threads will be useful going forward. We denote by $L_P = \bigcup_{t \in T} L_t$ the disjoint union of the thread locations. Whenever P is clear

Table 1. Basic statements $cmd_{V,T}$ over variables V and threads T

Command	Description
`skip`	Do nothing
`x := e`	Assign the value of expression e to variable $x \in V$
`assume`(b)	Enabled only if expression b evaluates to *true*, acts like `skip`
`create(t)`	Enable thread $t \in T$ for execution
`disableint`	Disable interrupts and context switches
`enableint`	Enable interrupts and context switches
`suspendsch`	Suspend the scheduler (other task threads cannot preempt the current thread); Also sets `ssflag` variable
`resumesch`	Resume the scheduler (other task threads can now preempt the current thread); Also unsets `ssflag` variable

from the context we will drop the subscript of P from L_P and its decorations. For a location $l \in L$ we denote by $tid(l)$ the thread t which contains location l. We denote the set of instructions of P by $inst_P = \bigcup_{t \in T} inst_t$. For an instruction $\iota \in inst_t$, we will also write $tid(\iota)$ to mean the thread t. For an instruction $\iota = \langle l, c, l' \rangle$, we call l the *source* location, and l' the *target* location of ι.

We denote the set of commands appearing in program P by $cmd(P)$. We will consider an assignment `x := e` as a *write-access* to x, and as a *read-access* to every variable that appears in the expression e. Similarly, `assume`(b) is considered to be a read-access of every variable that occurs in expression b. We say two accesses are *conflicting* accesses if they are read/write accesses to the same variable, and at least one of them is a write. We assume that the control-flow graph of each thread comes from a well-structured program. Finally, we assume that the *main* thread begins by initializing the variables to constant values. Figure 2 shows an example program and the control-flow-graphs of its threads.

We define the operational semantics of an interrupt-driven program using a labeled transition system (LTS). Let $P = (V, T)$ be a program. We define an LTS $\mathcal{T}_P = (Q, \Sigma, s, \Rightarrow)$ corresponding to P, where:

- Q is a set of states of the form $(pc, \phi, enab, rt, it, id, ss)$, where $pc \in T \to L$ is the program counter giving the current location of each thread, $\phi \in V \to \mathbb{Z}$ is a valuation for the variables, $enab \subseteq T$ is the set of enabled threads, $rt \in T$ is the currently running thread; $it \in T$ is the task thread which is interrupted when the scheduler is suspended; and id and ss are Boolean values telling us whether interrupts are disabled ($id = true$) or not ($id = false$) and whether the scheduler is suspended ($ss = true$) or not ($ss = false$).
- The set of labels Σ is the set of instructions $inst_P$ of P.
- The initial state s is $(\lambda t.s_t, \lambda x.0, \{main\}, main, main, false, false)$. Thus all threads are at their entry locations, the initial environment sets all variables to 0, only the main thread is enabled and running, the interrupted task is

```
main:
1. x := 0;
2. y := 0;
3. t := 0;
4. create(t1);
5. create(t2);
6.

t1:
7. x := x + 1;
8.

t2:
9. disableint;
10. y := t;
11. t := x;
12. if(t > 0) {
13.     y := y + 1;
14. }
15. else {
16.     t := t + 1;
17. }
18. enableint;
19.
```

(a) Example program

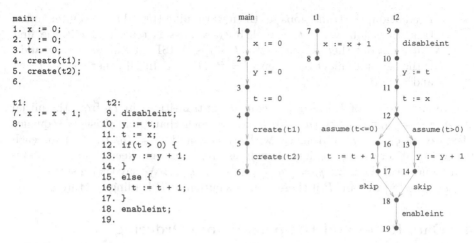

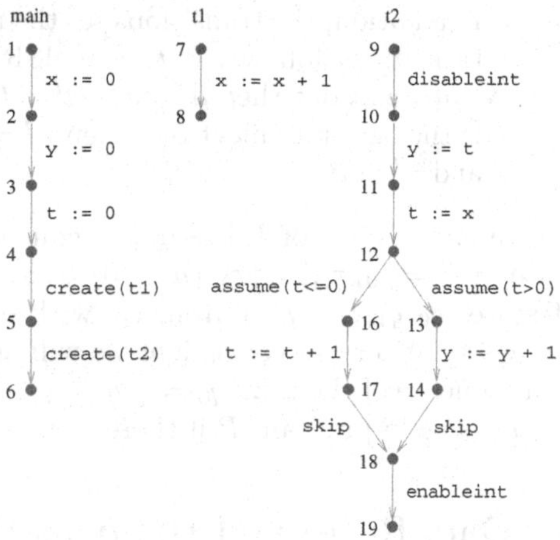

(b) Control-flow-graph representation

Fig. 2. An example program and its CFG representation.

set to *main* (this is a dummy value as it is used only when the scheduler is suspended), interrupts are enabled, and the scheduler is not suspended.

- For an instruction $\iota = \langle l, c, l' \rangle$ in $inst_P$, with $tid(\iota) = t$, we define

$$(pc, \phi, enab, rt, it, id, ss) \Rightarrow_\iota (pc', \phi', enab', rt', it', id', ss')$$

iff the following conditions are satisfied:
  - $t \in enab$; $pc(t) = l$; $pc' = pc[t \mapsto l']$;
  - if id is true or rt is an ISR then $t = rt$;
  - if ss is true, then either $t = rt$ or t is an ISR thread;
  - Based on the command c, the following conditions must be satisfied:
    * If c is the **skip** command then $\phi' = \phi$, $enab' = enab$, $id' = id$, and $ss' = ss$.
    * If c is an assignment statement of the form $x := e$ then $\phi' = \phi[x \mapsto [\![e]\!]_\phi]$, $enab' = enab$, $id' = id$, and $ss' = ss$.
    * If c is a command of the form **assume**(b) then $[\![b]\!]_\phi = true$, $\phi' = \phi$, $enab' = enab$, $id' = id$, and $ss' = ss$.
    * If c is a **create**(u) command then $t = main$, $\phi' = \phi$, $enab' = enab \cup \{u\}$, $id' = id$, and $ss' = ss$.
    * If c is the **disableint** command then $\phi' = \phi$, $enab' = enab$, $id' = true$, and $ss' = ss$.
    * If c is the **enableint** command then $\phi' = \phi$, $enab' = enab$, $id' = false$, and $ss' = ss$.
    * If c is the **suspendsch** command then $\phi' = \phi[ssflag \mapsto 1]$, $enab' = enab$, $id' = id$, and $ss' = true$.
    * If c is the **resumesch** command then $\phi' = \phi[ssflag \mapsto 0]$, $enab' = enab$, $id' = id$, and $ss' = false$.

- In addition, the transitions set the new running thread rt' and interrupted task it' as follows. If t is an ISR thread, ss is true, and ι is the first statement of t then $it' = rt$, $rt' = t$. If t is an ISR thread, ss is true, and ι is the last statement of t then $it' = it$, $rt' = it$. In all other cases, $rt' = t$ and $it' = it$.

An execution σ of P is a finite sequence of transitions in $\mathcal{T}_P$ from the initial state s: $\sigma = \tau_0, \tau_1, \ldots, \tau_n$ $(n \geq 0)$ from $\Rightarrow$, such that there exists a sequence of states $q_0, q_1, \ldots, q_{n+1}$ from Q, with $q_0 = s$ and $\tau_i = (q_i, \iota_i, q_{i+1})$ for each $0 \leq i \leq n$. Wherever convenient we will also represent an execution like σ above as a sequence of the form $q_0 \Rightarrow_{\iota_0} q_1 \Rightarrow_{\iota_1} \cdots \Rightarrow_{\iota_n} q_{n+1}$. We say that a state $q \in Q$ is *reachable* in program P if there is an execution of P leading to state q.

4 Data Races and Happens-Before Ordering

In this section we propose a definition of a data race which has general applicability, and also define a natural happens-before order for interrupt-driven programs.

4.1 Data Races

Data races have typically been defined in the literature in terms of a *happens-before* order on program executions. In the classical setting of lock-based synchronization, the happens-before relation is a partial order on the instructions in an execution, that is reflexive-transitive closure of the union of the *program-order* relation between two instructions in the same thread, and the *synchronizes-with* relation which relates a release of a lock in a thread to the next acquire of the same lock in another thread. Two instructions in an execution are then defined to be involved in a data race if they are conflicting accesses to a shared variable and are *not* ordered by the happens-before relation.

We feel it is important to have a definition of a data race that is based on the operational semantics of the class of programs we are interested in, and not on a happens-before relation. Such a definition would more tangibly capture what it is that a programmer typically tries to avoid when dealing with shared variables whose consistency she is worried about. Moreover, when coming up with a definition of the happens-before order (the synchronizes-with relation in particular) for non-standard concurrent programs like interrupt-driven programs, it is useful to have a reference notion to relate to. For instance, one could show that a proposed happens-before order is strong enough to ensure the absence of races.

We propose to define a race between two conflicting statements in a program in terms of whether two imaginary blocks enclosing each of these statements can *overlap* in an execution. Let us consider a multi-threaded program P in a class of concurrent programs with a certain operational execution semantics. Consider a block of contiguous instructions in a thread t of a program P and another block in thread t' of P. We say that these two blocks are involved in a *high-level race* in an execution of P if they *overlap* with each other during the execution, in that one block begins *in between* the beginning and ending of the other. We say two conflicting statements s and t in P are involved in a *data race* (or are *racy*), if the following condition is true: Consider the program P' which is obtained from P by replacing the statement s by the block "**skip**; s; **skip**", and similarly for statement t. Then there is an execution of P' in which the two blocks containing s and t are involved in a high-level race. The definition is illustrated in Fig. 3. We say a program P is *race-free* if no pair of instructions in it are racy.

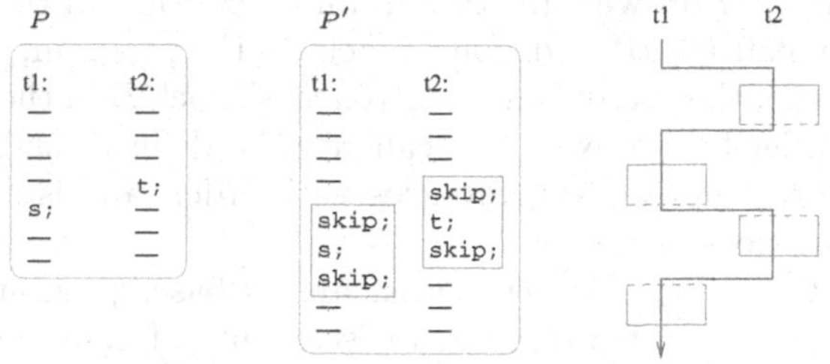

Fig. 3. Illustrating the definition of a data race on statements s and t. A program P, its transformation P', and an execution of P' in which the blocks overlap.

The rationale for this definition is that the concerned statements s and t may be compiled down to a sequence of instructions (represented by the blocks with **skip**'s around s and t) depending on the underlying processor and compiler, and if these instructions interleave in an execution, it may lead to undesirable results.

To illustrate the definition, consider the program in Fig. 2a. The accesses to x in line 7 and line 11 can be seen to be racy, since there is an execution of the augmented program P' in which *t1* performs the **skip** followed by the increment to x at line 7, followed by a context switch to thread *t2* which goes on to execute lines 9 and 10 and then the read of x in line 11. On the other hand, the version of the program in which line 7 is enclosed in a **disableint-enableint** block, does *not* contain a race.

We note that for classical concurrent programs, it might suffice to define a race as *consecutive* occurrences of conflicting accesses in an execution, as done in [4,17]. However, this definition is not general enough to apply to interrupt-driven programs. By this definition, the statements in lines 7 and 11 of the program in Fig. 2a are *not* racy, as there is *no* execution in which they happen consecutively. This is because the **disableint-enableint** block containing the access in line 11 is "atomic" in that the statements in the block must happen contiguously in any execution, and hence the instructions corresponding to line 7 and line 11 can never happen immediately one after another.

4.2 Disjoint Blocks and the Happens-Before Relation

Now that we have a proposed definition of races, we can proceed to give a principled way to define the happens-before relation for our class of interrupt-driven programs. The main question is how does one define the synchronizes-with relation. Our insight here is that the key to defining the synchronizes-with relation lies in identifying what we call *disjoint blocks* for the class of programs. Disjoint blocks are statically identifiable pairs of path segments in the CFGs of different threads, which are guaranteed by the execution semantics of the class of programs never to *overlap* in an execution of the program. Disjoint block structures – for example in the form of blocks enclosed between locks/unlocks of the same lock – are the primary mechanism used by developers to ensure race-freedom. The synchronizes-with relation in an execution can then be defined as relating, for every pair (A, B) of disjoint blocks in the program, the end of block A to the beginning of the succeeding occurrence of block B in the execution. The happens-before order for an execution can now be defined, as before, in terms of the program order and the synchronizes-with order, and is easily seen to be sufficient to ensure non-raciness.

Let us illustrate this hypothesis on classical lock-based programs. The disjoint block pairs for this class of programs are segments of code enclosed between acquires and releases of the *same* lock; or the portion of a thread's code before it spawns a thread t, and the whole of thread t's code; and similarly for joins. The synchronizes-with relation between instructions in an execution essentially goes from a release to the succeeding acquire of the same lock. If two accesses are related by the resulting happens-before order, they clearly cannot be involved in a race.

We now focus on defining a happens-before relation based on disjoint blocks for our class of interrupt-driven programs. We have identified eight pairs of disjoint block patterns for this class of programs, which are depicted in Fig. 4. We use the following types of blocks to define the pairs. A block of type D is a path segment in a task thread that begins with a `disableint` and ends with an `enableint` with no intervening `enableint` in between. A block of type S is a path segment in a task thread that begins with a `suspendsch` and ends with a `resumesch` with no intervening `resumesch`. An I block is an initial and terminating path segment in an ISR thread (i.e. begins with the first instruction and ends with a terminating instruction). Similarly, for a task thread t, T_t is an initial and terminating path in t, while M_t is an initial segment of the main thread that ends with a `create`(t) command. A block of type C_{ssflag} is a path segment in an ISR thread corresponding to the `then` block of a conditional that checks if $ssflag = 0$. For a synchronization flag f, C_f is the path segment in an ISR thread corresponding to the `then` block of a conditional that checks if $f = 0$. Finally F_f is a segment between statements that set f to 1 and back to 0, in a task thread. We also require that an F_f segment be within the scope of a `suspendsch` command.

We can now describe the pairs of disjoint blocks depicted in Fig. 4. Case (a) says that two D blocks in different task threads are disjoint. Clearly two such blocks can never overlap in an execution, since once one of the blocks begins execution no context-switch can occur until interrupts are enabled again. Case (b) says that D and I blocks are disjoint. Once again this is because once the D block

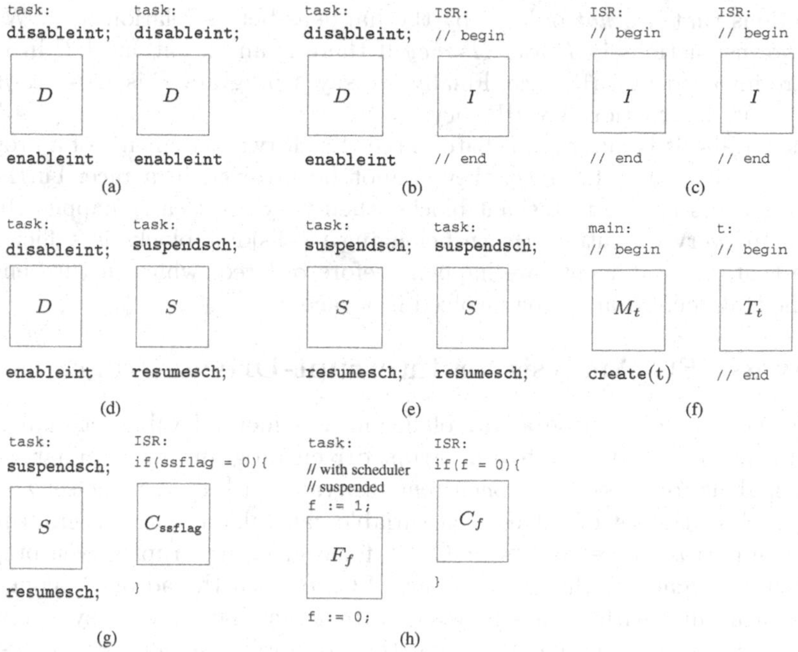

Fig. 4. Disjoint blocks in an interrupt-driven program.

begins execution no ISR can run until interrupts are enabled again, and once an ISR begins execution it runs to completion without any context-switches. Case (e) says that S blocks in different task threads are disjoint, because once the scheduler is suspended no context-switch to another task thread can occur. Case (f) says that M_t and T_t blocks are disjoint, since a thread cannot begin execution before it is created in main. Case (g) says that an S block is disjoint from a $C_{\mathtt{ssflag}}$ block. This is because once the scheduler is suspended by the `suspendsch` command, and even if a context-switch to an ISR occurs, the `then` block of the `if` statement will not execute. Conversely, if the ISR is running there can be no context-switch to another thread. Finally, case (h) is similar to case (g). We note that the disjoint block pairs are not ordered (the relation is symmetric).

We can now define the synchronizes-with relation as follows. Let $\sigma = q_0 \Rightarrow_{\iota_0} q_1 \Rightarrow_{\iota_1} \cdots \Rightarrow_{\iota_n} q_{n+1}$ be an execution of P. We say instruction ι_i *synchronizes-with* an instruction ι_j of P in σ, if $i < j$, $tid(\iota_i) \neq tid(\iota_j)$, and there exists a pair of disjoint blocks A and B, with ι_i ending block A and ι_j beginning block B. As usual we say ι_i is *program-order* related to ι_j iff $i < j$ and $tid(\iota_i) = tid(\iota_j)$. We define the *happens-before* relation on σ as the reflexive-transitive closure of the union of the program-order and synchronizes-with relations for σ.

We can now define a *HB-race* in an execution σ of P as follows: we say that two instructions ι_i and ι_j in σ are involved in a *HB-race* if they are conflicting instructions that are *not* ordered by the happens-before relation in σ. We say that two instructions in P are *HB-racy* if there is an execution of P in which they are involved in a HB-race. Finally, we say a program P is *HB-race-free* if no two of its instructions are HB-racy.

Once again, it is fairly immediate to see that if two statements of a program are not involved in a HB-race, they cannot be involved in a race. Further, if two statements belong to disjoint blocks, then they are clearly happens-before ordered in every execution. Hence belonging to disjoint blocks is sufficient to ensure that the statements are happens-before ordered, which in turn ensures that the statements cannot be involved in a race.

5 Sync-CFG Analysis for Interrupt-Driven Programs

In this section we describe a way of lifting a sequential value-set analysis in a sound way for a HB-race free interrupt-driven program, in a similar way to how it is done for lock-based concurrent programs in [11]. A value-set analysis keeps track of the set of values each variable can take at each program point. The basic idea is to create a "sync-CFG" for a given interrupt-driven program P, which is essentially the union of the CFGs of each thread of P, along with "may-synchronize-with" edges between statements that may be synchronizes-with related in an execution of P, and then perform the value-set analysis on the resulting graph. Whenever the given program is *HB-race free*, the result of the analysis is guaranteed to be sound, in a sense made clear in Theorem 1.

5.1 Sync-CFG

We begin by defining the "sync-CFG" for an interrupt-driven program. It is on this structure that we will do the value-set analysis. Let $P = (V, T)$ be an interrupt-driven program, and let G be the disjoint union (over threads $t \in T$) of the CFGs G_t. We define a set of *may-synchronize-with* edges in G, denoted $MSW(G)$, as follows. The edges correspond to the pairs of disjoint blocks depicted in Fig. 4, in that they connect the ending of one block to the beginning of the other block in the pair. Consider two instructions $\iota = \langle l, c, m \rangle \in inst_t$ and $\kappa = \langle l', c', m' \rangle \in inst_{t'}$, with $t \neq t'$. We add the edge (m, l') in $MSW(G)$, iff for some pair of disjoint blocks (A, B), ι ends a block of type A in thread t and κ begins a block of type B in thread t'. For example, corresponding to a (D, D) pair of disjoint blocks, we add the edge (m, l') when c is an `enableint` command, and c' is a `disableint` command.

The sync-CFG induced by P is the control flow graph given by G along with the additional edges in MSW(G). Figure 6 shows a program P_2 and its induced sync-CFG.

5.2 Value Set Analysis

We first spell out the particular form of abstract interpretation we will be using. It is similar to the standard formulation of [9], except that it is a little more general to accommodate non-standard control-flow graphs like the sync-CFG.

An *abstract interpretation* of a program $P = (V, T)$ is a structure of the form $\mathcal{A} = (D, \leq, d_o, F)$ where

- D is the set of *abstract states*.
- $(D, \leq)$ forms a complete lattice. We denote the join (least upper bound) in this lattice by $\sqcup_{\leq}$, or simply $\sqcup$ when the ordering is clear from the context.
- $d_0 \in D$ is the initial abstract state.
- $F : inst_P \rightarrow (D \rightarrow D)$ associates a *transfer function* $F(\iota)$ (or simply F_ι) with each instruction ι of P. We require each transfer function F_ι to be *monotonic*, in that whenever $d \leq d'$ we have $F_\iota(d) \leq F_\iota(d')$.

An abstract interpretation $\mathcal{A} = (D, \leq, d_0, F)$ of P induces a "global" transfer function $\mathcal{F}_{\mathcal{A}} : D \rightarrow D$, given by $\mathcal{F}_{\mathcal{A}}(d) = d_0 \sqcup \bigsqcup_{\iota \in inst_P} F_\iota(d)$. This transfer function can also be seen to be monotonic. By the Knaster-Tarski theorem [28], $\mathcal{F}_{\mathcal{A}}$ has a least fixed point (*LFP*) in D, which we denote by $LFP(\mathcal{F}_{\mathcal{A}})$, and refer to as the resulting value of the analysis.

A *value set* for a set of variables V is a map $vs : V \rightarrow 2^{\mathbb{Z}}$, associating a set of integer values with each variable in V. A value set vs induces a set of environments Φ_{vs} in a natural way: $\Phi_{vs} = \{\phi \mid \text{for all } x \in V,\ \phi(x) \in vs(x)\}$ (i.e. essentially the Cartesian product of the values sets). Conversely, a set of environments Φ for V, induces a value set $valset(\Phi)$ given by $valset(\Phi)(x) = \{v \in \mathbb{Z} \mid \exists \phi \in \Phi,\ \phi(x) = v\}$, which is the "projection" of the environments to each variable $x \in V$. Finally, we define a point-wise ordering on value sets as follows: $vs \preceq vs'$ iff $vs(x) \subseteq vs'(x)$ for each variable x in V. We denote the least element in this ordering by $vs_\perp = \lambda x.\emptyset$.

We can now define the value-set analysis $\mathcal{A}_{vset}$ for an interrupt-driven program $P = (V, T)$ as follows. Let $\mathcal{A}_{vset} = (D, \leq, d_0, F)$ where

- D is the set $L_P \rightarrow (V \rightarrow 2^{\mathbb{Z}})$ (thus an element of D associates a value-set with each program location)
- The ordering $d \leq d'$ holds iff $d(l) \preceq d'(l)$ for each $l \in L_P$
- The initial abstract value d_0 is given by:

$$d_0 = \lambda l. \begin{cases} \lambda x.\{0\} & \text{if } l = s_{main} \\ vs_\perp & \text{otherwise.} \end{cases}$$

- The transfer functions are given as follows. Given an abstract value d, and a location $l \in L_P$, we define vs_l^d to be the join of the value-set at l, and the value-set at all may-synchronizes-with edges coming into l. Thus $vs_l^d = d(l) \sqcup_{\preceq} \bigsqcup_{(n,l) \in MSW(G)} d(n)$. Below we will use Φ as an abbreviation of the set $\Phi_{vs_l^d}$ of environments induced by vs_l^d. Let $\iota = \langle l, c, l' \rangle$ be an instruction in P.
  - If c is the command `x := e` then $F_\iota(d) = d'$ where

$$d'(m) = \begin{cases} vs_l^d[x \mapsto [\![e]\!]_\Phi] & \text{if } m = l' \\ vs_\perp & \text{otherwise.} \end{cases}$$

- If c is the command `assume`(b), then $F_\iota(d) = d'$ where

$$d'(m) = \begin{cases} valset([\![b]\!]_\Phi) & \text{if } m = l' \\ vs_\bot & \text{otherwise.} \end{cases}$$

- If c is any other command (`skip`, `disableint`, `enableint`, `suspendsch`, `resumesch`, or `create`) then $F_\iota(d) = d'$ where

$$d'(m) = \begin{cases} vs_l^d & \text{if } m = l' \\ vs_\bot & \text{otherwise.} \end{cases}$$

Figure 6 shows the results of a value-set analysis on the sync-CFG of program P_2. The data-flow facts are shown just before a statement, at selected points in the program.

Soundness. The value-set analysis is sound in the following sense: if P is a *HB-race free* program, and we have a reachable state of P at a location l in a thread where a variable x is *read*; then the value of x in this state is contained in the value-set for x, obtained by the analysis at point l. More formally:

Theorem 1. *Let $P = (V, T)$ be an HB-race free interrupt-driven program, and let d^* be the result of the analysis $\mathcal{A}_{vset}$ on P. Let l be a location in a thread $t \in T$ where a variable x is read (i.e. P contains an instruction of the form $\langle l, c, l' \rangle$ where c is a read access of x). Let ϕ be an environment at l reachable via some execution of P. Then $\phi(x) \in d^*(l)(x)$.*

The proof of this theorem is similar to the one for classical concurrent programs in [11] (see [10] for a more accurate proof). The soundness claim can be extended to locations where a variable is "owned" (which includes locations where it is read). We say a variable x is *owned* by a thread t at location l, if an inserted read of x at this point is non-HB-racy in the resulting program.

Region-Based Analysis. One problem with the value-set analysis is that it may not be able to prove *relational* invariants (like $x \leq y$) for a program. One way to remedy this is to exploit the fact that concurrent programs often ensure race-free access to a *region* of variables, and to essentially do a region-based value-set analysis, as originally done in [21]. More precisely, let us say we have a partition of the set of variables V of a program P into a set of regions $R_1, \ldots, R_n$. We classify each read (write) access to a variable x in a region R, as an read (write) access to region R. We say that two instructions in an execution of P are involved in a *HB-region-race*, if the two instructions are conflicting accesses to the same region R, and are *not* happens-before ordered in the execution. A program is *HB-region-race free* if none of its executions contain a HB-region-race.

We can now define a region-based version of the value-set analysis for a program P, which we call $\mathcal{A}_{rvset}$. The value-set for a region R is a set of valuations (or sub-environments) for the variables in R. The transfer functions are defined in an analogous way to the value-set analysis. The analogue of Theorem 1 for regions gives us that for a HB-region-race free program, at any location where a region R is accessed, the region-value-set computed by the analysis at that point will contain every sub-environment of R reachable at that point.

6 Translation to Classical Lock-Based Programs

In this section we address the question of why an execution-preserving translation to a classical lock-based program is not a fruitful route to take. In a nutshell, such a translation would not preserve races and would induce a sync-CFG with many unnecessary MSW edges, leading to much more imprecise facts than the analysis on the native sync-CFG described in the previous section. We also describe how our approach can be viewed as a *lightweight* translation of an interrupt-driven program to a classical lock-based one. The translation is "lightweight" in the sense that it does *not* attempt to preserve the execution semantics of the given interrupt-driven program, but instead preserves races and the sync-CFG structure of the original program.

6.1 Execution-Preserving Lock Translation

One could try to translate a given interrupt-driven program P into a classical lock-based program P^L in a way that preserves the interleaved execution semantics of P. By this we mean that every execution of P has a corresponding execution in P^L that follows essentially the same sequence of interleaved instructions from the different threads (modulo of course the synchronization statements which may differ); and vice-versa. For example, to capture the semantics of `disableint-enableint`, one could introduce an "execution" lock E which is acquired in place of disabling interrupts, and released in place of enabling interrupts. Every instruction in a task thread outside a `disableint-enableint` block must also acquire and release E immediately before and after the instruction. Note that the latter step is necessary if we want to capture the fact that once a thread disables interrupts it cannot be preempted by any thread. Figure 5a shows an interrupt-driven program P_1 and its lock translation P_1^L in Fig. 5b. There are still issues with the translation related to re-entrancy of locks and it is not immediately clear how one would handle flag-based synchronization – but let us keep this aside for now.

The first problem with this translation is that it does not preserve race information. Consider the program P_1 in Fig. 5a and its translation P_1^L. The original program clearly has a race on x in statements 4 and 9. However the translation P_1^L does *not* have a race as the accesses are protected by the lock E. Hence checking for races in P^L does not substitute for checking in P. An alternative around this would be to first construct P' (recall that this is the version of P in which we introduce the `skip`-blocks around statements we want to check for races), then construct its lock translation $(P')^L$, and check this program for *high-level* races on the introduced `skip`-blocks. However this is expensive as it involves a 3x blow-up in going from P to P' and another 3x blow-up in going from P' to $(P')^L$. Further, checking for high-level races (for example using a lock-set analysis) is more expensive than just checking for races. In contrast, as we show next, our lock-set analysis on the native program P does not incur any of these expenses.

```
main:
1. x := y := t := 0;
2. create(t1);
3. create(t2);

t1:                    t2:
4. x := x + 1;         8. disableint;
5. disableint;         9. t := x;
6. x := y;             10. enableint;
7. enableint;
```

(a) Example program P_1

```
main:
1. x := y := t := 0;
2. spawn(t1);
3. spawn(t2);

t1:                    t2:
4. lock(E)             10. lock(E);
5. x := x + 1;         11. t := x;
6. unlock(E)           12. unlock(E);
7. lock(E)
8. x := y;
9. unlock(E)
```

(b) Exec-preserving trans. P_1^L

```
main:
1. x := y := t := 0;
2. spawn(t1);
3. spawn(t2);

t1:                    t2:
4. x := x + 1;         8. lock(A);
5. lock(A);            9. t := x;
6. x := y;             10. unlock(A);
7. unlock(A);
```

(c) Lightweight trans. P_1^W

Fig. 5. Example program P_1, and its lock and lightweight translations P_1^L, P_1^W.

The second problem with a precise lock translation is that the sync-CFG of the translated program has many unnecessary MSW-edges, leading to imprecision in the ensuing analysis. Consider the program P_2 in Fig. 6, and its lock translation P_2^L in Fig. 7. P_2 is similar to P_1 except that line 4 is now an increment of y instead of x, and the resulting program is race-free (in fact HB-race-free). Notice that the may-sync-with edges from line 13 to 4, and line 6 to 10 in the sync-CFG of P_2^L in Fig. 7 are *unnecessary* (they are not present in the native sync-CFG) and lead to imprecise facts in an interval analysis on this graph. Some of the final facts in an interval analysis on these graphs are shown alongside the programs in Figs. 6 and 7. In particular the analysis on P_2^L is unable to prove the assertion in line 10 of the original program.

6.2 A Lightweight Lock-Translation

Our disjoint block-based approach of Sect. 5 can be viewed as a *lightweight* lock translation which does not attempt to preserve execution semantics, but preserves disjoint blocks and hence also races and the sync-CFG structure of the original interrupt-driven program.

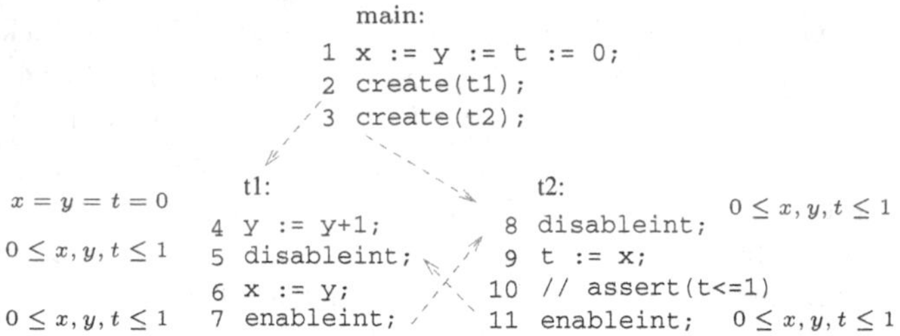

Fig. 6. Program P_2 with its Sync-CFG and facts from an interval analysis

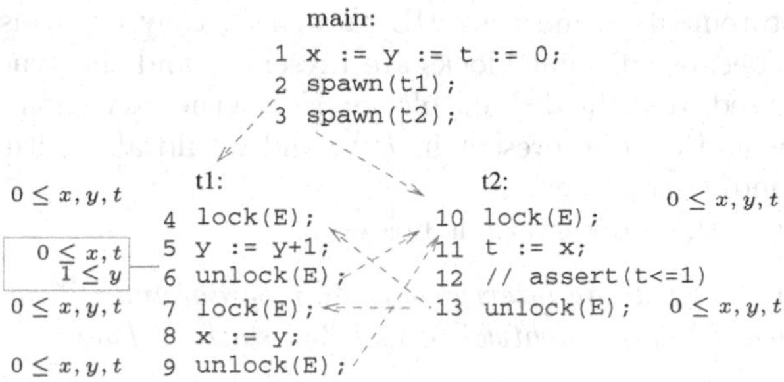

Fig. 7. Lock translation P_2^L of P_2, with its Sync-CFG and interval analysis facts

Let us first spell out the translation. Let us fix an interrupt-driven program $P = (V, T)$. The idea is simply to introduce a lock corresponding to each pattern of disjoint block pairs listed in Fig. 4, and to insert at the entry and exit to these blocks an acquire and release (respectively) of the corresponding lock. For each of the cases (a) through (h) we introduce locks named A through H, with some exceptions. Firstly, for case (f) regarding the `create` of a thread t, we simply translate these as a `spawn`(t) command in a classical lock-based programming language, which has a standard acquire-release semantics. Secondly, for case (h), we need a copy of H for *each* thread t, which we call H_t. This is because the concerned blocks (say between a set and unset of the flag f) are *not* disjoint across *task* threads, but only with the "then" block of an ISR thread statement that checks if $f = 0$. The ISR thread now acquires the set of locks $\{H_t \mid t \in T\}$ at the beginning of the "then" block of the `if` statement, and releases them at the end of that block. We call the resulting classical lock-based program P^W. Figure 5c shows this translation for the program P_1.

Figure 8 shows this translation along with the sync-CFG edges and some of the final facts in an interval analysis for the program P_2.

It is not difficult to see that P^W allows all executions that are possible in P. However it also allows more: for example the execution of P_1^W (Fig. 5c) in which thread $t1$ preempts $t2$ at line 9 to execute the statement at line 4, is *not* allowed in P_1. Thus it only *weakly* captures the execution semantics of P. However, every race in P is also a race in P^W. To see this, suppose we have a race on statements s and t in P. This means there is a high-level race on the two skip blocks around s and t in the augmented program P'. Since an execution exhibiting the high-level race on these blocks would also be present in $(P')^W$ which is identical to $(P^W)'$, it follows that the corresponding statements are racy in P^W as well.

Further, since our translation preserves disjoint blocks by construction, if s and t are in disjoint blocks in P, the corresponding statements will be in disjoint blocks in P^W; and vice-versa. It follows that the sync-CFGs induced by P and P^W are essentially isomorphic (modulo the synchronization statements). As a result, any value-set-based analysis will produce identical results on the two graphs.

Finally, if statements s and t are HB-racy in P, they must also be HB-racy in P^W. This is because disjoint blocks are preserved and the synchronizes-with relation is inherited from the disjoint blocks. Hence the execution witnessing the HB-race in P would also be present in P^W, and would also witness a HB-race on the corresponding statements.

We summarize these observations below:

Proposition 1. *Let P be an interrupt-driven program and P^W the classical lock program obtained using our lightweight lock translation. Then:*

1. *If statements s and t are racy in P, the corresponding statements are racy in P^W as well.*
2. *If statements s and t are HB-racy in P, the corresponding statements are HB-racy in P^W as well.*
3. *The sync-CFGs induced by P and P^W are essentially isomorphic. As a result the final facts in a value-set-based analysis on these graphs will be identical.*

□

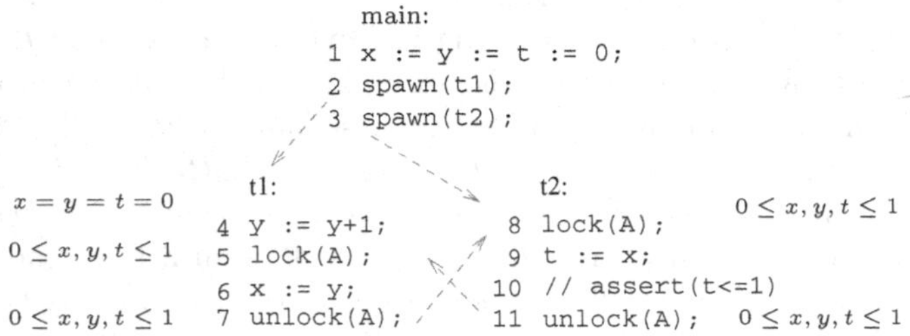

Fig. 8. Our lightweight translation P_2^W of P_2, with its Sync-CFG and interval analysis facts

6.3 Lockset Analysis for Race Detection

For classical lock-based programs, the lockset analysis [24] essentially tracks whether two statements are in disjoint blocks. Here two blocks are disjoint if they hold the same lock for the duration of the block. When two statements are in disjoint blocks, they are necessarily happens-before ordered, and hence this gives us a way to declare pairs of statements to be non-HB-racy.

A lockset analysis computes the set of locks held at each program point as follows: at program entry it is assumed that no locks are held. When a call to acquire(l) is encountered, the analysis adds the lock l at the *out* point of the call. When a call to release(l) is encountered the lockset at the *out* point of the call is the lockset computed at the *in* point with the lock l removed. For any other statement, the lockset from the *in* point of the statement is copied to its *out* point. The *join* operation is the simple intersection of the input locksets. Once locksets are computed at each point, a pair of conflicting statements s and

t in different threads are declared to *may* HB-race if the locksets held at these points have no lock in common.

Using our lock translation above, we can detect races as follows. Given an interrupt-driven program P, we first translate it to the lock-based program P^W, and do a lockset analysis on P^W. If any pair of conflicting statements s and t are found to be may-HB-racy in P^W, we declare them to be may-HB-racy in P. By Proposition 1(2), it follows that this is a sound analysis for interrupt-driven programs.

7 Analyzing the FreeRTOS Kernel Library

We now perform an experimental evaluation of the proposed race detection algorithm and sync-CFG-based relational analysis for interrupt-driven programs. We use the FreeRTOS kernel library [3], on which our interrupt-driven program semantics are based, to perform our evaluation. FreeRTOS is a collection of functions mostly written in C, that an application developer compiles with and invokes in the application code. We view the FreeRTOS kernel library as an interrupt-driven program as follows: we build an interrupt-driven program out of the FreeRTOS kernel as shown in the figure alongside. The main thread is responsible for initializing the kernel data structures and then creating two threads: a *task* thread which branches out calling each task kernel API function, and loops on this; and an *ISR* thread which similarly branches and loops on the ISR kernel API functions. FreeRTOS provides versions of API functions that can be called from interrupt service routines. These functions have "FromISR" appended to their name. While it is sufficient to have one ISR thread, we assume (in the analysis) that there could be any number of task threads running. To achieve this we simply add sync-edges *within* each task kernel function, in addition to the usual sync-edges between task functions. We used FreeRTOS version 10.0.0 for our experiments. We conducted these experiments on an Intel Core i7 machine with 32 GB RAM running Ubuntu 16.04.

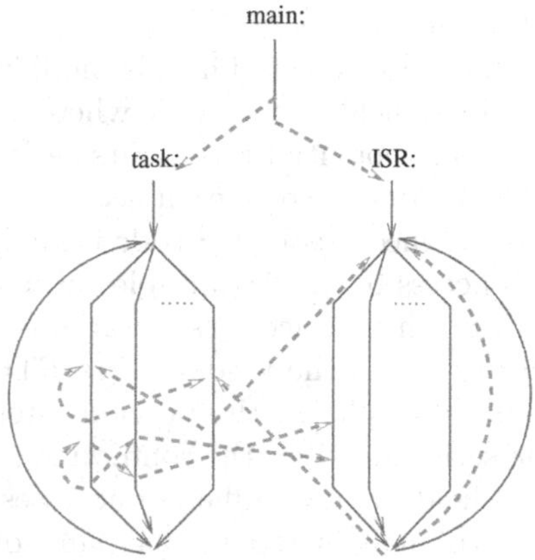

7.1 Race Detection

We consider 49 task and queue API functions that can be called from an application (termed top-level functions) for race detection. The functions operating on semaphores and mutexes were not considered.

We prepared the API functions for analysis, in two steps: (1) inlining and (2) lock insertion, as follows: The function `vTaskStartScheduler` and the queue initialization code in the function `xQueueGenericCreate` were treated as part of the main thread, which initializes kernel data structures. All the helper function calls made inside the top-level functions were inlined. After inlining, the functions are modified to acquire and release locks using the strategy explained in Sect. 6.2. We consider each pair of disjoint blocks as taking the same distinct lock. For example, the pair of disjoint blocks protected by `disableint-enableint` take lock A. That is `disableint` is replaced with `acquire`(A) and `enableint` is replaced with `release`(A). A total of 9 locks corresponding to disjoint blocks were employed in the modification of the FreeRTOS code. The two steps outlined above are automated. Inlining is achieved using the `inline` pass in the CIL framework [22]. Lock insertion is accomplished using a script.

The modified code, which has over 3.5K lines of code, is used for race detection. We tracked 24 variables and check whether the statements accessing them are racy. These variables include fields in the queue data-structure, task control block, and queue registry, as well as variables related to tasks. FreeRTOS maintains lists for the states of the tasks like "ready", "suspended", "waiting to send", etc. The pointers to these lists are also analysed. Access to any portion of a list (like the delayed list) is treated as an access of a corresponding variable of the same name.

Races are detected in this modified FreeRTOS code in three steps - (1) compute locks held, (2) identify whether access of a variable is a read or write, and (3) report potential races. First a lockset analysis, as explained in Sect. 6.3, to compute locks held at each access to variables, is implemented as a pass in CIL. The modified FreeRTOS code is analyzed using this new pass and the lockset at each access to the 24 variables of interest is computed. Then, a `writes` pass to identify whether accesses to variables are "read" or "write", also implemented in CIL, is run on the modified FreeRTOS code. Finally, a shell script to interpret both the results in the previous steps and report potential races is employed. The script identifies the conflicting access pairs (using the `writes` pass) and the locks held by the conflicting accesses (using lockset pass).

Our analysis reports 64 pairs of conflicting accesses as being potentially racy. On manual inspection we classified 18 of them are real races and the rest as false positives. Table 2 summarizes our findings. The second column in the table lists the variables of interest involved in the race, like various task list pointers, queue registry fields `pcQueueName` and `xHandle`, task variable `uxCurrentNumberOfTasks`, tick count `xTickCount`, etc. The third column lists the functions in which the conflicting accesses are made and the fourth gives the number of racing pairs. The fifth column assesses the potential races based on our manual inspection of the code. The analysis took 3.91 s.

The false positives were typically due to the fact that we had abstracted data-structures (like the delayed list which is a linked-list) by a synonymous variable. Thus even if the accesses were to different parts of the structure (like the container field of a list item and the next pointer of a different list item) our analysis flagged them as races.

We were in touch with the developers of FreeRTOS regarding the 18 pairs we classified as true positives. The 14 races on the queue registry were deemed to be non-issues as the queue delete function is usually invoked only once the application is about to terminate. The 2 races on `uxCurrentNumberOfTasks` are known (going by comments in the code) but are considered benign as the variable is of "base type". The remaining couple of races on the delayed task lists appear to be real issues as they have been fixed (independent of our work) in v10.1.1.

7.2 Region-Based Relational Analysis

Our aim here is to do a region-based interval and polyhedral analysis of a region-race-free subset of the FreeRTOS kernel APIs, and to prove some simple assertions about the kernel variables in each region.

We first identified six regions for this purpose. One region corresponds to variables protected by disabling interrupts (like `xTickCount`, `xNextTaskUnblockTime`, etc.), while variables protected by suspend and resume scheduler commands (like `uxPendedTicks`, `xPendingReadyList`, etc.) are in another region. Fields of the queue structure like `pcHead`, `pcTail`, etc. are in a third region, while the waiting lists for a queue form another region. The queue registry fields like `pcQueueName` and `xHandle` are in region 5. The pointer variable `pxCurrentTCB`, pointing to the current Task Control Block (TCB), is put in the sixth region.

The FreeRTOS code was modified further to reflect access to regions. For this new variables $R_1, \ldots, R_6$, are declared. Wherever there is a write (or read) access to a variable in region i an assignment statement that defines (or reads from) variable R_i is inserted just before the access. This is done using a script which takes the result of the `writes` pass to find where in the source code an appropriate assignment statement has to be inserted. We selected 15 APIs that did not contain any region races.

Next, we prepared the API functions for the analysis in two steps. They are described below:

Abstraction of FreeRTOS API Functions. We abstracted the FreeRTOS source code to prepare it for the relational analysis. In this abstraction, we basically model the various lists (ready list, delayed list) by their lengths and the value at the head of the list (if required). Using this abstraction, we are able to convert list operations to operations on integers.

Similarly, to model insertion into a list, we abstract it by incrementing the variable which represents the length of the list. We abstracted all the API functions in a similar fashion.

Creation of the Sync-CFG. The next step is to create a sync-CFG out of the abstracted program. For doing this, we used the abstracted version of the FreeRTOS code (along with acquire-release added as explained in Sect. 7.1).

Table 2. Potential races

Variables	Functions	#Race pairs	Remark
pxDelayedTaskList	eTaskGetState xTaskIncrementTick	1	Real race. Read of pxDelayedTaskList in eTaskGetState while it is written to in xTaskIncrementTick
pxOverflowDelayedTaskList	eTaskGetState xTaskIncrementTick	1	Real race. (similar as above)
uxCurrentNumberOfTasks	xTaskCreate uxTaskGetNumberOfTasks	2	Real race. Unprotected read in uxTaskGetNumberOfTasks while it is written to in xTaskCreate
pcQueueName xHandle	vQueueDelete pcQueueGetName vQueueAddToRegistry	14	Real race. Unprotected accesses in queue registry functions
xTasksWaitingToSend xTasksWaitingToReceive	eTaskGetState xQueueGenericReset	2	False positive. Initialization of vars when queue is created
pxDelayedTaskList pxOverflowDelayedTaskList xSuspendedTaskList pxCurrentTCB	9 functions like xTaskCreate, eTaskGetState, etc.	11	False positive. Initialization of vars when the first task is created
pxDelayedTaskList pxOverflowDelayedTaskList xSuspendedTaskList xTasksWaitingToSend xTasksWaitingToReceive	13 functions like vTaskDelay, eTaskGetState, etc.	33	False positive. The accesses are to disjoint portions of the lists

Next, we used a script to insert non-deterministic gotos from the point of release of a lock to the acquire of the same lock. Since we are using gotos for creation of sync-CFG, we keep all the API functions in main itself and evaluate a non-deterministic "if" condition before entering the code for an API function.

Results. For the purpose of analysis we listed out some numerical relations between kernel variables in the same region, which we believed should hold. We identified a total of 15 invariants including 4 invariants which involve relations between kernel variables. We then inserted assertions for these invariants at the key points in our source code like the exit of a block protecting a region.

We have implemented an interval-based value-set analysis and a region-based octagon and polyhedral analysis for C programs using CIL [22] as the front-end and the Apron library (version 0.9.11) [16]. We represent the sync-with edges of the sync-CFG of a program using goto statements from the source (release) to the target (acquire) of the may-synchronizes-with (MSW) edges.

We ran our implementation on the abstracted version of the FreeRTOS kernel library, with the aim of checking how many of the invariants it was able to prove. The abstracted code along with addition of gotos is about 1500 lines of code. We did a preliminary interval analysis on this abstracted sync-CFG and were able to prove 11 out of these 15 invariants. With a widening threshold of 30, the interval analysis takes under 5 min to run. As expected, the interval analysis could not prove the relational invariants.

We then did a region-based polyhedral analysis using the six regions identified above. For the region-based analysis, we used convex polyhedra domain with a widening threshold of 30. It is able to prove all the assertions we believed to be true. The analysis takes about 30 min to complete with the convex polyhedra domain and about 20 min with the octagon domain.

The results obtained by our analysis are shown in Table 3.

Table 3. Relational analysis results

Assertion	Interval Anal	Region Anal (Oct/Polyhedral)
xTickCount $\leq$ xNextTaskUnblockTime	No	Yes
head(pxDelayedTaskList) = xNextTaskUnblockTime	No	Yes
head(pxDelayedTaskList) $\geq$ TickCount	No	Yes
uxMessagesWaiting $\leq$ uxLength	No	Yes
uxMessagesWaiting ≥ 0	Yes	Yes
uxCurrentNumberOfTasks ≥ 0	Yes	Yes
lenpxReadyTasksLists ≥ 0	Yes	Yes
uxTopReadyPriority ≥ 0	Yes	Yes
lenpxDelayedTaskList ≥ 0	Yes	Yes
lenxPendingReadyList ≥ 0	Yes	Yes
lenxSuspendedTaskList ≥ 0	Yes	Yes
cRxLock ≥ -1	Yes	Yes
cTxLock ≥ -1	Yes	Yes
lenxTasksWaitingToSend ≥ 0	Yes	Yes
lenxTasksWaitingToReceive ≥ 0	Yes	Yes

8 Related Work

We classify related work based on the main topics touched upon in this paper.

Data Races. Adve and Hill [1] introduce the notion of a data race using a happens-before relation, and identify instructions that form release-acquire pairs, for low-level concurrent programs. Boehm and Adve [4] define races in terms of consecutive occurrences in a sequentially consistent execution, as well as using a happens-before order, in the context of the C++ semantics. They show their notions are equivalent as far as race-free programs go. As pointed out earlier, the definition of races as consecutive occurrences is inadequate in our setting. Schwarz *et al.* [26] define a notion of data race for priority-based interrupt-driven programs, where there is a single main task and multiple ISRs. A race occurs when the main thread is accessing a variable at a certain dynamic priority, and an ISR thread with higher priority also accesses the variable. Our definition can be seen to be stronger and more accurately captures racy situations. In particular, if the ISR thread with higher priority does not actually execute the conflicting access, due to say a condition not being enabled, then we would *not* call it a race. The term "high-level" race was coined by Artho *et al.* [2]. Our definition of a high-level race follows that of [20].

Analysis of Interrupt-Driven Programs. Regehr and Cooprider [23] describe a source-to-source translation of an interrupt-driven program to a standard multi-threaded program, and analyze the translated program for races. Their translation is inadequate for our setting in many ways: in particular, disable-enable of interrupts is translated by acquiring and releasing all ISR-specific locks; however this does not prevent interaction with another task while one task has disabled interrupts. In [8] they also describe an analysis framework for constant-propagation analysis on TinyOS applications. They use a similar idea of adding "control-flow" edges between disable-enable blocks and ISRs. However no soundness argument is given, and other kinds of blocks (suspend/resume, flag-based synchronization) are not handled. The works in [5,6,13] analyze timing properties, interrupt-latency, and stack sizes for interrupt-driven programs, using model-checking, algebraic, and algorithmic approaches. Schwarz *et al.* [25,26] give analyses for race-detection and invariants based on linear-equalities for their aforementioned class of priority-based interrupt-driven programs. Our work differs in several ways: Their analysis is directed towards *applications* (we target *libraries* where task priorities do not matter), their analyses are specific (we provide a basis for carrying out a variety of value-set and relational analyses, targeting race-free programs), they consider priority and flag-based synchronization (but not disable-enable and suspend-resume based synchronization). Sung and others [27] consider interrupt-driven applications in the form of ISRs with different priorities, and perform interval-based static analysis for checking assertions. They do not handle libraries and do not leverage race-freedom. Finally, [20] uses a model-checking approach to find all high-level races in FreeRTOS with a completeness guarantee.

Analysis of Race-Free Programs. Chugh *et al.* [7] use race information to do thread-modular null-dereference analysis, by killing facts at a point whenever a notional read of a variable is found to be racy. De *et al.* [11] propose the sync-CFG and value-set analysis for race-free programs, while Mukherjee *et al.* [21] extend the framework to region and relational analyses. Gotsman *et al.* [12] and Miné *et al.* [18,19] define relational shape/value analyses for concurrent programs that exploit race-freedom and lock invariants respectively. All these works are for classical lock-based synchronization while we target interrupt-driven programs.

9 Conclusion

In this paper our aim has been to give efficient static analyses for classes of non-standard concurrent programs like interrupt-driven kernels, that exploit the property of race-freedom. Towards this goal, we have proposed a definition of data races which we feel is applicable to general concurrent programs. We have also proposed a general principle for defining synchronizes-with edges, which is the key ingredient of a happens-before relation, based on the notion of disjoint blocks. We have implemented our theory to perform sound and effective static analysis for race-detection and invariant inference, on the popular real-time kernel FreeRTOS.

We feel this framework should be applicable to other kinds of concurrent systems, like other embedded kernels (for example TI-RTOS [14]) and application programs, and event-driven programs. There are additional challenges in these systems like priority-based preemption and priority inheritance conventions which need to be addressed. Apart from investigating these systems we would like to apply this theory to perform other static analyses like null-dereference, points-to, and shape analysis, for these non-standard classes of concurrent programs.

References

1. Adve, S.V., Hill, M.D.: A unified formalization of four shared-memory models. IEEE Trans. Parallel Distrib. Syst. **4**(6), 613–624 (1993)
2. Artho, C., Havelund, K., Biere, A.: High-level data races. J. Softw. Test. Verif. Reliab. **13**, 207–227 (2003)
3. Barry, R.: The FreeRTOS kernel, v10.0.0 (2017). https://freertos.org
4. Boehm, H., Adve, S.V.: Foundations of the C++ concurrency memory model. In: Proceedings of the ACM SIGPLAN 2008 Conference on Programming Language Design and Implementation, Tucson, USA, pp. 68–78. ACM (2008)
5. Brylow, D., Damgaard, N., Palsberg, J.: Static checking of interrupt-driven software. In: Proceedings of the 23rd International Conference on Software Engineering, ICSE 2001, Toronto, Ontario, Canada, 12–19 May 2001, pp. 47–56 (2001)
6. Chatterjee, K., Ma, D., Majumdar, R., Zhao, T., Henzinger, T.A., Palsberg, J.: Stack size analysis for interrupt-driven programs. In: Cousot, R. (ed.) SAS 2003. LNCS, vol. 2694, pp. 109–126. Springer, Heidelberg (2003). https://doi.org/10.1007/3-540-44898-5_7
7. Chugh, R., Voung, J.W., Jhala, R., Lerner, S.: Dataflow analysis for concurrent programs using data race detection. In: Proceedings of the ACM SIGPLAN 2008 Conference on Programming Language Design and Implementation, Tucson, AZ, USA, 7–13 June 2008, pp. 316–326 (2008)
8. Cooprider, N., Regehr, J.: Pluggable abstract domains for analyzing embedded software. In: Proceedings of the ACM SIGPLAN/SIGBED Conference on Languages, Compilers, and Tools for Embedded Systems (LCTES 2006), Ottawa, Canada, 14–16 June 2006, pp. 44–53 (2006)
9. Cousot, P., Cousot, R.: Abstract interpretation: a unified lattice model for static analysis of programs by construction or approximation of fixpoints. In: Proceedings of the ACM SIGACT-SIGPLAN Symposium on Principles of Programming Languages, pp. 238–252. ACM (1977)
10. De, A.: Access path based dataflow analysis for sequential and concurrent programs. Ph.D. thesis, Indian Institute of Science, Bangalore, December 2012

11. De, A., D'Souza, D., Nasre, R.: Dataflow analysis for data race-free programs. In: Proceedings of the 20th European Symposium on Programming ESOP 2011, Saarbrücken, Germany, 26 March – 3 April 2011, pp. 196–215 (2011)
12. Gotsman, A., Berdine, J., Cook, B., Sagiv, M.: Thread-modular shape analysis. In: Proceedings of the ACM SIGPLAN 2007 Conference on Programming Language Design and Implementation, San Diego, California, USA, 10–13 June 2007, pp. 266–277 (2007)
13. Huang, Y., Zhao, Y., Shi, J., Zhu, H., Qin, S.: Investigating time properties of interrupt-driven programs. In: Gheyi, R., Naumann, D. (eds.) SBMF 2012. LNCS, vol. 7498, pp. 131–146. Springer, Heidelberg (2012). https://doi.org/10.1007/978-3-642-33296-8_11
14. Texas Instruments: TI-RTOS: A Real-Time Operating System for Microcontrollers (2017). http://www.ti.com/tool/ti-rtos
15. Jeannet, B., Miné, A.: Apron: a library of numerical abstract domains for static analysis. In: Bouajjani, A., Maler, O. (eds.) CAV 2009. LNCS, vol. 5643, pp. 661–667. Springer, Heidelberg (2009). https://doi.org/10.1007/978-3-642-02658-4_52
16. Jeannet Bertrand, M.A.: Apron numerical abstract domain library (2009). http://apron.cri.ensmp.fr/library/
17. Kini, D., Mathur, U., Viswanathan, M.: Dynamic race prediction in linear time. In: Proceedings of the 38th ACM SIGPLAN Conference on Programming Language Design and Implementation, PLDI 2017, pp. 157–170. ACM, New York (2017)
18. Miné, A.: Relational thread-modular static value analysis by abstract interpretation. In: McMillan, K.L., Rival, X. (eds.) VMCAI 2014. LNCS, vol. 8318, pp. 39–58. Springer, Heidelberg (2014). https://doi.org/10.1007/978-3-642-54013-4_3
19. Monat, R., Miné, A.: Precise thread-modular abstract interpretation of concurrent programs using relational interference abstractions. In: Bouajjani, A., Monniaux, D. (eds.) VMCAI 2017. LNCS, vol. 10145, pp. 386–404. Springer, Cham (2017). https://doi.org/10.1007/978-3-319-52234-0_21
20. Mukherjee, S., Kumar, A., D'Souza, D.: Detecting all high-level dataraces in an RTOS kernel. In: Bouajjani, A., Monniaux, D. (eds.) VMCAI 2017. LNCS, vol. 10145, pp. 405–423. Springer, Cham (2017). https://doi.org/10.1007/978-3-319-52234-0_22
21. Mukherjee, S., Padon, O., Shoham, S., D'Souza, D., Rinetzky, N.: Thread-local semantics and its efficient sequential abstractions for race-free programs. In: Ranzato, F. (ed.) SAS 2017. LNCS, vol. 10422, pp. 253–276. Springer, Cham (2017). https://doi.org/10.1007/978-3-319-66706-5_13
22. Necula, G.: CIL – infrastructure for c program analysis and transformation (v. 1.3.7) (2002). http://people.eecs.berkeley.edu/~necula/cil/
23. Regehr, J., Cooprider, N.: Interrupt verification via thread verification. Electr. Notes Theor. Comput. Sci. **174**(9), 139–150 (2007)
24. Savage, S., Burrows, M., Nelson, G., Sobalvarro, P., Anderson, T.E.: Eraser: a dynamic data race detector for multithreaded programs. ACM Trans. Comput. Syst. **15**(4), 391–411 (1997)
25. Schwarz, M.D., Seidl, H., Vojdani, V., Apinis, K.: Precise analysis of value-dependent synchronization in priority scheduled programs. In: McMillan, K.L., Rival, X. (eds.) VMCAI 2014. LNCS, vol. 8318, pp. 21–38. Springer, Heidelberg (2014). https://doi.org/10.1007/978-3-642-54013-4_2
26. Schwarz, M.D., Seidl, H., Vojdani, V., Lammich, P., Müller-Olm, M.: Static analysis of interrupt-driven programs synchronized via the priority ceiling protocol. In: Proceedings of the ACM SIGPLAN-SIGACT Principles of Programming Languages (POPL), pp. 93–104 (2011)

27. Sung, C., Kusano, M., Wang, C.: Modular verification of interrupt-driven software. In: Proceedings of the 32nd IEEE/ACM International Conference on Automated Software Engineering, ASE 2017, Urbana, IL, USA, 30 October – 3 November 2017, pp. 206–216 (2017)
28. Tarski, A., et al.: A lattice-theoretical fixpoint theorem and its applications. Pac. J. Math. **5**, 285–309 (1955)

An Abstract Domain for Trees with Numeric Relations

Matthieu Journault[1(✉)], Antoine Miné[1,2(✉)], and Abdelraouf Ouadjaout[1(✉)]

[1] Sorbonne Université, CNRS, Laboratoire d'Informatique de Paris 6, LIP6, 75005 Paris, France
{matthieu.journault,antoine.mine,abdelraouf.ouadjaout}@lip6.fr
[2] Institut universitaire de France, Paris, France

Abstract. We present an abstract domain able to infer invariants on programs manipulating trees. Trees considered in the article are defined over a finite alphabet and can contain unbounded numeric values at their leaves. Our domain can infer the possible shapes of the tree values of each variable and find numeric relations between: the values at the leaves as well as the size and depth of the tree values of different variables. The abstract domain is described as a product of (1) a symbolic domain based on a tree automata representation and (2) a numerical domain lifted, for the occasion, to describe numerical maps with potentially infinite and heterogeneous definition set. In addition to abstract set operations and widening we define concrete and abstract transformers on these environments. We present possible applications, such as the ability to describe memory zones, or track symbolic equalities between program variables. We implemented our domain in a static analysis platform and present preliminary results analyzing a tree-manipulating toy-language.

1 Introduction

The abstract interpretation framework [5] enables the development of sound static analyzers by inferring and proving invariants on reachable states of programs. Invariants in the scope of abstract interpretation are elements of a lattice called an abstract domain. Most domains focus on numeric or pointer variables. By contrast, we propose an abstract domain for variables whose values are tree data-structures. Tree values appear natively in some languages (such as OCaml) and applications (such as the DOM in web programming) or can be encoded through pointer manipulations (as in C). Trees can abstract terms in logic programming. A tree domain can also be useful to collect symbolic expressions appearing in a program.

This work is supported by the European Research Council under Consolidator Grant Agreement 681393 – MOPSA.

L. Caires (Ed.): ESOP 2019, LNCS 11423, pp. 724–751, 2019.
https://doi.org/10.1007/978-3-030-17184-1_26

```
typedef struct node
{
  int data;
  struct node* next;
} node;

node* append(node* head, int data)
{
  if (head==NULL) {
    return (create(data, NULL));
  } else {
    node *cursor=head;
    while(cursor->next != NULL)
      cursor=cursor->next;
    node* new_node=create(data,NULL);
    cursor->next=new_node;
    return head;
  }
}
```

Program 1: Append to list in C

```
float golden_ratio(int n) {
  int i = 0;
  float r = 1;
  while (i < n) {
    r = 1 + 1 / r;
    i += 1;
  }
  return r;
}
```

Program 2: Golden ratio in C

```
let rec f x n =
  match n with
  | 0 -> []
  | _ -> (x+1)::(x-1)::(f x (n-1))

let () =
  (*Assume x:int and n:int>=0*)
  let t = f x n in
  match t with
  | [] -> ()
  | p :: q when p > x -> ()
  | _ -> assert false
```

Program 3: List type in OCaml

Used Memory Zones. Program 1 describes an `append` function defined in the C language, this function adds an integer at the end of a linked list. The infinite set of unbounded terms of the form `*(*( ...*(head + 4) ...+ 4) + 4)` represents memory zones that are used by the `append` function. Our analyzer is able to infer and represent such sets of terms. This provides the information that Program 1 does not use any of the `data` field of the linked list. Such a function would be fairly commonly called in a real-life project. In a classical top-down static analysis by abstract interpretation, function calls are inlined at each call site. A way to improve scalability is to design modular analyzers able to reuse previous analysis results (as emphasized in [7]). In order to be able to successfully reuse function body analysis, input states must be unified. Moreover the cost of performing the analysis of the body of functions grows with the number of variables that need to be tracked. A common way to deal with both problems is to use framing on the inputs of the functions (as in separation logic [25]). This improves (1) precision: as we know that they are not modified by the function call, (2) body analysis efficiency: as the input state is reduced and finally (3) modularity: as constraints on the usage of the first analysis are relaxed by the removal of constraints.

Symbolic Relations. Program 2 is a C function computing an approximation of the golden ration (as it is the limit of the sequence $r_0 = 1$, $r_{n+1} = 1 + \frac{1}{r_n}$). As classical numerical domains can not represent such numerical relations, methods were proposed to track symbolic equality between expressions (see [23]). However such methods can not handle the unbounded iteration of Program 2. The set of reachable states at the end of Program 2 can be expressed by $\mathtt{r} = 1 + 1/(1 + 1/\ldots 1 \ldots)$ with depth $\mathtt{n}$. Please note that to infer such results we need to express numerical relations between the size of trees and the numeric variables from the program.

Numerical Environment. Consider now the OCaml Program 3, we want to prove that the `assert false` expression is never reached. This program builds a list of size $2 * \mathtt{n}$ with alternating values $\mathtt{x}+1$ and $\mathtt{x}-1$. The assertion states that the head of the list is $\mathtt{x}+1$. After the definition of `t` there are two types of reachable states. (1) Those that have not gone through the loop ($\mathtt{t} \mapsto \mathtt{[]}, \mathtt{x} \mapsto \mathbb{Z}, \mathtt{n} \mapsto 0$), and (2) those that have gone through at least one iteration of the loop: ($\mathtt{t} \mapsto \mathtt{[}a_1\mathtt{;}a_2\mathtt{;}a_3\mathtt{;}\ \ \mathtt{...]}, x \mapsto \alpha, \mathtt{n} > 0, a_1 \mapsto \alpha+1, a_2 \mapsto \alpha-1, a_3 \mapsto \alpha+1$), where $\alpha \in \mathbb{Z}$. Therefore we need to be able to keep numerical relations between the parametric and unbounded number of numeric values appearing in `t` and numeric variables from the program. Classical numeric domains do not provide out-of-the-box abstractions for sets of partially defined numerical functions, therefore we define such an abstraction. As an example of analysis result, the memory representation obtained by our analysis for `t` describes the set of trees of the form: $\mathtt{Cons(}a\mathtt{,\ Cons(}b\mathtt{,\ Cons(}a\mathtt{,\ ...,\ Nil)\ ...))}$ where $a = \mathtt{x}+1$ and $b = \mathtt{x}-1$. Therefore we are able to prove that the `assert false` expression is never reached.

Contributions. The main contributions of the article are threefold: (1) The extension of results on tree automata to the abstract interpretation framework by definition of a widening operator, in order to represent the set of tree shapes that a variable can contain. (2) The definition of a numerical domain built upon classical abstract domains able to represent sets of partial numerical maps with heterogeneous and unbounded definition sets. This is necessary to represent the numeric values at the leaves of a set of trees, as trees are unbounded and can contain a different number of leaves. (3) The definition of a novel abstraction for trees that can contain numerical values at their leaves. This last domain combines the abstractions (1) and (2). Moreover it is relational as it can express relations between numerical values found in trees and in the rest of the program, and relations between trees. Finally all results were implemented in an existing framework and experimented on a toy-language.

Limitations. At this point, analyses can only be performed on the toy language presented thereinafter, not on real life code, therefore we do not present any benchmark results, even though examples of analysis results will be put forth. Indeed Programs 1, 2 and 3 were precisely analyzed once encoded into our toy-language (see Programs 4 and 5).

Outline. We start, in Sect. 2, by presenting the concrete semantic we want to abstract. In Sect. 3 we build a first abstraction which forgets numerical values and focuses on abstracting tree shapes. Section 4 presents a novel numerical abstract domain required for the definition of the abstract domain of Sect. 5, which aims at precisely representing numerical constraints between trees and program variables. In Sect. 6 we provide remarks on the implementation and results of the analyzer. Finally Sect. 7 mentions related works while Sect. 8 concludes.

Notations. Classical Galois connections (see [5]) are denoted $(A, \subseteq_A) \underset{\alpha}{\overset{\gamma}{\leftrightarrows}} (B, \subseteq_B)$. When no best abstraction can be defined, we use the *representation* framework (as defined by Bourdoncle in [3], also known as concretization only framework), representations are denoted by $(A, \subseteq_A) \overset{\gamma}{\leftarrow} (B, \subseteq_B)$. $A \twoheadrightarrow B$ denotes the set of partial maps from A to B, and $\lambda_{|A}x.f(x) \in B$ denotes the map in $A \to B$ that associates $f(x)$ to x. Finally when $f \in A \to C$ and $g \in B \to C$, with $A \cap B = \emptyset$, $f \uplus g$ is the function defined on $A \cup B$, that associates $f(x)$ (resp. $g(x)$) to x whenever $x \in A$ (resp. $x \in B$).

2 Syntax and Concrete Semantics

Definition 1. *An* alphabet *$\mathcal{F}$ is a finite set, a* ranked alphabet *is a pair $\mathcal{R} = (\mathcal{F}, a)$ where $\mathcal{F}$ is an alphabet and $a \in \mathcal{F} \to \mathbb{N}$. For $f \in \mathcal{F}$, we call* arity *of f the value $a(f)$. We assume that $\mathbb{Z}$ and $\mathcal{F}$ are disjoint and we define the set of* natural terms *over $\mathcal{R}$ (denoted $T_{\mathbb{Z}}(\mathcal{R})$) to be the smallest set defined by:*

- $\mathbb{Z} \subseteq T_{\mathbb{Z}}(\mathcal{R})$
- $\forall p \geq 0,\ f \in \mathcal{F}, t_1,\ \ldots, t_p \in T_{\mathbb{Z}}(\mathcal{R}),\ a(f) = p \Rightarrow f(t_1, \ldots, t_p) \in T_{\mathbb{Z}}(\mathcal{R})$

Moreover when $\mathcal{R}$ contains at least one symbol of arity 0, we define terms *over $\mathcal{R}$ (denoted $T(\mathcal{R})$) to be the smallest set defined by:*

- $\forall p \geq 0,\ f \in \mathcal{F}, t_1,\ \ldots, t_p \in T(\mathcal{R}),\ a(f) = p \Rightarrow f(t_1, \ldots, t_p) \in T(\mathcal{R})$

*In the following, $\mathcal{F}_n$ denotes the subset of $\mathcal{F}$ of arity n. Moreover given a term $t \in T(\mathcal{R})$ we denote $f =$ **head**$(t) \in \mathcal{F}$ and **sons**(t) a possibly empty tuple $(t_1, \ldots, t_n)$ of elements of $T(\mathcal{R})$ such that $t = f(t_1, \ldots, t_n)$.*

Remark 1. Numerical leaves are defined to contain integers, however this could be modified to rationals, real numbers or floats. We are parametric in the type of numeric values, as they are delegated to an underlying numerical domain.

Example 1. Consider the ranked alphabet $\mathcal{R} = \{$`*`(1), `&`(1), `+`(2), `x`(0)$\}$, $u(n)$ means that symbol u has arity n. Then `&x` $\in T(\mathcal{R})$, but `*(&x+4)` $\in T_{\mathbb{Z}}(\mathcal{R})$, and `*(&x+4)` $\notin T(\mathcal{R})$. Using this alphabet we can model C pointer arithmetic.

Example 2. $U = \{+(x, y) \mid x \leq y\}$ and $V = \{+(x, +(z, y)) \mid x \leq y \wedge z \leq y\}$ are two sets of natural terms over $\mathcal{R} = \{+(2)\}$ which we use as running examples.

$$
\begin{aligned}
\textit{tree-expr} &\triangleq \mid \texttt{make\_symbolic}(\mathcal{F}, \textit{tree-expr}, \ldots, \textit{tree-expr}) \\
&\quad \mid \texttt{make\_integer}(\textit{expr}) \\
&\quad \mid \texttt{get\_son}(\textit{tree-expr}, \textit{expr}) \\
\textit{stmt} &\triangleq \ldots \\
&\quad \mid \mathcal{T} \texttt{ = } \textit{tree-expr} \\
\textit{sym-expr} &\triangleq \mid \texttt{get\_sym\_head}(\textit{tree-expr}) \\
\textit{expr} &\triangleq \ldots \\
&\quad \mid \texttt{get\_num\_head}(\textit{tree-expr}) \\
&\quad \mid \texttt{is\_symbol}(\textit{tree-expr}) \\
&\quad \mid \textit{sym-expr} \texttt{ == } \mathcal{F}
\end{aligned}
$$

Fig. 1. Syntax extension of the language

$$
\begin{aligned}
&\mathbb{E}[\![\texttt{make\_symbolic}(s \in \mathcal{F}_m, T_1, \ldots, T_m)]\!](E, F) = \{s(t_1, \ldots, t_m) \mid \forall i,\ t_i \in \mathbb{E}[\![T_i]\!](E, F)\} \\
&\mathbb{E}[\![\texttt{make\_integer}(e \in \textit{expr})]\!](E, F) = \mathbb{E}[\![e]\!](E, F) \\
&\mathbb{E}[\![\texttt{is\_symbol}(T)]\!](E, F) = \{\texttt{true} \mid \exists t \in \mathbb{E}[\![T]\!](E, F), \exists f \in \mathcal{R},\ t = f(\ldots)\} \\
&\qquad\qquad \cup \{\texttt{false} \mid \exists t \in \mathbb{E}[\![T]\!](E, F), t \in \mathbb{Z}\} \\
&\mathbb{E}[\![\texttt{get\_son}(T, e)]\!](E, F) = \{t \mid \exists i \in \mathbb{E}[\![e]\!](E, F),\ t' \in \mathbb{E}[\![T]\!](E, F), f \in \mathcal{F}_{m>i}, \\
&\qquad\qquad t' = f(t_0, \ldots, t_{m-1}) \wedge t_i = t\} \\
&\mathbb{E}[\![\texttt{get\_num\_head}(T)]\!](E, F) = \{i \in \mathbb{Z} \mid \exists t \in \mathbb{E}[\![T]\!](E, F),\ t = i\} \\
&\mathbb{E}[\![\texttt{get\_sym\_head}(T)]\!](E, F) = \{s \in \mathcal{R} \mid \exists t \in \mathbb{E}[\![T]\!](E, F),\ t = s(\ldots)\}
\end{aligned}
$$

Fig. 2. Concrete operations on natural terms

```
int i;
int n;
tree y;
assume(n >= 0);
i = 0;
y = make_symbolic("p",{});
while (i < n) {
  y = make_symbolic("*",
           {make_symbolic("+",
                 {y,
                  make_integer(4)
                 })
           });
  i = i+1;
}
```

Program 4: `*(p+4)` iterated

```
int n; int i; int x; int rep;
tree t;
assume(n>=0);
i = 0;
t = make_symbolic("Nil",{});
while (i < n) {
  t = make_symbolic("Cons",
        {make_integer(x-1), t});
  t = make_symbolic("Cons",
        {make_integer(x+1), t});
  i = i + 1;
 };
if (get_sym_head(t) != "Nil") {
    rep = get_num_head(get_son(t,0));
    assert(rep > x);
 }
```

Program 5: List manipulation

Syntax of the Language and Concrete Operations. We assume already defined a small imperative language and extend it (in Fig. 1) with statements, tree expressions (*tree-expr*) which are expressions that are evaluated to trees, and simple symbol expressions (*sym-expr*) which enable the manipulation of symbols. We add the ability to build a tree which contains only a numerical leaf: $\texttt{make\_integer}(e)$, the ability to read the i-th son of a tree t: $\texttt{get\_son}(t, i)$, ... Figure 2 defines concrete operations over the set $\wp(T_{\mathbb{Z}}(\mathcal{R}))$. Figure 2 assumes given a set of program numerical variables $\mathcal{V}$, a set of numerical expressions (over $\mathcal{V}$) denoted *expr*, a set of statements *stmt*, a notion of numerical environment $E \in \mathfrak{E} = \mathcal{V} \to \mathbb{Z}$, a set of tree program variables $\mathcal{T}$, a notion of tree environment $F \in \mathfrak{F} = \mathcal{T} \to \wp(T_{\mathbb{Z}}(\mathcal{R}))$, $D = E \times F$ is our concrete domain. Finally we assume already partially defined on numerical expressions an evaluation function $\mathbb{E}[\![e \in \mathit{expr}]\!](E \in \mathcal{V} \to \mathbb{Z}, F \in \mathcal{T} \to \wp(T_{\mathbb{Z}}(\mathcal{R}))) \in \wp(\mathbb{Z})$. Using this operator we are able to define Program 4 which computes the memory zones used by **append** from Program 1, and Program 5 that simulates the behavior of Program 3.

3 Natural Term Abstraction by Tree Automata

In this section we start by defining a value abstraction for tree sets (in Sect. 3.1), which is then lifted to an environment abstraction (in Sect. 3.2).

3.1 Value Abstraction

As a first abstraction for natural terms, we put aside numerical values and define an abstraction able to describe sets of tree shapes. Tree automata enable the description of set of terms built upon a finite ranked alphabet. The ranked alphabet of the language we want to analyze is extend with the □ symbol to denote potential positions of numerical values.

Definition 2 (Finite tree automata). *A finite tree automaton (FTA) over a ranked alphabet $\mathcal{R}$ is a tuple $(Q, \mathcal{R}, Q_f, \delta)$, where Q is a (finite) set of states, $Q_f \subseteq Q$ is the set of final states, and $\delta \in \wp(\bigcup_{n\in\mathbb{N}} \mathcal{F}_n \times Q^n \times Q)$ is the set of transitions. We define $\overline{\delta} : (\bigcup_{n\in\mathbb{N}} \mathcal{F}_n \times Q^n) \to \wp(Q)$ by: $\overline{\delta}(f, \overrightarrow{q}) = \{q' \mid (f, \overrightarrow{q}, q') \in \delta\}$. When $\overline{\delta}$ is such that, $\forall n \in \mathbb{N}$, $f \in \mathcal{F}_n$, $\overrightarrow{q} \in Q^n$, $|\overline{\delta}(f, \overrightarrow{q})| = 1$, we say that the automaton is complete and deterministic (CDFTA). We then abuse notations and denote by $\delta(f, \overrightarrow{q})$ the unique element in the set $\overline{\delta}(f, \overrightarrow{q})$.*

Definition 3 (Reachability). *Given a FTA $\mathcal{A} = (Q, \mathcal{R}, Q_f, \delta)$ we define, a reachability function* $\text{REACH}_{\mathcal{A}} : T(\mathcal{R}) \to \wp(Q)$

$$\text{REACH}_{\mathcal{A}}(t) = \textbf{let } t_1, \ldots, t_n = \textbf{sons}(t) \textbf{ in} \bigcup_{(q_1,\ldots,q_n)\in(\text{REACH}_{\mathcal{A}}(t_1),\ldots,\text{REACH}_{\mathcal{A}}(t_n))} \overline{\delta}(\textbf{head}(t), (q_1, \ldots, q_n))$$

If **sons**(t) *is the empty tuple (which is the case when t is a constant a), the union is made over a unique element (which is the empty tuple), which then boils down to: $\overline{\delta}(a, ())$. If* **sons**(t) *is not the empty tuple and for some i, $\text{REACH}_{\mathcal{A}}(t_i)$ is empty, then $\text{REACH}_{\mathcal{A}}(t)$ is also empty.*

Example 3. Consider the ranked alphabet $\mathcal{R} = \{f(2), a(0)\}$, and the automaton $\mathcal{A} = (\{u, v\}, \mathcal{R}, \{v\}, \{a() \to u, f(v, v) \to v, f(u, u) \to u, f(u, u) \to v\})$. Then $\text{REACH}_{\mathcal{A}}(a) = \{u\}$, $\text{REACH}_{\mathcal{A}}(f(a, a)) = \{u, v\}$, $\text{REACH}_{\mathcal{A}}(f(f(a, a), a)) = \{u, v\}$.

Definition 4 (Acceptance). *Given a FTA $\mathcal{A} = (Q, \mathcal{R}, Q_f, \delta)$, a term t, we say that t is* accepted *by the automaton if* $\text{REACH}_{\mathcal{A}}(t) \cap Q_f \neq \emptyset$. *$\mathcal{L}(\mathcal{A})$ denotes the set of terms accepted by automaton $\mathcal{A}$.*

Example 4. With the definition of Example 3, $\mathcal{L}(\mathcal{A})$ is the set of terms over $\mathcal{R}$ that contain at least one f.

Definition 5 (Tree regular languages). *A set of terms $\mathcal{T}$ over a ranked alphabet $\mathcal{R}$ is called* tree regular *if there exists a FTA $\mathcal{A}$ over $\mathcal{R}$ such that $\mathcal{L}(\mathcal{A}) = \mathcal{T}$. The set of such languages is denoted TReg($\mathcal{R}$).*

Remark 2. As for regular languages, for all $\mathcal{A} \in$ FTA there exists $\mathcal{A}' \in$ CDFTA such that $\mathcal{L}(\mathcal{A}) = \mathcal{L}(\mathcal{A}')$, moreover $\mathcal{A}'$ is computable (see [4]).

Example 5.
- As proved in Example 4 the set of all terms over $\{f(2), a(0)\}$ that contain at least one f is tree regular.
- Consider now the ranked alphabet $\{a(1), b(1), \epsilon(0)\}$ and the set of terms $\mathcal{T} = \{\epsilon, a(b(\epsilon)), a(a(b(b(\epsilon)))), \dots\}$. We can prove (in a similar way as for $a^n b^n$ in regular languages) that $\mathcal{T}$ is not tree regular.
- On every ranked alphabet $\mathcal{R}$: every finite language, the empty language and $T(\mathcal{R})$ are tree regular.

Proposition 1. *$(TReg(\mathcal{R}), \subseteq, \cap, \cup, .^c, \emptyset, T(\mathcal{R}))$ is a complemented lattice with infinite height, moreover it is not complete. $\subseteq, \cap, \cup$ and complementation $(.^c)$ are computable operations on tree automata [4].*

We denote by $\mathcal{R}^\square$ the ranked alphabet $\mathcal{R}$ after adding the symbol $\square$ of arity 0 (we assume that $\square \notin \mathcal{R}$). Given a natural term t, we define $t^\square$ to be the term obtained by replacing every integer with the $\square$ symbol.

Proposition 2. *$(\wp(T_{\mathbb{Z}}(\mathcal{R})), \subseteq) \xleftarrow{\gamma} (TReg(\mathcal{R}^\square), \subseteq)$ where $\gamma(\mathcal{A}) = \{t \mid t^\square \in \mathcal{L}(\mathcal{A})\}$ is a representation. Moreover with such a γ definition, $\cup$, $\cap$ soundly represent the union and the intersection.*

Remark 3. We only have a representation and not a Galois connection as language $\mathcal{T}$ of Example 5 does not have a best tree regular over approximation.

Example 6. Let $\mathcal{R} = \{+(2)\}$ and $\mathcal{A} = (\{0,1\}, \mathcal{R}^\square, \{0,1\}, \{(\square() \to 0, +(0,0) \to 1, +(0,1) \to 1)\})$. Examples of terms recognized by $\mathcal{A}$ are shown on Fig. 3. Natural terms from our running example U and V (defined in Example 2) are also contained in $\gamma(\mathcal{A})$. Moreover as we do not provide numerical constraints: $1 + (3 + 4)$, 23, $1 + (2 + (3 + 4))$ are also elements in $\gamma(\mathcal{A})$.

Due to the infinite height of the lattice, a widening operator is required. In the following, we assume given a constant $w \in \mathbb{N}$, this constant will be used to stabilize increasing chains, the greater the constant, the more precise our widening operator will be.

Definition 6. *Let $\mathcal{A} = (Q, \mathcal{R}, Q_f, \delta) \in FTA$, and $\sim$ be an equivalence relation on Q, such that $p \sim q \wedge p \in Q_f \Rightarrow q \in Q_f$. We define $\mathcal{A}/\sim = (Q/\sim, \mathcal{R}, Q_f/\sim, \bigcup_{(f,q_1,\ldots,q_n,q)\in\delta}\{(f, q_1^{\sim}, \ldots, q_n^{\sim}, q^{\sim})\})$ where $q^{\sim}$ is the equivalence class of q in $\sim$.*

Proposition 3. *For every $\mathcal{A} \in FTA$ and every $\sim$ equivalence relation on its states, $\mathcal{L}(\mathcal{A}) \subseteq \mathcal{L}(\mathcal{A}/\sim)$.*

Therefore following the idea from [9] and in [11], we define a widening operation by quotienting states of automata by an equivalence relation of finite index. We define by induction a special sequence of equivalence relations on states of tree automata: $\sim_1 = \{Q_f, Q \setminus Q_f\}$ and $\sim_{k+1}$ is $\sim_k$ where we split equivalence classes not satisfying the following condition: $\forall f \in \mathcal{F}_n$, $\forall p_1, \ldots, p_n \in Q$, $\forall q_1, \ldots, q_n \in Q, (\bigwedge_{i=1}^{n} p_i \sim_k q_i) \Rightarrow \delta(f, p_1, \ldots, p_n) \sim_k \delta(f, q_1, \ldots, q_n)$ and $\forall q \in Q_f$, $q^{\sim_k} \subseteq Q_f$. This sequence of equivalence relations is the Myhill-Nerode sequence (see [4]). This sequence is of length at most the number of states of the automaton (before stabilization). Let $\phi(w) = \max\{i \leq |Q| \mid \text{index of } \sim_i \leq w\}$ (given an integer w, ϕ yields the index of the most precise of the equivalence relationships in the Myhill-Nerode sequence, that contains at most w equivalence classes) and $[\mathcal{A}]_w = \mathcal{A}/\sim_{\phi(w)}$. $[\mathcal{A}]_w$ is therefore a FTA with at most w states such that $\mathcal{L}(\mathcal{A}) \subseteq \mathcal{L}([\mathcal{A}]_w)$. As for regular languages, for every CDFTA a equivalent minimal CDFTA (in the sense of the number of states, and unique modulo state renaming) can be obtained by quotienting the automaton by $\sim_{|Q|}$. Therefore we define a widening operator on CDFTAs, which is then lifted to tree regular languages.

Definition 7 (Widening operator $\triangledown$). $\mathcal{A} \triangledown \mathcal{A}' = [\mathcal{A} \cup \mathcal{A}']_w$.

Proposition 4. *This widening is sound and stabilizes infinite sequences.*

Remark 4. Consider the two following complete and deterministic tree automata: $\mathcal{A} = (\{a, b, h\}, \{+(2)\}, \{a\}, \{\square() \to b, +(b, b) \to a\})$ and $\mathcal{B} = (\{a, b, c, h\}, \{+(2)\}, \{a\}, \{\square() \to b, +(b, b) \to c, +(b, c) \to a\})$ (unmentioned transitions go to h). $\mathcal{A}$ (resp. $\mathcal{B}$) recognizes the tree $+(\square, \square)$ (resp. $+(\square, +(\square, \square))$), it over-approximates U (resp. V) from our running example. $\mathcal{A} \cup \mathcal{B}$ is recognized by the following complete and deterministic tree automaton: $\mathcal{C} = (\{a, b, c, h\}, \{+(2)\}, \{a, c\}, \{\square() \to b, +(b, b) \to c, +(b, c) \to a\})$. If we want to widen $\mathcal{A}$ and $\mathcal{B}$ with parameter 3, the following equivalence relation is computed: $\{\{h\}, \{b\}, \{a, c\}\}$. Merging equivalent states produces $(\{a, b, h\}, \{+(2)\}, \{a\}, \{\square() \to b, +(b, b) \to a, +(b, a) \to a\})$, which contains a loop and over-approximates the union.

3.2 Environment Abstraction

Now that we are given an abstraction for natural term sets, let us show how this is lifted to a notion of abstract natural term environments mapping variables to natural terms. Given a set of natural term variables $\mathcal{T}$, consider $\mathfrak{F}^\sharp = (\mathcal{T} \rightarrow \text{TReg}(\mathcal{R}^\square)) \cup \{\bot\}$ and the set operators defined by the point-wise lifting of operators on $\text{TReg}(\mathcal{R}^\square)$. We also lift the concretization function $\wp(T_\mathbb{Z}(\mathcal{R})) \leftarrow \text{TReg}(\mathcal{R}^\square)$ to $\mathfrak{F} \leftarrow \mathfrak{F}^\sharp$. We assume given an abstract numerical environment $E^\sharp$ and an abstract evaluator $\mathbb{E}[\![e]\!]^\sharp$. Abstract transformers $[\![\texttt{make\_symbolic}]\!]^\sharp$, $[\![\texttt{is\_symbol}]\!]^\sharp$, $[\![\texttt{get\_son}(e)]\!]^\sharp$, $[\![\texttt{get\_sym\_head}]\!]^\sharp$ and $[\![\texttt{get\_num\_head}]\!]^\sharp$ are simple tree automata operations. For concision Fig. 4 only provides definitions of two of these operators. Please note that these definitions require all states of the automata to be reachable. An example of use of the `is_symbol` operator can be found in Example 7. Other abstract operators are similar.

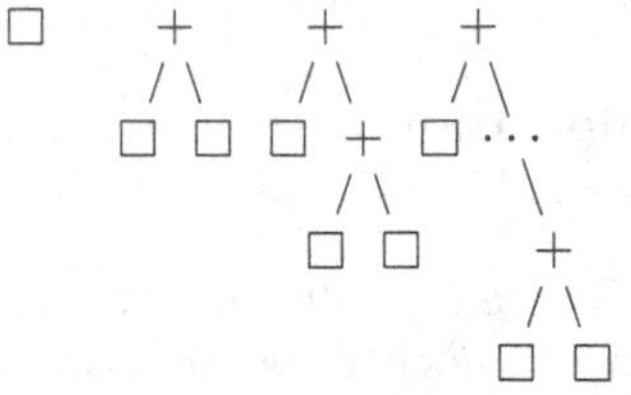

Fig. 3. Example of accepted trees from Example 6

$$\mathbb{E}^\sharp[\![\texttt{make\_integer}(e \in \mathit{expr})]\!](E^\sharp, F^\sharp) = \langle\{a\}, \mathcal{R}, \{a\}, \{\square() \rightarrow a\}\rangle$$

$$\mathbb{E}^\sharp[\![\texttt{get\_son}(T, e \in \mathit{expr})]\!](E^\sharp, F^\sharp) =$$

$$\bigcup_{\substack{(Q,\mathcal{R},Q_f,\delta) \in \mathbb{E}^\sharp[\![T]\!](E^\sharp,F^\sharp) \\ i \in \mathbb{E}^\sharp[\![e]\!](E^\sharp) \cap \{0,\ldots,m-1\}}} (Q, \mathcal{R}, \{q \in Q \mid \exists p \in Q_f,\ \exists s(p_0, \ldots, p_{m-1}) \rightarrow p \in \delta \wedge p_i = q\}, \delta)$$

Fig. 4. Abstract operators

Example 7. Consider the tree automaton $\mathcal{A}$ of Example 6, (Fig. 3), with $F^\sharp = (x \mapsto \mathcal{A})$: $[\![\texttt{get\_sym\_head}(x)]\!]^\sharp(E^\sharp, F^\sharp) = \{+\}$ and $[\![\texttt{get\_num\_head}(x)]\!]^\sharp(E^\sharp, F^\sharp) = \top$.

4 Numerical Abstractions

As emphasized in the introductory example, we rely on numerical domains to introduce constraints on numerical variables found in trees. In a classical numeric abstraction (e.g. intervals [6], octagons [22], polyhedra [8], ...), each abstract element represents a set of maps $\mathcal{V} \rightarrow \mathbb{R}$ for a fixed, finite set of variables $\mathcal{V}$. In contrast, our numeric variables are leaves of a possibly infinite set of trees of unbounded size. Hence before starting the presentation of the numerical abstraction for natural terms, we show how to extend in a generic way an abstract element in two steps. Firstly we want to be able to represent a set of maps, where each map is defined over a (possibly different) finite subset of an infinite set of variables (this is done in Sect. 4.1). Secondly, we use summarization variables to relax the finiteness constraint, so as to represent sets of maps over heterogeneous maps over infinitely many variables (done in Sect. 4.2).

4.1 Heterogeneous Support

We define $\mathfrak{M} \triangleq \wp(\mathcal{V} \nrightarrow \mathbb{R})$, the set of partial maps from $\mathcal{V}$, to $\mathbb{R}$. $\mathfrak{M}$ is ordered by the inclusion relation $\subseteq$. In the following $\mathbf{def}(f)$ denotes the definition set of f. We assume defined a representation $(\wp(\mathcal{S} \to \mathbb{R}), \subseteq) \overset{\gamma_0^{\mathcal{S}}}{\longleftarrow} (N_{\mathcal{S}}, \sqsubseteq_0^{\mathcal{S}})$, for every finite set $\mathcal{S} \subseteq \mathcal{V}$ (such as octagons in $|S|$ dimensions). $N_{\mathcal{S}}$ comes with the usual abstract set operator $\sqcap_0^{\mathcal{S}}$, $\sqcup_0^{\mathcal{S}}$. Moreover if $x \in \mathcal{S}$, $y \notin \mathcal{S}$, $\mathcal{S}'$ is another finite set and $N^\sharp \in N_{\mathcal{S}}$ then $N^\sharp[x \mapsto y] \in N_{\mathcal{S} \cup \{y\} \setminus \{x\}}$ is the abstract element obtained by renaming x into y, $N^\sharp_{|\mathcal{S}'} \in N_{\mathcal{S}'}$ is obtained by existentially quantifying dimensions associated to elements in $\mathcal{S}$ and not in $\mathcal{S}'$ and adding unconstrained dimensions for elements in $\mathcal{S}'$ and not in $\mathcal{S}$. From now on we assume that this last operator is exact (as for intervals, octagons, polyhedra over $\mathbb{R}$). However results from this section can be extended to numerical domains that are able, given $N^\sharp \in N_{\mathcal{S}}$, $N^{\sharp\prime} \in N_{\mathcal{S}'}$, to check if $\gamma_0^{\mathcal{S}}(N^\sharp) \subseteq \gamma_0^{\mathcal{S}'}(N^{\sharp\prime})_{|\mathcal{S}}$. The precision of the extension defined in this subsection would then depend upon the precision of this test in the underlying domain. Finally $[\![.]\!]_0^{\mathcal{S}}$ (resp. $[\![.]\!]_0^{\sharp,\mathcal{S}}$) refers to the classical concrete (resp. abstract) semantic of operators on sets of numerical maps (resp. abstract elements). A classical method for the abstraction of heterogeneous maps is the use of a partitioning of the concrete element according to the definition set of its represented maps. However partitioning induces an increase in numerical operation cost (exponential in the number of variable) which we would like to avoid. Therefore in order to abstract sets of maps with heterogeneous definition sets, we start by abstracting the potential definition set. We choose a simple lower-bound/upper-bound abstraction (l and u in the following definition). Moreover we need to abstract the potential mappings given a definition set: this is done using a classical numerical domain. Contrary to partitioning, we will use only one numerical abstract element, defined on the upper-bound u, to represent all environments (instead of one abstract element by definition set). We also add a $\top$ element, used in the case where the upper bound u is infinite.

Definition 8 (Numerical abstraction). *Let us define the following set:* $\mathfrak{M}^\sharp \triangleq \{\langle N^\sharp, l, u\rangle \mid l, u \in \wp(V) \wedge l$ *and* u *are finite* $\wedge l \subseteq u \wedge N^\sharp \in N_u \wedge N^\sharp \neq \bot_0^u\} \cup \{\top, \bot\}$. *An element of* $\mathfrak{M}^\sharp$ *is therefore: either* $\top$, $\bot$ *or a triple* $\langle N^\sharp, l, u\rangle$ *where* l *and* u *are finite sets of variables such that* $N^\sharp$ *is defined over* u.

Definition 9 (Concretization function). *Abstract elements from* $\mathfrak{M}^\sharp$ *are mapped to* $\mathfrak{M}$ *thanks to the following concretization function:* $\gamma(\bot) = \emptyset$, $\gamma(\top) = \mathfrak{M}$ *and* $\gamma(\langle N^\sharp, l, u\rangle) = \{\rho \in \mathcal{S} \to \mathbb{Z} \mid l \subseteq \mathcal{S} \subseteq u \wedge \rho \in \gamma_0^{\mathcal{S}}(N^\sharp)_{|\mathcal{S}})\}$.

Example 8. As an example consider $\gamma(\langle\{x = y, x \leq 3, z = 0\}, \{x\}, \{x, y, z\}\rangle) = \{(x \mapsto a) \mid a \leq 3\} \cup \{(x \mapsto a, y \mapsto a) \mid a \leq 3\} \cup \{(x \mapsto a, z \mapsto 0) \mid a \leq 3\} \cup \{(x \mapsto a, y \mapsto a, z \mapsto 0) \mid a \leq 3\}$. As intended, the resulting set of maps contains maps with different definition sets.

Definition 10 (Order). *On* $\mathfrak{M}^\sharp$ *we define the following comparison operator:* $\langle N^\sharp, l, u\rangle \sqsubseteq \langle N^{\sharp\prime}, l', u'\rangle \Leftrightarrow l' \subseteq l \subseteq u \subseteq u' \wedge N^\sharp \sqsubseteq_0^u N^{\sharp\prime}_{|u}$*, this comparison is trivially extended to* $\top$ *(resp.* $\bot$*) as being the biggest (resp. smallest) element in* $\mathfrak{M}^\sharp$*. In the following* $\mathfrak{M}^\sharp_\mathfrak{p}$ *denotes the subset of* $\mathfrak{M}^\sharp$ *where* $u = \mathfrak{p}$ *extended with* $\top$ *and* $\bot$*.*

Proposition 5. γ *is monotonic for* $\sqsubseteq$*.*

Figure 5 provides the definition of the concrete and abstract semantics of the classical numerical statements, `Assume` and `Assign` (denoted $x \leftarrow e$). We denote $\mathbf{vars}(e)$ the set of variables appearing in e. We recall that $[\![\texttt{Assume}(c)]\!]_0^{\mathcal{S}}(E \in \wp(\mathcal{S} \to \mathbb{R})) = \{f \in E \mid \texttt{true} \in \mathbb{E}[\![c]\!](f)\}$ and $[\![x \leftarrow e]\!]_0^{\mathcal{S}}(E \in \wp(\mathcal{S} \to \mathbb{R})) = \{f[x \mapsto e'] \mid f \in E \wedge e' \in \mathbb{E}[\![e]\!](f)\}$. In order to ease the lifting of these classical operators we define $[\![\texttt{stmt}]\!]_0(\mathcal{M} \in \mathfrak{M}) \triangleq \cup_{\mathcal{S} \text{ finite} \subseteq \mathcal{V}} [\![\texttt{stmt}]\!]_0^{\mathcal{S}}(\mathcal{M} \cap (\mathcal{S} \to \mathbb{R}))$, for every statement `stmt`. Moreover we assume the existence of the following abstract operators: $[\![\texttt{Assume}(c)]\!]_0^{\sharp,u}(N^\sharp)$ and $[\![x \leftarrow e]\!]_0^{\sharp,u} N^\sharp$ abstracting soundly their respective concrete transformers. Note that the concrete semantic of `Assume`(c) (resp. $x \leftarrow e$) enforces that maps are defined at least on the variables appearing in c (resp. in e and on x). Abstract operators from Fig. 5 are sound with respect to γ and their concrete operators.

$$[\![\texttt{Assume}(c)]\!](\mathcal{M}) = [\![\texttt{Assume}(c)]\!]_0(\{f \mid f \in \mathcal{M} \wedge \mathbf{vars}(c) \subseteq \mathbf{def}(f)\})$$
$$[\![\texttt{Assume}(c)]\!]^\sharp(\langle N^\sharp, l, u\rangle) = \langle [\![\texttt{Assume}(c)]\!]_0^{\sharp,u}(N^\sharp), l \cup \mathbf{vars}(c), u\rangle$$
$$[\![x \leftarrow e]\!](\mathcal{M}) = [\![x \leftarrow e]\!]_0(\{f \mid f \in \mathcal{M} \wedge \mathbf{vars}(e) \cup \{x\} \subseteq \mathbf{def}(f)\})$$
$$[\![x \leftarrow e]\!]^\sharp(\langle N^\sharp, l, u\rangle) = \langle [\![x \leftarrow e]\!]_0^{\sharp,u}(N^\sharp), l \cup \mathbf{vars}(e) \cup \{x\}, u\rangle$$

Fig. 5. Concrete and abstract semantic of usual numerical operators

We now need to define $\sqcup$ that abstracts the classic set operator $\cup$. We can not directly apply the corresponding abstract operator on the numerical component of the abstractions as they might have different definition sets. A first naive solution would be to extend their respective definition set and to perform the abstract operation on the resulting elements: $N^\sharp_{|u \cup u'} \sqcup_0^{u \cup u'} N^{\sharp\prime}_{|u \cup u'}$. However consider $M = \langle \{x = y\} (= U^\sharp), \{x, y\}, \{x, y\}\rangle$ and $N = \langle \{x = z\} (= V^\sharp), \{x, z\}, \{x, z\}\rangle$, where the underlying domain is the octagon domain where elements are represented as a set of linear constraints (e.g. $\{x = y\}$). We have $U^\sharp_{|\{x,y,z\}} = \{x = y\}$ and $V^\sharp_{|\{x,y,z\}} = \{x = z\}$, hence $U^\sharp_{|\{x,y,z\}} \sqcup_0^{\{x,y,z\}} V^\sharp_{|\{x,y,z\}} = \top$. Consider now the abstract element in $\mathfrak{M}^\sharp$: $R = \langle \{x = y, x = z\} (= W^\sharp), \{x\}, \{x, y, z\}\rangle$. The concretization of R over-approximates the union of the concretization of M and N, and its numerical component is more precise than $\top$. We note that the numerical constraints appearing in $W^\sharp$ could be found in $U^\sharp$ or $V^\sharp$, therefore in order to remove the aforementioned imprecision we define a refined abstract union operator, denoted as $\boxed{\star}$, that uses constraints found in the inputs in order to refine its

Algorithm 1. strengthening operator

Input : $X^\sharp$, C: a set of constraints, $U^\sharp \in N_u$: a soundness threshold on environment u, $V^\sharp \in N_v$: a soundness threshold on environment v
Output: $Z^\sharp$ an abstract element over-approximating $U^\sharp$ on u and $V^\sharp$ on v

```
Z♯ ← X♯;
foreach c ∈ C do
    T♯ ← [[Assume(c)]]♯,u∪v_0 (Z♯);
    if U♯ ⊑^u_0 T♯_|u ∧ V♯ ⊑^v_0 T♯_|v then
        Z♯ ← T♯;
    end
return Z♯;
```

result. This is done using the **strenghtening** operator of Algorithm 1 which adds constraints from C that do not make the projection of $X^\sharp$ to u (resp. v) lower than the threshold $U^\sharp$ (resp. $V^\sharp$). We assume that, given an abstract element $U^\sharp$, we can extract a finite set of constraints satisfied by $U^\sharp$, those are denoted **constraints**($U^\sharp$) (the more constraints can be extracted, the more precise the result will be). For example if the numerical domain is the interval domain, constraints have the form $\pm x \geq a$. If the numerical domain is the octagon domain the **constraints** operator yields all the linear relations among variables that define the octagon.

Definition 11 ($\boxast$ operator). *Let $U^\sharp \in N_u$, $V^\sharp \in N_v$ be two numerical environments, let $X^\sharp \in N_{u\cup v}$, let C be a sequence of numerical constraints over $u \cup v$, let $\mathfrak{c} = u \cap v$ we define:*

$$U^\sharp \boxast V^\sharp = \textbf{let } X^\sharp = (U^\sharp_{|\mathfrak{c}} \sqcup^{\mathfrak{c}}_0 V^\sharp_{|\mathfrak{c}})_{|u\cup v} \textbf{ in}$$
$$\textbf{let } C = \textbf{constraints}(U^\sharp) \cup \textbf{constraints}(V^\sharp) \textbf{ in}$$
$$\textbf{strengthening}(X^\sharp, C, U^\sharp, V^\sharp)$$

Remark 5.
- The precision of $\boxast$ depends upon the order of iteration over constraints $c \in C$ in Algorithm 1. Our implementation currently iterates in the order in which constraints are returned from the abstract domains. More clever heuristics will be considered in future work.
- $U^\sharp \boxast V^\sharp$ starts by performing the join over the domain $\mathfrak{c}$, the result is then strengthened. Other **strenghtening**($X^\sharp, U^\sharp \in N_u, V^\sharp \in N_v$) operator could be defined, however in order to ensure soundness of $\boxast$, it must satisfy the following constraints: $U^\sharp \sqsubseteq^u_0$ **strenghtening**($X^\sharp, U^\sharp, V^\sharp$) and $V^\sharp \sqsubseteq^v_0$ **strenghtening**($X^\sharp, U^\sharp, V^\sharp$).

Example 9. Let us now consider the example introduced thereinbefore $U^\sharp \boxast V^\sharp = \{x = y, y = z\} \in N_{\{x,y,z\}}$. Indeed using the notations of Definition 11: $Z^\sharp \triangleq X^\sharp = \top \in N_{\{x,y,z\}}$, $C = \{x = y, y = z\}$, moreover $[\![\mathtt{Assume}(x = y)]\!]^{\sharp,u\cup v}_0(\top) =$

$\{x = y\}(\triangleq T^\sharp)$, $U^\sharp \sqsubseteq_0^{\{x,y\}} \{x = y\} = T^\sharp_{|\{x,y\}}$ and $V^\sharp \sqsubseteq_0^{\{x,z\}} \top = T^\sharp_{|\{x,z\}}$. Therefore constraint $x = y$ is added to $Z^\sharp$. At the next loop iteration: $[\![\texttt{Assume}(x = z)]\!]_0^{\sharp,u\cup v}(\{x = y\}) = \{x = y, x = z\}(\triangleq T^\sharp)$, $U^\sharp \sqsubseteq_0^{\{x,y\}} \{x = y\} = T^\sharp_{|\{x,y\}}$ and $V^\sharp \sqsubseteq_0^{\{x,z\}} \{x = z\} = T^\sharp_{|\{x,z\}}$. Therefore constraint $x = z$ is added to $Z^\sharp$.

Proposition 6 (Soundness of $\boxast$). *let* $U^\sharp \in N_u$ *and* $V^\sharp \in N_v$*, then* $\gamma_0^u(U^\sharp) \subseteq (\gamma_0^{u\cup v}(U^\sharp \boxast V^\sharp))_{|u}$ *and* $\gamma_0^v(V^\sharp) \subseteq (\gamma_0^{u\cup v}(U^\sharp \boxast V^\sharp))_{|v}$.

Definition 12 (Union abstract operators). *We define the following abstract set operator:* $\langle N^\sharp, l, u\rangle \sqcup \langle N^{\sharp\prime}, l', u'\rangle \triangleq \langle N^\sharp \boxast N^{\sharp\prime}, l \cap l', u \cup u'\rangle$. *This operator soundly abstracts the union. Moreover in order to ensure the stabilization of infinitely increasing chains in* $\mathfrak{M}^\sharp$ *we define the following widening operator:*

$$\langle N^\sharp, l, u\rangle \triangledown \langle N^{\sharp\prime}, l', u'\rangle = \begin{cases} \langle N^\sharp \triangledown_0^u N^{\sharp\prime}_{|u}, l, u\rangle & \textit{when } l \subseteq l' \wedge u' \subseteq u \\ \langle N^\sharp \boxast N^{\sharp\prime}, l', u\rangle & \textit{when } l' \subset l \wedge u' \subseteq u \\ \top & \textit{otherwise} \end{cases}$$

Remark 6. This widening operator over-approximates to $\top$ whenever the upper-bound on the definition set is growing. This yields a huge loss of information however this numerical domain is designed as a tool domain used by a higher level abstraction in charge of stabilizing the environment before applying the widening, so that this case will not be used in practice.

Subsequent tree abstractions require the definition of the following operators:

- $\langle N^\sharp, l, u\rangle_{|-x} \triangleq \langle N^\sharp_{|u\setminus\{x\}}, l \setminus \{x\}, u \setminus \{x\}\rangle$ and $\langle N^\sharp, l, u\rangle_{|+x} \triangleq \langle N^\sharp_{|u\cup\{x\}}, l \cup \{x\}, u \cup \{x\}\rangle$ which respectively removes (adds) a variable to the numerical environment.
- $\langle N^\sharp, l, u\rangle_{|\mathcal{S}}$ is computed by adding variables in $\mathcal{S}$ and not in u and removing variables in u that are not in $\mathcal{S}$.

4.2 Representation of Maps over Potentially Unbounded Sets

In this subsection we focus on the problem of defining abstract numerical environments on potentially infinite environments. A classical method we use here is variable summarization (see [13]). This is based on the folding of several concrete objects (a potentially infinite number) to an abstract element which summarizes all concrete objects. The folding is encoded in a function f mapping summarized variables to the set of concrete variables they abstract. Given an abstract numerical environment $N^\sharp$ and a mapping from summary variables: $\mathcal{V}'$ to sets of concrete variables $f \in \mathcal{V}' \rightarrow \wp(\mathcal{V})$ where $f(v_1) \cap f(v_2) \neq \emptyset \Rightarrow v_1 = v_2$, we define the collapsing of a partial map $\rho \in \mathcal{V} \nrightarrow \mathbb{Z}$ under a summarizing function f:

$$\begin{aligned}\downarrow_f(\rho) = \{\rho' \in \mathcal{V}' \nrightarrow \mathbb{Z} \mid & \forall v' \in \mathcal{V}',\ (f(v') \cap \mathbf{def}(\rho) = \emptyset \wedge \rho'(v') = \mathbf{undefined}) \\ & \vee (\exists v \in \mathcal{V},\ v \in f(v') \cap \mathbf{def}(\rho) \wedge \rho'(v') = \rho(v))\}\end{aligned}$$

Example 10. Consider $\mathcal{V}' = \{x, y, z, t\}$ and $\mathcal{V} = \{a, b, c, d, g, h\}$, the environment $\rho = (a \mapsto 0, b \mapsto 1, c \mapsto 2, d \mapsto 3)$ and finally the summarizing function $f = (x \mapsto \{a\}, y \mapsto \{b, c\}, z \mapsto \{d\}, t \mapsto \{g\})$. Collapsing environment ρ under f yields the set of environments: $(x \mapsto 0, y \mapsto 1, z \mapsto 3)$ and $(x \mapsto 0, y \mapsto 2, z \mapsto 3)$.

Given a summarizing function f we can now define an extension of the concretization function γ of the previous subsection in the following manner:

$$\gamma[f](N^\sharp) = \{\rho \in \mathcal{V} \nrightarrow \mathbb{Z} \mid \downarrow_f (\rho) \subseteq \gamma(N^\sharp)\}$$

Example 11. Going back to Example 10 and considering the numerical abstract element: $N^\sharp = \langle\{x \leq y\}, \{x\}, \{x, y\}\rangle$, we have: $\gamma(N^\sharp) = \{(x \mapsto \alpha) \mid \alpha \in \mathbb{Z}\} \cup \{(x \mapsto \alpha, y \mapsto \beta) \mid \alpha \leq \beta\}$. We have: $m \in \gamma[f](N^\sharp) \Leftrightarrow \downarrow_f (m) \subseteq \gamma(N^\sharp) \Rightarrow \{x\} \subseteq \mathbf{def}(\downarrow_f (m)) \subseteq \{x, y\}$. Therefore if we assume m defined on d then $f(z) \cap \mathbf{def}(m) \neq \emptyset$ hence there would be an element in $\downarrow_f (m)$ defined on z. Hence m is not defined on d, similarly for g. Moreover $\{x\} \subseteq \mathbf{def}(\downarrow_f (m))$ implies that m is defined on a. Finally: defining $S = \{(a \mapsto \alpha) \mid \alpha \in \mathbb{Z}\} \cup \{(a \mapsto \alpha, b \mapsto \beta) \mid \alpha \leq \beta\} \cup \{(a \mapsto \alpha, c \mapsto \beta) \mid \alpha \leq \beta\} \cup \{(a \mapsto \alpha, b \mapsto \beta, c \mapsto \gamma) \mid \alpha \leq \beta \wedge \alpha \leq \gamma\}$. We have: $\gamma[f](N^\sharp) = S \cup (\bigcup_{f \in S}\{f \uplus (h \mapsto \delta) \mid \delta \in \mathbb{Z}\})$.

The abstract domains we will define in the following sections will employ this summarization framework. The manipulation of summarized variables requires the definition of a $\mathbf{fold}(E, x, \mathcal{S})$ (resp. $\mathbf{expand}(E, x, \mathcal{S})$) operator yielding a new environment where x is used as a summary variable for $\mathcal{S}$ (resp. where a summary variable x is desummarized into a set of variables $\mathcal{S}$). Let $\mathcal{S}$ and $\mathcal{S}'$ be two finite sets of elements such that $\mathcal{S}' \cap \mathcal{S} \subseteq \{x\}$, we define: $\mathbf{expand}_0(N^\sharp, x, \mathcal{S}'') = \bigsqcap_{v \in \mathcal{S}''} N^\sharp[x \mapsto v]_{|(\mathcal{S} \setminus \{x\}) \cup \mathcal{S}''}$ and $\mathbf{fold}_0(N^\sharp, x, \mathcal{S}'') = \bigsqcup_{v \in \mathcal{S}''} N^\sharp[v \mapsto x]_{|(\mathcal{S} \setminus \mathcal{S}'') \cup \{x\}}$ (which generalize the one introduced in [13]). These operations are lifted as operators on elements of $\mathfrak{M}^\sharp$:

$$\mathbf{expand}(\langle N^\sharp, l, u\rangle, x, \mathcal{S}) \triangleq \langle \mathbf{expand}_0(N^\sharp, x, \mathcal{S}), l \setminus \{x\}, (u \setminus \{x\}) \cup \mathcal{S}\rangle$$

$$\mathbf{fold}(\langle N^\sharp, l, u\rangle, x, \mathcal{S}) \triangleq \langle \mathbf{fold}_0(N^\sharp, x, \mathcal{S}), \begin{cases} (l \setminus \mathcal{S}) \cup \{x\} & \text{if } \mathcal{S} \subseteq l \\ (l \setminus \mathcal{S}) & \text{otherwise} \end{cases}, (u \setminus \mathcal{S}) \cup \{x\}\rangle$$

5 Natural Term Abstraction by Numerical Constraints

We are now able to represent sets of maps with heterogeneous supports and to lift their concretization (modulo a summarization function) to sets of maps with infinite and heterogeneous supports. Given a tree shape (in the sense of Sect. 3), we can associate a numeric variable to each numeric leaf, and use a numeric abstract element to represent the possible values of these leaves. We will name the variable of each leaf as the path from the root to the leaf, i.e., $\mathcal{V}$ is a set of words in $\{0, ..., n-1\}$ where n is the maximum arity of the considered ranked alphabet. In order to avoid confusion such paths will be denoted $\wr 0, 1, 1 \wr$ for the word $(0, 1, 1)$. A summarized variable then represents a set of such paths. We will abstract such sets as regular expressions. Using the summarization extended to heterogeneous supports presented in the previous section, it will be possible to represent, using a single numeric abstract element, a set of contraints over the numeric leaves of an infinite set of unbounded trees of arbitrary shape.

5.1 Hole Positions and Numerical Constraints

The presentation of our computable abstraction able to represent numerical values in trees is broken down (for presentation purposes) into two consecutive abstractions. The first one is not computable, as natural terms are abstracted as partial environments over tree paths to numerical values. This abstraction looses most of the tree shapes but focuses on their numerical environment. A second abstraction will show how partial environments over paths are abstracted into numerical abstract elements defined over a regular expression environment.

In the following, when $\mathcal{R}$ is a ranked alphabet of maximum arity n, we call *words* sequences of integers, $w = (w_0, \ldots, w_{p-1}) \in \{0, \ldots, (n-1)\}^p$ will be called a word of length p (denoted $|w|$), w_i denotes the i-th integer of the sequence, $\overline{w} = (w_1, \ldots, w_{p-1})$ is the tail of word w, $\mathcal{W}(\mathcal{R}) = \{0, \ldots, (n-1)\}^\star$ is the set of all words over $\{0, \ldots, n-1\}$ of arbitrary size.

Definition 13 (Position in a term). *Given a natural term t and a word w we inductively define the subterm of t at position w (denoted $t_{|w}$) to be:*

$$t_{|w} = \begin{cases} (t_{w_0})_{|\overline{w}} & \textit{when } |w| > 0 \wedge t = f(t_0, \ldots, t_{p-1}) \textit{ with } w_0 < p \\ t & \textit{when } |w| = 0 \\ \textbf{undefined} & \textit{otherwise} \end{cases}$$

Moreover we denote by $\textbf{numeric}(t) = \{w \in \mathbb{N}^\star \mid t_{|w} \in \mathbb{Z}\}$.

Definition 14 (Positioning lattice with exact numerical constraints). *We define $\mathcal{C}(\mathcal{R}) \triangleq \wp(\mathcal{W}(\mathcal{R}) \nrightarrow \mathbb{Z})$, an element of $\mathcal{C}(\mathcal{R})$ is therefore a set of partial maps that are acceptable bindings of positions to integers.*

Proposition 7 (Galois connection with natural terms). *When t is a natural term, $t_{\mathbb{Z}}$ is the partial map: $\lambda_{|\textbf{numeric}(t)} w.t_w$. We have the following Galois connection: $(\wp(T_{\mathbb{Z}}(\mathcal{R})), \subseteq) \underset{\alpha_{\mathcal{C}(\mathcal{R})}}{\overset{\gamma_{\mathcal{C}(\mathcal{R})}}{\leftrightarrows}} (\mathcal{C}(\mathcal{R}), \subseteq)$, with:*

$$\gamma_{\mathcal{C}(\mathcal{R})}(\Gamma) = \{t \in T_{\mathbb{Z}}(\mathcal{R}) \mid t_{\mathbb{Z}} \in \Gamma\} \quad \alpha_{\mathcal{C}(\mathcal{R})}(T) = \{t_{\mathbb{Z}} \mid t \in T\}$$

Example 12. Consider our running example (introduced in Example 2), $V = \{+(x, +(z, y)) \mid x \leq y \wedge z \leq y\}$, we have $\alpha_{\mathcal{C}(\mathcal{R})}(V) = \{\wr 0 \int \mapsto \alpha, \wr 1, 0 \int \mapsto \gamma, \wr 1, 1 \int \mapsto \beta \mid \alpha \leq \beta \wedge \gamma \leq \beta\}$. The concretization of which is exactly V.

Example 13. Consider however the ranked alphabet $\{f(2), g(2), a(0)\}$, and the tree a. Its abstraction contains only the empty map, the concretization of which is the set of all terms that do not contain any numerical value. For example: $f(g(a, a), a), g(a, a), \ldots$. This emphasizes that we loose information on:

- the labels in the natural terms: we only have the path from the root of the term to leaves with numerical labels, not the actual symbols along the path.
- the shape of the natural terms: we do not keep any information on subterms that do not contain numerical values.

Now that we have abstracted away the shape of the terms, we are left with numerical environments with potentially infinite dimensions (that are words over the alphabet $\{0,\ldots,n-1\}$) and different definition sets. Therefore following the idea of Sect. 4 we want to define a summarization for sets of words over the alphabet $\{0,\ldots,n-1\}$. A summarization of such a language can be expressed as a partition into sub-languages. The set of regular languages over the alphabet $\{0,\ldots,n-1\}$ is a subset of the set of languages over this alphabet, that is closed under common set operations. Hence given a set $\{r_1,\ldots,r_m\}$ of regular expressions (with respective recognized language $\{L_1,\ldots,L_m\}$), we summarize all words in L_i inside a common variable r_i and therefore $\uparrow\{r_1,\ldots,r_m\}$ denotes the summarization function: $\lambda r_i.L_i$. In the following, Reg_n denotes the set of regular expressions over the alphabet $A_n = \{0,\ldots,n-1\}$. As for tree regular expressions, $(\mathrm{Reg}_n, \subset, \cap, \cup, .^c, \emptyset, A_n^\star)$ is a (non complete) complemented lattice of infinite height, upon which we can define a widening operator $\triangledown$ (see [10]) in a similar manner as for tree regular expressions (this widening is also parameterized by an integer constant). We recall moreover that operators $\subset, \cap, \cup$ and complementation $(.^c)$ are computable, and that every finite set of words is regular. Moreover we have the following representation: $(A_n^\star, \sqsubseteq) \xleftarrow{\gamma_{\mathrm{Reg}_n}=Id} (\mathrm{Reg}_n, \sqsubseteq)$. Finally in order to disambiguate regular expressions from integers we will typeset them within $\lfloor . \rfloor$ in a bold font as in: $\lfloor \mathbf{0}+\mathbf{0.1}^\star \rfloor$.

Example 14. Using notations from Sect. 4.2, $\mathcal{V}' = \mathrm{Reg}_n$ and $\mathcal{V} = \mathcal{W}(\mathcal{R})$. Consider our running example (introduced in Example 2), natural terms from $V = \{+(x,+(z,y)) \mid x \le y \wedge z \le y\}$ contain three paths to numerical values: $\wr 0 \int$, $\wr 1,0 \int$ and $\wr 1,1 \int$. Numerical constraints on $\wr 0 \int$ and $\wr 1,0 \int$ are similar, therefore the two paths are summarized into one regular expression: $\lfloor \mathbf{0}+\mathbf{1.0} \rfloor$, $\wr 1,1 \int$ is left alone in its regular expression: $\lfloor \mathbf{1.1} \rfloor$. The two constraints $x \le y \wedge z \le y$ can now be expressed as one: $\lfloor \mathbf{0}+\mathbf{1.0} \rfloor \le \lfloor \mathbf{1.1} \rfloor$.

In Example 14, we saw that tree paths with similar numerical constraints can be summarized in one regular expression. However, for precision purposes, we do not want to summarize all tree paths into one regular expression. Hence, we will keep several disjoint regular expressions, which we call a subpartitioning.

Definition 15 (Subpartitioning). *Given a regular expression s, a subpartitioning of s is a set $\{s_1,\ldots,s_n\}$ of regular expressions such that $\forall i \neq j,\ s_i \cap s_j = \emptyset$ and $\bigcup_{i=1}^n s_i \subseteq s$. We note $P(s)$ the set of all subpartitioning of s. Moreover if $S = \{s_1,\ldots,s_n\}$ is a set of regular expressions, $[S]_\emptyset = S \setminus \{\emptyset\}$.*

Remark 7. Contrary to a partitioning of s, we do not require that the set of partitions covers s. Indeed when a set of tree paths is unconstrained we can just remove it from the partitioning, therefore no dimension in the numerical abstract environment will be allocated for this path.

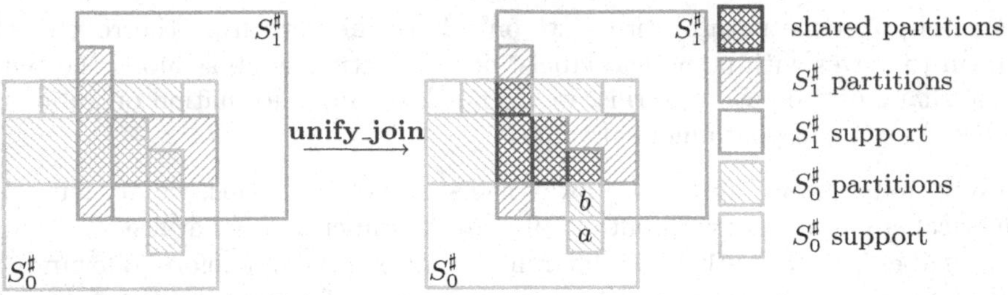

Fig. 6. Unification operator

Definition 16 (Positioning lattice with numerical abstraction). *Given a ranked alphabet* $\mathcal{R}$*, where the maximum arity of symbols is* n*, we define* $\mathcal{C}^\sharp(\mathcal{R}) = \{\langle s, \mathfrak{p}, R^\sharp \rangle \mid s \in Reg_n, \mathfrak{p} \in P(s), R^\sharp \in \mathfrak{M}^\sharp_{\mathfrak{p}}\}$*. Therefore* $\mathcal{C}^\sharp(\mathcal{R})$ *are triples containing:*

- s*: (called support) a regular expression coding for positions at which numerical values can be located.*
- $\mathfrak{p}$*: a subpartitioning of* s*. Elements of the same partition are subject to the same numerical constraints. Note that these partitions are regular.*
- $R^\sharp$*: an abstract numeric element where a dimension is associated to each partition, this dimension plays the role of a summary dimension.*

Remark 8. In the following, numerical abstract elements described in the form $\{c\}$, where c is a set of constraints, refer to $\langle c, \mathbf{vars}(c), \mathbf{vars}(c) \rangle \in \mathfrak{M}^\sharp$.

Algorithm 2. unify_join operator

Input : $\langle s, \{p_1, \ldots, p_n\}, R^\sharp \rangle, \langle s', \{p'_1, \ldots, p'_m\}, R^{\sharp\prime} \rangle$ two abstract elements
Output: two unified abstract elements

$(\underline{c_{i,j}})_{i \le n, j \le m} \leftarrow p_i \cap p'_j$;
$(\underline{p_i})_{i \le n} \leftarrow p_i \cap s'^c$;
$(\underline{p'_j})_{j \le m} \leftarrow p'_j \cap s^c$;
$(\underline{q_i})_{i \le n} \leftarrow p_i \cap s' \cap (\cup_{j \le m} \underline{c_{i,j}})^c$;
$(\underline{q'_j})_{j \le m} \leftarrow p'_j \cap s \cap (\cup_{i \le n} \underline{c_{i,j}})^c$;
$\underline{R^\sharp} \leftarrow R^\sharp$;
$\underline{R^{\sharp\prime}} \leftarrow R^{\sharp\prime}$;
for $i = 1$ **to** n **do**
  $R^\sharp \leftarrow \mathbf{expand}(R^\sharp, p_i, [\{\underline{c_{i,j}}\}_{j \le m} \cup \{\underline{p_i}\} \cup \{\underline{q_i}\}]_\emptyset)$;
for $j = 1$ **to** m **do**
  $R^{\sharp\prime} \leftarrow \mathbf{expand}(R^{\sharp\prime}, p'_j, [\{\underline{c_{i,j}}\}_{i \le n} \cup \{\underline{p'_j}\} \cup \{\underline{q'_j}\}]_\emptyset)$;
return $\langle s, \bigcup_{i \le n, j \le m} [\{\underline{q_i}, \underline{p_i}, \underline{c_{i,j}}\}]_\emptyset, \underline{R^\sharp} \rangle, \langle s', \bigcup_{i \le n, j \le m} [\{\underline{q'_i}, \underline{p'_j}, \underline{c_{i,j}}\}]_\emptyset, \underline{R^{\sharp\prime}} \rangle$;

Unification. The previous definition shows that two elements $U^\sharp = \langle s, \mathfrak{p}, R^\sharp\rangle$ and $V^\sharp = \langle s', \mathfrak{p}', R^{\sharp\prime}\rangle$ can have different subpartitionings ($\mathfrak{p}$ and $\mathfrak{p}'$). However the partitions in $\mathfrak{p}$ and in $\mathfrak{p}'$ might overlap, thus giving constraints to similar tree paths. Therefore in order to define the classical operators: $\sqsubseteq, \sqcup$ and $\triangledown$, we need to unify the two abstract elements ($U^\sharp$ and $V^\sharp$) so that given a tree path and the partition in which it is contained in $U^\sharp$, it is contained in the same partition in $V^\sharp$. This will enable us to rely on abstract operators on the numerical domain. In order to perform unification, we rely on the **expand** and **fold** operators. Indeed consider our running example, $U^\sharp = \langle \lfloor \mathbf{0}+\mathbf{1}\rfloor, \{\lfloor \mathbf{0}\rfloor, \lfloor \mathbf{1}\rfloor\}, \{\lfloor \mathbf{0}\rfloor \leq \lfloor \mathbf{1}\rfloor\}\rangle$ and $V^\sharp = \langle \lfloor \mathbf{0}+\mathbf{1}.(\mathbf{0}+\mathbf{1})\rfloor, \{\lfloor \mathbf{0}+\mathbf{1.0}\rfloor, \lfloor \mathbf{1.1}\rfloor\}, \{\lfloor \mathbf{0}+\mathbf{1.0}\rfloor \leq \lfloor \mathbf{1.1}\rfloor\}\rangle$. We see that constraints on tree path $\wr 0 \int$ is given: in $U^\sharp$ by partition $\lfloor \mathbf{0}\rfloor$ and in $V^\sharp$ by partition $\lfloor \mathbf{0}+\mathbf{1.0}\rfloor$. However we can split the partition $\lfloor \mathbf{0}+\mathbf{1.0}\rfloor$ into two partitions: $\lfloor \mathbf{0}\rfloor$ and $\lfloor \mathbf{1.0}\rfloor$, and expand variable $\lfloor \mathbf{0}+\mathbf{1.0}\rfloor$ into the two variables $\lfloor \mathbf{0}\rfloor$ and $\lfloor \mathbf{1.0}\rfloor$ in the numeric component: $\mathbf{expand}(\{\lfloor \mathbf{0}+\mathbf{1.0}\rfloor \leq \lfloor \mathbf{1.1}\rfloor\}, \lfloor \mathbf{0}+\mathbf{1.0}\rfloor, \{\lfloor \mathbf{0}\rfloor, \lfloor \mathbf{1.0}\rfloor\}) = \{\lfloor \mathbf{0}\rfloor \leq \lfloor \mathbf{1.1}\rfloor, \lfloor \mathbf{1.0}\rfloor \leq \lfloor \mathbf{1.1}\rfloor\}$. Once $U^\sharp$ and $V^\sharp$ are unified we can rely on the numerical join to soundly abstract the union. Note that splitting partitions is more precise than merging them. Indeed, consider the example where: in $U^\sharp$ we have $\lfloor \mathbf{0}\rfloor \geq 0$ and $\lfloor \mathbf{1}\rfloor \leq 0$ and in $V^\sharp$ we have $\lfloor \mathbf{0}+\mathbf{1}\rfloor = 0$. Splitting partition in $V^\sharp$ yields: $\lfloor \mathbf{0}\rfloor = 0, \lfloor \mathbf{1}\rfloor = 0$, after joining we get $\lfloor \mathbf{0}\rfloor \geq 0, \lfloor \mathbf{1}\rfloor \leq 0$. Whereas merging partitions in $U^\sharp$ yields $\lfloor \mathbf{0}+\mathbf{1}\rfloor$ unconstrained, after joining we also get that $\lfloor \mathbf{0}+\mathbf{1}\rfloor$ is unconstrained. However unifying by splitting or merging partitions in both abstract elements might result in an over-approximation of the initial elements. This does not pose a threat to the soundness of the join operator, but it does for the inclusion test. Unifying by splitting partitions induces an increase in the number of partitions which we want to avoid when trying to stabilize abstract elements in the widening. Hence, we define three unification operators:

- An operator **unify_join** that splits partitions from $U^\sharp$ and $V^\sharp$, this operator might induce an over-approximation for both $U^\sharp$ and $V^\sharp$ and is used in the join operation. This operator is presented in Algorithm 2, and illustrated in Fig. 6.
- An operator **unify_subset** that does not modify $V^\sharp$ (in order to avoid over-approximated it), we only split and merge (using the **fold** operator) partitions from $U^\sharp$ as, if the over-approximated $U^\sharp$ is smaller than $V^\sharp$, then so is the original $U^\sharp$.
- An operator **unify_widen** that unifies $U^\sharp$ and $V^\sharp$ by only merging partitions so that the number of partitions does not increase. This operator is used in the widening definition.

Operators **unify_subset** and **unify_widen** are very similar to **unify_join**.

Definition 17 (Comparison $\sqsubseteq_{\mathcal{C}^\sharp(\mathcal{R})}$). *Using* **unify_subset** *we define a relation on $\mathcal{C}^\sharp(\mathcal{R})$: $\sqsubseteq_{\mathcal{C}^\sharp(\mathcal{R})} = \{(U^\sharp, V^\sharp) \mid (\langle s, \mathfrak{p}, N^\sharp\rangle, \langle s', \mathfrak{p}', N^{\sharp\prime}\rangle) =$ **unify_subset**$(U^\sharp, V^\sharp) \Rightarrow s \subseteq s' \wedge \forall b \in \mathfrak{p}', (b \subseteq s^c \vee \exists! a \in \mathfrak{p}, b \cap s = a) \wedge N^\sharp \sqsubseteq N^{\sharp\prime}[\phi]\}$ where ϕ is the renaming from $\mathfrak{p}'$ into $\mathfrak{p}$ that renames b to a when such an a exists.*

Example 15. Going back to our running example: $U^\sharp = \langle \lfloor \mathbf{0}+\mathbf{1} \rfloor, \{\lfloor \mathbf{0} \rfloor, \lfloor \mathbf{1} \rfloor\}, \{\lfloor \mathbf{0} \rfloor \leq \lfloor \mathbf{1} \rfloor\}(=A^\sharp)\rangle$ and $V^\sharp = \langle \lfloor \mathbf{0}+\mathbf{1}.(\mathbf{0}+\mathbf{1}) \rfloor, \{\lfloor \mathbf{0}+\mathbf{1.0} \rfloor, \lfloor \mathbf{1.1} \rfloor\}, \{\lfloor \mathbf{0}+\mathbf{1.0} \rfloor \leq \lfloor \mathbf{1.1} \rfloor\}\rangle$. We have $s \not\subseteq s'$ hence $U^\sharp \not\sqsubseteq V^\sharp$. However if we now consider $W^\sharp$: $\langle \lfloor (\epsilon+\mathbf{1}).(\mathbf{0}+\mathbf{1}) \rfloor, \{\lfloor (\epsilon+\mathbf{1}).\mathbf{0} \rfloor, \lfloor (\epsilon+\mathbf{1}).\mathbf{1} \rfloor\}, \{\lfloor (\epsilon+\mathbf{1}).\mathbf{0} \rfloor \leq \lfloor (\epsilon+\mathbf{1}).\mathbf{1} \rfloor\}(=B^\sharp)\rangle$. $W^\sharp$ is already unified with $U^\sharp$, we have $s \subseteq s'$ and $\phi : (\lfloor (\epsilon+\mathbf{1}).\mathbf{0} \rfloor \mapsto \mathbf{0}, \lfloor (\epsilon+\mathbf{1}).\mathbf{1} \rfloor \mapsto \lfloor \mathbf{1} \rfloor)$. Moreover $A^\sharp \sqsubseteq B^\sharp[\phi] = \{\lfloor \mathbf{0} \rfloor \leq \lfloor \mathbf{1} \rfloor\}$. Hence $U^\sharp \sqsubseteq W^\sharp$.

Proposition 8. *We have:* $(\mathcal{C}(\mathcal{R}), \sqsubseteq_{\mathcal{C}(\mathcal{R})}) \xleftarrow{\gamma_1} (\mathcal{C}^\sharp(\mathcal{R}), \sqsubseteq_{\mathcal{C}^\sharp(\mathcal{R})})$, *where:* $\gamma_1(\langle s, \mathfrak{p}, R^\sharp\rangle) = \{f \mid \mathbf{def}(f) \subseteq \gamma_{Reg_n}(s) \wedge f \in \gamma[\uparrow \mathfrak{p}](R^\sharp)\}$. *By composition we get:* $(\wp(T_{\mathbb{Z}}(\mathcal{R})), \subseteq) \xleftarrow{\gamma_2} (\mathcal{C}^\sharp(\mathcal{R}), \sqsubseteq_{\mathcal{C}^\sharp\mathcal{R}})$, *with* $\gamma_2 = \gamma_{\mathcal{C}(\mathcal{R})} \circ \gamma_1$.

Example 16. Going back to our running example: $V^\sharp = \langle \lfloor \mathbf{0}+\mathbf{1}.(\mathbf{0}+\mathbf{1}) \rfloor, \{\lfloor \mathbf{0}+\mathbf{1.0} \rfloor, \lfloor \mathbf{1.1} \rfloor\}, \{\lfloor \mathbf{0}+\mathbf{1.0} \rfloor \leq \lfloor \mathbf{1.1} \rfloor\}\rangle$. We have: $\uparrow \mathfrak{p} = (\lfloor \mathbf{0}+\mathbf{1.0} \rfloor \mapsto \{\wr 0 \int, \wr 1,0 \int\}, \lfloor \mathbf{1} \rfloor \mapsto \wr 1 \int)$. Hence, $\gamma_1(V^\sharp) = \{(\wr 0 \int \mapsto \alpha, \wr 1 \int \mapsto \beta) \mid \alpha \leq \beta\} \cup \{(\wr 1,0 \int \mapsto \alpha, \wr 1 \int \mapsto \beta) \mid \alpha \leq \beta\} \cup \{(\wr 0 \int \mapsto \alpha, \wr 1,0 \int \mapsto \gamma, \wr 1 \int \mapsto \beta) \mid \alpha \leq \beta \wedge \gamma \leq \beta\}$. The product with tree automata refines this result so that only the last set is left.

We now define the $\sqcup$ operator that relies on the **unify_join** operator of Algorithm 2. Once elements are unified we can distinguish three kinds of partitions: (1) Partitions found in both abstract elements (e.g. ❁ in Fig. 6). (2) Partitions found in only one of the two, which do not overlap over the support of the other abstract element (denoted u^o), these are outer-partitions. Information on such partitions can be soundly kept when joining two abstract elements (e.g. partition a in Fig. 6). (3) Partitions found in only one of the two, which overlap over the support of the other abstract element, these are inner-partitions. Information on such partitions can not be soundly kept when joining two abstract elements. (e.g. partition b in Fig. 6). Therefore in the following definition of the join operator, we compute (once elements are unified) the common partitions and both outer-partitions and merge them to form the resulting subpartitioning.

Definition 18 (Union abstract operator). *Given* $U^\sharp, V^\sharp \in \mathcal{C}^\sharp(\mathcal{R})$, *if* $(\langle s, \mathfrak{p}, R^\sharp\rangle, \langle s', \mathfrak{p}', R^{\sharp\prime}\rangle) = \mathbf{unify\_join}(U^\sharp, V^\sharp)$, *let* $\mathfrak{c}$ *be* $\mathfrak{p} \cup \mathfrak{p}'$, *let* u^o *(*$U^\sharp$ *outer-partition) be* $\{e \in \mathfrak{p} \mid e \subseteq s'^c\}$, *let* v^o *(*$V^\sharp$ *outer-partition) be* $\{e \in \mathfrak{p}' \mid e \subseteq s^c\}$, *we then define:*

$$U^\sharp \sqcup_{\mathcal{C}^\sharp(\mathcal{R})} V^\sharp = \langle s \cup s', \mathfrak{c} \cup u^o \cup v^o, R^\sharp_{|\mathfrak{c} \cup u^o} \sqcup R^{\sharp\prime}_{|\mathfrak{c} \cup v^o}\rangle$$

Proposition 9. *We have:* $\gamma_1(U^\sharp) \cup \gamma_1(V^\sharp) \subseteq \gamma_1(U^\sharp \sqcup_{\mathcal{C}^\sharp(\mathcal{R})} V^\sharp)$.

Example 17. Consider the two following abstract elements (this is the particular case of our running example where all numerical values are equal): $V^\sharp = \langle \lfloor \mathbf{0}+\mathbf{1}.(\mathbf{0}+\mathbf{1}) \rfloor (=s), \{\lfloor \mathbf{0}+\mathbf{1.0} \rfloor (=a), \lfloor \mathbf{1.1} \rfloor (=b), \{a=b\}\}\rangle$, and $U^\sharp = \langle \lfloor \mathbf{0}+\mathbf{1} \rfloor (=s'), \{\lfloor \mathbf{0} \rfloor (=c), \lfloor \mathbf{1} \rfloor (=d)\}, \{c=d\}\rangle$. Intuitively $U^\sharp$ could encode the term $(x+x)$ and $V^\sharp$ the term $(x+(x+x))$. The unification of those two elements is: $V_1^\sharp = \langle s, \{c, b, \lfloor \mathbf{1.0} \rfloor (=e)\}, R^\sharp\rangle$ where $R^\sharp = \langle \{c=b, e=b\}, \{b\}, \{c, b, e\}\rangle$ and $U_1^\sharp = U^\sharp$, moreover the common environment ($\mathfrak{c}$ in previous definition) is: $\{c\}$,

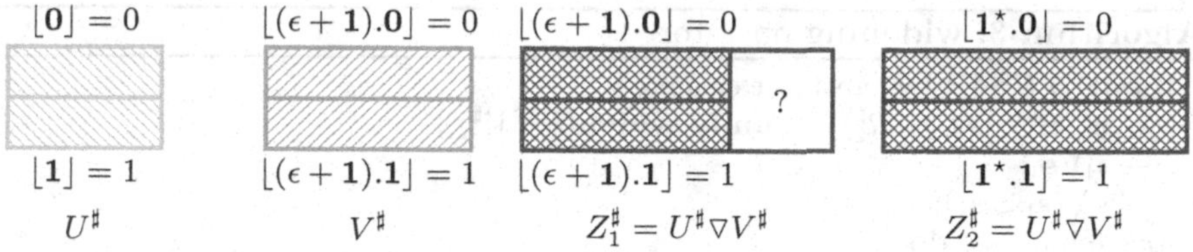

Fig. 7. Widening illustration

$V^\sharp$ outer-partitioning is $\{e, f\}$, $U^\sharp$ outer-partitioning is $\{d\}$. Hence: the numerical component resulting of the join is: $\langle\{c = d\}, \{c, d\}, \{c, d\}\rangle \sqcup \langle\{c = b, e = b\}, \{b\}, \{c, b, e\}\rangle$ which is: $\langle\{c = b, e = b, c = d\}, \emptyset, \{c, d, e, b\}\rangle$. We see here that using a naive numerical join operator, we would not have been able to get such a precise result (the numerical join would have yielded $\top$).

unify_widen $\mathcal{C}^\sharp(\mathcal{R})$ contains infinite increasing chains, therefore, we need to provide a widening operator. As for the other operators, widening is computed on unified abstract elements. A **unify_widen** operator is defined: it produces $U^\sharp$ and $V^\sharp$, over-approximations of its inputs with the same number of partitions. Moreover it ensures that each partition of $U^\sharp$ intersects exactly one partition of $V^\sharp$. This can be obtained by iterative merging partitions that overlap in both arguments until the abstract elements have the exact same partitions. Therefore from the result of **unify_widen** we can extract a list of pairs (a, b) where a is a partition from $U^\sharp$, b is a partition from $V^\sharp$ and $a \cap b \neq \emptyset$. This defines a bijection from partitions of $U^\sharp$ onto partitions of $V^\sharp$.

compose. In order to ensure stabilization we first need to stabilize the supports on which abstract elements are defined. This is easily done using the automaton widening ($s_1 \nabla s_2$ in Algorithm 3). Figure 7 illustrates the following simple example: $U^\sharp$ is an abstract element with support $\lfloor \mathbf{0} + \mathbf{1} \rfloor$, two partitions $u = \lfloor \mathbf{0} \rfloor$ and $u' = \lfloor \mathbf{1} \rfloor$, and numerical constraints $u' = 1$ and $u = 0$. $V^\sharp$ is an abstract element with support $\lfloor (\epsilon + \mathbf{1}).(\mathbf{0} + \mathbf{1}) \rfloor$, two partitions $v = \lfloor (\epsilon + \mathbf{1}).\mathbf{0} \rfloor$ and $v' = \lfloor (\epsilon + \mathbf{1}).\mathbf{1} \rfloor$ with the numerical constraints that $v = 0$ and $v' = 1$. Supports are unstable, therefore we start by widening them, which yields a new support: $\lfloor \mathbf{1}^\star.(\mathbf{0} + \mathbf{1}) \rfloor$. The unification of $U^\sharp$ and $V^\sharp$ leaves subpartitionings unchanged and yields the bijection $(u \mapsto v, u' \mapsto v')$. Given this information we now need to provide a new subpartitioning for the result of the widening. We see in this example that we could soundly use the subpartitioning from $V^\sharp$, this would produce the abstract element $Z_1^\sharp$ depicted in Fig. 7. However due to the widening of the support, paths of the form $\wr 1, 1, 1, 0 \int$ are in the support of the result but are left unconstrained as they are not in any of the partitions. Therefore we need to use the opportunity of the extension of the support to place constraints on the newly added paths. In order to do so we would like to force the extension of the existing partitions from $U^\sharp$ and $V^\sharp$ into the new support. Therefore we need to define a **compose** operator that produces a sound new partition, given: (1) a pair a, b of partitions (such as the one produced by

Algorithm 3. widening operator

Input : $U^\sharp, V^\sharp$ two abstract elements
$(\langle s_1, \mathfrak{p}_1, R_1^\sharp\rangle, \langle s_2, \mathfrak{p}_2, R_2^\sharp\rangle) \leftarrow$ **unify_widen**$(U^\sharp, V^\sharp)$;
$s \leftarrow s_1 \nabla s_2$;
$r \leftarrow s \setminus (s_1 \cup s_2)$;
foreach $a \in \mathfrak{p}_1$ **do**
  $b \leftarrow$ the unique element from $\mathfrak{p}_2$ such that $b \cap a \neq \emptyset$;
  $p \leftarrow$ **compose**(a, b, s_1, s_2, r);
  $\mathfrak{p} \leftarrow \{p\} \cup \mathfrak{p}$;
  $R_1^{\sharp\star} \leftarrow R_1^{\sharp\star}[a \mapsto p]$;
  $R_2^{\sharp\star} \leftarrow R_1^{\sharp\star}[b \mapsto p]$;
  $r \leftarrow r \setminus p$;
if $\mathfrak{p} = \mathfrak{p}_1$ **then**
  return $\langle s, \mathfrak{p}, R_1^{\sharp\star} \nabla R_2^{\sharp\star}\rangle$;
else
  return $\langle s, \mathfrak{p}, R_1^{\sharp\star} \sqcup R_2^{\sharp\star}\rangle$;

unify_widen), (2) the support s_1 (resp s_2) in which a (resp. b) lives and (3) a space to occupy r. The following criteria must be verified by the resulting partition p in order to be sound and to terminate: $p \cap s_1 = a$, $p \cap s_2 = b$ and $p \setminus (s_1 \cup s_2) \subseteq r$. A variety of **compose** operators could be defined, we chose: **compose**$(a, b, s_1, s_2, r) = a \cup (b \cap (s_2 \setminus s_1)) \cup ((a \nabla (a \cup b)) \cap r)$. The idea is the following: we keep a (as it is always sound thanks to the definition of the **unify_widen** operator), we keep the part from b that satisfies the soundness condition, and we extend into the space left to occupy according to the automata widening of a and $a \cup b$. In our example, considering the pair (u, v), this would translate as: $a = \mathbf{0}$, $b \cap (s_2 \setminus s_1) = \lfloor \mathbf{1.0} \rfloor$ and $(a \nabla (a \cup b)) \cap r = \lfloor \mathbf{0} \rfloor \nabla \lfloor (\epsilon + 1).\mathbf{0} \rfloor \cap \lfloor \mathbf{1}^{\geq 2}(\mathbf{0}+\mathbf{1}) \rfloor = \lfloor \mathbf{1}^{\geq 2}.\mathbf{0} \rfloor$. We get the new partition: $\lfloor \mathbf{1}^\star.\mathbf{0} \rfloor$. Doing the same with the pair (v, v') yields $\lfloor \mathbf{1}^\star.\mathbf{1} \rfloor$. Finally we get the abstract element $Z_2^\sharp$ from Fig. 7, which is more precise than $Z_1^\sharp$.

Definition 19 (Widening). *Algorithm 3 provides the definition of a widening operator using the* **unify_widen** *operator and parameterized by a* **compose** *function.*

Widening Stabilization. Our abstraction contains three components: (1) a support that describes the set of paths (2) a subpartitioning of this support and (3) a numerical component giving constraints on partitions in the subpartitioning. We show how the widening operator stabilizes all three components.

- Regular expression widening is used on supports when widening is called. Therefore ensuring support stabilization.
- Once supports are stable (this means $s_2 \subseteq s_1$), we have $p = a$ for every pair (a, b) of partitions. Meaning that once shapes stabilize, the only modifications

allowed on the subpartitionings are those made by the **unify_widen** operator. Each partition resulting from the operator is the union of input partitions, hence the subpartitioning will stabilize.
- Once subpartitionings are stable ($\mathfrak{p}_1 = \mathfrak{p}$ in Algorithm 3) numerical widening is applied on the numerical component in order to ensure stabilization.

Example 18 (Numerical example). Consider the simple example where: $\mathcal{R} = \{f(2)\}$, $U^\sharp = \langle \lfloor \mathbf{0}+\mathbf{1} \rfloor, \{\lfloor \mathbf{0} \rfloor, \lfloor \mathbf{1} \rfloor\}, \{\lfloor \mathbf{1} \rfloor = \lfloor \mathbf{0} \rfloor\}\rangle$ and $V^\sharp = \langle \lfloor \mathbf{0}+\mathbf{1} \rfloor, \{\lfloor \mathbf{0} \rfloor, \lfloor \mathbf{1} \rfloor\}, \{\lfloor \mathbf{1} \rfloor \geq \lfloor \mathbf{0} \rfloor, \lfloor \mathbf{1} \rfloor \leq \lfloor \mathbf{0} \rfloor + 1\}\rangle$. $U^\sharp$ and $V^\sharp$ have the same shape, therefore widening will be performed on the numerical component of the abstraction, therefore: $U^\sharp \nabla V^\sharp = \langle \lfloor \mathbf{0}+\mathbf{1} \rfloor, \{\lfloor \mathbf{0} \rfloor, \lfloor \mathbf{1} \rfloor\}, \{\lfloor \mathbf{1} \rfloor \geq \lfloor \mathbf{0} \rfloor\}\rangle$.

Reducing Dimensionality and Improving Precision. As emphasized by the previous examples, definitions and illustrations, the numerical component of an abstract state is used as a container for constraints on regular expressions, every node in a regular expression must then satisfy all numerical constraints on the underlying regular expression. Therefore when two nodes of a tree satisfy the same constraints, they should be stored in the same partition so as to reduce the dimension of the numerical domain (thus improving efficiency). Moreover the widening operator provided in Algorithm 3 relies (for precision) on the fact that partitions are built by similarity of constraints, therefore partition merging, when it does not result in an over-approximation, also leads to a precision gain. The unification operator defined in Algorithm 2 tends to split partitions whereas the widening operator defined in Algorithm 3 tends to merge them. In order to reduce dimensionality, we would like to define a **reduce** : $\mathcal{C}^\sharp(\mathcal{R}) \to \mathcal{C}^\sharp(\mathcal{R})$ operator, that folds variables with similar constraints into one. Please note that $\forall S \cap S' \subseteq \{x\}$, $x \in S$ and $R^\sharp \in N_S$, we have that $R^\sharp \sqsubseteq_{N_S}$ $\mathbf{expand}(\mathbf{fold}(R^\sharp, x, S'), x, S')$. This means that when variables are folded into one, expanding them afterwards would yield a bigger abstract element. For example, consider the octagon $R^\sharp = \{x \geq 2, y \geq 2, x = y\}$ then $\mathbf{fold}(R^\sharp, z, \{x, y\}) = \{z \geq 2\}(\triangleq R^{\sharp\prime})$ and $\mathbf{expand}(R^{\sharp\prime}, z, \{x, y\}) = \{x \geq 2, y \geq 2\}$. However if we consider $R^\sharp = \{x \geq 2, y \geq 2\}$ then $\mathbf{fold}(\mathbf{expand}(R^\sharp, z, \{x, y\}), z, \{x, y\}) = R^\sharp$. Therefore if we assume given a score function $\mathbf{score}(R^\sharp, x, S')$ ranging in $[0, 1]$ such that $\mathbf{score}(R^\sharp, x, S') = 1 \Leftrightarrow R^\sharp = \mathbf{expand}(\mathbf{fold}(R^\sharp, x, S'), x, S')$, we are able to define a generic **reduce** operator parameterized by a value α. This **reduce** operator merges partitions until no more set of partitions has a high enough score according to the **score** function. Finding a good **score** function is a work in progress. As a first approximation we used the following trivial one: $\mathbf{score}_0(R^\sharp, S) = 1$ when $\mathbf{expand}(\mathbf{fold}(R^\sharp, x, S), x, S) = R^\sharp$ and 0 otherwise. This $\mathbf{score}_0$ guarantees there is no loss of precision, but can miss opportunities for simplification.

Example 19. Consider the following example: $U^\sharp = \langle \lfloor \mathbf{0}+\mathbf{1} \rfloor, \{\lfloor \mathbf{0} \rfloor, \lfloor \mathbf{1} \rfloor\}, \{\lfloor \mathbf{0} \rfloor = 0, \lfloor \mathbf{1} \rfloor = 0\}\rangle$. Relations on $\lfloor \mathbf{0} \rfloor$ and $\lfloor \mathbf{1} \rfloor$ can be expressed in one relation using the summarizing variable $\lfloor \mathbf{0}+\mathbf{1} \rfloor$. This yields: $\mathbf{reduce}(U^\sharp) = \langle \lfloor \mathbf{0}+\mathbf{1} \rfloor, \{\lfloor \mathbf{0}+\mathbf{1} \rfloor\}, \{\lfloor \mathbf{0}+\mathbf{1} \rfloor = 0\}\rangle$. Note that $\mathbf{expand}(\{\lfloor \mathbf{0}+\mathbf{1} \rfloor = 0\}, \lfloor \mathbf{0}+\mathbf{1} \rfloor, \{\lfloor \mathbf{1} \rfloor, \lfloor \mathbf{0} \rfloor\}) = \{\lfloor \mathbf{0} \rfloor = 0, \lfloor \mathbf{1} \rfloor = 0\}$. Therefore no information is lost.

Abstract Semantic of Operators. As for tree automata, abstract semantic of operators defined in Sect. 2 can be defined as simple transformations on regular automata. Indeed the `make_symbolic`($s \in \mathcal{R}$) (resp. `get_son`) operator, amounts to adding (resp. removing) an integer letter to: (1) the partitions in the subpartitioning and (2) the support. `make_integer`($e \in expr$) amounts to building an abstract element with support $\lfloor \epsilon \rfloor$ and a subpartitioning containing only $\{\lfloor \epsilon \rfloor\}$, on which we put the constraint that it is equal to e. `is_symbol` needs only split the support and each partition, in the two language $L = \{\epsilon\}$ and $A_n^\star \setminus L$. Indeed in order to restrict to terms having only an integer as root, the support must be reduced to ϵ. The `get_sym_head` operator always yields the whole ranked alphabet (as this was abstracted away and will be refined by the automaton abstraction). Finally for `get_num_head`: (1) if the empty path $\wr\int$ is in the support we produce the set of integers satisfying the numerical constraints on the partition containing ϵ, and $\top$ in case no such partition could be found, and (2) otherwise we know that no numerical value is produced.

5.2 Product of Tree Automata and Numerical Constraints

The abstraction by tree automata defined in Sect. 3 and the abstraction by numerical constraints on tree paths defined in Sect. 5.1 provide non comparable information on the set of terms they abstract. Indeed the former describes precisely the shape of the term but can not express numerical constraints whereas the latter abstracts away most of the shape and focuses on numerical constraints. To benefit from both kinds of information, we use a reduced product between the two domains. Both abstractions in the product contain information on potential integer positions. The position of the $\square$ symbol in the tree automaton abstraction and the support in the numerical constraints abstractions both yield this information. We remove the support component from the product as the information can be retrieved from the tree abstraction. The definitions of the abstract operators in Sect. 5.1 require the support to be a regular language. We show in this subsection how to retrieve the support of a tree automaton with holes and that it is regular.

Given a FTA$(Q, \mathcal{R}, Q_f, \delta)$ over a ranked alphabet $\mathcal{R}$ with maximum arity n. We assume that every node in Q is reachable. Consider the following system over variables v_p for $p \in Q$ with values in the set of languages over the alphabet A_n (. designates the classical concatenation operator lifted to languages):

$$\{v_p = \bigcup_{(s,(q_1,\ldots,q_m),q)\in\delta | q_i = p} v_q.\{i\} \cup \begin{cases} \{\epsilon\} \text{ if } p \in Q_f \\ \emptyset \quad \text{otherwise} \end{cases} \mid p \in Q\}$$

Every language $\{i\}$ for $i \in \mathbb{N}$ is regular and does not contain ϵ, moreover $\emptyset$ and $\{\epsilon\}$ are regular languages. By application of Arden's rule (see [18]) and Gauss elimination we can compute the unique solution of this system, moreover every v_p is regular. Variable v_p is defined so that: $w \in v_p$ if and only if there exists a tree t recognized by the automaton such that $p \in \text{REACH}(t_{|w})$. If $\square \in \mathcal{R}$ we have that the regular language: $\cup_{(\square,(),p)\in\delta} v_p$ represents exactly the potential positions of integers in trees accepted by the tree automaton.

Height and Size. The product is enriched with a simple height and size abstraction: numerical variables (encoding heights and sizes) are added to the numerical component of the abstraction.

5.3 Environment Abstraction

In the previous section, we designed abstractions for sets of trees. However in order to be able to tackle the examples from the introductory section (Sect. 1) we need to design an abstraction able to represent maps from a set of variables to natural terms. In Sect. 3 we have shown how to lift abstractions on natural terms to abstractions of environments over a given finite set of finite term variables $\mathcal{T}$. We apply the same mechanism here to lift the product presented in Sect. 5.2. However lifting the product would result in abstract environments being maps from natural term variables to abstractions containing a numerical environment. In order to be able to express numerical relations between two sets of natural terms or even between numerical program variables and numerical values of natural terms we factor away the numerical environment so that it is shared by all natural term abstractions in the term environment and by the program variables in the numerical environment. Therefore the final abstraction is a pair $(m, R^\sharp)$ where: (1) m is a map from $\mathcal{T}$ to an abstract element that is a product of the automaton abstraction and the hole positioning abstraction. Moreover as all the numerical constraints are stored in a common numerical environment the product abstraction amounts to a pair $(\mathcal{A}, \mathfrak{p})$ where $\mathcal{A}$ is an element of the automaton abstraction and $\mathfrak{p}$ is a partitioning of its support. (2) $R^\sharp$ is an element of $\mathfrak{M}^\sharp$ binding in the same numerical element: numerical program variables and all partitions found in the mapping m.

6 Implementation and Example

6.1 Implementation

The analyzer was implemented in OCaml (~5000 loc) in the novel and still in development MOPSA framework (see [21]). MOPSA enables a modular development of static analyzers defined by abstract interpretation. An analyzer is built by choosing abstract domains, and combining them according to the user specification. MOPSA comes with pre-existing iterators and domains (e.g. interprocedural analysis, loop iterators, numerical domains, ...), and new ones can be added (e.g. tree abstract domain). A key feature of MOPSA is the ability of an abstract domain to use the abstract knowledge it maintains to transform dynamically expressions into other expressions that can be manipulated more easily by further domains, providing a flexible way to combine relational domains. For instance, assume that a domain abstracts arrays by associating a scalar variable a_0, a_1, ..., to each element $a[0]$, $a[1]$, ..., of an array a, and delegating the abstraction of the array contents to a numeric domain for scalars. It can then evaluate $\mathbb{E}^\sharp[\![2 * a[i] + i]\!](i \mapsto [0, 1])$ into the disjunction

$(2 * a_0 + i, i \mapsto [0,0]) \vee (2 * a_1 + i, i \mapsto [1,1])$, indicating that $2 * a[i] + i$ is equivalent to $2 * a_0 + i$ in the sub-environment where $i = 0$ and to $2 * a_1 + i$ in the sub-environment where $i = 1$. Each term of the disjunction contains an array-free expression that can be handled by the scalar domain in the corresponding sub-environment. In the abstract, expressions can be evaluated by induction on the syntax into symbolic expressions to retain the full power of relational domains and disjunctive reasoning (see [21] for more details). We exploit this feature in our implementation to combine our tree abstractions. We implemented (in the MOPSA framework) libraries for regular and tree regular languages that offer the usual lattice interface enriched with a widening operator. These libraries can be reused for the definition of other abstract domains. The overall complexity of the analysis is driven by the complexity of the lattice operations in the regular and tree regular libraries. These are exponential in the number of states of the considered automata, which is bounded by the widening parameter.

6.2 Examples of Analysis

Numerical variables of the form $\texttt{t}.x$, where $\texttt{t}$ is a natural term variable, represent a variable allocated for tree $\texttt{t}$. For example: $\texttt{t}.r$ where r is a regular expression is the variable allocated for partition r in tree $\texttt{t}$.

C Introductory Example. Let us consider the introductory example Program 4. The loop invariant inferred with our analysis is the following abstract element: $U^\sharp = (\texttt{y} \mapsto (\mathcal{A}, \{\lfloor \mathbf{0}.(\mathbf{0}.\mathbf{0})^\star.\mathbf{1} \rfloor (= r)\}), R^\sharp)$, with $\mathcal{A} = \langle \{a,b,c,d\}, \{*(1), +(2), \Box(0), (p,0)\}, \{c\}, \{*(d) \to c, +(c,a) \to d, \Box() \to a, p \to c\} \rangle$, and $R^\sharp$ satisfies the constraints: $\{\texttt{i} \geq 0, \texttt{i} \leq \texttt{n}, \texttt{y}.r = 4\}$. This describes precisely the set of terms of the form: $p, *(p{+}4), *(*(p{+}4){+}4), \ldots$. As mentioned in Sect. 6.1 evaluations of tree expressions yield pairs containing an expression and an abstract environment. Tree expressions are pairs $(\mathcal{A}, \mathfrak{p})$, partitions in $\mathfrak{p}$ are bound by the adjoined environment. Let us now present the result of the evaluation of the `make_integer(4)` expression in the abstract environment $U^\sharp$. Here we get the expression $(\mathcal{A}', \{\lfloor \epsilon \rfloor\})$ (where $\mathcal{A}'$ recognizes only $\Box$) in the environment: $(\texttt{y} \mapsto (\mathcal{A}, \{r\}), R^{\sharp\prime})$ where $R^{\sharp\prime} = R^\sharp \cup \{\lfloor \epsilon \rfloor = 4\}$. This emphasizes how the environment is used to give constraints on the adjoined expression. This transports numerical relations from the leafs of the expression up to the assigned variable $\texttt{t}$.

OCaml Introductory Example. Let us now consider the introductory example Program 5. The inferred loop invariant is the following ($r = \lfloor (\mathbf{1}.\mathbf{1})^\star.\mathbf{0} \rfloor$ and $r' = \lfloor (\mathbf{1}.\mathbf{1})^\star.\mathbf{1}.\mathbf{0} \rfloor$): $(\texttt{t} \mapsto (\mathcal{A}, \{r, r'\}), R^\sharp)$ and $R^\sharp$ satisfies the constraints: $\{\texttt{t}.r' = \texttt{x} - 1, \texttt{t}.r = \texttt{t}.r' + 2, i \geq 0, i \leq \texttt{n}\}$ and $\mathcal{A} = (\{a,b,c,d\}, \{\texttt{Cons}(2), \texttt{Nil}(0), \Box(0)\}, \{a\}, \{\texttt{Cons}(c,a) \to d, \texttt{Cons}(c,d) \to a, \texttt{Nil} \to a, \Box \to c\})$. Please note that at the end of the `while` loops the two numerical environments that need to be joined are not defined over the same set of variables (in the environments that have not gone through the loop, variables $\texttt{t}.r'$ and $\texttt{t}.r$ are not present). However thanks to the $\boxtimes$ operator, we do not have to loose the numerical relations between these variables and x. Hence we are able to prove that the assertion holds.

The analyzer was able to successfully analyze and infer the expected invariants for both examples.

7 Related Works

Previous works on sets of trees abstractions [20] were able to recognize larger classes of tree languages than tree automata. However we focused here on the abstraction of trees labeled with numerical values, therefore the work closest to ours would be [12]. Indeed it defines tree automata where leaves can be elements of a lattice (for example an interval). They are therefore able to represent sets of natural terms, but can not express numerical relations between the leaves of trees. Moreover they rely on a partitioning of the leaf lattice for tree automata operations. In [1] (and [2]) tree automata and regular automata are used for the model checking of programs manipulating C pointers and structures. Other uses have been made of tree automata in verification: shape analysis of C programs as in [15], computation of an over-approximation of terms computable by attackers of cryptographic protocols as in [24]. Widening regular languages by the computation of an equivalence relation of bounded index is also done in [9] and in [11]. As mentioned, variable summarization is often used to represent unbounded memory locations as in [17] or [14]. Moreover numerical abstract domains able to handle optional variables have been defined such as [19]. Finally termination analyses have been proposed for the analysis of programs manipulating tree structures (AVL, red-black trees) see [16].

8 Conclusion

In this article we presented a relational abstract environment for sets of trees over a finite algebra, with numerically labeled leaves. We emphasized the potential applications of being able to describe such trees: description of reachable memory zones, tracking symbolic equalities between program variables, description of tree like structures. In order to improve the precision of the analysis while not blowing up its cost we defined a novel abstraction for sets of maps with heterogeneous supports. This numeric abstraction is able to represent optional dimensions in numerical domains without losing relations with optional variables. All domains presented in the article were implemented as a library in the Mopsa framework.

References

1. Bouajjani, A., Habermehl, P., Rogalewicz, A., Vojnar, T.: Abstract regular tree model checking of complex dynamic data structures. In: Yi, K. (ed.) SAS 2006. LNCS, vol. 4134, pp. 52–70. Springer, Heidelberg (2006). https://doi.org/10.1007/11823230_5
2. Bouajjani, A., Habermehl, P., Vojnar, T.: Abstract regular model checking. In: Alur, R., Peled, D.A. (eds.) CAV 2004. LNCS, vol. 3114, pp. 372–386. Springer, Heidelberg (2004). https://doi.org/10.1007/978-3-540-27813-9_29
3. Bourdoncle, F.: Sémantiques des Langages Impératifs d'Ordre Supérieur et Interprétation Abstraite. Ph.D. thesis, Ecole polytechnique (1992)
4. Comon, H., et al.: Tree automata techniques and applications (2007). Release October, 12th 2007
5. Cousot, P., Cousot, R.: Abstract interpretation: a unified lattice model for static analysis of programs by construction or approximation of fixpoints. In: Proceedings of POPL, pp. 238–252. ACM (1977)
6. Cousot, P., Cousot, R.: Static determination of dynamic properties of generalized type unions. In: Language Design for Reliable Software, pp. 77–94 (1977)
7. Cousot, P., Cousot, R.: Modular static program analysis. In: Horspool, R.N. (ed.) CC 2002. LNCS, vol. 2304, pp. 159–179. Springer, Heidelberg (2002). https://doi.org/10.1007/3-540-45937-5_13
8. Cousot, P., Halbwachs, N.: Automatic discovery of linear restraints among variables of a program. In: Proceedings of POPL, pp. 84–96. ACM Press (1978)
9. Feret, J.: Abstract interpretation-based static analysis of mobile ambients. In: Cousot, P. (ed.) SAS 2001. LNCS, vol. 2126, pp. 412–430. Springer, Heidelberg (2001). https://doi.org/10.1007/3-540-47764-0_24
10. Le Gall, T.: Abstract lattices for the verification of systèmes with stacks and queues. Ph.D. thesis, University of Rennes 1, France (2008)
11. Le Gall, T., Jeannet, B., Jéron, T.: Verification of communication protocols using abstract interpretation of FIFO queues. In: Johnson, M., Vene, V. (eds.) AMAST 2006. LNCS, vol. 4019, pp. 204–219. Springer, Heidelberg (2006). https://doi.org/10.1007/11784180_17
12. Genet, T., Le Gall, T., Legay, A., Murat, V.: Tree regular model checking for lattice-based automata. CoRR, abs/1203.1495 (2012)
13. Gopan, D., DiMaio, F., Dor, N., Reps, T., Sagiv, M.: Numeric domains with summarized dimensions. In: Jensen, K., Podelski, A. (eds.) TACAS 2004. LNCS, vol. 2988, pp. 512–529. Springer, Heidelberg (2004). https://doi.org/10.1007/978-3-540-24730-2_38
14. Gopan, D., Reps, T.W., Sagiv, S.: A framework for numeric analysis of array operations. In: Proceedings of POPL, pp. 338–350. ACM (2005)
15. Habermehl, P., Holík, L., Rogalewicz, A., Šimáček, J., Vojnar, T.: Forest automata for verification of heap manipulation. In: Gopalakrishnan, G., Qadeer, S. (eds.) CAV 2011. LNCS, vol. 6806, pp. 424–440. Springer, Heidelberg (2011). https://doi.org/10.1007/978-3-642-22110-1_34
16. Habermehl, P., Iosif, R., Rogalewicz, A., Vojnar, T.: Proving termination of tree manipulating programs. In: Namjoshi, K.S., Yoneda, T., Higashino, T., Okamura, Y. (eds.) ATVA 2007. LNCS, vol. 4762, pp. 145–161. Springer, Heidelberg (2007). https://doi.org/10.1007/978-3-540-75596-8_12
17. Halbwachs, N., Péron, M.: Discovering properties about arrays in simple programs. In: Proceedings of PLDI, pp. 339–348. ACM (2008)

18. Hopcroft, J.E., Motwani, R., Ullman, J.D.: Introduction to Automata Theory, Languages, and Computation, 3rd edn. Addison-Wesley Longman Publishing Co., Inc, Boston (2006)
19. Liu, J., Rival, X.: Abstraction of optional numerical values. In: Feng, X., Park, S. (eds.) APLAS 2015. LNCS, vol. 9458, pp. 146–166. Springer, Cham (2015). https://doi.org/10.1007/978-3-319-26529-2_9
20. Mauborgne, L.: Representation of sets of trees for abstract interpretation. Ph.D. thesis, Ecole polytechnique (1999)
21. Miné, A., Ouadjaout, A., Journault, M.: Design of a modular platform for static analysis. In: The Ninth Workshop on Tools for Automatic Program Analysis (TAPAS 2018), Fribourg-en-Brisgau, Germany, August 2018. https://hal.sorbonne-universite.fr/hal-01870001/file/mine-al-tapas18.pdf
22. Miné, A.: The octagon abstract domain. In: Proceedings of WCRE, p. 310. IEEE Computer Society (2001)
23. Miné, A.: Symbolic methods to enhance the precision of numerical abstract domains. In: Emerson, E.A., Namjoshi, K.S. (eds.) VMCAI 2006. LNCS, vol. 3855, pp. 348–363. Springer, Heidelberg (2005). https://doi.org/10.1007/11609773_23
24. Monniaux, D.: Abstracting cryptographic protocols with tree automata. In: Cortesi, A., Filé, G. (eds.) SAS 1999. LNCS, vol. 1694, pp. 149–163. Springer, Heidelberg (1999). https://doi.org/10.1007/3-540-48294-6_10
25. Reynolds, J.C.: Separation logic: a logic for shared mutable data structures. In: Proceedings of 17th IEEE (LICS 2002), pp. 55–74. IEEE Computer Society (2002)

A Static Higher-Order Dependency Pair Framework

Carsten Fuhs[1(✉)] and Cynthia Kop[2(✉)]

[1] Department of Computer Science and Information Systems, Birkbeck, University of London, London, UK
carsten@dcs.bbk.ac.uk

[2] Department of Software Science, Radboud University Nijmegen, Nijmegen, The Netherlands
c.kop@cs.ru.nl

Abstract. We revisit the static dependency pair method for proving termination of higher-order term rewriting and extend it in a number of ways: (1) We introduce a new rewrite formalism designed for general applicability in termination proving of higher-order rewriting, Algebraic Functional Systems with Meta-variables. (2) We provide a syntactically checkable soundness criterion to make the method applicable to a large class of rewrite systems. (3) We propose a modular dependency pair *framework* for this higher-order setting. (4) We introduce a fine-grained notion of *formative* and *computable* chains to render the framework more powerful. (5) We formulate several existing and new termination proving techniques in the form of processors within our framework.

The framework has been implemented in the (fully automatic) higher-order termination tool WANDA.

1 Introduction

Term rewriting [3,48] is an important area of logic, with applications in many different areas of computer science [4,11,18,23,25,36,41]. *Higher-order* term rewriting – which extends the traditional *first-order* term rewriting with higher-order types and binders as in the λ-calculus – offers a formal foundation of functional programming and a tool for equational reasoning in higher-order logic. A key question in the analysis of both first- and higher-order term rewriting is *termination*; both for its own sake, and as part of confluence and equivalence analysis.

In first-order term rewriting, a hugely effective method for proving termination (both manually and automatically) is the *dependency pair (DP) approach* [2]. This approach has been extended to the *DP framework* [20,22], a highly modular methodology which new techniques for proving termination *and non-termination* can easily be plugged into in the form of *processors*.

In higher-order rewriting, two DP approaches with distinct costs and benefits are used: *dynamic* [31,45] and *static* [6,32–34,44,46] DPs. Dynamic DPs are more broadly applicable, yet static DPs often enable more powerful analysis techniques. Still, neither approach has the modularity and extendability of

L. Caires (Ed.): ESOP 2019, LNCS 11423, pp. 752–782, 2019.
https://doi.org/10.1007/978-3-030-17184-1_27

the DP framework, nor can they be used to prove non-termination. Also, these approaches consider different styles of higher-order rewriting, which means that for all results certain language features are not available.

In this paper, we address these issues for the *static* DP approach by extending it to a full higher-order *dependency pair framework* for both termination and non-termination analysis. For broad applicability, we introduce a new rewriting formalism, *AFSMs*, to capture several flavours of higher-order rewriting, including *AFSs* [26] (used in the annual Termination Competition [50]) and *pattern HRSs* [37,39] (used in the annual Confluence Competition [10]). To show the versatility and power of this methodology, we define various processors in the framework – both adaptations of existing processors from the literature and entirely new ones.

Detailed Contributions. We reformulate the results of [6,32,34,44,46] into a DP framework for AFSMs. In doing so, we instantiate the applicability restriction of [32] by a very liberal syntactic condition, and add two new flags to track properties of DP problems: one completely new, one from an earlier work by the authors for the *first-order* DP framework [16]. We give eight *processors* for reasoning in our framework: four translations of techniques from static DP approaches, three techniques from first-order or dynamic DPs, and one completely new.

This is a *foundational* paper, focused on defining a general theoretical framework for higher-order termination analysis using dependency pairs rather than questions of implementation. We have, however, implemented most of these results in the fully automatic termination analysis tool WANDA [28].

Related Work. There is a vast body of work in the first-order setting regarding the DP approach [2] and framework [20,22,24]. We have drawn from the ideas in these works for the core structure of the higher-order framework, but have added some new features of our own and adapted results to the higher-order setting.

There is no true higher-order DP *framework* yet: both static and dynamic approaches actually lie halfway between the original "DP approach" of first-order rewriting and a full DP framework as in [20,22]. Most of these works [30–32,34,46] prove "non-loopingness" or "chain-freeness" of a set $\mathcal{P}$ of DPs through a number of theorems. Yet, there is no concept of *DP problems*, and the set $\mathcal{R}$ of rules cannot be altered. They also fix assumptions on dependency chains – such as minimality [34] or being "tagged" [31] – which frustrate extendability and are more naturally dealt with in a DP framework using flags.

The static DP approach for higher-order term rewriting is discussed in, e.g., [34,44,46]. The approach is limited to *plain function passing (PFP)* systems. The definition of PFP has been made more liberal in later papers, but always concerns the position of higher-order variables in the left-hand sides of rules. These works include non-pattern HRSs [34,46], which we do not consider, but do not employ formative rules or meta-variable conditions, or consider non-termination, which we do. Importantly, they do not consider strictly positive inductive types, which could be used to significantly broaden the PFP restriction. Such types *are* considered in an early paper which defines a variation of static higher-order dependency pairs [6] based on a computability closure [7,8]. However, this work carries different restrictions (e.g., DPs must be type-preserving and not introduce fresh variables) and considers only one analysis technique (reduction pairs).

Definitions of DP approaches for *functional programming* also exist [32,33], which consider applicative systems with ML-style polymorphism. These works also employ a much broader, semantic definition than PFP, which is actually more general than the syntactic restriction we propose here. However, like the static approaches for term rewriting, they do not truly exploit the computability [47] properties inherent in this restriction: it is only used for the initial generation of dependency pairs. In the present work, we will take advantage of our exact computability notion by introducing a `computable` flag that can be used by the computable subterm criterion processor (Theorem 63) to handle benchmark systems that would otherwise be beyond the reach of static DPs. Also in these works, formative rules, meta-variable conditions and non-termination are not considered.

Regarding *dynamic* DP approaches, a precursor of the present work is [31], which provides a halfway framework (methodology to prove "chain-freeness") for dynamic DPs, introduces a notion of formative rules, and briefly translates a basic form of static DPs to the same setting. Our formative *reductions* consider the shape of reductions rather than the rules they use, and they can be used as a flag in the framework to gain additional power in other processors. The adaptation of static DPs in [31] was very limited, and did not for instance consider strictly positive inductive types or rules of functional type.

For a more elaborate discussion of both static and dynamic DP approaches in the literature, we refer to [31] and the second author's PhD thesis [29].

Organisation of the Paper. Section 2 introduces higher-order rewriting using AFSMs and recapitulates computability. In Sect. 3 we impose restrictions on the input AFSMs for which our framework is soundly applicable. In Sect. 4 we define static DPs for AFSMs, and derive the key results on them. Section 5 formulates the DP framework and a number of DP processors for existing and new termination proving techniques. Section 6 concludes. Detailed proofs for all results in this paper and an experimental evaluation are available in a technical report [17]. In addition, many of the results have been informally published in the second author's PhD thesis [29].

2 Preliminaries

In this section, we first define our notation by introducing the AFSM formalism. Although not one of the standards of higher-order rewriting, AFSMs combine features from various forms of higher-order rewriting and can be seen as a form of IDTSs [5] which includes application. We will finish with a definition of *computability*, a technique often used for higher-order termination methods.

2.1 Higher-Order Term Rewriting Using AFSMs

Unlike first-order term rewriting, there is no single, unified approach to higher-order term rewriting, but rather a number of similar but not fully compatible systems aiming to combine term rewriting and typed λ-calculi. For generality, we will use *Algebraic Functional Systems with Meta-variables*: a formalism which admits translations from the main formats of higher-order term rewriting.

Definition 1 (Simple types). *We fix a set $\mathcal{S}$ of* sorts. *All sorts are simple types, and if σ, τ are simple types, then so is $\sigma \to \tau$.*

We let $\to$ be right-associative. Note that all types have a unique representation in the form $\sigma_1 \to \ldots \to \sigma_m \to \iota$ with $\iota \in \mathcal{S}$.

Definition 2 (Terms and meta-terms). *We fix disjoint sets $\mathcal{F}$ of* function symbols, *$\mathcal{V}$ of* variables *and $\mathcal{M}$ of* meta-variables, *each symbol equipped with a type. Each meta-variable is additionally equipped with a natural number. We assume that both $\mathcal{V}$ and $\mathcal{M}$ contain infinitely many symbols of all types. The set $\mathcal{T}(\mathcal{F}, \mathcal{V})$ of* terms over *$\mathcal{F}, \mathcal{V}$ consists of expressions s where $s : \sigma$ can be derived for some type σ by the following clauses:*

(V) $x : \sigma$ if $x : \sigma \in \mathcal{V}$ (@) $s\ t : \tau$ if $s : \sigma \to \tau$ and $t : \sigma$

(F) $\mathtt{f} : \sigma$ if $\mathtt{f} : \sigma \in \mathcal{F}$ (Λ) $\lambda x.s : \sigma \to \tau$ if $x : \sigma \in \mathcal{V}$ and $s : \tau$

Meta-terms *are expressions whose type can be derived by those clauses and:*

(M) $Z\langle s_1, \ldots, s_k\rangle : \sigma_{k+1} \to \ldots \to \sigma_m \to \iota$

if $Z : (\sigma_1 \to \ldots \to \sigma_k \to \ldots \to \sigma_m \to \iota,\ k) \in \mathcal{M}$ and $s_1 : \sigma_1, \ldots, s_k : \sigma_k$

The λ binds variables as in the λ-calculus; unbound variables are called free, *and $FV(s)$ is the set of free variables in s. Meta-variables cannot be bound; we write $FMV(s)$ for the set of meta-variables occurring in s. A meta-term s is called* closed *if $FV(s) = \emptyset$ (even if $FMV(s) \neq \emptyset$). Meta-terms are considered modulo α-conversion. Application (@) is left-associative; abstractions (Λ) extend as far to the right as possible. A meta-term s* has type *σ if $s : \sigma$; it* has base type *if $\sigma \in \mathcal{S}$. We define $\mathsf{head}(s) = \mathsf{head}(s_1)$ if $s = s_1\ s_2$, and $\mathsf{head}(s) = s$ otherwise.*

A (meta-)term s has a sub-(meta-)term *t, notation $s \trianglerighteq t$, if either $s = t$ or $s \triangleright t$, where $s \triangleright t$ if (a) $s = \lambda x.s'$ and $s' \trianglerighteq t$, (b) $s = s_1\ s_2$ and $s_2 \trianglerighteq t$ or (c) $s = s_1\ s_2$ and $s_1 \trianglerighteq t$. A (meta-)term s has a* fully applied sub-(meta-)term *t, notation $s \blacktriangleright\!\!\!\!\underline{\ \ } t$, if either $s = t$ or $s \blacktriangleright t$, where $s \blacktriangleright t$ if (a) $s = \lambda x.s'$ and $s' \blacktriangleright\!\!\!\!\underline{\ \ } t$, (b) $s = s_1\ s_2$ and $s_2 \blacktriangleright\!\!\!\!\underline{\ \ } t$ or (c) $s = s_1\ s_2$ and $s_1 \blacktriangleright t$ (so if $s = x\ s_1\ s_2$, then x and $x\ s_1$ are not fully applied subterms, but s and both s_1 and s_2 are).*

For $Z : (\sigma, k) \in \mathcal{M}$, we call k the arity *of Z, notation $arity(Z)$.*

Clearly, all fully applied subterms are subterms, but not all subterms are fully applied. Every term s has a form $t\ s_1 \cdots s_n$ with $n \geq 0$ and $t = \mathsf{head}(s)$ a variable, function symbol, or abstraction; in meta-terms t may also be a meta-variable application $F\langle s_1, \ldots, s_k\rangle$. *Terms* are the objects that we will rewrite; *meta-terms* are used to define rewrite rules. Note that all our terms (and meta-terms) are, by definition, well-typed. For rewriting, we will employ *patterns*:

Definition 3 (Patterns). *A meta-term is a* pattern *if it has one of the forms* $Z\langle x_1,\ldots,x_k\rangle$ *with all* x_i *distinct variables;* $\lambda x.\ell$ *with* $x \in \mathcal{V}$ *and* ℓ *a pattern; or* $a\ \ell_1 \cdots \ell_n$ *with* $a \in \mathcal{F} \cup \mathcal{V}$ *and all* ℓ_i *patterns* $(n \geq 0)$*.*

In rewrite rules, we will use meta-variables for *matching* and variables only with *binders*. In terms, variables can occur both free and bound, and meta-variables cannot occur. Meta-variables originate in very early forms of higher-order rewriting (e.g., [1,27]), but have also been used in later formalisms (e.g., [8]). They strike a balance between matching modulo β and syntactic matching. By using meta-variables, we obtain the same expressive power as with Miller patterns [37], but do so without including a reversed β-reduction as part of matching.

Notational Conventions: We will use x, y, z for variables, X, Y, Z for meta-variables, b for symbols that could be variables or meta-variables, $\mathtt{f}, \mathtt{g}, \mathtt{h}$ or more suggestive notation for function symbols, and s, t, u, v, q, w for (meta-)terms. Types are denoted σ, τ, and ι, κ are sorts. We will regularly overload notation and write $x \in \mathcal{V}$, $\mathtt{f} \in \mathcal{F}$ or $Z \in \mathcal{M}$ without stating a type (or minimal arity). For meta-terms $Z\langle\rangle$ we will usually omit the brackets, writing just Z.

Definition 4 (Substitution). *A* meta-substitution *is a type-preserving function* γ *from variables and meta-variables to meta-terms. Let the* domain *of* γ *be given by:* $\mathtt{dom}(\gamma) = \{(x : \sigma) \in \mathcal{V} \mid \gamma(x) \neq x\} \cup \{(Z : (\sigma, k)) \in \mathcal{M} \mid \gamma(Z) \neq \lambda y_1 \ldots y_k.Z\langle y_1,\ldots,y_k\rangle\}$*; this domain is allowed to be infinite. We let* $[b_1 := s_1,\ldots,b_n := s_n]$ *denote the meta-substitution* γ *with* $\gamma(b_i) = s_i$ *and* $\gamma(z) = z$ *for* $(z : \sigma) \in \mathcal{V} \setminus \{b_1,\ldots,b_n\}$*, and* $\gamma(Z) = \lambda y_1 \ldots y_k.Z\langle y_1,\ldots,y_k\rangle$ *for* $(Z : (\sigma, k)) \in \mathcal{M} \setminus \{b_1,\ldots,b_n\}$*. We assume there are infinitely many variables* x *of all types such that (a)* $x \notin \mathtt{dom}(\gamma)$ *and (b) for all* $b \in \mathtt{dom}(\gamma)$*:* $x \notin FV(\gamma(b))$*.*

A substitution *is a meta-substitution mapping everything in its domain to terms. The result* $s\gamma$ *of applying a meta-substitution* γ *to a term* s *is obtained by:*

$$x\gamma = \gamma(x) \text{ if } x \in \mathcal{V} \qquad (s\ t)\gamma = (s\gamma)\ (t\gamma)$$
$$\mathtt{f}\gamma = \mathtt{f} \quad \text{if } \mathtt{f} \in \mathcal{F} \qquad (\lambda x.s)\gamma = \lambda x.(s\gamma) \quad \text{if } \gamma(x) = x \wedge x \notin \bigcup_{y \in \mathtt{dom}(\gamma)} FV(\gamma(y))$$

For meta-terms, the result $s\gamma$ *is obtained by the clauses above and:*

$$Z\langle s_1,\ldots,s_k\rangle\gamma = \gamma(Z)\langle s_1\gamma,\ldots,s_k\gamma\rangle \quad \text{if } Z \notin \mathtt{dom}(\gamma)$$
$$Z\langle s_1,\ldots,s_k\rangle\gamma = \gamma(Z)\langle\langle s_1\gamma,\ldots,s_k\gamma\rangle\rangle \quad \text{if } Z \in \mathtt{dom}(\gamma)$$
$$(\lambda x_1 \ldots x_k.s)\langle\langle t_1,\ldots,t_k\rangle\rangle = s[x_1 := t_1,\ldots,x_k := t_k]$$
$$(\lambda x_1 \ldots x_n.s)\langle\langle t_1,\ldots,t_k\rangle\rangle = s[x_1 := t_1,\ldots,x_n := t_n]\ t_{n+1} \cdots t_k \quad \text{if } n < k \text{ and } s \text{ is not an abstraction}$$

Note that for fixed k, any term has exactly one of the two forms above ($\lambda x_1 \ldots x_n.s$ with $n < k$ and s not an abstraction, or $\lambda x_1 \ldots x_k.s$).

Essentially, applying a meta-substitution that has meta-variables in its domain combines a substitution with (possibly several) β-steps. For example, we have that: $\mathtt{deriv}\ (\lambda x.\mathtt{sin}\ (F\langle x\rangle))[F := \lambda y.\mathtt{plus}\ y\ x]$ equals $\mathtt{deriv}\ (\lambda z.\mathtt{sin}\ (\mathtt{plus}\ z\ x))$. We also have: $X\langle 0, \mathtt{nil}\rangle[X := \lambda x.\mathtt{map}\ (\lambda y.x)]$ equals $\mathtt{map}\ (\lambda y.0)\ \mathtt{nil}$.

Definition 5 (Rules and rewriting). *Let $\mathcal{F}, \mathcal{V}, \mathcal{M}$ be fixed sets of function symbols, variables and meta-variables respectively. A* rule *is a pair $\ell \Rightarrow r$ of closed meta-terms of the same type such that ℓ is a pattern of the form $\mathtt{f}\ \ell_1 \cdots \ell_n$ with $\mathtt{f} \in \mathcal{F}$ and $FMV(r) \subseteq FMV(\ell)$. A set of rules $\mathcal{R}$ defines a rewrite relation $\Rightarrow_{\mathcal{R}}$ as the smallest monotonic relation on terms which includes:*

(Rule) $\ell\delta \Rightarrow_{\mathcal{R}} r\delta$ *if $\ell \Rightarrow r \in \mathcal{R}$ and $\mathtt{dom}(\delta) = FMV(\ell)$*

(Beta) $(\lambda x.s)\ t \Rightarrow_{\mathcal{R}} s[x := t]$

We say $s \Rightarrow_\beta t$ if $s \Rightarrow_{\mathcal{R}} t$ is derived using a (Beta) step. A term s is terminating *under $\Rightarrow_{\mathcal{R}}$ if there is no infinite reduction $s = s_0 \Rightarrow_{\mathcal{R}} s_1 \Rightarrow_{\mathcal{R}} \dots$, is* in normal form *if there is no t such that $s \Rightarrow_{\mathcal{R}} t$, and is* β-normal *if there is no t with $s \Rightarrow_\beta t$. Note that we are allowed to reduce at any position of a term, even below a λ. The relation $\Rightarrow_{\mathcal{R}}$ is terminating if all terms over $\mathcal{F}, \mathcal{V}$ are terminating. The set $\mathcal{D} \subseteq \mathcal{F}$ of* defined symbols *consists of those $(\mathtt{f} : \sigma) \in \mathcal{F}$ such that a rule $\mathtt{f}\ \ell_1 \cdots \ell_n \Rightarrow r$ exists; all other symbols are called* constructors.

Note that $\mathcal{R}$ is allowed to be infinite, which is useful for instance to model polymorphic systems. Also, right-hand sides of rules do not have to be in β-normal form. While this is rarely used in practical examples, non-β-normal rules may arise through transformations, and we lose nothing by allowing them.

Example 6. Let $\mathcal{F} \supseteq \{\mathtt{0} : \mathtt{nat},\ \mathtt{s} : \mathtt{nat} \to \mathtt{nat},\ \mathtt{nil} : \mathtt{list}, \mathtt{cons} : \mathtt{nat} \to \mathtt{list} \to \mathtt{list},\ \mathtt{map} : (\mathtt{nat} \to \mathtt{nat}) \to \mathtt{list} \to \mathtt{list}\}$ and consider the following rules $\mathcal{R}$:

$$\mathtt{map}\ (\lambda x.Z\langle x\rangle)\ \mathtt{nil} \Rightarrow \mathtt{nil}$$
$$\mathtt{map}\ (\lambda x.Z\langle x\rangle)\ (\mathtt{cons}\ H\ T) \Rightarrow \mathtt{cons}\ Z\langle H\rangle\ (\mathtt{map}\ (\lambda x.Z\langle x\rangle)\ T)$$

Then $\mathtt{map}\ (\lambda y.\mathtt{0})\ (\mathtt{cons}\ (\mathtt{s}\ \mathtt{0})\ \mathtt{nil}) \Rightarrow_{\mathcal{R}} \mathtt{cons}\ \mathtt{0}\ (\mathtt{map}\ (\lambda y.\mathtt{0})\ \mathtt{nil}) \Rightarrow_{\mathcal{R}} \mathtt{cons}\ \mathtt{0}\ \mathtt{nil}$. Note that the bound variable y does not need to occur in the body of $\lambda y.\mathtt{0}$ to match $\lambda x.Z\langle x\rangle$. However, a term like $\mathtt{map}\ \mathtt{s}\ (\mathtt{cons}\ \mathtt{0}\ \mathtt{nil})$ *cannot* be reduced, because $\mathtt{s}$ does not instantiate $\lambda x.Z\langle x\rangle$. We could alternatively consider the rules:

$$\mathtt{map}\ Z\ \mathtt{nil} \Rightarrow \mathtt{nil}$$
$$\mathtt{map}\ Z\ (\mathtt{cons}\ H\ T) \Rightarrow \mathtt{cons}\ (Z\ H)\ (\mathtt{map}\ Z\ T)$$

Where the system before had $(Z : (\mathtt{nat} \to \mathtt{nat}, 1)) \in \mathcal{M}$, here we assume $(Z : (\mathtt{nat} \to \mathtt{nat}, 0)) \in \mathcal{M}$. Thus, rather than meta-variable application $Z\langle H\rangle$ we use explicit application $Z\ H$. Then $\mathtt{map}\ \mathtt{s}\ (\mathtt{cons}\ \mathtt{0}\ \mathtt{nil}) \Rightarrow_{\mathcal{R}} \mathtt{cons}\ (\mathtt{s}\ \mathtt{0})\ (\mathtt{map}\ \mathtt{s}\ \mathtt{nil})$. However, we will often need explicit β-reductions; e.g., $\mathtt{map}\ (\lambda y.\mathtt{0})\ (\mathtt{cons}\ (\mathtt{s}\ \mathtt{0})\ \mathtt{nil}) \Rightarrow_{\mathcal{R}} \mathtt{cons}\ ((\lambda y.\mathtt{0})\ (\mathtt{s}\ \mathtt{0}))\ (\mathtt{map}\ (\lambda y.\mathtt{0})\ \mathtt{nil}) \Rightarrow_\beta \mathtt{cons}\ \mathtt{0}\ (\mathtt{map}\ (\lambda y.\mathtt{0})\ \mathtt{nil})$.

Definition 7 (AFSM). *An* AFSM *is a tuple $(\mathcal{F}, \mathcal{V}, \mathcal{M}, \mathcal{R})$ of a signature and a set of rules built from meta-terms over $\mathcal{F}, \mathcal{V}, \mathcal{M}$; as types of relevant variables and meta-variables can always be derived from context, we will typically just refer to the AFSM $(\mathcal{F}, \mathcal{R})$. An AFSM implicitly defines the abstract reduction system $(\mathcal{T}(\mathcal{F}, \mathcal{V}), \Rightarrow_{\mathcal{R}})$: a set of terms and a rewrite relation on this set. An AFSM is terminating if $\Rightarrow_{\mathcal{R}}$ is terminating (on all terms in $\mathcal{T}(\mathcal{F}, \mathcal{V})$).*

Discussion: The two most common formalisms in termination analysis of higher-order rewriting are *algebraic functional systems* [26] (AFSs) and *higher-order rewriting systems* [37,39] (HRSs). AFSs are very similar to our AFSMs, but use variables for matching rather than meta-variables; this is trivially translated to the AFSM format, giving rules where all meta-variables have arity 0, like the "alternative" rules in Example 6. HRSs use matching modulo β/η, but the common restriction of *pattern HRSs* can be directly translated into AFSMs, provided terms are β-normalised after every reduction step. Even without this β-normalisation step, termination of the obtained AFSM implies termination of the original HRS; for second-order systems, termination is equivalent. AFSMs can also naturally encode CRSs [27] and several applicative systems (cf. [29, Chapter 3]).

Example 8 (Ordinal recursion). A running example is the AFSM $(\mathcal{F}, \mathcal{R})$ with $\mathcal{F} \supseteq \{\mathtt{0} : \mathtt{ord},\ \mathtt{s} : \mathtt{ord} \to \mathtt{ord}, \mathtt{lim} : (\mathtt{nat} \to \mathtt{ord}) \to \mathtt{ord},\ \mathtt{rec} : \mathtt{ord} \to \mathtt{nat} \to (\mathtt{ord} \to \mathtt{nat} \to \mathtt{nat}) \to ((\mathtt{nat} \to \mathtt{ord}) \to (\mathtt{nat} \to \mathtt{nat}) \to \mathtt{nat}) \to \mathtt{nat}\}$ and $\mathcal{R}$ given below. As all meta-variables have arity 0, this can be seen as an AFS.

$$\begin{aligned} \mathtt{rec}\ \mathtt{0}\ K\ F\ G &\Rightarrow K \\ \mathtt{rec}\ (\mathtt{s}\ X)\ K\ F\ G &\Rightarrow F\ X\ (\mathtt{rec}\ X\ K\ F\ G) \\ \mathtt{rec}\ (\mathtt{lim}\ H)\ K\ F\ G &\Rightarrow G\ H\ (\lambda m.\mathtt{rec}\ (H\ m)\ K\ F\ G) \end{aligned}$$

Observant readers may notice that by the given constructors, the type `nat` in Example 8 is not inhabited. However, as the given symbols are only a subset of $\mathcal{F}$, additional symbols (such as constructors for the `nat` type) may be included. The presence of additional function symbols does not affect termination of AFSMs:

Theorem 9 (Invariance of termination under signature extensions). *For an AFSM $(\mathcal{F}, \mathcal{R})$ with $\mathcal{F}$ at most countably infinite, let $\mathtt{funs}(\mathcal{R}) \subseteq \mathcal{F}$ be the set of function symbols occurring in some rule of $\mathcal{R}$. Then $(\mathcal{T}(\mathcal{F}, \mathcal{V}), \Rightarrow_{\mathcal{R}})$ is terminating if and only if $(\mathcal{T}(\mathtt{funs}(\mathcal{R}), \mathcal{V}), \Rightarrow_{\mathcal{R}})$ is terminating.*

Proof. Trivial by replacing all function symbols in $\mathcal{F} \setminus \mathtt{funs}(\mathcal{R})$ by corresponding variables of the same type. □

Therefore, we will typically only state the types of symbols occurring in the rules, but may safely assume that infinitely many symbols of all types are present (which for instance allows us to select unused constructors in some proofs).

2.2 Computability

A common technique in higher-order termination is Tait and Girard's *computability* notion [47]. There are several ways to define computability predicates; here we follow, e.g., [5,7–9] in considering *accessible meta-terms* using strictly positive inductive types. The definition presented below is adapted from these works, both to account for the altered formalism and to introduce (and obtain termination of) a relation $\Rrightarrow_C$ that we will use in the "computable subterm criterion processor" of Theorem 63 (a termination criterion that allows us to handle systems that would otherwise be beyond the reach of static DPs). This allows for a minimal presentation that avoids the use of ordinals that would otherwise be needed to obtain $\Rrightarrow_C$ (see, e.g., [7,9]).

To define computability, we use the notion of an *RC-set:*

Definition 10. *A* set of reducibility candidates, *or* RC-set, *for a rewrite relation* $\Rightarrow_{\mathcal{R}}$ *of an AFSM is a set* I *of base-type terms* s *such that: every term in* I *is terminating under* $\Rightarrow_{\mathcal{R}}$*;* I *is closed under* $\Rightarrow_{\mathcal{R}}$ *(so if* $s \in I$ *and* $s \Rightarrow_{\mathcal{R}} t$ *then* $t \in I$*); if* $s = x\ s_1 \cdots s_n$ *with* $x \in \mathcal{V}$ *or* $s = (\lambda x.u)\ s_0 \cdots s_n$ *with* $n \geq 0$*, and for all* t *with* $s \Rightarrow_{\mathcal{R}} t$ *we have* $t \in I$*, then* $s \in I$ *(for any* $u, s_0, \ldots, s_n \in \mathcal{T}(\mathcal{F}, \mathcal{V})$*).*

We define I*-computability for an RC-set* I *by induction on types. For* $s \in \mathcal{T}(\mathcal{F}, \mathcal{V})$*, we say that* s *is* I*-computable if either* s *is of base type and* $s \in I$*; or* $s : \sigma \rightarrow \tau$ *and for all* $t : \sigma$ *that are* I*-computable,* $s\ t$ *is* I*-computable.*

The traditional notion of computability is obtained by taking for I the set of all terminating base-type terms. Then, a term s is computable if and only if (a) s has base type and is terminating; or (b) $s : \sigma \rightarrow \tau$ and for all computable $t : \sigma$ the term $s\ t$ is computable. This choice is simple but, for reasoning, not ideal: we do not have a property like: "if $\mathtt{f}\ s_1 \cdots s_n$ is computable then so is each s_i". Such a property would be valuable to have for generalising termination proofs from first-order to higher-order rewriting, as it allows us to use computability where the first-order proof uses termination. While it is not possible to define a computability notion with this property alongside case (b) (as such a notion would not be well-founded), we can come *close* to this property by choosing a different set for I. To define this set, we will use the notion of *accessible arguments*, which is used for the same purpose also in the *General Schema* [8], the *Computability Path Ordering* [9], and the *Computability Closure* [7].

Definition 11 (Accessible arguments). *We fix a quasi-ordering* $\succeq^{\mathcal{S}}$ *on* $\mathcal{S}$ *with well-founded strict part* $\succ^{\mathcal{S}} := \succeq^{\mathcal{S}} \setminus \preceq^{\mathcal{S}}$.[1] *For a type* $\sigma \equiv \sigma_1 \rightarrow \ldots \rightarrow \sigma_m \rightarrow \kappa$ *(with* $\kappa \in \mathcal{S}$*) and sort* ι*, let* $\iota \succeq^{\mathcal{S}}_+ \sigma$ *if* $\iota \succeq^{\mathcal{S}} \kappa$ *and* $\iota \succ^{\mathcal{S}}_- \sigma_i$ *for all* i*, and let* $\iota \succ^{\mathcal{S}}_- \sigma$ *if* $\iota \succ^{\mathcal{S}} \kappa$ *and* $\iota \succeq^{\mathcal{S}}_+ \sigma_i$ *for all* i.[2]

For $\mathtt{f} : \sigma_1 \rightarrow \ldots \rightarrow \sigma_m \rightarrow \iota \in \mathcal{F}$*, let* $Acc(\mathtt{f}) = \{i \mid 1 \leq i \leq m \wedge \iota \succeq^{\mathcal{S}}_+ \sigma_i\}$*. For* $x : \sigma_1 \rightarrow \ldots \rightarrow \sigma_m \rightarrow \iota \in \mathcal{V}$*, let* $Acc(x) = \{i \mid 1 \leq i \leq m \wedge \sigma_i$ *has the form* $\tau_1 \rightarrow \ldots \rightarrow \tau_n \rightarrow \kappa$ *with* $\iota \succeq^{\mathcal{S}} \kappa\}$*. We write* $s \trianglerighteq_{\mathsf{acc}} t$ *if either* $s = t$*, or* $s = \lambda x.s'$ *and* $s' \trianglerighteq_{\mathsf{acc}} t$*, or* $s = a\ s_1 \cdots s_n$ *with* $a \in \mathcal{F} \cup \mathcal{V}$ *and* $s_i \trianglerighteq_{\mathsf{acc}} t$ *for some* $i \in Acc(a)$ *with* $a \notin FV(s_i)$*.*

With this definition, we will be able to define a set C such that, roughly, s is C-computable if and only if (a) $s : \sigma \rightarrow \tau$ and $s\ t$ is C-computable for all C-computable t, or (b) s has base type, is terminating, and if $s = \mathtt{f}\ s_1 \cdots s_m$ then s_i is C-computable for all *accessible* i (see Theorem 13 below). The reason that $Acc(x)$ for $x \in \mathcal{V}$ is different is proof-technical: computability of $\lambda x.x\ s_1 \cdots s_m$

[1] Well-foundedness is immediate if $\mathcal{S}$ is finite, but we have not imposed that requirement.

[2] Here $\iota \succeq^{\mathcal{S}}_+ \sigma$ corresponds to "ι occurs only positively in σ" in [5,8,9].

implies the computability of more arguments s_i than computability of $\mathtt{f}\ s_1 \cdots s_m$ does, since x can be instantiated by anything.

Example 12. Consider a quasi-ordering $\succeq^{\mathcal{S}}$ such that $\mathtt{ord} \succ^{\mathcal{S}} \mathtt{nat}$. In Example 8, we then have $\mathtt{ord} \succeq^{\mathcal{S}}_{+} \mathtt{nat} \rightarrow \mathtt{ord}$. Thus, $1 \in \mathit{Acc}(\mathtt{lim})$, which gives $\mathtt{lim}\ H \trianglerighteq_{\mathsf{acc}} H$.

Theorem 13. *Let* $(\mathcal{F}, \mathcal{R})$ *be an AFSM. Let* $\mathtt{f}\ s_1 \cdots s_m \Rrightarrow_I s_i\ t_1 \cdots t_n$ *if both sides have base type,* $i \in \mathit{Acc}(\mathtt{f})$*, and all* t_j *are* I*-computable. There is an RC-set* C *such that* $C = \{s \in \mathcal{T}(\mathcal{F}, \mathcal{V}) \mid s$ *has base type* $\wedge$ s *is terminating under* $\Rightarrow_{\mathcal{R}} \cup \Rrightarrow_C \wedge$ *if* $s \Rightarrow^*_{\mathcal{R}} \mathtt{f}\ s_1 \cdots s_m$ *then* s_i *is* C*-computable for all* $i \in \mathit{Acc}(\mathtt{f})\}$.

Proof (sketch). Note that we cannot *define* C as this set, as the set relies on the notion of C-computability. However, we *can* define C as the fixpoint of a monotone function operating on RC-sets. This follows the proof in, e.g., [8,9]. □

The complete proof is available in [17, Appendix A].

3 Restrictions

The termination methodology in this paper is restricted to AFSMs that satisfy certain limitations: they must be *properly applied* (a restriction on the number of terms each function symbol is applied to) and *accessible function passing* (a restriction on the positions of variables of a functional type in the left-hand sides of rules). Both are syntactic restrictions that are easily checked by a computer (mostly; the latter requires a search for a sort ordering, but this is typically easy).

3.1 Properly Applied AFSMs

In *properly applied AFSMs*, function symbols are assigned a certain, minimal number of arguments that they must always be applied to.

Definition 14. *An AFSM* $(\mathcal{F}, \mathcal{R})$ *is* properly applied *if for every* $\mathtt{f} \in \mathcal{D}$ *there exists an integer* k *such that for all rules* $\ell \Rightarrow r \in \mathcal{R}$*: (1) if* $\ell = \mathtt{f}\ \ell_1 \cdots \ell_n$ *then* $n = k$*; and (2) if* $r \trianglerighteq \mathtt{f}\ r_1 \cdots r_n$ *then* $n \geq k$*. We denote* $\mathit{minar}(\mathtt{f}) = k$*.*

That is, every occurrence of a function symbol in the *right-hand* side of a rule has at least as many arguments as the occurrences in the *left-hand* sides of rules. This means that partially applied functions are often not allowed: an AFSM with rules such as $\mathtt{double}\ X \Rightarrow \mathtt{plus}\ X\ X$ and $\mathtt{doublelist}\ L \Rightarrow \mathtt{map}\ \mathtt{double}\ L$ is not properly applied, because double is applied to one argument in the left-hand side of some rule, and to zero in the right-hand side of another.

This restriction is not as severe as it may initially seem since partial applications can be replaced by λ-abstractions; e.g., the rules above can be made properly applied by replacing the second rule by: $\mathtt{doublelist}\ L \Rightarrow \mathtt{map}\ (\lambda x.\mathtt{double}\ x)\ L$. By using η-expansion, we can transform any AFSM to satisfy this restriction:

Definition 15 **($\mathcal{R}^{\uparrow}$).** *Given a set of rules $\mathcal{R}$, let their* η-expansion *be given by* $\mathcal{R}^{\uparrow} = \{(\ell\ Z_1 \cdots Z_m){\uparrow}^{\eta} \Rightarrow (r\ Z_1 \cdots Z_m){\uparrow}^{\eta} \mid \ell \Rightarrow r \in \mathcal{R}$ *with* $r : \sigma_1 \to \ldots \to \sigma_m \to \iota$, $\iota \in \mathcal{S}$, *and* $Z_1, \ldots, Z_m$ *fresh meta-variables*$\}$, *where*

- $s{\uparrow}^{\eta} = \lambda x_1 \ldots x_m.\overline{s}\ (x_1{\uparrow}^{\eta}) \cdots (x_m{\uparrow}^{\eta})$ *if s is an application or element of* $\mathcal{V} \cup \mathcal{F}$, *and* $s{\uparrow}^{\eta} = \overline{s}$ *otherwise;*
- $\overline{\mathtt{f}} = \mathtt{f}$ *for* $\mathtt{f} \in \mathcal{F}$ *and* $\overline{x} = x$ *for* $x \in \mathcal{V}$, *while* $\overline{Z\langle s_1, \ldots, s_k\rangle} = Z\langle \overline{s_1}, \ldots, \overline{s_k}\rangle$ *and* $\overline{(\lambda x.s)} = \lambda x.(s{\uparrow}^{\eta})$ *and* $\overline{s_1\ s_2} = \overline{s_1}\ (s_2{\uparrow}^{\eta})$.

Note that $\ell{\uparrow}^{\eta}$ is a pattern if ℓ is. By [29, Thm. 2.16], a relation $\Rightarrow_{\mathcal{R}}$ is terminating if $\Rightarrow_{\mathcal{R}^{\uparrow}}$ is terminating, which allows us to transpose any methods to prove termination of properly applied AFSMs to all AFSMs.

However, there is a caveat: this transformation can introduce non-termination in some special cases, e.g., the terminating rule $\mathtt{f}\ X \Rightarrow \mathtt{g}\ \mathtt{f}$ with $\mathtt{f} : \mathtt{o} \to \mathtt{o}$ and $\mathtt{g} : (\mathtt{o} \to \mathtt{o}) \to \mathtt{o}$, whose η-expansion $\mathtt{f}\ X \Rightarrow \mathtt{g}\ (\lambda x.(\mathtt{f}\ x))$ is non-terminating. Thus, for a properly applied AFSM the methods in this paper apply directly. For an AFSM that is not properly applied, we can use the methods to prove *termination* (but not non-termination) by first η-expanding the rules. Of course, if this analysis leads to a *counterexample* for termination, we may still be able to verify whether this counterexample applies in the original, untransformed AFSM.

Example 16. Both AFSMs in Example 6 and the AFSM in Example 8 are properly applied.

Example 17. Consider an AFSM $(\mathcal{F}, \mathcal{R})$ with $\mathcal{F} \supseteq \{\mathtt{sin}, \mathtt{cos} : \mathtt{real} \to \mathtt{real}, \mathtt{times} : \mathtt{real} \to \mathtt{real} \to \mathtt{real}, \mathtt{deriv} : (\mathtt{real} \to \mathtt{real}) \to \mathtt{real} \to \mathtt{real}\}$ and $\mathcal{R} = \{\mathtt{deriv}\ (\lambda x.\mathtt{sin}\ F\langle x\rangle) \Rightarrow \lambda y.\mathtt{times}\ (\mathtt{deriv}\ (\lambda x.F\langle x\rangle)\ y)\ (\mathtt{cos}\ F\langle y\rangle)\}$. Although the one rule has a functional output type ($\mathtt{real} \to \mathtt{real}$), this AFSM is properly applied, with `deriv` having always at least 1 argument. Therefore, we do not need to use $\mathcal{R}^{\uparrow}$. However, if $\mathcal{R}$ were to additionally include some rules that did not satisfy the restriction (such as the `double` and `doublelist` rules above), then η-expanding *all* rules, including this one, would be necessary. We have: $\mathcal{R}^{\uparrow} = \{\mathtt{deriv}\ (\lambda x.\mathtt{sin}\ F\langle x\rangle)\ Y \Rightarrow (\lambda y.\mathtt{times}\ (\mathtt{deriv}\ (\lambda x.F\langle x\rangle)\ y)\ (\mathtt{cos}\ F\langle y\rangle))\ Y\}$. Note that the right-hand side of the η-expanded `deriv` rule is not β-normal.

3.2 Accessible Function Passing AFSMs

In *accessible function passing* AFSMs, variables of functional type may not occur at arbitrary places in the left-hand sides of rules: their positions are restricted using the sort ordering $\succeq^{\mathcal{S}}$ and accessibility relation $\trianglerighteq_{\mathtt{acc}}$ from Definition 11.

Definition 18 (Accessible function passing). *An AFSM $(\mathcal{F}, \mathcal{R})$ is* accessible function passing (AFP) *if there exists a sort ordering $\succeq^{\mathcal{S}}$ following Definition 11 such that: for all* $\mathtt{f}\ \ell_1 \cdots \ell_n \Rightarrow r \in \mathcal{R}$ *and all* $Z \in FMV(r)$: *there are variables $x_1, \ldots, x_k$ and some i such that* $\ell_i \trianglerighteq_{\mathtt{acc}} Z\langle x_1, \ldots, x_k\rangle$.

The key idea of this definition is that computability of each ℓ_i implies computability of all meta-variables in r. This excludes cases like Example 20 below. Many common examples satisfy this restriction, including those we saw before:

Example 19. Both systems from Example 6 are AFP: choosing the sort ordering $\succeq^{\mathcal{S}}$ that equates $\mathtt{nat}$ and $\mathtt{list}$, we indeed have $\mathtt{cons}\ H\ T \trianglerighteq_{\mathsf{acc}} H$ and $\mathtt{cons}\ H\ T \trianglerighteq_{\mathsf{acc}} T$ (as $\mathit{Acc}(\mathtt{cons}) = \{1, 2\}$) and both $\lambda x.Z\langle x\rangle \trianglerighteq_{\mathsf{acc}} Z\langle x\rangle$ and $Z \trianglerighteq_{\mathsf{acc}} Z$. The AFSM from Example 8 is AFP because we can choose $\mathtt{ord} \succ^{\mathcal{S}} \mathtt{nat}$ and have $\mathtt{lim}\ H \trianglerighteq_{\mathsf{acc}} H$ following Example 12 (and also $\mathtt{s}\ X \trianglerighteq_{\mathsf{acc}} X$ and $K \trianglerighteq_{\mathsf{acc}} K$, $F \trianglerighteq_{\mathsf{acc}} F$, $G \trianglerighteq_{\mathsf{acc}} G$). The AFSM from Example 17 is AFP, because $\lambda x.\mathtt{sin}\ F\langle x\rangle \trianglerighteq_{\mathsf{acc}} F\langle x\rangle$ for any $\succeq^{\mathcal{S}}$: $\lambda x.\mathtt{sin}\ F\langle x\rangle \trianglerighteq_{\mathsf{acc}} F\langle x\rangle$ because $\mathtt{sin}\ F\langle x\rangle \trianglerighteq_{\mathsf{acc}} F\langle x\rangle$ because $1 \in \mathit{Acc}(\mathtt{sin})$.

In fact, *all* first-order AFSMs (where all fully applied sub-meta-terms of the left-hand side of a rule have base type) are AFP via the sort ordering $\succeq^{\mathcal{S}}$ that equates all sorts. Also (with the same sort ordering), an AFSM $(\mathcal{F}, \mathcal{R})$ is AFP if, for all rules $\mathtt{f}\ \ell_1 \cdots \ell_k \Rightarrow r \in \mathcal{R}$ and all $1 \le i \le k$, we can write: $\ell_i = \lambda x_1 \ldots x_{n_i}.\ell'$ where $n_i \ge 0$ and all fully applied sub-meta-terms of ℓ' have base type.

This covers many practical systems, although for Example 8 we need a non-trivial sort ordering. Also, there are AFSMs that cannot be handled with *any* $\succeq^{\mathcal{S}}$.

Example 20 (Encoding the untyped λ-calculus). Consider an AFSM with $\mathcal{F} \supseteq \{\mathtt{ap} : \mathtt{o} \to \mathtt{o} \to \mathtt{o},\ \mathtt{lm} : (\mathtt{o} \to \mathtt{o}) \to \mathtt{o}\}$ and $\mathcal{R} = \{\mathtt{ap}\ (\mathtt{lm}\ F) \Rightarrow F\}$ (note that the only rule has type $\mathtt{o} \to \mathtt{o}$). This AFSM is not accessible function passing, because $\mathtt{lm}\ F \trianglerighteq_{\mathsf{acc}} F$ cannot hold for any $\succeq^{\mathcal{S}}$ (as this would require $\mathtt{o} \succ^{\mathcal{S}} \mathtt{o}$).

Note that this example is also not terminating. With $t = \mathtt{lm}\ (\lambda x.\mathtt{ap}\ x\ x)$, we get this self-loop as evidence: $\mathtt{ap}\ t\ t \Rightarrow_{\mathcal{R}} (\lambda x.\mathtt{ap}\ x\ x)\ t \Rightarrow_{\beta} \mathtt{ap}\ t\ t$.

Intuitively: in an accessible function passing AFSM, meta-variables of a higher type may occur only in "safe" places in the left-hand sides of rules. Rules like the ones in Example 20, where a higher-order meta-variable is lifted out of a base-type term, are not admitted (unless the base type is greater than the higher type).

In the remainder of this paper, we will refer to a *properly applied, accessible function passing* AFSM as a PA-AFP AFSM.

Discussion: This definition is strictly more liberal than the notions of "plain function passing" in both [34] and [46] as adapted to AFSMs. The notion in [46] largely corresponds to AFP if $\succeq^{\mathcal{S}}$ equates all sorts, and the HRS formalism guarantees that rules are properly applied (in fact, all fully applied sub-meta-terms of both left- and right-hand sides of rules have base type). The notion in [34] is more restrictive. The current restriction of PA-AFP AFSMs lets us handle examples like ordinal recursion (Example 8) which are not covered by [34,46]. However, note that [34,46] consider a different formalism, which does take rules whose left-hand side is not a pattern into account (which we do not consider). Our restriction also quite resembles the "admissible" rules in [6] which are defined using a pattern computability closure [5], but that work carries additional restrictions.

In later work [32,33], Kusakari extends the static DP approach to forms of polymorphic functional programming, with a very liberal restriction: the definition is parametrised with an *arbitrary* RC-set and corresponding accessibility ("safety") notion. Our AFP restriction is actually an instance of this condition (although a more liberal one than the example RC-set used in [32,33]). We have chosen a specific instance because it allows us to use dedicated techniques for the RC-set; for example, our *computable subterm criterion processor* (Theorem 63).

4 Static Higher-Order Dependency Pairs

To obtain sufficient criteria for both termination and non-termination of AFSMs, we will now transpose the definition of static dependency pairs [6,33,34,46] to AFSMs. In addition, we will add the new features of *meta-variable conditions*, *formative reductions*, and *computable chains*. Complete versions of all proof sketches in this section are available in [17, Appendix B].

Although we retain the first-order terminology of dependency *pairs*, the setting with meta-variables makes it more suitable to define DPs as *triples*.

Definition 21 ((Static) Dependency Pair). *A* dependency pair (DP) *is a triple $\ell \Rrightarrow p\ (A)$, where ℓ is a closed pattern $\mathtt{f}\ \ell_1 \cdots \ell_k$, p is a closed meta-term $\mathtt{g}\ p_1 \cdots p_n$, and A is a set of* meta-variable conditions*: pairs $Z : i$ indicating that Z regards its ith argument. A DP is* conservative *if $FMV(p) \subseteq FMV(\ell)$.*

A substitution γ respects *a set of meta-variable conditions A if for all $Z : i$ in A we have $\gamma(Z) = \lambda x_1 \ldots x_j.t$ with either $i > j$, or $i \leq j$ and $x_i \in FV(t)$. DPs will be used only with substitutions that respect their meta-variable conditions.*

For $\ell \Rrightarrow p\ (\emptyset)$ (so a DP whose set of meta-variable conditions is empty), we often omit the third component and just write $\ell \Rrightarrow p$.

Like the first-order setting, the static DP approach employs *marked function symbols* to obtain meta-terms whose instances cannot be reduced at the root.

Definition 22 (Marked symbols). *Let $(\mathcal{F}, \mathcal{R})$ be an AFSM. Define $\mathcal{F}^\sharp := \mathcal{F} \uplus \{\mathtt{f}^\sharp : \sigma \mid \mathtt{f} : \sigma \in \mathcal{D}\}$. For a meta-term $s = \mathtt{f}\ s_1 \cdots s_k$ with $\mathtt{f} \in \mathcal{D}$ and $k = minar(\mathtt{f})$, we let $s^\sharp = \mathtt{f}^\sharp\ s_1 \cdots s_k$; for s of other forms $s^\sharp$ is not defined.*

Moreover, we will consider *candidates*. In the first-order setting, candidate terms are subterms of the right-hand sides of rules whose root symbol is a defined symbol. Intuitively, these subterms correspond to function calls. In the current setting, we have to consider also meta-variables as well as rules whose right-hand side is not β-normal (which might arise for instance due to η-expansion).

Definition 23 (β-reduced-sub-meta-term, $\trianglerighteq_\beta$, $\trianglerighteq_A$). *A meta-term s has a fully applied* β-reduced-sub-meta-term *t (shortly,* BRSMT*), notation $s \trianglerighteq_\beta t$, if there exists a set of meta-variable conditions A with $s \trianglerighteq_A t$. Here $s \trianglerighteq_A t$ holds if:*

- *$s = t$, or*
- *$s = \lambda x.u$ and $u \trianglerighteq_A t$, or*

- $s = (\lambda x.u)\ s_0 \cdots s_n$ *and some* $s_i \trianglerighteq_A t$, *or* $u[x := s_0]\ s_1 \cdots s_n \trianglerighteq_A t$, *or*
- $s = a\ s_1 \cdots s_n$ *with* $a \in \mathcal{F} \cup \mathcal{V}$ *and some* $s_i \trianglerighteq_A t$, *or*
- $s = Z\langle t_1, \ldots, t_k\rangle\ s_1 \cdots s_n$ *and some* $s_i \trianglerighteq_A t$, *or*
- $s = Z\langle t_1, \ldots, t_k\rangle\ s_1 \cdots s_n$ *and* $t_i \trianglerighteq_A t$ *for some* $i \in \{1, \ldots, k\}$ *with* $(Z : i) \in A$.

Essentially, $s \trianglerighteq_A t$ means that t can be reached from s by taking β-reductions at the root and "subterm"-steps, where $Z : i$ is in A whenever we pass into argument i of a meta-variable Z. BRSMTs are used to generate *candidates*:

Definition 24 (Candidates). *For a meta-term* s, *the set* $\mathsf{cand}(s)$ *of candidates of* s *consists of those pairs* $t\ (A)$ *such that (a)* t *has the form* $\mathtt{f}\ s_1 \cdots s_k$ *with* $\mathtt{f} \in \mathcal{D}$ *and* $k = minar(\mathtt{f})$, *and (b) there are* $s_{k+1}, \ldots, s_n$ *(with* $n \geq k$*) such that* $s \trianglerighteq_A t\ s_{k+1} \cdots s_n$, *and (c)* A *is minimal: there is no subset* $A' \subsetneq A$ *with* $s \trianglerighteq_{A'} t$.

Example 25. In AFSMs where all meta-variables have arity 0 and the right-hand sides of rules are β-normal, the set $\mathsf{cand}(s)$ for a meta-term s consists exactly of the pairs $t\ (\emptyset)$ where t has the form $\mathtt{f}\ s_1 \cdots s_{minar(\mathtt{f})}$ and t occurs as part of s. In Example 8, we thus have $\mathsf{cand}(G\ H\ (\lambda m.\mathtt{rec}\ (H\ m)\ K\ F\ G)) = \{\mathtt{rec}\ (H\ m)\ K\ F\ G\ (\emptyset)\}$.

If some of the meta-variables *do* take arguments, then the meta-variable conditions matter: candidates of s are pairs $t\ (A)$ where A contains exactly those pairs $Z : i$ for which we pass through the ith argument of Z to reach t in s.

Example 26. Consider an AFSM with the signature from Example 8 but a rule using meta-variables with larger arities:

$$\begin{array}{c}\mathtt{rec}\ (\mathtt{lim}\ (\lambda n.H\langle n\rangle))\ K\ (\lambda x.\lambda n.F\langle x,n\rangle)\ (\lambda f.\lambda g.G\langle f,g\rangle)\ \Rightarrow \\ G\langle \lambda n.H\langle n\rangle,\ \lambda m.\mathtt{rec}\ H\langle m\rangle\ K\ (\lambda x.\lambda n.F\langle x,n\rangle)\ (\lambda f.\lambda g.G\langle f,g\rangle)\rangle\end{array}$$

The right-hand side has one candidate:

$$\mathtt{rec}\ H\langle m\rangle\ K\ (\lambda x.\lambda n.F\langle x,n\rangle)\ (\lambda f.\lambda g.G\langle f,g\rangle)\ (\{G : 2\})$$

The original static approaches define DPs as pairs $\ell^\sharp \Rrightarrow p^\sharp$ where $\ell \Rightarrow r$ is a rule and p a subterm of r of the form $\mathtt{f}\ r_1 \cdots r_m$ – as their rules are built using terms, not meta-terms. This can set variables bound in r free in p. In the current setting, we use candidates with their meta-variable conditions and implicit β-steps rather than subterms, and we replace such variables by meta-variables.

Definition 27 (*SDP*). *Let* s *be a meta-term and* $(\mathcal{F}, \mathcal{R})$ *be an AFSM. Let* $metafy(s)$ *denote* s *with all free variables replaced by corresponding meta-variables. Now* $SDP(\mathcal{R}) = \{\ell^\sharp \Rrightarrow metafy(p^\sharp)\ (A) \mid \ell \Rightarrow r \in \mathcal{R} \wedge p\ (A) \in \mathsf{cand}(r)\}$.

Although static DPs always have a pleasant form $\mathtt{f}^\sharp\ \ell_1 \cdots \ell_k \Rrightarrow \mathtt{g}^\sharp\ p_1 \cdots p_n\ (A)$ (as opposed to the *dynamic* DPs of, e.g., [31], whose right-hand sides can have a meta-variable at the head, which complicates various techniques in the framework), they have two important complications not present in first-order DPs: the right-hand side p of a DP $\ell \Rrightarrow p\ (A)$ may contain meta-variables that do not occur in the left-hand side ℓ – traditional analysis techniques are not really equipped for this – and the left- and right-hand sides may have different types. In Sect. 5 we will explore some methods to deal with these features.

Example 28. For the non-η-expanded rules of Example 17, the set $SDP(\mathcal{R})$ has one element: $\mathtt{deriv}^\sharp\ (\lambda x.\mathtt{sin}\ F\langle x\rangle) \Rrightarrow \mathtt{deriv}^\sharp\ (\lambda x.F\langle x\rangle)$. (As `times` and `cos` are not defined symbols, they do not generate dependency pairs.) The set $SDP(\mathcal{R}^\uparrow)$ for the η-expanded rules is $\{\mathtt{deriv}^\sharp\ (\lambda x.\mathtt{sin}\ F\langle x\rangle)\ Y \Rrightarrow \mathtt{deriv}^\sharp\ (\lambda x.F\langle x\rangle)\ Y\}$. To obtain the relevant candidate, we used the β-reduction step of BRSMTs.

Example 29. The AFSM from Example 8 is AFP following Example 19; here $SDP(\mathcal{R})$ is:

$$\mathtt{rec}^\sharp\ (\mathtt{s}\ X)\ K\ F\ G \Rrightarrow \mathtt{rec}^\sharp\ X\ K\ F\ G\ (\emptyset)$$
$$\mathtt{rec}^\sharp\ (\mathtt{lim}\ H)\ K\ F\ G \Rrightarrow \mathtt{rec}^\sharp\ (H\ M)\ K\ F\ G\ (\emptyset)$$

Note that the right-hand side of the second DP contains a meta-variable that is not on the left. As we will see in Example 64, that is not problematic here.

Termination analysis using dependency pairs importantly considers the notion of a *dependency chain.* This notion is fairly similar to the first-order setting:

Definition 30 (Dependency chain). *Let $\mathcal{P}$ be a set of DPs and $\mathcal{R}$ a set of rules. A (finite or infinite)* $(\mathcal{P},\mathcal{R})$-dependency chain *(or just $(\mathcal{P},\mathcal{R})$-chain) is a sequence $[(\ell_0 \Rrightarrow p_0\ (A_0), s_0, t_0), (\ell_1 \Rrightarrow p_1\ (A_1), s_1, t_1), \ldots]$ where each $\ell_i \Rrightarrow p_i\ (A_i) \in \mathcal{P}$ and all s_i, t_i are terms, such that for all i:*

1. *there exists a substitution γ on domain $FMV(\ell_i) \cup FMV(p_i)$ such that $s_i = \ell_i\gamma$, $t_i = p_i\gamma$ and for all $Z \in \mathtt{dom}(\gamma)$: $\gamma(Z)$ respects A_i;*
2. *we can write $t_i = \mathtt{f}\ u_1 \cdots u_n$ and $s_{i+1} = \mathtt{f}\ w_1 \cdots w_n$ and each $u_j \Rightarrow^*_{\mathcal{R}} w_j$.*

Example 31. In the (first) AFSM from Example 6, we have $SDP(\mathcal{R}) = \{\mathtt{map}^\sharp\ (\lambda x.Z\langle x\rangle)(\mathtt{cons}\ H\ T) \Rrightarrow \mathtt{map}^\sharp\ (\lambda x.Z\langle x\rangle)\ T\}$. An example of a finite dependency chain is $[(\rho, s_1, t_1), (\rho, s_2, t_2)]$ where ρ is the one DP, $s_1 = \mathtt{map}^\sharp\ (\lambda x.\mathtt{s}\ x)\ (\mathtt{cons}\ 0\ (\mathtt{cons}\ (\mathtt{s}\ 0)\ (\mathtt{map}\ (\lambda x.x)\ \mathtt{nil})))$ and $t_1 = \mathtt{map}^\sharp\ (\lambda x.\mathtt{s}\ x)\ (\mathtt{cons}\ (\mathtt{s}\ 0)\ (\mathtt{map}\ (\lambda x.x)\ \mathtt{nil}))$ and $s_2 = \mathtt{map}^\sharp\ (\lambda x.\mathtt{s}\ x)\ (\mathtt{cons}\ (\mathtt{s}\ 0)\ \mathtt{nil})$ and $t_2 = \mathtt{map}^\sharp\ (\lambda x.\mathtt{s}\ x)\ \mathtt{nil}$.

Note that here t_1 reduces to s_2 in a single step ($\mathtt{map}\ (\lambda x.x)\ \mathtt{nil} \Rightarrow_{\mathcal{R}} \mathtt{nil}$).

We have the following key result:

Theorem 32. *Let $(\mathcal{F},\mathcal{R})$ be a PA-AFP AFSM. If $(\mathcal{F},\mathcal{R})$ is non-terminating, then there is an infinite $(SDP(\mathcal{R}),\mathcal{R})$-dependency chain.*

Proof (sketch). The proof is an adaptation of the one in [34], altered for the more permissive definition of *accessible function passing* over *plain function passing* as well as the meta-variable conditions; it also follows from Theorem 37 below. □

By this result we can use dependency pairs to prove termination of a given properly applied and AFP AFSM: if we can prove that there is no infinite $(SDP(\mathcal{R}), \mathcal{R})$-chain, then termination follows immediately. Note, however, that the reverse result does *not* hold: it is possible to have an infinite $(SDP(\mathcal{R}), \mathcal{R})$-dependency chain even for a terminating PA-AFP AFSM.

Example 33. Let $\mathcal{F} \supseteq \{\mathtt{0}, \mathtt{1} : \mathtt{nat},\ \mathtt{f} : \mathtt{nat} \to \mathtt{nat},\ \mathtt{g} : (\mathtt{nat} \to \mathtt{nat}) \to \mathtt{nat}\}$ and $\mathcal{R} = \{\mathtt{f}\ \mathtt{0} \Rightarrow \mathtt{g}\ (\lambda x.\mathtt{f}\ x), \mathtt{g}\ (\lambda x.F\langle x \rangle) \Rightarrow F\langle \mathtt{1} \rangle\}$. This AFSM is PA-AFP, with $SDP(\mathcal{R}) = \{\mathtt{f}^\sharp\ \mathtt{0} \Rrightarrow \mathtt{g}^\sharp\ (\lambda x.\mathtt{f}\ x),\ \mathtt{f}^\sharp\ \mathtt{0} \Rrightarrow \mathtt{f}^\sharp\ X\}$; the second rule does not cause the addition of any dependency pairs. Although $\Rightarrow_{\mathcal{R}}$ is terminating, there is an infinite $(SDP(\mathcal{R}), \mathcal{R})$-chain $[(\mathtt{f}^\sharp\ \mathtt{0} \Rrightarrow \mathtt{f}^\sharp\ X, \mathtt{f}^\sharp\ \mathtt{0}, \mathtt{f}^\sharp\ \mathtt{0}), (\mathtt{f}^\sharp\ \mathtt{0} \Rrightarrow \mathtt{f}^\sharp\ X, \mathtt{f}^\sharp\ \mathtt{0}, \mathtt{f}^\sharp\ \mathtt{0}), \ldots]$.

The problem in Example 33 is the *non-conservative* DP $\mathtt{f}^\sharp\ \mathtt{0} \Rrightarrow \mathtt{f}^\sharp\ X$, with X on the right but not on the left. Such DPs arise from *abstractions* in the right-hand sides of rules. Unfortunately, abstractions are introduced by the restricted η-expansion (Definition 15) that we may need to make an AFSM properly applied. Even so, often all DPs are conservative, like Examples 6 and 17. There, we do have the inverse result:

Theorem 34. *For any AFSM* $(\mathcal{F}, \mathcal{R})$*: if there is an infinite* $(SDP(\mathcal{R}), \mathcal{R})$*-chain* $[(\rho_0, s_0, t_0), (\rho_1, s_1, t_1), \ldots]$ *with all* ρ_i *conservative, then* $\Rightarrow_{\mathcal{R}}$ *is non-terminating.*

Proof (sketch). If $FMV(p_i) \subseteq FMV(\ell_i)$, then we can see that $s_i \Rightarrow_{\mathcal{R}} \cdot \Rightarrow_\beta^* t_i'$ for some term t_i' of which t_i is a subterm. Since also each $t_i \Rightarrow_{\mathcal{R}}^* s_{i+1}$, the infinite chain induces an infinite reduction $s_0 \Rightarrow_{\mathcal{R}}^+ t_0' \Rightarrow_{\mathcal{R}}^* s_1' \Rightarrow_{\mathcal{R}}^+ t_1'' \Rightarrow_{\mathcal{R}}^* \cdots$. □

The core of the dependency pair *framework* is to systematically simplify a set of pairs $(\mathcal{P}, \mathcal{R})$ to prove either absence or presence of an infinite $(\mathcal{P}, \mathcal{R})$-chain, thus showing termination or non-termination as appropriate. By Theorems 32 and 34 we can do so, although with some conditions on the non-termination result. We can do better by tracking certain properties of dependency chains.

Definition 35 (Minimal and Computable chains). *Let* $(\mathcal{F}, \mathcal{U})$ *be an AFSM and* $C_{\mathcal{U}}$ *an RC-set satisfying the properties of Theorem 13 for* $(\mathcal{F}, \mathcal{U})$*. Let* $\mathcal{F}$ *contain, for every type* σ*, at least countably many symbols* $\mathtt{f} : \sigma$ *not used in* $\mathcal{U}$*.*

A $(\mathcal{P}, \mathcal{R})$*-chain* $[(\rho_0, s_0, t_0), (\rho_1, s_1, t_1), \ldots]$ *is* $\mathcal{U}$-computable *if:* $\Rightarrow_{\mathcal{U}} \supseteq \Rightarrow_{\mathcal{R}}$*, and for all* $i \in \mathbb{N}$ *there exists a substitution* γ_i *such that* $\rho_i = \ell_i \Rrightarrow p_i\ (A_i)$ *with* $s_i = \ell_i\gamma_i$ *and* $t_i = p_i\gamma_i$*, and* $(\lambda x_1 \ldots x_n.v)\gamma_i$ *is* $C_{\mathcal{U}}$*-computable for all* v *and* B *such that* $p_i \trianglerighteq_B v$*,* γ_i *respects* B*, and* $FV(v) = \{x_1, \ldots, x_n\}$*.*

A chain is minimal *if the strict subterms of all* t_i *are terminating under* $\Rightarrow_{\mathcal{R}}$*.*

In the first-order DP framework, *minimal* chains give access to several powerful techniques to prove absence of infinite chains, such as the *subterm criterion* [24] and *usable rules* [22,24]. *Computable* chains go a step further, by building on the computability inherent in the proof of Theorem 32 and the notion of *accessible function passing* AFSMs. In computable chains, we can require that (some of) the subterms of all t_i are *computable* rather than merely *terminating*.

This property will be essential in the *computable subterm criterion processor* (Theorem 63).

Another property of dependency chains is the use of *formative rules*, which has proven very useful for dynamic DPs [31]. Here we go further and consider *formative reductions*, which were introduced for the first-order DP framework in [16]. This property will be essential in the *formative rules processor* (Theorem 58).

Definition 36 (Formative chain, formative reduction). *A $(\mathcal{P}, \mathcal{R})$-chain $[(\ell_0 \Rrightarrow p_0\ (A_0), s_0, t_0), (\ell_1 \Rrightarrow p_1\ (A_1), s_1, t_1), \ldots]$ is* formative *if for all i, the reduction $t_i \Rightarrow_{\mathcal{R}}^* s_{i+1}$ is ℓ_{i+1}-formative. Here, for a pattern ℓ, substitution γ and term s, a reduction $s \Rightarrow_{\mathcal{R}}^* \ell\gamma$ is ℓ-*formative *if one of the following holds:*

- *ℓ is not a fully extended linear pattern; that is: some meta-variable occurs more than once in ℓ or ℓ has a sub-meta-term $\lambda x.C[Z\langle s\rangle]$ with $x \notin \{s\}$*
- *ℓ is a meta-variable application $Z\langle x_1, \ldots, x_k\rangle$ and $s = \ell\gamma$*
- *$s = a\ s_1 \cdots s_n$ and $\ell = a\ \ell_1 \cdots \ell_n$ with $a \in \mathcal{F}^\sharp \cup \mathcal{V}$ and each $s_i \Rightarrow_{\mathcal{R}}^* \ell_i\gamma$ by an ℓ_i-formative reduction*
- *$s = \lambda x.s'$ and $\ell = \lambda x.\ell'$ and $s' \Rightarrow_{\mathcal{R}}^* \ell'\gamma$ by an ℓ'-formative reduction*
- *$s = (\lambda x.u)\ v\ w_1 \cdots w_n$ and $u[x := v]\ w_1 \cdots w_n \Rightarrow_{\mathcal{R}}^* \ell\gamma$ by an ℓ-formative reduction*
- *ℓ is not a meta-variable application, and there are $\ell' \Rightarrow r' \in \mathcal{R}$, meta-variables $Z_1 \ldots Z_n$ $(n \geq 0)$ and δ such that $s \Rightarrow_{\mathcal{R}}^* (\ell'\ Z_1 \cdots Z_n)\delta$ by an $(\ell'\ Z_1 \cdots Z_n)$-formative reduction, and $(r'\ Z_1 \cdots Z_n)\delta \Rightarrow_{\mathcal{R}}^* \ell\gamma$ by an ℓ-formative reduction.*

The idea of a formative reduction is to avoid redundant steps: if $s \Rightarrow_{\mathcal{R}}^* \ell\gamma$ by an ℓ-formative reduction, then this reduction takes only the steps needed to obtain an instance of ℓ. Suppose that we have rules $\mathtt{plus}\ \mathtt{0}\ Y \Rightarrow Y$, $\mathtt{plus}\ (\mathtt{s}\ X)\ Y \Rightarrow \mathtt{s}\ (\mathtt{plus}\ X\ Y)$. Let $\ell := \mathtt{g}\ \mathtt{0}\ X$ and $t := \mathtt{plus}\ \mathtt{0}\ \mathtt{0}$. Then the reduction $\mathtt{g}\ t\ t \Rightarrow_{\mathcal{R}} \mathtt{g}\ \mathtt{0}\ t$ is ℓ-formative: we must reduce the first argument to get an instance of ℓ. The reduction $\mathtt{g}\ t\ t \Rightarrow_{\mathcal{R}} \mathtt{g}\ t\ \mathtt{0} \Rightarrow_{\mathcal{R}} \mathtt{g}\ \mathtt{0}\ \mathtt{0}$ is not ℓ-formative, because the reduction in the second argument does not contribute to the non-meta-variable positions of ℓ. This matters when we consider ℓ as the left-hand side of a rule, say $\mathtt{g}\ \mathtt{0}\ X \Rightarrow \mathtt{0}$: if we reduce $\mathtt{g}\ t\ t \Rightarrow_{\mathcal{R}} \mathtt{g}\ t\ \mathtt{0} \Rightarrow_{\mathcal{R}} \mathtt{g}\ \mathtt{0}\ \mathtt{0} \Rightarrow_{\mathcal{R}} \mathtt{0}$, then the first step was redundant: removing this step gives a shorter reduction to the same result: $\mathtt{g}\ t\ t \Rightarrow_{\mathcal{R}} \mathtt{g}\ \mathtt{0}\ t \Rightarrow_{\mathcal{R}} \mathtt{0}$. In an infinite reduction, redundant steps may also be postponed indefinitely.

We can now strengthen the result of Theorem 32 with two new properties.

Theorem 37. *Let $(\mathcal{F}, \mathcal{R})$ be a* properly applied, accessible function passing *AFSM. If $(\mathcal{F}, \mathcal{R})$ is non-terminating, then there is an infinite $\mathcal{R}$-computable* formative *$(SDP(\mathcal{R}), \mathcal{R})$-dependency chain.*

Proof (sketch). We select a *minimal non-computable (MNC)* term $s := \mathtt{f}\ s_1 \cdots s_k$ (where all s_i are $C_{\mathcal{R}}$-computable) and an infinite reduction starting in s. Then we stepwise build an infinite dependency chain, as follows. Since s is non-computable but each s_i terminates (as computability implies termination), there exist a rule

$\mathtt{f}\ \ell_1 \cdots \ell_k \Rrightarrow r$ and substitution γ such that each $s_i \Rrightarrow^*_{\mathcal{R}} \ell_i\gamma$ and $r\gamma$ is non-computable. We can then identify a candidate t (A) of r such that γ respects A and $t\gamma$ is a MNC subterm of $r\gamma$; we continue the process with $t\gamma$ (or a term at its head). For the *formative* property, we note that if $s \Rrightarrow^*_{\mathcal{R}} \ell\gamma$ and u is terminating, then $u \Rrightarrow^*_{\mathcal{R}} \ell\delta$ by an ℓ-formative reduction for substitution δ such that each $\delta(Z) \Rrightarrow^*_{\mathcal{R}} \gamma(Z)$. This follows by postponing those reduction steps not needed to obtain an instance of ℓ. The resulting infinite chain is $\mathcal{R}$-computable because we can show, by induction on the definition of $\trianglerighteq_{\mathtt{acc}}$, that if $\ell \Rrightarrow r$ is an AFP rule and $\ell\gamma$ is a MNC term, then $\gamma(Z)$ is $C_{\mathcal{R}}$-computable for all $Z \in FMV(r)$. □

As it is easily seen that all $C_{\mathcal{U}}$-computable terms are $\Rrightarrow_{\mathcal{U}}$-terminating and therefore $\Rrightarrow_{\mathcal{R}}$-terminating, every $\mathcal{U}$-computable $(\mathcal{P}, \mathcal{R})$-dependency chain is also minimal. The notions of $\mathcal{R}$-computable and formative chains still do not suffice to obtain a true inverse result, however (i.e., to prove that termination implies the absence of an infinite $\mathcal{R}$-computable chain over $SDP(\mathcal{R})$): the infinite chain in Example 33 is $\mathcal{R}$-computable.

To see why the two restrictions that the AFSM must be *properly applied* and *accessible function passing* are necessary, consider the following examples.

Example 38. Consider $\mathcal{F} \supseteq \{\mathtt{fix} : ((\mathsf{o} \to \mathsf{o}) \to \mathsf{o} \to \mathsf{o}) \to \mathsf{o} \to \mathsf{o}\}$ and $\mathcal{R} = \{\mathtt{fix}\ F\ X \Rrightarrow F\ (\mathtt{fix}\ F)\ X\}$. This AFSM is not properly applied; it is also not terminating, as can be seen by instantiating F with $\lambda y.y$. However, it does not have any static DPs, since $\mathtt{fix}\ F$ is not a candidate. Even if we altered the definition of static DPs to admit a dependency pair $\mathtt{fix}^\sharp\ F\ X \Rrightarrow \mathtt{fix}^\sharp\ F$, this pair could not be used to build an infinite dependency chain.

Note that the problem does not arise if we study the η-expanded rules $\mathcal{R}^\uparrow = \{\mathtt{fix}\ F\ X \Rrightarrow F\ (\lambda z.\mathtt{fix}\ F\ z)\ X\}$, as the dependency pair $\mathtt{fix}^\sharp\ F\ X \Rrightarrow \mathtt{fix}^\sharp\ F\ Z$ does admit an infinite chain. Unfortunately, as the one dependency pair does not satisfy the conditions of Theorem 34, we cannot use this to prove non-termination.

Example 39. The AFSM from Example 20 is not accessible function passing, since $Acc(\mathtt{lm}) = \emptyset$. This is good because the set $SDP(\mathcal{R})$ is empty, which would lead us to falsely conclude termination without the restriction.

Discussion: Theorem 37 transposes the work of [34,46] to AFSMs and extends it by using a more liberal restriction, by limiting interest to *formative*, *$\mathcal{R}$-computable* chains, and by including meta-variable conditions. Both of these new properties of chains will support new termination techniques within the DP framework.

The relationship with the works for functional programming [32,33] is less clear: they define a different form of chains suited well to polymorphic systems, but which requires more intricate reasoning for non-polymorphic systems, as DPs can be used for reductions at the head of a term. It is not clear whether there are non-polymorphic systems that can be handled with one and not the other. The notions of formative and $\mathcal{R}$-computable chains are not considered there; meta-variable conditions are not relevant to their λ-free formalism.

5 The Static Higher-Order DP Framework

In first-order term rewriting, the DP *framework* [20] is an extendable framework to prove termination and non-termination. As observed in the introduction, DP analyses in higher-order rewriting typically go beyond the initial DP *approach* [2], but fall short of the full *framework*. Here, we define the latter for static DPs. Complete versions of all proof sketches in this section are in [17, Appendix C].

We have now reduced the problem of termination to non-existence of certain chains. In the DP framework, we formalise this in the notion of a *DP problem*:

Definition 40 (DP problem). *A* DP problem *is a tuple* $(\mathcal{P}, \mathcal{R}, m, f)$ *with* $\mathcal{P}$ *a set of DPs,* $\mathcal{R}$ *a set of rules,* $m \in \{\mathtt{minimal}, \mathtt{arbitrary}\} \cup \{\mathtt{computable}_{\mathcal{U}} \mid$ *any set of rules* $\mathcal{U}\}$*, and* $f \in \{\mathtt{formative}, \mathtt{all}\}$.[3]

A DP problem $(\mathcal{P}, \mathcal{R}, m, f)$ *is* finite *if there exists no infinite* $(\mathcal{P}, \mathcal{R})$*-chain that is* $\mathcal{U}$*-computable if* $m = \mathtt{computable}_{\mathcal{U}}$*, is minimal if* $m = \mathtt{minimal}$*, and is formative if* $f = \mathtt{formative}$*. It is* infinite *if* $\mathcal{R}$ *is non-terminating, or if there exists an infinite* $(\mathcal{P}, \mathcal{R})$*-chain where all DPs used in the chain are conservative.*

To capture the levels of permissiveness in the m *flag, we use a transitive-reflexive relation* $\succeq$ *generated by* $\mathtt{computable}_{\mathcal{U}} \succeq \mathtt{minimal} \succeq \mathtt{arbitrary}$.

Thus, the combination of Theorems 34 and 37 can be rephrased as: an AFSM $(\mathcal{F}, \mathcal{R})$ is terminating if $(\mathit{SDP}(\mathcal{R}), \mathcal{R}, \mathtt{computable}_{\mathcal{R}}, \mathtt{formative})$ is finite, and is non-terminating if $(\mathit{SDP}(\mathcal{R}), \mathcal{R}, m, f)$ is infinite for some $m \in \{\mathtt{computable}_{\mathcal{U}}, \mathtt{minimal}, \mathtt{arbitrary}\}$ and $f \in \{\mathtt{formative}, \mathtt{all}\}$.[4]

The core idea of the DP framework is to iteratively simplify a set of DP problems via *processors* until nothing remains to be proved:

Definition 41 (Processor). *A* dependency pair processor *(or just* processor*) is a function that takes a DP problem and returns either* NO *or a set of DP problems. A processor Proc is* sound *if a DP problem M is finite whenever Proc(M)* $\neq$ NO *and all elements of Proc(M) are finite. A processor Proc is* complete *if a DP problem M is infinite whenever Proc(M)* $=$ NO *or contains an infinite element.*

To prove finiteness of a DP problem M with the DP framework, we proceed analogously to the first-order DP framework [22]: we repeatedly apply sound DP processors starting from M until none remain. That is, we execute the following rough procedure: (1) let $A := \{M\}$; (2) while $A \neq \emptyset$: select a problem $Q \in A$ and a sound processor *Proc* with $\mathit{Proc}(Q) \neq \mathtt{NO}$, and let $A := (A \setminus \{Q\}) \cup \mathit{Proc}(Q)$. If this procedure terminates, then M is a finite DP problem.

---

[3] Our framework is implicitly parametrised by the signature $\mathcal{F}^\sharp$ used for term formation. As none of the processors we present modify this component (as indeed there is no need to by Theorem 9), we leave it implicit.

[4] The processors in this paper do not *alter* the flag m, but some *require* minimality or computability. We include the `minimal` option and the subscript $\mathcal{U}$ for the sake of future generalisations, and for reuse of processors in the *dynamic* approach of [31].

To prove termination of an AFSM $(\mathcal{F}, \mathcal{R})$, we would use as initial DP problem $(\mathit{SDP}(\mathcal{R}), \mathcal{R}, \mathtt{computable}_{\mathcal{R}}, \mathtt{formative})$, provided that $\mathcal{R}$ is properly applied and accessible function passing (where η-expansion following Definition 15 may be applied first). If the procedure terminates – so finiteness of M is proved by the definition of soundness – then Theorem 37 provides termination of $\Rightarrow_{\mathcal{R}}$.

Similarly, we can use the DP framework to prove infiniteness: (1) let $A := \{M\}$; (2) while $A \neq \mathtt{NO}$: select a problem $Q \in A$ and a complete processor *Proc*, and let $A := \mathtt{NO}$ if $\mathit{Proc}(Q) = \mathtt{NO}$, or $A := (A \setminus \{Q\}) \cup \mathit{Proc}(Q)$ otherwise. For non-termination of $(\mathcal{F}, \mathcal{R})$, the initial DP problem should be $(\mathit{SDP}(\mathcal{R}), \mathcal{R}, m, f)$, where m, f can be any flag (see Theorem 34). Note that the algorithms coincide while processors are used that are both sound *and* complete. In a tool, automation (or the user) must resolve the non-determinism and select suitable processors.

Below, we will present a number of processors within the framework. We will typically present processors by writing "for a DP problem M satisfying X, Y, Z, $\mathit{Proc}(M) = \dots$". In these cases, we let $\mathit{Proc}(M) = \{M\}$ for any problem M not satisfying the given properties. Many more processors are possible, but we have chosen to present a selection which touches on all aspects of the DP framework:

- processors which map a DP problem to NO (Theorem 65), a singleton set (most processors) and a non-singleton set (Theorem 42);
- changing the set $\mathcal{R}$ (Theorems 54, 58) and various flags (Theorem 54);
- using specific values of the f (Theorem 58) and m flags (Theorems 54, 61, 63);
- using term orderings (Theorems 49, 52), a key part of many termination proofs.

5.1 The Dependency Graph

We can leverage reachability information to *decompose* DP problems. In first-order rewriting, a graph structure is used to track which DPs can possibly follow one another in a chain [2]. Here, we define this *dependency graph* as follows.

Definition 42 (Dependency graph). *A DP problem $(\mathcal{P}, \mathcal{R}, m, f)$ induces a graph structure DG, called its* dependency graph, *whose nodes are the elements of $\mathcal{P}$. There is a (directed) edge from ρ_1 to ρ_2 in DG iff there exist s_1, t_1, s_2, t_2 such that $[(\rho_1, s_1, t_1), (\rho_2, s_2, t_2)]$ is a $(\mathcal{P}, \mathcal{R})$-chain with the properties for m, f.*

Example 43. Consider an AFSM with $\mathcal{F} \supseteq \{\mathtt{f} : (\mathtt{nat} \to \mathtt{nat}) \to \mathtt{nat} \to \mathtt{nat}\}$ and $\mathcal{R} = \{\mathtt{f}\ (\lambda x.F\langle x\rangle)\ (\mathtt{s}\ Y) \Rightarrow F\langle \mathtt{f}\ (\lambda x.\mathtt{0})\ (\mathtt{f}\ (\lambda x.F\langle x\rangle)\ Y)\rangle\}$. Let $\mathcal{P} := \mathit{SDP}(\mathcal{R}) =$

$$\left\{\begin{array}{ll} (1)\ \mathtt{f}^\sharp\ (\lambda x.F\langle x\rangle)\ (\mathtt{s}\ Y) \Rrightarrow \mathtt{f}^\sharp\ (\lambda x.\mathtt{0})\ (\mathtt{f}\ (\lambda x.F\langle x\rangle)\ Y) & (\{F:1\}) \\ (2)\ \mathtt{f}^\sharp\ (\lambda x.F\langle x\rangle)\ (\mathtt{s}\ Y) \Rrightarrow \mathtt{f}^\sharp\ (\lambda x.F\langle x\rangle)\ Y & (\{F:1\}) \end{array}\right\}$$

The dependency graph of $(\mathcal{P}, \mathcal{R}, \mathtt{minimal}, \mathtt{formative})$ is:

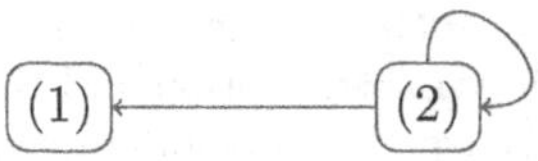

There is no edge from (1) to itself or (2) because there is no substitution γ such that $(\lambda x.\mathtt{0})\gamma$ can be reduced to a term $(\lambda x.F\langle x\rangle)\delta$ where $\delta(F)$ regards its first argument (as $\Rightarrow_{\mathcal{R}}^*$ cannot introduce new variables).

In general, the dependency graph for a given DP problem is undecidable, which is why we consider *approximations.*

Definition 44 (Dependency graph approximation [31]**).** *A finite graph G_θ approximates DG if θ is a function that maps the nodes of DG to the nodes of G_θ such that, whenever DG has an edge from ρ_1 to ρ_2, G_θ has an edge from $\theta(\rho_1)$ to $\theta(\rho_2)$. (G_θ may have edges that have no corresponding edge in DG.)*

Note that this definition allows for an *infinite* graph to be approximated by a *finite* one; infinite graphs may occur if $\mathcal{R}$ is infinite (e.g., the union of all simply-typed instances of polymorphic rules).

If $\mathcal{P}$ is finite, we can take a graph approximation $G_{\mathtt{id}}$ with the same nodes as DG. A simple approximation may have an edge from $\ell_1 \Rrightarrow p_1\ (A_1)$ to $\ell_2 \Rrightarrow p_2\ (A_2)$ whenever both p_1 and ℓ_2 have the form $\mathtt{f}^\sharp\ s_1 \cdots s_k$ for the same $\mathtt{f}$ and k. However, one can also take the meta-variable conditions into account, as we did in Example 43.

Theorem 45 (Dependency graph processor). *The processor $Proc_{G_\theta}$ that maps a DP problem $M = (\mathcal{P}, \mathcal{R}, m, f)$ to $\{(\{\rho \in \mathcal{P} \mid \theta(\rho) \in C_i\}, \mathcal{R}, m, f) \mid 1 \leq i \leq n\}$ if G_θ is an approximation of the dependency graph of M and $C_1, \ldots, C_n$ are the (nodes of the) non-trivial strongly connected components (SCCs) of G_θ, is both sound and complete.*

Proof (sketch). In an infinite $(\mathcal{P}, \mathcal{R})$-chain $[(\rho_0, s_0, t_0), (\rho_1, s_1, t_1), \ldots]$, there is always a path from ρ_i to ρ_{i+1} in DG. Since G_θ is finite, every infinite path in DG eventually remains in a cycle in G_θ. This cycle is part of an SCC. □

Example 46. Let $\mathcal{R}$ be the set of rules from Example 43 and G be the graph given there. Then $Proc_G(SDP(\mathcal{R}), \mathcal{R}, \mathtt{computable}_{\mathcal{R}}, \mathtt{formative}) = \{(\{\mathtt{f}^\sharp\ (\lambda x.F\langle x\rangle)\ (\mathtt{s}\ Y) \Rrightarrow \mathtt{f}^\sharp\ (\lambda x.F\langle x\rangle)\ Y\ (\{F : 1\})\}, \mathcal{R}, \mathtt{computable}_{\mathcal{R}}, \mathtt{formative})\}$.

Example 47. Let $\mathcal{R}$ consist of the rules for $\mathtt{map}$ from Example 6 along with $\mathtt{f}\ L \Rightarrow \mathtt{map}\ (\lambda x.\mathtt{g}\ x)\ L$ and $\mathtt{g}\ X \Rightarrow X$. Then $SDP(\mathcal{R}) = \{(1)\ \mathtt{map}^\sharp\ (\lambda x.Z\langle x\rangle)\ (\mathtt{cons}\ H\ T) \Rrightarrow \mathtt{map}^\sharp\ (\lambda x.Z\langle x\rangle)\ T,\ (2)\ \mathtt{f}^\sharp\ L \Rrightarrow \mathtt{map}^\sharp\ (\lambda x.\mathtt{g}\ x)\ L,\ (3)\ \mathtt{f}^\sharp\ L \Rrightarrow \mathtt{g}^\sharp\ X\}$. DP (3) is not conservative, but it is not on any cycle in the graph approximation $G_{\mathtt{id}}$ obtained by considering head symbols as described above:

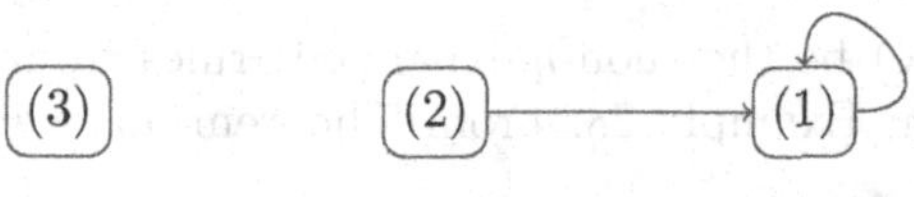

As (1) is the only DP on a cycle, $Proc_{SDP_{G_{\mathtt{id}}}}(SDP(\mathcal{R}), \mathcal{R}, \mathtt{computable}_{\mathcal{R}}, \mathtt{formative}) = \{\ (\{(1)\}, \mathcal{R}, \mathtt{computable}_{\mathcal{R}}, \mathtt{formative})\ \}$.

Discussion: The dependency graph is a powerful tool for simplifying DP problems, used since early versions of the DP approach [2]. Our notion of a dependency graph approximation, taken from [31], strictly generalises the original notion in [2], which uses a graph on the same node set as DG with possibly further edges. One can get this notion here by using a graph $G_{\mathtt{id}}$. The advantage of our definition is that it ensures soundness of the dependency graph processor also for *infinite* sets of DPs. This overcomes a restriction in the literature [34, Corollary 5.13] to dependency graphs without non-cyclic infinite paths.

5.2 Processors Based on Reduction Triples

At the heart of most DP-based approaches to termination proving lie well-founded orderings to delete DPs (or rules). For this, we use *reduction triples* [24,31].

Definition 48 (Reduction triple). *A* reduction triple $(\succsim, \succcurlyeq, \succ)$ *consists of two quasi-orderings* $\succsim$ *and* $\succcurlyeq$ *and a well-founded strict ordering* $\succ$ *on meta-terms such that* $\succsim$ *is monotonic, all of* $\succsim, \succcurlyeq, \succ$ *are meta-stable (that is,* $\ell \succsim r$ *implies* $\ell\gamma \succsim r\gamma$ *if* ℓ *is a closed pattern and* γ *a substitution on domain* $FMV(\ell) \cup FMV(r)$*, and the same for* $\succcurlyeq$ *and* $\succ$*),* $\Rightarrow_\beta \subseteq \succsim$*, and both* $\succsim \circ \succ \subseteq \succ$ *and* $\succcurlyeq \circ \succ \subseteq \succ$.

In the first-order DP framework, the reduction pair processor [20] seeks to orient all rules with $\succsim$ and all DPs with either $\succsim$ or $\succ$; if this succeeds, those pairs oriented with $\succ$ may be removed. Using reduction *triples* rather than pairs, we obtain the following extension to the higher-order setting:

Theorem 49 (Basic reduction triple processor). *Let* $M = (\mathcal{P}_1 \uplus \mathcal{P}_2, \mathcal{R}, m, f)$ *be a DP problem. If* $(\succsim, \succcurlyeq, \succ)$ *is a reduction triple such that*

1. *for all* $\ell \Rightarrow r \in \mathcal{R}$*, we have* $\ell \succsim r$*;*
2. *for all* $\ell \Rrightarrow p\ (A) \in \mathcal{P}_1$*, we have* $\ell \succ p$*;*
3. *for all* $\ell \Rrightarrow p\ (A) \in \mathcal{P}_2$*, we have* $\ell \succcurlyeq p$*;*

then the processor that maps M *to* $\{(\mathcal{P}_2, \mathcal{R}, m, f)\}$ *is both sound and complete.*

Proof (sketch). For an infinite $(\mathcal{P}_1 \uplus \mathcal{P}_2, \mathcal{R})$-chain $[(\rho_0, s_0, t_0), (\rho_1, s_1, t_1), \dots]$ the requirements provide that, for all i: (a) $s_i \succ t_i$ if $\rho_i \in \mathcal{P}_1$; (b) $s_i \succcurlyeq t_i$ if $\rho_i \in \mathcal{P}_2$; and (c) $t_i \succsim s_{i+1}$. Since $\succ$ is well-founded, only finitely many DPs can be in $\mathcal{P}_1$, so a tail of the chain is actually an infinite $(\mathcal{P}_2, \mathcal{R}, m, f)$-chain. □

Example 50. Let $(\mathcal{F}, \mathcal{R})$ be the (non-η-expanded) rules from Example 17, and $SDP(\mathcal{R})$ the DPs from Example 28. From Theorem 49, we get the following ordering requirements:

$$\mathtt{deriv}\ (\lambda x.\mathtt{sin}\ F\langle x\rangle) \succsim \lambda y.\mathtt{times}\ (\mathtt{deriv}\ (\lambda x.F\langle x\rangle)\ y)\ (\mathtt{cos}\ F\langle y\rangle)$$
$$\mathtt{deriv}^\sharp\ (\lambda x.\mathtt{sin}\ F\langle x\rangle) \succ \mathtt{deriv}^\sharp\ (\lambda x.F\langle x\rangle)$$

We can handle both requirements by using a polynomial interpretation $\mathcal{J}$ to $\mathbb{N}$ [15,43], by choosing $\mathcal{J}_{\mathtt{sin}}(n) = n+1$, $\mathcal{J}_{\mathtt{cos}}(n) = 0$, $\mathcal{J}_{\mathtt{times}}(n_1, n_2) = n_1$, $\mathcal{J}_{\mathtt{deriv}}(f) = \mathcal{J}_{\mathtt{deriv}^\sharp}(f) = \lambda n.f(n)$. Then the requirements are evaluated to: $\lambda n.f(n) + 1 \geq \lambda n.f(n)$ and $\lambda n.f(n) + 1 > \lambda n.f(n)$, which holds on $\mathbb{N}$.

Theorem 49 is not ideal since, by definition, the left- and right-hand side of a DP may have different types. Such DPs are hard to handle with traditional techniques such as HORPO [26] or polynomial interpretations [15,43], as these methods compare only (meta-)terms of the same type (modulo renaming of sorts).

Example 51. Consider the toy AFSM with $\mathcal{R} = \{\mathtt{f}\ (\mathtt{s}\ X)\ Y \Rightarrow \mathtt{g}\ X\ Y,\ \mathtt{g}\ X \Rightarrow \lambda z.\mathtt{f}\ X\ z\}$ and $\mathit{SDP}(\mathcal{R}) = \{\mathtt{f}^\sharp\ (\mathtt{s}\ X)\ Y \Rrightarrow \mathtt{g}^\sharp\ X,\ \mathtt{g}^\sharp\ X \Rrightarrow \mathtt{f}^\sharp\ X\ Z\}$. If $\mathtt{f}$ and $\mathtt{g}$ both have a type $\mathtt{nat} \rightarrow \mathtt{nat} \rightarrow \mathtt{nat}$, then in the first DP, the left-hand side has type $\mathtt{nat}$ while the right-hand side has type $\mathtt{nat} \rightarrow \mathtt{nat}$. In the second DP, the left-hand side has type $\mathtt{nat} \rightarrow \mathtt{nat}$ and the right-hand side has type $\mathtt{nat}$.

To be able to handle examples like the one above, we adapt [31, Thm. 5.21] by altering the ordering requirements to have base type.

Theorem 52 (Reduction triple processor). *Let* Bot *be a set* $\{\bot_\sigma : \sigma \mid \sigma \text{ a type}\} \subseteq \mathcal{F}^\sharp$ *of unused constructors,* $M = (\mathcal{P}_1 \uplus \mathcal{P}_2, \mathcal{R}, m, f)$ *a DP problem and* $(\succsim, \succcurlyeq, \succ)$ *a reduction triple such that: (a) for all* $\ell \Rightarrow r \in \mathcal{R}$*, we have* $\ell \succsim r$*; and (b) for all* $\ell \Rrightarrow p\ (A) \in \mathcal{P}_1 \uplus \mathcal{P}_2$ *with* $\ell : \sigma_1 \rightarrow \ldots \rightarrow \sigma_m \rightarrow \iota$ *and* $p : \tau_1 \rightarrow \ldots \rightarrow \tau_n \rightarrow \kappa$ *we have, for fresh meta-variables* $Z_1 : \sigma_1, \ldots, Z_m : \sigma_m$*:*

- $\ell\ Z_1 \cdots Z_m \succ p\ \bot_{\tau_1} \cdots \bot_{\tau_n}$ *if* $\ell \Rrightarrow p\ (A) \in \mathcal{P}_1$
- $\ell\ Z_1 \cdots Z_m \succcurlyeq p\ \bot_{\tau_1} \cdots \bot_{\tau_n}$ *if* $\ell \Rrightarrow p\ (A) \in \mathcal{P}_2$

Then the processor that maps M *to* $\{(\mathcal{P}_2, \mathcal{R}, m, f)\}$ *is both sound and complete.*

Proof (sketch). If $(\succsim, \succcurlyeq, \succ)$ is such a triple, then for $R \in \{\succcurlyeq, \succ\}$ define R' as follows: for $s : \sigma_1 \rightarrow \ldots \rightarrow \sigma_m \rightarrow \iota$ and $t : \tau_1 \rightarrow \ldots \rightarrow \tau_n \rightarrow \kappa$, let $s\ R'\ t$ if for all $u_1 : \sigma_1, \ldots, u_m : \sigma_m$ there exist $w_1 : \tau_1, \ldots, w_n : \tau_n$ such that $s\ u_1 \cdots u_m\ R\ t\ w_1 \cdots w_n$. Now apply Theorem 49 with the triple $(\succsim, \succcurlyeq', \succ')$. □

Here, the elements of Bot take the role of minimal terms for the ordering. We use them to flatten the type of the right-hand sides of ordering requirements, which makes it easier to use traditional methods to generate a reduction triple.

While $\succ$ and $\succcurlyeq$ may still have to orient meta-terms of distinct types, these are always *base* types, which we could collapse to a single sort. The only relation required to be monotonic, $\succsim$, regards pairs of meta-terms of the *same* type. This makes it feasible to apply orderings like HORPO or polynomial interpretations.

Both the basic and non-basic reduction triple processor are difficult to use for *non-conservative* DPs, which generate ordering requirements whose right-hand side contains a meta-variable not occurring on the left. This is typically difficult for traditional techniques, although possible to overcome, by choosing triples that do not regard such meta-variables (e.g., via an argument filtering [35,46]):

Example 53. We apply Theorem 52 on the DP problem $(\mathit{SDP}(\mathcal{R}), \mathcal{R}, \mathtt{computable}_{\mathcal{R}}, \mathtt{formative})$ of Example 51. This gives for instance the following ordering requirements:

$$\begin{array}{rr} \mathtt{f}\ (\mathtt{s}\ X)\ Y \succsim \mathtt{g}\ X\ Y & \mathtt{f}^\sharp\ (\mathtt{s}\ X)\ Y \succ \mathtt{g}^\sharp\ X\ \bot_{\mathtt{nat}} \\ \mathtt{g}\ X \succsim \lambda z.\mathtt{f}\ X\ z & \mathtt{g}^\sharp\ X\ Y \succcurlyeq \mathtt{f}^\sharp\ X\ Z \end{array}$$

The right-hand side of the last DP uses a meta-variable Z that does not occur on the left. As neither $\succ$ nor $\succcurlyeq$ are required to be monotonic (only $\succsim$ is), function symbols do not have to regard all their arguments. Thus, we can use a polynomial interpretation $\mathcal{J}$ to $\mathbb{N}$ with $\mathcal{J}_{\bot_{\mathtt{nat}}} = 0$, $\mathcal{J}_{\mathtt{s}}(n) = n + 1$ and $\mathcal{J}_{\mathtt{h}}(n_1, n_2) = n_1$ for $\mathtt{h} \in \{\mathtt{f}, \mathtt{f}^\sharp, \mathtt{g}, \mathtt{g}^\sharp\}$. The ordering requirements then translate to $X + 1 \geq X$ and $\lambda y.X \geq \lambda z.X$ for the rules, and $X + 1 > X$ and $X \geq X$ for the DPs. All these inequalities on $\mathbb{N}$ are clearly satisfied, so we can remove the first DP. The remaining problem is quickly dispersed with the dependency graph processor.

5.3 Rule Removal Without Search for Orderings

While processors often simplify only $\mathcal{P}$, they can also simplify $\mathcal{R}$. One of the most powerful techniques in first-order DP approaches that can do this are *usable rules*. The idea is that for a given set $\mathcal{P}$ of DPs, we only need to consider a *subset* $\mathit{UR}(\mathcal{P}, \mathcal{R})$ of $\mathcal{R}$. Combined with the dependency graph processor, this makes it possible to split a large term rewriting system into a number of small problems.

In the higher-order setting, simple versions of usable rules have also been defined [31,46]. We can easily extend these definitions to AFSMs:

Theorem 54. *Given a DP problem $M = (\mathcal{P}, \mathcal{R}, m, f)$ with $m \succeq \mathtt{minimal}$ and $\mathcal{R}$ finite, let $\mathit{UR}(\mathcal{P}, \mathcal{R})$ be the smallest subset of $\mathcal{R}$ such that:*

- *if a symbol $\mathtt{f}$ occurs in the right-hand side of an element of $\mathcal{P}$ or $\mathit{UR}(\mathcal{P}, \mathcal{R})$, and there is a rule $\mathtt{f}\ \ell_1 \cdots \ell_k \Rightarrow r$, then this rule is also in $\mathit{UR}(\mathcal{P}, \mathcal{R})$;*
- *if there exists $\ell \Rightarrow r \in \mathcal{R}$ or $\ell \Rrightarrow r\ (A) \in \mathcal{P}$ such that $r \trianglerighteq F\langle s_1, \dots, s_k \rangle\ t_1 \cdots t_n$ with $s_1, \dots, s_k$ not all distinct variables or with $n > 0$, then $\mathit{UR}(\mathcal{P}, \mathcal{R}) = \mathcal{R}$.*

Then the processor that maps M to $\{(\mathcal{P}, \mathit{UR}(\mathcal{P}, \mathcal{R}), \mathtt{arbitrary}, \mathtt{all})\}$ is sound.

For the proof we refer to the very similar proofs in [31,46].

Example 55. For the set $\mathit{SDP}(\mathcal{R})$ of the ordinal recursion example (Examples 8 and 29), all rules are usable due to the occurrence of $H\ M$ in the second DP. For the set $\mathit{SDP}(\mathcal{R})$ of the map example (Examples 6 and 31), there are no usable rules, since the one DP contains no defined function symbols or applied meta-variables.

This higher-order processor is much less powerful than its first-order version: if any DP or usable rule has a sub-meta-term of the form $F\ s$ or $F\langle s_1, \dots, s_k \rangle$ with $s_1, \dots, s_k$ not all distinct variables, then *all* rules are usable. Since applying a higher-order meta-variable to some argument is extremely common in higher-order rewriting, the technique is usually not applicable. Also, this processor imposes a heavy price on the flags: minimality (at least) is required, but is lost; the formative flag is also lost. Thus, usable rules are often combined with reduction triples to temporarily disregard rules, rather than as a way to permanently remove rules.

To address these weaknesses, we consider a processor that uses similar ideas to usable rules, but operates from the *left-hand* sides of rules and DPs rather than the right. This adapts the technique from [31] that relies on the new *formative* flag. As in the first-order case [16], we use a semantic characterisation of formative rules. In practice, we then work with over-approximations of this characterisation, analogous to the use of dependency graph approximations in Theorem 45.

Definition 56. *A function FR that maps a pattern ℓ and a set of rules $\mathcal{R}$ to a set $FR(\ell,\mathcal{R}) \subseteq \mathcal{R}$ is a* formative rules approximation *if for all s and γ: if $s \Rightarrow_{\mathcal{R}}^{*} \ell\gamma$ by an ℓ-formative reduction, then this reduction can be done using only rules in $FR(\ell,\mathcal{R})$.*

We let $FR(\mathcal{P},\mathcal{R}) = \bigcup\{FR(\ell_i,\mathcal{R}) \mid \mathtt{f}\ \ell_1 \cdots \ell_n \Rrightarrow p\,(A) \in \mathcal{P} \wedge 1 \leq i \leq n\}$.

Thus, a formative rules approximation is a subset of $\mathcal{R}$ that is *sufficient* for a formative reduction: if $s \Rightarrow_{\mathcal{R}}^{*} \ell\gamma$, then $s \Rightarrow_{FR(\ell,\mathcal{R})}^{*} \ell\gamma$. It is allowed for there to exist other formative reductions that do use additional rules.

Example 57. We define a simple formative rules approximation: (1) $FR(Z,\mathcal{R}) = \emptyset$ if Z is a meta-variable; (2) $FR(\mathtt{f}\ \ell_1 \cdots \ell_m,\mathcal{R}) = FR(\ell_1,\mathcal{R}) \cup \cdots \cup FR(\ell_m,\mathcal{R})$ if $\mathtt{f} : \sigma_1 \to \ldots \to \sigma_m \to \iota$ and no rules have type ι; (3) $FR(s,\mathcal{R}) = \mathcal{R}$ otherwise. This is a formative rules approximation: if $s \Rightarrow_{\mathcal{R}}^{*} Z\gamma$ by a Z-formative reduction, then $s = Z\gamma$, and if $s \Rightarrow_{\mathcal{R}}^{*} \mathtt{f}\ \ell_1 \cdots \ell_m$ and no rules have the same output type as s, then $s = \mathtt{f}\ s_1 \cdots s_m$ and each $s_i \Rightarrow_{\mathcal{R}}^{*} \ell_i\gamma$ (by an ℓ_i-formative reduction).

The following result follows directly from the definition of formative rules.

Theorem 58 (Formative rules processor). *For a formative rules approximation FR, the processor $Proc_{FR}$ that maps a DP problem $(\mathcal{P},\mathcal{R},m,\mathtt{formative})$ to $\{(\mathcal{P},FR(\mathcal{P},\mathcal{R}),m,\mathtt{formative})\}$ is both sound and complete.*

Proof (sketch). A processor that only removes rules (or DPs) is always complete. For soundness, if the chain is formative then each step $t_i \Rightarrow_{\mathcal{R}}^{*} s_{i+1}$ can be replaced by $t_i \Rightarrow_{FR(\mathcal{P},\mathcal{R})}^{*} s_{i+1}$. Thus, the chain can be seen as a $(\mathcal{P},FR(\mathcal{P},\mathcal{R}))$-chain. □

Example 59. For our ordinal recursion example (Examples 8 and 29), *none* of the rules are included when we use the approximation of Example 57 since all rules have output type $\mathtt{ord}$. Thus, $Proc_{FR}$ maps $(SDP(\mathcal{R}),\mathcal{R},\mathtt{computable}_{\mathcal{R}},\mathtt{formative})$ to $(SDP(\mathcal{R}),\emptyset,\mathtt{computable}_{\mathcal{R}},\mathtt{formative})$. *Note:* this example can also be completed without formative rules (see Example 64). Here we illustrate that, even with a simple formative rules approximation, we can often delete all rules of a given type.

Formative rules are introduced in [31], and the definitions can be adapted to a more powerful formative rules approximation than the one sketched in Example 59. Several examples and deeper intuition for the first-order setting are given in [16].

5.4 Subterm Criterion Processors

Reduction triple processors are powerful, but they exert a computational price: we must orient all rules in $\mathcal{R}$. The subterm criterion processor allows us to remove DPs without considering $\mathcal{R}$ at all. It is based on a *projection function* [24], whose higher-order counterpart [31,34,46] is the following:

Definition 60. *For $\mathcal{P}$ a set of DPs, let* $\mathtt{heads}(\mathcal{P})$ *be the set of all symbols* $\mathtt{f}$ *that occur as the head of a left- or right-hand side of a DP in* $\mathcal{P}$. *A* projection function *for* $\mathcal{P}$ *is a function* $\nu : \mathtt{heads}(\mathcal{P}) \to \mathbb{N}$ *such that for all DPs* $\ell \Rrightarrow p\ (A) \in \mathcal{P}$, *the function* $\overline{\nu}$ *with* $\overline{\nu}(\mathtt{f}\ s_1 \cdots s_n) = s_{\nu(\mathtt{f})}$ *is well-defined both for* ℓ *and for* p.

Theorem 61 (Subterm criterion processor). *The processor* $Proc_{\mathtt{subcrit}}$ *that maps a DP problem* $(\mathcal{P}_1 \uplus \mathcal{P}_2, \mathcal{R}, m, f)$ *with* $m \succeq \mathtt{minimal}$ *to* $\{(\mathcal{P}_2, \mathcal{R}, m, f)\}$ *if a projection function* ν *exists such that* $\overline{\nu}(\ell) \rhd \overline{\nu}(p)$ *for all* $\ell \Rrightarrow p\ (A) \in \mathcal{P}_1$ *and* $\overline{\nu}(\ell) = \overline{\nu}(p)$ *for all* $\ell \Rrightarrow p\ (A) \in \mathcal{P}_2$, *is sound and complete.*

Proof (sketch). If the conditions are satisfied, every infinite $(\mathcal{P}, \mathcal{R})$-chain induces an infinite $\unrhd \cdot \Rightarrow_{\mathcal{R}}^*$ sequence that starts in a strict subterm of t_1, contradicting minimality unless all but finitely many steps are equality. Since every occurrence of a pair in $\mathcal{P}_1$ results in a strict $\rhd$ step, a tail of the chain lies in $\mathcal{P}_2$. □

Example 62. Using $\nu(\mathtt{map}^\sharp) = 2$, $Proc_{\mathtt{subcrit}}$ maps the DP problem $(\{(1)\}, \mathcal{R}, \mathtt{computable}_{\mathcal{R}}, \mathtt{formative})$ from Example 47 to $\{(\emptyset, \mathcal{R}, \mathtt{computable}_{\mathcal{R}}, \mathtt{formative})\}$.

The subterm criterion can be strengthened, following [34,46], to also handle DPs like the one in Example 28. Here, we focus on a new idea. For *computable* chains, we can build on the idea of the subterm criterion to get something more.

Theorem 63 (Computable subterm criterion processor). *The processor* $Proc_{\mathtt{statcrit}}$ *that maps a DP problem* $(\mathcal{P}_1 \uplus \mathcal{P}_2, \mathcal{R}, \mathtt{computable}_{\mathcal{U}}, f)$ *to* $\{(\mathcal{P}_2, \mathcal{R}, \mathtt{computable}_{\mathcal{U}}, f)\}$ *if a projection function* ν *exists such that* $\overline{\nu}(\ell) \sqsupset \overline{\nu}(p)$ *for all* $\ell \Rrightarrow p\ (A) \in \mathcal{P}_1$ *and* $\overline{\nu}(\ell) = \overline{\nu}(p)$ *for all* $\ell \Rrightarrow p\ (A) \in \mathcal{P}_2$, *is sound and complete. Here,* $\sqsupset$ *is the relation on base-type terms with* $s \sqsupset t$ *if* $s \neq t$ *and (a)* $s \unrhd_{\mathtt{acc}} t$ *or (b) a meta-variable* Z *exists with* $s \unrhd_{\mathtt{acc}} Z\langle x_1, \ldots, x_k\rangle$ *and* $t = Z\langle t_1, \ldots, t_k\rangle\ s_1 \cdots s_n$.

Proof (sketch). By the conditions, every infinite $(\mathcal{P}, \mathcal{R})$-chain induces an infinite $(\Rrightarrow_{C_{\mathcal{U}}} \cup \Rightarrow_\beta)^* \cdot \Rightarrow_{\mathcal{R}}^*$ sequence (where $C_{\mathcal{U}}$ is defined following Theorem 13). This contradicts computability unless there are only finitely many inequality steps. As pairs in $\mathcal{P}_1$ give rise to a strict decrease, they may occur only finitely often. □

Example 64. Following Examples 8 and 29, consider the projection function ν with $\nu(\mathtt{rec}^\sharp) = 1$. As $\mathtt{s}\ X \unrhd_{\mathtt{acc}} X$ and $\mathtt{lim}\ H \unrhd_{\mathtt{acc}} H$, both $\mathtt{s}\ X \sqsupset X$ and $\mathtt{lim}\ H \sqsupset H\ M$ hold. Thus $Proc_{\mathtt{statc}}(\mathcal{P}, \mathcal{R}, \mathtt{computable}_{\mathcal{R}}, \mathtt{formative}) = \{(\emptyset, \mathcal{R}, \mathtt{computable}_{\mathcal{R}}, \mathtt{formative})\}$. By the dependency graph processor, the AFSM is terminating.

The computable subterm criterion processor fundamentally relies on the new $\mathtt{computable}_{\mathcal{U}}$ flag, so it has no counterpart in the literature so far.

5.5 Non-termination

While (most of) the processors presented so far are complete, none of them can actually return NO. We have not yet implemented such a processor; however, we can already provide a general specification of a *non-termination processor.*

Theorem 65 (Non-termination processor). *Let $M = (\mathcal{P}, \mathcal{R}, m, f)$ be a DP problem. The processor that maps M to* NO *if it determines that a sufficient criterion for non-termination of $\Rightarrow_{\mathcal{R}}$ or for existence of an infinite conservative $(\mathcal{P}, \mathcal{R})$-chain according to the flags m and f holds is sound and complete.*

Proof. Obvious. □

This is a very general processor, which does not tell us *how* to determine such a sufficient criterion. However, it allows us to conclude non-termination as part of the framework by identifying a suitable infinite chain.

Example 66. If we can find a finite $(\mathcal{P}, \mathcal{R})$-chain $[(\rho_0, s_0, t_0), \dots, (\rho_n, s_n, t_n)]$ with $t_n = s_0\gamma$ for some substitution γ which uses only conservative DPs, is formative if $f = \texttt{formative}$ and is $\mathcal{U}$-computable if $m = \texttt{computable}_{\mathcal{U}}$, such a chain is clearly a sufficient criterion: there is an infinite chain $[(\rho_0, s_0, t_0), \dots, (\rho_0, s_0\gamma, t_0\gamma), \dots, (\rho_0, s_0\gamma\gamma, t_0\gamma\gamma), \dots]$. If $m = \texttt{minimal}$ and we find such a chain that is however not minimal, then note that $\Rightarrow_{\mathcal{R}}$ is non-terminating, which also suffices.

For example, for a DP problem $(\mathcal{P}, \mathcal{R}, \texttt{minimal}, \texttt{all})$ with $\mathcal{P} = \{\texttt{f}^\sharp\ F\ X \Rrightarrow \texttt{g}^\sharp\ (F\ X),\ \texttt{g}^\sharp\ X \Rrightarrow \texttt{f}^\sharp\ \texttt{h}\ X\}$, there is a finite dependency chain: $[(\texttt{f}^\sharp\ F\ X \Rrightarrow \texttt{g}^\sharp\ (F\ X),\ \texttt{f}^\sharp\,\texttt{h}\,x,\ \texttt{g}^\sharp\,(\texttt{h}\,x)),\ (\texttt{g}^\sharp\ X \Rrightarrow \texttt{f}^\sharp\,\texttt{h}\,X,\ \texttt{g}^\sharp\,(\texttt{h}\,x),\ \texttt{f}^\sharp\,\texttt{h}\,(\texttt{h}\,x))]$. As $\texttt{f}^\sharp\,\texttt{h}\,(\texttt{h}\,x)$ is an instance of $\texttt{f}^\sharp\ \texttt{h}\ x$, the processor maps this DP problem to NO.

To instantiate Theorem 65, we can borrow non-termination criteria from first-order rewriting [13,21,42], with minor adaptions to the typed setting. Of course, it is worthwhile to also investigate dedicated higher-order non-termination criteria.

6 Conclusions and Future Work

We have built on the static dependency pair approach [6,33,34,46] and formulated it in the language of the DP *framework* from first-order rewriting [20,22]. Our formulation is based on AFSMs, a dedicated formalism designed to make termination proofs transferrable to various higher-order rewriting formalisms.

This framework has two important additions over existing higher-order DP approaches in the literature. First, we consider not only arbitrary and minimally non-terminating dependency chains, but also minimally *non-computable* chains; this is tracked by the $\texttt{computable}_{\mathcal{U}}$ flag. Using the flag, a dedicated processor allows us to efficiently handle rules like Example 8. This flag has no counterpart in the first-order setting. Second, we have generalised the idea of formative rules in [31] to a notion of formative *chains*, tracked by a `formative` flag. This makes it possible to define a corresponding processor that permanently removes rules.

Implementation and Experiments. To provide a strong formal groundwork, we have presented several processors in a general way, using semantic definitions of, e.g., the dependency graph approximation and formative rules rather than syntactic definitions using functions like *TCap* [21]. Even so, most parts of the DP framework for AFSMs have been implemented in the open-source termination prover WANDA [28], alongside a dynamic DP framework [31] and a mechanism to delegate some ordering constraints to a first-order tool [14]. For reduction triples, polynomial interpretations [15] and a version of HORPO [29, Ch. 5] are used. To solve the constraints arising in the search for these orderings, and also to determine sort orderings (for the accessibility relation) and projection functions (for the subterm criteria), WANDA employs an external SAT-solver. WANDA has won the higher-order category of the International Termination Competition [50] four times. In the International Confluence Competition [10], the tools ACPH [40] and CSI^ho [38] use WANDA as their "oracle" for termination proofs on HRSs.

We have tested WANDA on the *Termination Problems Data Base* [49], using AProVE [19] and MiniSat [12] as back-ends. When no additional features are enabled, WANDA proves termination of 124 (out of 198) benchmarks with static DPs, versus 92 with only a search for reduction orderings; a 34% increase. When all features except static DPs are enabled, WANDA succeeds on 153 benchmarks, versus 166 with also static DPs; an 8% increase, or alternatively, a 29% decrease in failure rate. The full evaluation is available in [17, Appendix D].

Future Work. While the static and the dynamic DP approaches each have their own strengths, there has thus far been little progress on a *unified* approach, which could take advantage of the syntactic benefits of both styles. We plan to combine the present work with the ideas of [31] into such a unified DP framework.

In addition, we plan to extend the higher-order DP framework to rewriting with *strategies*, such as implicit β-normalisation or strategies inspired by functional programming languages like OCaml and Haskell. Other natural directions are dedicated automation to detect non-termination, and reducing the number of term constraints solved by the reduction triple processor via a tighter integration with usable and formative rules with respect to argument filterings.

References

1. Aczel, P.: A general Church-Rosser theorem. Unpublished Manuscript, University of Manchester (1978)
2. Arts, T., Giesl, J.: Termination of term rewriting using dependency pairs. Theor. Comput. Sci. **236**(1–2), 133–178 (2000). https://doi.org/10.1016/S0304-3975(99)00207-8
3. Baader, F., Nipkow, F.: Term Rewriting and All That. Cambridge University Press, Cambridge (1998)
4. Bachmair, L., Ganzinger, H.: Rewrite-based equational theorem proving with selection and simplification. J. Logic Comput. **4**(3), 217–247 (1994). https://doi.org/10.1093/logcom/4.3.217

5. Blanqui, F.: Termination and confluence of higher-order rewrite systems. In: Bachmair, L. (ed.) RTA 2000. LNCS, vol. 1833, pp. 47–61. Springer, Heidelberg (2000). https://doi.org/10.1007/10721975_4
6. Blanqui, F.: Higher-order dependency pairs. In: Proceedings of the WST 2006 (2006)
7. Blanqui, F.: Termination of rewrite relations on λ-terms based on Girard's notion of reducibility. Theor. Comput. Sci. **611**, 50–86 (2016). https://doi.org/10.1016/j.tcs.2015.07.045
8. Blanqui, F., Jouannaud, J., Okada, M.: Inductive-data-type systems. Theor. Comput. Sci. **272**(1–2), 41–68 (2002). https://doi.org/10.1016/S0304-3975(00)00347-9
9. Blanqui, F., Jouannaud, J., Rubio, A.: The computability path ordering. Logical Methods Comput. Sci. **11**(4) (2015). https://doi.org/10.2168/LMCS-11(4:3)2015
10. Community. The International Confluence Competition (CoCo) (2018). http://project-coco.uibk.ac.at/
11. Dershowitz, N., Kaplan, S.: Rewrite, rewrite, rewrite, rewrite, rewrite. In: Conference Record of the Sixteenth Annual ACM Symposium on Principles of Programming Languages, Austin, Texas, USA, 11–13 January 1989, pp. 250–259. ACM Press (1989). https://doi.org/10.1145/75277.75299
12. Eén, N., Sörensson, N.: An extensible SAT-solver. In: Giunchiglia, E., Tacchella, A. (eds.) SAT 2003. LNCS, vol. 2919, pp. 502–518. Springer, Heidelberg (2004). https://doi.org/10.1007/978-3-540-24605-3_37
13. Emmes, F., Enger, T., Giesl, J.: Proving non-looping non-termination automatically. In: Gramlich, B., Miller, D., Sattler, U. (eds.) IJCAR 2012. LNCS (LNAI), vol. 7364, pp. 225–240. Springer, Heidelberg (2012). https://doi.org/10.1007/978-3-642-31365-3_19
14. Fuhs, C., Kop, C.: Harnessing first order termination provers using higher order dependency pairs. In: Tinelli, C., Sofronie-Stokkermans, V. (eds.) FroCoS 2011. LNCS (LNAI), vol. 6989, pp. 147–162. Springer, Heidelberg (2011). https://doi.org/10.1007/978-3-642-24364-6_11
15. Fuhs, C., Kop, C.: Polynomial interpretations for higher-order rewriting. In: Tiwari, A. (ed.) 23rd International Conference on Rewriting Techniques and Applications (RTA 2012) , RTA 2012. LIPIcs, vol. 15, Nagoya, Japan, 28 May–2 June 2012. pp. 176–192. Schloss Dagstuhl - Leibniz-Zentrum fuer Informatik (2012). https://doi.org/10.4230/LIPIcs.RTA.2012.176
16. Fuhs, C., Kop, C.: First-order formative rules. In: Dowek, G. (ed.) RTA 2014. LNCS, vol. 8560, pp. 240–256. Springer, Cham (2014). https://doi.org/10.1007/978-3-319-08918-8_17
17. Fuhs, C., Kop, C.: A static higher-order dependency pair framework (extended version). Technical report arXiv:1902.06733 [cs.LO], CoRR (2019)
18. Fuhs, C., Kop, C., Nishida, N.: Verifying procedural programs via constrained rewriting induction. ACM Trans. Comput. Logic **18**(2), 14:1–14:50 (2017). https://doi.org/10.1145/3060143
19. Giesl, J., et al.: Analyzing program termination and complexity automatically with AProVE. J. Autom. Reasoning **58**(1), 3–31 (2017). https://doi.org/10.1007/s10817-016-9388-y
20. Giesl, J., Thiemann, R., Schneider-Kamp, P.: The dependency pair framework: combining techniques for automated termination proofs. In: Baader, F., Voronkov, A. (eds.) LPAR 2005. LNCS (LNAI), vol. 3452, pp. 301–331. Springer, Heidelberg (2005). https://doi.org/10.1007/978-3-540-32275-7_21

21. Giesl, J., Thiemann, R., Schneider-Kamp, P.: Proving and disproving termination of higher-order functions. In: Gramlich, B. (ed.) FroCoS 2005. LNCS (LNAI), vol. 3717, pp. 216–231. Springer, Heidelberg (2005). https://doi.org/10.1007/11559306_12
22. Giesl, J., Thiemann, R., Schneider-Kamp, P., Falke, S.: Mechanizing and improving dependency pairs. J. Autom. Reasoning **37**(3), 155–203 (2006). https://doi.org/10.1007/s10817-006-9057-7
23. Haftmann, F., Nipkow, T.: Code generation via higher-order rewrite systems. In: Blume, M., Kobayashi, N., Vidal, G. (eds.) FLOPS 2010. LNCS, vol. 6009, pp. 103–117. Springer, Heidelberg (2010). https://doi.org/10.1007/978-3-642-12251-4_9
24. Hirokawa, N., Middeldorp, A.: Tyrolean termination tool: techniques and features. Inf. Comput. **205**(4), 474–511 (2007). https://doi.org/10.1016/j.ic.2006.08.010
25. Hoe, J.C., Arvind: Hardware synthesis from term rewriting systems. In: Silveira, L.M., Devadas, S., Reis, R. (eds.) VLSI: Systems on a Chip. IFIPAICT, vol. 34, pp. 595–619. Springer, Boston (2000). https://doi.org/10.1007/978-0-387-35498-9_52
26. Jouannaud, J., Rubio, A.: The higher-order recursive path ordering. In: 14th Annual IEEE Symposium on Logic in Computer Science, Trento, Italy, 2–5 July 1999, pp. 402–411. IEEE Computer Society (1999). https://doi.org/10.1109/LICS.1999.782635
27. Klop, J., Oostrom, V.V., Raamsdonk, F.V.: Combinatory reduction systems: introduction and survey. Theor. Comput. Sci. **121**(1–2), 279–308 (1993). https://doi.org/10.1016/0304-3975(93)90091-7
28. Kop, C.: WANDA - a higher-order termination tool. http://wandahot.sourceforge.net/
29. Kop, C.: Higher order termination. Ph.D. thesis, VU Amsterdam (2012)
30. Kop, C., van Raamsdonk, F.: Higher order dependency pairs for algebraic functional systems. In: Schmidt-Schauß, M. (ed.) Proceedings of the 22nd International Conference on Rewriting Techniques and Applications, RTA 2011. LIPIcs, vol. 10, Novi Sad, Serbia, 30 May–1 June 2011, pp. 203–218. Schloss Dagstuhl - Leibniz-Zentrum fuer Informatik (2011). https://doi.org/10.4230/LIPIcs.RTA.2011.203
31. Kop, C., van Raamsdonk, F.: Dynamic dependency pairs for algebraic functional systems. Logical Methods Comput. Sci. **8**(2), 10:1–10:51 (2012). https://doi.org/10.2168/LMCS-8(2:10)2012
32. Kusakari, K.: Static dependency pair method in rewriting systems for functional programs with product, algebraic data, and ML-polymorphic types. IEICE Trans. **96-D**(3), 472–480 (2013). https://doi.org/10.1587/transinf.E96.D.472
33. Kusakari, K.: Static dependency pair method in functional programs. IEICE Trans. Inf. Syst. **E101.D**(6), 1491–1502 (2018). https://doi.org/10.1587/transinf.2017FOP0004
34. Kusakari, K., Isogai, Y., Sakai, M., Blanqui, F.: Static dependency pair method based on strong computability for higher-order rewrite systems. IEICE Trans. Inf. Syst. **92**(10), 2007–2015 (2009). https://doi.org/10.1587/transinf.E92.D.2007
35. Kusakari, K., Nakamura, M., Toyama, Y.: Argument filtering transformation. In: Nadathur, G. (ed.) PPDP 1999. LNCS, vol. 1702, pp. 47–61. Springer, Heidelberg (1999). https://doi.org/10.1007/10704567_3
36. Meadows, C.A.: Applying formal methods to the analysis of a key management protocol. J. Comput. Secur. **1**(1), 5–36 (1992). https://doi.org/10.3233/JCS-1992-1102

37. Miller, D.: A logic programming language with lambda-abstraction, function variables, and simple unification. J. Logic Comput. **1**(4), 497–536 (1991). https://doi.org/10.1093/logcom/1.4.497
38. Nagele, J.: CoCo 2018 participant: CSI^ho 0.2 (2018). http://project-coco.uibk.ac.at/2018/papers/csiho.pdf
39. Nipkow, T.: Higher-order critical pairs. In: Proceedings of the Sixth Annual Symposium on Logic in Computer Science (LICS 1991), Amsterdam, The Netherlands, 15–18 July 1991, pp. 342–349. IEEE Computer Society (1991). https://doi.org/10.1109/LICS.1991.151658
40. Onozawa, K., Kikuchi, K., Aoto, T., Toyama, Y.: ACPH: system description for CoCo 2017 (2017). http://project-coco.uibk.ac.at/2017/papers/acph.pdf
41. Otto, C., Brockschmidt, M., von Essen, C., Giesl, J.: Automated termination analysis of Java Bytecode by term rewriting. In: Lynch, C. (ed.) Proceedings of the 21st International Conference on Rewriting Techniques and Applications, RTA 2010. LIPIcs, vol. 6, Edinburgh, Scottland, UK, 11–13 July 2010, pp. 259–276. Schloss Dagstuhl - Leibniz-Zentrum fuer Informatik (2010). https://doi.org/10.4230/LIPIcs.RTA.2010.259
42. Payet, É.: Loop detection in term rewriting using the eliminating unfoldings. Theor. Comput. Sci. **403**(2–3), 307–327 (2008). https://doi.org/10.1016/j.tcs.2008.05.013
43. van de Pol, J.: Termination of higher-order rewrite systems. Ph.D. thesis, University of Utrecht (1996)
44. Sakai, M., Kusakari, K.: On dependency pair method for proving termination of higher-order rewrite systems. IEICE Trans. Inf. Syst. **E88-D**(3), 583–593 (2005)
45. Sakai, M., Watanabe, Y., Sakabe, T.: An extension of the dependency pair method for proving termination of higher-order rewrite systems. IEICE Trans. Inf. Syst. **E84-D**(8), 1025–1032 (2001)
46. Suzuki, S., Kusakari, K., Blanqui, F.: Argument filterings and usable rules in higher-order rewrite systems. IPSJ Trans. Program. **4**(2), 1–12 (2011)
47. Tait, W.: Intensional interpretation of functionals of finite type. J. Symbolic Logic **32**(2), 187–199 (1967)
48. Terese: Term Rewriting Systems. Cambridge Tracts in Theoretical Computer Science, vol. 55. Cambridge University Press, Cambridge (2003)
49. Wiki: Termination Problems DataBase (TPDB). http://termination-portal.org/wiki/TPDB
50. Wiki: The International Termination Competition (TermComp) (2018). http://termination-portal.org/wiki/Termination_Competition

Coinduction in Uniform: Foundations for Corecursive Proof Search with Horn Clauses

Henning Basold[1(✉)], Ekaterina Komendantskaya[2(✉)], and Yue Li[2]

[1] CNRS, ENS Lyon, Lyon, France
henning.basold@ens-lyon.fr
[2] Heriot-Watt University, Edinburgh, UK
{ek19,yl55}@hw.ac.uk

Abstract. We establish proof-theoretic, constructive and coalgebraic foundations for proof search in coinductive Horn clause theories. Operational semantics of coinductive Horn clause resolution is cast in terms of *coinductive uniform proofs*; its constructive content is exposed via soundness relative to an intuitionistic first-order logic with recursion controlled by the later modality; and soundness of both proof systems is proven relative to a novel coalgebraic description of complete Herbrand models.

Keywords: Horn clause logic · Coinduction · Uniform proofs · Intuitionistic logic · Coalgebra · Fibrations · Löb modality

1 Introduction

Horn clause logic is a Turing complete and constructive fragment of first-order logic, that plays a central role in verification [22], automated theorem proving [52, 53, 57] and type inference. Examples of the latter can be traced from the Hindley-Milner type inference algorithm [55, 73], to more recent uses of Horn clauses in Haskell type classes [26, 51] and in refinement types [28, 43]. Its popularity can be attributed to well-understood fixed point semantics and an efficient semi-decidable resolution procedure for automated proof search.

According to the standard fixed point semantics [34, 52], given a set P of Horn clauses, the *least Herbrand model* for P is the set of all (finite) ground atomic formulae *inductively entailed* by P. For example, the two clauses below define the set of natural numbers in the least Herbrand model.

$$\kappa_{\mathbf{nat}0} : \mathbf{nat}\, 0$$
$$\kappa_{\mathbf{nat}s} : \forall x.\, \mathbf{nat}\, x \to \mathbf{nat}\, (s\, x)$$

This work is supported by the European Research Council (ERC) under the EU's Horizon 2020 programme (CoVeCe, grant agreement No. 678157) and by the EPSRC research grants EP/N014758/1, EP/K031864/1-2.

L. Caires (Ed.): ESOP 2019, LNCS 11423, pp. 783–813, 2019.
https://doi.org/10.1007/978-3-030-17184-1_28

Formally, the least Herbrand model for the above two clauses is the set of ground atomic formulae obtained by taking a (forward) closure of the above two clauses. The model for **nat** is given by $\mathcal{N} = \{\mathbf{nat}\, 0,\ \mathbf{nat}\, (s\, 0),\ \mathbf{nat}\, (s\, (s\, 0)), \ldots\}$.

We can also view Horn clauses coinductively. The *greatest complete Herbrand model* for a set P of Horn clauses is the largest set of finite and infinite ground atomic formulae *coinductively entailed* by P. For example, the greatest complete Herbrand model for the above two clauses is the set

$$\mathcal{N}^{\infty} = \mathcal{N} \cup \{\mathbf{nat}\, (s\, (s\, (\cdots)))\},$$

obtained by taking a backward closure of the above two inference rules on the set of all finite and infinite ground atomic formulae. The *greatest Herbrand model* is the largest set of *finite* ground atomic formulae *coinductively entailed* by P. In our example, it would be given by $\mathcal{N}$ already. Finally, one can also consider the *least complete Hebrand model*, which interprets entailment inductively but over potentially infinite terms. In the case of **nat**, this interpretation does not differ from $\mathcal{N}$. However, finite paths in coinductive structures like transition systems, for example, require such semantics.

The need for coinductive semantics of Horn clauses arises in several scenarios: the Horn clause theory may explicitly define a coinductive data structure or a coinductive relation. However, it may also happen that a Horn clause theory, which is not explicitly intended as coinductive, nevertheless gives rise to infinite inference by resolution and has an interesting coinductive model. This commonly happens in type inference. We will illustrate all these cases by means of examples.

Horn Clause Theories as Coinductive Data Type Declarations. The following clause defines, together with $\kappa_{\mathbf{nat}0}$ and $\kappa_{\mathbf{nat}s}$, the type of streams over natural numbers.

$$\kappa_{\mathbf{stream}} : \forall x y.\, \mathbf{nat}\, x \wedge \mathbf{stream}\, y \to \mathbf{stream}\, (\mathrm{scons}\, x\, y)$$

This Horn clause does not have a meaningful inductive, i.e. least fixed point, model. The greatest Herbrand model of the clauses is given by

$$\mathcal{S} = \mathcal{N}^{\infty} \cup \{\mathbf{stream}(\mathrm{scons}\, x_0\, (\mathrm{scons}\, x_1\, \cdots)) \mid \mathbf{nat}\, x_0, \mathbf{nat}\, x_1, \ldots \in \mathcal{N}^{\infty}\}$$

In trying to prove, for example, the goal ($\mathbf{stream}\, x$), a goal-directed proof search may try to find a substitution for x that will make ($\mathbf{stream}\, x$) valid relative to the coinductive model of this set of clauses. This search by resolution may proceed by means of an infinite reduction $\underline{\mathbf{stream}\, x} \overset{\kappa_{\mathbf{stream}}:[\mathrm{scons}\ y\ x'/x]}{\rightsquigarrow} \mathbf{nat}\, y \wedge \mathbf{stream}\, x' \overset{\kappa_{\mathbf{nat}0}:[0/y]}{\rightsquigarrow} \underline{\mathbf{stream}\, x'} \overset{\kappa_{\mathbf{stream}}:[\mathrm{scons}\ y'\ x''/x']}{\rightsquigarrow} \cdots$, thereby generating a stream Z of zeros via composition of the computed substitutions: $Z = (\mathrm{scons}\, 0\, x')[\mathrm{scons}\, 0\, x''/x'] \cdots$. Above, we annotated each resolution step with the label of the clause it resolves against and the computed substitution. A method to compute an answer for this infinite sequence of reductions was given by Gupta et al. [41] and Simon et al. [69]: the underlined loop gives rise to the circular unifier $x = \text{scons}\, 0\, x$ that corresponds to the infinite term Z. It is proven that, if a loop and a corresponding circular unifier are detected, they provide an answer that is sound relative to the greatest complete Herbrand model of the clauses. This approach is known under the name of CoLP.

Horn Clause Theories in Type Inference. Below clauses give the typing rules of the simply typed λ-calculus, and may be used for type inference or type checking:

$$\kappa_{t1} : \forall x\, \Gamma\, a.\, \mathbf{var}\, x \wedge \mathbf{find}\, \Gamma\, x\, a \;\; \rightarrow \mathbf{typed}\, \Gamma\, x\, a$$
$$\kappa_{t2} : \forall x\, \Gamma\, a\, m\, b.\, \mathbf{typed}\, [x : a|\Gamma]\, m\, b \rightarrow \mathbf{typed}\, \Gamma\, (\lambda\, x\, m)\, (a \rightarrow b)$$
$$\kappa_{t3} : \forall \Gamma\, a\, m\, n\, b.\, \mathbf{typed}\, \Gamma\, m\, (a \rightarrow b) \wedge \mathbf{typed}\, \Gamma\, n\, a \rightarrow \mathbf{typed}\, \Gamma\, (\mathrm{app}\, m\, n)\, b$$

It is well known that the Y-combinator is not typable in the simply-typed λ-calculus and, in particular, self-application $\lambda x.\, x\, x$ is not typable either. However, by switching off the occurs-check in Prolog or by allowing circular unifiers in CoLP [41,69], we can resolve the goal "$\mathbf{typed}\, []\, (\lambda\, x\, (\mathrm{app}\, x\, x))\, a$" and would compute the circular substitution: $a = b \rightarrow c, b = b \rightarrow c$ suggesting that an infinite, or circular, type may be able to type this λ-term. A similar trick would provide a typing for the Y-combinator. Thus, a coinductive interpretation of the above Horn clauses yields a theory of infinite types, while an inductive interpretation corresponds to the standard type system of the simply typed λ-calculus.

Horn Clause Theories in Type Class Inference. Haskell type class inference does not require circular unifiers but may require a cyclic resolution inference [37,51]. Consider, for example, the following mutually defined data structures in Haskell.

```
data OddList  a  =  OCons a (EvenList  a)
data EvenList a  =  Nil | ECons a (OddList a)
```

This type declaration gives rise to the following equality class instance declarations, where we leave the, here irrelevant, body out.

```
instance(Eq a, Eq (EvenList a)) => Eq (OddList a) where
instance(Eq a, Eq (OddList  a)) => Eq (EvenList a) where
```

The above two type class instance declarations have the shape of Horn clauses. Since the two declarations mutually refer to each other, an instance inference for, e.g., **Eq** (OddList **Int**) will give rise to an infinite resolution that alternates between the subgoals **Eq** (OddList **Int**) and **Eq** (EvenList **Int**). The solution is to terminate the computation as soon as the cycle is detected [51], and this method has been shown sound relative to the greatest Herbrand models in [36]. We will demonstrate this later in the proof systems proposed in this paper.

The diversity of these coinductive examples in the existing literature shows that there is a practical demand for coinductive methods in Horn clause logic, but it also shows that no unifying proof-theoretic approach exists to allow for a generic use of these methods. This causes several problems.

Problem 1. The existing proof-theoretic coinductive interpretations of cycle and loop detection are unclear, incomplete and not uniform.

Table 1. Examples of greatest (complete) Herbrand models for Horn clauses γ_1, γ_2, γ_3. The signatures are $\{a\}$ for the clause γ_1 and $\{a, f\}$ for the others.

Horn clauses	$\gamma_1 : \forall x. p\,x \to p\,x$	$\gamma_2 : \forall x. p(f\,x) \to p\,x$	$\gamma_3 : \forall x. p\,x \to p(f\,x)$
Greatest Herbrand model:	$\{p\,a\}$	$\{p(a), p(f\,a), p(f(f\,a)), \ldots\}$	$\emptyset$
Greatest complete Herbrand model:	$\{p\,a\}$	$\{p(a), p(f\,a), p(f(f\,a), \ldots, p(f(f \ldots)\}$	$\{p(f(f \ldots)\}$
CoLP substitution for query $p\,a$	*id*	fails	fails
CoLP substitution for query $p\,x$	*id*	$x = f\,x$	$x = f\,x$

To see this, consider Table 1, which exemplifies three kinds of circular phenomena in Horn clauses: The clause γ_1 is the easiest case. Its coinductive models are given by the finite set $\{p\,a\}$. On the other extreme is the clause γ_3 that, just like $\kappa_{\mathbf{stream}}$, admits only an infinite formula in its coinductive model. The intermediate case is γ_2, which could be interpreted by an infinite set of finite formulae in its greatest Herbrand model, or may admit an infinite formula in its greatest complete Herbrand model. Examples like γ_1 appear in Haskell type class resolution [51], and examples like γ_2 in its experimental extensions [37]. Cycle detection would only cover computations for γ_1, whereas γ_2, γ_3 require some form of loop detection[1]. However, CoLP's loop detection gives confusing results here. It correctly fails to infer $p\,a$ from γ_3 (no unifier for subgoals $p\,a$ and $p\,(f\,a)$ exists), but incorrectly fails to infer $p\,a$ from γ_2 (also failing to unify $p\,a$ and $p\,(f\,a)$). The latter failure is misleading bearing in mind that $p\,a$ is in fact in the coinductive model of γ_2. Vice versa, if we interpret the CoLP answer $x = f\,x$ as a declaration of an infinite term $(f\,f\,\ldots)$ in the model, then CoLP's answer for γ_3 and $p\,x$ is exactly correct, however the same answer is badly incomplete for the query involving $p\,x$ and γ_2, because γ_2 in fact admits other, finite, formulae in its models. And in some applications, e.g. in Haskell type class inference, a finite formula would be the only acceptable answer for any query to γ_2.

This set of examples shows that loop detection is too coarse a tool to give an operational semantics to a diversity of coinductive models.

Problem 2. Constructive interpretation of coinductive proofs in Horn clause logic is unclear. Horn clause logic is known to be a constructive fragment of FOL. Some applications of Horn clauses rely on this property in a crucial way. For example, inference in Haskell type class resolution is constructive: when a certain formula F is inferred, the Haskell compiler in fact constructs a proof term that inhabits F seen as type. In our earlier example **Eq** (OddList **Int**) of the Haskell type classes, Haskell in fact captures the cycle by a fixpoint term t and proves that t inhabits the type **Eq** (OddList **Int**).

[1] We follow the standard terminology of [74] and say that two formulae F and G form a cycle if $F = G$, and a loop if $F[\theta] = G[\theta]$ for some (possibly circular) unifier θ.

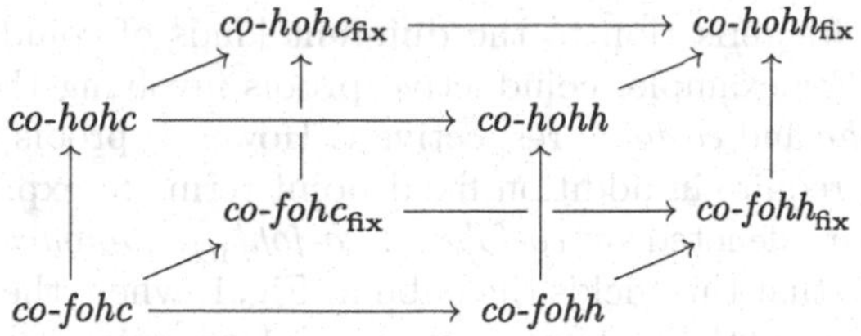

Fig. 1. Cube of logics covered by CUP

Although we know from [36] that these computations are sound relative to greatest Herbrand models of Horn clauses, the results of [36] do not extend to Horn clauses like γ_3 or $\kappa_{\mathbf{stream}}$, or generally to Horn clauses modelled by the greatest *complete* Herbrand models. This shows that there is not just a need for coinductive proofs in Horn clause logic, but *constructive* coinductive proofs.

Problem 3. Incompleteness of circular unification for irregular coinductive data structures. Table 1 already showed some issues with incompleteness of circular unification. A more famous consequence of it is the failure of circular unification to capture irregular terms. This is illustrated by the following Horn clause, which defines the infinite stream of successive natural numbers.

$$\kappa_{\mathbf{from}} : \forall x\, y.\, \mathbf{from}\,(s\,x)\,y \to \mathbf{from}\,x\,(\mathrm{scons}\,x\,y)$$

The reductions for $\mathbf{from}\,0\,y$ consist only of irregular (non-unifiable) formulae:

$$\mathbf{from}\ 0\ y \overset{\kappa_{\mathbf{from}}:[\mathrm{scons}\ 0\ y'/y]}{\rightsquigarrow} \mathbf{from}\ (s\,0)\ y' \overset{\kappa_{\mathbf{from}}:[\mathrm{scons}\ (s\,0)\ y''/y']}{\rightsquigarrow} \cdots$$

The composition of the computed substitutions would suggest an infinite term as answer: $\mathbf{from}\,0\,(\mathrm{scons}\ 0\ (\mathrm{scons}\ (s\,0)\ \ldots))$. However, circular unification no longer helps to compute this answer, and CoLP fails. Thus, there is a need for more general operational semantics that allows irregular coinductive structures.

A New Theory of Coinductive Proof Search in Horn Clause Logic

In this paper, we aim to give a principled and *general* theory that resolves the three problems above. This theory establishes a *constructive* foundation for coinductive resolution and allows us to give proof-theoretic characterisations of the approaches that have been proposed throughout the literature.

To solve Problem 1, we follow the footsteps of the *uniform proofs* by Miller et al. [53,54], who gave a general proof-theoretic account of resolution in first-order Horn clause logic (*fohc*) and three extensions: first-order hereditary Harrop clauses (*fohh*), higher-order Horn clauses (*hohc*), and higher-order hereditary Harrop clauses (*hohh*). In Sect. 3, we extend uniform proofs with a general coinduction proof principle. The resulting framework is called *coinductive uniform proofs (CUP)*. We show how the coinductive extensions of the four logics of Miller et al., which we name *co-fohc*, *co-fohh*, *co-hohc* and *co-hohh*, give a precise proof-theoretic characterisation to the different kinds of coinduction described in the literature. For example, coinductive proofs involving the clauses γ_1 and γ_2 belong to *co-fohc* and *co-fohh*, respectively. However, proofs involving clauses like γ_3 or $\kappa_{\mathbf{stream}}$ require in addition fixed point terms to express infinite data. These extentions are denoted by *co-fohc*$_{\text{fix}}$, *co-fohh*$_{\text{fix}}$, *co-hohc*$_{\text{fix}}$ and *co-hohh*$_{\text{fix}}$.

Section 3 shows that this yields the cube in Fig. 1, where the arrows show the increase in logical strength. The invariant search for regular infinite objects done in CoLP is fully described by the logic *co-fohc*$_{\text{fix}}$, including proofs for clauses like γ_3 and $\kappa_{\mathbf{stream}}$. An important consequence is that CUP is complete for γ_1, γ_2, and γ_3, e.g. $p\,a$ is provable from γ_2 in CUP, but not in CoLP.

In tackling Problem 3, we will find that the irregular proofs, such as those for $\kappa_{\mathbf{from}}$, can be given in *co-hohh*$_{\text{fix}}$. The stream of successive numbers can be defined as a higher-order fixed point term $s_{\text{fr}} = \text{fix}\, f.\, \lambda x.\, \text{scons}\, x\, (f\, (s\, x))$, and the proposition $\forall x.\, \mathbf{from}\, x\, (s_{\text{fr}}\, x)$ is provable in *co-hohh*$_{\text{fix}}$. This requires the use of higher-order syntax, fixed point terms and the goals of universal shape, which become available in the syntax of Hereditary Harrop logic.

In order to solve Problem 2 and to expose the constructive nature of the resulting proof systems, we present in Sect. 4 a coinductive extension of first-order intuitionistic logic and its sequent calculus. This extension ($\mathbf{iFOL}_{\blacktriangleright}$) is based on the so-called later modality (or Löb modality) known from provability logic [16,71], type theory [8,58] and domain theory [20]. However, our way of using the later modality to control recursion in first-order proofs is new and builds on [13,14]. In the same section we also show that CUP is sound relative to $\mathbf{iFOL}_{\blacktriangleright}$, which gives us a handle on the constructive content of CUP. This yields, among other consequences, a constructive interpretation of CoLP proofs.

Section 5 is dedicated to showing soundness of both coinductive proof systems relative to *complete Herbrand models* [52]. The construction of these models is carried out by using coalgebras and category theory. This frees us from having to use topological methods and will simplify future extensions of the theory to, e.g., encompass typed logic programming. It also makes it possible to give original and constructive proofs of soundness for both CUP and $\mathbf{iFOL}_{\blacktriangleright}$ in Sect. 5. We finish the paper with discussion of related and future work.

Originality of the Contribution

The results of this paper give a comprehensive characterisation of coinductive Horn clause theories from the point of view of proof search (by expressing coinductive proof search and resolution as coinductive uniform proofs), constructive proof theory (via a translation into an intuitionistic sequent calculus), and coalgebraic semantics (via coinductive Herbrand models and constructive soundness results). Several of the presented results have never appeared before: the coinductive extension of uniform proofs; characterisation of coinductive properties of Horn clause theories in higher-order logic with and without fixed point operators; coalgebraic and fibrational view on complete Herbrand models; and soundness of an intuitionistic logic with later modality relative to complete Herbrand models.

2 Preliminaries: Terms and Formulae

In this section, we set up notation and terminology for the rest of the paper. Most of it is standard, and blends together the notation used in [53] and [11].

Definition 1. We define the sets $\mathbb{T}$ of *types* and $\mathbb{P}$ of *proposition types* by the following grammars, where ι and o are the *base type* and *base proposition type*.

$$\mathbb{T} \ni \sigma, \tau ::= \iota \mid \sigma \to \tau \qquad \mathbb{P} \ni \rho ::= o \mid \sigma \to \rho, \quad \sigma \in \mathbb{T}$$

We adapt the usual convention that $\to$ binds to the right.

$$\frac{c : \tau \in \Sigma}{\Gamma \vdash c : \tau} \qquad \frac{x : \tau \in \Gamma}{\Gamma \vdash x : \tau} \qquad \frac{\Gamma \vdash M : \sigma \to \tau \qquad \Gamma \vdash N : \sigma}{\Gamma \vdash M\, N : \tau}$$

$$\frac{\Gamma, x : \sigma \vdash M : \tau}{\Gamma \vdash \lambda x.\, M : \sigma \to \tau} \qquad \frac{\Gamma, x : \tau \vdash M : \tau}{\Gamma \vdash \mathrm{fix}\, x.\, M : \tau}$$

Fig. 2. Well-formed terms

$$\frac{(p : \tau_1 \to \cdots \to \tau_n \to o) \in \Pi \qquad \Gamma \vdash M_1 : \tau_1 \quad \cdots \quad \Gamma \vdash M_n : \tau_n}{\Gamma \Vdash p\, M_1 \cdots M_n}$$

$$\frac{}{\Gamma \Vdash \top} \qquad \frac{\Gamma \Vdash \varphi \qquad \Gamma \Vdash \psi \qquad \Box \in \{\wedge, \vee, \to\}}{\Gamma \Vdash \varphi \,\Box\, \psi} \qquad \frac{\Gamma, x : \tau \Vdash \varphi}{\Gamma \Vdash \forall x : \tau.\, \varphi} \qquad \frac{\Gamma, x : \tau \Vdash \varphi}{\Gamma \Vdash \exists x : \tau.\, \varphi}$$

Fig. 3. Well-formed formulae

Definition 2. A *term signature* Σ is a set of pairs $c : \tau$, where $\tau \in \mathbb{T}$, and a *predicate signature* is a set Π of pairs $p : \rho$ with $\rho \in \mathbb{P}$. The elements in Σ and Π are called *term symbols* and *predicate symbols*, respectively. Given term and predicate signatures Σ and Π, we refer to the pair (Σ, Π) as *signature*. Let Var be a countable set of variables, the elements of which we denote by $x, y, \ldots$ We call a finite list Γ of pairs $x : \tau$ of variables and types a *context*. The set Λ_Σ of *(well-typed) terms* over Σ is the collection of all M with $\Gamma \vdash M : \tau$ for some context Γ and type $\tau \in \mathbb{T}$, where $\Gamma \vdash M : \tau$ is defined inductively in Fig. 2. A term is called *closed* if $\vdash M : \tau$, otherwise it is called *open*. Finally, we let Λ_Σ^- denote the set of all terms M that do not involve fix.

Definition 3. Let (Σ, Π) be a signature. We say that φ is a *(first-order) formula* in context Γ, if $\Gamma \Vdash \varphi$ is inductively derivable from the rules in Fig. 3.

Definition 4. The *reduction relation* $\longrightarrow$ on terms in Λ_Σ is given as the compatible closure (reduction under applications and binders) of β- and fix-reduction:

$$(\lambda x.\, M)N \longrightarrow M\,[N/x] \qquad \text{fix}\, x.\, M \longrightarrow M\,[\text{fix}\, x.\, M/x]$$

We denote the reflexive, transitive closure of $\longrightarrow$ by $\twoheadrightarrow$. Two terms M and N are called *convertible*, if $M \equiv N$, where $\equiv$ is the equivalence closure of $\longrightarrow$. Conversion of terms extends to formulae in the obvious way: if $M_k \equiv M'_k$ for $k = 1, \ldots, n$, then $p\, M_1 \cdots M_n \equiv p\, M'_1 \cdots M'_n$.

We will use in the following that the above calculus features subject reduction and confluence, cf. [61]: if $\Gamma \vdash M : \tau$ and $M \equiv N$, then $\Gamma \vdash N : \tau$; and $M \equiv N$ iff there is a term P, such that $M \twoheadrightarrow P$ and $N \twoheadrightarrow P$.

The *order* of a type $\tau \in \mathbb{T}$ is given as usual by $\text{ord}(\iota) = 0$ and $\text{ord}(\sigma \to \tau) = \max\{\text{ord}(\sigma) + 1, \text{ord}(\tau)\}$. If $\text{ord}(\tau) \leq 1$, then the arity of τ is given by $\text{ar}(\iota) = 0$ and $\text{ar}(\iota \to \tau) = \text{ar}(\tau) + 1$. A signature Σ is called *first-order*, if for all $f : \tau \in \Sigma$ we have $\text{ord}(\tau) \leq 1$. We let the arity of f then be $\text{ar}(\tau)$ and denote it by $\text{ar}(f)$.

Definition 5. The set of *guarded base terms* over a first-order signature Σ is given by the following type-driven rules.

$$\frac{x : \tau \in \Gamma \qquad \text{ord}(\tau) \leq 1}{\Gamma \vdash_g x : \tau} \qquad \frac{f : \tau \in \Sigma}{\Gamma \vdash_g f : \tau} \qquad \frac{\Gamma \vdash_g M : \sigma \to \tau \qquad \Gamma \vdash_g N : \sigma}{\Gamma \vdash_g M\, N : \tau}$$

$$\frac{f : \sigma \in \Sigma \qquad \text{ord}(\tau) \leq 1 \qquad \Gamma, x : \tau, y_1 : \iota, \ldots, y_{\text{ar}(\tau)} : \iota \vdash_g M_i : \iota \qquad 1 \leq i \leq \text{ar}(f)}{\Gamma \vdash_g \text{fix}\, x.\, \lambda \vec{y}.\, f\, \vec{M} : \tau}$$

General *guarded terms* are terms M, such that all fix-subterms are guarded base terms, which means that they are generated by the following grammar.

$$G ::= M \text{ (with } \vdash_g M : \tau \text{ for some type } \tau) \mid c \in \Sigma \mid x \in \text{Var} \mid G\, G \mid \lambda x.G$$

Finally, M is a *first-order* term over Σ with $\Gamma \vdash M : \tau$ if $\text{ord}(\tau) \leq 1$ and the types of all variables occurring in Γ are of order 0. We denote the set of guarded first-order terms M with $\Gamma \vdash M : \iota$ by $\Lambda_\Sigma^{G,1}(\Gamma)$ and the set of guarded terms in Γ by $\Lambda_\Sigma^G(\Gamma)$. If Γ is empty, we just write $\Lambda_\Sigma^{G,1}$ and Λ_Σ^G, respectively.

Note that an important aspect of guarded terms is that no free variable occurs under a fix-operator. *Guarded base terms* should be seen as specific fixed point terms that we will be able to unfold into potentially infinite trees. *Guarded terms* close guarded base terms under operations of the simply typed λ-calculus.

Example 6. Let us provide a few examples that illustrate (first-order) guarded terms. We use the first-order signature $\Sigma = \{\text{scons} \colon \iota \to \iota \to \iota, s \colon \iota \to \iota, 0 : \iota\}$.

1. Let $s_{\text{fr}} = \text{fix}\, f.\, \lambda x.\, \text{scons}\ x\ (f\ (s\ x))$ be the function that computes the streams of numerals starting at the given argument. It is easy to show that $\vdash_g s_{\text{fr}} : \iota \to \iota$ and so $s_{\text{fr}}\ 0 \in \Lambda_\Sigma^{G,1}$.

2. For the same signature Σ we also have $x : \iota \vdash_g x : \iota$. Thus $x \in \Lambda_{\Sigma}^{G,1}(x : \iota)$ and $s\,x \in \Lambda_{\Sigma}^{G,1}(x : \iota)$.
3. We have $x : \iota \to \iota \vdash_g x\,0 : \iota$, but $(x\,0) \notin \Lambda_{\Sigma}^{G,1}(x : \iota \to \iota)$.

The purpose of guarded terms is that these are productive, that is, we can reduce them to a term that either has a function symbol at the root or is just a variable. In other words, guarded terms have head normal forms: We say that a term M is in *head normal form*, if $M = f\,\overrightarrow{N}$ for some $f \in \Sigma$ or if $M = x$ for some variable x. The following lemma is a technical result that is needed to show in Lemma 8 that all guarded terms have a head normal form.

Lemma 7. *Let M and N be guarded base terms with $\Gamma, x : \sigma \vdash_g M : \tau$ and $\Gamma \vdash_g N : \sigma$. Then $M\,[N/x]$ is a guarded base term with $\Gamma \vdash_g M\,[N/x] : \tau$.*

Lemma 8. *If M is a first-order guarded term with $M \in \Lambda_{\Sigma}^{G,1}(\Gamma)$, then M reduces to a unique head normal form. This means that either (i) there is a unique $f \in \Sigma$ and terms $N_1, \ldots, N_{\mathrm{ar}(f)}$ with $\Gamma \vdash_g N_k : \iota$ and $M \twoheadrightarrow f\,\overrightarrow{N}$, and for all L if $M \twoheadrightarrow f\,\overrightarrow{L}$, then $\overrightarrow{N} \equiv \overrightarrow{L}$; or (ii) $M \twoheadrightarrow x$ for some $x : \iota \in \Gamma$.*

We end this section by introducing the notion of an atom and refinements thereof. This will enable us to define the different logics and thereby to analyse the strength of coinduction hypotheses, which we promised in the introduction.

Definition 9. A formula φ of the shape $\top$ or $p\,M_1 \cdots M_n$ is an *atom* and a

- *first-order atom*, if p and all the terms M_i are first-order;
- *guarded atom*, if all terms M_i are guarded; and
- *simple atom*, if all terms M_i are non-recursive, that is, are in Λ_{Σ}^{-}.

First-order, guarded and simple atoms are denoted by At_1, At_{ω}^{g} and At_{ω}^{s}. We denote conjunctions of these predicates by $\mathrm{At}_1^{g} = \mathrm{At}_1 \cap \mathrm{At}_{\omega}^{g}$ and $\mathrm{At}_1^{s} = \mathrm{At}_1 \cap \mathrm{At}_{\omega}^{s}$.

Note that the restriction for At_{ω}^{g} only applies to fixed point terms. Hence, any formula that contains terms without fix is already in At_{ω}^{g} and $\mathrm{At}_{\omega}^{g} \cap \mathrm{At}_{\omega}^{s} = \mathrm{At}_{\omega}^{s}$. Since these notions are rather subtle, we give a few examples

Example 10. We list three examples of first-order atoms.

1. For $x : \iota$ we have **stream** $x \in \mathrm{At}_1$, but there are also "garbage" formulae like "**stream** $(\mathrm{fix}\,x.\,x)$" in At_1. Examples of atoms that are not first-order are $p\,M$, where $p : (\iota \to \iota) \to o$ or $x : \iota \to \iota \vdash M : \tau$.
2. Our running example "**from** $0\ (s_{\mathrm{fr}}\ 0)$" is a first-order guarded atom in At_1^{g}.
3. The formulae in At_1^{s} may not contain recursion and higher-order features. However, the atoms of Horn clauses in a logic program fit in here.

3 Coinductive Uniform Proofs

This section introduces the eight logics of the coinductive uniform proof framework announced and motivated in the introduction. The major difference of uniform proofs with, say, a sequent calculus is the "uniformity" property, which means that the choice of the application of each proof rule is deterministic and all proofs are in normal form (cut free). This subsumes the operational semantics of resolution, in which the proof search is always goal directed. Hence, the main challenge, that we set out to solve in this section, is to extend the uniform proof framework with coinduction, while preserving this valuable operational property.

We begin by introducing the different goal formulae and definite clauses that determine the logics that were presented in the cube for coinductive uniform proofs in the introduction. These clauses and formulae correspond directly to those of the original work on uniform proofs [53] with the only difference being that we need to distinguish atoms with and without fixed point terms. The general idea is that goal formulae (G-formulae) occur on the right of a sequent, thus are the *goal* to be proved. Definite clauses (D-formulae), on the other hand, are selected from the context as assumptions. This will become clear once we introduce the proof system for coinductive uniform proofs.

Definition 11. Let D_i be generated by the following grammar with $i \in \{1, \omega\}$.

$$D_i ::= \mathrm{At}_i^s \mid G \to D \mid D \wedge D \mid \forall x : \tau .\, D$$

Table 2. D- and G-formulae for coinductive uniform proofs.

	Definite Clauses	Goals
co-fohc	D_1	$G ::= \mathrm{At}_1^s \mid G \wedge G \mid G \vee G \mid \exists x : \tau .\, G$
co-hohc	D_ω	$G ::= \mathrm{At}_\omega^s \mid G \wedge G \mid G \vee G \mid \exists x : \tau .\, G$
co-fohh	D_1	$G ::= \mathrm{At}_1^s \mid G \wedge G \mid G \vee G \mid \exists x : \tau .\, G \mid D \to G \mid \forall x : \tau .\, G$
co-hohh	D_ω	$G ::= \mathrm{At}_\omega^s \mid G \wedge G \mid G \vee G \mid \exists x : \tau .\, G \mid D \to G \mid \forall x : \tau .\, G$

The sets of definite clauses (D-formulae) and goals (G-formulae) of the four logics *co-fohc*, *co-fohh*, *co-hohc*, *co-hohh* are the well-formed formulae of the corresponding shapes defined in Table 2. For the variations *co-fohh*$_{\mathrm{fix}}$ etc. of these logics with fixed point terms, we replace upper index "s" with "g" everywhere in Table 2. A D-formula of the shape $\forall \vec{x}.\, A_1 \wedge \cdots \wedge A_n \to A_0$ is called *H-formula* or *Horn clause* if $A_k \in \mathrm{At}_1^s$, and *H^g-formula* if $A_k \in \mathrm{At}_1^g$. Finally, a *logic program* (or *program*) P is a set of H-formulae. Note that any set of D-formulae in *fohc* can be transformed into an intuitionistically equivalent set of H-formulae [53].

We are now ready to introduce the coinductive uniform proofs. Such proofs are composed of two parts: an outer coinduction that has to be at the root of a proof tree, and the usual the usual uniform proofs by Miller et al. [54]. The latter are restated in Fig. 4. Of special notice is the rule DECIDE that mimics the operational behaviour of resolution in logic programming, by choosing a clause D from the given program to resolve against. The coinduction is started by the rule CO-FIX in Fig. 5. Our proof system mimics the typical recursion with a guard condition found in coinductive programs and proofs [5,8,19,31,40]. This guardedness condition is formalised by applying the guarding modality $\langle \_ \rangle$ on the formula being proven by coinduction and the proof rules that allow us to distribute the guard over certain logical connectives, see Fig. 5. The guarding modality may be discharged only if the guarded goal was resolved against a clause in the initial program or any hypothesis, except for the coinduction hypotheses. This is reflected in the rule DECIDE$\langle\rangle$, where we may only pick a clause from P, and is in contrast to the rule DECIDE, in which we can pick *any* hypothesis. The proof may only terminate with the INITIAL step if the goal is no longer guarded.

Note that the CO-FIX rule introduces a goal as a new hypothesis. Hence, we have to require that this goal is also a definite clause. Since coinduction hypotheses play such an important role, they deserve a separate definition.

Definition 12. Given a language L from Table 2, a formula φ is a *coinduction goal* of L if φ simultaneously is a D- and a G-formula of L.

Note that the coinduction goals of *co-fohc* and *co-fohh* can be transformed into equivalent H- or H^g-formulae, since any coinduction goal is a D-formula.

Let us now formally introduce the coinductive uniform proof system.

$$\frac{\Sigma; P; \Delta \overset{D}{\Rightarrow} A \quad D \in P \cup \Delta}{\Sigma; P; \Delta \Longrightarrow A}\ \text{DECIDE} \qquad \frac{A \equiv A'}{\Sigma; P; \Delta \overset{A'}{\Rightarrow} A}\ \text{INITIAL} \qquad \frac{}{\Sigma; P; \Delta \Longrightarrow \top}\ \top R$$

$$\frac{\Sigma; P; \Delta \overset{D}{\Rightarrow} A \qquad \Sigma; P; \Delta \Longrightarrow G}{\Sigma; P; \Delta \xRightarrow{G \to D} A}\ {\to}L \qquad \frac{\Sigma; P, D; \Delta \Longrightarrow G}{\Sigma; P; \Delta \Longrightarrow D \to G}\ {\to}R$$

$$\frac{\Sigma; P; \Delta \xRightarrow{D_x} A \qquad x \in \{1,2\}}{\Sigma; P; \Delta \xRightarrow{D_1 \wedge D_2} A}\ \wedge L \qquad \frac{\Sigma; P; \Delta \Longrightarrow G_1 \qquad \Sigma; P; \Delta \Longrightarrow G_2}{\Sigma; P; \Delta \Longrightarrow G_1 \wedge G_2}\ \wedge R$$

$$\frac{\Sigma; P; \Delta \xRightarrow{D[N/x]} A \qquad \varnothing \vdash_g N : \tau}{\Sigma; P; \Delta \xRightarrow{\forall x.\, D} A}\ \forall L \qquad \frac{c : \tau, \Sigma; P; \Delta \Longrightarrow G[c/x] \qquad c : \tau \notin \Sigma}{\Sigma; P; \Delta \Longrightarrow \forall x : \tau.\, G}\ \forall R$$

$$\frac{\Sigma; P; \Delta \Longrightarrow G[N/x] \qquad \varnothing \vdash_g N : \tau}{\Sigma; P; \Delta \Longrightarrow \exists x : \tau.\, G}\ \exists R \qquad \frac{\Sigma; P; \Delta \Longrightarrow G_x \qquad x \in \{1,2\}}{\Sigma; P; \Delta \Longrightarrow G_1 \vee G_2}\ \vee R$$

Fig. 4. Uniform proof rules

$$\frac{\Sigma; P; \varphi \Longrightarrow \langle \varphi \rangle}{\Sigma; P \looparrowright \varphi}\ \text{CO-FIX}$$

$$\frac{\Sigma; P; \Delta \overset{D}{\Longrightarrow} A \quad D \in P}{\Sigma; P; \Delta \Longrightarrow \langle A \rangle}\ \text{DECIDE}\langle\rangle \qquad \frac{c : \tau, \Sigma; P; \Delta \Longrightarrow \langle \varphi\,[c/x] \rangle \quad c : \tau \notin \Sigma}{\Sigma; P; \Delta \Longrightarrow \langle \forall x : \tau.\, \varphi \rangle}\ \forall R\langle\rangle$$

$$\frac{\Sigma; P; \Delta \Longrightarrow \langle \varphi_1 \rangle \qquad \Sigma; P; \Delta \Longrightarrow \langle \varphi_2 \rangle}{\Sigma; P; \Delta \Longrightarrow \langle \varphi_1 \wedge \varphi_2 \rangle}\ \wedge R\langle\rangle \qquad \frac{\Sigma; P; \Delta, \varphi_1 \Longrightarrow \langle \varphi_2 \rangle}{\Sigma; P; \Delta \Longrightarrow \langle \varphi_1 \to \varphi_2 \rangle}\ {\to} R\langle\rangle$$

Fig. 5. Coinductive uniform proof rules

Definition 13. Let P and Δ be finite sets of, respectively, definite clauses and coinduction goals, over the signature Σ, and suppose that G is a goal and φ is a coinduction goal. A *sequent* is either a *uniform provability sequent* of the form $\Sigma; P; \Delta \Longrightarrow G$ or $\Sigma; P; \Delta \overset{D}{\Longrightarrow} A$ as defined in Fig. 4, or it is a *coinductive uniform provability sequent* of the form $\Sigma; P \looparrowright \varphi$ as defined in Fig. 5. Let L be a language from Table 2. We say that φ is *coinductively provable* in L, if P is a set of D-formulae in L, φ is a coinduction goal in L and $\Sigma; P \looparrowright \varphi$ holds.

The logics we have introduced impose different syntactic restrictions on D- and G-formulae, and will therefore admit coinduction goals of different strength. This ability to explicitly use stronger coinduction hypotheses within a goal-directed search was missing in CoLP, for example. And it allows us to account for different coinductive properties of Horn clauses as described in the introduction. We finish this section by illustrating this strengthening.

The first example is one for the logic *co-fohc*, in which we illustrate the framework on the problem of type class resolution.

Example 14. Let us restate the Haskell type class inference problem discussed in the introduction in terms of Horn clauses:

$$\begin{aligned}
\kappa_{\mathrm{i}} &: \mathbf{eq}\ \mathrm{i} \\
\kappa_{\mathrm{odd}} &: \forall x.\, \mathbf{eq}\ x \wedge \mathbf{eq}\ (\mathrm{even}\ x) \to \mathbf{eq}\ (\mathrm{odd}\ x) \\
\kappa_{\mathrm{even}} &: \forall x.\, \mathbf{eq}\ x \wedge \mathbf{eq}\ (\mathrm{odd}\ x) \ \ \to \mathbf{eq}\ (\mathrm{even}\ x)
\end{aligned}$$

To prove $\mathbf{eq}$ (odd i) for this set of Horn clauses, it is sufficient to use this formula directly as coinduction hypothesis, as shown in Fig. 6. Note that this formula is indeed a coinduction goal of *co-fohc*, hence we find ourselves in the simplest scenario of coinductive proof search. In Table 1, γ_1 is a representative for this kind of coinductive proofs with simplest atomic goals.

It was pointed out in [37] that Haskell's type class inference can also give rise to irregular corecursion. Such cases may require the more general coinduction

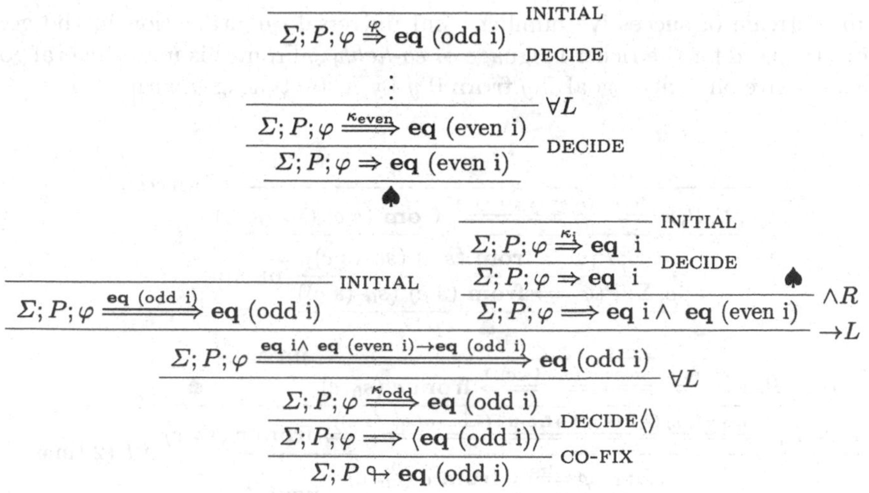

Fig. 6. The *co-fohc* proof for Horn clauses arising from Haskell Type class examples. φ abbreviates the coinduction hypothesis **eq** (odd i). Note its use in the branch ♠.

hypothesis (e.g. universal and/or implicative) of *co-fohh* or *co-hohh*. The below set of Horn clauses is a simplified representation of a problem given in [37]:

$$\begin{aligned}
&\kappa_{\mathrm{i}} : \mathbf{eq}\ \mathrm{i}\\
&\kappa_s : \forall x.\, (\mathbf{eq}\ x) \wedge \mathbf{eq}\ (s\ (g\ x)) \to \mathbf{eq}\ (s\ x)\\
&\kappa_g : \forall x.\, \mathbf{eq}\ x \qquad\qquad\qquad\qquad \to \mathbf{eq}\ (g\ x)
\end{aligned}$$

Trying to prove **eq** $(s$ i) by using **eq** $(s$ i) directly as a coinduction hypothesis is deemed to fail, as the coinductive proof search is irregular and this coinduction hypothesis would not be applicable in any guarded context. But it is possible to prove **eq** $(s$ i) as a corollary of another theorem: $\forall x.\, (\mathbf{eq}\ x) \to \mathbf{eq}\ (s\ x)$. Using this formula as coinduction hypothesis leads to a successful proof, which we omit here. From this more general goal, we can derive the original goal by instantiating the quantifier with i and eliminating the implication with κ_{i}. This second derivation is sound with respect to the models, as we show in Theorem 34.

We encounter γ_2 from Table 1 in a similar situation: To prove $p a$, we first have to prove $\forall x.\, p\ x$ in *co-fohh*, and then obtain $p\ a$ as a corollary by appealing to Theorem 34. The next example shows that we can cover all cases in Table 1 by providing a proof in *co-hohh*$_{\mathrm{fix}}$ that involves irregular recursive terms.

Example 15. Recall the clause $\forall x\ y.\, \mathbf{from}\ (s\ x)\ y \to \mathbf{from}\ x\ (\mathrm{scons}\ x\ y)$ that we named $\kappa_{\mathbf{from}}$ in the introduction. Proving $\exists y.\, \mathbf{from}\ 0\ y$ is again not possible directly. Instead, we can use the term $s_{\mathrm{fr}} = \mathrm{fix}\, f.\, \lambda x.\, \mathrm{scons}\ x\ (f\ (s\ x))$ from Example 6 and prove $\forall x.\, \mathbf{from}\ x\ (s_{\mathrm{fr}}\ x)$ coinductively, as shown in Fig. 7. This formula gives a coinduction hypothesis of sufficient generality. Note that the correct coinduction hypothesis now requires the fixed point definition of an infinite stream of successive numbers and universal quantification in the goal. Hence the need for the richer language of *co-hohh*$_{\text{fix}}$. From this more general goal we can derive our initial goal $\exists\, y.\textbf{from}\ 0\ y$ by instantiating y with $s_{\text{fr}}\ 0$.

$$
\spadesuit \;:=\; \dfrac{\dfrac{\dfrac{}{c, \Sigma; P; \varphi \xRightarrow{\textbf{from}\ (s\ c)\ (s_{\text{fr}}\ (s\ c))} \textbf{from}\ (s\ c)\ (s_{\text{fr}}\ (s\ c))}\ \text{INITIAL}}{c, \Sigma; P; \varphi \overset{\varphi}{\Rrightarrow} \textbf{from}\ (s\ c)\ (s_{\text{fr}}\ (s\ c))}\ \forall L}{c, \Sigma; P; \varphi \Longrightarrow \textbf{from}\ (s\ c)\ (s_{\text{fr}}\ (s\ c))}\ \text{DECIDE}
$$

$$
\dfrac{\dfrac{\dfrac{\dfrac{\dfrac{\dfrac{}{c, \Sigma; P; \varphi \xRightarrow{\textbf{from}\ c\ (\text{scons}\ c\ (s_{\text{fr}}\ (s\ c)))} \textbf{from}\ c\ (s_{\text{fr}}\ c)}\ \text{INITIAL} \qquad \spadesuit}{c, \Sigma; P; \varphi \xRightarrow{\textbf{from}\ (s\ c)\ (s_{\text{fr}}\ (s\ c)) \to \textbf{from}\ c\ (\text{scons}\ c\ (s_{\text{fr}}\ (s\ c)))} \textbf{from}\ c\ (s_{\text{fr}}\ c)}\ {\to}L}{c, \Sigma; P; \varphi \xRightarrow{\kappa_{\textbf{from}}} \textbf{from}\ c\ (s_{\text{fr}}\ c)}\ \forall L\,(2\text{ times})}{c, \Sigma; P; \varphi \Longrightarrow \langle \textbf{from}\ c\ (s_{\text{fr}}\ c) \rangle}\ \text{DECIDE}\langle\rangle}{\Sigma; P; \varphi \Longrightarrow \langle \forall x.\, \textbf{from}\ x\ (s_{\text{fr}}\ x) \rangle}\ \forall R\langle\rangle}{\Sigma; P \looparrowright \forall x.\, \textbf{from}\ x\ (s_{\text{fr}}\ x)}\ \text{CO-FIX}
$$

Fig. 7. The *co-hohh*$_{\text{fix}}$ proof for $\varphi = \forall x.\,\textbf{from}\ x\ (s_{\text{fr}}\ x)$. Note that the last step of the leftmost branch involves $\textbf{from}\ c\ (\text{scons}\ c\ (s_{\text{fr}}\ (s\ c))) \equiv \textbf{from}\ c\ (s_{\text{fr}}\ c)$.

There are examples of coinductive proofs that require a fixed point definition of an infinite stream, but do not require the syntax of higher-order terms or hereditary Harrop formulae. Such proofs can be performed in the *co-fohc*$_{\text{fix}}$ logic. A good example is a proof that the stream of zeros satisfies the Horn clause theory defining the predicate **stream** in the introduction. The goal (**stream** s_0), with $s_0 = \text{fix}\, x.\,\text{scons}\ 0\ x$ can be proven directly by coinduction. Similarly, one can type self-application with the infinite type $a = \text{fix}\, t.\, t \to b$ for some given type b. The proof for **typed** $[x : a]$ $(\text{app}\ x\ x)$ b is then in *co-fohc*$_{\text{fix}}$. Finally, the clause γ_3 is also in this group. More generally, circular unifiers obtained from CoLP's [41] loop detection yield immediately guarded fixed point terms, and thus CoLP corresponds to coinductive proofs in the logic *co-fohc*$_{\text{fix}}$. A general discussion of Horn clause theories that describe infinite objects was given in [48], where the above logic programs were identified as being productive.

4 Coinductive Uniform Proofs and Intuitionistic Logic

In the last section, we introduced the framework of coinductive uniform proofs, which gives an operational account to proofs for coinductively interpreted logic programs. Having this framework at hand, we need to position it in the existing ecosystem of logical systems. The goal of this section is to prove that coinductive uniform proofs are in fact constructive. We show this by first introducing an extension of intuitionistic first-order logic that allows us to deal with recursive

$$\frac{\Gamma \Vdash \Delta \quad \varphi \in \Delta}{\Gamma \mid \Delta \vdash \varphi}\ \textbf{(Proj)} \qquad \frac{\Gamma \mid \Delta \vdash \varphi' \quad \varphi \equiv \varphi'}{\Gamma \mid \Delta \vdash \varphi}\ \textbf{(Conv)} \qquad \frac{\Gamma \Vdash \Delta}{\Gamma \mid \Delta \vdash \top}\ \textbf{(}\top\textbf{-I)}$$

$$\frac{\Gamma \mid \Delta \vdash \varphi \qquad \Gamma \mid \Delta \vdash \psi}{\Gamma \mid \Delta \vdash \varphi \wedge \psi}\ \textbf{(}\wedge\textbf{-I)} \qquad \frac{\Gamma \mid \Delta \vdash \varphi_1 \wedge \varphi_2 \qquad i \in \{1,2\}}{\Gamma \mid \Delta \vdash \varphi_i}\ \textbf{(}\wedge_i\textbf{-E)}$$

$$\frac{\Gamma \mid \Delta \vdash \varphi_i \qquad \Gamma \Vdash \varphi_j \qquad j \neq i}{\Gamma \mid \Delta \vdash \varphi_1 \vee \varphi_2}\ \textbf{(}\vee_i\textbf{-I)} \qquad \frac{\Gamma \mid \Delta, \varphi_1 \vdash \psi \qquad \Gamma \mid \Delta, \varphi_2 \vdash \psi}{\Gamma \mid \Delta, \varphi_1 \vee \varphi_2 \vdash \psi}\ \textbf{(}\vee\textbf{-E)}$$

$$\frac{\Gamma \mid \Delta, \varphi \vdash \psi}{\Gamma \mid \Delta \vdash \varphi \to \psi}\ \textbf{(}\to\textbf{-I)} \qquad \frac{\Gamma \mid \Delta \vdash \varphi \to \psi \qquad \Gamma \mid \Delta \vdash \varphi}{\Gamma \mid \Delta \vdash \psi}\ \textbf{(}\to\textbf{-E)}$$

$$\frac{\Gamma, x : \tau \mid \Delta \vdash \varphi \qquad x \notin \Gamma}{\Gamma \mid \Delta \vdash \forall x : \tau .\, \varphi}\ \textbf{(}\forall\textbf{-I)} \qquad \frac{\Gamma \mid \Delta \vdash \forall x : \tau .\, \varphi \qquad M : \tau \in \Lambda^{G}_{\Sigma}(\Gamma)}{\Gamma \mid \Delta \vdash \varphi[M/x]}\ \textbf{(}\forall\textbf{-E)}$$

$$\frac{M : \tau \in \Lambda^{G}_{\Sigma}(\Gamma) \quad \Gamma \mid \Delta \vdash \varphi[M/x]}{\Gamma \mid \Delta \vdash \exists x : \tau .\, \varphi}\ \textbf{(}\exists\textbf{-I)} \qquad \frac{\Gamma \Vdash \psi \quad \Gamma, x : \tau \mid \Delta, \varphi \vdash \psi \quad x \notin \Gamma}{\Gamma \mid \Delta, \exists x : \tau .\, \varphi \vdash \psi}\ \textbf{(}\exists\textbf{-E)}$$

Fig. 8. Intuitionistic rules for standard connectives

proofs for coinductive predicates. Afterwards, we show that coinductive uniform proofs are sound relative to this logic by means of a proof tree translation. The model-theoretic soundness proofs for both logics will be provided in Sect. 5.

We begin by introducing an extension of intuitionistic first-order logic with the so-called *later modality*, written $\blacktriangleright$. This modality is the essential ingredient that allows us to equip proofs with a controlled form of recursion. The later modality stems originally from provability logic, which characterises transitive, well-founded Kripke frames [30,72], and thus allows one to carry out induction without an explicit induction scheme [16]. Later, the later modality was picked up by the type-theoretic community to control recursion in coinductive programming [8,9,21,56,58], mostly with the intent to replace syntactic guardedness checks for coinductive definitions by type-based checks of well-definedness.

Formally, the logic $\textbf{iFOL}_{\blacktriangleright}$ is given by the following definition.

Definition 16. The formulae of $\textbf{iFOL}_{\blacktriangleright}$ are given by Definition 3 and the rule:

$$\frac{\Gamma \Vdash \varphi}{\Gamma \Vdash \blacktriangleright \varphi}$$

Conversion extends to these formulae in the obvious way. Let φ be a formula and Δ a sequence of formulae in $\textbf{iFOL}_{\blacktriangleright}$. We say φ is *provable in context* Γ *under the assumptions* Δ in $\textbf{iFOL}_{\blacktriangleright}$, if $\Gamma \mid \Delta \vdash \varphi$ holds. The *provability relation* $\vdash$ is thereby given inductively by the rules in Figs. 8 and 9.

$$\frac{\Gamma \mid \Delta \vdash \varphi}{\Gamma \mid \Delta \vdash \blacktriangleright \varphi}\ \textbf{(Next)} \qquad \frac{\Gamma \mid \Delta \vdash \blacktriangleright(\varphi \to \psi)}{\Gamma \mid \Delta \vdash \blacktriangleright \varphi \to \blacktriangleright \psi}\ \textbf{(Mon)} \qquad \frac{\Gamma \mid \Delta, \blacktriangleright \varphi \vdash \varphi}{\Gamma \mid \Delta \vdash \varphi}\ \textbf{(Löb)}$$

Fig. 9. Rules for the later modality

The rules in Fig. 8 are the usual rules for intuitionistic first-order logic and should come at no surprise. More interesting are the rules in Fig. 9, where the rule **(Löb)** introduces recursion into the proof system. Furthermore, the rule **(Mon)** allows us to to distribute the later modality over implication, and consequently over conjunction and universal quantification. This is essential in the translation in Theorem 18 below. Finally, the rule **(Next)** gives us the possibility to proceed without any recursion, if necessary.

Note that so far it is not possible to use the assumption $\blacktriangleright \varphi$ introduced in the **(Löb)**-rule. The idea is that the formulae of a logic program provide us the obligations that we have to prove, possibly by recursion, in order to prove a coinductive predicate. This is cast in the following definition.

Definition 17. Given an H^g-formula φ of the shape $\forall \vec{x}. (A_1 \wedge \cdots \wedge A_n) \to \psi$, we define its *guarding* $\overline{\varphi}$ to be $\forall \vec{x}. (\blacktriangleright A_1 \wedge \cdots \wedge \blacktriangleright A_n) \to \psi$. For a logic program P, we define its guarding $\overline{P}$ by guarding each formula in P.

The translation given in Definition 17 of a logic program into formulae that admit recursion corresponds unfolding a coinductive predicate, cf. [14]. We show now how to transform a coinductive uniform proof tree into a proof tree in $\mathbf{iFOL}_{\blacktriangleright}$, such that the recursion and guarding mechanisms in both logics match up.

Theorem 18. *If P is a logic program over a first-order signature Σ and the sequent $\Sigma; P \looparrowright \varphi$ is provable in co-hohh$_{\text{fix}}$, then $\overline{P} \vdash \varphi$ is provable in* $\mathbf{iFOL}_{\blacktriangleright}$.

To prove this theorem, one uses that each coinductive uniform proof tree starts with an initial tree that has an application of the CO-FIX-rule at the root and that eliminates the guard by using the rules in Fig. 5. At the leaves of this tree, one finds proof trees that proceed only by means of the rules in Fig. 4. The initial tree is then translated into a proof tree in $\mathbf{iFOL}_{\blacktriangleright}$ that starts with an application of the **(Löb)**-rule, which corresponds to the CO-FIX-rule, and that simultaneously transforms the coinduction hypothesis and applies introduction rules for conjunctions etc. This ensures that we can match the coinduction hypothesis with the guarded formulae of the program P.

The results of this section show that it is irrelevant whether the guarding modality is used on the right (CUP-style) or on the left ($\mathbf{iFOL}_{\blacktriangleright}$-style), as the former can be translated into the latter. However, CUP uses the guarding on the right to preserve proof uniformity, whereas $\mathbf{iFOL}_{\blacktriangleright}$ extends a general sequent calculus. Thus, to obtain the reverse translation, we would have to have an admissible cut rule in CUP. The main ingredient to such a cut rule is the ability to prove several coinductive statements simultaneously. This is possible in CUP by proving the conjunction of these statements. Unfortunately, we cannot eliminate such a conjunction into one of its components, since this would require non-deterministic guessing in the proof construction, which in turn breaks uniformity. Thus, we leave a solution of this problem for future work.

5 Herbrand Models and Soundness

In Sect. 4 we showed that coinductive uniform proofs are sound relative to the intuitionistic logic **iFOL**$_\blacktriangleright$. This gives us a handle on the constructive nature of coinductive uniform proofs. Since **iFOL**$_\blacktriangleright$ is a non-standard logic, we still need to provide semantics for that logic. We do this by interpreting in Sect. 5.4 the formulae of **iFOL**$_\blacktriangleright$ over the well-known (complete) Herbrand models and prove the soundness of the accompanying proof system with respect to these models. Although we obtain soundness of coinductive uniform proofs over Herbrand models from this, this proof is indirect and does not give a lot of information about the models captured by the different calculi *co-fohc* etc. For this reason, we will give in Sect. 5.3 a direct soundness proof for coinductive uniform proofs. We also obtain coinduction invariants from this proof for each of the calculi, which allows us to describe their proof strength.

5.1 Coinductive Herbrand Models and Semantics of Terms

Before we come to the soundness proofs, we introduce in this section (complete) Herbrand models by using the terminology of final coalgebras. We then utilise this description to give operational and denotational semantics to guarded terms. These semantics show that guarded terms allow the description and computation of potentially infinite trees.

The coalgebraic approach has been proven very successful both in logic and programming [1,75,76]. We will only require very little category theoretical vocabulary and assume that the reader is familiar with the category **Set** of sets and functions, and functors, see for example [12,25,50]. The terminology of algebras and coalgebras [4,47,64,65] is given by the following definition.

Definition 19. A *coalgebra* for a functor $F\colon \mathbf{Set} \to \mathbf{Set}$ is a map $c\colon X \to FX$. Given coalgebras $d : Y \to FY$ and $c\colon X \to FX$, we say that a map $h : Y \to X$ is a *homomorphism* $d \to c$ if $Fh \circ d = c \circ h$. We call a coalgebra $c\colon X \to FX$ *final*, if for every coalgebra d there is a unique homomorphism $h\colon d \to c$. We will refer to h as the *coinductive extension* of d.

The idea of (complete) Herbrand models is that a set of Horn clauses determines for each predicate symbol a set of potentially infinite terms. Such terms are (potentially infinite) trees, whose nodes are labelled by function symbols and whose branching is given by the arity of these function symbols. To be able to deal with open terms, we will allow such trees to have leaves labelled by variables. Such trees are a final coalgebra for a functor determined by the signature.

Definition 20. Let Σ be first-order signature. The *extension* of a first-order signature Σ is a (polynomial) functor [38] $[\![\Sigma]\!] : \mathbf{Set} \to \mathbf{Set}$ given by

$$[\![\Sigma]\!](X) = \coprod_{f \in \Sigma} X^{\mathrm{ar}(f)},$$

where $\mathrm{ar}\colon \Sigma \to \mathbb{N}$ is defined in Sect. 2 and X^n is the n-fold product of X. We define for a set V a functor $[\![\Sigma]\!]+V\colon \mathbf{Set} \to \mathbf{Set}$ by $([\![\Sigma]\!]+V)(X) = [\![\Sigma]\!](X)+V$, where $+$ is the coproduct (disjoint union) in **Set**.

To make sense of the following definition, we note that we can view Π as a signature and we thus obtain its extension $[\![\Pi]\!]$. Moreover, we note that the final coalgebra of $[\![\Sigma]\!] + V$ exists because $[\![\Sigma]\!]$ is a polynomial functor.

Definition 21. Let Σ be a first-order signature. The *coterms* over Σ are the final coalgebra $\text{root}_V : \Sigma^\infty(V) \to [\![\Sigma]\!](\Sigma^\infty(V)) + V$. For brevity, we denote the coterms with no variables, i.e. $\Sigma^\infty(\emptyset)$, by $\text{root} : \Sigma^\infty \to [\![\Sigma]\!](\Sigma^\infty)$, and call it the *(complete) Herbrand universe* and its elements *ground* coterms. Finally, we let the *(complete) Herbrand base* $\mathcal{B}^\infty$ be the set $[\![\Pi]\!](\Sigma^\infty)$.

The construction $\Sigma^\infty(V)$ gives rise to a functor $\Sigma^\infty : \mathbf{Set} \to \mathbf{Set}$, called the *free completely iterative monad* [5]. If there is no ambiguity, we will drop the injections κ_i when describing elements of $\Sigma^\infty(V)$. Note that $\Sigma^\infty(V)$ is final with property that for every $s \in \Sigma^\infty(V)$ either there are $f \in \Sigma$ and $\overrightarrow{t} \in (\Sigma^\infty(V))^{\text{ar}(f)}$ with $\text{root}_V(s) = f(\overrightarrow{t})$, or there is $x \in V$ with $\text{root}_V(s) = x$. Finality allows us to specify unique maps into $\Sigma^\infty(V)$ by giving a coalgebra $X \to [\![\Sigma]\!](X) + V$. In particular, one can define for each $\theta : V \to \Sigma^\infty$ the substitution $t[\theta]$ of variables in the coterm t by θ as the coinductive extension of the following coalgebra.

$$\Sigma^\infty(V) \xrightarrow{\text{root}_V} [\![\Sigma]\!](\Sigma^\infty(V)) + V \xrightarrow{[\text{id}, \text{root} \circ \theta]} [\![\Sigma]\!](\Sigma^\infty(V))$$

Now that we have set up the basic terminology of coalgebras, we can give semantics to guarded terms from Definition 5. The idea is that guarded terms guarantee that we can always compute with them so far that we find a function symbol in head position, see Lemma 8. This function symbol determines then the label and branching of a node in the tree generated by a guarded term. If the computation reaches a constant or a variable, then we stop creating the tree at the present branch. This idea is captured by the following lemma.

Lemma 22. *There is a map* $[\![-]\!]_1 : \Lambda^{G,1}_\Sigma(\Gamma) \to \Sigma^\infty(\Gamma)$ *that is unique with*

1. *if* $M \equiv N$, *then* $[\![M]\!]_1 = [\![N]\!]_1$, *and*
2. *for all* M, *if* $M \twoheadrightarrow f\, \overrightarrow{N}$ *then* $\text{root}_\Gamma([\![M]\!]_1) = f\big(\overrightarrow{[\![N]\!]_1}\big)$, *and if* $M \twoheadrightarrow x$ *then* $\text{root}_\Gamma([\![M]\!]_1) = x$.

Proof (sketch). By Lemma 8, we can define a coalgebra on the quotient of guarded terms by convertibility $c : \Lambda^{G,1}_\Sigma(\Gamma)/_\equiv \to [\![\Sigma]\!]\Big(\Lambda^{G,1}_\Sigma(\Gamma)/_\equiv\Big) + \Gamma$ with $c[M] = f[\overrightarrow{N}]$ if $M \twoheadrightarrow f\, \overrightarrow{N}$ and $c[M] = x$ if $M \twoheadrightarrow x$. This yields a homomorphism $h : \Lambda^{G,1}_\Sigma(\Gamma)/_\equiv \to \Sigma^\infty(\Gamma)$ and we can define $[\![-]\!]_1 = h \circ [-]$. The rest follows from uniqueness of h.

5.2 Interpretation of Basic Intuitionistic First-Order Formulae

In this section, we give an interpretation of the formulae in Definition 3, in which we restrict ourselves to guarded terms. This interpretation will be relative to models in the complete Herbrand universe. Since we later extend these models to Kripke models to be able to handle the later modality, we formulate these models already now in the language of fibrations [17,46].

Definition 23. Let $p\colon \mathbf{E} \to \mathbf{B}$ be a functor. Given an object $I \in \mathbf{B}$, the *fibre* $\mathbf{E}_I$ above I is the category of objects $A \in \mathbf{E}$ with $p(A) = I$ and morphisms $f\colon A \to B$ with $p(f) = \mathrm{id}_I$. The functor p is a *(split) fibration* if for every morphism $u\colon I \to J$ in $\mathbf{B}$ there is functor $u^*\colon \mathbf{E}_J \to \mathbf{E}_I$, such that $\mathrm{id}_I^* = \mathrm{Id}_{\mathbf{E}_I}$ and $(v \circ u)^* = u^* \circ v^*$. We call u^* the *reindexing along* u.

To give an interpretation of formulae, consider the following category **Pred**.

$$\mathbf{Pred} = \begin{cases} \text{objects}: & (X, P) \text{ with } X \in \mathbf{Set} \text{ and } P \subseteq X \\ \text{morphisms}: & f : (X, P) \to (Y, Q) \text{ is a map } f : X \to Y \text{ with } f(P) \subseteq Q \end{cases}$$

The functor $\mathbb{P}\colon \mathbf{Pred} \to \mathbf{Set}$ with $\mathbb{P}(X, P) = X$ and $\mathbb{P}(f) = f$ is a split fibration, see [46], where the reindexing functor for $f\colon X \to Y$ is given by taking preimages: $f^*(Q) = f^{-1}(Q)$. Note that each fibre $\mathbf{Pred}_X$ is isomorphic to the complete lattice of predicates over X ordered by set inclusion. Thus, we refer to this fibration as the *predicate fibration.*

Let us now expose the logical structure of the predicate fibration. This will allow us to conveniently interpret first-order formulae over this fibration, but it comes at the cost of having to introduce a good amount of category theoretical language. However, doing so will pay off in Sect. 5.4, where we will construct another fibration out of the predicate fibration. We can then use category theoretical results to show that this new fibration admits the same logical structure and allows the interpretation of the later modality.

The first notion we need is that of fibred products, coproducts and exponents, which will allow us to interpret conjunction, disjunction and implication.

Definition 24. A fibration $p\colon \mathbf{E} \to \mathbf{B}$ has *fibred finite products* $(\mathbf{1}, \times)$, if each fibre $\mathbf{E}_I$ has finite products $(\mathbf{1}_I, \times_I)$ and these are preserved by reindexing: for all $f\colon I \to J$, we have $f^*(\mathbf{1}_J) = \mathbf{1}_I$ and $f^*(A \times_J B) = f^*(A) \times_I f^*(B)$. Fibred finite coproducts and exponents are defined analogously.

The fibration $\mathbb{P}$ is a so-called first-order fibration, which allows us to interpret first-order logic, see [46, Def. 4.2.1].

Definition 25. A fibration $p\colon \mathbf{E} \to \mathbf{B}$ is a *first-order fibration* if[2]

- $\mathbf{B}$ has finite products and the fibres of p are preorders;
- p has fibred finite products $(\top, \wedge)$ and coproducts $(\bot, \vee)$ that distribute;
- p has fibred exponents $\to$; and
- p has existential and universal quantifiers $\exists_{I,J} \dashv \pi_{I,J}^* \dashv \forall_{I,J}$ for all projections $\pi_{I,J}\colon I \times J \to I$.

A *first-order λ-fibration* is a first-order fibration with Cartesian closed base $\mathbf{B}$.

[2] Technically, the quantifiers should also fulfil the Beck-Chevalley and Frobenius conditions, and the fibration should admit equality. Since these are fulfilled in all our models and we do not need equality, we will not discuss them here.

The fibration $\mathbb{P}\colon \mathbf{Pred} \to \mathbf{Set}$ is a first-order λ-fibration, as all its fibres are posets and $\mathbf{Set}$ is Cartesian closed; $\mathbb{P}$ has fibred finite products $(\top, \cap)$, given by $\top_X = X$ and intersection; fibred distributive coproducts $(\emptyset, \cup)$; fibred exponents $\Rightarrow$, given by $(P \Rightarrow Q) = \{\vec{t} \mid \text{if } \vec{t} \in P, \text{ then } \vec{t} \in Q\}$; and universal and existential quantifiers given for $P \in \mathbf{Pred}_{X \times Y}$ by

$$\forall_{X,Y} P = \{x \in X \mid \forall y \in Y.\, (x, y) \in P\} \quad \exists_{X,Y} P = \{x \in X \mid \exists y \in Y.\, (x, y) \in P\}.$$

The purpose of first-order fibrations is to capture the essentials of first-order logic, while the λ-part takes care of higher-order features of the term language. In the following, we interpret types, contexts, guarded terms and formulae in the fibration $\mathbb{P}\colon \mathbf{Pred} \to \mathbf{Set}$: We define for types τ and context Γ sets $[\![\tau]\!]$ and $[\![\Gamma]\!]$; for guarded terms M with $\Gamma \vdash M : \tau$ we define a map $[\![M]\!]\colon [\![\Gamma]\!] \to [\![\tau]\!]$ in $\mathbf{Set}$; and for a formula $\Gamma \Vdash \varphi$ we give a predicate $[\![\varphi]\!] \in \mathbf{Pred}_{[\![\Gamma]\!]}$.

The semantics of types and contexts are given inductively in the Cartesian closed category $\mathbf{Set}$, where the base type ι is interpreted as coterms, as follows.

$$[\![\iota]\!] = \Sigma^\infty \qquad\qquad [\![\emptyset]\!] = \mathbf{1}$$
$$[\![\tau \to \sigma]\!] = [\![\sigma]\!]^{[\![\tau]\!]} \qquad\qquad [\![\Gamma, x : \tau]\!] = [\![\Gamma]\!] \times [\![\tau]\!]$$

We note that a coterm $t \in \Sigma^\infty(V)$ can be seen as a map $(\Sigma^\infty)^V \to \Sigma^\infty$ by applying a substitution in $(\Sigma^\infty)^V$ to t: $\sigma \mapsto t[\sigma]$. In particular, the semantics of a guarded first-order term $M \in \Lambda_\Sigma^{G,1}(\Gamma)$ is equivalently a map $[\![M]\!]_1\colon [\![\Gamma]\!] \to \Sigma^\infty$. We can now extend this map inductively to $[\![M]\!]\colon [\![\Gamma]\!] \to [\![\tau]\!]$ for all guarded terms $M \in \Lambda_\Sigma^G(\Gamma)$ with $\Gamma \vdash M : \tau$ by

$$\begin{aligned}
[\![M]\!](\gamma)(\vec{t}) &= [\![M\, \vec{x}]\!]_1([\vec{x} \mapsto \vec{t}]) \qquad \vdash_g M : \tau \text{ with } \operatorname{ar}(\tau) = |\vec{t}| = |\vec{x}| \\
[\![c]\!](\gamma)(\vec{t}) &= c\, \vec{t} \\
[\![x]\!](\gamma) &= \gamma(x) \\
[\![M\, N]\!](\gamma) &= [\![M]\!](\gamma)([\![N]\!](\gamma)) \\
[\![\lambda x.\, M]\!](\gamma)(t) &= [\![M]\!](\gamma[x \mapsto t])
\end{aligned}$$

Lemma 26. *The mapping $[\![-]\!]$ is a well-defined function from guarded terms to functions, such that $\Gamma \vdash M : \tau$ implies $[\![M]\!]\colon [\![\Gamma]\!] \to [\![\tau]\!]$.*

Since $\mathbb{P}\colon \mathbf{Pred} \to \mathbf{Set}$ is a first-order fibration, we can interpret inductively all logical connectives of the formulae from Definition 3 in this fibration. The only case that is missing is the base case of predicate symbols. Their interpretation will be given over a Herbrand model that is constructed as the largest fixed point of an operator over all predicate interpretations in the Herbrand base. Both the operator and the fixed point are the subjects of the following definition.

Definition 27. We let the set of *interpretations* $\mathcal{I}$ be the powerset $\mathcal{P}(\mathcal{B}^\infty)$ of the complete Herbrand base. For $I \in \mathcal{I}$ and $p \in \Pi$, we denote by $I|_p$ the interpretation of p in I (the fibre of I above p)

$$I|_p = \{\vec{t} \in (\Sigma^\infty)^{\operatorname{ar}(p)} \mid p(\vec{t}) \in I\}.$$

Given a set P of H^g-formulae, we define a monotone map $\Phi_P : \mathcal{I} \to \mathcal{I}$ by

$$\Phi_P(I) = \{[\![\psi]\!]_1[\theta] \mid (\forall \vec{x}.\ \bigwedge_{k=1}^{n} \varphi_k \to \psi) \in P, \theta : |\vec{x}| \to \Sigma^\infty, \forall k.\ [\![\varphi_k]\!]_1[\theta] \in I\},$$

where $[\![-]\!]_1[\theta]$ is the extension of semantics and substitution from coterms to the Herbrand base by functoriality of $[\![\Pi]\!]$. The *(complete) Herbrand model* $\mathcal{M}_P$ of P is the largest fixed point of Φ_P, which exists because $\mathcal{I}$ is a complete lattice.

Given a formula φ with $\Gamma \Vdash \varphi$ that contains only guarded terms, we define the semantics of φ in **Pred** from an interpretation $I \in \mathcal{I}$ inductively as follows.

$$\begin{aligned}
[\![\Gamma \Vdash p\,\vec{M}]\!]_I &= \left([\![\vec{M}]\!]\right)^*(I|_p) && \\
[\![\Gamma \Vdash \top]\!]_I &= \top_{[\![\Gamma]\!]} && \\
[\![\Gamma \Vdash \varphi \,\Box\, \psi]\!]_I &= [\![\Gamma \Vdash \varphi]\!]_I \,\Box\, [\![\Gamma \Vdash \psi]\!]_I && \Box \in \{\wedge, \vee, \to\} \\
[\![\Gamma \Vdash Qx : \tau.\, \varphi]\!]_I &= Q_{[\![\Gamma]\!],[\![\tau]\!]}\, [\![\Gamma, x : \tau \Vdash \varphi]\!]_I && Q \in \{\forall, \exists\}
\end{aligned}$$

Lemma 28. *The mapping $[\![-]\!]_I$ is a well-defined function from formulae to predicates, such that $\Gamma \Vdash \varphi$ implies $[\![\varphi]\!]_I \subseteq [\![\Gamma]\!]$ or, equivalently, $[\![\varphi]\!]_I \in$* **Pred**$_{[\![\Gamma]\!]}$.

This concludes the semantics of types, terms and formulae. We now turn to show that coinductive uniform proofs are sound for this interpretation.

5.3 Soundness of Coinductive Uniform Proofs for Herbrand Models

In this section, we give a direct proof of soundness for the coinductive uniform proof system from Sect. 3. Later, we will obtain another soundness result by combining the proof translation from Theorem 18 with the soundness of **iFOL**$_\blacktriangleright$ (Theorems 39 and 42). The purpose of giving a direct soundness proof for uniform proofs is that it allows the extraction of a coinduction invariant, see Lemma 32.

The main idea is as follows. Given a formula φ and a uniform proof π for $\Sigma; P \looparrowright \varphi$, we construct an interpretation $I \in \mathcal{I}$ that validates φ, i.e. $[\![\varphi]\!]_I = \top$, and that is contained in the complete Herbrand model $\mathcal{M}_P$. Combining these two facts, we obtain that $[\![\varphi]\!]_{\mathcal{M}_P} = \top$, and thus the soundness of uniform proofs.

To show that the constructed interpretation I is contained in $\mathcal{M}_P$, we use the usual coinduction proof principle, as it is given in the following definition.

Definition 29. An *invariant for* $K \in \mathcal{I}$ is a set $I \in \mathcal{I}$, such that $K \subseteq I$ and I is a Φ_P-invariant, that is, $I \subseteq \Phi_P(I)$. If K has an invariant, then $K \subseteq \mathcal{M}_P$.

Thus, our goal is now to construct an interpretation together with an invariant. This invariant will essentially collect and iterate all the substitutions that appear in a proof. For this we need the ability to compose substitutions of coterms, which we derive from the monad [5] $(\Sigma^\infty, \eta, \mu)$ with $\mu : \Sigma^\infty \Sigma^\infty \Rightarrow \Sigma^\infty$.

Definition 30. A *(Kleisli-)substitution* θ from V to W, written $\theta : V \twoheadrightarrow W$, is map $V \to \Sigma^\infty(W)$. Composition of $\theta : V \twoheadrightarrow W$ and $\delta : U \twoheadrightarrow V$ is given by

$$\theta \circledcirc \delta = U \xrightarrow{\delta} \Sigma^\infty(V) \xrightarrow{\Sigma^\infty(\theta)} \Sigma^\infty(\Sigma^\infty(W)) \xrightarrow{\mu_W} \Sigma^\infty(W).$$

The notions in the following definition will allow us to easily organise and iterate the substitutions that occur in a uniform proof.

Definition 31. Let S be a set with $S = \{1, \ldots, n\}$ for some $n \in \mathbb{N}$. We call the set S^* of lists over S the set of *substitution identifiers.* Suppose that we have substitutions $\theta_0 : V \twoheadrightarrow \emptyset$ and $\theta_k : V \twoheadrightarrow V$ for each $k \in S$. Then we can define a map $\Theta : S^* \to (\Sigma^\infty)^V$, which turns each substitution identifier into a substitution, by iteration from the right:

$$\Theta(\varepsilon) = \theta_0 \quad \text{and} \quad \Theta(w : k) = \Theta(w) \circledcirc \theta_k$$

After introducing these notations, we can give the outline of the soundness proof for uniform proofs relative to the complete Herbrand model. Given an H^g-formula $\forall \vec{x}. \varphi$, we note that a uniform proof π for $\Sigma; P \looparrowright \forall \vec{x}. \varphi$ starts with

$$\cfrac{\cfrac{\vec{c} : \iota, \Sigma; P; \Delta \Longrightarrow \langle \varphi[\vec{c}/\vec{x}] \rangle \qquad \vec{c} : \iota \notin \Sigma}{\Sigma; P; \forall \vec{x}. \varphi \Longrightarrow \langle \forall \vec{x}. \varphi \rangle}\ \forall R\langle\rangle}{\Sigma; P \looparrowright \forall \vec{x}. \varphi}\ \text{CO-FIX}$$

where the eigenvariables in $\vec{c}$ are all distinct. Let Σ^c be the signature $\vec{c} : \iota, \Sigma$ and C the set of variables in $\vec{c}$. Suppose the following is a valid subtree of π.

$$\cfrac{\cfrac{\Sigma^c; P; \Delta \xrightarrow{\varphi[\vec{N}/\vec{x}]} A}{\Sigma^c; P; \Delta \xrightarrow{\forall \vec{x}. \varphi \in \Delta} A}\ \forall L}{\Sigma^c; P; \Delta \Longrightarrow A}\ \text{DECIDE}$$

This proof tree gives rise to a substitution $\delta : C \twoheadrightarrow C$ by $\delta(c) = [\![N_c]\!]$, which we call an *agent* of π. We let $D \subseteq \mathrm{At}_1^g$ be the set of atoms that are proven in π:

$$D = \{A \mid \Sigma^c; P; \Delta \Longrightarrow \langle A \rangle \text{ or } \Sigma^c; P; \Delta \Longrightarrow A \text{ appears in } \pi\}$$

From the agents and atoms in π we extract an invariant for the goal formula.

Lemma 32. *Suppose that φ is an H^g-formula of the form $\forall \vec{x}. A_1 \wedge \cdots \wedge A_n \to A_0$ and that there is a proof π for $\Sigma; P \looparrowright \varphi$. Let D be the proven atoms in π and $\theta_0, \ldots, \theta_s$ be the agents of π. Define $A_k^c = A_k[\vec{c}/\vec{x}]$ and suppose further that I_1 is an invariant for $\{A_k^c[\Theta(\varepsilon)] \mid 1 \leq k \leq n\}$. If we put*

$$I_2 = \bigcup_{w \in S^*} D\left[\Theta\left(w\right)\right]$$

then $I_1 \cup I_2$ is an invariant for $A_0^c[\Theta(\varepsilon)]$.

Once we have Lemma 32 the following soundness theorem is easily proven.

Theorem 33. *If φ is an H^g-formula and $\Sigma; P \looparrowright \varphi$, then $[\![\varphi]\!]_{\mathcal{M}_P} = \top$.*

Finally, we show that extending logic programs with coinductively proven lemmas is sound. This follows easily by coinduction.

Theorem 34. *Let φ be an H^g-formula of the shape $\forall \vec{x}.\, \psi_1 \to \psi_2$, such that, for all substitutions θ if $[\![\psi_1]\!]_1[\theta] \in \mathcal{M}_{P,\varphi}$, then $[\![\psi_1]\!]_1[\theta] \in \mathcal{M}_P$. Then $\Sigma; P \looparrowright \varphi$ implies $\mathcal{M}_{P\cup\{\varphi\}} = \mathcal{M}_P$, that is, $P \cup \{\varphi\}$ is a conservative extension of P with respect to the Herbrand model.*

As a corollary we obtain that, if there is a proof for $\Sigma; P \looparrowright \varphi$, then a proof for $\Sigma; P, \varphi \looparrowright \psi$ is sound with respect to $\mathcal{M}_P$. Indeed, by Theorem 34 we have that $\mathcal{M}_P = \mathcal{M}_{P\cup\varphi}$ and by Theorem 33 that $\Sigma; P, \varphi \looparrowright \psi$ is sound with respect to $\mathcal{M}_{P\cup\{\varphi\}}$. Thus, the proof of $\Sigma; P, \varphi \looparrowright \psi$ is also sound with respect to $\mathcal{M}_P$. We use this property implicitly in our running examples, and refer the reader to [15,49] for proofs, further examples and discussion.

5.4 Soundness of iFOL$_\blacktriangleright$ over Herbrand Models

In this section, we demonstrate how the logic **iFOL**$_\blacktriangleright$ can be interpreted over Herbrand models. Recall that we obtained a fixed point model from the monotone map Φ_P on interpretations. In what follows, it is crucial that we construct the greatest fixed point of Φ_P by iteration, c.f. [6,32,77]: Let **Ord** be the class of all ordinals equipped with their (well-founded) order. We denote by $\mathbf{Ord}^{\mathrm{op}}$ the class of ordinals with their reversed order and define a monotone function $\overleftarrow{\Phi_P} \colon \mathbf{Ord}^{\mathrm{op}} \to \mathcal{I}$, where we write the argument ordinal in the subscript, by

$$\left(\overleftarrow{\Phi_P}\right)_\alpha = \bigcap_{\beta<\alpha} \Phi_P\left(\overleftarrow{\Phi_P}_\beta\right).$$

Note that this definition is well-defined because $<$ is well-founded and because Φ_P is monotone, see [14]. Since $\mathcal{I}$ is a complete lattice, there is an ordinal α such that $\overleftarrow{\Phi_P}_\alpha = \Phi_P\left(\overleftarrow{\Phi_P}_\alpha\right)$, at which point $\overleftarrow{\Phi_P}_\alpha$ is the largest fixed point $\mathcal{M}_P$ of Φ_P. In what follows, we will utilise this construction to give semantics to **iFOL**$_\blacktriangleright$.

The fibration $\mathbb{P} \colon \mathbf{Pred} \to \mathbf{Set}$ gives rise to another fibration as follows. We let $\overline{\mathbf{Pred}}$ be the category of functors (monotone maps) with fixed predicate domain:

$$\overline{\mathbf{Pred}} = \begin{cases} \text{objects:} & u \colon \mathbf{Ord}^{\mathrm{op}} \to \mathbf{Pred}, \text{such that } \mathbb{P} \circ u \text{ is constant} \\ \text{morphisms:} & u \to v \text{ are natural transformations } f \colon u \Rightarrow v, \\ & \text{such that } \mathbb{P}f \colon \mathbb{P} \circ u \Rightarrow \mathbb{P} \circ v \text{ is the identity} \end{cases}$$

The fibration $\overline{\mathbb{P}} \colon \overline{\mathbf{Pred}} \to \mathbf{Set}$ is defined by evaluation at any ordinal (here 0), i.e. by $\overline{\mathbb{P}}(u) = \mathbb{P}(u(0))$ and $\overline{\mathbb{P}}(f) = (\mathbb{P}f)_0$, and reindexing along $f \colon X \to Y$ by applying the reindexing of $\mathbb{P}$ point-wise, i.e. by $f^{\#}(u)_\alpha = f^*(u_\alpha)$.

Note that there is a (full) embedding $K \colon \mathbf{Pred} \to \overline{\mathbf{Pred}}$ that is given by $K(X, P) = (X, \overline{P})$ with $\overline{P}_\alpha = P$. One can show [14] that $\overline{\mathbb{P}}$ is again a first-order fibration and that it models the later modality, as in the following theorem.

Theorem 35. *The fibration $\overline{\mathbb{P}}$ is a first-order fibration. If necessary, we denote the first-order connectives by $\dot{\top}$, $\dot{\wedge}$ etc. to distinguish them from those in* **Pred**. *Otherwise, we drop the dots. Finite (co)products and quantifiers are given point-wise, while for $X \in$* **Set** *and $u, v \in \overline{\mathbf{Pred}}_X$ exponents are given by*

$$(v \mathrel{\dot{\Rightarrow}} u)_\alpha = \bigcap_{\beta\leq\alpha} (v_\beta \Rightarrow u_\beta).$$

There is a fibred functor $\blacktriangleright\colon \overline{\mathbf{Pred}} \to \overline{\mathbf{Pred}}$ *with* $\overline{\pi} \circ \blacktriangleright = \overline{\pi}$ *given on objects by*

$$(\blacktriangleright u)_\alpha = \bigcap\nolimits_{\beta<\alpha} u_\beta$$

and a natural transformation next: Id $\Rightarrow \blacktriangleright$ *from the identity functor to* $\blacktriangleright$*. The functor* $\blacktriangleright$ *preserves reindexing, products, exponents and universal quantification:* $\blacktriangleright(f^{\#}u) = f^{\#}(\blacktriangleright u)$, $\blacktriangleright(u \wedge v) = \blacktriangleright u \wedge \blacktriangleright v$, $\blacktriangleright(u^v) \to (\blacktriangleright u)^{\blacktriangleright v}$, $\blacktriangleright(\overline{\forall}_n u) = \overline{\forall}_n(\blacktriangleright u)$. *Finally, for all* $X \in \mathbf{Set}$ *and* $u \in \overline{\mathbf{Pred}}_X$*, there is* löb: $(\blacktriangleright u \mathrel{\dot\Rightarrow} u) \to u$ *in* $\overline{\mathbf{Pred}}_X$.

Using the above theorem, we can extend the interpretation of formulae to $\mathbf{iFOL}_\blacktriangleright$ as follows. Let $u\colon \mathbf{Ord}^{\mathrm{op}} \to \mathcal{I}$ be a descending sequence of interpretations. As before, we define the restriction of u to a predicate symbol $p \in \Pi$ by $(u|_p)_\alpha = u_\alpha|_p = \{\vec{t} \mid p(\vec{t}) \in u_\alpha\}$. The semantics of formulae in $\mathbf{iFOL}_\blacktriangleright$ as objects in $\overline{\mathbf{Pred}}$ is given by the following iterative definition.

$$\begin{aligned}
[\![\Gamma \Vdash p\,\vec{M}]\!]_u &= \left(\overrightarrow{[\![M]\!]}\right)^{\#}(u|_p) \\
[\![\Gamma \Vdash \top]\!]_u &= \dot{\top}_{[\![\Gamma]\!]} \\
[\![\Gamma \Vdash \varphi \mathbin{\Box} \psi]\!]_u &= [\![\Gamma \Vdash \varphi]\!]_u \mathbin{\Box} [\![\Gamma \Vdash \psi]\!]_u && \Box \in \{\wedge, \vee, \to\} \\
[\![\Gamma \Vdash Qx : \tau.\, \varphi]\!]_u &= Q_{[\![\Gamma]\!],[\![\tau]\!]}\, [\![\Gamma, x : \tau \Vdash \varphi]\!]_u && Q \in \{\forall, \exists\} \\
[\![\Gamma \Vdash \blacktriangleright \varphi]\!]_u &= \blacktriangleright [\![\Gamma \Vdash \varphi]\!]_u
\end{aligned}$$

The following lemma is the analogue of Lemma 28 for the interpretation of formulae without the later modality.

Lemma 36. *The mapping* $[\![-]\!]_u$ *is a well-defined map from formulae in* $\mathbf{iFOL}_\blacktriangleright$ *to sequences of predicates, such that* $\Gamma \Vdash \varphi$ *implies* $[\![\varphi]\!]_u \in \overline{\mathbf{Pred}}_{[\![\Gamma]\!]}$.

Lemma 37. *All rules of* $\mathbf{iFOL}_\blacktriangleright$ *are sound with respect to the interpretation* $[\![-]\!]_u$ *of formulae in* $\overline{\mathbf{Pred}}$*, that is, if* $\Gamma \mid \Delta \vdash \varphi$*, then* $\left(\bigwedge_{\psi\in\Delta}[\![\psi]\!]_u \mathrel{\dot\Rightarrow} [\![\varphi]\!]_u\right) = \dot{\top}$. *In particular,* $\Gamma \vdash \varphi$ *implies* $[\![\varphi]\!]_u = \dot{\top}$.

The following lemma shows that the guarding of a set of formulae is valid in the chain model that they generate.

Lemma 38. *If* φ *is an H-formula in P, then* $[\![\overline{\varphi}]\!]_{\overleftarrow{\Phi_P}} = \dot{\top}$.

Combining this with soundness from Lemma 37, we obtain that provability in $\mathbf{iFOL}_\blacktriangleright$ relative to a logic program P is sound for the model of P.

Theorem 39. *For all logic programs P, if* $\Gamma \mid \overline{P} \vdash \varphi$ *then* $[\![\varphi]\!]_{\overleftarrow{\Phi_P}} = \dot{\top}$.

The final result of this section is to show that the descending chain model, which we used to interpret formulae of $\mathbf{iFOL}_\blacktriangleright$, is sound and complete for the fixed point model, which we used to interpret the formulae of coinductive uniform proofs. This will be proved in Theorem 42 below. The easiest way to prove this result is by establishing a functor $\overline{\mathbf{Pred}} \to \mathbf{Pred}$ that maps the chain $\overleftarrow{\Phi_P}$ to the model $\mathcal{M}_P$, and that preserves and reflects truth of first-order formulae (Proposition 41). We will phrase the preservation of truth of first-order formulae by a functor by appealing to the following notion of fibrations maps, cf. [46, Def. 4.3.1].

Definition 40. Let $p\colon \mathbf{E} \to \mathbf{B}$ and $q\colon \mathbf{D} \to \mathbf{A}$ be fibrations. A *fibration map* $p \to q$ is a pair $(F\colon \mathbf{E} \to \mathbf{D}, G\colon \mathbf{B} \to \mathbf{A})$ of functors, s.t. $q \circ F = G \circ p$ and F preserves Cartesian morphisms: if $f\colon X \to Y$ in $\mathbf{E}$ is Cartesian over $p(f)$, then $F(f)$ is Cartesian over $G(p(f))$. (F, G) is a map of *first-order (λ-)fibrations*, if p and q are first-order (λ-)fibrations, and F and G preserve this structure.

Let us now construct a first-order λ-fibration map $\overline{\mathbf{Pred}} \to \mathbf{Pred}$. We note that since every fibre of the predicate fibration is a complete lattice, for every chain $u \in \overline{\mathbf{Pred}}_X$ there exists an ordinal α at which u stabilises. This means that there is a limit $\lim u$ of u in $\mathbf{Pred}_X$, which is the largest subset of X, such that $\forall \alpha.\ \lim u \subseteq u_\alpha$. This allows us to define a map $L\colon \overline{\mathbf{Pred}} \to \mathbf{Pred}$ by

$$L(X, u) = (X, \lim u)$$
$$L(f\colon (X, u) \to (Y, v)) = f.$$

In the following proposition, we show that L gives us the ability to express first-order properties of limits equivalently through their approximating chains. This, in turn, provides soundness and completeness for the interpretation of the logic $\mathbf{iFOL}_{\blacktriangleright}$ over descending chains with respect to the largest Herbrand model.

Proposition 41. *$L\colon \overline{\mathbf{Pred}} \to \mathbf{Pred}$, as defined above, is a map of first-order fibrations. Furthermore, L is right-adjoint to the embedding $K\colon \mathbf{Pred} \to \overline{\mathbf{Pred}}$. Finally, for each $p \in \Pi$ and $u \in \overline{\mathbf{Pred}}_{\mathcal{B}^\infty}$, we have $L(u|_p) = L(u)|_p$.*

We get from Proposition 41 soundness and completeness of $\overleftarrow{\Phi_P}$ for Herbrand models. More precisely, if φ is a formula of plain first-order logic ($\blacktriangleright$-free), then its interpretation in the coinductive Herbrand model is true if and only if its interpretation over the chain approximation of the Herbrand model is true.

Theorem 42. *If φ is $\blacktriangleright$-free (Definition 3) then $[\![\varphi]\!]_{\overleftarrow{\Phi_P}} = \dot{\top}$ if and only if $[\![\varphi]\!]_{\mathcal{M}_P} = \top$.*

Proof (sketch). First, one shows for all $\blacktriangleright$-free formulae φ that $L([\![\varphi]\!]_{\overleftarrow{\Phi_P}}) = [\![\varphi]\!]_{\mathcal{M}_P}$ by induction on φ and using Proposition 41. Using this identity and $K \dashv L$, the result is then obtained from the following adjoint correspondence.

$$\frac{\dot{\top} = K(\top) \longrightarrow [\![\varphi]\!]_{\overleftarrow{\Phi_P}} \quad \text{in } \overline{\mathbf{Pred}}}{\top \longrightarrow L([\![\varphi]\!]_{\overleftarrow{\Phi_P}}) = [\![\varphi]\!]_{\mathcal{M}_P} \quad \text{in } \mathbf{Pred}}$$

□

6 Conclusion, Related Work and the Future

In this paper, we provided a comprehensive theory of resolution in coinductive Horn-clause theories and coinductive logic programs. This theory comprises of a uniform proof system that features a form of guarded recursion and that provides operational semantics for proofs of coinductive predicates. Further, we showed how to translate proofs in this system into proofs for an extension of intuitionistic FOL with guarded recursion, and we provided sound semantics for both proof systems in terms of coinductive Herbrand models. The Herbrand models and semantics were thereby presented in a modern style that utilises coalgebras and fibrations to provide a conceptual view on the semantics.

Related Work. It may be surprising that automated *proof search for coinductive predicates* in first-order logic does not have a coherent and comprehensive theory, even after three decades [3,60], despite all the attention that it received as programming [2,29,42,44] and proof [33,35,39,40,45,59,64–67] method. The work that comes close to algorithmic proof search is the system CIRC [63], but it cannot handle general coinductive predicates and corecursive programming. Inductive and coinductive data types are also being added to SMT solvers [24,62]. However, both CIRC and SMT solving are inherently based on classical logic and are therefore not suited to situations where proof objects are relevant, like programming, type class inference or (dependent) type theory. Moreover, the proposed solutions, just like those in [41,69] can only deal with regular data, while our approach also works for irregular data, as we saw in the **from**-example.

This paper subsumes Haskell type class inference [37,51] and exposes that the inference presented in those papers corresponds to coinductive proofs in *co-fohc* and *co-hohh*. Given that the proof systems proposed in this paper are constructive and that uniform proofs provide proofs (type inhabitants) in normal form, we could give a propositions-as-types interpretation to all eight coinductive uniform proof systems. This was done for *co-fohc* and *co-hohh* in [37], but we leave the remaining cube from the introduction for future work.

Future Work. There are several directions that we wish to pursue in the future. First, we know that CUP is incomplete for the presented models, as it is intuitionistic and it lacks an admissible cut rule. The first can be solved by moving to Kripke/Beth-models, as done by Clouston and Goré [30] for the propositional part of $\mathbf{iFOL}_{\blacktriangleright}$. However, the admissible cut rule is more delicate. To obtain such a rule one has to be able to prove several propositions simultaneously by coinduction, as discussed at the end of Sect. 4. In general, completeness of recursive proof systems depends largely on the theory they are applied to, see [70] and [18]. However, techniques from cyclic proof systems [27,68] may help. We also aim to extend our ideas to other situations like higher-order Horn clauses [28,43] and interactive proof assistants [7,10,23,31], typed logic programming, and logic programming that mix inductive and coinductive predicates.

Acknowledgements. We would like to thank Damien Pous and the anonymous reviewers for their valuable feedback.

References

1. Abbott, M., Altenkirch, T., Ghani, N.: Containers: constructing strictly positive types. TCS **342**(1), 3–27 (2005). https://doi.org/10.1016/j.tcs.2005.06.002
2. Abel, A., Pientka, B., Thibodeau, D., Setzer, A.: Copatterns: programming infinite structures by observations. In: POPL 2013, pp. 27–38 (2013). https://doi.org/10.1145/2429069.2429075
3. Aczel, P.: Non-well-founded sets. Center for the Study of Language and Information, Stanford University (1988)
4. Aczel, P.: Algebras and coalgebras. In: Backhouse, R., Crole, R., Gibbons, J. (eds.) Algebraic and Coalgebraic Methods in the Mathematics of Program Construction. LNCS, vol. 2297, pp. 79–88. Springer, Heidelberg (2002). https://doi.org/10.1007/3-540-47797-7_3
5. Aczel, P., Adámek, J., Milius, S., Velebil, J.: Infinite trees and completely iterative theories: a coalgebraic view. TCS **300**(1–3), 1–45 (2003). https://doi.org/10.1016/S0304-3975(02)00728-4
6. Adámek, J.: On final coalgebras of continuous functors. Theor. Comput. Sci. **294**(1/2), 3–29 (2003). https://doi.org/10.1016/S0304-3975(01)00240-7
7. P.L. group on Agda: Agda Documentation. Technical report, Chalmers and Gothenburg University (2015). http://wiki.portal.chalmers.se/agda/, version 2.4.2.5
8. Appel, A.W., Melliès, P.A., Richards, C.D., Vouillon, J.: A very modal model of a modern, major, general type system. In: POPL, pp. 109–122. ACM (2007). https://doi.org/10.1145/1190216.1190235
9. Atkey, R., McBride, C.: Productive coprogramming with guarded recursion. In: ICFP, pp. 197–208. ACM (2013). https://doi.org/10.1145/2500365.2500597
10. Baelde, D., et al.: Abella: a system for reasoning about relational specifications. J. Formaliz. Reason. **7**(2), 1–89 (2014). https://doi.org/10.6092/issn.1972-5787/4650
11. Barendregt, H., Dekkers, W., Statman, R.: Lambda Calculus with Types. Cambridge University Press, Cambridge (2013)
12. Barr, M., Wells, C.: Category Theory for Computing Science. Prentice Hall International Series in Computer Science, 2nd edn. Prentice Hall, Upper Saddle River (1995). http://www.tac.mta.ca/tac/reprints/articles/22/tr22abs.html
13. Basold, H.: Mixed inductive-coinductive reasoning: types, programs and logic. Ph.D. thesis, Radboud University Nijmegen (2018). http://hdl.handle.net/2066/190323
14. Basold, H.: Breaking the Loop: Recursive Proofs for Coinductive Predicates in Fibrations. ArXiv e-prints, February 2018. https://arxiv.org/abs/1802.07143
15. Basold, H., Komendantskaya, E., Li, Y.: Coinduction in uniform: foundations for corecursive proof search with horn clauses. Extended version of this paper. CoRR abs/1811.07644 (2018). http://arxiv.org/abs/1811.07644
16. Beklemishev, L.D.: Parameter free induction and provably total computable functions. TCS **224**(1–2), 13–33 (1999). https://doi.org/10.1016/S0304-3975(98)00305-3
17. Bénabou, J.: Fibered categories and the foundations of naive category theory. J. Symb. Logic **50**(1), 10–37 (1985). https://doi.org/10.2307/2273784
18. Berardi, S., Tatsuta, M.: Classical system of Martin-Löf's inductive definitions is not equivalent to cyclic proof system. In: Esparza, J., Murawski, A.S. (eds.) FoSSaCS 2017. LNCS, vol. 10203, pp. 301–317. Springer, Heidelberg (2017). https://doi.org/10.1007/978-3-662-54458-7_18

19. Birkedal, L., Møgelberg, R.E.: Intensional type theory with guarded recursive types qua fixed points on universes. In: LICS, pp. 213–222. IEEE Computer Society (2013). https://doi.org/10.1109/LICS.2013.27
20. Birkedal, L., Møgelberg, R.E., Schwinghammer, J., Støvring, K.: First steps in synthetic guarded domain theory: step-indexing in the topos of trees. In: Proceedings of LICS 2011, pp. 55–64. IEEE Computer Society (2011). https://doi.org/10.1109/LICS.2011.16
21. Bizjak, A., Grathwohl, H.B., Clouston, R., Møgelberg, R.E., Birkedal, L.: Guarded dependent type theory with coinductive types. In: Jacobs, B., Löding, C. (eds.) FoSSaCS 2016. LNCS, vol. 9634, pp. 20–35. Springer, Heidelberg (2016). https://doi.org/10.1007/978-3-662-49630-5_2. https://arxiv.org/abs/1601.01586
22. Bjørner, N., Gurfinkel, A., McMillan, K., Rybalchenko, A.: Horn clause solvers for program verification. In: Beklemishev, L.D., Blass, A., Dershowitz, N., Finkbeiner, B., Schulte, W. (eds.) Fields of Logic and Computation II. LNCS, vol. 9300, pp. 24–51. Springer, Cham (2015). https://doi.org/10.1007/978-3-319-23534-9_2
23. Blanchette, J.C., Meier, F., Popescu, A., Traytel, D.: Foundational nonuniform (co)datatypes for Higher-Order Logic. In: LICS 2017, pp. 1–12. IEEE Computer Society (2017). https://doi.org/10.1109/LICS.2017.8005071
24. Blanchette, J.C., Peltier, N., Robillard, S.: Superposition with datatypes and codatatypes. In: Galmiche, D., Schulz, S., Sebastiani, R. (eds.) IJCAR 2018. LNCS (LNAI), vol. 10900, pp. 370–387. Springer, Cham (2018). https://doi.org/10.1007/978-3-319-94205-6_25
25. Borceux, F.: Handbook of Categorical Algebra. Basic Category Theory, vol. 1. Cambridge University Press, Cambridge (2008)
26. Bottu, G., Karachalias, G., Schrijvers, T., Oliveira, B.C.D.S., Wadler, P.: Quantified class constraints. In: Haskell Symposium, pp. 148–161. ACM (2017). https://doi.org/10.1145/3122955.3122967
27. Brotherston, J., Simpson, A.: Sequent calculi for induction and infinite descent. J. Log. Comput. **21**(6), 1177–1216 (2011). https://doi.org/10.1093/logcom/exq052
28. Burn, T.C., Ong, C.L., Ramsay, S.J.: Higher-order constrained horn clauses for verification. PACMPL **2**(POPL), 11:1–11:28 (2018). https://doi.org/10.1145/3158099
29. Capretta, V.: General Recursion via Coinductive Types. Log. Methods Comput. Sci. **1**(2), July 2005. https://doi.org/10.2168/LMCS-1(2:1)2005
30. Clouston, R., Goré, R.: Sequent calculus in the topos of trees. In: Pitts, A. (ed.) FoSSaCS 2015. LNCS, vol. 9034, pp. 133–147. Springer, Heidelberg (2015). https://doi.org/10.1007/978-3-662-46678-0_9
31. Coquand, T.: Infinite objects in type theory. In: Barendregt, H., Nipkow, T. (eds.) TYPES 1993. LNCS, vol. 806, pp. 62–78. Springer, Heidelberg (1994). https://doi.org/10.1007/3-540-58085-9_72
32. Cousot, P., Cousot, R.: Constructive versions of Tarski's fixed point theorems. Pac. J. Math. **82**(1), 43–57 (1979). http://projecteuclid.org/euclid.pjm/1102785059
33. Dax, C., Hofmann, M., Lange, M.: A proof system for the linear time μ-calculus. In: Arun-Kumar, S., Garg, N. (eds.) FSTTCS 2006. LNCS, vol. 4337, pp. 273–284. Springer, Heidelberg (2006). https://doi.org/10.1007/11944836_26
34. van Emden, M., Kowalski, R.: The semantics of predicate logic as a programming language. J. Assoc. Comput. Mach. **23**, 733–742 (1976). https://doi.org/10.1145/321978.321991
35. Endrullis, J., Hansen, H.H., Hendriks, D., Polonsky, A., Silva, A.: A coinductive framework for infinitary rewriting and equational reasoning. In: RTA 2015, pp. 143–159 (2015). https://doi.org/10.4230/LIPIcs.RTA.2015.143

36. Farka, F., Komendantskaya, E., Hammond, K.: Coinductive soundness of corecursive type class resolution. In: Hermenegildo, M.V., Lopez-Garcia, P. (eds.) LOPSTR 2016. LNCS, vol. 10184, pp. 311–327. Springer, Cham (2017). https://doi.org/10.1007/978-3-319-63139-4_18
37. Fu, P., Komendantskaya, E., Schrijvers, T., Pond, A.: Proof relevant corecursive resolution. In: Kiselyov, O., King, A. (eds.) FLOPS 2016. LNCS, vol. 9613, pp. 126–143. Springer, Cham (2016). https://doi.org/10.1007/978-3-319-29604-3_9
38. Gambino, N., Kock, J.: Polynomial functors and polynomial monads. Math. Proc. Cambridge Phil. Soc. **154**(1), 153–192 (2013). https://doi.org/10.1017/S0305004112000394
39. Giesl, J., et al.: Analyzing program termination and complexity automatically with AProVE. J. Autom. Reason. **58**(1), 3–31 (2017). https://doi.org/10.1007/s10817-016-9388-y
40. Giménez, E.: Structural recursive definitions in type theory. In: Larsen, K.G., Skyum, S., Winskel, G. (eds.) ICALP 1998. LNCS, vol. 1443, pp. 397–408. Springer, Heidelberg (1998). https://doi.org/10.1007/BFb0055070
41. Gupta, G., Bansal, A., Min, R., Simon, L., Mallya, A.: Coinductive logic programming and its applications. In: Dahl, V., Niemelä, I. (eds.) ICLP 2007. LNCS, vol. 4670, pp. 27–44. Springer, Heidelberg (2007). https://doi.org/10.1007/978-3-540-74610-2_4
42. Hagino, T.: A typed lambda calculus with categorical type constructors. In: Pitt, D.H., Poigné, A., Rydeheard, D.E. (eds.) Category Theory and Computer Science. LNCS, vol. 283, pp. 140–157. Springer, Heidelberg (1987). https://doi.org/10.1007/3-540-18508-9_24
43. Hashimoto, K., Unno, H.: Refinement type inference via horn constraint optimization. In: Blazy, S., Jensen, T. (eds.) SAS 2015. LNCS, vol. 9291, pp. 199–216. Springer, Heidelberg (2015). https://doi.org/10.1007/978-3-662-48288-9_12
44. Howard, B.T.: Inductive, coinductive, and pointed types. In: Harper, R., Wexelblat, R.L. (eds.) Proceedings of ICFP 1996, pp. 102–109. ACM (1996). https://doi.org/10.1145/232627.232640
45. Hur, C.K., Neis, G., Dreyer, D., Vafeiadis, V.: The power of parameterization in coinductive proof. In: Proceedings of POPL 2013, pp. 193–206. ACM (2013). https://doi.org/10.1145/2429069.2429093
46. Jacobs, B.: Categorical Logic and Type Theory. Studies in Logic and the Foundations of Mathematics, vol. 141. North Holland, Amsterdam (1999)
47. Jacobs, B.: Introduction to Coalgebra: Towards Mathematics of States and Observation. Cambridge Tracts in Theoretical Computer Science, vol. 59. Cambridge University Press, Cambridge (2016). https://doi.org/10.1017/CBO9781316823187. http://www.cs.ru.nl/B.Jacobs/CLG/JacobsCoalgebraIntro.pdf
48. Komendantskaya, E., Li, Y.: Productive corecursion in logic programming. J. TPLP (ICLP 2017 post-proc.) **17**(5–6), 906–923 (2017). https://doi.org/10.1017/S147106841700028X
49. Komendantskaya, E., Li, Y.: Towards coinductive theory exploration in horn clause logic: Position paper. In: Kahsai, T., Vidal, G. (eds.) Proceedings 5th Workshop on Horn Clauses for Verification and Synthesis, HCVS 2018, Oxford, UK, 13th July 2018, vol. 278, pp. 27–33 (2018). https://doi.org/10.4204/EPTCS.278.5
50. Lambek, J., Scott, P.J.: Introduction to Higher-Order Categorical Logic. Cambridge University Press, Cambridge (1988)
51. Lämmel, R., Peyton Jones, S.L.: Scrap your boilerplate with class: extensible generic functions. In: ICFP 2005, pp. 204–215. ACM (2005). https://doi.org/10.1145/1086365.1086391

52. Lloyd, J.W.: Foundations of Logic Programming, 2nd edn. Springer, Heidelberg (1987). https://doi.org/10.1007/978-3-642-83189-8
53. Miller, D., Nadathur, G.: Programming with Higher-order logic. Cambridge University Press, Cambridge (2012)
54. Miller, D., Nadathur, G., Pfenning, F., Scedrov, A.: Uniform proofs as a foundation for logic programming. Ann. Pure Appl. Logic **51**(1–2), 125–157 (1991). https://doi.org/10.1016/0168-0072(91)90068-W
55. Milner, R.: A theory of type polymorphism in programming. J. Comput. Syst. Sci. **17**(3), 348–375 (1978). https://doi.org/10.1016/0022-0000(78)90014-4
56. Møgelberg, R.E.: A type theory for productive coprogramming via guarded recursion. In: CSL-LICS, pp. 71:1–71:10. ACM (2014). https://doi.org/10.1145/2603088.2603132
57. Nadathur, G., Mitchell, D.J.: System description: Teyjus—a compiler and abstract machine based implementation of λProlog. CADE-16. LNCS (LNAI), vol. 1632, pp. 287–291. Springer, Heidelberg (1999). https://doi.org/10.1007/3-540-48660-7_25
58. Nakano, H.: A modality for recursion. In: LICS, pp. 255–266. IEEE Computer Society (2000). https://doi.org/10.1109/LICS.2000.855774
59. Niwinski, D., Walukiewicz, I.: Games for the μ-Calculus. TCS **163**(1&2), 99–116 (1996). https://doi.org/10.1016/0304-3975(95)00136-0
60. Park, D.: Concurrency and automata on infinite sequences. In: Deussen, P. (ed.) GI-TCS 1981. LNCS, vol. 104, pp. 167–183. Springer, Heidelberg (1981). https://doi.org/10.1007/BFb0017309
61. Plotkin, G.D.: LCF considered as a programming language. Theor. Comput. Sci. **5**(3), 223–255 (1977). https://doi.org/10.1016/0304-3975(77)90044-5
62. Reynolds, A., Kuncak, V.: Induction for SMT solvers. In: D'Souza, D., Lal, A., Larsen, K.G. (eds.) VMCAI 2015. LNCS, vol. 8931, pp. 80–98. Springer, Heidelberg (2015). https://doi.org/10.1007/978-3-662-46081-8_5
63. Roşu, G., Lucanu, D.: Circular coinduction: a proof theoretical foundation. In: Kurz, A., Lenisa, M., Tarlecki, A. (eds.) CALCO 2009. LNCS, vol. 5728, pp. 127–144. Springer, Heidelberg (2009). https://doi.org/10.1007/978-3-642-03741-2_10
64. Rutten, J.: Universal coalgebra: a theory of systems. TCS **249**(1), 3–80 (2000). https://doi.org/10.1016/S0304-3975(00)00056-6
65. Sangiorgi, D.: Introduction to Bisimulation and Coinduction. Cambridge University Press, New York (2011)
66. Santocanale, L.: A calculus of circular proofs and its categorical semantics. In: Nielsen, M., Engberg, U. (eds.) FoSSaCS 2002. LNCS, vol. 2303, pp. 357–371. Springer, Heidelberg (2002). https://doi.org/10.1007/3-540-45931-6_25
67. Santocanale, L.: μ-bicomplete categories and parity games. RAIRO - ITA **36**(2), 195–227 (2002). https://doi.org/10.1051/ita:2002010
68. Shamkanov, D.S.: Circular proofs for the Gödel-Löb provability logic. Math. Notes **96**(3), 575–585 (2014). https://doi.org/10.1134/S0001434614090326
69. Simon, L., Bansal, A., Mallya, A., Gupta, G.: Co-logic programming: extending logic programming with coinduction. In: Arge, L., Cachin, C., Jurdziński, T., Tarlecki, A. (eds.) ICALP 2007. LNCS, vol. 4596, pp. 472–483. Springer, Heidelberg (2007). https://doi.org/10.1007/978-3-540-73420-8_42
70. Simpson, A.: Cyclic arithmetic is equivalent to Peano arithmetic. In: Esparza, J., Murawski, A.S. (eds.) FoSSaCS 2017. LNCS, vol. 10203, pp. 283–300. Springer, Heidelberg (2017). https://doi.org/10.1007/978-3-662-54458-7_17
71. Smoryński, C.: Self-Reference and Modal Logic. Universitext. Springer, New York (1985). https://doi.org/10.1007/978-1-4613-8601-8

72. Solovay, R.M.: Provability interpretations of modal logic. Israel J. Math. **25**(3), 287–304 (1976). https://doi.org/10.1007/BF02757006
73. Sulzmann, M., Stuckey, P.J.: HM(X) type inference is CLP(X) solving. J. Funct. Program. **18**(2), 251–283 (2008). https://doi.org/10.1017/S0956796807006569
74. Terese: Term Rewriting Systems. Cambridge University Press, Cambridge (2003)
75. Turner, D.A.: Elementary strong functional programming. In: Hartel, P.H., Plasmeijer, R. (eds.) FPLE 1995. LNCS, vol. 1022, pp. 1–13. Springer, Heidelberg (1995). https://doi.org/10.1007/3-540-60675-0_35
76. van den Berg, B., de Marchi, F.: Non-well-founded trees in categories. Ann. Pure Appl. Logic **146**(1), 40–59 (2007). https://doi.org/10.1016/j.apal.2006.12.001
77. Worrell, J.: On the final sequence of a finitary set functor. Theor. Comput. Sci. **338**(1–3), 184–199 (2005). https://doi.org/10.1016/j.tcs.2004.12.009

Author Index

Printed in the United States
By Bookmasters